MANAGERIAL ACCOUNTING

Twelfth Canadian Edition

Ray H. Garrison, D.B.A., CPA
Professor Emeritus
Brigham Young University

Theresa Libby, Ph.D., FCPA, FCA
University of Central Florida

Alan Webb, Ph.D., FCPA, FCA
University of Waterloo

Eric W. Noreen, Ph.D., CMA
(Co-Author, U.S. Edition)
Professor Emeritus
University of Washington

Peter C. Brewer, Ph.D., CPA
(Co-Author, U.S. Edition)
Wake Forest University

MANAGERIAL ACCOUNTING
Twelfth Canadian Edition

ISBN-13: 978-1-26-019327-5
ISBN-10: 1-26-019327-6

4 5 6 7 8 TCP 24 23 22

Printed and bound in Canada.

Care has been taken to trace ownership of copyright material contained in this text; however, the publisher will welcome any information that enables it to rectify any reference or credit for subsequent editions.

Director of Product: Rhondda McNabb
Senior Portfolio Manager: Alwynn Pinard
Senior Marketing Manager: Loula March
Senior Content Developer: Amy Rydzanicz
Portfolio Associate: Christine Albert
Senior Supervising Editor: Jessica Barnoski
Photo/Permissions Editor: Nadine Bachan
Copy Editor: Kelli Howey
Plant Production Coordinator: Heitor Moura
Manufacturing Production Coordinator: Jason Stubner
Cover Design: Dianne Reynolds
Cover Images: Lighthouse: Shutterstock; Graph: © Artistdesign29/Shutterstock
Interior Design: Lightbox Visual Communications, Inc.
Composition: Aptara®, Inc.
Printer: Transcontinental Printing Group

Dedication

To our families, and the students and instructors who will use this book.

About the Authors

Ray H. Garrison is Emeritus Professor of Accounting at Brigham Young University, Provo, Utah. He received his B.S. and M.S. degrees from Brigham Young University and his D.B.A. degree from Indiana University. As a certified public accountant, Professor Garrison has been involved in management consulting work with both national and regional accounting firms. He has published articles in *The Accounting Review, Management Accounting*, and other professional journals. Innovation in the classroom has earned Professor Garrison the Karl G. Maeser Distinguished Teaching Award from Brigham Young University.

Theresa Libby is the EY Professor of Accounting in the Kenneth G. Dixon School of Accounting at the University of Central Florida. She received her Ph.D. from the University of Waterloo and a B.Comm. from the University of Windsor. Her research interests include the manager's use of accounting information for decision making, the effects of budgeting processes on performance, and accounting ethics. She has published in leading research journals including *The Accounting Review, Contemporary Accounting Research, Journal of Business Ethics*, and the *Journal of Management Accounting Research*. Professor Libby has presented her work throughout North America, Europe, and Australia. Professor Libby was awarded the L. S. Rosen Outstanding Educator Award by the Canadian Academic Accounting Association and was named as a Fellow of the Institute of Chartered Professional Accountants of Ontario in recognition of outstanding career accomplishments.

Alan Webb is the Deloitte Professor in the School of Accounting and Finance at the University of Waterloo. He is a graduate of Mount Allison University and the University of Alberta, with B.Comm. and Ph.D. degrees. His primary research interests are in the areas of incentives, goal setting, and performance measurement. Professor Webb has presented his work throughout North America and is currently the Editor-in-Chief at *Contemporary Accounting Research*. His research publications appear in *The Accounting Review, Journal of Accounting Research, Journal of Management Accounting Research, Contemporary Accounting Research, Accounting, Organizations and Society*, and *Issues in Accounting Education*. Professor Webb was awarded the L. S. Rosen Outstanding Educator Award by the Canadian Academic Accounting Association and was named a Fellow of the Institute of Chartered Professional Accountants of Ontario for his outstanding career accomplishments.

Eric W. Noreen (Co-author, U.S. Edition) is a globe-trotting academic who has held appointments at institutions in the United States, Europe, and Asia and has taught at INSEAD in France and the Hong Kong Institute of Science and Technology. He is emeritus professor of accounting at the University of Washington. Currently, he is the Accounting Circle Professor of Accounting, Fox School of Business, Temple University. He received his B.A. degree from the University of Washington and M.B.A. and Ph.D. degrees from Stanford University. A Certified Management Accountant, he was awarded a Certificate of Distinguished Performance by the Institute of Certified Management Accountants.

Peter C. Brewer (Co-author, U.S. Edition) is a Lecturer in the Department of Accountancy at Wake Forest University. Prior to joining the faculty at Wake Forest, he was an accounting professor at Miami University for 19 years. He holds a B.S. degree in accounting from Penn State University, an M.S. degree in accounting from the University of Virginia, and a Ph.D. from the University of Tennessee. He has published more than 35 articles in a variety of journals including *Management Accounting Research*, the *Journal of Information Systems*, *Cost Management*, *Strategic Finance*, the *Journal of Accountancy*, *Issues in Accounting Education*, and the *Journal of Business Logistics*. Professor Brewer has received Miami University's Richard T. Farmer School of Business Teaching Excellence Award and has been recognized on two occasions by the Miami University Associated Student Government for "making a remarkable commitment to students and their educational development." He is a leader in undergraduate management accounting curriculum innovation and the use of the case method for teaching undergraduate management accounting courses. He is a leading thinker in undergraduate management accounting curriculum innovation and is a frequent presenter at various professional and academic conferences.

Brief Contents

Contents

Chapter Eight
Variable Costing: A Tool for Management 304

SECTION 3
Planning and Control 338

Chapter Nine
Budgeting 339

SECTION 4
Short-Term and Long-Term Decisions   538

Chapter Twelve
Relevant Costs for Decision Making   539

ENHANCING PRODUCT OFFERINGS TO STAY COMPETITIVE AT WESTJET   539

COST CONCEPTS FOR DECISION MAKING   540

ANALYSIS OF VARIOUS DECISION SITUATIONS   546

UTILIZATION OF A CONSTRAINED RESOURCE   559

Chapter Thirteen
Capital Budgeting Decisions   603

GOING FOR GOLD   603

CAPITAL BUDGETING—PLANNING INVESTMENTS   604

DISCOUNTED CASH FLOWS—THE NET PRESENT VALUE METHOD   605

DISCOUNTED CASH FLOWS—THE INTERNAL RATE OF RETURN METHOD   614

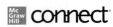

Garrison/Libby/Webb:

For centuries, the lighthouse has stood as a beacon of guidance for mariners at sea. More than an aid to navigation, the lighthouse symbolizes safety, permanence, reliability, and the comforts of the familiar.

For this reason, we continue to illustrate the twelfth Canadian edition of our flagship accounting publication, *Managerial Accounting* by Garrison, Libby, and Webb, with an image that we feel encapsulates the greatest strengths of this market-leading text.

Garrison is your guide through the challenges of learning managerial accounting. It identifies the three functions that managers must perform within their organizations—plan operations, control activities, and make decisions—and explains the managerial accounting information necessary for these functions; how to collect, prepare, or analyze it; and, just as importantly, how to interpret that information. To achieve this, the twelfth Canadian edition of *Managerial Accounting* focuses, now as in the past, on three qualities: relevance, balance, and clarity.

Your guide through the challenges of learning managerial accounting

Relevance. Every effort is made to help students relate the concepts in this book to the decisions made by actual managers in practice. With chapter openers based on real-world scenarios, in-chapter examples providing practical applications, beyond the bottom line features, knowledge in action summaries, and extensive end-of-chapter material, a student reading Garrison should never have to ask, "Why am I learning this?"

Balance. Garrison provides extensive examples and end-of-chapter material covering the full breadth of business types found in practice, including manufacturing, service, tech sector, retail, and not-for-profit entities. Moreover, we feature a range of small to large companies to show the relevance of management accounting to organizations of differing size and complexity.

Clarity. Generations of students have praised Garrison for its accessibility and readability, but that's just the beginning. Discussions of technical material have been further simplified and made more concise where possible, and the entire book has been thoroughly revised with the objective of making learning and teaching from Garrison as easy as possible. Key term definitions and icons signifying ethics, writing, and Excel assignments continue to add clarity for both students and instructors. In addition, students and instructors will work with clear, well-written supplements that employ consistent terminology.

The authors' steady focus on these three core elements has led to tremendous results.

What makes Garrison such a powerful learning tool?

Managerial Accounting is full of pedagogy designed to make studying productive. Here you will see the kind of engaging, helpful pedagogical features that make Garrison a favourite among both instructors and students.

Section Overviews
The twelfth Canadian edition is divided into five sections. One-page summaries at the beginning of each section map the chapters included and how they are related.

Opening Vignettes
These short chapter openers, based on real-world scenarios, highlight some of the issues, concepts, and decisions faced by managers that are discussed in the ensuing pages.

SECTION 2

COSTING

Chapters 5 through 8

Chapters 5 through 8 provide a comprehensive description of how costs are associated with manufacturing activities. In addition, these costing systems can be applied to service organizations and not-for-profit organizations. To permit costing for such specialized situations, two costing systems, job-order costing and process costing, can be mixed and matched.

Chapter 5 begins with the most basic and widely used costing system, *job-order costing*. Job-order costing permits costs to be assigned to specific outcomes, termed *jobs*, so that costs can be accumulated for what a company produces. In addition, manufacturing overhead—a term often shortened to just *overhead*—is assigned by a process of averaging to estimate its amount before actual overhead costs are known.

Chapter 6 introduces an averaging calculation used for costing similar units of product, termed *process costing*. The ordering of costs learned in financial accounting (namely, average and FIFO) can be applied. The idea of equivalent units is explained, so that partially finished work in process can be valued in inventory. Chapter 6 also presents an elaboration of overhead methods so that overhead can be divided up between departments (the cost object in this case) to permit better management control of overhead and more accurate costing.

Chapter 7 introduces activity-based costing, another way to divide up overhead and non-manufacturing costs. Cost objects are defined as activities, and activities are costed by identifying a relevant cost driver. By doing this, overhead costing can be improved and management can focus on managing activities rather than outcomes. Given the increasing importance of overhead costs incurred in some types of organizations, methods to improve the management of overhead costs are important.

Chapter 8 completes the costing segment by describing variable costing. Variable costing assigns only variable manufacturing costs to production as opposed to all manufacturing costs, as was described in earlier chapters under the term *absorption costing*.

CHAPTER 5

SYSTEMS DESIGN: JOB-ORDER COSTING

LEARNING OBJECTIVES

After studying Chapter 5, you should be able to

1. Distinguish between process costing and job-order costing, and identify the production or service processes that fit with each costing method.

2. Recognize the flow of costs through a job-order costing system.

3. Compute predetermined overhead rates, and explain why estimated overhead costs (rather than actual overhead costs) are used in the costing process.

4. Record the journal entries that reflect the flow of costs in a job-order costing system.

5. Apply overhead cost to work in process using a predetermined overhead rate.

6. Prepare schedules of cost of goods manufactured and cost of goods sold.

7. Compute underapplied or overapplied overhead cost, and prepare the journal entry to close the balance in

JOB COSTING AT ACCENTURE

Cavan Images / Getty Images

Accenture is one of the world's largest consulting firms, with annual revenues greater than $34 billion. Because the firm does not manufacture a physical product and therefore does not have any inventory on its balance sheet, it might be tempting to conclude that it does not need a job-order costing system. However, that is not true.

Accenture pays its consultants more than $23 billion per year to provide services for clients. Job-order costing enables the firm to compare each client's revenues to the costs of serving those clients. It also enables the firm to determine what portion of their consulting capacity was billable to clients and what portion was not billed to specific clients.

In this chapter, we will examine methods of accurately estimating the total cost by job for specifically identifiable manufactured products and services, and we will explore why this information is key to setting prices, valuing inventory, and identifying opportunities for cost control for many firms.

Source: Accenture Annual Report 2017.

Learning Aids
These pedagogical boxes emphasize and summarize key content for students.

LEARNING AID

Key Formulas for Contribution Format Income Statements

Operating income = (Unit CM × Q) – Fixed expenses
CM = Sales – Variable expenses
CM per unit = Per unit sales – Per unit variable expenses
CM ratio = Total CM ÷ Total sales or CM ratio = Per unit CM ÷ Per unit sales
Variable expense ratio = Variable expenses ÷ Sales

In these formulas, CM = contribution margin and Q = quantity of goods sold in units.

IN BUSINESS

Smaller Internet service providers such as Seaside Wireless Communications Inc., based in Nova Scotia, do not have their own broadband networks but instead pay for access to networks owned by larger telecommunication companies such as Bell Canada and Rogers Communications Inc. These smaller companies pay for access to the broadband network on a per end-user (customer) basis. Seaside's cost to access a broadband network owned by another company will therefore vary in direct proportion to the number of customers they have. Moreover, the rate per user that the owners of the broadband networks are allowed to charge companies such as Seaside is regulated by the Canadian Radio-television and Telecommunications Commission (CRTC). Since those rates are reviewed only periodically by the CRTC, companies such as Seaside will know with certainty what their variable cost will be for providing each customer with access to a broadband network.

In Business
These helpful boxed features provide examples of how some of the concepts discussed in the chapter arise in actual companies. Every chapter contains one or more of these current examples.

Knowledge in Action
These summaries provide examples of how key concepts covered in the chapter are applied by managers in practice. They are intended to reinforce the practical relevance of the material being learned.

KNOWLEDGE IN ACTION

Managers can apply their knowledge of cost terms, concepts, and classifications when:

- Preparing financial statements
- Determining selling prices for products or services
- Predicting costs when activity levels change
- Developing budgets
- Assigning costs to cost objects such as products, customers, jobs, or departments
- Deciding among various alternative courses of action
- Determining whether or not costs are relevant to a decision being made

BEYOND THE BOTTOM LINE

Some managers believe that extrinsic incentives "crowd out" employees' intrinsic motivation. That is, they think that paying people based on their performance can actually reduce the extent to which they enjoy doing their job. To avoid this possibility, some companies pay only salaries to their employees and have no performance-based pay. Management in these companies believes that if employees are paid a fair salary and enjoy their job, intrinsic motivation will be high and performance-based extrinsic incentives will be unnecessary.

Beyond the Bottom Line
This feature focuses on qualitative issues about ethics and corporate social responsibility related to one or more of the topics covered in the chapter. They are intended to highlight issues that arise in many organizations that extend beyond concerns about profitability.

Managerial Accounting has earned a reputation for the best practice material of any text on the market. The twelfth Canadian edition includes both new and revised exercises, problems, and cases. Features include:

Instant Quizzes
These short questions are designed to allow students to test their understanding of key topics as they work through each chapter. Each question is intended to take only a few minutes at most to complete. Several instant quizzes are included in each chapter starting with Chapter 2. To provide feedback for the instant quizzes, solutions for all questions are provided at the end of each chapter.

INSTANT QUIZ 2-3
If a merchandising company has cost of goods sold of $250,000, purchases of $270,000 during the period, and ending merchandise inventory of $30,000, calculate the amount of beginning merchandise inventory.

REVIEW PROBLEM: COST–VOLUME–PROFIT RELATIONSHIPS

Review Problems and Solutions

Voltar Company manufactures cordless home telephones. The company's contribution format income statement for the most recent year is given below:

	Total	Per Unit	Percentage of Sales
Sales (20,000 units)	$1,200,000	$60	100%
Less variable expenses	900,000	45	?%
Contribution margin	300,000	$15	?%
Less fixed expenses	240,000		
Operating income	$ 60,000		

Discussion Cases

These short cases focus on one or more of the concepts covered in the chapter. They are designed to provoke deeper thought about key topics and to generate in-class discussion. One case has been developed for each chapter.

DISCUSSION CASE

Discussion Case 3–1

Further to the information provided in Review Problem 2, assume that all of the fixed costs pertain to the two full-time staff members who process each patient being admitted to the hospital. Each staff member is paid a salary of $4,750 per month. The variable cost per admission relates to items such as the patient identification bracelet issued to each patient, the medical history form that must be completed by each patient, and so on. You can also assume that the maximum number of patients that the two staff members can admit during any given month is 2,000. Further, if fewer than 1,000 patients were to be admitted per month on an ongoing basis, only one full-time staff member would be required.

Required:
What is the relevant range of activity for which the cost formula you calculated in Review Problem 2 applies? Discuss how management at Red Deer Hospital could use the additional information provided above to estimate costs if the number of admissions is expected to exceed 2,000 on a regular basis or to fall below 1,000 on a recurring basis.

QUESTIONS

Questions

2–1 Would costs related to the building used only by administrative personnel, such as heat and lights, property taxes, and insurance, be considered part of manufacturing overhead? Why or why not?

2–2 What are the three basic categories of manufacturing costs?

2–3 Are product costs always expensed in the period in which they are incurred? Explain.

2–4 What are administrative costs? How are they treated on the income statement?

2–5 What is the difference between raw materials inventory and work in process inventory? Are they included on the balance sheet or income statement?

2–6 If a company automates its production processes, would you expect that to increase or decrease prime costs? Why?

2–7 What is the difference between total manufacturing costs incurred and the cost of goods manufactured?

Foundational Exercises

Each chapter of the text from Chapter 2 on contains one set of foundational exercises that include "building block" questions related to one concise set of data. These exercises can be used for in-class discussion or as homework assignments. Foundational exercises are also available on Connect.

FOUNDATIONAL EXERCISES

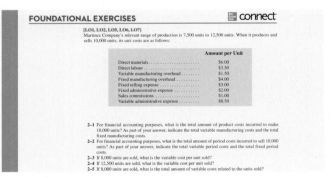

[LO1, LO2, LO5, LO6, LO7]

Martinez Company's relevant range of production is 7,500 units to 12,500 units. When it produces and sells 10,000 units, its unit costs are as follows:

	Amount per Unit
Direct materials	$6.00
Direct labour	$3.50
Variable manufacturing overhead	$1.50
Fixed manufacturing overhead	$4.00
Fixed selling expense	$3.00
Fixed administrative expense	$2.00
Sales commissions	$1.00
Variable administrative expense	$0.50

2–1 For financial accounting purposes, what is the total amount of product costs incurred to make 10,000 units? As part of your answer, indicate the total variable manufacturing costs and the total fixed manufacturing costs.

2–2 For financial accounting purposes, what is the total amount of period costs incurred to sell 10,000 units? As part of your answer, indicate the total variable period costs and the total fixed period costs.

2–3 If 8,000 units are sold, what is the variable cost per unit sold?

2–4 If 12,500 units are sold, what is the variable cost per unit sold?

2–5 If 8,000 units are sold, what is the total amount of variable costs related to the units sold?

EXERCISES

Exercises

EXERCISE 2–1 Classifying Manufacturing Costs [LO1]

The costs below all relate to Sounds Good, a company based in Alberta that manufactures high-end audio equipment such as speakers, receivers, CD players, turntables, and home theatre systems. The company owns all of the manufacturing facilities (building and equipment) but rents the space used by the non-manufacturing employees (accounting, marketing, sales, human resources).

Required:
For each cost, indicate whether it would most likely be classified as a direct labour, direct material, manufacturing overhead, marketing and selling, or administrative cost.

Problems and Check Figures

We provide Check Figures for some problems to help students confirm their calculations for key requirements.

PROBLEMS

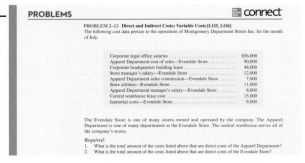

PROBLEM 2–13 Direct and Indirect Costs; Variable Costs [LO5, LO6]

The following cost data pertain to the operations of Montgomery Department Stores Inc. for the month of July.

Corporate legal office salaries	$56,000
Apparel Department cost of sales—Evendale Store	90,000
Corporate headquarters building lease	48,000
Store manager's salary—Evendale Store	12,000
Apparel Department sales commission—Evendale Store	7,000
Store utilities—Evendale Store	11,000
Apparel Department manager's salary—Evendale Store	8,000
Central warehouse lease cost	15,000
Janitorial costs—Evendale Store	9,000

The Evendale Store is one of many stores owned and operated by the company. The Apparel Department is one of many departments at the Evendale Store. The central warehouse serves all of the company's stores.

Required:
1. What is the total amount of the costs listed above that are direct costs of the Apparel Department?
2. What is the total amount of the costs listed above that are direct costs of the Evendale Store?

Excel Simulations

Simulated Excel questions, assignable within Connect, allow students to practise their Excel skills—such as using basic formulas and formatting—within the context of managerial accounting. These questions feature animated, narrated Help and Show Me tutorials (when enabled), as well as automatic feedback and grading for both students and professors.

Applying Excel

This feature links the power of Excel with managerial accounting concepts by illustrating how Excel functionality can be used to better understand accounting data. Applying Excel goes beyond plugging numbers into a template by providing students with an opportunity to build their own Excel worksheets and formulas. Students are then asked "what if" questions in which they analyze not only how related pieces of accounting data affect each other, but also what they do. Applying Excel is integrated within Connect allowing students to practise their skills online with algorithmically generated data sets.

Data Analytics Exercises

New Data Analytics Exercises teach students how to use software tools to derive managerial insights and communicate them to stakeholders. These new exercises, which appear in Connect, are linked to a diverse range of learning objectives that span numerous chapters. Some of these exercises require students to use various Microsoft Excel–based tools, such as Goal Seek, Pivot Tables, and Solver, to analyze data sets to derive solutions. Other exercises also teach students how to use a variety of data visualization techniques, such as charts, graphs, and maps, to communicate their findings in succinct and compelling ways. Additionally, some of these exercises will enable students to interpret data visualizations depicted in Tableau. Students will not need to learn Tableau to complete these exercises; rather, they will be given the opportunity to acquire the value-added skill of interpreting Tableau visualizations.

CASES ——————————— Cases

 CASE 2–28 [LO1, LO2, LO3, LO4]
John Ranton, president and founder of Running Mate, could hardly contain his excitement over the operating results for his company's second year of operations. Running Mate is an online retailer of a GPS running watch that records distance, time, speed, heart rate, and a number of other statistics. Ranton's company does not manufacture the watches, but instead purchases them directly from the manufacturer based in China and resells them through its online shopping site. During the first two years of operation, Ranton decided to hold the selling price of the watch constant at $100 per unit in an effort to attract business. He was also able to negotiate a deal with the supplier to hold Running Mate's cost per watch constant at $80 per unit for the two years.

Connecting Concepts ————————————

These challenging cases appear at the end of each of the first four sections of the book and illustrate how numerous concepts covered in each chapter can be applied to a single company. The four cases each use the same company setting and often require integration of multiple concepts from the chapters included in the section.

CONNECTING CONCEPTS

SECTION 1

COST BEHAVIOUR AND COST-VOLUME-PROFIT ANALYSIS
Easy Learning (EL) develops online learning platforms for companies using gamification techniques to make the learning experience engaging. Research shows that employees are far more likely to use learning platforms if they are easy and fun to use. EL's approach is to embed the learning content, usually a series of multiple choice questions, in the games they use in their platform. EL works with company management to develop the learning content and their platforms have been used in a wide variety of functional areas such as manufacturing, sales, customer service, distribution, and product development. EL has developed a strong reputation for being the most creative and reliable developer of online learning platforms and the company has clients across Canada and the United States.

Competition has increased considerably over the past five years, with several start-up companies offering their own versions of online learning platforms. Given this, EL is placing increased emphasis on its customer acquisition activities, which range from attending tech conventions, developing webinars, presenting their research at conferences, follow-up meetings and calls with prospective customers, and online advertising. Annual recurring revenue (ARR) for use of the learning platform from each customer averages $100,000, so acquiring and retaining customers is critical to EL's success.

 ————— Writing Assignments

These encourage students to practise critical thinking and effective writing.

 ————— Ethics Assignments

These serve as a reminder that in business ethical conduct is just as important as profits.

Focus on the Twelfth Canadian Edition

Book Philosophy and Structure

The twelfth Canadian edition uses the framework established by Garrison, Noreen, and Brewer in the seventeenth U.S. edition as a starting point. However, our text is very much unique in that it is tailored to the Canadian business and education setting. The text was written with two main goals in mind: (1) to facilitate learning through clear and concise discussion of each topic, provision of detailed examples, and extensive end-of-chapter material; and (2) to provide the flexibility necessitated by the requirements of our Canadian users. The text can be covered in a single-term course but also provides students with a valuable resource for subsequent courses in managerial accounting.

Based on positive feedback from reviewers, the order of topics in the twelfth Canadian edition has not changed. The first two chapters describe the key responsibilities of managers, their need for managerial accounting information, the role of professional ethics for management accountants, and the growing impact of big data and corporate social responsibility on managers' decision making. We also address the major differences between financial and managerial accounting and introduce key cost terms, concepts, and classifications that are used throughout the remainder of the text. The following six chapters cover topics that provide the foundation for understanding the tools and concepts covered in later chapters. Chapters 3 and 4 focus on cost behaviour patterns, cost prediction models, and cost–volume–profit analysis. The remaining foundational material is covered in Chapters 5 through 8, which collectively examine the major types of costing systems used by organizations.

Chapters 9 through 11 apply the foundational material to a variety of topics and concepts that collectively represent the major planning and control activities managers perform in organizations. Chapters 9 and 10 examine, respectively, managers' development and use of budgets, and the role of standard costs both for planning purposes and as a tool to evaluate and understand past performance. Chapter 11 examines management control techniques such as the use of responsibility centres within the organization to establish accountability and evaluation, and the design and use of performance measurement systems.

Chapters 12 and 13 present the second major application of the foundational material and focus, respectively, on short-term and long-term decision analysis and the relevant information required by managers for each. Chapter 12 introduces the concept of relevant costs and examines the approach managers *should* use for different types of decisions that involve cash inflows and outflows for a relatively short period of time. Chapter 13 focuses on longer-term decisions that typically require a significant capital expenditure at the beginning of a project and involve cash inflows and outflows over several years. We conclude with online Chapter 14, which covers financial statement analysis from the perspective of the needs and objectives of different stakeholders of the organization.

In keeping with our first major goal in writing the text, every chapter provides detailed in-chapter examples and quizzes, extensive end-of-chapter review problems, short-answer questions, exercises, problems, and cases that cover manufacturing, service, tech, and not-for-profit organizations. To accomplish our second major goal, we organize the material in the text and use appendices to cover more advanced or specialized topics in a way that will facilitate different approaches by instructors to designing course content. Moreover, our end-of-chapter material ranges considerably in difficulty to allow instructors flexibility with respect to the depth of understanding they want their students to achieve for the various topics.

What's New and Improved in the Twelfth Canadian Edition

The twelfth Canadian edition builds on the strengths of our previous editions but we continue to identify areas for improvements. Reviewer suggestions have been incorporated in the new edition as have changes identified by the authors consistent with accomplishing our two main goals identified above. Based on user feedback, we have retained all of the key features introduced in the past two editions such as in-chapter instant quizzes, Beyond the Bottom line features, Knowledge in Action summaries, Discussion Cases, Foundational Exercises, and Connecting Concepts at the end of each major section of the text. We have also added content for new CPA Canada technical competencies related to big data, data integrity and data quality, and others. As described in more detail below, we also made extensive revisions throughout the text designed to make the discussion of key concepts even more understandable for students and to update examples where needed. Based on reviewer feedback we have also removed outdated content and other material no longer considered necessary for an introductory management accounting text. As always, we have extensively updated the end-of-chapter exercises, problems, and cases, with more than one-third of the content reflecting either new or revised material.

An overview of specific improvements in each chapter of the twelfth Canadian edition is detailed below:

- **Chapter 1** includes a new section on big data and its use by managers when making decisions. New In Business examples have been added. To enhance focus on key material we have shortened the section on strategic management and removed content on lean production. The end-of-chapter material has been extensively revised.

- **Chapter 2** has been extensively rewritten to make the discussion more concise in several sections. A new chapter opener has been created and the In Business examples have been updated. The review problem has been revised and end-of-chapter material has been extensively updated with new and revised content.

- **Chapter 3** has a new chapter opener that focuses on the tech sector to demonstrate the broad relevance of management accounting. The chapter content has been updated to discuss the impact of artificial intelligence and machine learning on the cost structure in many organizations. A new In Business example has been created and several sections have been revised to make the content more concise. A new review problem has been created and the end-of-chapter material has been extensively revised.

- **Chapter 4** has a new in-chapter example on cost structure and sales mix. The discussion of indifference analysis has been removed given its limited relevance in an introductory textbook. A new In Business example has been added. The review problem has been revised and extensive updates have been made to the end-of-chapter material.

- **Chapter 5** includes a new chapter opener and In Business examples illustrating real-world applications of job-order costing in the service industry. The end-of-chapter material has been revised and reorganized so that the problem difficulty flows more naturally from easy through medium to difficult exercises and problems.

- **Chapter 6** includes an updated In Business example about process costing at the Coca-Cola Company. The end-of-chapter material has been extensively revised including the addition of more problems at a medium level of difficulty.

- **Chapter 7** includes revised In Business examples updated for currency. End-of-chapter material has been extensively revised including the addition of more problems of medium difficulty. A new appendix has also been added covering time-driven activity-based costing, which is being used more extensively in practice.

- **Chapter 8** includes a revised chapter opener, revised In Business examples, and a revised Beyond the Bottom Line feature. These revisions help to focus the chapter material on variable costing as a way to improve internal decision making and avoid incentives to overproduce. In addition, a new Learning Aid has been added to this chapter. End-of-chapter material has been extensively revised.

- **Chapter 9** has a new chapter opener based on the same company introduced in the chapter opener for Chapter 3. A new Learning Aid has been created that summarizes key assumptions managers typically make when preparing a budget. A new section on the use of forecasts has been added. The discussion of participative budgeting has been shortened and the section on budgeting in government and non-profit settings has been removed given its limited relevance in an introductory textbook. Extensive revisions have been made to the end-of-chapter material.

- **Chapter 10** includes revisions to the body of the chapter as well as the chapter opener, In Business, and Beyond the Bottom Line features to make them easier to read. End-of-chapter material has been extensively revised including reorganizing the exercises and problems to more rationally link to the chapter learning objectives.

- **Chapter 11** includes a new chapter opener and In Business feature as well as a new section on corporate social responsibility and the balanced scorecard. Appendix 11A has been streamlined to improve readability. End-of-chapter material has been extensively revised.

- **Chapter 12** has a revised chapter opener concerning relevant costing in the airline industry. In addition, a new section has been added to the appendix covering the uses of cost-based information for pricing including value-based pricing and the concept of economic value to the customer. End-of-chapter material has been extensively revised.

- **Chapter 13** has a new section on the role of data quality and integrity in capital budgeting decisions. A new In Business example has been added. The writing has been streamlined throughout the chapter to improve readability. Back by popular demand from users, present value tables are now included in Appendix 13A. End-of-chapter material has been extensively revised.

- In **Chapter 14**, an online chapter, examples have been updated.

Award-Winning Technology

McGraw Hill Connect® McGraw Hill *Connect®* is an award-winning digital teaching and learning solution that empowers students to achieve better outcomes and enables instructors to improve efficiency with course management. Within Connect, students have access to SmartBook®, McGraw Hill's adaptive learning and reading resource. SmartBook prompts students with questions based on the material they are studying. By assessing individual answers, SmartBook learns what each student knows and identifies which topics they need to practise, giving each student a personalized learning experience and path to success.

Connect's key features also include analytics and reporting, simple assignment management, smart grading, the opportunity to post your own resources, and the Connect Instructor Library, a repository for additional resources to improve student engagement in and out of the classroom.

Instructor Resources for Garrison Twelfth Canadian Edition

The following instructor resources are available online on Connect:

Instructor's Manual The *Instructor's Manual* includes chapter overviews, assignment grids featuring levels of difficulty, and chapter-by-chapter lists of service examples.

Solutions Manual This supplement contains completely worked out solutions to all assignment material and a general discussion of the use of group exercises.

In addition, the manual contains suggested course outlines and a listing of exercises, problems, and cases scaled according to difficulty.

Computerized Test Bank Nearly 2,000 questions are organized by chapter and include true/false, multiple-choice, and essay questions, plus computational problems. Use it to make different versions of the same test, change the answer order, edit and add questions, and conduct online testing. Technical support for this software is available. The files are also available in RTF for printing.

Microsoft® PowerPoint® Slides Available on Connect, these slides offer a great visual complement for your lectures. A complete set of slides covers each chapter.

Microsoft® Excel® Templates These are the solutions to the Microsoft Excel templates offered online.

End-of-Chapter Problems

Connect for Garrison *Managerial Accounting* twelfth Canadian edition provides assignable, gradable end-of-chapter content to help students learn how to solve problems and apply concepts. Advanced algorithms allow students to practise problems multiple times to ensure full comprehension of each problem.

Excel Simulation Problems

Excel Simulation Problems allow students to master their Excel skills within the context of managerial accounting. The problems feature animated and narrated Help and Show Me tutorials for students, with automatic feedback and grading.

Effective. Efficient. Easy to Use.

McGraw-Hill Connect is an award-winning digital teaching and learning solution that empowers students to achieve better outcomes and enables instructors to improve course-management efficiency.

Personalized & Adaptive Learning

Connect's integrated SmartBook helps students study more efficiently, highlighting where in the text to focus and asking review questions to give each student a personalized learning experience and path to success.

High-Quality Course Material

Our trusted solutions are designed to help students actively engage in course content and develop critical higher-level thinking skills, while offering you the flexibility to tailor your course to meet your needs.

Analytics & Reporting

Monitor progress and improve focus with Connect's visual and actionable dashboards. Reporting features empower instructors and students with real-time performance analytics.

Seamless Integration

Link your Learning Management System with Connect for single sign-on and gradebook synchronization, with all-in-one ease for you and your students.

Impact of Connect on Pass Rates

72.5%

Without Connect

85.2%

With Connect

SMARTBOOK

NEW SmartBook 2.0 builds on our market-leading adaptive technology with enhanced capabilities and a streamlined interface that deliver a more usable, accessible and mobile learning experience for both students and instructors.

Available on mobile smart devices – with both online and offline access – the ReadAnywhere app lets students study anywhere, anytime.

SUPPORT AT EVERY STEP

McGraw-Hill ensures you are supported every step of the way. From course design and set up, to instructor training, LMS integration and ongoing support, your Digital Success Consultant is there to make your course as effective as possible.

Learn more about Connect at mheducation.ca

Reviewers

The efforts of many people are needed to develop and improve a text. Among these people are the reviewers and consultants who point out areas of concern, cite areas of strength, and make recommendations for change. In this regard, the professors named on this page provided feedback that was enormously helpful in preparing the twelfth Canadian edition of *Managerial Accounting*.

Suggestions have been received from many of our colleagues across Canada and throughout the world who have used the prior editions of *Managerial Accounting*. This is vital feedback that we rely on in each edition. Each of those who have offered comments and suggestions has our thanks.

Robert Chapman, *Mount Royal University*
Elliott Currie, *University of Guelph*
Kalinga Jagoda, *University of Guelph*
Amy Kwan, *University of Toronto*
Darlene Lowe, *MacEwan University*
Joe Toste, *Centennial College*

Acknowledgements

The twelfth Canadian edition of *Managerial Accounting* has benefited from the assistance of numerous individuals and groups. This assistance was invaluable in providing us with materials, review comments and suggestions, and technical assistance. Commissioned reviewers across Canada assisted with suggestions and clarifications that reflect their views of the materials they examined.

Materials were provided by the American Accounting Association, CGA-Canada and CMA-Canada (both now part of CPA Canada), and SAP Canada. In each case, an acknowledgement is included when the material is used in the textbook. The U.S. authors acknowledge materials provided by the AICPA, the Institute of Certified Management Accountants, and the Chartered Institute of Management Accountants (United Kingdom).

We also received invaluable input and support through the years from present and former colleagues and students. We are indebted to the following individuals who helped adapt, critique, and shape the ancillary package for the Canadian market: Shannon Butler, *Carleton University*; Robert Chapman, *Mount Royal University*; Heather Cornish, *NAIT*; Robert Ducharme, *University of Waterloo*; Kathy Falk, *University of Toronto*; Kalinga Jagoda, *University of Guelph*; Debra Lee Hue, *Centennial College* and *Durham College*; Marc Seguin, *Algonquin College*.

The extraordinary efforts of a talented group of individuals at McGraw Hill made all of this come together. We especially thank Alwynn Pinard, for her guidance throughout this project; Amy Rydzanicz, for initiating the developmental work for this edition and for tirelessly following the whole process through until the final printing; Jessica Barnoski, who managed the final production of this book; and all the marketing and sales people who helped bring this book to both instructors and students. We also thank all those who worked behind the scenes to ensure the successful completion of this book. Special thanks to Kelli Howey for her careful editing and proofreading of the entire textbook.

Despite the assistance we received, we acknowledge our responsibility for the contents of this book. We appreciate suggestions and questions from our users.

Learning Aids

Chapter 2

- Summary of Cost Classifications
- Summary of Variable and Fixed Cost Behaviour

Chapter 4

- Key Formulas for Contribution Format Income Statements
- Cost–Volume–Profit Analysis
- Single-Product CVP Analysis
- Multi-Product CVP Analysis

Chapter 5

- Summary of Overhead Concepts

Appendix 6A

- Comparison of Process Costing Methods

Chapter 7

- Activity-Based Costing versus Traditional Product Costing

Chapter 8

- Variable Costing versus Absorption Costing
- Comparative Income Effects of Absorption and Variable Costing

Chapter 9

- Estimates and Assumptions for a Master Budget

Chapter 10

- Summary of Variance Formulas for Variable Costs

Chapter 11

- Elements of Return on Investment

Appendix 11A

- Range of Negotiated Transfer Prices

Chapter 12

- Keep or Drop a Product/Segment
- Make or Buy
- Accept or Reject a Special Order
- Sell or Process Further

Chapter 13

- WACC as a Screening Tool
- Net Present Value and Internal Rate of Return Methods

Appendix 13B

- Tax Adjustments Required in a Capital Budgeting Analysis
- Net Present Value and Internal Rate of Return Methods (with Taxes)

Online Chapter 14

- Summary of Ratios

SECTION

1

OVERVIEW AND FOUNDATION

Chapters 1 through 4

Chapters 1 and 2 present background material and also introduce information on topics appearing in later chapters. Chapters 3 and 4 focus on cost behaviour patterns, cost prediction models, and cost–volume–profit analysis. These topics provide the foundation for later chapters on costing techniques, budgeting, standard costs, and decision analysis. Thus, it is important to study these chapters carefully to be prepared for what comes later!

Chapter 1 describes managers' key responsibilities and how managerial accounting can help in fulfilling them. The chapter highlights the key differences between financial and managerial accounting. The importance of ethics and corporate social responsibility for accountants are also covered, and some key managerial concepts important in today's organizations are discussed.

Chapter 2 begins by describing how costs are classified and explains the distinction between product and period costs. Next, the steps involved in calculating cost of goods sold and the cost of goods manufactured are presented. These calculations provide the structure for the costing methods covered in subsequent chapters. Chapter 2 also presents a basic discussion of cost behaviour, which is important to numerous topics in later chapters. The chapter concludes with a discussion of cost classifications for assigning costs to cost objects and for decision making.

Chapter 3 describes the different types of cost behaviour and how costs that contain a mix of behaviours can be identified and analyzed. Importantly, approaches to estimating mixed costs are also illustrated. The chapter also presents an alternative way of presenting revenue and expense information, the contribution format, which subsequent chapters will show is very useful in evaluating the impact of short-term decisions on operating income.

Chapter 4 builds on the concept of cost behaviour and incorporates revenues to provide commonly used tools for analysis and short-term decision making, including cost–volume–profit analysis and break-even analysis with and without corporate income taxes.

CHAPTER 1

MANAGERIAL ACCOUNTING AND THE BUSINESS ENVIRONMENT

■ THE ROLE OF THE PROFESSIONAL ACCOUNTANT IN CREATING AND SUSTAINING VALUE

Caia Image / Glow Images

The role of accountants in organizations has evolved considerably over the past 10 years. No longer considered to be just "bean-counters" who compile and report information internally in organizations, today's professional accountants working in industry are expected to have expertise in management accounting, finance, strategy and governance. Moreover, they play a key leadership role in decision making and managing employees across the various functional areas of an organization. From operational-level decisions related to quality control to strategic planning decisions about the products to offer and the markets in which the company will compete, professional accountants can add value. In Canada, the Chartered Professional Accountant (CPA) is highly regarded by employers and CPAs often hold senior management positions such as Chief Financial Officer, Treasurer and Vice-President.

Managerial accounting primarily concerns providing information to people inside an organization who direct and control its operations. In contrast, **financial accounting** primarily concerns providing information to shareholders, creditors, and others who are outside an organization. Managerial accounting provides data that help organizations run more efficiently. Financial accounting provides the scorecard by which a company's past performance is judged.

Managerial accounting concerns developing information and analysis to help managers make business decisions that satisfy customers and other stakeholders while continuously monitoring costs and improving efficiencies. This requires management accountants to prepare a variety of reports. Some reports compare actual results to plans and to benchmarks focusing on how well managers or business units have performed. Other reports provide timely updates on key non-financial and financial indicators, such as orders received, customer acquisition costs, customer satisfaction, and sales. Reports may also be prepared as needed to help investigate specific problems, such as a decline in profitability of a product line, or to help decide whether to outsource some of the business operations. In contrast, financial accounting focuses on a limited set of specific quarterly and annual financial statements prepared in accordance with generally accepted accounting principles (GAAP) and government regulations.

Because managerial accounting is manager-oriented, its study must be preceded by some understanding of what managers do, the information managers need, and the general business environment. Accordingly, the purpose of this chapter is to briefly examine these subjects.

■ THE WORK OF MANAGERS AND THEIR NEED FOR MANAGERIAL ACCOUNTING INFORMATION

Every organization—large and small—has managers who perform several major activities—*planning*, *directing and motivating*, *controlling*, and *decision making*. **Planning** involves establishing goals and specifying how to achieve them. **Directing and motivating** involve mobilizing people to carry out plans and run routine operations. **Controlling** involves gathering feedback to ensure that the plan is being properly executed or modified as circumstances change. **Decision making** involves selecting a course of action from competing alternatives. Managerial accounting information plays a vital role in these basic management activities; below we take a closer look at each.

Planning

Assume that you work for Scotiabank and that you are in charge of the company's campus recruiting for all undergraduate accounting majors. In this example, your planning process begins by establishing a goal such as this: to recruit the best and brightest university and college graduates. The next stage of the planning process requires specifying how to achieve this goal by answering numerous questions:

- How many students do we need to hire in total?
- What schools do we plan to include in our recruiting efforts?
- How will we compare students to one another to decide who will be extended job offers?
- What salary will we offer our new hires?
- How much money can we spend on our recruiting efforts?

Plans are often accompanied by a **budget**. A budget is a detailed plan for the future that is usually expressed in formal quantitative terms. As the head of campus recruiting at Scotiabank, your budget includes two key components. First, you must work with other managers inside the company to establish a budgeted amount of total salaries that can be offered to all new hires. Second, you must create a budget that quantifies how much you intend to spend on your campus recruiting activities. Chapter 9 examines the budget preparation process in detail.

Managerial accounting
Purpose is to provide information to managers for use in planning and controlling operations and for decision making.

Financial accounting
Purpose is to provide information to shareholders, creditors, and other stakeholders outside the organization.

LEARNING OBJECTIVE
Describe the functions performed by managers.

Planning
Developing goals and specifying how to achieve them.

Directing and motivating
Mobilizing people to carry out plans and run routine operations.

Controlling
Gathering feedback to ensure that the plan is being properly executed or modified as necessary.

Decision making
Selecting a course of action from among alternatives.

Budget
A quantitative plan for acquiring and using financial and other resources over a specified future time period.

Directing and Motivating

In addition to planning for the future, managers must oversee day-to-day activities and keep the organization functioning smoothly. This requires motivating and directing people. Managers assign tasks to employees, arbitrate disputes, answer questions, solve on-the-spot problems, and make many small decisions that affect customers and employees. For example, managers at Scotiabank need to assign specific employees the task of scheduling and conducting student interviews. Other employees are charged with determining the appropriate salary level for new hires. Moreover, managers need to establish procedures for resolving differences in opinion that inevitably arise when deciding which students should receive job offers. In effect, directing is the part of managers' activities that deals with the routine and the here and now. Managerial accounting data are often used in this type of day-to-day decision making.

Controlling

Once you have established and started implementing Scotiabank's recruiting plan, you transition to the control process. This process involves gathering, evaluating, and responding to feedback to ensure that this year's recruiting process meets expectations. It also includes evaluating the feedback to find ways to run a more effective recruiting campaign next year. The control process involves answering questions such as these:

- Did we succeed in hiring the planned number of students at each school?
- Is our method of comparing students to one another working?
- Did we stay within our budget for spending on recruiting activities?

As you can see, many questions need to be answered as part of the control process. When answering these questions, your goal is to go beyond simple yes or no answers to find out why performance exceeded or failed to meet expectations. Part of the control process includes preparing **performance reports**. A performance report compares budgeted data to actual data on a periodic basis, usually monthly, to identify and learn from excellent performance and to identify and eliminate sources of unsatisfactory performance. Performance reports can also be used as one of many inputs to help evaluate and reward employees. Chapters 9, 10, and 11 include examples of different types of performance reports used by organizations.

Performance reports Detailed reports prepared on a periodic basis that compare budgeted data to actual data.

Although our example focused on Scotiabank's campus recruiting efforts, we could have described how planning enables companies such as BCE, Rogers, and Telus to continuously improve their wireless networks, or how it helped NAD Electronics develop and market its home audio systems. We could have discussed how the control process helps Pfizer and Eli Lilly ensure that their pharmaceutical drugs are produced in conformance with rigorous quality standards, or how Sobeys relies on the control process to keep its grocery shelves stocked with top-selling products. We could also have looked at planning and control failures such as Boeing's recent problems with the anti-stall system in its 737 Max aircraft. In short, all managers perform planning and controlling activities.

IN BUSINESS

Companies are increasingly using wearable technology such as smartwatches, scanners, and smart glasses to improve employee productivity. In a very real sense this technology is being used as part of the organization's control system. For example, at GE Aviation, mechanics use smart glasses that allow them to check reference manuals without needing to interrupt their work. However, a UK study shows that some workers have concerns that wearable technology allows their employers to engage in excessive monitoring of their behaviour and may lead to discriminatory practices using health data tracked by some wearable devices. Best practices suggest that companies need to be mindful not only of the enhanced control benefits that can arise from the use of wearable technology, but also of the potential costs that may come in the form of employee concerns about how the technology will be used.

Decision Making

Perhaps the most basic managerial skill is the ability to make intelligent, data-driven decisions. Broadly speaking, many of those decisions revolve around the following three questions. *What* should we be selling? *Whom* should we be serving? *How* should we execute? Exhibit 1–1 provides examples of decisions pertaining to each of these three categories.

The left-hand column of Exhibit 1–1 suggests that every company must make decisions related to the products and services that it sells. For example, each year Rogers must decide how to allocate its marketing budget across the various products and services it sells. Air Canada must decide what ticket prices to establish for each of its approximately 1,600 flights per day. Paradigm Electronics must decide whether to discontinue certain models of home theatre speakers.

The middle column of Exhibit 1–1 indicates that all companies must make decisions related to the customers that they serve. For example, Hudson's Bay Company must decide how to allocate its marketing budget between products that tend to appeal to male versus female customers. FedEx must decide whether to expand its services into new markets across the globe. Royal Bank of Canada must decide whether to discontinue customers that may be unprofitable.

The right-hand column of Exhibit 1–1 shows that companies also make decisions related to how they execute. For example, Bombardier must decide whether to rely on outside vendors to manufacture many of the parts used to make its trains. In an economic downturn, a manufacturer might have to decide whether to eliminate one eight-hour shift at each of three plants or to close one plant. Finally, all companies have to decide among competing improvement opportunities. For example, a company may have to decide whether to implement a new software system, to upgrade a piece of equipment, or to provide extra training to its employees.

Big Data

Increasingly, companies are making the types of decisions described in the previous section using analytical approaches that employ extensive amounts of data from a variety of sources. Experts estimate that every second of every day we are creating 1.7 megabytes of new information per person. Given our global population of more than 7.5 billion people, this is a truly astonishing rate of data generation. However, less than 0.5% of these data are currently being analyzed and used to support decision making, thereby suggesting that business managers have an extraordinary opportunity to harness what is known as the *big data* phenomenon. **Big data** refers to large collections of data that are gathered from inside or outside a company to provide opportunities for ongoing reporting and analysis. Big data can be both "structured," such as memos and reports, and "unstructured," such as videos, pictures, audio, and other digital forms.

Big data
Large collections of data that are gathered from inside or outside a company to provide opportunities for ongoing reporting and analysis.

EXHIBIT 1–1   Examples of Decisions

What should we be selling?	Whom should we be serving?	How should we execute?
What products and services should be the focus of our marketing efforts?	Who should be the focus of our marketing efforts?	How should we market our products and services and through what mediums?
What new products and services should we offer?	Whom should we start serving with these new products and services?	How should we expand our capacity to produce these new products and deliver the new services?
What prices should we charge for our products and services?	Who should pay price premiums or receive price discounts?	How should we determine the appropriate premiums and discounts?
What products and services should we discontinue?	Whom should we stop serving?	How should we reduce our capacity?

Big data is often discussed in terms of five Vs. The first three of those Vs—variety, volume, and velocity—refine the definition of big data. *Variety* refers to the data formats in which information is stored. This includes traditional forms and digital formats, including social media as well as click-streams on a webpage, sensor-enabled feedback, and Internet-based audio/video files. *Volume* refers to the continuously expanding quantity of data that companies must gather, cleanse, organize, and analyze. For larger companies, this can be hundreds of petabytes of data (where one petabyte equals one million gigabytes). *Velocity* speaks to the rate at which data are received and acted on by organizations. This is particularly important where the data have a limited shelf life. For example, retailers can better match supply with demand if they are receiving and responding to sales data in seconds or minutes rather than days or weeks.

The remaining Vs—value and veracity—define users' expectations with respect to big data. The concept of *value* implies that the expenditure of time and money by organizations to analyze big data needs to result in insights that are valued by stakeholders. For example, shareholders expect big data analysis to translate into financial benefits, such as rising sales, increased return on investment, and a higher stock price. *Veracity* refers to the fact that users expect their data to be accurate and trustworthy. For management accounting professionals, veracity may be the most important of the five Vs because their analysis and opinions, which are relied on by numerous stakeholders (such as managers, investors, and regulators), must be supported by verifiable data.

From a managerial accounting standpoint, the goal for managers is to use *data analytics* to derive value from big data. **Data analytics** refers to the process of analyzing data with the aid of specialized systems and software to draw conclusions about the information they contain. Managers often communicate the findings from their data analysis to others through the use of *data visualization* techniques, such as graphs, charts, maps, and diagrams.

Data analytics can be used for descriptive, diagnostic, predictive, and prescriptive purposes. *Descriptive analytics* are used to answer the question: What happened? For example, managers may use them to better understand historical trends in revenues and expenses. *Diagnostic analytics* are used to answer the question: Why did it happen? For example, managers may analyze economic indicators, such as changes in the unemployment rate, to help explain why sales increased or decreased. *Predictive analytics* are used to answer the question: What will happen? For example, managers can use predictive techniques, such as regression analysis, to estimate sales or expenses for the next month, quarter, or year. Finally, *prescriptive analytics* can be used to answer the question: What should I do? For example, managers may use prescriptive analytics to decide which products should be promoted, de-emphasized, or discontinued.

Data analytics
The process of analyzing data with aid of specialized systems and software to draw conclusions about the information they contain.

The Planning and Control Cycle

Planning and control cycle
The flow of management activities through planning, directing and motivating, and controlling, and then back to planning again.

The work of management discussed in this part of the chapter is summarized in the model shown in Exhibit 1–2. The model, which depicts the **planning and control cycle**, illustrates

EXHIBIT 1–2   The Planning and Control Cycle

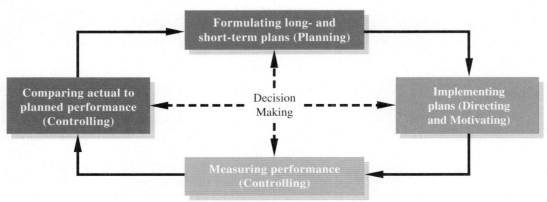

the smooth flow of management activities from planning through directing and motivating, controlling, and then back to planning again. All of these activities involve decision making, so it is depicted as the hub around which the other activities revolve.

Managerial accounting can help serve the information needs of managers in all phases of the planning and control cycle. The management accountant can prepare detailed reports that managers need to make both day-to-day and long-term decisions, and also prepare budgets to help direct resources toward the organization's goals. Later, the management accountant compares actual costs and revenues with the budgeted figures and prepares reports to inform management about any significant variances from budget. Management information needs vary from business to business, but as you work your way through this book, you will be introduced to many of the tools that management accountants use to meet these needs.

Strategic Management

As a fundamental element of the planning and control cycle, companies must have a viable long-run strategy for succeeding in the marketplace. A **strategy** is a game plan that enables a company to attract and retain customers by distinguishing itself from competitors. The focal point of a company's strategy should be its target customers. A company can succeed only if it creates a reason for customers to repeatedly choose it over the competition. These reasons, or what are more formally called *customer value propositions*, are the essence of strategy. Value propositions typically focus on providing customers with one of the following: products or services with exceptional quality and innovation, operational excellence (i.e., low-cost products or services with reliable service), or outstanding customer service.

Managerial accounting plays a critical role in providing information to management to facilitate strategy implementation and monitoring. For example, many companies employ sophisticated performance measurement systems, such as the balanced scorecard (discussed in Chapter 11), that track performance on key metrics that management believes are critical to the success of the chosen strategy. For example, if product quality and innovation is central to the value proposition, then measures of customer satisfaction with quality or the number of new features added to existing products could be used.

Strategy
A game plan that enables a company to attract and retain customers by distinguishing itself from competitors.

■ COMPARISON OF FINANCIAL AND MANAGERIAL ACCOUNTING

Financial accounting reports are prepared for external parties, such as shareholders and creditors, whereas managerial accounting reports are typically prepared for individuals inside the organization. This distinction in the users of the information results in a number of major differences between financial and managerial accounting, even though both financial and managerial accounting typically rely on the same underlying financial data. These differences are summarized in Exhibit 1–3.

As shown in Exhibit 1–3, in addition to the reports being prepared for different users, financial and managerial accounting also differ in their emphasis between the past and the future, in the type of data provided to users, and in several other ways. These differences are discussed in the following sections.

LEARNING OBJECTIVE **2**
Identify the major differences and similarities between financial and managerial accounting.

Emphasis on the Future

Since *planning* is such an important part of the manager's job, managerial accounting has a strong future orientation. In contrast, financial accounting primarily summarizes past financial transactions. These summaries may be useful in planning, but only to a point. Changes are constantly taking place in economic conditions, customer needs and desires, competitive conditions, and so on. All of these changes require that managers' planning be based in large part on estimates of what will happen rather than on summaries of what has already happened.

EXHIBIT 1–3   Comparison of Financial and Managerial Accounting

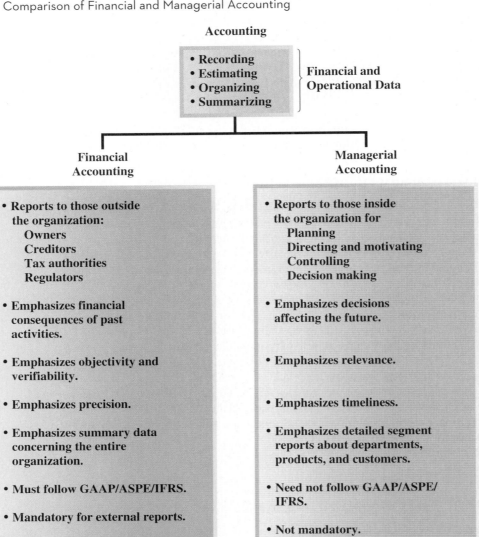

Relevance of Data

Financial accounting data are expected to be objective and verifiable. However, for internal use, managers need information that is relevant even if it is not completely objective or verifiable. By relevant, we mean *appropriate for the decision being made*. For example, it is difficult to verify estimated sales volumes for a new product, but this is exactly the type of information that is most useful to managers in their decision making. Managerial accounting should be flexible enough to provide whatever data are relevant for a particular decision.

Less Emphasis on Precision

Making sure that amounts are highly accurate can take time and effort. While a high degree of accuracy is required for external reports, most managers would rather have timely information than have to wait for more accurate information. Moreover, some decisions such as product pricing or major investments are highly time sensitive and need to be made quickly. For this reason, management accounting often places less emphasis on precision than financial accounting. For example, in a decision involving hundreds of millions of dollars, estimates that are rounded to the nearest million dollars are probably good enough.

Segments of an Organization

Financial accounting is primarily concerned with reporting for the company as a whole. By contrast, managerial accounting focuses much more on the parts, or **segments**, of a company. These segments can be evaluated independently from other parts of the organization and may be product lines, individual customers, sales territories, divisions, departments, or any other categorization of the company's activities for which management finds it useful to have financial data. Financial accounting does require some breakdowns of revenues and costs by major segments in external reports, but this is a secondary emphasis. In managerial accounting, segment analysis and reporting is the primary emphasis.

Segments
Any parts of an organization that can be evaluated independently of other parts and about which the manager seeks financial or non-financial data.

Generally Accepted Accounting Principles

Financial accounting statements prepared for external users must be prepared in accordance with generally accepted accounting principles (GAAP). External users must have some assurance that the reports have been prepared in accordance with some common set of standards. In Canada, public companies are required to use International Financial Reporting Standards (IFRS) when preparing financial statements for external use. The purpose of IFRS is to enhance the comparability and clarity of financial information on a global basis. Private companies and not-for-profit organizations are not required to adopt IFRS but instead can use accounting standards for private enterprises (ASPE). While the common ground rules established by IFRS enhance comparability across external reporting jurisdictions, they do not necessarily lead to the type of reports that would be most useful in internal decision making since they are still based on historical information.

Because managerial accounting is not bound by GAAP, managers have flexibility to determine the content and form of internal reports to best suit the needs of the organization. The only constraint is that the expected benefits from using the information should outweigh the costs of collecting, analyzing, and summarizing the data.

Managerial Accounting—Not Mandatory

Financial accounting is mandatory; that is, it must be done using the rules established as part of the IFRS. Various outside parties, such as the provincial and territorial securities regulators and the tax authorities, require periodic financial statements. Managerial accounting, on the other hand, is not mandatory. No regulatory bodies or other outside agencies specify the information that has to be compiled, analyzed, or reported internally. Since managerial accounting is completely optional, before compiling, analyzing, and reporting information internally managers must always ask themselves "Will the information be beneficial?" rather than "Is the information required?" Because of this, there is considerable variation in practice regarding the extent to which the tools and techniques covered in this book are used by companies. Smaller and younger companies tend to rely on a limited number of management accounting techniques such as budgets and basic cost allocation approaches, while larger more established companies employ more sophisticated techniques such as the balanced scorecard, activity-based costing, and discounted cash flow analysis.

◼ MANAGERIAL ACCOUNTING: THE BROADER CONTEXT

It is important to understand that managers apply the concepts and tools covered in the subsequent chapters in a broad business context. This broad context includes enterprise risk management, ethics, corporate social responsibility, and leadership. Each of these contextual factors is briefly described below.

LEARNING OBJECTIVE ❸
Explain the basic concept of enterprise risk management.

EXHIBIT 1–4   Business Functions Making Up the Value Chain

Research and Development	Product Design	Manufacturing	Marketing	Distribution	Customer Service

Enterprise Risk Management

Business process
A series of steps that are followed to carry out some task or activity in a business.

A key challenge for managers is to continuously improve the *business processes* that are required to deliver products or services to the company's customers. A **business process** is a series of steps that are followed to carry out some task or activity in a business. It is quite common for the linked set of steps making up a business process to span departmental boundaries. The term *value chain* is often used when we look at how the functional departments of an organization interact with one another to form business processes. A **value chain**, as shown in Exhibit 1–4, consists of the major business functions that add value to a company's products and services. The customer's needs are most effectively met by coordinating the business processes that span these functions.

Value chain
Consists of the major business functions that add value to a company's products and services.

Enterprise risk management
A process used by a company to proactively identify and manage foreseeable risks.

Every business strategy or decision involves risks. **Enterprise risk management** is an approach used by companies to manage, protect, and improve business processes by proactively identifying and managing risks. Some risks are foreseeable. For example, a company could reasonably be expected to foresee the possibility of a natural disaster or a fire destroying its centralized data storage facility. Companies respond to this type of risk by maintaining off-site backup data storage facilities.

Companies should identify foreseeable risks before they occur rather than react to unfortunate events that have already happened. The left-hand column of Exhibit 1–5 provides

EXHIBIT 1–5   Identifying and Controlling Business Risks

Examples of Business Risks	Examples of Controls to Reduce Business Risks
• Customer information being stolen from computer files	• Create firewalls that prohibit computer hackers from corrupting or stealing customer information.
• Products harming customers	• Develop a formal and rigorous new product-testing program.
• Losing market share due to the unforeseen actions of competitors	• Develop an approach for legally gathering information about competitors' plans and practices.
• A website malfunctioning	• Thoroughly test the website before going live on the Internet.
• A supplier strike halting the availability of raw materials for production	• Establish a relationship with two or more companies capable of providing needed raw materials.
• A poorly designed incentive scheme causing employees to make bad or high-risk decisions	• Establish an appropriate level of performance-based pay in conjunction with other employee benefits not dependent on performance.
• An employee stealing assets	• Segregate duties so that the same employee does not have physical custody of an asset and the responsibility of accounting for it.
• An employee accessing unauthorized information from databases	• Create password-protected data access or use encryption techniques to prevent employees from obtaining information not needed to do their jobs.
• Inaccurate budget estimates causing inefficient use of resources	• Implement a rigorous budget review process.
• Failing to comply with equal employment opportunity laws	• Create a report that tracks key metrics related to compliance with the laws.

10 examples of business risks. This list is not exhaustive; rather, its purpose is to illustrate the diverse nature of business risks that companies face. Whether the risks relate to the weather, computer hackers, complying with the law, employee theft, financial reporting, or strategic decision making, they all have one thing in common: if the risks are not managed effectively, they can impair a company's ability to meet its goals.

Once a company identifies its risks it can respond to them in various ways, such as accepting, avoiding, sharing, or reducing the risk. Perhaps the most common risk management tactic is to reduce risks by implementing specific controls. The right-hand column of Exhibit 1–5 provides an example of a control that could be implemented to help reduce each of the risks mentioned in the left-hand column of the exhibit.

In conclusion, a sophisticated enterprise risk management system cannot guarantee that all risks are eliminated. Nonetheless, many companies understand that managing risks is superior to reacting, perhaps too late, to unfortunate events.

■ ETHICS

LEARNING OBJECTIVE 4
Explain the nature and importance of ethics for accountants.

A series of high-profile financial scandals in the public and private sectors have raised deep concerns about ethics in business and government. There are good reasons for companies to be concerned about their ethical reputation. A company that is not trusted by its customers, employees, and suppliers will eventually suffer. In the short run virtue is sometimes its own reward, but in the long run business ethics should be taken seriously because the very survival of the company may depend on the level of trust held by its stakeholders.

Professional accounting organizations are given the right of association and certain rights of self-government by provincial and territorial governments in Canada. One inherent requirement of such rights is an expression of public service in the form of a code of ethics. Typically, these codes outline professional behaviour in terms of how members should conduct themselves in their dealings with the public, their association, and other members. Professional accountants must be familiar with their code of ethics because the rules for professional behaviour, competence, confidentiality, integrity, and objectivity are complex in real situations.

Businesses are organizations comprising employees pursuing goals and objectives. These organizations have formal relationships among their employees, but informal relationships and activities are also present that must focus on achieving the objectives of a wide group of people known as *stakeholders*. Stakeholders are people within and outside the organization who have an interest in the activities of the organization. Employees, shareholders, and creditors have an obvious interest in what the organization does, but so do the customers, the suppliers, the competitors, and the communities in which the organization operates. All of these stakeholders can benefit from the organization's undertakings, but they can also be harmed by these activities.

To reduce the likelihood that employees will engage in undesirable activities that may harm various stakeholders, many companies prepare a formal code of conduct to reflect their values and moral system. The document specifies what is expected of permanent and temporary employees in their dealings with the various stakeholders. Thus, the code reflects what the company stands for when it interacts through its employees with other stakeholders. Public companies often make their code of conduct available online. For example, the code of conduct for the Canadian Imperial Bank of Commerce (CIBC) provides standards for honesty and integrity, respect, conflicts of interest, community activities, and safeguarding information and assets. Moreover, codes of conduct often contain guidance on what employees should do upon observing a violation of one or more standards by a co-worker or superior. Through its code of conduct, a company can provide its employees with specific guidance as to how their activities should be conducted to reflect the values needed to achieve the objectives of the organization.

Corporate Social Responsibility

LEARNING OBJECTIVE 5
Explain the elements of corporate social responsibility.

Companies are responsible for producing financial results that satisfy shareholders, but this must be balanced against the need to conduct operations and dealings in an ethical and morally responsible fashion. Organizations have a corporate social responsibility to serve other

Corporate social responsibility (CSR)
A concept whereby organizations consider the needs of all stakeholders when making decisions.

stakeholders—such as customers, employees, suppliers, communities, and environmental and human rights advocates—whose interests are directly or indirectly affected by the company's performance. **Corporate social responsibility (CSR)** is a concept whereby organizations consider the needs of a broad set of stakeholders when making decisions. CSR extends beyond legal compliance to include voluntary actions that satisfy stakeholder expectations. Numerous companies, such as the Royal Bank of Canada, Mountain Equipment Co-op, and Canadian Tire, prominently describe issues related to environmental sustainability and social responsibility initiatives on their websites and prepare annual CSR reports that provide extensive details regarding these activities. These reports often include measures of environmental and social performance such as electricity usage, water consumption, employee safety, employee training, charitable donations, and so on.

Exhibit 1–6 presents examples of CSRs that are of interest to six stakeholder groups. Many companies are paying increasing attention to these types of broadly defined responsibilities for several reasons. First, socially responsible investors control trillions of investment capital dollars. Companies that want access to this capital must have good social performance. Second, a growing number of employees want to work for a company that recognizes and responds to its social responsibilities. Third, many customers seek to purchase products and services from socially responsible companies. Fourth, non-government organizations (NGOs) and activists are more capable than ever of tarnishing a company's reputation by publicizing its environmental or human rights missteps using social media. Given these factors, it is important to understand that a company's social performance can affect its financial performance and thus managers must establish plans, implement controls, and make decisions that consider the consequences for all key stakeholders.[1]

EXHIBIT 1–6
Examples of Corporate Social Responsibilities

Companies should provide *customers* with
- Safe products that are fairly priced.
- Competent, courteous, and rapid delivery of products and services.
- Full disclosure of product-related risks.
- Easy-to-use information systems for shopping and tracking orders.

Companies should provide *suppliers* with
- Fair contract terms and prompt payments.
- Reasonable time to prepare orders.
- Hassle-free acceptance of timely and complete deliveries.
- Cooperative rather than unilateral actions.

Companies should provide *shareholders* with
- Competent management and effective governance.
- Easy access to complete and accurate financial information.
- Full disclosure of risks.
- Honest answers to knowledgeable questions.

Companies and their suppliers should provide *employees* with
- Safe and comfortable working conditions.
- Non-discriminatory treatment and the right to organize and file grievances.
- Fair compensation.
- Opportunities for training, promotion, and personal development.

Companies should provide *communities* with
- Payment of fair taxes.
- Honest information about long-term plans, such as plant closings.
- Resources that support charities, schools, and civic activities.
- Reasonable access to media sources.

Companies should provide *environmental and human rights advocates* with
- Greenhouse gas emissions data.
- Recycling and resource conservation data.
- Child labour transparency.
- Full disclosure of suppliers located in developing countries.

IN BUSINESS

It has become standard practice for companies to regularly report on their CSR activities because of the demand for this information by internal (e.g., employees) and external (e.g., investors) stakeholders. For example, Canadian Tire reports metrics on factory worker safety, ethical sourcing of goods, business social compliance, and charity programs such as Jumpstart. CSR performance has become so important that numerous agencies now exist that rate and rank companies on how well they are doing with respect to social and environmental performance. For example, in 2018 Mountain Equipment Co-op and Canadian Tire were the top-rated Canadian companies with respect to CSR performance according to CR Rep Trak.

■ LEADERSHIP

LEARNING OBJECTIVE 6
Explain how intrinsic motivation, extrinsic incentives, and cognitive biases affect employee behaviour.

As noted in the chapter opener, increasingly management accountants are playing a key role as leaders in organizations given their breadth of expertise. Important to the role of leaders is managing employees. An organization's employees bring diverse needs, beliefs, and goals to the workplace. Leaders must be able to unite the behaviours of employees around two common themes—pursuing strategic goals and making optimal decisions. To fulfill this responsibility, leaders need to understand how *intrinsic motivation*, *extrinsic incentives*, and *cognitive biases* influence human behaviour.

Intrinsic Motivation

Intrinsic motivation refers to motivation that comes from within us. Stop for a moment to identify the greatest accomplishment of your life. Then ask yourself what motivated you to achieve this goal. In all likelihood, you achieved it because you wanted to, not because someone forced you to do it. In other words, you were intrinsically motivated. Similarly, an organization is more likely to prosper when its employees are intrinsically motivated to pursue its interests. A leader who employees perceive as credible and respectful of their value to the organization can increase the extent to which those employees are intrinsically motivated to pursue their individual goals. As your career evolves, to be perceived as a credible leader you'll need to possess three attributes—technical competence, personal integrity (in terms of work ethic and honesty), and strong communication skills (oral and written). To be perceived as a leader who is respectful of your co-workers' value to the organization, you'll need to possess three more attributes—strong mentoring skills to help others realize their potential, strong listening skills to learn from your co-workers and be responsive to their needs, and personal humility in terms of deferring recognition to all employees who contribute to the organization's success. If you possess these six traits, then you'll have the potential to become a leader who inspires others to readily and energetically channel their efforts toward achieving organizational goals.

Extrinsic Incentives

Many organizations use extrinsic incentives to highlight important goals and to motivate employees to achieve them. For example, assume a company establishes the goal of reducing the time needed to perform a task by 20%. In addition, assume the company agrees to pay bonus compensation to its employees if they achieve the goal within three months. In this example, the company is using a type of extrinsic incentive known as a bonus to highlight a particular goal and presumably to motivate employees to achieve it.

While proponents of extrinsic incentives rightly assert that these types of rewards can have a powerful influence on employee behaviour, they can also produce dysfunctional consequences. For example, suppose the employees mentioned above earned their bonuses by achieving the 20% time reduction goal within three months. However, let's also assume that during those three months the quality of the employees' output plummeted, thereby causing a spike in the company's repair costs, product returns, and customer defections. In this instance, did the extrinsic incentive work properly? The answer is yes and no. The bonus system did motivate employees to attain the time-reduction goal. However, it also had the unintended consequence of causing employees to neglect product quality, thereby increasing repair costs, product returns, and customer defections. In other words, what was a well-intended extrinsic incentive actually produced dysfunctional results for the company. This example highlights an important leadership challenge—designing financial compensation systems that fairly reward employees for their efforts without inadvertently creating extrinsic incentives that motivate them to take actions that harm the company.

Cognitive Biases

Leaders need to be aware that all people (including themselves) possess cognitive biases, or distorted thought processes, that can adversely affect planning, controlling, and decision making. To illustrate how cognitive bias works, let's consider the scenario of a television "infomercial" where someone is selling a product with a proclaimed value of $200 for $19.99 if viewers call within the next 30 minutes. Why do you think the seller claims that the product has a $200 value even though it is highly likely the true value is considerably less? The seller is relying on a cognitive bias called *anchoring bias* in an effort to convince viewers that a $180 discount is simply too good to pass up. The "anchor" is the false assertion that the product is actually worth $200. If viewers erroneously attach credibility to this contrived piece of information, their analysis of the situation may cause them to spend $19.99 on an item whose true economic value is much less than that amount.

While cognitive biases cannot be eliminated, effective leaders should take two steps to reduce their negative impacts. First, they should acknowledge their own susceptibility to cognitive bias. For example, a leader's judgment might be clouded by optimism bias, which pertains to being overly optimistic in assessing the likelihood of future outcomes. Second, they should acknowledge the presence of cognitive bias in others and introduce techniques to minimize their adverse consequences. For example, *confirmation bias* is where people pay greater attention to information that confirms their preconceived notions while devaluing information that contradicts them. To counteract this bias a leader may routinely appoint independent teams of employees to assess the credibility of recommendations set forth by other individuals and groups.

BEYOND THE BOTTOM LINE

Some managers believe that extrinsic incentives "crowd out" employees' intrinsic motivation. That is, they think that paying people based on their performance can actually reduce the extent to which they enjoy doing their job. To avoid this possibility, some companies pay only salaries to their employees and have no performance-based pay. Management in these companies believes that if employees are paid a fair salary and enjoy their job, intrinsic motivation will be high and performance-based extrinsic incentives will be unnecessary.

SUMMARY

- Managerial accounting assists managers in carrying out their responsibilities, which include planning, directing and motivating, controlling, and decision making. **[LO1]**
- Managerial accounting differs substantially from financial accounting in that it is oriented more toward the future, emphasizes relevant data, places less emphasis on precision, emphasizes segments of an organization (rather than the organization as a whole), is not governed by generally accepted accounting principles, and is not mandatory. **[LO2]**

- Enterprise risk management involves proactively identifying and managing key risks faced by an organization. **[LO3]**
- Many organizations prepare a code of conduct to reflect their values and the moral system under which they operate. Professional accounting organizations also have their own code of professional ethics to provide guidance for members, regardless of their place of employment. **[LO4]**
- As an extension of the concept of organizational ethics, many companies have embraced corporate social responsibility, whereby the needs of various stakeholders are considered when making decisions. **[LO5]**
- As part of their role in managing employees, it is important for management accountants to understand how behaviour is influenced by intrinsic motivation, extrinsic incentives, and cognitive biases. **[LO6]**

DISCUSSION CASE

DISCUSSION CASE 1–1

Companies such as CIBC have developed a detailed code of conduct for their employees and often make this information publicly available by providing a copy of the code online. For example, the CIBC code of conduct can be found at http://www.cibc.com/ca/inside-cibc/governance/governance-practices/code-of-conduct.html.

Required:

If you are an employee at CIBC, what are some benefits of having such a detailed code of conduct? Might there be any disadvantages to CIBC in having such a detailed code of conduct?

QUESTIONS

1–1 Why is timeliness of information so important for managerial accounting?

1–2 What is the difference between directing activities and controlling activities?

1–3 What is a budget?

1–4 For what purposes might predictive analytics be used by managers?

1–5 What is a performance report and how might it be useful to managers?

1–6 Pick any large company and explain three ways it could segment its companywide performance.

1–7 What is the role of managerial accounting in strategic management?

1–8 Why do management accountants need to understand their company's strategy?

1–9 What are the six business functions that make up the value chain?

1–10 What are some examples of things socially responsible organizations should provide for their employees?

1–11 Provide three examples of how a company's risks can influence its planning, controlling, and decision-making activities.

1–12 Why should companies be careful to maintain a good ethical reputation?

1–13 Why do companies prepare a code of conduct?

1–14 Why are leadership skills important to managers?

1–15 Identify a control a company could use to reduce the risk that environmental protection laws related to pollution are violated.

1–16 What is the difference between intrinsic motivation and extrinsic incentives?

EXERCISES

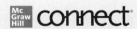

EXERCISE 1–1 Functions Performed by Managers [LO1]

Each of the following independent examples involves one or more of the four major activities carried out by managers at Sights and Sounds, a manufacturer of high-quality televisions and audio equipment for home use: planning, directing and motivating, controlling, and decision making.

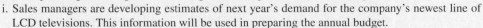

i. Sales managers are developing estimates of next year's demand for the company's newest line of LCD televisions. This information will be used in preparing the annual budget.

ii. In reviewing the monthly quality control reports, the production manager for home theatre systems has noticed that an unusually high number of units were discovered to have manufacturing defects. She is putting together a team of employees to investigate the problem.

   iii. Managers in the research and development department are developing a recommendation as to which of two alternative design choices the company should use for its line of floor speakers.

   iv. The most recent monthly performance report shows disappointing results for sales of the company's line of OLED televisions in May. Sales are well below budget, and the product manager for OLED televisions is evaluating several issues including how retailers can be motivated to improve sales; the production schedule for the next three months; and, longer term, the possibility of discontinuing this product line.

Required:

For each example, select which of the four activities managers are carrying out and briefly explain the basis for your choice(s). Some examples may include more than one type of activity.

EXERCISE 1–2 Financial and Managerial Accounting [LO2]

Each of the following is primarily either financial accounting or managerial accounting in nature.

   i. Preparing an income statement for use in filing the company's annual corporate tax return with Canada Revenue Agency.

   ii. Preparing an analysis of the profitability of each of the company's three major product lines for the past three months. The analysis will be used to make decisions related to resource allocation, potential changes in marketing strategy, and production scheduling.

   iii. Preparing a detailed schedule of accounts receivable balances that are more than 120 days past due to determine the allowance for doubtful accounts to be used in the year-end financial statements.

   iv. Estimating customer satisfaction by calculating the dollar value of all products returned in the past month and comparing it to returns in the same month last year.

   v. Preparing a detailed schedule of accounts receivable balances that are more than 120 days past due for only those customers who regularly purchase the company's products. The purpose of the analysis is to identify potential changes to the credit terms offered to regular customers (e.g., payment due dates, interest on overdue balances).

Required:

For each item above, briefly explain whether it is primarily financial accounting or primarily managerial accounting in nature.

EXERCISE 1–3 Enterprise Risk Management [LO3]

The table below refers to seven industries.

Required:

For each industry, identify one important risk faced by the companies that compete within that industry. Also, describe one control that companies could use to reduce the risk that you have identified.

	Type of Risk	**Control**
1. Light rail transit (e.g., Bombardier)		
2. Beer and alcohol (e.g., Labatt)		
3. Newspaper (e.g., Globe Media Group)		
4. Sports and entertainment (e.g., Maple Leaf Sports and Entertainment)		
5. Solar energy (e.g., Canadian Solar)		
6. Software as a service (e.g., Dropbox)		
7. Motorcycles (e.g., Honda)		

PROBLEMS

PROBLEM 1–4 Cognitive Biases [LO6]

In the 1970s, one million college-bound students were surveyed and asked to compare themselves to their peers. Some of the key findings of the survey were as follows:

   a. Seventy percent of the students rated themselves as above average in leadership ability, while only 2% rated themselves as below average in this regard.

   b. With respect to athletic skills, 60% of the students rated their skills as above the median and only 6% of students rated themselves as below the median.

   c. Sixty percent of the students rated themselves in the top 10% in terms of their ability to get along with others, while 25% of the students felt that they were in the top 1% in terms of this interpersonal skill.

Required:

What type of cognitive bias reveals itself in the data mentioned above? How might this cognitive bias adversely influence a manager's planning, controlling, and decision-making activities? What steps could managers take to reduce the possibility that this cognitive bias would adversely influence their actions?

PROBLEM 1–5 Planning and Control Activities [LO1]

The Sports Network (TSN), a Canadian television network, broadcasts a variety of content, including sporting events (e.g., baseball, basketball, football, golf, hockey), feature programs (e.g., *That's Hockey*), and news broadcasts (e.g., *Sports Desk*). Managing a major television network such as TSN very frequently involves planning, directing and motivating, controlling, and decision making. Indeed, networks such as TSN deliver new program content to viewers on a daily basis, with some content, such as sports news broadcasts, changing as the day unfolds. Managing this type of organization is highly challenging and dynamic.

Required:

For each of the four functions performed by managers (planning, directing and motivating, controlling, and decision making), identify three examples of activities managers at a television network such as TSN would likely engage in.

PROBLEM 1–6 Ethics in Business [LO4]

Assume that you are the chairman of the Department of Accountancy at Central Manitoba University. One of the accounting professors in your department, Dr. Smith, has been uniformly regarded by students as an awful teacher for more than 10 years. Other accounting professors within your department have observed Dr. Smith's classroom teaching and they concur that his teaching skills are very poor. However, Dr. Smith was granted tenure 15 years ago, thereby ensuring him life-long job security at Central Manitoba University.

Much to your surprise, today you received a phone call from an accounting professor at B.C. University. During this phone call you are informed that B.C. University is on the verge of making a job offer to Dr. Smith. However, before extending the job offer, the faculty at B.C. University wants your input regarding Dr. Smith's teaching effectiveness while at Central Manitoba University.

Required:

How would you respond to the professor from B.C. University? What would you say about Dr. Smith's teaching ability? Would you describe your answer to this inquiry as being ethical? Why?

PROBLEM 1–7 Corporate Social Responsibility [LO3, LO5]

It is now common for companies to regularly report their corporate social responsibility performance. Such CSR reports include information on environmental performance (e.g., emissions, water consumption, recycling initiatives, use of green suppliers, etc.) and social performance (e.g., workplace safety training, diversity hiring practices, involvement with local charities, etc.). This trend is generally considered to be a very positive change relative to a sole focus on financial performance. However, critics have suggested that some companies are engaging in "greenwashing," whereby they are using CSR reports to appear more environmentally responsible than they actually are, or to exaggerate claims about the extent of their social responsibility. These concerns have merit, because unlike financial reporting CSR reporting is not regulated by law or subject to mandatory audits by a third party.

Required:

1. What incentives do companies have to engage in greenwashing or to overstate their claims about being socially responsible?
2. What controls could management put in place to increase the likelihood that the company actually engages in environmentally and socially responsible activities?

PROBLEM 1–8 Extrinsic Incentives [LO3, LO6]

Providing extrinsic rewards such as bonuses for achieving or exceeding expected levels of performance can be a powerful motivator. Not surprisingly, the use of extrinsic rewards is pervasive in companies. However, a key concern with using extrinsic rewards is that while they can motivate desired behaviour, they can also result in unintended consequences that may have negative effects on the company. Two examples of the use of extrinsic rewards follow below.

Example 1: A manager of a manufacturing business division receives a significant bonus if her division meets or exceeds the profit target established at the beginning of the year. Assume she is responsible for all aspects of the value chain depicted in Exhibit 1–4.

Example 2: A salesperson at a large electronics retailer receives a commission on all customer sales. Assume each retail outlet has multiple sales staff all eligible for sales commissions and have some discretion to offer discounts to customers to secure a sale.

Required:
1. For each of the above examples, identify two unintended consequences that could have harmful effects for the company longer term that may arise as the result of the extrinsic incentives employed.
2. For each of the above examples, identify some controls a company could put in place to reduce the likelihood that the unintended consequences you identified in requirement 1 will occur.

PROBLEM 1–9 Value Chain Analysis [LO3]
Some companies that manufacture multiple products perform a comprehensive assessment of individual product profitability by collecting the costs incurred for each of the major business functions in the value chain and comparing them to the revenues generated by each of their major product offerings. For example, a manufacturer of home electronics equipment employing this type of analysis would separately track the research and development, product design, manufacturing, marketing, distribution, and customer service costs for each of its major product lines, such as televisions, home theatre systems, and speakers. Revenues for each of these product lines would also be separately identified, allowing managers to calculate profitability on a product-by-product basis.

Required:
1. Identify some benefits and challenges of performing the type of value chain analysis described above in a company that has multiple product lines.
2. What might cause some of the costs for the specific functions making up the value chain to increase or decrease over the life of a product (i.e., from the early to mature stages of a product's life)?

ENDNOTES

1. The insights presented in this paragraph and many of the examples in Exhibit 1–6 were drawn from Ronald W. Clement, "The Lessons from Stakeholder Theory for U.S. Business Leaders," *Business Horizons,* May/June 2005, pp. 255–264; and Terry Leap and Misty L. Loughry, "The Stakeholder-Friendly Firm," *Business Horizons,* March/April 2004, pp. 27–32.

COST TERMS, CONCEPTS, AND CLASSIFICATIONS

After studying Chapter 2, you should be able to

1 Identify each of the three basic manufacturing cost categories.

2 Distinguish between product costs and period costs.

3 Prepare an income statement, including the calculation of cost of goods sold.

4 Prepare a schedule of cost of goods manufactured.

5 Explain the differences between variable and fixed costs.

6 Identify the differences between direct and indirect costs.

7 Describe the cost classifications used in making decisions: differential costs, opportunity costs, and sunk costs.

■ COST CONCEPTS IN PRACTICE

Shutterstock / guteksk7

Experts predict that the cost of the batteries used in electric vehicles will continue to decline. For example, in 2015 the battery alone represented 57% of the total cost of an electric vehicle. However, by 2025 the battery could be as little as 20% of the total vehicle cost. This reduction in battery costs could dramatically reduce manufacturers' selling prices for electric vehicles, thereby increasing the number of vehicles purchased by consumers.

From a management accounting standpoint, electric vehicle manufacturers such as Tesla would view the cost of their batteries as a direct material cost, a product cost, and a variable cost. It would be a direct material cost because the cost of each battery can be easily traced to a specific vehicle. It would be a product cost because installing one battery in each vehicle is a necessary part of the manufacturing process. It would be a variable cost because the battery cost per vehicle is constant whereas the total costs of batteries increase as more units are produced.

The chapter builds on this example by examining the different ways of classifying costs, the flow of costs through the financial statements, cost behaviour basics, and additional cost concepts that are critical to effective decision making.

LEARNING OBJECTIVE ❶

Identify each of the three basic manufacturing cost categories.

■ GENERAL COST CLASSIFICATIONS

All types of organizations incur costs—businesses such as manufacturing, merchandising, or service companies; not-for-profit organizations such as Hockey Canada; and government agencies such as Statistics Canada. Managerial accounting is applicable to all types of organizations. For this reason, our discussion of cost characteristics considers a variety of organizations—manufacturing, merchandising, and service. Service organizations such as KPMG use cost concepts in analyzing and costing their services. Software as a service (SaaS) companies such as Axonify use costs incurred to acquire specific customers to determine the profits generated by that customer. This type of cost analysis provides data for planning and controlling service delivery functions in the same way that manufacturing cost analysis provides data for planning and controlling manufacturing functions.

Our primary focus in this chapter is on manufacturing companies, since their basic activities include most of the activities found in other types of business organizations. Manufacturing companies such as Mega Brands Inc., Bombardier, and CCM Hockey acquire raw materials, produce finished goods, market, distribute, bill customers, and incur costs. Therefore, an understanding of costs in a manufacturing company can be very helpful in understanding costs in other types of organizations.

Manufacturing Costs

Most manufacturing companies divide manufacturing costs into three broad categories: direct materials, direct labour, and manufacturing overhead. A discussion of each category follows.

Direct Materials

The materials that go into the final product are called *raw materials*. Raw materials refers to any materials that are used in the final product, and the finished product of one company can become the raw materials of another company. For example, car mirrors produced by Magna International are a raw material used by automobile manufacturers such as Ford.

Raw materials may include both direct and indirect materials. **Direct materials** are those materials that become an integral part of the finished product and that can be easily (i.e., physically and conveniently) traced to that product. Examples include the seats Bombardier purchases from subcontractors to install in its passenger trains, and the components NAD Electronics uses in its stereo amplifiers.

Sometimes it is not worth the expense to trace the costs of relatively insignificant materials to the finished products. An example is the solder used to make electrical connections in a Sony television. Materials such as solder are **indirect materials** and are included as part of manufacturing overhead, which is discussed below. Indirect materials are still raw materials, but they are not treated as direct materials because the costs of directly tracing them to the finished products exceed the benefits of doing so.

Direct Labour

Direct labour consists of labour costs that can be easily traced to individual units of product. The labour costs of assembly-line workers at Bauer Hockey, for example, are direct labour costs, as are the labour costs of welders at Irving Shipbuilding.

Labour costs that cannot be physically traced to individual products, or that can be traced only at a significant cost, are called **indirect labour** and treated as part of manufacturing overhead. Indirect labour includes the labour costs of factory janitors, production supervisors, and materials handlers. Although these workers are involved in the production process, it would be either impractical or impossible to accurately trace their costs to specific units of product.

Manufacturing Overhead

Manufacturing overhead, the third element of manufacturing costs, includes all costs of manufacturing except direct materials and direct labour. Manufacturing overhead includes items such as indirect materials, indirect labour, maintenance and repairs on production equipment, heat and light, property taxes, depreciation, and insurance on manufacturing facilities.

Direct materials
Those materials that become an integral part of a finished product and can be conveniently traced to it.

Indirect materials
Small items of material that may become an integral part of a finished product but whose costs of tracing exceed the benefits.

Direct labour
Those factory labour costs that can be traced easily to individual units of product.

Indirect labour
The labour costs of janitors, supervisors, materials handlers, and other factory workers that cannot be conveniently traced directly to particular products.

Manufacturing overhead
All costs associated with manufacturing except direct materials and direct labour.

A company also incurs costs associated with its selling and administrative functions (utilities, property taxes, insurance, depreciation, etc.), but these costs are not included in manufacturing overhead. Only costs associated with *operating the production facility (factory)* are included in the manufacturing overhead category. Various terms are used to describe manufacturing overhead, such as *indirect manufacturing cost*, *factory overhead*, and *factory burden*. All of these terms are synonymous with *manufacturing overhead*.

Manufacturing overhead combined with direct labour is called **conversion cost**. This term stems from the fact that direct labour costs and overhead costs are incurred to convert materials into finished products. Direct labour combined with direct materials is called **prime cost**, which, following from the discussion above about direct and indirect costs, groups the two types of direct costs into one category.

Conversion cost
Direct labour cost plus manufacturing overhead cost.

Prime cost
Direct materials cost plus direct labour cost.

Classification of Manufacturing Costs

The appropriate classification of idle time and overtime premiums of production workers whose normal wages are considered direct labour is important to consider. For example, if three hours of a production worker's time are idle (i.e., not spent on production activities) and each hour costs $20, then $60 of idle time cost is usually charged to overhead if management feels that the cost is a general cost of all production. However, if a specific job results in idle time, such as waiting for materials because of a product design change demanded by the customer, then the idle time could be charged to the direct labour costs of that job. Whether the customer will pay for the charge will most likely depend on the details of the sales contract that typically contains provisions about the extent to which non-recurring costs incurred by the manufacturer can be billed to the client.

Overtime premiums represent the extra hourly wage rate paid to production workers who are required to work additional hours beyond their standard employment contract (e.g., 40 hours per week). For example, a worker with a normal workweek of 40 hours who works 45 hours in a particular week might be paid time and a half for five overtime hours. Thus, if $30 is the base hourly rate, the five hours will have an overtime premium of $15 per hour × 5 hours, or $75. Classification of the overtime as direct labour or overhead depends on the cause of the overtime. Overtime incurred for a job-specific reason (e.g., a rush order for a customer) would be classified as direct labour. Conversely, overtime costs resulting from general conditions, such as peak production needs across numerous customers, would be classified as overhead to be allocated to all products produced during that period.

Overtime premiums
The extra hourly wage rate paid to workers who must work more than their normal time requirements.

Non-manufacturing Costs

Generally, non-manufacturing costs are divided into two categories: (1) marketing or selling costs and (2) administrative costs.

Marketing or selling costs include all costs necessary to secure customer orders and get the finished product or service to the customer. These costs are often called *order-getting* and *order-filling costs*. Examples of marketing costs are order-getting costs such as those for advertising, sales travel, and sales salaries or commissions. Order-filling costs include packing, shipping, and the costs of finished goods warehouses.

Administrative costs include all executive, organizational, and clerical costs associated with the *general management* and *support* of an organization rather than with manufacturing, marketing, or selling. Examples of administrative costs are executive compensation; costs of administrative support functions such as accounting, human resources, and risk management; and other costs involved in the administration of the organization *as a whole*.

Marketing or selling costs
All costs necessary to secure customer orders and get the finished product or service to the customer.

Administrative costs
All executive, organizational, and clerical costs associated with the general management of an organization rather than with manufacturing, marketing, or selling.

INSTANT QUIZ 2–1
Would the wages of a supervisor responsible for overseeing the handling of incoming raw material shipments for all products be classified as: (a) direct materials; (b) direct labour; (c) indirect labour; or (d) manufacturing overhead? You can choose more than one classification.

IN BUSINESS

Equinor is a Norwegian company that recently "hired" Roberta to work in its treasury department. The interesting thing about Roberta is that she has no last name—and, for that matter, she has no arms, legs, or face. She is a robot designed to perform time-consuming and repetitive clerical tasks more efficiently and effectively than human beings.

The Hackett Group estimates that 67% of global companies will cut their labour and outsourcing costs by 20 to 35% over the next few years by automating "some or most of their finance-department tasks." In addition to cutting costs, Elie Girard, the finance chief at Atos SE, plans to use robots to better enable his employees to perform complex, decision-oriented work. He says that using robots to complete his department's tedious tasks will cause the job descriptions of his remaining employees to evolve very quickly.

Source: Tatyana Shumsky, "Firms Leave Bean Counting to the Robots," *The Wall Street Journal*, October 23, 2017, p. B5.

LEARNING OBJECTIVE ❷

Distinguish between product costs and period costs.

◼ PRODUCT COSTS VERSUS PERIOD COSTS

Costs can also be classified as either *product costs* or *period costs*. To understand the difference between product costs and period costs, the matching principle from financial accounting is helpful.

Generally, costs are recognized as expenses on the income statement in the same periods that benefits from the cost are realized. For example, if a company pays for two years of building insurance in advance, the entire amount is not considered an expense of the year in which the payment is made. Instead, one-half of the cost is recognized as an expense each year. The reason is that both years—not just the first year—benefit from the insurance payment. The unexpensed portion of the insurance payment is carried on the balance sheet as an asset called *prepaid insurance*. The *matching principle* is based on the accrual concept and states that *costs incurred to generate revenue should be recognized as expenses in the same period that the revenue is recognized*. This means that if a cost is incurred to acquire or produce something that will eventually be sold, then the cost should be recognized as an expense only when the sale takes place. Such costs are called *product costs*.

Product Costs

Product costs
All costs that are involved in the purchase or manufacture of goods. In the case of manufactured goods, these costs consist of direct materials, direct labour, and manufacturing overhead. They are also called inventoriable costs.

For financial accounting purposes, **product costs** include all costs involved in acquiring or making a product. In the case of manufactured goods, these costs consist of direct materials, direct labour, and manufacturing overhead. Product costs "attach" to units of product as the goods are purchased or manufactured, and they remain attached as the goods go into inventory awaiting sale. Product costs are initially assigned to an inventory account on the balance sheet. When the goods are sold, the costs are released from inventory as expenses (typically called *cost of goods sold*) and matched against revenue for that period. Since product costs are initially assigned to inventories, they are also known as *inventoriable costs*. This means that a product cost such as direct materials or direct labour might be incurred during one period but not expensed until a following period when the completed product is sold. Thus, product costs will be present in inventories and cost of goods sold.

Period Costs

Period costs
All costs that are expensed on the income statement in the period in which they are incurred or accrued. Selling (marketing) and administrative expenses are period costs.

Period costs are all those costs not included in product costs. These costs are expensed on the income statement in the period in which they are incurred, using the usual rules of accrual accounting. Period costs are not included as part of the cost of either purchased or manufactured goods. Accounting department costs and advertising are examples of period costs. Neither are included as part of the cost of purchased or manufactured goods. Rather, both items are treated as expenses on the income statement in the period in which they are incurred.

INSTANT QUIZ 2–2
Are the wages of a production supervisor of a manufacturing company considered a product cost or a period cost? What about the wages of the marketing manager—product cost or period cost?

As discussed above, *all selling and administrative expenses are period costs.* Therefore, advertising, executive salaries, sales commissions, public relations, and other non-manufacturing costs discussed earlier are all period costs. They will appear on the income statement as expenses in the period in which they are incurred. Careful analysis of the purpose of costs is necessary to separate product from period costs. Exhibit 2–1 summarizes the cost terms that we have introduced so far.

EXHIBIT 2–1   Summary of Cost Terms

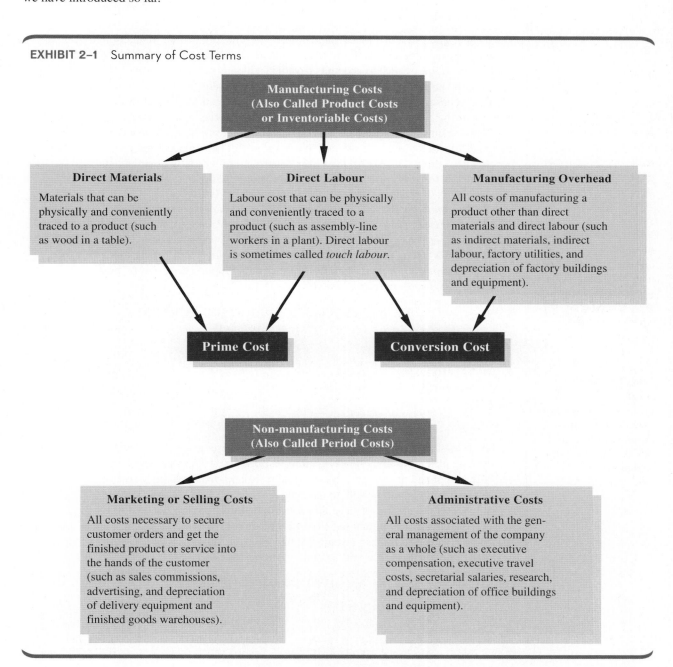

■ COST CLASSIFICATIONS ON FINANCIAL STATEMENTS

In this section, we examine the cost classifications used on the financial statements of manufacturing and merchandising companies. Financial statements prepared by a *manufacturing* company are more complex than the statements prepared by a merchandising or service company because the manufacturing company must account for the production of its goods as well as for the marketing of them. The production process gives rise to many costs that do not exist in a merchandising or service company, and these costs must be accounted for on the manufacturing company's financial statements. Conversely, merchandising companies such as retail stores simply purchase goods from suppliers for resale to customers. In this section, we focus on how accounting similarities and differences between manufacturing and merchandising companies affect the details included in the balance sheet and income statement.

The Balance Sheet

Raw (direct) materials inventory
Materials used to make a product that have not yet been placed into production.

Work in process inventory
Inventory consisting of units of product that are only partially complete and will require further work before they are ready for sale to a customer.

Finished goods inventory
Inventory consisting of units of product that have been completed but have not yet been sold to customers.

The balance sheet of a manufacturing company is generally similar to that of a merchandising company. For example, both have assets such as cash, accounts receivable, and prepaid expenses and liabilities such as accounts payable and loans payable. However, the key difference relates to the inventory accounts. A merchandising company has only one class of inventory—goods purchased from suppliers, that have not yet been sold to customers. By contrast, manufacturing companies have three classes of inventories—raw (direct) materials, work in process, and finished goods. **Raw (direct) materials inventory**, discussed earlier, represents the materials used to make a product that have not yet been placed into production. **Work in process inventory** consists of units of product that are partially complete and require additional work before they are ready to sell to a customer. **Finished goods inventory** consists of complete units of product that have not yet been sold to customers.

We use two hypothetical companies—Darden Manufacturing and Reston Bookstore—to illustrate the concepts discussed in this section. Darden Manufacturing is located in Sherbrooke, Quebec, and makes navigation systems for automobile manufacturers. Reston Bookstore is a small bookstore in Moncton, New Brunswick, specializing in selling books about Atlantic Canada.

The footnotes to Darden Manufacturing's annual report reveal the following information concerning its inventories:

DARDEN MANUFACTURING CORPORATION
Inventory Accounts

	Beginning Balance	Ending Balance
Raw Materials	$ 60,000	$ 50,000
Work in Process	90,000	60,000
Finished Goods	125,000	175,000
Total inventory accounts	$275,000	$285,000

Darden Manufacturing's raw materials inventory consists of electronic components and materials (e.g., plastic) used in the navigation systems. The work in process inventory consists of partially completed navigation systems. The finished goods inventory consists of navigation systems that are ready to be sold to customers.

In contrast, the Inventory account at Reston Bookstore consists entirely of the costs of books the company has purchased from publishers for resale to the public. In merchandising companies like Reston, these inventories may be called *merchandise inventories*. The beginning and ending balances in this account appear as follows:

RESTON BOOKSTORE
Inventory Account

	Beginning Balance	Ending Balance
Merchandise inventory	$100,000	$150,000

The Income Statement

LEARNING OBJECTIVE 3

Prepare an income statement, including the calculation of cost of goods sold.

Exhibit 2–2 compares the income statements of Reston Bookstore and Darden Manufacturing. For illustration purposes, these statements contain more detail about cost of goods sold than you will generally find in financial statements.

The income statements of merchandising and manufacturing firms like Reston Bookstore and Darden Manufacturing are very similar. The only apparent difference is in the labels of some of the entries that go into the computation of the cost of goods sold figure. In Exhibit 2–2, the computation of cost of goods sold relies on the following basic equation for inventory accounts:

Basic Equation for Inventory Accounts

$$\text{Beginning balance} + \text{Additions to inventory} = \text{Ending balance} + \text{Withdrawals from inventory}$$

The logic of this equation, which applies to any inventory account, is illustrated in Exhibit 2–3. At the beginning of the period, the inventory contains a beginning balance. During the period, additions are made to the inventory through purchases or other means. The sum of the beginning balance and the additions to the account is the total amount of inventory available for sale. During the period, withdrawals are made from inventory. Whatever is left at the end of the period after these withdrawals is the ending balance. At the end of the

---

EXHIBIT 2–2 Comparative Income Statements: Merchandising and Manufacturing Companies

MERCHANDISING COMPANY
Reston Bookstore

Sales		$1,000,000
Cost of goods sold:		
Beginning merchandise inventory	$100,000	
Add: Purchases..	650,000	
Goods available for sale...	750,000	
Deduct: Ending merchandise inventory..................	150,000	
Cost of goods sold..		600,000
Gross margin..		400,000
Less operating expenses:		
Selling expense	100,000	
Administrative expense...	200,000	300,000
Operating income...		$ 100,000

Cost of merchandise inventory purchased from outside suppliers during the period

MANUFACTURING COMPANY
Darden Manufacturing

Sales		$1,500,000
Cost of goods sold:		
Beginning finished goods inventory	$125,000	
Add: Cost of goods manufactured	850,000	
Goods available for sale...	975,000	
Deduct: Ending finished goods inventory...............	175,000	
Cost of goods sold..		800,000
Gross margin..		700,000
Less operating expenses:		
Selling expense	250,000	
Administrative expense...	300,000	550,000
Operating income...		$ 150,000

Manufacturing costs associated with goods that were finished during the period (see Exhibit 2–4 for details)

Note: Operating income is income before interest and taxes. Interest and income taxes are ignored here.

EXHIBIT 2–3   Inventory Flow

Beginning balance + Additions   =   Total available   –   Withdrawals   =   Ending balance

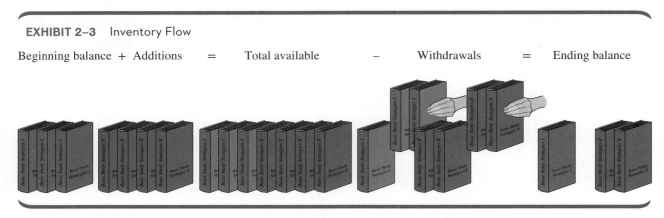

period, all of the inventory that was available for sale during the period must either still be in ending inventory or have been withdrawn from the inventory account.

These concepts are applied to determine the cost of goods sold for a merchandising company like Reston Bookstore as follows:

$$\text{Cost of goods sold} = \text{Beginning merchandise inventory} + \text{Purchases} - \text{Ending merchandise inventory}$$

EXHIBIT 2–4   Darden Manufacturing Schedule of Cost of Goods Manufactured

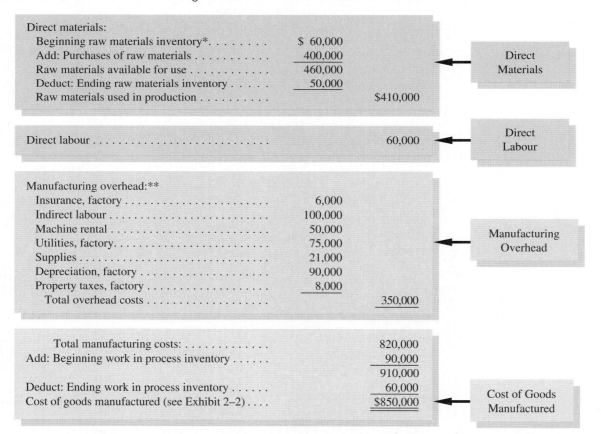

Direct materials:		
Beginning raw materials inventory*.	$ 60,000	
Add: Purchases of raw materials	400,000	
Raw materials available for use	460,000	
Deduct: Ending raw materials inventory	50,000	
Raw materials used in production		$410,000
Direct labour		60,000
Manufacturing overhead:**		
Insurance, factory	6,000	
Indirect labour	100,000	
Machine rental	50,000	
Utilities, factory.	75,000	
Supplies	21,000	
Depreciation, factory	90,000	
Property taxes, factory	8,000	
Total overhead costs		350,000
Total manufacturing costs:	820,000	
Add: Beginning work in process inventory	90,000	
	910,000	
Deduct: Ending work in process inventory	60,000	
Cost of goods manufactured (see Exhibit 2–2)	$850,000	

Labels on right side: Direct Materials; Direct Labour; Manufacturing Overhead; Cost of Goods Manufactured

*We assume in this example that the Raw Materials Inventory account contains only direct materials and that indirect materials are carried in a separate Supplies account. Using a Supplies account for indirect materials is common practice among companies. In Chapter 5, we discuss the procedure to be followed if both direct and indirect materials are carried in a single account.

**In Chapter 5 we will see that the manufacturing overhead section of the schedule of cost of goods manufactured can be simplified considerably by using what is called a *predetermined overhead rate*.

The cost of goods sold for a manufacturing company like Darden Manufacturing is determined as follows:

$$\text{Cost of goods sold} = \text{Beginning finished goods inventory} + \text{Cost of goods manufactured} - \text{Ending finished goods inventory}$$

To determine the cost of goods sold in a manufacturing company like Darden Manufacturing, we need to know the *cost of goods manufactured* and the beginning and ending balances in the finished goods inventory account. The **cost of goods manufactured** consists of the manufacturing costs associated with goods that were *finished* during the period. The cost of goods manufactured figure for Darden Manufacturing is derived in Exhibit 2–4, which contains a *schedule of cost of goods manufactured*.

> **Cost of goods manufactured**
> Costs that include the direct materials, direct labour, and manufacturing overhead used for the products finished during the period.

■ SCHEDULE OF COST OF GOODS MANUFACTURED

The **schedule of cost of goods manufactured** in Exhibit 2–4 contains all three elements of product costs discussed earlier—direct materials, direct labour, and manufacturing overhead.

The direct materials cost is not the cost of materials purchased during the period—rather it is the cost of materials *used* during the period. The purchases of raw materials are added to the beginning inventory of raw materials to determine the cost of raw materials available for use. The ending raw materials inventory is deducted from this amount to arrive at the cost of raw materials used in production. The sum of the three cost elements—materials, direct labour, and manufacturing overhead—is the **total manufacturing costs** of $820,000. However, this is *not* the same thing as the cost of goods manufactured for the period of $850,000. The distinction between the *total manufacturing cost* and the *cost of goods manufactured* is very easy to miss. Some of the materials, direct labour, and manufacturing overhead costs incurred during the period relate to goods that are not yet completed. As stated above, the cost of goods manufactured consists of the manufacturing cost associated with the goods that were *finished* during the period. Consequently, adjustments need to be made to the total manufacturing costs incurred during the period for partially completed goods that were in process at the beginning and at the end of the period. The costs that relate to goods that are not yet completed are shown in the work in process inventory figures at the bottom of the schedule. Note that the beginning work in process inventory must be added to the manufacturing costs for the period, and the ending work in process inventory must be deducted, to arrive at the cost of goods manufactured. The $30,000 decline in the Work in Process account during the year ($90,000 – $60,000) explains the $30,000 difference between the total manufacturing cost and the cost of goods manufactured.

> **LEARNING OBJECTIVE** ❹
> Prepare a schedule of cost of goods manufactured.

> **Schedule of cost of goods manufactured**
> A schedule showing the direct materials, direct labour, and manufacturing overhead costs incurred for a period and assigned to work in process and completed goods.

> **Total manufacturing costs**
> Costs that represent the direct materials, direct labour, and manufacturing overhead used to perform the production work for finished or unfinished products for the period.

Product Costs—A Closer Look

To understand product costs more fully, it is helpful to look briefly at the flow of costs in a manufacturing company. This will help us understand how product costs move through the various accounts and how they affect the balance sheet and the income statement.

Exhibit 2–5 illustrates how costs flow in a manufacturing company. Raw materials purchases are recorded in the raw materials inventory account. When raw materials are used in production, their costs are transferred to the Work in Process Inventory account as direct materials. Notice that direct labour cost and manufacturing overhead cost are added

EXHIBIT 2–5 Cost Flows and Classifications in a Manufacturing Company

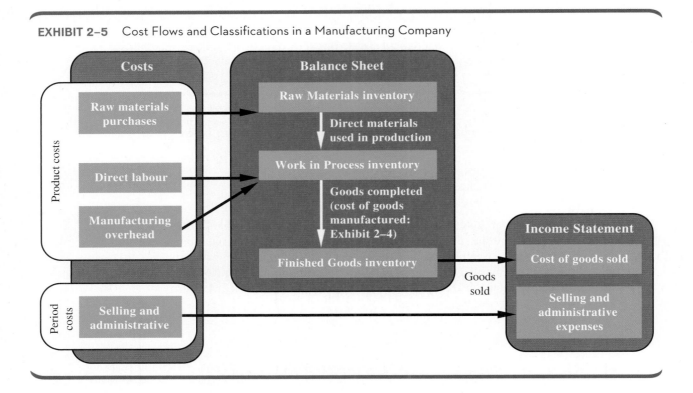

directly to work in process. Work in process can be viewed as products on an assembly line. The direct materials, direct labour, and manufacturing overhead costs added to work in process in Exhibit 2–5 are the costs needed to complete these products as they move along this assembly line.

Notice from Exhibit 2–5 that as goods are completed, their cost is transferred from work in process to finished goods, where they remain until the goods are sold to a customer. As goods are sold, their cost is transferred from finished goods to cost of goods sold. At this point, the total costs required to make the product are finally recorded as an expense.

BEYOND THE BOTTOM LINE

Some companies are strategic about how they classify period costs for external reporting purposes. For example, Coca-Cola did not separately report any research and development expenses for the years ended December 31, 2015–2018. However, the company came out with new products during that same period. Some claim companies do this to avoid tipping their hand to competitors regarding the extent of their R&D activities. However, it is questionable as to whether this approach to strategically classifying expenses is appropriate since it involves withholding information from external stakeholders such as shareholders.

An Example of Cost Flows

Exhibit 2–6 builds on Exhibit 2–5 by providing an example of cost flows through the balance sheet and income statement in a manufacturing company using T-accounts for the key accounts involved. As goods are being worked on, costs for direct materials, direct labour, and manufacturing overhead are debited to work in process inventory. In our example, we show the total amount debited to work in process of $800,000, but in practice individual entries are

EXHIBIT 2–6   An Example of Cost Flows in a Manufacturing Company

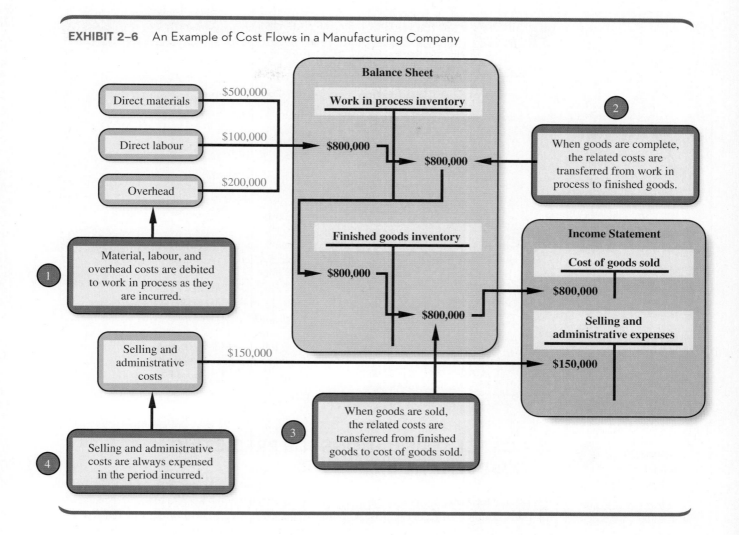

made as expenditures are incurred for each of the three categories of manufacturing costs. Once the goods are complete, work in process inventory is credited for $800,000, with the corresponding debit to finished goods inventory. Finally, when the goods are sold, finished goods inventory is credited for the cost of the items, with the corresponding debit to cost of goods sold, an income statement account. The $150,000 of selling and administrative expenses are expensed immediately to the income statement in the period incurred.

INSTANT QUIZ 2–4

Calculate the cost of goods manufactured for a company that has direct materials costs of $410,000, direct labour costs of $60,000, manufacturing overhead costs of $350,000, beginning work in process inventory of $90,000, and ending work in process inventory of $60,000.

So far, we have been mainly concerned with classifications of manufacturing costs to determine inventory valuations on the balance sheet and cost of goods sold on the income statement. However, costs are used for many purposes, which often require different classifications of costs. We consider several different purposes for cost classifications in the remaining sections of this chapter. To help keep the big picture in mind, we suggest that you refer to the Learning Aid below as you progress through the rest of this chapter.

LEARNING AID

Summary of Cost Classifications

Purpose of Cost Classification	Cost Classifications

Preparing external financial statements	• Product costs (inventoriable)
	  • Direct materials
	  • Direct labour
	  • Manufacturing overhead
	• Period costs (expensed)
	  • Non-manufacturing costs
	    • Marketing or selling costs
	    • Administrative costs

Predicting cost behaviour in response to changes in activity	• Variable cost (proportional to activity) • Fixed cost (constant in total)
Assigning costs to cost objects such as departments or products	• Direct cost (can easily be traced) • Indirect cost (cannot easily be traced; must be allocated)
Making decisions	• Differential cost (differs between alternatives) • Sunk cost (past cost not affected by a decision) • Opportunity cost (forgone benefit)

LEARNING OBJECTIVE 5
Explain the differences between variable and fixed costs.

Cost behaviour
The way in which a cost reacts or responds to changes in the level of activity.

■ COST CLASSIFICATIONS FOR PREDICTING COST BEHAVIOUR

It is often necessary to predict how a certain cost will behave in response to a change in activity. For example, managers will want to know how costs will change if sales increase or decrease. **Cost behaviour** refers to how a cost reacts or responds to changes in the level of activity. As the activity level rises and falls, a particular cost may rise and fall as well—or it may remain constant. For planning purposes, a manager must be able to anticipate which of these will happen, and if a cost can be expected to change, the manager must know by how much it will change. To help make such distinctions, costs are often categorized as *variable* or *fixed*. As you will see throughout the textbook, understanding cost behaviour is critical for management accountants when preparing reports for internal decision-making purposes (Chapter 3), analyzing the impact of changes in sales volume on profits (Chapter 4), developing budgets (Chapter 9), and making short-term (Chapter 12) and long-term (Chapter 13) decisions. We briefly introduce the topic of cost behaviour in this chapter but return to it in greater detail in Chapter 3.

Variable Cost

Variable cost
A cost that varies, in total, in direct proportion to changes in the level of activity. A variable cost is constant per unit.

A **variable cost** varies, in total, in direct proportion to changes in the level of activity. The activity can be expressed in many ways, such as units produced, units sold, kilometres driven, beds occupied, lines of print, or hours worked. A good example of a variable cost is direct materials. The cost of direct materials used during a period will vary, in total, in direct proportion to the number of units that are produced. To illustrate this idea, consider the Nova Bus Corporation. Each bus requires one battery. As the output of buses increases and decreases, the number of batteries used will increase and decrease proportionately. If bus production goes up 10%, then the number of batteries used will also go up 10%. The concept of a variable cost is shown graphically in Exhibit 2–7.

EXHIBIT 2–7   Variable and Fixed Cost Behaviour

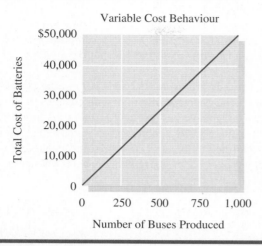

Variable Cost Behaviour

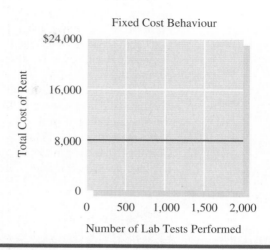

Fixed Cost Behaviour

The graph on the left-hand side of Exhibit 2–7 illustrates that the *total variable* cost rises and falls as the activity level rises and falls. This idea is presented below, assuming that a battery costs $50:

Number of Buses Produced	Cost per Battery	Total Variable Cost—Batteries
1	$50	$ 50
500	50	25,000
1,000	50	50,000

Although total variable costs change as the activity level changes, a variable cost is constant if expressed on a *per unit* basis. That is, the per unit cost of batteries remains constant at $50 even though the total cost of the batteries increases and decreases with activity levels.

Many examples exist of costs that are variable with respect to the products and services provided by a company. In a manufacturing company, variable costs include items such as direct materials, shipping costs, sales commissions, and some elements of manufacturing overhead, such as indirect materials. In a merchandising company, variable costs include items such as cost of goods sold and commissions to salespeople. In service companies such as a law firm, variable costs would include utilities based on consumption or use (e.g., kilowatt hours of electricity, litres of water) and part-time wages paid on an hourly basis.

Fixed Cost

A **fixed cost** is a cost that remains constant, in total, regardless of changes in the level of activity. Examples of fixed costs are insurance, property taxes, Internet access, supervisory salaries, administrative salaries, and advertising. As the activity level rises and falls, the fixed costs remain constant in total amount unless influenced by some outside force, such as price changes. Rent is a good example of a fixed cost. Suppose the Saskatchewan Health Clinic rents a machine for $8,000 per month that tests blood samples for the presence of leukaemia cells. The $8,000 monthly rental cost is incurred regardless of the number of tests performed during the month. The concept of a fixed cost is shown graphically on the right-hand side of Exhibit 2–7.

Very few costs are completely fixed. Most will change if there is a large enough change in activity. For example, suppose that the capacity of the leukaemia diagnostic machine at the

Fixed cost
A cost that remains constant, in total, regardless of changes in the level of activity within the relevant range. If a fixed cost is expressed on a per unit basis, it varies inversely with the level of activity.

Relevant range
The range of activity within which assumptions about variable and fixed cost behaviour are valid.

Saskatchewan Health Clinic is 2,000 tests per month. If the clinic needs to perform more than 2,000 tests in a month, it will be necessary to rent an additional machine, which will cause an increase in the fixed costs. When we say a cost is fixed, we mean it is fixed within some *relevant range* of activity. The **relevant range** is the range of activity within which the assumptions about variable and fixed costs are valid. For example, the assumption that the rent for diagnostic machines is $8,000 per month is valid within the relevant range of 0 to 2,000 tests per month.

Fixed costs can create confusion if they are expressed on a per unit basis because the average fixed cost per unit will increase and decrease *inversely* with changes in activity. For the Saskatchewan Health Clinic, the average cost per test *decreases* as the number of tests performed *increases*. This is because the $8,000 rental cost is spread over more tests. Conversely, as the number of tests performed in the clinic declines, the average cost per test rises as the $8,000 rental cost is spread over fewer tests. This concept is illustrated in the table below:

Monthly Rental Cost	Number of Tests Performed	Average Cost per Test
$8,000	10	$800
8,000	500	16
8,000	2,000	4

Note that if the Saskatchewan Health Clinic performs only 10 tests each month, the rental cost of the equipment averages $800 per test. But if 2,000 tests are performed each month, the average cost drops to only $4 per test.

INSTANT QUIZ 2–5

Using the information from the Saskatchewan Health Clinic example, if 1,000 tests are performed in a month, calculate the total monthly machine rental costs and average machine rental costs per test. If 3,000 tests are performed in a month, calculate the total monthly machine rental costs.

Mixed Costs
Costs that contain both variable and fixed cost elements.

Some costs contain variable and fixed cost elements; these are called **mixed costs**. An example is the total wages paid to sales staff. A portion of these wages is usually a fixed salary and does not vary with the level of selling activity. However, quite often a portion (sales commissions) of the total wages varies directly with the amount of sales generated by the salesperson. Mixed costs are quite common, but we defer further discussion of their behaviour and analysis until Chapter 3.

A summary of both variable and fixed cost behaviour is presented in the Learning Aid below.

LEARNING AID

Summary of Variable and Fixed Cost Behaviour

Cost	Behaviour of the Cost (within the relevant range)	
	In Total	**Per Unit**
Variable cost	Total variable cost increases and decreases in proportion to changes in the activity level.	Variable costs remain constant per unit.
Fixed cost	Total fixed cost is not affected by changes in the activity level within the relevant range.	Fixed costs decrease per unit as the activity level rises and increase per unit as the activity level falls.

■ COST CLASSIFICATIONS FOR ASSIGNING COSTS TO COST OBJECTS

LEARNING OBJECTIVE ⑥
Identify the differences between direct and indirect costs.

Costs are assigned to objects for a variety of purposes including pricing, profitability analysis, and cost management. A **cost object** is any unit of analysis for which cost data are desired—including products, customers, jobs, and organizational subunits. For assigning costs to cost objects, costs are classified as either *direct* or *indirect*.

Direct Cost

A **direct cost** is a cost that can be easily and conveniently traced to the particular cost object under consideration. The concept of direct cost extends beyond just direct materials and direct labour discussed earlier in this chapter. For example, if Roots Canada is assigning costs to its various regional and national sales offices, then the salary of the sales manager in its Alberta office is a direct cost of that office.

Indirect Cost

An **indirect cost** is a cost that cannot be easily and conveniently traced to the particular cost object under consideration. For example, a Moosehead Breweries factory may produce many varieties of beer. The factory manager's salary is an indirect cost of a particular variety, such as Premium Dry. This is because the factory manager's salary is not caused by any one variety of beer but rather is incurred as a consequence of running the entire factory. When the cost object is a product, as discussed earlier in the chapter, indirect costs such as indirect materials and indirect labour are included in manufacturing overhead. *To be directly traced to a cost object such as a particular product, the cost must be caused by the cost object.* The factory manager's salary is called a *common cost* of producing the various products of the factory. A **common cost** is a cost that is incurred to support a number of cost objects but cannot be traced to any of them individually.

A particular cost may be direct or indirect, depending on the cost object. While the salary of the manager of the Moosehead Breweries factory is an *indirect* cost of manufacturing Premium Dry beer, it is a *direct* cost of the manufacturing division. In the first case, the cost object is the brand of beer. In the second case, the cost object is the entire manufacturing division.

Cost object
Any unit of analysis for which cost data are desired.

Direct cost
A cost that can be easily and conveniently traced to the particular cost object under consideration.

Indirect cost
A cost that cannot be easily and conveniently traced to the particular cost object under consideration.

Common cost
A cost that is incurred to support a number of cost objects but cannot be traced to any of them individually.

INSTANT QUIZ 2-6
Would the research and development costs incurred by BMW for new and existing vehicle models be considered a direct or indirect cost of a particular model in their automobile product line, such as the X5 SUV?

■ COST CLASSIFICATIONS FOR DECISION MAKING

LEARNING OBJECTIVE ⑦
Describe the cost classifications used in making decisions: differential costs, opportunity costs, and sunk costs.

Costs are an important feature of many business decisions. In making decisions, it is essential to have a clear understanding of the concepts of *differential cost*, *opportunity cost*, and *sunk cost*.

Differential Cost and Revenue

Decisions involve choosing among alternatives. In business decisions, each alternative has certain costs and benefits that must be compared to the costs and benefits of the other available alternatives. A difference in costs between any two alternatives is known as a

Differential cost
A difference in cost between any two alternatives.

Differential revenue
A difference in revenue between any two alternatives.

differential cost. A difference in revenues between any two alternatives is known as **differential revenue**.

To illustrate how the concept of differential revenues and costs can be used for decision making, assume that Nature Way Cosmetics Inc. is thinking about changing its marketing method from distribution through retailers to distribution by a network of neighbourhood sales representatives. Present costs and revenues are compared to projected costs and revenues in the following table:

	Retailer Distribution (present)	Sales Representatives (proposed)	Differential Costs and Revenues
Revenues.................	$700,000	$800,000	$100,000
Cost of goods sold (V).........	350,000	400,000	50,000
Advertising (F)..............	80,000	45,000	(35,000)
Commissions (V)............	–0–	40,000	40,000
Warehouse depreciation (F).....	50,000	80,000	30,000
Other expenses (F)...........	60,000	60,000	–0–
Total....................	540,000	625,000	85,000
Operating income............	$160,000	$175,000	$ 15,000

V = Variable; F = Fixed

According to the preceding analysis, the differential revenue is $100,000 and the differential costs total $85,000, leaving a positive differential operating income of $15,000 under the proposed marketing plan.

The decision of whether Nature Way Cosmetics should stay with the present retail distribution or switch to sales representatives could be made on the basis of the operating incomes of the two alternatives. As we see in the above analysis, the operating income under the present distribution method is $160,000, whereas the operating income under sales representatives is estimated to be $175,000. Therefore, using sales representatives is preferred, since it would result in $15,000 higher operating income.

In general, only the differences between alternatives are relevant in decisions. Those items that are the same under all alternatives and that are not affected by the decision can be ignored. For example, in the Nature Way Cosmetics example, the Other Expenses category, which is $60,000 under both alternatives, can be ignored since it has no effect on the decision. This is an extremely important principle in managerial accounting that we will return to in later chapters.

Opportunity Cost

Opportunity cost
The potential benefit that is given up when one alternative is selected over another.

Opportunity cost is the potential benefit that is given up when one alternative is selected over another. To illustrate this important concept, consider the following examples:

Example 1

Vicki, a university student, has a part-time job that pays her $300 per week. She would like to spend a week at the beach during the study break, and her employer has agreed to give her the time off, but without pay. The $300 in forgone wages would be an opportunity cost of taking the week off to be at the beach.

Example 2

Suppose that Hudson's Bay Company is considering investing a large sum of money in land that may be a site for a future store. Rather than invest the funds in land, the company could deposit the funds in an interest-bearing account with its bank. If the land is acquired, the opportunity cost will be the interest income that could have been earned if the funds had been deposited at the bank.

Example 3

Steve is employed with a company that pays him a salary of $60,000 per year. He is thinking about leaving the company and returning to school. Since returning to school would require that he give up his $60,000 salary, the forgone salary is an opportunity cost of getting further education.

INSTANT QUIZ 2–7
A company needs land on which to build a new head office building. Management is considering using a parking lot it owns that generates a small loss of $10,000 per year. What is the opportunity cost of using the parking lot for the new head office building?

Opportunity costs are not usually entered in the accounting records of an organization, but they must be explicitly considered in many decisions managers make. Virtually every alternative has an associated opportunity cost. In Example 3 above, for instance, if Steve decides to stay at his job, an opportunity cost is still involved—the higher income that potentially could be earned in future years as a result of returning to school.

Sunk Cost

A **sunk cost** is a cost *that has already been incurred* and that cannot be changed by any decision made now or in the future. Since sunk costs cannot be changed and thus will never differ under any alternative courses of action being considered, they are not differential costs. And because only differential costs are relevant in a decision, sunk costs should *always* be ignored.

Sunk cost
Any cost that has already been incurred and that cannot be changed by any decision made now or in the future.

INSTANT QUIZ 2–8
In deciding wither to keep or sell old production equipment, is its potential salvage value an opportunity cost or a sunk cost?

To illustrate a sunk cost, assume that a company paid $50,000 several years ago for a special-purpose machine. The machine was used to make a product that is now obsolete and can no longer be sold at a price sufficient to generate a profit. Even though in hindsight the purchase of the machine may have been unwise, the $50,000 cost has been incurred and cannot be undone. In short, the $50,000 originally paid for the machine is a sunk cost that should be ignored in current decisions.

KNOWLEDGE IN ACTION

Managers can apply their knowledge of cost terms, concepts, and classifications when:

- Preparing financial statements
- Determining selling prices for products or services
- Predicting costs when activity levels change
- Developing budgets
- Assigning costs to cost objects such as products, customers, jobs, or departments
- Deciding among various alternative courses of action
- Determining whether or not costs are relevant to a decision being made

SUMMARY

- Manufacturing costs can be divided into three broad categories: direct materials, direct labour, and manufacturing overhead. Non-manufacturing costs are usually classified as either marketing/selling costs or administrative costs. **[LO1]**
- When valuing inventories and determining expenses for the balance sheet and income statement, costs are classified as either product costs or period costs. Product costs are assigned to inventory and considered assets until the products are sold. At the point of sale, product costs become cost of goods sold on the income statement. In contrast, period costs are expensed in the period in which they are incurred. **[LO2]**
- In a manufacturing company, cost of goods sold is calculated by adding cost of goods manufactured to beginning finished goods inventory and then deducting the ending finished goods inventory. In a merchandising company, cost of goods sold is calculated by adding cost of goods purchased to beginning merchandise inventory and then deducting the ending merchandise inventory. Selling and administrative expenses are treated as period costs for both manufacturing and merchandising companies. **[LO3]**
- For manufacturing companies, the cost of goods manufactured must be calculated as part of the determination of cost of goods sold. Total manufacturing cost incurred is the sum of direct materials used in production, direct labour incurred, and total overhead costs for the period. Total manufacturing cost is added to beginning work in process inventory, and ending work in process inventory is then deducted to arrive at the cost of goods manufactured for the period. Work in process consists of goods started but not yet complete. **[LO4]**
- To predict cost behaviour, managers commonly classify costs into two categories, variable and fixed. Variable costs, in total, are strictly proportional to activity, but variable cost per unit is constant within a relevant range. Total fixed costs remain the same for changes in activity occurring within the relevant range. However, average fixed cost per unit decreases (increases) as the number of units increases (decreases). **[LO5]**
- To assign costs to cost objects such as products or departments, costs are classified as direct or indirect. Direct costs can conveniently be traced to the cost objects. Indirect costs cannot conveniently be traced to cost objects. **[LO6]**
- Differential costs and revenues are those that differ between alternatives. An opportunity cost is the benefit that is forgone when one alternative is selected over another. A sunk cost occurred in the past and cannot be changed in the future. Differential cost and opportunity cost should be carefully considered in decisions. Sunk costs are always irrelevant in decision making and should be ignored. **[LO7]**

REVIEW PROBLEM 1: COST TERMS

Many new cost terms have been introduced in this chapter. It will take you some time to learn what each term means and how to properly classify costs in an organization. Consider the following example: Porter Company manufactures furniture, including tables. Selected costs are given below:

1. The tables are made of wood that costs $100 per table.
2. The tables are assembled by workers at a wage cost of $40 per table.
3. Workers assembling the tables are supervised by a factory supervisor who is paid $45,000 per year.
4. Electrical costs are $2 per machine-hour. Four machine-hours are required to produce a table.
5. The depreciation on the machines used to make the tables totals $10,000 per year. The machines have no resale value and do not wear out through use.
6. The salary of the president of the company is $200,000 per year.
7. The company spends $250,000 per year to advertise its products.
8. Salespersons are paid a commission of $30 for each table sold.
9. Instead of producing the tables, the company could rent its factory space for $50,000 per year.
10. Overtime premiums for production staff were $10,000 during a one-month period when customer demand was high across all product lines.

Carefully study the classification of each cost. If you don't understand why a particular cost is classified the way it is, reread the section of the chapter discussing the particular cost term. The terms *variable cost* and *fixed cost* refer to how costs behave with respect to the number of tables produced in a year.

Solution to Review Problem 1

Selected Cost	Variable Cost	Fixed Cost	Period (Selling and Administrative) Cost	Product Cost			To Units of Product		Sunk Cost	Opportunity Cost
				Direct Materials	Direct Labour	Manufacturing Overhead	Direct	Indirect		
1. Wood used for the tables ($100 per table)	X			X			X			
2. Labour cost to assemble a table ($40 per table)	X				X		X			
3. Salary of the factory supervisor ($45,000 per year)		X				X		X		
4. Cost of electricity to produce tables ($2 per machine-hour)	X					X		X		
5. Depreciation of machines used to produce tables ($10,000 per year)		X				X		X	X*	
6. Salary of the company president ($200,000 per year)		X	X							
7. Advertising expense ($250,000 per year)		X	X							
8. Commissions paid to salespersons ($30 per table sold)	X		X							
9. Rental income forgone on factory space ($50,000 per year)										X‡
10. Overtime premiums ($10,000)		X				X		X		

*This is a sunk cost, since the outlay for the equipment on which the depreciation is based was made in a previous period.

‡This is an opportunity cost, since it represents the potential benefit that is lost or sacrificed as a result of using the manufacturing facilities to produce tables. Opportunity cost is a special category of cost that is not ordinarily recorded in an organization's accounting books. To avoid possible confusion with other costs, we will not attempt to classify this cost in any other way except as an opportunity cost.

REVIEW PROBLEM 2: SCHEDULE OF COST OF GOODS MANUFACTURED AND INCOME STATEMENT

Fisher Limited is a manufacturer that produces a single product. The following information has been taken from the company's production, sales, and cost records for the just-completed year:

Production in units	30,000
Sales in units	?
Ending finished goods inventory in units	?
Sales in dollars	$650,000
Costs:	
Advertising	$ 50,000
Direct labour	$ 80,000
Indirect labour	$ 60,000
Raw materials purchased	$160,000
Building rent (production uses 80% of the space; administrative and sales offices use the rest)	$ 50,000
Utilities, factory	$ 35,000
Royalty paid for use of production patent, $1 per unit produced	?
Maintenance, factory	$ 25,000
Rent for special production equipment, $6,000 per year plus $0.10 per unit produced	?
Selling and administrative salaries	$140,000
Other factory overhead costs	$ 11,000
Other selling and administrative expenses	$ 20,000

	Beginning of Year	End of Year
Inventories:		
Raw materials	$20,000	$10,000
Work in process	$30,000	$40,000
Finished goods	$ 0	?

The finished goods inventory is being carried at the average unit production cost for the year. The selling price of the product is $25 per unit.

Required:
1. Prepare a schedule of cost of goods manufactured for the year.
2. Compute the following:
    a. The number of units in the finished goods inventory at the end of the year.
    b. The cost of the units in the finished goods inventory at the end of the year.
3. Prepare an income statement for the year.

Solution to Review Problem 2

1.

FISHER LIMITED **Schedule of Cost of Goods Manufactured** **For the Year Ended xxxx**		
Direct materials:		
Raw materials inventory, beginning	$ 20,000	
Add: Purchases of raw materials	160,000	
Raw materials available for use	180,000	
Deduct: Raw materials inventory, ending	10,000	
Raw materials used in production		$170,000
Direct labour		80,000

FISHER LIMITED
Schedule of Cost of Goods Manufactured
For the Year Ended xxxx

Manufacturing overhead:		
Indirect labour..	60,000	
Building rent (80% × $50,000)............................	40,000	
Utilities, factory	35,000	
Royalty on patent ($1 per unit × 30,000 units)...............	30,000	
Maintenance, factory.....................................	25,000	
Rent on equipment: $6,000 + ($0.10 per unit × 30,000 units).......	9,000	
Other factory overhead costs...........................	11,000	
Total overhead costs		210,000
Total manufacturing costs...............................		460,000
Add: Work in process inventory, beginning		30,000
		490,000
Deduct: Work in process inventory, ending		40,000
Cost of goods manufactured		$450,000

2.   *a.*   To compute the number of units in the finished goods inventory at the end of the year, we must first compute the number of units sold during the year:

$$\frac{\text{Total sales}}{\text{Unit selling price}} = \frac{\$650,000}{\$25 \text{ per unit}} = 26,000 \text{ units sold}$$

Units in the finished goods inventory, beginning	0
Units produced during the year..	30,000
Units available for sale	30,000
Units sold during the year (above)	26,000
Units in the finished goods inventory, ending...............................	4,000

   b.   The average production cost per unit during the year is

$$\frac{\text{Cost of goods manufactured}}{\text{Number of units produced}} = \frac{\$450,000}{30,000 \text{ units}} = \$15 \text{ per unit}$$

Thus, the cost of the units in the finished goods inventory at the end of the year is 4,000 units × $15 per unit = $60,000.

3.

FISHER LIMITED
Income Statement
For the Year Ended xxxx

Sales		$650,000
Cost of goods sold:		
Finished goods inventory, beginning	$ 0	
Add: Cost of goods manufactured	450,000	
Goods available for sale	450,000	
Finished goods inventory, ending........................	60,000	390,000
Gross margin..		260,000
Selling and administrative expenses:		
Advertising	50,000	
Building rent (20% × $50,000)...........................	10,000	
Selling and administrative salaries	140,000	
Other selling and administrative expense....................	20,000	220,000
Operating income		$ 40,000

DISCUSSION CASE

DISCUSSION CASE 2–1
Understanding cost terms and concepts is considerably more important in larger organizations with complex operations and multiple products or services being offered. In smaller and simpler companies that manufacture or sell only a single product, or for companies that have only a single service, the topics covered in this chapter have limited importance or relevance.

Required:
Do you agree with this statement? Why or why not?

QUESTIONS

2–1 Would costs related to the building used only by administrative personnel, such as heat and lights, property taxes, and insurance, be considered part of manufacturing overhead? Why or why not?

2–2 What are the three basic categories of manufacturing costs?

2–3 Are product costs always expensed in the period in which they are incurred? Explain.

2–4 What are administrative costs? How are they treated on the income statement?

2–5 What is the difference between raw materials inventory and work in process inventory? Are they included on the balance sheet or income statement?

2–6 If a company automates its production processes, would you expect that to increase or decrease prime costs? Why?

2–7 What is the difference between total manufacturing costs incurred and the cost of goods manufactured?

2–8 Which two classes of inventory does a manufacturing company have that a merchandising or service company does not?

2–9 A company pays its employees a weekly salary based on working 40 hours per week and pays $20 per hour for time worked in excess of 40 hours. In terms of cost behaviour, what type of cost is total wages for this company?

2–10 As the level of activity increases, on a per unit basis, explain what happens to variable costs and fixed costs.

2–11 Assume your mobile plan provides you with 5 GB of data for $50 per month and charges you $5 for every 200 MB of data you use in excess of that. What type of cost is this?

2–12 Why is manufacturing overhead considered an indirect cost of a unit of product?

2–13 In deciding whether to replace an existing machine with a newer, more cost-effective machine, the original cost of the existing machine should be compared to the cost of the new machine. Do you agree? Explain.

2–14 You are looking at options for a new mobile plan. Instead of selling the iPhone 8 that your parents gave you for your birthday last year, you decide to keep it to reduce the cost of a new plan by signing up for a "bring your own phone" option. Is there an opportunity cost of this choice? Why or why not?

2–15 Should overtime premiums paid to employees to complete a rush order for a specific customer be classified as overhead or as direct labour? Explain.

2–16 Is it possible for a company to have $0 in cost of goods manufactured but $100,000 in cost of goods sold? Explain.

FOUNDATIONAL EXERCISES

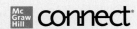

[LO1, LO2, LO5, LO6, LO7]
Martinez Company's relevant range of production is 7,500 units to 12,500 units. When it produces and sells 10,000 units, its unit costs are as follows:

	Amount per Unit
Direct materials.....................	$6.00
Direct labour.......................	$3.50
Variable manufacturing overhead........	$1.50
Fixed manufacturing overhead	$4.00
Fixed selling expense	$3.00
Fixed administrative expense	$2.00
Sales commissions	$1.00
Variable administrative expense	$0.50

2–1 For financial accounting purposes, what is the total amount of product costs incurred to make 10,000 units? As part of your answer, indicate the total variable manufacturing costs and the total fixed manufacturing costs.

2–2 For financial accounting purposes, what is the total amount of period costs incurred to sell 10,000 units? As part of your answer, indicate the total variable period costs and the total fixed period costs.

2–3 If 8,000 units are sold, what is the variable cost per unit sold?

2–4 If 12,500 units are sold, what is the variable cost per unit sold?

2–5 If 8,000 units are sold, what is the total amount of variable costs related to the units sold?

2–6 If 12,500 units are sold, what is the total amount of variable costs related to the units sold?

2–7 If 8,000 units are produced, what is the average fixed manufacturing cost per unit produced?

2–8 If 12,500 units are produced, what is the average fixed manufacturing cost per unit produced?

2–9 If 8,000 units are produced, what is the total amount of fixed manufacturing cost incurred to support this level of production?

2–10 If 12,500 units are produced, what is the total amount of fixed manufacturing cost incurred to support this level of production?

2–11 If 8,000 units are produced, what is the total amount of manufacturing overhead cost incurred to support this level of production? What is this total amount expressed on a per unit basis?

2–12 If 12,500 units are produced, what is the total amount of manufacturing overhead cost incurred to support this level of production? What is this total amount expressed on a per unit basis?

2–13 If 11,000 units are produced, what are the total amounts of direct and indirect manufacturing costs incurred to support this level of production?

2–14 What total incremental cost will Martinez incur if it increases production from 10,000 to 10,001 units?

EXERCISES

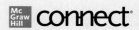

EXERCISE 2–1 Classifying Manufacturing Costs [LO1]

The costs below all relate to Sounds Good, a company based in Alberta that manufactures high-end audio equipment such as speakers, receivers, CD players, turntables, and home theatre systems. The company owns all of the manufacturing facilities (building and equipment) but rents the space used by the non-manufacturing employees (accounting, marketing, sales, human resources).

Required:

For each cost, indicate whether it would most likely be classified as a direct labour, direct material, manufacturing overhead, marketing and selling, or administrative cost.

1. Depreciation, taxes, and insurance on the manufacturing facilities.
2. Rent on the office space used by the non-manufacturing staff.
3. Salaries paid to the employees who produce the audio equipment.
4. Cost of the glue used to fasten the company's logo to the grill used on all of its speakers.
5. The cost of online advertising.
6. Salaries paid to the accounting employees.
7. Salary paid to the production manager who supervises the manufacturing activities for all products.
8. Cost of the plastic used for turntable dust covers.
9. Bonuses paid to sales staff for meeting their monthly sales goals.
10. Salary paid to the manager of the human resources department.

EXERCISE 2–2 Classification of Costs as Period or Product Costs [LO2]

Precision Electronics manufactures wearable devices that incorporate Global Positioning System technology. Their devices are used by runners, cyclists, golfers, hikers, etc. The following are some costs incurred by Precision Electronics:

1. The cost of components used in the devices.
2. Factory heating costs.
3. Factory equipment maintenance costs.
4. Training costs for new administrative employees.
5. The cost of solder used in assembling the devices.
6. The travel costs of the company's Chief Financial Officer.
7. Wages and salaries of factory security personnel.
8. Utility costs for the building used exclusively for administrative personnel.
9. Wages and salaries in the department responsible for customer billing.

10. Depreciation on fitness centre equipment used only by factory employees.
11. Telephone expenses for the manager of the production facility.
12. The costs of shipping devices to customers.
13. The wages of employees who assemble the devices.
14. The Chief Executive Officer's salary.
15. Overtime paid to administrative staff in the accounts payable department.

Required:
Classify the above costs as either product (inventoriable) costs or period (non-inventoriable) costs.

EXERCISE 2–3   Constructing an Income Statement [LO3]

Home Entertainment, a retailer of CDs and DVDs, provided the following information for the month of June:

Sales	$150,000
Selling expenses	40,000
Administrative expenses	25,000
Merchandise inventory, beginning balance	12,000
Merchandise inventory, ending balance	22,000
Merchandise purchases	90,000

CHECK FIGURE
Goods available for sale—$102,000; Gross margin—$70,000; Operating income—$5,000.

Required:
Prepare an income statement for the company for the month.

EXERCISE 2–4   Prepare a Schedule of Cost of Goods Manufactured [LO4]

Classic Sound is a start-up company that produces vinyl records for numerous record labels worldwide. The company has two full-time employees working in the production department while the CEO splits her time 80/20% between developing new business and overseeing the production process. Information taken from the accounting records for the first three months of operations is shown below.

Beginning raw materials inventory	$ 0
Purchases of raw materials	50,000
Ending raw materials inventory	25,000
Direct labour	40,000
Manufacturing overhead	30,000
Beginning work in process inventory	0
Ending work in process inventory	5,000
Purchase of production equipment	100,000
Rent for production facility	9,000

Required:
1. Prepare a schedule of cost of goods manufactured for the company for the month.
2. What types of expenses are likely included in the total manufacturing overhead cost of $30,000 incurred for the first three months of operation?

EXERCISE 2–5   Fixed and Variable Costs [LO5]

Mike's Radiator Services specializes in the repair and replacement of radiators for passenger vehicles. Variable and fixed costs related to installation activities for the most recent month (January) are listed below:

Item	
Number of radiators replaced	100
Variable expenses:	
Direct materials (new radiators)	$50,000
Direct labour (2 hours per installation)	5,000
Indirect materials	500
Fixed expenses:	
Installation supervisor's wages	$ 8,000
Equipment depreciation	1,000
Insurance and utilities for garage	700

Required:

1. Calculate the per unit amounts for each of the variable expense and fixed expense items in January.
2. Mike expects that 80 radiators will be installed in February and that this level of activity is within the relevant range for all variable and fixed expenses. Calculate
    a. The total expense for each of the variable and fixed cost items above.
    b. The per unit amounts for each of the variable and fixed cost items above. Explain any differences in the per unit amounts between January and February.
3. Which, if any, of the costs shown above would be considered sunk costs? Why?

EXERCISE 2–6 Identifying Direct and Indirect Costs [LO6]

Northwest Hospital is a full-service hospital that provides everything from major surgery and emergency room care to outpatient clinics.

Required:

For each cost incurred at Northwest Hospital, indicate whether it would most likely be a direct cost or an indirect cost of the specified cost object by placing an X in the appropriate column.

	Cost Object	Direct Cost	Indirect Cost
Ex. Catered food served to patients	A particular patient		X
1. The wages of pediatric nurses	The pediatric department		
2. Prescription drugs	A particular patient		
3. Heating the hospital	The pediatric department		
4. The salary of the head of pediatrics	The pediatric department		
5. The salary of the head of pediatrics	A particular patient		
6. Hospital chaplain's salary	A particular patient		
7. Lab tests by outside contractor	A particular patient		
8. Lab tests by outside contractor	A particular department		

EXERCISE 2–7 Differential, Opportunity, and Sunk Costs [LO7]

Performance Edge (PE) is a consulting firm that helps companies develop employee recognition programs. It maintains a large inventory of prizes companies can give to deserving employees. Because of growth in demand for its services, PE is considering selling its existing warehouse used for storing the prize inventory and leasing a new, larger warehouse facility. The existing warehouse has a large parking lot that was newly paved last year and PE rents about 30% of the parking spots to occupants of adjacent properties. The new warehouse is expected to be much more energy efficient and is larger than PE currently requires to store inventory. As a result, if they make the move management plans to sublet about 15% of the space for the next three years. The new warehouse is also expected to require less maintenance but because of the additional size two new warehouse employees will be hired.

Required:

For each of the items below, indicate by placing an X in the appropriate column whether it should be considered a differential cost, an opportunity cost, or a sunk cost in the decision to move into the new warehouse. If none of the categories apply for a particular item, leave all columns blank. The first item has been completed as an example:

Item	Differential Revenue	Differential Cost	Opportunity Cost	Sunk Cost
Ex. Cost of electricity for the warehouses		X		
1. Sublet revenue for the new warehouse				
2. Lease payments for the new warehouse				
3. Net book value of the existing warehouse				

(Continued on next page)

(Continued from previous page)

Item	Differential Revenue	Differential Cost	Opportunity Cost	Sunk Cost
4. Sales proceeds from selling the existing warehouse				
5. Warehouse maintenance costs				
6. Warehouse staff wages				
7. Paving costs for the parking lot of the existing warehouse				
8. Parking lot revenues for the existing warehouse				

EXERCISE 2–8 Opportunity Costs and Sunk Costs [LO7]

Johnson Company manufactures sporting goods. One of its products is generating very low operating income, and management is trying to decide whether it should keep or drop that product. Five years ago, the company paid $1,500,000 for the building in which the product is manufactured and $500,000 for the land. The net book value (original cost less accumulated depreciation) for the building is $1,375,000. Management paid the annual property taxes and insurance on the building two weeks ago ($30,000 total). The manufacturing equipment used to make the product was also purchased five years ago at a cost of $300,000 and has a net book value of $150,000. Management was recently approached by an individual who offered to pay $1,000,000 for the land, building, and equipment. Two weeks later, a second individual contacted management and offered to rent the manufacturing facilities for $20,000 per month.

Required:

Which of the above costs are opportunity costs with respect to deciding whether or not to continue to manufacture the product, and which are sunk costs? Explain your answers.

EXERCISE 2–9 Product Cost Flows; Product versus Period Costs [LO2, LO3]

Running Data began operations on February 1. The company produces GPS watches designed for runners. On February 15, the company purchased 1,000 DVD discs to include with each running watch it sells. The DVD is preloaded with product setup information, an instruction manual including video examples, and warranty details. Each disc costs Running Data $2.00.

During February, 200 discs were taken from the raw materials inventory. Of these, 20 were taken by the sales manager to sales meetings with prospective retailers to carry the watches and handed out as advertising. The remaining discs were included with the GPS watches that were being manufactured in February. Of the watches that were bundled with the discs during February, 75% were completed and transferred from work in process to finished goods. Of the watches completed during the month, 60% were sold and shipped to customers.

CHECK FIGURE
Cost of discs in: Raw materials—$1,600; Work in process—$90; Finished goods—$108; Cost of goods sold—$162; Advertising expense—$40.

Required:

1. Determine the cost of discs that would be in each of the following accounts at February 28:
   a.   Raw Materials.
   b.   Work in Process.
   c.   Finished Goods.
   d.   Cost of Goods Sold.
   e.   Advertising Expense.
2. Specify whether each of the above accounts would appear on the balance sheet or on the income statement at February 28.

EXERCISE 2–10 Preparation of a Schedule of Cost of Goods Manufactured and Cost of Goods Sold [LO1, LO3, LO4]

The following details are from the accounting records of Gulf Shore Limited for the year ended April 30:

Costs incurred:

Direct labour......................................	$ 70,000
Raw material purchases	118,000
Indirect labour....................................	30,000
Maintenance, factory equipment......................	6,000
Advertising expense	90,000
Insurance, factory equipment	800
Sales staff salaries................................	50,000
Rent, factory facilities.............................	20,000
Supplies, factory	4,200
Depreciation, office equipment......................	3,000
Depreciation, factory equipment.....................	19,000

	Beginning of Year	End of Year
Inventories:		
Raw materials	$ 7,000	$15,000
Work in process.....................	10,000	5,000
Finished goods	20,000	35,000

Required:
1. Prepare a schedule of cost of goods manufactured for the year ended April 30.
2. Prepare the cost of goods sold section of Gulf Shore Limited's income statement for the year ended April 30.
3. Why does the cost of goods manufactured differ from cost of goods sold?

EXERCISE 2–11 Classification of Costs as Variable or Fixed [LO5]
Below are listed various costs that may be found in a variety of organizations.
1. Small glass plates used for lab tests in a hospital.
2. Straight-line depreciation of a building.
3. Senior management salaries.
4. Advertising of products and services.
5. Electrical costs of operating production equipment.
6. Batteries used in motorcycle manufacturing.
7. Commissions paid to sales staff.
8. Liability insurance paid by a dentist.
9. Subscription fee paid for use of cloud-based analytics software.

Required:
Classify each cost as either variable or fixed with respect to the volume of goods or services produced and sold by the organization.

	Cost Behaviour	
Cost Item	**Variable**	**Fixed**

EXERCISE 2–12 Classification of Labour Costs [LO1]
Jan Davis is employed by Wesley Limited. Last week she worked 48 hours assembling one of the company's products. Wesley's employees work a 40-hour week and Davis is paid $24 per hour. Employees are paid time and a half for any hours worked in excess of the standard 40 hours. Assume the overtime is the result of an overall increase in demand for all products.

Required:
1. Allocate Davis's wages for the week between direct labour cost and manufacturing overhead cost.
2. How would your answer to part (1) have changed if the overtime was incurred to meet a rush order for a particular customer?
3. Now assume that in a different 40-hour week, Davis had 35 hours where she was actually working but was idle 5 hours due to scheduled maintenance on the production equipment. Allocate Davis's wages for the week between direct labour cost and manufacturing overhead cost.

PROBLEMS

PROBLEM 2–13 Direct and Indirect Costs; Variable Costs [LO5, LO6]

The following cost data pertain to the operations of Montgomery Department Stores Inc. for the month of July.

Corporate legal office salaries	$56,000
Apparel Department cost of sales—Evendale Store	90,000
Corporate headquarters building lease	48,000
Store manager's salary—Evendale Store	12,000
Apparel Department sales commission—Evendale Store	7,000
Store utilities—Evendale Store	11,000
Apparel Department manager's salary—Evendale Store	8,000
Central warehouse lease cost	15,000
Janitorial costs—Evendale Store	9,000

The Evendale Store is one of many stores owned and operated by the company. The Apparel Department is one of many departments at the Evendale Store. The central warehouse serves all of the company's stores.

Required:
1. What is the total amount of the costs listed above that are direct costs of the Apparel Department?
2. What is the total amount of the costs listed above that are direct costs of the Evendale Store?
3. What is the total amount of the Apparel Department's direct costs that are also variable costs with respect to total departmental sales?

PROBLEM 2–14 Classification of Labour Costs [LO1]

Big Sky Equipment manufactures and sells camping equipment. Employees in the production department are paid $30 per hour but receive $45 per hour for each hour worked in excess of 40 hours per week.

Required:
1. Calculate the total wages for the week if an employee works 50 hours. Of the total, how much would the company allocate to direct labour cost? To manufacturing overhead cost?
2. In a different week, suppose an employee works 45 hours but is idle for 3 hours during the week due to a shortage of direct materials used in production. Calculate the employee's total wages for the week. How much of this amount would be allocated to direct labour cost? To manufacturing overhead cost?
3. Big Sky provides employee benefits that cost $9 for each hour the employee works (either regular time or overtime). During a particular week, an employee works 52 hours but is idle for 6 hours due to an equipment breakdown. Calculate the employee's total wages and employee benefits for the week. If employee benefits are considered by the company to be part of manufacturing overhead cost, how much of the total wages and employee benefits for the week would be allocated to direct labour cost? To manufacturing overhead cost?
4. Refer to the data in (3) above. If the company treats that part of employee benefits relating to direct labour as added direct labour cost, how much of the wages and employee benefits for the week will be allocated to direct labour cost? To manufacturing overhead cost?

PROBLEM 2–15 Cost Classification [LO1, LO2, LO5, LO7]

Robyn Blake has invented a new type of fly swatter. After thinking it through carefully, she has decided to quit her $5,000 per month job with a start-up tech company to produce and sell the fly swatters full time. Robyn will rent a garage that will be used as a production plant. The rent will be $300 per month. She will also rent production equipment at a cost of $1,000 per month.

The cost of materials for each fly swatter will be $0.60. Robyn will hire workers to produce the fly swatters. They will be paid $1.00 for each completed unit. Robyn will rent a room in the house next door for use as her sales office. The rent will be $150 per month. She will add extended voicemail to her mobile plan to ensure she gets after-hours messages from customers. The feature will cost $5 per month.

Robyn has savings that are earning her interest of $2,000 per year. She plans to withdraw all of her savings to use in getting the business started for the first year. Robyn plans to advertise her product in numerous trade publications at a cost of $400 per month. She plans to pay her sales staff a commission of $0.20 for each fly swatter sold.

She does not plan to take any salary from the new company for the first year. Robyn has already paid the legal fees required to incorporate her new company at a total cost of $1,000.

Required:
1. Prepare an answer sheet with the following column headings:

Name of the Cost	Variable Cost	Fixed Cost	Product Cost			Period (Selling and Administrative) Cost	Opportunity Cost	Sunk Cost
			Direct Materials	Direct Labour	Manufacturing Overhead			

List the different costs associated with the new product decision down the left column (under Name of the Cost). Then place an X under each heading that describes the type of cost involved. Several column headings may have an X under them for a single cost. (For example, a cost may be a fixed cost, a period cost, and a sunk cost; you would place an X under each of these column headings opposite the cost.)
2. All of the costs you should have listed above, except one, would be differential costs between the alternatives of Robyn setting up her company or staying at her job with the tech company. Which item is not a differential cost? Explain.

PROBLEM 2–16 Classification of Costs as Variable or Fixed and Direct or Indirect [LO1, LO2, LO5, LO6]

Listed below are costs found in various organizations.
 1. Depreciation, executive jet.
 2. Costs of shipping finished goods to customers.
 3. Wood used in manufacturing furniture.
 4. Sales manager's salary.
 5. Electricity used in manufacturing furniture.
 6. Salary of the secretary to the company president.
 7. Aerosol attachment placed on a spray can produced by the company.
 8. Costs of billing customers.
 9. Packing supplies for shipping products overseas.
10. Sand used in manufacturing concrete.
11. Supervisor's salary, factory.
12. Executive life insurance.
13. Sales commissions.
14. Employee benefits, assembly-line workers.
15. Advertising costs.
16. Property taxes on warehouses used to store finished goods.
17. Lubricants for production equipment.

Required:
Prepare an answer sheet with column headings as shown below. For each cost item, indicate whether it would be variable or fixed with respect to the number of units produced and sold, and then whether it would be a selling cost, an administrative cost, or a product cost. If it is a product cost, indicate whether it would typically be treated as a direct or an indirect cost with respect to units of product. Three sample answers are provided for illustration:

Cost Item	Variable or Fixed	Selling Cost	Administrative Cost	Product Cost	
				Direct	Indirect
Direct labour	V			X	
Executive salaries	F		X		
Factory rent	F				X

PROBLEM 2–17 Schedule of Cost of Goods Manufactured; Income Statement; Cost Behaviour [LO1, LO2, LO3, LO4, LO5]
The following information pertains to the most recent quarter at Precious Production Limited.

Purchases of raw materials	$ 360,000
Raw materials inventory, beginning	40,000
Raw materials inventory, ending.	68,000
Depreciation, factory.	168,000
Insurance, factory	20,000
Direct labour	240,000
Maintenance, factory.	120,000
Administrative expenses	280,000
Sales	1,800,000
Utilities, factory	108,000
Supplies, factory	4,000
Selling expenses	320,000
Indirect labour.	260,000
Work in process inventory, beginning.	28,000
Work in process inventory, ending	120,000
Finished goods inventory, beginning	40,000
Finished goods inventory, ending	160,000

Required:
1. Prepare a schedule of cost of goods manufactured.
2. Prepare an income statement.
3. Assume that the company produced the equivalent of 10,000 units of product during the year. What was the average cost per unit for direct labour? What was the average cost per unit for factory insurance?
4. Assume that the company expects to produce 12,000 units of product during the coming year. What average cost per unit and what total cost would you expect the company to incur for direct materials at this level of activity? For factory insurance? (In preparing your answer, assume that direct materials is a variable cost and that depreciation is a fixed cost; also assume that depreciation is computed on a straight-line basis.)
5. As the manager responsible for production costs, explain to the president any difference in the average costs per unit between (3) and (4) above.
6. Assuming the company produced 20,000 fully and partially finished units during the year, determine the cost components of the finished goods inventory, which is composed of 4,000 finished units.

> **CHECK FIGURE**
> Cost of goods manufactured—$1,160,000; Gross margin—$760,000; Operating income—$160,000; Direct labour cost per unit for 12,000 units—$24; Insurance cost per unit for 12,000 units—$1.67.

PROBLEM 2–18 Sunk Costs and Opportunity Costs [LO7]
You have just started a new part-time job at Learning Solutions, a company that develops online training platforms for corporate clients and provides content support on a subscription basis. Learning Solutions is considering upgrading the computers used by its graphic design department. The five computers being replaced cost $12,000 two years ago and now have a net book value of $4,000 based on using straight-line depreciation, a three-year useful life, and $0 salvage value. Your analysis indicates you can likely get about $500 per computer if you advertise them online.

The new computers being considered will cost $15,000 in total and will also have a three-year useful life, with an estimated salvage value of $0. The new machines each include annual licences for graphic design software for which Learning Solutions is currently paying a total of $500 per year, per machine.

Required:
1. You prepared an analysis of the financial effects of keeping the old machines versus buying the new machines that ignored the $4,000 book value of the old machines but included the potential salvage proceeds of $500 per computer. Your supervisor has politely told you that it was a mistake to exclude the $4,000 since it will have to be written off for financial reporting purposes if Learning Solutions goes ahead and purchases the new computers. Your supervisor noted, "You should have included a loss of $1,500 in your analysis: the $2,500 salvage value ($500 × 5) less the $4,000 net book value to be written off." Who is correct, and why?

2. Your analysis also shows that under the option to keep the existing computers there are two opportunity costs: (a) the salvage value of $500 for each of the old computers, and (b) the $500 per machine in software licence cost savings that would have been realized if the new machines had been purchased. Again, your supervisor has politely told you that including these costs under the alternative to keep the old machines is wrong since in neither case are there any out-of-pocket costs incurred by Learning Solutions. Who is correct, and why?

PROBLEM 2–19 Classification of Various Costs [LO1, LO2, LO5, LO7]

RTW Company manufactures acoustic and electric guitars. Selected costs from the most recent year of operations follow below.

1. The guitars use metal for the frets and tuning knobs that costs $10 per guitar.
2. Wages for employees who handcraft the guitars total $175 per guitar.
3. Insurance on the manufacturing facilities totals $5,000 per year.
4. Glue used in the assembly process amounts to $3 per guitar.
5. The annual depreciation cost of the machines used to cut and finish the wood used in the guitars totals $15,000.
6. The salary of the vice president of marketing is $150,000 per year.
7. The salary of the manager of manufacturing operations is $120,000 per year.
8. The total cost of an advertising campaign paid at the beginning of the year just ended was $75,000.
9. Instead of producing acoustic guitars, RTW Company could use the manufacturing facilities to increase production of electric guitars that would generate operating income of $100,000 per year.
10. Overtime premiums for production staff were $1,000 during a one-month period to meet a rush order on a specific model of guitar for a single large customer.

Required:

Prepare an answer sheet with the following column headings:

			Product Cost			Period (Selling and Administrative) Cost	To Units of Product		Opportunity Cost	Sunk Cost
Name of the Cost	Variable Cost	Fixed Cost	Direct Materials	Direct Labour	Manufacturing Overhead		Direct	Indirect		

List the different costs associated with the company down the left column (under Name of the Cost). Then place an X under each heading that describes the type of cost involved. Several column headings may have an X under them for a single cost. (That is, a cost may be a fixed cost, a period cost, and a sunk cost; you would place an X under each of these column headings opposite the cost.) Under the variable cost column, list only those costs that would be variable with respect to the number of guitars that are produced and sold.

PROBLEM 2–20 Cost Classification and Cost Behaviour [LO1, LO2, LO5, LO6]

The Outdoor Dining Company specializes in producing a set of wood patio furniture consisting of a table and four chairs. The set enjoys great popularity, and the company has ample orders to keep production going at its full capacity of 2,000 sets per year. Annual cost data at full capacity follow:

Direct labour	$118,000
Advertising	50,000
Factory supervision	40,000
Property taxes, factory building	3,500
Sales commissions	80,000
Insurance, factory	2,500
Depreciation, administrative office equipment	4000
Lease cost, factory equipment	12,000
Indirect materials, factory	6,000
Depreciation, factory	10,000
Administrative office supplies	3,000
Direct materials used (wood, bolts, etc.)	94,000
Utilities, factory	20,000

Required:

1. Prepare an answer sheet with the column headings shown below. Enter each cost item on your answer sheet, placing the dollar amount under the appropriate headings. As an example, this has already been done for the first item in the list above. Note that each cost item is classified in two ways: first, as either variable or fixed with respect to the number of units produced and sold, and second, as either a selling and administrative cost or a product cost. (If the item is a product cost, it should also be classified as either direct or indirect, as shown.)

	Cost Behaviour		Selling or	Product Cost	
Cost Item	Variable	Fixed	Administrative Cost	Direct	Indirect*
Direct labour	$118,000			$118,000	

*To units of product

2. Total the dollar amounts in each of the columns in (1) above. Compute the average product cost per patio set.
3. Due to reduced demand, assume that production drops to only 1,000 sets per year. Would you expect the average product cost per patio set to increase, decrease, or remain unchanged? Explain. No computations are necessary.
4. Refer to the original data. The president's sister has considered making herself a patio set and has priced the necessary materials at a building supply store. As an alternative, she has asked the president whether she could purchase a patio set from the Outdoor Dining Company "at cost," and the president has agreed to let her do so.
   a. Would you expect any disagreement between the two over the price the sister should pay? Explain. What price does the president probably have in mind? The sister?
   b. Since the company is operating at full capacity, what cost term used in the chapter might be justification for the president to charge the full regular price to his sister and still be selling "at cost"? Explain.

PROBLEM 2–21 Variable and Fixed Costs; Subtleties of Direct and Indirect Costs [LO5, LO6]
Madison Seniors Care Centre is a non-profit organization that provides a variety of health services to the elderly. The centre is organized into a number of departments, one of which is the Meals-on-Wheels program that delivers hot meals to seniors in their homes on a daily basis. Below are listed a number of costs of the centre and the Meals-on-Wheels program.

Example: The cost of groceries used in meal preparation
a. The cost of leasing the Meals-on-Wheels van.
b. The cost of incidental supplies such as salt, pepper, napkins, and so on.
c. The cost of gasoline consumed by the Meals-on-Wheels van.
d. The rent on the facility that houses Madison Seniors Care Centre, including the Meals-on-Wheels program.
e. The salary of the part-time manager of the Meals-on-Wheels program.
f. Depreciation on the kitchen equipment used in the Meals-on-Wheels program.
g. The hourly wages of the caregiver who drives the van and delivers the meals.
h. The costs of complying with health and safety regulations in the kitchen.
i. The costs of mailing letters soliciting donations to the Meals-on-Wheels program.

Required:
For each cost listed above, indicate whether it is a direct or indirect cost of the Meals-on-Wheels program, whether it is a direct or indirect cost of particular seniors served by the program, and whether it is variable or fixed with respect to the number of seniors served. Use the form below for your answer.

	Direct or Indirect Cost of the Meals-on-Wheels Program		Direct or Indirect Cost of Particular Seniors Served by the Meals-on-Wheels Program		Variable or Fixed with Respect to the Number of Seniors Served by the Meals-on-Wheels Program	
Item Description	Direct	Indirect	Direct	Indirect	Variable	Fixed
Example: The cost of groceries used in meal preparation	X		X		X	

PROBLEM 2–22 Schedule of Cost of Goods Manufactured; Income Statement
[LO1, LO2, LO3, LO4]

Cost and sales information for the most recent fiscal year are shown below:

WALLACE RIVER COMPANY Cost and Sales Information For the Year Ended December 31	
Purchases of raw materials	$ 90,000
Raw materials inventory, beginning	10,000
Raw materials, ending	17,000
Depreciation, factory	42,000
Insurance, factory	5,000
Direct labour	60,000
Maintenance, factory	30,000
Administrative expense	70,000
Sales	450,000
Utilities, factory	27,000
Supplies, factory	1,000
Selling expense	80,000
Advertising expense	20,000
Indirect labour, factory	65,000
Work in process inventory, beginning	7,000
Work in process inventory, ending	30,000
Finished goods inventory, beginning	10,000
Finished goods inventory, ending	40,000

Required:

1. Prepare a schedule of cost of goods manufactured.
2. Prepare an income statement.
3. Assume that the company produced 10,000 units of product during the year. What was the average cost per unit for direct materials? What was the average cost per unit for factory depreciation?
4. Assume that the company expects to produce and sell 15,000 units of product during the coming year. What average cost per unit and what total cost would you expect the company to incur for direct materials and for factory depreciation at this level of activity? Assume that raw materials costs charged by suppliers will not change next year. For factory depreciation, assume that the company uses straight-line depreciation and that the factory equipment has five years of useful life remaining.
5. Explain any difference in the average cost per unit between requirements (3) and (4) above.

PROBLEM 2–23 Ethics and the Manager [LO2]

M. K. Gallant is president of Kranbrack Corporation, a company whose stock is traded on a national exchange. In a meeting with investment analysts at the beginning of the year, Gallant had predicted that the company's earnings would grow by 20% this year. Unfortunately, sales have been less than expected for the year, and Gallant concluded within two weeks of the end of the fiscal year that it would be impossible to report an increase in earnings as large as predicted unless some drastic action was taken. Accordingly, Gallant has ordered that wherever possible, expenditures should be postponed to the new year—including cancelling or postponing orders with suppliers, delaying planned maintenance and training, and cutting back on end-of-year advertising and travel. Additionally, Gallant ordered the company's controller to carefully scrutinize all costs that are currently classified as period costs and re-classify as many as possible as product costs. The company is expected to have substantial inventories at the end of the year.

Required:

1. Why would reclassifying period costs as product costs increase this period's reported earnings?
2. Do you believe Gallant's actions are ethical? Why or why not?

PROBLEM 2–24 Schedule of Cost of Goods Manufactured; Income Statement; Cost Behaviour [LO1, LO2, LO3, LO4, LO5]

Carlton Manufacturing Company provided the following details about operations in February:

Purchases of raw materials	$130,000
Maintenance, factory.	37,000
Direct labour	32,500
Depreciation, factory equipment.	55,000
Indirect materials, factory	3,000
Selling and administrative salaries	42,500
Utilities, factory	26,000
Sales commissions	17,500
Insurance, factory equipment	4,000
Depreciation, sales equipment	20,000
Advertising expenses	107,500
Rent, factory building	?

The company also provided details regarding the balances in the inventory accounts at the beginning and end of the month as follows:

	Beginning of Month	End of Month
Raw materials	$25,000	?
Work in process.	24,000	?
Finished goods	15,000	?

Raw materials used in production cost $135,000, total overhead costs for the year were $170,000, the goods available for sale totalled $360,000, and the cost of goods sold totalled $317,500.

Required:
1. Prepare a schedule of cost of goods manufactured and the cost of goods sold section of the company's income statement for the year.
2. Assume that the dollar amounts given above are for the equivalent of 15,000 units produced during the year. Compute the average cost per unit for direct materials used, and compute the average cost per unit for rent on the factory building.
3. Assume that in the following year the company expects to produce 20,000 units. What average cost per unit and total cost would you expect to be incurred for direct materials, and for rent on the factory building? Direct materials are a variable cost and rent is a fixed cost.
4. As the manager in charge of production costs, explain to the president the reason for any difference in the average costs per unit between (2) and (3) above.

PROBLEM 2–25 Different Cost Classifications for Different Purposes [LO2, LO4, LO5, LO6]

Dozier Company produced and sold 1,000 units during its first month of operations. It reported the following costs and expenses for the month:

Item	Amount
Direct materials.	$69,000
Direct labour	35,000
Variable manufacturing overhead (indirect materials)	15,000
Fixed manufacturing overhead (depreciation, equipment)	28,000
Variable selling expense (commissions).	12,000
Fixed selling expense (sales staff salaries)	18,000
Variable administrative expense (part-time staff, hourly wages)	4,000
Fixed administrative expense (full-time staff, salaries)	25,000

Required:
1. With respect to cost classifications for preparing financial statements: (a) What is the total product cost? (b) What is the total period cost?

2. With respect to cost classifications for assigning costs to cost objects: (a) What is the total direct manufacturing cost? (b) What is the total indirect manufacturing cost?

3. With respect to cost classifications for manufacturers: (a) What is the total manufacturing cost (assume there are no opening or closing balances for work in process inventories)? (b) What is the total non-manufacturing cost? (c) What is the total conversion cost and prime cost?

4. With respect to cost classifications for predicting cost behaviour: (a) What is the total variable manufacturing cost? (b) What is the total fixed cost for the company as a whole? (c) What is the variable cost per unit produced and sold?

5. If Dozier produced 1,100 units instead of 1,000 units, how much incremental manufacturing cost would they incur to make the additional 100 units?

PROBLEM 2–26 Income Statement; Schedule of Cost of Goods Manufactured [LO1, LO2, LO3, LO4]

The following information was taken from the accounting records of Mitchell Company for last year:

Selling expenses	$ 140,000
Raw materials inventory, January 1	90,000
Raw materials inventory, December 31	60,000
Utilities, factory	36,000
Direct labour cost	150,000
Depreciation, factory	162,000
Purchases of raw materials	750,000
Sales	2,500,000
Insurance, factory	40,000
Supplies, factory	15,000
Administrative expenses	270,000
Indirect labour	300,000
Maintenance, factory	87,000
Work in process inventory, January 1	180,000
Work in process inventory, December 31	100,000
Finished goods inventory, January 1	260,000
Finished goods inventory, December 31	210,000

Management wants to organize these data into a better format so that financial statements can be prepared for the year.

Required:
1. Prepare a schedule of cost of goods manufactured as in Exhibit 2–4.
2. Compute the cost of goods sold.
3. Using data as needed from (1) and (2) above, prepare an income statement.
4. Assuming production of finished and semi-finished goods amounted to 412,500 units for the past year, calculate the cost components of the ending finished goods inventory of 55,176 units. (*Hint:* The categories of costs in the ending inventory are the same as the total manufacturing costs; only the amounts are different.)

> **CHECK FIGURE**
> Cost of goods manufactured—$1,650,000; Cost of goods sold—$1,700,000; Gross margin—$800,000; Operating income—$390,000.

PROBLEM 2–27 Differential Costs, Sunk Costs, and Opportunity Costs [LO7]

Lilly Martin is a third-year university student who has operated her own lawn care business for the past four years. She has one employee, her younger brother, whom she pays $15 per hour. He has worked an average of 600 hours per season since Lilly started her business. She is planning on giving him a raise of $2 per hour for the fifth season of her business, which will amount to additional wages of about $1,200. When Lilly first started operations, she borrowed $1,000 from her parents to purchase two lawn mowers for $500 each. Because Lilly is an accounting major, she decided to prepare financial statements at the end of each lawn care season so she would know how much she earned. For accounting purposes she assumed each lawn mower would have a five-year life with $25 salvage value. As of the end of her fourth year of operations, each lawn mower had a net book value of $120. Lilly estimates she could sell each mower now for $40 each.

Lilly is beginning to plan for the fifth year of operations and recently learned of a company that leases lawn mowers to small businesses. The company is currently offering one-year leases on a mower similar to the type Lilly currently uses for $200. In addition, the company charges an up-front administration fee of $25 to process the lease agreement. As part of the lease agreement, the company will perform two oil changes and sharpen the mower blades twice during the year. Lilly's accounting records show that she has paid about $100 in total per season for having the oil changed and blades sharpened twice for each of her two mowers. However, Lilly estimates that she will have to forgo about $75 in total lawn care revenue for the season related to having to take the two leased lawnmowers in to the company during regular business hours to have the oil changed and blades sharpened. Her father has always changed the oil and sharpened the blades on the existing mowers on Sundays when Lilly wasn't using them. Given other time commitments of both Lilly and her brother, she cannot foresee being able to work extra hours to make up the time lost for the oil changes and blade sharpening.

Lilly would be responsible to pay for any repairs arising from use of the mowers such as broken wheels, damaged blades, broken cables, etc. Given the high amount of usage, repair costs have averaged about $150 per season for each of her two existing mowers and she estimates they will be similar in the fifth year even if she leases the two mowers. After finishing her fourth season of operations Lilly paid about $100 in total for each mower to replace the wheels and install new starter cords.

The new mowers are more fuel efficient and Lilly's research shows they will use about 7.5% less gas than her current mowers. Lilly's existing mowers each use about 4 litres of gas per hour, which amounts to about 2,400 litres per season at an average of $1.00 per litre.

Lilly has never increased her billing rate of $30 per hour since she started her company but plans to raise her rates to $32 per hour, which will generate additional revenue of about $2,400 in the fifth year.

Required:
1. Should Lilly sell her old mowers and lease two new mowers for her fifth season of operations? Show all calculations.
2. For any of the amounts above not used in your analysis, briefly explain why it was excluded.

CASES

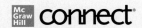

CASE 2–28 [LO1, LO2, LO3, LO4]

John Ranton, president and founder of Running Mate, could hardly contain his excitement over the operating results for his company's second year of operations. Running Mate is an online retailer of a GPS running watch that records distance, time, speed, heart rate, and a number of other statistics. Ranton's company does not manufacture the watches, but instead purchases them directly from the manufacturer based in China and resells them through its online shopping site. During the first two years of operation, Ranton decided to hold the selling price of the watch constant at $100 per unit in an effort to attract business. He was also able to negotiate a deal with the supplier to hold Running Mate's cost per watch constant at $80 per unit for the two years.

Operating expenses for each of the first two years of operation consist only of advertising expenses and the salaries paid to the website designer/administrator and the company's bookkeeper. Because Ranton is busy with his numerous other business ventures, the bookkeeper also looks after the day-to-day operations of Running Mate and has sole signing authority to make expenditures on the company's behalf. To motivate his website designer to create a website that is easy to use and appealing to customers, Ranton decided to pay her a commission equal to 1% of annual sales in both 2020 and 2021. The salaries paid to the website administrator and the bookkeeper were the same in both years and totalled $92,000. Annual advertising expenses of $8,000 were also the same in both years.

After reviewing the operating results for 2020 (shown below), Ranton roughly calculated the expected sales and expenses for 2021 based on anticipated sales of 10,000 watches at a price of $100 per unit and a cost of $80 per unit. He calculated expected operating expenses in 2021 based on the 2020 cost per unit of $13.50 ($108,000 ÷ 8,000). Based on his calculations (shown below), Ranton expected a 25% improvement in 2021 operating income, in keeping with the increase in unit sales. So, when Running Mate's bookkeeper provided Ranton with the actual results shown below for 2021, he was thrilled. Operating income had improved over 44% compared to 2020 on sales growth of 25%.

	2020	2021 Expected	2021 Actual
Sales (units)	8,000	10,000	10,000
Sales	$800,000	$1,000,000	$1,000,000
Cost of goods sold	640,000	800,000	800,000
Gross margin	160,000	200,000	200,000
Operating expenses	108,000	135,000	125,000
Operating income	$ 52,000	$ 65,000	$ 75,000

Ranton has always been an entrepreneur at heart but has no formal training in financial accounting or management accounting. He has always had the bookkeeper prepare annual financial statements.

Required:

1. Explain the nature of the error made by Ranton when calculating expected operating income for 2021.
2. Based on the information provided in the case, recalculate the expected results for 2021. For Ranton's benefit, provide details on the specific items included in operating expenses (advertising, salaries, and commissions). Based on your calculations of the expected results for 2021, are the actual results for 2021 as good as Ranton originally thought? Explain.
3. Compare the expected operating expenses per your calculations in (2) to the actual results shown above for 2021. If you were Ranton, what follow-up questions would you have for the bookkeeper about 2021 operations?

CASE 2–29 Differential Revenues and Costs, Opportunity Costs, and Sunk Costs [LO7]

Performance Edge (PE) is a consulting company with offices in all major Canadian cities; its corporate headquarters are in Hamilton, Ontario. The company specializes in developing employee reward and recognition programs for its clients, which range from manufacturing companies to reservation centres for hotel chains. One of the most popular programs developed by PE involves working with its clients' management teams to establish performance goals for employees. Once the performance goals are established, PE develops a reward program whereby employees receive points instead of cash for attaining the goals set by management. The more difficult the goal, the greater the number of points received by the employee for goal attainment. The points can be redeemed for prizes such as bicycles; barbecues; computers; cameras; vacations; and gift certificates to restaurants, clothing and jewellery stores, and so on. PE has developed a catalogue of prizes that is distributed to employees so that they can see what they will be able to redeem their points for should they attain their performance goals for the period.

As part of the service offered to its clients, PE maintains an inventory of the prizes that can be purchased by its clients' employees with their points. PE purchases the prizes directly from manufacturers and wholesalers but maintains a reasonably large inventory of most items offered in its catalogue to ensure that they are available to clients on a timely basis. The inventory is kept in a warehouse at Stoney Creek, a community that is part of the city of Hamilton. The warehouse was purchased several years ago, and PE has grown considerably since then. Indeed, in recent months, delays have occurred in getting prizes to some clients because the warehouse is no longer large enough to maintain sufficient quantities of all items.

About a month ago, Reg White, the facilities manager at PE, became aware of a larger warehouse in nearby Burlington that is available for a long-term lease. The lease would qualify as an operating lease, so the monthly lease payments would be expensed. Although the warehouse in Burlington is larger than the current facility in Stoney Creek, White estimates that the utility costs will be lower because it is more modern and energy efficient. Another benefit of moving to the new warehouse will be that PE won't have to pay property taxes or building insurance since it won't own the building. Also, because the new warehouse is larger than PE currently requires to maintain an adequate inventory of prizes, it will be able to sublet about 15% of the total space to another tenant, at least for the next few years until it needs to take over the entire facility.

White also believes that it shouldn't be too hard to sell the existing warehouse in Stoney Creek based on conversations he has had with a commercial property real estate agent who already has clients interested in making an offer. Because the existing warehouse isn't yet fully depreciated, White also thinks that selling it will help PE's bottom line because the company will no longer have to charge the depreciation expense to the income statement. Another benefit of selling the existing warehouse is that PE will no longer incur the maintenance and repair costs, or the salary of the building maintenance manager, who will be let go if the company decides to rent the new facility. Maintenance costs of the new warehouse will be paid by the building's owner, unless the repairs are the result of damage caused by PE, in which case PE will be responsible for the costs. White thinks that insurance on the inventory of prizes and the costs of security personnel on-site 24/7 will not change if PE decides to move to the new warehouse.

One drawback in selling the existing warehouse is that PE will no longer earn the operating income associated with the small parking lot it had on one corner of the property. PE rented parking spaces to employees of a business on an adjacent property that did not have its own parking. Net of the annual costs of maintaining the parking lot (snow removal, repairs, security cameras, etc.), PE made a small operating profit each year.

Required:
1. Identify the differential revenues and costs related to keeping the existing warehouse in Stoney Creek versus renting the new facility in Burlington.
2. Are there any opportunity costs associated with selling the old warehouse?
3. What kind of cost is the depreciation expense on the old warehouse? Should it be considered in deciding whether to stay in the existing location or rent the new facility? Why or why not?

INSTANT QUIZ SOLUTIONS

2–1
The wages would be included as indirect labour since it would be difficult to trace these costs directly to units of the product. As indirect labour the costs are also part of manufacturing overhead.

2–2
The production supervisor's wages are considered a product cost because he or she is directly involved in the production of the product. The marketing manager's wages are a period cost because he or she is not involved in manufacturing the product but instead has responsibilities relating to creating awareness of the product.

2–3
Cost of goods sold = Beginning inventory + Purchases − Ending inventory
Rearranging to solve for ending finished goods inventory:
Beginning inventory = Cost of goods sold − Purchases + Ending inventory
Given the facts in the question:
$250,000 − $270,000 + $30,000 = $10,000

2–4
Cost of goods manufactured = Direct materials + Direct labour + Manufacturing overhead + Beginning work in process inventory − Ending work in process inventory $410,000 + $60,000 + $350,000 + $90,000 − $60,000 = $850,000

2–5
Total machine rental costs: $8,000 Average machine rental costs per test: $8,000 ÷ 1,000 tests = $8 per test Total machine rental costs if number of tests is 3,000 per month will likely be
$16,000 ($8,000 × 2 machines). Two machines will be needed, since each machine can perform only 2,000 tests per month.

2–6
The research and development costs would be considered an indirect cost of the X5 model since they are incurred in an effort to improve all BMW vehicles.

2–7
In this case the company will be better off by $10,000 per year to use the parking lot space for the new building. So, there is no opportunity cost.

2–8
The salvage value is an opportunity cost of keeping the equipment since it represents a potential benefit that would be given up if the equipment were not sold. That is, salvage value is received only if the equipment is sold.

COST BEHAVIOUR: ANALYSIS AND USE

LEARNING OBJECTIVES

After studying Chapter 3, you should be able to

1 Describe how fixed and variable costs behave and how to use them to predict costs.

2 Analyze mixed costs using various approaches.

3 Prepare an income statement using the contribution format.

4 (Appendix 3A) Analyze a mixed cost using the least-squares regression method.

■ COST BEHAVIOUR IN THE KNOWLEDGE ECONOMY

Source: Axonify

Given the rise of the knowledge economy an increasing number of companies' costs are largely fixed in the form of employee salaries. This is because the service these companies provide is heavily dependent on employees with specialized knowledge or skills. However, even in such companies there will still be some costs that vary in proportion to certain activities. Thus managers' ability to understand how costs behave is still relevant and important.

For example, in software as a service (SaaS) companies such as Axonify, based in Waterloo, Ontario, understanding how customer acquisition costs (CAC) behave is extremely important. Axonify develops customized online learning platforms for organizations, with the service provided on a subscription fee basis. CAC pertain to those expenses incurred to identify and secure new customers. Some CAC are fixed and relate to the salaries of employees whose job it is to acquire new customers. However, CAC also includes costs that vary in proportion to the activities required to identify and acquire new customers. Such costs would include trips to trade shows, development of online content such as webinars to demonstrate product features, or visits to potential customers. Understanding the fixed and variable elements of CAC improves managers' ability at SaaS companies such as Axonify to predict costs in future periods, set prices for the services provided, and make planning decisions.

In Chapter 2, we explained that costs can be classified by behaviour. *Cost behaviour* refers to how a cost will react or change as changes take place in the level of business activity. An understanding of cost behaviour is key to many decisions in an organization. The descriptions and techniques presented in this chapter are simplified so that they are easily understandable, but the ideas are appropriate for analyzing more complex situations that will appear in later chapters.

This chapter briefly reviews the definitions of variable costs and fixed costs and then discusses the behaviour of these costs in greater depth than in Chapter 2. We also discuss in greater detail a cost behaviour pattern, known as a *mixed* or *semi-variable* cost. All three cost behaviour patterns—variable, fixed, and mixed—are found in most organizations. The relative proportion of each type of cost present in a firm represents the firm's **cost structure**. In Chapter 4, we will more fully discuss how cost structure can affect decision making. We conclude the chapter by introducing a new income statement format—called the *contribution format*—in which costs are organized by behaviour rather than by the traditional functions of production, sales, and administration.

Cost structure
The relative proportion of fixed, variable, and mixed costs found in an organization.

LEARNING OBJECTIVE ❶
Describe how fixed and variable costs behave and how to use them to predict costs.

■ TYPES OF COST BEHAVIOUR PATTERNS

Variable Costs

As explained in Chapter 2, a variable cost is one whose *total dollar* amount varies in direct proportion to changes in the activity level. This means that if the activity level doubles, the total dollar amount of the variable costs also doubles. If the activity level increases by only 10% then the total dollar amount of the variable costs increases by 10% as well, and so on.

Recall from Chapter 2 that a variable cost remains constant if expressed on a *per unit* basis. For example, consider Sledding Adventures, a small company based in Whistler, British Columbia, that provides dog sled tours. After every tour, which lasts about two hours, the company gives each customer a drink (coffee, tea, or hot chocolate) and a light snack. The drinks and snacks ("refreshments") cost Sledding Adventures $10 per person. If we look at the cost of the refreshments on a *per person* basis, the cost is constant at $10. This $10 cost per person will not change, regardless of how many customers are served by Sledding Adventures. The behaviour of this variable cost, on both a per unit and a total basis, is tabulated as follows:

Number of Customers	Refreshment Cost per Customer	Total Cost of Refreshments
100	$10	$1,000
200	10	2,000
400	10	4,000
800	10	8,000

The idea that a variable cost is constant per unit but varies in total with the activity level is crucial to an understanding of cost behaviour patterns. However, it is possible for the variable cost per unit to change once activity levels are outside the relevant range. In the above example, if Sledding Adventures needed 1,500 refreshments, the unit cost might drop below $10 per refreshment if a quantity discount is provided by the supplier of the drinks or snacks. Similarly, if fewer than 100 refreshments were required, the unit cost per refreshment might be more than $10.

Exhibit 3–1 illustrates variable cost behaviour graphically. Note that the graph of the total refreshment costs slopes upward to the right. This is because the total cost of refreshments is directly proportional to the number of customers. In contrast, the graph of the per unit cost of refreshments is flat because the cost of refreshments per customer is constant at $10.

EXHIBIT 3–1 Variable Cost Behaviour

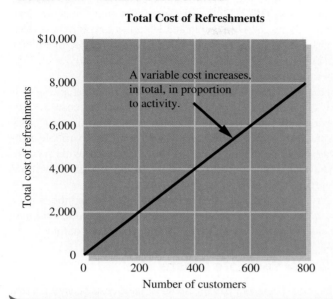

Total Cost of Refreshments

A variable cost increases, in total, in proportion to activity.

Total cost of refreshments

Number of customers

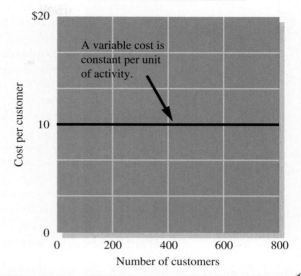

Per Unit Cost of Refreshments

A variable cost is constant per unit of activity.

Cost per customer

Number of customers

The Activity Base

For a cost to be variable, it must be variable *with respect to something*. That "something" is its *activity base*. An **activity base** is a measure of whatever causes a variable cost to be incurred. Some of the most common activity bases are direct labour-hours, machine-hours, units produced, and units sold. Other examples of activity bases are the number of kilometres driven by salespeople, the number of loads of laundry processed by a hotel, the number of bicycles repaired by a bike shop, and the number of occupied beds in a hospital.

Whether a cost is considered to be variable depends on whether it is caused by the activity under consideration. For example, if a manager is analyzing the cost of service calls for a product warranty, the relevant activity measure is the number of service calls made. Those costs that vary in total with the number of service calls made are the variable costs of making service calls.

For the purposes of this chapter, unless stated otherwise you can assume that the activity base under consideration is the total volume of goods and services produced or sold by the organization. So, for example, if we ask whether the cost of direct materials at Cervélo, a bicycle manufacturer, is a variable cost, the answer is yes, since the cost of direct materials is variable with respect to Cervélo's total volume of production. We will specify the activity base only when it is something other than total production or sales.

Activity base
A measure of whatever causes a variable cost to be incurred. For example, the total cost of direct materials in a bicycle manufacturing company will increase as the number of bicycles produced increases. Therefore, the number of bicycles produced is an activity base for explaining the total cost of direct materials.

IN BUSINESS

Smaller Internet service providers such as Seaside Wireless Communications Inc., based in Nova Scotia, do not have their own broadband networks but instead pay for access to networks owned by larger telecommunication companies such as Bell Canada and Rogers Communications Inc. These smaller companies pay for access to the broadband network on a per end-user (customer) basis. Seaside's cost to access a broadband network owned by another company will therefore vary in direct proportion to the number of customers they have. Moreover, the rate per user that the owners of the broadband networks are allowed to charge companies such as Seaside is regulated by the Canadian Radio-television and Telecommunications Commission (CRTC). Since those rates are reviewed only periodically by the CRTC, companies such as Seaside will know with certainty what their variable cost will be for providing each customer with access to a broadband network.

Extent of Variable Costs

The extent and type of variable costs incurred by an organization depend on the organization's structure and activities. A public utility like Hydro One, with large investments in equipment, tends to have few variable costs. Most of the costs are associated with its plant, and these costs tend to be insensitive to changes in levels of service provided. A manufacturing company like Paradigm, by contrast, often has many variable costs; these costs are associated with both manufacturing and distributing its products to customers.

In most merchandising companies, such as Canadian Tire, the cost of merchandise purchased for resale, a variable cost, constitutes a very large component of total cost. Service companies, by contrast, vary considerably with respect to the nature of their cost structures. Some service companies, such as the fast food chain Harvey's, have significant variable costs because of their raw material costs. Other companies, such as Deloitte, that provide services requiring specialized knowledge, have a high proportion of fixed costs in the form of facilities and highly trained salaried employees.

Some frequently encountered variable costs are listed in Exhibit 3–2. This exhibit is not a complete listing of all costs that can be considered variable, but provides a useful list of many of the costs that are normally considered variable with respect to the volume of output.

True Variable versus Step-Variable Costs

Not all variable costs have exactly the same behaviour pattern. Some variable costs behave in a *true variable* or *proportionately variable* pattern. Other variable costs behave in a *step-variable* pattern.

True Variable Costs

Direct materials represent a true variable cost because the amount used during a period varies in direct proportion to the level of production activity. Moreover, as discussed in Chapter 2, materials purchased but not sold in the form of a final product that period are carried forward to the next period as inventory either as raw materials, work in process, or finished goods.

Step-Variable Costs

Step-variable cost
A cost (such as the cost of a maintenance worker) that is obtainable only in large amounts and that increases and decreases only in response to fairly wide changes in the activity level.

The cost of a resource that is obtainable only in large amounts and that increases or decreases only in response to fairly wide changes in activity is known as a **step-variable cost**. For example, the wages of full-time salaried maintenance workers are often considered to be a variable cost, but this labour cost doesn't behave in quite the same way as direct materials. Unlike direct materials, the time of maintenance workers is obtainable only in large blocks (e.g., 35 hours per week). Moreover, any maintenance worker time not spent actually working cannot be stored as inventory and carried forward to the next period. Furthermore, a maintenance crew can work at a fairly leisurely pace if there is limited work to do but intensify its efforts if things get busy. For this reason, small changes in the level of production may have no effect on the number of maintenance workers employed by the company.

EXHIBIT 3–2
Examples of Variable Costs

Type of Organization	Costs That Are Normally Variable with Respect to Volume of Output
Merchandising company	Cost of goods (merchandise) sold

Manufacturing company	Manufacturing costs:
	     Direct materials
	     Indirect materials, such as lubricants
	     or supplies
	     Power

Both merchandising and manufacturing companies	Selling, general, and administrative costs:
	     Sales commissions
	     Shipping costs

Service organizations	Supplies, travel, part-time employee hourly wages

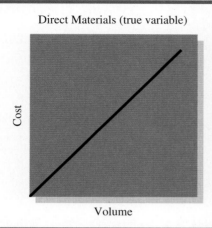

Direct Materials (true variable)

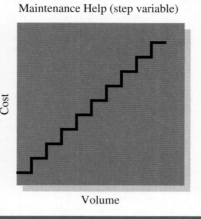

Maintenance Help (step variable)

EXHIBIT 3–3
True Variable versus
Step-Variable Costs

The behaviour of a step-variable cost is contrasted with the behaviour of a true variable cost in Exhibit 3–3. Notice that the need for maintenance help changes only with fairly wide changes in volume, and that when additional maintenance time is obtained it comes in relatively large, indivisible chunks. For example, if we assume a full-time maintenance worker's salary is based on working 35 hours per week, then the company is committed to paying the full salary for that worker regardless of how many hours are actually spent working. Thus, management's objective when dealing with step-variable costs should be to obtain the fullest use of services possible for each separate step.

INSTANT QUIZ 3–1
Assume you pay to your mobile service provider $7 for each 100 MB of data overages. Are these data overage charges a true variable cost or a step-variable cost? Explain.

The Linearity Assumption and the Relevant Range

In dealing with variable costs, we have assumed a strictly linear relationship between cost and volume, except in the case of step-variable costs. However, many costs classified as variable actually behave in a *curvilinear* fashion. The behaviour of **curvilinear costs** is shown in Exhibit 3–4.

Curvilinear costs
Costs that show a curved relationship between cost and activity rather than a straight-line relationship.

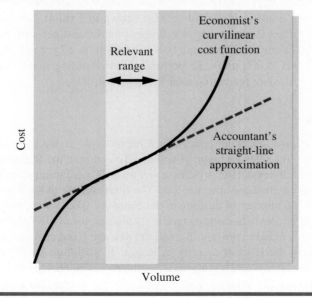

EXHIBIT 3–4
Curvilinear Costs and the Relevant Range

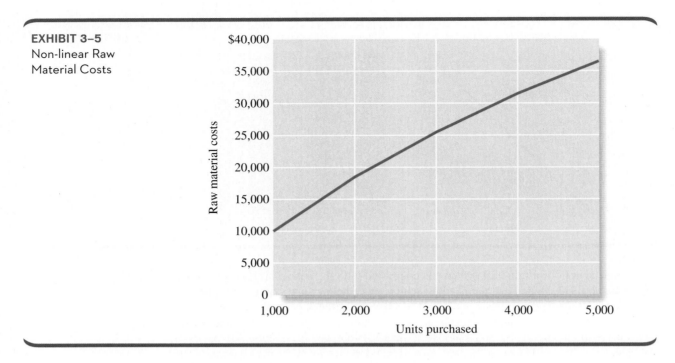

EXHIBIT 3–5
Non-linear Raw
Material Costs

Although many costs are not strictly linear, a curvilinear cost can be reasonably approximated with a straight line within the band of activity known as the *relevant range*. The relevant range is that range of activity within which the assumptions made about cost behaviour are valid. For example, note that the dashed line in Exhibit 3–4 can be used as an accurate approximation to the curvilinear cost within the shaded relevant range. However, outside the relevant range, this particular straight line is a poor approximation to the curvilinear cost relationship.

Some variable costs are predictably non-linear over the relevant range of activity. A **non-linear variable cost** is one where the per unit amount changes (increases or decreases) as the activity level changes. For example, the unit cost of raw materials used by manufacturing companies often decreases as the quantity of materials purchased increases. Conversely, per-dollar sales commissions often increase as the volume of sales increases to strengthen the motivation for sales staff to keep selling more products or services.

An example of a non-linear variable cost is shown in Exhibit 3–5. Total raw material costs on the *y*-axis reflect the following non-linearity in the cost per unit: 0–1,000 units, $10 per unit; 1,001–2,000 units, $8.50 per unit; 2,001–3,000 units, $7 per unit; 3,001–4,000 units, $6 per unit; and 4,001–5,000 units, $5 per unit. Understanding non-linearity in unit cost behaviour is important when predicting total variable costs.

Non-linear variable cost

A variable cost where the per unit amount increases or decreases as the activity level changes.

Fixed Costs

In our discussion of cost behaviour patterns in Chapter 2, we stated that total fixed costs remain constant within the relevant range of activity. To continue the Sledding Adventures example, assume the company decides to lease a van for $400 per month to pick up customers at their hotel and return them there after the tour. The *total* amount of the lease payments is the same regardless of the number of customers the company takes on its sledding tours during any given month. This cost behaviour pattern is shown graphically in Exhibit 3–6.

Since fixed costs remain constant in total, the average fixed cost *per unit* becomes progressively smaller as the level of activity increases. If Sledding Adventures has only 100 customers in a month, the $400 fixed rental cost amounts to an average of $4 per customer. If there are 800 customers, the fixed rental cost averages only 50 cents per customer. This aspect

EXHIBIT 3–6   Fixed Cost Behaviour

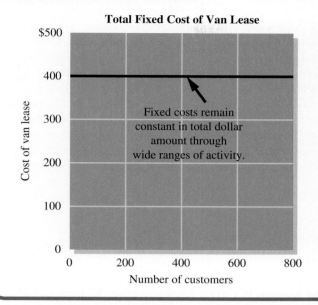

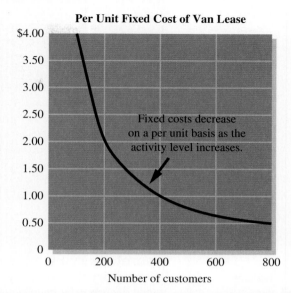

of the behaviour of fixed costs is also displayed in Exhibit 3–6. Note that as the number of customers increases, the average unit cost drops, but it drops at a decreasing rate. The first customers have the greatest impact on the average fixed costs per unit.

INSTANT QUIZ 3–2
Based on Exhibit 3–6, what is the average lease cost per customer if there are 600 customers in a month? What are the total lease costs if there are 600 customers in a month?

Types of Fixed Costs

Fixed costs are sometimes referred to as *capacity costs*, since they result from outlays made for buildings, equipment, skilled employees, and other resources required to provide the basic capacity for sustained operations. For planning purposes, fixed costs can be viewed as being either *committed* or *discretionary*.

Committed Fixed Costs

Committed fixed costs are those investments in facilities, equipment, and the basic elements of operating any business that cannot be significantly reduced, even for short time periods, without making fundamental changes that might impair a firm's ability to attain its long-term objectives. Examples are depreciation of buildings and equipment, property taxes, insurance expenses, financial statement audits, data security, and salaries of top management and operating personnel. Even if operations are temporarily interrupted or activity levels reduced, committed fixed costs remain largely unchanged in the short term. Once a decision is made to acquire committed fixed resources, the company may be locked into that decision for many years. Consequently, such commitments should be made only after carefully analyzing the available alternatives. The analysis of long-term investment decisions involving committed fixed costs will be examined in Chapter 13.

Committed fixed costs
Fixed costs that are difficult to change in the short term and that relate to the investment in facilities, equipment, and the basic elements of operating any business.

Discretionary Fixed Costs

Discretionary fixed costs
Fixed costs arising from annual decisions by management to spend in certain areas, such as advertising and research.

Discretionary fixed costs, often called *managed fixed costs*, are those costs that arise from annual decisions by management to spend in certain fixed cost areas. Examples of discretionary fixed costs are advertising, research and development, and management training programs.

Two key differences exist between discretionary and committed fixed costs. First, the planning horizon for a discretionary fixed cost is short term—usually a single year. By contrast, committed fixed costs usually have a planning horizon that extends several years. As such, a discretionary fixed cost can be adjusted year to year, or even during a fiscal period if necessary. Second, relative to committed costs, some discretionary fixed costs can be reduced in the short run with fewer negative effects on long-run organizational objectives. For example, spending on management training programs can be reduced if the company is not performing well. Although some unfavourable consequences may result from such a reduction, they are unlikely to be as severe as those that would result if the company decided to reduce committed fixed costs by laying off key personnel.

The Trend toward Fixed Costs

The trend in many companies is now more than ever toward greater fixed costs relative to variable costs. Numerous tasks that used to be performed by humans, often paid hourly wages, have been automated. An early example of the rise of automation and the resultant increase in fixed costs was the advent of ATM machines, which first appeared in Canada in the late 1960s. As another example, automobile manufacturers began automating certain aspects of the manufacturing process using robotics in the 1970s. More recently, grocery stores have installed self-checkout stations, as have other retailers such as Walmart and Home Depot. Two broad factors have contributed to increased automation. First, global competition in many industries has created pressure to give customers more value for their money (e.g., through faster or more accurate service), which often can be satisfied only by automating business processes. Second, rapid advances in technology have facilitated an ever-increasing degree of automation. These advances include the rise of artificial intelligence, whereby devices or systems are designed to function intelligently in performing tasks where until very recently human intervention was required. These include tasks such as stock trading, operating equipment, or even providing travel advice! This trend toward companies having a higher proportion of committed fixed costs is likely to accelerate rapidly in the future given exciting developments in machine learning and quantum computing.

IN BUSINESS

For software development companies such as TextNow, based in Waterloo, Ontario, knowing that the majority of their expenses are the fixed wages paid to their developers makes developing accurate expense budgets quite easy. This is because unless new developers are hired or existing ones leave, the majority of TextNow's expenses will stay the same from one month to the next. However, a big challenge for companies like TextNow is deciding how many developers to hire, particularly when the business is first starting to grow. When dealing with committed fixed costs related to knowledge workers, hiring the appropriate number of employees is critical to the success of an organization. In particular, given how difficult it is to reduce committed fixed costs such as salaries in the short run, determining and maintaining appropriate staffing levels has become a very important issue for companies in the tech sector.

Fixed Costs and the Relevant Range

The concept of the relevant range discussed earlier is also important in understanding fixed costs. The relevant range of activity for a fixed cost is the range of activity over which the graph of the cost is flat, as in Exhibit 3–7. As a company expands its level of activity it may outgrow its facilities, or the number of employees may need to be increased. The result, of course, will be increased committed fixed costs as larger facilities are built and as new management positions are created.

The fixed cost pattern depicted in Exhibit 3–7 appears similar to step-variable costs depicted in Exhibit 3–3. However, there are two major differences between the step-variable costs and the fixed costs depicted in Exhibit 3–7. First, a step-variable cost such as maintenance labour can easily be adjusted upward or downward in the short term by hiring and laying off maintenance workers. By contrast, once a company has signed a lease for a building, it is locked into that level of lease cost for the life of the contract.

Second, the *width of the steps* depicted for step-variable costs is much narrower than the width of the steps depicted for the fixed costs in Exhibit 3–7. The width of the steps relates to the volume or level of activity. For step-variable costs, the width of a step may be 40 hours of activity or less when dealing with a cost such as maintenance labour. However, for fixed costs, the width of a step may be *thousands* or even *tens of thousands* of hours of activity when dealing with a committed cost related to production equipment. Because the width of the steps

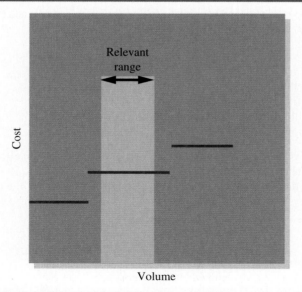

EXHIBIT 3–7
Fixed Costs and the Relevant Range

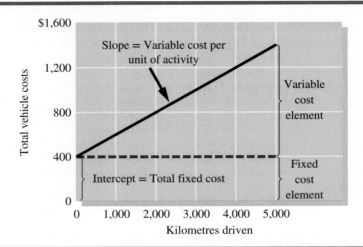

for step-variable costs is generally so narrow, these costs can be treated as variable costs for most purposes. Conversely, the width of the steps for fixed costs is so wide that these costs must generally be treated as being fixed within the entire relevant range of activity.

Mixed Costs

As discussed in Chapter 2, mixed costs contain both variable and fixed cost elements. Mixed costs are also known as *semi-variable costs*. To continue the Sledding Adventures example, the company pays $400 per month in van lease payments plus $0.20 per kilometre to operate the van. If the company drives 1,000 kilometres in a month, the total vehicle costs will be $600, made up of $400 in fixed cost plus $200 in variable cost. Exhibit 3–8 shows the behaviour of this mixed cost.

Even if Sledding Adventures has no customers in a particular month and does not use the van, it will still have to pay the $400 fixed lease cost. This is why the cost line in Exhibit 3–8 intersects the vertical cost axis at the $400 point. For every kilometre the van is driven, costs will increase by $0.20. Therefore, the total cost line slopes upward as the variable cost element is added to the fixed cost element.

Since the mixed cost in Exhibit 3–8 is represented by a straight line, the following equation for a straight line can be used to express the relationship between mixed cost and the level of activity:

$$Y = a + bX$$

In this equation,

Y = The total mixed cost
a = The total fixed cost (the vertical intercept of the line)
b = The variable cost per unit of activity (the slope of the line)
X = The level of activity

Because the variable cost per unit equals the slope of the straight line, the steeper the slope, the higher the variable cost per unit.

In the case of the total vehicle cost paid by Sledding Adventures, the equation is written as follows:

$$Y = \$400 + \$0.20X$$

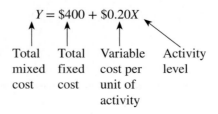

Total   Total   Variable   Activity
mixed   fixed   cost per   level
cost   cost   unit of
                      activity

This equation makes it very easy to calculate what the total mixed cost would be for any level of activity within the relevant range. For example, suppose that the company expects to drive the van 3,000 kilometres next month. Then the total vehicle costs will be $1,000, calculated as follows:

$$Y = \$400 + (\$0.20 \text{ per kilometre} \times 3,000 \text{ kilometres})$$
$$= \$1,000$$

INSTANT QUIZ 3-3

GolfTech pays all sales staff a fixed salary of $5,000 per month plus a 2% commission on sales. What will total wages be for a sales staff member who generates $200,000 in sales for a month?

■ ANALYZING MIXED COSTS

LEARNING OBJECTIVE ❷
Analyze mixed costs using various approaches.

Estimating Cost Behaviour

How does management go about actually estimating the fixed and variable components of a mixed cost? Common methods used in practice are *account analysis*, the *engineering approach*, the *high–low method*, and *regression analysis*. The first three methods are discussed below, and Appendix 3A demonstrates how to use Microsoft Excel to perform least-squares regression analysis.

Account Analysis

In **account analysis**, each account under consideration is qualitatively identified as either variable, fixed, or mixed based on the analyst's prior knowledge of how the cost in the account behaves, which is often developed by analyzing past records of cost and activity data. For accounts such as vehicle costs for Sledding Adventures shown in Exhibit 3–8, the analyst would need to identify the fixed (lease costs) and variable (gas, oil, etc.) components of the total costs recorded in that account. The total fixed cost is the sum of the costs for the accounts that have been classified as fixed. The variable cost per unit is estimated by dividing the sum of the costs for the accounts that have been classified as variable by the total activity.

Account analysis
A method for analyzing cost behaviour in which each account under consideration is classified as either variable or fixed based on the analyst's prior knowledge of how the cost in the account behaves.

Engineering Approach

The **engineering approach** to cost analysis involves a detailed analysis of what cost behaviour *should* be, typically based on an evaluation of the physical quantity of inputs such as direct materials and direct labour required to produce a unit of output. For example, Pizza Hut might use the engineering approach to estimate the cost of serving a particular take-out pizza. The cost of the pizza is estimated by carefully costing the specific quantity of ingredients used to make the pizza, the time required to prepare the pizza, and the amount of power consumed to cook the pizza. The engineering approach can be very time consuming and is typically used in situations where no past experience is available on activity and costs. Moreover, the engineering approach is often used only for direct materials and labour. That is because it is simply too time consuming to attempt to identify physical input–output relationships for indirect items such as the salt used to make pizza dough at Pizza Hut.

Engineering approach
A detailed analysis of cost behaviour based on an industrial engineer's evaluation of the physical inputs required to produce a unit of output and of the costs of those inputs.

Using the High–Low Method

The **high–low method** is a simple method of separating a mixed cost into its fixed and variable elements. The first step in properly applying the high–low method is to visually diagnose cost behaviour with a scattergraph plot. We will use the example below to illustrate its use.

High–low method
A method of separating a mixed cost into its fixed and variable elements by analyzing the change in cost between the high and low levels of activity.

Assume that Hamilton Hotel has the following cost and activity data for electrical costs for the most recent 12 months as follows:

Month	Activity Level: Occupancy-Days	Electrical Costs
January	2,600	$6,260
February	2,850	6,550
March	3,530	8,000
April	1,440	4,000
May	540	2,300
June	1,120	3,600
July	3,160	7,300
August	3,610	8,100
September	1,260	3,700
October	190	1,773
November	1,080	3,320
December	2,050	5,200

The first step in analyzing the cost and activity data is to plot the data on a scattergraph. This plot immediately reveals any non-linearities or other problems with the data. Scattergraphs can easily be produced using software packages such as Microsoft Excel. The scattergraph of electrical costs versus occupancy-days at the Hamilton Hotel is reproduced in the first panel of Exhibit 3–9. Note two things about this scattergraph:

Dependent variable
A variable that responds to some causal factor; total cost is the dependent variable, as represented by the letter Y in the equation $Y = a + bX$.

1. The total electrical cost, Y, is plotted on the vertical axis. Cost is known as the **dependent variable**, since the amount of cost incurred during a period depends on the level of activity for the period.
2. The activity, X (occupancy-days in this case), is plotted on the horizontal axis. Activity is known as the **independent variable**, since it causes variations in the cost.

Independent variable
A variable that acts as a causal factor; activity is the independent variable, as represented by the letter X in the equation $Y = a + bX$.

From the scattergraph, it is evident that the relationship between electrical costs and occupancy-days is approximately *linear*. That is, the points lie more or less along a straight line. Such a straight line has been drawn in the second panel of Exhibit 3–9 using the *add trendline* chart option in Excel. **Linear cost behaviour** occurs whenever a straight line is a reasonable approximation for the relationship between cost and activity.

As another example, suppose we had been interested in the relationship between total cleaning staff wages and the number of occupancy-days at the hotel. The permanent, full-time cleaning staff can handle up to 1,500 occupancy-days in a month. Beyond that level of activity, part-time cleaning staff must be utilized. The cost and activity data for cleaning are plotted on the scattergraph in Exhibit 3–10. Looking at that scattergraph, it is evident that two straight lines would do a much better job of fitting the data than a single straight line. Up to 1,500 occupancy-days, total cleaning staff wages are essentially a fixed cost. Above 1,500 occupancy-days, total cleaning staff wages are a mixed cost. This happens because, as stated above, the permanent full-time cleaning staff can handle up to 1,500 occupancy-days in a month. Above that level, part-time cleaning staff are called in to help, which adds to the cost. Consequently, two straight lines are used to represent total cleaning staff wages—one for the relevant range of 0 to 1,500 occupancy-days and one for the relevant range of 1,501 to 4,000 occupancy-days.

Linear cost behaviour
Cost behaviour where the relationship between cost and activity can be reasonably approximated by a straight line.

Assuming that the scattergraph plot indicates a linear relationship between cost and activity, the fixed and variable cost elements of a mixed cost can be estimated using the *high–low method* or the *least-squares regression method*. The high–low method is based on the rise-over-run formula for the slope of a straight line. If the relationship between cost and activity can be represented by a straight line, then the slope of the straight line is equal to the variable cost per unit of activity. Consequently, the following formula, using basic algebra, can be used to estimate the variable cost:

$$\text{Variable cost per unit of activity} = \text{Slope of the line} = \frac{\text{Rise}}{\text{Run}} = \frac{Y_2 - Y_1}{X_2 - X_1}$$

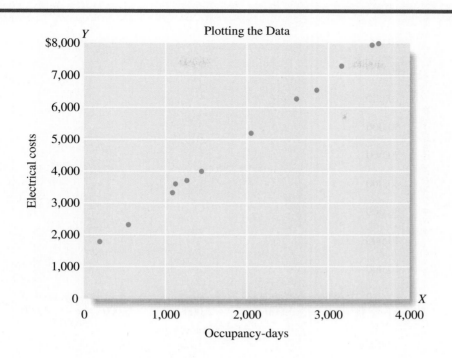

EXHIBIT 3–9
Scattergraph
Analysis

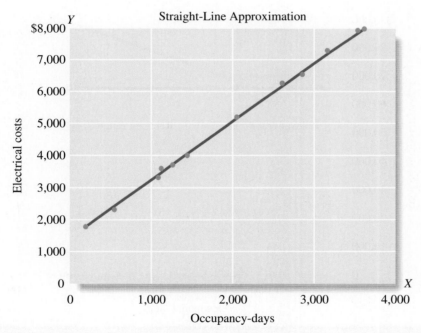

To analyze mixed costs with the high–low method, begin by identifying the period with the lowest level of activity and the period with the highest level of activity. For the above formula, select the period with the lowest activity as the first point and the period with the highest activity as the second point. Consequently, the formula becomes

$$\text{Variable cost per unit} = \frac{Y_2 - Y_1}{X_2 - X_1} = \frac{\text{Cost at high activity level} - \text{Cost at low activity level}}{\text{High activity level} - \text{Low activity level}}$$

or

$$\text{Variable cost per unit of activity} = \frac{\text{Change in cost}}{\text{Change in activity}}$$

EXHIBIT 3–10
More Than One
Relevant Range

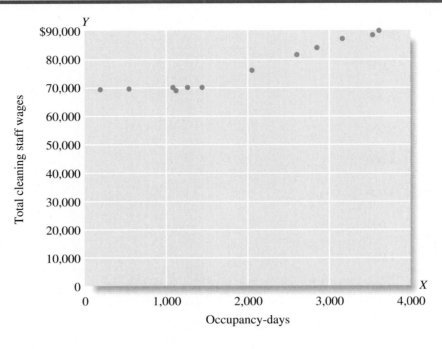

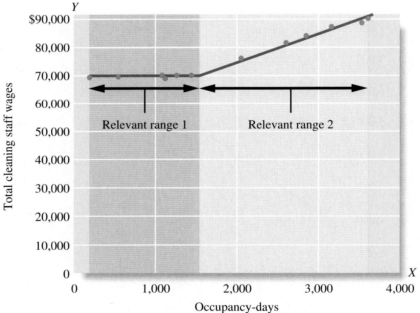

As shown by the formula, when the high–low method is used, the variable cost per unit of activity is estimated by dividing the difference in cost between the high and low levels of activity by the change in activity between those two points.

Using the high–low method to analyze the relation between electrical costs and occupancy-days, we first identify the periods with the highest and lowest *activity*—in this case, August and October, per the data in the table. We then use the activity and cost data from these two periods to estimate the variable cost component as follows:

	Occupancy-Days	Electrical Cost Incurred
High activity level (August)	3,610	$8,100
Low activity level (October)	190	1,773
Change	3,420	$6,327

$$\text{Variable cost per unit of activity} = \$1.85 \text{ per occupancy-day} = \frac{\text{Change in cost}}{\text{Change in activity}} = \frac{\$6,327}{3,420}$$

Having determined that the variable rate for electrical costs is $1.85 per occupancy-day, we can now determine the amount of fixed cost. This is done by taking total cost at *either* the high or the low activity level and deducting the variable cost element. In the computation below, total cost at the high activity level is used to compute the fixed cost element:

$$\text{Fixed cost element} = \text{Total cost} - \text{Variable cost element}$$
$$= \$8,100 - (\$1.85 \text{ per occupancy-day} \times 3,610 \text{ occupancy-days})$$
$$= \$1,421.50$$

The electrical costs can be expressed as $1,421.50 per month plus $1.85 per occupancy-day. The total electrical costs can also be expressed in terms of the equation for a straight line as follows:

$$Y = \$1,421.50 + \$1.85X$$

Total electrical cost   Total occupancy-days

Sometimes the high and low levels of activity don't coincide with the high and low amounts of cost. For example, the period that has the highest level of activity may not have the highest amount of cost. Nevertheless, the highest and lowest levels of *activity* should be used to analyze a mixed cost under the high–low method. This is because the analyst would like to use data that reflect the greatest possible variation in activity.

The high–low method is very simple to apply, but because it uses only two data points it may not produce accurate estimates of the cost equation. For example, the periods with the highest and lowest activity may be unusual in that they represent the two extremes. A cost formula that is estimated solely using data from these unusual periods may misrepresent the true cost relationship that holds during normal periods. Accordingly, if greater accuracy is needed for cost estimation, other methods utilizing all available data such as *least-squares regression* can be used. Regression analysis is discussed in the appendix to this chapter. However, if managers choose to use the high–low method, they should do so with full awareness of its limitations.

INSTANT QUIZ 3-4

Using the equation for total electrical costs developed for the Hamilton Hotel, predict total electrical costs for a month when total occupancy-days are expected to be 500.

■ THE CONTRIBUTION FORMAT

Separating costs into fixed and variable elements helps to predict costs and, as we will see in later chapters, is often crucial in making decisions. The distinction between fixed and variable costs is at the heart of the **contribution approach** to producing income statements. The contribution approach provides managers with an income statement that clearly distinguishes between fixed and variable costs.

Contribution approach
An income statement format where costs are separated into variable and fixed categories.

LEARNING OBJECTIVE

Prepare an income statement using the contribution format.

Why a New Income Statement Format?

An income statement prepared using the *traditional approach*, as illustrated in Chapter 2, is organized in a "functional" format—emphasizing the functions of production, administration, and sales. No attempt is made to distinguish between fixed and variable costs. Under the heading Administrative Expense, for example, both variable and fixed costs are lumped together.

Although an income statement prepared in the functional format may be useful for external reporting, it has serious limitations when used for internal purposes. As we will see in later chapters, presenting cost data on the income statement in a fixed and variable format can better facilitate certain decisions managers need to make. For example, decisions related to budgeting, product or service pricing, the utilization of scarce resources (e.g., shelf space by a retailer), and make internally versus outsourcing all require an identification of fixed and variable cost elements. The contribution approach to the income statement was developed in response to this need.

The Contribution Approach

Exhibit 3–11 illustrates the contribution approach to the income statement with a simple example based on assumed data, along with the traditional approach discussed in Chapter 2.

Contribution margin
The amount remaining from sales revenues after all variable expenses have been deducted.

Notice that the contribution approach separates costs into fixed and variable categories, first deducting variable expenses from sales to obtain the *contribution margin*. The **contribution margin** is the amount remaining from sales revenues after variable expenses have been deducted. This amount *contributes* toward covering fixed expenses and then toward profits for the period.

INSTANT QUIZ 3–5
Based on Exhibit 3–11, what would you expect total variable costs to be if sales were $36,000? What would you expect total fixed costs to be if sales were $24,000?

EXHIBIT 3–11
Comparison of the Contribution Income Statement with the Traditional Income Statement

Traditional Approach (costs organized by function)			Contribution Approach (costs organized by behaviour)		
Sales		$12,000	Sales.		$12,000
Less cost of goods sold . . .		6,000*	Less variable expenses:		
Gross margin.		6,000	Variable production	$2,000	
Less operating expenses:. .			Variable selling	600	
Selling	$3,100*		Variable administrative .	400	3,000
Administrative.	1,900*	5,000	Contribution margin.		9,000
Operating income		$ 1,000	Less fixed expenses:		
			Fixed production	4,000	
			Fixed selling.	2,500	
			Fixed administrative. . . .	1,500	8,000
			Operating income.		$ 1,000

*Contains both variable and fixed expenses. This is the income statement for a manufacturing company; thus, when the income statement is placed in the contribution format, the cost of goods sold figure is divided between variable production costs and fixed production costs. If this were the income statement for a *merchandising* company (which simply purchases completed goods from a supplier), then the cost of goods sold would be *all* variable.

KNOWLEDGE IN ACTION

Managers can apply their knowledge about cost behaviour when:

- Predicting costs at different levels of activity
- Calculating sales needed to achieve break-even profit levels
- Estimating sales needed to achieve desired profit targets
- Estimating the impact of sales volume changes on profit
- Costing products
- Preparing budgets and analyzing differences between actual and budgeted results
- Deciding whether to keep or drop a product
- Deciding whether to make a product internally or outsource production*

*Many of these applications will become clearer after working through the material in subsequent chapters.

SUMMARY

- Three major classifications of costs were discussed in this chapter: variable, fixed, and mixed. **[LO1]**
- Mixed costs are a combination of variable and fixed elements and can be expressed in equation form as $Y = a + bX$, where Y is the cost, a is the fixed cost element, b is the variable cost per unit of activity, and X is the activity. **[LO1]**
- The first step in analyzing a mixed cost is to prepare a scattergraph to permit a visual assessment of the relationship between the cost and the activity. Costs are plotted on the vertical axis and activity levels on the horizontal axis of the scattergraph. **[LO2]**
- If the scattergraph indicates that the relationship between cost and activity is approximately linear, the variable and fixed components of the mixed cost can be estimated using the high–low method or the regression method (see Appendix 3A). **[LO2]**
- The high–low method estimates the variable and fixed cost components by analyzing the change in cost between the high and low levels of activity. The method is based on the rise-over-run formula for the slope of a straight line. **[LO2]**
- To facilitate decision making, the income statement can be prepared in a contribution format. The contribution format classifies costs on the income statement by cost behaviour (i.e., variable versus fixed) rather than by functional areas such as production, administration, and sales. **[LO3]**

REVIEW PROBLEM 1: COST BEHAVIOUR

James Company manufactures and sells a single product. A partially completed schedule of the company's total and per unit costs over a relevant range of 120,000 to 200,000 units produced and sold annually is shown below:

	Units Produced and Sold		
	120,000	160,000	200,000
Total costs:			
Variable costs	$ 300,000	$?	$?
Fixed costs.	720,000	?	?
Total costs	$1,020,000	$?	$?
Cost per unit:			
Variable cost	$?	$?	$?
Fixed cost	?	?	?
Total cost per unit	$?	$?	$?

Required:
Compute the missing amounts, assuming that cost behaviour patterns remain unchanged within the relevant range of 120,000 to 200,000 units.

Solution to Review Problem 1

The variable cost per unit can be computed as follows:

$$300,000 \div 120,000 \text{ units} = \$2.50 \text{ per unit}$$

Therefore, the missing amounts are as follows:

	Units Produced and Sold		
	120,000	**160,000**	**200,000**
Total costs:			
Variable costs (@ $2.50 per unit)	$ 300,000	$ 400,000	$ 500,000
Fixed costs.	720,000	720,000	720,000
Total costs	$1,020,000	$1,120,000	$1,220,000
Cost per unit:			
Variable cost	$ 2.50	$ 2.50	$ 2.50
Fixed cost	6.00	4.50	3.60
Total cost per unit	$ 8.50	$ 7.00	$ 6.10

Observe that the total variable costs increase in proportion to the number of units produced and sold, but that these costs remain constant at $2.50 if expressed on a per unit basis.

In contrast, the total fixed costs do not change with changes in the level of activity. They remain constant at $720,000 within the relevant range. With increases in activity, however, the fixed cost per unit decreases, dropping from $6.00 per unit when 120,000 units are produced to only $3.60 per unit when 200,000 units are produced. *Because of this troublesome aspect of fixed costs, they are most easily (and most safely) dealt with on a total basis, rather than on a unit basis, in cost analysis work.*

REVIEW PROBLEM 2: HIGH–LOW METHOD

The Controller at the Red Deer Hospital has asked for a cost formula that separates the fixed and variable components of the costs for the Patient Admissions Department. Monthly costs and the number of patients admitted for the past 10 months are shown below:

Month	Number of Patients Admitted	Admissions Department Costs
January	1,800	$14,700
February	1,900	$15,200
March	1,700	$13,700
April	1,600	$14,000
May	1,500	$14,300
June	1,300	$13,100
July	1,100	$12,800
August	1,200	$13,000
September	1,400	$14,200
October	1,650	$14,300
November	1,825	$15,000
December	1,375	$13,150

Required:
1. Use the high–low method to establish the fixed and variable components of patient admissions costs.
2. Express the fixed and variable components of admissions costs as a cost formula in the form $Y = a + bX$.

Solution to Review Problem 2

1. The first step in the high–low method is to identify the periods of the lowest and highest activity. These periods are July (1,100 admissions) and February (1,900 admissions).

    The second step is to compute the variable cost per unit using those two data points:

Month	Admissions	Costs
High activity level (February)	1,900	$15,200
Low activity level (July)	1,100	12,800
Change	800	$ 2,400

$$\text{Variable cost per admission} = \$3.00 \text{ per admission} = \frac{\text{Change in cost}}{\text{Change in activity}} = \frac{\$2,400}{800}$$

The third step is to compute the fixed cost element by deducting the variable cost element from the total cost at either the high or low activity level. In the computation below, the high point of activity is used:

$$\text{Fixed cost element} = \text{Total cost} - \text{Variable cost element}$$
$$= \$15,200 - (\$3.00 \text{ per admission} \times 1,900 \text{ admissions})$$
$$= \$9,500$$

2. The cost formula is $Y = \$9,500 + \$3.00X$.

DISCUSSION CASE

Discussion Case 3–1
Further to the information provided in Review Problem 2, assume that all of the fixed costs pertain to the two full-time staff members who process each patient being admitted to the hospital. Each staff member is paid a salary of $4,750 per month. The variable cost per admission relates to items such as the patient identification bracelet issued to each patient, the medical history form that must be completed by each patient, and so on. You can also assume that the maximum number of patients that the two staff members can admit during any given month is 2,000. Further, if fewer than 1,000 patients were to be admitted per month on an ongoing basis, only one full-time staff member would be required.

Required:
What is the relevant range of activity for which the cost formula you calculated in Review Problem 2 applies? Discuss how management at Red Deer Hospital could use the additional information provided above to estimate costs if the number of admissions is expected to exceed 2,000 on a regular basis or to fall below 1,000 on a recurring basis.

QUESTIONS

3–1 Identify some examples of variable costs for a restaurant.
3–2 What effect does an increase in volume have on
  a. Unit fixed costs?
  b. Unit variable costs?
  c. Total fixed costs?
  d. Total variable costs?
3–3 What is the activity base? What would be a likely activity base for the cost of sales commissions paid to sales staff?
3–4 What is a non-linear variable cost?
3–5 What is the difference between a true variable and a step-variable cost?
3–6 Describe a non-linear variable cost and give an example.
3–7 What is a mixed cost? Give some examples.
3–8 Classify the following fixed costs as normally being either committed or discretionary:
  a. Depreciation on buildings.
  b. Property taxes.
  c. Research and development.

  d. Maintenance on production equipment.
  e. Office equipment leases.
  f. Professional development courses.

3–9 How could knowledge of the relevant range for a fixed cost help a manager when making planning decisions requiring cost estimates?

3–10 Identify one advantage and one disadvantage of using the account analysis approach to estimating cost behaviour.

3–11 What is the purpose of preparing a scattergraph?

3–12 Why is it potentially problematic that the high–low method uses only two data points to determine the cost function?

3–13 Give the general formula for a mixed cost. Which term represents the variable cost per unit? The fixed cost?

3–14 For a manufacturing company, what is the difference between how the gross margin and contribution margin are calculated?

FOUNDATIONAL EXERCISES

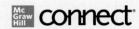

[LO2, LO3]

Phillips Company manufactures air-conditioning units for commercial buildings and has noticed considerable variation in shipping expenses from month to month as per the data below:

Month	Units Shipped	Total Shipping Expense
January	4	$2,200
February	4	$3,100
March	5	$2,600
April	2	$1,500
May	3	$2,200
June	6	$3,000
July	8	$3,600

3–1 Which two months should be used if Phillips wants to estimate the behaviour of shipping expenses using the high–low method?

3–2 Using the high–low method, what is the variable cost per unit to ship air conditioners?

3–3 What is the fixed cost of shipping air conditioners?

3–4 What is the cost formula for shipping expenses?

3–5 If seven air conditioners are shipped in August, estimate the total shipping expenses.

3–6 If nine air conditioners are shipped in September, estimate the fixed shipping expenses.

3–7 If 10 air conditioners are shipped in October, estimate the variable shipping expenses.

3–8 If the air conditioners have an average sales price of $5,000, variable manufacturing costs are $2,500 per unit, variable manufacturing overhead is $500 per unit, and variable selling and administration costs (excluding shipping) are $200 per unit, what is the contribution margin per unit?

3–9 Given the facts in part 3–8, estimate the total contribution margin for August if seven air conditioners are produced and sold.

3–10 Given the facts in part 3–8, if total fixed costs (excluding shipping) are $3,000 per month, estimate operating income for August if seven air conditioners are produced and sold.

3–11 By how much would the total contribution margin decrease in August if Phillips decides to offer its customers a 5% price discount on the seven units?

3–12 By how much would operating income decrease in August if Phillips decides to offer its customers a 5% price discount on the seven units?

3–13 Estimate variable shipping expenses to ship 12 air conditioners if the shipping company reduces the variable cost per unit by 10% for each unit shipped in excess of 10 units.

3–14 Given the facts in part 3–13, estimate total shipping expenses for 12 air conditioners.

3–15 Given the facts in part 3–13, are variable shipping expenses linear or non-linear? Explain.

EXERCISES

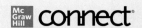

EXERCISE 3–1 Fixed and Variable Cost Behaviour [LO1]

Goes-Down-Smooth operates a number of smoothie bars in busy suburban malls. The fixed weekly expense of a smoothie bar is $2,500, and the variable cost per smoothie served is $0.75.

Required:
1. Fill in the following table with your estimates of total costs and cost per smoothie at the indicated levels of activity for a smoothie bar. Round off the cost of a smoothie to the nearest tenth of a cent.

	Smoothies Served in a Week		
	2,100	2,800	3,500
Fixed cost	?	?	?
Variable cost....................	?	?	?
Total cost	?	?	?
Cost per smoothie served..........	?	?	?

2. Does the cost per smoothie increase, decrease, or remain the same as the number of smoothies served in a week increases? Explain.

EXERCISE 3–2 Scattergraph Analysis [LO2]

Cool-It Company is a wholesaler of custom-built air conditioning units for commercial buildings. The data below show the number of units shipped and the total shipping expenses for the past eight months.

Month	Number of Units Shipped	Total Shipping Expenses
January	3	$3,600
February	6	$4,600
March	4	$3,400
April	5	$4,000
May	7	$4,600
June	8	$5,400
July	2	$2,400
August	1	$1,200

Required:
1. Use Microsoft Excel to prepare a scattergraph using the above data. Shipping expenses should be on the vertical axis and number of units shipped should be on the horizontal axis.
2. Does the relation between shipping expenses and the number of units shipped appear to be linear? Explain your response.
3. Based on a visual inspection of the scattergraph, do you think shipping expense is a true variable cost or a mixed cost? Explain your response.

EXERCISE 3–3 High–Low Method [LO2]

Refer to the data in Exercise 3–2 for the Cool-It Company.

Required:
1. Using the high–low method, estimate the fixed shipping expenses per month and the variable cost of shipping each unit.
2. Express the fixed and variable components of total monthly shipping expenses as a cost formula.
3. If Cool-It Company expects to ship 20 units next month, would you feel comfortable using the cost formula from part 2 to estimate total shipping expenses? Why or why not?

> **CHECK FIGURE**
> Variable cost =
> $600 per unit
> shipped;
> Fixed cost = $600.

EXERCISE 3–4 Contribution Format Income Statement [LO3]

Crazy Canucks is a small, family-owned retailer specializing in alpine ski and snowboard equipment located in Squamish, B.C. An income statement for the ski department's most recent month is shown below.

CRAZY CANUCKS Income Statement—Crazy Canucks For the Month Ended January 31		
Sales		$300,000
Cost of goods sold.		180,000
Gross margin.		120,000
Selling and administrative expenses:		
Selling expenses	$60,000	
Administrative expenses	20,000	80,000
Operating income		$ 40,000

Skis sell, on average, for $1,500 per pair. Variable selling expenses are $150 per pair of skis sold. The remaining selling expenses are fixed. The administrative expenses are 20% variable and 80% fixed. The company purchases its skis from several suppliers at an average cost of $900 per pair.

Required:
1. Prepare an income statement for the month using the contribution approach.
2. For every pair of skis sold during January, what was the contribution toward covering fixed expenses and toward earning profits?
3. What would the total contribution margin be in a month where 150 pairs of skis were sold? Do not prepare a new contribution format income statement to determine your answer.

EXERCISE 3–5 Cost Behaviour; Contribution Format Income Statement [LO1, LO3]

Wave Runners is a boat rental business that has the following costs over the relevant range of 12,000 to 18,000 operating hours for its boats:

	Operating Hours			
	12,000	14,000	16,000	18,000
Total costs:				
Variable costs	$ 54,000	?	?	?
Fixed costs.	504,000	?	?	?
Total costs	$558,000	?	?	?
Cost per unit:				
Variable cost	?	?	?	?
Fixed cost	?	?	?	?
Total cost per hour	?	?	?	?

Required:
1. Complete the schedule of the company's total and unit costs above.
2. Assume that Wave Runners rents its boats for $40 per hour and had 15,000 hours of rentals last year. Prepare a contribution format income statement for the year.

EXERCISE 3–6 Account Analysis Method [LO2]

Anand Limited manufactures drones for industrial use. Most of their costs are either true variable costs or fixed costs. However, an account analysis shows the following items are mixed costs.

Account	Analysis	2019 Total Cost
Production supervision	80% fixed	$150,000
Utilities	20% fixed	$ 60,000
Sales staff wages*	70% fixed	$200,000
Quality control inspections**	90% fixed	$ 40,000

*The 30% variable portion relates to sales commissions based on total sales.
**50% of manufactured units are inspected each year.

In 2019 Anand Limited produced and sold 500 drones at $2,000 each.

Required:
1.   Management expects to sell 700 drones in 2020, does not anticipate any cost increases due to inflation, and plans to maintain the sales price of $2,000 per drone. Estimate total costs for each of the mixed cost items above. Be sure to show the variable and fixed components of the total cost.
2.   In addition to the facts per requirement 1, assuming that direct material costs are $500 per unit and direct labour costs are $250 per unit, calculate the expected contribution margin for 2020 based on sales of 700 drones.

EXERCISE 3–7 Cost Behaviour; High–Low Method [LO2]
We Deliver operates a fleet of delivery trucks in Halifax. Analysis shows that if a truck is driven 105,000 kilometres during a year, the average operating cost is 11.4 cents ($0.114) per kilometre. If a truck is driven only 70,000 kilometres during a year, the average operating cost increases to 13.4 cents ($0.134) per kilometre.

Required:
1.   Using the high–low method, estimate the variable and fixed cost elements of the annual cost of truck operation.
2.   Express the variable and fixed costs in the form $Y = a + bX$.
3.   If a truck were driven 80,000 kilometres during a year, what total cost would you expect to be incurred?

EXERCISE 3–8 High–Low Method; Predicting Cost [LO2]
The number of blood tests performed and the related costs over the last nine months in Brentline Hospital are given below:

Month	Blood Tests Performed	Blood Test Costs
January	3,125	$14,000
February	3,500	$14,500
March	2,500	$11,500
April	2,125	$10,000
May	2,250	$11,000
June	1,500	$ 8,500
July	1,550	$ 8,400
August	2,750	$12,000
September	2,875	$13,000

Required:
1.   Using the high–low method, estimate the cost formula for blood tests.
2.   Using the cost formula you derived above, what blood test costs would you expect to be incurred during a month in which 2,300 blood tests are performed?

EXERCISE 3–9 Scattergraph Analysis; High–Low Method [LO2]
Refer to the data in Exercise 3–8 for Brentline Hospital.

Required:
1.   Using Microsoft Excel, prepare a scattergraph using the data from Exercise 3–8. Plot cost on the vertical axis and activity on the horizontal axis. Use the "add trendline" feature of Microsoft Excel to fit a line through the points on your scattergraph.
2.   Scrutinize the points on your graph, and explain why the high–low method would or would not yield an accurate cost formula in this situation.

EXERCISE 3–10 High–Low Method; Predicting Cost [LO2]
Prairie Motels has a total of 4,000 rooms in its chain of motels located in eastern Canada. On average, 80% of the rooms are occupied each day. The company's operating costs are $84 per occupied room per day at this occupancy level, assuming a 30-day month. This $84 contains both variable and fixed cost elements. During April, the occupancy rate dropped to only 40%. A total of $6,000,000 in operating cost was incurred during April.

Required:
1.   Estimate the variable cost per occupied room per day.
2.   Estimate the total fixed operating costs per month.
3.   Assume that the occupancy rate increases to 60% during May. What total operating costs would you expect the company to incur in May?

PROBLEMS

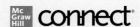

PROBLEM 3–11 High–Low Method; Cost of Goods Manufactured [LO2]

Sarnia Ltd. is a manufacturing company that produces a single product. The company keeps meticulous records of manufacturing activities from which the following information has been extracted:

	March—Low	June—High
Number of units produced....................	6,000	9,000
Cost of goods manufactured...................	$168,000	$257,000
Work in process inventory, beginning............	$9,000	$32,000
Work in process inventory, ending	$15,000	$21,000
Direct materials cost per unit	$6	$6
Direct labour cost per unit.....................	$10	$10
Manufacturing overhead cost, total..............	?	?

> **CHECK FIGURE**
> June total manufacturing overhead—$102,000; Cost of goods manufactured—$198,000.

The company's manufacturing overhead cost consists of both variable and fixed cost elements. To have data available for planning, management wants to determine how much of the overhead cost varies with the number of units produced versus how much is fixed per month.

Required:
1. For both March and June, estimate the amount of manufacturing overhead cost added to production.
2. Using the high-low method, estimate a cost formula for manufacturing overhead.
3. If 7,000 units are produced during a month, what would be the cost of goods manufactured? Assume that work in process inventories do not change.

PROBLEM 3–12 Traditional and Contribution Format Income Statement [LO3]

Winter Leisure is a retailer of snowboards. The information below is for the quarter ended December 31:

	Amount
Total sales revenue.............................	$1,600,000
Selling price per snowboard......................	800
Variable selling expense per snowboard	100
Variable administrative expense per snowboard	40
Total fixed selling expense.......................	300,000
Total fixed administrative expense	240,000
Merchandise inventory, beginning balance	60,000
Merchandise inventory, ending balance..............	90,000
Merchandise purchases	640,000

Required:
1. Prepare a traditional income statement for the quarter ended December 31.
2. Prepare a contribution format income statement for the quarter ended December 31.
3. What was the contribution toward fixed expenses and profits for each snowboard sold during the quarter? (State this figure in a single dollar amount per snowboard.)
4. What would operating income be if only 1,500 snowboards were sold in a quarter? You can assume no change to fixed expenses will occur if sales decline to 1,500 snowboards. (*Hint:* You don't need to prepare a new income statement to determine the answer.)

PROBLEM 3–13 Identifying Cost Behaviour Patterns [LO1]

A number of scattergraphs displaying cost behaviour patterns are shown below. The vertical axis on each graph represents total cost, and the horizontal axis represents the level of activity (volume).

Required:

1. For each of the following situations, identify the graph that illustrates the cost behaviour pattern involved. Any graph may be used more than once.

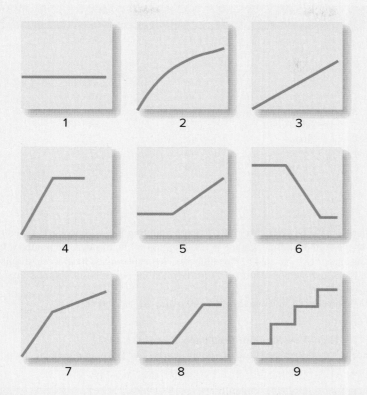

a. Charges for data usage on a smartphone plan—a flat fixed charge for the first 500 MB, plus a variable cost per megabyte for usage above 500 MB.
b. Wages for software development staff, all of whom are paid a fixed monthly salary.
c. Licensing fees paid to the provincial government to operate dog sled tours. A fee of $10 per tour is paid for the first 1,000 tours, with no additional fees paid if tours exceed 1,000.
d. Cost of raw materials, where the cost starts at $7.50 per unit and then decreases by 5 cents per unit for each of the first 100 units purchased, after which it remains constant at $2.50 per unit.
e. Cost of a monthly high-speed Internet plan, where $50 is charged for 0–250 MB usage, $75 for 251 to 500 MB usage, $100 for 501 to 750 MB usage, and $125 for 751 MB usage and above.
f. Wage expense paid to tree planters who receive $0.10 per tree planted.
g. Rent on a factory building donated by the county, where the agreement calls for rent of $100,000 less $1 for each direct labour-hour worked in excess of 200,000 hours, but a minimum rental payment of $20,000 must be paid.
h. Wages paid to sales staff who receive a fixed salary per month and sales commissions equal to 5% of sales for every sales dollar they generate above $250,000. No additional commissions are paid for sales above $1,000,000.
i. Raw materials costs, where the first 1,000 units cost $1 per unit, with the unit cost dropping to $0.80 per unit for quantities above 1,000.

2. How would a knowledge of cost behaviour patterns such as those above help a manager analyze the cost structure of his or her company?

(CPA, adapted)

PROBLEM 3–14 High–Low Method; Scattergraph Analysis [LO2]
Travis Metals heats copper ingots to a high temperature by placing them in a large oven. The heated ingots are then run through a shaping machine that forms them into wire. Due to the length of time it takes the oven to heat up, it is never turned off. When the ingots are placed in the oven the temperature is raised to a higher level. Once they are done being heated the oven temperature is turned back down until

a new batch of ingots is ready to be heated. The following information shows the ingots processed and the power costs over the past 10 months.

Month	Ingots	Power Cost
January	110	$5,500
February	90	$4,500
March	80	$4,400
April	100	$5,000
May	130	$6,000
June	120	$5,600
July	70	$4,000
August	60	$3,200
September	50	$3,400
October	40	$2,400

Required:
1. Using Microsoft Excel, prepare a scattergraph by plotting ingots processed and power costs on a graph. Use the Add Trendline feature in Excel to plot a line through the points of the graph. Do power costs appear to be related to the number of ingots processed in a month? Explain.
2. Using the high–low method, estimate a cost formula for power costs. Express the formula in the form $Y = a + bX$.
3. Predict total power costs in a month when 140 ingots are processed.

PROBLEM 3–15 High–Low Method; Predicting Cost [LO1, LO2]
Crosshill Company's total overhead costs at various levels of activity are presented below:

Month	Machine-Hours	Total Overhead Cost
April	70,000	$198,000
May	60,000	$174,000
June	80,000	$222,000
July	90,000	$246,000

Assume that the overhead cost above consists of utilities, supervisory salaries, and maintenance. The breakdown of these costs at the 60,000-machine-hour level of activity in May is as follows:

Utilities (variable)	$ 48,000
Supervisory salaries (fixed)..................	21,000
Maintenance (mixed).......................	105,000
Total overhead cost	$174,000

The company wants to break down the maintenance cost into its variable and fixed cost elements.

Required:
1. Estimate how much of the $246,000 of overhead cost in July was maintenance cost. (*Hint:* To do this, first determine how much of the $246,000 consisted of utilities and supervisory salaries. Think about the behaviour of variable and fixed costs within the relevant range.)
2. Using the high–low method, estimate a cost formula for maintenance.
3. Express the company's total overhead cost in the form $Y = a + bX$.
4. What total overhead cost would you expect to be incurred at an activity level of 75,000 machine-hours?

PROBLEM 3–16 Cost Behaviour; High–Low Method; Contribution Format Income Statement [LO1, LO2, LO3]

Skate World is a merchandising company that sells skateboards both at its retail store and its online store. Results for the most recent three months are shown below.

	July	August	September
Sales in units..................................	4,000	4,500	5,000
Sales	$400,000	$450,000	$500,000
Cost of goods sold..........................	240,000	270,000	300,000
Gross margin.................................	160,000	180,000	200,000
Selling and administrative expenses			
Advertising expense	21,000	21,000	21,000
Shipping expense	34,000	36,000	38,000
Salaries and commissions..............	78,000	84,000	90,000
Insurance expense........................	6,000	6,000	6,000
Depreciation expense	15,000	15,000	15,000
Total selling and administrative	154,000	162,000	170,000
Operating income	$ 6,000	$ 18,000	$ 30,000

CHECK FIGURE
Variable shipping expense—$4 per unit; Variable salaries and commissions expense—$12 per unit; Contribution margin—$120,000.

Required:

1. Identify each of the company's expenses (including cost of goods sold) as either variable, fixed, or mixed.
2. Using the high–low method, separate each mixed expense into variable and fixed elements. State the cost formula for each mixed expense.
3. Redo the company's income statement for September using the contribution format.

PROBLEM 3–17 High–Low Method; Predicting Cost [LO1, LO2]

Colby Limited is a manufacturing company whose total factory overhead costs fluctuate somewhat from year to year, according to the number of machine-hours worked in its production facility. These costs at high and low levels of activity over recent years are given below:

	Level of Activity	
	Low	High
Machine-hours..................	50,000	75,000
Total factory overhead costs	$14,250,000	$17,625,000

The factory overhead costs above consist of indirect materials, rent, and maintenance. The company has analyzed these costs at the 50,000 machine-hours level of activity as follows:

Indirect materials (variable).................	$ 5,000,000
Rent (fixed)	6,000,000
Maintenance (mixed).......................	3,250,000
Total factory overhead costs	$14,250,000

For planning purposes, the company wants to break down the maintenance cost into its variable and fixed cost elements.

Required:

1. Estimate how much of the factory overhead cost of $17,625,000 at the high level of activity consists of maintenance cost.
2. Using the high–low method, estimate a cost formula for maintenance.
3. What *total* overhead costs would you expect the company to incur at an operating level of 70,000 machine-hours?

PROBLEM 3–18 Step-Variable Costs; Non-Linear Variable Costs; Cost Prediction [LO1, LO2]
Learn Fast specializes in developing online training modules for its clients. Most of its costs are fixed but some have unusual cost behaviour patterns. For example, because of the intense competition from other companies providing a similar service, Learn Fast pays its sales staff a fixed salary of $80,000 plus sales commissions using the following scheme:

Sales Level	Commission %
$1–$100,000	5%
$101,000–$150,000	7%
$151,000–$200,000	9%
> $200,000	15%

Learn Fast has grown rapidly over the past three years, with similar growth in the number of new clients expected for the next few years. As a result of the growth, Learn Fast's customer support department is struggling to keep up with requests from customers for technical support. The two customer support employees are both paid an annual salary of $75,000 and are paid $60 per hour for time worked in excess of the 35 standard hours per week. In the most recent annual period the two customer support employees worked a combined total of 1,000 overtime hours. Management believes this is the maximum number of overtime hours the two employees can cope with and is considering hiring a third full-time staff member for the customer support department at a starting salary of $70,000 per year.

Required:
1. In terms of cost behaviour, what type of cost do sales staff wages represent? Be specific in your description.
2. Estimate total wages for a salesperson who generates $210,000 in sales for a year.
3. Discuss any potential negative behavioural consequences among sales staff that the sales commission structure used by Learn Fast might induce.
4. In terms of cost behaviour, what type of cost do customer support staff wages represent? Be specific in your description.
5. Write a cost formula for a single customer support employee's weekly wages, assuming no change to the salary or overtime rate described above. Assume the annual salary is based on working 50 weeks per year.
6. Calculate the total customer support staff wages for the most recent annual period. Estimate total wages for the next annual period if a new staff member is hired. What are the advantages and disadvantages of hiring the additional staff member?

CASES

CASE 3–19 Scattergraph Analysis; Selection of an Activity Base; High–Low Method [LO2]
Waverley Welding Company provides welding services for a variety of industrial customers in the manufacturing, aerospace, and electronics industries. The number of jobs completed from one month to the next varies considerably, and jobs differ in terms of the complexity of the welding requirements. More complex jobs can take significantly longer to complete. Management knows that overhead costs have a fixed and a variable component but, until now, has not attempted to determine which measure of activity should be used for planning and forecasting.

The table below shows data for the most recent fiscal year. Management believes that either the number of jobs completed each month or the number of direct labour-hours incurred each month could be used as the activity base. However, they are not sure which is more appropriate:

Month	Overhead	Direct Labour-Hours	Jobs
January	$ 75,045	4,781	500
February	$ 69,491	3,548	350
March	$ 71,993	3,990	400
April	$ 81,217	5,466	550
May	$ 60,162	1,914	200
June	$ 68,364	3,157	250
July	$ 78,351	5,000	500
August	$ 81,582	6,114	600
September	$ 77,691	5,108	500
October	$ 68,355	3,624	350
November	$ 69,886	3,900	400
December	$ 83,434	5,700	510

Overhead includes costs such as the maintenance supervisor's salary, depreciation on the welding equipment, and indirect materials used on each job. Electricity costs are also included in overhead and are significant since welding equipment consumes a relatively high amount of energy. Waverley Welding also employs a mix of experienced and inexperienced welders. Experienced welders are paid a higher hourly wage but are more efficient and tend to incur less wastage of indirect materials. Inexperienced welders are of course paid less on a per hour basis but work more slowly and use more indirect materials.

Required:
1. Prepare a scattergraph with overhead costs on the vertical axis and direct labour-hours on the horizontal axis.
2. Prepare a scattergraph with overhead costs on the vertical axis and number of jobs on the horizontal axis.
3. Which activity measure should be used as the activity base for predicting overhead costs?
4. For the activity measure you recommended in (3) above, use the high–low method to estimate a cost formula for maintenance.

CASE 3–20 Mixed Cost Analysis and the Relevant Range [LO1, LO2]

The Ramon Company is a manufacturer that is interested in developing a cost formula to estimate the fixed and variable components of its monthly manufacturing overhead costs. The company wishes to use machine-hours as its measure of activity and has gathered the data below for this year and last year:

Month	Last Year Machine-Hours	Last Year Overhead Costs	This Year Machine-Hours	This Year Overhead Costs
January	21,000	$84,000	21,000	$86,000
February	25,000	99,000	24,000	93,000
March	22,000	89,500	23,000	93,000
April	23,000	90,000	22,000	87,000
May	20,500	81,500	20,000	80,000
June	19,000	75,500	18,000	76,500
July	14,000	70,500	12,000	67,500
August	10,000	64,500	13,000	71,000
September	12,000	69,000	15,000	73,500
October	17,000	75,000	17,000	72,500
November	16,000	71,500	15,000	71,000
December	19,000	78,000	18,000	75,000

The company leases all of its manufacturing equipment. The lease arrangement calls for a flat monthly fee up to 19,500 machine-hours. If the machine-hours used exceed 19,500, then the fee becomes strictly variable with respect to the total number of machine-hours used during the month. Lease expense is a major element of overhead cost.

Required:

1. Using the high–low method, estimate a manufacturing overhead cost formula.
2. Prepare a scattergraph using all of the data for the two-year period. Describe the cost behaviour pattern revealed by your scattergraph plot.
3. Based on (2), do you have any concerns about the accuracy of the high–low estimates that you computed?
4. Assume that the company consumes 22,500 machine-hours during a month. Using the high–low method, estimate the total overhead cost that would be incurred at this level of activity. Be sure to consider only the data points contained in the relevant range of activity when performing your computations.

INSTANT QUIZ SOLUTIONS

3–1

It is a step-variable cost since the amount paid only changes in steps of 100 MB of data overage. Another way to look at it is that for overages of 1 MB to 100 MB the cost is fixed at $7. But if the overage is 101 MB then the cost increases by another $7 to $14, and so on.

3–2

The average lease cost per customer is $0.67 ($400 ÷ 600 customers). Total lease costs are $400 when there are 600 customers, as the lease represents a fixed monthly cost.

3–3

Total wages will be $5,000 + (2% × $200,000) = $9,000.

3–4

The cost equation is $Y = \$1,421.50 + \$1.85X$. When total occupancy-days are 500, electrical costs will be $1,421.50 + $1.85(500) = $2,346.50.

3–5

Total variable costs are 25% of sales: $3,000 ÷ $12,000. If sales are $36,000, total variable costs will be $9,000 ($36,000 × 0.25). In the absence of information that $24,000 is outside the relevant range of activity, total fixed costs will be $8,000, as per the contribution format income statement.

■ APPENDIX 3A: LEAST-SQUARES REGRESSION CALCULATIONS

LEARNING OBJECTIVE **4**

Analyze a mixed cost using the least-squares regression method.

Least-squares regression method

A method of separating a mixed cost into its fixed and variable elements by fitting a regression line that minimizes the sum of the squared errors.

Unlike the high–low method discussed in the chapter, the **least-squares regression method** uses all available data to separate a mixed cost into its fixed and variable components. The regression method is being used more than ever by organizations as part of a trend to perform sophisticated analysis of large data sets to facilitate better planning and decision making. A *regression line* of the form $Y = a + bX$ is fitted to the data, where a represents the total fixed cost and b represents the variable cost per unit of activity. The basic idea of the least-squares regression method is illustrated in Exhibit 3A–1 using hypothetical data points. Notice from the exhibit that the deviations from the plotted points to the regression line are measured vertically on the graph. These vertical deviations are called the *regression errors* (or *residuals*) and represent the difference between the estimated cost and the actual cost at a given level of activity. A regression line that perfectly explains the relationship between X and Y has all the points exactly on the line. The least-squares regression method computes the regression line that minimizes the sum of these squared errors.

Statistical software packages such as R, SPSS, and SAS are widely available that quickly and accurately perform the calculations automatically. Spreadsheet software, such as Microsoft Excel, can also be used to do least-squares regressions. In addition to estimates of the intercept (fixed cost) and slope (variable cost per unit), least-squares regression software ordinarily provides a number of other very useful statistics. One of these statistics is the R^2, which is a measure of *goodness of fit*. The R^2 fit statistic represents the percentage of the variation in the dependent variable (e.g., cost) that is explained by variation in the independent variable (activity). R^2 varies from 0% to 100%; the higher the percentage, the better. A regression line that fits the data perfectly would have an R^2 of 1 (100%), but R^2 would be 0 (0%) in a situation where no fit was achieved by the regression line.

To illustrate how Microsoft Excel can be used to calculate the intercept a, the slope b, and the R^2 statistic, we use the Hamilton Hotel data for electrical costs that appear in Exhibit 3A–2. The table in Exhibit 3A–2 reproduces the data and shows the results of the regression analysis conducted using Microsoft Excel.

The slope, intercept, and R^2 are computed using Microsoft Excel. According to the calculations carried out by Microsoft Excel, the fixed electrical cost (Intercept) is $1,364 per month and the variable cost (Slope) is $1.86 per occupancy-day. Therefore, the cost formula for electrical cost is

$$Y = a + bX$$
$$Y = \$1,364 + \$1.86X$$

Note the R^2 (RSQ) of 99.9% which is very high, indicating that nearly all of the variation in electrical costs is explained by the variation in occupancy-days. This is almost a perfect fit of the regression line to the actual data. Such a good fit would be very rare in practice.

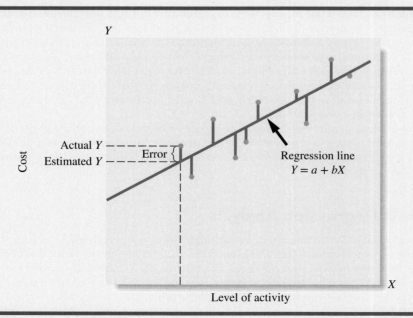

EXHIBIT 3A–1
The Concept of Least-Squares Regression

EXHIBIT 3A–2
The Least-Squares Regression Worksheet for the Hamilton Hotel

Month	Occupancy-Days	Electrical Costs
January	2,600	$6,260
February	2,850	6,550
March	3,530	8,000
April	1,440	4,000
May	540	2,300
June	1,120	3,600
July	3,160	7,300
August	3,610	8,100
September	1,260	3,700
October	190	1,773
November	1,080	3,320
December	2,050	5,200
Intercept	$1,364	
Slope	$ 1.86	
R^2	99.9%	

Even when using the regression method you should always plot the data in a scattergraph to assess the extent to which the relationship between the cost and activity level is approximately linear. A quick look at the scattergraph can reveal the strength of the relationship between the cost and the activity, or that the relationship is something other than a simple straight line. In such cases, additional analysis is required.

Economic Plausibility

Economic plausibility
A qualitative assessment of whether the relationship between the independent and dependent variables in a cost estimation model makes sense from an economic perspective.

Statistical software packages and spreadsheets such as Excel can readily perform the calculations required for the least-squares regression method and provide fit statistics such as R^2 that permit evaluation of the model fit. But managers must also carefully consider the **economic plausibility** of the relationship between the activity chosen as the independent variable and the cost being predicted. The question that managers must think about in assessing economic plausibility is whether it makes sense that a change in the activity level of the independent variable would cause a change in the dependent variable. In our example above, it is economically plausible that an increase in occupancy-days would cause an increase in electrical costs at the Hamilton Hotel. More occupancy-days would lead to increased use of the various electronic devices in a hotel room, such as the lights, television, radio, air conditioner, and heater, which of course would increase the use of electricity. However, using the number of cleaning staff employed at the hotel as the independent variable would have lower economic plausibility. One would not expect a strong association between electrical costs and the number of cleaning staff. That said, the R^2 of a regression model using the number of cleaning staff as the independent variable instead of the number of occupancy-days might still be quite high. Why? Because as the number of occupancy-days increases, more cleaning staff will eventually need to be hired, making it appear that the number of cleaning staff causes an increase in electrical costs. However, the real driver of electrical costs in this example is occupancy-days.

Because it is easy to generate cost estimation models with tools such as Microsoft Excel, managers might be tempted to use a "see what works" approach when selecting activities to use as independent variables. Therefore, applying the economic plausibility criterion, in addition to statistical criteria such as R^2, is always a good idea.

Multiple Regression Analysis

Multiple regression
An analytical method required in those situations where variations in a dependent variable are caused by more than one activity.

In the discussion thus far, we have assumed that a single factor, such as occupancy-days, drives the variable cost component of a mixed cost. This assumption is acceptable for many mixed costs, but in some situations there may be more than one causal factor driving the variable cost element. For example, shipping costs may depend on both the number of units shipped *and* the weight of the units. In a situation such as this, *multiple regression* is more appropriate to use. **Multiple regression** is used when the dependent variable (e.g., cost) is caused by more than one activity. Although adding more activities, or independent variables, makes the computations more complex, the principles involved are the same as in the simple least-squares regression approach discussed above. The same statistical software packages used for simple regression with one independent variable can also perform multiple regression analysis.

For multiple regression analysis instead of R^2, adjusted R^2 is used, which represents the amount of variation in the dependent variable explained by the *set* of independent variables adjusting for the number variables included in the set. Adjusted R^2 also ranges from 0 to 100. Managers should also consider the economic plausibility of each independent variable included in the cost estimation model.

■ APPENDIX 3A SUMMARY

- The least-squares method is the best approach for cost estimation because it incorporates all available data points in the analysis. Computer software such as SPSS and SAS can perform the calculations required by the least-squares regression method, as can Microsoft Excel. Regression analysis software also calculates other useful statistics, such as R^2, which quantifies the amount of variation in the dependent variable explained by the independent variable. **[LO4]**
- In addition to examining fit statistics such as R^2 and preparing a scattergram to visually assess the relationship between the independent and dependent variables, managers should also consider the economic plausibility of the relationship. This involves qualitatively assessing whether it makes sense for the independent and dependent variables to be causally related. **[LO4]**
- Multiple regression analysis involves the use of more than one independent variable in predicting the behaviour of a dependent variable. Fit statistics such as adjusted R^2 can be computed for multiple regression analysis, and economic plausibility is still important to evaluate. **[LO4]**

■ APPENDIX 3A EXERCISES AND PROBLEMS

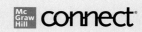

EXERCISE 3A–1 Least-Squares Regression [LO2, LO4]

The head of the radiology department at Majestic River Hospital in Woodstock, New Brunswick, believes the utility costs incurred in her department are a mixed cost. She thinks that utility costs are likely related to how many patients per month receive a CAT scan. The scanner uses a large amount of electricity and can't be turned off because of how long it takes to warm up for each use on a patient. When the scanner is used on a patient a burst of electricity is consumed. After each use on a patient, the scanner goes into a sleep mode and consumes a small amount of electricity. Data on the number of scans per month and monthly utility costs for the past year are provided below.

Month	Number of Scans	Utility Costs
January	60	$2,200
February	70	$2,600
March	90	$2,900
April	120	$3,300
May	100	$3,000
June	130	$3,600
July	150	$4,000
August	140	$3,600
September	110	$3,100
October	80	$2,500
November	160	$4,500
December	50	$1,850

Required:
1. Prepare a scattergraph plot. Is the number of CAT scans likely a good predictor of total utility costs?
2. Using least-squares regression, estimate the fixed cost and variable cost elements of monthly utility costs. Estimate the fixed cost element to the nearest dollar and the variable cost element to the nearest cent.

EXERCISE 3A–2 Least-Squares Regression [LO4]
Cycle Accessories manufacturers cellphone holders that can be mounted on the handle bars of most motorcycles. The manufacturing process is highly automated and management feels that machine-hours are likely the main driver of overhead costs. Data from the most recent year are shown below.

Month	Machine-Hours	Overhead Costs
January	1,500	$48,400
February	1,560	47,620
March	1,800	52,800
April	2,520	56,320
May	2,700	58,960
June	3,300	62,480
July	3,900	65,120
August	4,500	67,750
September	4,200	66,000
October	2,700	59,840
November	1,860	54,560
December	3,900	64,240

Required:
1. Using least-squares regression, estimate the fixed cost and variable cost elements of monthly overhead costs. Estimate the fixed cost element to the nearest dollar and the variable cost element to the nearest cent.
2. If the company expects to use 3,000 machine-hours next month, estimate total overhead costs.
3. If the company receives a special order that will require 8,000 machine-hours next month, would you be confident using the estimates from part (1) to predict overhead costs? Why or why not?

EXERCISE 3A–3 Least-Squares Regression [LO4]
Serenity Living manufactures gas fireplaces for home use. Each unit produced goes through a complex quality control process. The company has observed quality control costs as follows over the past 16 weeks:

Week	Units Produced	Total Quality Control Costs
1	24	$540
2	15	$400
3	30	$620
4	12	$380
5	18	$480
6	27	$580
7	20	$500
8	21	$511
9	17	$442
10	19	$469
11	22	$521
12	29	$616
13	26	$569
14	14	$391
15	16	$430
16	28	$602

For planning purposes, the company's management wants to know the amount of variable quality control costs per unit and the total fixed quality control costs per week.

Required:
1. Using the least-squares regression method, estimate the variable and fixed elements of the quality control cost.
2. If the company produces 20 gas fireplaces next week, what are the expected total quality control costs?
3. Evaluate the economic plausibility of using units produced to predict total quality control costs.

PROBLEM 3A–4 Cost Behaviour; Least-Squares Regression Method [LO4]
Mary Ellis owns a small manufacturing company and would like to develop more accurate estimates for overhead expenses when making planning decisions. She is pretty sure that overhead is a mixed cost that varies with direct labour-hours but she would like to do a proper analysis to determine the variable and fixed components. She collected the following information for the past 12 months on direct labour-hours incurred and total overhead expenses.

Month	Direct Labour-Hours	Total Overhead Costs
January	1,500	$44,000
February	1,680	$47,200
March	1,800	$48,000
April	2,520	$51,200
May	2,700	$53,600
June	3,300	$56,800
July	3,900	$59,200
August	4,500	$61,600
September	4,200	$60,000
October	2,700	$54,400
November	1,860	$49,600
December	3,900	$58,400

Required:
1. Using the least-squares regression method, estimate the variable overhead cost per direct labour-hour and the total fixed overhead cost per month.
2. Express the cost data derived in part (1) above in the form $Y = a + bX$.
3. Using the cost formula stated in part 2, estimate total overhead costs for a month where direct labour-hours are expected to be 3,900. Why does your estimate differ from the actual amount of overhead in December when there were 3,900 direct labour-hours?

PROBLEM 3A–5 Least-Squares Regression Analysis; Pricing Decision [LO4]
Tom Davis runs a guiding company, Chief Adventures, based in Squamish, British Columbia, that takes customers on guided tours 12 months a year. During peak season, Davis employs up to 30 guides, all of whom are paid on an hourly basis at an average rate of $20 per hour. While there is some variation, tours are typically three hours in length. Chief Adventures has considerable fixed costs, including insurance, vehicle rentals, property taxes on its office building and warehouse, provincial licensing fees, utilities, wireless communications, administrative staff, and advertising. Each guided tour also results in variable costs, such as snacks for the customers, tour booklets, and other minor expenses. Other than the wages paid to guides, Tom has been recording all of these other fixed and variable costs as guiding expenses.

For planning purposes, Tom would like to be able to separate the variable and fixed components of guiding expenses. He thinks that the variable costs related to each guided tour are likely to be closely related to the number of customers served during a month. To begin the analysis Tom has compiled monthly data for 2021 below. (*Note:* The guiding expenses exclude the hourly wages paid to guides.)

Month	Number of Customers	Guiding Expenses
January	1,500	$ 44,000
February	1,680	47,400
March	1,800	48,000
April	2,520	51,400
May	2,700	53,600
June	3,300	56,800
July	3,900	59,400
August	4,500	61,600
September	4,200	60,000
October	2,700	54,600
November	1,860	49,600
December	3,900	58,400
Total	34,560	$644,800

Required:

1. Prepare a scattergraph that plots the number of customers on the *x*-axis and guiding expenses on the *y*-axis. What insights are revealed by your scattergraph?
2. Is it economically plausible for variable guiding expenses to be related to the number of customers? Explain.
3. Use the least-squares regression method to estimate the fixed and variable components of guiding expenses.
4. Assume that a small group of six tourists wants to go on a three-hour tour that will require two guides. What is the minimum amount Chief Adventures can charge the group to cover the variable expenses of the tour?

PROBLEM 3A–6 Least-Squares Regression; Scattergraph; Comparison of Activity Bases [LO2, LO4]

Green Care Limited (GCL) manufactures environmentally friendly electric lawn mowers, and demand has been growing rapidly. Management would like to develop cost formulas for planning and decision making. The company's cost analyst has concluded that utilities cost is a mixed cost, and she is attempting to find an activity base with which the cost might be closely related. The controller has suggested that units produced might be a good base to use in developing a cost formula. The production superintendent disagrees; he thinks that direct labour-hours would be a better base since different lawn mower models have different production requirements. The cost analyst has decided to try both bases and has assembled the following information for the past eight months:

Month	Units Produced	Direct Labour-Hours	Utilities Cost
January	60,000	15,000	$200,000
February	44,000	9,000	180,000
March	84,000	12,000	240,000
April	48,000	18,000	300,000
May	72,000	30,000	400,000
June	100,000	27,000	420,000
July	120,000	24,000	340,000
August	112,000	33,000	480,000

Required:

1. Using units produced as the independent (*X*) variable:
   a. Determine a cost formula for utilities cost using the least-squares regression method.
   b. Prepare a scattergraph and plot the units produced and utilities cost. (Plot cost on the vertical axis and units produced on the horizontal axis.)
2. Using direct labour-hours as the independent (*X*) variable, repeat 1(*a*) and (*b*) above.
3. Would you recommend that the company use units produced or direct labour-hours as a base for planning utilities cost?
4. Evaluate the economic plausibility of using units produced or direct labour-hours to predict utilities cost.

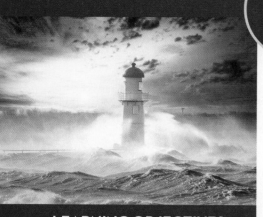

CHAPTER 4

COST–VOLUME–PROFIT RELATIONSHIPS

■ MOBILE COMPUTATIONS

Photo courtesy of Alan Webb

Mobile dog grooming businesses are becoming popular in urban centres across Canada. These companies use specially equipped vans to provide grooming services at customers' homes.

Such companies will incur a number of variable costs for each grooming session, including the hourly wages paid to the groomer, grooming supplies such as shampoo, and fuel costs to drive the van to the customer's home. Fixed costs include insurance, licensing, depreciation and maintenance for the vans, depreciation on the dog grooming equipment, advertising, and so on.

Although the business model for mobile dog grooming is quite simple, careful analysis is still required to understand how changes in the volume of activity will impact operating income, the number of customers required to break even, and how changes in pricing or costs (variable and fixed) will affect profitability. Building on Chapter 3, these and other issues related to understanding key relationships among cost, volume, and profit are the focus of this chapter.

Cost–volume–profit (CVP) analysis helps managers understand the relationships among cost, volume, and profit. CVP analysis focuses on how profits are affected by the following five elements:

1.   Prices of products or services.
2.   Volume or level of activity.
3.   Per unit variable costs.
4.   Total fixed costs.
5.   Mix of products or services sold for multi-product companies.

CVP is a vital tool in many business decisions. These decisions include which products to manufacture and services to offer, the prices to charge, the marketing strategy to adopt, and the cost structures to implement.

To illustrate the use of CVP analysis in business decisions, we will use a hypothetical company, Acoustic Concepts Inc. Our focus will be on a new speaker the company has designed for automobile sound systems.

■ THE BASICS OF CVP ANALYSIS

LEARNING OBJECTIVE 1
Explain how changes in activity affect contribution margin and operating income.

One of the most common applications of CVP analysis is to examine how changes in activity levels, selling prices, variable costs per unit, or fixed costs will impact profits. Preparing a contribution income statement introduced in Chapter 3 is a useful first step for this type of analysis. The Acoustic Concepts Inc. contribution income statement for the most recent month is shown below:

ACOUSTIC CONCEPTS INC.
Contribution Income Statement
For the Month of June

	Total	Per Unit
Sales (400 speakers)	$100,000	$ 250
Less variable expenses	60,000	150
Contribution margin	40,000	$ 100
Less fixed expenses	35,000	
Operating income	$ 5,000	

As noted in Chapter 3, the contribution format income statement is typically prepared for management's internal use in decision making and planning and would not ordinarily be made available to external stakeholders such as creditors, shareholders, or tax authorities. We ignore income taxes throughout most of this chapter so that we can more easily focus on the central issues of CVP analysis.

Contribution Margin

As explained in Chapter 3, contribution margin (CM) is the amount remaining from sales revenue after variable expenses have been deducted. Thus, it is the amount available to cover fixed expenses and then to provide profits for the period. If the CM is not sufficient to cover the fixed expenses, then a loss occurs for the period. To illustrate with an extreme example, assume that by the middle of a particular month Acoustic Concepts has sold only one speaker. At that point, the company's income statement will appear as follows:

	Total	Per Unit	Percentage of Sales
Sales (1 speaker)...............	$ 250	$250	100%
Less variable expenses	150	150	60%
Contribution margin	100	$100	40%
Less fixed expenses..............	35,000		
Operating loss..................	$(34,900)		

For each additional speaker that the company sells during the month, $100 more in CM will become available to help cover the fixed expenses. If a second speaker is sold, for example, then the total CM will increase by $100 (to a total of $200) and the company's operating loss will decrease by $100, to $34,800:

	Total	Per Unit	Percentage of Sales
Sales (2 speakers)...............	$ 500	$250	100%
Less variable expenses	300	150	60%
Contribution margin	200	$100	40%
Less fixed expenses..............	35,000		
Operating loss..................	$(34,800)		

If enough speakers are sold to generate $35,000 in CM, then all of the fixed costs will be covered and the company will have managed to at least *break even* for the month—that is, to show neither profit nor loss but just cover all of its expenses. To reach the break-even point, the company has to sell 350 speakers in a month, since each speaker sold yields $100 in CM:

	Total	Per Unit	Percentage of Sales
Sales (350 speakers).............	$87,500	$250	100%
Less variable expenses	52,500	150	60%
Contribution margin	35,000	$100	40%
Less fixed expenses..............	35,000		
Operating income	$ –0–		

Computation of the break-even point is discussed in detail later in the chapter; for now, note that the **break-even point** is the level of sales at which profit is zero.

Once the break-even point is reached, operating income will increase by the CM per unit for each additional unit sold. If 351 speakers are sold in a month, for example, then we can expect the operating income for the month to be $100, since the company will have sold one speaker more than the number required to break even:

	Total	Per Unit	Percentage of Sales
Sales (351 speakers).............	$87,750	$250	100%
Less variable expenses	52,650	150	60%
Contribution margin	35,100	$100	40%
Less fixed expenses..............	35,000		
Operating income	$ 100		

Break-even point
The level of sales at which profit is zero. The break-even point can also be defined as the point where total sales equals total expenses, or as the point where total contribution margin equals total fixed expenses. Sales − variable expenses − fixed expenses = $0.

If 352 speakers are sold (two speakers above the break-even point), then the operating income for the month will be $200, and so on. To estimate profit at any sales level above the break-even point, simply multiply the number of units sold in excess of the break-even point by the unit CM. The result represents the anticipated operating income for the period. Or, to estimate the effect of an increase in sales on profits, the manager can simply multiply the increase in units sold by the unit CM. The result will be the expected increase in operating income. To illustrate, if Acoustic Concepts is currently selling 400 speakers per month and hopes to increase sales to 425 speakers per month, the anticipated effect on operating profits can be computed as follows:

Increased number of speakers to be sold	25
Contribution margin per speaker	× $100
Increase in operating income	$2,500

These calculations can be verified as follows:

	Sales Volume			
	400 Speakers	**425 Speakers**	**Difference 25 Speakers**	**Per Unit**
Sales	$100,000	$106,250	$6,250	$250
Less variable expenses	60,000	63,750	3,750	150
Contribution margin	40,000	42,500	2,500	$100
Less fixed expenses.	35,000	35,000	–0–	
Operating income	$ 5,000	$ 7,500	$2,500	

INSTANT QUIZ 4–1
Calculate the decrease in operating income if Acoustic Concepts sells 300 speakers per month instead of 400.

To summarize, if sales are zero, the company's operating loss equals its fixed expenses. Each unit that is sold reduces the loss by the amount of the unit CM. Once the break-even point has been reached, each additional unit sold increases the company's operating profit by the amount of the unit CM.

The income statements shown above for Acoustic Concepts illustrate the fundamentals of CVP analysis but are based on some simplifying assumptions. We assumed that selling price per unit, variable expenses per unit, and total fixed expenses remained constant even for large changes in sales volumes. Simplifications such as these make the analysis easier to prepare and permit a preliminary examination of the profit effects of alternative scenarios. However, a more complex examination of CVP relationships that relaxes the simplifying assumptions can easily be handled by computer spreadsheet programs that permit more sophisticated forms of "what if" analysis.

Cost–volume–profit (CVP) graph
The relationships among revenues, costs, and level of activity presented in graphic form.

LEARNING OBJECTIVE ❷
Prepare and interpret a cost-volume-profit graph.

■ CVP RELATIONSHIPS IN GRAPHIC FORM

Relationships among revenue, cost, profit, and volume can be expressed graphically by preparing a **cost–volume–profit (CVP) graph**. A CVP graph highlights CVP relationships over wide ranges of activity.

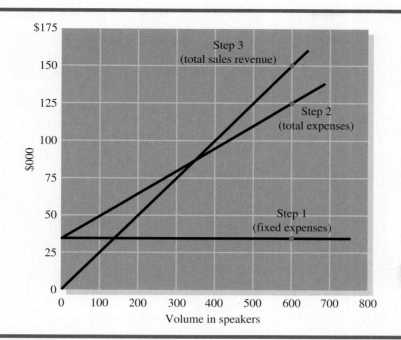

EXHIBIT 4–1
Preparing the CVP Graph

Preparing the CVP Graph

In a CVP graph (sometimes called a *break-even chart*), unit volume is commonly represented on the horizontal *x*-axis and dollars on the vertical *y*-axis. Preparing a CVP graph involves three steps, as depicted in Exhibit 4–1, and can easily be accomplished using software such as Microsoft Excel.

1. Plot the line parallel to the volume axis that represents total fixed expenses. For Acoustic Concepts, total fixed expenses are $35,000.
2. Plot the line representing total expenses (fixed plus variable) at various activity levels. For example, in Exhibit 4–1, total expenses at an activity level of 600 speakers are calculated as follows:

Fixed expenses	$ 35,000
Variable expenses (600 speakers × $150).	90,000
Total expenses.	$125,000

   Total expenses at other activity levels are calculated using this approach.
3. Plot the line representing total sales dollars at various activity levels. For example, in Exhibit 4–1, sales at an activity level of 600 speakers are $150,000 (600 speakers × $250 per speaker). Total sales at other activity levels are calculated using this approach.

The interpretation of the completed CVP graph is given in Exhibit 4–2. The anticipated profit or loss at any given level of sales is measured by the vertical distance between the total revenue line (sales) and the total expenses line (variable expenses plus fixed expenses).

The break-even point is where the total revenue and total expenses lines intersect. The break-even point of 350 speakers in Exhibit 4–2 agrees with the break-even point computed earlier.

As discussed earlier, when sales are below the break-even point—in this case, 350 units—the company incurs a loss, the amount of which increases as sales further decrease below the break-even point. When sales are above the break-even point, the company earns a profit and

EXHIBIT 4–2
The Completed
CVP Graph

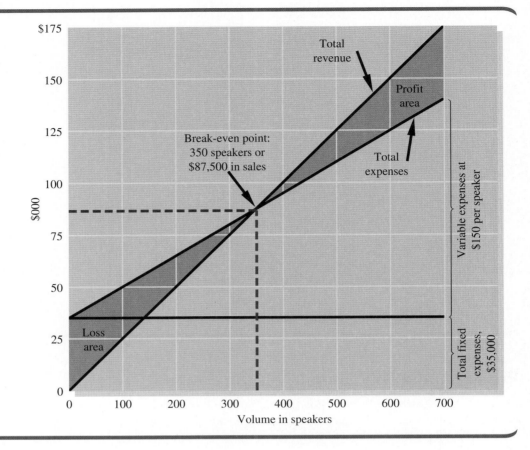

the amount of the profit (represented by the vertical distance between the total revenue and total expense lines) increases as sales increase.

A simpler form of the CVP graph, called a *profit graph*, is presented in Exhibit 4–3. That graph is based on the following equation:

$$\text{Profit} = \text{Unit CM} \times Q - \text{Fixed expenses}$$

where Q is the quantity of items sold.

In the case of Acoustic Concepts, the equation can be expressed as

$$\text{Profit} = \$100 \times Q - \$35,000$$

INSTANT QUIZ 4-2
Using the profit equation, verify that Acoustic Concepts will have a profit of $25,000, as shown in Exhibit 4-2, if sales volume is 600 speakers.

Because this is a linear equation, it plots profit as a single straight line. To plot the line, simply compute the profit at different sales volumes. For example, when the sales volume is zero (i.e., $Q = 0$), the profit is −$35,000 (= $100 × 0 − $35,000). When Q is 700, the profit is $35,000 (= $100 × 700 − $35,000). Profit or loss at other sales volume levels is similarly calculated.

The break-even point on the profit graph is the volume of sales at which profit is zero and is indicated by the vertical dashed line on the graph.

EXHIBIT 4–3   The Profit Graph

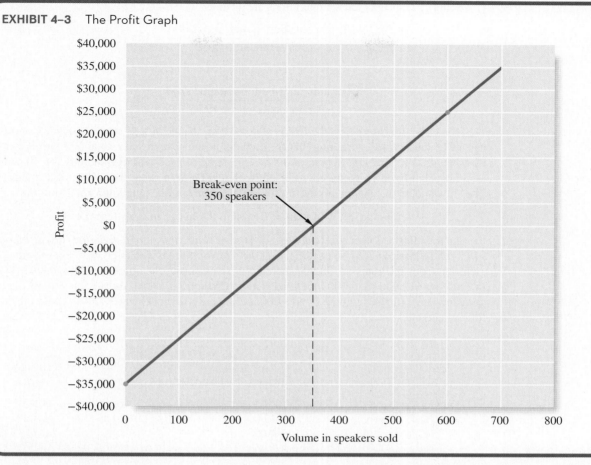

Break-even point: 350 speakers

CONTRIBUTION MARGIN AND VARIABLE EXPENSE RATIOS

Contribution Margin Ratio

In the previous section, we explored how CVP relationships can be visualized by using a CVP graph. In this section, we show how the CM ratio can be used in CVP calculations. As the first step, we have added a column to Acoustic Concepts' contribution income statement, in which sales revenues, variable expenses, and CM are expressed as a percentage of sales:

	Total	Per Unit	Percentage of Sales
Sales (400 speakers)	$100,000	$250	100%
Less variable expenses	60,000	150	60%
Contribution margin	40,000	$100	40%
Less fixed expenses	35,000		
Operating income	$ 5,000		

The CM expressed as a percentage of total sales is referred to as the **contribution margin (CM) ratio**. This ratio is computed as follows:

$$\text{CM ratio} = \frac{\text{Contribution margin}}{\text{Sales}}$$

LEARNING OBJECTIVE 3
Calculate the contribution margin ratio and the variable expense ratio. Use the contribution margin ratio to compute changes in contribution margin and operating income resulting from changes in sales volume.

Contribution margin (CM) ratio
The contribution margin as a percentage of total sales.

For Acoustic Concepts, the computations are as follows:

$$\frac{\text{Total contribution margin: } 40,000}{\text{Total sales: } \$100,000} = 40\%$$

or

$$\frac{\text{Per unit contribution margin: } \$100}{\text{Per unit sales price: } \$250} = 40\%$$

The CM ratio shows how the CM is affected by a change in total sales. Acoustic Concepts has a CM ratio of 40%, meaning that for each dollar increase in sales, total CM will increase by 40 cents ($1 sales × CM ratio of 40%). Operating income will also increase by 40 cents, assuming that fixed costs are not affected by the increase in sales. The effect of a change in sales revenue on the change in CM dollars can be expressed in equation form as follows:

Change in CM dollars = CM ratio × Change in sales revenue

As this illustration suggests, *the effect on operating income of any dollar change in total sales can be computed by simply applying the CM ratio to the dollar change.* For example, if Acoustic Concepts plans a $30,000 increase in sales during the coming month, the CM will increase by $12,000 ($30,000 increased sales × CM ratio of 40%). As we noted above, operating income will also increase by $12,000 if fixed costs do not change. This is verified by the following table:

	Sales Level			Percentage of Sales
	Current	**Expected**	**Increase**	
Sales......................	$100,000	$130,000	$30,000	100%
Less variable expenses.......	60,000	78,000*	18,000	60%
Contribution margin.........	40,000	52,000	12,000	40%
Less fixed expenses	35,000	35,000	–0–	
Operating income...........	$ 5,000	$ 17,000	$12,000	

*$130,000 expected sales ÷ $250 per unit = 520 units. 520 units × $150 per unit = $78,000.

INSTANT QUIZ 4–3
Calculate the effect on operating income if Acoustic Concepts has a $30,000 increase in sales, assuming fixed costs do not increase.

Some managers prefer to work with the CM ratio rather than the unit CM. The CM ratio is particularly valuable when tradeoffs must be made between more dollar sales of one product and more dollar sales of another. Generally speaking, when trying to increase sales, products that yield the greatest amount of CM per dollar of sales should be emphasized. We will come back to this idea later in the chapter.

Variable Expense Ratio

Variable expense ratio
The ratio of variable expenses to sales.

Another useful concept is the **variable expense ratio**, which is the ratio of variable expenses to sales. It is computed by dividing the total variable expenses by the total sales, or, in a single-product analysis, it is computed by dividing the variable expenses per unit by the unit selling price. In the case of Acoustic Concepts, the variable expense ratio is 0.60; that is, variable expense is 60% of sales. Expressed as an equation, the variable expense ratio is:

$$\text{Variable expense ratio} = \frac{\text{Variable expenses}}{\text{Sales}}$$

This leads to a useful equation that relates the CM ratio to the variable expense ratio as follows:

$$\text{CM ratio} = \frac{\text{Contribution margin}}{\text{Sales}}$$

$$\text{CM ratio} = \frac{\text{Sales} - \text{Variable expenses}}{\text{Sales}}$$

$$\text{CM ratio} = 1 - \text{Variable expense ratio}$$

Understanding how the CM ratio and variable expense ratio are calculated and how they are related will be helpful in the next section where we apply the concepts.

■ SOME APPLICATIONS OF CVP CONCEPTS

Having now covered the basics of CVP analysis we can turn to examining how changes to costs, prices, and volume will impact estimated profits. The Learning Aid below summarizes the key concepts and formulas covered so far that we will use in the examples that follow.

LEARNING AID

Key Formulas for Contribution Format Income Statements

Operating income = (Unit CM × Q) − Fixed expenses
CM = Sales − Variable expenses
CM per unit = Per unit sales − Per unit variable expenses
CM ratio = Total CM ÷ Total sales or CM ratio = Per unit CM ÷ Per unit sales
Variable expense ratio = Variable expenses ÷ Sales

In these formulas, CM = contribution margin and Q = quantity of goods sold in units.

Example 1: Change in Fixed Cost and Sales Volume

Acoustic Concepts is currently selling 400 speakers per month at $250 per speaker, for total monthly sales of $100,000. The sales manager feels that a $10,000 increase in the monthly advertising budget would increase monthly sales by $30,000 to a total of $130,000. Should the advertising budget be increased? The following table shows the effect of the proposed change in monthly advertising budget:

| | Sales Volume | | | |
	Current Sales	Sales with Additional Advertising Budget	Difference	Percentage of Sales
Sales	$100,000	$130,000*	$30,000	100%
Less variable expenses . .	60,000	78,000†	18,000	60%
Contribution margin	40,000	52,000	12,000	40%
Less fixed expenses.	35,000	45,000‡	10,000	
Operating income	$ 5,000	$ 7,000	$ 2,000	

*New unit sales: $130,000 ÷ $250 per unit = 520 units
†520 units × $150 per unit = $78,000 or $130,000 × 60% (variable expense ratio) = $78,000
‡$35,000 plus additional $10,000 monthly advertising budget = $45,000

Assuming no other factors need to be considered, the increase in the advertising budget should be approved since it would lead to an increase in operating income of $2,000. There are two shorter ways to present this solution. The first alternative solution follows:

Alternative Solution 1

Expected total contribution margin: $130,000 × 40% CM ratio	$52,000
Current total contribution margin: $100,000 × 40% CM ratio.	40,000
Incremental contribution margin.	12,000
Less incremental advertising expense.	10,000
Increased operating income	$ 2,000

Since in this case only the fixed costs and the sales volume change, the solution can be presented in an even shorter format, as follows:

Alternative Solution 2

Incremental contribution margin: $30,000 × 40% CM ratio	$12,000
Less incremental advertising expense.	10,000
Increased operating income	$ 2,000

Incremental
An analytical approach that focuses only on those items of revenue, cost, and volume that will change as a result of a decision.

Notice that this approach does not require a knowledge of previous sales. Also notice that it is unnecessary under either alternative approach to prepare an income statement. Both approaches involve an **incremental** that considers only those items of revenue, cost, and volume that will change if the new program is implemented.[1] Although in each case a new income statement could have been prepared, the incremental approach is simpler and focuses attention on the specific items involved in the decision. In the remaining examples we use the incremental approach rather than preparing new income statements.

Example 2: Change in Variable Costs and Sales Volume

Refer to the original data. Recall that Acoustic Concepts is currently selling 400 speakers per month. Management is contemplating the use of higher-quality components, which would increase variable costs (and thereby reduce the CM) by $10 per speaker. However, the sales manager predicts that the higher overall quality would increase sales to 480 speakers per month. Should the higher-quality components be used? The $10 increase in variable costs will decrease the unit CM by $10 from $100 to $90.

Solution

Expected total contribution margin with higher-quality components:	
480 speakers × $90 per speaker	$43,200
Current total contribution margin:	
400 speakers × $100 per speaker	40,000
Increase in total contribution margin	$ 3,200

According to this incremental analysis, the higher-quality components should be used. Since fixed costs will not change, the $3,200 increase in CM shown above should result in a $3,200 increase in operating income.

Example 3: Change in Fixed Costs, Selling Price, and Sales Volume

Refer to the original data and recall again that the company is currently selling 400 speakers per month. To increase sales, the sales manager would like to reduce the selling price by $20 per speaker and increase the advertising budget by $15,000 per month. The sales manager argues that if these two actions are taken, unit sales will increase by 50% to 600 speakers per month. Should the changes be made? A decrease of $20 per speaker in the selling price will cause the unit CM to decrease from $100 to $80.

Solution

Expected total contribution margin with lower selling price:	
600 speakers × $80 per speaker	$48,000
Current total contribution margin:	
400 speakers × $100 per speaker	40,000
Incremental contribution margin	8,000
Change in fixed costs:	
Incremental advertising expense	15,000
Reduction in operating income	$ (7,000)

According to this incremental analysis, the changes should not be made.

Example 4: Change in Variable Cost, Fixed Cost, and Sales Volume

Refer to the original data. As before, the company is currently selling 400 speakers per month. The sales manager would like to pay the salespeople a commission of $15 per speaker sold, rather than the flat salaries that now total $6,000 per month. The sales manager is confident that the change will increase monthly sales by 15% to 460 speakers per month. Should the change be made?

Solution
Changing the sales staff from a salaried basis to a commission basis will affect both fixed and variable costs. Fixed costs will decrease by $6,000, from $35,000 to $29,000. Variable costs per unit will increase by $15, from $150 to $165, and the unit CM will decrease from $100 to $85:

Expected total contribution margin with sales staff on commission:	
460 speakers × $85 per speaker	$39,100
Current total contribution margin:	
400 speakers × $100 per speaker	40,000
Decrease in total contribution margin	(900)
Change in fixed costs:	
Salary expense saved if sales commissions are paid	6,000
Increase in operating income	$ 5,100

According to this incremental analysis, the change should be made.

IN BUSINESS

Perhaps the biggest flop of the dot-com era was an online grocer called Webvan. The company burned through $800 million in cash before filing for bankruptcy in 2001 and halting operations. Part of Webvan's downfall was a cost structure heavily skewed toward fixed costs. For example, Webvan stored huge amounts of inventory in refrigerated warehouses that cost $40 million each to build. The company had 4,500 salaried employees with benefits (including warehouse workers and delivery personnel) and a fleet of its own delivery trucks.

Fast forward more than 15 years, and now Instacart Inc. is trying to become a profitable online grocer. Only this time Instacart is avoiding the kinds of huge fixed cost investments that plagued Webvan. Instead of hiring salaried employees with benefits, Instacart uses drivers who are independent contractors to deliver groceries to customers. The company pays its drivers $10 per order delivered plus additional compensation based on order size and delivery speed. Since the drivers use their own vehicles to pick up groceries directly from the supermarket, it eliminates the need for a fleet of delivery trucks, as well as the need for expensive refrigerated warehouses and the associated working capital tied up in perishable inventories.

Source: Greg Benninger, "Rebuilding History's Biggest Dot-Com Bust," *The Wall Street Journal,* January 13, 2015, pp. B1–B2.

Importance of the Contribution Margin

As stated in the introduction to this chapter, CVP analysis seeks the most profitable combination of variable costs, fixed costs, selling price, and sales volume. The above examples show that the effect on the CM is a major consideration in deciding on the most profitable combination of these factors. The Learning Aid below summarizes some basic decision rules that follow from these examples.

LEARNING AID

Cost–Volume–Profit Analysis

Potential Changes Affecting:
- Selling price per unit
- Variable unit costs
- Fixed costs
- Volume

Decision Rule:

Make change if	Increase in contribution margin > Increase in fixed costs *or*
	Decrease in contribution margin < Decrease in fixed costs
Do not make change if	Increase in contribution margin < Increase in fixed costs *or*
	Decrease in contribution margin > Decrease in fixed costs

LEARNING OBJECTIVE 5
Compute the break-even point in unit sales and sales dollars.

■ BREAK-EVEN ANALYSIS

Break-Even Computations

Earlier we defined the break-even point to be the level of sales at which the company's profit (operating income) is zero. The contribution format income statement can be stated in simple equation form as follows:

$$\text{Profits} = (\text{Sales} - \text{Variable expenses}) - \text{Fixed expenses}$$

or

$$\text{Profits} = [P \times Q] - [VC \times Q] - \text{Fixed expenses}$$

Where: P = selling price per unit; Q = number of units sold; and VC = variable costs per unit.

Recognizing that the difference between the selling price per unit and the variable cost per unit represents the unit contribution margin (CM), we can further simplify the profit equation as follows:

$$\text{Profits} = [CM \times Q] - \text{Fixed expenses}$$

We will use rearranged versions of this profit equation as a means of calculating the break-even point in units and in sales dollars as described next.

Break-Even Units

At the break-even point, profits are zero. Therefore, the break-even point in units sold is where the total contribution margin equals total fixed expenses. Rearranging the simplified profit equation above yields the formula for calculating the number of units that must be sold to break even:

$$\text{Break-even point in units sold} = \frac{\text{Fixed expenses}}{\text{Unit contribution margin}}$$

At Acoustic Concepts Inc., each speaker generates a CM of $100 ($250 selling price – $150 variable expenses) and total fixed expenses are $35,000. So, using the formula we determine that they must sell 350 speakers to break even.

$$\frac{\text{Fixed expenses}}{\text{Unit contribution margin}} = \frac{\$35,000}{\$100 \text{ per speaker}} = 350 \text{ speakers}$$

Break-Even Sales Dollars

A variation of the break-even formula using the CM ratio instead of the unit CM is shown below. The result using this formula is the break-even in total sales dollars rather than in total units sold:

$$\text{Break-even point in total sales dollars} = \frac{\text{Fixed expenses}}{\text{CM ratio}}$$

We can use this formula for Acoustic Concepts Inc., which has a CM ratio of 40% ($100 / $250) as follows:

$$\frac{\text{Fixed expenses}}{\text{CM ratio}} = \frac{\$35,000}{40\%} = \$87,500$$

Alternatively, the break-even point in sales dollars can be computed by multiplying the break-even level of unit sales by the selling price per unit:

$$350 \text{ speakers} \times \$250 = \$87,500$$

INSTANT QUIZ 4–4

Calculate the break-even point in units and sales dollars assuming Acoustic Concepts' fixed costs are $40,000 and the CM remains the same at $100 per unit.

BEYOND THE BOTTOM LINE

Social enterprises have been referred to as "double-bottom-line" organizations that, while seeking to earn a profit or at least break even, more importantly exist to "fulfill a social mission" (http://www.socialenterprise.ca/social-enterprise). Rather than relying on public donations or government grants to sustain their ability to deliver the social mission, these organizations use business strategies similar to for-profit organizations to generate revenue. These revenues are then used to maintain or expand activities related to the social mission.

For example, Toms is a company in New Brunswick that sells eyewear and shoes. For every pair of eyewear sold, part of the profit goes toward a program that helps restore the sight of individuals in developing countries (http://www.ponddesh-pande.ca/sociale-enterprise-examples).

The types of CVP analysis examined in this chapter are equally applicable to social enterprises. In particular, these organizations need a good understanding of the break-even level of operations and the impact of changes to prices, variable costs, or fixed costs on operating income.

■ TARGET OPERATING PROFIT ANALYSIS

CVP formulas can also be used to determine the sales volume needed to achieve a target operating profit. As with break-even analysis the focus can be on estimating either the unit sales or the total sales dollars required to generate a particular profit target. Both approaches are shown below.

LEARNING OBJECTIVE **6**

Determine the level of sales needed to achieve a desired target profit.

Unit Sales

Suppose that Acoustic Concepts would like to earn a target operating profit of $40,000 per month. How many speakers would have to be sold?

The key to target profit analysis is recognizing that instead of solving for the unit sales where operating profits are zero, you instead solve for the unit sales where operating profits are $40,000. As such the simplified profit equation introduced in the previous section is again relevant:

$$\text{Profits} = [\text{CM} \times Q] - \text{Fixed expenses}$$

However, instead of solving the equation with $0 profits we include the target profit amount. This results in the slightly modified formula shown below that adds the target operating profit to the numerator in the expression on the right-hand side of the equation:

$$\text{Units sold to attain the target profit} = \frac{\text{Fixed expenses} + \text{Target operating profit}}{\text{Unit contribution margin}}$$

Using this formula for Acoustic Concepts Inc. shows they must sell 750 speakers to generate $40,000 operating profit.

$$\frac{\$35,000 \text{ fixed expenses} + \$40,000 \text{ target operating profit}}{\$100 \text{ contribution margin per speaker}} = 750 \text{ speakers}$$

The following check shows selling 750 speakers will indeed lead to $40,000 in operating profit:

$$\$100(750) - \$35,000 = \$40,000$$

Sales Dollars

If instead we want to calculate the dollar sales level required to achieve a target operating profit, a similar modification to the formula introduced in the previous section is required. The revised formula is as follows:

$$\text{Dollar sales to attain target profit} = \frac{\text{Fixed expenses} + \text{Target operating profit}}{\text{CM ratio}}$$
$$= \frac{\$35,000 + \$40,000}{0.40}$$
$$= \$187,500$$

Alternatively, we could simply multiply the number of speakers required to achieve $40,000 in operating profit by the selling price of $250 to get the same result:

$$\$250 \times 750 = \$187,500$$

INSTANT QUIZ 4–5

Calculate the sales units and sales dollars required if Acoustic Concepts has a target profit of $80,000. Assume fixed costs are $45,000, the sales price per unit is $250, and variable costs per unit are $150.

After-Tax Analysis

Operating profit in the preceding analysis has ignored income taxes, but for-profit organizations are required to pay corporate income taxes on any income they generate. In general, operating profit after taxes can be computed as a fixed percentage of income before taxes. To calculate income taxes, we multiply the tax rate (t) by the operating profit before taxes (B). Therefore, after-tax profit is equal to profit before taxes $\times (1 - t)$ and is derived as follows:

$$\text{Profit after taxes} = \text{Before-tax profit} - \text{Taxes}$$
$$= B - t(B)$$
$$= B(1 - t)$$

Dividing both sides by $(1 - t)$, income before taxes is equal to profit after taxes divided by 1 minus the tax rate $(1 - t)$:

$$B = \frac{\text{Profit after taxes}}{(1 - t)}$$

Using the previous example, assume that the tax rate is 30% and the target operating profit is $49,000 *after* taxes. The target profit can be achieved by selling 1,050 speakers. The appropriate formula to use is:

$$\frac{\text{Fixed expenses} + [(\text{Target after-tax profit}) / (1 - \text{Tax rate})]}{\text{Contribution margin per unit}}$$

$$\frac{\$35,000 + [\$49,000 / (1 - 0.3)]}{\$100} = 1{,}050 \text{ speakers}$$

The Learning Aid below summarizes the key formulas used in break-even and target profit analysis.

LEARNING AID

Single-Product CVP Analysis

Break-Even

• Unit Sales:

$$\text{Break-even point in units sold} = \frac{\text{Fixed expenses}}{\text{Unit contribution margin}}$$

• Sales Dollars:

$$\text{Break-even point in total sales dollars} = \frac{\text{Fixed expenses}}{\text{CM ratio}}$$

Target Operating Profit*

• Unit Sales:

$$\text{Units sold to attain target profit} = \frac{\text{Fixed expenses} + \left[\dfrac{\text{Target after-tax profit}}{1 - \text{Tax rate}}\right]}{\text{Unit contribution margin}}$$

• Sales Dollars:

$$\text{Dollar sales to attain target profit} = \frac{\text{Fixed expenses} + \left[\dfrac{\text{Target after-tax profit}}{1 - \text{Tax rate}}\right]}{\text{CM ratio}}$$

*In cases where taxes are ignored, replace "Target after-tax profit/(1 − Tax rate)" with "Target profit."

INSTANT QUIZ 4–6

How many speakers must Acoustic Concepts sell to earn an after-tax profit of $56,000? Assume fixed expenses are $35,000, CM is $100 per unit, and the tax rate is 30%.

Margin of safety
The excess of budgeted (or actual) sales over the break-even volume of sales.

■ THE MARGIN OF SAFETY

The **margin of safety** is the excess of budgeted (or actual) sales over the break-even level of sales. It states the amount by which sales can drop before losses begin to occur. The higher the margin of safety, the lower the risk of not breaking even. The formula for calculating the margin of safety is as follows:

$$\text{Margin of safety} = \text{Total budgeted (or actual) sales} - \text{Break-even sales}$$

The margin of safety can also be expressed in percentage form. This percentage is obtained by dividing the margin of safety in dollar terms by total sales:

$$\text{Margin of safety percentage} = \frac{\text{Margin of safety in dollars}}{\text{Total budgeted (or actual) sales}}$$

The calculations for the margin of safety for Acoustic Concepts are as follows:

Sales (at the current volume of 400 speakers) (a)	$100,000
Break-even sales (350 speakers)	87,500
Margin of safety (in dollars) (b)	$ 12,500
Margin of safety as a percentage of sales, (b) ÷ (a)	12.5%

This margin of safety means that with the company's current prices and costs, a reduction in sales of $12,500, or 12.5% from the current level, would result in just breaking even.

In a single-product firm like Acoustic Concepts, the margin of safety can also be expressed in terms of the number of units sold by dividing the margin of safety in dollars by the selling price per unit. In this case, the margin of safety is 50 speakers ($12,500 ÷ $250 per speaker = 50 speakers).

INSTANT QUIZ 4–7
Assume Acoustic Concepts has a current sales volume of $120,000 and break-even sales of $100,000. Calculate the margin of safety in dollars and the margin of safety percentage.

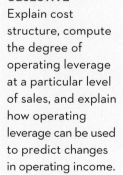

■ CVP CONSIDERATIONS IN CHOOSING A COST STRUCTURE

Cost structure refers to the relative proportion of fixed and variable costs incurred by an organization. An organization often has some latitude in trading off between fixed and variable costs. For example, investments in automated equipment can reduce variable labour costs. In this section, we discuss the choice of a cost structure, focusing on the effect of cost structure on profit stability, in which *operating leverage* plays a key role.

Cost Structure and Profit Stability

Which cost structure is better—high variable costs and low fixed costs, or the opposite? No single answer to this question is possible: either structure has its advantages. To show what we mean, refer to the contribution format income statements given below for two family-owned businesses that both manufacture custom furniture. Northumberland Ltd. has automated some of its production processes but still relies on manual labour for several processes. Conversely, Wasaga Inc. has automated almost all production processes. Consequently, Northumberland has higher variable costs, but Wasaga has higher fixed costs. Results for the most recent year are shown below.

	Northumberland Ltd.		Wasaga Inc.	
	Total	Percentage	Total	Percentage
Sales	$500,000	100%	$500,000	100%
Less variable expenses	250,000	50%	100,000	20%
Contribution margin	250,000	50%	400,000	80%
Less fixed expenses.........	200,000		350,000	
Operating income	$ 50,000		$ 50,000	

Which company has the better cost structure? The answer depends on many factors, including the long-run trend in sales, year-to-year fluctuations in the level of sales, and the attitude of the owners toward risk. If sales are expected to be above $500,000 in the future, then Wasaga Inc. probably has the better cost structure. This is because its CM ratio is higher, and its operating income will therefore increase more rapidly as sales increase. To illustrate, assume that each company experiences a 20% increase in sales without any increase in fixed costs. The new income statements are as follows:

	Northumberland Ltd.		Wasaga Inc.	
	Total	Percentage	Total	Percentage
Sales	$600,000	100%	$600,000	100%
Less variable expenses	300,000	50%	120,000	20%
Contribution margin	300,000	50%	480,000	80%
Less fixed expenses........	200,000		350,000	
Operating income	$100,000		$130,000	

Wasaga Inc. has experienced a greater increase in operating income due to its higher CM ratio, even though the increase in sales was the same for both companies.

What if sales drop below $500,000? What are the break-even points of the two companies? What are their margins of safety? The computations needed to answer these questions are carried out as follows:

	Northumberland Ltd.	Wasaga Inc.
Fixed expenses	$200,000	$350,000
Contribution margin ratio......................	÷50%	÷80%
Break-even in total sales dollars	$400,000	$437,500
Total current sales (a).........................	$500,000	$500,000
Break-even sales	400,000	437,500
Margin of safety in sales dollars (b)	$100,000	$ 62,500
Margin of safety as a percentage of sales, (b) ÷ (a) ...	20%	12.5%

Northumberland is less vulnerable to sales decreases than Wasaga for two reasons. First, due to its lower fixed expenses, Northumberland has a lower break-even point and a higher margin of safety, as shown by the computations above. Therefore, it will not incur losses as quickly as Wasaga in periods of sharply declining sales. Second, due to its lower CM ratio, Northumberland will not lose CM as rapidly as Wasaga when sales do drop. Thus, we can say that Northumberland's income will be less volatile in response to a change in sales. We saw earlier that this is a drawback when sales increase, but it provides more protection when sales drop. And, because its break-even point is lower, Northumberland can suffer a larger sales decline before losses emerge.

To summarize, without knowing future sales increases or decreases, it is not obvious which cost structure is better. Wasaga Inc., with its higher fixed costs and lower variable costs, will experience wider swings in operating income as sales change, with greater profits in good years and greater losses in bad years. Northumberland Ltd., with its lower fixed costs and higher variable costs, will enjoy greater operating income stability and will be more protected from losses during bad years, but at a cost of lower operating income in good years.

Operating Leverage

Operating leverage
A measure of how sensitive operating income is to a given percentage change in sales. It is computed by dividing the contribution margin by operating income.

Operating leverage is a measure of how sensitive operating income is to percentage changes in sales. Operating leverage acts as a multiplier. If operating leverage is high, a small percentage increase in sales can produce a much larger percentage increase in operating income.

Operating leverage can be illustrated by returning to the data given above for the two furniture manufacturers. We previously showed that a 20% increase in sales (from $500,000 to $600,000 for each company) results in a 160% increase in the operating income for Wasaga (from $50,000 to $130,000) versus a 100% increase in the operating income for Northumberland (from $50,000 to $100,000). Thus, for a 20% increase in sales, Wasaga experiences a much greater percentage increase in profits than Northumberland. Therefore, we would say Wasaga has greater operating leverage than Northumberland.

Degree of operating leverage
A measure, at a given level of sales, of how a percentage change in sales volume will affect profits. The degree of operating leverage is computed by dividing contribution margin by operating income.

The **degree of operating leverage** is a measure, at a given level of sales, of how a percentage change in sales volume will affect profits. It is computed by the following formula:

$$\text{Degree of operating leverage} = \frac{\text{Contribution margin}}{\text{Operating income}}$$

To illustrate, the degree of operating leverage for the two companies at a $500,000 sales level is as follows:

$$\text{Northumberland} = \frac{\$250,000}{\$50,000} = 5$$

$$\text{Wasaga} = \frac{\$400,000}{\$50,000} = 8$$

Since the degree of operating leverage for Northumberland is 5, the company's operating income grows five times as fast as its sales. Similarly, Wasaga's operating income grows eight times as fast as its sales. Thus, if sales increase by 20%, then we can expect the operating income of Northumberland to increase by 100%, and the operating income of Wasaga to increase by 160%. In general, this relation between the percentage change in operating income is given by the following formula:

% change in operating income = Degree of operating leverage × % change in sales

Examples:

Northumberland: % change in operating income = 5 × 20% = 100%

Wasaga: % change in operating income = 8 × 20% = 160%

What is responsible for the higher operating leverage at Wasaga? The only difference between the two companies is their cost structure. If two companies have the same total revenue and same total expense but different cost structures, then the company with the higher proportion of fixed costs in its cost structure will have higher operating leverage. Referring back to the original example, while both companies have sales of $500,000 and total expenses of $450,000, 44% of Northumberland's costs are fixed but 78% of Wasaga's costs are fixed. As a consequence, Wasaga's degree of operating leverage is higher than Northumberland's.

The degree of operating leverage is greatest at sales levels near the break-even point and decreases as sales and profits rise. The following table shows the degree of operating leverage for Northumberland at various sales levels. (Data used earlier for Northumberland are shown in colour.)

Sales	$400,000	$450,000	$500,000	$600,000	$800,000
Less variable expenses	200,000	225,000	250,000	300,000	400,000
Contribution margin (a)	200,000	225,000	250,000	300,000	400,000
Less fixed expenses.	200,000	200,000	200,000	200,000	200,000
Operating income (b)	$ –0–	$ 25,000	$ 50,000	$100,000	$200,000
Degree of operating leverage, (a) ÷ (b)	∞	9	5	3	2

Thus, a 20% increase in sales increases operating profits by only 40% (20% × 2) if the company is operating at a $800,000 sales level, as compared to the 100% increase we computed earlier at the $500,000 sales level. The degree of operating leverage continues to decrease the more the company increases sales from its break-even point.

INSTANT QUIZ 4–8

Assume Northumberland has current sales of $600,000 and a degree of operating leverage of 3, as shown in the table. If sales increase by 10%, calculate the percentage change in operating income, and calculate the new operating income in dollars.

■ SALES MIX

LEARNING OBJECTIVE 9
Compute the break-even point for a multi-product company and explain the effects of changes in the sales mix on the contribution margin and the break-even point.

Before concluding our discussion of CVP concepts, we consider the effect of changes in sales mix on a firm's profits.

The Definition of Sales Mix

The term **sales mix** refers to the relative proportions in which a company's products are sold. Managers try to achieve the combination, or mix, that will yield the greatest amount of profits. Most companies have several products, and often these products are not equally profitable; therefore, profits depend to some extent on the company's sales mix. Profits will be greater if high-margin rather than low-margin items make up a relatively large proportion of total sales.

Changes in the sales mix can cause considerable variation in a company's profits. A shift in the sales mix from high-margin items to low-margin items can cause total profits to decrease even though total sales may increase. Conversely, a shift in the sales mix from low-margin items to high-margin items can cause the opposite effect—total profits may increase even though total sales decrease. It is one thing to achieve a particular sales volume, but it is quite another to sell the most profitable mix of products.

Sales mix
The relative proportions in which a company's products are sold. Sales mix is computed by expressing the sales of each product as a percentage of total sales.

Sales Mix and Break-Even Analysis

If a company sells more than one product, break-even analysis is somewhat more complex than in a single-product company. This is because different products typically have different selling prices, different costs, and different CMs. Consequently, the break-even point depends on the mix in which the various products are sold. As with the single product analysis covered earlier in the chapter, multi-product break-even analysis can be expressed in total sales dollars or units. We present both approaches below.

Break-Even Sales Dollars

To illustrate, consider Canadiana, a small company that produces two products. *Majestic Mountains* is a DVD that provides a stunning video tour of the Rocky Mountains in Alberta. *Maritime History* is an audio book recounting major historical events in Maritime Canada during the 19th and 20th centuries. Because production of a DVD involves raw material inputs (e.g., the disc), variable costs are high relative to production of an audio book.

The company's July sales, expenses, and contribution margin for each product are shown below along with the total fixed expenses for the company and total operating income.

	Majestic Mountains		Maritime History		Total	
	Amount	Percentage	Amount	Percentage	Amount	Percentage
Sales	$100,000	100%	$400,000	100%	$500,000	100%
Variable expenses	75,000	75%	200,000	50%	275,000	55%
Contribution margin	$ 25,000	25%	$200,000	50%	$225,000	45%
Fixed expenses					135,000	
Operating income					$ 90,000	

The break-even point for the company as a whole can be calculated as follows:

$$\frac{\text{Fixed expenses}}{\text{Overall CM ratio}} = \frac{\$135,000}{.45} = \$300,000$$

The break-even level of sales for each product can be determined as shown below.

	Majestic Mountains	Maritime History	Total
Current dollar sales.	$100,000	$400,000	$500,000
Percentage of total dollar sales	20%	80%	100%
Sales at the break-even point*.	$60,000	$240,000	$300,000
	*($300,000 × 20%)	*($300,000 × 80%)	

We can verify that $300,000 is indeed the break-even level of sales for the company as a whole by preparing new income statements at the break-even level of sales for each product. Note that at the break-even level of sales, the company's contribution margin ratio remains 45% because the sales mix of 20% *Majestic Mountains* and 80% *Maritime History* is unchanged.

	Majestic Mountains		Maritime History		Total	
	Amount	Percentage	Amount	Percentage	Amount	Percentage
Sales	$60,000	100%	$240,000	100%	$300,000	100%
Variable expenses	45,000	75%	120,000	50%	165,000	55%
Contribution margin	$15,000	25%	$120,000	50%	$135,000	45%
Fixed expenses					135,000	
Operating income					$ 0	

Break-Even Units

Exhibit 4–4 shows an approach to calculating the break-even point in units when a company sells more than one product. The approach is based on calculating a weighted-average CM per unit for the multiple products based on the existing unit sales mix and the individual CM per unit for each product. For Canadiana, the weighted-average CM of $12.16 (rounded) per unit is based on the existing product sales mix of 13.5% (rounded) *Majestic Mountains* (2,500 units) and 86.5% (rounded) *Maritime History* (16,000 units), and the individual CM per unit of the two products respectively of $10.00 and $12.50, as shown in Exhibit 4–4. Note that the sales mix percentages are based on the unit sales of each product as a percentage of total sales. For example, the sales mix percentage for *Majestic Mountains* of 13.5% (rounded) is calculated as 2,500 ÷ 18,500.

EXHIBIT 4–4 Multi-Product Break-Even Analysis in Units

	Majestic Mountains		Maritime History		
	Total (2,500 units)	Per Unit	Total (16,000 units)	Per Unit	Total (18,500 units)
Sales	$100,000	$ 40.00	$ 400,000	$ 25.00	$ 500,000
Less variable expenses	75,000	30.00	200,000	12.50	275,000
Contribution margin	$ 25,000	$ 10.00	$ 200,000	$ 12.50	225,000
Less fixed expenses.					135,000
Operating income					$ 90,000
	(1)	(2)	(3) (1) × (2)	(4) Total	(4) ÷ (3)
	CM Per Unit	Sales Mix %	Weighted CM Per Unit	Fixed Expenses	Break-Even Units
Majestic Mountains.	$10.00	13.5%* (2,500 ÷ 18,500)	$ 1.35		
Maritime History.	$12.50	86.5%* (16,000 ÷ 18,500)	$ 10.81*		
Total			$ 12.16	$135,000	11,102*

*Rounded

While the approach used in in Exhibit 4–4 provides the intuition underlying the weighted-average CM concept, it can be calculated more easily by simply dividing the total contribution margin at the current level of sales by the total number of units sold at that level as follows:

$$\text{Weighted-average CM} = \frac{\text{Total contribution margin}}{\text{Total unit sales}} = \frac{\$225,000}{18,500} = \$12.16 \text{ per unit}$$

To determine the total number of units that must be sold at the current sales mix, the final step is to divide total fixed costs by the weighted-average CM per unit. As shown in Exhibit 4–4, for Canadiana the total number of units that must be sold to break even for both products is 11,102 ($135,000 ÷ $12.16). The number of units of each product that must be sold to break even at the current sales mix can then be calculated as follows:

Majestic Mountains: 11,102 × 13.5% = 1,499 units (rounded)

Maritime History: 11,102 × 86.5% = 9,603 units (rounded)

Also, the sales in dollars of each product that must be sold to break even at the current sales mix can be calculated as follows:

Majestic Mountains: 1,499 × $40 per unit = $ 59,960

Maritime History: 9,603 × $25 per unit = $240,075

Note that these sales dollars amounts are almost exactly the same as shown earlier, which uses the formula approach to calculate break-even sales dollars in total and then determines sales amounts for each product. The small differences in each case are due to rounding the units to the nearest whole number in the first step. The two methods of calculating break-even values (total sales dollars or total units) in a multi-product company are both valid approaches. The method that managers adopt will likely be a function of whether they prefer to think about break-even amounts in units or in dollars.

Effects of a Sales Mix Change

The $300,000 in sales dollars represents the break-even point for Canadiana as long as the sales mix does not change. *If the sales mix changes, then the break-even point (dollars or units) will also change.* This is illustrated by the results for December, in which the sales mix

EXHIBIT 4–5   Multi-Product Break-Even Analysis: A Shift in Sales Mix

CANADIANA
Contribution Income Statement
For the Month of October

	Majestic Mountains		Maritime History		Total	
Units	10,000		4,000		14,000	
	Amount	Percentage	Amount	Percentage	Amount	Percentage
Sales........................	$400,000	100%	$100,000	100%	$500,000	100%
Less variable expenses.........	300,000	75%	50,000	50%	350,000	70%
Contribution margin...........	$100,000	25%	$ 50,000	50%	150,000	30%
Less fixed expenses					135,000	
Operating income.............					$ 15,000	

Computation of the break-even point in total sales dollars:

$$\frac{\text{Fixed expenses}}{\text{Overall CM ratio}} = \frac{\$135,000}{0.30} = \$450,000$$

Computation of the break-even point in total unit sales:*

$$\frac{\text{Fixed expenses}}{\text{Weighted-average CM per unit}} = \frac{\$135,000}{(\$150,000 \div 14,000)} = 12,600 \text{ units}$$

*The only difference from Exhibit 4–4 is the change in sales mix to reflect 71.4% (10,000 ÷ 14,000) for Majestic Mountains and 28.6% (4,000 ÷ 14,000) for Maritime History.

shifted away from the more profitable *Maritime History* (which has a 50% CM ratio) toward the less profitable *Majestic Mountains* (which has only a 25% CM ratio). These results appear in Exhibit 4–5.

INSTANT QUIZ 4-9
Assume that the sales mix for Canadiana changes such that unit sales are 40% from *Majestic Mountains* and 60% from *Maritime History*. Fixed costs and the CM per unit for each product are the same as per Exhibit 4-4. Calculate the new weighted-average CM per unit and the total number of units that need to be sold to break even.

In Exhibit 4–5, although total sales have remained unchanged at $500,000, the sales mix is very different compared to Exhibit 4–4, with most of the sales now coming from the less profitable *Majestic Mountains* product. Notice that this shift in the sales mix has caused both the overall CM ratio and total profits to drop sharply from July. The overall CM ratio has dropped from 45% in July to only 30% in December, and operating income has dropped from $90,000 to only $15,000. In addition, with the drop in the overall CM ratio, the company's break-even point is no longer $300,000 in sales. Since the company is now realizing a lower average CM per dollar of sales, it takes more total sales to cover the same amount of fixed costs. Thus, the break-even point has increased from $300,000 to $450,000 in sales per year, or from 12,000 total units to 18,000 total units.

In preparing a break-even analysis, some assumptions must be made concerning the sales mix. If the manager expects that changes in the operating environment (consumer preferences, market share, competitors' actions, etc.) are likely to cause changes in the sales mix, then these factors must be explicitly considered in any CVP computations. Otherwise, the manager may make decisions on the basis of outdated data.

LEARNING AID

Multi-Product CVP Analysis

Overall Contribution Margin Ratio

$$\text{Overall CM ratio} = \frac{\text{Total CM all products}}{\text{Total sales all products}}$$

Weighted-Average Contribution Margin per Unit

(Product 1: CM per unit × Sales mix %) +
(Product 2: CM per unit × Sales mix %) + ⋯ for each product

or

Total CM all products ÷ Total unit sales all products

Break-Even

Total Sales Dollars

$$\text{Total sales dollars to break even} = \frac{\text{Fixed expenses}}{\text{Overall CM ratio}}$$

Total Sales Units

$$\text{Total sales units to break even} = \frac{\text{Fixed expenses}}{\text{Weighted-average CM per unit}}$$

Target Operating Profit

Total Sales Dollars

$$\text{Dollar sales to attain target profit} = \frac{\text{Fixed expenses} + \left[\dfrac{\text{Target after-tax profit}}{1 - \text{Tax rate}}\right]}{\text{Overall CM ratio}}$$

◼ ASSUMPTIONS OF CVP ANALYSIS

A number of assumptions typically underlie CVP analysis:

1. Selling price is constant throughout the entire relevant range. The price of a product or service does not change as volume changes.
2. Costs are linear throughout the entire relevant range, and they can accurately be divided into variable and fixed elements.
3. Variable costs per unit are constant, and fixed costs are constant in total over the entire relevant range.
4. In multi-product companies, the sales mix is constant.
5. In manufacturing companies, inventories do not change. The number of units produced equals the number of units sold (this assumption is considered further in Chapter 8).

While some of these assumptions may be violated in practice, the results of CVP analysis are often precise enough to be useful for decision-making purposes. For example, in most multi-product companies, the sales mix is stable enough that the results of CVP analysis are reasonably accurate. Moreover, if managers have reason to believe that assumptions regarding prices or costs need to be revised, the examples used in this chapter illustrate how readily the CVP analysis can be revised to incorporate different assumptions.

KNOWLEDGE IN ACTION

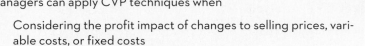

Managers can apply CVP techniques when

- Considering the profit impact of changes to selling prices, variable costs, or fixed costs
- Identifying how cost structure affects the relation between changes in sales and changes in profit
- Calculating sales levels required to break even or achieve target profits in single- or multi-product settings
- Considering the profit impact of changes to the sales mix in a multi-product setting
- Considering the profit impact of adding new products or discontinuing existing products
- Preparing budgets

SUMMARY

- Cost–volume–profit (CVP) analysis is based on a simple model of how contribution margin (CM) and operating income respond to changes in selling prices, costs, and volume. The analysis is based on the contribution income statement approach and requires a detailed understanding of cost behaviour. **[LO1]**
- A CVP graph depicts the relationships between sales volume in units and fixed expenses, variable expenses, total expenses, total sales, and profits. The CVP graph is useful for developing intuition about how costs and profits respond to changes in sales volume. **[LO2]**
- The CM ratio is the ratio of the total CM to total sales. This ratio can be used to estimate the effect of a change in total sales on operating income. The variable expense ratio is the ratio of total variable expenses to total sales. **[LO3]**
- The techniques of CVP analysis can be used to estimate the effects on CM and operating profit of changes to sales volume, fixed costs, variable costs per unit, and selling prices. **[LO4]**
- The break-even point is the level of sales (in units or in dollars) at which the company generates zero profits. The break-even point can be computed using a simple formula derived from the simple profit equation. **[LO5]**
- The formula approach can also be used to compute the level of sales required to attain a target profit. **[LO6]**
- The margin of safety is the amount by which the company's current sales exceed break-even sales. **[LO7]**
- The degree of operating leverage measures the effect of a percentage change in sales on the company's operating income. The higher the degree of operating leverage, the more sensitive operating income will be to a change in sales. **[LO8]**
- The profits of a multi-product company are affected by its sales mix. Changes in the sales mix can affect the break-even point, margin of safety, and other critical measures. **[LO9]**

REVIEW PROBLEM: COST–VOLUME–PROFIT RELATIONSHIPS

Voltar Company manufactures cordless home telephones. The company's contribution format income statement for the most recent year is given below:

	Total	Per Unit	Percentage of Sales
Sales (20,000 units).	$1,200,000	$60	100%
Less variable expenses	900,000	45	?%
Contribution margin	300,000	$15	?%
Less fixed expenses.	240,000		
Operating income	$ 60,000		

Management believes operating income can be further improved and would like you to prepare the following analysis.

Required:

1. Compute the company's CM ratio and variable expense ratio.
2. Compute the company's break-even point in both units and sales dollars.
3. Assume that sales increase by $400,000 next year. If cost behaviour patterns remain unchanged, by how much will the company's operating income increase? Use the CM ratio to determine your answer.
4. Refer to the original data. Assume that next year, management wants the company to earn a minimum profit of $90,000. How many units will have to be sold to meet this target profit figure? Ignore taxes.
5. Refer to the original data. Compute the company's margin of safety in both dollar and percentage form.
6. *a.* Compute the company's degree of operating leverage at the current level of sales.
   b. Assume that, through a more intense effort by the sales staff, the company's sales increase by 8% next year. By what percentage would you expect operating income to increase? Use the operating leverage concept to obtain your answer.
   c. Verify your answer to (*b*) by preparing a new income statement showing an 8% increase in sales.
7. In an effort to increase sales and profits, management is considering using a higher-quality speaker in the phone. The higher-quality speaker would increase variable costs by $3 per unit, but management could eliminate one part-time quality inspector, who is paid a salary of $30,000 per year. The sales manager estimates that the higher-quality speaker would increase annual sales by at least 20%.
   a. Assuming that changes are made as described above, prepare a projected contribution format income statement for next year. Show data on a total, per unit, and percentage basis.
   b. Compute the company's new break-even point in both units and dollars of sales.
   c. Would you recommend that the changes be made? Why or why not?

Solutions to Review Problem

1. CM ratio: Variable expense ratio:

   $$\frac{\text{CM}}{\text{Selling price}} = \frac{\$15}{\$60} = 25\% \qquad \frac{\text{Variable expenses}}{\text{Selling price}} = \frac{\$45}{\$60} = 75\%$$

2. $$\text{Break-even units} = \frac{\text{Fixed expenses}}{\text{CM per unit}} = \frac{\$240,000}{\$15} = 16,000 \text{ units}$$

   $$\text{Break-even dollars} = \frac{\text{Fixed expenses}}{\text{CM ratio}} = \frac{\$240,000}{.25} = \$960,000$$

3. Increase in sales $400,000
   Multiply by the contribution margin ratio . . . .   × 25%
   Expected increase in contribution margin $100,000

   Since the fixed expenses are not expected to change, operating income will increase by the entire $100,000 increase in CM computed above.

4. $$\frac{\text{Fixed expenses} + \text{Target profit}}{\text{CM per unit}} = \frac{\$240,000 + \$90,000}{\$15} = 22,000 \text{ units}$$

5. Total sales − Break-even sales = Margin of safety in dollars
   $1,200,000 − $960,000   = $240,000

   $$\frac{\text{Margin of safety in dollars}}{\text{Total sales}} = \frac{\$240,000}{\$1,200,000} = 20\%$$

6. *a.* $$\frac{\text{CM}}{\text{Operating income}} = \frac{\$300,000}{\$60,000} = 5 \text{ times}$$
   b. Expected increase in sales 8%
   Degree of operating leverage . . . .   × 5
   Expected increase in operating income 40%

   c. If sales increase by 8%, then 21,600 units (20,000 × 1.08) will be sold next year. The new income statement will be as follows:

	Total	Per Unit	Percentage of Sales
Sales (21,600 units)...................	$1,296,000	$60	100%
Less variable expenses	972,000	45	75%
Contribution margin	324,000	$15	25%
Less fixed expenses...................	240,000		
Operating income	$ 84,000		

The $84,000 expected operating income for next year represents a 40% increase over the $60,000 operating income earned during the current year. This corresponds to the calculation in part *b* above.

7. *a.* A 20% increase in sales would result in 24,000 units being sold next year: 20,000 units × 1.20 = 24,000 units.

	Total	Per Unit	Percentage of Sales
Sales (24,000 units).................	$1,440,000	$60	100%
Less variable expenses	1,152,000	48*	80%*
Contribution margin	288,000	$12	20%
Less fixed expenses..................	210,000†		
Operating income	$ 78,000		

*$45 + $3 = $48; $48 ÷ $60 = 80%
†$240,000 − $30,000 = $210,000

Note that the change in per unit variable expenses results in a change in both the per unit CM and the CM ratio.

b. Break-even point in units:

$$\frac{\text{Fixed expenses}}{\text{CM per unit}} = \frac{\$210,000}{\$12} = 17,500 \text{ units}$$

Break-even point in sales dollars:

$$\frac{\text{Fixed expenses}}{\text{CM ratio}} = \frac{\$210,000}{0.20} = \$1,050,000$$

c. Yes. Based on these data, the changes should be made. The company's operating income will increase from the current $60,000 to $78,000 per year. Although the changes will result in a higher break-even point (17,500 units compared to the current 16,000 units), the margin of safety will be higher than the current $240,000. The new margin of safety will be:

Margin of safety in dollars = Total sales − Break-even sales
$1,440,000 − $1,050,000   = $390,000

Overall, this change would be good for the company.

DISCUSSION CASE

DISCUSSION CASE 4–1

Critics of CVP analysis claim that the assumptions underlying the analysis are almost certain to be violated in practice, thus severely limiting the practical value of the various techniques covered in this chapter. Moreover, say the critics, in the highly competitive environment in which many companies operate the assumptions necessary for CVP analysis are even more likely to be violated. Arguably, companies that face stiff competition and thus could benefit most from CVP analysis may be the least likely to be able to use the techniques because of the restrictive assumptions.

Required:

Do you agree with the claims made by the critics of CVP analysis regarding its limited value in practice? Why or why not?

QUESTIONS

4–1 What is the contribution margin ratio? How is this value useful in planning business operations?

4–2 What determines the slope of a profit graph?

4–3 What is meant by an incremental analysis? What is the key advantage of using this approach to decision making?

4–4 In all respects, Company A and Company B are identical except that Company A's costs are mostly variable, whereas Company B's costs are mostly fixed. When sales increase, which company will tend to realize the greatest increase in profits? Explain.

4–5 What does it mean to have a *margin of safety* of 20%?

4–6 If a company experiences an increase in the contribution margin per unit, what will be the impact on its break-even level of sales?

4–7 Name the two approaches to break-even analysis. Briefly explain how each approach works.

4–8 In a profit graph, what is the impact on the break-even level of sales if the slope of the profit line gets flatter? What is the impact on the break-even level of unit sales if the slope of the profit line stays the same but the line moves up to intersect the vertical axis at a higher point (i.e., closer to $0)?

4–9 What effect would an increase in the income tax rate from 25% to 30% have on the break-even level of sales (dollars or units), assuming no change to price per unit, variable cost per unit, or fixed expenses?

4–10 What is meant by the term *cost structure*?

4–11 Companies X and Y are in the same industry. Company X is highly automated, whereas Company Y relies primarily on labour to make its products. If sales and total expenses in the two companies are about the same, which company would you expect to have the lower margin of safety? Why?

4–12 How is the weighted-average contribution margin per unit calculated for companies that sell two or more products?

4–13 Assume that Company Z, which sells two products, has changed its sales mix so that it sells a lower proportion of the product with the higher CM. What will be the impact on the break-even level of unit sales? Explain your answer.

FOUNDATIONAL EXERCISES

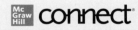

[LO1, LO3, LO4, LO5, LO6, LO7, LO8]

Oslo Company prepared the following contribution format income statement based on a sales volume of 1,000 units (the relevant range of production is 500 units to 1,500 units):

Sales	$20,000
Variable expenses	12,000
Contribution margin	8,000
Fixed expenses	6,000
Operating income	$ 2,000

Answer each question independently and refer to the original data unless otherwise instructed.

4–1 What is the contribution margin per unit?

4–2 What is the contribution margin ratio?

4–3 What is the variable expense ratio?

4–4 If sales increase to 1,001 units, what would be the increase in operating income?

4–5 If sales decline to 900 units, what would be the operating income?

4–6 If the selling price increases by $2 per unit and the sales volume decreases by 100 units, what would be the operating income?

4–7 If the variable cost per unit increases by $1, spending on advertising increases by $1,500, and unit sales increase by 250 units, what would be the operating income?

4–8 What is the break-even point in unit sales?

4–9 What is the break-even point in dollar sales?

4–10 How many units must be sold to achieve a target profit of $5,000?

4–11 What is the margin of safety in dollars? What is the margin of safety percentage?

4–12 What is the degree of operating leverage?

4–13 Using the degree of operating leverage, what is the estimated percent increase in operating income of a 5% increase in sales?

4–14 Assume that the amounts of the company's total variable expenses and total fixed expenses were reversed. In other words, assume that the total variable expenses are $6,000 and the total fixed expenses are $12,000. Under this scenario and assuming that total sales remain the same, what is the degree of operating leverage?

4–15 Using the degree of operating leverage that you computed in the previous question, what is the estimated percent increase in operating income of a 5% increase in sales?

EXERCISES

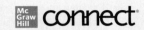

EXERCISE 4–1 The Effect of Changes in Sales Volume on Operating Income [LO1]
Whirly's contribution format income statement for the most recent month is shown below:

	Total	Per Unit
Sales (10,000 units).................................	$350,000	$35.00
Variable expenses	200,000	20.00
Contribution margin	150,000	$15.00
Fixed expenses	135,000	
Operating income	$ 15,000	

Required:
Consider each case independently. You need not prepare a new income statement. Instead, use the incremental approach where possible.
1. What would be the revised operating income per month if the sales volume increases by 100 units?
2. What would be the revised operating income per month if the sales volume decreases by 200 units?
3. What would be the revised operating income per month if the sales volume is 9,000 units?

EXERCISE 4–2 Prepare a Profit Graph [LO2]
Capricio Enterprises distributes a single product whose selling price is $19 and whose variable expense is $15 per unit. The company's fixed expense is $12,000 per month.

Required:
1. Prepare a profit graph for the company up to a sales level of 4,000 units.
2. Estimate the company's break-even point in unit sales using your profit graph.

EXERCISE 4–3 Computing and Using the Contribution Margin Ratio; Computing the Break-Even Point [LO3, LO5]
In March, James Electronics had sales of $2,500,000 (25,000 units), total variable expenses of $1,500,000, and total fixed expenses of $800,000.

Required:
1. What is the company's CM ratio?
2. Using the CM ratio, calculate the break-even level of sales in dollars.
3. What is the break-even level of sales in units?
4. Estimate the change in the company's operating income if it increased its total sales by $600,000.

EXERCISE 4–4 Changes in Variable Costs, Fixed Costs, and Volume [LO4]
Information for Drone On Limited is shown below:

	Per Unit	Percentage of Sales
Selling price	$1,000	100%
Variable expenses	800	80%
Contribution margin	$ 200	20%

Total fixed expenses are $100,000 per month, and Drone On Limited is selling 1,000 drones per month.

Required:
1. The marketing manager argues that a $5,000 increase in the monthly budget to prepare webinars would increase monthly sales by 50 drones. Should the webinar budget be increased?
2. Refer to the original data. Management is considering using higher-quality components that would increase the variable cost by $80 per unit. The marketing manager believes the higher-quality product would increase sales by 15% per month. Should the higher-quality components be used?

EXERCISE 4–5 Compute the Break-Even Point [LO5]
Mauro Products distributes a single product, a scarf; its selling price is $15 and its variable cost is $12 per unit. The company's monthly fixed expense is $4,200.

Required:
1. Solve for the company's break-even point in unit sales.
2. Solve for the company's break-even point in sales dollars.
3. If Mauro Products decides to drop its selling price to $14 with no change to the variable cost per unit or fixed expenses, what will be the new break-even point in unit sales?

> **CHECK FIGURE**
> Break-even units before price drop—1,400; Break-even units after price drop—2,100.

EXERCISE 4–6 Compute the Level of Sales Required to Attain a Target Profit [LO6]
Fox Harbour Limited produces and sells a single product; its selling price is $200 and its variable cost is $150 per unit. The company's monthly fixed expense is $200,000.

Required:
1. Solve for the unit sales that are required to earn a target profit before taxes of $20,000.
2. Solve for the dollar sales that are required to earn a target profit before taxes of $60,000.
3. Calculate the number of units that need to be sold to earn an after-tax income of $120,000, assuming a tax rate of 25%.

EXERCISE 4–7 Break-Even Analysis [LO5]; Margin of Safety [LO7]
James House is planning on starting a cleaning services business but has not decided whether he should focus on residential clients or commercial clients. His estimates of revenue, variable expenses, and fixed expenses are shown below.

	Residential	Commercial
Revenue..........................	$25 per hour	$35 per hour
Variable expense..................	$15 per hour	$20 per hour
Fixed expense	$500 per month	$825 per month

Required:
1. Calculate the number of break-even hours for residential clients and commercial clients.
2. Assume that James decides to focus on commercial clients and his business is operating at 120 hours per month. Calculate the margin of safety both in dollars and as a percentage of sales.

EXERCISE 4–8 Compute and Use the Degree of Operating Leverage [LO8]
Engberg Company installs lawn sod in home yards. The company's most recent monthly contribution format income statement appears below:

	Amount	Percentage of Sales
Sales	$80,000	100%
Variable expenses	32,000	40%
Contribution margin	48,000	60%
Fixed expenses	38,000	
Operating income	$10,000	

Required:
1. Compute the company's degree of operating leverage.
2. Using the degree of operating leverage, estimate the impact on operating income of a 5% increase in sales.
3. Verify your estimate from (2) above by constructing a new contribution format income statement for the company, assuming a 5% increase in sales.

EXERCISE 4–9 Compute the Break-Even Point for a Multi-Service Company; Compute Sales for a Target Profit [LO6, LO9]

Gulf Shore Lawn and Garden Maintenance provides two general outdoor services: lawn maintenance and garden maintenance. The company charges customers $15 per hour for each type of service, but lawn maintenance has higher variable costs ($7 per hour) than garden maintenance ($3 per hour) because of fuel expenses incurred to operate lawn-mowing equipment. All employees are paid a fixed monthly salary. A contribution format income statement for a recent month for the two services appears below. During the month, 6,000 hours of lawn maintenance services and 2,000 hours of garden maintenance were provided.

	Lawn Maintenance	Per Hour	Garden Maintenance	Per Hour	Total
Sales	$90,000	$15	$30,000	$15	$120,000
Variable expenses	42,000	7	6,000	3	48,000
Contribution margin . . .	$48,000	$ 8	$24,000	$12	72,000
Fixed expenses					54,000
Operating income					$ 18,000

Required:
1. Compute the overall CM ratio for the company.
2. Compute the overall break-even point for the company in sales dollars.
3. Compute the weighted-average CM per hour for the company.
4. Calculate the overall break-even point for the company in hours.
5. At the overall break-even point in total hours, how many hours of each service must be provided for the company to break even?
6. Calculate the overall sales in dollars required to earn an after-tax profit of $42,000 if the tax rate is 30%.

EXERCISE 4–10 Break-Even and Target Profit Analysis [LO3, LO4, LO5, LO6]

Super Sales Company is the exclusive distributor for a high-quality knapsack. The product sells for $60 per unit and has a CM ratio of 40%. The company's fixed expenses are $360,000 per year. The company plans to sell 17,000 knapsacks this year.

CHECK FIGURE
Break-even point in units, 15,000 and sales dollars, $900,000; Unit sales required to earn $90,000 with 25% tax rate, 20,000.

Required:
1. What are the variable expenses per unit?
2. Determine the following:
   a. What is the break-even point in units and in sales dollars?
   b. What sales level in units and in sales dollars is required to earn an annual profit of $90,000?
   c. What sales level in units is required to earn an annual after-tax profit of $90,000 if the tax rate is 25%?
   d. Assume that through negotiation with the manufacturer, Super Sales Company is able to reduce its variable expenses by $3 per unit. What is the company's new break-even point in units and in sales dollars?

EXERCISE 4–11 Break-Even Analysis; Cost–Volume–Profit Graphing [LO2, LO4, LO5]

The Saint John SPCA is preparing for its annual dinner-dance fundraiser. The planning committee has put together the following expected costs for the event:

Dinner (per person)	$ 18
Program (per person)	$ 2
Band	$2,800
Ballroom rental.	$ 900
Entertainment post-dinner	$1,000
Tickets and advertising.	$1,300

The committee members would like to charge $35 per person for the event.

Required:
1. Compute the break-even point for the event in terms of the number of people that must attend.
2. Assume only 300 people attended the dinner-dance last year. If the same number attend this year, what price per ticket must be charged to break even?
3. Refer to the original data ($35 per ticket). Prepare a CVP graph for the event from 0 tickets up to 600 tickets sold.

EXERCISE 4–12 Using a Contribution Format Income Statement [LO1, LO4]

Kelly Company's most recent contribution format income statement is shown below:

	Total	Per Unit
Sales (60,000 units)	$600,000	$10
Variable expenses.	360,000	6
Contribution margin	240,000	$ 4
Fixed expenses	100,000	
Operating income	$140,000	

Required:
Prepare a new contribution format income statement under each of the following conditions (consider each case independently):
1. The number of units sold increases by 30%.
2. The selling price decreases by $1 per unit, and the number of units sold increases by 20%.
3. The selling price increases by $1 per unit, fixed expenses increase by $20,000, and the number of units sold decreases by 10%.
4. Variable expenses increase by 60 cents per unit, the selling price increases by 15%, and the number of units sold decreases by 15%.

EXERCISE 4–13 Missing Data; Basic Cost–Volume–Profit Concepts [LO1, LO2]

Fill in the missing amounts in each of the eight case situations below. Each case is independent of the others. (*Hint:* One way to find the missing amounts is to prepare a contribution format income statement for each case, enter the known data, and then compute the missing items.)

    a.   Assume that only one product is being sold in each of the following four case situations:

Case	Units Sold	Sales	Variable Expenses	Contribution Margin per Unit	Fixed Expenses	Operating Income (Loss)
1	15,000	$180,000	$120,000	?	$ 50,000	?
2	?	$100,000	?	$10	$ 32,000	$ 8,000
3	10,000	?	$ 70,000	$13	?	$ 12,000
4	6,000	$300,000	?	?	$100,000	$(10,000)

    b.   Assume that more than one product is being sold in each of the following four case situations:

Case	Sales	Variable Expenses	Average Contribution Margin (percentage)	Fixed Expenses	Operating Income (Loss)
1	$500,000	$?	20%	$?	$ 7,000
2	$400,000	$ 260,000	?	$ 100,000	?
3	?	?	60%	$ 130,000	$20,000
4	$600,000	$ 420,000	?	?	$(5,000)

EXERCISE 4–14 Break-Even and Target Profit Analysis [LO3, LO4, LO5, LO6]

New Tech Limited manufactures and sells wireless phone chargers. The product sells for $30 per unit and has a CM ratio of 50%. The company's fixed expenses are $450,000 per year.

Required:
1. What are the variable expenses per unit?
2. What is the annual break-even point in units and in sales dollars?
3. What annual sales level in units and in sales dollars is required to earn target operating income of $150,000? Ignore taxes.
4. Assume that New Tech is able to reduce variable costs by $3 per unit but to do so will increase fixed costs by $54,000. What is the company's new annual break-even point in units?
5. Referring to the original data, what sales level in dollars is required to earn an annual target profit of $100,000 after taxes if the company's tax rate is 20%?

EXERCISE 4–15 Operating Leverage [LO4, LO8]

Magic Realm Inc. has developed a new fantasy board game. The company sold 15,000 games last year at a selling price of $20 per game. Fixed expenses associated with the game total $182,000 per year, and variable expenses are $6 per game. Production of the game is entrusted to a printing contractor. Variable expenses consist mostly of payments to this contractor.

Required:
1. Prepare a contribution format income statement for the company at the current level of sales, and compute the degree of operating leverage.
2. Management is confident that the company can sell 18,000 games next year (an increase of 3,000 games, or 20%, over current sales). Compute the following:
    a. The expected percentage increase in operating income for next year.
    b. The expected operating income for next year. (Do not prepare an income statement; use the degree of operating leverage to compute your answer.)

EXERCISE 4–16 Break-Even and Target Profit Analysis [LO4, LO5, LO6]

Outback Outfitters sells recreational equipment. One of the company's products, a small camp stove, sells for $50 per unit. Variable expenses are $32 per stove, and fixed expenses associated with the stove total $108,000 per month.

Required:
1. Compute the company's break-even point in unit sales and in total sales dollars.
2. If the variable expenses per stove increase as a percentage of the selling price, will it result in a higher or a lower break-even point? Why? (Assume that the fixed expenses remain unchanged.)
3. At present, the company is selling 8,000 stoves per month. The sales manager is convinced that a 10% reduction in the selling price would result in a 25% increase in monthly sales of stoves. There would be no change to fixed costs. Using an incremental approach, calculate the effect on operating income of this change. (*Hint:* When determining the incremental effect on operating income, re-member to also consider the impact of the 10% decline in selling price given the current level of sales of 8,000 stoves per month.)
4. Refer to the data in (3) above. How many stoves would have to be sold at the new selling price to attain a target profit of $35,000 per month? Ignore taxes.

EXERCISE 4–17 Multi-Product Break-Even Analysis [LO9]

Gogan Company manufactures and sells two products: Basic and Deluxe. Monthly sales, CM ratios, and the CM per unit for the two products are shown below:

	Product		
	Basic	**Deluxe**	**Total**
Sales	$600,000	$400,000	$1,000,000
Contribution margin ratio	60%	35%	?
Contribution margin per unit	$ 9.00	$ 11.50	?

The company's fixed expenses total $400,000 per month.

Required:
1. Prepare a contribution format income statement for the company as a whole.
2. Compute the overall break-even point in dollars for the company based on the current sales mix.
3. Compute the overall break-even point in units for the company based on the current sales mix.

4.   If sales increase by $50,000 per month, by how much would you expect operating income to increase? What are your assumptions?

5.   If sales increase by 5,000 units per month, by how much would you expect operating income to increase? What are your assumptions?

PROBLEMS

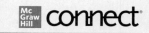

PROBLEM 4–18   Cost–Volume–Profit Analysis; Degree of Operating Leverage [LO1, LO3, LO4, LO5, LO8]

Feather Friends Inc. distributes a high-quality wooden birdhouse that sells for $20 per unit. Variable expenses are $8 per unit, and fixed expenses total $180,000 per year. Its operating results for last year were as follows:

Sales (20,000 units)	$400,000
Variable expenses	160,000
Contribution margin	240,000
Fixed expenses	180,000
Operating income	$ 60,000

Required:

Answer the following independent questions:

1.   What is the product's CM ratio?

2.   Use the CM ratio to determine the break-even point in sales dollars.

3.   Assume this year's total sales increase by $75,000. If the fixed expenses do not change, how much will operating income increase?

4.   Assuming that the operating results for last year were as above:

   a.   Compute the degree of operating leverage based on last year's sales.

   b.   The president expects sales to increase by 20% next year. Using the degree of operating leverage from last year, what percentage increase in operating income will the company realize this year? Calculate the dollar increase in operating income.

5.   The sales manager is convinced that a 10% reduction in the selling price, combined with a $30,000 increase in advertising, would increase this year's unit sales by 25%. If the sales manager is right, what would be this year's operating income if his ideas are implemented? Do you recommend implementing the sales manager's suggestions? Why?

6.   The president does not want to change the selling price. Instead, he wants to increase the sales commission by $1 per unit. He thinks that this move, combined with some increase in advertising, would increase this year's unit sales by 25%. How much could the president increase this year's advertising expense and still earn the same $60,000 operating income as last year?

PROBLEM 4–19   Break-Even Analysis; Pricing [LO1, LO3, LO5]

Minden Company introduced a new product last year for which it is trying to find an optimal selling price. Marketing studies suggest that the company can increase sales by 5,000 units for each $2 reduction in the selling price. The company's present selling price is $70 per unit, and variable expenses are $40 per unit. Fixed expenses are $540,000 per year. The present annual sales volume (at the $70 selling price) is 15,000 units.

Required:

1.   What is the present yearly operating income or loss?

2.   What is the present break-even point in unit sales and in dollar sales?

3.   Assuming that the marketing studies are correct, what is the maximum annual profit that the company can earn? At how many units and at what selling price per unit would the company generate this profit?

4.   What would be the break-even point in unit sales and in dollar sales using the selling price you determined in (3) above (e.g., the selling price at the level of maximum profits)? Why is this break-even point different from the break-even point you computed in (2) above?

> **CHECK FIGURE**
> Present operating loss—($90,000);
> Unit sales to break even—18,000;
> Maximum annual profit—$270,000.

PROBLEM 4–20 Sales Mix; Multi-Product Break-Even Analysis [LO9]
Smithen Company, a wholesale distributor, has been operating for only a few months. The company sells three products—sinks, mirrors, and vanities. Budgeted sales by product and in total for the coming month are shown below based on planned unit sales as follows:

	Units	Percentage
Sinks........................	1,000	50%
Mirrors	500	25%
Vanities.....................	500	25%
Total	2,000	100%

	Product							
	Sinks		**Mirrors**		**Vanities**		**Total**	
Percentage of total sales	48%		20%		32%		100%	
Sales	$ 240,000	100%	$100,000	100%	$160,000	100%	$500,000	100%
Variable expenses	72,000	30%	80,000	80%	88,000	55%	240,000	48%
Contribution margin	$ 168,000	70%	$ 20,000	20%	$ 72,000	45%	260,000	52%
Contribution margin per unit ...	$ 168		$ 40		$ 144			
Fixed expenses							223,600	
Operating income							$ 36,400	

$$\text{Break-even point in sales dollars} = \frac{\text{Fixed expenses}}{\text{Overall CM ratio}} = \frac{\$223,600}{0.52} = \$430,000$$

Break-even point in unit sales:

$$\frac{\text{Total fixed expenses}}{\text{Weighted-average CM per unit}} = 1,720 \text{ units} = \frac{\$223,600}{\$130^*}$$

$$*(\$168 \times 0.50) + (\$40 \times 0.25) + (\$144 \times 0.25)$$

As shown by these data, operating income is budgeted at $36,400 for the month, break-even sales dollars at $430,000, and break-even unit sales at 1,720.

Assume that actual sales for the month total $504,000 (2,100 units), with the CM ratio and per unit amounts the same as budgeted. Actual fixed expenses are the same as budgeted, $223,600. Actual sales by product are as follows: sinks, $126,000 (525 units); mirrors, $210,000 (1,050 units); and vanities, $168,000 (525 units).

Required:
1. Prepare a contribution format income statement for the month based on actual sales data. Present the income statement in the format shown above.
2. Compute the break-even point in sales dollars for the month, based on the actual data.
3. Calculate the break-even point in unit sales for the month, based on the actual data.
4. Considering the fact that the company exceeded its $500,000 sales budget for the month, the president is shocked at the results shown on your income statement in (1) above. Prepare a brief memo for the president explaining why both the operating results and the break-even point in sales dollars are different from what was budgeted.

PROBLEM 4–21 Basic Cost–Volume–Profit Analysis; Break-Even Point; Cost Structure; Target Sales [LO1, LO2, LO4, LO5, LO6, LO8]
Northwood Company manufactures basketballs. The company has a ball that sells for $25. At present, the ball is manufactured in a small plant that relies heavily on direct-labour workers. Thus, variable expenses are high, totalling $15 per ball, of which 60% is direct labour cost.

Last year the company sold 30,000 of these balls, with the following results:

Sales	$750,000
Variable expenses	450,000
Contribution margin	300,000
Fixed expenses	210,000
Operating income	$ 90,000

Required:

1. Compute (a) the CM ratio and the break-even point in balls, and (b) the degree of operating leverage at last year's sales level.

2. Due to an increase in labour rates, the company estimates that variable expenses will increase by $3 per ball next year. If this change takes place and the selling price per ball remains constant at $25, what will be the new CM ratio and break-even point in balls?

3. Refer to the data in (2) above. If the expected change in variable expenses takes place, how many balls will have to be sold next year to earn the same operating income, $90,000, as last year?

4. Refer again to the data in (2) above. The president feels that the company must raise the selling price of its basketballs. If Northwood Company wants to maintain the same CM ratio as last year, what selling price per ball must it charge next year to cover the increased labour costs?

5. Refer to the original data. The company is discussing the construction of a new, automated manufacturing plant. The new plant would slash variable expenses per ball by 40%, but it would cause fixed expenses per year to double. If the new plant is built, what would be the company's new CM ratio and new break-even point in balls?

6. Refer to the data in (5) above.
   a. If the new plant is built, how many balls will have to be sold next year to earn the same net operating income, $90,000, as last year?
   b. Assume the new plant is built and that next year the company manufactures and sells 30,000 balls (the same number as sold last year). Prepare a contribution format income statement and compute the degree of operating leverage.
   c. If you were a member of top management, would you have been in favour of constructing the new plant? Explain.

PROBLEM 4–22 Break-Even Analysis; Target Profit Analysis; Margin of Safety; CM Ratio [LO1, LO3, LO5, LO6, LO7]

Menlo Company distributes a single product. The company's sales and expenses for last month follow:

	Total	Per Unit
Sales	$450,000	$30
Variable expenses	180,000	12
Contribution margin	270,000	$18
Fixed expenses	216,000	
Operating income	$ 54,000	

Required:

1. What is the monthly break-even point in unit sales and in dollar sales?

2. Without resorting to computations, what is the total contribution margin at the break-even point?

3. How many units would have to be sold each month to earn a target profit of $90,000? Verify your answer by preparing a contribution format income statement at the target sales level.

4. Refer to part 3 and now assume that the tax rate is 30%. How many units would need to be sold each month for an after-tax target profit of $90,000?

5. Refer to the original data. Compute the company's margin of safety in both dollar and percentage terms.

6. What is the company's CM ratio? If sales increase by $50,000 per month and there is no change in fixed expenses, by how much would you expect monthly net operating income to increase?

PROBLEM 4–23 Graphing; Incremental Analysis; Operating Leverage
[LO2, LO4, LO5, LO6, LO8]

The Fashion Shoe Company operates a chain of women's shoe shops that carry many styles of shoes that are all sold at the same price. Sales personnel in the shops are paid a sales commission on each pair of shoes sold plus a small base salary.

The following data pertain to Shop 48:

	Per Pair of Shoes
Sales price	$ 60.00
Variable expenses:	
Invoice cost.	$ 27.00
Sales commission.	9.00
Total variable expenses	$ 36.00
Fixed expense per year:	
Advertising.	$ 60,000
Rent	40,000
Salaries.	200,000
Total fixed expenses.	$300,000

Required:

1. What is Shop 48's annual break-even point in unit sales and dollar sales?
2. Prepare a CVP graph showing cost and revenue data for Shop 48 from zero shoes up to 17,000 pairs of shoes sold each year. Clearly indicate the break-even point on the graph.
3. If 12,000 pairs of shoes are sold in a year, what would be Shop 48's operating income (loss)?
4. The company is considering paying the Shop 48 store manager an incentive commission of $4 per pair of shoes (in addition to the salesperson's commission). If this change is made, what will be the new break-even point in unit sales?
5. Refer to the original data. As an alternative to (4) above, the company is considering paying the Shop 48 store manager $4.00 commission on each pair of shoes sold in excess of the break-even point. If this change is made, what will be Shop 48's operating income (loss) if 15,000 pairs of shoes are sold?
6. Refer to the original data. The company is considering eliminating sales commissions entirely in its shops and increasing fixed salaries by $60,000 annually. If this change is made, what will be Shop 48's new break-even point in dollar sales?

PROBLEM 4–24 Break-Even and Target Profit Analysis [LO5, LO6]

The Shirt Works sells a large variety of T-shirts and sweatshirts. Steve Hooper, the owner, is thinking of expanding his sales by hiring high school students, on a commission basis, to sell sweatshirts bearing the name and mascot of the local high school.

These sweatshirts would have to be ordered from the manufacturer six weeks in advance, and they could not be returned because of the unique printing required. The sweatshirts would cost Hooper $8 each with a minimum order of 75 sweatshirts. Any additional sweatshirts would have to be ordered in increments of 75.

Since Hooper's plan would not require any additional facilities, the only costs associated with the project would be the costs of the sweatshirts and the costs of the sales commissions. The selling price of the sweatshirts would be $13.50 each. Hooper would pay the students a commission of $1.50 for each shirt sold.

Required:

1. To make the project worthwhile, Hooper would require a $1,200 profit for the first three months of the venture. What level of unit sales and dollar sales would be required to reach this target net operating income? Show all computations.
2. Assume that the venture is undertaken and an order is placed for 75 sweatshirts. What would be Hooper's break-even point in unit sales and in dollar sales? Show computations and explain the reasoning behind your answer.

CHECK FIGURE
300 sweatshirts to achieve target profit of $1,200; Break-even in units— 50 sweatshirts.

PROBLEM 4–25 Sales Mix; Multi-Product Break-Even Analysis; Target Profit; Margin of Safety [LO6, LO7, LO9]

Warm Hands, a small company based in Prince Edward Island, manufactures and sells two types of lightweight gloves for runners—Warm and Cozy. Current revenue, cost, and unit sales data for the two products appear below:

	Warm	Cozy
Selling price per pair	$8.00	$12.00
Variable expenses per pair	$2.00	$ 6.00
Number of pairs sold monthly	600 units	200 units

Fixed expenses are $2,250 per month.

Required:
1. Assuming the sales mix above, do the following:
    a. Prepare a contribution format income statement showing both dollars and percentage columns for each product and for the company as a whole.
    b. Compute the break-even point in sales dollars for the company as a whole and the margin of safety in both dollars and percentage of sales.
    c. Compute the break-even point in units for the company as a whole and the margin of safety in both units (pairs of gloves) and percentage of sales.
    d. Compute how many pairs of gloves must be sold overall if the company wants to make an after-tax target profit of $4,725 and the tax rate is 30%. Assume that the sales mix remains the same as shown above.
2. The company has developed another type of gloves that provide better protection in extreme cold, Toasty, which the company plans to sell for $20 per pair. At this price, the company expects to sell 200 pairs per month of the product. The variable expense would be $16 per pair. The company's fixed expenses would not change.
    a. Prepare another contribution format income statement, including sales of Toasty (sales of the other two products would not change).
    b. Compute the company's new break-even point in sales dollars for the company as a whole and the new margin of safety in both dollars and percentage of sales.
3. The president of the company is puzzled by your analysis. He does not understand why the break-even point has gone up even though there has been no increase in fixed expenses and the addition of the new product has increased the total CM. Explain to the president what happened.

PROBLEM 4–26 Sales Mix; Multi-Product Break-Even Analysis [LO9]

Active Life manufactures wearable technology for a variety of purposes. The Athletics Division produces three models of a watch that monitors heart rate, steps taken, calories burned, distance covered, and other metrics related to personal health. Data for the three models are shown below:

	Basic	Advanced	Elite
Selling price per watch	$160.00	$240.00	$360.00
Variable expenses per watch:			
Production	88.00	108.00	126.00
Sales commissions	32.00	24.00	36.00
Total variable expenses	120.00	132.00	162.00
Contribution margin per watch:	$ 40.00	$108.00	$198.00

The Athletics Division has the following fixed costs:

	Per Month
Fixed production costs	$180,000
Advertising expense	150,000
Administrative salaries	78,000
Total	$408,000

Sales, in units, over the past two months are shown below. The increased in total watches sold is attributable to a special advertising campaign focused on the Basic model. The manager of the Athletics Division believed there was an opportunity to boost sales for that model during the busy holiday season. The one-time advertising campaign in December cost $10,000.

	Basic	Advanced	Elite	Total
November	2,000	2,000	4,000	8,000
December	6,000	2,000	2,000	10,000

Required:
1. Without preparing an income statement, calculate operating income in both November and December.
2. Explain why operating income differs between the two months. Was the advertising campaign a success? Why or why not?
3. Compute the Athletics Division's break-even point in unit sales for November.
4. Has December's break-even point in units gone up or down from November's break-even point? Explain without calculating the actual break-even point for December.
5. Assume the sales mix stays the same in January as it was in December. Calculate the total contribution margin if 12,000 units are sold. Assume no change to the contribution margin per unit for any of the models in January.

PROBLEM 4–27 Changes in Cost Structure; Break-Even Analysis; Operating Leverage; Margin of Safety [LO4, LO5, LO6, LO7, LO8]
Frieden Company's contribution format income statement for last month is shown below:

Sales (40,000 units)	$800,000
Variable expenses...........................	560,000
Contribution margin.........................	240,000
Fixed expenses	192,000
Operating income...........................	$ 48,000

Competition is intense, and Frieden Company's profits vary considerably from one year to the next. Management is exploring opportunities to increase profitability.

Required:
1. Frieden's management is considering a major upgrade to the manufacturing equipment, which would result in fixed expenses increasing by $240,000 per month. However, variable expenses would decrease by $6 per unit. Selling price would not change. Prepare two contribution format income statements, one showing current operations and one showing how operations would appear if the upgrade is completed. Show an Amount column, a Per Unit column, and a Percentage column on each statement. Do not show percentages for the fixed expenses.
2. Refer to the income statements in (1) above. For both current operations and the proposed new operations, compute (*a*) the degree of operating leverage, (*b*) the break-even point in dollars, and (*c*) the margin of safety in both dollar and percentage terms.
3. Calculate the unit sales per month at which Frieden management will be indifferent between doing the major upgrade to the manufacturing equipment and not doing the upgrade. Based on this analysis, should Frieden proceed with the major upgrade? Why or why not?
4. Refer to the original data. Instead of doing the major upgrade to the equipment, management is considering introducing a new advertising campaign that will increase fixed expenses by $20,000 per month. Management believes the new advertisements will increase monthly unit sales by 10%. Should Frieden proceed with the new advertising campaign?

PROBLEM 4–28 Interpretive Questions on the Cost–Volume–Profit Graph [LO2, LO5]
A CVP graph, as illustrated below, is a useful tool for showing relationships between an organization's costs, volume, and profits:

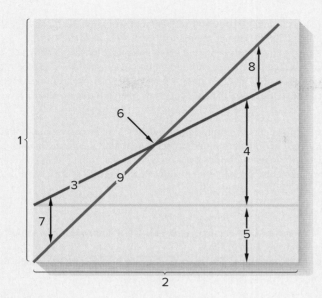

Required:
1. Identify the numbered components in the CVP graph.
2. State the effect of each of the following actions on line 3, line 9, and the break-even point. For line 3 and line 9, state whether the action will cause the line to
   • Remain unchanged.
   • Shift upward.
   • Shift downward.
   • Have a steeper slope (i.e., rotate upward).
   • Have a flatter slope (i.e., rotate downward).
   • Shift upward *and* have a steeper slope.
   • Shift upward *and* have a flatter slope.
   • Shift downward *and* have a steeper slope.
   • Shift downward *and* have a flatter slope.

In the case of the break-even point, state whether the action will cause the break-even point to
   • Remain unchanged.
   • Increase.
   • Decrease.
   • Probably change, but the direction is uncertain.

Treat each case independently.
Example: Fixed costs are decreased by $90,000 each period.
Answer (see choices above):   Line 3: Shift downward.
                                   Line 9: Remain unchanged.
                                   Break-even point: Decrease.

a.   The unit selling price increases from $100 to $110.
b.   The per unit variable costs decrease from $40 to $36.
c.   The total fixed costs increase by $80,000.
d.   Two thousand more units are sold during the period than were budgeted.
e.   Due to paying salespeople a commission rather than a flat salary, fixed costs decrease by $21,000 per period, and unit variable costs increase by $6.
f.   As a result of an increase in the cost of materials, both unit variable costs and the selling price increase by $6.
g.   Advertising costs increase by $50,000 per period, but unfortunately the number of units sold does not change.
h.   Upgrades to manufacturing equipment increase fixed costs by $40,000 per period, but variable costs per unit decrease by $2 per unit.

PROBLEM 4–29 Changes in Fixed and Variable Costs; Break-Even and Target Profit Analysis [LO4, LO5, LO6]
Neptune Company produces toys and other items for use in beach and resort areas. A small, inflatable toy has come onto the market that the company is anxious to produce and sell. The new toy will sell for $3 per unit. Enough capacity exists in the company's plant to produce 16,000 units of the toy each

month. Variable expenses to manufacture and sell one unit would be $1.25, and fixed expenses associated with the toy would total $35,000 per month.

The company's marketing department predicts that demand for the new toy will exceed the 16,000 units that the company is able to produce. Additional manufacturing space can be rented from another company at a fixed expense of $1,000 per month. Variable expenses in the rented facility would total $1.40 per unit, due to somewhat less efficient operations than in the main plant.

Required:
1. Compute the monthly break-even point for the new toy in units and in total dollar sales.
2. How many units must be sold each month to make a monthly operating income of $12,000?
3. If the sales manager receives a bonus of 10 cents for each unit sold in excess of the break-even point, how many units must be sold each month to earn a return of 25% on the monthly investment in fixed costs?

PROBLEM 4–30 Changes in Cost Structure; Break-Even Analysis; Operating Leverage; Margin of Safety [LO4, LO5, LO7, LO8]
Lawson Manufacturing Company's (LMC) contribution format income statement for the most recent month is given below:

Sales (15,000 units)	$450,000
Variable expenses	315,000
Contribution margin	135,000
Fixed expenses	90,000
Operating income	$ 45,000

LMC's operating income is highly sensitive to changes in the operating environment, and management is considering ways to stabilize earnings and improve profitability.

Required:
1. New equipment has come on the market that would allow LMC to automate a portion of its operations. Variable costs would be reduced by $9 per unit. However, fixed costs would increase to a total of $225,000 each month. Prepare two contribution format income statements, one showing current operations and one showing how operations would appear if the new equipment is purchased. Show an Amount column, a Per Unit column, and a Percentage column on each statement. Do not show percentages for the fixed costs.
2. Refer to the income statements in (1) above. For both current operations and the proposed new operations, compute (*a*) the degree of operating leverage, (*b*) the break-even point in dollars, and (*c*) the margin of safety in both dollar and percentage terms.
3. Refer again to the data in (1) above. As a manager, what factor would be paramount in your mind in deciding whether to purchase the new equipment? (You may assume that ample funds are available to make the purchase.)
4. Refer to the original data. Rather than purchase new equipment, the marketing manager argues that the company's marketing strategy should be changed. Instead of paying sales commissions, which are included in variable expenses, the marketing manager suggests that salespeople be paid fixed salaries and that the company invest heavily in advertising. The marketing manager claims that this new approach would increase unit sales by 30% without any change in selling price, the company's new monthly fixed expenses would be $180,000, and its operating income would increase by 20%. Compute the break-even point in dollar sales for the company under the new marketing strategy. Do you agree with the marketing manager's proposal?
5. What level of sales under the new marketing strategy would generate the same operating income as the most recent month?

PROBLEM 4–31 CVP Applications; Contribution Margin Ratio: Degree of Operating Leverage [LO3, LO5, LO6, LO8]
Dog Dandy distributes a dog collar made of wooden beads that sells for $40 per unit. Variable expenses are $20 per unit, and fixed expenses total $120,000 per year. Its operating results for last year were as follows:

Sales	$400,000
Variable expenses...........................	200,000
Contribution margin........................	200,000
Fixed expenses	120,000
Operating income..........................	$ 80,000

Required:

Answer each of the following independent questions based on the original data.

1. What is the product's CM ratio?
2. Use the CM ratio to determine the break-even point in dollar sales.
3. Assume this year's unit sales and total sales decrease by $50,000. If the fixed expenses do not change, how much will operating income decrease?
4. What is the degree of operating leverage based on last year's sales?
5. Assume the this year's unit sales will decrease by 20% next year. Using the degree of operating leverage from last year, what percentage decrease in operating income will the company incur this year?
6. The sales manager is convinced that a 10% reduction in the selling price, combined with a $20,000 increase in advertising, would increase this year's unit sales by 40%. If the sales manager is right, what would be this year's operating income if his ideas are implemented? Do you recommend implementing the sales manager's suggestions? Why?

PROBLEM 4–32 Changes in Cost Structure; Break-Even Analysis; Target Profit [LO5, LO6, LO8]

Alliance Enterprises is considering extensively modifying its manufacturing equipment. The modifications will result in less wastage of materials, which will reduce variable manufacturing costs and introduce changes to the production process that will improve product quality. This will allow Alliance to increase the selling price of the product. Annual fixed costs are expected to increase to $750,000 if the modifications are made. Expected fixed and variable costs as well as the selling prices are shown below:

Cost Item	Existing Equipment	Modified Equipment
Selling price per unit.............	$36	$40
Variable cost per unit	$28	$25
Fixed costs.....................	$330,000	$750,000

Required:

1. Determine Alliance Enterprises' break-even point in units with the existing equipment and with the modified equipment.
2. Determine the sales level in units at which the modified equipment will achieve a 25% target profit-to-sales ratio (ignore taxes).
3. Determine the sales level in units at which the modified equipment will achieve $63,000 in after-tax operating income. Assume a tax rate of 30%.
4. Determine the sales level at which profits will be the same for either the existing or modified equipment.

PROBLEM 4–33 CVP Analysis; Cost Structure [LO3, LO4, LO8]

Due to erratic sales of its sole product—a high-capacity battery for laptop computers—PEM Inc. has been experiencing difficulty for some time. The company's contribution format income statement for the most recent month is given below:

Sales (19,500 × $30 per unit)..................	$585,000
Variable expenses...........................	409,500
Contribution margin........................	175,500
Fixed expenses	180,000
Operating loss..............................	$ (4,500)

Required:

1. Compute the company's CM ratio and its break-even point in both unit sales and dollar sales.
2. The president believes that a $16,000 increase in the monthly advertising budget, combined with an intensified effort by the sales staff, will result in an $80,000 increase in monthly sales. If the president is right, what will be the effect on the company's monthly net operating income or loss? (Use the incremental approach in preparing your answer.)
3. Refer to the original data. The sales manager is convinced that a 10% reduction in the selling price, combined with an increase of $60,000 in the monthly advertising budget, will double unit sales. What will the new contribution format income statement look like if these changes are adopted?
4. Refer to the original data. The marketing department thinks that a fancy new package for the laptop computer battery would help sales. The new package would increase packaging costs by 75 cents per unit. Assuming no other changes, how many units would have to be sold each month to earn a profit of $9,750?
5. Refer to the original data. By automating, the company could reduce variable expenses by $3 per unit. However, fixed expenses would increase by $72,000 each month.
   a. Compute the new CM ratio and the new break-even point in both unit sales and dollar sales.
   b. Assume that the company expects to sell 26,000 units next month. Prepare two contribution format income statements, one assuming that operations are not automated and one assuming that they are. (Show data on a per unit and percentage basis, as well as in total, for each alternative.)
   c. At what number of unit sales would the company be indifferent between automating operations versus not automating? Would you recommend that the company automate its operations? Explain.

CASES

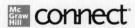

CASE 4–34 Cost Structure; Break-Even and Target Profit Analysis [LO5, LO6, LO8]

Pittman Company is a small but growing manufacturer of telecommunications equipment. The company has no sales force of its own; rather, it relies completely on independent sales agents to market its products. These agents are paid a sales commission of 15% for all items sold.

Barbara Cheney, Pittman's controller, has just prepared the company's budgeted income statement for next year as follows:

PITTMAN COMPANY		
Budgeted Income Statement		
For the Year Ended December 31		
Sales		$16,000,000
Manufacturing expenses:		
Variable	$7,200,000	
Fixed	2,340,000	9,540,000
Gross margin		6,460,000
Selling and administrative expenses		
Sales commissions	2,400,000	
Fixed marketing expenses*	120,000	
Fixed administrative expenses	1,800,000	4,320,000
Operating income		2,140,000
Interest expense		540,000
Income before income taxes		1,600,000
Income taxes (30%)		480,000
Net income		$ 1,120,000

*Primarily depreciation on storage facilities

As Barbara handed the statement to Karl Vecci, Pittman's president, she commented, "I went ahead and used the agents' 15% commission rate in completing these statements, but we've just learned that they refuse to handle our products next year unless we increase the commission rate to 20%."

"That's the last straw," Karl replied angrily. "Those agents have been demanding more and more, and this time they've gone too far. How can they possibly defend a 20% commission rate?"

"They claim that after paying for advertising, travel, and the other costs of promotion, there's nothing left over for profit," replied Barbara.

"I say it's just plain robbery," retorted Karl. "And I also say it's time we dumped those guys and got our own sales force. Can you get your people to work up some cost figures for us to look at?"

"We've already worked them up," said Barbara. "Several companies we know about pay a 7.5% commission to their own salespeople, along with a small salary. Of course, we would have to handle all promotion costs, too. We figure our fixed expenses would increase by $2,400,000 per year, but that would be more than offset by the $3,200,000 (20% × $16,000,000) that we would avoid on agents' commissions."

The breakdown of the $2,400,000 cost follows:

Salaries:	
Sales manager.	$ 100,000
Salespersons	600,000
Travel and entertainment	400,000
Advertising	1,300,000
Total	$2,400,000

"Super," replied Karl. "And I noticed that the $2,400,000 equals what we're paying the agents under the old 15% commission rate."

"It's even better than that," explained Barbara. "We can actually save $75,000 a year because that's what we're paying our auditors to check out the agents' reports. So our overall administrative expenses would be less."

"Pull all of these numbers together and we'll show them to the executive committee tomorrow," said Karl. "With the approval of the committee, we can move on the matter immediately."

Required:
1. Compute Pittman Company's break-even point in dollar sales for next year assuming:
   a. The agents' commission rate remains unchanged at 15%.
   b. The agents' commission rate is increased to 20%.
   c. The company employs its own sales force.
2. Assume that Pittman Company decides to continue selling through agents and pays the 20% commission rate. Determine the dollar sales that would be required to generate the same net income as contained in the budgeted income statement for next year.
3. Determine the dollar sales at which net income would be equal regardless of whether Pittman Company sells through agents (at a 20% commission rate) or employs its own sales force.
4. Compute the degree of operating leverage that the company would expect to have at the end of next year assuming:
   a. The agents' commission rate remains unchanged at 15%.
   b. The agents' commission rate is increased to 20%.
   c. The company employs its own sales force.
   Use income *before* income taxes in your operating leverage computation.
5. Based on the data in (1) through (4) above, make a recommendation as to whether the company should continue to use sales agents (at a 20% commission rate) or employ its own sales force. Give reasons for your answer.

CASE 4–35 Break-Even Levels for Individual Products in a Multi-Product Company [LO6, LO9]
Jasmine Richards met her boss, Rick McNeil, at the pop machine in the lobby. McNeil is the vice president of marketing at Down East Lures Corporation. Richards was puzzled by some calculations she had been doing, so she initiated this conversation:

Richards: Rick, I'm not sure how to go about answering the questions that came up at the meeting with the president yesterday.

McNeil: What's the problem?

Richards: The president wanted to know the break-even point for each of the company's products, but I'm having trouble figuring them out.

McNeil: I'm sure you can handle it, Jasmine. And, by the way, I need your analysis on my desk tomorrow morning at 8:00 A.M. sharp so I can look at it before the follow-up meeting at 9:00.

Down East Lures makes three fishing lures in its manufacturing facility in Prince Edward Island. Data concerning these products appear below:

	Frog	Minnow	Worm
Normal annual sales volume (units)	100,000	200,000	300,000
Unit selling price.	$2.00	$1.40	$0.80
Variable cost per unit	$1.20	$0.80	$0.50

Total fixed expenses for the entire company are $282,000 per year. All three products are sold in highly competitive markets, so the company is unable to raise its prices without losing unacceptable numbers of customers. The company has no work in process or finished goods inventories due to an extremely effective lean manufacturing system.

Required:
1. What is the company's overall break-even point in total sales dollars?
2. Of the total fixed costs of $282,000, $18,000 relate directly to the Frog lure product, $96,000 relate directly to the Minnow lure product, and $60,000 relate directly to the Worm lure product. The remaining fixed expenses of $108,000 consist of common fixed costs such as administrative salaries, rent on the factory building, and advertising expenses for the company as a whole. These common fixed expenses are not directly related to any particular product but must be incurred as part of operating the business.
    a. What is the break-even point in units for each product? *Note:* Management insists that Richards separately calculate the break-even point for each product using its CM per unit and only the fixed expenses that relate directly to that product.
    b. If the company sells exactly the break-even quantity of each product calculated in (*a*), calculate the overall profit of the company. Explain this result to management.
    c. Calculate the company's overall break-even point in units using the weighted-average CM approach. How many units of each product must be sold at the break-even level? Comment on any significant differences you see between these results and those of (*a*) above.

CONNECTING CONCEPTS

SECTION 1

COST BEHAVIOUR AND COST-VOLUME-PROFIT ANALYSIS

Easy Learning (EL) develops online learning platforms for companies using gamification techniques to make the learning experience engaging. Research shows that employees are far more likely to use learning platforms if they are easy and fun to use. EL's approach is to embed the learning content, usually a series of multiple choice questions, in the games they use in their platform. EL works with company management to develop the learning content and their platforms have been used in a wide variety of functional areas such as manufacturing, sales, customer service, distribution, and product development. EL has developed a strong reputation for being the most creative and reliable developer of online learning platforms and the company has clients across Canada and the United States.

Competition has increased considerably over the past five years, with several start-up companies offering their own versions of online learning platforms. Given this, EL is placing increased emphasis on its customer acquisition activities, which range from attending tech conventions, developing webinars, presenting their research at conferences, follow-up meetings and calls with prospective customers, and online advertising. Annual recurring revenue (ARR) for use of the learning platform from each customer averages $100,000, so acquiring and retaining customers is critical to EL's success.

For the next fiscal period, Claire Jackson, EL's CEO and founder, has told the senior management team that she wants to acquire 40 new customers compared to the 20 new customers that were acquired in the fiscal period just ended. Jackson believes that it is reasonable to expect the marketing department to spend in total the equivalent of about one year's ARR that will be generated by the number of new customers acquired in that year.

The total number of monthly follow-up activities with prospective clients (e.g., calls, meetings, product demos, etc.) and the total marketing department costs for last year are shown below:

	Number of Client Follow-Up Activities	Total Cost
January	500	$175,000
February	450	$160,500
March	320	$122,800
April	600	$204,000
May	305	$118,450
June	480	$169,200
July	530	$183,700
August	370	$137,300
September	415	$150,350
October	550	$189,500
November	625	$211,250
December	510	$177,900
Total	**5,655**	**$1,999,950**

Required:

1. Assuming no change to the cost behaviour implied by the data from last year and no increase in costs due to inflation or other factors, estimate the total spending that will be required by the marketing department to acquire 40 new customers next year. You can further assume that the relationship between the number of follow-up activities with prospective clients and the number of new customers actually acquired next year, the conversion ratio, will be the same as it was last year (i.e., 20/5,655, or 0.35%).

2. Given your answer to part (1), is Jackson likely to approve the estimated total spending by the marketing department next year? Show your calculations.

3. The vice-president of marketing estimates that the conversion ratio can be improved to 0.40% by paying a $10,000 bonus to employees for "converting" a customer and by increasing the amount spent on follow-up activities with prospective customers to $350 per activity. Is Jackson likely to approve these estimated increases? Show your calculations.

4. Given the increase in costs described in part (3) above, what would the new conversion ratio need to be in order for Jackson to be indifferent between making the suggested changes and doing nothing? Show your calculations.

INSTANT QUIZ SOLUTIONS

4–1

$(400 - 300) \times \$100$ per speaker = $10,000 decrease in operating income

4–2

Profit = Unit CM $\times Q$ − Fixed expenses
Profit = ($100 $\times$ 600) − $35,000
Profit = $25,000

4–3

Change in CM = CM ratio $\times$ Change in sales
Change in CM = 40% $\times$ $30,000
Change in CM = $12,000

4–4

Break-even point in units sold	$= \dfrac{\text{Fixed expenses}}{\text{Unit CM}}$
Break-even point in units sold	= $40,000 ÷ $100
Break-even point in units sold	= 400
Break-even point in total sales dollars	$= \dfrac{\text{Fixed expenses}}{\text{CM ratio}}$
Break-even in total sales dollars	= $40,000 ÷ 40%
Break-even in total sales dollars	= $100,000

4–5

$$\text{Units sold to attain the target profit} = \frac{\text{Fixed expenses} + \text{Target operating profit}}{\text{Unit CM}}$$

$$= \frac{\$45,000 + \$80,000}{\$100} = 1,250$$

$$\text{Dollar sales to attain target profit} = \frac{\text{Fixed expenses} + \text{Target operating profit}}{\text{CM ratio}}$$

$$= \frac{\$45,000 + \$80,000}{40\%} = \$312,500$$

4–6

$$\text{Units sold to attain target profit} = \frac{\text{Fixed expenses} + \left[\dfrac{\text{Target after-tax profit}}{1 - \text{Tax rate}}\right]}{\text{Unit CM}}$$

$$= \frac{\$35,000 + [\$56,000/(1 - 0.3)]}{\$100} = 1,150 \text{ speakers}$$

4–7

Margin of safety = Total budgeted (or actual) sales − Break-even sales
Margin of safety = \$120,000 − \$100,000
Margin of safety = \$20,000

$$\text{Margin of safety percentage} = \frac{\text{Margin of safety in dollars}}{\text{Total budgeted (or actual) sales}}$$

Margin of safety percentage = \$20,000 ÷ \$120,000
Margin of safety percentage = 16.7%

4–8

Percentage change in operating income = Degree of operating leverage × Percentage change in sales
Percentage change in operating income = 3 × 10%
Percentage change in operating income = 30%
New operating income in dollars: \$100,000 + (\$100,000 × 30%) = \$130,000

4–9

Weighted-average CM per unit: (0.4 × \$10.00) + (0.6 × \$12.50) = \$10 per unit

$$\text{Total sales units to break even} = \frac{\text{Fixed expenses}}{\text{Weighted-average CM per unit}}$$

$$\text{Total sales units to break even} = \frac{\$135,000}{\$11.50} = 11,739$$

ENDNOTES

1. In economics, incremental analysis is often termed *marginal analysis* because of the assumptions used in economics about the behaviour of revenues and costs. Accountants tend to use a more general term, *incremental,* so that less restrictive assumptions about the behaviour of revenues and costs can be made, for example, step-variable costs.

COSTING

Chapters 5 through 8

Chapters 5 through 8 provide a comprehensive description of how costs are associated with manufacturing activities. In addition, these costing systems can be applied to service organizations and not-for-profit organizations. To permit costing for such specialized situations, two costing systems, job-order costing and process costing, can be mixed and matched.

Chapter 5 begins with the most basic and widely used costing system, *job-order costing*. Job-order costing permits costs to be assigned to specific outcomes, termed *jobs*, so that costs can be accumulated for what a company produces. In addition, manufacturing overhead—a term often shortened to just *overhead*—is assigned by a process of averaging to estimate its amount before actual overhead costs are known.

Chapter 6 introduces an averaging calculation used for costing similar units of product, termed *process costing*. The ordering of costs learned in financial accounting (namely, average and FIFO) can be applied. The idea of equivalent units is explained, so that partially finished work in process can be valued in inventory. Chapter 6 also presents an elaboration of overhead methods so that overhead can be divided up between departments (the cost object in this case) to permit better management control of overhead and more accurate costing.

Chapter 7 introduces activity-based costing, another way to divide up overhead and non-manufacturing costs. Cost objects are defined as activities, and activities are costed by identifying a relevant cost driver. By doing this, overhead costing can be improved and management can focus on managing activities rather than outcomes. Given the increasing importance of overhead costs incurred in some types of organizations, methods to improve the management of overhead costs are important.

Chapter 8 completes the costing segment by describing variable costing. Variable costing assigns only variable manufacturing costs to production as opposed to all manufacturing costs, as was described in earlier chapters under the term *absorption costing*.

SYSTEMS DESIGN: JOB-ORDER COSTING

■ JOB COSTING AT ACCENTURE

Cavan Images / Getty Images

Accenture is one of the world's largest consulting firms, with annual revenues greater than $34 billion. Because the firm does not manufacture a physical product and therefore does not have any inventory on its balance sheet, it might be tempting to conclude that it does not need a job-order costing system. However, that is not true.

Accenture pays its consultants more than $23 billion per year to provide services for clients. Job-order costing enables the firm to compare each client's revenues to the costs of serving those clients. It also enables the firm to determine what portion of their consulting capacity was billable to clients and what portion was not billed to specific clients.

In this chapter, we will examine methods of accurately estimating the total cost by job for specifically identifiable manufactured products and services, and we will explore why this information is key to setting prices, valuing inventory, and identifying opportunities for cost control for many firms.

Source: Accenture Annual Report 2017.

Understanding how products and services are costed is vital to managers because costing methods can have an important impact on reported profits and on key management decisions such as pricing, planning, forecasting, and outsourcing decisions. Nevertheless, external financial reporting standards and tax reporting regulations heavily influence how costs are accumulated and summarized in both the external financial reports and internal managerial reports. Managers believe it is easier and less expensive to use a single method of costing for both external and internal purposes. Since these external financial reporting standards and tax-based regulations require use of absorption costing to determine product costs, it has become the most popular costing approach.

In **absorption costing**, *all* manufacturing costs, fixed and variable, are assigned to units of product—units are said to *fully absorb manufacturing costs*. All non-manufacturing costs are treated as **period costs** and are not assigned to units of product. Instead, they often appear as selling, general, and administrative costs on the financial statements. The absorption costing approach is also known as **full costing**. Two main types of absorption costing systems are *process costing* and *job-order costing*.

Later, in Chapter 8, we look at product costing from a different point of view called *variable costing*. In Chapter 8 we also discuss the strengths and weaknesses of the two approaches.

■ JOB-ORDER AND PROCESS COSTING

In computing the cost of a product or a service, managers face a difficult problem. Many costs (such as rent) do not change much from month to month, while production levels will go up in one month and then down in another. In addition to variations in the level of production, several different products or services may be produced in the same period. Under these conditions, how is it possible to accurately determine the cost of a product or service? In practice, assigning costs to products and services involves averaging some cost types across time periods and across products or services. The way this averaging is carried out depends heavily on the method used to produce the product or provide the service.

Process Costing

A **process costing system** is used in situations where the company produces many units of a single product (such as frozen orange juice concentrate). Examples are mixing cement at St. Marys Cement, refining oil at Petro-Canada, mixing and bottling beverages at Coca-Cola, and making paper towels at Royale (a division of Irving Consumer Products). All of these industries are characterized by an essentially homogeneous product that flows evenly through the production process on a continuous basis.

Process costing systems accumulate costs in a particular operation or department for an entire period (month, quarter, or year) and then divide this total cost by the number of units produced during the period. The basic formula for process costing is as follows:

$$\frac{\text{Unit product cost}}{\text{(per litre, kilogram, bottle)}} = \frac{\text{Total manufacturing cost}}{\text{Total units produced (litres, kilograms, bottles)}}$$

Since one unit of product (litre, kilogram, bottle) is indistinguishable from any other unit of product, each unit is assigned the same average cost. This costing technique results in a broad average unit cost figure that applies to identical units flowing in a continuous stream out of the production process.

Job-Order Costing

A **job-order costing system** is used in situations where many *different* products or services are produced each period. For example, a Levi Strauss clothing factory may make many different types of jeans for both men and women during a month. A particular order might consist of 1,000 stonewashed men's blue denim jeans, style number A312. This order of

Absorption costing
A costing method that includes all manufacturing costs—direct materials, direct labour, and both variable and fixed overhead—as part of the cost of a finished unit of product; synonymous with *full costing*.

Period costs
All costs that are expensed on the income statement in the period in which they are incurred or accrued. Selling (marketing) and administrative expenses are period costs.

Full costing
Another name for *absorption costing*.

LEARNING OBJECTIVE
Distinguish between process costing and job-order costing, and identify the production or service processes that fit with each costing method.

Process costing system
A costing system used in those manufacturing situations where a single, homogeneous product (such as cement or oil) flows in a continuous stream out of the production process.

Job-order costing system
A costing system used in situations where many different products, jobs, or services are produced each period.

1,000 jeans is called a *job*. In a job-order costing system, costs are traced and allocated to jobs, and then the costs of the job are divided by the number of units in the job to arrive at an average cost per unit.

Other examples of situations where job-order costing is used are large-scale construction projects managed by Bechtel Corporation, commercial aircraft produced by Bombardier, greeting cards designed and printed by Hallmark, and airline meals prepared by Cara. All of these examples are characterized by diverse outputs. Each Bechtel project is different from every other—the company could be simultaneously constructing a dam in Zaire and a bridge in Indonesia. Likewise, each airline orders a different meal choices from Cara's catering service.

Job-order costing is also used extensively in service industries and not-for-profit organizations. Hospitals, social service agencies, law firms, movie studios, accounting firms, and advertising agencies all use a variation of job-order costing to accumulate costs for accounting, billing, financial reporting, and internal management purposes including budgeting and forecasting and evaluation of employees' performance relative to budgets/targets. For example, the production of the British Open golf broadcast by TSN and the accumulation of treatment-related costs for each patient admitted to hospital are both suitable job-order costing projects.

Although the detailed example of job-order costing provided in the following section deals with a manufacturing firm, the same basic concepts and procedures are used by many service organizations. The essential difference for service organizations is the lack of raw materials in the cost of their services. For example, a public accounting firm has cost elements involving direct labour and overhead but not raw materials, because the firm does not make a physical item. However, to avoid duplicating the discussion that follows, the more comprehensive manufacturing environment will be presented, with the service application addressed in exercises and problems.

INSTANT QUIZ 5–1
Identify which of the following products is likely to be costed using a job-order costing system and which by a process costing system: bottled water, architectural services, house paint, custom homes, gasoline, tax return preparation services, litres of milk.

The record-keeping and cost assignment problems are more complex when a company sells many different products and services than when it has only a single product. Since the products are different, the costs are typically different. Consequently, cost records must be maintained for each distinct job. For example, a lawyer in a large criminal law practice would ordinarily keep separate records of the costs of advising and defending each of her clients. The Levi Strauss factory mentioned earlier would keep the costs of filling orders for particular styles, sizes, and colours of jeans separately. Thus, a job-order costing system requires more effort than a process costing system. Nevertheless, job-order costing is used by more than half the manufacturers in North America.

In this chapter, we focus on the design of a job-order costing system. In the following chapter, we focus on process costing and also look more closely at the similarities and differences between the two costing methods.

■ JOB-ORDER COSTING—AN OVERVIEW

LEARNING OBJECTIVE ❷
Recognize the flow of costs through a job-order costing system.

To introduce job-order costing, we will follow a specific job as it progresses through the manufacturing process. This job consists of two experimental couplings that ABY Precision Machining has agreed to produce for Loops Unlimited, a manufacturer of roller coasters. Couplings connect the cars on the roller coaster and are a critical component in the performance and safety of the ride. Before we begin our discussion, recall from Chapter 2 that companies generally classify manufacturing costs into three broad categories: (1) direct materials,

(2) direct labour, and (3) manufacturing overhead. As we study the operation of a job-order costing system, we will see how each of these three types of costs is recorded and accumulated. You may wish to refer to the summary of document flows presented in Exhibit 5–5 later in the chapter as you work through the example below.

Measuring Direct Materials Cost

ABY Precision Machining requires four G7 connectors and two M46 housings to make the two experimental couplings for Loops Unlimited. If this were a standard product, there would be a *bill of materials* for the product. A **bill of materials** is a record that lists the type and quantity of each item of the materials needed to complete a unit of product. In this case, ABY's production staff determined from the blueprints that each coupling requires two connectors and one housing; therefore, to make two couplings, four connectors and two housings are required.

A *production order* is issued when an agreement has been reached with the customer concerning the quantities, prices, and shipment date for the order. The Production Department then prepares a *materials requisition form*. The **materials requisition form** is a document that (1) specifies the type and quantity of materials to be drawn from the storeroom and (2) identifies the job to which the costs of the materials are to be charged. The form controls the flow of materials into production and also makes entries in the accounting records. A sample materials requisition form is provided in Exhibit 5–1.

The ABY Precision Machining materials requisition form in Exhibit 5–1 shows that the company's Milling Department has requisitioned two M46 housings and four G7 connectors for the Loops Unlimited order, which has been designated as Job 2B47.

Previously, we used the terms *direct materials* and *raw materials*. This distinction should be clarified. **Direct materials** represent materials that are directly traced to the product or service. Raw materials are ingredients that are converted into a finished product. Semi-finished materials, or supplies for a service job, could be considered direct materials if they were important enough to be directly traced to the job, but they are not raw materials. In summary, raw materials can be direct materials, but not all direct materials are necessarily raw materials.

Job Cost Sheet

After being notified that the production order has been issued, the Accounting Department prepares a *job cost sheet* similar to the one presented in Exhibit 5–2. A **job cost sheet** is a form prepared for each separate job that records the materials, labour, and overhead costs charged to the job.

Bill of materials
A record that lists the type and quantity of each major item of the materials required to make a product.

Materials requisition form
A detailed source document that specifies the type and quantity of materials that are to be drawn from the storeroom and identifies the job to which the costs of materials are to be charged.

Direct materials
Those materials that become an integral part of a finished product and can be conveniently traced to it.

Job cost sheet
A form prepared for each job that records the materials, labour, and overhead costs charged to the job.

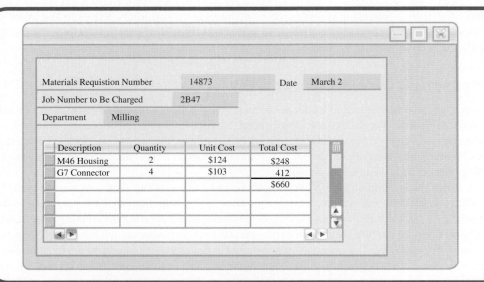

EXHIBIT 5–1
Materials Requisition Form

EXHIBIT 5–2
Job Cost Sheet

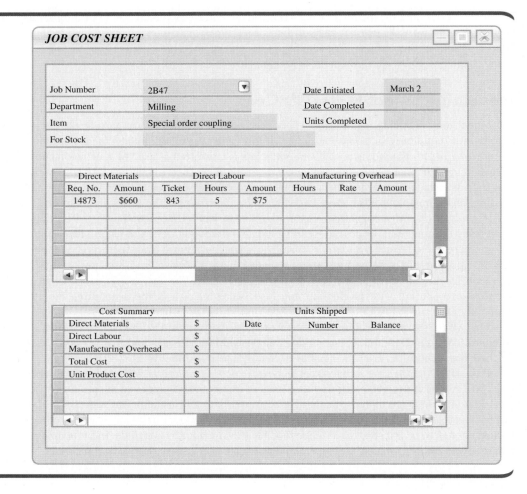

JOB COST SHEET

Job Number	2B47		Date Initiated	March 2
Department	Milling		Date Completed	
Item	Special order coupling		Units Completed	
For Stock				

Direct Materials		Direct Labour			Manufacturing Overhead		
Req. No.	Amount	Ticket	Hours	Amount	Hours	Rate	Amount
14873	$660	843	5	$75			

Cost Summary		Units Shipped		
Direct Materials	$	Date	Number	Balance
Direct Labour	$			
Manufacturing Overhead	$			
Total Cost	$			
Unit Product Cost	$			

After direct materials are issued, the Accounting Department's job-order costing software automatically generates a job cost sheet like the one in Exhibit 5–2. Note that the $660 cost for direct materials shown earlier on the materials requisition form has been charged to Job 2B47 on its job cost sheet. The requisition number 14873 is also recorded on the job cost sheet to make it easier to identify the source for the direct materials charge.

In addition to serving as a means for charging costs to jobs, the job cost sheet is also a key part of a firm's accounting records. Job cost sheets are a subsidiary ledger to the Work in Process account because the detailed records that they provide for the jobs in process add up to the balance in Work in Process.

Measuring Direct Labour Cost

Direct labour cost is handled in much the same way as direct materials cost. Direct labour consists of labour charges that are easily traced to a particular job. Labour charges that cannot be easily traced directly to any job are treated as part of manufacturing overhead. As discussed in Chapter 2, this category of labour costs is termed *indirect labour* and includes tasks such as maintenance, supervision, and cleanup.

Today many companies rely on computerized systems (rather than paper and pencil) to maintain employee *time tickets*. A completed **time ticket** is an hour-by-hour summary of the employee's activities throughout the day. One computerized approach to creating time tickets uses bar codes to capture data. Each employee and each job has a unique bar code. When beginning work on a job, the employee scans three bar codes using a handheld device much like the bar code readers at grocery store checkout stands. The first bar code indicates that a job is being started, the second is the unique bar code on the employee's identity badge, and the

Time ticket
A detailed source document that is used to record an employee's hour-by-hour activities during a day.

EXHIBIT 5–3   Employee Time Ticket

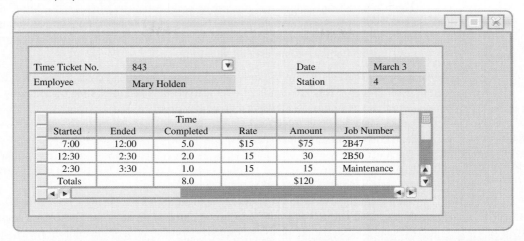

		Time			
Started	Ended	Completed	Rate	Amount	Job Number
7:00	12:00	5.0	$15	$75	2B47
12:30	2:30	2.0	15	30	2B50
2:30	3:30	1.0	15	15	Maintenance
Totals		8.0		$120	

Time Ticket No. 843   Date March 3
Employee Mary Holden   Station 4

third is the unique bar code of the job itself. This information is fed automatically via an electronic network to a computer that notes the time and records all of the data. When the task is completed, the employee scans a bar code indicating the task is complete, the bar code on his or her identity badge, and the bar code attached to the job. This information is relayed to the computer, which again notes the time, and a time ticket, such as the one shown in Exhibit 5–3, is automatically prepared. Because all of the source data are already in computer files, the labour costs can be automatically posted to job cost sheets. For example, Exhibit 5–3 shows $75 of direct labour cost related to Job 2B47. This amount is automatically posted to the job cost sheet shown in Exhibit 5–2. The time ticket in Exhibit 5–3 also shows $15 of indirect labour costs related to performing maintenance. This cost is treated as part of manufacturing overhead and does not get posted on a job cost sheet.

Computers, coupled with technology such as bar codes and radio-frequency identification devices (RFIDs), can eliminate many routine bookkeeping activities while at the same time increasing timeliness and accuracy.

IN BUSINESS

Radio-frequency identification devices (RFIDs) are now replacing bar code scanning systems in many business applications. The addition of RFID tags can be costly but can increase workflow efficiency. For example, Air Canada Cargo RFID-tags each piece of cargo that it ships. The tags allow the company to track cargo through the warehouse, out on the tarmac, and inside each plane. RFID tagging allows Air Canada Cargo to be more efficient and to track valuable data that can be used to improve customer service.

Indirect cost
A cost that cannot be easily and conveniently traced to the particular cost object under consideration.

■ COMPUTING PREDETERMINED OVERHEAD RATES

LEARNING OBJECTIVE
Compute predetermined overhead rates, and explain why estimated overhead costs (rather than actual overhead costs) are used in the costing process.

Manufacturing overhead must be included with direct materials and direct labour on the job cost sheet, since manufacturing overhead is also a product cost. However, assigning manufacturing overhead to units of product can be a difficult task. There are four reasons for this:

1. Manufacturing overhead costs are **indirect** costs. This means that it is either impossible or difficult to trace these costs directly to a particular product or job.
2. Manufacturing overhead consists of many different types of costs, ranging from the grease used in machines, an example of variable overhead, to the annual salary of the production manager, an example of fixed overhead.

3. Even though output may fluctuate due to seasonal or other factors, manufacturing overhead costs tend to remain relatively constant due to the presence of fixed costs.

4. The timing of payment of manufacturing overhead costs often varies. Some items, such as property taxes for the land on which the factory is built, may be paid once per year, while other items are paid for quarterly, monthly, or as acquired. But the company produces finished items continuously all year long.

Given these problems, about the only way to assign overhead costs to products is to use an allocation process. This allocation of overhead costs is accomplished by selecting an *allocation base* that is common to all of the company's products and services. An **allocation base** is a measure, such as direct labour-hours (DLH) or machine-hours (MH), that is used to apply overhead costs to products and services.

The most widely used allocation bases are direct labour-hours and direct labour cost, with machine-hours and even units of product (where a company has only a single product) also used to some extent.

Manufacturing overhead is commonly applied to products using a *predetermined overhead rate*. The **predetermined overhead rate** is computed by dividing the total estimated manufacturing overhead cost for the period by the estimated total amount of the allocation base as follows:

$$\text{Predetermined overhead rate} = \frac{\text{Estimated total manufacturing overhead cost}}{\text{Estimated total units in the allocation base}}$$

Note that the predetermined overhead rate is based on *estimated* rather than actual results. This is because the *predetermined* overhead rate is computed *before* the period begins and is used to *apply* overhead cost to jobs throughout the period. The process of assigning overhead cost to jobs is called **overhead application**. The formula for determining the amount of overhead cost to apply to a particular job is

$$\begin{array}{c}\text{Overhead applied to} \\ \text{a particular job}\end{array} = \begin{array}{c}\text{Predetermined} \\ \text{overhead rate}\end{array} \times \begin{array}{c}\text{Amount of the allocation} \\ \text{base incurred by the job}\end{array}$$

For example, if the predetermined overhead rate is $8 per direct labour-hour, then $8 of overhead is *applied* to a job for each direct labour-hour incurred by the job. When the allocation base is direct labour-hours, the formula becomes

$$\begin{array}{c}\text{Overhead applied to} \\ \text{a particular job}\end{array} = \begin{array}{c}\text{Predetermined} \\ \text{overhead rate}\end{array} \times \begin{array}{c}\text{Actual direct labour-hours} \\ \text{charged to the job}\end{array}$$

Using the Predetermined Overhead Rate

To illustrate the steps involved in computing and using a predetermined overhead rate, let's return to ABY Precision Machining. The company has estimated its total manufacturing overhead costs will be $320,000 for the year and its total direct labour-hours will be 40,000. Its predetermined overhead rate for the year is $8 per direct labour-hour, shown as follows:

$$\text{Predetermined overhead rate} = \frac{\text{Estimated total manufacturing overhead cost}}{\text{Estimated total units in the allocation base}}$$

$$\frac{\$320,000}{40,000 \text{ direct labour-hours}} = \$8 \text{ per direct labour-hour}$$

The job cost sheet in Exhibit 5–4 indicates that 27 direct labour-hours were charged to Job 2B47. Therefore, a total of $216 of overhead cost is applied to the job:

$$\begin{array}{c}\text{Overhead applied to} \\ \text{Job 2B47}\end{array} = \begin{array}{c}\text{Predetermined} \\ \text{overhead rate}\end{array} \times \begin{array}{c}\text{Actual direct labour-hours} \\ \text{charged to Job 2B47}\end{array}$$

$216 of overhead applied to Job 2B47 = $8/DLH ×27 direct labour-hours

---

Allocation base
A measure of activity, such as direct labour-hours or machine-hours, that is used to assign costs to cost objects.

Predetermined overhead rate
A rate used to charge overhead costs to jobs; the rate is established in advance for each period using estimates of total manufacturing overhead cost and of the total allocation base for the period.

Overhead application
The process of charging manufacturing overhead cost to job cost sheets and to the Work in Process account.

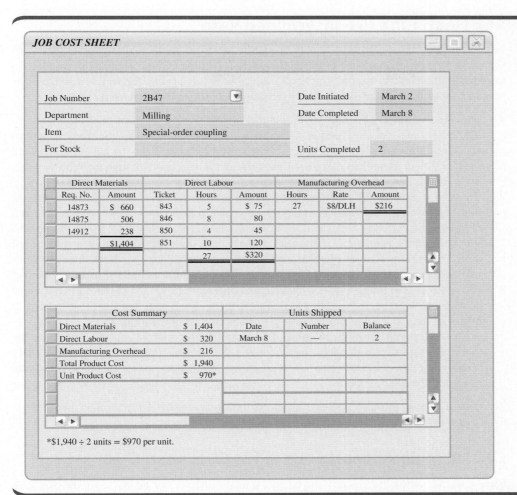

EXHIBIT 5–4
A Completed Job
Cost Sheet

This amount of overhead has been entered on the job cost sheet in Exhibit 5–4. Note that this is *not* the actual amount of overhead caused by the job. There is no attempt to trace actual overhead costs to jobs—if that could be done, the costs would be direct costs, not overhead. The overhead assigned to the job is simply a share of the total overhead that was estimated at the beginning of the year. When a company applies overhead cost to jobs as we have done—that is, by multiplying actual activity by the predetermined overhead rate—it is called a **normal cost system**.

The overhead may be applied when direct labour-hours are charged to jobs, or all of the overhead can be applied at once when the job is completed. The choice is up to the company. If a job is not completed at year-end, however, overhead should be applied to jobs so as to value the work in process inventory for financial reporting purposes.

Normal cost system
A costing system in which overhead costs are applied to jobs by multiplying a predetermined overhead rate by the actual amount of the allocation base incurred by the job.

INSTANT QUIZ 5-2

The managers at Automated Systems Inc. (ASI) estimate that $350,000 of overhead cost will be incurred this year related to 4,000 hours of run time for specialized machinery and equipment. Assuming ASI uses machine-hours as the allocation base, calculate the predetermined overhead rate that will be used to apply overhead to jobs. If the specialized machinery is run for 250 hours to produce the components making up Job 427B, calculate the amount of overhead that will be applied to that job.

The Need for a Predetermined Rate

Instead of using a predetermined rate based on estimates, a company could wait until the end of the accounting period to compute an actual overhead rate based on the actual total manufacturing costs and the actual total units in the allocation base for the period. However, managers cite several reasons for using predetermined overhead rates instead of actual overhead rates:

1. Managers would like to know the accounting system's valuation of completed jobs *before* the end of the accounting period. Suppose, for example, that ABY Precision Machining waits until the end of the year to compute its overhead rate. Then the cost of goods sold for Job 2B47 will not be known until the close of the year, even though the job was completed and shipped to the customer in March.

2. If actual overhead rates are computed frequently, seasonal factors in overhead costs or in the allocation base can produce fluctuations in the overhead rates. For example, the costs of heating and cooling a production facility in Halifax will be highest in the winter and summer months and lowest in the spring and fall. If an overhead rate is computed each month or each quarter, the predetermined overhead rate will go up in the winter and summer and down in the spring and fall. Two identical jobs, one completed in the winter and one completed in the spring, will be assigned different costs if the overhead rate is computed on a monthly or quarterly basis. Managers generally feel that such fluctuations in overhead rates and costs serve no useful purpose and are misleading.

3. The use of a predetermined overhead rate simplifies record-keeping. To determine the overhead cost to apply to a job, the accounting staff at ABY Precision Machining simply multiply the direct labour-hours recorded for the job by the predetermined overhead rate of $8 per direct labour-hour.

For these reasons, most companies use predetermined overhead rates rather than actual overhead rates in their cost accounting systems.

Choice of an Allocation Base for Overhead Cost

Cost driver
A factor that causes overhead costs, such as machine-hours, beds occupied, computer time, or flight-hours.

Ideally, the allocation base used in the predetermined overhead rate should *drive* the overhead cost. A **cost driver** is a factor that causes overhead costs, such as machine-hours, beds occupied, computer time, or flight-hours. If a base is used to compute overhead rates that does not "drive" overhead costs, then the result will be inaccurate overhead rates and distorted product costs. For example, if direct labour-hours are used to allocate overhead, but in reality overhead has little to do with the number of direct labour-hours used on that job, then products with high direct labour-hour requirements will be allocated too much overhead and will be overcosted.

In the past, direct labour accounted for up to 60% of the cost of many products, with overhead cost making up only a small portion of the remainder. This situation has been changing for two reasons. First, sophisticated automated equipment has taken over functions that used to be performed by direct labour workers. Since the costs of acquiring and maintaining such equipment are classified as overhead, this increases overhead while decreasing direct labour. Second, products are themselves becoming more sophisticated and complex and change more frequently. This increases the need for highly skilled indirect workers such as engineers. As a result of these two trends, direct labour cost is decreasing relative to overhead as a component of product costs.

In companies where direct labour and overhead costs have been moving in opposite directions, it is difficult to argue that direct labour "drives" overhead costs. Accordingly, in recent years, managers in some companies have used *activity-based costing* principles to redesign their cost accounting systems. Activity-based costing is a costing technique that is designed to reflect more accurately the demands that products, customers, and other cost objects make on overhead resources. The activity-based approach is discussed in more detail in Chapter 7.

Although direct labour may not be an appropriate allocation base in some industries, in others it continues to be a significant driver of manufacturing overhead. Indeed, many manufacturing companies in North America continue to use direct labour as the primary or secondary allocation base for manufacturing overhead. The key point is that the allocation base used by the company should really drive, or cause, overhead costs, and direct labour is sometimes but not always an appropriate allocation base.

Computation of Unit Costs

With the application of ABY Precision Machining's $216 manufacturing overhead to the job cost sheet in Exhibit 5–4, the job cost sheet is almost complete. There are two final steps. First, the totals for direct materials, direct labour, and manufacturing overhead are transferred to the Cost Summary section of the job cost sheet and added together to obtain the total cost for the job. Then the total cost ($1,940) is divided by the number of units (2) to obtain the unit cost ($970). As indicated earlier, *this unit cost is an average cost and should not be interpreted as the cost that would actually be incurred if another unit was produced*. Much of the actual overhead would not change at all if another unit were produced, so the incremental cost of an additional unit is something less than the average unit cost of $970.

INSTANT QUIZ 5-3
Explain why some production costs must be assigned to products through an allocation process.

The completed job cost sheet will serve as the basis for valuing unsold units in ending inventory and determining cost of goods sold.

Summary of Document Flows

The sequence of events discussed above is summarized in Exhibit 5–5. A careful study of the flow of documents in this exhibit provides a good overview of the overall operation of a job-order costing system.

EXHIBIT 5–5 The Flow of Documents in a Job-Order Costing System

Sales order	Production order	Materials requisition form / Direct labour time ticket / Predetermined overhead rates	Job cost sheet
A sales order is prepared as a basis for issuing a…	A production order initiates work on a job, whereby costs are charged through…	These production costs are accumulated on a form, prepared by the accounting department, known as a…	The job cost sheet forms the basis for computing product and unit costs that are used to value ending inventories and to determine cost of goods sold for units sold.

LEARNING OBJECTIVE ❹
Record the journal entries that reflect the flow of costs in a job-order costing system.

■ JOB-ORDER COSTING—THE FLOW OF COSTS THROUGH THE ACCOUNTING SYSTEM

We are now ready to take a more detailed look at the flow of costs through the company's formal accounting system. To illustrate, we will consider a single month's activity for Rand Company, a producer of gold and silver commemorative medallions. We will work through the example step by step and then summarize our work in Exhibits 5–9, 5–10, and 5–11.

Rand Company has two jobs in process during April, the first month of its fiscal year. Job A, a special minting of 1,000 gold medallions commemorating the 75th anniversary of D-Day and the Battle of Normandy, was started during March and had $30,000 in manufacturing costs already accumulated on April 1. Job B, an order for 10,000 of these same medallions in silver, was started in April.

The Purchase and Issue of Materials

On April 1, Rand Company had $7,000 in raw materials on hand. During the month, the company purchased an additional $60,000 in raw materials. The purchase is recorded in journal entry (1) below:

(1)

Raw Materials Inventory	60,000	
Accounts Payable		60,000

As explained in Chapter 2, Raw Materials Inventory is an asset account. Thus, when raw materials are purchased, they are initially recorded as an asset—not as an expense.

Issue of Direct and Indirect Materials

During April, $52,000 in raw materials was requisitioned from the storeroom for use in production. These raw materials include $50,000 of direct materials and $2,000 of indirect materials. Entry (2) records the issue of the materials to the production departments:

(2)

Work in Process Inventory	50,000	
Manufacturing Overhead	2,000	
Raw Materials Inventory		52,000

The materials charged to Work in Process Inventory represent direct materials for specific jobs. As these materials are entered into the Work in Process account, they are also recorded on the appropriate job cost sheets. This point is illustrated in Exhibit 5–6, where $28,000 of the $50,000 in direct materials is charged to Job A's cost sheet and the remaining $22,000 is charged to Job B's cost sheet. (In this example, all data are presented in summary form, and the job cost sheet is abbreviated.)

The $2,000 charged to Manufacturing Overhead in entry (2) represents indirect materials used in production during April. Observe that the Manufacturing Overhead account is separate from the Work in Process account. The purpose of the Manufacturing Overhead account is to accumulate all manufacturing overhead costs as they are incurred during a period.

Before leaving Exhibit 5–6, note that the job cost sheet for Job A contains a beginning balance of $30,000. We stated earlier that this balance represents the cost of work done during March that has been carried forward to April. Also note that the Work in Process account contains the same $30,000 balance. *The reason the $30,000 appears in both places is that the Work in Process account is a control account and the job cost sheets form a subsidiary ledger. Thus, the Work in Process account contains a summarized total of all costs appearing on the individual job cost sheets for all jobs in process at any given point in time.* (Since Rand Company had only Job A in process at the beginning of April, Job A's $30,000 balance on that date is equal to the balance in the Work in Process account.)

EXHIBIT 5–6   Raw Materials Cost Flows

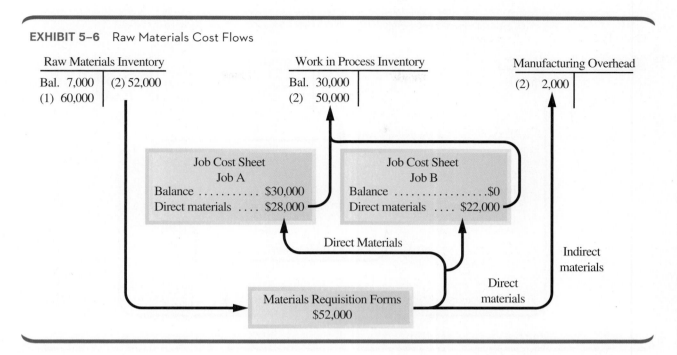

Issue of Direct Materials Only

Sometimes the materials drawn from the Raw Materials Inventory account are all direct materials. In this case, the entry to record the issue of the materials into production is as follows:

Work in Process Inventory	XXX	
Raw Materials Inventory		XXX

Labour Cost

As work is performed in various departments of Rand Company from day to day, employees' time worked is recorded and forwarded to the Accounting Department. In the Accounting Department, the hours worked are costed according to the various employee wage rates, and the resulting costs are classified as either direct or indirect labour. In April, $60,000 was recorded for direct labour and $15,000 for indirect labour, resulting in the following summary entry:

(3)

Work in Process Inventory	60,000	
Manufacturing Overhead	15,000	
Salaries and Wages Payable		75,000

Only direct labour is added to the Work in Process account. For Rand Company, this amounted to $60,000 for April.

At the same time that direct labour costs are added to Work in Process, they are also added to the individual job cost sheets, as shown in Exhibit 5–7. During April, $40,000 of direct labour cost was charged to Job A, and the remaining $20,000 was charged to Job B.

The labour costs charged to Manufacturing Overhead ($15,000) represent the indirect labour costs of the period, such as supervision, janitorial work, and maintenance.

Manufacturing Overhead Costs

Recall that all costs of operating the factory other than direct materials and direct labour are classified as manufacturing overhead costs. These costs are entered directly into the

EXHIBIT 5–7   Labour Cost Flows

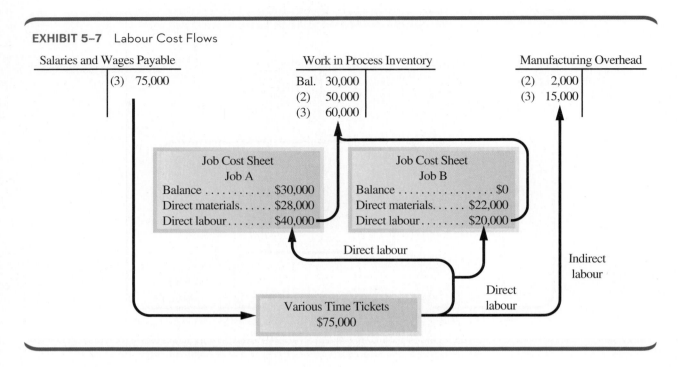

Manufacturing Overhead account as they are incurred. To illustrate, assume that Rand Company incurred the following general factory costs during April:

Utilities (heat, water, and power)	$21,000
Rent on factory equipment	16,000
Miscellaneous factory costs	3,000
Total	$40,000

The following entry records that these costs were incurred:

(4)

Manufacturing Overhead	40,000	
Accounts Payable		40,000

In addition, assume that during April, Rand Company recognized $13,000 in accrued property taxes and that $7,000 in prepaid insurance expired on factory buildings and equipment. The following entry records these items:

(5)

Manufacturing Overhead	20,000	
Property Taxes Payable		13,000
Prepaid Insurance		7,000

Finally, assume that the company recognized $18,000 in depreciation on factory equipment during April. The following entry records the accrual of this depreciation:

(6)

Manufacturing Overhead	18,000	
Accumulated Depreciation		18,000

In short, *all* manufacturing overhead costs are recorded directly into the Manufacturing Overhead account as they are incurred day by day throughout a period. It is important to understand that Manufacturing Overhead is a control account for many—perhaps thousands of—subsidiary accounts, such as Indirect Materials, Indirect Labour, and Factory Utilities. As the Manufacturing Overhead account is debited for costs during a period, the various subsidiary accounts are also debited. In the example above and also in the assignment material for this chapter, we omit the entries to the subsidiary accounts for the sake of brevity.

■ THE APPLICATION OF MANUFACTURING OVERHEAD

LEARNING OBJECTIVE **5**

Apply overhead cost to work in process using a predetermined overhead rate.

Since actual manufacturing overhead costs are charged to the Manufacturing Overhead control account rather than to Work in Process, how are manufacturing overhead costs assigned to Work in Process? The answer is, by means of the predetermined overhead rate. Recall from our discussion earlier in the chapter that a predetermined overhead rate is established at the beginning of each year. The rate is calculated by dividing the estimated total manufacturing overhead cost for the year by the estimated total units in the allocation base (measured in machine-hours, direct labour-hours, or some other base). The predetermined overhead rate is then used to apply overhead costs to jobs. For example, if direct labour-hours is the allocation base, overhead cost is applied to each job by multiplying the number of direct labour-hours charged to the job by the predetermined overhead rate.

To illustrate, assume that Rand Company has used machine-hours in computing its predetermined overhead rate and that this rate is $6 per machine-hour. Also assume that during April, 10,000 machine-hours were worked on Job A and 5,000 machine-hours were worked on Job B (a total of 15,000 machine-hours). Thus, $90,000 in overhead cost (15,000 machine-hours × $6 = $90,000) would be applied to Work in Process. The following entry records the application of Manufacturing Overhead to Work in Process:

(7)

Work in Process..	90,000	
Manufacturing Overhead		90,000

The flow of costs through the Manufacturing Overhead account is detailed in Exhibit 5–8.

The "actual overhead costs" in the Manufacturing Overhead account shown in Exhibit 5–8 are the costs that were added to the account in entries (2) through (6). Observe that recording these actual overhead costs [entries (2) through (6)] and the application of overhead to Work in Process [entry (7)] represent two separate and entirely distinct processes.

EXHIBIT 5–8 The Flow of Costs in Overhead Application

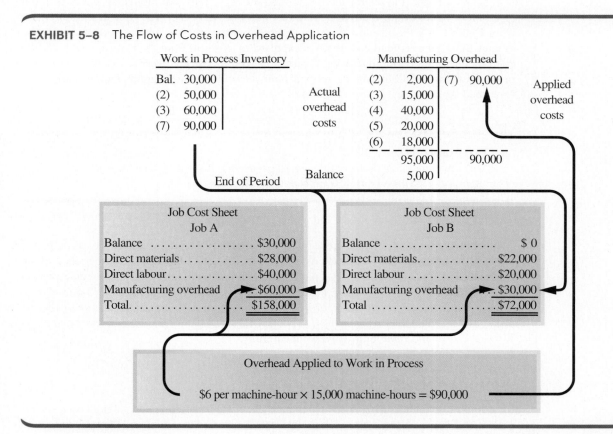

The Concept of a Clearing Account

The Manufacturing Overhead account operates as a clearing account. As we have noted, actual factory overhead costs are debited to the accounts as they are incurred day by day throughout the year. At certain intervals during the year, usually when a job is completed, overhead cost is released from the Manufacturing Overhead account and is applied to the Work in Process account by means of the predetermined overhead rate. Work in Process is debited and Manufacturing Overhead is credited. This sequence of events is illustrated as follows:

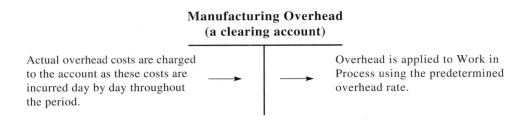

Manufacturing Overhead
(a clearing account)

Actual overhead costs are charged to the account as these costs are incurred day by day throughout the period.

Overhead is applied to Work in Process using the predetermined overhead rate.

The actual overhead costs incurred and shown as debits in the Manufacturing Overhead account are a result of many different types of overhead costs. A brief list of some of the different types is presented in the journal entries, numbers 4, 5 and 6, or in the schedule of cost of goods manufactured, shown in Exhibit 5–11 or previously in Exhibit 2–4. The clearing account concept actually represents a general ledger control account for a subsidiary ledger that contains the detailed information on each type of overhead cost.

As we emphasized earlier, the predetermined overhead rate is based entirely on estimates of what overhead costs are *expected* to be, and it is established before the year begins. As a result, the overhead cost applied during a year will almost certainly turn out to be more or less than the overhead cost that is actually incurred. For example, notice from Exhibit 5–8 that Rand Company's actual overhead costs for the period are $5,000 greater than the overhead cost that was applied to Work in Process, resulting in a $5,000 debit balance in the Manufacturing Overhead account. We will reserve discussion of what to do with this $5,000 balance until a later section in this chapter, Complications of Overhead Application.

INSTANT QUIZ 5–4
Explain why companies use predetermined overhead rates rather than actual manufacturing overhead costs to apply overhead to jobs.

For the moment, we can conclude by noting from Exhibit 5–8 that the cost of a completed job consists of the actual materials cost of the job, the actual labour cost of the job, and the overhead cost *applied* to the job. Pay particular attention to the following subtle but important point: *Actual overhead costs are not charged to jobs; actual overhead costs do not appear on the job cost sheet, nor do they appear in the Work in Process account. Only the applied overhead cost, based on the predetermined overhead rate, appears on the job cost sheet and in the Work in Process account.* Study this point carefully.

Non-manufacturing Costs

In addition to manufacturing costs, companies also incur marketing and selling costs. As explained in Chapter 2, these costs should be treated as period expenses and charged directly to the income statement. *Non-manufacturing costs should not go into the Manufacturing Overhead account.* To illustrate the correct treatment of non-manufacturing costs, assume that Rand Company incurred $30,000 of selling and administrative salaries during April. The following entry records these salaries:

(8)

Salaries Expense..	30,000	
Salaries and Wages Payable		30,000

Assume that depreciation on office equipment during April was $7,000. The entry is as follows:

(9)

Depreciation Expense	7,000	
Accumulated Depreciation		7,000

Pay particular attention to the difference between this entry and entry (6), where we recorded depreciation on factory equipment. In journal entry (6), depreciation on factory equipment was debited to Manufacturing Overhead and is therefore a product cost. In journal entry (9) above, depreciation on office equipment was debited to Depreciation Expense. Depreciation on office equipment is considered to be a period expense rather than a product cost.

Finally, assume that advertising was $42,000 and that other selling and administrative expenses in April total $8,000. The following entry records these items:

(10)

Advertising Expense..	42,000	
Other Selling and Administrative Expense......................	8,000	
Accounts Payable*		50,000

*Other accounts, such as Cash, may be credited.

Because the amounts in entries (8) through (10) all go directly into expense accounts, they have no effect on product costs. The same is true of any other selling and administrative expenses incurred during April, including sales commissions, depreciation on sales equipment, rent on office facilities, insurance on office facilities, and related costs.

◼ COST OF GOODS MANUFACTURED

LEARNING OBJECTIVE **6**
Prepare schedules of cost of goods manufactured and cost of goods sold.

When a job is completed, the finished output is transferred from the production departments to the finished goods warehouse. By this time, the Accounting Department will have charged the job with direct materials and direct labour cost, and manufacturing overhead will have been applied using the predetermined rate. A transfer of these costs must be made within the costing system that *parallels* the physical transfer of the goods to the finished goods warehouse. The costs of the completed job are transferred out of the Work in Process account and into the Finished Goods account. The sum of all amounts transferred between these two accounts represents the cost of goods manufactured for the period.

In the case of Rand Company, assume that Job A was completed during April. The following entry transfers the cost of Job A from Work in Process to Finished Goods:

(11)

Finished Goods Inventory....................................	158,000	
Work in Process Inventory..................................		158,000

The $158,000 represents the completed cost of Job A, as shown on the job cost sheet in Exhibit 5–8. Since Job A was the only job completed during April, the $158,000 also represents the cost of goods manufactured for the month.

Job B was not completed by month-end, so its cost will remain in the Work in Process account and carry over to the next month. If a balance sheet is prepared at the end of April, the cost accumulated thus far on Job B will appear as "Work in Process Inventory" in the assets section.

Cost of Goods Sold

As units in finished goods are shipped to customers, their cost is transferred from the Finished Goods account into the Cost of Goods Sold account. If a complete job is shipped, as in the case where a job has been done to a customer's specifications, then it is a simple matter to transfer the entire cost appearing on the job cost sheet into the Cost of Goods Sold account. In most cases, however, only a portion of the units involved in a particular job will be immediately sold. In these situations, the unit cost must be used to determine how much product cost should be removed from Finished Goods and charged to Cost of Goods Sold.

For Rand Company, we will assume that 750 of the 1,000 gold medallions in Job A were shipped to customers by the end of the month, for total sales revenue of $225,000. Since 1,000 units were produced and the total cost of the job from the job cost sheet was $158,000, the unit product cost was $158. The following journal entries record the sale (all sales are on account):

(12)

Accounts Receivable...	225,000	
Sales...		225,000

(13)

Cost of Goods Sold..	118,500	
Finished Goods Inventory................................		118,500
($158 per unit × 750 units = $118,500)		

With entry (13), the flow of costs through our job-order costing system is completed.

Summary of Cost Flows

To pull the entire Rand Company example together, journal entries (1) through (13) are summarized in Exhibit 5–9. The flow of costs through the accounts is presented in T-account form in Exhibit 5–10.

Exhibit 5–11 presents a schedule of cost of goods manufactured, a schedule of cost of goods sold and and Income Statement for Rand Company. Note particularly from Exhibit 5–11 that the manufacturing overhead cost on the schedule of cost of goods manufactured is the overhead applied to jobs during the month—not the actual manufacturing overhead costs incurred. The reason for this can be traced back to journal entry (7) and the T-account for Work in Process that appears in Exhibit 5–10. Under a normal costing system as illustrated in this chapter, applied—not actual—overhead costs are assigned to jobs and thus to Work in Process Inventory. In contrast, in Chapter 2, actual overhead costs were assigned to Work in Process and included in the schedule of cost of goods manufactured. This is because we had not introduced the concept of normal costing in that chapter. Note also that the cost of goods manufactured for the month ($158,000) agrees with the amount transferred from Work in Process to Finished Goods for the month, as recorded earlier in entry (11). Also note that this $158,000 figure is used in computing the cost of goods sold for the month. Observe that the cost of goods sold figure on the Income Statement for April ($123,500) is carried down from the schedule of cost of goods sold.

EXHIBIT 5–9
Summary of Rand
Company Journal
Entries

(1)

Raw Materials	60,000	
Accounts Payable		60,000

(2)

Work in Process	50,000	
Manufacturing Overhead	2,000	
Raw Materials		52,000

(3)

Work in Process	60,000	
Manufacturing Overhead	15,000	
Salaries and Wages Payable		75,000

(4)

Manufacturing Overhead	40,000	
Accounts Payable		40,000

(5)

Manufacturing Overhead	20,000	
Property Taxes Payable		13,000
Prepaid Insurance		7,000

(6)

Manufacturing Overhead	18,000	
Accumulated Depreciation		18,000

(7)

Work in Process	90,000	
Manufacturing Overhead		90,000

(8)

Salaries Expense	30,000	
Salaries and Wages Payable		30,000

(9)

Depreciation Expense	7,000	
Accumulated Depreciation		7,000

(10)

Advertising Expense	42,000	
Other Selling and Administrative Expense	8,000	
Accounts Payable		50,000

(11)

Finished Goods	158,000	
Work in Process		158,000

(12)

Accounts Receivable	225,000	
Sales		225,000

(13)

Cost of Goods Sold	118,500	
Finished Goods		118,500

EXHIBIT 5–10   Summary of Cost Flows—Rand Company

Raw Materials			
Bal.	7,000	(2)	52,000
(1)	60,000		
Bal.	15,000		

Work in Process			
Bal.	30,000	(11)	158,000
(2)	50,000		
(3)	60,000		
(7)	90,000		
Bal.	72,000		

Finished Goods			
Bal.	10,000	(13)	118,500
(11)	158,000		
Bal.	49,500		

Manufacturing Overhead			
(2)	2,000	(7)	90,000
(3)	15,000		
(4)	40,000		
(5)	20,000		
(6)	18,000		
Bal.	5,000		

Accumulated Depreciation			
		XX	
		(6)	18,000
		(9)	7,000

Cost of Goods Sold		
(13)	118,500	

Accounts Payable			
		XX	
		(1)	60,000
		(4)	40,000
		(10)	50,000

Salaries and Wages Payable			
		XX	
		(3)	75,000
		(8)	30,000

Property Taxes Payable			
		XX	
		(5)	13,000

Accounts Receivable		
XX*		
(12)	225,000	

Prepaid Insurance			
XX			
		(5)	7,000

Capital Stock		
		XX

Retained Earnings		
		XX

Sales			
		(12)	225,000

Salaries Expense		
(8)	30,000	

Depreciation Expense		
(9)	7,000	

Advertising Expense		
(10)	42,000	

Other Selling and Administrative Expense		
(10)	8,000	

Explanation of entries:
(1) Raw materials purchased.
(2) Direct and indirect materials issued into production.
(3) Direct and indirect factory labour cost incurred.
(4) Utilities and other factory costs incurred.
(5) Property taxes and insurance incurred on the factory.
(6) Depreciation recorded on factory assets.
(7) Overhead cost applied to Work in Process.

(8) Administrative salaries expense incurred.
(9) Depreciation recorded on office equipment.
(10) Advertising and other expense incurred.
(11) Cost of goods manufactured transferred into finished goods.
(12) Sale of job A recorded.
(13) Cost of goods sold recorded for job A.

*XX = Normal balance in the account (for example, Accounts Receivable normally carries a debit balance).

Cost of Goods Manufactured
Direct materials:

Raw materials inventory, beginning.............	$ 7,000	
Add: Purchases of raw materials	60,000	
Total raw materials available	67,000	
Deduct: Raw materials inventory, ending	15,000	
Raw materials used in production	52,000	
Less indirect materials included in manufacturing overhead...........................	2,000	$ 50,000
Direct labour		60,000
Manufacturing overhead applied to work in process ...		90,000
Total manufacturing costs		200,000
Add: Beginning work in process inventory		30,000
		230,000
Deduct: Ending work in process inventory		72,000
Cost of goods manufactured		$158,000

Cost of Goods Sold

Finished goods inventory, beginning...............	$ 10,000
Add: Cost of goods manufactured	158,000
Goods available for sale.........................	168,000
Deduct: Finished goods inventory, ending..........	49,500
Unadjusted cost of goods sold	118,500
Add: Underapplied overhead*	5,000
Adjusted cost of goods sold	$ 123,500

*The underapplied overhead is added to cost of goods sold. If overhead was overapplied, it would be deducted from costs of goods sold.

RAND COMPANY
Income Statement
For the Month Ending April 30

Sales.......................................		$225,000
Less cost of goods sold ($118,500 + $5,000)		123,500
Gross margin		101,500
Less selling and administrative expenses:		
Salaries expense................................	$30,000	
Depreciation expense............................	7,000	
Advertising expense.............................	42,000	
Other expense..................................	8,000	87,000
Net income....................................		$ 14,500

EXHIBIT 5–11
Schedules of Cost of Goods Manufactured, Cost of Goods Sold, and Income Statement

LEARNING OBJECTIVE 7

Compute under-applied or over-applied overhead cost, and prepare the journal entry to close the balance in manufacturing overhead to the appropriate accounts.

■ COMPLICATIONS OF OVERHEAD APPLICATION

We need to consider two complications relating to overhead application. These are (1) the computation of underapplied and overapplied overhead and (2) the disposition of any balance remaining in the Manufacturing Overhead account at the end of a period.

Underapplied and Overapplied Overhead

Since the predetermined overhead rate is established before a period begins and is based entirely on estimated data, there will generally be a difference between the amount of overhead cost applied to Work in Process and the amount of overhead cost actually incurred during a period. In the case of Rand Company, for example, the predetermined overhead rate of $6 per hour resulted in $90,000 of overhead cost being applied to Work in Process, whereas actual overhead costs for April proved to be $95,000 (as shown in Exhibit 5–8). The difference between the overhead cost applied to Work in Process and the actual overhead costs of a period is termed either **underapplied overhead** or **overapplied overhead**. For Rand Company, overhead was underapplied because the applied cost ($90,000) was $5,000 less than the actual cost ($95,000). If the situation had been reversed and the company had applied $95,000 in overhead cost to Work in Process while incurring actual overhead costs of only $90,000, then the overhead would have been overapplied.

What causes underapplied or overapplied overhead? Recall that the predetermined overhead rate is calculated at the beginning of the year based on the manager's best estimate of the total cost of overhead for the year (the numerator in the predetermined overhead rate calculation) as well as their best estimate of the volume of the cost driver activity—for example, direct labour-hours or machine-hours (the denominator in the predetermined overhead rate calculation). If, for example, the predetermined overhead rate is $6 per machine-hour, then it is assumed that actual overhead costs incurred will be $6 for every machine-hour that is actually worked. There are at least two reasons why this may not be the case. First, much of the overhead consists of fixed costs that do not change as the number of machine-hours incurred goes up or down. Second, spending on overhead items may or may not be under control. Therefore, it is not unusual for the total amount of overhead applied using the predetermined rate to be different from the actual overhead that should have been applied. A fuller explanation of the causes of underapplied and overapplied overhead is covered in Chapter 10.

To illustrate what can happen, suppose that two companies—Turbo Crafters and Black & Howell—have prepared the following estimated data for the coming year:

	Company	
	Turbo Crafters	**Black & Howell**
Predetermined overhead rate based on:	Machine-hours	Direct materials cost
Estimated manufacturing overhead (a).	$300,000	$120,000
Estimated amount of allocation base (b)	75,000	80,000
Predetermined overhead rate, (a) ÷ (b).	$4 per machine-hour	150% of direct materials cost

Note that when the allocation base is dollars—such as direct materials cost in the case of Black & Howell—the predetermined overhead rate is a *percentage* of the allocation base. When dollars are divided by dollars, the result is a *percentage*.

Now assume that because of unexpected changes in overhead spending and changes in demand for the companies' products, the *actual* overhead cost and the *actual* activity recorded during the year in each company are as follows:

	Company	
	Turbo Crafters	**Black & Howell**
Actual manufacturing overhead costs.	$290,000	$130,000
Actual amount of allocation base	68,000	$ 90,000

For each company, note that the actual data for both cost and the allocation base differ from the estimates used in computing the predetermined overhead rate. This results in underapplied and overapplied overhead as follows:

	Company	
	Turbo Crafters	**Black & Howell**
Actual manufacturing overhead cost	$290,000	$130,000
Manufactured overhead cost applied to Work in Process during the year:		
Predetermined overhead rate (a).	$4 per machine-hour	150% of direct material cost
Actual total amount of allocation base (b) . .	68,000 machine-hours	$90,000 direct material cost
Manufacturing overhead applied (a) × (b)	$ 272,000	$135,000
Underapplied (overapplied) manufacturing overhead	$ 18,000	$ (5,000)

For Turbo Crafters, notice that the amount of overhead cost applied to Work in Process ($272,000) is less than the actual overhead cost for the year ($290,000). Therefore, overhead is underapplied. Also notice that the original estimate of overhead in Turbo Crafters ($300,000) is not directly involved in this computation. Its impact is felt only through the $4 predetermined overhead rate that is used.

For Black & Howell, the amount of overhead cost applied to Work in Process ($135,000) is greater than the actual overhead cost for the year ($130,000), so overhead is overapplied.

Disposition of Underapplied or Overapplied Overhead Balances

What disposition should be made of any underapplied or overapplied balance remaining in the Manufacturing Overhead account at the end of a period? Under current accounting standards applicable in Canada (IAS 2):

> *Unallocated overheads are recognised as an expense in the period in which they are incurred. In periods of abnormally high production, the amount of fixed overhead allocated to each unit of production is decreased so that inventories are not measured above cost.*

Note that IAS 2 is a financial reporting standard that is not necessarily required to be followed for internal purposes. Even so, most companies treat accounting for inventory costs consistently for both financial reporting and internal management decision making for simplicity's sake. Thus, the balance in the account must be treated in one of two ways depending on whether it was under- or overapplied during the year:

1. If overhead was underapplied, the remaining balance is closed out to Cost of Goods Sold.
2. If overhead was overapplied, the remaining balance is allocated among Work in Process, Finished Goods, and Cost of Goods Sold in proportion to the overhead applied during the current period in the ending balances of these accounts.

INSTANT QUIZ 5–5
Explain conceptually why it makes sense to close out underapplied overhead to Cost of Goods Sold but then to allocate overapplied overhead between Work in Process and Finished Goods Inventory accounts on the Balance Sheet and Cost of Goods Sold on the Income Statement.

Close Out Underapplied Overhead to Cost of Goods Sold
As mentioned above, closing out the balance in Manufacturing Overhead to Cost of Goods Sold is simpler than the allocation method. Returning to the example of

Rand Company, the entry to close the $5,000 of underapplied overhead to Cost of Goods Sold is as follows:

(14)

Cost of Goods Sold.	5,000	
Manufacturing Overhead		5,000

Note that since there is a debit balance in the Manufacturing Overhead account, Manufacturing Overhead must be credited to close out the account. This has the effect of increasing Cost of Goods Sold for April to $123,500:

Unadjusted cost of goods sold [from entry (13)]	$118,500
Add underapplied overhead [entry (14) above]	5,000
Adjusted cost of goods sold	$123,500

After this adjustment is made, Rand Company's income statement for April will appear as was shown earlier in Exhibit 5–11.

Allocate Overapplied Overhead among Accounts

Allocation of overapplied overhead assigns overhead costs to where they would have gone in the first place had it not been for the errors in the estimates going into the predetermined overhead rate.

For illustrative purposes, assume the $5,000 remaining balance in the Manufacturing Overhead account of Rand Company was overapplied. First, it is necessary to determine the amount of overhead applied during April in each of the accounts. The computations are as follows:

Overhead applied in work in process inventory, April 30	$30,000	33.33%
Overhead applied in finished goods inventory, April 30		
($60,000 ÷ 1,000 units = $60 per unit) × 250 units.	15,000	16.67%
Overhead applied in cost of goods sold, April		
($60,000 ÷ 1,000 units = $60 per unit) × 750 units.	45,000	50.00%
Total overhead applied	$90,000	100.00%

Based on the above percentages, the overapplied overhead (i.e., a credit balance in Manufacturing Overhead) is allocated as in the following journal entry:

Manufacturing Overhead	5,000.00	
Work in Process (33.33% × $5,000).		1,666.50
Finished Goods (16.67% × $5,000)		833.50
Cost of Goods Sold (50.00% × $5,000)		2,500.00

Note that the first step in the allocation was to determine the amount of overhead applied in each account. For Finished Goods, for example, the total amount of overhead applied to Job A, $60,000, was divided by the total number of units in Job A, 1,000 units, to arrive at the average overhead applied of $60 per unit. Since 250 units from Job A were still in ending finished goods inventory, the amount of overhead applied in the Finished Goods Inventory account was $60 per unit multiplied by 250 units, or $15,000 in total.

A summary of the concepts discussed in this section is presented in the following Learning Aid.

A General Model of Product Cost Flows

The flow of costs in a product costing system is presented in the form of a T-account model in Exhibit 5–12. This model applies as much to a process costing system as it does to a job-order costing system. Examination of this model can be very helpful in gaining a perspective as to how costs enter a system, flow through it, and finally end up as Cost of Goods Sold on the income statement.

LEARNING AID

Summary of Overhead Concepts

At the beginning of the period:

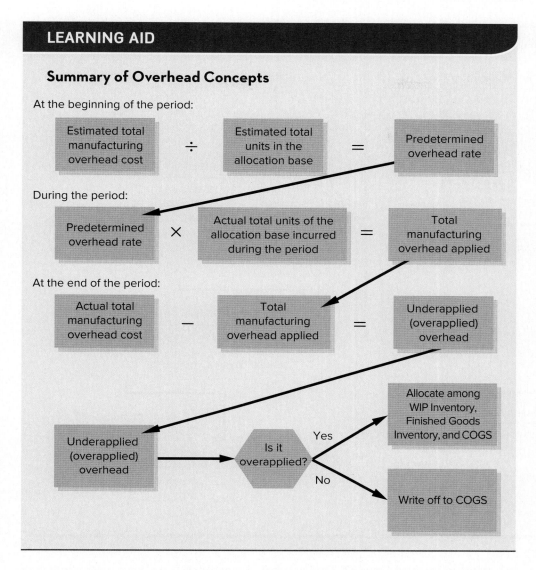

At the end of the period:

Allocate among WIP Inventory, Finished Goods Inventory, and COGS

Write off to COGS

Variations from the General Model of Product Cost Flow

Costing systems can vary from what is reflected by the general model. While the general model is the most complete description, circumstances may make such a complete system too costly. For example, a system variation known as *backflush costing* can permit labour charges to be made directly to manufacturing overhead. Then overhead is applied to the cost of completed jobs along with raw materials, so that the need to keep work in process records can be avoided. Such a minimal treatment of work in process is justified in a mechanized lean manufacturing (JIT) environment. Cost of completed jobs still reflects the material and overhead (including labour), but the record-keeping system reflects the simplified needs of the production environment.

Multiple Predetermined Overhead Rates

Our discussion of overhead in this chapter has assumed that there is a single predetermined overhead rate for an entire factory called a **plantwide overhead rate**. This is, in fact, common practice—particularly in smaller companies. But in larger companies, *multiple predetermined overhead rates* are often used. In a **multiple predetermined overhead rate** system, there is usually a different overhead rate for each production department. Such a system, while more complex, is considered to be more accurate because it can reflect differences across departments in how overhead costs are incurred. For example, overhead might be allocated based on direct labour-hours in departments that are relatively labour intensive and based on machine-hours in departments that are relatively machine intensive. When multiple

Plantwide overhead rate
A single predetermined overhead rate used throughout a plant.

Multiple predetermined overhead rate
A costing system in which there are multiple overhead cost pools with a different predetermined rate for each cost pool, rather than a single predetermined overhead rate for the entire company. Frequently, each production department is treated as a separate overhead cost pool.

EXHIBIT 5–12 A General Model of Cost Flows

Raw Materials	
Debited for the cost of materials purchased	Credited for direct materials added to Work in Process Credited for indirect materials added to Manufacturing Overhead

Salaries and Wages Payable	
	Credited for direct labour added to Work in Process Credited for indirect labour added to Manufacturing Overhead

Manufacturing Overhead	
Debited for actual overhead costs incurred	Credited for overhead cost applied to Work in Process
Underapplied overhead cost	Overapplied overhead cost

Work in Process	
Debited for the cost of direct materials, direct labour, and manufacturing overhead applied	Credited for the cost of goods manufactured

Finished Goods	
Debited for the cost of goods manufactured	Credited for the cost of goods sold

Cost of Goods Sold	
Debited for the cost of goods sold	

predetermined overhead rates are used, overhead is applied in each department according to its own overhead rate as a job proceeds through the department.

To illustrate, refer to the data in the following table, where Cook Company has two departments (A and B) and several jobs in process. Data are provided for two of these jobs (X and Y). If the company uses a plantwide overhead rate of $12 ($336,000 ÷ 28,000 DLH), then the overhead costs applied to Job X and Job Y will be $8,400 ($12 × 700 hours + $12 × 0) and $12 ($12 × 0 hours + $12 × 1 hour), respectively. However, if overhead is applied using department overhead rates, then Job X will be assigned $2,800 ($4 × 700 direct labour-hours) and Job Y will be assigned $8,400 ($12 × 700 machine-hours):

Cook Company	Department A	Department B	Total
Overhead cost	$84,000	$252,000	$336,000
Direct labour-hours	21,000	7,000	28,000 DLH
Machine-hours	7,000	21,000	28,000 MH
Overhead cost driver	21,000 DLH	21,000 MH	
Overhead rate: Plantwide			$12 per DLH
Overhead rate: By department	$ 4/DLH	$12/MH	
Direct labour-hours—Job X	700	0	
Direct labour-hours—Job Y	0	1	
Machine-hours—Job X	1	0	
Machine-hours—Job Y	0	700	

The decision to use a plantwide rate versus separate rates for each department comes down to costs versus benefits. It is cheaper to use a plantwide rate, since the costs of gathering and analyzing information are lower, but separate rates are more informative when the activities that drive overhead costs differ among departments. Improved decision making resulting from more accurate overhead data can justify the added costs of gathering separate departmental overhead data.

INSTANT QUIZ 5–6

Are plantwide or multiple overhead rates more accurate? Why? And why would a company choose to use the less accurate rate?

■ JOB-ORDER COSTING IN SERVICE COMPANIES

Job-order costing is used in service and non-profit organizations, such as accounting firms, hospitals, airlines, and repair shops, as well as in manufacturing companies. In an accounting firm, for example, different services provided to each client are classified as a "job" in our manufacturing example. Costs of providing that service (e.g., auditing financial statements, preparing tax returns, valuing a division for sale) are accumulated day by day on a job cost sheet as the service is being provided. The most significant cost categories in a service firm are direct labour (i.e., number of hours and cost per hour of the staff assigned to the job) and overhead, for example the cost of rent, depreciation of office equipment, salaries of secretarial staff, and so forth. These two cost categories are often blended into a "charge-out rate" for the staff providing service. The charge-out rate represents the total cost, including salaries and estimated overhead, of one hour of that staff person's time. Clients are often invoiced for the number of hours of services provided multiplied by the applicable charge-out rates.

In manufacturing firms job-order costing is used to assign costs to units of product, which becomes the cost of goods sold or the value at which unsold goods are recognized as inventory on the balance sheet. Service firms produce services, not inventoriable products. Even so, the cost of producing services is key to decisions about pricing (Will my prices cover my costs and allow for a profit margin? Are my prices competitive?) and cost control (Are my services provided as efficiently as my competitors?). In sum, job-order costing is a versatile and widely used costing method that may be encountered in virtually any organization that provides diverse products or services.

BEYOND THE BOTTOM LINE

In professional accounting firms, prices are often quoted based on estimated time to complete the work. If the work actually takes more time than estimated, the accounting firm will have to renegotiate the price with the client, which can be difficult to do after the fact, or accept a lower profit margin on the job. For these reasons, professional staff may think it is better to avoid reporting that the work took more time than was initially estimated.

Professional accounting firms typically have a policy against underreporting time because they see this practice as a first step down the "slippery slope" of unethical behaviour. First of all, underreporting is untruthful and reporting untruthfully is contrary to organizational and professional codes of conduct. In addition, if this year's actual time spent completing the work is used as the basis for next year's time estimate, then underreporting this year will put pressure on the budget in the following years. Staff may be tempted to cut corners to meet these unrealistic time budgets in future periods, which can lead to poor-quality work.

IN BUSINESS

Streaming services like Netflix and Amazon Prime make significant investments in producing original content to attract and retain subscribers. In fact, recent estimates indicate that Amazon has budgeted more than $200 million per season to produce five seasons of a new Lord of the Rings series. With this much money at stake, cost tracking and cost control are essential. Each series, season, or even each episode within a season produced by the streaming service can be considered a "job," and costs of direct materials (costumes, props, film, etc.) and direct labour (actors, directors, and extras) are charged to each show's job cost sheet. A share of the studio's overhead costs, such as utilities, depreciation of equipment, wages of maintenance workers, and so forth, is also charged to each series.

■ USE OF INFORMATION TECHNOLOGY

Earlier in the chapter, we discussed how bar code technology can be used to record labour time—reducing the drudgery in that task and increasing accuracy. Bar codes have many other uses.

In a company with a well-developed bar code system, the manufacturing cycle begins with the receipt of a customer's order in electronic form. Until very recently, the order would have been received via electronic data interchange (EDI), which involves a network of computers linking organizations. An EDI network allows companies to electronically exchange business documents and other information that extends into all areas of business activity, from ordering raw materials to shipping completed goods. EDI was developed in the 1980s and requires significant investment in programming and networking hardware. Recently, EDI has been challenged by far cheaper Internet-based alternatives—XML (Extensible Markup Language), which is an extension of HTML (Hypertext Markup Language), and JSON (JavaScript Object Notation). HTML tells the browser how to display information on your screen, but the computer doesn't know what the information is—it just displays it. XML and JSON provide additional tags that identify the kind of information that is being exchanged. For example, price data might be coded as <price> 14.95 <price>. When the computer reads this piece of data and sees the tag <price> surrounding 14.95, it immediately knows that this is a price. These tags can designate many different kinds of information—customer orders, medical records, bank statements, and so on—and the tags indicate to the computer how to display, store, and retrieve the information.

Once an order has been received via EDI or over the Internet in the form of an XML or JSON file, the computer draws up a list of required raw materials and sends out electronic purchase orders to suppliers. When materials arrive at the company's plant from the suppliers, bar codes that have been applied by the suppliers are scanned to update inventory records and to trigger payment for the materials.

Goods ready to be shipped are packed into containers, which are bar-coded with information that includes the customer number, the type and quantity of goods being shipped, and the order number. This bar code is then used to prepare billing information and track the packed goods until they are placed on a carrier for shipment to the customer. Some customers require that the packed goods be bar-coded with point-of-sale labels that can be scanned at retail checkout counters. These scans allow the retailer to update inventory records, verify price, and generate a customer receipt.

In short, bar code technology is being integrated into all areas of business activity. When combined with EDI or web-based data interchange, it eliminates a lot of clerical drudgery and allows companies to capture and exchange more data and to analyze and report information much more quickly and completely and with less error than with manual systems.

An enterprise resource planning (ERP) system represents a real-time computer system using a single uniform database that is coupled with modules for accounting, logistics, and human resources. Full use of these modules permits an integrated system response for

Internet-based orders in XML or JSON, supplier purchases and payables, inventory management, production, sales and receivables, treasury, and capital (fixed) assets management. Major suppliers of such ERP systems include Oracle, SAP, and Epicor. Other companies provide certified software that is compatible with these systems.

KNOWLEDGE IN ACTION

Managers can apply their knowledge about job-order costing when

- Calculating the product/service cost when many different products/services are produced in the year
- Setting prices to ensure the price exceeds the cost to produce the product or service
- Estimating the amount of overhead cost to apply to each of the various products or services produced
- Calculating the value of inventory included on the Balance Sheet and the Cost of Goods Sold disclosed on the Income Statement

SUMMARY

- Job-order costing and process costing are widely used to track costs. Job-order costing is used in situations where the organization offers many different products or services, such as in furniture manufacturers, hospitals, and legal firms. **[LO1]**
- Process costing is used where units of product are homogeneous, such as in flour milling or cement production. **[LO1]**
- Materials requisition forms and labour time tickets are used to assign direct materials and direct labour costs to jobs in a job-order costing system. Manufacturing overhead costs are assigned to jobs through use of a predetermined overhead rate. These costs are recorded in the general ledger using journal entries that reflect the cost flows through the job-order system. **[LO2, LO3, LO4]**
- The predetermined overhead rate is established before the period begins by dividing the estimated total manufacturing overhead cost for the period by the estimated total allocation base for the period. The most frequently used allocation bases are direct labour-hours and machine-hours. Overhead is applied to jobs by multiplying the predetermined overhead rate by the actual amount of the allocation base used by the job. **[LO3, LO5]**
- Since the predetermined overhead rate is based on estimates, the actual overhead cost incurred during a period may be more or less than the amount of overhead cost applied to production. Such a difference is referred to as *underapplied* or *overapplied overhead*. **[LO7]**
- The schedules of Cost of Goods Manufactured and Cost of Goods Sold summarize the flow of costs through the job-order costing system. Any under- or overapplied overhead for a period can be (1) closed out to Cost of Goods Sold; (2) allocated among Work in Process, Finished Goods, and Cost of Goods Sold; or (3) carried forward to the end of the year. **[LO6, LO7]**
- When overhead is underapplied, manufacturing overhead costs have been understated and therefore expenses must be adjusted upward. When overhead is overapplied, manufacturing overhead costs have been overstated and therefore inventories and/or expenses must be adjusted downward. **[LO7]**

REVIEW PROBLEM: JOB-ORDER COSTING

Hogle Company is a manufacturing firm that uses job-order costing. On January 1, the beginning of its fiscal year, the company's inventory balances were as follows:

Raw materials....................................	$20,000
Work in process.................................	15,000
Finished goods..................................	30,000

The company applies overhead cost to jobs on the basis of machine-hours worked. For the current year, the company estimated that it would work 75,000 machine-hours and incur $450,000 in manufacturing overhead cost. The following transactions were recorded for the year:

a.   Raw materials were purchased on account: $410,000.

b.   Raw materials were requisitioned for use in production: $380,000 ($360,000 direct materials and $20,000 indirect materials).

c.   The following costs were incurred for employee services: direct labour, $75,000; indirect labour, $110,000; sales commissions, $90,000; and administrative salaries, $200,000.

d.   Sales travel costs were incurred: $17,000.

e.   Utility costs were incurred in the factory: $43,000.

f.   Advertising costs were incurred: $180,000.

g.   Depreciation was recorded for the year: $350,000 (80% relates to factory operations, and 20% relates to selling and administrative activities).

h.   Insurance expired during the year: $10,000 (70% relates to factory operations, and the remaining 30% relates to selling and administrative activities).

i.   Manufacturing overhead was applied to production. Due to greater than expected demand for its products, the company worked 80,000 machine-hours during the year.

j.   Goods costing $900,000 to manufacture according to their job cost sheets were completed during the year.

k.   Goods were sold on account to customers during the year at a total selling price of $1,500,000. The goods cost $870,000 to manufacture according to their job cost sheets.

Required:

1.   Prepare journal entries to record the preceding transactions.

2.   Post the entries in (1) above to T-accounts (don't forget to enter the opening balances in the inventory accounts).

3.   Is Manufacturing Overhead underapplied or overapplied for the year?

4.   Prepare a Schedule of Cost of Goods Manufactured and Cost of Goods Sold for the year. Prepare the appropriate journal entry to dispose of under/overapplied overhead at year-end. If overhead is overapplied, allocate based on the entire cost of manufacturing in each of Work in Process, Finished Goods, and Cost of Goods Sold.

5.   Prepare an Income Statement for the year.

Solution to Review Problem

1.   *a.* Raw Materials   410,000

         Accounts Payable   410,000

    b. Work in Process.   360,000

         Manufacturing Overhead   20,000

         Raw Materials   380,000

    c. Work in Process.   75,000

         Manufacturing Overhead   110,000

         Sales Commissions Expense.   90,000

         Administrative Salaries Expense.   200,000

         Salaries and Wages Payable   475,000

    d. Sales Travel Expense.   17,000

         Accounts Payable   17,000

    e. Manufacturing Overhead   43,000

         Accounts Payable   43,000

    f. Advertising Expense.   180,000

         Accounts Payable   180,000

    g. Manufacturing Overhead   280,000

         Depreciation Expense   70,000

         Accumulated Depreciation   350,000

    h. Manufacturing Overhead   7,000

         Insurance Expense.   3,000

         Prepaid Insurance   10,000

    i. The predetermined overhead rate for the year is computed as follows:

$$\frac{\text{Estimated manufacturing overhead, \$450,000}}{\text{Estimated machine-hours, 75,000}} = \$6 \text{ per machine-hour}$$

Based on the 80,000 machine-hours actually worked during the year, the company would apply $480,000 in overhead cost to production: 80,000 machine-hours × $6 = $480,000. The following entry records this application of overhead cost:

Work in Process......................................	480,000	
Manufacturing Overhead...........................		480,000
j. Finished Goods.....................................	900,000	
Work in Process....................................		900,000
k. Accounts Receivable...............................	1,500,000	
Sales		1,500,000
Cost of Goods Sold................................	870,000	
Finished Goods		870,000

2.

Raw Materials

Bal.	20,000	(b)	380,000
(a)	410,000		
Bal.	50,000		

Work in Process

Bal.	15,000	(j)	900,000
(b)	360,000		
(c)	75,000		
(i)	480,000		
Bal.	30,000		

Finished Goods

Bal.	30,000	(k)	870,000
(j)	900,000		
Bal.	60,000		

Cost of Goods Sold

(k)	870,000	

Manufacturing Overhead

(b)	20,000	(i)	480,000
(c)	110,000		
(e)	43,000		
(g)	280,000		
(h)	7,000		
	460,000		480,000
		Bal.	20,000

Prepaid Insurance

		(h)	10,000

Sales Commissions Expense

(c)	90,000	

Accumulated Depreciation

		(g)	350,000

Accounts Receivable

(k)	1,500,000	

Administrative Salary Expense

(c)	200,000	

Sales Travel Expense

(d)	17,000	

Accounts Payable

		(a)	410,000
		(d)	17,000
		(e)	43,000
		(f)	180,000

Sales

		(k)	1,500,000

Advertising Expense

(f)	180,000	

Depreciation Expense

(g)	70,000	

Salaries and Wages Payable

		(c)	475,000

Insurance Expense

(h)	3,000	

3.   Manufacturing overhead is overapplied for the year.

4.   **HOGLE COMPANY**
        Schedule of Cost of Goods Manufactured and Cost of Goods Sold
                      For the Year Ended December 31

Cost of Goods Manufactured
Direct Materials:
Raw materials inventory, January 1	$ 20,000	
Add: Purchases of raw materials	410,000	
Total raw materials available	430,000	
Deduct: Raw materials inventory, December 31	50,000	
Raw materials used in production	380,000	
Less: Indirect materials	20,000	
Direct materials used in production.		$360,000
Direct labour		75,000
Manufacturing overhead applied to work in process . . .		480,000
Total manufacturing costs.		915,000
Add: Beginning work in process inventory.		15,000
		930,000
Deduct: Ending work in process inventory.		(30,000)
Cost of goods manufactured		$900,000

Cost of Goods Sold
Finished goods inventory, January 1		$ 30,000
Add: Cost of goods manufactured.		900,000
Goods available for sale		930,000
Deduct: Finished goods inventory, December 31		(60,000)
Unadjusted cost of goods sold.		870,000
Deduct: Overapplied overhead*		(18,000)
Adjusted cost of goods sold		$852,000

*The entry to dispose of the overapplied overhead is as follows:

Work in Process Inventory, December 31		$30,000	3%
Finished Goods Inventory, December 31		$60,000	7%
Unadjusted Cost of Goods Sold	$870,000		
Less Work in Process Inventory, January 1	$ (15,000)		90%
Less Finished Goods Inventory, January 1	$(30,000)	$825,000	
Total		$915,000	100%
Manufacturing Overhead	$20,000		
Work in Process ($20,000 × 3%)		$ 600	
Finished Goods ($20,000 × 7%)		1,400	
Cost of Goods Sold ($20,000 × 90%)		18,000	

5.   **HOGLE COMPANY**
                             Income Statement
                      For the Year Ended December 31

Sales.		$1,500,000
Less cost of goods sold		852,000
Gross margin		648,000
Less selling and administrative expenses:		
Sales commissions expense.	$ 90,000	
Administrative salaries expense.	200,000	
Sales travel expense.	17,000	
Advertising expense.	180,000	
Depreciation expense.	70,000	
Insurance expense	3,000	560,000
Operating income		$ 88,000

DISCUSSION CASE

DISCUSSION CASE 5–1

Although job-order costing was originally developed for use in manufacturing environments, it is equally applicable in organizations that provide services rather than manufactured goods. A public accounting firm is one such organization.

Required:

Develop a list of "products" provided by the employees and partners of a typical public accounting office in your area. Choose one of those products to examine further. Next, develop a list of costs that would be incurred to provide that product/service. Consider which of these costs are direct and which are indirect (i.e., overhead), and identify an appropriate cost driver for each overhead type. How might this information be used to determine the price to charge one client of the public accounting firm for your selected product in the coming year?

QUESTIONS

5–1 Why aren't actual overhead costs traced to jobs just as direct materials and direct labour costs are traced to jobs?

5–2 When would job-order costing be used instead of process costing?

5–3 What is the purpose of the job cost sheet in a job-order costing system?

5–4 What is a predetermined overhead rate, and how is it computed?

5–5 Explain how a sales order, a production order, a job cost sheet, a materials requisition form, and a labour time ticket are involved in producing and costing products.

5–6 What factors should be considered in selecting a base to be used in computing the predetermined overhead rate?

5–7 Define the term *cost driver* and indicate how it is used in job-order costing.

5–8 If a company fully allocates all of its overhead costs to jobs, does this guarantee that a profit will be earned for the period?

5–9 What account is credited when overhead cost is applied to work in process? Would you expect the amount applied for a period to equal the actual overhead costs of the period? Why or why not?

5–10 What is underapplied overhead? Overapplied overhead? What disposition is made of these amounts at the end of the period?

5–11 Provide two reasons why overhead might be underapplied in a given year.

5–12 What adjustment is made for underapplied overhead on the schedule of cost of goods sold? What adjustment is made for overapplied overhead?

5–13 Gorman Company applies overhead cost to jobs on the basis of direct labour cost. Job A, which was started and completed during the current period, shows charges of $6,000 for direct materials, $15,000 for direct labour, and $7,500 for overhead on its job cost sheet. Job B, which is still in process at year-end, shows charges of $2,500 for direct materials and $4,000 for direct labour. Should any overhead cost be added to Job B at year-end? Explain and calculate the amount, if necessary.

5–14 A company assigns overhead cost to completed jobs on the basis of 150% of direct labour cost. The job cost sheet for Job 313 shows that $12,000 in direct materials was used on the job and that $16,000 in direct labour cost was incurred. If 750 units were produced in Job 313, what is the unit product cost?

5–15 What is a plantwide overhead rate? Why are multiple overhead rates, rather than a plantwide overhead rate, used in some companies?

5–16 Under what conditions would direct labour be a poor allocation base to use in allocating manufacturing overhead?

5–17 "Predetermined overhead rates smooth product costs." Do you agree? Why?

5–18 Explain clearly why a portion of overapplied overhead for an interim period should be carried to the balance sheet. What conceptual factor is assumed in the argument?

5–19 Why does the calculation of the percentages for overapplied overhead reduce the costs of goods sold by the opening inventories? What would happen if such a deduction were not made?

FOUNDATIONAL EXERCISES

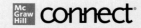

[LO2, LO3, LO5, LO6]

Sweeten Company had no jobs in progress at the beginning of March and no beginning inventories. The company has two manufacturing departments—Moulding and Fabrication. It started, completed, and sold only two jobs during March: Job P and Job Q. The following additional information is available for the company as a whole and for Jobs P and Q (all data and questions relate to the month of March):

	Moulding	Fabrication	Total
Estimated total machine-hours used	2,500	1,500	4,000
Estimated total fixed manufacturing overhead . . .	$10,000	$15,000	$25,000
Estimated variable manufacturing overhead per machine-hour	$1.40	$2.20	

	Job P	Job Q
Direct materials	$13,000	$8,000
Direct labour cost.	$21,000	$7,500
Actual machine hours used:		
Moulding	1,700	800
Fabrication	600	900
Total.	2,300	1,700

Sweeten Company had no underapplied or overapplied manufacturing overhead costs during the month.

For questions 5–1 through 5–9, assume that Sweeten Company uses departmental predetermined overhead rates with machine-hours as the allocation base in both departments. For questions 5–10 through 5–15, assume that the company uses a plantwide predetermined overhead rate with machine-hours as the allocation base.

5–1 What is the company's predetermined overhead rate in Moulding and Fabrication?

5–2 How much manufacturing overhead from Moulding was applied to Job P and to Job Q?

5–3 How much manufacturing overhead was applied from Fabrication to Job P and to Job Q?

5–4 What was the total manufacturing cost assigned to Job P?

5–5 If Job P included 20 units, what was its unit product cost?

5–6 What was the total manufacturing cost assigned to Job Q?

5–7 If Job Q included 30 units, what was its unit product cost?

5–8 Assume that Sweeten Company used cost-plus pricing (and a markup percentage of 80% of total manufacturing cost) to establish selling prices for all of its jobs. What selling price would the company have established for Jobs P and Q? What are the selling prices for both jobs when stated on a per unit basis?

5–9 What was Sweeten Company's cost of goods sold for March?

5–10 What was the company's plantwide predetermined overhead rate?

5–11 How much manufacturing overhead was applied to Job P and how much was applied to Job Q?

5–12 If Job P included 20 units, what was its unit product cost?

5–13 If Job Q included 30 units, what was its unit product cost?

5–14 Assume that Sweeten Company used cost-plus pricing (and a markup percentage of 80% of total manufacturing cost) to establish selling prices for all of its jobs. What selling price would the company have established for Jobs P and Q? What are the selling prices for both jobs when stated on a per unit basis?

5–15 What was Sweeten Company's cost of goods sold for March?

EXERCISES

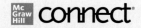

EXERCISE 5–1 Process Costing and Job-Order Costing [LO1]

Which would be more appropriate in each of the following organizations—job-order costing or process costing?

a. A custom home builder.

b. A music producer.

c. A website designer.

d. A business consultant.

e. An airline.

f.   A paper towel manufacturer.
g.   An auto repair shop.
h.   A dairy processing plant.
i.   A real estate developer.
j.   A pulp and paper manufacturer.
k.   A law firm.
l.   A sunscreen manufacturer.

EXERCISE 5–2 Computing Job Costs [LO2]

Weaver Company's predetermined overhead rate is $20.00 per direct labour-hour, and its direct labour wage rate is $15.00 per hour. The following information pertains to Job A-200:

Direct materials	$200
Direct labour	$150

Required:
1.   What is the total manufacturing cost assigned to Job A-200?
2.   If Job A-200 consists of 50 units, what is the average cost assigned to each unit included in the job?

EXERCISE 5–3 Compute the Predetermined Overhead Rate [LO3]

Logan Products computes its predetermined overhead rate annually on the basis of machine-hours. At the beginning of the year, it estimated that its total manufacturing overhead would be $250,000 and machines would be run a total of 10,000 hours. Its actual total manufacturing overhead for the year was $236,400 and its actual total machine-hours was 16,500 hours.

Required:
Compute the company's predetermined overhead rate for the year.

EXERCISE 5–4 Prepare Journal Entries [LO4]

Lancaster Company recorded the following transactions for the just-completed month:
a. $45,000 in raw materials was purchased on account.
b. $125,000 in raw materials was requisitioned for use in production. Of this amount, $70,000 was for direct materials and the remainder was for indirect materials.
c.   Total labour wages of $212,000 were incurred. Of this amount, $183,000 was for direct labour and the remainder was for indirect labour.
d.   Additional manufacturing overhead costs of $189,000 were incurred.

Required:
Record the above transactions in journal entries.

EXERCISE 5–5 Apply Overhead [LO5, LO7]

Carera Corporation uses a predetermined overhead rate of $18 per direct labour-hour. This predetermined rate was based on 15,000 estimated direct labour-hours and $270,000 of estimated total manufacturing overhead.

The company incurred actual total manufacturing overhead costs of $230,000 and 12,500 total direct labour-hours during the period.

Required:
1.   Determine the amount of manufacturing overhead applied to units of product during the period as well as the amount of over- or underapplied overhead for the period.
2.   Prepare the journal entry to dispose of over- or underapplied overhead.

EXERCISE 5–6 Apply Overhead Cost to Jobs [LO5]

Luthan Company uses a plantwide predetermined overhead rate of $23.40 per direct labour-hour. This predetermined rate was based on a cost formula that estimated $257,400 of total manufacturing overhead cost for an estimated activity level of 11,000 direct labour-hours.

The company incurred actual total manufacturing overhead cost of $249,000 and 10,800 total direct labour-hours during the period.

Required:
Determine the amount of manufacturing overhead cost that would have been applied to all jobs during the period.

EXERCISE 5–7 Schedules of Cost of Goods Manufactured and Cost of Goods Sold [LO6]
Primare Corporation has provided the following data concerning last month's manufacturing operations.

Purchase of raw materials...	$30,000
Indirect materials included in manufacturing overhead	$ 5,000
Direct labour..	$58,000
Manufacturing overhead applied to work in process	$87,000
Underapplied overhead	$ 4,000

Inventories	Beginning	Ending
Raw materials................................	$12,000	18,000
Work in process	56,000	65,000
Finished goods...............................	35,000	42,000

Required:
1. Prepare a schedule of cost of goods manufactured for the month.
2. Prepare a schedule of cost of goods sold for the month.

EXERCISE 5–8 Prepare T-Accounts [LO4, LO6]
Granger Products recorded the following transactions for the just-completed month. The company had no beginning inventories:
a. $75,000 in raw materials was purchased for cash.
b. $73,000 in raw materials was requisitioned for use in production. Of this amount, $67,000 was for direct materials and the remainder was for indirect materials.
c. Total wages of $152,000 were incurred and paid. Of this amount, $134,000 was for direct labour and the remainder was for indirect labour.
d. Additional manufacturing overhead costs of $126,000 were incurred and paid.
e. Manufacturing overhead costs of $178,000 were applied to jobs using the company's predetermined overhead rate.
f. All of the jobs in process at the end of the month were completed and shipped to customers.
g. If overhead is underapplied in the period, it is closed out to cost of goods sold. If overhead is overapplied in the period, it is based on the basis of the amount of allocated overhead that is in the ending balances in each account.

Required:
1. Post the above transactions to T-accounts.
2. Determine the cost of goods sold for the period.

EXERCISE 5–9 Underapplied and Overapplied Overhead [LO7]
Cretin Enterprises uses a predetermined overhead rate of $8 per direct labour-hour. This predetermined rate was based on 40,000 estimated direct labour-hours and $320,000 of estimated total manufacturing overhead.

The company incurred actual total manufacturing overhead costs of $298,000 and 38,500 total direct labour-hours during the period. There were no beginning inventories, and all goods produced in the period were shipped out to customers before period-end.

Required:
1. Determine the amount of underapplied or overapplied manufacturing overhead for the period.
2. What is the effect on gross margin for the period?

EXERCISE 5–10 Schedules of Cost of Goods Manufactured and Cost of Goods Sold [LO6]
The following data from the just-completed year are taken from the accounting records of Eccles Company:

Sales	$643,000
Direct labour cost	90,000
Raw material purchases	132,000
Selling expenses	100,000
Administrative expenses	43,000
Manufacturing overhead applied to work in process ...	210,000
Actual manufacturing overhead costs	220,000

Inventory	Beginning of Year	End of Year
Raw materials	$ 8,000	$10,000
Work in process....................................	5,000	20,000
Finished goods	70,000	25,000

Required:
1. Prepare a schedule of cost of goods manufactured. Assume all raw materials used in production were direct materials.
2. Prepare a schedule of cost of goods sold.

EXERCISE 5–11 Varying Predetermined Overhead Rates [LO3, LO5]

Jacarda Company makes a composting bin that is subject to wide seasonal variations in demand. Unit product costs are computed on a quarterly basis by dividing each quarter's manufacturing costs (materials, labour, and overhead) by the quarter's production in units. The company's estimated costs, by quarter, for the coming year are given below:

	Quarter			
	First	**Second**	**Third**	**Fourth**
Direct materials	$240,000	$120,000	$ 60,000	$180,000
Direct labour	96,000	48,000	24,000	72,000
Manufacturing overhead	228,000	204,000	192,000	216,000
Total manufacturing costs	$564,000	$372,000	$276,000	$468,000
Number of units to be produced......	80,000	40,000	20,000	60,000
Estimated unit product cost	$ 7.05	$ 9.30	$ 13.80	$ 7.80

Management finds the variation in unit product costs to be confusing and difficult to work with. It has been suggested that the problem lies with manufacturing overhead, since it is the largest element of cost. Accordingly, you have been asked to find a more appropriate way of assigning manufacturing overhead cost to units of product. After some analysis, you have determined that the company's overhead costs are mostly fixed and therefore show little sensitivity to changes in the level of production.

Required:
1. The company uses a job-order costing system. How would you recommend that manufacturing overhead cost be assigned to production? Be specific, and show computations.
2. Recompute the company's unit product costs in accordance with your recommendations in (1) above.

EXERCISE 5–12 Departmental Overhead Rates [LO3, LO5]

Grange Company has two departments, Stamping and Assembly. The company uses a job-order costing system and computes a predetermined overhead rate in each department. The Stamping Department bases its rate on machine-hours, and the Assembly Department bases its rate on direct labour cost. At the beginning of the year, the company made the following estimates:

| | Department | |
	Stamping	Assembly
Direct labour-hours	40,000	125,000
Machine-hours.	300,000	15,000
Manufacturing overhead cost.	$2,550,000	$4,000,000
Direct labour cost.	$ 360,000	$3,200,000

Required:
1.   Compute the predetermined overhead rate to be used in each department.
2.   Assume that the overhead rates you computed in (1) above are in effect. The job cost sheet for Job 407, which was started and completed during the year, shows the following:

| | Department | |
	Stamping	Assembly
Direct labour-hours	25	100
Machine-hours.	450	20
Materials requisitioned.	$400	$1,850
Direct labour cost.	$250	$ 800

CHECK FIGURE
Stamping = $8.50 per machine-hour; Assembly = 125% of direct labour cost. Total manufacturing overhead cost applied = $4,825.

Compute the total overhead cost applied to Job 407.
3.   Would you expect substantially different amounts of overhead cost to be charged to some jobs if the company used a plantwide overhead rate based on direct labour cost instead of using departmental rates? Explain. No computations are necessary.

EXERCISE 5–13 Overhead Application [LO3, LO5]
Sportway Inc. produces high-quality tennis racquets and golf clubs using a patented forming process and high-quality hand-finishing. Products move through two production departments: Forming and Finishing. The company uses departmental overhead rates to allocate overhead costs. Overhead is allocated based on machine-hours in Forming and direct labour cost in Finishing. Information related to costs for last year is provided below:

	Tennis Racquets	Golf Clubs
Annual production and sales (units). .	5,000	8,000
Direct materials cost per unit	$4.50	$3.50
Direct labour cost per unit:		
Forming Department	$3.00	$2.50
Finishing Department.	$6.00	$4.00
Machine hours per unit:		
Forming Department	0.25	0.25
Finishing Department.	—	0.50

In addition, the firm budgets manufacturing overhead at $35,750 in the Forming Department and $46,500 in the Finishing Department.

Required:
1.   Determine the overhead application rate for each department.
2.   Determine the total cost per unit of tennis racquets and golf clubs.

PROBLEMS

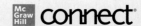

PROBLEM 5–14 Plantwide and Departmental Predetermined Overhead Rates; Overhead Application [LO3, LO4, LO5]

Wilmington Company has two manufacturing departments—Assembly and Fabrication. It considers all of its manufacturing overhead costs to be fixed costs. The first set of data that is shown below is based on estimates from the beginning of the year. The second set of data relates to one particular job completed during the year—Job Bravo.

	Assembly	Fabrication	Total
Manufacturing overhead costs	$600,000	$800,000	$1,400,000
Direct labour-hours....................	50,000	30,000	80,000
Machine-hours	20,000	100,000	120,000

Job Bravo	Assembly	Fabrication
Direct labour-hours...........................	11	3
Machine-hours	3	6

Required:
1. If Wilmington used a plantwide predetermined overhead rate based on direct labour-hours, how much manufacturing overhead would be applied to Job Bravo?
2. If Wilmington uses departmental predetermined overhead rates with direct labour-hours as the allocation base in Assembly and machine-hours as the allocation base in Fabrication, how much manufacturing overhead would be applied to Job Bravo?

> **CHECK FIGURE**
> Predetermined overhead rate based on direct labour-hours = $12 per DLH.

PROBLEM 5–15 Applying Overhead in a Service Company [LO2, LO3, LO5]

Scott's Outdoor Design began operations on January 2. The company designs outdoor commercial spaces. The following activity was recorded in the company's Work in Process account for the first month of operations:

Work in Process			
Costs of subcontracted work	50,000	To completed projects	350,000
Direct staff costs	125,000		
Studio overhead	250,000		

Scott's Outdoor Design is a service firm, so the names of the accounts it uses are different from the names used in manufacturing companies. Costs of Subcontracted Work is comparable to Direct Materials, Direct Staff Costs is equivalent to Direct Labour, Studio Overhead is equivalent to Manufacturing Overhead, and Completed Projects is equivalent to Finished Goods. Apart from the difference in terms, the accounting methods used by the company are identical to the methods used by manufacturing companies.

The company uses a job-order costing system and applies studio overhead to Work in Process on the basis of direct staff costs. At the end of January, only one job was still in process. This job (the XYZ Corporation Headquarters project) had been charged with $20,800 in direct staff costs.

Required:
1. Compute the predetermined overhead rate that was in use during January.
2. Complete the following job cost sheet for the partially completed XYZ Corporation Headquarters project:

Job Cost Sheet
XYZ Corporation Headquarters Project
As of January 31

Costs of subcontracted work..	$?
Direct staff costs	?
Studio overhead..	?
Total cost to January 31	$?

PROBLEM 5–16 Applying Overhead in a Service Company [LO3, LO4, LO5]

Speedy Auto Repairs uses a job-order costing system. The company's direct materials consist of replacement parts installed in customer vehicles, and its direct labour consists of the mechanics' hourly wages. Speedy's overhead costs include various items such as the shop manager's salary, depreciation of equipment, utilities, insurance, and magazine subscriptions and refreshments for the waiting room.

The company applies all of its overhead costs to jobs based on direct labour-hours. At the beginning of the year, it made the following estimates:

Direct labour-hours required to support estimated output	20,000
Fixed overhead costs.	$350,000
Variable overhead costs per direct labour-hour.	$1

During the year, Mr. Wilkes brought in his vehicle to replace his brakes, spark plugs, and tires. The following information was available with respect to his job:

Direct materials.	$590
Direct labour cost	$109
Direct labour-hours used.	6

Required:
1. Compute the predetermined overhead rate.
2. Compute Mr. Wilkes's total job cost.
3. If Speedy establishes its selling prices using a markup percentage of 40% of its total job cost, then how much would it have charged Mr. Wilkes?

PROBLEM 5–17 Applying Overhead; Journal Entries; Disposition of Underapplied or Overapplied Overhead [LO4, LO5, LO7]

The following information is taken from the accounts of Foster Corp. The entries in the T-accounts are summaries of the transactions that affected those accounts during the year:

Manufacturing Overhead				**Work in Process**			
(a)	380,000	*(b)*	410,000	Bal.	105,000	*(c)*	760,000
		Bal.	30,000		210,000		
					115,000		
				(b)	410,000		
				Bal.	80,000		

Finished Goods				**Cost of Goods Sold**			
Bal.	160,000	*(d)*	820,000	*(d)*	820,000		
(c)	760,000						
Bal.	100,000						

The overhead applied to production during the year is distributed among the ending balances in the accounts as follows:

Work in Process, ending	$ 32,800
Finished Goods, ending.	41,000
Cost of Goods Sold.	336,200
Overhead applied	$410,000

For example, of the $80,000 ending balance in Work in Process, $32,800 was overhead applied during the year.

Required:
a.   Identify the reasons for entries (*a*) through (*d*).
b.   The company allocates any balance in the Manufacturing Overhead account to the other accounts in proportion to the overhead applied during the year that is in the ending balance in each account. Prepare the necessary journal entry, with supporting computations.

PROBLEM 5–18   Applying Overhead; T-Accounts; Journal Entries [LO3, LO4, LO5, LO7]
Medusa Products uses a job-order costing system. Overhead costs are applied to jobs on the basis of machine-hours. At the beginning of the year, management estimated that the company would incur $170,000 in manufacturing overhead costs for the year and work 85,000 machine-hours.

Required:
1.   Compute the company's predetermined overhead rate.
2.   Assume that during the year the company actually works only 80,000 machine-hours and incurs the following costs in the Manufacturing Overhead and Work in Process accounts:

Manufacturing Overhead				Work in Process		
Utilities	14,000	?		Direct materials	530,000	
Insurance	9,000			Direct labour	85,000	
Maintenance	33,000			Overhead	?	
Indirect materials	7,000					
Indirect labour	65,000					
Depreciation	40,000					

Copy the data in the T-accounts above onto your answer sheet. Compute the amount of overhead cost that would be applied to Work in Process for the year, and make the entry in your T-accounts.
3.   Compute the amount of underapplied or overapplied overhead for the year, and show the balance in your Manufacturing Overhead T-account. Prepare a journal entry to properly dispose of the balance.
4.   Explain why the manufacturing overhead was underapplied or overapplied for the year.

PROBLEM 5–19   Journal Entries; T-Accounts; Cost Flows [LO4, LO5, LO7]
Ravsten Company uses a job-order costing system. On January 1, the beginning of the current year, the company's inventory balances were as follows:

Raw Materials	$16,000
Work in Process	$10,000
Finished Goods.	$30,000

The company applies overhead cost to jobs on the basis of machine-hours. For the current year, the company estimated that it would work 36,000 machine-hours and incur $153,000 in manufacturing overhead cost. The following transactions were recorded for the year:
a.   Raw materials were purchased on account: $200,000.
b.   Raw materials were requisitioned for use in production: $190,000 (80% direct and 20% indirect).
c.   The following costs were incurred for employee services:

Direct labour	$160,000
Indirect labour	$ 27,000
Sales commissions	$ 36,000
Administrative salaries.	$ 80,000

d.   Heat, power, and water costs were incurred in the factory: $42,000.
e.   Prepaid insurance expired during the year: $10,000 (90% relates to factory operations, and 10% relates to selling and administrative activities).
f.   Advertising costs were incurred, $50,000.
g.   Depreciation was recorded for the year: $60,000 (85% relates to factory operations, and 15% relates to selling and administrative activities).

h.   Manufacturing overhead cost was applied to production. The company recorded 40,000 machine-hours for the year.

i.   Goods that cost $480,000 to manufacture according to their job cost sheets were transferred to the finished goods warehouse.

j.   Sales for the year totalled $700,000 and were all on account. The total cost to manufacture these goods according to their job cost sheets was $475,000.

Required:

1.   Prepare journal entries to record the transactions given above.

2.   Prepare T-accounts for inventories, Manufacturing Overhead, and Cost of Goods Sold. Post relevant data from your journal entries to these T-accounts (don't forget to enter the opening balances in your inventory accounts). Compute an ending balance in each account.

3.   Is Manufacturing Overhead underapplied or overapplied for the year? Prepare a journal entry to properly dispose of any balance in the Manufacturing Overhead account.

4.   Prepare an income statement for the year. (Do not prepare a schedule of cost of goods manufactured; all of the information needed for the income statement is available in the journal entries and T-accounts you have prepared.)

PROBLEM 5–20 T-Accounts; Applying Overhead [LO3, LO5, LO7]
Durham Company's trial balance as of January 1, the beginning of the current year, is shown below:

Cash.	$ 8,000	
Accounts Receivable.	13,000	
Raw Materials.	7,000	
Work in Process	18,000	
Finished Goods.	20,000	
Prepaid Insurance	4,000	
Plant and Equipment.	230,000	
Accumulated Depreciation.		$ 42,000
Accounts Payable		30,000
Capital Stock.		150,000
Retained Earnings.		78,000
Total	$300,000	$300,000

Durham Company uses a job-order costing system. During the year, the following transactions took place:

a.   Raw materials were purchased on account: $45,000.

b.   Raw materials were requisitioned for use in production: $40,000 (80% direct and 20% indirect).

c.   Factory utility costs were incurred: $14,600.

d.   Depreciation was recorded on plant and equipment: $28,000. Three-fourths of the depreciation relates to factory equipment, and the remainder relates to selling and administrative equipment.

e.   Costs for salaries and wages were incurred as follows:

Direct labour.	$40,000
Indirect labour.	$18,000
Sales commissions	$10,400
Administrative salaries.	$25,000

f.   Prepaid insurance expired during the year: $3,000 (80% relates to factory operations, and 20% relates to selling and administrative activities).

g.   Miscellaneous selling and administrative expenses were incurred: $18,000.

h.   Manufacturing overhead was applied to production. The company applies overhead on the basis of 150% of direct labour cost.

i.   Goods that cost $130,000 to manufacture according to their job cost sheets were transferred to the finished goods warehouse.

j.   Goods that had cost $120,000 to manufacture according to their job cost sheets were sold on account for $200,000.

k.   Collections from customers during the year totalled $197,000.

l.   Payments to suppliers on account during the year totalled $100,000; payments to employees for salaries and wages totalled $90,000.

Required:
1. Prepare a T-account for each account in the company's trial balance, and enter the opening balances shown above.
2. Record the transactions above directly into the T-accounts. Prepare new T-accounts as needed. Key your entries to the letters (*a*) through (*l*) above. Find the ending balance in each account.
3. Is manufacturing overhead underapplied or overapplied for the year? Make an entry in the T-accounts to properly dispose of any balance in the Manufacturing Overhead account.
4. Prepare an income statement for the year. (Do not prepare a schedule of cost of goods manufactured; all of the information needed for the income statement is available in the T-accounts you have prepared.)

PROBLEM 5–21 Cost Flows; T-Accounts; Income Statement [LO3, LO5, LO7]
PQB Inc. designs and fabricates movie props such as mock-ups of star fighters and cybernetic robots. The company's balance sheet as of January 1, the beginning of the current year, appears below.

Since each prop is a unique design and may require anything from a few hours to a month or more to complete, PQB uses a job-order costing system. Overhead in the fabrication shop is charged to props on the basis of direct labour cost. The company estimated that it would incur $80,000 in manufacturing overhead and $100,000 in direct labour cost during the year. The following transactions were recorded during the year:
a. Raw materials, such as wood, paints, and metal sheeting, were purchased on account: $80,000.
b. Raw materials were issued to production: $90,000 ($5,000 of this amount was for indirect materials).
c. Payroll costs were incurred and paid: direct labour, $120,000; indirect labour, $30,000; and selling and administrative salaries, $75,000.
d. Fabrication shop utilities costs were incurred: $12,000.
e. Depreciation was recorded for the year: $30,000 ($5,000 on selling and administrative assets; $25,000 on fabrication shop assets).
f. Prepaid insurance expired: $4,800 ($4,000 related to fabrication shop operations, and $800 related to selling and administrative activities).
g. Shipping expenses were incurred: $40,000.
h. Other manufacturing overhead costs were incurred: $17,000 (credit Accounts Payable).
i. Manufacturing overhead was applied to production. Overhead is applied on the basis of direct labour cost.
j. Movie props that cost $310,000 to produce according to their job cost sheets were completed.
k. Sales for the year totalled $450,000 and were all on account. The total cost to produce these movie props was $300,000 according to their job cost sheets.
l. Collections on account from customers totalled $445,000.
m. Payments on account to suppliers totalled $150,000.

	PQB Inc. Balance Sheet January 1	
Assets		
Current assets:		
Cash.....................................		$ 15,000
Accounts receivable		40,000
Inventories:		
Raw materials................................	$ 25,000	
Work in process................................	30,000	
Finished goods (props awaiting shipment)	45,000	100,000
Prepaid insurance		5,000
Total current assets..................................		160,000
Buildings and equipment.............................	500,000	
Less accumulated depreciation........................	210,000	290,000
Total assets..		$450,000
Liabilities and Shareholders' Equity		
Accounts payable....................................		$ 75,000
Capital stock.......................................	$250,000	
Retained earnings...................................	125,000	375,000
Total liabilities and shareholders' equity...............		$450,000

Required:
1. Prepare a T-account for each account on the company's balance sheet, and enter the beginning balances.
2. Make entries directly into the T-accounts for the transactions given above. Create new T-accounts as needed. Determine an ending balance for each T-account.
3. Was manufacturing overhead underapplied or overapplied for the year? Assume that the company allocates any overhead balance among the Work in Process, Finished Goods, and Cost of Goods Sold accounts, using the overall balances in each account. Prepare a journal entry to show the allocation. (Round allocation percentages to one decimal place.)
4. Prepare an income statement for the year. (Do not prepare a schedule of cost of goods manufactured; all of the information needed for the income statement is available in the T-accounts.)

PROBLEM 5–22 T-Accounts; Overhead Rates; Journal Entries [LO3, LO4, LO5, LO7]
Kenworth Company uses a job-order costing system. Only three jobs—Job 105, Job 106, and Job 107—were worked on during November and December. Job 105 was completed on December 10; the other two jobs were still in production on December 31, the end of the company's operating year. Data from the job cost sheets of the three jobs follow:

	Job Cost Sheet		
	Job 105	Job 106	Job 107
November costs incurred:			
Direct materials.	$16,500	$ 9,300	$ 0
Direct labour.	$13,000	$ 7,000	$ 0
Manufacturing overhead.	$20,800	$11,200	$ 0
December costs incurred:			
Direct materials.	$ 0	$ 8,200	$21,300
Direct labour.	$ 4,000	$ 6,000	$10,000
Manufacturing overhead.	?	?	?

The following additional information is available: Manufacturing overhead is applied to jobs on the basis of direct labour cost.
Balances in the inventory accounts at November 30 were as follows:

Raw Materials.	$40,000
Work in Process.	?
Finished Goods.	$85,000

Required:
1. Prepare T-accounts for Raw Materials, Work in Process, Finished Goods, and Manufacturing Overhead. Enter the November 30 inventory balances given above; in the case of Work in Process, compute the November 30 balance and enter it into the Work in Process T-account.
2. Prepare journal entries for *December* as follows:
   a. Prepare an entry to record the issue of materials into production, and post the entry to appropriate T-accounts. (In the case of direct materials, it is not necessary to make a separate entry for each job.) Indirect materials used during December totalled $4,000.
   b. Prepare an entry to record the incurrence of labour cost, and post the entry to appropriate T-accounts. (In the case of direct labour cost, it is not necessary to make a separate entry for each job.) Indirect labour cost totalled $8,000 for December.
   c. Prepare an entry to record the incurrence of $19,000 in various actual manufacturing overhead costs for December (credit Accounts Payable). Post this entry to the appropriate T-accounts.
3. What apparent predetermined overhead rate does the company use to assign overhead cost to jobs? Using this rate, prepare a journal entry to record the application of overhead cost to jobs for December (it is not necessary to make a separate entry for each job). Post this entry to the appropriate T-accounts.
4. As stated earlier, Job 105 was completed during December. Prepare a journal entry to show the transfer of this job off the production line and into the finished goods warehouse. Post the entry to the appropriate T-accounts.
5. Determine the balance at December 31 in the Work in Process inventory account. How much of this balance consists of costs charged to Job 106? Job 107?

PROBLEM 5–23 Plantwide versus Multiple Predetermined Overhead Rates: Service Industry [LO2, LO3, LO5]

McCullough Regional Medical Centre uses a job-order costing system to assign costs to its patients. Its direct materials include a variety of items such as pharmaceutical drugs, heart valves, artificial hips, and pacemakers. Its direct labour costs (e.g., surgeons, anesthesiologists, radiologists, and nurses) associated with specific surgical procedures and tests are traced to individual patients. All other costs, such as depreciation of medical equipment, insurance, utilities, incidental medical supplies, and the labour costs associated with around-the-clock monitoring of patients, are treated as overhead costs.

Historically, McCullough has used one predetermined overhead rate based on the number of patient-days (each night that a patient spends in the hospital counts as one patient-day) to allocate overhead costs to patients. Recently a member of the hospital's accounting staff has suggested using two predetermined overhead rates (allocated based on the number of patient-days) to improve the accuracy of the costs allocated to patients. The first overhead rate would include all overhead costs within the Intensive Care Unit (ICU) and the second overhead rate would include all Other overhead costs. Information pertaining to the hospital's estimated number of patient-days, its estimated overhead costs, and two of its patients—Patient A and Patient B—is provided below:

	ICU	Other
Estimated number of patient-days.............	2,000	18,000
Estimated fixed overhead cost.................	$3,200,000	$14,000,000
Estimated variable overhead cost per patient-day..	$ 236	$ 96
	Patient A	**Patient B**
Direct materials............................	$ 4,500	$ 6,200
Direct labour..............................	$ 25,000	$ 36,000
Total number of patient days (including ICU)	14	21
Number of patient days spent in ICU	0	7

Required:
1. Assuming McCullough continues to use only one predetermined overhead rate, calculate:
    a. The predetermined overhead rate.
    b. The total cost, including direct materials, direct labour, and applied overhead, assigned to Patient A and Patient B.
2. Assuming McCullough calculates two overhead rates as recommended by the staff accountant, calculate:
    a. The ICU and Other overhead rates.
    b. The total cost, including direct materials, direct labour, and applied overhead, assigned to Patient A and Patient B.
3. What insights are revealed by the staff accountant's approach?

PROBLEM 5–24 Journal Entries; T-Accounts; Disposition of Underapplied or Overapplied Overhead; Income Statement [LO3, LO4, LO5, LO7]

Heavenly Displays Inc. puts together large-scale fireworks displays—primarily for Canada Day celebrations sponsored by corporations and municipalities. The company assembles and orchestrates complex displays using pyrotechnic components purchased from suppliers throughout the world. The company has built a reputation for safety and for the awesome power and brilliance of its computer-controlled shows. Heavenly Displays builds its own launch platforms and its own electronic controls. Because of the company's reputation, customers order shows up to a year in advance. Since each show is different in terms of duration and components used, Heavenly Displays uses a job-order costing system.

Heavenly Displays' trial balance as of January 1, the beginning of the current year, is given below:

Cash...	$ 9,000	
Accounts Receivable..........................	30,000	
Raw Materials................................	16,000	
Work in Process	21,000	
Finished Goods...............................	38,000	
Prepaid Insurance	7,000	
Buildings and Equipment	300,000	
Accumulated Depreciation		$128,000
Accounts Payable		60,000
Salaries and Wages Payable		3,000
Capital Stock.................................		200,000
Retained Earnings.............................		30,000
Total	$421,000	$421,000

The company charges manufacturing overhead costs to jobs on the basis of direct labour-hours. (Each customer order for a complete fireworks display is a separate job.) Management estimated that the company would incur $135,000 in manufacturing overhead costs in the fabrication and electronics shops and would work 18,000 direct labour-hours during the year. The following transactions occurred during the year:

a.   Raw materials, consisting mostly of skyrockets, mortar bombs, flares, wiring, and electronic components, were purchased on account: $820,000.

b.   Raw materials were issued to production: $830,000 ($13,000 of this amount was for indirect materials, and the remainder was for direct materials).

c.   Fabrication and electronics shop payrolls were accrued: $200,000 (70% direct labour and 30% indirect labour). A total of 20,800 direct labour-hours were worked during the year.

d.   Selling and administrative salaries were accrued: $150,000.

e.   The company prepaid additional insurance premiums of $38,000 during the year. Prepaid insurance expiring during the year was $40,000 (only $600 relates to selling and administrative; the other $39,400 relates to the fabrication and electronics shops because of the safety hazards involved in handling fireworks).

f.   Marketing cost was incurred: $100,000.

g.   Depreciation charges for the year totalled $40,000 (70% relates to fabrication and electronics shop assets, and 30% relates to selling and administrative assets).

h.   Property taxes were accrued on the shop buildings: $12,600 (credit Accounts Payable).

i.   Manufacturing overhead cost was applied to jobs.

j.   Jobs completed during the year had a total production cost of $1,106,000 according to their job cost sheets.

k.   Revenue (all on account) was $1,420,000. Cost of Goods Sold (before any adjustment for underapplied or overapplied overhead) was $1,120,000.

l.   Cash collections on account from customers totalled $1,415,000.

m.   Cash payments on accounts payable totalled $970,000. Cash payments to employees for salaries and wages totalled $348,000.

Required:

1.   Prepare journal entries for the year's transactions.

2.   Prepare a T-account for each account in the company's trial balance, and enter the opening balances given above. Post your journal entries to the T-accounts. Prepare new T-accounts as needed. Compute the ending balance in each account.

3.   Is manufacturing overhead underapplied or overapplied for the year? Prepare the necessary journal entry to dispose of the balance in the Manufacturing Overhead account.

4.   Prepare an income statement for the year. (Do not prepare a statement of cost of goods manufactured; all of the information needed for the income statement is available in the T-accounts.)

PROBLEM 5–25 Multiple Departments; Applying Overhead [LO3, LO5, LO7]
WoodGrain Technology makes home office furniture from fine hardwoods. The company uses a job-order costing system and predetermined overhead rates to apply manufacturing overhead cost to jobs. The predetermined overhead rate in the Preparation Department is based on machine-hours, and the rate in the Fabrication Department is based on direct materials cost. At the beginning of the year, the company's management made the following estimates for the year:

	Department	
	Preparation	**Fabrication**
Machine-hours	80,000	21,000
Direct labour-hours	35,000	65,000
Direct materials cost	$190,000	$400,000
Direct labour cost	$280,000	$530,000
Manufacturing overhead cost	$416,000	$720,000

Job 127 was started on April 1 and completed on May 12. The company's cost records show the following information concerning the job:

	Department	
	Preparation	Fabrication
Machine-hours	350	70
Direct labour-hours	80	130
Direct materials cost	$940	$1,200
Direct labour cost	$710	$ 980

Required:

1. Compute the predetermined overhead rate used during the year in the Preparation Department. Compute the rate used in the Fabrication Department.
2. Compute the total overhead cost applied to Job 127.
3. What would be the total cost recorded for Job 127? If the job contained 25 units, what would be the unit product cost?
4. At the end of the year, the records of WoodGrain Technology revealed the following *actual* cost and operating data for all jobs worked on during the year:

	Department	
	Preparation	Fabrication
Machine-hours	73,000	24,000
Direct labour-hours	30,000	68,000
Direct materials cost	$165,000	$420,000
Manufacturing overhead cost	$390,000	$740,000

What was the amount of underapplied or overapplied overhead in each department at the end of the year?

> **CHECK FIGURE**
> Predetermined overhead rate for preparation = $520 per machine-hour; Total overhead cost applied = $3,980; Total cost of Job 127 = $7,810.

PROBLEM 5–26 T-Account Analysis of Cost Flows [LO3, LO6, LO7]

Selected ledger accounts for Realm Company are given below for the just-completed year:

Raw Materials

Bal. 1/1	30,000	Credits	?
Debits	420,000		
Bal. 31/12	60,000		

Manufacturing Overhead

Debits	385,000	Credits	?

Work in Process

Bal. 1/1	70,000	Credits	810,000
Direct materials	320,000		
Direct labour	110,000		
Overhead	400,000		
Bal. 31/12	?		

Factory Wages Payable

Debits	179,000	Bal. 1/1	10,000
		Credits	175,000
		Bal. 31/12	6,000

Finished Goods

Bal. 1/1	40,000	Credits	?
Debits	?		
Bal. 31/12	130,000		

Cost of Goods Sold

Debits	?	

Required:

1. What was the cost of raw materials put into production during the year?
2. How much of the materials in (1) consisted of indirect materials?
3. How much of the factory labour cost for the year consisted of indirect labour?
4. What was the cost of goods manufactured for the year?
5. What was the cost of goods sold for the year (before considering underapplied or overapplied overhead)?
6. If overhead is applied to production on the basis of direct materials cost, what rate was in effect during the year?
7. Was manufacturing overhead underapplied or overapplied? By how much?
8. Compute the ending balance in the Work in Process inventory account. Assume that this balance consists entirely of goods started during the year. If $32,000 of this balance is direct materials cost, how much of it is direct labour cost? Manufacturing overhead cost?

PROBLEM 5–27 Schedule of Cost of Goods Manufactured; Overhead Analysis
[LO3, LO5, LO6, LO7]

Calgary Injection Moulding operates a job-order costing system and applies overhead cost to jobs on the basis of machine-hours. In computing an overhead rate for the year, the company's estimates were as follows: manufacturing overhead cost, $248,000, and machine-hours, 40,000. The company has provided the data in the following table:

	Beginning	Ending
Raw Materials.	$21,000	$16,000
Work in Process	$44,000	$40,000
Finished Goods.	$68,000	$60,000

The following actual costs were incurred during the year:

Purchase of raw materials (all direct)	$133,000
Direct labour	$ 80,000
Machine-hours	42,000
Manufacturing overhead costs	$264,000

Required:

1. *a.* Compute the predetermined overhead rate for the year.
   b. Compute the amount of underapplied or overapplied overhead for the year. How is overapplied (underapplied) overhead disposed of at year-end?
2. Prepare a schedule of cost of goods manufactured for the year.
3. Compute the cost of goods sold for the year. (Do not include any underapplied or overapplied overhead in your cost of goods sold figure.)
4. Job 137 was started and completed during the year. What price would have been charged to the customer if the job required $3,200 in materials, $4,200 in direct labour cost, and required 350 machine-hours to complete? Assume the company prices its jobs at 40% above the job's cost according to the accounting system.
5. Direct labour made up $8,000 of the $40,000 ending Work in Process inventory balance. A total of 2,050 machine-hours had been applied to the incomplete units of product included in Work in Process inventory at year-end. Supply the information missing below:

Direct materials.	$?
Direct labour	8,000
Manufacturing overhead	?
Work in process inventory	$40,000

PROBLEM 5–28 Predetermined Overhead Rate; Disposition of Underapplied or Overapplied Overhead [LO3, LO5, LO7]

Gordon Company is highly automated and uses computerized controllers in manufacturing operations. The company uses a job-order costing system and applies manufacturing overhead cost to products on the basis of the time recorded to complete each job by the computerized controllers attached to each machine. The following estimates were used in preparing the predetermined overhead rate at the beginning of the year:

Machine time in hours.	4,000
Manufacturing overhead cost	$230,000

A severe economic recession resulted in cutting back production and a buildup of inventory in the company's warehouse. The company's cost records revealed the following actual cost and operating data for the year:

Machine time in hours.	3,150
Manufacturing overhead cost	$228,000
Inventories at year-end:	
Raw Materials	$ 20,000
Work in Process	$ 32,000
Finished Goods	$530,000
Cost of Goods Sold	$428,000

Required:
1. Compute the company's predetermined overhead rate for the year.
2. Compute the underapplied or overapplied overhead for the year.
3. Prepare the journal entry to show the disposal of under/overapplied overhead.
4. Discuss the impact of an unexpected economic recession on the application of manufacturing overhead.

PROBLEM 5–29 Comprehensive Problem [LO2, LO3, LO4, LO5, LO7]
Gold Nest Company of Hong Kong is a family-owned enterprise that makes souvenirs for the tourist market. The company sells through an extensive network of trading companies that receive commissions on their sales. Transactions occur in Hong Kong dollars ($).

The company uses a job-order costing system in which overhead is applied to jobs on the basis of direct labour cost. It budgeted $330,000 of manufacturing overhead and estimated direct labour cost to be $200,000 in total this fiscal year. On July 1, the start of the company's fiscal year, inventory account balances were as follows:

Raw Materials	$25,000
Work in Process	$10,000
Finished Goods	$40,000

During the year, the following transactions were completed:
a. Raw materials were purchased on account: $275,000.
b. Raw materials were requisitioned for use in production: $280,000 (materials costing $220,000 were chargeable directly to jobs; the remaining materials were indirect).
c. Costs for employee services were incurred as follows:

Direct materials.	$180,000
Indirect labour.	$ 72,000
Sales commissions	$ 63,000
Administrative salaries	$ 90,000

d. Rent during the year: $75,000 ($60,000 of this amount related to factory operations, and the remainder related to administrative activities).
e. Utility costs were incurred in the factory: $57,000.
f. Advertising costs were incurred: $14,000.
g. Depreciation was recorded on equipment: $100,000 ($88,000 of this amount was on equipment used in factory operations; the remaining $12,000 was on equipment used in selling and administrative activities).

h.   Manufacturing overhead cost was applied to jobs: $_____?
i.   Goods that had cost $675,000 to manufacture according to their job cost sheets were completed.
j.   Sales (all on account) to customers during the year totalled $1,250,000. These goods cost $700,000 to manufacture according to their job cost sheets.

Required:
1.   Prepare journal entries to record the transactions for the year.
2.   Prepare T-accounts for inventories, Manufacturing Overhead, and Cost of Goods Sold. Post relevant data from your journal entries to these T-accounts (don't forget to enter the opening balances in your inventory accounts). Compute an ending balance in each account.
3.   Is Manufacturing Overhead underapplied or overapplied for the year? Prepare a journal entry to properly dispose of any balance in the Manufacturing Overhead account. If overhead is overapplied, use the entire cost of manufacturing to allocate the overapplied portion to the appropriate accounts.
4.   Prepare an income statement for the year. (Do not prepare a schedule of cost of goods manufactured; all of the information needed for the income statement is available in the journal entries and T-accounts you have prepared.)

> **CHECK FIGURE**
> Predetermined
> overhead rate =
> 165% of direct
> labour cost;
> Manufacturing over-
> head underapplied
> by $40,000.

PROBLEM 5–30 Comprehensive Problem: Journal Entries; T-Accounts; Financial Statements [LO3, LO4, LO5, LO6, LO7]

Oil Field Equipment Company is a small company that manufactures specialty heavy equipment for use in Alberta oil-fields. The company uses a job-order costing system and applies manufacturing overhead cost to jobs on the basis of the direct labour-hours. At the beginning of the current year, the following estimates were made to compute the predetermined overhead rate: manufacturing overhead cost, $360,000, and 900 direct labour-hours. The following transactions took place during the year (all purchases and services were acquired on account):

a.   Raw materials were purchased for use in production: $200,000.
b.   Raw materials were requisitioned for use in production (all direct materials): $185,000.
c.   Utility bills were incurred in the factory: $70,000 (90% related to factory operations and the remaining related to administrative activities).
d.   Costs for salaries and wages were incurred as follows:

Direct labour (975 hours)	$230,000
Indirect labour.	$ 90,000
Selling and administrative salaries	$110,000

e.   Maintenance costs were incurred in the factory: $54,000.
f.   Advertising costs were incurred: $136,000.
g.   Depreciation was recorded for the year: $95,000 (80% relates to factory assets, and the remainder relates to selling and administrative equipment).
h.   Rental cost was incurred on buildings: $120,000 (85% of the space is occupied by the factory, and the remainder is related to selling and administration facilities).
i.   Manufacturing overhead cost was applied to jobs: $_____?
j.   Cost of goods manufactured for the year was $770,000.
k.   Sales for the year (all on account) totalled $1,200,000. These goods cost $800,000 according to their job cost sheets.

The balances in the inventory accounts at the beginning of the year were as follows:

Raw Materials.	$30,000
Work in Process	$21,000
Finished Goods	$60,000

Required:
1.   Prepare journal entries to record the above data.
2.   Post your entries to T-accounts. (Don't forget to enter the opening inventory balances above.) Determine the ending balances in the inventory accounts and in the Manufacturing Overhead account.
3.   Prepare a schedule of cost of goods manufactured.
4.   Prepare a journal entry to properly dispose of any balance in the Manufacturing Overhead account. Prepare a schedule of cost of goods sold.

5. Prepare an income statement for the year.
6. Job 412 was one of many jobs started and completed during the year. The job required $8,000 in direct materials and 39 hours of direct labour time at a total direct labour cost of $9,200. The job contained only four units. If the company billed at a price of 60% above the unit product cost on the job cost sheet, what price per unit would have been charged to the customer?

PROBLEM 5–31 Plantwide versus Departmental Overhead Rates; Underapplied or Overapplied Overhead [LO3, LO5, LO7]

"Don't tell me we've lost another bid!" exclaimed Janice Hudson, president of Prime Products Inc. "I'm afraid so," replied Doug Martin, the operations vice president. "One of our competitors underbid us by about $10,000 on the Hastings job." "I just can't figure it out," said Hudson. "It seems we're either too high to get the job or too low to make any money on half the jobs we bid. What's happened?"

Prime Products manufactures specialized goods to customers' specifications and operates a job-order costing system. Manufacturing overhead cost is applied to jobs on the basis of direct labour cost. The following estimates were made at the beginning of the year:

	Cutting	Machining	Assembly	Total Plant
		Department		
Direct labour	$300,000	$200,000	$400,000	$ 900,000
Manufacturing overhead	$540,000	$800,000	$100,000	$1,440,000

Jobs require varying amounts of work in the three departments. The Hastings job, for example, would have required manufacturing costs in the three departments as follows:

	Cutting	Machining	Assembly	Total Plant
		Department		
Direct material	$12,000	$ 900	$ 5,600	$18,500
Direct labour	$ 6,500	$1,700	$13,000	$21,200
Manufacturing overhead	?	?	?	?

The company uses a plantwide overhead rate to apply manufacturing overhead cost to jobs.

Required:
1. Assuming the use of a plantwide overhead rate:
    a. Compute the rate for the current year.
    b. Determine the amount of manufacturing overhead cost that would have been applied to the Hastings job.
2. Suppose that instead of using a plantwide overhead rate, the company had used a separate predetermined overhead rate in each department. Under these conditions:
    a. Compute the rate for each department for the current year.
    b. Determine the amount of manufacturing overhead cost that would have been applied to the Hastings job.
3. Explain the difference between the manufacturing overhead that would have been applied to the Hastings job using the plantwide rate in 1(b) above and using the departmental rates in 2(b).
4. Assume that it is customary in the industry to bid jobs at 150% of total manufacturing cost (direct materials, direct labour, and applied overhead). What was the company's bid price on the Hastings job? What would the bid price have been if departmental overhead rates had been used to apply overhead cost?
5. At the end of the year, the company assembled the following *actual* cost data relating to all jobs worked on during the year:

	Cutting	Machining	Assembly	Total Plant
		Department		
Direct material	$760,000	$ 90,000	$410,000	$1,260,000
Direct labour	$320,000	$210,000	$340,000	$ 870,000
Manufacturing overhead	$560,000	$830,000	$ 92,000	$1,482,000

Compute the underapplied or overapplied overhead for the year (*a*) assuming that a plantwide overhead rate is used, and (*b*) assuming that departmental overhead rates are used.

PROBLEM 5–32 Comprehensive Problem [LO3, LO4, LO5, LO7]
Mountain Manufacturing Company produces custom stamped metal parts for a variety of customers in Western Canada. During January, the company had two jobs in process. Job A was an order for 1,200 stamped parts and was started in December. Job A had $12,000 of manufacturing costs already accumulated on January 1. Job B was an order for 1,000 stamped parts and was started in January.

The company used a job-order costing system. Total manufacturing overhead for the year was estimated to be $576,000. Mountain Manufacturing uses direct labour-hours as the allocation base to establish its predetermined overhead rate. A total of 19,200 direct labour-hours are expected to be worked during the year. On January 1, the start of the company's fiscal year, inventory account balances were as follows:

Raw Materials......................................	$15,000
Work in Process	$12,000
Finished Goods....................................	$10,000

During the month of January, the following transactions were completed:
a. Raw materials were purchased for $30,000.
b. Raw materials were requisitioned for use in production in the amount of $35,000. Of this amount, $25,000 was related to manufacturing ($5,000 for Job A and $20,000 for Job B) and the rest were indirect materials.
c. In January, $32,000 of direct labour ($7,000 for Job A and $25,000 for Job B). In addition, $2,000 of indirect labour costs were incurred.
d. In January, the company incurred the following general factory costs: Utilities expense of $8,000, rent on factory equipment of $8,000, and insurance costs of $1,900.
e. The company recognized $10,000 in depreciation on factory equipment.
f. The company applied manufacturing overhead to Job A and Job B. A total of 350 direct labour-hours were spent completing Job A and 1,250 direct labour-hours were recorded for Job B.
g. Administrative salaries of $30,000 were paid in January.
h. Selling expenses totalled $6,000 in January.
i. Job A was completed in January. The completed cost of Job A according to the job cost sheet was $34,500. Job B remains in process at the end of January.
j. Sales of all 1,200 units in Job A were recorded on account in the amount of $48,300 in January.

Required:
1. Prepare journal entries to record the transactions for January.
2. Prepare T-accounts. Determine ending balances in the inventory accounts and in the Manufacturing Overhead account.
3. Prepare a schedule of cost of goods manufactured.
4. Prepare a journal entry to properly dispose of any balance in the Manufacturing Overhead account. Determine the adjusted Cost of Goods Sold.
5. Prepare an income statement for the month of January.

CASES

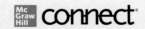

CASE 5–33 Critical Thinking; Interpretation of Manufacturing Overhead Rates [LO3, LO5]
Sharpton Fabricators Corporation manufactures a variety of parts for the automotive industry. The company uses a job-order costing system with a plantwide predetermined overhead rate based on direct labour-hours. On December 10, 2019, the company's controller made a preliminary estimate of the predetermined overhead rate for 2020. The new rate was based on the estimated total manufacturing overhead cost of $3,402,000 and the estimated 63,000 total direct labour-hours for 2020:

$$\text{Predetermined overhead rate} = \frac{\$3,402,000}{63,000 \text{ hours}}$$
$$= \$54 \text{ per direct labour-hour}$$

This new predetermined overhead rate was communicated to top managers in a meeting on December 11. The rate did not cause any comment because it was within a few cents of the overhead rate that had been used during 2019. One of the subjects discussed at the meeting was a proposal by the production manager to purchase an automated milling machine centre built by Central Robotics. The president of Sharpton Fabricators, Kevin Reynolds, agreed to meet with the regional sales representative from Central Robotics to discuss the proposal.

On the day following the meeting, Reynolds met with Jay Warner, Central Robotics' sales representative. The following discussion took place:

Reynolds: Lisa Winter, our production manager, asked me to meet with you since she's interested in installing an automated milling machine centre. Frankly, I'm skeptical. You're going to have to show me this isn't just another expensive toy for Lisa's people to play with.

Warner: That shouldn't be too difficult, Kevin. The automated milling machine centre has three major advantages. First, it's much faster than the manual methods you're using. It can process about twice as many parts per hour as your current milling machines. Second, it's much more flexible. There are some up-front programming costs, but once those have been incurred, almost no setup is required on the machines for standard operations. You just punch in the code of the standard operation, load the machine's hopper with raw material, and the machine does the rest.

Reynolds: Yeah, but what about cost? Having twice the capacity in the milling machine area won't do us much good. That centre is idle much of the time, anyway.

Warner: I was getting there. The third advantage of the automated milling machine centre is lower cost. Winter and I looked over your present operations, and we estimated that the automated equipment would eliminate the need for about 6,000 direct labour-hours a year. What is your direct labour cost per hour?

Reynolds: The wage rate in the milling area averages about $32 per hour. Fringe benefits raise that figure to about $41 per hour.

Warner: Don't forget your overhead.

Reynolds: Next year the overhead rate will be about $54 per direct labour-hour.

Warner: So including fringe benefits and overhead, the cost per direct labour-hour is about $95.

Reynolds: That's right.

Warner: Since you can save 6,000 direct labour-hours per year, the cost savings would amount to about $570,000 a year, and our 60-month lease plan would require payments of only $348,000 per year.

Reynolds: Sold! When can you install the equipment?

Shortly after this meeting, Reynolds informed the company's controller of the decision to lease the new equipment, which would be installed over the Christmas vacation period. The controller realized that this decision would require a recomputation of the predetermined overhead rate for 2020, since the decision would affect both the manufacturing overhead and the direct labour-hours for the year. After talking with both the production manager and the sales representative from Central Robotics, the controller discovered that in addition to the annual lease cost of $348,000, the new machine would also require a skilled technician/programmer who would have to be hired at a cost of $50,000 per year to maintain and program the equipment. Both of these costs would be included in factory overhead. There would be no other changes in total manufacturing overhead cost, which is almost entirely fixed. The controller assumed that the new machine would result in a reduction of 6,000 direct labour-hours for the year from the levels that had initially been planned.

When the revised predetermined overhead rate for 2020 was circulated among the company's top managers, there was considerable dismay.

Required:
1. Recompute the predetermined rate assuming that the new machine will be installed. Explain why the new predetermined overhead rate is higher (or lower) than the rate that was originally estimated for 2020.
2. What effect (if any) would this new rate have on the cost of jobs that do not use the new automated milling machine?
3. Why would managers be concerned about the new overhead rate?
4. After seeing the new predetermined overhead rate, the production manager admitted that he probably wouldn't be able to eliminate all of the 6,000 direct labour-hours. He had been hoping to accomplish the reduction by not replacing workers who retire or quit, but that would not be possible. As a result, the real labour savings would only be about 2,000 hours—one worker. In the light of this additional information, evaluate the original decision to acquire the automated milling machine from Central Robotics.

CASE 5–34 Single versus Multiple Overhead Application Rates [LO3, LO5]

Foster Appliance Repair has developed a reputation over many years of providing high-quality, reliable repair services at a fair price. The company has grown from a two-person operation (run by Victor Foster and his wife Sally Jones) to a much larger company employing Foster and Jones as well as four skilled repair personnel and two service technicians. Jones manages the front office and prepares all accounting-related records for the company. Recently, Jones has noticed a decline in profits generated by the repair business. Foster has also noticed some decline in the number of repairs completed over the past few months. He believes this reduction may be due to increased competition from a new repair shop in the area. Since pricing is based to a large degree on the cost of repairs, Foster asked Jones to spend some time analyzing how repair costs were charged to jobs, to better understand the problem. He was quick to remind Jones that he was committed to keeping all personnel on fixed salaries since he believes this allows him to keep good employees and encourages loyalty to the company.

Jones collected the following information about the costing system:

- Direct materials used in repairs are charged directly to the job.
- The four repair personnel are paid a fixed salary of $50,000 per year, and the two technicians are paid a fixed salary of $38,000 per year. Jones estimates that each of the six repair personnel works 1,750 hours per year on customer jobs.
- Other budgeted indirect support costs for the year (e.g., rent, insurance, utilities, supplies, repair van maintenance, repair van depreciation) total $178,450, including Foster's and Jones's salaries.
- The price for each job is calculated on a cost-plus basis. Customers pay the total cost to complete the job plus a markup of 10%.
- The total cost for each job is calculated as follows: total direct material cost plus the "shop rate" × number of repair hours to complete the job. The shop rate is applied to all types of repair jobs. The shop rate is calculated as the sum of the repair personnel salaries plus budgeted indirect support costs for the year divided by the estimated total hours to be worked on customer jobs for the year.
- Jones noted that about 65% of total indirect costs related to complex repairs over the last couple of years, while the other 35% of total indirect costs related to simpler repairs. Even so, about half of the total time worked on customer jobs by repair personnel and technicians was related to complex repairs, while the other half was related to simple repairs. While Jones believed this was important information, she realized it was not taken into account when calculating the overall shop rate for the year.

Required:
1. Calculate the shop rate for the year based on the above information gathered by Jones.
2. Use the information gathered by Jones about the proportion of complex and simple repairs each year to calculate different shop rates that could be applied to complex and simple repair work.
3. Consider Job 1246 completed by Foster Appliance Repair last month. The job cost sheet indicates $115 cost of direct materials plus 6 hours of labour time × the shop rate.
   a. Calculate the total price charged to the customer, assuming a 10% markup on cost.
   b. By doing a little more digging, Jones was able to determine that 2 of the 6 hours spent on Job 1246 were related to complex repairs, while 4 of the 6 hours spent on the job were related to simple repairs. Use this information and the two shop rates calculated in (2) above to estimate the price that would have been charged for Job 1246 under this new system.
4. Using all of the information gathered to this point, explain why Foster Appliance Repair may be selling fewer repairs, resulting in lower profitability.

INSTANT QUIZ SOLUTIONS

5–1
Job-order: architectural services, custom homes, tax return preparation services; Process: bottled water, house paint, gasoline, litres of milk.

5–2
Predetermined overhead rate = $350,000 ÷ 4,000 MH = $87.50 per MH. Overhead applied to Job 427B = 250 MH × $87.50 = $21,875.

5–3
Some production costs, such as a factory manager's salary, cannot be traced to a particular product or job but rather are incurred as a result of overall production activities. In addition, some production costs, such as indirect materials, cannot easily be traced to jobs. If these costs are to be assigned to products, they must be allocated to the products.

5–4

If actual manufacturing overhead cost is applied to jobs, then the company must wait until the end of the accounting period to apply overhead and to cost jobs. If the company computes actual overhead rates more frequently to get around this problem, the rates may fluctuate widely. Overhead cost tends to be incurred somewhat evenly from month to month (due to the presence of fixed costs), whereas production activity often fluctuates. The result is high overhead rates in periods with low activity and low overhead rates in periods with high activity. For these reasons, most companies use predetermined overhead rates to apply manufacturing overhead costs to jobs. In addition, applying overhead via a predetermined rate is relatively easy to apply and simplifies record-keeping.

5–5

When actual overhead turns out to be less than estimated (i.e., overhead is overapplied), this amount should not all be charged to income this period since inventory will be undervalued on the balance sheet. These actual costs, if allocated to WIP and Finished Goods inventory, will then be charged against income when the related goods are sold, better satisfying the matching principle.

5–6

Multiple predetermined overhead rates are typically more accurate than plantwide overhead rates. Even so, a manager may choose to use the plantwide (less accurate) rate if the cost of collecting and maintaining the data required to keep track of the multiple rates is expected to be greater than the benefits of doing so. Benefits in this case are usually judged by answering the question "Would my decisions change if I had the more detailed information?" If no, then the cost to collect and report such information would be considered greater than the benefit.

■ APPENDIX 5A: THE PREDETERMINED OVERHEAD RATE AND CAPACITY

LEARNING OBJECTIVE 8

Explain the implications of basing the predetermined overhead rate on activity at full capacity rather than on estimated activity for the period.

Companies typically base their predetermined overhead rates on the estimated, or budgeted, amount of the allocation base for the upcoming period. This is the method that is used in the chapter, but it is a practice that has recently come under severe criticism. An example will be very helpful in understanding why. Harmony Corporation manufactures music CDs for local recording studios. The company has a CD-duplicating machine that can produce a new CD every 10 seconds from a master CD. The company leases the CD-duplicating machine for $180,000 per year, and this is the company's only manufacturing overhead. With allowances for setups and maintenance, the machine is theoretically capable of producing up to 900,000 CDs per year. However, due to weak retail sales of CDs, the company's commercial customers are unlikely to order more than 600,000 CDs next year. The company uses machine time as the allocation base for applying manufacturing overhead. These data are summarized below:

Harmony Corporation Data	
Total manufacturing overhead cost.....................	$180,000 per year
Allocation base: Machine time per CD.................	10 seconds per CD
Capacity	900,000 CDs per year
Budgeted output for next year........................	600,000 CDs

If Harmony follows common practice and computes its predetermined overhead rate using estimated, or budgeted, figures, then its predetermined overhead rate for next year will be $0.03 per second of machine time, computed as follows:

$$\frac{\text{Estimated total manufacturing overhead cost, \$180,000}}{\text{Estimated total units in the allocation base, 600,000 CDs} \times 10 \text{ seconds per CD}} = \$0.03 \text{ per second}$$

Since each CD requires 10 seconds of machine time, each CD will be charged $0.30 of overhead cost.

Critics charge that there are two problems with this procedure. First, if predetermined overhead rates are based on budgeted activity, then the unit product costs will fluctuate, depending on the budgeted level of activity for the period. For example, if the budgeted output for the year was only 300,000 CDs, the predetermined overhead rate would be $0.06 per second of machine time or $0.60 per CD rather than $0.30 per CD. In general, if budgeted output falls, the overhead cost per unit will increase; it will appear that the CDs cost more to make. Managers may then be tempted to increase prices at the worst possible time—just as demand is falling.

Second, critics charge that under the traditional approach, products are charged for resources that they do not use. When the fixed costs of capacity are spread over estimated activity, the units produced must shoulder the costs of unused capacity. That is why the applied overhead cost per unit increases as the level of activity falls. The critics argue that products should be charged only for the capacity that they use; they should not be charged for the capacity they do not use. This can be accomplished by basing the predetermined overhead rate on capacity as follows:

$$\frac{\text{Total manufacturing overhead cost at capacity, \$180,000}}{\text{Total units in the allocation base at capacity, 900,000 CDs} \times 10 \text{ seconds per CD}} = \$0.02 \text{ per second}$$

Since the predetermined overhead rate is $0.02 per second, the overhead cost applied to each CD will be $0.20. This charge is constant and is not affected by the level of activity during a period. If output falls, the charge will still be $0.20 per CD.

The use of capacity will almost certainly result in underapplied overhead. If actual output at Harmony Corporation is 600,000 CDs, then only $120,000 of overhead cost will be applied to products ($0.20 per CD × 600,000 CDs). Since the actual overhead cost is $180,000, there will be underapplied overhead of $60,000. In another departure from tradition, the critics suggest that the underapplied overhead that results from idle capacity should be separately disclosed on the income statement as the Cost of Unused Capacity—a period expense. Disclosing this cost as a lump sum on the income statement, rather than burying it in Cost of Goods Sold or ending inventories, makes it much more visible to managers.

Official pronouncements (IAS 2) prohibit basing predetermined overhead rates on capacity for external reports, although predetermined overhead rates based on capacity could be used for internal reporting. If so, managers would need to judge the benefits in terms of improved decision making against the potential cost of having to calculate inventory values and the Cost of Goods Sold using one method for external reporting and a different method for internal reporting.

■ APPENDIX 5A SUMMARY

- In this appendix, we have calculated the overhead application rate using a denominator equal to budgeted or estimated amount of the allocation base for the period. **[LO8]**
- Critics argue that this means the application rate for manufacturing overhead will fluctuate as the budgeted amount of the allocation base fluctuates from period to period. **[LO8]**
- Instead, it is suggested that the predetermined overhead rate should be based on total units of the allocation base at capacity. **[LO8]**
- The result will almost always be underapplied overhead, since most firms do not operate at full capacity all of the time. **[LO8]**
- Managers may wish to separate out underapplied overhead resulting from idle capacity in the income statement as the Cost of Unused Capacity, making it much more visible to managers and reminding them that unused capacity could be managed better in the next period. **[LO8]**

■ APPENDIX 5A QUESTIONS, EXERCISES, PROBLEMS, AND CASES

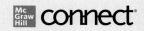

5A–1   If the plant is operated at less than capacity and the predetermined overhead rate is based on the estimated total units in the allocation base at capacity, will overhead ordinarily be overapplied or underapplied?

5A–2   Define the Cost of Unused Capacity and discuss why it might be calculated.

EXERCISE 5A–1 Overhead Rates and Capacity Issues [LO3, LO5, LO7, LO8]
Estate Pension Services helps clients set up and administer pension plans that comply with tax laws and regulatory requirements. The firm uses a job-order costing system in which overhead is applied to clients' accounts on the basis of professional staff-hours charged to the accounts. Data concerning two previous years appear below:

	20X1	20X2
Estimated professional staff-hours to be charged to clients' accounts	2,400	2,250
Estimated overhead cost	$144,000	$144,000
Professional staff-hours available	3,000	3,000

"Professional staff-hours available" is a measure of the capacity of the firm. Any hours available that are not charged to clients' accounts represent unused capacity.

Required:
1. Jennifer Miyami is an established client whose pension plan was set up many years ago. In both 20X1 and 20X2, only five hours of professional staff time were charged to Miyami's account. If the company bases its predetermined overhead rate on the estimated overhead cost and the estimated professional staff-hours to be charged to clients, how much overhead cost would have been applied to Miyami's account in 20X1? In 20X2?
2. Suppose that the company bases its predetermined overhead rate on the estimated overhead cost and the estimated professional staff-hours to be charged to clients as in (1) above. Also suppose that the actual professional staff-hours charged to clients' accounts and the actual overhead costs turn out to be exactly as estimated in both years. By how much would the overhead be underapplied or overapplied in 20X1? In 20X2?
3. Refer back to the data concerning Miyami in (1) above. If the company bases its predetermined overhead rate on the estimated overhead cost and the professional staff-hours available, how much overhead cost would have been applied to Miyami's account in 20X1? In 20X2?

4. Suppose that the company bases its predetermined overhead rate on the estimated overhead cost and the professional staff-hours available as in (3) above. Also suppose that the actual professional staff-hours charged to clients' accounts and the actual overhead costs turn out to be exactly as estimated in both years. By how much would the overhead be underapplied or overapplied in 20X1? In 20X2?

PROBLEM 5A–2 Predetermined Overhead Rate and Capacity [LO3, LO5, LO7, LO8]

Alderberry Recording Inc. is a small audio recording studio. The company handles work for advertising agencies—primarily for radio ads—and has a few singers and bands as clients. Alderberry Recording handles all aspects of recording, from editing to making a digital master. The competition in the audio recording industry has always been tough, but it has been getting even tougher over the last several years. The studio has been losing customers to newer studios that are equipped with more up-to-date equipment and are able to offer very attractive prices and excellent service. Summary data concerning the last two years of operations follow:

	20X1	20X2
Estimated hours of studio service	1,000	750
Estimated studio overhead cost	$90,000	$90,000
Actual hours of studio service provided	900	600
Actual studio overhead cost incurred	$90,000	$90,000
Hours of studio service at capacity	1,800	1,800

The company applies studio overhead to recording jobs on the basis of the hours of studio service provided. For example, 30 hours of studio time were required to record, edit, and master the *Fire* album for a local band. All of the studio overhead is fixed, and the actual overhead cost incurred was exactly as estimated at the beginning of the year in both 20X1 and 20X2.

Required:

1. Alderberry Recording computes its predetermined overhead rate at the beginning of each year based on the estimated studio overhead and the estimated hours of studio service for the year. How much overhead would have been applied to the *Fire* job if it had been done in 20X1? In 20X2? By how much would overhead have been underapplied or overapplied in 20X1? In 20X2?

2. The president of Alderberry Recording has heard that some companies in the industry have changed to a system of computing the predetermined overhead rate at the beginning of each year based on the estimated studio overhead for the year and the hours of studio service that could be provided at capacity. He would like to know what effect this method would have on job costs. How much overhead would have been applied using this method to the *Fire* job if it had been done in 20X1? In 20X2? By how much would overhead have been underapplied or overapplied in 20X1 using this method? In 20X2?

3. How would you interpret the underapplied or overapplied overhead that results from using studio-hours at capacity to compute the predetermined overhead rate?

4. What fundamental business problem is Alderberry Recording facing? Which method of computing the predetermined overhead rate is likely to be more helpful in facing this problem? Explain.

CASE 5A–3 Ethics; Predetermined Overhead Rate and Capacity [LO5, LO8]

Melissa Loester, the new controller of PowerDrives Inc., has just returned from a seminar on the choice of the activity level in the predetermined overhead rate. Even though the subject did not sound exciting at first, she found that there were some important ideas presented that should get a hearing at her company. After returning from the seminar, she arranged a meeting with the production manager, Jan Laird, and the assistant production manager, Lonny Lee.

Loester: I ran across an idea that I wanted to check out with both of you. It's about the way we compute predetermined overhead rates.

Laird: We're all ears.

Loester: We compute the predetermined overhead rate by dividing the estimated total factory overhead for the coming year by the estimated total units produced for the coming year.

Lee: We've been doing that as long as I've been with the company.

Laird: And it has been done that way at every other company I've worked at, except at most places they divide by direct labour-hours.

Loester: We use units because it is simpler and we basically make one product with minor variations. But, there's another way to do it. Instead of dividing the estimated total factory overhead by the estimated total units produced for the coming year, we could divide by the total units produced at capacity.

Lee: Oh, the Marketing Department will love that. It will drop the costs on all of our products. They'll go wild over there cutting prices.

Loester: That is a worry, but I wanted to talk to both of you first before going over to Marketing.

Laird: Aren't you always going to have a lot of underapplied overhead?

Loester: That's correct, but let me show you how we would handle it. Here's an example based on our budget for next year:

Budgeted (estimated) production............................	80,000 units
Budgeted sales..	80,000 units
Capacity...	100,000 units
Selling price...	$70 per unit
Variable manufacturing cost	$18 per unit
Total manufacturing overhead cost (all fixed).............	$2,000,000
Selling and administrative expenses (all fixed)...........	$1,950,000
Beginning inventories	$0

Traditional approach to computing the predetermined overhead rate:

$$\text{Predetermined overhead rate} = \frac{\text{Estimated total manufacturing overhead cost}}{\text{Estimated total amount of the allocation base}}$$

$$= \frac{\$2,000,000}{80,000 \text{ units}} = \$25 \text{ per unit}$$

Budgeted Income Statement

Revenue (80,000 units × $70 per unit)......................	$5,600,000	
Cost of goods sold:		
Variable manufacturing		
(80,000 units × $18 per unit)	$1,440,000	
Manufacturing overhead		
applied (80,000 units × $25 per unit)....................	2,000,000	3,440,000
Gross margin...	2,160,000	
Selling and administrative expenses........................	1,950,000	
Operating income	$ 210,000	

New approach to computing the predetermined overhead rate using capacity in the denominator:

$$\text{Predetermined overhead rate} = \frac{\text{Estimated total manufacturing overhead cost at capacity}}{\text{Estimated total amount of the allocation base at capacity}}$$

$$= \frac{\$2,000,000}{100,000 \text{ units}} = \$20 \text{ per unit}$$

Budgeted Income Statement

Revenue (80,000 units × $70 per unit)......................	$5,600,000	
Cost of goods sold:		
Variable manufacturing		
(80,000 units × $18 per unit)	$1,440,000	
Manufacturing overhead applied		
(80,000 units × $20 per unit)	1,600,000	3,040,000
Gross margin...	2,560,000	
Cost of unused capacity		
[(100,000 units − 80,000 units) × $20 per unit]	400,000	
Selling and administrative expenses........................	1,950,000	
Operating income	$ 210,000	

Laird: Whoa!! I don't think I like the looks of that "Cost of unused capacity." If that thing shows up on the income statement, someone from headquarters is likely to come down here looking for some people to lay off.

Lee: I'm worried about something else, too. What happens when sales are not up to expectations? Can we pull the "hat trick"?

Loester: I'm sorry, I don't understand.

Laird: Lonny's talking about something that happens fairly regularly. When sales are down and profits look like they are going to be lower than the president told the owners they were going to be, the president comes down here and asks us to deliver some more profits.

Lee: And we pull them out of our hat.

Laird: Yeah, we just increase production until we get the profits we want.

Loester: I still don't understand. You mean you increase sales?

Laird: Nope, we increase production. We're the production managers, not the sales managers.

Loester: I get it. Since you have produced more, the sales force has more units it can sell.

Laird: Nope, the marketing people don't do a thing. We just build inventories and that does the trick.

Required:

In all of the questions below, assume that the predetermined overhead rate under the traditional method is $25 per unit, and under the new method it is $20 per unit. Also assume that under the traditional method (used for internal reporting), any underapplied or overapplied overhead is taken directly to the income statement as an adjustment to Cost of Goods Sold. Assume the company has decided to use these overhead methods for internal reporting.

1. Suppose actual production is 80,000 units. Compute the operating incomes that would be realized under the traditional and new methods if actual sales are 75,000 units and everything else turns out as expected.

2. How many units would have to be produced under each of the methods in order to realize the budgeted operating income of $210,000 if actual sales are 75,000 units and everything else turns out as expected?

3. What effect does the new method based on capacity have on the volatility of operating income?

4. Will the "hat trick" be easier or harder to perform if the new method based on capacity is used?

5. Do you think the "hat trick" is ethical?

SYSTEMS DESIGN: PROCESS COSTING

After studying Chapter 6, you should be able to

1. Record the flow of materials, labour, and overhead through a process costing system.

2. Compute the equivalent units of production using the weighted-average method.

3. Compute the cost per equivalent unit using the weighted-average method.

4. Assign costs to units using the weighted-average method.

5. Prepare a cost reconciliation report accounting for the costs transferred out and the costs in work in process inventory at the end of the period using the weighted-average method.

6. (Appendix 6A) Compute the equivalent units of production using the FIFO method.

7. (Appendix 6A) Compute the cost per equivalent unit using the FIFO method.

8. (Appendix 6A) Prepare a cost reconciliation report accounting for the costs transferred out and the costs in work in process inventory at the end of the period using the FIFO method.

9. (Online Appendix 6B) Compute the cost of lost units or shrinkage.

■ COSTING THE "QUICKER-PICKER-UPPER"

Shutterstock / Bukhanovskyy

Procter & Gamble (P&G) manufactures Bounty paper towels in two main processing departments—Paper Making and Paper Converting. In this type of manufacturing environment, costs cannot be readily traced to individual rolls of Bounty; however, given the homogeneous nature of the product, the total costs incurred in each department can be spread uniformly across the number of cases of Bounty produced. P&G uses a similar costing approach for many of its products, such as Tide laundry detergent, Crest toothpaste, and Pringles chips.

A s explained in Chapter 5, there are two basic costing systems in use: job-order costing and process costing. A job-order costing system is used in situations where many different jobs or products are worked on each period. Examples of industries that typically use job-order costing are furniture manufacturers; special-order printers; shipbuilders; and many types of service organizations, such as repair shops and professional accounting services.

By contrast, process costing is most commonly used in industries that produce essentially homogeneous (i.e., uniform) products on a continuous basis, such as bricks, corn flakes, pop, and paper. Process costing is particularly used in companies that convert basic raw materials into homogeneous products, such as Alcan (aluminum ingots), Kimberly-Clark (toilet paper), Dover Industries (flour), Imperial Oil (gasoline and lubricating oils), and Christie (crackers). A form of process costing may also be used by utilities that produce gas, water, and electricity. In the service sector, process costing is also applied in settings where a large number of similar transactions are processed in bulk. For example, Visa could use process costing to understand the cost of processing credit card transactions, Sun Life could use process costing to understand the cost of processing simple health benefit claims, and Canada Post could use process costing to understand the cost to ship each kilogram of mail to different regions of the country. As suggested by the length of this list, process costing is in very wide use.

Our purpose in this chapter is to extend the discussion of product costing to include a process costing system.

■ COMPARISON OF JOB-ORDER AND PROCESS COSTING

Much of what you learned in the preceding chapter about costing and cost flows applies equally well to process costing in this chapter. We are not throwing out all that you have learned about costing and starting from scratch with a whole new system. The similarities that exist between job-order and process costing can be summarized as follows:

1.   Both systems have the same basic purposes—to assign materials, labour, and overhead costs to products and to provide a mechanism for computing unit costs.
2.   Both systems use the same basic manufacturing accounts, including Manufacturing Overhead, Raw Materials, Work in Process, and Finished Goods.
3.   The flow of costs through the manufacturing accounts is basically the same in both systems.

The differences between job-order and process costing arise from two factors. The first is that the flow of units in a process costing system is more or less continuous, and the second is that these units are indistinguishable from one another. Under process costing, it makes no sense to try to identify materials, labour, and overhead costs with a particular order from a customer (as we did with job-order costing), since each order is just one of many that are filled from a continuous flow of virtually identical units from the production line. Under process costing, we accumulate costs *by department*, rather than by order, and assign these costs equally to all units that pass through the department during a period.

A further difference between the two costing systems is that the job cost sheet is not used in process costing, since the focal point of that method is departments. Instead of using job cost sheets, a document known as a **production report** is prepared for each department in which work is done on products. The production report serves several functions. It summarizes the number of units moving through a department during a period, and it also provides a computation of unit costs. In addition, it shows what costs were charged to the department and how these costs were disposed. The department production report is the key document in a process costing system.

Production report
A report that summarizes all activity in a department's Work in Process account during a period and that contains three parts: a quantity schedule and a computation of equivalent units, a computation of total and unit costs, and a cost reconciliation.

Job-Order Costing	Process Costing
1. Many different jobs are worked on during each period, with each job having different production requirements.	1. A single product is produced either on a continuous basis or in long production runs. All units of product are identical.
2. Costs are accumulated by individual job, regardless of the accounting period during which the work is done.	2. Costs are accumulated by department, during an accounting period.
3. The *job cost sheet* is the key document controlling the accumulation of costs by a job.	3. The *department production report* is the key document showing the accumulation and disposition of costs by a department.
4. Unit costs are computed *by job* on the job cost sheet.	4. Unit costs are computed *by department* on the department production report.

EXHIBIT 6–1
Differences between Job-Order and Process Costing

The major differences between job-order and process costing are summarized in Exhibit 6–1.

INSTANT QUIZ 6–1
Smith Paper Mill has two main product lines: newsprint that is produced and sold in standard rolls to newspaper publishers, and specialty papers that are made to order with special colours or finishes as defined by customers' needs. What costing system would you advise the company to use for these product lines: job order or process costing? Why?

■ PROCESS COST FLOWS

Before presenting a detailed example of process costing, it is useful to see how manufacturing costs flow through a process costing system.

Processing Departments

A **processing department** is part of an organization where work is performed on a product and where materials, labour, or overhead costs are added to the product. For example, a potato chip factory operated by Frito-Lay might have three processing departments—one for preparing potatoes, one for cooking, and one for inspecting and packaging. A brick factory might have two processing departments—one for mixing and moulding clay into brick form and one for firing the moulded brick. A company can have as many or as few processing departments as are needed to complete a product or service. Some products and services may go through several processing departments, while others may go through only one or two. Regardless of the number of departments involved, all processing departments have two essential features: First, the activity performed in the processing department must be performed uniformly on all of the units passing through it. Second, the output of the processing department must be identical.

Products in a process costing environment, such as bricks or potato chips, typically flow in a sequence from one department to another, as shown in Exhibit 6–2.

Processing department
Any location in an organization where work is performed on a product and where materials, labour, or overhead costs are added to the product.

EXHIBIT 6–2 Sequential Processing Departments

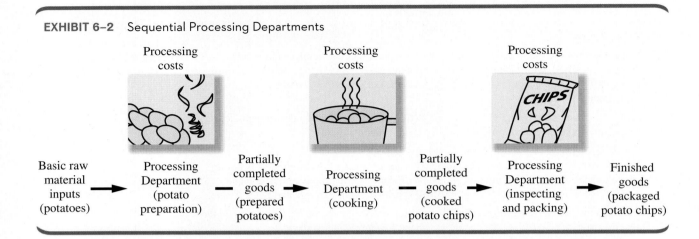

Processing costs

Processing costs

Processing costs

Basic raw material inputs (potatoes) → Processing Department (potato preparation) — Partially completed goods (prepared potatoes) → Processing Department (cooking) — Partially completed goods (cooked potato chips) → Processing Department (inspecting and packing) → Finished goods (packaged potato chips)

IN BUSINESS

The Coca-Cola Company produces and sells drink concentrates, flavour bases, and syrups to both company-owned and outside bottlers that mix, fill, label, and ship the final product to customers in more than 200 countries. The process of creating a drink concentrate or syrup includes adding raw materials like sugar, flavourings, caffeine, and filtered water using proprietary recipes known only to a select few people at Coca-Cola. Conversion costs include the labour required to identify, measure, and add the appropriate raw materials as well as the cost to run the machines utilized to develop the concentrate or syrup to its proper consistency and to package it for shipment to bottling plants.

Coca-Cola's manufacturing process for drink concentrates, flavour bases, and syrups is well suited for process costing because it produces a continuous stream of identical units of product. The material costs and conversion costs incurred at the various stages of the production process can be assigned to products by spreading them evenly over the total production volume.

LEARNING OBJECTIVE ❶

Record the flow of materials, labour, and overhead through a process costing system.

The Flow of Materials, Labour, and Overhead Costs

Cost accumulation is simpler in a process costing system than in a job-order costing system. In a process costing system, instead of having to trace costs to hundreds of different jobs, costs are traced to only a few processing departments. In a process costing system, production costs are not identified with specific units or batches of product. Instead, an average unit cost is computed by dividing total production costs for the period by the number of units produced during the same period.

A T-account model of materials, labour, and overhead cost flows in a process costing system is given in Exhibit 6–3. Several key points should be noted from this exhibit. First, note that a separate Work in Process account is maintained for *each processing department*. In contrast, in a job-order costing system there may be only a single Work in Process account for the entire company. Second, note that the completed production of the first processing department (Department A in the exhibit) is transferred into the Work in Process account of the second processing department (Department B), where it undergoes further work. After this further work, the completed units are transferred into Finished Goods. (In Exhibit 6–3 we show only two processing departments, but a company may have many processing departments.)

EXHIBIT 6–3   T-Account Model of Process Costing Flows

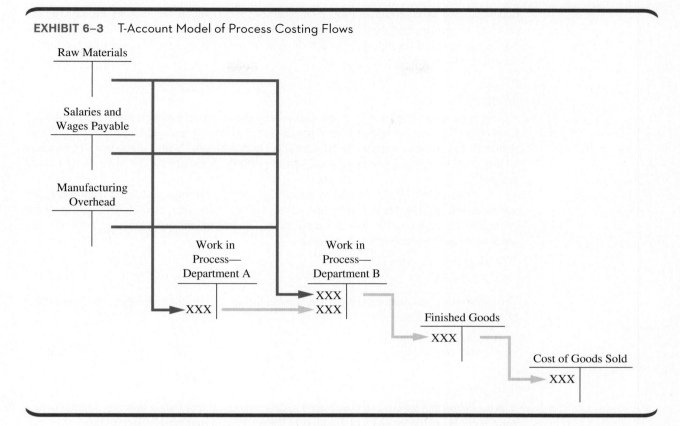

Finally, note that materials, labour, and overhead costs can be added in *any* processing department—not just the first. Costs in Department B's Work in Process account consist of the materials, labour, and overhead costs incurred in Department B plus the costs attached to partially completed units transferred in from Department A (called **transferred-in costs**).

Transferred-in costs Costs attached to products that have been received from a prior processing department.

Materials, Labour, and Overhead Cost Entries

To complete our discussion of cost flows in a process costing system, in this section we show journal entries relating to materials, labour, and overhead costs at Standard Products Co., a producer of Green Clean, a multi-purpose household cleaner. The company has two processing departments—Mixing and Filling. In the Mixing Department, the various ingredients are checked for quality and then mixed to create bulk liquid cleaner. In the Filling Department, bottles are checked for defects, filled with cleaner, capped, and labelled, and then the bottles are packed for shipping.

Materials Costs

As in job-order costing, materials are drawn from the storeroom using a materials requisition form. Materials can be added in any processing department, although it is not unusual for materials to be added only in the first processing department, with subsequent departments adding only labour and overhead costs as the partially completed units move along toward completion.

At Standard Products Co., some materials (water, cleaning agents, and fragrances) are added in the Mixing Department, and other materials (bottles, caps, labels, and packing materials) are added in the Filling Department. The journal entry for placing materials into process in the first department is as follows:

Work in Process—Mixing	20,000	
Raw Materials..		20,000

The journal entry to record the materials used in the second processing department, the Filling Department, is as follows:

Work in Process—Filling.....................................	10,000	
Raw Materials..		10,000

Labour Costs

In process costing, labour costs are traced to departments, not to individual jobs. The following entry records the labour costs in the Mixing Department at Standard Products Co.:

Work in Process—Mixing	7,500	
Salaries and Wages Payable		7,500

Overhead Costs

If production is stable from period to period and if overhead costs are incurred uniformly over the year, actual overhead costs can be charged to departments. However, if production levels fluctuate or if overhead costs are not incurred uniformly, charging products with actual overhead costs will result in unit product costs that vary randomly from one period to the next. In such a situation, predetermined overhead rates should be used to charge overhead cost to products, the same as in job-order costing. When predetermined overhead rates are used, each department has its own separate rate, with the rates being computed as discussed in Chapter 5. Overhead cost is then applied to units of product as the units move through the various departments. Since predetermined overhead rates are widely used in process costing, we will assume their use throughout the remainder of this chapter.

The following journal entry is used to apply overhead costs to units of product for the Mixing Department:

Work in Process—Mixing	12,000	
Manufacturing Overhead		12,000

Completing the Cost Flows

Once processing has been completed in a department the product units are transferred to the next department for further processing, as illustrated earlier in the T-accounts in Exhibit 6–3. The following journal entry is used to transfer the costs of partially completed units from the Mixing Department to the Filling Department:

Work in Process—Filling.....................................	39,500	
Work in Process—Mixing		39,500

After processing has been completed in the Filling department, the costs of the completed units are then transferred to the Finished Goods inventory account:

Finished Goods..	49,500	
Work in Process—Filling................................		49,500

Finally, when a customer's order is filled and units are sold, the cost of the units is transferred to Cost of Goods Sold:

Cost of Goods Sold......................................	49,500	
Finished Goods..		49,500

To summarize, the cost flows between accounts are basically the same in a process costing system as they are in a job-order costing system. The only noticeable difference at this point is that a process costing system has a separate Work in Process account for each department.

INSTANT QUIZ 6–2
Even though process costing is different from job-order costing, the calculation of the predetermined overhead rate is the same under both methods. True or false?

We now turn our attention to Tropic Breeze, a company that manufactures two models of an efficient and reliable industrial fan for use in large factory spaces. Tropic Breeze uses process costing to determine its unit product cost. The company's production process includes three processing departments, the Housings Department, the Electrics and Testing Department, and the Inspection and Packing Department. The basic idea in process costing is to add together all of the costs incurred in a department during a period and then spread these costs uniformly across the units processed in that department during that period. As we will see, applying this simple idea involves a few complications.

■ EQUIVALENT UNITS OF PRODUCTION

LEARNING OBJECTIVE ❷
Compute the equivalent units of production using the weighted-average method.

After materials, labour, and overhead costs have been accumulated in a department, the department's output must be determined so that unit costs can be computed. In the simplest case, average unit cost can be computed by dividing total manufacturing costs by the number of units produced during a given time period. The difficulty is that a department usually has some partially completed units in its ending inventory. This is because the production schedule does not necessarily match the accounting schedule. Companies want to value their inventory on hand at the end of each accounting period (typically, each month), but production scheduling is tied more directly to customer orders than to accounting periods. Therefore, there will typically be incomplete units in inventory at the end of an accounting period; we deal with this issue by counting them in "equivalent units." It does not seem reasonable to count these partially completed units as equivalent to fully completed units when counting the department's output. Therefore, Tropic Breeze mathematically converts these partially completed units into an *equivalent* number of fully completed units. In process costing, this is done using the following formula:

Equivalent units = Number of partially completed units × Percentage completion

As the formula states, **equivalent units** are defined as the product of the number of partially completed units and the percentage completion of those units. Equivalent units are the number of complete units that could have been obtained from the materials and effort that went into the partially completed units.

Equivalent units
The product of the number of partially completed units and their percentage of completion with respect to a particular cost. Equivalent units are the number of complete whole units one could obtain from the materials and effort contained in partially completed units.

For example, suppose the Housings Department at Tropic Breeze has 500 units in its ending work in process inventory that are 60% complete. These 500 partially complete units are equivalent to 300 fully complete units (500 × 60% = 300). Therefore, the ending work in process inventory contains 300 equivalent units. These equivalent units are added to any fully completed units to determine the period's output for the department—called the *equivalent units of production*.

Equivalent units of production for a period can be computed in two different ways. Accounting standards (IAS 2) allow for inventory costing using either the weighted-average or the FIFO method. In this chapter, we discuss the *weighted-average method*. In Appendix 6A, we discuss the *FIFO (first in, first out) method*. In the **FIFO method** of process costing, equivalent units and unit costs relate only to work done during the current period. In contrast, the **weighted-average method** blends together units and costs from the current period with units and costs from the prior period. The **equivalent units of production (weighted-average method)** for a department are the number of units transferred to the next department (or to finished goods) plus the equivalent units in the department's ending work in process inventory.

FIFO method
A method of accounting for cost flows in a process costing system in which equivalent units and unit costs relate only to work done during the current period.

Weighted-average method
A method of process costing that blends together units and costs from both the current and prior periods.

Equivalent units of production (weighted-average method)
The units transferred to the next department (or to finished goods) during the period plus the equivalent units in the department's ending work in process inventory.

INSTANT QUIZ 6–3
Suppose there are 5,000 full-time students and 1,250 part-time students (taking approximately half of the regular class load) in the Faculty of Management at Westly University. Using the concept of equivalent units, how many full-time equivalent students are enrolled in the Faculty of Management?

Weighted-Average Method

Under the weighted-average method, a department's equivalent units are computed as follows:

Weighted-Average Method
(a separate calculation is made for each cost category in
each processing department)

$$\text{Equivalent units of production} = \text{Units transferred to the next department or to finished goods} + \text{Equivalent units in ending work in process inventory}$$

Note that computation of the equivalent units of production involves adding the number of units transferred out of the department to the equivalent units in the department's ending inventory. There is no need to compute the equivalent units for the units transferred out of the department—they are 100% complete with respect to the work done in that department or they would not be transferred out. In other words, each unit transferred out of the department is counted as one equivalent unit.

Consider the Electrics and Testing Department at Tropic Breeze. This department uses computerized machines to ensure the electrical integrity of the industrial fans produced. Efficiency and reliability are a key to Tropic Breeze's competitive advantage; the company has invested in specialized testing equipment to ensure customer satisfaction with the end product. The following activity took place in the department in May:

Electrics and Testing Department	Units	Percentage Completed Materials	Conversion
Work in process, May 1	200	55%	30%
Units started into production during May	5,000		
Units completed during May and transferred to the next department	4,800	100%*	100%*
Work in process, May 31	400	40%	25%

*It is always assumed that units transferred out of a department are 100% complete with respect to the processing done in that department.

	Materials	Conversion
Units transferred to the next department.	4,800	4,800
Work in process, May 31:		
400 units × 40% complete with respect to materials	160	
400 units × 25% complete with respect to conversion		100
Equivalent units of production	4,960	4,900

EXHIBIT 6–4
Equivalent Units of Production: Weighted-Average Method

Note the use of the term *conversion* in the above table. Conversion cost, as defined in Chapter 2, is direct labour cost plus manufacturing overhead cost. In process costing, conversion cost is often—but not always—treated as a single element of product cost.

Note that the May 1 beginning work in process was 55% complete with respect to materials costs and 30% complete with respect to conversion costs. This means that 55% of the materials costs required to complete the units had already been incurred. Likewise, 30% of the conversion costs required to complete the units had already been incurred.

Two equivalent unit figures must be computed—one for materials and one for conversion. These computations are shown in Exhibit 6–4.

Note that the computations in Exhibit 6–4 ignore the fact that the units in the beginning work in process inventory were partially complete. For example, the 200 units in beginning inventory were already 30% complete with respect to conversion costs. The 4,800 units transferred to the next department consist of 200 units in the beginning inventory plus 4,600 units started and completed during the current period. The weighted-average method is concerned only with the equivalent units that are in the ending inventories and in units transferred to the next department—it is not concerned with the fact that the beginning inventory was already partially complete. In other words, the 4,900 equivalent units computed using the weighted-average method include work that was accomplished in prior periods. This is a key point regarding the weighted-average method, and it is easy to overlook.

INSTANT QUIZ 6–4
Of materials, labour, and overhead, which types of cost make up conversion costs?

Averages, in general, hide the details of the elements that make up the average. For example, the average of 2 + 4 is 3. The average of 1 + 5 is 3. If the manager is not interested in the details of the elements, then the average provides all of the information needed. If costs from one period to the next are approximately equal (for example, 3 + 3), the average is also a reasonable representation of the results. A third explanation for the use of the average approach is the relative size of the beginning inventory of work in process compared to the current production. For example, if the beginning inventory is only one-tenth of the current production, the average (weighted) of $\left(\frac{1}{10}\right)(1) + \left(\frac{9}{10}\right)(5) = 4.60$ is very accurate. In addition to the advantage of ease of computation, another advantage of the weighted-average method is that it generates very accurate results when costs are relatively stable from one period to the next or when the size of current production dominates the beginning inventory. All of these factors are common characteristics of process costing environments!

Exhibit 6–5 provides an alternative way of looking at the computation of equivalent units of production. Study this exhibit carefully before going on.

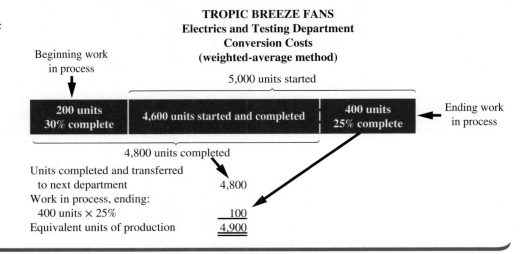

EXHIBIT 6–5
Visual Perspective of Equivalent Units of Production

TROPIC BREEZE FANS
Electrics and Testing Department
Conversion Costs
(weighted-average method)

Units completed and transferred to next department	4,800
Work in process, ending:	
400 units × 25%	100
Equivalent units of production	4,900

LEARNING OBJECTIVE ③

Compute the cost per equivalent unit using the weighted-average method.

■ COMPUTE AND APPLY COSTS

In the last section we computed the equivalent units of production for materials and for conversion at Tropic Breeze Fans. In this section, we will compute the cost per equivalent unit for materials and for conversion. We will then use these costs to value ending work in process and finished goods inventories. Exhibit 6–6 displays all of the data concerning May's operations in the Electrics and Testing Department that we will need to complete these tasks.

Cost per Equivalent Unit—Weighted-Average Method

In the weighted-average method, the cost per equivalent unit is computed as follows:

Weighted-Average Method
(a separate calculation is made for each cost category in each processing department)

$$\text{Cost per equivalent unit} = \frac{\text{Cost of beginning work in process inventory} + \text{Cost added during the period}}{\text{Equivalent units of production}}$$

EXHIBIT 6–6
Electrics and Testing Department Data for May Operations

Work in process, beginning:	
Units in process	200
Stage of completion with respect to materials	55%
Stage of completion with respect to conversion	30%
Costs in the beginning inventory:	
Materials cost	$ 9,600
Conversion cost	5,575
Total cost in the beginning inventory	$ 15,175
Units started into production during the period	5,000
Units completed and transferred out	4,800
Costs added to production during the period:	
Materials cost	$ 368,600
Conversion cost	350,900
Total cost added in the department	$ 719,500
Work in process, ending:	
Units in process	400
Stage of completion with respect to materials	40%
Stage of completion with respect to conversion	25%

Note that the numerator is the sum of the cost of beginning work in process inventory and the cost added during the period. Thus, the weighted-average method blends together costs from the prior and current periods. That is why it is called the weighted-average method: it averages together units and costs from both the prior and current periods.

The costs per equivalent unit for materials and for conversion are computed below for the Electrics and Testing Department for May:

<table>
<thead>
<tr><th colspan="3">Electrics and Testing Department
Costs per Equivalent Unit</th></tr>
<tr><th></th><th>Materials</th><th>Conversion</th></tr>
</thead>
<tbody>
<tr><td>Cost of beginning work in process inventory . . . .</td><td>$ 9,600</td><td>$ 5,575</td></tr>
<tr><td>Costs added during the period . . . .</td><td>368,600</td><td>350,900</td></tr>
<tr><td>Total cost (a) . . . .</td><td>$378,200</td><td>$ 356,475</td></tr>
<tr><td>Equivalent units of production (see the
   computations in Exhibit 6–4) (b) . . . .</td><td>4,960</td><td>4,900</td></tr>
<tr><td>Cost per equivalent unit (a) ÷ (b) . . . .</td><td>$ 76.25</td><td>$ 72.75</td></tr>
</tbody>
</table>

INSTANT QUIZ 6–5

Mike Jones, Director of Accounting at Acme Brands, has calculated that there are 6,250 equivalent units of production for materials in the Mixing Department at the end of the current month. Assuming beginning work in process inventory costs for materials were $7,250, and $10,750 of additional materials costs were added in the period, calculate the cost per equivalent unit for materials for the Mixing Department using the weighted-average method.

■ APPLYING COSTS—WEIGHTED-AVERAGE METHOD

LEARNING OBJECTIVE 4
Assign costs to units using the weighted-average method.

The costs per equivalent unit are used to value units in ending inventory and units that are transferred to the next department. For example, each unit transferred out of Tropic Breeze's Electrics and Testing Department to the Inspection and Packing Department will carry with it a cost of $149 ($76.25 for materials cost and $72.75 for conversion cost). Since 4,800 units were transferred out in May to the next department, the total cost assigned to these units is $715,200 (4,800 units × $149 per unit).

A complete accounting of the costs of both ending work in process inventory and the units transferred out follows:

<table>
<thead>
<tr><th colspan="4">Electrics and Testing Department
Costs of Ending Work in Process Inventory and the Units Transferred Out</th></tr>
<tr><th></th><th>Materials</th><th>Conversion</th><th>Total</th></tr>
</thead>
<tbody>
<tr><td>Ending work in process inventory:</td><td></td><td></td><td></td></tr>
<tr><td> Equivalent units of production (a)</td><td></td><td></td><td></td></tr>
<tr><td> 400 units × 40% complete with respect to materials</td><td>160</td><td></td><td></td></tr>
<tr><td> 400 units × 25% complete with respect to conversion</td><td></td><td>100</td><td></td></tr>
<tr><td> Cost per equivalent unit (see above) (b)</td><td>$ 76.25</td><td>$ 72.75</td><td></td></tr>
<tr><td> Cost of ending work in process inventory (a) × (b)</td><td>$ 12,200</td><td>$ 7,275</td><td>$ 19,475</td></tr>
<tr><td>Units completed and transferred out:</td><td></td><td></td><td></td></tr>
<tr><td> Units transferred to the next department (a)</td><td>4,800</td><td>4,800</td><td></td></tr>
<tr><td> Cost per equivalent unit (see above) (b)</td><td>$ 76.25</td><td>$ 72.75</td><td></td></tr>
<tr><td> Cost of units transferred out (a) × (b)</td><td>$366,000</td><td>$349,200</td><td>$715,200</td></tr>
</tbody>
</table>

In each case, the equivalent units are multiplied by the cost per equivalent unit to determine the cost assigned to the units. This is done for each cost category—in this case, materials and conversion. The equivalent units for the units completed and transferred out are simply the number of units transferred to the next department because they would not have been transferred unless they were complete.

BEYOND THE BOTTOM LINE

In the examples presented in this chapter, we provide the percentage of completion of the product for materials and conversion costs on which the calculation of equivalent units is based. In reality, managers need to estimate the percentage of completion at the end of each month based on observation and judgment. Increasing the estimated percentage of completion can increase operating income by reducing the cost of goods sold. The impact on cost of goods sold is achieved through the calculation of cost per unit. If the firm can recognize the inventory costs incurred over a higher percentage of completion of the product, then the cost of each unit sold recorded under a process costing system in the current period will also be low. If managers are paid a bonus based on achievement of profit targets, they may feel pressure to be less conservative in their estimates of percentage of completion. Recognize this can be only a short-term benefit to the manager, though, as the recognized cost per unit will necessarily be higher in the following month.

LEARNING OBJECTIVE 5

Prepare a cost reconciliation report accounting for the costs transferred out and the costs in work in process inventory at the end of the period using the weighted-average method.

The costs assigned to ending work in process inventory and to the units transferred out reconcile with the costs we started with in Exhibit 6–6, as shown below:

Electrics and Testing Department
Cost Reconciliation

Costs to be accounted for:	
Cost of beginning work in process inventory (Exhibit 6–6)	$ 15,175
Costs added to production during the period (Exhibit 6–6)	719,500
Total cost to be accounted for	$ 734,675
Costs accounted for as follows:	
Cost of ending work in process inventory (see above)	$ 19,475
Cost of units transferred out (see above)	715,200
Total cost accounted for	$ 734,675

The $715,200 cost of the units transferred to the next department, Inspection and Packing, is accounted for in that department as "costs transferred in." It is treated in the process costing system as just another category of costs, like materials or conversion costs. The only difference is that the costs transferred in are always 100% complete with respect to the work done in the Inspection and Packing Department. When the products are completed in this last department, their costs are transferred to finished goods.

Summary of Tropic Breeze Fans Costing

Exhibit 6–7 displays a production report for the Electrics and Testing Department costs calculated on the previous pages. The production activity in units is displayed in the Quantity Schedule. This schedule summarizes the activity for the month of May and is used to begin the calculation of equivalent units of production. The schedule of costs per equivalent unit

EXHIBIT 6–7   Production Report—Weighted-Average Method

TROPIC BREEZE FANS
Electrics and Testing Department Production Report
(weighted-average method)

Quantity Schedule and Equivalent Units

	Quantity Schedule	Materials	Conversion
Units to be accounted for:			
Work in process, May 1 (materials 55% complete; conversion 30% complete)	200		
Started into production	5,000		
Total units	5,200		

| | Quantity Schedule | **Equivalent Units (EU)** | |
		Materials	**Conversion**
Units accounted for as follows:			
Transferred to the next department	4,800	4,800	4,800
Work in process, May 31 (materials 40% complete; conversion 25% complete)	400	160*	100†
Total units and equivalent units of production (see Exhibit 6–4)	5,200	4,960	4,900

Costs per Equivalent Unit

	Total Cost	Materials	Conversion	Whole Unit
Cost to be accounted for:				
Work in process, May 1	$ 15,175	$ 9,600	$ 5,575	
Cost added in the Electrics and Testing Department	719,500	368,600	350,900	
Total cost (a)	$ 734,675	$378,200	$356,475	
Equivalent units of production (b) (see above)		4,960	4,900	
Cost per EU,‡ (a) ÷ (b)		$ 76.25	+ $ 72.75	= $149.00

Cost Reconciliation

	Total Cost	Materials	Conversion
Cost accounted for as follows:			
Transferred to next department:			
4,800 units × $149.00 each	$ 715,200	4,800	4,800
Work in process, May 31:			
Materials, at $76.25 per EU	12,200	160	
Conversion, at $72.75 per EU	7,275		100
Total work in process, May 31	19,475		
Total cost	$ 734,675		

*40% × 400 units = 160 equivalent units
†25% × 400 units = 100 equivalent units
‡EU = Equivalent unit

summarizes the production costs for the month of May plus the beginning work in process for May. These costs are used together with the equivalent units from the quantity schedule to compute the weighted unit costs. Finally, the production report is completed by computing the cost reconciliation. The total costs to be accounted for are tested against the total of the cost of units transferred to the next department and the work in process costs at May 31 to ensure all costs have been properly accounted for.

EXHIBIT 6–8
Schedule of
Cost of Goods
Manufactured

TROPIC BREEZE FANS Schedule of Cost of Goods Manufactured	
Cost of goods manufactured:	
Total manufacturing costs...	$719,500
Add: Beginning work in process inventory................................	15,175
	734,675
Deduct: Ending work in process inventory...............................	19,475
Cost of goods manufactured	$715,200

It is worth noting at this point the relationship of the costs reflected in the production report to the schedules of cost of goods manufactured presented in Chapters 2 and 5 and the work in process general ledger account. Exhibit 5–11 in Chapter 5 will help you picture the relationships.

Exhibit 6–8 provides an example calculation of the cost of goods manufactured for Tropic Breeze Fans. The cost of the beginning work in process inventory, $15,175, is the beginning general ledger balance for work in process. The total manufacturing costs of $719,500 represent the cost of raw material used, the cost of direct labour used, and the manufacturing overhead applied during May. These three types of costs, at $719,500, increase the Work in Process account for May. The cost of goods manufactured is $715,200, which represents what is transferred out of work in process for May, leaving the ending work in process balance in the general ledger of $19,475. A careful tracing of the description of these costs to the schedule of costs of goods manufactured as shown in Exhibit 5–11 will help you visualize how the costs from the production report for process costs link to the general ledger.

■ OPERATION COSTING

The costing systems discussed in Chapter 5 and in this chapter represent the two ends of a continuum. On one end, we have job-order costing, which is used by companies that produce many different items—generally to customer specifications. On the other end, we have process costing, which is used by companies that produce basically homogeneous products in large quantities. Between these two extremes, there are many hybrid systems that include characteristics of both job-order and process costing. One of these hybrids is called *operation costing*.

Operation costing
A hybrid costing system used when products are manufactured in batches and when the products have some common characteristics and some individual characteristics. This system handles materials the same way as in job-order costing and labour and overhead the same way as in process costing.

Operation costing is used in situations where products have some common characteristics and also some individual characteristics. Shoes, for example, have common characteristics in that all styles involve cutting and sewing that can be done on a repetitive basis, using the same equipment and following the same basic procedures. Shoes also have individual characteristics—some are made of expensive leathers and others may be made using inexpensive synthetic materials. In a situation such as this, where products have some common characteristics but also must be handled individually, operation costing may be used to determine product costs.

As mentioned above, operation costing is a hybrid system that employs aspects of both job-order and process costing. Products are typically handled in batches when operation costing is in use, with each batch charged for its own specific materials. In this sense, operation costing is similar to job-order costing. However, labour and overhead costs are accumulated by operation or by department, and these costs are assigned to units as in process costing. If shoes are being produced, for example, each shoe is charged the same per-unit conversion cost regardless of the style involved, but it is charged with its specific materials cost. Thus, the company is able to distinguish between styles in terms of materials, but it is able to employ the simplicity of a process costing system for labour and overhead costs.

Examples of other products for which operation costing may be used are electronic equipment (such as semiconductors), textiles, clothing, and jewellery (such as rings, bracelets, and medallions). Products of this type are typically produced in batches, but they can vary considerably from model to model or from style to style in terms of the cost of raw material inputs. Therefore, an operation costing system is well suited for providing cost data.

■ FLEXIBLE MANUFACTURING SYSTEMS

A plant that uses a flexible manufacturing system (FMS) is heavily automated, and its activities are organized around cells, or islands, of automated equipment. The FMS concept is having a major impact on costing in several ways. One of these is through allowing companies to switch their systems from the more costly job-order approach to a less costly process or operation approach. This switching is made possible because FMS is proving to be highly efficient in reducing the setup time required between products and jobs. With setup time only a small fraction of previous levels, companies are able to move between products and jobs with about the same speed as if they were working in a continuous, process-type environment. The result is that these companies are able to employ process costing techniques in situations that previously required job-order costing. As the use of FMS grows (and becomes even more efficient), some managers predict that job-order costing will slowly disappear except in a few select industries.

A further impact of FMS is through its focus on cells rather than on departments. Although production reports are still prepared in FMS settings, these reports are either much broader, including the entire production process (many cells), or much narrower, including only a single cell or workstation. If JIT is practised, then the production report becomes greatly simplified, regardless of the level at which it is prepared.

KNOWLEDGE IN ACTION

Managers can apply their knowledge about process costing when

- Calculating the product/service cost when many units of relatively uniform products/services are produced in the year
- Setting prices to ensure the price exceeds the cost to produce the product or service
- Calculating the value of inventory included on the balance sheet and the cost of goods sold disclosed on the income statement

---

SUMMARY

- Process costing is used in situations where homogeneous products or services are produced on a continuous basis. Costs flow through the manufacturing accounts in basically the same way in a process costing system as in a job-order costing system. However, costs are accumulated by department rather than by job in process costing. **[LO1]**
- In process costing, the equivalent units of production must be determined for each cost category in each department. Under the weighted-average method, the equivalent units of production equals the number of units transferred out to the next department or to finished goods plus the equivalent units in ending work in process inventory. The equivalent units in ending inventory equal the product of the number of partially completed units in ending work in process inventory and their percentage of completion with respect to the specific cost category. **[LO2]**

- Under the weighted-average method, the cost per equivalent unit for a specific cost category is computed by adding the cost of beginning work in process inventory and the cost added during the period and then dividing the result by the equivalent units of production (i.e., calculating the average). [LO3]
- The cost per equivalent unit is then used to value the ending work in process inventory and the units transferred out to the next department or to finished goods. [LO4]
- Costs are transferred from one department to the next until the last processing department. At that point, the cost of completed units is transferred to finished goods. At the end of the period, a cost reconciliation is prepared to account for the costs transferred out and costs in work in process inventory at the end of the period. [LO5]

REVIEW PROBLEM 1: PROCESS COST FLOWS AND REPORTS

Lanyard Home Paint Company produces exterior latex paint, which it sells in four-litre containers. The company has two processing departments—Base Fab and Finishing. White paint, which is used as a base for all of the company's paints, is mixed from raw ingredients in the Base Fab Department. In the Finishing Department, pigments are added to the basic white paint, the pigmented paint is squirted under pressure into four-litre containers, and the containers are labelled and packed for shipping. Information relating to the company's operations for April is as follows:

a. Raw materials were issued for use in production: Base Fab Department, $851,000; Finishing Department, $629,000.

b. Direct labour costs were incurred: Base Fab Department, $330,000; Finishing Department, $270,000.

c. Manufacturing overhead cost was applied: Base Fab Department, $665,000; Finishing Department, $405,000.

d. Paint that had been prepared for shipping was transferred from the Finishing Department to Finished Goods: $3,200,000.

Required:

1. Prepare journal entries to record items (*a*) through (*d*) above.

2. Post the journal entries from (1) above to T-accounts. The balance in the Base Fab Department's Work in Process account on April 1 was $150,000; the balance in the Finishing Department's Work in Process account was $70,000. After posting entries to the T-accounts, find the ending balance in each department's Work in Process account.

3. Prepare a production report for the Base Fab Department for April. The following additional information is available regarding production in the Base Fab Department during April:

Production data for four-litre containers of paint:	
Units (containers) in process, April 1: 100% complete as to materials, 60% complete as to labour and overhead.	30,000
Units (containers) started into production during April	420,000
Units (containers) completed and transferred to the Finishing Department .	370,000
Units (containers) in process, April 30: 50% complete as to materials, 25% complete as to labour and overhead.	80,000
Cost data:	
Work in process inventory, April 1:	
Materials	$ 92,000
Labour	21,000
Overhead	37,000
Total cost	$150,000
Cost added during April:	
Materials	$851,000
Labour	330,000
Overhead	665,000

4. Prepare the journal entry to record the transfer of basic white paint from the Base Fab Department to the Finishing Department, and post it to the appropriate T-accounts. (*Hint:* The dollar amount of the transfer was determined in (3) above.)

Solution to Review Problem 1

1. *a.* Work in Process—Base Fab Department 851,000
           Work in Process—Finishing Department 629,000
              Raw Materials   1,480,000
    b. Work in Process—Base Fab Department 330,000
           Work in Process—Finishing Department 270,000
              Salaries and Wages Payable........................   600,000
    c. Work in Process—Base Fab Department 665,000
           Work in Process—Finishing Department 405,000
              Manufacturing Overhead..........................   1,070,000
    d. Finished Goods 3,200,000
           Work in Process—Finishing Department   3,200,000

2.

Raw Materials		
Bal. XXX	(a)	1,480,000

Salaries and Wages Payable		
	(b)	600,000

Work in Process— Base Fab Department		
Bal. 150,000	(Part 4)	1,850,000
(a) 851,000		
(b) 330,000		
(c) 665,000		
Bal. 146,000		

Manufacturing Overhead		
(Various actual costs)	(c)	1,070,000

Work in Process— Finishing Department		
Bal. 70,000	(d)	3,200,000
(a) 629,000		
(b) 270,000		
(c) 405,000		
(Part 4) 1,850,000		
Bal. 24,000		

Finished Goods	
Bal. XXX	
(d) 3,200,000	

3.

LANYARD HOME PAINT COMPANY
Production Report—Base Fab Department
For the Month Ended April 30

Quantity Schedule and Equivalent Units

	Quantity Schedule
Units (four-litre containers) to be accounted for:	
Work in process, April 1	
(all materials, 60% labour and	
overhead added last month)	30,000
Started into production.........................	420,000
Total units.................................	450,000

		Equivalent Units (EU)		
		Materials	Labour	Overhead
Units (four-litre containers) accounted for as follows:				
Transferred to Finishing				
Department	370,000	370,000	370,000	370,000
Work in process, April 30 (materials				
50% complete; labour and				
overhead 25% complete)	80,000	40,000*	20,000*	20,000*
Total units and equivalent				
units of production.	450,000	410,000	390,000	390,000

*Materials: 80,000 units × 50% = 40,000 equivalent units; labour and overhead: 80,000 units × 25% = 20,000 equivalent units

Costs per Equivalent Unit (EU)

	Total Cost	Materials	Labour	Overhead	Whole Unit
Cost to be accounted for:					
Work in process, April 1	$ 150,000	$ 92,000	$ 21,000	$ 37,000	
Cost added by the Base Fab					
Department	1,846,000	851,000	330,000	665,000	
Total cost (a)	$1,996,000	$943,000	$351,000	$702,000	
Equivalent units of production (b)	–	410,000	390,000	390,000	
Cost per EU, (a) ÷ (b)	–	$2.30 +	$0.90 +	$1.80 =	$5.00

Cost Reconciliation

	Total Cost	Materials	Labour	Overhead
Cost accounted for as follows:				
Transferred to Finishing Department:				
370,000 units, at $5.00 each	$1,850,000	370,000	370,000	370,000
Work in process, April 30:				
Materials, at $2.30 per EU.	92,000	40,000		
Labour, at $0.90 per EU	18,000		20,000	
Overhead, at $1.80 per EU	36,000			20,000
Total work in process.	146,000			
Total cost	$1,996,000			

4.	Work in Process—Finishing		
	Department	1,850,000	
	Work in Process—Base Fab		
	Department		1,850,000

REVIEW PROBLEM 2: UNITS AND COST ASSIGNMENT

Power Company passes its product through several departments, the last of which is the Finishing Department. Conversion costs are added evenly throughout the process in this department. One-fourth of direct materials is added at the beginning of the process, and the remaining three-fourths is added when the process is 50% complete with respect to conversion costs.

During June, 475,000 units of product were transferred to finished goods. Of these units, 100,000 units were 40% complete with respect to conversion costs at the beginning of the period and 375,000 were started and completed during the period. At the end of June, the work in process inventory comprised 225,000 units that were 30% complete with respect to conversion costs. Total costs to account for include $949,375 for conversion costs and $616,250 for direct materials.

Required:
1. Determine the equivalent units of production with respect to conversion costs and with respect to direct materials for the Finishing Department.
2. Compute the conversion cost and the direct materials cost per equivalent unit.
3. Compute the amount of conversion cost and the amount of the direct materials cost assigned to the units completed and to the ending work in process inventory.

Solution to Review Problem 2

1. Equivalent unit calculations:

		Equivalent Units (EU)	
		Materials	Conversion
Units accounted for as follows:			
Transferred to the next department	475,000	475,000	475,000
Work in process, June 30:			
Material, 25% complete; conversion, 30% complete ..	225,000	56,250	67,500
Total units accounted for	700,000	531,250	542,500

2. Unit cost calculations:

Conversion cost per equivalent unit $= \$949{,}375 \div 542{,}500 \text{ units} = \$1.75$
Direct materials cost per equivalent unit $= \$616{,}250 \div 531{,}250 \text{ units} = \$1.16$

3. Allocation of materials and conversion cost to products:

	Equivalent Units	Per Unit Cost	Allocated Cost
Transferred out:			
Materials	475,000	$1.16	$ 551,000
Conversion costs	475,000	1.75	831,250
			$1,382,250 (a)
Work in Process			
Materials (225,000 × 0.25)	56,250	$1.16	$ 65,250
Conversion (225,000 × 0.3)...............	67,500	1.75	118,125
			183,375 (b)
Total cost accounted for: (a) + (b)............			$1,565,625

DISCUSSION CASE

DISCUSSION CASE 6–1

Process costing methods rely extensively on managers' estimates of percentage of completion for both costing products and calculating equivalent units of production. While most managers understand the importance of accurate estimates to the integrity of their process costing systems, they also have incentives to produce profits for their shareholders.

Required:
Discuss how incorrect estimates could be used to artificially boost profits, considering the issue from the perspectives of both managers and shareholders.

QUESTIONS

6–1   Under what conditions is it appropriate to use a process costing system?
6–2   In what ways are job-order and process costing different?
6–3   Why is cost accumulation easier in a process costing system than it is in a job-order costing system?
6–4   How many Work in Process accounts are maintained in a company that uses process costing?
6–5   Assume that a company has two processing departments—Mixing and Firing. Prepare a journal entry to show a transfer of partially completed units from the Mixing Department to the Firing Department.

6–6   Assume that a company has two processing departments—Mixing followed by Firing. Explain what costs might be added to the Firing Department's Work in Process account during a period.

6–7   What is meant by the term *equivalent units of production* when the weighted-average method is used?

6–8   "The increasing use of flexible manufacturing systems will result in a reduction in the importance of process costing over time." Do you agree or disagree and why?

6–9   If FIFO is a more accurate costing method, why would a manager choose to use the weighted-average method instead? List at least three reasons.

FOUNDATIONAL EXERCISES

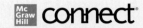

[LO1, LO2, LO3, LO4, LO5]

Clopack Company manufactures one product that goes through one processing department called Mixing. All raw materials are introduced at the start of work in the Mixing Department. The company uses the weighted-average method to account for units and costs. Its Work in Process T-account for the Mixing Department for June follows (all forthcoming questions pertain to June):

Work in Process—Mixing Department			
June 1—balance	$28,000	Completed and transferred to finished goods	?
Materials	120,000		
Direct labour	79,500		
Overhead	97,000		
June 30—balance	?		

The June 1 work in process inventory consisted of 5,000 kilograms with $16,000 in materials cost and $12,000 in conversion cost. The June 1 work in process inventory was 100% complete with respect to materials and 50% complete with respect to conversion. During June, 37,500 kilograms were started into production. The June 30 work in process inventory consisted of 8,000 kilograms that were 100% complete with respect to materials and 40% complete with respect to conversion.

Required:

6–1   Prepare the journal entries to record the raw materials used in production and the direct labour cost incurred.

6–2   Prepare the journal entry to record the overhead cost applied to production.

6–3   How many units were completed and transferred to finished goods during the period?

6–4   Compute the equivalent units of production for materials.

6–5   Compute the equivalent units of production for conversion.

6–6   What is the amount of the cost of beginning work in process inventory plus the cost added during the period for materials?

6–7   What is the amount of the cost of beginning work in process inventory plus the cost added during the period for conversion?

6–8   What is the cost per equivalent unit for materials?

6–9   What is the cost per equivalent unit for conversion?

6–10   What is the cost of ending work in process inventory for materials?

6–11   What is the cost of ending work in process inventory for conversion?

6–12   What is the cost of materials transferred to finished goods?

6–13   What is the amount of conversion cost transferred to finished goods?

6–14   Prepare the journal entry to record the transfer of costs from Work in Process to Finished Goods.

6–15   What is the total cost to be accounted for? What is the total cost accounted for?

EXERCISES

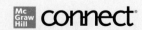

EXERCISE 6–1   Process Costing Journal Entries [LO1]
Arizona Brick Corporation produces bricks in two processing departments—Moulding and Firing. Information relating to the company's operations in March follows:

a.   Raw materials were issued for use in production: Moulding Department, $28,000; Firing Department, $5,000.

b.   Direct labour costs were incurred: Moulding Department, $18,000; Firing Department, $5,000.

c. Manufacturing overhead was applied: Moulding Department, $24,000; Firing Department, $37,000.

d. Unfired, moulded bricks were transferred from the Moulding Department to the Firing Department. According to the company's process costing system, the cost of the unfired, moulded bricks was $67,000.

e. Finished bricks were transferred from the Firing Department to the finished goods warehouse. According to the company's process costing system, the cost of the finished bricks was $108,000.

f. Finished bricks were sold to customers. According to the company's process costing system, the cost of the finished bricks sold was $106,000.

Required:

Prepare journal entries to record items (*a*) through (*f*) above.

EXERCISE 6–2 Computation of Equivalent Units—Weighted-Average Method [LO2]

Handy Products Company manufactures a product that goes through three processing departments. Information relating to activity in the first department during October is given below:

	Units	Percentage Completed	
		Materials	Conversion
Work in process, October 1.	25,000	90%	60%
Work in process, October 31.	15,000	100%	50%

The department started 195,000 units into production during the month and transferred 205,000 completed units to the next department.

Required:

Compute the equivalent units of production for the first department for October, assuming that the company uses the weighted-average method of accounting for units and costs.

CHECK FIGURE
Equivalent units are 220,000 for materials and 212,500 for conversion.

EXERCISE 6–3 Cost per Equivalent Unit—Weighted-Average Method [LO3]

Ainsley Industries uses the weighted-average method in its process costing system. Data for the Assembly Department for May appear below:

	Materials	Labour	Overhead
Work in process, May 1	$28,000	$22,000	$117,500
Cost added during May.	$52,000	$18,500	$ 63,600
Equivalent units of production	1,500	800	1,200

Required:

Compute the cost per equivalent unit for materials, for labour, for overhead, and in total.

EXERCISE 6–4 Assigning Costs to Units—Weighted-Average Method [LO4]

Data concerning a recent period's activity in the Prep Department, the first processing department in a company that uses process costing, appear below:

	Materials	Conversion
Equivalent units in ending work-in-process inventory	2,000	800
Cost per equivalent unit	$13.86	$4.43

A total of 20,100 units were completed and transferred to the next processing department during the period.

Required:

1. Compute the cost of ending work in process inventory for materials, conversion, and in total.
2. Compute the cost of the units completed and transferred out for materials, conversion, and in total.

EXERCISE 6–5 Process Costing Journal Entries [LO1]

Tasty Bakery uses a process costing system for its single product—a popular rye bread. Tasty has two processing departments—Mixing and Baking. The T-accounts below show the flow of costs through the two departments in April:

Work in Process—Mixing			
Balance, April 1	5,000	Transferred out	60,000
Direct materials	25,000		
Direct labour	15,000		
Overhead	20,000		

Work in Process—Baking			
Balance April 1	10,000	Transferred out	100,000
Transferred in	60,000		
Direct labour	12,000		
Overhead	30,000		

Required:

Prepare journal entries showing the flow of costs through the two processing departments during April.

EXERCISE 6–6 Equivalent Units and Cost per Equivalent Unit—Weighted-Average Method [LO2, LO3]

Healthcheck Corp. manufactures an antacid product that passes through two departments. Data for June for the first department follow:

	Litres	Materials	Labour	Overhead
Work in process, June 1	80,000	$ 68,600	$ 30,000	$ 48,000
Litres started in process	760,000			
Litres transferred out.	790,000			
Work in process, June 30	50,000			
Cost added during June.		$907,200	$370,000	$592,000

CHECK FIGURE

Cost per equivalent unit = $1.19 for materials, $0.50 for labour, and $0.80 for overhead.

The beginning work in process inventory was 80% complete with respect to materials and 75% complete with respect to labour and overhead. The ending work in process inventory was 60% complete with respect to materials and 20% complete with respect to labour and overhead.

Required:

Assume that the company uses the weighted-average method of accounting for units and costs.
1. Compute the equivalent units for June's activity for the first department.
2. Determine the costs per equivalent unit for June.

EXERCISE 6–7 Equivalent Units—Weighted-Average Method [LO2]

Green House Inc. processes cleaning fluid used as a base for household cleaning products produced by various distributors. Two departments are involved: Mixing and Heating. Data relating to litres of cleaning fluid processed in the Mixing Department during October are provided below:

	Litres of Cleaning Fluid	Percentage Completed*
Work in process, October 1.	25,000	35%
Work in process, October 31.	5,000	70%
*Labour and overhead only		

A total of 25,000 litres of cleaning fluid were started into processing during October. All materials are added at the beginning of processing in the Mixing Department.

Required:

Compute the equivalent units for October for the Mixing Department, assuming that the company uses the weighted-average method of accounting for units.

EXERCISE 6–8 Equivalent Units and Cost per Equivalent Unit—Weighted-Average Method [LO2, LO3, LO4, LO5]

Grand River Company produces a high-quality insulation material that passes through two production processes. Data for November for the first process follow:

	Units	Completion with Respect to Materials	Completion with Respect to Conversion
Work in process inventory, November 1.......	80,000	50%	25%
Work in process inventory, November 30......	60,000	45%	20%
Materials cost in work in process inventory, November 1	$ 76,600		
Conversion cost in work in process inventory, November 1	$ 34,900		
Units started into production...............	300,000		
Units transferred to the next process..........	320,000		
Materials cost added during November	$410,000		
Conversion cost added during November......	$234,500		

Required:

1. Assume that the company uses the weighted-average method of accounting for units and costs. Determine the equivalent units for November for the first process.
2. Compute the costs per equivalent unit for November for the first process.
3. Determine the total cost of ending work in process inventory and the total cost of units transferred to the next process in November.

EXERCISE 6–9 Cost Reconciliation—Weighted-Average Method [LO5]

United Claim Processors provides claims processing services for major insurance companies. The Winnipeg location processes all health benefit claims for various insurance benefit providers. Claims are received electronically or by mail in the Initial Review Department. Employees in this department sort claims into simple and complex categories and note any missing documentation that may be required. Simple claims are then passed on to the Processing Department where skilled claims processors match information from the claim with each individual's accounts in the database and then estimate the value of the benefit payment to be paid. Complex claims go to a separate processing centre for further examination. The next stage in the simple claims process is the Approval and Payment Department, where final approvals and payments to claimants are initiated and completed.

During March, the Initial Review Department transferred 3,500 simple claims to the Processing Department. At the end of March, 500 claims remained in the Initial Review Department that were 90% complete with respect to conversion. The cost per equivalent unit for the month was $1.75 per claim processed, and total costs incurred in the Initial Review Department during the month totalled $6,913. (Note that there are only conversion costs in this process; no raw materials are added at any point.)

Required:

Prepare the cost reconciliation portion of the Initial Review Department's production report for March.

PROBLEMS

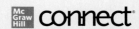

PROBLEM 6–10 Equivalent Units, Cost per Equivalent Unit, Assigning Costs—Weighted-Average Method [LO2, LO3, LO4, LO5]

CloverSweet Inc. manufactures a product that goes through two departments prior to completion. The information shown in the table below is available about work in the first department, the Mixing Department, during June:

		Percentage Complete	
	Units	Materials	Conversion
Work in process, beginning............	50,000	75%	30%
Started into production	430,000		
Completed and transferred out	380,000		
Work in process, ending	100,000	60%	40%

	Materials	Conversion
Work in process, beginning............	$ 45,500	$ 25,000
Costs added during June...............	$425,500	$145,000

Required:

Assume that the company uses the weighted-average method.

1. Determine the equivalent units for June for the first process.
2. Compute the costs per equivalent unit for June for the first process.
3. Determine the total cost of ending work in process inventory and the total cost of units transferred to the next process in June.
4. Prepare a report that reconciles the total costs assigned to the ending work in process inventory and the units transferred out with the costs in beginning inventory and costs added during the period.

PROBLEM 6–11 Equivalent Units; Assigning Costs—Weighted-Average Method
[LO2, LO3, LO4, LO5]

The WireOne Company manufactures high-quality coated electrical wire in two departments, Weaving and Coating. Materials are introduced at various points during work in the Weaving Department. After the weaving is completed, the materials are transferred into the Coating Department, where specialty plastic coating is applied.

Selected data relating to the Weaving Department during May are given below:

Production data:	
Kilograms in process, May 1 (materials 100% complete; conversion 80% complete)	85,000
Kilograms started into production during May............................	365,000
Kilograms completed and transferred to Coating...........................	?
Kilograms in process, May 31 (materials 65% complete; conversion 30% complete)	55,000
Cost data:	
Work in process inventory, May 1:	
Materials cost	$101,000
Conversion cost...	$ 51,000
Cost added during May:	
Materials cost	$462,000
Conversion cost...	$213,000

The company uses the weighted-average method.

Required:

CHECK FIGURE
Cost per EU for May = $1.31 for materials and $0.64 for conversion.

1. Compute the equivalent units of production.
2. Compute the costs per equivalent unit for May.
3. Determine the cost of ending work in process inventory and of the units transferred to the Coating Department.
4. Prepare a cost reconciliation between the costs determined in (3) above and the cost of beginning inventory and costs added during the period.

PROBLEM 6–12 Interpreting a Report—Weighted-Average Method [LO2, LO3, LO4]
Parandah Electronics Ltd., located in England, assembles a standard electrical component from parts it purchases from various suppliers. The production process consists of several steps, starting with assembly, which takes place in the Assembly Department. The company recently hired a new accountant, who prepared the following report for the department for May, using the weighted-average method:

Quantity Schedule

Units to be accounted for:	
Work in process, May 1 (materials 90% complete; conversion 80% complete)	8,000
Started into production	26,000
Total units	34,000
Units accounted for as follows:	
Transferred to next department	28,000
Work in process, May 31 (materials 75% complete; conversion 50% complete)	6,000
Total units	34,000

Cost Reconciliation

Cost to be accounted for:	
Work in process, May 1	£ 13,400
Cost added in the department	87,800
Total cost to be accounted for	£101,200
Cost accounted for as follows:	
Work in process, May 31	£ 12,450
Transferred to next department	88,750
Total cost accounted for	£101,200

The company's management would like some additional information about May's operation in the Assembly Department. (The currency in England is the pound, denoted by the symbol £.)

Required:
1. How many units were started and completed during May?
2. What were the equivalent units for May for materials and conversion costs?
3. What were the costs per equivalent unit for May? The following additional data are available concerning the department's costs:

	Materials	Conversion	Total
Work in process, May 1	£ 9,000	£ 4,400	£13,400
Costs added during May	£56,000	£31,250	£87,250

4. Verify the accountant's ending work in process inventory figure (£12,450) given in the report.
5. The new manager of the Assembly Department is asked to estimate the incremental cost of processing an additional 1,000 units through the department. He takes the unit cost for an equivalent whole unit that you computed in (3) above and multiplies this figure by 1,000. Will this method yield a valid estimate of incremental cost? Explain.

PROBLEM 6–13 Comprehensive Problem; Second Production Department—Weighted-Average Method [LO2, LO3, LO4, LO5]
Old Country Links Inc. produces sausages in three production departments: Mixing, Casing and Curing, and Packaging. In the Mixing Department, meats are prepared and ground and then mixed with spices. The spiced meat mixture is then transferred to the Casing and Curing Department, where the mixture is force-fed into casings and then hung and cured in climate-controlled smoking chambers. In the

Packaging Department, the cured sausages are sorted, packed, and labelled. The company uses the weighted-average method in its process costing system. Data for September for the Casing and Curing Department follow:

	Units	Mixing	Materials	Conversion
Work in process inventory, September 1	1	100%	90%	80%
Work in process inventory, September 30	1	100%	80%	70%

	Mixing	Materials	Conversion
Work in process inventory, September 1	$ 1,670	$ 90	$ 605
Costs added during September	$81,460	$6,006	$42,490

Mixing cost represents the costs of the spiced meat mixture transferred in from the Mixing Department. The spiced meat mixture is processed in the Casing and Curing Department in batches; each unit in the above table is a batch, and one batch of spiced meat mixture produces a set amount of sausages that are passed on to the Packaging Department. During September, 50 batches (i.e., units) were completed and transferred to the Packaging Department.

Required:
1. Determine the Casing and Curing Department's equivalent units of production for mixing, materials, and conversion for the month of September. Do not round off your computations.
2. Compute the Casing and Curing Department's cost per equivalent unit for mixing, materials, and conversion for the month of September.
3. Compute the Casing and Curing Department's cost of ending work in process inventory for mixing, materials, conversion, and in total for September.
4. Compute the Casing and Curing Department's cost of units transferred out to the Packaging Department for mixing, materials, conversion, and in total for September.
5. Prepare a cost reconciliation report for the Casing and Curing Department for September.

PROBLEM 6–14 Equivalent Units; Costing of Inventories; Journal Entries—Weighted-Average Method [LO1, LO2, LO3, LO4]
Tambin Inc. produces a gasoline additive that, when added to the gas tank of the average automobile, is designed to increase gas mileage by 10%. The company's controller suspects that the year-end dollar balances shown below in the inventory accounts may be incorrect.

	Units	Costs
Work in process, December 31 (materials 100% complete; conversion 50% complete)	25,000	$ 60,000
Finished goods, December 31	30,000	$113,500

There were no finished goods inventories at the beginning of the year. The company uses the weighted-average method of process costing. There is only one processing department.

A review of the company's inventory and cost records shows the following:

		Costs	
	Units	Materials	Conversion
Work in process, beginning of year (materials 100% complete; conversion 80% complete)	20,000	$ 22,000	$ 48,000
Started into production	685,000		
Costs added during the year		$750,000	$2,000,000
Units completed during the year	680,000		

Required:
1. Determine the equivalent units and the costs per equivalent unit for materials and conversion for the year.
2. Determine the amount of cost that should be assigned to the ending work in process and finished goods inventories.
3. Prepare the necessary correcting journal entry to adjust the work in process and finished goods inventories to the correct balances as of December 31.

CHECK FIGURE
Corrected cost per equivalent unit is $1.10 for materials and $2.96 for conversion.

PROBLEM 6–15 Comprehensive Process Costing Problem [LO1, LO2, LO3, LO4, LO5]

Fryer's Choice produces a specially blended vegetable oil widely used in restaurant deep fryers. The blending process creates a cooking oil that can be heated to a high temperature, but does not smoke or smell. The oil is produced in two departments: Blending and Bottling. Raw materials are introduced at various points in the Blending Department.

The following incomplete Work in Process T-account is available for the Blending Department for March:

Work in Process—Blending

March 1 balance (20,000 litres; materials 100% complete; labour and overhead 90% complete)	$ 38,000	Completed and transferred to Bottling (___?___ litres)	___$???___
March costs added:			
Oils (390,000 litres)	495,000		
Direct labour	72,000		
Overhead	181,000		
March 31 inventory (40,000 litres; materials 75% complete, labour and overhead 25% complete)	$???		

The March 1 beginning inventory in the Blending Department consists of the following cost elements: raw materials, $25,000; direct labour, $4,000; and overhead, $9,000.

Costs incurred during March in the Bottling Department were materials used, $115,000; direct labour, $18,000; and overhead cost applied to production, $42,000. The company uses the weighted-average method in its process costing.

Required:
1. Prepare journal entries to record the cost incurred in both the Blending Department and the Bottling Department during March. Key your entries to the items (*a*) through (*f*) below:
   a. Raw materials were issued for use in production.
   b. Direct labour costs were incurred.
   c. Manufacturing overhead costs for the entire factory were incurred: $225,000. (*Hint:* Credit Accounts Payable.)
   d. Manufacturing overhead cost was applied to production using a predetermined overhead rate.
   e. Units that were complete with respect to processing in the Bottling Department were transferred to finished goods: $950,000.
   f. Completed units were sold on account: $1,500,000. The cost of goods sold was $890,000.
2. Post the journal entries from (1) above to T-accounts. The following account balances existed at the beginning of March. (*Note:* The beginning balance in the Blending Department's Work in Process account is given above.)

Raw materials	$681,000
Work in Process—Bottling Department	65,000
Finished goods	20,000

After posting the entries to the T-accounts, find the ending balance in the inventory accounts and the manufacturing overhead accounts.
3. Prepare a production report for the Blending Department for March.
4. Prepare the journal entry to record the transfer of finished goods from the Blending Department to the Bottling Department and post to the appropriate T-accounts prepared in (2) above.

PROBLEM 6–16 Interpreting a Report—Weighted-Average Method [LO2, LO3, LO4]
Cooperative San José of southern Sonora state in Mexico makes a unique syrup using cane sugar and local herbs. The syrup is sold in small bottles and is prized as a flavouring for drinks and for use in desserts. The bottles are sold to customers in Canada for $12 each. The first stage in the production process is carried out in the Mixing Department, which removes foreign matter from the raw materials and mixes them in the proper proportions in large vats. The company uses the weighted-average method in its process costing system.

    A hastily prepared report for the Mixing Department for April appears below:

Units to be accounted for:	
Work in process, April 1 (materials 90% complete; conversion 80% complete)	30,000
Started into production	200,000
Total units to be accounted for	230,000
Units accounted for as follows:	
Transferred to next department...............................	190,000
Work in process, April 30 (materials 75% complete; conversion 60% complete) ...	40,000
Total units accounted for.....................................	230,000

Cost Reconciliation

Cost to be accounted for:	
Work in process, April 1.......................................	$ 98,000
Cost added during the month	827,000
Total cost to be accounted for	$925,000
Cost accounted for as follows:	
Work in process, April 30.....................................	$119,400
Transferred to next department................................	805,600
Total costs accounted for.....................................	$925,000

Management would like some additional information about Cooperative San José's operations.

Required:
1. What were the equivalent units for the month?
2. What were the costs per equivalent unit for the month? The beginning inventory consisted of the following costs: materials, $67,800, and conversion cost, $30,200. The costs added during the month consisted of materials, $579,000, and conversion cost, $248,000.
3. How many of the units transferred to the next department were started and completed during the month?
4. The manager of the Mixing Department stated, "Materials prices jumped from about $2.50 per unit in March to $3 per unit in April, but due to good cost control I was able to hold our materials cost to less than $3 per unit for the month." Should this manager be rewarded for good cost control? Explain.

PROBLEM 6–17 Comprehensive Process Costing Problem [LO2, LO3, LO4, LO5]
Sunspot Beverages Ltd. of Fiji makes blended tropical fruit drinks in two stages. Fruit juices are extracted from fresh fruits and then blended in the Blending Department. The blended juices are then bottled and packed for shipping in the Bottling Department. The following information pertains to the operations of the Blending Department for June.

		Percent Complete	
	Units	**Materials**	**Conversion**
Work in process, beginning..................	20,000	100%	75%
Started into production	180,000		
Completed and transferred out	160,000		
Work in process, ending	40,000	100%	25%
Costs		**Materials**	**Conversion**
Work in process, beginning..................		$ 25,200	$ 24,800
Cost added during June.....................		$334,800	$238,700

Required:
Assume that the company uses the weighted-average method.
1.   Determine the equivalent units for June for the Blending Department.
2.   Compute the costs per equivalent unit for the Blending Department.
3.   Determine the total cost of ending work in process inventory and the total cost of units transferred to the Bottling Department.
4.   Prepare a cost reconciliation report for the Blending Department for June.

PROBLEM 6–18 Equivalent Units; Assigning Costs; Cost Reconciliation—Weighted-Average Method [LO2, LO3, LO4, LO5]

Superior Micro Products uses the weighted-average method in its process costing system. During January, the Delta Assembly Department completed its processing of 25,000 units and transferred them to the next department. The cost of beginning work in process inventory and the costs added during January amounted to $599,780 in total. The ending work in process inventory in January consisted of 3,000 units, which were 80% complete with respect to materials and 60% complete with respect to labour and overhead. The costs per equivalent unit for the month were as follows:

	Materials	Labour	Overhead
Cost per equivalent unit........................	$12.50	$3.20	$6.40

Required:
1.   Compute the equivalent units of materials, labour, and overhead in the ending work in process inventory for the month.
2.   Compute the cost of ending work in process inventory for materials, labour, overhead, and in total for January.
3.   Compute the cost of the units transferred to the next department for materials, labour, overhead, and in total for January.
4.   Prepare a cost reconciliation for January. (*Note:* You will not be able to break the cost to be accounted for into the cost of beginning work in process inventory and costs added during the month.)

PROBLEM 6–19 Comprehensive Problem; Second Production Department—Weighted-Average Method [LO2, LO3, LO4, LO5]

Scribners Corporation produces fine papers in three production departments—Pulping, Drying, and Finishing. In the Pulping Department, raw materials such as wood fibre and rag cotton are mechanically and chemically treated to separate their fibres. The result is a thick slurry of fibres. In the Drying Department, the wet fibres transferred from the Pulping Department are laid down on porous webs, pressed to remove excess liquid, and dried in ovens. In the Finishing Department, the dried paper is coated, cut, and spooled onto reels. The company uses the weighted-average method in its process costing system. Data for March for the Drying Department follow:

	Units	Percent Complete Pulping	Percent Complete Conversion
Work in process inventory, March 1	5,000	100%	20%
Work in process inventory, March 31	8,000	100%	25%
Pulping cost in work in process inventory, March 1		$ 4,800	
Conversion cost in work in process inventory, March 1		$ 500	
Units transferred to the next production department		157,000	
Pulping costs added during March		$102,450	
Conversion costs added during March		$ 31,300	

No materials are added in the Drying Department. Pulping cost represents the costs of the wet fibres transferred in from the Pulping Department. Wet fibre is processed in the Drying Department in batches; each unit in the above table is a batch, and one batch of wet fibres produces a set amount of dried paper that is passed on to the Finishing Department.

Required:
1. Compute the Drying Department's equivalent units of production for pulping and conversion in March.
2. Compute the Drying Department's cost per equivalent unit for pulping and conversion in March.
3. Compute the Drying Department's cost of ending work in process inventory for pulping, conversion, and in total for March.
4. Compute the Drying Department's cost of units transferred out to the Finishing Department for pulping, conversion, and in total in March.
5. Prepare a cost reconciliation report for the Drying Department for March.

CASES

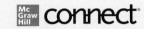

CASE 6–20 Effect of Incorrect Costing across Departments—Weighted-Average Method
[LO2, LO3, LO4, LO5]

Tavia Limited manufactures a plastic gasket that is used in automobile engines. The gaskets go through three processing departments: Mixing, Forming, and Stamping. The company's accountant (who is very inexperienced) has prepared a summary of production and costs for the Forming Department for October, as follows:

Work in process inventory, October 1 (8,000 units; materials 100% complete; conversion $7/8$ complete)	$ 22,420*
Costs transferred in from the Mixing Department	81,480
Material added during October (added when processing is 50% complete in the Forming Department)	27,600
Conversion costs added during October	96,900
Total departmental costs	$228,400
Forming Department costs assigned to:	
Units completed and transferred to the Stamping Department (100,000 units at $2.284 each)	$228,400
Work in process inventory, October 31 (5,000 units, conversion $2/5$ complete)	
Total departmental costs assigned	$228,400

*Consists of cost transferred in, $8,820; materials cost, $3,400; and conversion costs, $10,200

After mulling over the data above, Tavia's president commented, "I can't understand what's happening here. Despite a concentrated effort at cost reduction, our unit cost actually went up in the Forming Department last month. With that kind of performance, year-end bonuses are out of the question for the people in that department."

The company uses the weighted-average method in its process costing.

Required:
1. Prepare a report for the Forming Department for October showing how much cost should have been assigned to the units completed and transferred to the Stamping Department and to the ending work in process inventory.
2. Explain to the president why the unit cost appearing on the report prepared by the accountant is so high.

CASE 6–21 Inventory Valuation under Process Costing—Weighted-Average Method
[LO2, LO3, LO4, LO5]

Using an old family recipe, Rachel Archer started a company that produces root beer. Archer opened the doors of Rachel's Real Root Beer on January 1. The company struggled for the first few months, but by the end of September, the customer list was expanding rapidly. Archer realized that bottling by hand was becoming more and more difficult as the orders continued to come in. To purchase the automated equipment needed to expand further, Archer realized it would be necessary to borrow money.

Archer was disappointed to find that few banks were willing to make a loan to such a small company, but she finally found a bank that would consider her loan application. However, Archer was informed that she would have to supply up-to-date financial statements with her loan application.

Archer had not bothered with formal financial statements so far—she felt that as long as the balance in the company's chequing account kept increasing, the company was doing fine. She wondered how she was going to determine the value of the root beer in the work in process and finished goods inventories to put on her company's balance sheet.

Archer approached Ed Switzer, an old friend currently working for a local accounting firm. After talking with Archer and touring her production facility, Switzer suggested a process costing system (using the weighted-average method) since Archer's company produces only one standard product in a continuous production process. During the plant tour, Switzer noted that Archer ran the operation as one department. At the beginning of the process, the various ingredients were checked for quality and then mixed and injected with carbon dioxide to create bulk root beer. Then bottles were checked for defects, filled with root beer, capped, visually inspected again for defects, and then packed into cases (12 bottles per case) for shipping. At this point, completed cases were transferred to finished goods.

Archer asked Switzer to help her calculate the work in process and finished goods inventory cost to put on the company balance sheet at the end of August. To get started, Switzer asked Archer to collect several pieces of information. Details collected by Archer are listed below:

a. Approximately 75% of raw materials cost is added at the beginning of the process, and 25% is added when the product is 85% complete. Conversion costs are added evenly throughout the process.
b. Archer estimated there were 550 units of product that were 75% complete for raw materials and 60% complete for conversion on August 1. From her bank records, she calculated that the raw materials cost included in the opening inventory was about $650 and conversion cost was about $430.
c. During August, 3,000 units of product were started into production, and 2,400 were completed and transferred to finished goods. Costs added to production during August were $3,840 for materials and $3,480 for conversion.
d. At the end of August, the work in process inventory was made up of 1,150 units that were 75% complete for materials and 50% complete for conversion costs.

Using this information, Switzer agreed to prepare a report indicating the cost of both work in process and finished goods inventory that Archer would need to report on her balance sheet as at August 30.

Required:
Take on the role of Switzer and prepare the report for Archer. Be sure to provide all details, including a full production report, to help Archer understand how costs were calculated.

INSTANT QUIZ SOLUTIONS

6–1
Process costing can be used for the newsprint product line since it involves many identical units and is produced and sold in large batches. The custom paper product line would use a job order costing system since different customers are likely to request different weights and finishes in their orders.

6–2
The answer to this question is true. Both process costing and job-order costing use the same method to calculate the predetermined overhead rate.

6–3
The number of full-time equivalent students is $5,000 + (50\% \times 1,250) = 5,625$.

6–4
Recall from Chapter 2 that conversion costs include labour and overhead added during production.

6–5
Cost per equivalent unit $= (\$7,250 + \$10,750) \div 6,250 = \$2.88$.

■ APPENDIX 6A: FIFO METHOD

The FIFO method of process costing differs from the weighted-average method in two ways: (1) the computation of equivalent units, and (2) the way in which costs of beginning inventory are treated. The FIFO method is generally considered to be more accurate than the weighted-average method, but it is more complex. The complexity is not a problem for computers, but the FIFO method is a little more difficult to understand and to learn than the weighted-average method.

Equivalent Units—FIFO Method

The computation of equivalent units under the FIFO (or first in, first out) method differs in two ways from computation under the weighted-average method.

First, the "units transferred out" is divided into two parts. One part consists of the units from the beginning inventory that were completed and transferred out, and the other part consists of the units that were both *started* and *completed* during the current period.

Second, full consideration is given to the amount of work expended during the current period on units in the *beginning* work in process inventory as well as on units in the ending inventory. Thus, under the FIFO method, both beginning and ending inventories are converted to an equivalent units basis. For the beginning inventory, the equivalent units represent the work done to *complete* the units; for the ending inventory, the equivalent units represent the work done to bring the units to a stage of partial completion at the end of the period (the same as with the weighted-average method).

The formula for computing the equivalent units of production under the FIFO method is more complex than under the weighted-average method:

> *FIFO Method*
> *(a separate calculation is made for each cost category in each processing department)*
>
> Equivalent units of production = Equivalent units to complete beginning work in process inventory*
> + Units started and completed during the period
> + Equivalent units in ending work in process inventory
>
> $$\begin{matrix} \text{*Equivalent units to} \\ \text{complete beginning work} \\ \text{in process inventory} \end{matrix} = \begin{matrix} \text{Units in beginning} \\ \text{work in process} \\ \text{inventory} \end{matrix} \times \left(100\% - \begin{matrix} \text{Percentage completion} \\ \text{of beginning work in} \\ \text{process inventory} \end{matrix} \right)$$

The equivalent units of production can also be determined as follows:

> Equivalent units of production = Units transferred out
> + Equivalent units in ending work in process inventory
> − Equivalent units in beginning work in process inventory

To illustrate the FIFO method, refer again to the data for the Electrics and Testing Department at Tropic Breeze Fans. The department completed and transferred 4,800 units to the Inspection and Packing Department during May. Since 200 of these units came from the beginning inventory, the Electrics and Testing Department must have started and completed 4,600 units during May. The 200 units in the beginning inventory were 55% complete with respect to materials and only 30% complete with respect to conversion costs when the month started. Thus, to complete these units the department must have added another 45% of materials costs (100% − 55% = 45%) and another 70% of conversion costs (100% − 30% = 70%). Following this line of reasoning, the equivalent units for the department for May are computed as shown in Exhibit 6A–1.

Comparison of Equivalent Units of Production under the Weighted-Average and FIFO Methods

Stop at this point and compare the data in Exhibit 6A–1 with the data in Exhibit 6–4 in the chapter, which shows the computation of equivalent units under the weighted-average method. Also refer to Exhibit 6A–2, which compares the two methods.

	Materials	Conversion
To complete beginning work in process:		
Materials: 200 units × (100% − 55%*).....................	90	
Conversion: 200 units × (100% − 30%*)		140
Units started and completed during the period...................	4,600†	4,600†
Ending work in process:		
Materials: 400 units × 40% complete......................	160	
Conversion: 400 units × 25% complete		100
Equivalent units of production	4,850	4,840

*This is the work needed to complete the units in beginning inventory.
†5,000 units started − 400 units in ending work in process = 4,600 units started and completed. This can also be computed as 4,800 units completed and transferred to the next department − 200 units in beginning work in process inventory. The FIFO method assumes that the units in beginning inventory are finished first.

EXHIBIT 6A–1
Equivalent Units of Production: FIFO Method

EXHIBIT 6A–2   Visual Perspective of Equivalent Units of Production—Conversion

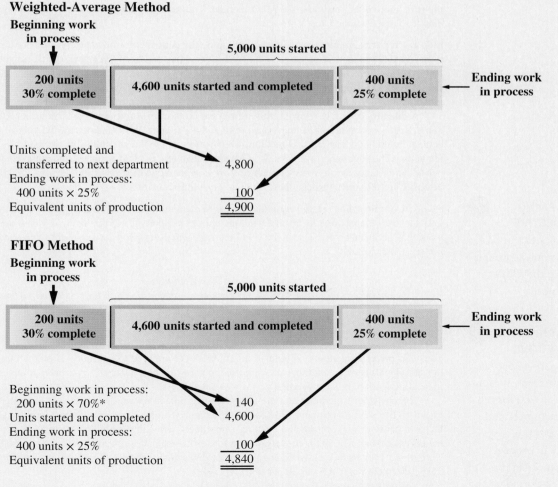

TROPIC BREEZE FANS
Electrics and Testing Department
Conversion Costs

Weighted-Average Method
Beginning work in process

5,000 units started

| 200 units 30% complete | 4,600 units started and completed | 400 units 25% complete | Ending work in process |

Units completed and
  transferred to next department   4,800
Ending work in process:
  400 units × 25%   100
Equivalent units of production   4,900

FIFO Method
Beginning work in process

5,000 units started

| 200 units 30% complete | 4,600 units started and completed | 400 units 25% complete | Ending work in process |

Beginning work in process:
  200 units × 70%*   140
Units started and completed   4,600
Ending work in process:
  400 units × 25%   100
Equivalent units of production   4,840

*100% − 30% = 70%. This 70% represents the work needed to complete the units in the beginning inventory.

The essential difference between the two methods is that the weighted-average method blends work and costs from the prior period with work and costs in the current period, whereas the FIFO method separates the two periods. To see this more clearly, consider the following reconciliation of the two calculations of equivalent units:

Electrics and Testing Department	Materials	Conversion
Equivalent units—weighted-average method	4,960	4,900
Less equivalent units in beginning inventory:		
200 units × 55%	110	
200 units × 30%		60
Equivalent units of production—FIFO method	4,850	4,840

From the above, it is evident that the FIFO method removes the equivalent units that were already in beginning inventory from the equivalent units as defined using the weighted-average method. Thus, the FIFO method isolates the equivalent units due to work performed during the current period. The weighted-average method, on the other hand, blends the equivalent units already in beginning inventory with the equivalent units due to work performed in the current period.

■ PRODUCTION REPORT—FIFO METHOD

The steps followed to prepare a production report under the FIFO method are the same as those discussed earlier for the weighted-average method. However, since the FIFO method distinguishes between units in the beginning inventory and units started during the year, the cost reconciliation portion of the report is more complex under the FIFO method. To illustrate the FIFO method, we will again use the data for Tropic Breeze Fans.

Step 1: Prepare a quantity schedule and compute the equivalent units. There is only one difference between a quantity schedule prepared under the FIFO method and one prepared under the weighted-average method. This difference relates to units transferred out. As explained earlier in our discussion of equivalent units, the FIFO method divides units transferred out into two parts. One part consists of the units in the beginning inventory, and the other part consists of the units started and completed during the current period.

A quantity schedule showing this format for units transferred out is presented in Exhibit 6A–3, along with a computation of equivalent units for the month. We explained earlier that in computing equivalent units under the FIFO method, we must first show the amount of work required *to complete* the units in the beginning inventory. We then show the number of units started and completed during the period, and finally we show the amount of work *completed* on the units still in process at the end of the period. Carefully trace through these computations in Exhibit 6A–3.

LEARNING OBJECTIVE 7

Compute the cost per equivalent unit using the FIFO method.

Step 2: Compute the cost per equivalent unit. In computing unit costs under the FIFO method, we use only those costs that were incurred during the current period, and we ignore any costs in the beginning work in process inventory. Under the FIFO method, *unit costs relate only to work done during the current period* as follows:

> *FIFO Method*
> *(a separate calculation is made for each cost category in each processing department)*
>
> $$\text{Cost per equivalent unit} = \frac{\text{Cost added during the period}}{\text{Equivalent units of production}}$$

LEARNING OBJECTIVE 8

Prepare a cost reconciliation report accounting for the costs transferred out and the costs in work in process inventory at the end of the period using the FIFO method.

The costs per equivalent unit computed in Exhibit 6A–3 are used to cost units of product transferred to the next department; in addition, they are used to show the cost attached to partially completed units in the ending work in process inventory.

The costs per equivalent unit are used to value units in ending inventory and units that are transferred to the next department. For example, each unit transferred out of the Electrics and Testing Department to the Inspection and Packing Department will carry with it a cost of $148.50: $76.00 for materials cost and $72.50 for conversion cost for work done in the current period. Since 4,600 units were started and transferred out in May to the next department, the total cost assigned to these units is $683,100 (4,600 units × $148.50 per unit).

Step 3: Prepare a cost reconciliation. The purpose of the cost reconciliation is to show how the costs charged to a department during a period are accounted for. With the FIFO method, two cost elements are

EXHIBIT 6A–3   Production Report—FIFO Method

TROPIC BREEZE FANS
Electrics and Testing Department Production Report
(FIFO method)

Quantity Schedule and Equivalent Units

	Quantity Schedule
Units to be accounted for:	
Work in process, May 1 (materials 55% complete; conversion 30% complete)	200
Started into production	5,000
Total units	5,200

	Quantity Schedule	Equivalent Units (EU) Materials	Equivalent Units (EU) Conversion
Units accounted for as follows:			
Transferred to the next department			
From beginning inventory*	200	90	140
Started and completed in the month†	4,600	4,600	4,600
Work in process, May 31 (materials 40% complete; conversion 25% complete)	400	160	100
Total units and equivalent units of production	5,200	4,850	4,840

Costs per Equivalent Unit

	Total Cost	Materials	Conversion	Whole Unit
Cost to be accounted for:				
Work in process, May 1	$ 15,175			
Cost added in the department (a)	719,500	368,600	350,900	
Total cost	$734,675			
Equivalent units of production (b) (see above)		4,850	4,840	
Cost per EU, (a) ÷ (b)		$76.00 +	$72.50 =	$148.50

Cost Reconciliation

	Total Cost	Equivalent Units Materials	Equivalent Units Conversion
Cost accounted for as follows:			
Transferred to next department:			
From beginning inventory:			
Cost in beginning inventory	$ 15,175		
Cost to complete these units			
Materials at $76.00 per EU	6,840	90	
Conversion at $72.50 per EU	10,150		140
Total cost from beginning inventory	$ 32,165		
Units started and completed this month at $148.50 per EU	$683,100	4,600	4,600
Total cost transferred out	$715,265		
Work in process, May 31:			
Materials, at $76.00 per EU	$ 12,160	160	
Conversion, at $72.50 per EU	7,250		100
Total work in process, May 31	19,410		
Total cost	$734,675		

*Materials: 200 × (100% − 55%) = 90 EU. Conversion: 200 × (100% − 30%) = 140 EU.
†5,000 units started − 400 units in ending inventory = 4,600 units started and completed.

associated with the units in the beginning work in process inventory. The first element is the cost carried over from the prior period ($15,175 from Exhibit 6A–3). The second element is the cost needed to complete these units ($6,840 of materials plus $10,150 of conversion costs in Exhibit 6A–3).

For units started and completed in the month, we simply multiply the number of units started and completed by the total cost per unit to determine the amount transferred out. This is $683,100 for the department (see Exhibit 6A–3).

Finally, the amount of cost attached to the ending work in process inventory is computed by multiplying the cost per equivalent unit figures for the month by the number of equivalent units for materials and conversion costs in ending inventory.

Note that the $715,265 cost of the units transferred to the next department, Inspection and Packing, are accounted for in that department as "costs transferred in." As in the weighted-average method, this cost is treated in the process costing system as just another category of costs, like materials or conversion costs. The only difference is that the costs transferred in are always 100% complete with respect to the work done in the Inspection and Packing Department. Costs are passed on from one department to the next in this fashion, until they are transferred to finished goods.

A Comparison of Costing Methods

In most situations, the weighted-average and FIFO methods produce very similar unit costs. If there are never any ending inventories, as in an ideal lean production (JIT) environment, the two methods will produce identical results. This is because, without any ending inventories, no costs can be carried forward into the next period, and the weighted-average method bases the unit costs on only the current period's costs—just as in the FIFO method. If there *are* ending inventories, either erratic input prices or erratic production levels are also required to generate much of a difference in unit costs under the two methods. This is because the weighted-average method blends the unit costs from the prior period with the unit costs of the current period. Unless these unit costs differ greatly, the blending does not make much difference.

Nevertheless, from the standpoint of cost control, the FIFO method is superior to the weighted-average method. Current performance should be measured in relation to costs of the current period only, and the weighted-average method mixes costs of the current period with costs of the prior period. Thus, under the weighted-average method, the manager's apparent performance in the current period is influenced by what happened in the prior period. This problem does not arise under the FIFO method because the FIFO method makes a clear distinction between costs of prior periods and costs incurred during the current period. For the same reason, the FIFO method also provides more up-to-date cost data for decision making.

On the other hand, the weighted-average method is simpler to apply than the FIFO method, but computers can handle the additional calculations with ease once they have been appropriately programmed. A detailed comparison of the weighted-average and FIFO methods is provided in the Learning Aid that follows:

LEARNING AID

Comparison of Process Costing Methods

Weighted Average	FIFO
1. Equivalent units of production are calculated at the end of each period by adding together the completed units transferred out and the equivalent units in ending work in process inventory.	1. Equivalent units of production are calculated at the end of each period by adding together the completed units transferred out and the equivalent units in ending work in process inventory *less equivalent units in beginning work in process inventory.*
2. Cost per equivalent unit is calculated by adding the cost of beginning work in process inventory and the costs added during the period and dividing the total by the equivalent units of production (i.e., taking the weighted average).	2. Cost per equivalent unit is calculated by dividing the costs added during the period by the equivalent units of production.
3. Total cost for the period is calculated as the cost per equivalent unit times the equivalent units of production.	3. Total cost for the period is calculated as the cost per equivalent unit times the equivalent units of production.

■ APPENDIX 6A SUMMARY

- Under the FIFO method of process costing, both beginning and ending inventories are converted to an equivalent-units basis. For the beginning inventory, the equivalent units represent the work done to *complete* the units; for the ending inventory, the equivalent units represent the work done to bring the units to a stage of partial completion at the end of the period (the same as with the weighted-average method). **[LO6]**
- Under the FIFO method, for the cost per equivalent unit we use only those costs that were incurred during the current period, and we ignore any costs in the beginning work in process inventory. Under the FIFO method, *unit costs relate only to work done during the current period.* **[LO7]**
- The cost per equivalent unit is then used to value the ending work in process inventory and the units transferred out to the next department or to finished goods. Costs are transferred from one department to the next until the last processing department. At that point, the cost of completed units is transferred to finished goods. At the end of the period, a cost reconciliation is prepared to account for the costs transferred out and costs in work in process inventory at the end of the period. **[LO8]**

■ APPENDIX 6A QUESTIONS, EXERCISES, PROBLEMS, AND CASES

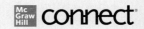

6A–1 How does the computation of equivalent units under the FIFO method differ from the computation of equivalent units under the weighted-average method?

6A–2 From the standpoint of cost control, why is the FIFO method superior to the weighted-average method?

EXERCISE 6A–1 Computation of Equivalent Units—FIFO Method [LO6]
QualityCo produces wine bottles for vintners in a process that starts in the Melt and Mould Department. Data concerning that department's operations in the most recent period appear below:

Beginning work in process:	
Units in process..	400
Stage of completion with respect to materials	75%
Stage of completion with respect to conversion	25%
Units started into production during the month	42,600
Units completed and transferred out............................	42,500
Ending work in process:	
Units in process..	500
Stage of completion with respect to materials	80%
Stage of completion with respect to conversion	30%

Required:
QualityCo uses the FIFO method in its process costing system. Compute the equivalent units of production for the period for the Melt and Mould Department.

EXERCISE 6A–2 Cost per Equivalent Unit—FIFO Method [LO7]
Tolerin Company uses the FIFO method in its process costing system. Data for the Assembly Department for May appear below:

	Materials	Labour	Overhead
Cost added during May........................	$41,280	$26,460	$66,150
Equivalent units of production	8,000	7,000	7,000

Required:
Compute the cost per equivalent unit for materials, for labour, for overhead, and in total.

EXERCISE 6A–3 Assigning Costs to Units—FIFO Method [LO8]
Data concerning a recent period's activity in the Mixing Department, the first processing department in a company that uses process costing, appear below:

	Materials	Conversion
Cost of work in process inventory at the beginning of the period	$2,700	$380
Equivalent units of production in the ending work in process inventory	800	200
Equivalent units of production required to complete the beginning work in process inventory	400	700
Cost per equivalent unit for the period	$4.40	$1.30

A total of 8,000 units were completed and transferred to the next processing department during the period. Beginning work in process inventory consisted of 1,000 units, and ending work in process inventory consisted of 2,000 units.

Required:
Compute the FIFO cost of the units transferred to the next department during the period and the cost of ending work in process inventory.

EXERCISE 6A–4 Equivalent Units and Cost per Equivalent Unit—FIFO Method [LO6, LO7]
Refer to the data for Healthcheck Corp. in Exercise 6–6.

Required:
Assume that the company uses the FIFO method of accounting for units and costs.

1. Compute the equivalent units for June's activity for the first processing department.
2. Determine the costs per equivalent unit for June.

EXERCISE 6A–5 Equivalent Units; Assigning Costs—FIFO Method [LO6, LO7]
Krollon Company uses the FIFO method in its process costing system. The following data are for the most recent month of operations in one of the company's processing departments:

Units in beginning inventory	400
Units started into production	4,300
Units in ending inventory	300
Units transferred to the next department	4,400

	Materials	Conversion
Percentage completion of beginning inventory	70%	30%
Percentage completion of ending inventory	80%	40%

The cost of beginning inventory according to the company's costing system was $7,886, of which $4,897 was for materials and the remainder was for conversion cost. The costs added during the month amounted to $181,652. The costs per equivalent unit for the month were as follows:

	Materials	Conversion
Cost per equivalent unit	$18.20	$23.25

Required:
1. Compute the total cost per equivalent unit for the month.
2. Compute the equivalent units of material and of conversion costs in the ending inventory.
3. Compute the equivalent units of material and of conversion costs that were required to complete the beginning inventory.
4, Determine the number of units started and completed during the month.
5. Determine the costs of ending inventory and units transferred out.

EXERCISE 6A–6 Equivalent Units—FIFO Method [LO6]
Refer to the data for Green House Inc. in Exercise 6–7.

Required:

Compute the equivalent units for October for the Cleaning Department, assuming that the company uses the FIFO method of accounting for units.

PROBLEM 6A–7 Equivalent Units; Cost per Equivalent Unit; Assigning Costs—FIFO Method [LO6, LO7, LO8]

Refer to the data for the Mixing Department in CloverSweet Inc. in Problem 6–10. Assume that the company uses the FIFO method rather than the weighted-average method in its process costing system.

Required:

1. Determine the equivalent units for June for the first process.
2. Compute the costs per equivalent unit for June for the first process.
3. Determine the total cost of ending work in process inventory and the total cost of units transferred to the next process in June.
4. Prepare a report that reconciles the total costs assigned to the ending work in process inventory and the units transferred out with the costs in beginning inventory and costs added during the period.

PROBLEM 6A–8 Equivalent Units; Applying Costs—FIFO Method [LO6, LO7, LO8]

Jones Company manufactures a single product and uses process costing (FIFO method). The company's product goes through two processing departments, Etching and Wiring. The following activity was recorded in the Etching Department during July:

Production data:	
Units in process, July 1 (materials 60% complete; conversion 30% complete)	50,000
Units started into production.	500,000
Units in process, July 31 (materials 80% complete; conversion 40% complete)	60,000
Cost data:	
Work in process inventory, July 1:	
Materials cost	$ 17,000
Conversion cost.	$ 3,000
Cost added during July:	
Materials cost	$457,200
Conversion cost.	$349,300

Materials are added at several stages during the etching process. The company uses the FIFO method.

Required:

1. Compute the equivalent units of production.
2. Compute the costs per equivalent unit for July.
3. Determine the cost of ending work in process inventory and of the units transferred to the Wiring Department.
4. Prepare a cost reconciliation between the costs determined in (3) above and the cost of beginning inventory and costs added during the period.

PROBLEM 6A–9 Equivalent Units; Costs per Equivalent Unit; Applying Costs—FIFO Method [LO6, LO7, LO8]

Refer to the data for the Blending Department of Sunspot Beverages Ltd. in Problem 6–17. Assume that the company uses the FIFO method rather than the weighted-average method in its process costing system.

Required:

1. Determine the equivalent units for June for the Blending Department.
2. Compute the costs per equivalent unit for June for the Blending Department.
3. Determine the total cost of ending work in process inventory and the total cost of units transferred to the next process for the Blending Department in June.
4. Prepare a cost reconciliation report for the Blending Department for June.

CASE 6A–10 Effect of Incorrect Costing across Departments—FIFO Method [LO6, LO7, LO8]
Refer to the data for Tavia Limited in Case 6–20. Assume that the company uses the FIFO method.

Required:
1. Prepare a report for the Forming Department for October showing how much cost should have been assigned to the units completed and transferred to the Stamping Department and to the ending work in process inventory.
2. Assume that in order to remain competitive the company undertook a major cost-cutting program during October. Would the effects of this cost-cutting program tend to show up more under the weighted-average method or under the FIFO method? Explain your answer.

CASE 6A–11 Inventory Valuation under Process Costing—FIFO Method [LO6, LO7, LO8]
Refer to the data for Rachel's Real Root Beer in Case 6–21. Assume the company uses the FIFO method.

Required:
Take on the role of Switzer and prepare the report for Archer. Be sure to provide all details, including a full production report, to help Archer understand how costs were calculated.

ACTIVITY-BASED COSTING: A TOOL TO AID DECISION MAKING

LEARNING OBJECTIVES

After studying Chapter 7, you should be able to

1 Explain the activity-based costing model and how it differs from a traditional costing system.

2 Assign costs to cost pools using a first-stage allocation, and compute activity rates.

3 Assign costs to a cost object using a second-stage allocation.

4 Use activity-based costing to compute product and customer margins.

5 Compare product costs computed using traditional and activity-based costing methods.

6 (Appendix 7A) Use activity-based costing techniques to compute unit product costs for external reports.

7 (Appendix 7B) Use time-driven activity-based costing to assign costs to cost objects.

■ MEASURING THE COST OF PRODUCT COMPLEXITY

McGraw-Hill Education / Mark Dierker

Increasing product variety and supply chain complexity can lead to increased fixed as well as variable costs. Fixed overhead costs, such as procurement costs, material handling costs, and inventory control costs, all increase as product variety and supply chain complexity increase. Toyota Motor Corp. identified this issue as a key target for cost control initiatives. For example, Toyota decided to use 21 rather than 100 different types of radiators across its product line. According to estimates from Toyota, a program to narrow down the number of different components used in vehicles as well as sourcing more components from fewer suppliers has reduced time and cost to create new models by at least 30%. Traditional job-order and process costing systems can mask the increased cost due to product variety and product complexity. To the contrary, activity-based costing (ABC) is designed to provide managers with cost information that can be used to manage both manufacturing-related and non-manufacturing-related overhead costs.

Activity-based costing (ABC)
A costing method based on activities that is designed to provide managers with cost information for strategic and other decisions that potentially affect capacity and therefore fixed costs.

This chapter introduces the concept of *activity-based costing*, which has been embraced by manufacturing, service, and not-for-profit organizations including Purolator courier and Toronto's The Hospital for Sick Children. **Activity-based costing (ABC)** is a costing method that is designed to provide managers with cost information for strategic and other decisions that potentially affect capacity and therefore fixed as well as variable costs. ABC is typically used as a supplement to, rather than as a replacement for, a company's usual costing system. Most organizations that use ABC have two costing systems—the official costing system, which is used to prepare external financial reports, and the ABC system, which is used for internal decision making and for managing activities.

This chapter focuses primarily on ABC applications in manufacturing to contrast with the material presented in earlier chapters. More specifically, Chapters 4, 5, and 6 focused on traditional absorption costing systems used by manufacturing companies to calculate unit product costs for valuing inventories and determining cost of goods sold for external financial reports. In contrast, this chapter explains how manufacturing companies can use ABC rather than traditional methods to calculate unit product costs for managing overhead and making decisions. Because of the broad role that ABC can play in facilitating decisions related to product pricing, cost management, capacity utilization, and customer profitability, it is important that both accountants and non-accountants understand its purpose and application.

LEARNING OBJECTIVE 1
Explain the activity-based costing model and how it differs from a traditional costing system.

THE TREATMENT OF COSTS UNDER THE ACTIVITY-BASED COSTING MODEL

As noted above, traditional absorption costing is designed to provide data for external financial reports. In contrast, ABC is designed for use in internal decision making. As a consequence, ABC differs from traditional cost accounting in several ways. In ABC,

1. Non-manufacturing as well as manufacturing costs may be assigned to products, but only on a cause-and-effect basis.
2. Some manufacturing costs may be excluded from product costs.
3. Numerous **overhead cost pools** are used, each of which is allocated to products and other cost objects using its own unique measure of activity.
4. Overhead rates, or activity rates, may be based on the level of activity at capacity rather than on the budgeted level of activity.

Overhead cost pools
Groups of overhead cost elements.

Each of these departures from traditional cost accounting practices will be discussed in turn.

Non-manufacturing Costs and Activity-Based Costing

In traditional cost accounting, only manufacturing costs are assigned to products. Selling and administrative expenses are treated as period expenses and are not assigned to products. However, many of these non-manufacturing costs are also part of the costs of producing, selling, distributing, and servicing products. For example, commissions paid to salespeople, shipping costs, and warranty repair costs can easily be traced to individual products. In this chapter, we will use the term *overhead* to refer to non-manufacturing costs as well as to indirect manufacturing costs. In ABC, products are assigned all of the overhead costs—non-manufacturing as well as manufacturing—that they can reasonably be estimated to have caused. In essence, we will be determining the entire cost of a product rather than just its manufacturing cost. The focus in Chapters 5 and 6 was on determining just the manufacturing cost of a product.

Manufacturing Costs Excluded under Activity-Based Costing

In traditional cost accounting, *all* manufacturing costs are assigned to products—even manufacturing costs that are not caused by the products. For example, in Chapter 5 we learned that a predetermined plantwide overhead rate is computed by dividing all budgeted manufacturing overhead costs by a measure of budgeted activity such as direct labour-hours. This approach spreads *all* manufacturing overhead costs across products based on each product's direct labour-hours (commonly called the "peanut butter–spreading" approach). In contrast, ABC systems assign costs to a product only if there is good reason to believe that the cost would be affected by decisions concerning the product. Recall that manufacturing overhead costs include all costs of manufacturing other than direct materials and direct labour. Some of these costs, for example the plant controller's salary or the factory security guard's wages, are actually unaffected by product-related decisions and are therefore treated as period expenses instead of product costs under ABC.

Additionally, in a traditional absorption costing system, the costs of unused, or idle, capacity are assigned to products. If the budgeted level of activity declines, the overhead rate and unit product costs increase as the increasing costs of idle capacity are spread over a smaller base. In contrast, in ABC products are only charged for the costs of the capacity they use—not for the costs of the capacity they don't use. This provides more stable unit product costs and is consistent with the goal of assigning to products only the costs of the resources that they use. Instead of assigning the costs of idle capacity to products, in ABC these costs are considered to be period costs that flow through to the income statement as an expense of the current period. This treatment highlights the cost of idle capacity rather than burying it in inventory and cost of goods sold.

As will be seen in the example presented in this chapter, this departure from traditional costing approaches represents one of the key benefits of ABC, as it results in better information for decision making.

Overhead Cost Pools, Allocation Bases, and Activity-Based Costing

Throughout the 19th and early 20th centuries, costing system designs were simple and satisfactory. Typically, either one plantwide overhead cost pool or a number of departmental overhead cost pools were used to assign overhead costs to products. The plantwide and departmental approaches always had one thing in common—they relied on allocation bases such as direct labour-hours and machine-hours to allocate overhead costs to products. In labour-intensive production processes, direct labour was the most common choice for an overhead allocation base because it represented a large component of product costs; direct labour-hours were closely tracked; and many managers believed that direct labour-hours, the total volume of units produced, and overhead costs were highly correlated. Given that most companies at the time were producing a very limited variety of products that required similar resources to produce, allocation bases such as direct labour-hours, or even machine-hours, worked fine because in fact there was probably little difference in the overhead costs attributable to different products.

In the early 1990s, conditions began to change. Many tasks previously done by direct labourers were being performed by automated equipment—a component of overhead. Companies began creating new products and services at an ever-accelerating rate that differed in volume, batch size, and complexity. Managing and sustaining this product diversity required investing in many more overhead resources, such as production schedulers and product design engineers, that had no obvious connection to direct labour-hours or machine-hours. In this new environment, continuing to rely exclusively on a limited number of overhead cost pools and traditional allocation bases posed the risk that reported unit product costs would be distorted and, therefore, misleading when used for decision making. Thanks to advances in information technology that make more complex costing systems feasible, the ABC approach has appeal in today's business environment. ABC uses more cost pools and unique measures of activity to better understand the costs of managing and sustaining product diversity.

Exhibit 7–1 provides a visual representation of the differences between traditional and activity-based costing discussed above. Traditional costing treats all manufacturing costs as product costs and all other costs as period costs. Activity-based costing recognizes both indirect manufacturing and indirect non-manufacturing costs as overhead and allocates overhead costs that change with levels of production activity as product costs and overhead costs that do not change with levels of production activity as period costs.

EXHIBIT 7–1   Differences between Traditional and Activity-Based Costing

Traditional Absorption Costing:

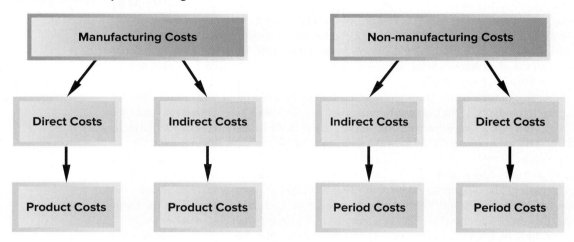

Activity-Based Costing:

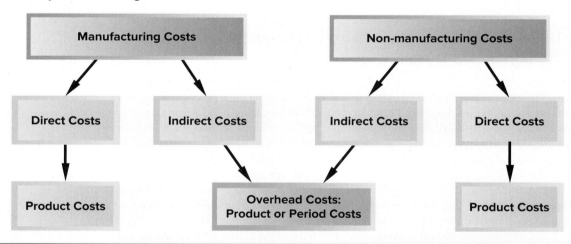

Activity

Any event that causes the consumption of overhead resources.

Activity cost pool

A "bucket" in which costs are accumulated that relate to a single activity measure in the activity-based costing system.

Activity measure

An allocation base in an activity-based costing system; ideally, a measure of the amount of activity that drives the costs in an activity cost pool; also called a cost *driver*.

     In ABC, an **activity** is any event that causes the consumption of overhead resources. An **activity cost pool** is a "bucket" in which costs are accumulated that relate to a single activity measure in the ABC system. An **activity measure** is an allocation base in an ABC system. The term *cost driver* is also used to refer to an activity measure because the activity measure should "drive" the cost being allocated. The two most common types of activity measures are *transaction drivers* and *duration drivers*. A **transaction driver** is a simple count of the number of times an activity occurs, such as the number of bills sent out to customers. A **duration driver** measures the amount of time required to perform an activity, such as the time spent preparing individual bills for customers. In general, duration drivers are more accurate measures of resource consumption than transaction drivers, but they take more effort to record. For that reason, transaction drivers are more often used in practice.

INSTANT QUIZ 7–1

Identify and explain the four main differences between ABC and traditional product costing approaches.

Many companies throughout the world continue to base overhead allocations on cost drivers that vary with volume of production or service provided. In situations where overhead costs and direct labour-hours are highly correlated or in situations where the goal of the overhead allocation process is mainly to prepare external financial reports, this practice makes sense. However, if plantwide overhead costs do not move in tandem with plantwide direct labour-hours or machine-hours, product costs will be distorted. ABC addresses this issue by defining five levels of activity—unit-level, batch-level, product-level, customer-level, and organization-sustaining—which largely do *not* relate to the volume of units produced or services provided. These levels are described as follows:

1. **Unit-level activities** are performed each time a unit is produced. The costs of unit-level activities should be proportional to the number of units produced. For example, providing power to run processing equipment is a unit-level activity since power tends to be consumed in proportion to the number of units produced.
2. **Batch-level activities** are performed each time a batch is handled or processed, regardless of how many units are in the batch. For example, tasks such as placing purchase orders, setting up equipment, and arranging for shipments to customers are batch-level activities. They are incurred once for each batch (or customer order). Costs at the batch level depend on the number of batches processed rather than on the number of units produced, the number of units sold, or other measures of volume. For example, the cost of setting up a machine for batch processing is the same regardless of whether the batch contains 100 or 10,000 items.
3. **Product-level activities** relate to specific products and typically must be carried out regardless of how many batches are run or units of product are produced or sold. For example, activities such as designing a product, advertising a product, and maintaining a product manager and staff are all product-level activities.
4. **Customer-level activities** relate to specific customers and include activities such as sales calls, catalogue mailings, and general technical support that are not tied to any specific product.
5. **Organization-sustaining activities** are carried out regardless of which customers are served, which products are produced, how many batches are run, or how many units are made. This category includes activities such as heating the factory, cleaning executive offices, providing a computer network, arranging for loans, and preparing annual reports to shareholders.

IN BUSINESS

Canadian River Expeditions runs river rafting trips on the Nahanni River. A seven-day trip down the Nahanni River in the Northwest Territories is one of the most popular. Guests travel over 240 kilometres from Virginia Falls to Nahanni Butte. The company runs trips of one or two rafts, with a guaranteed ratio of one guide for every four guests. The company provides all meals on the trip.

Image Source/Javier Perini CM

In terms of the hierarchy of activities, a guest can be considered as a unit and a raft as a batch. In that context, the wages paid to the guides are a batch-level cost because each raft requires a guide regardless of the number of guests in the raft. Imagine that each guest is given a mug to use during the trip and to take home at the end of the trip as a souvenir. The cost of the mug is a unit-level cost because the number of mugs given away is strictly proportional to the number of guests on a trip.

What about the costs to attract new customers or to provide advice to customers about which guided rafting tour to take? These would be product-level costs, while the cost to receive and record customer payments and complete other necessary financial record-keeping would be an organization-level cost.

Transaction driver
A simple count of the number of times an activity occurs.

Duration driver
A measure of the amount of time required to perform an activity.

Unit-level activities
Activities that arise as a result of the total volume of goods produced and services performed each time a unit is produced.

Batch-level activities
Activities performed each time a batch of goods is handled or processed, regardless of how many units are in a batch. The amount of resources consumed depends on the number of batches run rather than on the number of units in the batch.

Product-level activities
Activities that relate to specific products that must be carried out regardless of how many units are produced and sold or batches run.

Customer-level activities
Activities that are carried out to support customers but that are not related to any specific product.

Organization-sustaining activities
Activities that are carried out regardless of which customers are serviced, which products are produced, how many batches are run, or how many units are made.

Activity Rates Based on Capacity, Not Budget

In a traditional absorption costing system, predetermined overhead rates are computed by dividing budgeted overhead costs by a measure of budgeted activity such as budgeted direct labour-hours. This practice results in applying the costs of unused, or idle, capacity to products, and it results in unstable unit product costs. If budgeted activity falls, the overhead rate increases because the fixed components of overhead are spread over a smaller base, resulting in increased unit product costs.

INSTANT QUIZ 7–2
Provide one specific example of a unit-level, a batch-level, a product-level, a customer-level, and an organization-sustaining activity.

In ABC, products are charged for the costs of capacity they use—not for the costs of capacity they do not use. In other words, the costs of idle capacity are not charged to products. This results in more stable unit costs and is consistent with the objective of assigning only those costs to products that are actually caused by the products. Instead of assigning the costs of idle capacity to products, in ABC these costs are considered to be period costs that flow through to the income statement as an expense of the current period. This treatment highlights the cost of idle capacity rather than burying it in inventory and cost of goods sold.

■ DESIGNING AN ACTIVITY-BASED COSTING SYSTEM

There are three essential characteristics of a successful ABC implementation. First, top managers must strongly support the implementation because their leadership is instrumental in properly motivating all employees to accept the need for change. Second, top managers should ensure that ABC data are linked to how people are evaluated and rewarded. If employees continue to be evaluated and rewarded using traditional (non-ABC) cost data, they will quickly get the message that ABC is not important and will ignore the information provided by the system. Third, a cross-functional team should be created to design and implement the ABC system. The team should include representatives from each area that will use ABC data, such as marketing, production, engineering, and accounting departments. These cross-functional employees possess detailed knowledge of many parts of an organization's operations that is crucial for designing an effective ABC system. Moreover, utilizing the knowledge of cross-functional managers reduces their resistance to change because they feel involved in the ABC implementation process. Time after time, when accountants have attempted to implement an ABC system on their own without top-management support and cross-functional involvement, the results have been ignored.

To illustrate the design and use of an ABC system, we use Classic Brass Inc., a company that makes two main product lines for luxury yachts—standard stanchions and custom compass housings. The president of the company, John Towers, is concerned about the company's poor financial results (see Exhibit 7–2). He is concerned that the price for standard stanchions might be too high, but Tom Olafson, the marketing manager, believes competitors may be setting their prices very low, maybe even below cost, in order to increase market share. Mary Johns, the accounting manager, wonders if Classic Brass is incorrectly calculating the cost of standard stanchions and thinks ABC might help. Like most other ABC implementations, the new ABC system would supplement, rather than replace, the existing cost accounting system, which would continue to be used for external financial reports. The new ABC system would be used to prepare special reports for management decisions such as bidding on new business.

The accounting manager drew the chart in Exhibit 7–3 to explain the general structure of the ABC model. Cost objects, such as products, give rise to activities. For example, a customer order for a compass housing requires the activity of preparing a production order. Such

EXHIBIT 7–2
Classic Brass Income Statement

CLASSIC BRASS
Income Statement
Year Ended December 31, 2021

Sales.......................................		$3,200,000
Cost of goods sold:		
Direct materials	$ 975,000	
Direct labour	351,250	
Manufacturing overhead*	1,000,000	2,326,250
Gross margin		873,750
Selling and administrative expenses:		
Shipping expenses	65,000	
Marketing expenses..................................	300,000	
General administrative expenses	510,000	875,000
Operating income....................................		$ (1,250)

*The company's traditional costing system allocates manufacturing overhead to products using a plantwide overhead rate and machine-hours as the allocation base. Inventory levels did not change during the year.

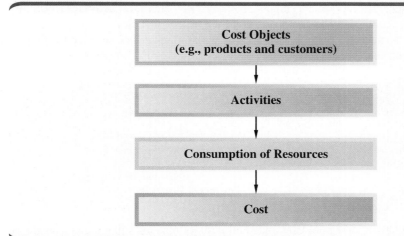

EXHIBIT 7–3
The Activity-Based Costing Model

an activity consumes resources. A production order uses a sheet of paper and takes time to fill out, and the consumption of resources causes costs. The greater the number of sheets used to fill out production orders and the greater the amount of time devoted to filling out such orders, the greater the cost. ABC analyzes these types of relationships to identify how products and customers affect costs.

As in most companies, the ABC team at Classic Brass felt that the company's traditional cost accounting system adequately measured the direct material and direct labour costs of products since these costs are directly traced to products. Therefore, the ABC system would be concerned solely with manufacturing overhead and selling and administrative costs.

The team felt it was important to carefully plan how it would go about implementing the new ABC system at Classic Brass. Accordingly, the implementation process was broken down into five basic steps:

1. Identify and define activities, activity cost pools, and activity measures.
2. Assign overhead costs to activity cost pools.
3. Calculate activity rates.
4. Assign overhead costs to cost objects using the activity rates and activity measures.
5. Prepare management reports.

Step 1: Identify and Define Activities, Activity Cost Pools, and Activity Measures

The first major step is to identify the activities that will form the foundation for the system. This can be difficult and time-consuming and involves a great deal of judgment. A common procedure is for the individuals on the ABC implementation team to interview people who work in overhead departments and ask them to describe their major activities. Ordinarily, this results in a very long list of activities.

The length of such lists can be a problem. On one hand, the greater the number of activities tracked in the ABC system, the more accurate the costs are likely to be. On the other hand, it is costly to design, implement, maintain, and use a complex system involving large numbers of activities. Consequently, the original lengthy list of activities is usually reduced to a smaller number by combining similar activities. For example, several actions may be involved in handling and moving raw materials—from receiving raw materials on the loading dock to sorting them into the appropriate bins in the storeroom. All of these activities might be combined into a single activity called *materials handling*.

When combining activities in an ABC system, activities should be grouped together at the appropriate level. Batch-level activities should not be combined with unit-level activities, or product-level activities with batch-level activities, and so on. In general, it is best to combine only those activities that are highly correlated with each other within a level. For example, the number of customer orders received is likely to be highly correlated with the number of completed customer orders shipped, so these two batch-level activities (receiving and shipping orders) can usually be combined with little loss of accuracy.

At Classic Brass, the ABC team, in consultation with top managers, selected the following *activity cost pools* and *activity measures*:

Activity Cost Pools at Classic Brass	
Activity Cost Pool	**Activity Measure**
Customer Orders	Number of customer orders
Product Design	Number of product designs
Order Size	Machine-hours
Customer Relations	Number of active customers
Other	Not applicable

The Customer Orders cost pool is assigned all costs of resources that are consumed by taking and processing customer orders, including costs of processing paperwork and any costs involved in setting up machines for specific orders. The activity measure for this cost pool is simply the number of customer orders received. This is a *batch-level activity*, since each order generates work that occurs regardless of whether the order is for 1 unit or 1,000 units.

The Product Design cost pool is assigned all costs of resources consumed in designing products. The activity measure for this cost pool is the number of products designed. This is a *product-level activity*, since the amount of design work on a new product does not depend on the number of units ultimately ordered or batches ultimately run.

The Order Size cost pool is assigned all costs of resources consumed as a consequence of the number of units produced, including the costs of miscellaneous factory supplies, power to run machines, and some equipment depreciation. This is a *unit-level activity*, since each unit requires some of these resources. The activity measure for this cost pool is machine-hours.

The Customer Relations cost pool is assigned all costs associated with maintaining relations with customers, including the costs of sales calls and the costs of entertaining customers. The activity measure for this cost pool is the number of customers the company has on its active customer list. The Customer Relations cost pool represents a *customer-level* activity.

The Other cost pool is assigned all overhead costs that are not associated with customer orders, product design, production units, or customer relations. These costs mainly consist of *organization-sustaining costs* and the *costs of unused, idle capacity*. Recall that these types of costs should *not* be assigned to products since they represent resources that are *not* consumed by products.

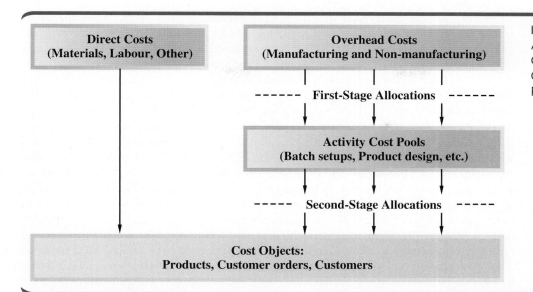

EXHIBIT 7–4
Activity-Based
Costing Two-Stage
Cost Allocation
Process

Step 2: Assign Overhead Costs to Activity Cost Pools

LEARNING OBJECTIVE **2**
Assign costs to cost pools using a first-stage allocation, and compute activity rates.

After the ABC system is designed, the team is ready to begin the process of actually computing the costs of products, customers, and other objects of interest. As shown in Exhibit 7–4, assigning costs to cost objects under ABC is a two-stage process. In the first stage, manufacturing and non-manufacturing overhead is allocated to the activity cost pools. In the second stage, the costs for the activities are allocated to the various cost objects. As with the traditional costing systems discussed in Chapters 5 and 6, direct costs are traced directly to cost objects. We begin our discussion of the mechanics of ABC with the first-stage allocations.

Exhibit 7–5 shows the annual overhead costs (both manufacturing and non-manufacturing) that Classic Brass intends to assign to its activity cost pools. Notice that the data in the exhibit are organized by department (e.g., Production, General Administrative, and Marketing). This is because the data have been extracted from the company's general ledger. General ledgers usually classify costs within the departments where the costs are incurred. For example, salaries, supplies, rent, and so forth incurred in the marketing department are charged to that department. The functional orientation of the general ledger mirrors the presentation of costs in the absorption income statement in Exhibit 7–2. In fact, you'll notice that the total costs for the Production Department in Exhibit 7–5 ($1,000,000) equal the total manufacturing overhead costs from the income statement in Exhibit 7–2. Similarly, the total costs for the General Administrative and Marketing Departments in Exhibit 7–5 ($510,000 and $300,000) equal the marketing and general and administrative expenses shown in Exhibit 7–2.

Production Department:		
Indirect factory wages	$500,000	
Factory equipment depreciation	300,000	
Factory utilities	120,000	
Factory building lease	80,000	$1,000,000
General Administrative Department:		
Administrative wages and salaries	400,000	
Office equipment depreciation	50,000	
Administrative building lease	60,000	510,000
Marketing Department:		
Marketing wages and salaries	250,000	
Selling expenses	50,000	300,000
Total overhead cost		$1,810,000

EXHIBIT 7–5
Annual Overhead
Costs (Both
Manufacturing and
Non-manufacturing)
at Classic Brass

First-stage allocation
The process by which overhead costs are assigned to activity cost pools in an activity-based costing system.

Three costs included in the income statement in Exhibit 7–2—direct materials, direct labour, and shipping—are excluded from the costs shown in Exhibit 7–5. The ABC team purposely excluded these costs from Exhibit 7–5 because the existing costing system can accurately trace direct materials, direct labour, and shipping costs to products.

Classic Brass's ABC system will divide the nine types of overhead costs in Exhibit 7–5 among its activity cost pools via an allocation process called *first-stage allocation*. The **first-stage allocation** in an ABC system is the process of assigning functionally organized overhead costs derived from a company's general ledger to the activity cost pools.

First-stage allocations are usually based on the results of interviews with employees who have first-hand knowledge of the activities. For example, Classic Brass needs to allocate $500,000 of indirect factory wages to its five activity cost pools. These allocations will be more accurate if the employees who are classified as indirect factory workers (e.g., supervisors, engineers, and quality inspectors) are asked to estimate what percentage of their time is spent dealing with customer orders, with product design, with processing units of product (i.e., order size), and with customer relations. Departmental managers are typically interviewed to determine how the non-personnel costs should be distributed across the activity cost pools. For example, the Classic Brass production manager would be interviewed to determine how the $300,000 of factory equipment depreciation (shown in Exhibit 7–5) should be allocated to the activity cost pools. The key question that the production manager would need to answer is, "What percentage of the available machine capacity is consumed by each activity, such as the number of customer orders or the number of units processed (i.e., size of orders)?"

The results of the interviews at Classic Brass are displayed in Exhibit 7–6. For example, factory equipment depreciation is distributed 20% to Customer Orders, 60% to Order Size, and 20% to the Other cost pool. The resource in this instance is machine time. According to the estimates made by the production manager, 60% of the total available machine time was used to actually process units to fill orders. This percentage is entered in the Order Size column. Each customer order requires setting up, which also requires machine time. This activity consumes 20% of the total available machine time and is entered under the Customer Orders column. The remaining 20% of available machine time represents idle time and is entered under the Other column.

We will not go into the details of how all of the percentages in Exhibit 7–6 were determined. However, note that 100% of the factory building lease has been assigned to the Other cost pool. Classic Brass has a single production facility. It has no plans to expand or to sublease any excess space. The cost of this production facility is treated as an organization-sustaining cost because there is no way to avoid even a portion of this cost if a particular product or customer is dropped. (Remember that organization-sustaining costs are assigned to the Other cost pool and are not allocated to products.) In contrast, some companies have separate facilities for manufacturing specific products. The costs of these separate facilities could be directly traced to the specific products.

Once the percentage distributions in Exhibit 7–6 have been established, it is easy to allocate costs to the activity cost pools. The results of this first-stage allocation are displayed in Exhibit 7–7. Each cost is allocated across the activity cost pools by multiplying it by the percentages in Exhibit 7–6. For example, the indirect factory wages of $500,000 are multiplied by the 25% entry under Customer Orders in Exhibit 7–6 to arrive at the $125,000 entry under Customer Orders in Exhibit 7–7. Similarly, the indirect factory wages of $500,000 are multiplied by the 40% entry under Product Design in Exhibit 7–6 to arrive at the $200,000 entry under Product Design in Exhibit 7–7. All of the entries in Exhibit 7–7 are computed in this way.

Now that the first-stage allocations to the activity cost pools have been completed, the next step is to compute the activity rates.

INSTANT QUIZ 7-3
Using Exhibit 7–6 and Exhibit 7–7, explain how the $40,000 of administrative wages and salaries allocated to the Order Size activity cost pool in Exhibit 7-7 was determined.

EXHIBIT 7–6   Results of Interviews: Distribution of Resource Consumption across Activity Cost Pools

	Activity Cost Pools					
	Customer Orders	Product Design	Order Size	Customer Relations	Other	Totals
Production Department:						
Indirect factory wages	25%	40%	20%	10%	5%	100%
Factory equipment depreciation.	20%	0%	60%	0%	20%	100%
Factory utilities	0%	10%	50%	0%	40%	100%
Factory building lease	0%	0%	0%	0%	100%	100%
General Administrative Department:						
Administrative wages and salaries. . . .	15%	5%	10%	30%	40%	100%
Office equipment depreciation.	30%	0%	0%	25%	45%	100%
Administrative building lease	0%	0%	0%	0%	100%	100%
Marketing Department:						
Marketing wages and salaries	22%	8%	0%	60%	10%	100%
Selling expenses.	10%	0%	0%	70%	20%	100%

EXHIBIT 7–7   First-Stage Allocations to Activity Cost Pools

	Activity Cost Pools					Totals Taken from General Ledger
	Customer Orders	Product Design	Order Size	Customer Relations	Other	
Production Department:						
Indirect factory wages	$125,000	$200,000	$100,000	$ 50,000	$ 25,000	$ 500,000
Factory equipment depreciation.	60,000	0	180,000	0	60,000	300,000
Factory utilities	0	12,000	60,000	0	48,000	120,000
Factory building lease	0	0	0	0	80,000	80,000
General Administrative Department:						
Administrative wages and salaries. . .	60,000	20,000	40,000	120,000	160,000	400,000
Office equipment depreciation.	15,000	0	0	12,500	22,500	50,000
Administrative building lease	0	0	0	0	60,000	60,000
Marketing Department:						
Marketing wages and salaries	55,000	20,000	0	150,000	25,000	250,000
Selling expenses.	5,000	0	0	35,000	10,000	50,000
Total	$320,000	$252,000	$380,000	$367,500	$490,500	$1,810,000

Exhibit 7–6 shows that Customer Orders consume 25% of the resources represented by the $500,000 of indirect factory wages:

$$25\% \times \$500,000 = \$125,000$$

Other entries in the spreadsheet are computed in a similar fashion.

EXHIBIT 7–8
Computation of
Activity Rates

Activity Cost Pools	(a) Total Cost*	(b) Total Activity	(a) ÷ (b) Activity Rate
Customer orders........	$320,000	1,000 orders	$320 per order
Product design	$252,000	400 designs	$630 per design
Order size............	$380,000	20,000 MHs	$19 per MH
Customer relations......	$367,500	250 customers	$1,470 per customer
Other	$490,500	Not applicable	Not applicable

*From Exhibit 7–7.

Step 3: Calculate Activity Rates

The activity rates that will be used for assigning overhead costs to products and customers are computed in Exhibit 7–8. The ABC team determined the total activity for each cost pool that would be required to produce the company's current product mix and to serve its present customers. These numbers are listed in Exhibit 7–8. For example, the ABC team found that 400 new product designs are required each year to serve the company's current customers. The activity rates are computed by dividing the *total* cost for each activity by its *total* activity. For example, the $320,000 total annual cost for the Customer Orders cost pool is divided by the total of 1,000 customer orders per year to arrive at the activity rate of $320 per customer order. Similarly, the $252,000 *total* cost for the Product Design cost pool is divided by the *total* number of designs (i.e., 400 product designs) to determine the activity rate of $630 per design. Note that activity rates are not computed for the Other category of costs. This is because the Other cost pool consists of organization-sustaining costs and costs of idle capacity that are not allocated to products and customers.

The entries in Exhibit 7–8 indicate that on average a customer order consumes resources that cost $320, a product design consumes resources that cost $630, an order consumes resources that cost $19 per machine-hour, and maintaining relations with a customer consumes resources that cost $1,470. Note that these are *average* figures. Some members of the ABC design team at Classic Brass argued that it would be unfair to charge all new products the same $630 product design cost regardless of how much design time they actually require. After discussing the pros and cons, the team concluded that it would not be worth the effort to keep track of actual design time spent on each new product. They felt that the benefits of increased accuracy would not be great enough to justify the higher cost of implementing and maintaining the more detailed costing system. Similarly, some team members were uncomfortable assigning the same $1,470 cost to each customer because different customers place different demands on the resources of the company. However, while everyone agreed with this concern, the data that would be required to measure individual customers' demands on resources were not currently available. Rather than delay implementation of the ABC system, the team decided to defer such refinements.

INSTANT QUIZ 7–4

Vikram Company identified $25,200 of overhead costs to be assigned to the order-processing cost pool. A total of 350 orders were processed in the year. Calculate the activity rate to be used to assign costs from this cost pool to the customer orders cost object.

Before proceeding, it would be helpful to review the overall process of assigning costs to products and other cost objects in an ABC system. Exhibit 7–9 summarizes the ABC system at Classic Brass. We recommend that you carefully go over this exhibit. In particular, two things about Exhibit 7–9 are important to keep in mind. First, direct materials, direct labour, and shipping costs are included because they are all direct costs of the cost objects and must be considered when analyzing total costs related to products, customer orders, and customers. These

EXHIBIT 7–9   The Activity-Based Costing Model at Classic Brass

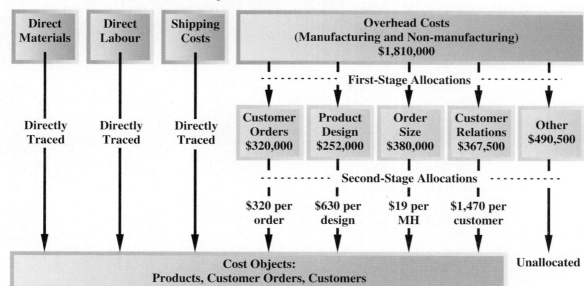

costs were not included in the first-stage allocations because that process deals with assigning overhead costs to activity cost pools. Second, the Other category, which contains organization-sustaining costs and costs of idle capacity, is not allocated to products or customers.

■ SECOND-STAGE ALLOCATION OF OVERHEAD COSTS

The fourth step in the implementation of ABC is called *second-stage allocation*. In the **second-stage allocation**, activity rates are used to apply overhead costs to products and customers.

Step 4: Assign Overhead Costs to Cost Objects Using the Activity Rates and Activity Measures

First, we will illustrate how to assign costs to products, followed by an example of how to assign costs to customers. The data needed by the ABC team to assign overhead costs to Classic Brass's two products—standard stanchions and custom compass housings—are as follows:

Standard Stanchions

1. This product line does not require any new design resources.
2. 30,000 units were ordered during the year, making up 600 separate orders.
3. Each stanchion requires 35 minutes of machine time, for a total of 17,500 machine-hours.

Custom Compass Housings

1. This is a custom product that requires new design resources.
2. There were 400 orders for custom compass housings. Orders for this product are placed separately from orders for standard stanchions.
3. There were 400 custom designs prepared. One custom design was prepared for each order.
4. Since some orders were for more than one unit, a total of 1,250 custom compass housings were produced during the year. A custom compass housing requires an average of two machine-hours, for a total of 2,500 machine-hours.

LEARNING OBJECTIVE 3
Assign costs to a cost object using a second-stage allocation.

Second-stage allocation
The process by which activity rates are used to apply costs to products and customers in activity-based costing.

EXHIBIT 7–10
Assigning Overhead
Costs to Products

Overhead Cost for the Standard Stanchions

Activity Cost Pools	(a) Activity Rate*	(b) Activity	(a) × (b) ABC Cost
Customer orders..............	$320 per order	600 orders	$192,000
Product design	$630 per design	0 designs	0
Order size...................	$ 19 per MH	17,500 MHs	332,500
Total......................			$524,500

Overhead Cost for the Custom Compass Housing

Activity Cost Pools	(a) Activity Rate*	(b) Activity	(a) × (b) ABC Cost
Customer orders..............	$320 per order	400 orders	$128,000
Product design	$630 per design	400 designs	252,000
Order size...................	$ 19 per MH	2,500 MHs	47,500
Total......................			$427,500

*From Exhibit 7–8

Notice that 600 customer orders were placed for standard stanchions and 400 customer orders were placed for custom compass housings, for a total of 1,000 customer orders. All 400 product designs related to custom compass housings; none related to standard stanchions. Producing 30,000 standard stanchions required 17,500 machine-hours, and producing 1,250 custom compass housings required 2,500 machine-hours, for a total of 20,000 machine-hours.

Exhibit 7–10 illustrates how overhead costs are assigned to the standard stanchions and custom compass housings. For example, the exhibit shows that $192,000 of overhead costs is assigned from the Customer Orders activity cost pool to the standard stanchions ($320 per order × 600 orders). Similarly, $128,000 of overhead costs is assigned from the Customer Orders activity cost pool to the custom compass housings ($320 per order × 400 orders). The Customer Orders cost pool contained a total of $320,000 (see Exhibit 7–7 or 7–8), and this total amount has been assigned to the two products ($192,000 + $128,000 = $320,000).

INSTANT QUIZ 7-5
The following activity data relate to overhead-related activities used to produce Product Q43 this period: 120 direct labour-hours at $7 per DLH, 43 machine-hours at $2 per MH, 4 machine setups at $63 per setup, and 5 shipments at $12 per shipment. Determine the total overhead cost that should be assigned to this product under an ABC system.

Exhibit 7–10 shows that a total of $952,000 of overhead costs is assigned to Classic Brass's two product lines—$524,500 to standard stanchions and $427,500 to custom compass housings. This amount is less than the $1,810,000 of overhead costs included in the ABC system. Why? The total amount of overhead assigned to products does not match the total amount of overhead cost in the ABC system, because the ABC team purposely did not assign the $367,500 of Customer Relations and $490,500 of Other costs to products. The Customer Relations activity is a customer-level activity and the Other activity is an organization-sustaining activity—neither activity is caused by products. As shown below, when the Customer Relations and Other activity costs are added to the $952,000 of overhead costs assigned to products, the total is $1,810,000:

	Standard Stanchions	Custom Compass Housings	Total
Overhead Costs Assigned to Products			
Customer orders	$192,000	$128,000	$ 320,000
Product design	–0–	252,000	252,000
Order size	332,500	47,500	380,000
Subtotal	$524,500	$427,500	952,000
Overhead Costs Not Assigned to Products			
Customer relations			367,500
Other			490,500
Subtotal			858,000
Total overhead cost			$1,810,000

Next, we describe another aspect of second-stage allocations—assigning activity costs to customers. The data needed by the design team to assign overhead costs to one of its company's customers—Windward Yachts—are as follows:

Windward Yachts

1. The company placed a total of three orders.
   a. Two orders were for 150 standard stanchions per order.
   b. One order was for a single custom compass housing unit.
2. A total of 177 machine-hours were used to fulfill the three customer orders.
   a. The 300 standard stanchions required 175 machine-hours.
   b. The custom compass housing required 2 machine-hours.
3. Windward Yachts is one of 250 customers served by Classic Brass.

As shown in Exhibit 7–11, the ABC team calculated that $6,423 of overhead costs should be assigned to Windward Yachts. The exhibit shows that Windward Yachts is assigned $960 ($320 per order × 3 orders) of overhead costs from the Customer Orders activity cost pool, $630 ($630 per design × 1 design) from the Product Design cost pool, $3,363 ($19 per machine-hour × 177 machine-hours) from the Order Size cost pool, and $1,470 ($1,470 per customer × 1 customer) from the Customer Relations cost pool.

With second-stage allocations complete, the ABC design team was ready to turn its attention to creating reports that would help explain the company's first-ever operating loss.

Overhead Cost for Windward Yachts

Activity Cost Pools	(a) Activity Rate*	(b) Activity	(a) × (b) ABC Cost
Customer orders	$ 320 per order	3 orders	$ 960
Product design	$ 630 per design	1 design	630
Order size	$ 19 per MH	177 MHs	3,363
Customer relations	$1,470 per customer	1 customer	1,470
Total overhead cost assigned to customer			$6,423

*From Exhibit 7–8

EXHIBIT 7–11
Assigning Overhead Costs to Customers

LEARNING OBJECTIVE ④

Use activity-based costing to compute product and customer margins.

■ PRODUCT AND CUSTOMER MARGINS

The most common management reports prepared with ABC data are product and customer profitability reports. These reports help companies channel their resources to their most profitable growth opportunities, while at the same time highlighting products and customers that drain profits. We begin by illustrating a product profitability report, followed by a customer profitability report.

Step 5: Prepare Management Reports

The Classic Brass ABC team realized that the profit from a product, also called the *product margin*, is a function of the product's sales and the direct and indirect costs that the product incurs. The ABC cost allocations shown in Exhibit 7–10 summarize only each product's indirect (i.e., overhead) costs. Therefore, to compute a product's profit (i.e., product margin), the design team needed to gather each product's sales and direct costs in addition to the overhead costs previously computed. The pertinent sales and direct cost data for each product are shown below. Notice that the numbers in the total column agree with the income statement in Exhibit 7–2:

	Standard Stanchions	Custom Compass Housings	Total
Sales.................	$2,660,000	$540,000	$3,200,000
Direct costs:			
Direct materials	905,500	69,500	975,000
Direct labour	263,750	87,500	351,250
Shipping................	60,000	5,000	65,000

Having gathered the above data, the design team created the product profitability report shown in Exhibit 7–12. The report reveals that standard stanchions are profitable, with a positive product margin of $906,250, whereas the custom compass housings are unprofitable, with a negative product margin of $49,500. Keep in mind that the product profitability report purposely does not include the costs in the Customer Relations and Other activity cost pools. These costs, which total $858,000, are excluded from the report because they are not caused by the products. Customer Relations costs are caused by customers, not products. The Other costs are organization-sustaining costs that are not caused by any particular product or customer.

EXHIBIT 7–12
Product Margins—
Activity-Based
Costing

	Standard Stanchions	Custom Compass Housings
Sales.................................	$2,660,000	$540,000
Costs:		
Direct materials	$905,500	$ 69,500
Direct labour	263,750	87,500
Shipping costs	60,000	5,000
Customer orders (from Exhibit 7–10)	192,000	128,000
Product design (from Exhibit 7–10)		252,000
Order size (from Exhibit 7–10)	332,500	47,500
Total cost.............................	1,753,750	589,500
Product margin	$ 906,250	$ (49,500)

The product margins can be reconciled with the company's operating income as follows:

	Standard Stanchions	Custom Compass Housings	Total
Sales (see Exhibit 7–12)	$2,660,000	$540,000	$3,200,000
Total costs (see Exhibit 7–12).................	1,753,750	589,500	2,343,250
Product margins (see Exhibit 7–12)	$ 906,250	$ (49,500)	856,750
Overhead costs not assigned to products:			
Customer relations (see Exhibit 7–8)			367,500
Other (see Exhibit 7–8).....................			490,500
Total......................................			858,000
Operating income			$ (1,250)

Next, the design team created a customer profitability report for Windward Yachts. Similar to the product profitability report, the design team needed to gather data concerning sales to Windward Yachts and the direct material, direct labour, and shipping costs associated with those sales. These data are presented below:

	Windward Yachts
Sales......................	$11,350
Direct costs:	
Direct material costs	2,123
Direct labour costs	1,900
Shipping costs	205

Using these data and the data from Exhibit 7–11, the design team created the customer profitability report shown in Exhibit 7–13. The report revealed that the customer margin for Windward Yachts is $699. A similar report could be prepared for each of Classic Brass's 250 customers, thereby enabling the company to cultivate relationships with its most profitable customers, while taking steps to reduce the negative impact of unprofitable customers.

INSTANT QUIZ 7–6

Household Supply Company produces and sells a variety of natural home cleaning products. This year, Mitchell Hardware has ordered 1,200 cases (50 cases per order) of ZipClean, Household Supply's most popular all-purpose cleaner. Each case contains 24 bottles of ZipClean and sells for $72. Each bottle contains $0.95 of direct materials and $0.40 of direct labour. Overhead is assigned on the basis of $1.10 per bottle and $250 per order processed. Compute the customer margin for Mitchell Hardware.

	Windward Yachts	
Sales		$11,350
Costs:		
Direct materials...	$2,123	
Direct labour	1,900	
Shipping	205	
Customer orders (from Exhibit 7–11).....................	960	
Product design (from Exhibit 7–11)	630	
Order size (from Exhibit 7–11).........................	3,363	
Customer relations (from Exhibit 7–11)...................	1,470	10,651
Customer margin.......................................		$ 699

EXHIBIT 7–13
Customer Margin—
Activity-Based
Costing

In addition to customer costs and margins, many firms today are using activity-based costing to calculate *supplier* costs and margins. Just like customers, suppliers can impact costs accumulated within the firm. For example, the cost of a purchased component should include the price paid to the supplier plus any related costs of reliability, quality, late delivery of components, etc. When selecting longer-term suppliers, all of these potential costs are relevant.

Activity cost pools related to supplier costs might be set up to include purchasing, receiving, inspection of incoming components, warranty and rework costs due to poor quality components, and expedited manufacturing due to late delivery of components. Once these costs are accumulated in activity cost pools, they can be assigned to particular suppliers based on the cost drivers selected. Cost drivers might include units purchased or dollar value of products purchased from each supplier.

<table>
<tr><td>

LEARNING OBJECTIVE ⑤

Compare product costs computed using traditional and activity-based costing methods.

</td></tr>
</table>

■ COMPARISON OF TRADITIONAL AND ACTIVITY-BASED COSTING PRODUCT COSTS

The ABC team used a two-step process to compare its traditional and ABC product costs. First, the team reviewed the product margins reported by the traditional costing system. Then they looked at the differences between the traditional and ABC product margins.

Product Margins Computed Using the Traditional Costing System

Classic Brass's traditional costing system assigns only manufacturing costs to products—this includes direct materials, direct labour, and manufacturing overhead. Selling and administrative costs are not assigned to products. Exhibit 7–14 shows the product margins reported by Classic Brass's traditional costing system. We will explain how these margins were calculated in three steps. First, the sales and direct materials and direct labour cost data are the same numbers used by the ABC team to prepare Exhibit 7–12. In other words, the traditional costing system and the ABC system treat these three pieces of revenue and cost data identically.

Second, the traditional costing system uses a plantwide overhead rate to assign manufacturing overhead costs to products. The numerator for the plantwide overhead rate is $1,000,000, which is the total amount of manufacturing overhead shown on the income statement in Exhibit 7–2. The footnote in Exhibit 7–2 mentions that the traditional costing

EXHIBIT 7–14 Product Margins—Traditional Costing System

Product Margins—Traditional Costing System			Custom Compass Housings		Total	
	Standard Stanchions					
Sales		$2,660,000		$540,000		$3,200,000
Cost of goods sold:						
Direct materials...............	$905,500		$ 69,500		$ 975,000	
Direct labour	263,750		87,500		351,250	
Manufacturing overhead	875,000	2,044,250	125,000	282,000	1,000,000	2,326,250
Product margin		$ 615,750		$258,000		873,750
Selling and administrative.......						875,000
Operating income						$ (1,250)

system uses machine-hours to assign manufacturing overhead costs to products. The Order Size activity in Exhibit 7–8 used 20,000 machine-hours as its level of activity. These same 20,000 machine-hours would be used in the denominator of the plantwide overhead rate, which is computed as follows:

$$\text{Plantwide overhead rate} = \frac{\text{Total estimated manufacturing overhead}}{\text{Total estimated machine-hours}}$$

$$= \frac{\$1,000,000}{20,000 \text{ machine-hours}}$$

$$= \$50 \text{ per machine-hour}$$

Since 17,500 machine-hours were worked on standard stanchions, this product line is assigned $875,000 (17,500 machine-hours × $50 per machine-hour) of manufacturing overhead cost. Similarly, the custom compass housings required 2,500 machine-hours, so this product line is assigned $125,000 (2,500 machine-hours × $50 per machine-hour) of manufacturing overhead cost. The sales of each product minus its cost of goods sold equals the product margin of $615,750 for standard stanchions and $258,000 for custom compass housings.

Notice that the operating loss of $1,250 shown in Exhibit 7–14 agrees with the loss reported in the income statement in Exhibit 7–2. The company's *total* sales, *total* costs, and resulting operating loss are the same regardless of whether you are looking at the absorption income statement in Exhibit 7–2 or the traditional product profitability analysis in Exhibit 7–14. Although the "total pie" remains constant across the traditional and ABC systems, what differs is how the pie is divided between the two product lines. The traditional product margin calculations suggest that standard stanchions are generating a product margin of $615,750 and the custom compass housings a product margin of $258,000. However, these product margins differ from the ABC product margins reported in Exhibit 7–12. Indeed, the traditional costing system is sending misleading signals to Classic Brass's managers about each product's profitability. We explain why in the next section.

The Differences between Activity-Based Costs and Traditional Product Costs

The changes in product margins caused by switching from the traditional costing system to the ABC system are shown below:

	Standard Stanchions	Custom Compass Housings
Product margins—traditional (from Exhibit 7–14).	$615,750	$ 258,000
Product margins—ABC (from Exhibit 7–12).	906,250	(49,500)
Change in reported product margins.	$290,500	$(307,500)

The traditional costing system overcosts the standard stanchions and consequently reports an artificially low product margin for this product. The switch to an activity-based view of product profitability increases the product margin on standard stanchions by $290,500. In contrast, the traditional costing system undercosts the custom compass housings and reports an artificially high product margin for this product. The switch to ABC decreases the product margin on custom compass housings by $307,500.

The reasons for the change in reported product margins between the two costing methods are revealed in Exhibit 7–15. The top portion of the exhibit shows each product's direct and indirect cost assignments as reported by the traditional costing system in Exhibit 7–14. For example, Exhibit 7–15 includes the following costs for standard stanchions: direct materials, $905,500; direct labour, $263,750; and manufacturing overhead, $875,000. Each of these

EXHIBIT 7–15 A Comparison of Traditional and Activity-Based Cost Assignments

	Standard Stanchions		Custom Compass Housings		Total
	(a) Amount	(a) ÷ (c) %	(b) Amount	(b) ÷ (c) %	(c) Amount
Traditional Costing System					
Direct materials....................	$ 905,500	92.9%	$ 69,500	7.1%	$ 975,000
Direct labour	263,750	75.1%	87,500	24.9%	351,250
Manufacturing overhead	875,000	87.5%	125,000	12.5%	1,000,000
Total cost assigned to products	$2,044,250		$282,000		2,326,250
Selling and administrative............					875,000
Total cost.........................					$3,201,250
ABC System					
Direct costs:					
Direct materials..................	$ 905,500	92.9%	$ 69,500	7.1%	$ 975,000
Direct labour	263,750	75.1%	87,500	24.9%	351,250
Shipping	60,000	92.3%	5,000	7.7%	65,000
Indirect costs:					
Customer orders	192,000	60.0%	128,000	40.0%	320,000
Product design..................	0	0.0%	252,000	100.0%	252,000
Order size	332,500	87.5%	47,500	12.5%	380,000
Total cost assigned to products	$1,753,750		$589,500		2,343,250
Costs not assigned to products:					
Customer relations.................					367,500
Other					490,500
Total cost.........................					$3,201,250

costs corresponds to those reported in Exhibit 7–14. Notice that the selling and administrative costs of $875,000 are purposely not allocated to products because these costs are considered to be period costs. Similarly, the bottom portion of Exhibit 7–15 summarizes the direct and indirect cost assignments as reported by the ABC system in Exhibit 7–12. The only new information in Exhibit 7–15 is shown in the two columns of percentages. The first column of percentages shows the percentage of each cost assigned to standard stanchions. For example, the $905,500 of direct materials cost traced to standard stanchions is 92.9% of the company's total direct materials cost of $975,000. The second column of percentages does the same thing for custom compass housings.

The traditional costing system and the ABC system report different product margins for three reasons:

1. The traditional costing system allocates *all* manufacturing costs to products regardless of whether they consumed those costs. The ABC system does not assign manufacturing overhead costs to products for either Customer Relations activities or Other (organization-sustaining) activities because they are not caused by any particular product. From an ABC point of view, assigning these costs to products is inherently arbitrary and counterproductive.

2. The traditional costing system allocates *all* manufacturing overhead costs using machine-hours, a volume-related allocation base that may or may not reflect what actually causes these costs. The ABC system uses unique activity measures (most of which are *not* volume-related) to allocate the cost of each activity cost pool selected on the basis of management's assessment of the driver of overhead costs for that activity. For example,

the traditional costing system assigns 87.5% of the Product Design activity to standard stanchions even though that product caused none of these costs. Conversely, all of the Product Design activity costs should be assigned to custom compass housings, not just the 12.5% under the traditional system. The overall effect is that traditional costing systems overcost high-volume products (such as custom compass housings) and undercost low-volume products (such as standard stanchions) because they assign batch-level and product-level costs using volume-related allocation bases (such as machine-hours).

3. The ABC system assigns non-manufacturing overhead costs such as shipping to products on a cause-and-effect basis. The traditional costing system excludes these costs because they are classified as period costs.

The ABC design team presented the results of its work in a meeting attended by all of the top managers of Classic Brass, including the president, John Towers; the production manager, Susan Richter; the marketing manager, Tom Olafson; and the accounting manager, Mary Goodman. The ABC team brought with them copies of the chart showing the ABC design (Exhibit 7–7) and the table comparing the traditional and ABC cost assignments (Exhibit 7–15). After the formal presentation by the ABC team, the following discussion took place:

Towers: I would like to personally thank the ABC team for all of the work they have done and for an extremely interesting presentation. I am now beginning to wonder about a lot of the decisions we have made in the past using our old cost accounting system. According to the ABC analysis, we had it all backward. We are losing money on the custom products and making a fistful on the standard products.

Goodman: I have to admit that I had no idea that the Product Design work for custom compass housings was so expensive! I knew burying these costs in our plantwide overhead rate was penalizing standard stanchions, but I didn't understand the magnitude of the problem.

Richter: I never did believe we were making a lot of money on the custom jobs. You ought to see all of the problems they create for us in production.

Olafson: I hate to admit it, but the custom jobs always seem to give us headaches in marketing, too.

Towers: If we are losing money on custom compass housings, why not suggest to our customers that they go elsewhere for that kind of work?

Olafson: Wait a minute, we would lose a lot of sales.

Richter: So what? We would save a lot more costs.

Goodman: Maybe yes, maybe no. Some of the costs would not disappear if we were to drop the custom business.

Olafson: Like what?

Goodman: Well Tom, I believe you said that about 10% of your time is spent dealing with new products. As a consequence, 10% of your salary was allocated to the Product Design cost pool. If we were to drop all of the products requiring design work, would you be willing to take a 10% pay cut?

Olafson: I trust you're joking.

Goodman: Do you see the problem? Just because 10% of your time is spent on custom products doesn't mean that the company would save 10% of your salary if the custom products were dropped. Before we take drastic action like dropping the custom products, we should identify which costs are really relevant.

Towers: I think I see what you are driving at. We wouldn't want to drop a lot of products only to find that our costs really haven't changed much. It is true that dropping the products would free up resources like Tom's time, but we had better be sure we have some good use for those resources *before* we take such an action.

As the discussion among Classic Brass managers illustrates, caution should be exercised before taking action based on an ABC analysis such as that shown in Exhibits 7–14 and 7–15. The product and customer margins computed in those exhibits are a useful starting point for further analysis, but managers need to know what costs are really affected before taking any action such as dropping a product or customer or changing the prices of products or services.

Targeting Process Improvements

Activity-based management (ABM)
A management approach that, in conjunction with activity-based costing, improves processes and reduces costs.

The ABC model illustrated in the preceding sections can readily be used to identify areas that would benefit from process improvements. Indeed, managers often cite this as the major benefit of ABC. **Activity-based management (ABM)** is used in conjunction with ABC to improve processes and reduce costs. ABM is used in organizations as diverse as manufacturing companies, hospitals, and the Canadian Coast Guard.

The first step in any improvement program is to decide what to improve. The theory of constraints approach, which is discussed in Chapter 12, is a powerful tool for targeting the area in an organization where improvement will yield the greatest benefit. ABM provides another approach. The activity rates computed in ABC can provide valuable clues concerning where there is waste and scope for improvement in an organization. For example, managers at Classic Brass were surprised at the high cost of customer orders. Some customer orders are for less than $100 worth of products, and yet it costs, on average, $320 to process an order according to the activity rates calculated in Exhibit 7–8. This seemed very expensive for an activity that adds no value to the product. As a consequence, the customer order processing activity was targeted for improvement.

Benchmarking
A systematic approach of comparing the performance of some aspect of an organization's operations to that of outstanding external companies or to other divisions within the same organization.

Benchmarking is another way to utilize the information in activity rates. **Benchmarking** is a systematic approach to identifying the activities with the greatest room for improvement. It is based on comparing the performance of some aspect of an organization's operations (e.g., quality control) with the performance of other, similar organizations known for their outstanding performance. Using outside organizations as the basis for comparison is known as *external benchmarking*. Some companies also use *internal benchmarking*, where one division's operations (e.g., customer order processing) is compared to other divisions that are performing well on that activity. If a particular part of the organization performs well below the external or internal benchmark, managers will likely target that area for improvement.

Activity-Based Costing and External Reports

Although ABC generally provides more accurate product costs than traditional costing methods, it is infrequently used for external reports for a number of reasons. First, external reports are less detailed than internal reports prepared for decision making. On the external reports, individual product costs are not reported. Cost of goods sold and inventory valuations are disclosed, but there is no breakdown of these accounts by product. If some products are under-costed and some are overcosted, the errors tend to offset each other when the product costs are added together.

Second, it is often very difficult to make changes in a company's accounting system. The official cost accounting systems in most large companies are usually embedded in complex computer applications that have been modified in-house over the course of many years. It is extremely difficult to make changes in such applications without causing numerous bugs, which can lead to errors in the resulting information.

Third, an ABC system such as the one described in this chapter does not conform to GAAP. As discussed in Chapter 2, product costs computed for external reports must include all of the manufacturing costs and only manufacturing costs; however, in an ABC system as described in this chapter, product costs exclude some manufacturing costs and include some non-manufacturing costs. It is possible to adjust the ABC data at the end of the period to conform to GAAP, but that requires more work. Appendix 7A presents an approach for using a modified form of ABC for external reporting purposes.

Fourth, auditors are likely to be uncomfortable with allocations based on interviews with the company's personnel. Such subjective data can easily be manipulated by management to make earnings and other key variables look more favourable.

For all of these reasons, most companies confine their ABC efforts to special studies for management and do not attempt to integrate ABC into their formal cost accounting systems.

LEARNING AID

Activity-Based Costing versus Traditional Product Costing

Item	ABC	Traditional
1. Number of cost pools	1. Numerous, based on key activities involved in product/service	1. Small number, based on key production/service departments
2. Treatment of manufacturing overhead (MOH)	2. Allocated to products only if *caused* by products	2. All MOH allocated to products
3. Activity measures used for applying overhead	3. Mix of unit-level (e.g., labour-hours) and non-unit-level (e.g., batches); vary by activity	3. Typically unit-level (e.g., labour-hours); vary by department
4. Treatment of non-manufacturing overhead (e.g., shipping costs)	4. Allocated to products or customers if *caused* by products or customers	4. Expensed as period costs
5. Treatment of direct materials and labour	5. Directly traced to cost objects	5. Directly traced to cost objects
6. Use for external financial reporting	6. Usually requires modification because of items 2 and 4 (see Appendix 7A)	6. Typically no modifications required as it conforms to GAAP

■ THE LIMITATIONS OF ACTIVITY-BASED COSTING

Implementing an ABC system is a major undertaking, requiring substantial resources. And, once implemented, an ABC system is more costly to maintain than a traditional costing system—data concerning numerous activity measures must be collected, checked, and entered into the system. The benefits of increased accuracy may not outweigh these costs.

ABC produces numbers, such as product margins, that may be at odds with the numbers produced by traditional costing systems. But managers are accustomed to using traditional costing systems to run their operations, and traditional costing systems are often used in performance evaluations. Essentially, ABC changes the rules of the game. It is well established that changes in organizations—particularly those that alter the rules of the game—inevitably face resistance. This underscores the importance of top-management support and the full participation of line managers, as well as the accounting staff, in any ABC initiative. If ABC is viewed as an accounting initiative that does not have the full support of top management, it is doomed to failure.

In practice, most managers insist on fully allocating all costs to products, customers, and other cost objects in an ABC system—including the costs of idle capacity and organization-sustaining costs. This results in overstated costs and understated margins and mistakes in pricing and other critical decisions.

ABC data can easily be misinterpreted and must be used with care in making decisions. Costs assigned to products, customers, and other cost objects are only *potentially* relevant. Before making any significant decisions using ABC data, managers must identify which costs are really relevant for the decision at hand.

As discussed in the previous section, reports generated by the best ABC systems do not conform to GAAP. Consequently, an organization involved in ABC should have two costing systems—one for internal use and one for preparing external reports. This is costlier than maintaining just one system and may cause confusion about which system is to be believed and relied on.

IN BUSINESS

In a survey of large manufacturing companies in Canada, nearly 66% of the respondents indicated they believed an ABC system could potentially add value to their organization. However, despite acknowledging its perceived usefulness, only 39% of the responding companies had actually implemented an ABC system across all business units in the organization. Kaplan and Anderson (2007) provide some possible reasons for this relatively low adoption rate:

- High implementation and maintenance costs of ABC systems.
- Inaccuracies in activity costs due to the need for subjective estimates of the amount of time spent on various activities.
- Inability of ABC systems to completely capture the complexity of actual operations.
- Difficulties integrating ABC data from multiple business units across the organization.

Although ABC offers the potential for more accurate product costs, managers must carefully consider all costs of implementing, maintaining, and using the system. Further, some of the reasons cited by Kaplan and Anderson (2007) suggest that implementing a more complex costing system will not automatically result in more accurate costs. Only if estimated benefits exceed all estimated costs should the ABC implementation proceed.

KNOWLEDGE IN ACTION

Managers can apply their knowledge about ABC when

- Calculating the product/service cost when the firm produces a variety of products or when products are highly customized and the design and production process is complex. These are the conditions under which applying overhead uniformly to products is likely to cause the greatest distortion in product/service cost.
- Setting prices to ensure the price exceeds the cost to produce the product or service.
- Identifying activities that would benefit from process improvement (e.g., eliminating waste, decreasing processing time, reducing defects and rework).

SUMMARY

- Under traditional cost accounting methods, all manufacturing costs—even those not caused by specific products—are allocated to products. Non-manufacturing costs that are caused by products are not assigned to products. Traditional costing methods also allocate the costs of idle capacity to products, which, in effect, charges them for resources not used. **[LO1]**
- Traditional costing methods rely on unit-level allocation bases, such as direct labour-hours and machine-hours. This results in overcosting high-volume products and undercosting low-volume products and can lead to mistakes when making decisions. **[LO1]**
- Activity-based costing (ABC) estimates the costs of the resources consumed by cost objects such as products and customers. The approach taken in ABC recognizes that cost objects generate the need for activities that in turn consume costly resources. Activities form the link between costs and cost objects. **[LO1, LO2]**
- ABC is concerned with overhead—both manufacturing overhead and selling and administrative overhead. The accounting for direct labour and direct materials is usually unaffected by the use of ABC. **[LO1, LO2]**

- To develop an ABC system, companies typically choose a small set of activities that summarize much of the work performed in overhead departments. Associated with each activity is an activity cost pool. Where possible, overhead costs are directly traced to these activity cost pools. Remaining overhead costs are assigned to the activity cost pools in the first-stage allocation. [LO2]
- An activity rate is computed for each cost pool by dividing the costs assigned to the cost pool by the measure of activity for the cost pool. In the second-stage allocation, activity rates are used to apply costs to cost objects such as products and customers. [LO3, LO4]
- Activity-based management (ABM) utilizes information from the ABC system to target activities in need of process improvements. Benchmarking performance against world-class organizations or other high-performing divisions within the same organization can help identify activities most in need of improvement. [LO4]
- Product costs computed under ABC are often quite different from the costs generated by a company's traditional cost accounting system because ABC assigns only costs caused by products, uses activity measures that are not necessarily volume related, and assigns non-manufacturing costs such as shipping on a cause-and-effect basis. [LO5]

REVIEW PROBLEM 1: ACTIVITY-BASED COSTING

Advanced Products Corporation produces a fire-resistant commercial filing cabinet that it sells to office furniture distributors. The company has a simple ABC system that it uses for internal decision-making purposes. The company has two overhead departments, whose costs are listed below:

Overhead Costs	
Manufacturing overhead	$500,000
Selling and administrative overhead	300,000
Total overhead costs.	$800,000

The company's ABC system has the following activity cost pools and activity measures:

Activity Cost Pool	Activity Measure
Assembling units	Number of units
Processing orders	Number of customer orders
Customer support.	Number of customers
Other	These costs are not allocated to products or customers

Costs assigned to the "Other" activity cost pool have no activity measure; they consist of the costs of unused capacity and organization-sustaining costs, neither of which are assigned to orders, customers, or the product.

Advanced Products distributes the costs of manufacturing overhead and selling and administrative overhead to the activity cost pools based on interviews with employees as reported below:

	Assembling Units	Processing Orders	Customer Support	Other	Total
Manufacturing overhead	50%	35%	5%	10%	100%
Selling and administrative overhead . . .	10%	45%	25%	20%	100%
Total activity	1,000 units	250 orders	100 customers		

Required:
1. Prepare a report showing the first-stage allocations of overhead costs to the activity cost pools. (Use Exhibit 7–7 as a guide.)
2. Compute the activity rates for the activity cost pools. (Use Exhibit 7–8 as a guide.)
3. Prepare a report showing the overhead costs attributable to Shenzhen Enterprises, one of Advanced Products' customers. Last year, Shenzhen ordered filing cabinets four different times. Shenzhen ordered 80 filing cabinets in total during the year. (Use Exhibit 7–11 as a guide.)
4. The selling price of a filing cabinet is $595. The cost of direct materials is $180 per filing cabinet, and direct labour is $50 per filing cabinet. What is the customer margin of Shenzhen Enterprises? (Use Exhibit 7–13 as a guide.)

Solution to Review Problem 1

1. The first-stage allocation is as follows:

	Assembling Units	Processing Orders	Customer Support	Other	Total
Manufacturing overhead	$250,000	$175,000	$ 25,000	$ 50,000	$500,000
Selling and administrative overhead . .	30,000	135,000	75,000	60,000	300,000
Total overhead costs	$280,000	$310,000	$100,000	$110,000	$800,000

Example: According to the distribution of resources across activities, 50% of the $500,000 manufacturing overhead cost is attributable to assembling units activities:

$$\$500,000 \times 50\% = \$250,000$$

Other entries in the table are determined in a similar manner.

2. Computation of activity rates:

Activity Cost Pools	(a) Total Cost	(b) Total Activity	(a) ÷ (b) Activity Rate
Assembling units.	$280,000	1,000 units	$ 280 per unit
Processing orders.	$310,000	250 orders	$1,240 per order
Customer support	$100,000	100 customers	$1,000 per customer

3. Computation of the overhead costs attributable to Shenzhen Enterprises:

Activity Cost Pools	(a) Activity Rate	(b) Activity	(a) × (b) ABC Cost
Assembling units.	$ 280 per unit	80 units	$22,400
Processing orders.	$1,240 per order	4 orders	4,960
Customer support	$1,000 per customer	1 customer	$ 1,000
Total.			$28,360

4. The customer margins for Shenzhen can be computed as follows:

Sales (80 units × $595 per unit).		$47,600
Costs:		
Direct materials (80 units × $180 per unit)	$14,400	
Direct labour (80 units × $50 per unit).	4,000	
Assembling units.	22,400	
Processing orders	4,960	
Customer support	1,000	46,760
Customer margin.		$ 840

REVIEW PROBLEM 2: COMPARISON OF TRADITIONAL COSTING AND ACTIVITY-BASED COSTING

Rocky Mountain Corporation makes two types of hiking boots—Xactive and Pathbreaker. Data concerning these two product lines appear below:

	Xactive	Pathbreaker
Selling price per unit	$127.00	$89.00
Direct materials per unit	$ 64.80	$51.00
Direct labour per unit	$ 18.20	$13.00
Direct labour-hours per unit	1.4 DLHs	1.0 DLHs
Estimated annual production and sales	25,000 units	75,000 units

The company has a traditional costing system in which manufacturing overhead is applied to units based on direct labour-hours. Data concerning manufacturing overhead and direct labour-hours for the upcoming year appear below:

Estimated total manufacturing overhead	$2,200,000
Estimated total direct labour-hours	110,000 DLHs

Required:
1. Using Exhibit 7–14 as a guide, compute the product margins for the Xactive and Pathbreaker products under the company's traditional costing system.
2. The company is considering replacing its traditional costing system with an ABC system that would assign its manufacturing overhead to the following four activity cost pools (the Other cost pool includes organization-sustaining costs and idle capacity costs):

	Estimated Overhead Cost	Expected Activity		
Cost Pools and Activity Measures		**Xactive**	**Pathbreaker**	**Total**
Supporting direct labour (direct labour-hours)	$ 797,500	35,000	75,000	110,000
Batch setups (setups)	680,000	250	150	400
Product-sustaining (number of products)	650,000	1	1	2
Other	72,500	NA	NA	NA
Total manufacturing overhead cost	$2,200,000			

Using Exhibit 7–12 as a guide, compute the product margins for the Xactive and Pathbreaker products under the ABC system.
3. Using Exhibit 7–15 as a guide, prepare a quantitative comparison of the traditional and activity-based cost assignments. Explain why the traditional and activity-based cost assignments differ.

Solution to Review Problem 2

1. Under the traditional direct labour-hour based costing system, manufacturing overhead is applied to products using the predetermined overhead rate computed as follows:

$$\text{Predetermined overhead rate} = \frac{\text{Estimated total manufacturing overhead cost}}{\text{Estimated total direct labour-hours}}$$

$$= \frac{\$2,200,000}{110,000 \text{ DLHs*}} = \$20.00 \text{ per DLH}$$

*25,000 units of Xactive @ 1.4 DLH per unit + 75,000 units of Pathbreaker @ 1.0 DLH per unit = 35,000 DLHs + 75,000 DLHs = 110,000 DLHs.

Consequently, the product margins using the traditional approach are computed as follows:

	Xactive	Pathbreaker	Total
Sales...................................	$3,175,000	$6,675,000	$9,850,000
Direct materials	1,620,000	3,825,000	5,445,000
Direct labour	455,000	975,000	1,430,000
Manufacturing overhead applied @ $20.00 per direct labour-hour	700,000	1,500,000	2,200,000
Total manufacturing cost	2,775,000	6,300,000	9,075,000
Product margin.........................	$ 400,000	$ 375,000	$ 775,000

Note that all of the manufacturing overhead cost is applied to the products under the company's traditional costing system.

2. The first step is to determine the activity rates:

Activity Cost Pools*	(a) Total cost	(b) Total Activity	(a) ÷ (b) Activity Rate
Supporting direct labour...........	$797,500	110,000 DLHs	$7.25 per DLH
Batch setups	$680,000	400 setups	$1,700 per setup
Product-sustaining	$650,000	2 products	$325,000 per product

*The Other activity cost pool is not shown above because it includes organization-sustaining and idle capacity costs that should not be assigned to products.

Under the ABC system, the product margins are computed as follows:

	Xactive	Pathbreaker	Total
Sales...................................	$3,175,000	$6,675,000	$9,850,000
Direct materials	1,620,000	3,825,000	5,445,000
Direct labour	455,000	975,000	1,430,000
Supporting direct labour	253,750	543,750	797,500
Batch setups............................	425,000	255,000	680,000
Product-sustaining	325,000	325,000	650,000
Total cost	3,078,750	5,923,750	9,002,500
Product margin.........................	$ 96,250	$ 751,250	$ 847,500

3. The quantitative comparison is as follows:

	Xactive		Pathbreaker		Total
Traditional Costing System	(a) Amount	(a) ÷ (c) %	(b) Amount	(b) ÷ (c) %	(c) Amount
Direct materials	$1,620,000	29.8%	$3,825,000	70.2%	$5,445,000
Direct labour.......................	455,000	31.8%	975,000	68.2%	1,430,000
Manufacturing overhead..............	700,000	31.8%	1,500,000	68.2%	2,200,000
Total cost assigned to products.........	$2,775,000		$6,300,000		$9,075,000
ABC System					
Direct costs:					
Direct materials	$1,620,000	29.8%	$3,825,000	70.2%	$5,445,000
Direct labour.....................	455,000	31.8%	975,000	68.2%	1,430,000
Indirect costs:					
Supporting direct labour............	253,750	31.8%	543,750	68.2%	797,500
Batch setups	425,000	62.5%	255,000	37.5%	680,000
Product-sustaining	325,000	50.0%	325,000	50.0%	650,000
Total cost assigned to products.........	$3,078,750		$5,923,750		9,002,500
Costs not assigned to products:					
Other..........................					72,500
Total cost					$9,075,000

The traditional and activity-based cost assignments differ for two reasons. First, the traditional system assigns all $2,200,000 of manufacturing overhead to products. The ABC system assigns only $2,127,500 of manufacturing overhead to products. The ABC system does not assign the $72,500 of Other activity costs to products because they represent organization-sustaining and idle capacity costs. Second, the traditional system uses one unit-level activity measure, direct labour-hours, to assign 31.8% of all overhead to the Xactive product line and 68.2% of all overhead to the Pathbreaker product line. The ABC system assigns 62.5% of batch setup costs (a batch-level activity) to the Xactive product line and 37.5% to the Pathbreaker product line. The ABC system assigns 50% of product-sustaining costs (a product-level activity) to each product line.

DISCUSSION CASE

DISCUSSION CASE 7–1
Implementing an ABC system should proceed only if management believes the benefits of doing so will exceed the costs. The costs of an ABC system are not difficult to quantify. They include identifying the key activities, developing an information system to record and report information, collecting data for activity measures, and maintaining the system. More difficult to quantify are the benefits of adopting an ABC system.

Required:
Can you identify some qualitative benefits of adopting ABC? Can any of these be quantified? How could management deal with uncertainty related to any potential benefits of adopting an ABC system?

QUESTIONS

7–1 How are non-manufacturing costs related to selling, shipping, and distribution activities treated under the ABC approach?

7–2 Why is direct labour a poor base for allocating overhead in many companies?

7–3 Why are overhead rates in ABC based on the level of activity at capacity rather than on the budgeted level of activity?

7–4 What is an activity cost pool?

7–5 What are unit-level, batch-level, product-level, customer-level, and organization-sustaining activities?

7–6 What types of costs should not be assigned to products in an ABC system?

7–7 Why are transaction drivers typically used more often than duration drivers in practice?

7–8 Why is the first stage of the allocation process in ABC often based on interviews?

7–9 What is benchmarking?

7–10 When ABC is used, why are manufacturing overhead costs often shifted from high-volume products to low-volume products?

7–11 What is the second-stage allocation in ABC?

7–12 What are the two chief limitations of ABC?

7–13 Why is ABC as described in the chapter unacceptable for external reporting purposes?

FOUNDATIONAL EXERCISES

[LO2, LO3, LO4, LO5]

Hickory Company manufactures two products—14,000 units of Product Y and 6,000 units of Product Z. The company uses a plantwide overhead rate based on direct labour-hours. It is considering implementing an activity-based costing (ABC) system that allocates all of its manufacturing overhead to four cost pools. The following additional information is available for the company as a whole and for Products Y and Z:

	Activity Measure	Estimated Overhead Cost	Expected Activity
Machining	Machine-hours	$200,000	10,000 MH
Machine setups.	Number of setups	$100,000	200 setups
Product design	Number of products	$ 84,000	2 products
General factory.	Direct labour-hours	$300,000	12,000 DLHs

	Product Y	Product Z
Machine-hours	7,000	3,000
Number of setups	50	150
Number of products	1	1
Direct labour-hours	8,000	4,000

7–1   What is the company's plantwide overhead rate?

7–2   Using the plantwide overhead rate, how much manufacturing overhead cost is allocated to Product Y? How much is allocated to Product Z?

7–3   What is the activity rate for the Machining activity cost pool?

7–4   What is the activity rate for the Machine Setups activity cost pool?

7–5   What is the activity rate for the Product Design activity cost pool?

7–6   What is the activity rate for the General Factory activity cost pool?

7–7   Which of the four activities is a batch-level activity? Why?

7–8   Which of the four activities is a product-level activity? Why?

7–9   Using the ABC system, how much total manufacturing overhead cost would be assigned to Product Y?

7–10   Using the ABC system, how much total manufacturing overhead cost would be assigned to Product Z?

7–11   Using the plantwide overhead rate, what percentage of the total overhead cost is allocated to Product Y? What percentage is allocated to Product Z?

7–12   Using the ABC system, what percentage of the Machining costs is assigned to Product Y? What percentage is assigned to Product Z? Are these percentages similar to those obtained in requirement 11? Why?

7–13   Using the ABC system, what percentage of Machine Setups cost is assigned to Product Y? What percentage is assigned to Product Z? Are these percentages similar to those obtained in requirement 11? Why?

7–14   Using the ABC system, what percentage of the Product Design cost is assigned to Product Y? What percentage is assigned to Product Z? Are these percentages similar to those obtained in requirement 11? Why?

7–15   Using the ABC system, what percentage of the General Factory cost is assigned to Product Y? What percentage is assigned to Product Z? Are these percentages similar to those obtained in requirement 11? Why?

EXERCISES

To help identify which exhibits to refer to when working on the exercises, problems, and cases, use the following guide: (*a*) first-stage allocations to activity cost pools: Exhibit 7–7; (*b*) computation of activity rates: Exhibit 7–8; (*c*) assigning overhead costs to products: Exhibit 7–10; (*d*) assigning overhead costs to customers: Exhibit 7–11; (*e*) product margins: Exhibit 7–12; and (*f*) customer margins: Exhibit 7–13.

EXERCISE 7–1 Activity-Based Costing Cost Hierarchy [LO1]
The following activities occur at Greenwich Corporation, a company that manufactures a variety of products:

a.   Manage the parts inventories.

b.   Issue purchase orders for a job.

c.   Human Resources department sets up payroll files for new production workers.

d.   The factory's general manager meets with other department heads, such as marketing, to coordinate plans.

e.   Direct labour workers assemble products.

f.   Design new products.

g.   Issue raw materials from inventory to be used in jobs.

h.   Perform periodic preventive maintenance on general-use equipment.

Classify each of the activities above as a unit-level, a batch-level, a product-level, or an organization-sustaining activity.

EXERCISE 7–2 First-Stage Allocation in a Service Company [LO2]

MobileCash Corporation operates a fleet of armoured cars that make scheduled pickups and deliveries for its customers. The company is implementing an ABC system that has four activity cost pools: Travel, Pickup and Delivery, Customer Service, and Other. The activity measures are kilometres for the Travel cost pool, number of pickups and deliveries for the Pickup and Delivery cost pool, and number of customers for the Customer Service cost pool. The Other cost pool has no activity measure. The following costs will be assigned using the ABC system:

Driver and guard wages	$ 840,000
Vehicle operating expense	270,000
Vehicle depreciation.	150,000
Customer representative salaries and expenses	180,000
Office expenses	40,000
Administrative expenses	340,000
Total cost	$1,820,000

The distribution of resource consumption across the activity cost pools is as follows:

	Travel	Pickup and Delivery	Customer Service	Other	Totals
Driver and guard wages.	40%	45%	10%	5%	100%
Vehicle operating expense.	75%	5%	0%	20%	100%
Vehicle depreciation	70%	10%	0%	20%	100%
Customer representative salaries and expenses.	0%	0%	85%	15%	100%
Office expenses.	0%	25%	35%	40%	100%
Administrative expenses	0%	5%	55%	40%	100%

Required:
Carry out the first-stage allocations of costs to activity cost pools as illustrated in Exhibit 7–7.

EXERCISE 7–3 First-Stage Allocation in a Manufacturing Company [LO2]

MovieTime Corporation produces furniture and fixtures for home theatre installations. John Jones, the owner of the company, recognized a trend in home theatre installations starting about three years ago and began working with local design firms and home builders to offer affordable yet high-quality furnishings for new construction and renovation markets. The company's most popular product is a leather upholstered recliner with a cup holder and snack tray built into each chair's arms. Last year, John decided to implement an ABC system to better understand the overall cost structure and to ensure he was charging competitive prices that would also allow the firm to remain profitable over the longer term.

The ABC system is designed to allow direct material and direct labour to be traced directly to each of the company's four main products. The system also includes four activity cost pools for overhead: Quality Control and Inspection, Order Processing, Delivery and Installation, and Other. The activity measures are units produced for Quality Control and Inspection, number of orders for Order Processing, and number of deliveries for Delivery and Installation. The Other cost pool has no activity measure. The following costs will be assigned using the ABC system:

Indirect factory salaries	$ 520,000
Delivery crew wages expense	140,000
Delivery vehicle operating expenses and depreciation	95,000
Procurement and order processing salaries and expenses	103,000
Office expenses	25,000
Other administrative expenses	225,000
Total cost	$1,108,000

The distribution of resource consumption across the activity cost pools is as follows:

	Quality Control and Inspection	Delivery and Installation	Order Processing	Other	Totals
Indirect factory salaries................................	50%	25%	20%	5%	100%
Delivery crew wages expense	0%	75%	10%	15%	100%
Delivery vehicle operating expenses and depreciation	0%	80%	10%	10%	100%
Procurement and order processing salaries and expenses.....	10%	10%	65%	15%	100%
Office expenses.......................................	15%	15%	35%	35%	100%
Other administrative expenses..........................	15%	5%	40%	40%	100%

Required:

Carry out the first-stage allocations of costs to activity cost pools as illustrated in Exhibit 7–7.

EXERCISE 7–4 Compute Activity Rates and Assign to a Cost Object [LO3]

(This exercise is a continuation of Exercise 7–3; it should be assigned *only* if Exercise 7–3 is also assigned.)
The ABC system at MovieTime contains the following activity cost pools and activity rates this year:

Activity	Total Activity
Quality control and inspection................	4,800 units produced
Delivery and installation	1,200 deliveries
Order processing	920 orders processed
Other	None

Activity data have also been supplied for the leather recliner product line:

Activity	Total Activity for the Leather Recliner Product Line
Quality control and inspection	1,200 units produced
Delivery and installation..............	300 deliveries
Order processing....................	230 orders processed

Required:

1. Using the first-stage allocation from Exercise 7–3 and the above data, compute the activity rates for the ABC system. (Use Exhibit 7–8 as a guide.) Round to the nearest whole cent.
2. Determine the total overhead cost that would be assigned to the leather recliner product line using the ABC system.

EXERCISE 7–5 Compute Activity Rates and Assign to a Cost Object [LO2, LO3]

Brookside Property Management is a property management service company for small shopping malls that uses ABC to estimate costs for pricing and other purposes. The owner of the company believes that costs are driven primarily by the area of outdoor maintenance (parking lots, sidewalks, and gardens), the area of indoor tenant space in the shopping mall, the distance to travel to the shopping mall, and the number of shopping malls managed. In addition, the costs of managing the indoor tenant space depend on whether the tenants are located on the main level or other levels of the mall. Accordingly, the company uses the five activity cost pools listed below:

Activity Cost Pool	Activity Measure
Management of outdoor areas	Square metres of outdoor areas
Management of indoor mall space—main level	Square metres of main level mall space
Management of indoor mall space—other levels	Square metres of non–main level mall space
Travel to jobs	Kilometres
Customer billing and service	Number of shopping malls

The company has already carried out its first-stage allocations of costs. The company's annual costs and activities are summarized as follows:

Activity Cost Pool	Estimated Overhead Cost	Expected Activity
Management of outdoor areas	$ 69,850	127,000 square metres of outdoor areas
Management of indoor mall space—main level	$114,400	104,000 square metres of main level mall space
Management of indoor mall space—other levels.......	$307,500	246,000 square metres of non–main level mall space
Travel to jobs	$ 6,600	22,000 kilometres
Customer billing and service	$ 13,800	8 shopping malls

Parker Hills Shopping Mall is one of Brookside's oldest clients. Details concerning the mall's layout, outdoor space, and distance from Brookside's head office are as follows:

Activity	Total Activity for Parker Hills Mall
Management of outdoor areas........................	16,000 square metres of outdoor areas
Management of indoor mall space—main level	25,000 square metres of main level mall space
Management of indoor mall space—other levels	0, as mall only has one level
Travel to jobs.....................................	2,500 kilometres travelled
Customer billing and service........................	1 shopping mall

Required:
1. Compute the activity rate for each of the activity cost pools.
2. Determine the total overhead cost that would be assigned to the Parker Hills Shopping Mall using the ABC system.

EXERCISE 7–6 Second-Stage Allocation [LO3]
Larner Corporation manufactures two types of light fixtures for industrial use, the J78 and the W52. The company's ABC system contains the following six activity cost pools and activity rates:

Activity Cost Pool	Activity Rates
Supporting direct labour	14.00 per direct labour-hour
Machine processing...................	$6.00 per machine-hour
Machine setups	$80.00 per setup
Production orders	$60.00 per order
Shipments	$40.00 per shipment
Product-sustaining...................	$400.00 per product

Activity data have been supplied for the following products:

	Total Expected Activity	
	J78	W52
Direct labour-hours	100	40
Machine-hours.............................	20	30
Machine setups	3	1
Production orders	2	1
Shipments	5	1
Product-sustaining.........................	1	1

Required:
Determine the total overhead cost that would be assigned to each of the products listed above in the ABC system.

EXERCISE 7–7 Product and Customer Profitability Analysis [LO3, LO4]

Colby Company makes cases for cell phones of all sizes and types for sale through specialty retailers. The company makes a standard model for the most recent iPhone as well as a deluxe model. Management has designed an ABC system with the following activity cost pools and activity rates for these models:

Activity Cost Pool	Activity Rates
Supporting manufacturing..................	$3 per direct labour-hour
Order processing........................	$15 per order
Customer service........................	$50 per customer

Management would like an analysis of the profitability of a particular customer, Cell City, which has ordered the following products over the last 12 months:

	Standard Model	Deluxe Model
Number of cases.........................	120	35
Number of orders........................	5	2
Direct labour-hours per case	0.20	0.40
Selling price per case.....................	$35	$55
Direct materials cost per case	$10	$12

The company's direct labour rate is $19 per hour.

Required:
Using the company's ABC system, compute the customer margin of Cell City.

EXERCISE 7–8 Activity Measures [LO1]

Various activities at Reservations Online, a hotel reservation call centre, are listed below:

Activity
a. Reservation specialists help customers who call in to the centre to make a hotel reservation.
b. Software technicians improve the system that automatically routes new calls to available reservation specialists.
c. Trainers develop webinars to inform reservation specialists about monthly specials as well as quizzes to ensure employees have understood the material.
d. Monthly invoices are prepared and sent out to hotels/hotel chains that use Reservation Online services.
e. Payments from customers that are received electronically are checked against the bank statement for the month.
f. Team leaders randomly listen in on phone calls answered by their team members and provide written feedback.
g. Health and safety training is provided to all employees in the company.

Required:
1. Classify each activity as unit-level, batch-level, product-level, customer-level, or organization-sustaining.
2. For each activity, provide an example of a cost driver that might be used in the Reservations Online ABC system.

EXERCISE 7–9 Computing Activity-Based Costing Product Costs [LO2, LO3]

Jamesway Corporation makes two types of replacement fittings for heavy construction equipment—screws and bolts. Data regarding the two products follow:

	Direct Labour-Hours per Unit	Annual Production
Screws	0.20	40,000 units
Bolts........................	0.10	60,000 units

Additional information about the company follows:

a.   Screws require $8 in direct materials per unit, and bolts require $6.
b.   The direct labour wage rate is $20 per hour.
c.   Screws are more complex to manufacture than bolts, and they require special equipment.
d.   The ABC system has the following activity cost pools:

Activity Cost Pool	Activity Measure	Estimated Overhead Cost	Activity		
			Screws	Bolts	Total
Machine setups.........	Number of setups	$ 18,000	80	40	120
Special processing	Machine-hours	$160,000	4,000	0	4,000
General factory.........	Direct labour-hours	$210,000	7,000	14,000	21,000

Required:
1.   Compute the activity rate for each activity cost pool.
2.   Determine the unit cost of each product according to the ABC system, including direct materials and direct labour.

EXERCISE 7–10   First-Stage Allocations [LO2]

The operations vice-president of the Regal Bank of Canada, Kristin Wu, has been interested in investigating the efficiency of the bank's operations. She has been particularly concerned about the costs of handling routine transactions at the bank and would like to compare these costs at the bank's various branches. If the branches with the most efficient operations can be identified, their methods can be studied and then replicated elsewhere. While the bank maintains meticulous records of wages and other costs, there has been no attempt thus far to show how those costs are related to the various services provided by the bank. Wu has asked for your help in conducting an ABC study of bank operations. In particular, she would like to know the cost of opening an account, the cost of processing deposits and withdrawals, and the cost of processing other customer transactions.

The Windsor branch of the Regal Bank of Canada submitted the following cost data for last year:

Teller wages....................	$150,000
Assistant branch manager salary	70,000
Branch manager salary...........	85,000
Total........................	$305,000

Virtually all of the other costs of the branch—rent, depreciation, utilities, and so on—are organization-sustaining costs that cannot be meaningfully assigned to individual customer transactions, such as depositing cheques.

In addition to the cost data above, the employees of the Windsor branch have been interviewed concerning how their time was distributed last year across the activities included in the ABC study. The results of those interviews appear below:

Distribution of Resource Consumption across Activities					
	Opening Accounts	Processing Deposits and Withdrawals	Processing Other Customer Transactions	Other Activities	Totals
Teller wages.......	0%	75%	15%	10%	100%
Assistant branch manager salary...	10%	15%	25%	50%	100%
Branch manager salary	0%	0%	20%	80%	100%

Required:
Prepare the first-stage allocation for Wu as illustrated in Exhibit 7–7.

EXERCISE 7–11 Computing and Interpreting Activity Rates [LO3]

(This exercise is a continuation of Exercise 7–10; it should be assigned *only* if Exercise 7–10 is also assigned.) The manager of the Windsor branch of the Regal Bank of Canada has provided the following data concerning the transactions of the branch during the past year:

Activity	Total Activity at the Windsor Branch
Opening accounts.........................	200 accounts opened
Processing deposits and withdrawals..........	50,000 deposits and withdrawals
Processing other customer transactions........	1,000 other customer transactions

The lowest costs reported by other branches for these activities are displayed below:

Activity	Lowest Cost among All Regal Bank of Canada Branches
Opening accounts.........................	$24.35 per account opened
Processing deposits and withdrawals.........	$2.72 per deposit or withdrawal
Processing other customer transactions.......	$48.90 per other customer transaction

Required:

1. Using the first-stage allocation from Exercise 7–10 and the above data, compute the activity rates for the ABC system. (Use Exhibit 7–8 as a guide.) Round all computations to the nearest whole cent.
2. What do these results suggest to you concerning operations at the Windsor branch?

EXERCISE 7–12 Activity Measures [LO1]

Various activities at Ming Corporation, a manufacturing company, are listed below. Each activity has been classified as a unit-level, batch-level, product-level, or customer-level activity.

Activity	Level of Activity in the Cost Hierarchy	Examples of Activity Measures
a. Direct labour workers assemble products	Unit level	
b. Products are designed by engineers	Product level	
c. Equipment is set up	Batch level	
d. Machines are used to shape and cut materials	Unit level	
e. Monthly bills are sent out to regular customers.....	Customer level	
f. Materials are moved from the receiving dock to production lines	Batch level	
g. All completed units are inspected for defects	Unit level	

Required:

Complete the table by providing an example of an activity measure for each activity.

EXERCISE 7–13 Cost Hierarchy [LO1]

Green Glider Corporation makes golf carts that it sells directly to golf courses throughout the world. Several basic models are available, which are modified to suit the needs of each particular golf course. A golf course located in British Columbia, for example, would typically specify that its golf carts come equipped with retractable rain-proof covers. In addition, each customer (i.e., golf course) customizes its golf carts with its own colour scheme and logo. The company typically makes all of the golf carts for a customer before starting work on the next customer's golf carts.

Below are listed a number of activities and costs at Green Glider Corporation:

a.   The purchasing department orders the colour of paint specified by the customer from the company's supplier.

b.   A steering wheel is installed in a golf cart.

c.   An outside lawyer draws up a new generic sales contract for the company, limiting Green Glider's liability in case of accidents that involve its golf carts.

d. The company's paint shop makes a stencil for a customer's logo.

e. A sales representative visits a previous customer to check on how the company's golf carts are working out and to try to make a new sale.

f. The accounts receivable department prepares the bill for a completed order.

g. Electricity is used to heat and light the factory and the administrative offices.

h. A golf cart is painted.

i. The company's engineer modifies the design of a model to eliminate a potential safety problem.

j. The marketing department has a catalogue printed and then mails copies to golf course managers.

k. Completed golf carts are individually tested on the company's test track.

l. A new model golf cart is shipped to the leading golfing trade magazine to be evaluated for the magazine's annual rating of golf carts.

Required:
Classify each of the costs or activities above as unit-level, batch-level, product-level, customer-level, or organization-sustaining. In this case, customers are golf courses, products are the various models of the golf cart, a batch is a specific order from a customer, and units are individual golf carts.

EXERCISE 7–14 Second-Stage Allocation and Margin Calculations [LO3, LO4]
Roll Board Inc. manufactures several models of high-quality skateboards. The company's ABC system has four activity cost pools, which are listed below along with their activity measures and activity rates:

Activity Cost Pool	Activity Measure	Activity Rate
Supporting direct labour	Number of direct labour-hours	$6 per direct labour-hour
Batch processing	Number of batches	$45 per batch
Order processing	Number of orders	$85 per order
Customer service	Number of customers	$72 per customer

The company just completed a single order from SkateCo for 1,200 entry-level skateboards. The order was produced in 12 batches. Each skateboard required 1.5 direct labour-hours. The selling price was $175 per skateboard, the direct materials cost was $68.50 per skateboard, and the direct labour cost was $20 per direct labour-hour. This was the only order from SkateCo for the year.

Required:
Using Exhibit 7–13 as a guide, prepare a report showing the customer margin on sales to SkateCo for the year.

EXERCISE 7–15 Activity-Based versus Traditional Costing [LO3, LO5]
Sandy's Fan Gear makes two different products sold to local sports clubs: baseball caps and lanyards. Products come in several different colours. Overhead costs are currently allocated based on direct labour-hours. During the year the company produced 2,000 caps and 1,500 lanyards. To produce one cap takes 0.4 direct labour-hours and to produce one lanyard takes 0.1 direct labour-hours. The owner, Sandy, has identified other activities that also drive costs and would like to change to an activity-based costing system. She has collected the following information:

Cost Driver	Total Cost of Activity	Cost Driver Volume Caps	Cost Driver Volume Lanyards
Number of machine setups	$12,000	16	12
Number of inspections	$ 800	12	8
Number of shipments	$10,000	80	60

Required:
1. Compute the amount of overhead to be allocated to each product using the traditional allocation method based on direct labour-hours.
2. Compute the amount of overhead to be allocated to each product using the activity-based information in the table.

EXERCISE 7–16 Comprehensive Activity-Based Costing Exercise [LO2, LO3, LO4]
Cancico Communications has supplied the following data for use in its ABC system:

Overhead Costs	
Wages and salaries........	$262,500
Other overhead costs	150,000
Total overhead costs.......	$412,500

Activity Cost Pool	Activity Measure	Total Activity
Direct labour support.........	Number of direct labour-hours	7,500 DLHs
Order processing	Number of orders	600 orders
Customer support...........	Number of customers	120 customers
Other	These costs are not allocated to products or customers.	NA

Distribution of Resource Consumption across Activity Cost Pools					
	Direct Labour Support	Order Processing	Customer Support	Other	Total
Wages and salaries....	20%	40%	30%	10%	100%
Other overhead costs...	15%	25%	25%	35%	100%

During the year, Cancico Communications completed an order for special telephone equipment for a new customer, HurnTel. This customer did not order any other products during the year. Data concerning that order follow:

Selling price......................	$220 per unit
Units ordered	115 units
Direct materials	$195 per unit
Direct labour-hours	0.6 DLH per unit
Direct labour rate	$22 per DLH

Required:
1. Using Exhibit 7–7 as a guide, prepare a report showing the first-stage allocations of overhead costs to the activity cost pools.
2. Using Exhibit 7–8 as a guide, compute the activity rates for the activity cost pools.
3. Prepare a report showing the overhead costs for the order from HurnTel, including customer support costs.
4. Using Exhibit 7–13 as a guide, prepare a report showing the customer margin for HurnTel.

EXERCISE 7–17 Calculating and Interpreting Activity-Based Costing Data [LO2, LO3]
Jane's Cookhouse is a popular restaurant located in a scenic setting. The owner of the restaurant has been trying to better understand costs at the restaurant and has hired a student intern to conduct an ABC study. The intern, in consultation with the owner, identified three major activities. The intern then completed the first-stage allocations of costs to the activity cost pools, using data from last month's operations. The results appear below:

Activity Cost Pool	Activity Measure	Total Cost	Total Activity
Serving a party of diners	Number of parties served	$12,000	5,000 parties
Serving a diner.............	Number of diners served	$90,000	12,000 diners
Serving a drink.............	Number of drinks ordered	$26,000	10,000 drinks

The above costs include all of the costs of the restaurant except for organization-sustaining costs such as rent, property taxes, and top-management salaries. A group of diners who ask to sit at the same table are counted as a party. Some costs, such as the costs of cleaning linen, are the same whether one person is at a table or the table is full. Other costs, such as washing dishes, depend on the number of diners served.

Prior to the ABC study, the owner knew very little about the costs of the restaurant. She knew that the total cost for the month (including organization-sustaining costs) was $180,000 and that 12,000 diners had been served. Therefore, the average cost per diner was $15.

Required:
1. According to the ABC system, what is the total cost of serving each of the following parties of diners?
   a. A party of four diners that orders three drinks in total.
   b. A party of two diners that does not order any drinks.
   c. A lone diner who orders two drinks.
2. Convert the total costs you computed in (1) above to costs per diner. In other words, what is the average cost per diner for serving each of the following parties?
   a. A party of four diners that orders three drinks in total.
   b. A party of two diners that does not order any drinks.
   c. A lone diner who orders two drinks.
3. Why do the costs per diner for the three different parties differ from each other and from the overall average cost of $15.00 per diner?

EXERCISE 7–18 Customer Profitability Analysis [LO3, LO4, LO5]

Quick Supply distributes office supplies to small to medium sized offices throughout the Region of Waterloo, Ontario. Quick Supply sets its prices by marking up its cost of goods sold by 5%. For example, if Quick Supply paid $100 to buy supplies from manufacturers, Quick Supply would charge its customers $105 to purchase these supplies.

For years, Quick Supply believed that the 5% markup covered its selling and administrative expenses and provided a reasonable profit. However, in the face of declining profits, Quick Supply decided to implement an ABC system to help improve its understanding of customer profitability. The company broke its selling and administrative expenses into five activities, as shown below:

Activity Cost Pool	Activity Measure	Total Cost	Total Activity
Customer deliveries	Number of deliveries	$ 400,000	5,000 deliveries
Manual order processing	Number of manual orders	300,000	4,000 orders
Electronic order processing	Number of electronic orders	200,000	12,500 orders
Line item picking	Number of line items picked	500,000	400,000 line items
Other organization-sustaining costs	NA	600,000	
Total selling and administrative expense		$2,000,000	

Quick Supply gathered the data below for two typical offices that it serves—City Office and County Office (both offices purchased a total quantity of office supplies that had cost Quick Supply $30,000 to buy from manufacturers):

	Activity	
Activity Measure	City Office	County Office
Number of deliveries	8	12
Number of manual orders.	0	15
Number of electronic orders	8	0
Number of line items picked	80	100

Required:
1. Compute the total revenue that Quick Supply would receive from City Office and County Office.
2. Compute the activity rate for each activity cost pool.
3. Compute the total activity costs that would be assigned to City Office and County Office.
4. Compute Quick Supply's customer margin for City Office and County Office. (*Hint:* Do not overlook the $30,000 cost of goods sold that Quick Supply incurred serving each office.)
5. Describe the purchasing behaviours that are likely to characterize Quick Supply's least profitable customers.

PROBLEMS

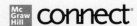

PROBLEM 7–19 Evaluating the Profitability of Services [LO2, LO3, LO4]

Kenosha Winter Services is a small, family-owned snow-removal business. For its services, the company has always charged a flat fee per hundred square metres of snow removal. The current fee is $12.75 per hundred square metres. However, there is some question about whether the company is actually making any money on jobs for some customers—particularly those located on more remote properties that require considerable travel time. The owner's daughter, home from school for the summer, has suggested investigating this question using ABC. After some discussion, a simple system consisting of four activity cost pools seemed to be adequate. The activity cost pools and their activity measures appear below:

Activity Cost Pool	Activity Measure	Activity for the Year
Snow removal	Square metres cleaned (00s)	32,000 hundred square metres
Travel to jobs.	Kilometres driven	15,000 kilometres
Job support	Number of jobs	400 jobs
Other (costs of idle capacity and organization-sustaining costs). . .	None	NA

The total cost of operating the company for the year is $390,000, which includes the following costs:

Wages	$150,000
Supplies.	40,000
Snow removal equipment depreciation.	20,000
Vehicle expenses.	40,000
Office expenses.	60,000
President's compensation	80,000
Total cost.	$390,000

Resource consumption is distributed across the activities as follows:

	Distribution of Resource Consumption across Activity Cost Pools				
	Snow Removal	Travel to Jobs	Job Support	Other	Total
Wages	80%	10%	0%	10%	100%
Supplies.	100%	0%	0%	0%	100%
Snow removal equipment depreciation.	80%	0%	0%	20%	100%
Vehicle expenses.	0%	60%	0%	40%	100%
Office expenses.	0%	0%	45%	55%	100%
President's compensation	0%	0%	40%	60%	100%

Job support consists of receiving calls from potential customers at the home office, scheduling jobs, billing, resolving issues, and so on.

Required:

1. Using Exhibit 7–7 as a guide, prepare the first-stage allocation of costs to the activity cost pools.
2. Using Exhibit 7–8 as a guide, compute the activity rates for the activity cost pools.
3. The company recently completed a 3,500-square-metre snow removal job at Hometown Hardware—a 75-kilometre round-trip journey from Kenosha's offices. Compute the cost of this job using the ABC system.
4. The revenue from the Hometown Hardware job was $446.25 (3,500 square metres at $12.75 per hundred square metres). Using Exhibit 7–13 as a guide, prepare a report showing the margin from this job.

5.   What do you conclude concerning the profitability of the Hometown Hardware job? Explain.
6.   What advice would you give the president concerning pricing jobs in the future?

PROBLEM 7–20 Activity-Based Costing and Bidding on Jobs [LO2, LO3]

Vance Asbestos Removal Company removes potentially toxic asbestos insulation and related products from buildings. The company's estimator has been involved in a long-simmering dispute with the on-site work supervisors. The on-site supervisors claim that the estimator does not adequately distinguish between routine work, such as removal of asbestos insulation around heating pipes in older homes, and non-routine work, such as removing asbestos-contaminated ceiling plaster in industrial buildings. The on-site supervisors believe that non-routine work is far more expensive than routine work and should bear higher customer charges. The estimator sums up his position in this way: "My job is to measure the area to be cleared of asbestos. As directed by top management, I simply multiply the square metres by $4,000 per thousand square metres to determine the bid price. Since our average cost is only $3,000 per thousand square metres, that leaves enough cushion to take care of the additional costs of non-routine work that shows up. Besides, it is difficult to know what is routine or not routine until you actually start tearing things apart."

To shed light on this controversy, the company initiated an ABC study of all of its costs. Data from the ABC system follow:

Activity Cost Pool	Activity Measure	Total Activity
Removing asbestos	Thousands of square metres	500,000 m²
Estimating and job setup.	Number of jobs	200 jobs*
Working on non-routine jobs	Number of non-routine jobs	25 non-routine jobs
Other (costs of idle capacity and organization-sustaining costs).	Not applicable; these costs are not allocated to jobs.	

*The total number of jobs includes non-routine jobs as well as routine jobs. Non-routine jobs as well as routine jobs require estimating and setup work.

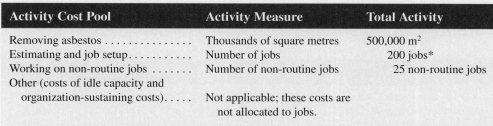

Wages and salaries	$ 200,000
Disposal fees.	600,000
Equipment depreciation	80,000
On-site supplies.	60,000
Office expenses.	190,000
Licensing and insurance	370,000
Total cost.	$1,500,000

	Distribution of Resource Consumption across Activity Cost Pools				
	Removing Asbestos	Estimating and Job Setup	Working on Non-routine Jobs	Other	Total
Wages and salaries	40%	10%	35%	15%	100%
Disposal fees.	70%	0%	30%	0%	100%
Equipment depreciation	50%	0%	40%	10%	100%
On-site supplies.	55%	15%	20%	10%	100%
Office expenses.	10%	40%	30%	20%	100%
Licensing and insurance	50%	0%	40%	10%	100%

Required:
1.   Using Exhibit 7–7 as a guide, perform the first-stage allocation of costs to the activity cost pools.
2.   Using Exhibit 7–8 as a guide, compute the activity rates for the activity cost pools.

3. Using the activity rates you have computed, determine the total cost and the average cost per thousand square metres of each of the following jobs according to the ABC system:
    a.   A routine 2,000-square-metre asbestos removal job.
    b.   A routine 4,000-square-metre asbestos removal job.
    c.   A non-routine 2,000-square-metre asbestos removal job.
4. Given the results you obtained in (3) above, do you agree with the estimator that the company's present policy for bidding on jobs is adequate?

PROBLEM 7–21 Second-Stage Allocations and Product Margins [LO3, LO4]

AnimPix Inc. is a small company that creates computer-generated animations for films and television. Much of the company's work consists of short commercials for television, but the company also does realistic computer animations for special effects in movies.

The young founders of the company have become increasingly concerned with the economics of the business—particularly since many competitors have sprung up recently in the local area. To help understand the company's cost structure, an ABC system has been designed. Three major activities are carried out in the company: animation concept, animation production, and contract administration. The animation concept activity is carried out at the contract proposal stage when the company bids on projects. This is an intensive activity that involves individuals from all parts of the company in creating storyboards and prototype stills to be shown to the prospective client. After the client has accepted a project, the animation goes into production and contract administration begins. Technical staff do almost all of the work involved in animation production, whereas administrative staff are largely responsible for contract administration. The activity cost pools and their activity measures and rates are listed below:

Activity Cost Pool	Activity Measure	Activity Rate
Animation concept	Number of proposals	$6,040 per proposal
Animation production	Minutes of animation	$7,725 per minute of animation
Contract administration.	Number of contracts	$6,800 per contract

These activity rates include all of the costs of the company, except for the costs of idle capacity and organization-sustaining costs. There are no direct labour or direct materials costs.

Preliminary analysis using these activity rates has indicated that the local commercials segment of the market may be unprofitable. This segment is highly competitive. Producers of local commercials may ask several companies like AnimPix to bid, which results in an unusually low ratio of accepted contracts to bids. Furthermore, the animation sequences tend to be much shorter for local commercials than for other work. Since animation work is billed at standard rates according to the running time of the completed animation, the revenues from these short projects tend to be below average. Data concerning activity in the local commercials market appear below:

Activity Measure	Local Commercials
Number of proposals.	25
Minutes of animation	5
Number of contracts	10

The total sales for local commercials amounted to $180,000.

Required:
1. Determine the cost of the local commercials market. (Think of the local commercials market as a product.)
2. Prepare a report showing the product margin of the local commercials market. (Remember, this company has no direct materials or direct labour costs.)
3. What would you recommend to management concerning the local commercials market?

PROBLEM 7–22 Activity Rates and Activity-Based Management [LO2, LO3]

Onassis Catering is a Greek company that provides passenger and crew meals to airlines operating out of two international airports in Athens and Corfu. The operations at the two airports are managed separately, and top management believes that there may be benefits to greater sharing of information between the two operations.

To better compare the two operations, an ABC system has been designed with the active participation of the managers at both airports. The ABC system is based on the following activity cost pools and activity measures:

Activity Cost Pool	Activity Measure
Meal preparation...	Number of meals
Flight-related activities.......................................	Number of flights
Customer service..	Number of customers
Other (costs of idle capacity and organization-sustaining costs)	NA

The operation at Athens International Airport (AIA) serves 1 million meals annually on 5,000 flights for 10 different airlines. (Each airline is considered one customer.) The annual cost of running the AIA airport operation, excluding only the costs of raw materials for meals, totals €3,675,000. (*Note:* The currency in Greece is the euro, denoted by €.)

Annual Cost of the AIA Operation	
Cooks and delivery personnel wages	€3,000,000
Kitchen supplies	37,500
Chef salaries	225,000
Equipment depreciation	75,000
Administrative wages and salaries	187,500
Building costs	150,000
Total cost..	€3,675,000

To help determine the activity rates, employees were interviewed and asked how they divided their time among the four major activities. The results of employee interviews at AIA are displayed below:

	Distribution of Resource Consumption across Activities at the AIA Operation				
	Meal Preparation	Flight-Related	Customer Service	Other	Total
Cooks and delivery personnel wages	75%	20%	0%	5%	100%
Kitchen supplies	100%	0%	0%	0%	100%
Chef salaries	30%	20%	40%	10%	100%
Equipment depreciation	60%	0%	0%	40%	100%
Administrative wages and salaries	0%	20%	60%	20%	100%
Building costs	0%	0%	0%	100%	100%

Required:
1. Perform the first-stage allocation of costs to the activity cost pools. (Use Exhibit 7–7 as a guide.)
2. Compute the activity rates for the activity cost pools. (Use Exhibit 7–8 as a guide.) Do not round off.
3. The Corfu operation has already concluded its ABC study and has reported the following activity rates: 2.48 per meal for meal preparation; 144.50 per flight for flight-related activities; and 12,000 for customer service. Comparing the activity rates for the AIA operation you computed in (2) above to the activity rates for Corfu, do you have any suggestions for the top management of Onassis Catering?

PROBLEM 7–23 Comparing Traditional and Activity-Based Costing Product Margins [LO1, LO3, LO4]

Modern Tools makes two types of chain saws—High Grade and Professional. Data concerning these two product lines appear below:

	High Grade	Professional
Selling price per unit..........................	$215.50	$387.00
Direct materials per unit	$ 83.50	$212.00
Direct labour per unit	$ 30.00	$ 45.00
Direct labour-hours per unit	1.0 DLHs	1.5 DLHs
Estimated annual production and sales..........	75,000 units	25,000 units

The company has a traditional costing system in which manufacturing overhead is applied to units based on direct labour-hours. Data concerning manufacturing overhead and direct labour-hours for the upcoming year appear below:

Estimated total manufacturing overhead.....	$1,350,000
Estimated total direct labour-hours.........	112,500 DLHs

Required:

1. Using Exhibit 7–14 as a guide, compute the product margins for the High Grade and the Professional products under the company's traditional costing system.
2. The company is considering replacing its traditional costing system with an ABC system that would assign its manufacturing overhead to the following four activity cost pools (the Other cost pool includes organization-sustaining costs and idle capacity costs):

		Expected Activity		
Activities and Activity Measures	**Estimated Overhead Cost**	**High Grade**	**Professional**	**Total**
Supporting direct labour (direct labour-hours)	$ 573,750	75,000	37,500	112,500
Batch setups (setups).................	621,250	75	275	350
Product-sustaining (number of products)...............	110,000	1	1	2
Other	45,000	NA	NA	NA
Total manufacturing overhead cost......	$1,350,000			

Using Exhibit 7–12 as a guide, compute the product margins for the High Grade and Professional products under the ABC system.

3. Explain why and how the traditional and activity-based cost assignments differ.

PROBLEM 7–24 Comparing Traditional and Activity-Based Product Margins [LO1, LO3, LO4, LO5]

Hi-Tek Manufacturing Inc. makes two types of industrial component parts—the B300 and the T500. An absorption costing income statement for the most recent period is shown below:

HI-TEK MANUFACTURING INC. Income Statement	
Sales	$2,100,000
Cost of goods sold.............................	1,600,000
Gross margin.................................	500,000
Sales and administrative expenses	550,000
Net operating loss	($50,000)

Hi-Tek produced and sold 70,000 units of B300 at a price of $20 per unit and 17,500 units of T500 at a price of $40 per unit. The company's traditional cost system allocates manufacturing overhead to products using a plantwide overhead rate and direct labour dollars as the allocation base. Additional information relating to the company's two product lines is shown below:

	B300	T500	Total
Direct materials.	$436,300	$251,700	$ 688,000
Direct labour .	$200,000	$104,000	$ 304,000
Manufacturing overhead .			$ 608,000
Cost of goods sold.			$1,600,000

The company has created an activity-based costing system to evaluate the profitability of its products. Hi-Tek's ABC implementation team concluded that $50,000 and $100,000 of the company's advertising expenses could be directly traced to B300 and T500, respectively. The remainder of the selling and administrative expenses were organization-sustaining in nature. The ABC team also distributed the company's manufacturing overhead to four activities as shown below:

Activity Cost Pool (and Activity Measures)	Manufacturing Overhead	Activity B300	Activity T500	Activity Total
Machining (machine-hours) .	$213,500	90,000	62,500	152,500
Setups (setup-hours) .	157,500	75	300	375
Product-sustaining (number of products).	120,000	1	1	2
Other (organization-sustaining costs) .	117,000	NA	NA	NA
Total manufacturing overhead costs .	$608,000			

Required:
1.   Using Exhibit 7–14 as a guide, compute the product margins for the B300 and T500 under the company's traditional costing system.
2.   Using Exhibit 7–12 as a guide, compute the product margins for B300 and T500 under the activity-based costing system.
3.   Using Exhibit 7–15 as a guide, prepare a quantitative comparison of the traditional and activity-based cost assignments. Explain why the traditional and activity-based cost assignments differ.

PROBLEM 7–25 Choice of Costing System [LO1, LO3, LO4, LO5]

Klein Company produces three types of bird feeders: Basic, Squirrel-Proof, and Deluxe. Currently, the company allocates overhead to products using machine-hours. This year, the company produced 1,000 Basic models, 2,000 Squirrel-Proof models, and 1,800 Deluxe models. Details for each product at the end of the current year are as follows:

	Basic	Squirrel-Proof	Deluxe
Revenue.	$30,000	$110,000	$117,000
Direct materials.	$12,000	$ 50,000	$ 54,000
Direct labour .	$ 7,500	$ 19,000	$ 22,500
Machine-hours per unit.	0.3 MH	0.5 MH	0.4 MH

The total overhead cost to be allocated to products is $28,000.

Required:
1.   Calculate the profit per unit for each product after allocated overhead costs using machine-hours.
2.   Use the activity-based information below to reallocate overhead costs to products. Compare product profitability under the two different overhead allocation methods.

Cost Driver	Cost	Basic	Squirrel-Proof	Deluxe
Number of machine setups .	$12,000	3 setups	4 setups	5 setups
Operating machines.	$ 4,000	.3 MH	.5 MH	.4 MH
Number of sales orders received.	$ 4,000	20 orders	40 orders	45 orders
Number of units shipped.	$ 8,000	1,000 units	2,000 units	1,800 units

CASES

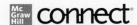

CASE 7–26 Comprehensive Activity-Based Costing [LO2, LO3, LO5]

Kolbec Community College (KCC) has 4,000 full-time students and offers a variety of academic programs in three areas: professional studies, arts, and technology. The professional studies programs prepare students for administrative and clerical jobs in a variety of professional settings, including accounting, medicine, and law. The arts program's offerings are wide ranging and include graphic design, digital animation, culinary arts, cosmetology, and music arts. The technology programs are also varied, including information technology, medical laboratory technology, electrical engineering technology, pharmacy technology, and natural resources technology.

The chief financial officer of KCC, Lynn Jones, has consistently emphasized to other members of the senior management team the importance of understanding the costs of delivering the various academic programs. To that end, the costing system used at KCC tracks the direct costs of each program, which are shown below on an annual basis, along with the number of full-time students:

Item	Professional Studies	Arts	Technology	Total
Full-time students	2,000	1,000	1,000	4,000
Professors' salaries	$1,260,000	$ 650,000	$ 780,000	$2,690,000
Administrative salaries	105,000	70,000	70,000	245,000
Supplies	40,000	150,000	50,000	240,000
Teaching support	160,000	100,000	80,000	340,000
Facilities	275,000	150,000	175,000	600,000
Total direct cost	$1,840,000	$1,120,000	$1,155,000	$4,115,000

It is very important to understand the overhead costs consumed by each academic program at KCC in determining the full cost of operating the programs. Central administration at KCC allocates financial resources to academic programs based on the estimated full cost per student of delivering the program. The overhead costs at KCC are significant, totalling over 60% of direct costs. Total annual overhead costs at KCC are as follows:

	Cost
Administrative salaries	$ 900,000
Facility costs	1,300,000
Office expenses	300,000
Total overhead costs	$2,500,000

Traditionally, KCC has allocated overhead costs to academic programs on the basis of the number of full-time students in each program. This approach was deemed appropriate since Jones reasoned that increasing the number of students at KCC would result in higher overhead costs (e.g., more facilities would be needed, more indirect support costs would be incurred, etc.). However, Jones is beginning to question the accuracy of the traditional approach since it results in a similar full cost per student for the arts and technology programs, which she feels doesn't make sense. Based on her knowledge of the programs, Jones feels that the technology program is probably more expensive to deliver than the arts program, but this does not come through in the traditional costing approach.

Jones recently attended a seminar on management techniques being used by leading educational institutions that, among other topics, covered the basics of the ABC approach. She likes the idea of being able to assign indirect costs to academic programs on the basis of how much of the support activity resources are consumed by each program. If Jones's instincts are correct in that some programs consume more resources of certain activities than others, this could have a significant impact on the overhead costs assigned to each under the ABC approach.

Upon returning to KCC, Jones decides to implement ABC. She, along with Assistant CFO James West, begins by identifying the key activities used to support the teaching programs. Rather than getting too detailed with respect to identifying activities in the initial implementation, Jones decides to keep the process manageable and comes up with six key activities. Next, based on a series of interviews with various KCC employees who work in the departments covered by the identified activities, Jones and West estimate the percentage of the total administrative, facility, and office expense resources consumed by each activity. Again, to keep the process efficient, Jones rounds all percentages to the nearest 5%, figuring that a "close enough" approach will suffice for this initial implementation and recognizing that the estimates are subjective to begin with. The results are shown below:

Activity	Resource Distribution across Activities		
	Administrative	Facilities	Office
Central administration....................	20%	5%	15%
Information systems technology............	20%	15%	15%
Student counselling services..............	5%	5%	10%
Human resources........................	10%	5%	10%
Library operations......................	20%	60%	30%
Registrar's office.......................	25%	10%	20%
Total	100%	100%	100%

Working with key personnel from each of the six activities shown above, Jones and West then identify the activity measure and the quantity of that measure used for each teaching program. Fortunately, KCC implemented an enterprise resource planning system a few years ago, which is already tracking much of the information needed regarding the activity measures and the specific quantities for each academic program:

Activity	Measure	Professional	Arts	Technology
Central administration..................	Hours spent on program	6,000	7,000	7,000
Information systems technology............	Processing hours	6,000	3,000	12,000
Student counselling services..............	Number of students counselled	180	115	205
Human resources.......................	Number of admin. staff and faculty members	21	15	14
Library operations.....................	Number of library circulations	6,000	3,000	3,000
Registrar's office.....................	Full-time students	2,000	1,000	1,000

Required:
1. Using the traditional approach to assigning overhead costs to academic programs:
   a. Calculate the predetermined overhead rate.
   b. Assign the overhead costs to each academic program using the predetermined rate.
   c. Calculate the total cost per student (direct costs plus overhead) of operating each academic program.
2. Using ABC, complete the following requirements:
   a. Using Exhibit 7–7 as a guide, complete the first-stage allocation of overhead costs to academic programs.
   b. Using Exhibit 7–8 as a guide, calculate the activity rates for each of the activity cost pools.
   c. Using the activity rates calculated in (b), complete the second-stage allocation of overhead to academic programs.
3. Based on the results of (2), calculate the total cost per student (direct costs plus overhead) of operating each academic program.
4. Draft a memo to Jones explaining the key reasons for differences in the total cost per student of operating each academic program that arise between the traditional costing approach and ABC.

CASE 7–27 Activity-Based Costing and Pricing [LO2, LO3, LO4, LO5]

Oxford Concrete Inc. (OCI) processes and distributes various types of cement. The company buys quarried local rock, limestone, and clay from around the world and mixes, blends, and packages the processed cement for resale. OCI offers a large variety of cement types that it sells in one-kilogram bags to local retailers for small do-it-yourself jobs. The major cost of the cement is raw materials. However, the company's predominantly automated mixing, blending, and packaging processes require a substantial amount of manufacturing overhead. The company uses relatively little direct labour.

Some of OCI's cement mixtures are very popular and sell in large volumes, while a few of the recently introduced cement mixtures sell in very low volumes. OCI prices its cements at manufacturing cost plus a 25% markup, with some adjustments made to keep the company's prices competitive.

For the coming year, OCI's budget includes estimated manufacturing overhead cost of $4,400,000. OCI assigns manufacturing overhead to products on the basis of direct labour-hours. The expected direct labour cost totals $1,200,000, which represents 100,000 hours of direct labour time. Based on the sales budget and expected raw materials costs, the company will purchase and use $10,000,000 of raw materials (mostly quarried rock, limestone, and clay) during the year.

The expected costs for direct materials and direct labour for one-kilogram bags of two of the company's cement products appear below:

	Normal Portland	High Sulphate Resistance
Direct materials..................	$9.00	$5.80
Direct labour (0.02 hours per bag)	$0.24	$0.24

OCI's controller believes that the company's traditional costing system may be providing misleading cost information. To determine whether this is the case, the controller has prepared an analysis of the year's expected manufacturing overhead costs, as shown in the following table:

Activity Cost Pool	Activity Measure	Expected Activity for the Year	Expected Cost for the Year
Purchasing...........	Purchase orders	4,000 orders	$1,120,000
Materials handling	Number of setups	2,000 setups	386,000
Quality control	Number of batches	1,000 batches	180,000
Mixing..............	Mixing-hours	190,000 mixing-hours	2,090,000
Blending	Blending-hours	64,000 blending-hours	384,000
Packaging	Packaging-hours	48,000 packaging-hours	240,000
Total manufacturing overhead cost.....			$4,400,000

Data regarding the expected production of Normal Portland and High Sulphate Resistance cement mixes are presented below:

	Normal Portland	High Sulphate Resistance
Expected sales..................	160,000 kilograms	8,000 kilograms
Batch size	10,000 kilograms	500 kilograms
Setups	4 per batch	4 per batch
Purchase order size	20,000 kilograms	500 kilograms
Mixing time per 100 kilograms......	3 mixing-hours	3 mixing-hours
Blending time per 100 kilograms	1 blending-hour	1 blending-hour
Packaging time per 100 kilograms ...	0.6 packaging-hours	0.6 packaging-hours

Required:
1. Using direct labour-hours as the base for assigning manufacturing overhead cost to products, do the following:
   a. Determine the predetermined overhead rate that will be used during the year.
   b. Determine the unit product cost of one kilogram of the Normal Portland cement and one kilogram of the High Sulphate Resistance cement.
2. Using ABC as the basis for assigning manufacturing overhead cost to products, do the following:
   a. Determine the total amount of manufacturing overhead cost assigned to the Normal Portland cement and to the High Sulphate Resistance cement for the year.
   b. Using the data developed in 2(a) above, compute the amount of manufacturing overhead cost per kilogram of the Normal Portland cement and the High Sulphate Resistance cement. Round all computations to the nearest whole cent.
   c. Determine the unit product cost of one kilogram of the Normal Portland cement and one kilogram of the High Sulphate Resistance cement.
3. Write a brief memo to the president of OCI explaining what you found in (1) and (2) above, and discuss the implications to the company of using direct labour as the base for assigning manufacturing overhead cost to products.

INSTANT QUIZ SOLUTIONS

7–1

The four main differences between traditional costing and ABC are (1) both manufacturing and non-manufacturing costs may be assigned to products on a cause-and-effect basis under ABC but not traditional product costing; (2) some manufacturing costs that would be included in the predetermined overhead rate under traditional costing would not be applied to cost objects under ABC because they do not drive the cost of that cost object; (3) while departmental or plantwide overhead rates are used in traditional costing, ABC uses many different cost pools that are based on activities that drive cost, not departmental organization; and (4) activity rates are often calculated based on activity at capacity, while under traditional costing, budgeted levels of activity are used in the denominator of predetermined overhead rates.

7–2

A specific example could be a company that produces and sells flat-screen TVs. A unit-level activity is installing the digital receiver in each TV produced. A batch-level activity is ordering stands in three different colours to use for each of three different models of TVs produced. A product-level activity is the design of a new model of TV with next-generation electronics. A customer-level activity is a salesperson visiting a customer to ensure he or she is pleased with the product quality and delivery specifications. An organization-sustaining activity is seeking outside legal advice on the terms of the top manager's employment contracts.

7–3

The $40,000 of administrative wages and salaries allocated to the Order Size activity cost pool is calculated as follows: $400,000 total administrative wages and salaries × 10% consumed per Exhibit 7–6: $40,000.

7–4

Total overhead costs related to order processing = $25,200. A total of 350 orders were processed in the year; therefore, the activity rate to assign order processing costs to the customer orders cost object is $25,200 ÷ 350 = $72 per order.

7–5

Total overhead applied to Product Q43 = (120 DLH × $7 per DLH) + (43 MH × $2 per MH) + (4 setups × $63 per setup) + (5 shipments × $12 per shipment) = $1,238.

7–6

Customer margin for Mitchell Hardware is as follows:

Revenue	1,200 cases × $72 per case	$86,400
Less expenses:		
Direct material	(1,200 cases × 24 bottles) × $0.95	27,360
Direct labour	(1,200 cases × 24 bottles) × $0.40	11,520
Unit-level overhead applied	(1,200 cases × 24 bottles) × 1.10	31,680
Order processing	1,200 cases at 50 cases per order = 24 orders ×	
	$250 per order	6,000
Customer margin	. . . .	$ 9,840

■ APPENDIX 7A: USING A MODIFIED FORM OF ACTIVITY-BASED COSTING TO DETERMINE PRODUCT COSTS FOR EXTERNAL REPORTS

LEARNING OBJECTIVE   **6**

Use activity-based costing techniques to compute unit product costs for external reports.

This chapter has emphasized using ABC information in internal decisions. However, a modified form of ABC can also be used to develop product costs for external financial reports. For this purpose, product costs include *all* manufacturing overhead costs—including organization-sustaining costs and the costs of idle capacity—and exclude all non-manufacturing costs, even costs that are clearly caused by the products.

The simplest absorption costing systems as described in Chapter 5 assign manufacturing overhead costs to products using a single plantwide predetermined overhead rate based on direct labour-hours or machine-hours. When ABC is used to assign manufacturing overhead costs to products, a predetermined overhead rate is computed for each activity cost pool. An example will make this difference clear.

Maxtar Industries manufactures high-quality smoker/barbecue units. The company has two product lines—Premium and Standard. The company has traditionally applied manufacturing overhead costs to these products using a plantwide predetermined overhead rate based on direct labour-hours. Exhibit 7A–1 details how the unit product costs of the two product lines are computed using the company's traditional costing system. The unit product cost of the Premium product line is $71.60, and the unit product cost of the Standard product line is $53.70, according to this traditional costing system.

Maxtar Industries has recently experimented with an ABC approach to determining its unit product costs for external reporting purposes. The company's ABC system has three activity cost pools: (1) Supporting direct labour, (2) setting up machines, and (3) parts administration. The top of Exhibit 7A–2 displays basic data concerning these activity cost pools. Note that the total estimated overhead cost in these three cost pools, $1,520,000, agrees with the total estimated overhead cost in the company's traditional costing system. The company's ABC system simply provides an alternative way to allocate the company's manufacturing overhead across the two products.

EXHIBIT 7A–1

Maxtar Industries' Traditional Costing System

Basic Data

Total estimated manufacturing overhead cost		$1,520,000
Total estimated direct labour-hours		400,000 DLHs

	Premium	**Standard**
Direct materials per unit	$40.00	$30.00
Direct labour per unit	$24.00	$18.00
Direct labour-hours per unit	2.0 DLHs	1.5 DLHs
Units produced	50,000 units	200,000 units

Computation of the Predetermined Overhead Rate

$$\text{Predetermined overhead rate} = \frac{\text{Total estimated manufacturing overhead}}{\text{Total estimated amount of the allocation base}}$$

$$= \frac{\$1,520,000}{400,000} = 3.80 \text{ per DLH}$$

Traditional Unit Product Costs

	Premium	**Standard**
Direct materials	$40.00	$30.00
Direct labour	24.00	18.00
Manufacturing overhead (2.0 DLHs × $3.80 per DLH; 1.5 DLHs × $3.80 per DLH)	7.60	5.70
Unit product cost	$71.60	$53.70

Basic Data

1. Activities and Activity Measures	Estimated Overhead Cost	Expected Activity		
		Premium	Standard	Total
Supporting direct labour (DLHs)	$ 800,000	100,000	300,000	400,000
Setting up machines (setups).	480,000	600	200	800
Parts administration (part types).	240,000	140	60	200
Total manufacturing overhead cost.	$1,520,000			

2. Computation of Activity Rates

Activities	(a) Estimated Overhead Cost	(b) Total Expected Activity	(a) ÷ (b) Activity Rate
Supporting direct labour	$800,000	400,000 DLHs	$2 per DLH
Setting up machines	$480,000	800 setups	$600 per setup
Parts administration	$240,000	200 part types	$1,200 per part type

3. Assigning Overhead Costs to Products

Overhead Cost for the Premium Product

Activity Cost Pools	(a) Activity Rate	(b) Activity	(a) × (b) ABC Cost
Supporting direct labour	$2 per DLH	100,000 DLHs	$200,000
Setting up machines	$600 per setup	600 setups	360,000
Parts administration	$1,200 per part type	140 part types	168,000
Total			$728,000

Overhead Cost for the Standard Product

Activity Cost Pools	(a) Activity Rate	(b) Activity	(a) × (b) ABC Cost
Supporting direct labour	$2 per DLH	300,000 DLHs	$600,000
Setting up machines	$600 per setup	200 setups	120,000
Parts administration	$1,200 per part type	60 part types	72,000
Total			$792,000

4. ABC Product Costs

	Premium	Standard
Direct materials.	$40.00	$30.00
Direct labour	24.00	18.00
Manufacturing overhead ($728,000 ÷ 50,000 units;		
$792,000 ÷ 200,000 units)	14.56	3.96
Unit product cost.	$78.56	$51.96

The activity rates for the three activity cost pools are computed in the second table in Exhibit 7A–2. For example, the total cost in the "Setting up machines" activity cost pool, $480,000, is divided by the total activity associated with that cost pool, 800 setups, to determine the activity rate of $600 per setup.

The activity rates are used to allocate overhead costs to the two products in the third table in Exhibit 7A–2. For example, the activity rate for the "Setting up machines" activity cost pool, $600 per setup, is multiplied by the Premium product line's 600 setups to determine the $360,000 machine setup cost allocated to the Premium product line. The overhead cost per unit is determined at the bottom of this table by dividing the total overhead cost by the number of units produced. For example, the Premium product line's total overhead cost of $728,000 is divided by 50,000 units to determine the $14.56 overhead cost per unit.

The table at the bottom of Exhibit 7A–2 displays the ABC unit product costs. Note that these unit product costs differ from those computed using the company's traditional costing system in Exhibit 7A–1. Because the ABC system contains both a batch-level (setting up machines) and a product-level (parts administration) activity cost pool, the unit product costs under ABC follow the usual pattern in which overhead costs are shifted from the high-volume to the low-volume product. The unit product cost of the Standard product line, the high-volume product, has gone down from $53.70 under the traditional costing system to $51.96 under ABC. In contrast, the unit product cost of the Premium product line, the low-volume product, has increased from $71.60 under the traditional costing system to $78.56 under ABC. Instead of arbitrarily assigning most of the costs of setting up machines and of parts administration to the high-volume product, the ABC system more accurately assigns these costs to the two products.

■ APPENDIX 7A SUMMARY

- A modified form of activity-based costing (ABC) can be used for external financial reporting. However, when used for external reports, product costs include only manufacturing costs and exclude all non-manufacturing costs. **[LO6]**

■ APPENDIX 7A PROBLEMS AND CASES

PROBLEM 7A–1 Activity-Based Costing Product Costs for External Reports [LO6]
Data concerning Cranur Architects Corporation's two major business lines are given below:

	Commercial	Residential
Direct materials per square metre	$6.00	$4.50
Direct labour per square metre	$48	$36
Direct labour-hours per square metre	0.1 DLHs	0.075 DLHs
Estimated annual output	40,000 m²	280,000 m²

The company has a traditional costing system in which architecture department overhead is applied to units (square metres of architectural drawings) based on direct labour-hours. Data concerning architecture department overhead and direct labour-hours for the upcoming year appear below:

Estimated total architecture department overhead	$670,000
Estimated total direct labour-hours	25,000 DLHs

Required:
1. Determine the unit costs of the Commercial and Residential products under the company's traditional costing system.
2. The company is considering replacing its traditional costing system for determining unit product costs for external reports with an ABC system. The ABC system would have the following three activity cost pools:

Activities and Activity Measures	Estimated Overhead Cost	Expected Activity		
		Commercial	Residential	Total
Supporting direct labour (direct labour-hours)	$600,000	4,000	21,000	25,000
Drawing software modifications (changes)	60,000	100	25	125
Quality review and technical checks (tests)	10,000	80	20	100
Total service department overhead cost	$670,000			

Determine the unit costs (cost per square metre of architectural drawings) of the Commercial and Residential lines of business under the ABC system.

PROBLEM 7A–2 Activity-Based Costing Product Costs for External Reports [LO6]
Krunkel Company makes two products and uses a traditional costing system in which a single plantwide predetermined overhead rate is computed based on direct labour-hours. Data for the two products for the upcoming year follow:

	Mercon	Wurcon
Direct materials cost per unit	$ 10.00	$ 8.00
Direct labour cost per unit.	$ 3.00	$ 3.75
Direct labour-hours per unit	0.20	0.25
Number of units produced.	10,000	40,000

These products are customized to some degree for specific customers.

Required:
1. The company's manufacturing overhead costs for the year are expected to be $336,000. Using the company's traditional costing system, compute the unit product costs for the two products.
2. Management is considering an ABC system in which half of the overhead would continue to be allocated on the basis of direct labour-hours and half would be allocated on the basis of engineering design time. The Mercon product and the Wurcon product are expected to need 4,000 engineering design hours each. Compute the unit product costs for the two products using the proposed ABC system.
3. Explain why the unit product costs differ between the two systems.

PROBLEM 7A–3 Activity-Based Costing as an Alternative to Traditional Product Costing [LO6]
Rehm Company manufactures a product that is available in both a deluxe model and a regular model. The company has manufactured the regular model for years. The deluxe model was introduced several years ago to tap a new segment of the market. Since introduction of the deluxe model, the company's profits have steadily declined, and management has become increasingly concerned about the accuracy of its costing system. Sales of the deluxe model have been increasing rapidly.

Manufacturing overhead is assigned to products on the basis of direct labour-hours. For the current year, the company has estimated that it will incur $6,000,000 in manufacturing overhead cost and produce 15,000 units of the deluxe model and 120,000 units of the regular model. The deluxe model requires 1.6 hours of direct labour time per unit, and the regular model requires 0.8 hours. Material and labour costs per unit are as follows:

	Model	
	Deluxe	Regular
Direct materials.	$154	$112
Direct labour	$ 16	$ 8

Required:
1. Using direct labour-hours as the base for assigning manufacturing overhead cost to products, compute the predetermined overhead rate. Using this rate and other data from the problem, determine the unit product cost of each model.
2. Management is considering using ABC to apply manufacturing overhead costs to products for external financial reports. The ABC system would have the following four activity cost pools:

Activity Cost Pool	Activity Measure	Estimated Overhead Costs
Purchase orders.	Number of purchase orders	$ 252,000
Scrap/rework orders	Number of scrap/rework orders	648,000
Product testing	Number of tests	1,350,000
Machine-related	Machine-hours	3,750,000
Total overhead cost		$6,000,000

Activity Measure	Expected Activity		
	Deluxe	Regular	Total
Number of purchase orders..........................	400	800	1,200
Number of scrap/rework orders......................	500	400	900
Number of tests...................................	6,000	9,000	15,000
Machine-hours	20,000	30,000	50,000

Using Exhibit 7–8 as a guide, compute the predetermined overhead rates (i.e., activity rates) for each of the four activity cost pools.

3. Using the predetermined overhead rates computed in (2) above, do the following:
   a. Compute the total amount of manufacturing overhead cost that would be applied to each model using the ABC system. After you have computed these totals, determine the amount of manufacturing overhead cost per unit for each model.
   b. Compute the unit product cost of each model (materials, labour, and manufacturing overhead).

4. From the data you developed in (1) through (3) above, identify factors that may account for the company's declining profits.

PROBLEM 7A–4 Activity-Based Costing as an Alternative to Traditional Product Costing [LO6]
For many years, Sinclair Graphic Design has provided design and digital-printing services for indoor banners. The nylon banners, which come in a standard size, are used for a variety of purposes, including trade shows, sporting events, and other promotional activities. Three years ago, the company introduced a second printing and production service for outdoor banners that has become increasingly popular. The outdoor banners are a more complex product than the indoor banners, requiring weatherproof vinyl materials and a different printing process to improve the visibility of the text and graphics content. Moreover, outdoor banners are printed in smaller production runs because of less frequent orders; the setup of the printing equipment takes longer; and, since higher durability is needed to withstand the elements, more quality inspections are needed. Under the traditional costing approach, overhead costs are assigned to the products on the basis of direct labour-hours.

Despite the introduction of the new outdoor banners, profits have declined steadily over the past three years. Management is beginning to believe that the company's costing system may be at fault. Unit costs for materials and labour for the two products follow:

	Indoor Banners	Outdoor Banners
Direct materials...........................	$ 9	$26
Direct labour ($20 per hour)................	$20	$60

Management estimates that the company will incur $600,000 in overhead costs during the current year and that 10,000 indoor banners and 2,000 outdoor banners will be produced and sold.

Required:
1. Compute the predetermined overhead rate assuming that the company continues to apply overhead cost to products on the basis of direct labour-hours. Using this rate and other data from the problem, determine the unit product cost of each product.
2. Management is considering using ABC to apply overhead cost to products for external financial reports. Some preliminary work has been done, and the data that have been collected are displayed below. Using these data, calculate the predetermined overhead rate for each activity cost pool identified below:

	Estimated Total Overhead Costs	Activity Measures		
		Indoor Banners	Outdoor Banners	Total
Order processing (orders received).........	$150,000	500	500	1,000
Print setup (number of batches)	50,000	800	200	1,000
Artwork and graphic design (labour-hours) ..	350,000	7,000	7,000	14,000
Quality control (number of inspections).....	50,000	400	400	800
Total overhead cost....................	600,000			

3. Using the predetermined manufacturing overhead rates that you computed in (2) above, do the following:

    a. Determine the total amount of manufacturing overhead cost that would be applied to each product using the ABC system. After you have computed these totals, determine the amount of overhead cost per unit of each product.

    b. Compute the unit product cost of each product.

4. Based on your calculations in (1) through (3) above, in terms of overhead cost, what factors make the outdoor banners more costly to produce than the indoor banners? Are the outdoor banners as profitable as the company thinks they are? Explain.

PROBLEM 7A–5 Activity-Based Costing as an Alternative to Traditional Product Costing [LO6]

Erte Inc. manufactures two models of high-pressure steam valves, the XR7 model and the ZD5 model. Data regarding the two products follow:

Product	Direct Labour-Hours	Annual Production	Total Direct Labour-Hours
XR7....................	0.2 DLHs per unit	20,000 units	4,000 DLHs
ZD5....................	0.4 DLHs per unit	40,000 units	16,000 DLHs
			20,000 DLHs

Additional information about the company follows:

a. Product XR7 requires $35 in direct materials per unit, and product ZD5 requires $25.

b. The direct labour rate is $20 per hour.

c. The company has always used direct labour-hours as the base for applying manufacturing overhead cost to products. Manufacturing overhead totals $1,480,000 per year.

d. Product XR7 is more complex to manufacture than product ZD5 and requires the use of a special milling machine.

e. Because of the special work required in (d) above, the company is considering the use of ABC to apply overhead cost to products. Three activity cost pools have been identified, and the first-stage allocations have been completed. Data concerning these activity cost pools appear below:

Activity Cost Pool	Activity Measure	Estimated Total Cost	Estimated Total Activity		
			XR7	ZD5	Total
Machine setups	Number of setups	$ 180,000	150	100	250
Special milling	Machine-hours	300,000	1,000	0	1,000
General factory	Direct labour-hours	1,000,000	4,000	16,000	20,000
		$1,480,000			

Required:

1. Assume that the company continues to use direct labour-hours as the base for applying overhead cost to products.

    a. Compute the predetermined overhead rate.

    b. Determine the unit product cost of each product.

2. Assume that the company decides to use ABC to apply overhead cost to products.

    a. Compute the activity rate for each activity cost pool. Also compute the amount of overhead cost that would be applied to each product.

    b. Determine the unit product cost of each product.

3. Explain why overhead cost shifted from the high-volume product to the low-volume product under ABC.

CASE 7A–6 Contrasting Activity-Based Costing and Traditional Costing [LO2, LO3, LO4, LO6]

"Wow! Is that R-92 model ever a loser! It's time to cut back its production and shift our resources toward the new T-95 model," said Graham Thomas, executive vice-president of Thomas Products Inc. "Just look at this income statement I've received from accounting. The T-95 is generating over eight times as much profit as the R-92 on one-sixth of the unit sales. I'm convinced that our future depends on the T-95." The year-end statement to which Thomas was referring is shown below:

		Model	
	Total	**R-92**	**T-95**
Sales	$11,125,000	$9,000,000	$2,125,000
Cost of goods sold	6,900,000	5,490,000	1,410,000
Gross margin	4,225,000	3,510,000	715,000
Less selling and administrative expenses	3,675,000	3,450,000	225,000
Operating income	$ 550,000	$ 60,000	$ 490,000
Number of units produced and sold		30,000	5,000

"The numbers sure look that way," replied Julie Williams, the company's sales manager. "But why isn't the competition more excited about the T-95? I know we've been producing the model for only three years, but I'm surprised that more of our competitors haven't recognized what a cash cow it is."

"I think it's our new automated plant," replied Thomas. "Now it takes only two direct labour-hours to produce a unit of the R-92 and three direct labour-hours to produce a unit of the T-95. That's considerably less than it used to take us."

"I agree that automation is wonderful," replied Williams. "I suppose that's how we're able to hold down the price of the T-95. Taylor Company in England tried to bring out a T-95 but discovered they couldn't touch our price. But Taylor is killing us on the R-92 by undercutting our price with some of our best customers. I suppose they'll pick up all of our R-92 business if we move out of that market. But who cares? We don't even have to advertise the T-95; it just seems to sell itself."

"My only concern about automation is how our manufacturing overhead rate has shot up," said Thomas. "Our total manufacturing overhead cost is $2,700,000. That comes out to be a hefty amount per direct labour-hour, but Dianne down in accounting has been using direct labour-hours as the base for computing overhead rates for years and doesn't want to change. I don't suppose it matters as long as costs get assigned to products."

"I've never understood that debit and credit stuff," replied Williams. "But I think you've got a problem in production. I had lunch with Janet, our plant manager, yesterday and she complained about how complex the T-95 is to produce. Apparently they have to do a lot of setups, special soldering, and other work on the T-95 just to keep production moving. And they have to inspect every single unit."

"It'll have to wait," said Thomas. "I'm writing a proposal to the board of directors to phase out the R-92. We've got to increase our bottom line or we'll all be looking for jobs."

Required:

1. Compute the predetermined overhead rate based on direct labour-hours that the company used during the year. (There was no underapplied or overapplied overhead for the year.)

2. Direct materials and direct labour costs per unit for the two products are as follows:

	R-92	T-95
Direct materials	$75	$120
Direct labour	$36	$ 54

Using these data and the rate computed in (1) above, determine the unit product cost of each product under the company's traditional costing system.

3. Assume that the company's $2,700,000 in manufacturing overhead cost can be assigned to six activity cost pools, as follows:

Activity Cost Pool (and Activity Measure)	Estimated Overhead Costs	Expected Activity		
		Total	R-92	T-95
Machine setups (number of setups)	$312,000	1,600	1,000	600
Quality control (number of inspections).	540,000	9,000	4,000	5,000
Purchase orders (number of orders)	135,000	1,200	840	360
Soldering (number of solder joints)	675,000	200,000	60,000	140,000
Shipments (number of shipments)	198,000	600	400	200
Machine-related (machine-hours).	840,000	70,000	30,000	40,000
	$2,700,000			

Given these data, would you support a recommendation to expand sales of the T-95? Explain your position.

4. From the data you prepared in (3) above, why do you suppose the T-95 "just seems to sell itself"?

5. If you were president of Thomas Products Inc., what strategy would you follow from this point forward to improve the company's overall profits?

■ APPENDIX 7B: TIME-DRIVEN ACTIVITY-BASED COSTING: A MICROSOFT EXCEL–BASED APPROACH

LEARNING OBJECTIVE ⑦
Use time-driven activity-based costing to assign costs to cost objects.

The purpose of this appendix is to introduce you to *time-driven activity-based costing* (TDABC). The approach demonstrated in this appendix overcomes two important limitations that accompany the activity-based costing (ABC) model described in the main body of the chapter. First, TDABC does not require extensive interviews with employees to perform stage one allocations. For a company that employs thousands of people, these interviews can be very time-consuming—which limits a company's ability to frequently update its cost model. Second, the ABC model assumes that employees will self-report their own idle time within the "Other" cost pool that is not allocated to products. In reality, most employees are very averse to reporting their own idle time because it may signal to management that the size of the labour force can be reduced.

This appendix will demonstrate how TDABC can be used to assign indirect costs to cost objects such as products and customers. We'll also explain how TDABC can be used for capacity analysis purposes. For simplicity, we limit the scope of this appendix to focus solely on labour costs. While TDABC systems can include other types of indirect costs such as equipment costs and utility costs, we purposely omit these kinds of costs to simplify our capacity analysis discussion.

Ridley Company: An Example

Ridley Company would like to improve its understanding of customer profitability and capacity utilization. As an initial pilot project, the company has decided to use TDABC to analyze its Customer Service Department labour costs. The goals of the project are to obtain a better understanding of how customer service labour costs are used by individual customers and to obtain a more informed basis for making employee staffing decisions within the department. In the past, the company has relied on "educated guesses" to make staffing decisions, which often resulted in an imbalance between the number of employees on the payroll and the number of employees needed to serve customers. Ridley hopes that TDABC will enable it to estimate the financial implications of better aligning its labour capacity with its customer demand.

The Data Inputs

Exhibit 7B–1 summarizes three types of data inputs for Ridley's TDABC model—resource data, activity data, and cost object data. The resource data includes the number of employees in the Customer Service Department (30), the average salary per employee ($29,952), the number of weeks in a year (52), the

EXHIBIT 7B–1 Ridley Company: The Data Inputs

	A	B	C	D	E
1			Ridley Company		
2			Customer Service Department		
3			Data Inputs		
4					
5	*Resource Data:*				
6	Number of employees	30			
7	Average salary per employee	$ 29,952			
8					
9	Weeks per year	52			
10	Minutes available per week (40 hours × 60 minutes)	2,400			
11	Practical capacity percentage	80%			
12					
13	*Activity Data:*	Order processing	Query resolution	Credit reviews	
14	Minutes per unit of the activity	10	30	40	
15					
16	*Cost Object Data:*	Customer A	Customer B	Customer C	All Customers
17	Number of orders processed	30	18	7	200,000
18	Number of customer queries	17	10	8	4,500
19	Number of credit reviews	1	1	1	8,900
20					

minutes available per week (2,400), and the practical capacity percentage (80%). The practical capacity percentage acknowledges that employees are not serving customers 100 percent of their available minutes. They spend some of their available time on vacation, on breaks, in training, attending to personal needs, etc. Thus, Ridley estimates that 80 percent of an employee's available minutes are spent actually serving customers.

The activity data contained in Exhibit 7B–1 specifies three activities within the Customer Service Department, namely order processing (cell B13), query resolution (cell C13), and credit reviews (cell D13). It also states the average number of minutes required to perform each activity one time. For example, on average it takes 10 minutes to process one order, 30 minutes to resolve one query from a customer, and 40 minutes to review one customer's creditworthiness.[1] The cost object data that are shown in Exhibit 7B–1 provide activity data for customers A, B, and C as well as all customers served by the Customer Service Department during the year. For example, customers A, B, and C placed 30, 18, and 7 orders, respectively. A total of 200,000 orders were placed by all of Ridley's customers during the year.

Customer Cost Analysis

Exhibit 7B–2 summarizes the three-step TDABC process that Ridley Company uses to assign Customer Service Department labour costs to customers A, B, and C. The first step is to divide the total cost of the resources supplied in cell B10 ($898,560) by the practical capacity of the resources supplied in cell B14 (2,995,200 minutes) to obtain the cost per minute of the resource supplied in cell B16 ($0.30). Notice that cell B12 shows a practical capacity per employee of 99,840 minutes. This amount is obtained by multiplying together three cells from the data inputs tab shown in Exhibit 7B–1—cell B9 (52 weeks), cell B10 (2,400 minutes per week), and cell B11 (80%).

The second step in Exhibit 7B–2 is to calculate the time-driven activity rate for each of the three activities. For example, the time-driven activity rate for the order processing activity of $3.00 per order (cell B21) is derived by multiplying 10 minutes per unit of the activity (cell B19) by the cost per minute of the resource supplied of $0.30 (cell B20). Similarly, the time-driven activity rate for the query resolution activity of $9.00 per query (cell C21) is derived by multiplying 30 minutes per unit of the activity (cell C19) by the cost per minute of the resource supplied of $0.30 (cell C20).

The third step in Exhibit 7B–2 is to assign customer service labour costs to customers A, B, and C. For example, the total customer service costs assigned to customer A of $255 (cell B36) is the sum of

EXHIBIT 7B–2   Ridley Company: Customer Cost Analysis

	A	B	C	D
1	Ridley Company			
2	Customer Service Department			
3	Customer Cost Analysis			
4				
5	Step 1: Calculate the cost per minute of the resource supplied			
6				
7	*Customer Service Department:*			
8	Number of employees (a)	30		
9	Average salary per employee (b)	$ 29,952		
10	Total cost of resources supplied (a) × (b)	$ 898,560		
11				
12	Practical capacity per employee (in minutes) (a)	99,840		
13	Number of employees (b)	30		
14	Practical capacity of resources supplied (in minutes) (a) × (b)	2,995,200		
15				
16	Cost per minute of the resource supplied	$ 0.30		
17				
18	Step 2: Calculate the time-driven activity rate	Order processing	Query resolution	Credit reviews
19	Minutes per unit of the activity (a)	10	30	40
20	Cost per minute of the resource supplied (b)	$ 0.30	$ 0.30	$ 0.30
21	Time-driven activity rate (a) × (b)	$ 3.00	$ 9.00	$ 12.00
22				
23	Step 3: Assign costs to cost objects	Customer A	Customer B	Customer C
24	Number of orders processed (a)	30	18	7
25	Time-driven activity rate (b)	$ 3.00	$ 3.00	$ 3.00
26	Order processing costs assigned (a) × (b)	$ 90.00	$ 54.00	$ 21.00
27				
28	Number of customer queries (a)	17	10	8
29	Time-driven activity rate (b)	$ 9.00	$ 9.00	$ 9.00
30	Query resolution costs assigned (a) × (b)	$ 153.00	$ 90.00	$ 72.00
31				
32	Number of credit checks (a)	1	1	1
33	Time-driven activity rate (b)	$ 12.00	$ 12.00	$ 12.00
34	Credit review costs assigned (a) × (b)	$ 12.00	$ 12.00	$ 12.00
35				
36	Total customer service costs assigned	$ 255.00	$ 156.00	$ 105.00
37				

the order processing costs of $90 (cell B26), the query resolution costs of $153 (cell B30), and the credit review costs of $12 (cell B34). Notice that the number of orders processed in cell B24 (30), the number of customer queries in cell B28 (17), and the number of credit reviews in cell B32 (1) are linked to cells B17 through B19 in the data inputs tab shown in Exhibit 7B–1.

The type of cost assignments summarized in Exhibit 7B–2 could be useful to Ridley Company in larger initiatives, such as measuring customer profitability and managing its customer mix based on those insights. Furthermore, the cost assignments shown in Exhibit 7B–2 were performed without having to interview the 30 employees within the Customer Services Department. Instead, Ridley Company only needed to make a reasonable estimate regarding its practical capacity percentage (80%) and to estimate the amount of time required to perform each activity one time in order to compute its time-driven activity rates.

However, the data in Exhibit 7B–2 do not help Ridley quantify and manage its used and unused capacity costs, nor do they enable the company to estimate the number of Customer Service Department employees that it would need to meet future customer demand. To glean these types of insights from Ridley's TDABC system, we turn our attention to the topic of capacity analysis.

EXHIBIT 7B–3   Ridley Company: Capacity Analysis

	A	B	C	D	E
1	Ridley Company				
2	Customer Service Department				
3	Capacity Analysis				
4					
5	Step 1: Calculate the used capacity in minutes	Order processing	Query resolution	Credit reviews	Total
6	Customer demand for each activity (a)	200,000	4,500	8,900	
7	Customer service minutes required per unit of each activity (b)	10	30	40	
8	Customer service minutes used to meet demand (a) × (b)	2,000,000	135,000	356,000	2,491,000
9					
10	Step 2: Calculate the unused capacity in minutes				
11	Total customer service minutes available to meet demand (a)	2,995,200			
12	Total customer service minutes used to meet demand (b)	2,491,000			
13	Unused capacity in minutes (a) − (b)	504,200			
14					
15	Step 3: Calculate the unused capacity in number of employees				
16	Unused capacity in minutes (a)	504,200			
17	Practical capacity per employee (in minutes) (b)	99,840			
18	Unused capacity in number of employees (a) ÷ (b)	5.05			
19					
20	Step 4: Calculate the financial impact of matching capacity with demand				
21	Potential adjustment in number of employees (rounded) (a)	(5.00)			
22	Average salary per employee (b)	$ 29,952			
23	Impact on expenses of matching capacity with demand (a) × (b)	$(149,760)			
24					
25	Note: Cell B21 uses the formula =If(B18>0,rounddown(-B18,0),roundup(-B18,0))				
26					

Capacity Analysis

Exhibit 7B–3 shows the four-step process that Ridley Company uses for capacity management purposes. It focuses on *all* of Ridley's customers rather than just customers A, B, and C. The first step is to calculate the total used capacity in minutes of 2,491,000 (= 2,000,000 + 135,000 + 356,000). The second step is to take the total minutes available of 2,995,200 from cell B11 (and as previously computed in cell B14 in Exhibit 7B–2) minus the minutes used of 2,491,000 (from cell B12) to derive the 504,200 minutes of unused capacity shown in cell B13.

The third step translates the unused capacity in minutes to unused capacity in terms of employees. We perform this calculation because customer service employees are a step-fixed cost rather than a variable cost. In other words, Ridley does not purchase customer service capacity by the minute. Instead, it hires individual employees who each provide 99,840 minutes of practical capacity per year. Because the unused capacity in minutes is 504,200 and the practical capacity of one employee is 99,840 minutes, the total unused capacity equates with 5.05 employees (= 504,200 ÷ 99,840).

The fourth step calculates the financial impact of matching capacity with demand. The key to this step is the formula in cell B21 of Exhibit 7B–3, which rounds the value reported in cell B18 to a whole number. We perform this rounding function because Ridley alters its step-fixed employee headcount in terms of whole employees, not portions of an employee. So, for example, cell B18 shows an unused capacity of 5.05 employees; however, Ridley cannot eliminate .05 employees. It could possibly eliminate five or six employees, but nothing in between. Since eliminating six employees would leave the Customer Service Department a little short-handed, we round down to five employees. Given the average salary per employee of $29,952, the impact on expenses of matching labour capacity with demand is a savings of $149,760 (= 5.00 × $29,952).

"What-If" Analysis

The data inputs in Exhibit 7B–1 also enable Ridley to answer some interesting "what if" questions. For example, what if the company were able to lower its credit review time from 40 minutes to 30 minutes?

EXHIBIT 7B–4 Ridley Company's Customer Cost Analysis: A "What If" Analysis

	A	B	C	D
1	Ridley Company			
2	Customer Service Department			
3	Customer Cost Analysis			
4				
5	Step 1: Calculate the cost per minute of the resource supplied			
6				
7	*Customer Service Department:*			
8	Number of employees (a)	30		
9	Average salary per employee (b)	$ 29,952		
10	Total cost of resources supplied (a) × (b)	$ 898,560		
11				
12	Practical capacity per employee (in minutes) (a)	99,840		
13	Number of employees (b)	30		
14	Practical capacity of resources supplied (in minutes) (a) × (b)	2,995,200		
15				
16	Cost per minute of the resource supplied	$ 0.30		
17				
		Order processing	Query resolution	Credit reviews
18	Step 2: Calculate the time-driven activity rate			
19	Minutes per unit of the activity (a)	10	30	30
20	Cost per minute of the resource supplied (b)	$ 0.30	$ 0.30	$ 0.30
21	Time-driven activity rate (a) × (b)	$ 3.00	$ 9.00	$ 9.00
22				
23	Step 3: Assign costs to cost objects	Customer A	Customer B	Customer C
24	Number of orders processed (a)	30	18	7
25	Time-driven activity rate (b)	$ 3.00	$ 3.00	$ 3.00
26	Order processing costs assigned (a) × (b)	$ 90.00	$ 54.00	$ 21.00
27				
28	Number of customer queries (a)	17	10	8
29	Time-driven activity rate (b)	$ 9.00	$ 9.00	$ 9.00
30	Query resolution costs assigned (a) × (b)	$ 153.00	$ 90.00	$ 72.00
31				
32	Number of credit checks (a)	1	1	1
33	Time-driven activity rate (b)	$ 9.00	$ 9.00	$ 9.00
34	Credit review costs assigned (a) × (b)	$ 9.00	$ 9.00	$ 9.00
35				
36	Total customer service costs assigned	$ 252.00	$ 153.00	$ 102.00
37				

How would this affect the costs assigned to customers A, B, and C? To answer this question, we would change cell D14 in Exhibit 7B–1 from 40 minutes to 30 minutes. The revised customer cost analysis that would be instantly generated is shown in Exhibit 7B–4.

Notice that cell D19 shows 30 minutes per credit review instead of the 40 minutes shown in the same cell in Exhibit 7B–2. This in turn lowers the cost per credit review to $9.00 (as shown in cell D21) rather than the $12.00 shown in the same cell in Exhibit 7B–2. The lower time-driven activity rate of $9.00 carries forward to cells B33 through D33 and in turn lowers each customer's total customer service costs by $3. For example, customer A's total customer service cost is $252 in cell B36 of Exhibit 7B–4, whereas the corresponding total in cell B36 of Exhibit 7B–2 is $255.

Let's further assume that Ridley Company wants to answer the question: What if we also increase the number of orders processed from 200,000 (as shown in cell E17 in Exhibit 7B–1) to 265,000? How would the projected increase in the number of orders processed affect our staffing needs in the Customer Service Department? After making the appropriate change in cell E17 of Exhibit 7B–1, Exhibit 7B–5 provides the answer to this question—Ridley Company would need to hire one more employee at an estimated cost of $29,952.

EXHIBIT 7B–5   Ridley Company's Capacity Analysis: A "What If" Analysis

	A	B	C	D	E
1	Ridley Company				
2	Customer Service Department				
3	Capacity Analysis				
4					
5	**Step 1: Calculate the used capacity in minutes**	Order processing	Query resolution	Credit reviews	**Total**
6	Customer demand for each activity (a)	265,000	4,500	8,900	
7	Customer service minutes required per unit of each activity (b)	10	30	30	
8	Customer service minutes used to meet demand (a) × (b)	2,650,000	135,000	267,000	3,052,000
9					
10	**Step 2: Calculate the unused capacity in minutes**				
11	Total customer service minutes available to meet demand (a)	2,995,200			
12	Total customer service minutes used to meet demand (b)	3,052,000			
13	Unused capacity in minutes (a) – (b)	(56,800)			
14					
15	**Step 3: Calculate the unused capacity in number of employees**				
16	Unused capacity in minutes (a)	(56,800)			
17	Practical capacity per employee (in minutes) (b)	99,840			
18	Unused capacity in number of employees (a) ÷ (b)	(0.57)			
19					
20	**Step 4: Calculate the financial impact of matching capacity with demand**				
21	Potential adjustment in number of employees (rounded) (a)	1.00			
22	Average salary per employee (b)	$ 29,952			
23	Impact on expenses of matching capacity with demand (a) × (b)	$ 29,952			
24					
25	Note: Cell B21 uses the formula =If(B18>0,rounddown(-B18,0),roundup(-B18,0))				
26					

To understand how this answer is derived, let's start with Step 1 within Exhibit 7B–5, which shows 265,000 orders processed in cell B6. This increase in the number of orders processed increases the number of customer service minutes needed to meet customer demand to 3,052,000 (cell E8). Step 2 shows that the total customer service minutes available of 2,995,200 (cell B11) is now less than the number of minutes used to meet demand of 3,052,000 (cell B12), which results in unused capacity of (56,800) minutes as shown in cell B13. Because the unused capacity is a negative number, it implies that Ridley does not have enough capacity available to satisfy the estimated customer demand. Step 3 in Exhibit 7B–5 translates the shortage in minutes to a shortfall stated in terms of number of employees—or (0.57) employees as shown in cell B18. Given that Ridley cannot hire slightly more than one-half of an employee, cell B21 rounds this number to 1.00 and then cell B23 translates the estimated cost of hiring one additional employee to $29,952.

TDABC helps companies estimate the financial impact of aligning capacity with demand, particularly with respect to step-fixed resources such as the customer service employees in the Ridley Company example.

■ APPENDIX 7B SUMMARY

- Time-based activity-based costing (TBABC) has several strengths compared to traditional activity-based costing as reviewed in this appendix. The strengths of this methodology include:
  - it is easy to update because it does not require employee interviews,
  - it quantifies unused capacity costs in an objective fashion that does not require employees to self-report their own idle time, and
  - it helps companies estimate the financial impact of aligning capacity with demand. **[LO7]**

■ APPENDIX 7B EXERCISES AND PROBLEMS

EXERCISE 7B–1 Time-Driven Activity-Based Costing [LO7]

Saratoga Company manufactures jobs to customer specifications. The company is conducting a time-driven activity-based costing study in its Purchasing Department to better understand how Purchasing Department labour costs are consumed by individual jobs. To aid the study, the company provided the following data regarding its Purchasing Department and three of its many jobs:

Number of employees	12
Average salary per employee	$28,000
Weeks of employment per year	52
Hours worked per week	40
Practical capacity percentage	85%

	Requisition Processing	Bid Evaluation	Inspection
Minutes per unit of the activity	15	45	30
	Job X	**Job Y**	**Job Z**
Number of requisitions processed	8	5	4
Number of bids evaluated	3	2	4
Number of inspections	6	2	6

Required:
1. Calculate the cost per minute of the resource supplied in the Purchasing Department.
2. Calculate the time-driven activity rate for each of Saratoga's three activities.
3. Calculate the total purchasing labour costs assigned to Job X, Job Y, and Job Z.

EXERCISE 7B–2 Time-Driven Activity-Based Costing [LO7]

Refer to the data in Exercise 7B–1. In addition, assume that Saratoga Company provided the following activity data for *all* jobs produced during the year:

	Requisition Processing	Bid Evaluation	Inspection
Activity demands for all jobs	7,000	9,400	10,000

Required:
1. Calculate Saratoga's used capacity in minutes.
2. Calculate Saratoga's unused capacity in minutes.
3. Calculate Saratoga's unused capacity in number of employees. (Do not round your answer to a whole number.)
4. Calculate the impact on expenses of matching capacity with demand. (Be sure to round your potential adjustment in the number of employees to a whole number.)

EXERCISE 7B–3 Time-Driven Activity-Based Costing [LO7]

Refer to the data in Exercises 7B–1 and 7B–2. Now assume that Saratoga Company would like to answer the following "what if" question using its time-driven activity-based costing system: Assuming our estimated activity demands for all jobs in the next period will be as shown below, how will this affect our job costs and our staffing levels within the Purchasing Department?

	Requisition Processing	Bid Evaluation	Inspection
Activity demands for all jobs	7,600	9,900	11,000

Required:

1. How will these revised activity demands affect the total Purchasing Department labour costs assigned to Job X, Job Y, and Job Z? No calculations are necessary.
2. Using the revised activity demands, calculate Saratoga's used capacity in minutes.
3. Using the revised activity demands, calculate Saratoga's unused capacity in minutes.
4. Using the revised activity demands, calculate Saratoga's unused capacity in number of employees. (Do not round your answer to a whole number.)
5. Based on the revised activity demands, calculate the impact on expenses of matching capacity with demand. (Be sure to round your potential adjustment in the number of employees to a whole number.)

PROBLEM 7B–4 Time-Driven Activity-Based Costing [LO7]

Stahl Company is conducting a time-driven activity-based costing study in its Shipping Department. To aid the study, the company provided the following data regarding its Shipping Department and the customers served by the department:

Number of employees	34
Average salary per employee	$34,000
Weeks of employment per year	52
Hours worked per week	40
Practical capacity percentage	80%

	Line-Item Picking	Packaging	Loading Deliveries
Minutes per unit of the activity	5	15	30

	Customer L	Customer M	Customer N	All Customers
Number of line items picked	280	160	90	335,000
Number of boxes packaged	50	20	15	46,800
Number of deliveries loaded	6	2	10	12,100

Required:

1. Using the customer cost analysis shown in Exhibit 7B–2 as your guide, compute the following:
   a. The cost per minute of the resource supplied in the Shipping Department.
   b. The time-driven activity rate for each of Stahl's three activities.
   c. The total labour costs consumed by Customer L, Customer M, and Customer N.
2. Using the capacity analysis shown in Exhibit 7B–3 as your guide, compute the following:
   a. The used capacity in minutes.
   b. The unused capacity in minutes.
   c. The unused capacity in number of employees. (Do not round your answer to a whole number.)
   d. The impact on expenses of matching capacity with demand. (Be sure to round your potential adjustment in the number of employees to a whole number.)

PROBLEM 7B–5 Time-Driven Activity-Based Costing [LO7]

Athens Company is conducting a time-driven activity-based costing study in its Engineering Department. To aid the study, the company provided the following data regarding its Engineering Department and the customers served by the department:

Average number of employees	10
Average salary per employee	$90,000
Weeks of employment per year	52
Hours worked per week	40
Practical capacity percentage	85%

	New Product Design	Engineering Change Orders	Product Testing
Hours per unit of activity	40	20	8

	Customer A	Customer B	Customer C	All Customers
Number of new products designed	3	2	4	180
Number of engineering change orders . . .	5	2	2	250
Number of products tested	8	4	6	160

Required:
1. Using the customer cost analysis shown in Exhibit 7B–2 as your guide, compute the following:
   a. The cost per hour of the resource supplied in the Engineering Department.
   b. The time-driven activity rate per hour for each of Athens three activities.
   c. The total engineering costs consumed by Customer A, Customer B, and Customer C.
2. Using the capacity analysis shown in Exhibit 7B–3 as your guide, compute the following:
   a. The used capacity in hours.
   b. The unused capacity in hours.
   c. The unused capacity in number of employees. (Do not round your answer to a whole number.)
   d. The impact on expenses of matching capacity with demand. (Be sure to round your potential adjustment in the number of employees to a whole number.)
3. Assume that Athens is considering expanding its business such that the estimated number of new products designed would increase to 250, the number of engineering change orders would jump to 320, and the number of products tested would rise to 240. Using these revised figures, calculate the following:
   a. The used capacity in hours.
   b. The unused capacity in hours.
   c. The unused capacity in number of employees. (Do not round your answer to a whole number.)
   d. The impact on expenses of matching capacity with demand. (Be sure to round your potential adjustment in the number of employees to a whole number.)

ENDNOTES

1. For simplicity, we assume that all orders, queries, and credit reviews consume the same amount of minutes per unit of the activity.

VARIABLE COSTING: A TOOL FOR MANAGEMENT

■ INCENTIVES TO OVERPRODUCE IN THE AUTO INDUSTRY

fotog / Tetra images RF / Getty Images

Automakers often react to downturns in the economy by flooding the market with more cars than they know can actually be sold. This may allow them to generate short-term profits even at the expense of long-term corporate stability. Why? Due to absorption costing methods required for financial reporting, when firms build inventory, fewer fixed expenses make their way onto the income statement. As we will discover in this chapter, *absorption costing*—the most widely used method of determining product costs—can lead to artificial increases in short-term profits when firms increase the quantity of goods produced. Where do these extra costs go? To the Balance Sheet Inventory accounts! Another approach, called *variable costing*, is therefore preferred by some managers for internal decision making. Ordinarily, absorption costing and variable costing produce different figures for operating income, and the difference can be quite large. In addition to showing how these two methods differ, we will consider the arguments for and against each costing method and show how management decisions can be affected by the costing method chosen.

n Chapters 3 and 4, we mainly assumed inventories were insignificant or that production equals sales at the end of the period. This assumption is reasonable in some situations, as will be shown later in this chapter when we discuss lean production. However, inventories are rarely zero, and the level of inventory held at the end of the period can have a significant effect on reported income under the absorption costing approach.

■ OVERVIEW OF ABSORPTION AND VARIABLE COSTING

In Chapters 3 and 4, we learned that the contribution format income statement and cost–volume–profit (CVP) analysis are valuable management tools for internal decision making. Both of these tools emphasize cost behaviour and require that managers carefully distinguish between variable and fixed costs. Absorption costing, which was discussed in Chapter 2 and used in Chapters 5 and 6 and Appendix 7A, is different in that it assigns both variable and fixed costs to products—mingling them in a way that makes it difficult for managers to distinguish between them. While absorption costing is useful, and it is actually required for external financial reporting, variable costing is often more useful for internal management decisions as it focuses on *cost behaviour*, clearly separating fixed from variable costs and making it easier to apply the CVP concepts (e.g., "how many units must we sell to break even?") discussed in the preceding chapters.

Absorption Costing

In Chapter 5, we learned that absorption costing treats *all* manufacturing costs as **product costs**, regardless of whether they are variable or fixed. The cost of a unit of product under the absorption costing method therefore consists of direct materials, direct labour, and *both* variable and fixed manufacturing overhead. Thus, absorption costing allocates a portion of fixed manufacturing overhead cost to each unit of product, along with the variable manufacturing costs. Because absorption costing includes all manufacturing costs as product costs, it is frequently referred to as full costing.

Variable Costing

Under **variable costing**, only those manufacturing costs that vary with output are treated as product costs. This generally includes direct materials, direct labour, and the variable portion of manufacturing overhead. Fixed manufacturing overhead is not treated as a product cost under this method. Rather, fixed manufacturing overhead is treated as a **period cost**, and, like selling and administrative expenses, it is expensed in its entirety against revenue each period. Consequently, the cost of a unit of product in inventory or in cost of goods sold under the variable costing method does not contain any fixed overhead cost.

Variable costing is sometimes referred to as **direct costing** or **marginal costing**. The term *direct costing* was popular for many years, but it is slowly disappearing from day-to-day use. The term *variable costing* is more descriptive of the way in which product costs are computed when a contribution format income statement is prepared.

Selling and Administrative Expenses

To complete this summary comparison of absorption and variable costing, we need to consider briefly the handling of selling and administrative expenses. These expenses are rarely treated as product costs, regardless of the costing method in use. Thus, under either absorption or variable costing, selling and administrative expenses are always treated as period costs (expenses) and deducted from revenues as incurred.

Exhibit 8–1 summarizes the classification of costs under both absorption and variable costing.

LEARNING OBJECTIVE ❶
Identify how variable costing differs from absorption costing, and compute unit product costs under each method.

Product costs
All costs that are involved in the purchase or manufacture of goods. In the case of manufactured goods, these costs consist of direct materials, direct labour, and manufacturing overhead. They are also called inventoriable costs.

Variable costing
A costing method that includes only variable manufacturing costs—direct materials, direct labour, and variable manufacturing overhead—in the cost of a unit of product.

Period costs
All costs that are expensed on the income statement in the period in which they are incurred or accrued. Selling (marketing) and administrative expenses are period costs.

Direct costing
Another name for *variable costing*.

Marginal costing
Another name for *variable costing*.

EXHIBIT 8–1
Cost Classifications:
Absorption versus
Variable Costing

Absorption Costing		Variable Costing
Product costs	Direct materials	Product costs
	Direct labour	
	Variable manufacturing overhead	
	Fixed manufacturing overhead	
Period costs	Variable selling and administrative expenses	Period costs
	Fixed selling and administrative expenses	

Unit Cost Computations

To illustrate the computation of unit product costs under both absorption and variable costing, consider Boley Company, a small company that produces a single product and has the following cost structure:

Number of units produced each year	6,000
Variable costs per unit:	
Direct materials	$ 2
Direct labour	4
Variable manufacturing overhead	1
Variable selling and administrative expenses	3
Fixed costs per year:	
Fixed manufacturing overhead.	30,000
Fixed selling and administrative expenses.	10,000

Under the absorption costing method, *all* manufacturing costs, variable and fixed, are included when determining the unit product cost. Thus, if the company sells a unit of product and absorption costing is being used, then $12 (consisting of $7 variable cost and $5 fixed cost) will be deducted on the income statement as cost of goods sold. Similarly, any unsold units will be carried as inventory on the balance sheet at $12 each:

Absorption Costing	
Direct materials	$ 2
Direct labour	4
Variable manufacturing overhead	1
Total variable production cost	7
Fixed manufacturing overhead ($30,000 ÷ 6,000 units of product).	5
Unit product cost	$12

Under the variable costing method, only the variable manufacturing costs are included in product costs. Therefore, if the company sells a unit of product, only $7 will be deducted as cost of goods sold, and unsold units will be carried in the balance sheet inventory account at only $7 each:

Variable Costing	
Direct materials	$2
Direct labour	4
Variable manufacturing overhead	1
Unit product cost	$7

(The $30,000 fixed manufacturing overhead in variable costing will be expensed in total against income as a period expense, along with the selling and administrative expenses.)

The flow of costs among the general ledger accounts, the income statement, and the balance sheet are summarized in the following Learning Aid.

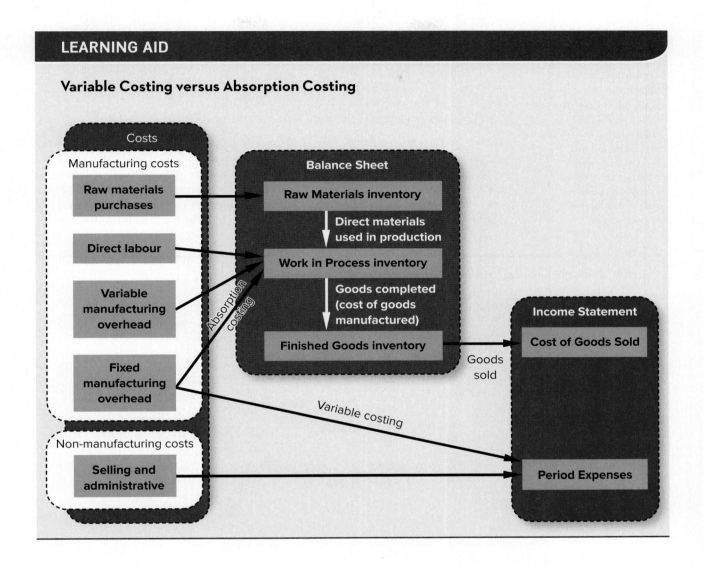

LEARNING AID

Variable Costing versus Absorption Costing

■ INCOME COMPARISON OF ABSORPTION AND VARIABLE COSTING

Income statements prepared under the absorption and variable costing approaches are shown in Exhibit 8–2. In preparing these statements, we use the data for Boley Company presented earlier, along with other information about the company, as given below:

LEARNING OBJECTIVE ② Prepare income statements using both variable and absorption costing.

Units in beginning inventory	–0–
Units produced	6,000
Units sold	5,000
Units in ending inventory	1,000
Selling price per unit	$ 20
Selling and administrative expenses:	
Variable per unit	$ 3
Fixed per year	$10,000

Unit cost computations for absorption and variable costing:	Absorption Costing	Variable Costing
Unit product cost:		
Direct materials	$ 2	$ 2
Direct labour.	4	4
Variable manufacturing overhead.	1	1
Fixed manufacturing overhead ($30,000 ÷ 6,000 units) . .	5	—
Unit product cost	$12	$ 7

Fixed manufacturing overhead cost deferred in inventory
The portion of the fixed manufacturing overhead cost of a period that goes into inventory under the absorption costing method as a result of production exceeding sales.

Several points can be made about the financial statements in Exhibit 8–2:

1. Under the absorption costing method, if there is an ending inventory balance the fixed manufacturing costs associated with this inventory will be carried forward as a balance sheet account, Inventory, rather than being treated as a period cost. Such a deferral of costs is known as **fixed manufacturing overhead cost deferred in inventory**. The process can be explained by referring to the data for Boley Company. During the current period, Boley Company produced 6,000 units but sold only 5,000 units, leaving

---

EXHIBIT 8–2 Comparison of Absorption and Variable Costing—Boley Company

Absorption Costing

Sales (5,000 units × $20 per unit)		$100,000
Less cost of goods sold:		
Beginning inventory	$ –0–	
Add cost of goods manufactured (6,000 units × $12 per unit)	72,000	
Goods available for sale.	72,000	
Deduct ending inventory (1,000 units × $12 per unit)	12,000	
Cost of goods sold		60,000
Gross margin		40,000
Less selling and administrative expenses (5,000 units × $3 variable per unit + $10,000 fixed).		25,000
Operating income		$ 15,000

Note the difference in ending inventories. Fixed manufacturing overhead cost at $5 per unit is included under the absorption approach. This explains the difference in ending inventory and in operating income (1,000 units × $5 per unit = $5,000).

Variable Costing

Sales (5,000 units × $20 per unit)		$100,000
Less variable expenses:		
Variable cost of goods sold:		
Beginning inventory	$ –0–	
Add variable manufacturing costs (6,000 units × $7 per unit)	42,000	
Goods available for sale	42,000	
Deduct ending inventory (1,000 units × $7 per unit)	7,000	
Variable cost of goods sold	35,000	
Variable selling and administrative expenses (5,000 units × $3 per unit) . . .	15,000	50,000
Contribution margin		50,000
Less fixed expenses:		
Fixed manufacturing overhead	30,000	
Fixed selling and administrative expenses	10,000	40,000
Operating income		$ 10,000

1,000 unsold units in the ending inventory. Under the absorption costing method, each unit produced is assigned $5 in fixed overhead cost (see the unit cost computations above). Therefore, each of the 1,000 units going into inventory at the end of the period has $5 in fixed manufacturing overhead cost attached to it, or a total of $5,000 for the 1,000 units. *This fixed manufacturing overhead cost of the current period is deferred in inventory to the next period, when, it is hoped, these units will be taken out of inventory and sold.* The deferral of $5,000 of fixed manufacturing overhead costs can be seen clearly by analyzing the ending inventory under the absorption costing method:

Variable manufacturing costs: 1,000 units × $7	$ 7,000
Fixed manufacturing overhead costs: 1,000 units × $5	5,000
Total inventory value	$12,000

In summary, under absorption costing, of the $30,000 in fixed manufacturing overhead costs incurred during the period only $25,000 (5,000 units sold × $5) has been included on the income statement in cost of goods sold. The remaining $5,000 (1,000 units *not* sold × $5) has been deferred in inventory to the next period.

2. Under the variable costing method, the entire $30,000 in fixed manufacturing overhead costs has been treated as an expense of the current period (see the bottom portion of the variable costing income statement).

3. The ending inventory figure under the variable costing method is $5,000 less than it is under the absorption costing method. This is because under variable costing, only the variable manufacturing costs are assigned to units of product and therefore included in inventory:

Variable manufacturing costs: 1,000 units × $7	$7,000

The $5,000 difference in ending inventories explains the difference in operating income reported between the two costing methods. Operating income is $5,000 *more* under absorption costing since, as already explained, $5,000 of fixed manufacturing overhead cost has been deferred in inventory to the next period under that costing method.

4. The absorption costing income statement makes no distinction between fixed and variable costs; therefore, it is not well suited for CVP computations, which are important for good planning and control. To generate data for CVP analysis, it is necessary to spend time reworking and reclassifying costs on the absorption statement.

5. The variable costing approach to costing units of product blends very well with the contribution approach to the income statement, since both concepts are based on the idea of classifying costs by behaviour. The variable costing data in Exhibit 8–2 can be used immediately in CVP computations.

It is important to note that the examples in this chapter will use *actual* overhead rates rather than *predetermined* ones as used in Chapter 5 in order to reduce unneeded complexity. What is illustrated about the effects of inventory on the difference in operating income will hold, regardless of the use of actual or predetermined overhead rates.

INSTANT QUIZ 8–1

Is fixed manufacturing overhead treated as a product or period cost under absorption costing? Under variable costing?

Essentially, the difference between the absorption costing method and the variable costing method centres on timing. Advocates of variable costing say that fixed manufacturing costs should be expensed immediately in total, whereas advocates of absorption costing say that fixed manufacturing costs should be charged against revenues bit by bit as units of product are sold. Any units of product not sold under absorption costing result in fixed costs being inventoried and carried forward as *assets* to the next period. We will defer discussing the arguments presented by each side in this dispute until after we have a better understanding of the two methods. Nevertheless, as we will see in the discussion of Emerald Isle Knitters, the use of absorption costing can sometimes produce strange effects on income statements.

LEARNING OBJECTIVE ❸

Reconcile variable costing and absorption costing operating incomes, and explain why the two amounts differ.

■ EXTENDED COMPARISON OF INCOME DATA

Emerald Isle Knitters Ltd., located in the Republic of Ireland, is a small company that manufactures traditional wool fishermen's sweaters. The company's basic data appear in the first part of Exhibit 8–3, and the absorption costing income statements as reported to the bank for the last three years appear in the first part of the conclusion of Exhibit 8–3. Sean MacLafferty, the company accountant, decided to try using the variable costing approach to see what effect that might have on operating income. The variable costing income statements for the last three years appear in the lower part of the conclusion of Exhibit 8–3.

Note that Emerald Isle Knitters maintained a steady rate of production per year of 25,000 sweaters. However, sales varied from year to year. In year 1, production and sales were equal. In year 2, production exceeded sales due to a cancelled order. In year 3, sales recovered and exceeded production. As a consequence, inventories did not change during year 1, inventories increased during year 2, and inventories decreased during year 3. *The change in inventories during the year is the key to understanding how absorption costing differs from variable costing.* Note that when inventories increase in year 2, absorption costing operating income exceeds variable costing operating income. When inventories decrease in year 3, the opposite

EXHIBIT 8–3   Absorption and Variable Costing Data—Emerald Isle Knitters Ltd.

Basic Data

Selling price per unit sold	€20
Variable manufacturing cost per unit produced	7
Fixed manufacturing overhead costs per year	150,000
Variable selling and administrative expenses per unit sold	1
Fixed selling and administrative expenses per year	90,000

	Year 1	Year 2	Year 3	Three Years Together
Units in beginning inventory	–0–	–0–	5,000	–0–
Units produced	25,000	25,000	25,000	75,000
Units sold	25,000	20,000	30,000	75,000
Units in ending inventory	–0–	5,000	–0–	–0–

Unit Product Costs

	Year 1	Year 2	Year 3
Under variable costing (variable manufacturing costs only)	€ 7	€ 7	€ 7
Under absorption costing:			
Variable manufacturing costs	€ 7	€ 7	€ 7
Fixed manufacturing overhead costs (€150,000 spread over the number of units produced in each year)	6	6	6
Total absorption cost per unit	€13	€13	€13

continued

EXHIBIT 8–3 *concluded*

Absorption Costing

	Year 1	Year 2	Year 3	Three Years Together
Sales	€500,000	€400,000	€600,000	€1,500,000
Less cost of goods sold:				
Beginning inventory	€ –0–	€ –0–	€ 65,000	€ –0–
Add cost of goods manufactured (25,000 units × €13 per unit)	325,000	325,000	325,000	975,000
Goods available for sale	325,000	325,000	390,000	975,000
Less ending inventory (5,000 units × €13 per unit)	–0–	65,000	–0–	–0–
Cost of goods sold	325,000	260,000	390,000	975,000
Gross margin	175,000	140,000	210,000	525,000
Less selling and administrative expenses	115,000*	110,000*	120,000*	345,000
Operating income	€ 60,000	€ 30,000	€ 90,000	€ 180,000

*The selling and administrative expenses are computed as follows:
Year 1: 25,000 units × €1 per unit variable + €90,000 fixed = €115,000.
Year 2: 20,000 units × €1 per unit variable + €90,000 fixed = €110,000.
Year 3: 30,000 units × €1 per unit variable + €90,000 fixed = €120,000.

Variable Costing

	Year 1	Year 2	Year 3	Three Years Together
Sales	€500,000	€400,000	€600,000	€1,500,000
Less variable expenses:				
Variable cost of goods sold:				
Beginning inventory	€ –0–	€ –0–	€ 35,000	€ –0–
Add variable manufacturing costs (25,000 units × €7 per unit)	175,000	175,000	175,000	525,000
Goods available for sale	175,000	175,000	210,000	525,000
Less ending inventory (5,000 units × €7 per unit)	–0–	35,000	–0–	–0–
Variable cost of goods sold	175,000*	140,000*	210,000*	525,000
Variable selling and administrative expenses (€1 per unit sold)	25,000	20,000	30,000	75,000
	200,000	160,000	240,000	600,000
Contribution margin	300,000	240,000	360,000	900,000
Less fixed expenses:				
Fixed manufacturing overhead	150,000	150,000	150,000	450,000
Fixed selling and administrative expenses	90,000	90,000	90,000	270,000
	240,000	240,000	240,000	720,000
Operating income	€ 60,000	€ –0–	€120,000	€ 180,000

*The variable cost of goods sold could have been computed more simply as follows:
Year 1: 25,000 units sold × €7 per unit = €175,000.
Year 2: 20,000 units sold × €7 per unit = €140,000.
Year 3: 30,000 units sold × €7 per unit = €210,000.

occurs—variable costing operating income exceeds absorption costing operating income. And when there is no change in inventories, as in year 1, there is no difference in operating income between the two methods. Why is this? The reasons are discussed below and are briefly summarized in the accompanying Learning Aid:

1. When production and sales are equal, as in year 1 for Emerald Isle Knitters, operating income will generally be the same regardless of whether absorption or variable costing is used. This is because the *only* difference that can exist between absorption and variable costing operating incomes is the amount of fixed manufacturing overhead recognized as expense on the income statement. When everything that is produced in the year is sold, all of the fixed manufacturing overhead assigned to units of product under absorption costing becomes part of the current year's cost of goods sold. Under variable costing, the total fixed manufacturing overhead flows directly to the income statement as an expense. So, under either method, when production equals sales (and hence there is no change in inventories), all of the fixed manufacturing overhead incurred during the year flows through to the income statement as expense. Therefore, the operating income under the two methods is the same.

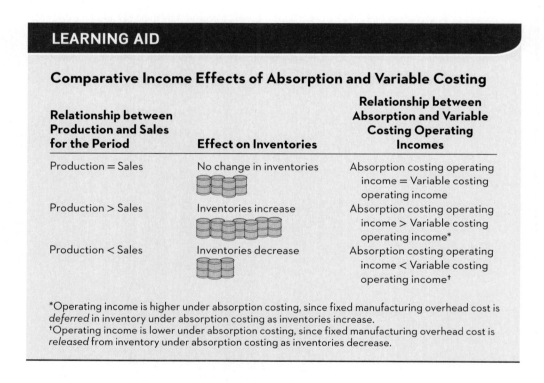

LEARNING AID

Comparative Income Effects of Absorption and Variable Costing

Relationship between Production and Sales for the Period	Effect on Inventories	Relationship between Absorption and Variable Costing Operating Incomes
Production = Sales	No change in inventories	Absorption costing operating income = Variable costing operating income
Production > Sales	Inventories increase	Absorption costing operating income > Variable costing operating income*
Production < Sales	Inventories decrease	Absorption costing operating income < Variable costing operating income†

*Operating income is higher under absorption costing, since fixed manufacturing overhead cost is *deferred* in inventory under absorption costing as inventories increase.
†Operating income is lower under absorption costing, since fixed manufacturing overhead cost is *released* from inventory under absorption costing as inventories decrease.

2. When production exceeds sales (see year 2 in Exhibit 8–3), the operating income reported under absorption costing will generally be greater than the operating income reported under variable costing. This occurs because under absorption costing, part of the fixed manufacturing overhead costs of the current period is deferred in inventory. In year 2, for example, €30,000 of fixed manufacturing overhead costs (5,000 units × €6 per unit) has been applied to units in ending inventory. These costs are excluded from cost of goods sold.

    Under variable costing, however, *all* of the fixed manufacturing overhead costs of year 2 have been immediately expensed. As a result, the operating income for year 2 under variable costing is €30,000 *less* than it is under absorption costing. Exhibit 8–4 contains a reconciliation of the variable costing and absorption costing operating income figures.

EXHIBIT 8–4   Reconciliation of Variable Costing and Absorption Costing—Operating Income Data from Exhibit 8-3

	Year 1	Year 2	Year 3
Variable costing operating income	€60,000	€ –0–	€120,000
Add fixed manufacturing overhead costs deferred in inventory under absorption costing (5,000 units × €6 per unit)	–0–	30,000	–0–
Deduct fixed manufacturing overhead costs released from inventory under absorption costing (5,000 units × €6 per unit)	–0–	–0–	(30,000)
Absorption costing operating income.	€60,000	€30,000	€ 90,000

3. When production is less than sales (see year 3 in Exhibit 8–3), the operating income reported under the absorption costing approach will generally be less than the operating income reported under the variable costing approach. This happens because as inventories are drawn down, the fixed manufacturing overhead costs that were previously deferred in inventory under absorption costing are released and charged against income (known as **fixed manufacturing overhead cost released from inventory**). In year 3, for example, the €30,000 in fixed manufacturing overhead costs deferred in inventory under the absorption approach from year 2 to year 3 is released from inventory because these units were sold. As a result, the cost of goods sold for year 3 contains not only all of the fixed manufacturing overhead costs for year 3 (since all that was produced in year 3 was sold in year 3) but €30,000 of fixed manufacturing overhead costs from year 2 as well.

> By contrast, under variable costing, only the fixed manufacturing overhead costs of year 3 have been charged against year 3. The result is that operating income under variable costing is €30,000 *more* than it is under absorption costing. Exhibit 8–4 reconciles the variable costing and absorption costing operating income figures for year 3.

> Careful reading of Exhibit 8–3 will raise the following question: Why is operating income not influenced by changes in inventories when variable costing is used? The reason is that variable costing releases variable costs from inventory to cost of goods sold in amounts that are based on the volume of sales. So production does not influence the cost of goods sold because fixed manufacturing overhead is fixed and not released as cost of goods sold as it was with absorption costing.

4. Over an *extended* period of time, the cumulative operating income figures reported under absorption costing and variable costing tend to be the same. This is because over the long run, sales cannot exceed production, nor can production much exceed sales. The shorter the time period, the more the operating income figures will tend to differ.

Fixed manufacturing overhead cost released from inventory
The portion of the fixed manufacturing overhead cost of a prior period that becomes an expense of the current period under the absorption costing method as a result of sales exceeding production.

INSTANT QUIZ 8-2
Parker Company had $5,000,000 in sales and reported a $300,000 profit in its annual report to shareholders. According to a CVP analysis prepared for management's use, $5,000,000 in sales is the break-even point for the company. Did the company's inventory level increase, decrease, or remain unchanged? Explain.

Effect of Changes in Production on Operating Income

In the Emerald Isle Knitters example in the preceding section, production was constant and sales fluctuated over the three-year period. Since sales fluctuated, the income statements that MacLafferty presented in Exhibit 8–3 allowed us to see the effect of changes in sales on operating income under both variable and absorption costing.

To further investigate the differences between variable and absorption costing, MacLafferty next put together the hypothetical example in Exhibit 8–5. In this example, sales are constant and production fluctuates (the opposite of Exhibit 8–3). The purpose of Exhibit 8–5 is to illustrate the effect of changes in *production* on operating income under both variable and absorption costing.

Variable Costing

Operating income is *not* affected by changes in production under variable costing. Notice from Exhibit 8–5 that operating income is the same for all three years under the variable costing approach, although production exceeds sales in one year and is less than sales in another year. In short, a change in production has no effect on operating income when variable costing is used.

Absorption Costing

Operating income *is* affected by changes in production under absorption costing. As shown in Exhibit 8–5, operating income under the absorption approach goes up in year 2, in response to the increase in production for that year, and then goes down in year 3, in response to the drop in production for that year. Note particularly that operating income goes up and down between these two years *even though the same number of units is sold in each year*. The reason for this effect can be traced to the shifting of fixed manufacturing overhead costs between periods under the absorption costing method as a result of changes in inventory.

As shown in Exhibit 8–5, production exceeds sales in year 2, resulting in an increase of 10,000 units in inventory. Each unit produced during year 2 has €6 in fixed manufacturing overhead costs attached to it (see the unit cost computations at the top of Exhibit 8–5). Therefore, €60,000 (10,000 units × €6) of the fixed manufacturing overhead costs of year 2 are not charged against that year but rather are added to the inventory account (along with the variable manufacturing costs). The operating income of year 2 rises sharply, because these

EXHIBIT 8–5 Sensitivity of Costing Methods to Changes in Production—Hypothetical Data

Basic Data

Selling price per unit sold	€ 25
Variable manufacturing cost per unit produced	10
Fixed manufacturing overhead costs per year	300,000
Variable selling and administrative expenses per unit sold	1
Fixed selling and administrative expenses per year	200,000

	Year 1	Year 2	Year 3
Units in beginning inventory	–0–	–0–	10,000
Units produced	40,000	50,000	30,000
Units sold	40,000	40,000	40,000
Units in ending inventory	–0–	10,000	–0–

Unit Product Costs

	Year 1	Year 2	Year 3
Under variable costing (variable manufacturing costs only)	€10.00	€10.00	€10.00
Under absorption costing:			
Variable manufacturing costs	€10.00	€10.00	€10.00
Fixed manufacturing overhead costs (€300,000 spread over the number of units produced in each year)	7.50	6.00	10.00
Total absorption cost per unit	€17.50	€16.00	€20.00

continued

EXHIBIT 8–5 *concluded*

Absorption Costing

	Year 1		Year 2		Year 3	
Sales (40,000 units)		€1,000,000		€1,000,000		€1,000,000
Less cost of goods sold:						
Beginning inventory	€ –0–		€ –0–		€160,000	
Add cost of goods manufactured	700,000*		800,000*		600,000*	
Goods available for sale	700,000		800,000		760,000	
Less ending inventory	–0–		160,000†		–0–	
Cost of goods sold		700,000		640,000		760,000
Gross margin		300,000		360,000		240,000
Less selling and administrative expenses (40,000 units × €1 per unit + €200,000)		240,000		240,000		240,000
Operating income		€ 60,000		€ 120,000		€ –0–

*Cost of goods manufactured:
Year 1: 40,000 units × €17.50 per unit = €700,000.
Year 2: 50,000 units × €16.00 per unit = €800,000.
Year 3: 30,000 units × €20.00 per unit = €600,000.
†Ending inventory, year 2: 10,000 units × €16 per unit = €160,000.

Variable Costing

	Year 1		Year 2		Year 3	
Sales (40,000 units)		€1,000,000		€1,000,000		€1,000,000
Less variable expenses:						
Variable cost of goods sold:						
Beginning inventory	€ –0–		€ –0–		€100,000	
Add variable manufacturing costs at €10 per unit produced	400,000		500,000		300,000	
Goods available for sale	400,000		500,000		400,000	
Less ending inventory	–0–		100,000*		–0–	
Variable cost of goods sold	400,000		400,000		400,000	
Variable selling and administrative expenses	40,000		40,000		40,000	
		440,000		440,000		440,000
Contribution margin		560,000		560,000		560,000
Less fixed expenses:						
Fixed manufacturing overhead	300,000		300,000		300,000	
Fixed selling and administrative expenses	200,000		200,000		200,000	
		500,000		500,000		500,000
Operating income		€ 60,000		€ 60,000		€ 60,000

*Ending inventory, year 2: 10,000 units × €10 per unit = €100,000.

EXHIBIT 8–6 Reconciliation of Variable Costing and Absorption Costing—Operating Income Data from Exhibit 8–5

	Year 1	Year 2	Year 3
Variable costing operating income	€60,000	€ 60,000	€ 60,000
Add fixed manufacturing overhead costs deferred in inventory under absorption costing (10,000 units × €6 per unit)	–0–	60,000	–0–
Deduct fixed manufacturing overhead costs released from inventory under absorption costing (10,000 units × €6 per unit)	–0–	–0–	(60,000)
Absorption costing operating income	€60,000	€120,000	€ –0–

costs are deferred in inventories, even though the same number of units is sold in year 2 as in the other years.

The reverse effect occurs in year 3. Since sales exceed production in year 3, that year is forced to cover all of its own fixed manufacturing overhead costs as well as the fixed manufacturing overhead costs carried forward in inventory from year 2. A substantial drop in operating income during year 3 results from the release of fixed manufacturing overhead costs from inventories, despite the fact that the same number of units is sold in that year as in the other years.

The variable costing and absorption costing operating incomes are reconciled in Exhibit 8–6. This exhibit shows that the differences in operating income can be traced to the effects of changes in inventories on absorption costing operating income. Under absorption costing, fixed manufacturing overhead costs are deferred in inventory when inventories increase and are released from inventory when inventory decreases.

INSTANT QUIZ 8–3

Fill in the blanks: Under variable costing _____ drives operating income, while under absorption costing _____ and _____ drive operating income.

LEARNING OBJECTIVE ④

Explain the advantages and disadvantages of both variable and absorption costing.

■ CHOOSING A COSTING METHOD

The Impact on the Manager

Opponents of absorption costing argue that shifting fixed manufacturing overhead cost between periods can be confusing and can lead to misinterpretations and even to faulty decisions. Look again at the data in Exhibit 8–5. A manager might wonder why operating income went up substantially in year 2 under absorption costing when sales remained the same as in the prior year. Was it a result of lower selling costs or more efficient operations, or was some other factor involved? A manager cannot determine this by simply looking at the absorption costing income statement. Then, in year 3, operating income drops sharply, even though again the same number of units is sold as in the other two years. Why would income rise in one year and then drop in the next? The figures seem erratic and contradictory and can lead to confusion and a loss of confidence in the integrity of the statement data.

By contrast, the variable costing income statements in Exhibit 8–5 are clear and easy to understand. Sales remain constant over the three-year period covered in the exhibit, so both contribution margin and operating income also remain constant. The statements are consistent with what managers would expect to happen under the circumstances, so they tend to generate confidence rather than confusion.

Under variable costing, revenue essentially drives operating income. Under absorption costing, both revenue and production drive operating income. The two drivers create confusion for the user of operating income because it is difficult to perceive income without first selling what is produced, something absorption costing does.

INSTANT QUIZ 8-4
Explain how fixed manufacturing overhead costs are shifted from one period to another under absorption costing.

To avoid mistakes when absorption costing is used, readers of financial statements should be alert to changes in inventory levels. Under absorption costing, if inventories increase, fixed manufacturing overhead costs are deferred in inventories and operating income increases. If inventories decrease, fixed manufacturing overhead costs are released from inventories and operating income decreases. Thus, fluctuations in operating income can be due to changes in inventories rather than to changes in sales.

CVP Analysis and Absorption Costing

Absorption costing is widely used for both internal and external reports. Many firms use the absorption approach exclusively because of its focus on *full* costing of units of product. A weakness of the method, however, is its inability to dovetail well with CVP analysis.

To illustrate, refer again to Exhibit 8–3. Let us compute the break-even point for Emerald Isle Knitters. To obtain the break-even point, we divide total fixed costs by the contribution margin per unit:

Selling price per unit	€	20
Variable costs per unit		8
Contribution margin per unit	€	12
Fixed manufacturing overhead costs		€150,000
Fixed selling and administrative costs		90,000
Total fixed costs		€240,000

$$\frac{\text{Total fixed costs}}{\text{Contribution margin per unit}} = \frac{€240,000}{€12} = 20,000 \text{ units}$$

The break-even point is 20,000 units. Notice from Exhibit 8–3 that in year 2 the firm sold exactly 20,000 units, the break-even volume. Under the contribution approach, using variable costing, the firm does break even in year 2, showing zero operating income. *Under absorption costing, however, the firm shows a positive operating income of €30,000 for year 2.* How can this be? How can absorption costing produce a positive operating income when the firm sold exactly the break-even volume of units?

The answer lies in the fact that €30,000 in fixed manufacturing overhead costs were deferred in inventory during year 2 under absorption costing and therefore did not appear as expenses. By deferring these fixed manufacturing overhead costs in inventory, the income statement shows a profit even though the company sold exactly the break-even volume of units. Absorption costing runs into similar kinds of difficulty in other areas of CVP analysis, which assumes that variable costing is being used.

Absorption break-even analysis requires the analysis of two drivers, sales and production. By determining various levels for each driver, a zero operating income could be determined. But as in mathematics, a single equation does not provide a unique solution when there are two unknowns. Various possible sales and production levels that can create a break-even operating income are what *break-even* means here. For example, see year 3 of Exhibit 8–5, where 40,000 units were sold and 30,000 units were produced. Operating income is zero, or break even.

Decision Making

A basic problem with absorption costing is that fixed manufacturing overhead costs appear to be variable with respect to the number of units sold, but they are not. For example, in Exhibit 8–3 the absorption unit product cost is €13, but the variable portion of this cost is only €7. Since the product costs are stated on a per unit basis, managers may mistakenly believe that if another unit is produced, it will cost the company €13.

The misperception that absorption unit product costs are variable can lead to many managerial problems, including inappropriate pricing decisions and decisions to drop products that are in fact profitable. We will discuss these problems with absorption costing product costs more fully in later chapters.

External Reporting, Income Taxes, and Management Performance Evaluation

Practically speaking, absorption costing is required for external reports in the United States and is the predominant method used in Canada. In Canada, *International Accounting Standard 2, Inventories* requires a company to assign to work in process and finished goods inventory the laid-down cost of materials plus the cost of direct labour and the applicable share of manufacturing overhead expenses. For income tax purposes in Canada, the Canada Revenue Agency's *Interpretation Bulletin IT473R, Inventory Valuation* permits both variable and absorption costing for determining taxable income.

Even if a company uses absorption costing for its external reports, a manager can use variable costing statements for internal reports. No particular accounting problems are created by using *both* costing methods—the variable costing method for internal reports and the absorption costing method for external reports. As we demonstrated earlier in Exhibits 8–5 and 8–6, the adjustment from variable costing operating income to absorption costing operating income is a simple one that can be made easily at year-end. Computer systems such as those described in Chapter 5 can make the conversion, as long as the information is contained in the supporting database.

Top executives of publicly held corporations are typically evaluated based on the earnings reported in the external financial reports presented to shareholders. This creates a problem for top executives who might otherwise favour using variable costing for internal reports. They may feel that since their performance evaluation and any potential bonuses they might earn are based on meeting profit targets and profits are defined using absorption costing, their everyday decisions should also be based on absorption costing data.

Advantages of Variable Costing and the Contribution Approach

As stated earlier, even if the absorption approach is used for external reporting purposes, variable costing, together with the contribution format income statement, is an appealing alternative for internal reports. The advantages of variable costing can be summarized as follows:

1. Data required for CVP analysis can be taken directly from a contribution format income statement. These data are not available on a conventional absorption costing statement.
2. Under variable costing, the profit for a period is not affected by changes in inventories. Other things remaining equal (e.g., selling prices, costs, sales mix), profits move in the same direction as sales when variable costing is used.
3. Managers often assume that unit product costs are variable costs. This is a problem under absorption costing because unit product costs are a combination of both fixed and variable costs. Under variable costing, unit product costs do not contain fixed costs.

4. The impact of fixed costs on profits is emphasized under the variable costing and contribution approach. The total amount of fixed costs appears explicitly on the income statement, highlighting that the whole amount of fixed costs must be covered for the company to be truly profitable. Under absorption costing, the fixed costs are mingled with the variable costs and are buried in cost of goods sold and in ending inventories.

5. Variable costing data make it easier to estimate the profitability of products, customers, and other segments of the business. With absorption costing, profitability is obscured by arbitrary allocations of fixed costs. We will discuss these issues in later chapters.

6. Variable costing ties in with cost control methods such as standard costs and flexible budgets, which we will cover in later chapters.

7. Variable costing operating income is closer to net cash flow than absorption costing operating income. This is particularly important for companies with potential cash flow problems.

With all of these advantages, one might wonder why absorption costing continues to be used almost exclusively for external reporting and why it is the predominant choice for internal reports as well. This is partly due to tradition, but absorption costing is also attractive to many accountants and managers because they believe it better matches costs with revenues—it is consistent with the matching principle.

Advocates of absorption costing argue that *all* manufacturing costs must be assigned to products to properly match the costs of producing units of product with the revenues from the units when they are sold. The fixed costs of depreciation, taxes, insurance, supervisory salaries, and so on, are just as essential to manufacturing products as are the variable costs.

Advocates of variable costing argue that fixed manufacturing costs are not really the costs of any particular unit of product. These costs are incurred in order to have the *capacity* to make products during a particular period and will be incurred even if nothing is made during the period. Moreover, whether a unit is made or not, the fixed manufacturing costs will be exactly the same. Therefore, variable costing advocates argue that fixed manufacturing costs are not part of the costs of producing a particular unit of product and thus the matching principle dictates that fixed manufacturing costs should be charged to the current period.

BEYOND THE BOTTOM LINE

A downside of absorption or full costing is that it can be used by an unethical manager to deliberately mislead others. This is possible because reported profits are affected by inventory buildups or draw-downs if fixed costs are included in inventory. During periods of inventory buildup, less than a year's fixed costs will be expensed, and during years in which inventory is reduced, more than a year's fixed costs will be expensed. An unethical manager whose bonus is based on operating income, for example, could make profits appear higher by simply building up inventory levels, since there is a direct relationship between ending inventory and operating income. Those responsible for performance evaluation should look beyond the bottom line to identify such abuses.

One restriction on the unethical use of absorption costing to increase operating income by building ending inventories is the application of the generally accepted accounting principle of "lower of cost or market." The ending inventory has to be examined for its saleability by determining its market value. If market value of the inventory is below cost, then a loss is recorded in the income statement of the current period. Thus, if the excess inventory could not be sold, a write-down is expected, which would reduce but not necessarily eliminate the operating income resulting from the inventory buildup.

At any rate, absorption costing is a generally accepted method for preparing mandatory external financial reports. Probably because of the cost and possible confusion of maintaining two separate costing systems—one for external reporting and one for internal reporting—most companies use absorption costing for both external and internal reports, although decreasing information processing costs may result in more firms using two costing systems in the future.

INSTANT QUIZ 8–5
What arguments can be advanced in favour of treating fixed manufacturing overhead costs as product costs?

There may also be important strategic reasons for using absorption costing. Senior management, for example, may fear that variable costing will result in an overemphasis on contribution margin and lead to insufficient attention to the management of fixed costs. Decision makers may focus too much on short-run profitability and bring long-run harm to the company. For example, long-term profitability will suffer if managers, lured by the attractiveness of high contribution margins, set product prices too low because of blindness to the existence of fixed costs. This is a particular risk in those industries in which the trend has been for cost structures to shift away from variable costs. Judging from the dominant use of absorption costing, it appears that managers have generally concluded that the incremental benefits of variable costing information are outweighed by these strategic factors and the additional costs of maintaining parallel systems.

■ IMPACT OF LEAN PRODUCTION

As discussed in this chapter, variable and absorption costing will produce different operating income figures whenever the number of units produced is different from the number of units sold—in other words, whenever there is a change in the number of units in inventory. We have also learned that the absorption costing operating income figure can be erratic, sometimes moving in a direction that is opposite from the movement in sales.

When companies use lean production methods, these problems are reduced. The erratic movement of operating income under absorption costing and the difference in operating income between absorption and variable costing occur because of changes in the number of units in inventory. As noted in Chapter 1, lean thinking only allows production in response to customer orders, so the number of units produced tends to equal the number of units sold, thereby resulting in minimal inventory. Under lean production, goods are produced to customers' orders, and the goal is to eliminate finished goods inventories entirely and reduce work in process inventory to almost nothing. In addition to minimizing inventory holding costs, lean production reduces the ability of an unethical manager to manage reported earnings by building inventory. Recall our discussion above indicating that when inventories build under absorption costing, less than a year's fixed costs will be expensed, thus artificially boosting income. If, on the other hand, there is very little inventory, then changes in inventories will be very small and both variable and absorption costing will show basically the same operating income figure. In that case, absorption costing operating income will move in the same direction as movements in sales.

Of course, the cost of a unit of product will still be different between variable and absorption costing, as explained earlier in the chapter. But when lean production is used, the differences in operating income will largely disappear.

INSTANT QUIZ 8–6
Explain the difference between lean and traditional manufacturing and why these differences lead to different measures of operating income under absorption costing.

IN BUSINESS

Conmed, a surgical device maker, switched to lean manufacturing by replacing its assembly lines with U-shaped production cells. It also started producing only enough units to satisfy customer demand (also known as **just-in-time production**) rather than producing as many units as possible and storing them in warehouses. The company calculated that its customers use one of its disposable surgical devices every 90 seconds, so that is precisely how often it produces a new unit. Its assembly area for fluid-injection devices used to occupy 300 square metres of space and contained $93,000 worth of parts. Now the company produces its fluid-injection devices in 60 square metres of space while maintaining only $6,000 of parts inventory.

ER productions Ltd / Blend Images

Just-in-time (JIT) production
A system in the lean production model where production is not initiated until a customer has ordered a product.

KNOWLEDGE IN ACTION

Managers can apply their knowledge about variable costing when

- Performing CVP analysis to determine the number of units of product or service that must be sold in order for the firm to break even
- Explaining changes to net operating income since variable costing income statements are not affected by changes in inventory levels
- Identifying additional variable costs that will be incurred to make one more unit of product, which is important information for managers to consider when making decisions about expanding production
- Examining the impact of fixed costs on profits by highlighting the total amount of fixed costs that must be covered for the company to be truly profitable

SUMMARY

- Variable and absorption costing are alternative methods of determining unit product costs. **[LO1]**
- Under variable costing, only those production costs that vary with output are treated as product costs. This includes direct materials; variable overhead; and, ordinarily, direct labour. Fixed manufacturing overhead is treated as a period cost and charged off against revenue as it is incurred, the same as selling and administrative expenses. **[LO1]**
- Under absorption costing, fixed manufacturing overhead is treated as a product cost, along with direct materials, direct labour, and variable overhead; therefore, a portion of fixed manufacturing overhead is assigned to each unit as it is produced. When some goods remain unsold at the end of the period, some of the fixed manufacturing overhead cost is held in inventory and deferred to the period in which the related units of product are sold. Thus, under absorption costing, it is possible to defer a portion of the fixed manufacturing overhead cost of one period to the next period through the inventory account. **[LO1]**
- When preparing variable costing income statements, fixed manufacturing costs are expensed immediately and in total. When preparing absorption costing income statements, fixed manufacturing costs are charged against revenues bit by bit as units of product are sold. Any unsold units of product under absorption costing carry a portion of fixed manufacturing overhead with them into inventory as assets to the next period. **[LO2]**
- The shifting of fixed manufacturing overhead cost between periods under absorption costing can cause operating income to fluctuate erratically and can result in confusion and unwise decisions on the part of management. To guard against mistakes when they interpret income statement data, managers should be alert to any changes that may have taken place in inventory levels or in unit product costs during the period. **[LO3]**

- Practically speaking, variable costing cannot be used externally for financial reporting purposes in certain jurisdictions mainly because it does not conform to the matching principle (i.e., that revenues should be matched with the cost of generating those revenues). However, variable costing may be used internally for planning and is particularly useful when applying cost–volume–profit (CVP) concepts in profit planning and decision making. **[LO4]**

REVIEW PROBLEM: CONTRASTING VARIABLE AND ABSORPTION COSTING

Dexter Company produces and sells a single product, a fan housing unit used in commercial heating and cooling systems. Selected cost and operating data relating to the product for two years are given below:

Selling price per unit.	$50
Manufacturing costs:	
Variable per unit produced:	
Direct materials.	11
Direct labour	6
Variable overhead	3
Fixed per year	120,000
Selling and administrative costs:	
Variable per unit sold	5
Fixed per year	70,000

	Year 1	Year 2
Units in beginning inventory.	–0–	2,000
Units produced during the year.	10,000	6,000
Units sold during the year.	8,000	8,000
Units in ending inventory	2,000	–0–

Required:
1. Assume that the company uses absorption costing.
   - *a.* Compute the unit product cost in each year.
   - *b.* Prepare an income statement for each year.
2. Assume that the company uses variable costing.
   - *a.* Compute the unit product cost in each year.
   - *b.* Prepare an income statement for each year.
3. Reconcile the variable costing and absorption costing operating incomes.

Solution to Review Problem

1. *a.* Under absorption costing, all manufacturing costs, variable and fixed, are included in unit product costs:

	Year 1	Year 2
Direct materials	$11	$11
Direct labour	6	6
Variable manufacturing overhead	3	3
Fixed manufacturing overhead		
($120,000 ÷ 10,000 units)	12	
($120,000 ÷ 6,000 units)		20
Unit product cost	$32	$40

b. The absorption costing income statements follow:

		Year 1		Year 2
Sales (8,000 units × $50 per unit)		$400,000		$400,000
Less cost of goods sold:				
Beginning inventory	$ –0–		$ 64,000	
Add cost of goods manufactured				
(10,000 units × $32 per unit)	320,000			
(6,000 units × $40 per unit)			240,000	
Goods available for sale	320,000		304,000	
Less ending inventory				
(2,000 units × $32 per unit; 0 units) . . .	64,000	256,000	–0–	304,000
Gross margin		144,000		96,000
Less selling and administrative				
expenses		110,000*		110,000*
Operating income		$ 34,000		$ (14,000)
*Selling and administrative expenses:				
Variable (8,000 units × $5 per unit)	$ 40,000			
Fixed per year	70,000			
Total	$110,000			

2. a. Under variable costing, only the variable manufacturing costs are included in unit product costs:

	Year 1	Year 2
Direct materials	$11	$11
Direct labour	6	6
Variable manufacturing overhead	3	3
Unit product cost	$20	$20

b. The variable costing income statements follow. Notice that the variable cost of goods sold is computed in a simpler, more direct manner than in the examples provided earlier. On a variable costing income statement, either approach to computing the cost of goods sold followed in this chapter is acceptable.

		Year 1		Year 2
Sales (8,000 units × $50 per unit).		$400,000		$400,000
Less variable expenses:				
Variable cost of goods sold				
(8,000 units × $20 per unit)	$160,000		$160,000	
Variable selling and administrative				
expenses (8,000 units × $5 per unit) . .	40,000		40,000	
Contribution margin		200,000		200,000
Less fixed expenses:				
Fixed manufacturing overhead	120,000		120,000	
Fixed selling and				
administrative expenses	70,000	190,000	70,000	190,000
Operating income		$ 10,000		$ 10,000

3.   The reconciliation of the variable and absorption costing operating incomes follows:

	Year 1	Year 2
Variable costing operating income	$10,000	$10,000
Add fixed manufacturing overhead costs deferred in inventory under absorption costing (2,000 units × $12 per unit)	24,000	
Deduct fixed manufacturing overhead costs released from inventory under absorption costing (2,000 units × $12 per unit). . .		24,000
Absorption costing operating income.	$34,000	$(14,000)

DISCUSSION CASE

DISCUSSION CASE 8–1

Tough times can bring out the worst in people. When companies are desperate to stay in business or to report more favourable earnings to the market, some managers just can't seem to resist the temptation to manipulate reported profits. Unfortunately, inventory is sometimes a tempting target of such manipulation. While some companies may boost their own inventories to report higher profits, other companies use inventory manipulation in a more roundabout way: they produce excess inventory but then find ways to induce their customers to buy more product than they really need (known as "channel stuffing" or "trade loading").

Required:
Using the concepts discussed in this chapter, consider how the requirement to report for financial accounting purposes under absorption costing might play a role. Could a firm with sales below the break-even point still report profits?

QUESTIONS

8–1 What is the basic difference between absorption costing and variable costing?

8–2 Why is variable costing a better support for short-term planning and decision making than absorption costing?

8–3 If production and sales are equal, which method would you expect to show the higher operating income, variable costing or absorption costing? Why?

8–4 If production exceeds sales, which method would you expect to show the higher operating income, variable costing or absorption costing? Why?

8–5 If fixed manufacturing overhead costs are released from inventory under absorption costing, what does this tell you about the level of production in relation to the level of sales?

8–6 Delone Industries had $1 25,000 in sales and reported a $75,000 profit in its annual report to shareholders. According to a CVP analysis prepared for management's use, $125,000 in sales is the break-even point for the company. Did the company's inventory level increase, decrease, or remain unchanged? Explain.

8–7 How is the use of variable costing limited?

8–8 How does lean production reduce or eliminate the difference in reported operating income between absorption and variable costing?

FOUNDATIONAL EXERCISES

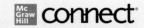

[LO1, LO2, LO3, LO4]

Diego Company manufactures one product that is sold for $80 per unit. The following information pertains to the company's first year of operations in which it produced 40,000 units and sold 35,000 units.

Variable costs per unit:	
Manufacturing:	
Direct materials.	$24
Direct labour	$14
Variable manufacturing overhead	$ 2
Variable selling and administrative.	$ 4
Fixed costs per year:	
Fixed manufacturing overhead	$800,000
Fixed selling and administrative expenses	$496,000

Required:

Answer each question independently based on the original data unless instructed otherwise.

8–1 What is the unit product cost under variable costing?

8–2 What is the unit product cost under absorption costing?

8–3 What is the company's total contribution margin under variable costing?

8–4 What is the company's net operating income under variable costing?

8–5 What is the company's total gross margin under absorption costing?

8–6 What is the company's net operating income under absorption costing?

8–7 What is the amount of the difference between the variable costing and absorption costing net operating incomes? What is the cause of this difference?

8–8 What is the company's break-even point in unit sales? Is it above or below the actual sales volume? Compare the break-even sales volume to your answer for question 6 and comment.

8–9 What would have been the company's variable costing net operating income if it had produced and sold 35,000 units? You do not need to perform any calculations to answer this question.

8–10 What would have been the company's absorption costing net operating income if it had produced and sold 35,000 units? You do not need to perform any calculations to answer this question.

8–11 If the company produces 5,000 fewer units than it sells in its second year of operations, will absorption costing net operating income be higher or lower than variable costing net operating income in Year 2? Why? No calculations are necessary.

EXERCISES

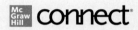

EXERCISE 8–1 Variable and Absorption Costing Unit Product Costs [LO1]

Ida Sidha Karya Company is a family-owned company located in the village of Gianyar on the island of Bali in Indonesia. The company produces a handcrafted Balinese musical instrument called a gamelan that is similar to a xylophone. The gamelans are sold to a Canadian importer for $850. Selected data for the company's operations last year follow:

Units in beginning inventory....................	0
Units produced..................................	500
Units sold......................................	450
Units in ending inventory......................	50
Variable costs per unit:	
Direct materials...............................	$150
Direct labour..................................	$270
Variable manufacturing overhead	$40
Variable selling and administrative...........	$25
Fixed costs:	
Fixed manufacturing overhead..................	$120,000
Fixed selling and administrative..............	$40,000

Required:

1. Assume that the company uses absorption costing. Compute the unit product cost for one gamelan.
2. Assume that the company uses variable costing. Compute the unit product cost for one gamelan.

EXERCISE 8–2 Variable Costing Income Statement; Explanation of Difference in Operating Income [LO2]

Refer to the data in Exercise 8–1 for Ida Sidha Karya Company. An absorption costing income statement prepared by the company's accountant appears below:

Sales	$382,500
Cost of goods sold........................	315,000
Gross margin..............................	67,500
Selling and administrative expenses........	51,250
Operating income	$ 16,250

Required:

1. Determine how much of the ending inventory consists of fixed manufacturing overhead cost deferred in inventory to the next period.
2. Prepare an income statement for the year using the variable costing method. Explain the difference in operating income between the two costing methods.

EXERCISE 8–3 Reconciliation of Absorption and Variable Costing Operating Incomes [LO3]
Sunrise Pools and Spas manufactures fibreglass forms for in-ground pools and swim spas for all-season use. The company uses variable costing for internal management reports and absorption costing for external reports to shareholders, creditors, and the government. The company has provided the data for their swim spa business in years 1, 2, and 3 shown below.
    The company's fixed manufacturing overhead per unit was constant at $2,500 for all three years:

	Year 1	Year 2	Year 3
Inventories:			
Beginning (units)	150	160	150
Ending (units)	160	150	200
Variable costing operating income	$292,400	$269,200	$251,800

Required:

1. Determine each year's absorption costing operating income. Present your answer in the form of a reconciliation report, such as the one shown in Exhibit 8–6.
2. In year 4, the company's variable costing operating income was $240,200 and its absorption costing operating income was $205,200. Did inventories increase or decrease during year 4? How much fixed manufacturing overhead cost was deferred or released from inventory during year 4?

EXERCISE 8–4 Evaluating Absorption and Variable Costing as Alternative Costing Methods [LO4]
The following questions involve the same manufacturing company in two different sets of circumstances. In both, the cost structure of the company is constant from year to year. Selling prices, unit variable costs, and total fixed costs are the same in every year. However, unit sales and/or unit production levels may vary from year to year.

Required:

1. Consider the following data for scenario A:

	Year 1	Year 2	Year 3
Variable costing operating income	$16,847	$16,847	$16,847
Absorption costing operating income	$16,847	$29,378	$ 6,018

   a. Were unit sales constant from year to year? Explain.
   b. What was the relationship between unit sales and unit production levels in each year? For each year, indicate whether inventories grew or shrank.

2. Consider the following data for scenario B:

	Year 1	Year 2	Year 3
Variable costing operating income (loss)	$16,847	$(18,153)	$(53,153)
Absorption costing operating income	$16,847	$ 17,583	$ 18,318

   a. Were unit sales constant from year to year? Explain.
   b. What was the relationship between unit sales and unit production levels in each year? For each year, indicate whether inventories grew or shrank.

3. Given the patterns of operating income in scenarios A and B above, which costing method, variable costing or absorption costing, do you believe provides a better reflection of economic reality? Explain.

EXERCISE 8–5 Variable Costing Unit Product Cost and Income Statement; Break-Even [LO1, LO2]

Waterloo Storage Products makes a four-drawer plastic storage cabinet on casters meant for use in garages and workshops. Each cabinet sells for $35. Data for last year's operations follow:

Units in beginning inventory.............................	0
Units produced	25,000
Units sold	21,500
Units in ending inventory	3,500
Variable costs per unit:	
Direct materials	$ 8
Direct labour......................................	10
Variable manufacturing overhead....................	2
Variable selling and administrative..................	4
Total variable cost per unit	$ 24
Fixed costs:	
Fixed manufacturing overhead	$ 75,000
Fixed selling and administrative.....................	110,000
Total fixed costs	$185,000

Required:

1. Assume that the company uses variable costing. Compute the unit product cost for one storage cabinet.
2. Assume that the company uses variable costing. Prepare a contribution format income statement for the year.
3. What is the company's break-even point in terms of units sold?

> **CHECK FIGURE**
> Unit product cost
> of one storage
> cabinet = $20.

EXERCISE 8–6 Absorption Costing Unit Product Cost; Income Statement [LO1, LO2]

Refer to the data in Exercise 8–5 for Waterloo Storage Products. Assume in this exercise that the company uses absorption costing.

Required:

1. Compute the unit product cost for one storage cabinet.
2. Prepare an income statement for the year.

EXERCISE 8–7 Variable and Absorption Costing Unit Product Costs; Income Statements [LO1, LO2]

Baxtell Company manufactures and sells a single product. The following costs were incurred during the company's first year of operations:

Variable costs per unit:	
Manufacturing:	
Direct materials....................................	$ 25
Direct labour......................................	12
Variable manufacturing overhead..................	3
Variable selling and administrative..................	5
Fixed costs per year:	
Fixed manufacturing overhead	200,000
Fixed selling and administrative expense	110,000

During the year, the company produced 25,000 units and sold 21,000 units. The selling price of the company's product is $65 per unit.

Required:

1. Assume that the company uses absorption costing.
    a. Compute the unit product cost.
    b. Prepare an income statement for the year.
2. Assume that the company uses variable costing.
    a. Compute the unit product cost.
    b. Prepare an income statement for the year.

EXERCISE 8–8 Inferring Costing Method; Unit Product Cost [LO1, LO4]

Sparn Limited incurs the following costs to produce and sell a single product:

Variable costs per unit:		
Direct materials	$	20
Direct labour......................................		10
Variable manufacturing overhead		4
Variable selling and administrative expenses		8
Fixed costs per year:		
Fixed manufacturing overhead		180,000
Fixed selling and administrative expenses		600,000

During the last year, 30,000 units were produced and 22,500 units were sold. The Finished Goods Inventory account at the end of the year shows a balance of $85,000 for the 2,500 unsold units.

Required:

1. Is the company using absorption costing or variable costing to cost units in the Finished Goods Inventory account? Show computations to support your answer.
2. Assume that the company wishes to prepare financial statements for the year to issue to its shareholders.
    a. Is the $85,000 figure for finished goods inventory the correct amount to use on these statements for external reporting purposes? Explain.
    b. At what dollar amount should the 2,500 units be carried in inventory for external reporting purposes?

EXERCISE 8–9 Variable Costing Income Statement; Reconciliation [LO2, LO3]

Morey Company has just completed its first year of operations. The company's absorption costing income statement for the year appears below:

MOREY COMPANY Income Statement		
Sales (40,000 units at $33.75 per unit)		$1,350,000
Cost of goods sold:		
Beginning inventory	$ 0	
Add cost of goods manufactured		
(50,000 units at $21 per unit)	1,050,000	
Goods available for sale	1,050,000	
Less ending inventory (10,000 units at $21 per unit)	210,000	840,000
Gross margin.....................................		510,000
Selling and administrative expenses		420,000
Operating income		$ 90,000

The company's selling and administrative expenses consist of $300,000 per year in fixed expenses and $3 per unit sold in variable expenses. The company's $21 per unit product cost given above is computed as follows:

Direct materials...	$10
Direct labour..	4
Variable manufacturing overhead.........................	2
Fixed manufacturing overhead ($250,000 ÷ 50,000 units).......	5
Unit product cost.......................................	$21

Required:
1. Redo the company's income statement in the contribution format using variable costing.
2. Reconcile any difference between the operating income on your variable costing income statement and the operating income on the absorption costing income statement above.

EXERCISE 8–10 Deducing Changes in Inventory [LO3]

Parker Products Inc., a manufacturer, reported $123 million in sales and a loss of $18 million in its annual report to shareholders. According to a CVP analysis prepared for management, the company's break-even point is $115 million in sales.

Required:
Assuming that the CVP analysis is correct, is it likely that the company's inventory level increased, decreased, or remained unchanged during the year? Explain.

PROBLEMS

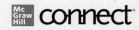

PROBLEM 8–11 Variable Costing Income Statement; Reconciliation [LO2, LO3]

During Durton Company's first two years of operations, the company reported variable costing operating income as shown below. Production and cost data for the two years are given:

	Year 1	Year 2
Units produced	25,000	25,000
Units sold	20,000	30,000

	Year 1	Year 2
Sales (at $50 per unit)	$1,000,000	$1,500,000
Variable expenses:		
Variable cost of goods sold (at $20 per unit)	400,000	600,000
Variable selling and administrative costs (at $3 per unit)	60,000	90,000
Total variable expenses	460,000	690,000
Contribution margin	540,000	810,000
Fixed expenses:		
Fixed manufacturing overhead	350,000	350,000
Fixed selling and administrative	250,000	250,000
Total fixed expenses	600,000	600,000
Operating income (loss)	$ (60,000)	$ 210,000

The company's $20 unit product cost is computed as follows:

Direct materials	$ 8
Direct labour	10
Variable manufacturing overhead	2
Unit product cost	$20

Required:
1. Prepare an absorption costing income statement for each year.
2. Reconcile the absorption costing and variable costing operating income figures for each year.

PROBLEM 8–12 Variable and Absorption Costing Unit Product Costs and Income Statements; Explanation of Difference in Operating Income [LO1, LO2, LO3]

Coverall Inc. produces and sells a unique type of case for a standard-size tablet computer that is guaranteed waterproof but still allows for regular functionality of the tablet. The company has just opened a new plant to manufacture these cases, and the following cost and revenue data have been provided for the first month of the plant's operation in the form of a worksheet:

Beginning inventory...........................	$ 0
Units produced................................	20,000
Units sold.....................................	15,000
Selling price per unit	$ 80
Selling and administrative expenses:	
Variable per unit............................	$ 6
Fixed (total)	$475,000
Manufacturing costs:	
Direct materials cost per unit...................	$ 12
Direct labour cost per unit	$ 9
Variable manufacturing overhead cost per unit	$ 5
Fixed manufacturing overhead cost (total).........	$600,000

Since the new case is unique in design, management is anxious to see how profitable it will be and has asked that an income statement be prepared for the month.

Required:

1. Assume that the company uses absorption costing.
    a. Determine the unit product cost.
    b. Prepare an income statement for the month.
2. Assume that the company uses variable costing.
    a. Determine the unit product cost.
    b. Prepare a contribution format income statement for the month.
3. Explain the reason for any difference in the ending inventory balances under the two costing methods and the impact of this difference on reported operating income.

PROBLEM 8–13 Comprehensive Problem with Labour Fixed [LO1, LO2, LO3, LO4]

Zurgot Inc. has just organized a new division to manufacture and sell specially designed computer tables, using select hardwoods. The division's monthly costs are shown in the schedule below:

Manufacturing costs:	
Variable costs per unit:	
Direct materials	$ 152
Variable manufacturing overhead	$ 10
Fixed manufacturing overhead costs (total).............	$340,000
Selling and administrative costs:	
Variable	15% of sales
Fixed (total)	$160,000

Zurgot regards all of its workers as full-time employees, and the company has a long-standing no-layoff policy. Furthermore, production is highly automated. Accordingly, the company includes its labour costs in its fixed manufacturing overhead. The tables sell for $400 each.

During the first month of operations, the following activity was recorded:

Units produced..........	4,000
Units sold	3,200

Required:
1. Compute the unit product cost under
    a.   Absorption costing.
    b.   Variable costing.
2. Prepare an income statement for the month using absorption costing.
3. Prepare a contribution format income statement for the month using variable costing.
4. Assume that the company must obtain additional financing. As a member of top management, which of the statements that you have prepared in (2) and (3) above would you prefer to have with you when you negotiate with the bank? Why?
5. Reconcile the absorption costing and variable costing operating income figures in (2) and (3) above.

> **CHECK FIGURE**
> Unit product cost
> under absorption
> costing = $247;
> Unit product cost
> under variable
> costing = $162.

PROBLEM 8–14 Absorption and Variable Costing; Production Constant, Sales Fluctuate [LO1, LO2, LO3, LO4]
Leander Office Products Inc. produces and sells small storage and organizational products for office use. During the first month of operations, the products sold well. Andrea Leander, the owner of the company, was surprised to see a loss for the month on her income statement. This statement was prepared by a local bookkeeping service recommended to her by her bank manager. The statement follows:

LEANDER OFFICE PRODUCTS INC. Income Statement		
Sales (40,000 units)		$200,000
Variable expenses:		
Variable cost of goods sold*	$80,000	
Variable selling and administrative expenses	30,000	110,000
Contribution margin		90,000
Fixed expenses:		
Fixed manufacturing overhead	75,000	
Fixed selling and administrative expenses	20,000	95,000
Operating loss		$ (5,000)

*Consists of direct materials, direct labour, and variable manufacturing overhead.

Leander is discouraged over the loss shown for the month, particularly since she had planned to use the statement to encourage investors to purchase shares in the new company. A friend who is an accountant insists that the company should be using absorption costing rather than variable costing. He argues that if absorption costing had been used, the company would probably have reported a profit for the month.

Selected cost data relating to the product and to the first month of operations follow:

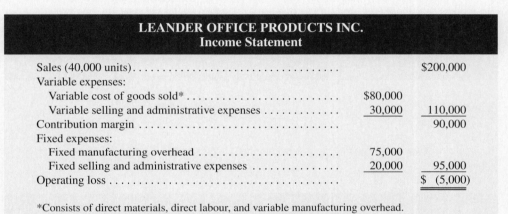

Units produced	50,000
Units sold	40,000
Variable costs per unit:	
Direct materials	$1.00
Direct labour	$0.80
Variable manufacturing overhead	$0.20
Variable selling and administrative expenses	$0.75

Required:
1. Complete the following.
    a.   Compute the unit product cost under absorption costing.
    b.   Redo the company's income statement for the month using absorption costing.
    c.   Reconcile the variable and absorption costing operating income (loss) figures.
2. Was the accountant correct in suggesting that the company really earned a "profit" for the month? Explain.
3. During the second month of operations, the company again produced 50,000 units but sold 60,000 units. (Assume no change in total fixed costs.)
    a.   Prepare a contribution format income statement for the month using variable costing.
    b.   Prepare an income statement for the month using absorption costing.
    c.   Reconcile the variable costing and absorption costing operating income figures.

PROBLEM 8–15 Prepare and Reconcile Variable Costing Statements [LO1, LO2, LO3, LO4]
Audiophonics Limited manufactures and sells high-quality and durable ear buds for use with personal electronics that are custom moulded to each customer's ear. Cost data for the product follow:

Variable costs per unit:		
Direct materials	$	12
Direct labour		24
Variable factory overhead		8
Variable selling and administrative		6
Total variable costs per unit	$	50
Fixed costs per month:		
Fixed manufacturing overhead		$240,000
Fixed selling and administrative		180,000
Total fixed costs per month		$420,000

The product sells for $80 per unit. Production and sales data for May and June, the first two months of operations, are as follows:

	Units Produced	Units Sold
May	15,000	13,000
June	15,000	17,000

Income statements prepared by the Accounting Department using absorption costing are presented below:

	May	June
Sales	$1,040,000	$1,360,000
Cost of goods sold:		
Beginning inventory	0	120,000
Add cost of goods manufactured	900,000	900,000
Goods available for sale	900,000	1,020,000
Less ending inventory	120,000	0
Cost of goods sold	780,000	1,020,000
Gross margin	260,000	340,000
Selling and administrative expenses	258,000	282,000
Operating income	$ 2,000	$ 58,000

Required:
1. Determine the unit product cost under
   a. Absorption costing.
   b. Variable costing.
2. Prepare variable costing income statements for May and June using the contribution approach.
3. Reconcile the variable costing and absorption costing operating income figures.
4. The company's Accounting Department has determined the break-even point to be 14,000 units per month, computed as follows:

$$\frac{\text{Fixed cost per month}}{\text{Unit contribution margin}} = \frac{\$420,000}{\$30 \text{ per unit}} = 14,000 \text{ units}$$

On receiving this figure, the president commented, "There's something peculiar here. The controller says that the break-even point is 14,000 units per month. Yet we sold only 13,000 units in May, and the income statement we received showed a $2,000 profit. Which figure do we believe?" Prepare a brief explanation of what happened on the May income statement.

CHECK FIGURE
Unit product cost under absorption costing = $60;
Unit product cost under variable costing = $44.

PROBLEM 8–16 Incentives Created by Absorption Costing; Ethics and the Manager [LO2, LO4]
Lydia Hartley, manager of UltraProducts' New Zealand Division, is trying to set the production schedule for the last quarter of the year. The New Zealand Division had planned to sell 100,000 units during the year, but current projections indicate sales will be only 78,000 units in total. By September 30, the following activity had been reported:

	Units
Inventory, January 1	0
Production	72,000
Sales	60,000
Inventory, September 30	12,000

Demand has been soft, and the sales forecast for the last quarter is only 18,000 units.

The division can rent warehouse space to store up to 30,000 units. The division should maintain a minimum inventory level of 1,500 units. Hartley is aware that production must be at least 6,000 units per quarter in order to retain a nucleus of key employees. Maximum production capacity is 45,000 units per quarter.

Due to the nature of the division's operations, fixed manufacturing overhead is a major element of product cost.

Required:
1. Assume that the division is using variable costing. How many units should be scheduled for production during the last quarter of the year? Show computations and explain your answer. Will the number of units scheduled for production affect the division's reported profit for the year? Explain.
2. Assume that the division is using absorption costing and that the divisional manager is given an annual bonus based on the division's operating income. If Hartley wants to maximize her division's operating income for the year, how many units should be scheduled for production during the last quarter? Explain.
3. Identify the ethical issues involved in the decision Hartley must make about the level of production for the last quarter of the year.

PROBLEM 8–17 Variable and Absorption Costing Unit Product Costs and Income Statements [LO1, LO2, LO3, LO4]
Haas Company manufactures and sells one product. The following information pertains to each of the company's first three years of operations:

Variable cost per unit:		
Manufacturing:		
Direct materials	$	30
Direct labour		18
Variable manufacturing overhead		6
Variable selling and administrative		3
Fixed costs per year:		
Fixed manufacturing overhead	$960,000	
Fixed selling and administrative expenses	$240,000	

During its first year of operations, Haas produced 60,000 units and sold 60,000 units. During its second year of operations, it produced 75,000 units and sold 50,000 units. In its third year, Haas produced 40,000 units and sold 65,000 units. The selling price of the company's product is $87 per unit.

Required:
1. Compute the company's break-even point in units sold.
2. Assume the company uses variable costing:
   a. Compute unit product costs for Year 1, Year 2, and Year 3.
   b. Prepare an income statement for Year 1, Year 2, and Year 3.
3. Assume the company uses absorption costing:
   a. Compute unit product costs for Year 1, Year 2, and Year 3.
   b. Prepare an income statement for Year 1, Year 2, and Year 3.
4. Compare net income operating income figures that you computed in requirements 2 and 3 to the break-even point calculated in requirement 1. Which net operating income figures seem counterintuitive? Why?

PROBLEM 8–18 Prepare and Interpret Statements; Changes in Both Sales and Production; Lean Production [LO1, LO2, LO3, LO4]

ElectronPlus manufactures and sells a unique electronic part. Operating results for the first three years of activity were as follows (absorption costing basis):

	Year 1	Year 2	Year 3
Sales.....................................	$1,000,000	$800,000	$1,000,000
Cost of goods sold:			
Beginning inventory.............................	0	0	280,000
Add cost of goods manufactured..................	800,000	840,000	760,000
Goods available for sale........................	800,000	840,000	1,040,000
Less ending inventory	0	280,000	190,000
Cost of goods sold	800,000	560,000	850,000
Gross margin	200,000	240,000	150,000
Selling and administrative expenses	170,000	150,000	170,000
Operating income (loss)..........................	$ 30,000	$ 90,000	$ (20,000)

Sales dropped by 20% during year 2 due to the entry of several foreign competitors into the market. ElectronPlus had expected sales to remain constant at 50,000 units for the year; production was set at 60,000 units in order to build a buffer against unexpected spurts in demand. By the start of year 3, management could see that spurts in demand were unlikely and that the inventory was excessive. To work off the excessive inventories, ElectronPlus cut back production during year 3, as shown below:

	Year 1	Year 2	Year 3
Production in units	50,000	60,000	40,000
Sales in units	50,000	40,000	50,000

Additional information about the company follows:

a. The company's plant is highly automated. Variable manufacturing costs (direct materials, direct labour, and variable manufacturing overhead) total only $4 per unit, and fixed manufacturing overhead costs total $600,000 per year.

b. Fixed manufacturing overhead costs are applied to units of product on the basis of each year's planned production. (That is, a new fixed overhead rate is computed each year, as in Exhibit 8–5.)

c. Variable selling and administrative expenses are $2 per unit sold. Fixed selling and administrative expenses total $70,000 per year.

d. The company uses a FIFO inventory flow assumption.

Management of ElectronPlus can't understand why profits tripled during year 2 when sales dropped by 20%, and why a loss was incurred during year 3 when sales recovered to previous levels.

Required:

1. Prepare a contribution format income statement for each year using variable costing.
2. Refer to the absorption costing income statements above.
    a. Compute the unit product cost in each year under absorption costing. (Show how much of this cost is variable and how much is fixed.)
    b. Reconcile the variable costing and absorption costing operating income figures for each year.
3. Refer again to the absorption costing income statements. Explain why operating income was higher in year 2 than it was in year 1 under the absorption approach, in light of the fact that fewer units were sold in year 2 than in year 1.
4. Refer again to the absorption costing income statements. Explain why the company suffered a loss in year 3 but reported a profit in year 1, although the same number of units was sold in each year.
5. *a.* Explain how operations would have differed in year 2 and year 3 if the company had been using lean production, with the result that ending inventory was zero.
    b. If lean production had been in use during year 2 and year 3, what would the company's operating income (or loss) have been in each year under absorption costing? Explain the reason for any differences between these income figures and the figures reported by the company in the statements above.

CASES

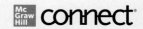

CASE 8–19 Absorption Costing and Ethics [LO1, LO2, LO3, LO4]

"There must be something wrong with these statements!" exclaimed Hugh Richards, president of Ajax Inc. "They just don't make sense. We sold the same number of units this year as we did last year, yet our profits have tripled! Who messed up the calculations?"

Ajax Inc. is a medium-sized supplier of plastic components to the automobile industry and has been in business for 25 years. Sales forecasting has been relatively easy to do in the past since Ajax has had long-term, single-sourcing relationships with most of its customers. In 2018, however, there was a threat of a strike at one of Ajax Inc.'s major raw materials suppliers. For that reason, Ajax management decided to purchase more raw materials and produce more components in 2018 than actually required, in anticipation of raw materials shortages in 2019. Manufacturing equipment was typically operated below capacity, so this boost in production was possible without incurring significant increased fixed manufacturing costs. The income statement and production reports to which Richards was referring are shown below:

	2017	2018
Sales (40,000 units each year)	$1,250,000	$1,250,000
Cost of goods sold	840,000	720,000
Gross margin	410,000	530,000
Selling and administrative expenses	350,000	350,000
Operating income	$ 60,000	$ 180,000

	2017	2018
Production in units	40,000	50,000
Sales in units	40,000	40,000
Variable manufacturing cost per unit produced	$ 6	$ 6
Variable selling and administrative expense per unit sold	$ 2	$ 2
Fixed manufacturing overhead costs (total)	$600,000	$600,000

Ajax Inc. uses absorption costing and applies fixed manufacturing overhead costs to its only product on the basis of each year's production. (Thus, a new fixed manufacturing overhead rate is computed each year, as in Exhibit 8–5.)

Required:

Take on the role of the CFO of Ajax Inc. Write a memo to Richards to explain why the operating income for 2018 was higher than for 2017 under absorption costing, although the same number of units was sold in each year. Make sure to include the following:

1. A contribution format income statement for each year, using variable costing. Be sure to reconcile the variable costing and absorption costing operating income figures for each year.
2. A brief discussion of the advantages and disadvantages of variable over absorption costing for internal reporting purposes.
3. A discussion of the ramifications of returning to the "normal" level of production in the coming year.
4. A recommendation: Should the company continue to "overproduce" in coming years to boost operating income?

CASE 8–20 Overproduction and Absorption Costing [LO2, LO3, LO4]

It is December 15 and Jane Jones, the plant manager at Acme Electric Fan Co., faces a difficult decision. The operation has been running steadily over the last 11 months. During that time, Jane worked with the production engineers to tweak the production machinery just enough to allow for a small increase in available capacity. The plant produced 18,000 fans between January and the end of November and is scheduled to produce 2,000 fans in the month of December. The sales manager indicates that all 20,000 fans will be sold by the end of the year. Jane realizes the extra investment in engineering costs will allow the plant to produce an extra 500 fans in December. Cost and pricing information are provided below:

Variable costs per unit:	
Raw material	$ 3
Direct labour	$ 2
Variable production costs	$ 1
Variable selling expenses	$ 1
Fixed manufacturing costs	$61,500
Beginning inventory	–0–
Selling price per unit	$ 12

Inventory holding costs are negligible, and customers have been known to place unexpected special orders that are typically difficult to fill. Jane figures a small safety stock of 500 fans would provide a cushion against future special orders. Even so, Jane is torn about the decision to produce the 500 additional fans. Her performance is evaluated mainly by the profit generated by the plant. In addition, her year-end bonus is based on profitability of the plant. Jane is worried that incurring the extra costs will have a negative effect on plant profitability.

Required:
Take on the role of the plant accountant and provide Jane with the analysis she needs to make an informed decision. Assuming the company utilizes absorption costing, analyze the effect of producing the additional 500 fans on plant profitability and on Jane's bonus, and recommend a course of action.

CONNECTING CONCEPTS

SECTION 2

COSTING

While many Easy Learning (EL) customers develop their own educational content to use with the EL online learning platforms, some prefer to hire EL to develop content for them. Custom online content is produced by the EL Educational Consulting Department. This department is made up of education specialists and web developers. In addition, EL subcontracts custom online content development to a group of independent topical specialists. This is necessary because EL's customers are involved in a wide range of specialities and industries. Having full-time content development staff to cover the wide variety of topical areas would not be feasible.

The Educational Consulting Department uses a job-order costing system. Each customer order for online content development is considered a "job." Costs of online content development fall into three main categories: costs of subcontracted work, direct in-house staff costs, and departmental overhead costs made up of other departmental costs that cannot be directly traced to a particular job. In-house staff are required to submit time sheets at the end of each week where they indicate total hours worked broken down by customer order. Direct costs including subcontracted work and direct in-house staff costs as well as an appropriate allocation of departmental overhead is charged against the revenue generated by each job as the jobs are completed. The department worked on several different jobs during the month. Information about two of these jobs, one for Smith & Valens and another for Walker & Chen, that were started and completed by the Educational Consulting Department this month is provided below:

	Smith & Valens	Walker & Chen
Cost of subcontracted work	$45,000	$85,000
Direct in-house staff costs	$12,500	$ 5,000
Total in-house staff hours worked	425 hrs	150 hrs

Overhead is allocated based on the actual costs incurred each month and the number of direct in-house staff hours worked. Total overhead costs incurred by the department this month were $115,000, and 625 total in-house staff hours were worked in the department during the month.

Claire Jackson, the CEO and founder of EL, is increasingly concerned with the economics of the business. Competition is increasing and she wants to make sure she understands the cost structure in each of the departments. To better understand how costs are accumulated and charged out to customers, Claire has identified the Educational Consulting Department as one of three departments where an ABC system will be implemented. An activity analysis indicates there are two main activities carried out within the Educational Consulting Department that generate overhead costs: technical support and administration. Technical support involves ensuring the content developed by outside subcontractors and the work carried out by in-house staff are integrated into a working product of high quality. Administration involves overseeing the work of in-house staff, ensuring deadlines are met and customer contracts are fulfilled as per agreed details. Activity cost pools and their measures are provided below:

Activity Cost Pool	Activity Measure	Activity Rate
Technical support	Dollars of subcontracted costs incurred	$0.50 per dollar of subcontracted cost
Administration	Number of in-house staff direct hours worked	$85 per in-house staff direct hour

Required:
1. Analyze the total cost of each job under each method of allocating overhead. How do the costs differ? Why?
2. What insights can the CEO gain from the ABC costing experiment? Would you recommend that ABC be rolled out across the organization? Why or why not?

INSTANT QUIZ SOLUTIONS

8–1
Fixed manufacturing overhead is treated as a product cost under absorption costing and a period cost under variable costing.

8–2
Inventory increased. The increase resulted in fixed manufacturing overhead cost being charged to ending inventory on the balance sheet. This reduced fixed manufacturing overhead cost, resulting in a profit even though the company operated at its break-even level of sales.

8–3
Under variable costing, *revenue* drives operating income, while under absorption costing, *revenue* and *production* drive operating income.

8–4
Under absorption costing, fixed manufacturing overhead costs are included in product costs, along with direct materials, direct labour, and variable manufacturing overhead. If some of the units are not sold by the end of the period, then they are carried into the next period as inventory. The fixed manufacturing overhead cost attached to the units in ending inventory follows the units into the next period. When the units are finally sold, the fixed manufacturing overhead cost that has been carried over with the units is included as part of that period's cost of goods sold.

8–5
Absorption costing advocates believe that absorption costing does a better job of matching costs with revenues than variable costing. They argue that all manufacturing costs must be assigned to products to properly match the costs of producing units of product with the revenues from the units when they are sold. They believe that no distinction should be made between variable and fixed manufacturing costs for matching costs and revenues.

8–6
Under lean production methods, little if any inventory is held on hand; thus, there is no ability to move fixed overhead costs on to the Balance Sheet at the end of each period. On the other hand, under traditional production methods, inventory tends to build during periods of low demand and is drawn down in periods of high demand. Inventory values on the Balance Sheet must include a portion of fixed manufacturing overhead and, thus, these costs are moved to the Balance Sheet rather than expensed on the Income Statement when inventory builds.

SECTION 3

PLANNING AND CONTROL

Chapters 9, 10, and 11

Every organization needs to plan on a regular basis. Chapter 9 describes the steps by which plans are translated into a master budget expressed in financial terms. Importantly, budgets are used to allocate resources and coordinate activities across the various functional areas within an organization. To evaluate whether the plan is being achieved, many organizations employ detailed performance reports comparing actual amounts to budget. Explanations are typically sought in cases where revenues and expenses differ significantly from the budget.

Standard costing, described in Chapter 10, is an example of a tool that managers can use to monitor and control cost performance. Chapter 10 also applies the concept of flexible budgeting (introduced in Chapter 9) to overhead costs, which for many companies is now a major expense given the rise of automation.

Chapter 11 completes our discussion of the approaches used by managers to control operations by introducing the concept of responsibility centres, which involves identifying subunits within the organization whose managers have well-defined control over costs, profits, and investment funds. In large organizations, responsibility centres often supply goods and services to each other, and Chapter 11 explores the pricing of these transactions. Key metrics used to evaluate the performance of responsibility centres are also presented in Chapter 11, as is the concept of the balanced scorecard, which incorporates both financial and non-financial measures.

BUDGETING

LEARNING OBJECTIVES

After studying Chapter 9, you should be able to

1 Explain why organizations budget, and describe the processes they use to create budgets.

2 Prepare the supporting components of a master budget and the budgeted financial statements.

3 Prepare a flexible budget, and explain the need for the flexible budget approach.

4 Prepare a performance report using the flexible budget approach.

5 (Online Appendix 9A) Compute the optimal inventory level and order size.

■ BUDGETING IN TECH COMPANIES

Source: Axonify

Budgeting is one of the most common management accounting tools used by organizations. Regardless of a company's size, age, industry, or business model, budgets are used as part of developing plans for future periods and they provide a benchmark in assessing actual performance in the current period.

Budgets are an important part of the planning process at Axonify, a software as a service (SaaS) company based in Waterloo, Ontario. Axonify develops and implements online learning platforms for companies to use in providing self-guided training for employees. Their business model is quite straightforward. Revenues are primarily earned on a subscription basis from their customers, usually annually. Costs mainly relate to product development, customer support, marketing, and customer acquisition.

For Axonify, preparing an annual budget is a key part of the planning process. For example, as part of developing the budget, they estimate how many new customers will be required to achieve revenue growth objectives based on assumptions about the subscription revenues likely to be received from each customer. Axonify also budgets the expected costs of acquiring new customers, developing new products, providing customer support, and marketing and other activities. During the year, Axonify compares actual revenues and expenses to the budget on a monthly basis and where possible takes corrective action to address any unfavourable departures from the plan.

Budgets are an important tool used by management of all types of organizations. Budgets are used to help communicate financial objectives for the future, allocate resources, and coordinate activities across the different functional areas within the organization. Budgets are also used by managers to periodically compare actual performance of revenues, expenses, and profits to the plan.

In this chapter, we focus on the major steps involved in preparing budgets as well as some of the issues that influence how managers use and respond to budgets.

LEARNING OBJECTIVE 1

Explain why organizations budget, and describe the processes they use to create budgets.

■ THE BASIC FRAMEWORK OF BUDGETING

A budget is a detailed plan for the future that is typically expressed in quantitative terms. The act of preparing a budget is called *budgeting*. The use of budgets to control a firm's activities is known as *budgetary control*.

The **master budget** summarizes a company's plans, setting specific targets for sales, production, distribution, customer support, new product development, and administrative and financing activities. It generally culminates in a cash budget, a budgeted income statement, and a budgeted balance sheet. We cover all of these in the sections below.

Why Organizations Create Budgets

Master budget

A summary of a company's plans in which specific targets are set for sales, production, distribution, administrative, and financing activities; it generally culminates in a cash budget, a budgeted income statement, and a budgeted balance sheet.

Budgets serve as both a planning tool and a control tool in organizations. Planning involves developing objectives and preparing various budgets to achieve these objectives. Control involves gathering feedback to assess the extent to which the objectives developed at the planning stage are being attained. An effective budgeting system provides for *both* planning and control.

As part of the planning process, budgets are used to:

1. Encourage managers to *think about* and *plan* for the future.
2. *Communicate* management's financial goals throughout the organization.
3. *Allocate resources* to those parts of the organization where they can be used most effectively.
4. *Coordinate* the plans and activities of managers in different departments.

As part of a control system, budgets are compared to actual results during the year to:

1. *Improve* the efficiency and effectiveness of operations.
2. *Evaluate* and *reward* employees.

Choosing a Budget Period

Continuous or perpetual budget

A 12-month budget that rolls forward one month (or quarter) as the current month (or quarter) is completed.

Operating budgets ordinarily cover a one-year period corresponding to the company's fiscal year. Many companies divide their budget year into four quarters and further break the budget down into monthly figures. *Continuous or perpetual budgets* are used by many organizations. A **continuous or perpetual budget** is a 12-month budget that rolls forward one month (or quarter) as the current month (or quarter) is completed. In other words, one month (or quarter) is added to the end of the budget as each month (or quarter) comes to a close. This approach always keeps managers focused at least one year ahead, which helps them from becoming too narrowly fixated on short-term results.

How Organizations Create Budgets

Participative budget

A method of preparing budgets in which managers prepare their own budget estimates. These budget estimates are then reviewed by the manager's supervisor, and any issues are resolved by mutual agreement, leading to a completed budget.

Companies usually create budgets by relying on some combination of top-down budgeting and *participative budgeting*. A **participative budget** involves managers from across the organization in developing budget estimates for their areas of responsibility.

With a top-down approach, top-level managers initiate the budgeting process by issuing overall profit targets. Lower-level managers are directed to prepare budgets comprising the detailed revenues and expenses necessary to meet those targets. This approach often demoralizes lower-level managers because it ignores their knowledge and experience. Furthermore, the targets imposed by top-level managers, who may possess strategic vision while lacking operational knowledge, may be unrealistically difficult or unknowingly too easy. If the targets are too difficult and top-level managers penalize lower-level managers for not meeting them, it will generate resentment rather than cooperation and commitment.

Because of these complications many companies choose to use a participative budgeting approach, involving lower-level managers in developing the budget because it:

1. Shows *respect* for their experience and opinions.
2. *Leverages* their knowledge and experience to provide more accurate estimates than those imposed by top-level managers who usually have less detailed knowledge of day-to-day operations.
3. Increases their *motivation* to achieve goals they had input in setting.
4. *Empowers* them to take ownership of the budget and to be accountable for deviations from it.

Budget estimates prepared by lower-level managers cannot simply be accepted without review by higher levels of management. If no review system is present, participative budgets may contain excessive **budgetary slack**. Slack is the difference between the revenues and expenses a manager expects can be achieved and the amounts included in the budget. Revenue budgets that are intentionally set at lower than expected levels and expense budgets that are set at higher than expected levels contain slack.[1] Managers may attempt to create slack to increase the likelihood of obtaining rewards that are contingent on meeting or beating the budget or to reduce how hard they have to work during the period to attain their budgets. Slack can result in the misallocation of resources, inefficiencies, and less effort by managers. Therefore, before budgets are finalized they should be carefully reviewed by the manager's immediate superior. If changes from the original budget seem desirable, the items in question should be discussed and revised by the mutual consent of the managers and their superiors.

Budgetary slack
The difference between the revenues and expenses a manager believes can actually be achieved and the amounts included in the budget. Slack will exist when revenue budgets are intentionally set below expected levels and expense budgets are set above expected levels.

BEYOND THE BOTTOM LINE

Intentionally creating budget slack can be considered unethical since it involves misstating budgeted revenues and expenses. In addition to being unethical, knowingly misstating budgeted revenues or expenses to increase one's chances of meeting or beating the budget can have negative consequences for an organization. An example is allocating more resources than appropriate to business units that include slack in their expense budgets. In turn, this can hurt performance if business units use these resources inefficiently. Moreover, it can result in other business units not having the resources required to perform to their potential.

As a means of limiting the creation of budget slack, many companies have a code of conduct that prohibits employees from intentionally misstating information used for internal decision-making purposes. By creating a culture of ethical behaviour, a code of conduct can help ensure that budgets represent managers' best estimates of expected revenues and expenses.

Benchmarking

An input to creating budgets that some companies use is the performance of competitors, "best-in-class" companies, or other business units in the same company. A best-in-class company is one known for achieving exceptional levels of performance on some aspect of their operations such as customer service, distribution, marketing, and so on. The approach of comparing revenue, cost, or process performance to other high-performing companies, or to other successful business units in the same company, is known as *benchmarking* (for more on benchmarking, see Chapter 7). The purpose of benchmarking is to identify the factors that allow other companies or business units to achieve superior performance and, to the extent possible, incorporate these factors into operations.

Benchmarking can influence the budgeting process by giving managers targeted levels of sales or expenses to aim for when setting the budget. For example, if a leading competitor is achieving better gross margins on similar products, this may lead managers to budget expenses that reflect the need for cost reductions. Alternatively, if competitors are achieving higher sales growth for similar products, this may lead managers to set more aggressive revenue budgets that reflect larger increases over prior periods.

Although benchmarking can provide useful information that can inform the budgeting process, as will be discussed below managers must still be careful not to set budget targets that are excessively difficult. To avoid this possibility, budgets could be set such that they reflect progress toward achieving revenue and expense performance being enjoyed by leading competitors.

Behavioural Factors in Budgeting

The remainder of the chapter deals with technical aspects of preparing budgets, but it is important to keep in mind that two important purposes of the budget are to motivate people and coordinate their efforts. These purposes can be undermined if the budget is used in an inflexible manner to control people. This relates to the idea of **responsibility accounting**, whereby managers are held responsible for those items—and *only* those items—that they can actually influence to a significant extent. Each revenue or cost item in the budget is the responsibility of a manager who is held responsible for subsequent deviations between budgeted goals and actual results. In effect, responsibility accounting *personalizes* accounting information by holding individuals responsible for revenues and costs. If managers were to be held accountable for revenues or expenses outside their control, this could become very demoralizing.

Another key issue related to the motivational aspect of budgets is the difficulty level of the budget targets for revenues and expenses. If budgets are too difficult, employees will eventually recognize that they are unattainable, and motivation and morale will likely suffer. If the budgets are too easy, inefficiencies or less effort will result. In practice, most companies try to set their budget targets at a *challenging but attainable* level. Such targets can usually be met by competent managers.

The difficulty level of budget targets becomes even more important when managers' bonuses are based on meeting or exceeding the budget. Under this type of compensation scheme, a bonus is paid only if the budget is attained. For obvious reasons, managers who work under such a bonus plan, or whose performance is evaluated based on meeting budget targets, usually prefer to have challenging but attainable budgets rather than highly difficult budgets.

> ### IN BUSINESS
>
> In addition to creating financial budgets for revenues and expenses, many companies also establish budgets or "targets" for non-financial measures of performance such as customer satisfaction, service delivery, new product development, and employee training. The rationale is that achieving the targets established for non-financial measures will help the company achieve its financial budgets for revenues and expenses.
>
> For example, many fast-food restaurants have targets for how long it takes to complete orders for both in-restaurant and drive-through customers. The idea behind setting these targets is that providing efficient (fast) customer service will enhance customer satisfaction. In turn, satisfied customers are more likely to visit the restaurant again in the future, which will help management attain its budgets for revenue and profits.
>
> Source: Personal conversations with Alykhan Damji and Nash Damji, A&W Canada franchisees.

■ THE MASTER BUDGET: AN OVERVIEW

The master budget consists of a number of separate but interdependent budgets. Exhibit 9–1 is an overview of the various parts of the master budget and how they are related. Preparing a master budget for a manufacturing company is somewhat more complex than for other types of organizations (e.g., service companies, merchandising companies), so we focus on that setting in the example below. However, many of the steps described below for developing sales budgets, selling and administrative budgets, cash budgets, and so on, follow a similar approach regardless of the type of organization.

The first step in the budgeting process is preparing a **sales budget**, which is a detailed schedule showing the expected sales for the budget period. An accurate sales budget is the key to the entire budgeting process. All of the other parts of the master budget depend on the sales budget in some way, as illustrated in Exhibit 9–1. So, if the sales budget is inaccurate, the rest of the budget will be inaccurate. The sales budget is based on the company's sales forecast,

Responsibility accounting
A system of accountability in which managers are held responsible for those items of revenue and cost over which they can exert significant influence—and only those items. Managers are held responsible for differences between budgeted and actual results.

LEARNING OBJECTIVE ❷
Prepare the supporting components of a master budget and the budgeted financial statements.

Sales budget
A detailed schedule showing the expected sales for coming periods; these sales are typically expressed in both dollars and units.

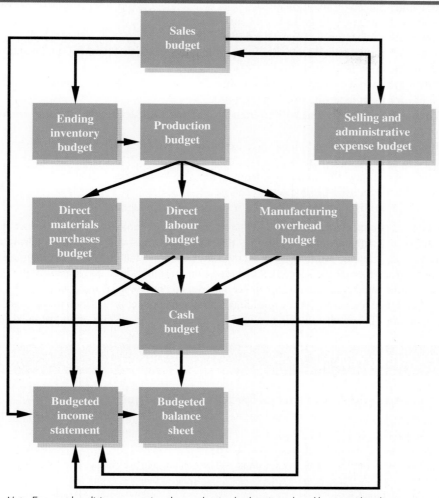

EXHIBIT 9–1
The Master Budget
Interrelationships

Note: For merchandising companies, the production budget is replaced by a merchandise purchases budget, and there is no manufacturing overhead budget.

Source: From SIROPOLIS. *SIROPOLIS SMALL BUS MGMT 5ED, 5E.* © 1994 South-Western, a part of Cengage Learning, Inc. Reproduced by permission. www.cengage.com/permissions.

which may require the use of sophisticated mathematical models and statistical tools that are beyond the scope of this book.

The sales budget influences the variable portion of the selling and administrative expense budget and it feeds into the production budget, which defines how many units need to be produced during the budget period. The production budget in turn is used to determine the direct materials, direct labour, and manufacturing overhead budgets. Once a company has prepared these three manufacturing cost budgets, it can prepare the ending finished goods inventory budget.

The master budget concludes with the preparation of a cash budget, income statement, and balance sheet. A **cash budget** is a detailed plan that shows how cash resources will be acquired and used over some specified time period. Observe from Exhibit 9–1 that all of the operating budgets have an impact on the cash budget. In the case of the sales budget, the impact comes from the planned cash receipts to be received from sales. In the case of the other budgets, the impact comes from the planned cash expenditures within the budgets themselves. The final schedule of the master budget is the balance sheet, which estimates a company's assets, liabilities, and shareholders' equity at the end of a budget period.

Cash budget
A detailed plan showing how cash resources will be acquired and used over a specified time period.

The Big Picture

The multitude of schedules contained in a master budget can be overwhelming. Therefore, it is important to see the big picture in two respects. First, a master budget for a manufacturing company is designed to answer 10 key questions as follows:

1. How much sales will we earn?
2. How much cash will we collect from customers?
3. How much raw material will we need to purchase?
4. How much manufacturing cost (including direct materials, direct labour, and manufacturing overhead) will we incur?
5. How much cash will we pay to our suppliers and our direct labourers, and how much will we pay for manufacturing overhead resources?
6. What is the total cost that will be transferred from finished goods inventory to cost of goods sold?
7. How much selling and administrative expense will we incur and how much cash will we pay related to those expenses?
8. How much money will we borrow from or repay to lenders, including interest?
9. How much operating income will we earn?
10. What will our balance sheet look like at the end of the budget period?

Second, it is important to understand that many of the schedules in a master budget depend on a variety of estimates and assumptions that managers must make when preparing those schedules. The Learning Aid below summarizes the questions that underlie these estimates and assumptions for seven of the schedules included in a master budget. As you study the budget schedules in the remainder of the chapter, keep these two "big picture" insights in mind: (1) the budget is designed to answer 10 key questions, and (2) the budget is based on various estimates and assumptions. Doing so will help you understand *why* and *how* a master budget is created.

LEARNING AID

Estimates and Assumptions for a Master Budget

Sales budget:
1. What are the budgeted unit sales?
2. What is the budgeted selling price per unit?
3. What percentage of accounts receivable will be collected in the current and subsequent period?

Production budget:
1. What percentage of next period's unit sales needs to be maintained in ending finished goods inventory?

Direct materials budget:
1. How many units of raw material are needed to make one unit of finished goods?
2. What is the budgeted cost for one unit of raw material?
3. What percentage of next period's production needs should be maintained in ending raw materials inventory?
4. What percentage of raw material purchases will be paid in the current and subsequent periods?

Direct labour budget:
1. How many direct labour-hours are required per unit of finished goods?
2. What is the budgeted direct labour wage rate per hour?

Manufacturing overhead budget:
1. What is the budgeted variable overhead cost per unit of the allocation base?
2. What is the total budgeted fixed overhead cost per period?
3. What is the budgeted depreciation expense on factory assets per period?

Selling and administrative expense budget:
1. What is the budgeted variable selling and administrative expense per unit sold?
2. What is the total budgeted fixed selling and administrative expense per period?
3. What is the budgeted depreciation expense on non-factory assets per period?

Cash budget:
1. What is the budgeted minimum cash balance?
2. What are our estimated expenditures for non-current asset purchases and dividends?
3. What is the estimated interest rate on borrowed funds?

Preparing the Master Budget

We use a hypothetical company, Patterson Framing Limited, to illustrate the preparation of a master budget. The company manufactures picture frames that it sells through an extensive distribution network in Canada and the United States. The following schedules will be prepared below in developing the master budget:

1. A sales budget, including a schedule of expected cash collections.
2. A production budget.
3. A direct materials purchases budget, including a schedule of expected cash disbursements for raw materials.
4. A direct labour budget.
5. A manufacturing overhead budget.
6. An ending finished goods inventory budget.
7. A selling and administrative expense budget.
8. A cash budget.
9. A budgeted income statement.
10. A budgeted balance sheet.

In the following sections, we will study each of these schedules. The balance sheet as at December 31, 2020 for Patterson Framing is shown below. As described below, some of these balance sheet amounts will be used in preparing the budget schedules for 2021:

PATTERSON FRAMING LIMITED
Balance Sheet December 31, 2020
Assets

Current assets:		
Cash	$ 50,000	
Accounts receivable	180,000	
Raw materials inventory (2,400 metres)	9,600	
Finished goods inventory (2,000 frames).	40,000	
Total current assets.		$ 279,600
Plant and equipment:		
Land	160,000	
Buildings and equipment	1,400,000	
Accumulated depreciation	(584,000)	
Plant and equipment, net		976,000
Total assets.		$1,255,600

Liabilities and Shareholders' Equity

Current liabilities:		
Accounts payable (raw materials)		$ 26,688
Shareholders' equity:		
Common shares	$ 600,000	
Retained earnings.	628,912	
Total shareholders' equity		1,228,912
Total liabilities and shareholders' equity		$1,255,600

Budget Assumptions

Before preparing the individual schedules that make up the master budget, managers from the various departments at Patterson Framing would need to develop the estimates and assumptions discussed above. The estimates and assumptions that we will use as we work through the creation of the master budget for Patterson Framing are shown below.

PATTERSON FRAMING
Budgeting Assumptions
For the Year Ending December 31, 2021

		Quarter			
	All 4 Quarters	**1**	**2**	**3**	**4**
Sales Budget					
Unit sales		20,000	60,000	80,000	40,000
Selling price per unit	$ 30				
% of sales collected in quarter of sale	60%				
% of sales collected in quarter after sale	40%				
Production Budget					
% of next quarter's sales in finished goods inventory	10%				
Direct Materials Budget					
Metres of raw material per unit	1				
Cost per metre of raw material.	$ 4				
% of next quarter's production needs in ending inventory	10%				
% of purchases paid in quarter purchased	70%				
% of purchases paid in quarter after purchase	30%				
Direct Labour Budget					
Direct labour hours per frame	0.5				
Direct labour cost per hour	$ 20				
Manufacturing Overhead Budget					
Variable manufacturing overhead per direct labour-hour	$ 2				
Fixed manufacturing overhead per quarter (excluding depreciation).	$221,250				
Depreciation per quarter	$ 30,000				
Selling and Administrative Budget					
Variable selling and administrative expense per frame	$ 2				
Fixed selling and administrative expense per quarter:					
Advertising.	$ 20,000				
Senior management salaries.	$ 50,000				
Insurance	$ 19,000				
Property tax	$ 9,000				
Depreciation.	$ 4,000				
Cash Budget					
Minimum cash balance	$ 50,000				
Equipment purchases per quarter.	$ 20,000				
Dividends per quarter.	$ 10,000				
Annual (quarterly) interest rate	4% (1%)				

The Sales Budget

The sales budget is the starting point in preparing the master budget. As shown earlier in Exhibit 9–1, all other items in the master budget, including production, purchases, inventories, and expenses, depend on it in some way.

The sales budget is constructed by multiplying the budgeted sales in units by the selling price. Schedule 1 contains the sales budget for Patterson Framing for the year 2021 by quarters. Notice from the schedule that the company plans to sell 200,000 picture frames during the year, with sales peaking in the third quarter.

INSTANT QUIZ 9–1
Calculate second-quarter cash collections from sales for a company that expects to have credit sales of $200,000 in quarter 1 and $300,000 in quarter 2, and collects 75% in the quarter of sale and the remaining 25% in the following quarter.

   A schedule of expected cash collections, such as the one that appears in Schedule 1 for Patterson Framing, is prepared after the sales budget. This schedule will be needed later to prepare the cash budget. Cash collections consist of collections on sales made to customers in prior periods plus collections on sales made in the current budget period. At Patterson Framing, experience has shown that 60% of sales is collected in the quarter in which the sale is made and the remaining 40% is collected in the following quarter. So, for example, 60% of the first-quarter sales of $600,000 (or $360,000) is collected during the first quarter and 40% (or $240,000) is collected during the second quarter.

SCHEDULE 1

PATTERSON FRAMING LIMITED
Sales Budget
For the Year Ending December 31, 2021

	Quarter				
	1	**2**	**3**	**4**	**Year**
Budgeted sales (units)	20,000	60,000	80,000	40,000	200,000
Selling price per unit	× $30	× $30	× $30	× $30	× $30
Total budgeted sales.	$600,000	$1,800,000	$2,400,000	$1,200,000	$6,000,000
Schedule of Expected Cash Collections					
Accounts receivable 31/12/20*	$180,000				$ 180,000
First-quarter sales:†					
($600,000 × 60%, 40%)	360,000	240,000			600,000
Second-quarter sales:					
($1,800,000 × 60%, 40%)		1,080,000	720,000		1,800,000
Third-quarter sales:					
($2,400,000 × 60%, 40%)			1,440,000	960,000	2,400,000
Fourth-quarter sales:‡					
($1,200,000 × 60%)				720,000	720,000
Total cash collections.	$540,000	$1,320,000	$2,160,000	$1,680,000	$5,700,000

*Cash collections from last year's fourth-quarter sales. See the December 31, 2020, balance sheet.
†Cash collections from sales are as follows: 60% collected in the quarter of sale, and the remaining 40% collected in the following quarter.
‡Uncollected fourth-quarter sales appear as accounts receivable on the company's end-of-year balance sheet (see Schedule 10).

The Production Budget

The **production budget** is prepared after the sales budget. The production budget lists the number of units that must be produced during each budget period to meet expected sales and to provide for the desired ending inventory. Production needs can be determined as follows:

Production budget
A detailed plan showing the number of units that must be produced during a period to meet both sales and inventory needs.

Budgeted sales in units	XXXX
Add desired ending inventory.	XXXX
Total needs	XXXX
Less beginning inventory	XXXX
Required production	XXXX

Schedule 2 contains the production budget for Patterson Framing.

SCHEDULE 2

PATTERSON FRAMING LIMITED
Production Budget
For the Year Ending December 31, 2021

			Quarter		
	1	**2**	**3**	**4**	**Year**
Budgeted sales (units)	20,000	60,000	80,000	40,000	200,000
Add desired ending inventory*	6,000	8,000	4,000	3,000†	3,000
Total needs	26,000	68,000	84,000	43,000	203,000
Less beginning inventory‡	2,000	6,000	8,000	4,000	2,000
Required production (units).	24,000	62,000	76,000	39,000	201,000

Note that production requirements for a quarter are influenced by the desired level of the ending inventory. At Patterson Framing, management believes that an ending inventory equal to 10% of the next quarter's sales strikes the appropriate balance

*Ten percent of the next quarter's sales.
†Estimated.
‡The same as the prior quarter's ending inventory.

INSTANT QUIZ 9-2
Calculate the required production for a company that expects to sell 8,000 units in quarter 4, and has a desired ending inventory of 1,000 units of finished goods and an opening inventory of 500 units.

Inventory Purchases—Merchandising Firm

Patterson Framing prepares a production budget, since it is a *manufacturing* firm. If it were a *merchandising* firm, then instead of a production budget it would prepare a merchandise purchases budget showing the amount of goods to be purchased from its suppliers during the period. The merchandise purchases budget is in the same basic format as the production budget except that it shows goods to be purchased rather than goods to be produced, as shown below:

Budgeted sales	XXXX
Add desired ending merchandise inventory	XXXX
Total needs	XXXX
Less beginning merchandise inventory.	XXXX
Required purchases.	XXXX

The merchandising firm prepares a merchandise purchases budget such as the one above for each item carried in inventory. The merchandise purchases budget can be expressed in terms of either units or the purchase cost of those units.

It is worth noting that for companies selling a service based on the expertise of its employees (e.g., consulting firms, law firms), or that develop products that do not require physical inputs (e.g., software development), neither a production budget nor a merchandise purchases budget is required.

The Direct Materials Purchases Budget

Direct materials purchases budget
A detailed plan showing the amount of raw materials that must be purchased during a period to meet both production and inventory needs.

After the production requirements have been computed, a **direct materials purchases budget** can be prepared. The direct materials purchases budget details the raw materials that must be purchased to meet the production budget and to provide for adequate inventories. The required purchases of raw materials are computed as follows:

Raw materials needed to meet the production schedule.........	XXXX
Add desired ending inventory of raw materials	XXXX
Total raw materials needs..............................	XXXX
Less beginning inventory of raw materials..................	XXXX
Raw materials to be purchased...........................	XXXX

Schedule 3 contains the direct materials purchases budget for Patterson Framing. The only raw material included in that budget is a wood composite, which is the major material used to make the frame. The remaining raw materials, such as glue and finishing nails, are relatively insignificant and are included in variable manufacturing overhead. Notice that materials requirements are first determined in units (metres, kilograms, litres, and so on) and then translated into dollars by multiplying by the appropriate unit cost. Also note that the management of Patterson Framing wants to maintain ending inventories of raw materials equal to 10% of the following quarter's production needs.

SCHEDULE 3

PATTERSON FRAMING LIMITED
Direct Materials Purchases Budget
For the Year Ending December 31, 2021

	Quarter				
	1	**2**	**3**	**4**	**Year**
Required production—units (Schedule 2).................	24,000	62,000	76,000	39,000	201,000
Raw materials needs per unit (1 metre)..................	1	1	1	1	1
Production needs (metres).......	24,000	62,000	76,000	39,000	201,000
Add desired ending inventory	6,200	7,600	3,900	3,000	3,000
Total needs (metres)............	30,200	69,600	79,900	42,000	204,000
Less beginning inventory........	2,400	6,200	7,600	3,900	2,400
Raw materials to be purchased....	27,800	63,400	72,300	38,100	201,600
Cost of raw materials to be purchased at $4.00 per metre...	$ 111,200	$ 253,600	$289,200	$152,400	$806,400

Schedule of Expected Cash Disbursements for Raw Materials

Accounts payable 31/12/20	$ 26,688				$ 26,688
First-quarter purchases: ($111,200 × 70%, 30%).......	77,840	$ 33,360			111,200
Second-quarter purchases: ($253,600 × 70%, 30%).......		177,520	$ 76,080		253,600
Third-quarter purchases: ($289,200 × 70%, 30%).......			202,440	$ 86,760	289,200
Fourth-quarter purchases: $152,400 × 70%)				106,680	106,680
Total cash disbursements........	$104,528	$ 210,880	$278,520	$193,440	$ 787,368

The first line in the direct materials purchases budget contains the required production for each quarter, which is taken directly from the production budget (Schedule 2). Looking at the first quarter, the key elements of the budget are as follows:

- Total production needs: 24,000 frames × 1 metre per frame = 24,000 metres
- Desired ending inventory: 10% × 62,000 metres (the following quarter's needs) = 6,200 metres
- Total needs: 24,000 metres (production) + 6,200 (inventory) = 30,200 metres
- Total purchases: 30,200 metres (total needed) − 2,400 (opening inventory) = 27,800 metres
- Total purchase cost: 27,800 metres × $4.00 per metre = $111,200

As with the production budget, the amounts listed under the Year column are not always the sum of the quarterly amounts. The desired ending inventory of raw materials for the year is the same as the desired ending inventory of raw materials for the fourth quarter. Likewise, the beginning inventory of raw materials for the year is the same as the beginning inventory of raw materials for the first quarter.

The direct materials purchases budget is usually accompanied by a schedule of expected cash disbursements for raw materials. This schedule is needed to prepare the overall cash budget. Disbursements for raw materials consist of payments for purchases on account in prior periods plus any payments for purchases in the current budget period. Schedule 3 contains such a schedule of cash disbursements.

INSTANT QUIZ 9–3

Calculate the total cash disbursements in the second quarter for a company that needs to purchase 31,000 kilograms of raw materials at a cost of $0.20 per kilogram, where 50% of purchases are paid in the quarter the purchase is made and the remainder in the following quarter. Assume that 57,000 kilograms of raw material were purchased in the first quarter at a cost of $0.20 per kilogram.

Ordinarily, companies do not immediately pay their suppliers. At Patterson Framing, the policy is to pay for 70% of purchases in the quarter in which the purchase is made and 30% in the following quarter. So, while the company intends to purchase $111,200 worth of wood composite materials in the first quarter, the company will pay for only 70%, $77,840, in the first quarter and the remaining 30% in the second quarter. The company will also pay $26,688 in the first quarter for wood composite that was purchased on account in the previous quarter, but not yet paid for. This is the beginning balance in the accounts payable. Therefore, the total cash disbursements for wood composite in the first quarter are $104,528.

The Direct Labour Budget

Direct labour budget
A detailed plan showing labour requirements over a specified time period.

The **direct labour budget** is also developed from the production budget. By knowing in advance what will be needed in terms of labour hours throughout the budget year, the company can plan to adjust the number of employees as required.

To compute direct labour requirements, the number of units of finished product to be produced each period (month, quarter, and so on) is multiplied by the number of direct labour-hours required to produce a single unit. For example, 24,000 frames are to be produced in the first quarter, and each frame requires 0.50 direct labour-hours, so a total of 12,000 direct labour-hours (24,000 frames × 0.50 direct labour-hours per frame) will be required. The direct labour requirements can then be translated into expected direct labour costs. How this is done will depend on the labour policy of the firm. In Schedule 4, the management of Patterson Framing has assumed that the direct labour force will be adjusted as the work requirements change from quarter to quarter. In that case, the total direct labour cost is computed simply by multiplying the direct labour-hour requirements by the direct labour rate per hour. For example, the direct labour cost in the first quarter is $240,000 (12,000 direct labour-hours × $20 per direct labour-hour).

SCHEDULE 4

PATTERSON FRAMING LIMITED
Direct Labour Budget
For the Year Ending December 31, 2021

	Quarter				
	1	**2**	**3**	**4**	**Year**
Units to be produced (Schedule 2)......	24,000	62,000	76,000	39,000	201,000
Direct labour time per unit (hours)	0.5	0.5	0.5	0.5	0.5
Total direct labour-hours needed	12,000	31,000	38,000	19,500	100,500
Direct labour cost per hour	$ 20.00	$ 20.00	$ 20.00	$ 20.00	$ 20.00
Total direct labour cost*	$240,000	$620,000	$760,000	$390,000	$2,010,000

*This schedule assumes that the direct labour workforce will be fully adjusted to the workload (i.e., "Total direct labour-hours needed") each quarter.

Many companies have employment policies or union contracts that prevent them from laying off and rehiring workers as needed. Suppose, for example, that Patterson Framing has 40 workers who are classified as direct labour and each of them is guaranteed at least 420 hours of pay each quarter at a rate of $20 per hour. In that case, the minimum direct labour cost for a quarter is as follows:

$$40 \text{ workers} \times 420 \text{ hours} \times \$20 = \$336,000$$

Note that in this case, the direct labour costs for the first quarter would increase to $336,000.

The Manufacturing Overhead Budget

The **manufacturing overhead budget** provides a schedule of all costs of production other than direct materials and direct labour. Schedule 5 shows the manufacturing overhead budget for Patterson Framing. Note how the production costs are separated into variable and fixed components. The variable component is $2 per direct labour-hour. The fixed component is $251,250 per quarter. Because the variable component of the manufacturing overhead depends on direct labour, the first line in the manufacturing overhead budget consists of the budgeted direct labour-hours from the direct labour budget (Schedule 4). The budgeted direct labour-hours in each quarter are multiplied by the variable overhead rate to determine the variable component of manufacturing overhead. For example, the variable manufacturing overhead for the first quarter is

$$\$24,000 = 12,000 \text{ direct labour-hours} \times \$2.00 \text{ per direct labour-hour}$$

This is added to the fixed manufacturing overhead for the quarter to determine the total manufacturing overhead for the quarter as follows: $275,250 = $24,000 (variable) + $251,250 (fixed).

> **Manufacturing overhead budget**
> A detailed plan showing the indirect production costs that will be incurred over a specified time period.

SCHEDULE 5

PATTERSON FRAMING LIMITED
Manufacturing Overhead Budget
For the Year Ending December 31, 2021

	Quarter				
	1	2	3	4	Year
Budgeted direct labour-hours (Schedule 4)	12,000	31,000	38,000	19,500	100,500
Variable overhead rate	$ 2.00	$ 2.00	$ 2.00	$ 2.00	$ 2.00
Variable manufacturing overhead	$ 24,000	$ 62,000	$ 76,000	$ 39,000	$ 201,000
Fixed manufacturing overhead.	251,250	251,250	251,250	251,250	1,005,000
Total manufacturing overhead	275,250	313,250	327,250	290,250	1,206,000
Less depreciation	(30,000)	(30,000)	(30,000)	(30,000)	(120,000)
Cash disbursements for manufacturing overhead.	$245,250	$283,250	$297,250	$260,250	$1,086,000
Total manufacturing overhead (a)					$1,206,000
Budgeted direct labour-hours (b).					100,500
Predetermined overhead rate for the year (a) ÷ (b)					$ 12.00

The last line of Schedule 5 for Patterson Framing shows its budgeted cash disbursements for manufacturing overhead. Since some of the overhead costs are not cash outflows, the total budgeted manufacturing overhead costs must be adjusted to determine the cash disbursements for manufacturing overhead. At Patterson Framing, the only significant non-cash manufacturing overhead cost is depreciation, which is $30,000 per quarter. These non-cash depreciation charges are deducted from the total budgeted manufacturing overhead to determine the expected cash disbursements. Patterson Framing pays all overhead costs involving cash disbursements in the quarter incurred. Note that the company's predetermined overhead rate for the year will be $12 per direct labour-hour, which is determined by dividing the total budgeted manufacturing overhead for the year by the total budgeted direct labour-hours for the year.

The Ending Finished Goods Inventory Budget

Ending finished goods inventory budget
A budget showing the dollar amount of cost expected to appear on the balance sheet for unsold units at the end of a period.

After Schedules 1 through 5 are completed, all of the data needed to compute unit product costs will be available. This computation is needed for two reasons: first, to determine cost of goods sold on the budgeted income statement, and second, to identify the amount to put on the balance sheet inventory account for unsold units. The carrying cost of the unsold units is computed on the **ending finished goods inventory budget**.

The unit product cost computations are shown in Schedule 6 based on absorption costing. For Patterson Framing, the absorption costing unit product cost is $20 per picture frame—consisting of $4 of direct materials, $10 of direct labour, and $6 of manufacturing overhead. For convenience, the manufacturing overhead is applied to units of product on the basis of direct labour-hours. The budgeted carrying cost of the expected ending inventory is $60,000.

SCHEDULE 6

PATTERSON FRAMING LIMITED
Ending Finished Goods Inventory Budget
(absorption costing basis)
For the Year Ending December 31, 2021

Item	Quantity	Cost	Total
Production cost per unit:			
Direct materials	1.0 metre	$ 4.00 per metre	$ 4.00
Direct labour	0.5 hours	$20.00 per hour	10.00
Manufacturing overhead	0.5 hours	$12.00 per hour	6.00
Unit product cost			$ 20.00
Budgeted finished goods inventory:			
Ending finished goods inventory in units			
(Schedule 2)			3,000
Unit product cost (see above)			× $20
Ending finished goods in dollars			$60,000

INSTANT QUIZ 9–4
Calculate the unit product cost where each unit (a) requires 40 kilograms of raw materials that cost $1.50 per kilogram, (b) needs 2 hours of direct labour at a cost of $30 per hour, and (c) has manufacturing overhead applied on the basis of direct labour-hours with an overhead rate of $25 per hour.

The Selling and Administrative Expense Budget

Selling and administrative expense budget
A detailed schedule of planned expenses that will be incurred in areas other than manufacturing during a budget period.

The **selling and administrative expense budget** includes budgeted expenses for areas other than manufacturing. Almost all organizations, regardless of their nature, will have a selling and administrative expense budget. In large organizations, this budget is a compilation of many smaller, individual budgets submitted by department heads and other people responsible for selling and administrative expenses. For example, the marketing manager in a large organization would submit a budget detailing the advertising expenses for each budget period.

Schedule 7 contains the selling and administrative expense budget for Patterson Framing. Like the manufacturing overhead budget, the selling and administrative expense budget is divided into variable and fixed cost components. For Patterson Framing, the variable selling and administrative expense is $2.00 per frame. Consequently, budgeted sales in frames for each quarter are entered at the top of the schedule. These data are taken from the sales budget (Schedule 1). The budgeted variable selling and administrative expenses are determined by multiplying the budgeted frames sold by the variable selling and administrative expense per frame. For example, the budgeted variable selling and administrative expense for the first quarter is $40,000 (20,000 frames × $2.00 per frame). The fixed selling and administrative expenses are then added to the variable selling and administrative expenses to arrive at the total budgeted selling and administrative expenses.

SCHEDULE 7

PATTERSON FRAMING LIMITED
Selling and Administrative Expense Budget
For the Year Ending December 31, 2021

	Quarter				
	1	**2**	**3**	**4**	**Year**
Budgeted sales in units (Schedule 1)...............	20,000	60,000	80,000	40,000	200,000
Variable selling and administrative expenses per frame*...........	$ 2.00	$ 2.00	$ 2.00	$ 2.00	$ 2.00
Budgeted variable expense.........	$ 40,000	$120,000	$160,000	$ 80,000	$400,000
Budgeted fixed selling and administrative expenses					
Advertising..................	20,000	20,000	20,000	20,000	80,000
Senior management salaries......	50,000	50,000	50,000	50,000	200,000
Insurance	19,000	19,000	19,000	19,000	76,000
Property taxes.................	9,000	9,000	9,000	9,000	36,000
Depreciation..................	4,000	4,000	4,000	4,000	16,000
Total budgeted fixed selling and administrative expenses.......	102,000	102,000	102,000	102,000	408,000
Total budgeted selling and administrative expenses.......	142,000	222,000	262,000	182,000	808,000
Less depreciation expense.......	(4,000)	(4,000)	(4,000)	(4,000)	(16,000)
Less insurance expense	(19,000)	(19,000)	(19,000)	(19,000)	(76,000)
Add insurance premium payment			76,000		76,000
Less property tax expense	(9,000)	(9,000)	(9,000)	(9,000)	(36,000)
Add property tax paid				36,000	36,000
Cash disbursements for selling and administrative expenses....	$110,000	$190,000	$306,000	$186,000	$792,000

*Commissions, clerical, and shipping

To determine the cash disbursements for selling and administrative expenses, the total budgeted expenses are adjusted by subtracting any non-cash items included in the budget and adding any cash expenditures not reflected in the budgeted amounts. As shown in Schedule 7, three items must be subtracted: depreciation of $4,000 per quarter because this is a non-cash expense; insurance of $19,000 per quarter because although this is an expense under accrual accounting, it does not represent an actual outflow of cash each quarter; and property taxes of $9,000 because this too is an expense under accrual accounting, but not a cash outflow each quarter. Two cash disbursements are added: the insurance premium payment of $76,000 in the third quarter, and the property tax payment of $36,000 in the fourth quarter. Each of these additions is necessary to reflect the actual timing of the cash outflows for insurance premiums and property taxes.

The Cash Budget

As illustrated in Exhibit 9–1, the cash budget integrates much of the data developed in the preceding steps. It is a good idea to review Exhibit 9–1 to get the big picture firmly in mind before moving on.

The cash budget is composed of four major sections:

1. Receipts section
2. Disbursements section
3. Cash excess or deficiency section
4. Financing section (borrowings, loan repayments, and interest expense)

The receipts section is a list of all of the cash inflows (except for financing) expected during the budget period. Usually, the major source of receipts is sales.

The disbursements section consists of all cash payments that are planned for the budget period. These payments include raw materials purchases (or inventory purchases for merchandising companies), direct labour payments, manufacturing overhead costs, and so on, as contained in their respective budgets. In addition, other cash disbursements are included, such as equipment purchases, dividends, and other cash withdrawals by owners.

The cash excess or deficiency section is computed as follows:

Cash balance, beginning.	XXXX
Add receipts	XXXX
Total cash available before financing	XXXX
Less disbursements.	XXXX
Excess (deficiency) of cash available over disbursements	XXXX

If there is a cash deficiency during any budget period, the company will need to borrow funds. If there is a cash excess during any budget period, after ensuring any targeted minimum cash balance is met, funds borrowed in previous periods may be repaid or the excess funds (i.e., above the targeted cash balance) can be invested.

The financing section provides a detailed account of the borrowings and loan repayments projected to take place during the budget period. It also includes the details of interest payments that will be due on money borrowed. Preparing a cash budget eliminates uncertainty as to what the cash surplus or shortfall will be in two months, six months, or a year from now.

The cash budget should be broken down into time periods that are short enough to capture major fluctuations in cash balances. While a monthly cash budget is most common, many firms budget cash on a weekly or even daily basis, particularly start-up companies where cash needs are particularly high in the early months (or years) of operation. The cash budget for Patterson Framing, prepared on a quarterly basis, appears in Schedule 8. The cash budget builds on the earlier schedules and uses additional data provided as follows:

- The beginning cash balance is $50,000.
- Management plans to spend $80,000 during the year on equipment purchases: $20,000 in each quarter.
- The board of directors has approved cash dividends of $10,000 per quarter.
- Management would like to have a cash balance of at least $50,000 at the beginning of each quarter for contingencies.
- Patterson Framing has an open line of credit with a bank that enables the company to borrow funds as needed at a 4% annual interest rate to a maximum total loan balance of $500,000. To simplify the calculations in the example, all borrowing occurs at the beginning of quarters and all repayments are made at the end of quarters. We also assume that interest on total outstanding loan balances is paid quarterly. However, in practice, banks and other creditors typically require interest payments each month based on the average loan balance outstanding for that period.

The cash budget is prepared one quarter at a time, starting with the first quarter. The first step is to enter the beginning cash balance of $50,000 for the first quarter. This amount represents the cash balance shown on the December 31, 2020, balance sheet. The $540,000 in cash collections from customers is added to the beginning balance to arrive at the total cash available of $590,000. Since the total disbursements are $819,178 and the total cash available is only $590,000, there is a shortfall of $229,178. As management would like to have a beginning cash balance of at least $50,000 for the second quarter, the company will need to borrow $281,998.

SCHEDULE 8

PATTERSON FRAMING LIMITED
Cash Budget
For the Year Ending December 31, 2021

	Schedule	Quarter 1	2	3	4	Year
Cash balance, beginning		$50,000	$50,000	$50,000	$55,514	$50,000
Add collections from sales	1		1,320,000	2,160,000	1,680,000	5,700,000
Total cash available		590,000	1,370,000	2,210,000	1,735,514	5,750,000
Less disbursements:						
Direct materials	3	104,528	210,880	278,520	193,440	787,368
Direct labour	4	240,000	620,000	760,000	390,000	2,010,000
Manufacturing overhead	5	245,250	283,250	297,250	260,250	1,086,000
Selling and administrative	7	110,000	190,000	306,000	186,000	792,000
Income taxes	9	89,400	89,400	89,400	89,400	357,600
Equipment purchases		20,000	20,000	20,000	20,000	80,000
Dividends		10,000	10,000	10,000	10,000	40,000
Total disbursements		819,178	1,423,530	1,761,170	1,149,090	5,152,968
Excess (deficiency) of cash available over disbursements		(229,178)	(53,530)	448,830	586,424	597,032
Financing:						
Borrowings (at beginning)		281,998	107,424	0	0	389,422
Repayment (at end)		0	0	(389,422)	0	(389,422)
Interest*		(2,820)	(3,894)	(3,894)	0	(10,608)
Total financing		279,178	103,530	(393,316)	0	(10,608)
Cash balance, ending		$50,000	$50,000	$55,514	$586,424	$586,424

*The interest payments relate to the total loan balance outstanding each quarter. Calculations for each quarter based on an annual interest rate of 4% are as follows:

Quarter 1: $281,998 \times 4\% \times 0.25 = \$2,820$

Quarters 2 and 3: $(\$281,998 \times 4\% \times 0.25) + (\$107,424 \times 4\% \times 0.25) = \$3,894$

Note that the borrowing of $281,998 takes into account the fact that interest of 1% (4% divided by 4) must be paid at the end of the quarter on the loan balance outstanding for the first quarter. Simple algebra can be used to solve for the borrowing required in the first quarter as follows:

$$\text{Excess cash (Deficiency)} + \text{Borrowing} - \text{Interest on borrowing}$$
$$= \text{Target cash balance}$$
$$\$(229,178) + X - 0.01X = \$50,000$$
$$X = \$281,998$$

Note that in the above formula, the amount of excess cash available in the period will be used whenever that amount is *less* than the target cash balance for the end of the period. For example, if excess cash available for Patterson Framing had been $40,000 at the end of the first quarter, that amount would have been used instead of the deficiency of $229,178. Also note that if there is excess cash available (but it is less than the target balance), that amount would be included in the above formula as a positive value whereas cash deficiency amounts are included as a negative value. Finally, in the above formula, X is the amount to be borrowed at the beginning of the quarter and $0.01X$ represents the interest (1% per quarter in our example) to be paid at the end of the quarter.

The second quarter of the cash budget is handled similarly. Note that the ending cash balance for the first quarter is brought forward as the beginning cash balance for the second quarter. Also note that additional borrowing is required in the second quarter because of the continuing cash shortfall. The same approach is used to solve for the required borrowing in the second quarter except that the amount of interest ($2,820) on the loan outstanding from the first quarter is now included in the formula below because it will have to be paid again at the end of the second quarter. The revised formula for solving the amount of required borrowing in the second quarter is as follows:

$$\$(53,530) - \$2,820 + X - 0.01X = \$50,000$$
$$X = \$107,424$$

In the third quarter, the cash flow situation improves dramatically and the excess cash available over disbursements is $448,830. This makes it possible for the company to repay its loans from the bank, which now total $389,422 ($281,998 + $107,424) along with the $3,894 interest for the third quarter ($389,422 × 1%), for a total of $393,316. The cash balance at the end of the third quarter after repaying the loans and the interest is $55,514, which exceeds the minimum required balance of $50,000.

INSTANT QUIZ 9–5

A company has an opening cash balance of $80,000, expects cash receipts of $800,000 and cash disbursements of $850,000 for the first quarter, and desires an ending cash balance of at least $80,000. Assume an interest rate of 1% per quarter and that interest on outstanding loans must be paid at the end of each quarter. How much cash will the company need to borrow at the beginning of the first quarter?

In the case of Patterson Framing, all loans have been repaid by year-end. If all loans are not repaid and a budgeted income statement or balance sheet is being prepared, then interest must be accrued on the outstanding loans for the period since the last interest payment was made. For example, if interest is normally paid on the 15th of each month and monthly budgeted financial statements are prepared, an interest accrual will be required for the period between the 16th day of the month and the end of the month. This interest will *not* appear on the cash budget (since it has not yet been paid), but it will appear as part of interest expense on the budgeted income statement and as a liability (interest payable) on the budgeted balance sheet.

As with the production and raw materials budgets, the amounts under the Year column in the cash budget are not always the sum of the amounts for the four quarters. In particular, the beginning cash balance for the year is the same as the beginning cash balance for the first quarter, and the ending cash balance is the same as the ending cash balance for the fourth quarter. Also, note that the beginning cash balance for any quarter is the same as the ending cash balance for the previous quarter.

INSTANT QUIZ 9–6

Given your answer to Instant Quiz 9–5, calculate the amount of interest expense for the first quarter.

The Budgeted Income Statement

A budgeted income statement can be prepared from the data developed in Schedules 1 to 8. *The budgeted income statement is one of the key schedules in the budget process.* It shows the company's planned net income for the upcoming budget period, and it stands as a benchmark against which actual company performance can be measured. Schedule 9 contains the budgeted income statement for Patterson Framing.

The Budgeted Balance Sheet

The budgeted balance sheet is developed using the actual balance sheet at the end of the most recent fiscal period as the starting point (e.g., December 31, 2020, for Patterson Framing) and adjusting it for the data contained in the other budgets. Patterson Framing's budgeted balance sheet is presented in Schedule 10. It is important to point out that not all companies that prepare a master budget will necessarily prepare a budgeted balance sheet since responsibility accounting, discussed earlier in the chapter, largely focuses on

PATTERSON FRAMING LIMITED
Budgeted Income Statement
For the Year Ending December 31, 2021

	Schedule	
Sales..	1	$6,000,000
Less cost of goods sold (200,000 frames at $20)........	6	4,000,000
Gross margin		2,000,000
Less selling and administrative expenses...............	7	808,000
Operating income (before taxes and interest)		1,192,000
Income taxes (30% × $1,192,000)*...................		357,600
Interest expense	8	10,608
Net income......................................		$ 823,792

*Income taxes would ordinarily be based on income *after* deducting interest expense. However, because income taxes are affected by the amount of interest expense, and both amounts affect the cash flow calculations in Schedule 8, we simplify the calculations by deducting interest expense after income taxes have been calculated on operating income.

PATTERSON FRAMING LIMITED
Budgeted Balance Sheet
December 31, 2021
Assets

Current assets:		
Cash	$ 586,424 (*a*)	
Accounts receivable.............................	480,000 (*b*)	
Raw materials inventory	12,000 (*c*)	
Finished goods inventory.........................	60,000 (*d*)	
Total current assets..........................		$1,138,424
Plant and equipment:		
Land...	160,000 (*e*)	
Buildings, furniture and equipment.................	1,480,000 (*f*)	
Accumulated depreciation	(720,000) (*g*)	
Plant and equipment, net		920,000
Total assets......................................		$2,058,424

Liabilities and Shareholders' Equity

Current liabilities:		
Accounts payable.................................	$ 45,720 (*h*)	
Shareholders' equity:		
Common shares	600,000 (*i*)	
Retained earnings................................	1,412,704 (*j*)	
Total shareholders' equity		2,012,704
Total liabilities and shareholders' equity..................		$2,058,424

Explanation of December 31, 2021, budgeted balance sheet figures:
a. The ending cash balance, as projected by the cash budget in Schedule 8.
b. Forty percent of fourth-quarter sales, from Schedule 1 ($1,200,000 × 40% = $480,000).
c. From Schedule 3, the ending raw materials inventory is 3,000 metres and costs $4.00 per metre. Therefore, the ending inventory in dollars is $12,000 (3,000 × $4).
d. From Schedule 6.
e. From the December 31, 2020, balance sheet (no change).
f. The December 31, 2020, balance sheet indicated a balance of $1,400,000. During 2021, $80,000 in additional equipment will be purchased (see Schedule 8), bringing the December 31, 2021, balance to $1,480,000.
g. The December 31, 2020, balance sheet indicated a balance of $584,000. During 2021, $136,000 of depreciation will be taken ($120,000 on Schedule 5 and $16,000 on Schedule 7), bringing the December 31, 2021, balance to $720,000.
h. Thirty percent of the fourth-quarter raw materials purchases, from Schedule 3 ($152,400 × 30% = $45,720).
i. From the December 31, 2020, balance sheet (no change).
j. December 31, 2020, balance.............. $ 628,912
      Add net income, from Schedule 9......... 823,792
                                              1,452,704
      Deduct dividends paid, from Schedule 8 ... 40,000
      December 31, 2021, balance.............. $1,412,704

comparing actual results for revenues and costs to budgeted amounts. As such, a budgeted income statement and a cash budget are commonly prepared, but practice varies with respect to budgeted balance sheets.

It is worth pointing out that we have simplified the treatment of income taxes on the income statement (Schedule 9) by assuming an effective rate of 30%. Most for-profit corporations in Canada are required to pay income taxes on taxable income, but calculating the effective rate is complex and is typically covered in introductory courses on taxation. However, companies that budget positive operating income calculate a budgeted effective tax rate and include income tax expense as an additional item on the budgeted income statement, as we have done in our example.

LEARNING OBJECTIVE ❸

Prepare a flexible budget, and explain the need for the flexible budget approach.

Static budget
A budget designed for only the planned level of activity.

Flexible budget
A budget that provides estimates of what revenues and costs should be for any level of activity within a specified range.

■ FLEXIBLE BUDGET

The budgets presented in Schedules 1 to 10 are often referred to as static budgets. A **static budget** is prepared only for the planned or budgeted level of activity. In our example, that level of activity was the forecast sales volume of 200,000 units. While this approach is suitable for planning, it can be inadequate for control if the actual level of activity during a period differs significantly from the budgeted level. Specifically, the problem that arises when a significant difference exists between actual and budgeted levels of activity is that it becomes very difficult to evaluate how well a manager did in generating revenues and controlling costs. For example, if actual activity levels are significantly higher than expected for Patterson Framing, actual revenues and variable costs will be considerably higher than static budget amounts. Should we conclude that the manager did a good job in generating revenues, but not so well in controlling costs? Clearly this is not a fair evaluation since the costs are above budget because the volume of actual activity exceeded the static budget amount. Thus, an alternative approach is needed to restore the usefulness of budgets as a control tool.

Flexible budgets take into account changes in revenues and costs expected to occur as a consequence of changes in actual activity. A **flexible budget** provides estimates of what revenues and costs should be for any level of activity within a specified range. When a flexible budget is used in performance evaluation, actual revenues and costs are compared to what the *revenues and costs should have been for the actual level of activity during the period* rather than to the planned budgeted revenues and costs from the static budget. This is a very important distinction—particularly for variable costs. If adjustments for the level of activity are not made, it is very difficult to interpret differences between actual and budgeted revenues and costs.

How a Flexible Budget Works

The basic idea of the flexible budget approach is that the budget is adjusted to show what revenues and costs *should be* for a specific level of activity. To illustrate how a flexible budget works, we build on the Patterson Framing master budget example to develop income statements for different levels of activity within a range of annual sales of 180,000 units to 220,000 units, or 10% below or above the static budget level. To simplify the example, we have omitted interest expense and income tax expense, although both could easily be included using the steps presented in preparing the static budget. Note that although Exhibit 9–2 presents an annual flexible budget, the same approach can be used in developing flexible budgets for shorter reporting periods, such as quarters or months. Also note that the flexible budget income statements in Exhibit 9–2 were prepared using the variable costing approach covered in Chapter 8. As a result, the operating income shown in Exhibit 9–2 for sales of 200,000 units is $1,187,000, while the operating income shown in Schedule 9 is $1,192,000. This difference of $5,000 arises because operating income in Schedule 9 was calculated using absorption costing and an additional 1,000 units of finished goods inventory were added in 2021 (Schedule 2). The additional manufacturing overhead deferred in finished goods inventory using absorption costing is $5,000: 1,000 units × $5.00 per unit of

EXHIBIT 9–2   Flexible Budget Income Statement

PATTERSON FRAMING LIMITED
Flexible Budget
For the Year Ending December 31, 2021

	Budgeted Amount per Unit	Sales in Units		
		180,000	200,000	220,000
Sales	$30.00	$5,400,000	$6,000,000	$6,600,000
Less variable expenses:				
Direct materials*	4.00	720,000	800,000	880,000
Direct labour*	10.00	1,800,000	2,000,000	2,200,000
Variable manufacturing overhead#	1.00	180,000	200,000	220,000
Selling and administrative†	2.00	360,000	400,000	440,000
Total variable expenses	17.00	3,060,000	3,400,000	3,740,000
Contribution margin	$13.00	2,340,000	2,600,000	2,860,000
Less fixed expenses:				
Manufacturing overhead**		1,005,000	1,005,000	1,005,000
Selling and administrative##		408,000	408,000	408,000
Total fixed expenses		1,413,000	1,413,000	1,413,000
Operating income		$ 927,000	$1,187,000	$1,447,000

*Per unit amount as per Schedule 6
#Variable overhead cost per hour (Schedule 5) multiplied by direct labour-hours per unit (Schedule 6): $2 × 0.5 = $1.00
†Per unit amount as per Schedule 7
**Total budgeted fixed overhead expense as per Schedule 5
##Total budgeted fixed selling and administrative expenses as per Schedule 7

fixed overhead ($10 per hour × 0.5 hours per unit). The rate of $10 per hour for fixed overhead is based on the total rate of $12 per hour (Schedule 6) less $2 per hour for variable overhead (Schedule 5). We use variable costing to emphasize the revenue and cost behaviour patterns expected over this relevant range of activity. Specifically, the selling price and variable costs per unit are expected to remain constant, while total fixed costs are not expected to change over the relevant range.

The calculation of the revenues and expenses in Exhibit 9–2 is straightforward. The amounts *per unit* for sales and variable expenses are multiplied by the activity level (units) to arrive at the totals for the year. For example, for an activity level of 180,000 units, total sales are calculated as $30.00 × 180,000 = $5,400,000. Each of the variable expense line items is calculated in a similar fashion. Fixed costs are not expected to change over the relevant range of activity, so they stay the same for each activity level shown in Exhibit 9–2. The flexible budget provides a useful tool in estimating operating income at different levels of activity using the cost–volume–profit concepts discussed in Chapter 4. As illustrated in Exhibit 9–2, a 20,000-unit change in sales volume above or below the budgeted level of 200,000 units causes a $260,000 change in operating income, which can be calculated as 20,000 units × $13.00 per unit contribution margin. Importantly, a flexible budget can be developed for any level of activity within the relevant range of activity. Thus, if actual sales volume for the year is 209,000 units, a flexible budget can be prepared showing what revenues and costs should have been for that level of activity.

Forecasts

A planning tool often used by companies is the **forecast**. Like a budget, a forecast represents management's estimates of revenues and expenses likely to occur in a future period.

Forecast
The quantification of future plans.

However, forecasts are typically prepared *after* a fiscal period has started and can cover periods as short as a week or a month or as long as several years. An advantage of using a forecast as a planning tool after the fiscal period has started is that it will be based on current information that may differ from the information used to prepare the static budget. For example, after the first six months of a fiscal period have been completed, managers can prepare a forecast for the final six months using up-to-date information about demand for products or services, consumer trends, competitors' recent product or service offerings, product or service costs, and so on.

The bigger the changes in a company's operating environment since the time the static budget was prepared, the more likely the forecast is to differ from the budget. Importantly, if these changes are big enough, the forecast will replace the static budget for purposes of making planning decisions over the forecast period. Decisions related to production scheduling, product or service pricing, development of new marketing campaigns, staffing decisions, and so on, may well differ from what was originally envisioned in the master budget. Similar to how a flexible budget allows for a more meaningful comparison of actual results to budget when activity levels have changed compared to the static budget, a forecast is a better planning tool than the static budget when a company's operating conditions have significantly changed after the year began.

Cash flow forecast
An estimation of future cash inflows and cash outflows from operating activities, investing activities, and financing activities.

A particularly common type of forecast used by many companies is a **cash flow forecast**. Using current information about expected revenues and expenses, cash flow forecasts represent management's best estimates of cash inflows and outflows related to operations, investing activities, and financing activities. The cash flow forecast is like the cash budget discussed earlier, but is based on more current information. For some companies, particularly those at the start-up phase, cash flow forecasts are prepared on a highly frequent basis, sometimes weekly. For companies at this early stage, it is critical that management frequently monitors expected cash inflows and outflows to ensure the company can meet its obligations to suppliers, creditors, employees, and other stakeholders.

LEARNING OBJECTIVE ❹
Prepare a performance report using the flexible budget approach.

Flexible budget variance
The difference between actual and flexible budget amounts for revenues and expenses.

◼ USING THE FLEXIBLE BUDGETING CONCEPT IN PERFORMANCE EVALUATION

To demonstrate the control benefits of using the flexible budgeting approach to evaluate performance, we continue with our example of Patterson Framing. The flexible budget performance report shown in Exhibit 9–3 has three main components. First, it presents actual revenues and expenses for the year, given an actual sales volume of 220,000 units. Second, it contains a flexible budget based on actual sales of 220,000 units, using the revenues and expenses from Exhibit 9–2. Third, it shows the **flexible budget variance**, the difference between actual results and the flexible budget, with unfavourable and favourable variances labelled "U" and "F," respectively. As shown in Exhibit 9–3, actual operating income for 2021 was $1,087,400, while the flexible budget indicates that at an actual volume of 220,000 unit sales $1,447,000 should have been earned. The flexible budget variances for the individual line items tell the story as to why the unfavourable operating income variance of $359,600 occurred. The largest contributing factor was the unfavourable sales variance of $330,000, so management will want to determine why the actual selling price of $28.50 per unit ($6,270,000 ÷ 220,000) differed from the budget of $30 per unit. Cost control also appears to have been a problem for many of the variable expenses at Patterson Framing, which in total were $28,600 above budget. As will be further explored in Chapter 10, the flexible budget variances for manufacturing costs (direct materials, direct labour, variable overhead) could have been caused by actual unit prices for production inputs differing from budget, or the actual quantities used in producing the 220,000 units differing from budget. Management will want to know the extent to which these two factors contributed to the variances shown in Exhibit 9–3.

EXHIBIT 9–3   Flexible Budget Performance Report

PATTERSON FRAMING LIMITED
Flexible Budget Performance Report
For the Year Ending December 31, 2021

	Budgeted Amount per Unit	Actual (220,000 units)	Flexible Budget (220,000 units)	Flexible Budget Variance††	
Sales...............................	$30.00	$6,270,000	$6,600,000	$330,000	U
Less variable expenses:					
Direct materials*....................	4.00	869,000	880,000	11,000	F
Direct labour*.....................	10.00	2,244,000	2,200,000	44,000	U
Variable manufacturing overhead#......	1.00	228,800	220,000	8,800	U
Selling and administrative†...........	2.00	426,800	440,000	13,200	F
Total variable expenses..............	17.00	3,768,600	3,740,000	28,600	U
Contribution margin...................	$13.00	2,501,400	2,860,000	358,600	U
Less fixed expenses:					
Manufacturing overhead**............		1,012,000	1,005,000	7,000	U
Selling and administrative##...........		402,000	408,000	6,000	F
Total fixed expenses.................		1,414,000	1,413,000	1,000	U
Operating income.....................		$1,087,400	$1,447,000	$359,600	U

*Per unit amount as per Schedule 6
#Variable overhead cost per hour (Schedule 5) multiplied by direct labour-hours per unit (Schedule 6): $2 × 0.5 = $1.00
†Per unit amount as per Schedule 7
**Total budgeted fixed overhead expense as per Schedule 5
##Total budgeted fixed selling and administrative expenses as per Schedule 7
††U = unfavourable variance; F = favourable variance

The value of the flexible budget performance report for control purposes can be further illustrated by examining Exhibit 9–4, which presents a static budget performance report. The **static budget variance** in Exhibit 9–4 represents the differences between actual results at an activity level of 220,000 units and the static budget amounts at an activity level of 200,000 units. The sales variance is $270,000 favourable, suggesting that Patterson Framing had a good year overall. However, this sales variance is very misleading as it is attributable to selling 20,000 more units than planned per the static budget. While selling more units than planned is a good thing from a revenue perspective, the static budget variances for the variable expense items are all unfavourable because of this difference between the static budget level of activity and actual sales. Accordingly, the static budget variances for variable expenses are not useful in evaluating how well managers did at controlling costs at actual levels of activity. Hence, the key benefit of the flexible budget performance report shown in Exhibit 9–3 is that it removes the effects of any volume differences between actual results and the static budget. This allows for a much more meaningful analysis of how well managers did in generating revenue and controlling costs.

Static budget variance
The difference between actual and static budget amounts for revenues and expenses.

INSTANT QUIZ 9-7
Assume a company prepares a static budget based on sales of 25,000 units and a contribution margin of $2.50 per unit. If actual sales are 20,000 units, calculate the contribution margin for the flexible budget.

EXHIBIT 9–4 Static Budget Performance Report

PATTERSON FRAMING LIMITED
Static Budget Performance Report
For the Year Ending December 31, 2021

	Budgeted Amount per Unit	Actual (220,000 units)	Static Budget (220,000 units)	Static Budget Variance††	
Sales...............................	$30.00	$6,270,000	$6,000,000	$270,000	F
Less variable expenses:					
Direct materials*....................	4.00	869,000	800,000	69,000	U
Direct labour*......................	10.00	2,244,000	2,000,000	244,000	U
Variable manufacturing overhead#.......	1.00	228,800	200,000	28,800	U
Selling and administrative†	2.00	426,800	400,000	26,800	U
Total variable expenses	17.00	3,768,600	3,400,000	368,600	U
Contribution margin..................	$13.00	2,501,400	2,600,000	98,600	U
Less fixed expenses:					
Manufacturing overhead**............		1,012,000	1,005,000	7,000	U
Selling and administrative##...........		402,000	408,000	6,000	F
Total fixed expenses.................		1,414,000	1,413,000	1,000	U
Operating income....................		$1,087,400	$1,187,000	$ 99,600	U

*Per unit amount as per Schedule 6
#Variable overhead cost per hour (Schedule 5) multiplied by direct labour-hours per unit (Schedule 6): $2 × 0.5 = $1.00
†Per unit amount as per Schedule 7
**Total budgeted fixed overhead expense as per Schedule 5
##Total budgeted fixed selling and administrative expenses as per Schedule 7
††U = unfavourable variance; F = favourable variance

Finally, some companies integrate the information contained in Exhibits 9–3 and 9–4 in preparing a comprehensive performance report that includes actual results along with both flexible and static budget amounts. An example of this type of report is shown in Exhibit 9–5. Note that the total unfavourable static budget variance of $99,600 is the same as calculated in Exhibit 9–4, but Exhibit 9–5 shows that it consists of two components: (1) an unfavourable flexible budget variance of $359,600 from Exhibit 9–3 and (2) a favourable $260,000 *sales volume variance*. The **sales volume variance** represents the difference between the flexible and static budget amounts for revenues and expenses caused by actual activity levels differing from the static budget amounts. Because both the flexible and static budgets are prepared using budgeted amounts per unit, the only difference that can arise between these two budgets relates to the actual level of activity differing from the static budget level. For example, the favourable sales volume variance of $600,000 for sales is calculated as follows: (220,000 units − 200,000 units) × $30 per unit. The sales volume variances for variable expenses are calculated in a similar fashion. Because total budgeted fixed expenses should be constant within the relevant range of activity, no differences between the flexible and static budgets arise for these items. The advantage of preparing a comprehensive report such as that shown in Exhibit 9–5 is that it helps managers isolate the part of the static budget variance caused solely by volume (activity) differences from the part caused by other factors, such as actual unit prices differing from budget. In Chapter 10, we will further explore the factors that can cause sales volume variances.

Sales volume variance
The difference between flexible and static budget amounts for revenues and expenses caused by actual activity levels differing from static budget amounts.

EXHIBIT 9–5   Comprehensive Performance Report

PATTERSON FRAMING LIMITED
Comprehensive Performance Report†
For the Year Ending December 31, 2021

	Actual (220,000 units)	Flexible Budget Variance*	Flexible Budget (220,000 units)	Sales Volume Variance*	Static Budget (200,000 units)
Sales	$6,270,000	$330,000 U	$6,600,000	$600,000 F	$6,000,000
Less variable expenses:					
Direct materials	869,000	11,000 F	880,000	80,000 U	800,000
Direct labour	2,244,000	44,000 U	2,200,000	200,000 U	2,000,000
Variable manufacturing overhead	228,800	8,800 U	220,000	20,000 U	200,000
Selling and administrative†	426,800	13,200 F	440,000	40,000 U	400,000
Total variable expenses	3,768,600	28,600 U	3,740,000	340,000 U	3,400,000
Contribution margin	2,501,400	358,600 U	2,860,000	260,000 F	2,600,000
Less fixed expenses:					
Manufacturing overhead	1,012,000	7,000 U	1,005,000	0	1,005,000
Selling and administrative	402,000	6,000 F	408,000	0	408,000
Total fixed expenses	1,414,000	1,000 U	1,413,000	0	1,413,000
Operating income	$1,087,400	$359,600 U	$1,447,000	$260,000 F	$1,187,000

$99,600 U
Total static budget variance

*U = unfavourable variance; F = favourable variance.
†All actual and flexible budget amounts as per Exhibit 9–3; all static budget amounts as per Exhibit 9–4.

INSTANT QUIZ 9–8
Given the details in Instant Quiz 9–7, calculate the flexible budget variance and sales volume variance if the actual contribution margin, based on selling 20,000 units, is $48,000.

KNOWLEDGE IN ACTION

Managers can apply their knowledge about budgeting when:

- Determining how difficult budget targets should be to attain and whether or not rewards should be linked to attainment of those targets
- Forecasting sales and estimating the impact sales levels will have on expenses
- Estimating operating income in future periods
- Making operational decisions such as planning inventory levels (see online Appendix 9A), staffing levels, allocating resources and production scheduling
- Estimating cash inflows and outflows and arranging in advance for any short-term borrowing
- Evaluating actual performance compared to static budget amounts or flexible budget amounts
- Identifying the causes of differences between actual results and budgeted amounts (more on this in Chapter 10)

SUMMARY

- Budgets play a dual role in organizations (planning and control) and offer several benefits. These include the communication of management's plans, allocation of resources, coordination of activities, and establishment of goals and objectives that can be used to evaluate subsequent performance. **[LO1]**
- Budgets represent a key element of responsibility accounting systems, whereby managers are held responsible for revenue and cost items over which they have significant influence. The comparison of actual and budgeted results is a common feature of such systems. **[LO1]**
- The preparation of a master budget involves numerous interrelated schedules and begins with the development of the sales budget, which is based on the sales forecast. For a manufacturing company, once the sales budget has been set, the production budget can be prepared since it depends on how many units are to be sold. The production budget determines how many units are to be produced. After it has been prepared, the various manufacturing cost budgets and selling and administrative budgets can be developed. **[LO2]**
- After the detailed budget schedules have been completed, the cash budget, budgeted income statement, and budgeted balance sheet can be prepared, which collectively provide an overall financial summary of the budget. **[LO2]**
- Some companies use flexible budgets to address the limitations that arise with static budgets when actual activity levels differ significantly from budgeted levels. Preparing flexible budgets involves restating the budget at the end of a reporting period using actual activity levels and budgeted per unit amounts for revenues and variable expenses. A flexible budget provides a better tool for evaluating managers' performance in generating revenue and controlling costs, given the actual volume of activity. **[LO3]**
- Preparing flexible budgets also permits companies to prepare performance reports that decompose the difference between actual results and the static budget into flexible budget variances and sales volume variances. This approach is helpful in isolating the cause of variances and forms the basis for further investigation. **[LO4]**

REVIEW PROBLEM: COMPLETING A MASTER BUDGET

The following data are for preparation of a second-quarter master budget for Soper Company, a wholesale distributor of consumer goods.

a.   At the end of the previous quarter (March 31), the organization's balance sheet showed the following account balances:

Cash	$ 8,000	
Accounts receivable	20,000	
Inventory	36,000	
Buildings and equipment (net)	120,000	
Accounts payable		$ 21,750
Common shares		150,000
Retained earnings		12,250
	$184,000	$184,000

b.   Actual sales for March and budgeted sales for April through July are as follows:

March (actual)	$50,000
April	$60,000
May	$72,000
June	$90,000
July	$48,000

c.   Sales are 60% for cash and 40% on credit. All payments on credit sales are collected in the month following the sale. The accounts receivable at March 31 are a result of March credit sales.

d.   The company's gross margin is 25% of sales.

e. Monthly expenses are as follows: commissions, 12% of sales; rent, $2,500 per month; other expenses (excluding depreciation), 6% of sales. Assume that these expenses are paid monthly. Depreciation is $900 per month (includes depreciation on new assets).

f. Each month's ending inventory should equal 80% of the following month's cost of goods sold.

g. Half of a month's inventory purchases are paid for in the month of purchase and half in the following month. The accounts payable at March 31 is the result of March purchases for inventory.

h. Equipment costing $1,500 will be purchased in April.

i. The company must maintain a minimum cash balance of $4,000. An open line of credit is available at a local bank. All borrowing is done at the beginning of a month, and all repayments are made at the end of a month. The monthly interest rate is 1%. Interest must be paid at the end of each month based on the total loans outstanding for that month.

Required:

Using the data above, complete the following statements and schedules for the second quarter:

1. Schedule of expected cash collections:

	April	May	June	Quarter
Schedule of Expected Cash Collections				
Cash sales....................................	$36,000			
Credit sales*.................................	20,000			
Total collections.............................	$56,000			

*40% of prior month's sales

2. *a.* Merchandise purchases budget:

	April	May	June	Quarter
Budgeted cost of goods sold	$45,000*	$54,000		
Add desired ending inventory	43,200†			
Total needs.................................	88,200			
Less beginning inventory....................	36,000			
Required purchases	$52,200			

*$60,000 sales × 75% = $45,000
†$54,000 × 80% = $43,200

b. Schedule of expected cash disbursements for merchandise purchases:

	April	May	June	Quarter
For March purchases	$21,750			$21,750
For April purchases	26,100	$26,100		52,200
For May purchases.........................				
For June purchases.........................				
Total cash disbursements for purchases.........	$47,850			

3. Schedule of expected cash disbursements for selling and administrative expenses:

	April	May	June	Quarter
Commissions	$ 7,200			
Rent	2,500			
Other expenses............................	3,600			
Total cash disbursements for selling and administrative expenses...................	$13,300			

4.   Cash budget:

	April	May	June	Quarter
Cash balance, beginning....................	$ 8,000			
Add cash collections.......................	56,000			
Total cash available.......................	64,000			
Less cash disbursements:				
For inventory purchases..................	47,850			
For selling and administrative expenses......	13,300			
For equipment purchases	1,500			
Total cash disbursements	62,650			
Excess (deficiency) of cash	$ 1,350			
Financing				
Borrowings*...........................	2,677			
Repayments...........................				
Interest**	(27)			
Total financing	2,650			
Cash balance, ending	$ 4,000			

*$1,350 + X − .01X = $4,000; X = $2,677 rounded
**$2,677 × 1%

5.   Prepare an absorption costing income statement for the quarter ending June 30, as shown in Schedule 9.

6.   Prepare a balance sheet as at June 30.

Solution to Review Problem

1.

Schedule of Expected Cash Collections				
	April	May	June	Quarter
Cash sales...............................	$36,000	$43,200	$54,000	$133,200
Credit sales*............................	20,000	24,000	28,800	72,800
Total collections........................	$56,000	$67,200	$82,800	$206,000

*40% of the preceding month's sales

2.   *a.*   Merchandise purchases budget:

	April	May	June	Quarter
Budgeted cost of goods sold	$45,000*	$ 54,000	$67,500	$166,500
Add desired ending inventory**	43,200	54,000	28,800	28,800
Total needs............................	88,200	108,000	96,300	195,300
Less beginning inventory.................	36,000	43,200	54,000	36,000
Required purchases	$52,200	$ 64,800	$42,300	$159,300

*$60,000 sales × 75% = $45,000
**April 30: $54,000 × 80%; June 30: July sales $48,000 × 75% cost ratio × 80%

b.   Schedule of cash disbursements for purchases:

	April	May	June	Quarter
For March purchases	$21,750			$ 21,750
For April purchases	26,100*	$26,100		52,200
For May purchases...................		32,400**	$32,400	64,800
For June purchases...................			21,150***	21,150
Total cash disbursements	$47,850	$58,500	$53,550	$159,900

*April purchases × 50%; May purchases × 50%; June purchases × 50%

3. Schedule of cash disbursements for selling and administrative expenses:

	April	May	June	Quarter
Commissions (12% of sales)	$ 7,200	$ 8,640	$10,800	$26,640
Rent (given)	2,500	2,500	2,500	7,500
Other expenses (6% of sales)	3,600	4,320	5,400	13,320
Total cash disbursements for selling and administrative expenses	$13,300	$15,460	$18,700	$47,460

4. Cash budget:

	April	May	June	Quarter
Cash balance, beginning	$ 8,000	$ 4,000	$ 4,000	$ 8,000
Add cash collections	56,000	67,200	82,800	206,000
Total cash available	64,000	71,200	86,800	214,000
Less disbursements:				
For inventory purchases	47,850	58,500	53,550	159,900
For selling and administrative expenses . .	13,300	15,460	18,700	47,460
For equipment purchases	1,500	0	0	1,500
Total disbursements	62,650	73,960	72,250	208,860
Excess (deficiency) of cash	1,350	(2,760)	14,550	5,140
Financing:				
Borrowings*	2,677	6,856	0	9,553
Repayments	0	0	(9,553)	(9,533)
Interest**	(27)	(96)	(96)	(219)
Total financing	2,650	6,760	(9,629)	(219)
Cash balance, ending	$ 4,000	$ 4,000	$ 4,921	$ 4,921

*April: $1,350 + X − .01X = $4,000; X = $2,677 rounded
 May: ($2,760) + X − .01X − $27 = $4,000; X = $6,856 (rounded)
**April: $2,677 × 1%; May and June ($2,677 + $6,856) × 1% = $96

5. Income statement:

SOPER COMPANY Income Statement For the Quarter Ended June 30		
Sales ($60,000 + $72,000 + $90,000)		$222,000
Cost of goods sold (CGS):		
Beginning inventory (given)	$ 36,000	
Add purchases (Part 2)	159,300	
Goods available for sale	195,300	
Ending inventory (Part 2)	28,800	166,500
Gross margin		55,500
Selling and administrative expenses:		
Commissions (Part 3)	26,640	
Rent (Part 3)	7,500	
Depreciation ($900 × 3)	2,700	
Other expenses (Part 3)	13,320	50,160
Operating income		5,340
Less interest expense (Part 4)		219
Net income		$ 5,121

Note: CGS can also be computed as follows: Sales of $225,000 × 75% = $166,500

6. Balance sheet:

SOPER COMPANY Balance Sheet June 30		
Assets		
Current assets:		
Cash (Part 4)...		$ 4,921
Accounts receivable (40% × $90,000)................................		36,000
Inventory (Part 2)...		28,800
Total current assets..		69,721
Buildings and equipment, net ($120,000 + $1,500 − $2,700).................		118,800
Total assets..		$188,521
Liabilities and Shareholders' Equity		
Current liabilities:		
Accounts payable (Part 2: 50% × $42,300).................		$ 21,150
Shareholders' equity:		
Common shares	$150,000	
Retained earnings*...................................	17,371	167,371
Total liabilities and shareholders' equity...................		$188,521
*Retained earnings, beginning...........................	$ 12,250	
Add net income......................................	5,121	
Retained earnings, ending...............................	$ 17,371	

DISCUSSION CASE

DISCUSSION CASE 9–1
Are there any circumstances under which creating some budget slack might be acceptable, or even desirable, from the organization's perspective? Explain your answer.

QUESTIONS

9–1 Give an example of how preparing a budget can lead to the coordination of activities between different functional areas in an organization.

9–2 As part of the control system, why are budget results compared to actual results?

9–3 What is a perpetual or continuous budget?

9–4 What is benchmarking?

9–5 Why is the sales forecast the starting point in budgeting?

9–6 What are some examples of estimates or assumptions required to prepare the master budget?

9–7 Why is depreciation not included in the cash budget?

9–8 What is a participative budget? What are the major advantages of participative budgets?

9–9 What is budget slack? Why might managers be tempted to build slack into their budgets?

9–10 What is a challenging but attainable budget?

9–11 What is the sales budget and why is it so important in the budgeting process?

9–12 For a professional services company such as a law firm, which type of expenses would likely make up the largest proportion of total expenses in their budget? Why?

9–13 Describe the difference between a static budget and a flexible budget.

9–14 What are some possible causes of an unfavourable flexible budget variance for direct labour?

9–15 What is the difference between a forecast and a static budget? What is the primary purpose of a forecast?

FOUNDATIONAL EXERCISES

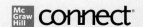

[LO2]

Morganton Company makes one product, and has provided the following information to help prepare the master budget for its first four months of operations:

a.   The budgeted selling price per unit is $70. Budgeted unit sales for June, July, August, and September are 8,400, 10,000, 12,000, and 13,000 units, respectively. All sales are on credit.

b.   Forty percent of credit sales are collected in the month of the sale and 60% in the following month.

c.   The ending finished goods inventory equals 20% of the following month's unit sales.

d.   The ending raw materials inventory equals 10% of the following month's raw materials production needs. Each unit of finished goods requires 5 kilograms of raw materials. The raw materials cost $2.00 per kilogram.

e.   Thirty percent of raw materials purchases are paid for in the month of purchase and 70% in the following month.

f.   The direct labour wage rate is $15 per hour. Each unit of finished goods requires two direct labour-hours.

g.   The variable selling and administrative expense per unit sold is $1.80. The fixed selling and administrative expense per month is $60,000.

9–1 What are the budgeted sales for July?

9–2 What are the expected cash collections for July?

9–3 What is the accounts receivable balance at the end of July?

9–4 According to the production budget, how many units should be produced in July?

9–5 If 61,000 kilograms of raw materials are needed to meet production in August, how many kilograms of raw materials should be purchased in July?

9–6 What is the estimated cost of raw materials purchases for July?

9–7 If the cost of raw material purchases in June is $88,880, what are the estimated cash disbursements for raw materials purchases in July?

9–8 What is the estimated accounts payable balance at the end of July?

9–9 What is the estimated raw materials inventory balance at the end of July?

9–10 What is the total estimated direct labour cost for July assuming the direct labour workforce is adjusted to match the hours required to produce the forecast number of units produced?

9–11 If the company always uses an estimated predetermined plantwide overhead rate of $10 per direct labour-hour, what is the estimated unit product cost?

9–12 What is the estimated finished goods inventory balance at the end of July?

9–13 What is the estimated cost of goods sold and gross margin for July?

9–14 What is the estimated total selling and administrative expense for July?

9–15 What is the estimated operating income for July?

EXERCISES

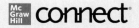

EXERCISE 9–1 Schedule of Expected Cash Collections [LO2]

Silver Company makes a product that is very popular as a Mother's Day gift. Thus, peak sales occur in May of each year, as shown in the company's sales budget for the second quarter given below:

	April	May	June	Total
Budgeted sales (all on account)	$300,000	$500,000	$200,000	$1,000,000

From past experience, the company has learned that 20% of a month's sales are collected in the month of sale, another 70% are collected in the month following sale, and the remaining 10% are collected in the second month following sale. Bad debts are negligible and can be ignored. February sales totalled $230,000, and March sales totalled $260,000.

Required:

a.   Prepare a schedule of expected cash collections from sales, by month and in total, for the second quarter.

b.   Assume that the company will prepare a budgeted balance sheet as of June 30. Compute the accounts receivable as of that date.

EXERCISE 9–2 Sales and Production Budget [LO2]

Fortin Limited produces and sells a single product, a wearable LED light for runners and cyclists. The analytics group at Fortin Limited has developed the following estimates for unit sales in the upcoming year.

	First Quarter	Second Quarter	Third Quarter	Fourth Quarter
Budgeted unit sales	24,000	22,500	21,000	22,000

The light sells for $40 per unit and all sales are on account. 75% of sales are expected to be collected in the month of sale, with the remainder in the following month. Accounts receivable at the beginning of the quarter were $184,000 and will all be collected during the first quarter of the year.

At the end of the previous quarter there were 2,400 units in finished goods inventory. The desired ending finished goods inventory at the end of each quarter is 10% of the next quarter's budgeted sales. Management expects sales in the fourth quarter of the upcoming year to be the same as the first quarter of the following year.

Required:
1. Prepare the company's sales budget and schedule of expected cash collections.
2. Prepare the company's production budget for the upcoming fiscal year.

EXERCISE 9–3 Direct Materials Purchases Budget [LO2]

Refer to the data in Exercise 9–2. Each light requires two separate LED bulbs, each of which costs $2. To ensure enough LED bulbs are on hand to support short-term production if a problem arises with the sole supplier, Fortin Limited maintains an ending inventory of 10% of the following quarter's production needs. A total of 4,800 LED bulbs will be on hand to start the first quarter of the upcoming fiscal year.

Required:
Prepare a direct materials purchases budget for LED bulbs, by quarter and in total, for the upcoming fiscal year. At the bottom of your budget, show the dollar amount of purchases for each quarter and for the year in total.

EXERCISE 9–4 Direct Labour Budget [LO2]

Refer to the data in Exercise 9–2. Each light requires 0.75 direct labour-hours for assembly and employees are paid $20 per hour.

Required:
Prepare the company's direct labour budget for the upcoming fiscal year, assuming that the direct labour workforce is adjusted each quarter to match the number of hours required to produce the forecast number of units.

CHECK FIGURE
1. Total direct labour cost 1st quarter = $357,740; 2. Total direct labour cost 3rd quarter = $316,500.

EXERCISE 9–5 Manufacturing Overhead Budget [LO2]

The direct labour budget of Yuvwell Corporation for the upcoming fiscal year contains the following details concerning budgeted direct labour-hours:

	1st Quarter	2nd Quarter	3rd Quarter	4th Quarter
Budgeted direct labour-hours	8,000	8,200	8,500	7,800

The company's variable manufacturing overhead rate is $3.25 per direct labour-hour and the company's fixed manufacturing overhead is $48,000 per quarter. The only non-cash item included in fixed manufacturing overhead is depreciation, which is $16,000 per quarter.

Required:
1. Construct the company's manufacturing overhead budget for the upcoming fiscal year.
2. Compute the company's manufacturing overhead rate (including both variable and fixed manufacturing overhead) for the upcoming fiscal year. Round off to the nearest whole cent.

EXERCISE 9–6 Selling and Administrative Expense Budget [LO2]

The budgeted unit sales of Weller Company for the upcoming fiscal year are provided below:

	1st Quarter	2nd Quarter	3rd Quarter	4th Quarter
Budgeted unit sales...........	15,000	16,000	14,000	13,000

The company's variable selling and administrative expense per unit is $2.50. Fixed selling and administrative expenses include advertising expenses of $8,000 per quarter, executive salaries of $35,000 per quarter, and depreciation of $20,000 per quarter. In addition, the company will make insurance payments of $5,000 in the first quarter and $5,000 in the third quarter. Finally, property taxes of $8,000 will be paid in the second quarter.

Required:

Prepare the company's selling and administrative expense budget for the upcoming fiscal year.

EXERCISE 9–7 Cash Budget Analysis [LO2]

A cash budget, by quarter, is given below for a retail company (000 omitted). The company requires a minimum cash balance of $5,000 to start each quarter.

Required:

Fill in the missing amounts in the table that follows:

	Quarter 1	2	3	4	Year
Cash balance, beginning.........................	$ 6	$?	$?	$?	$?
Add collections from customers	?	?	96	?	323
Total cash available	71	?	?	?	?
Less disbursements:					
Purchases of inventory.........................	35	45	?	35	?
Selling and administrative expenses	?	30	30	?	113
Equipment purchases	8	8	10	?	36
Dividends.....................................	2	2	2	2	?
Total disbursements	?	85	?	?	?
Excess (deficiency) of cash available over disbursements..........................	(2)	?	11	?	?
Financing:					
Borrowings....................................	?	15	—	—	?
Repayments*	—	—	(?)	(16)	(?)
Total financing.................................	?	?	?	?	?
Cash balance, ending	$?	$?	$?	$?	$?

*For this exercise assume there will be no interest on any borrowings.

EXERCISE 9–8 Preparing a Flexible Budget [LO3]

Auto Lavage is a Canadian company that owns and operates a large automatic carwash facility near Quebec. The following table provides data concerning the company's costs:

	Fixed Cost per Month	Cost per Car Washed
Cleaning supplies		$0.70
Electricity	$1,400	0.10
Maintenance		0.30
Wages and salaries	4,700	0.40
Depreciation	8,300	
Rent...	2,100	
Administrative expenses	1,800	0.05

The company expects to charge customers an average of $5.90 per car washed.

Required:
Using Exhibit 9–2 as your guide, prepare a flexible budget for October assuming either 8,000 or 9,000 cars are washed.

EXERCISE 9–9 Flexible Budget Performance Report [LO3, LO4]
Refer to the data in Exercise 9–8. Auto Lavage's actual level of activity was 8,100 cars. The actual revenues and expenses for October are given below:

	Actual Data for 8,100 Cars
Sales	$49,300
Variable expenses:	
Cleaning supplies	6,075
Electricity	891
Maintenance	2,187
Wages and salary	3,402
Administrative	486
Fixed expenses:	
Electricity	1,450
Wages and salaries	4,700
Depreciation	8,300
Rent	2,100
Administrative	1,745

Required:
1. Prepare a flexible budget performance report for October using Exhibit 9–3 as your guide.
2. Prepare a comprehensive performance report for October using Exhibit 9–5 as your guide. Assume that the static budget for October was based on an activity level of 8,000 cars.

EXERCISE 9–10 Flexible Budget Performance Report [LO4]
Vision and Audio is a small owner-managed business that specializes in the installation of television and audio equipment for customers with high-end home theatre systems. The company has provided the following data concerning its most recent month of operations:

	Budgeted Fixed Component per Month	Budgeted Variable Component per Installation	Actuals for October
Revenue		$550	$52,250
Installer wages	$17,200		16,900
Selling and administrative expenses	1,225	15	2,804
			(1,304 fixed)
Office expenses	5,400	3	5,416
			(5,112 fixed)
Marketing expenses	3,160		3,300
Insurance	300		300
Miscellaneous expenses	550	2	709
			(538 fixed)

The company uses the number of installations as its measure of activity. For example, selling and administrative expenses should be $1,225 plus $15 per job, and the actual selling and administrative expenses for October were $1,990. The company expected to do 100 installations in October, but actually did 95.

Required:
Prepare a comprehensive performance report for October using Exhibit 9–5 as your guide. Assume that the static budget for October was based on an activity level of 100 jobs.

CHECK FIGURE
Actual operating income = $22,821; Flexible budget operating income = $22,515; Static budget operating income = $25,165.

PROBLEMS

PROBLEM 9–11 Integration of Sales, Production, and Direct Materials Budgets [LO2]
Milo Company manufactures beach umbrellas. The company is preparing detailed budgets for the third quarter and has assembled the following information to assist in the budget preparation:

a.   The Marketing Department has estimated sales as follows for the remainder of the year (in units):

July	30,000
August	70,000
September	50,000
October	20,000
November	10,000
December	10,000

The selling price of the umbrellas is $12 each.

b.   All sales are on account. Based on past experience, sales are expected to be collected in the following pattern:

> 30% in the month of sale
> 65% in the month following sale
> 5% uncollectible

Sales for June were $300,000.

c.   The company maintains finished goods inventories equal to 15% of the following month's sales. This requirement will be met at the end of June.

d.   Each beach umbrella requires 1 metre of Gilden, a material that is sometimes hard to acquire. Therefore, the company requires that the ending inventory of Gilden be equal to 50% of the following month's production needs. The inventory of Gilden on hand at the beginning of the quarter is 18,000 metres.

e.   Gilden costs $3.20 per metre. One-half of a month's purchases of Gilden is paid for in the month of purchase; the remainder is paid for in the following month. The accounts payable on July 1 for purchases of Gilden during June will be $76,000.

Required:
1.   Calculate the estimated sales, by month and in total, for the third quarter.
2.   Calculate the expected cash collections, by month and in total, for the third quarter.
3.   Calculate the estimated quantity of beach umbrellas that need to be produced in July, August, September, and October.
4.   Calculate the quantity of Gilden (in metres) that needs to be purchased, by month and in total, for the third quarter.
5.   Calculate the cost of the raw material (Gilden) purchases, by month and in total, for the third quarter.
6.   Calculate the expected cash disbursements for raw material (Gilden) purchases, by month and in total, for the third quarter.

PROBLEM 9–12 Schedules of Expected Cash Collections and Disbursements [LO2]
You have been asked to prepare a December cash budget for Ashton Company, a distributor of exercise equipment. The following information is available about the company's operations:

a.   The cash balance on December 1 is $40,000.
b.   Actual sales for October and November and expected sales for December are shown below. Sales on account are collected over a three-month period as follows: 20% collected in the month of sale, 60% collected in the month following sale, and 18% collected in the second month following sale. The remaining 2% is uncollectible.

	October	November	December
Cash sales	$ 65,000	$ 70,000	$ 83,000
Sales on account	$400,000	$525,000	$600,000

c. Purchases of inventory will total $280,000 for December. Thirty percent of a month's inventory purchases are paid during the month of purchase. The accounts payable remaining from November's inventory purchases total $161,000, all of which will be paid in December.

d. Selling and administrative expenses are budgeted at $430,000 for December. Of this amount, $50,000 is for depreciation.

e. A new web server for the Marketing Department costing $76,000 will be purchased for cash during December, and dividends totalling $9,000 will be paid during the month.

f. The company maintains a minimum cash balance of $20,000. An open line of credit is available from the company's bank to bolster the cash position as needed.

Required:

1. Prepare a schedule of expected cash collections for December.
2. Prepare a schedule of expected cash disbursements during December for merchandise purchases.
3. Prepare a cash budget for December. Indicate in the financing section any borrowing that will be needed during the month. Assume that any interest will not be paid until the following month.

PROBLEM 9–13 Evaluating a Company's Budget Procedures [LO1]

Springfield Corporation operates on a calendar-year basis. It begins the annual budgeting process in late August, when the president establishes targets for total sales dollars and net operating income before taxes for the next year. The sales target is given to the Marketing Department, where the marketing manager formulates a sales budget by product line in both units and dollars. From this budget, sales quotas by product line in units and dollars are established for each of the corporation's sales districts. The marketing manager also estimates the cost of the marketing activities required to support the target sales volume and prepares a tentative marketing expense budget.

The executive vice president uses the sales and profit targets, the sales budget by product line, and the tentative marketing expense budget to determine the dollar amounts that can be devoted to manufacturing and corporate office expense. The executive vice president prepares the budget for corporate expenses, and then forwards to the Production Department the product-line sales budget in units and the total dollar amount that can be devoted to manufacturing.

The production manager meets with the factory managers to develop a manufacturing plan that will produce the required units when needed within the cost constraints set by the executive vice president. The budgeting process usually comes to a halt at this point because the Production Department does not consider the financial resources allocated to it to be adequate.

When this standstill occurs, the vice president of finance, the executive vice president, the marketing manager, and the production manager meet to determine the final budgets for each of the areas. This normally results in a modest increase in the total amount available for manufacturing costs, while the marketing expense and corporate office expense budgets are cut. The total sales and net operating income figures proposed by the president are seldom changed. Although the participants are seldom pleased with the compromise, these budgets are final. Each executive then develops a new detailed budget for the operations in his or her area.

None of the areas has achieved its budget in recent years. Sales often run below the target. When budgeted sales are not achieved, each area is expected to cut costs so that the president's profit target can still be met. However, the profit target is seldom met because costs are not cut enough. In fact, costs often run above the original budget in all functional areas. The president is disturbed that Springfield has not been able to meet the sales and profit targets. He hired a consultant with considerable relevant industry experience. The consultant reviewed the budgets for the past four years. He concluded that the product-line sales budgets were reasonable and that the cost and expense budgets were adequate for the budgeted sales and production levels.

Required:

1. Discuss how the budgeting process as employed by Springfield Corporation contributes to the failure to achieve the president's sales and profit targets.
2. Suggest how Springfield Corporation's budgeting process could be revised to correct the problem.
3. Should the functional areas be expected to cut their costs when sales volume falls below budget? Explain your answer.

(This material is reprinted with permission from CPA Canada. All rights reserved by copyright owner.)

PROBLEM 9–14 Production and Direct Materials Purchases Budgets [LO2]

Symphony Electronics produces wireless speakers for outdoor use on patios, decks, etc. Their most popular model is the All Weather and requires four separate XL12 components per unit. The company is now planning raw material needs for the second quarter. Sales of the All Weather are the highest in the second quarter of each year as customers prepare for the summer season. The company has the following inventory requirements:

a. The finished goods inventory on hand at the end of each month must be equal to 16,000 units plus 10% of the next month's sales. The finished goods inventory on March 31 is budgeted to be 28,000 units.

b. The raw materials inventory on hand at the end of each month must be equal to 20% of the following month's production needs for raw materials. The raw materials inventory on March 31 for XL 12 is budgeted to be 98,400 components.

c. The company maintains no work in process inventories.

A sales budget for the All Weather speaker is as follows:

	Budgeted Sales in Units
April	120,000
May	150,000
June	210,000
July	106,000
August	60,000

CHECK FIGURE
1. Total production (units) in May = 156,000;
3. Direct materials purchases (XL 12 components) June = 719,840.

Required:
1. Prepare a production budget for the All Weather for April, May, June and July.
2. Prepare a direct materials purchases budget showing the quantity of XL 12 components to be purchased for April, May and June and for the quarter in total.

PROBLEM 9–15 Direct Materials Purchases and Direct Labour Budgets [LO2]
The production department of Zan Corporation has submitted the following forecast of units to be produced by quarter for the upcoming fiscal year:

	1st Quarter	2nd Quarter	3rd Quarter	4th Quarter
Units to be produced	5,000	8,000	7,000	6,000

In addition, 6,000 grams of raw materials inventory is on hand at the start of the 1st quarter and the beginning accounts payable for the 1st quarter is $2,880.

Each unit requires 8 grams of raw material that costs $1.20 per gram. Management desires to end each quarter with an inventory of raw materials equal to 25% of the following quarter's production needs. The desired ending inventory for the 4th quarter is 8,000 grams. Management plans to pay for 60% of raw material purchases in the quarter acquired and 40% in the following quarter. Each unit requires 0.20 direct labour-hours and direct labourers are paid $11.50 per hour.

Required:
1. Prepare the company's direct materials purchases budget and schedule of expected cash disbursements for materials for the upcoming fiscal year.
2. Prepare the company's direct labour budget for the upcoming fiscal year, assuming that the direct labour workforce is adjusted each quarter to match the number of hours required to produce the forecast number of units produced.

PROBLEM 9–16 Direct Labour and Manufacturing Overhead Budgets [LO2]
The Bakery Department of Culbert Dessert Corporation has submitted the following forecast of fruit pies to be produced by quarter for the upcoming fiscal year.

	First Quarter	Second Quarter	Third Quarter	Fourth Quarter
Units to be produced	8,000	11,000	9,000	13,000

Each unit requires 0.30 direct labour-hours, and direct labour-hour workers are paid $10.50 per hour.

In addition, the variable manufacturing overhead rate is $1.50 per direct labour-hour. The fixed manufacturing overhead is $23,000 per quarter. The only non-cash element of manufacturing overhead is depreciation, which is $7,000 per quarter.

Required:
1. Prepare the company's direct labour budget for the upcoming fiscal year, assuming that the direct labour workforce is adjusted each quarter to match the number of hours required to produce the forecast number of units produced.
2. Prepare the company's manufacturing overhead budget. As per Schedule 5, your manufacturing overhead budget should also include the budgeted cash disbursements for overhead.

PROBLEM 9–17 Schedules of Expected Cash Collections and Disbursements; Balance Sheet [LO2]
Deacon Company is a merchandising company that is preparing a budget for the second quarter of the calendar year. The following information is available.

DEACON COMPANY
Balance Sheet
March 31

Assets

Cash.	$ 55,000
Accounts receivable	36,000
Inventory.	40,000
Plant and equipment, net of depreciation	100,000
Total assets	$231,000

Liabilities and Shareholders' Equity

Accounts payable	$ 51,300
Common shares.	70,000
Retained earnings	109,700
Total liabilities and shareholders' equity	$231,000

Budgeted Income Statements	April	May	June
Sales	$100,000	$110,000	$130,000
Cost of goods sold.	60,000	66,000	78,000
Gross margin.	40,000	44,000	52,000
Selling and administrative expenses	15,000	16,500	19,500
Operating income	$ 25,000	$ 27,500	$ 32,500

Budgeting assumptions:

a. Sixty percent of sales are cash sales and 40% of sales are credit sales. Twenty percent of all credit sales are collected in the month of sale and the remaining 80% are collected in the month subsequent to the sale.
b. Budgeted sales for July are $140,000.
c. 10% of merchandise inventory purchases are paid in cash at the time of the purchase. The remaining 90% of purchases are credit purchases. All purchases on credit are paid in the month subsequent to the purchase.
d. Each month's ending merchandise inventory should equal $10,000 plus 50% of the next month's cost of goods sold.
e. Depreciation expense is $1,000 per month. All other selling and administrative expenses are paid in full in the month the expense is incurred.

Required:
1. Calculate the expected cash collections for April, May, and June.
2. Calculate the budgeted merchandise purchases for April, May, and June.
3. Calculate the expected cash disbursements for merchandise purchases for April, May, and June.
4. Prepare a budgeted balance sheet at June 30. (*Hint:* You need to calculate the cash paid for selling and administrative expenses during April, May, and June to determine the cash balance in your June 30 balance sheet.)

PROBLEM 9–18 Cash Budget; Income Statement; Balance Sheet [LO2]

Minden Company is a wholesale distributor of premium European chocolates. The company's balance sheet as of April 30 is given below:

MINDEN COMPANY Balance Sheet April 30	
Assets	
Cash.	$ 9,000
Accounts receivable	54,000
Inventory	30,000
Buildings and equipment, net of depreciation	207,000
Total assets	$300,000
Liabilities and Shareholders' Equity	
Accounts payable	$ 63,000
Note payable	14,500
Common shares.	180,000
Retained earnings	42,500
Total liabilities and shareholders' equity	$300,000

The company is in the process of preparing a budget for May and has assembled the following data:

a. Sales are budgeted at $200,000 for May. Of these sales, $60,000 will be for cash; the remainder will be credit sales. One-half of a month's credit sales are collected in the month the sales are made, and the remainder is collected in the following month. All of the April 30 accounts receivable will be collected in May.

b. Purchases of inventory are expected to total $120,000 during May. These purchases will all be on account. Forty percent of all purchases are paid for in the month of purchase; the remainder are paid in the following month. All of the April 30 accounts payable to suppliers will be paid during May.

c. The May 31 inventory balance is budgeted at $40,000.

d. Selling and administrative expenses for May are budgeted at $72,000, exclusive of depreciation. These expenses will be paid in cash. Depreciation is budgeted at $2,000 for the month.

e. The note payable on the April 30 balance sheet will be paid during May, with $100 in interest. (All of the interest relates to May.)

f. New refrigerating equipment costing $6,500 will be purchased for cash during May.

g. During May, the company will borrow $20,000 from its bank by giving a new note payable to the bank for that amount. The new note will be due in one year.

Required:

1. Prepare a cash budget for May. Support your budget with a schedule of expected cash collections from sales and a schedule of expected cash disbursements for merchandise purchases.

2. Prepare a budgeted income statement for May. Use the absorption costing income statement format as shown in Schedule 9.

3. Prepare a budgeted balance sheet as of May 31.

PROBLEM 9–19 Integration of Sales, Production, and Direct Materials Purchases Budgets [LO2]

Water Sport Inc. manufactures a small personal water tube used for children learning to swim. Management is now preparing detailed budgets for the third quarter, July through September, and has assembled the following information to assist:

a. The Marketing Department has estimated sales as follows for the remainder of the year (number of water tubes):

July	6,500	October	3,000
August	5,000	November	2,500
September	4,000	December	2,000

The selling price of the water tubes is $60.

b. All sales are on account. Based on past experience, sales are expected to be collected in the following pattern:

> 50% in the month of sale
> 45% in the month following sale
> 5% uncollectible

The beginning accounts receivable balance (excluding uncollectible amounts) on July 1 will be $160,000.

c. The company maintains finished goods inventories equal to 20% of the following month's sales. The inventory of finished goods on July 1 will be 1,300 units.

d. Each water tube requires 3 kilograms of synthetic polyisoprene rubber compound. To prevent shortages, the company would like the inventory of synthetic rubber compound on hand at the end of each month to be equal to 20% of the following month's production needs. The inventory of synthetic rubber compound on hand on July 1 will be 3,720 kilograms.

e. The synthetic rubber compound costs $3.50 per kilogram. Water Sport pays for 70% of its purchases in the month of purchase; the remainder is paid for in the following month. The accounts payable balance for synthetic rubber compound purchases will be $11,400 on July 1.

Required:

1. Prepare a sales budget, by month and in total, for the third quarter. (Show your budget in both units of water tubes and dollars.) Also prepare a schedule of expected cash collections, by month and in total, for the third quarter.

2. Prepare a production budget for each of the months July through October.

3. Prepare a direct materials purchases budget for synthetic rubber compound, by month and in total, for the third quarter. Also prepare a schedule of expected cash disbursements for synthetic rubber compound, by month and in total, for the third quarter.

PROBLEM 9–20 Completing a Master Budget [LO2]

The following data relate to the second quarter operations of Leisure Sports, a wholesale distributor of consumer sporting goods, as of March 31:

Cash.....................................	$ 9,000
Accounts receivable	48,000
Inventory................................	12,600
Building and equipment, net................	214,100
Accounts payable	18,300
Common shares...........................	190,000
Retained earnings	75,400

a. Actual sales for March and budgeted sales for April through July are as follows:

March (actual)............................	$60,000
April	70,000
May	85,000
June......................................	90,000
July	50,000

b. Sales are 20% cash and 80% credit. Credit sales are collected in the month following sale. The accounts receivable at March 31 are a result of March credit sales.

c. The company's gross margin is 40% of sales.

d. Monthly expenses are as follows: salaries and wages $7,500 per month; shipping, 6% of sales; advertising, $6,000 per month; other expenses, 4% of sales. Depreciation, including depreciation on new assets acquired during the quarter, will be $6,000 in total for the quarter.

e. Each month's ending inventory should equal 30% of the following month's cost of goods sold.

f. One-half of a month's inventory purchases is paid for in the month of purchase; the other half is paid for in the following month.

g. Equipment costing $11,500 will be purchased for cash in April and $3,000 will be purchased for cash in May.

h. Dividends of $3,500 will be declared and paid in June.

i.   The company must maintain a minimum cash balance of $8,000. An open line of credit is available at a local bank. All borrowing is done at the beginning of a month, and all repayments are made at the end of a month. The monthly interest rate is 1%. Interest must be paid at the end of each month based on the total loans outstanding for that month.

Required:

Using the data above, complete the following:

1.   Sales budget and schedule of expected cash collections:

	March (actual)	April	May	June	July
Sales Budget					
Total sales	$60,000	$70,000			
Cash (20%).	$12,000	$14,000			
Credit (80%).	$48,000	$56,000	___	___	___

All credit sales are collected in the month following the sale.

	April	May	June	Total
Schedule of Expected Cash Collections				
Cash sales.	$14,000			
Credit sales.	48,000			
Total collections.	$62,000			

2.   Merchandise purchases budget:

	April	May	June	Quarter
Budgeted cost of goods sold	$42,000*	$51,000		
Add desired ending inventory	15,300†			
Total needs	57,300			
Less beginning inventory	12,600			
Required purchases	$44,700			

*For April sales: $70,000 sales × 60% cost ratio
†$51,000 × 30%

Schedule of expected cash disbursements—Merchandise purchases:

	April	May	June	Quarter
March purchases	$18,300			
April purchases	22,350	$22,350		
May purchases.				
June purchases.				
Total disbursements	$40,650			

3.   Schedule of expected cash disbursements—Selling and administrative expenses:

	April	May	June	Quarter
Salaries and wages	$ 7,500			
Shipping	4,200			
Advertising	6,000			
Other expenses	2,800			
Total disbursements	$20,500			

4.   Cash budget:

	April	May	June	Quarter
Cash balance, beginning	$ 9,000			
Add cash collections	62,000			
Total cash available	$71,000	____	____	____
Less cash disbursements				
For inventory purchases	40,650			
For selling and administrative				
expenses	20,500			
For equipment purchases	11,500	____	____	____
For dividend payments	0	____	____	____
Total cash disbursements	72,650	____	____	____
Excess (deficiency) of cash	$(1,650)			
Financing:				
Etc.				

5.   Prepare an absorption costing income statement, similar to the one shown in Schedule 9, for the quarter ended June 30.
6.   Prepare a balance sheet as of June 30.

PROBLEM 9–21 Cash Budget with Supporting Schedules [LO2]

Scott Products Inc. is a merchandising company that sells binders, paper, and other school supplies. The company is planning its cash needs for the third quarter. In the past, Scott Products has had to borrow money during the third quarter to support peak sales of back-to-school materials, which occur during August. The following information has been assembled to assist in preparing a cash budget for the quarter:

a.   Budgeted monthly absorption costing income statements for July through October are as follows:

	July	August	September	October
Sales	$40,000	$70,000	$50,000	$45,000
Cost of goods sold	24,000	42,000	30,000	27,000
Gross margin	16,000	28,000	20,000	18,000
Selling and administrative expenses:				
Selling expense	7,200	11,700	8,500	7,300
Administrative expense*	5,600	7,200	6,100	5,900
Total expenses	12,800	18,900	14,600	13,200
Operating income	$ 3,200	$ 9,100	$ 5,400	$ 4,800

*Includes $2,000 depreciation each month

b.   Sales are 20% for cash and 80% on credit.
c.   Credit sales are collected over a three-month period, with 10% collected in the month of sale, 70% in the month following sale, and 20% in the second month following sale. May sales totalled $30,000, and June sales totalled $36,000.
d.   Inventory purchases are paid for within 15 days. Therefore, 50% of a month's inventory purchases is paid for in the month of purchase. The remaining 50% is paid for in the following month. Accounts payable for inventory purchases at June 30 total $11,700.
e.   The company maintains its ending inventory levels at 75% of the cost of the merchandise to be sold in the following month. The merchandise inventory at June 30 is $18,000.
f.   Land costing $4,500 will be purchased in July.
g.   Dividends of $1,000 will be declared and paid in September.
h.   The cash balance on June 30 is $8,000; the company must maintain a cash balance of at least this amount at the end of each month.
i.   The company has an agreement with a local bank that allows the company to borrow up to a total loan balance of $40,000. The interest rate on these loans is 1% per month. All borrowing is done at the beginning of a month. The company would, as far as it is able, repay the loan at the end of each month. Interest must be paid at the end of each month based on the outstanding loans for that month. There are no loans outstanding as at June 30.

Required:

1. Prepare a schedule of expected cash collections for July, August, and September and for the quarter in total.
2. Prepare the following for merchandise inventory:
   a. A merchandise purchases budget for July, August, and September.
   b. A schedule of expected cash disbursements for merchandise purchases for July, August, and September and for the quarter in total.
3. Prepare a cash budget for July, August, and September and for the quarter in total.

CHECK FIGURE

1. Expected cash collections July = $36,160; 2a. Merchandise purchases August = $33,000; 3. Excess (deficiency) of cash available over disbursements September = $23,625.

PROBLEM 9–22 Cash Budget with Supporting Schedules; Changing Assumptions [LO2]

Refer to the data for Scott Products Inc. in Problem 9–21. The company's president is interested in knowing how reducing inventory levels and collecting accounts receivable sooner will impact the cash budget. He revises the cash collection and ending inventory assumptions as follows:

1. Sales continue to be 20% for cash and 80% on credit. However, credit sales from July, August, and September are collected over a three-month period, with 25% collected in the month of sale, 60% collected in the month following sale, and 15% in the second month following sale. Credit sales from May and June are collected during the third quarter using the collection percentages specified in Problem 9–21.
2. The company maintains its ending inventory levels for July, August, and September at 25% of the cost of merchandise to be sold in the following month. The merchandise inventory at June 30 remains $18,000 and accounts payable for inventory purchases at June 30 remains $11,700.

All other information from Problem 9–21 that is not referred to above remains the same.

Required:

1. Using the president's new assumptions in (1) above, prepare a schedule of expected cash collections for July, August, and September and for the quarter in total.
2. Using the president's new assumptions in (2) above, prepare the following for merchandise inventory:
   a. A merchandise purchases budget for July, August, and September.
   b. A schedule of expected cash disbursements for merchandise purchases for July, August, and September and for the quarter in total.
3. Using the president's new assumptions, prepare a cash budget for July, August, and September and for the quarter in total.
4. Briefly explain how the president's revised assumptions affect the cash budget.

PROBLEM 9–23 Integrated Operating Budgets [LO2]

The Western Division of Keltic Company manufactures a vital component that is used in one of Keltic's major product lines. The Western Division has been experiencing some difficulty in coordinating activities among its various departments, which has resulted in some shortages of the component at critical times. To overcome the shortages, the manager of the Western Division has decided to initiate a monthly budgeting system that is integrated among departments.

The first budget is to be for the second quarter of the current year. To assist in creating the budget, the divisional controller has accumulated the following information:

Sales. Sales through the first three months of the current year were 48,000 units. Actual sales in units for January, February, and March, and planned sales in units over the next five months, are given below:

January (actual)............................	9,000
February (actual)...........................	15,000
March (actual).............................	24,000
April (planned)	30,000
May (planned).............................	53,000
June (planned).............................	75,000
July (planned)	68,000
August (planned)...........................	45,000

In total, the Western Division expects to produce and sell 380,000 units during the current year.

Direct Materials. Two different materials are used in the production of the component. Data regarding these materials are given below:

Direct Materials	Units of Direct Materials per Finished Component	Cost per Unit	Inventory at March 31
No. 226	2 kilograms	$4.00	23,000 kilograms
No. 301	5 metres	$1.50	35,000 metres

Material No. 226 is sometimes in short supply. Therefore, the Western Division requires that enough of the material be on hand at the end of each month to provide for 60% of the following month's production needs. Material No. 301 is easier to obtain, so only 30% of the following month's production needs must be on hand at the end of each month.

Direct Labour. The Western Division has three departments through which the components must pass before they are completed. Information relating to direct labour in these departments is given below:

Department	Direct Labour-Hours per Finished Component	Cost per Direct Labour-Hour
Cutting.	0.15	$16.00
Assembly.	0.60	14.00
Finishing	0.10	18.00

Direct labour is adjusted to the workload each month.

Manufacturing Overhead. The Western Division manufactured 48,000 components during the first three months of the current year. The actual variable overhead costs incurred during this three-month period are shown below. The Western Division's controller believes that the variable overhead costs incurred during the last nine months of the year will be at the same rate per component as experienced during the first three months:

Utilities	$ 63,000
Indirect labour.	34,000
Supplies.	18,000
Other	9,800
Total variable overhead.	$124,800

The actual fixed manufacturing overhead costs incurred during the first three months totalled $1,287,000. The Western Division has budgeted fixed manufacturing overhead costs for the entire year as follows:

Supervision	$ 785,000
Property taxes	129,000
Depreciation	2,619,000
Insurance.	568,000
Other	65,000
Total fixed manufacturing overhead	$4,166,000

Finished Goods Inventory. The desired monthly ending finished goods inventory is 20% of the next month's estimated sales. The Western Division has 6,000 units in finished goods inventory on March 31.

Required:
1. Prepare a production budget for the Western Division for the second quarter ending June 30. Show computations by month and in total for the quarter.
2. Prepare a direct materials purchases budget for each type of material for the second quarter ending June 30. Again show computations by month and in total for the quarter.

3. Prepare a direct labour budget for the second quarter ending June 30. This time it is *not* necessary to show monthly figures; show quarterly totals only. Assume that the workforce is adjusted as work requirements change.

4. Assume that the company plans to produce a total of 380,000 units for the year. Prepare a manufacturing overhead budget for the nine-month period ending December 31. (Do not compute a predetermined overhead rate.) Again, it is *not* necessary to show monthly figures.

   (This material is reprinted with permission from CPA Canada. All rights reserved by copyright owner.)

PROBLEM 9–24 Completing a Master Budget [LO2]

The following data relate to the operations of Shilow Company, a wholesale distributor of consumer goods:

Current assets as of March 31:	
Cash	$ 8,000
Accounts receivable	20,000
Inventory	36,000
Buildings and equipment, net	120,000
Accounts payable	21,750
Common shares	150,000
Retained earnings	12,250

a. The gross margin is 25% of sales.
b. Actual and budgeted sales data are as follows:

March (actual)	$50,000
April	60,000
May	72,000
June	90,000
July	48,000

c. Sales are 60% for cash and 40% on credit. Credit sales are collected in the month following sale. The accounts receivable at March 31 are the result of March credit sales.
d. Each month's ending inventory should equal 80% of the following month's budgeted cost of goods sold.
e. One-half of a month's inventory purchases is paid for in the month of purchase; the other one-half is paid for in the following month. The accounts payable at March 31 are the result of March purchases of inventory.
f. Monthly expenses are as follows: commissions, 12% of sales; rent, $2,500; other expenses (excluding depreciation), 6% of sales. Assume that these expenses are paid monthly. Depreciation is $900 per month and includes depreciation on new assets.
g. Equipment will be acquired for cash: $1,500 in April.
h. Management would like to maintain a minimum cash balance of $4,000 at the end of each month. The company has an agreement with a local bank that allows the company to borrow as needed at the beginning of each month, up to a total loan balance of $20,000. The interest rate on these loans is 1% per month and for simplicity we will assume that interest is not compounded. The company would, as far as it is able, repay the loan plus accumulated interest at the end of the quarter.

Required:
Using the preceding data, complete the following:
1. Schedule of expected cash collections:

	April	May	June	Quarter
Cash sales	$36,000			
Credit sales	20,000			
Total collections	$56,000			

2. Merchandise purchases budget:

	April	May	June	Quarter
Budgeted cost of goods sold	$45,000*			
Add desired ending inventory	43,200†			
Total needs	88,200			
Less beginning inventory	36,000			
Required purchases	$52,200			

*$60,000 sales × 75%
†$54,000 × 80%

Schedule of expected cash disbursements—Merchandise purchases:

	April	May	June	Quarter
March purchases	$21,750			$21,750
April purchases	26,100	$26,100		52,200
May purchases				
June purchases				
Total disbursements	$47,850			

3. Complete the following cash budget:

	April	May	June	Quarter
Cash balance, beginning	$ 8,000			
Add cash collections	56,000			
Total cash available	64,000			
Less cash disbursements:				
For inventory	47,850			
For expenses	13,300			
For equipment	1,500			
Total cash disbursements	62,650			
Excess (deficiency) of cash	$ 1,350			
Financing:				
Etc.				

4. Prepare an absorption costing income statement, similar to the one shown in Schedule 9, for the quarter ended June 30.
5. Prepare a balance sheet as of June 30.

PROBLEM 9–25 Applying the Flexible Budget Approach [LO3, LO4]
Frank Weston, supervisor of the Freemont Corporation's Machining Department, was visibly upset after being reprimanded for his department's poor performance over the prior month. The department's cost control report is given below:

FREEMONT CORPORATION—MACHINING DEPARTMENT Cost Control Report For the Month Ended June 30			
	Actual	Static Budget	Static Budget Variance
Machine-hours	38,000	35,000	
Direct labour wages	$86,100	$80,500	$5,600 U
Supplies	23,100	21,000	2,100 U
Maintenance	137,300	134,000	3,300 U
Utilities	15,700	15,200	500 U
Supervision	38,000	38,000	0
Depreciation	80,000	80,000	0
Total	$380,200	$368,700	$11,500 U

"I just can't understand all of these unfavourable variances," Weston complained to the supervisor of another department. "When the boss called me in, I thought he was going to give me a pat on the back because I know for a fact that my department worked more efficiently last month than it has ever worked before. Instead, he tore me apart. I thought for a minute that it might be over the supplies that were stolen out of our warehouse last month. But they amounted to only a couple of hundred dollars, and just look at this report. Everything is unfavourable."

Direct labour wages and supplies are variable costs; supervision and depreciation are fixed costs; and maintenance and utilities are mixed costs. The fixed component of the budgeted maintenance cost is $92,000; the fixed component of the budgeted utilities cost is $11,700.

Required:
1. Evaluate the company's cost control report and explain why the variances were all unfavourable.
2. Using Exhibit 9–3 as your guide, prepare a performance report that will help Mr. Weston's superiors assess how well costs were controlled in the Machining Department.

PROBLEM 9–26 Critique a Report; Prepare a Performance Report [LO4]

TipTop Flight School offers flying lessons at a small municipal airport. The school's owner and manager has been attempting to evaluate performance and control costs using a variance report that compares the planning budget to actual results. A recent variance report appears below:

TIPTOP FLIGHT SCHOOL Variance Report For the Month Ended July 31			
	Actual Results	Static Budget	Variance
Lessons	155	150	
Revenue	$33,900	$33,000	$900 F
Expenses			
Instructor wages	$ 9,870	$ 9,750	$120 U
Aircraft depreciation	5,890	5,700	190 U
Fuel	2,750	2,250	500 U
Maintenance	2,450	2,330	120 U
Ground facility expense	1,540	1,550	10 F
Administration	3,320	3,390	70 F
Total expense	25,820	24,970	850 U
Operating income	$ 8,080	$ 8,030	$ 50 F

After several months of using such variance reports, the owner has become frustrated. For example, she is quite confident that instructor wages were very tightly controlled in July, but the report shows an unfavourable variance.

The static budget was developed using the following formulas, where q is the number of lessons sold:

	Cost Formulas
Revenue	$220q$
Instructor wages	$65q$
Aircraft depreciation	$38q$
Fuel	$15q$
Maintenance	$530 + $12q$
Ground facility expense	$1,250 + $2q$
Administration	$3,240 + $1q$

Required:
1. Should the owner feel frustrated with the variance reports? Explain.
2. Prepare a comprehensive performance report for the school for July. Use Exhibit 9–5 as your guide.
3. Evaluate the school's performance for July.

CASES

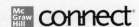

CASE 9–27 Master Budget with Supporting Schedules [LO2]

Knockoffs Unlimited, a nationwide distributor of low-cost imitation designer necklaces, has an exclusive franchise on the distribution of the necklaces, and sales have grown so rapidly over the past few years that it has become necessary to add new members to the management team. To date, the company's budgeting practices have been inferior, and at times the company has experienced a cash shortage. You have been given responsibility for all planning and budgeting. Your first assignment is to prepare a master budget for the next three months, starting April 1. You are eager to make a favourable impression on the president and have assembled the information below.

The necklaces are sold to retailers for $10 each. Recent and forecast sales in units are as follows:

January (actual)	20,000	June	50,000
February (actual)	26,000	July	30,000
March (actual)	40,000	August	28,000
April	65,000	September	25,000
May	100,000		

The large buildup in sales before and during May is due to Mother's Day. Ending inventories should be equal to 40% of the next month's sales in units.

The necklaces cost the company $4 each. Purchases are paid for as follows: 50% in the month of purchase and the remaining 50% in the following month. All sales are on credit, with no discount, and payable within 15 days. The company has found, however, that only 20% of a month's sales are collected by month-end. An additional 70% is collected in the following month, and the remaining 10% is collected in the second month following sale. Bad debts have been negligible.

The company's monthly selling and administrative expenses are given below:

Variable:	
Sales commissions	4% of sales
Fixed:	
Advertising	$200,000
Rent	18,000
Wages and salaries	106,000
Utilities	7,000
Insurance	3,000
Depreciation	14,000

All selling and administrative expenses are paid during the month, in cash, with the exception of depreciation and insurance. Insurance is paid on an annual basis, in November of each year. The company plans to purchase $16,000 in new equipment during May and $40,000 in new equipment during June; both purchases will be paid in cash. The company declares dividends of $15,000 each quarter, payable in the first month of the following quarter. The company's balance sheet at March 31 is given below:

Assets

Cash	$	74,000
Accounts receivable ($26,000 February sales; $320,000 March sales)		346,000
Inventory		104,000
Prepaid insurance		21,000
Fixed assets, net of depreciation		950,000
Total assets		$1,495,000

Liabilities and Shareholders' Equity

Accounts payable	$	100,000
Dividends payable		15,000
Common shares		800,000
Retained earnings		580,000
Total liabilities and shareholders' equity		$1,495,000

The company wants a minimum ending cash balance each month of $50,000. All borrowing is done at the beginning of the month, with any repayments made at the end of the month. The interest rate on these loans is 1% per month and must be paid at the end of each month based on the outstanding loan balance for that month.

Required:

Prepare a master budget for the three-month period ending June 30. Include the following detailed budgets:

1. *a.* A sales budget by month and in total.
   b. A schedule of expected cash collections from sales, by month and in total.
   c. A merchandise purchases budget in units and in dollars. Show the budget by month and in total.
   d. A schedule of expected cash disbursements for merchandise purchases, by month and in total.
2. A cash budget. Show the budget by month and in total.
3. A budgeted income statement for the three-month period ending June 30. Use the variable costing approach.
4. A budgeted balance sheet as of June 30.

CASE 9–28 Critiquing a Report; Preparing Spending Variances [LO3, LO4]

Farrar University offers an extensive continuing education program in many cities throughout the province. For the convenience of its faculty and administrative staff and to save costs, the university operates a motor pool. The motor pool operated with 20 vehicles until February, when an additional automobile was acquired at the request of the university administration. The motor pool furnishes gasoline, oil, and other supplies for its automobiles. A mechanic does routine maintenance and minor repairs. Major repairs are performed at a nearby commercial garage. Each year, the supervisor of the motor pool prepares an annual budget, which is reviewed by the university and approved after suitable modifications.

The following cost control report shows actual selling and administrative costs for March of the current year compared to 1/12 of the annual budget:

FARRAR UNIVERSITY MOTOR POOL			
Cost Control Report			
For the Month Ended March 31			
	Annual Budget	Monthly Budget (1/12 of Annual Budget)	March Actual	(Over) Under Budget
---	---	---	---	---
Kilometres	600,000	50,000	58,000	
Autos	20	20	21	
Gasoline	$ 96,000	$ 8,000	$ 8,970	$ (970)
Oil, minor repairs, parts	30,000	2,500	2,840	(340)
Outside repairs	9,600	800	980	(180)
Insurance	18,000	1,500	1,625	(125)
Salaries and benefits	103,320	8,610	8,610	0
Vehicle depreciation	48,000	4,000	4,200	(200)
Total	$304,920	$25,410	$27,225	$(1,815)

The annual budget was based on the following assumptions:

a. $0.16 per kilometre for gasoline.
b. $0.05 per kilometre for oil, minor repairs, and parts.
c. $480 per automobile per year for outside repairs.
d. $900 per automobile per year for insurance.
e. $8,610 per month for salaries and benefits.
f. $2,400 per automobile per year for depreciation.

The supervisor of the motor pool is unhappy with the report, claiming it paints an unfair picture of the motor pool's performance.

Required:

1. Prepare a flexible budget performance report for March. Use Exhibit 9–3 as a guide.
2. What are the deficiencies in the original cost control report? How does the report that you prepared in (1) above overcome these deficiencies?

(CMA, adapted)

CASE 9–29 Evaluating Budgeting Procedures [LO1]

Tom Emory and Jim Morris strolled back to their plant from the administrative offices of Ferguson & Son Manufacturing Company. Tom is manager of the machine shop in the company's factory; Jim is manager of the equipment maintenance department.

The men had just attended the monthly performance evaluation meeting for plant department heads. These meetings had been held on the third Tuesday of each month since Robert Ferguson, Jr., the president's son, had become plant manager a year earlier.

As they were walking, Tom Emory spoke: "Boy, I hate those meetings! I never know whether my department's accounting reports will show good or bad performance. I'm beginning to expect the worst. If the accountants say I saved the company a dollar, I'm called 'Sir,' but if I spend even a little too much—boy, do I get in trouble. I don't know if I can hold on until I retire."

Tom had just been given the worst evaluation he had ever received in his long career with Ferguson & Son. He was the most respected of the experienced machinists in the company. He had been with Ferguson & Son for many years and was promoted to supervisor of the machine shop when the company expanded and moved to its present location. The president (Robert Ferguson, Sr.) had often stated that the company's success was due to the high-quality work of machinists like Tom. As supervisor, Tom stressed the importance of craftsmanship and told his workers that he wanted no sloppy work coming from his department.

When Robert Ferguson, Jr., became the plant manager, he directed that monthly performance comparisons be made between actual and budgeted costs for each department. The departmental budgets were intended to encourage the supervisors to reduce inefficiencies and to seek cost reduction opportunities. The company controller was instructed to have his staff "tighten" the budget slightly whenever a department attained its budget in a given month; this was done to reinforce the plant manager's desire to reduce costs. The young plant manager often stressed the importance of continued progress toward attaining the budget; he also made it known that he kept a file of these performance reports for future reference when he succeeded his father.

Tom Emory's conversation with Jim Morris continued as follows:

Emory: I really don't understand. We've worked so hard to meet the budget, and the minute we do so they tighten it on us. We can't work any faster and still maintain quality. I think my men are ready to quit trying. Besides, those reports don't tell the whole story. We always seem to be interrupting the big jobs for all those small rush orders. All that setup and machine adjustment time is killing us. And quite frankly, Jim, you were no help. When our hydraulic press broke down last month, your people were nowhere to be found. We had to take it apart ourselves and got stuck with all that idle time.

Morris: I'm sorry about that, Tom, but you know my department has had trouble making budget, too. We were running well behind at the time of that problem, and if we'd spent a day on that old machine, we would never have made it up. Instead we made the scheduled inspections of the forklift trucks because we knew we could do those in less than the budgeted time.

Emory: Well, Jim, at least you have some options. I'm locked into what the scheduling department assigns to me and you know they're being harassed by sales for those special orders. Incidentally, why didn't your report show all the supplies you guys wasted last month when you were working in Bill's department?

Morris: We're not out of the woods on that deal yet. We charged the maximum we could to other work and haven't even reported some of it yet.

Emory: Well, I'm glad you have a way of getting out of the pressure. The accountants seem to know everything that's happening in my department, sometimes even before I do. I thought all that budget and accounting stuff was supposed to help, but it just gets me into trouble. It's all a big pain. I'm trying to put out quality work; they're trying to save pennies.

Required:

1. Identify the problems that appear to exist in Ferguson & Son Manufacturing Company's budgetary control system and explain how the problems are likely to reduce the effectiveness of the system.
2. Explain how Ferguson & Son Manufacturing Company's budgetary control system could be revised to improve its effectiveness.

INSTANT QUIZ SOLUTIONS

9–1

Cash collections from first-quarter sales: $200,000 × 25%   = $ 50,000
Cash collections from second-quarter sales: $300,000 × 75% =   225,000
Total cash collections in the second quarter $275,000

9–2

Budgeted unit sales	8,000
Add desired ending inventory	1,000
Total needs	9,000
Less beginning inventory	500
Required production	8500

9–3

Payment for first-quarter purchases: 31,000 × $0.20 × 50%   = $3,100
Payment for second-quarter purchases: 57,000 × $0.20 × 50% = 5,700
Total cash disbursements in the second quarter $8,800

9–4

Direct materials: 40 kilograms × $1.50 per kilogram $ 60.00
Direct labour: 2 hours × $30 per hour   60.00
Manufacturing overhead: 2 hours × $25 per hour   50.00
Unit product cost $170.00

9–5

Opening cash balance + Receipts − Disbursements = Excess cash (deficiency)
$80,000 + $800,000 − $850,000 = $30,000 excess
$30,000 is less than the target balance of $80,000, so they will need to borrow funds.
Formula:

$$\$30,000 + X - 0.01X = \$80,000$$
$$.99X = \$50,000$$
$$X = \$50,505 \text{ (rounded)}$$

9–6

$50,505 × 1% = $505 (rounded)

9–7

20,000 × $2.50 = $50,000

9–8

Flexible budget variance = $48,000 (20,000 × $2.40*) − $50,000 (20,000 × $2.50) = $2,000 unfavourable
Sales volume variance = $50,000 (20,000 × $2.50) − $62,500 (25,000 × $2.5) = $12,500 unfavourable

*$48,000/20,000

ENDNOTES

1.   Stan Davis, Todd De Zoort, and Lori Kopp, "The Effect of Obedience Pressure and Perceived Responsibility on Management Accountants' Creation of Budgetary Slack," *Behavioural Research in Accounting* 18, 2006, pp. 19–36.

STANDARD COSTS AND OVERHEAD ANALYSIS

■ MANAGING DISTRIBUTION COSTS

Comstock Images / Alamy

Rising fuel costs create pressure for companies like Catalyst Paper Corporation, a pulp and paper manufacturer based in British Columbia, to find ways to improve the management of the distribution function. At Catalyst Paper, analysts developed a model used to calculate the budgeted or "standard" cost for each shipment made to a customer. At the end of each month, company analysts compare the actual shipping costs to the standard amounts estimated by their model.

Variances between the actual and standard costs can be caused by several factors including bad weather, delays in production or differences between customers' budgeted and actual purchasing patterns. Once the causes of the variances have been identified, managers can take follow-up actions aimed at eliminating or reducing variances in future periods.

Chapter 10 continues our three-chapter study of planning, control, and performance measurement. Our study of performance measurement begins with the production function. In this chapter we see how various measures are used to control operations and to evaluate performance in this key operating area.

Companies in highly competitive industries, such as Cenovus Energy, WestJet, Tim Hortons, and West Fraser Timber Company, must be able to provide high-quality goods and services at market prices. If they do not, their customers will buy from lower priced (and potentially more efficient) competitors. Operationally, managers must obtain inputs such as raw materials and electricity at the lowest possible prices and use them as effectively as possible while maintaining or increasing the quality of what they sell. If inputs are purchased at prices that are too high or greater quantities are used than is really necessary, cost may be unnecessarily high. For many companies, the answer to this control problem lies at least partially in *standard costs*.

Standards represent specific elements of budgets (Chapter 9), such as direct materials or direct labour requirements, as well as projected overhead costs. As such, standards serve both a planning function and a control function. Whether or not organizations employ standard costs to formally cost jobs (Chapter 5) or processes (Chapter 6) is one of the decisions managers must make. If they decide to use actual costs for jobs or processes, they can still use standard costs for budgeting and operational planning.

Controlling overhead costs is also a major concern for managers in business, government, and not-for-profit organizations. Indeed, overhead is a major cost—if not *the* major cost—in many large organizations. Control of overhead costs poses special problems in part because they are more difficult to understand than direct materials and direct labour. Overhead is made up of numerous individual items, some of which are small in dollar amounts. Further, some overhead costs are variable and others are fixed. In this chapter we extend the concept of flexible budgets introduced in Chapter 9 to their use in controlling overhead costs. We also address the analysis and reporting of overhead costs within a standard costing system.

■ STANDARD COSTS—MANAGEMENT BY EXCEPTION

A *standard* is a benchmark or "norm" for measuring performance. Standards are found everywhere. Your doctor evaluates your weight using standards that have been set for individuals of your age, height, and gender. The food we eat in restaurants must be prepared under specified standards of cleanliness. The buildings we live in must conform to standards set in building codes. Standards are also widely used in managerial accounting, where they relate to the *quantity* and *cost* of inputs used in manufacturing goods or providing services.

Quantity and cost standards are set for each major input, such as raw materials and labour time. *Quantity standards* specify how much of an input should be used to make a unit of product or provide a unit of service. *Cost (price) standards* specify how much should be paid for each unit of the input. Actual quantities and actual costs of inputs are periodically compared to these standards. If either the quantity or the cost of inputs departs significantly from the standards, managers investigate the discrepancy to find and eliminate the cause of the problem. This process is called **management by exception**.

This basic approach to identifying and solving problems is used in the *variance analysis cycle*, which is illustrated in Exhibit 10–1. The cycle begins with the preparation of standard cost performance reports in the accounting department. These reports highlight the variances, which are the differences between actual results and what should have occurred according to the standards. The variances can raise numerous questions. Why did the variance occur? Why is this variance larger than it was last period? The significant variances are investigated to discover their root causes. Corrective actions are taken, and then the next period's operations are carried out.

Management by exception
A system of management in which standards are set for various operating activities that are then periodically compared to actual results. Any differences that are deemed significant are brought to the attention of management as "exceptions."

EXHIBIT 10–1 The Variance Analysis Cycle

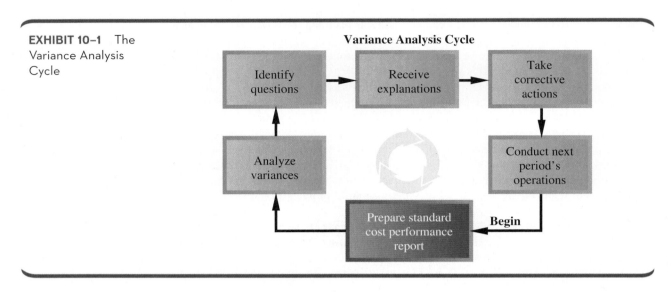

It is important to note that different individuals within the organization are usually called upon to help investigate and explain variances based on their specific responsibilities. For example, if raw materials cost is higher than the standard, the purchasing department manager is in the best position to help explain it. If a higher quantity of direct labour is used than the standard, both the production manager and the purchasing manager will be asked to help explain it. Perhaps the purchasing manager approved the purchase of lower quality materials at a lower cost, but this impacted the efficiency of the production process such that more direct labour per unit was required than dictated by the standard.

Once the variance has been investigated and explained and corrective action has been taken, the cycle begins again with the preparation of a new standard cost performance report for the most recent period. The emphasis should be on highlighting problems, finding their root causes, and taking corrective action. The goal is to improve operations—not to assign blame.

LEARNING OBJECTIVE ❶

Explain how direct materials standards and direct labour standards are set.

■ SETTING STANDARD COSTS

Setting price and quantity standards ideally combines the expertise of everyone who is responsible for purchasing and using inputs. In a manufacturing setting, this might include accountants, purchasing managers, engineers, production supervisors, line managers, and production workers. Past records of purchase prices and of input usage can be helpful in setting standards. In a service setting, time and service standards might also be set. However, the standards should be designed to encourage efficient *future* operations, not a repetition of *past* operations that may or may not have been efficient.

Who Uses Standard Costs?

Manufacturing, service, food, and not-for-profit organizations all use standards to some extent. Auto service centres like Canadian Tire, for example, often set specific labour time standards for the completion of certain auto repairs, such as installing a water pump or changing a tire, and then measure actual performance against these standards. Fast-food outlets such as Harvey's have exacting standards as to the quantity of meat put into a sandwich, as well as standards for the cost of the meat. Hospitals have standard costs (for food, laundry, and other items) for each occupied bed per day, as well as standard time allowances for certain routine activities, such as laboratory tests. In short, you are likely to run into standard costs in virtually any line of business.

Manufacturing companies often have highly developed standard costing systems in which standards relating to materials, labour, and overhead are developed in detail for each separate product. A **standard cost record** shows the standard quantities and costs of the inputs required to produce a unit of a specific product. The cost is calculated by multiplying the standard quantity of each input required to produce one unit of output by the price or rate for that input. These records are electronically created and maintained as part of the company's accounting information system. In this section, we provide a detailed example of how standard costs are set in preparing the standard cost record.

Ideal versus Practical Standards

Should standards be attainable all of the time, part of the time, or almost none of the time? Opinions vary, but standards tend to fall into one of two categories—either ideal or practical.

Ideal standards are those that can be attained only under the best circumstances. They allow for no machine breakdowns or other work interruptions, and they call for a level of effort that can be attained only by the most skilled and efficient employees working at peak effort 100% of the time. Some managers feel that such standards have motivational value. They argue that even though employees know they will rarely meet the standard, it is a constant reminder of the need for ever-increasing efficiency and effort. However, few firms use ideal standards because most managers feel they are discouraging for even the most diligent workers. Moreover, when ideal standards are used, variances from the standards have little meaning. Large variances from the ideal are normal, so it is difficult to manage by exception.

Practical standards are defined as standards that are tight but attainable. They allow for normal machine downtime and employee rest periods, and they can be attained through reasonable, although highly efficient, efforts by the average employee. Variances from practical standards typically signal a need for management attention because they represent deviations that fall outside normal operating conditions. In addition to signalling abnormal conditions, they can also be used to forecast cash flows and plan inventory. By contrast, ideal standards cannot be used in normal budgets or plans; they do not allow for normal inefficiencies, so they result in unrealistic planning and forecasting figures.

Throughout the remainder of this chapter, we will assume the use of practical rather than ideal standards.

Setting Direct Materials Standards

We will use the hypothetical Heirloom Pewter Company to illustrate the development and application of a standard costing system. The company was organized a year ago, and its only product is a reproduction of an 18th-century pewter bookend. The bookend is made largely by hand, using traditional metal-working tools. Consequently, the manufacturing process is very labour-intensive and requires a high level of skill.

Heirloom Pewter has recently expanded its workforce to take advantage of unexpected demand for the bookends as gifts. The company started with a small group of experienced pewter workers but has had to hire less experienced workers as a result of the expansion. The president of the company, J. D. Wriston, has called a meeting to discuss production problems. Attending the meeting are Tom Kuchel, the production manager; Janet Warner, the purchasing manager; and George Hanlon, the corporate controller.

Wriston: I've got a feeling that we aren't getting the production we should out of our new people.

Kuchel: Give us a chance. Some of the new people have been with the company for less than a month.

Warner: Let me add that production seems to be wasting an awful lot of material— particularly pewter. That stuff is very expensive.

Kuchel: What about the shipment of defective pewter that you bought—the one with the iron contamination? That caused us major problems.

Warner: How was I to know it was off-grade? Besides, it was a great deal.

Standard cost record
A detailed listing of the standard amounts of materials, labour, and overhead that should go into a unit of product or service, multiplied by the standard price or rate that has been set for each cost element.

Ideal standards
Standards that allow for no machine breakdowns or other work interruptions and that require peak efficiency at all times.

Practical standards
Standards that allow for normal machine downtime and other work interruptions and can be attained through reasonable, although highly efficient, efforts by the average employee.

Wriston: Calm down, everybody. Let's get the facts before we start attacking each other.

Kuchel: I agree. The more facts the better.

Wriston: Okay, George, it's your turn. Facts are the controller's department.

Hanlon: I'm afraid I can't provide the answers off the top of my head, but if you give me about a week I can set up a system that can routinely answer questions relating to worker productivity, material waste, and input prices.

Wriston: Let's mark it on our calendars.

Standard price per unit

The price that should be paid for a single unit of materials, including shipping, receiving, and other such costs, net of any discounts allowed.

Hanlon's first task was to prepare price and quantity standards for the company's only significant raw material, pewter ingots. The **standard price per unit** for direct materials should reflect the final, delivered cost of the materials including shipping, receiving, and other such costs, net of any discounts taken. After consulting with Warner, the purchasing manager, Hanlon prepared the following documentation for the standard price of a kilogram of pewter in ingot form:

Purchase price per kg, top-grade pewter	$3.60
Freight cost, by truck, from the supplier's warehouse	0.44
Receiving and handling cost	0.05
Less purchase discount.	(0.09)
Standard price per kilogram.	$4.00

Notice that the standard price reflects a particular grade of material (top-grade) delivered by a particular type of carrier (truck). Allowances have also been made for handling and discounts. If everything proceeds according to these expectations, the net standard price of a kilogram of pewter should therefore be $4.

Standard quantity per unit

The amount of materials that should be required to complete a single unit of product, including allowances for normal waste, spoilage, and other inefficiencies.

The **standard quantity per unit** for direct materials should reflect the amount of material required for each unit of finished product, as well as an allowance for unavoidable waste, spoilage, and other normal inefficiencies. After consulting with Kuchel, the production manager, Hanlon prepared the following documentation for the standard quantity of pewter required for a pair of bookends:

Materials requirements as specified in the bill of materials for a pair of bookends, in kilograms.	2.7
Allowance for waste and spoilage, in kilograms	0.2
Allowance for rejects, in kilograms	0.1
Standard quantity per pair of bookends, in kilograms	3.0

A bill of materials details the type and quantity of each item of material that should be used in a product. As shown above, it should be adjusted for waste and other factors when determining the standard quantity per unit of product. "Waste and spoilage" refers to materials that are wasted as a normal part of the production process or that spoil before they are used. "Rejects" refers to the direct materials contained in units that are defective and must be scrapped.

Although it is common to recognize allowances for waste, spoilage, and rejects when setting standard costs, this practice is often criticized because it contradicts the zero defects goal associated with improvement programs. If allowances for waste, spoilage, and rejects are built into the standard cost, the levels of those allowances should be periodically reviewed and reduced over time to reflect improved processes, better training, and better equipment.

Once the price and quantity standards have been set, the standard cost of materials per unit of finished product can be computed as

$$3.0 \text{ kilograms per unit} \times \$4 \text{ per kilogram} = \$12 \text{ per unit}$$

This $12 cost figure for a pair of bookends will appear as one item on the standard cost record of the product.

IN BUSINESS

Vale S.A., a Brazilian mining company, has built a fleet of 35 very large ships known as "Valemax" to carry iron ore mined in Brazil to ports in Asia. Vale initially built these ships to counteract the high cost of shipping iron ore, which at some points was higher per tonne ($88) than the average cost of a tonne of iron ore itself ($60). According to Tim Murray, an iron ore analyst with J Capital Research, shipping iron ore from Australia to China costs about $7 per tonne using a 180,000-tonne capacity ship, while the same-sized ship delivering from Brazil to China costs about $17 per tonne. By using the larger Valemax ships, Vale could reduce the shipping cost per tonne of iron ore from Brazil to China enough to allow it to compete with its Australian rivals.

INSTANT QUIZ 10–1
Identify the differences between practical and ideal standards.

Setting Direct Labour Standards

Direct labour price and quantity standards are usually expressed in terms of a labour rate and labour-hours. The **standard rate per hour** for direct labour includes not only wages earned but also employee benefits (e.g., Employment Insurance, extended medical insurance) and other labour costs. Using wage records and in consultation with the production manager, Hanlon determined the standard labour rate per hour at the Heirloom Pewter Company as follows:

Basic average wage rate per hour	$15.00
Employment taxes at 10% of the basic rate	1.50
Employee benefits at 30% of the basic rate	4.50
Standard rate per direct labour-hour	$21.00

Standard rate per hour
The labour rate that should be incurred per hour of labour time, including Employment Insurance, employee benefits, and other labour costs.

Many companies prepare a single standard rate for all employees in a department. This standard rate reflects the expected "mix" of workers, even though the actual wage rates may vary somewhat from individual to individual due to differing skills or seniority. According to the standard computed above, the direct labour rate for Heirloom Pewter should average $21 per hour.

The standard direct labour time required to complete a unit of product (generally called the **standard hours per unit**) is perhaps the single most difficult standard to determine. One approach for physical tasks is to break down each task into elemental body movements (such as reaching, pushing, and turning over). Published tables of standard times for such movements are available. Another approach is for an industrial engineer to do a time and motion study, which involves recording the time required for certain tasks. As stated earlier, the standard time should include allowances for breaks and personal needs of employees, cleanup, rejects, and machine downtime. After consulting with Kuchel, the production manager, Hanlon prepared the following documentation for the standard hours per unit:

Standard hours per unit
The amount of labour time that should be required to complete a single unit of product, including allowances for breaks, machine downtime, cleanup, rejects, and other normal inefficiencies.

Basic labour time per unit, in hours	1.9
Allowance for breaks and personal needs................	0.1
Allowance for cleanup and machine downtime	0.3
Allowance for rejects	0.2
Standard labour-hours per unit of product	2.5

Once the rate and time standards have been set, the standard labour cost per unit of product can be computed as

2.5 hours per unit × $21 per hour = $52.50 per unit

This $52.50 cost figure appears along with direct materials as one item on the standard cost record of the product.

Standard labour-hours have declined in relative importance for some organizations. This is particularly true in highly automated manufacturing firms. However, for many service organizations and numerous other construction and processing organizations, labour remains an important input to the production and service activities. For these organizations, standard labour-hours inform workers and managers what is expected and how labour should be used. More specifically, standards and the resulting comparisons to actual labour-hours may serve to motivate workers and managers. Labour standards can influence individuals in setting their own goals.

Setting Variable Manufacturing Overhead Standards

As with direct labour, the price and quantity standards for variable manufacturing overhead are generally expressed in terms of rate and hours. The rate represents *the variable portion of the predetermined overhead rate* first discussed in Chapter 5. Developing the rate requires estimating both the unit cost of the variable overhead items used in production (indirect supplies, indirect labour, etc.) and the quantity required for the planned level of production. The unit costs are relatively straightforward to estimate and can be based on prior-year amounts or existing contractual agreements with suppliers that lock in prices. The quantities for variable overhead items can be estimated using actual results from prior periods. The hours relate to whatever activity base is used to apply overhead to units of product (usually machine-hours or direct labour-hours). At Heirloom Pewter, the variable portion of the predetermined overhead rate is $3 per *direct labour-hour*. Therefore, the standard variable manufacturing overhead cost per unit is computed as

2.5 hours per unit × $3 per hour = $7.50 per unit

Standard cost per unit
The standard cost of a unit of product as shown on the standard cost card; it is computed by multiplying the standard quantity or hours by the standard price or rate for each cost element.

This $7.50 cost figure appears along with direct materials and direct labour as one item on the standard cost record for variable production costs in Exhibit 10–2. Observe that the **standard cost per unit** is computed by multiplying the standard quantity or hours by the standard price or rate. We expand our discussion of standard costs to include fixed manufacturing overhead later in this chapter.

Are Standards the Same as Budgets?

Standards and budgets are very similar. The major distinction between the two terms is that a standard is a *unit* amount, whereas a budget is a *total* amount. The standard cost for materials at Heirloom Pewter is $12 per pair of bookends. If 1,000 pairs of bookends are to be manufactured during a budgeting period, then the budgeted cost of materials will be $12,000. In effect, *a standard can be viewed as the budgeted cost for one unit of product.*

EXHIBIT 10–2
Standard Cost Record—Variable Production Cost

Inputs	(1) Standard Quantity or Hours	(2) Standard Price or Rate	(3) Standard Cost (1) × (2)
Direct materials	3.0 kilograms	$ 4.00	$12.00
Direct labour	2.5 hours	21.00	52.50
Variable manufacturing overhead	2.5 hours	3.00	7.50
Total standard variable cost per unit			$72.00

A General Model for Variance Analysis

An important reason for separating standards into two categories—price and quantity—is that different managers are usually responsible for buying and for using inputs, and these two activities occur at different times. In the case of raw materials, for example, the purchasing manager is responsible for the price, and this responsibility is exercised at the time of purchase. In contrast, the production manager is responsible for the amount of the raw materials used, and this responsibility is exercised when the materials are used in production, which may be many weeks or months after the purchase date. It is important, therefore, that we separate discrepancies due to deviations from price standards from those due to deviations from quantity standards. Differences between *standard* prices and *actual* prices and *standard* quantities and *actual* quantities are called variable cost **variances**. The act of computing and interpreting variances is called *variance analysis.*

A general model for computing standard cost variances for variable costs is presented in Exhibit 10–3. This model isolates price variances from quantity variances and shows how each of these variances is computed. We will use this model to compute variances for direct materials, direct labour, and variable manufacturing overhead. We will discuss the model for calculating and interpreting fixed overhead variances later in this chapter.

Four things should be noted from Exhibit 10–3. First, a price variance and a quantity variance can be computed for all three variable cost elements—direct materials, direct labour, and variable manufacturing overhead—even though the variance is not called by the same name in all cases. For example, a price variance is called a *materials price variance* in the case of direct materials but a *labour rate variance* in the case of direct labour and an *overhead spending variance* in the case of variable manufacturing overhead.

Second, although the price variance may be called different names it is computed in exactly the same way regardless of whether one is dealing with direct materials, direct labour, or variable manufacturing overhead. The same is true with the quantity variance.

Third, the inputs represent the actual quantity of direct materials, direct labour, and variable manufacturing overhead used; the output represents the good production of the period, expressed in terms of the *standard quantity (or the standard hours) allowed for the actual output* (see column 3 in Exhibit 10–3). The **standard quantity allowed** or **standard hours allowed** means the amount of direct materials, direct labour, or variable manufacturing overhead *that should have been used* to produce the actual output of the

Variances
The differences between standard prices and quantities and actual prices and quantities.

Standard quantity allowed
The amount of materials that should have been used to complete the period's output, as computed by multiplying the actual number of units produced by the standard quantity per unit.

Standard hours allowed
The time that should have been taken to complete the period's output, as computed by multiplying the actual number of units produced by the standard hours per unit.

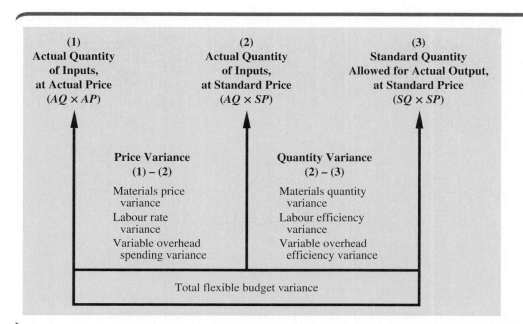

EXHIBIT 10–3
A General Model for Variance Analysis—Variable Production Costs

period. This could be more or less than the materials, labour, or overhead that were *actually* used, depending on the efficiency or inefficiency of operations. The standard quantity allowed is computed by multiplying the actual output in units by the standard input allowed per unit.

Fourth, note that the amount in column 3 ($SQ \times SP$) of Exhibit 10–3 represents the flexible budget for the period. In Chapter 9 we prepared a simplified version of a flexible budget based on the *actual* quantity of units produced for the period multiplied by the total *budgeted* cost per unit. When a standard costing system is being used, the flexible budget is based on the *standard quantity allowed* for the *actual* output achieved multiplied by the *standard price* per unit. As will be illustrated in the sections that follow, this revised approach to calculating the flexible budget permits the flexible budget variance introduced in Chapter 9 (Exhibit 9–3) for a period to be broken down into its price and quantity components.

With this general model as a foundation, we will now examine the price and quantity variances in more detail.

LEARNING OBJECTIVE ❷

Compute the direct materials price and quantity variances, and explain their significance.

■ USING STANDARD COSTS—DIRECT MATERIALS VARIANCES

After determining Heirloom Pewter Company's standard costs for direct materials, direct labour, and variable manufacturing overhead, Hanlon's next step was to compute the company's variances for June, the most recent month. As discussed in the preceding section, variances are computed by comparing standard costs to actual costs. To facilitate this comparison, Hanlon referred to the standard cost data contained in Exhibit 10–2. This exhibit shows that the standard cost of direct materials per unit of product is

$$3.0 \text{ kilograms per unit} \times \$4 \text{ per kilogram} = \$12 \text{ per unit}$$

Heirloom Pewter's purchasing records for June showed that 6,500 kilograms of pewter were purchased at a cost of $3.80 per kilogram. This cost figure included freight and handling and was net of the quantity discount. All of the materials purchased were used during June to manufacture 2,000 pairs of pewter bookends. Using these data and the standard costs from Exhibit 10–2, Hanlon computed the price and quantity variances shown in Exhibit 10–4.

EXHIBIT 10–4
Variance Analysis— Direct Materials

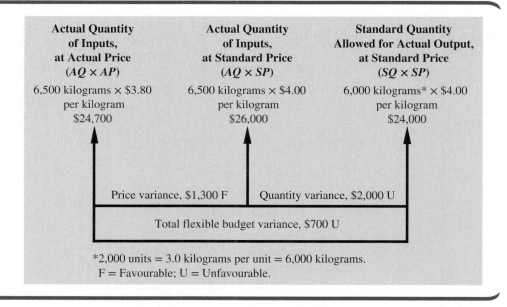

Actual Quantity of Inputs, at Actual Price ($AQ \times AP$)	Actual Quantity of Inputs, at Standard Price ($AQ \times SP$)	Standard Quantity Allowed for Actual Output, at Standard Price ($SQ \times SP$)
6,500 kilograms × $3.80 per kilogram $24,700	6,500 kilograms × $4.00 per kilogram $26,000	6,000 kilograms* × $4.00 per kilogram $24,000

Price variance, $1,300 F Quantity variance, $2,000 U

Total flexible budget variance, $700 U

*2,000 units = 3.0 kilograms per unit = 6,000 kilograms.
F = Favourable; U = Unfavourable.

The three arrows in Exhibit 10–4 point to three different total cost figures. The first, $24,700, refers to the actual total cost of the pewter purchased during June. The second, $26,000, refers to what the actual quantity of pewter would have cost if it had been purchased at the standard price of $4.00 per kilogram rather than the actual price of $3.80 per kilogram. The difference between these two figures, $1,300 ($26,000 − $24,700), is the price variance. It exists because the actual purchase price was $0.20 per kilogram less than the standard purchase price. This variance is labelled *favourable* (denoted by F), since the actual price was less than the standard price. A price variance is labelled *unfavourable* (denoted by U) if the actual price exceeds the standard price.

The third arrow in Exhibit 10–4 points to $24,000 (i.e., the flexible budget amount). This would have been the cost of pewter had it been purchased at the standard price and only the amount allowed by the standard quantity had been used. The standard calls for 3 kilograms of pewter per unit. Since 2,000 pairs of bookends were produced, 6,000 kilograms of pewter should have been used. This is referred to as the *standard quantity allowed for the actual output*. If 6,000 kilograms of pewter had been purchased at the standard price of $4.00 per kilogram, the company would have spent $24,000. The difference between this figure, $24,000, and the figure at the end of the middle arrow in Exhibit 10–4, $26,000, is the quantity variance of $2,000.

To understand the quantity variance, note that the actual amount of pewter used in production was 6,500 kilograms. However, the standard amount of pewter allowed for the actual output is only 6,000 kilograms. Therefore, in total, 500 kilograms too much pewter was used to produce the actual output. To express this in dollar terms, multiply 500 kilograms by the standard price of $4.00 per kilogram to yield the quantity variance of $2,000. Why is the standard price, rather than the actual price, of the pewter used in this calculation? The production manager is ordinarily responsible for the quantity variance. If the actual price was used in the calculation of the quantity variance, the production manager would also be held responsible for the performance of the purchasing manager who was unable to purchase the pewter at the standard price. Apart from being unfair, time-consuming debates between the production manager and purchasing manager could occur every time the actual price of an input is above its standard price. To avoid these debates, which can be an unproductive distraction to managers, the standard price is used when computing the quantity variance.

The quantity variance in Exhibit 10–4 is labelled *unfavourable* (denoted by U). This is because more pewter was used to produce the actual output than is called for by the standard. A quantity variance is labelled *favourable* if the actual quantity is less than the standard quantity.

The computations in Exhibit 10–4 reflect the fact that all of the material purchased during June was also used during June. How are the variances computed if a different amount of material is purchased than is used? To illustrate, assume that during June the company purchased 6,500 kilograms of materials, but used only 5,000 kilograms of material during the month and produced only 1,600 units. In this case, the price variance and quantity variance would be as shown in Exhibit 10–5.

There are two reasons that companies compute the materials price variance when materials are purchased rather than when they are used in production. First, delaying the computation of the price variance until the materials are used would result in less-timely variance reports if there is a time gap between the purchase of materials and their use in production. Second, by computing the price variance at the time of purchase, materials can be carried in the inventory accounts at their standard cost. This greatly simplifies bookkeeping. Appendix 10B at the end of the chapter explains how the simplified bookkeeping works in a standard costing system where inventories of direct materials exist.

Note from Exhibit 10–5 that the price variance is computed on the entire amount of material purchased (6,500 kilograms), as before, whereas the quantity variance is computed only on the portion of this material used in production during the month (5,000 kilograms). A quantity variance on the 1,500 kilograms of material purchased during the month but *not* used in production (6,500 kilograms purchased − 5,000 kilograms used = 1,500 kilograms unused)

EXHIBIT 10–5   Variance Analysis—Direct Materials, When the Amount Purchased Differs from the Amount Used

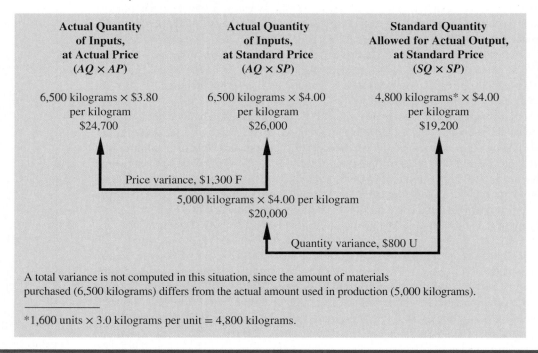

Actual Quantity of Inputs, at Actual Price (AQ × AP)	Actual Quantity of Inputs, at Standard Price (AQ × SP)	Standard Quantity Allowed for Actual Output, at Standard Price (SQ × SP)
6,500 kilograms × $3.80 per kilogram $24,700	6,500 kilograms × $4.00 per kilogram $26,000	4,800 kilograms* × $4.00 per kilogram $19,200

Price variance, $1,300 F

5,000 kilograms × $4.00 per kilogram
$20,000

Quantity variance, $800 U

A total variance is not computed in this situation, since the amount of materials purchased (6,500 kilograms) differs from the actual amount used in production (5,000 kilograms).

―――――――
*1,600 units × 3.0 kilograms per unit = 4,800 kilograms.

will be computed in a future period when these materials are drawn out of inventory and used in production. The situation illustrated in Exhibit 10–5 is common for companies that purchase materials well in advance of use and store the materials in warehouses while awaiting the production process.

Materials Price Variance—A Closer Look

Materials price variance
A measure of the difference between the actual unit price paid for an item and the standard price, multiplied by the quantity purchased.

A **materials price variance** measures the difference between what is paid for a given quantity of materials and what should have been paid according to the standard that has been set multiplied by the quantity purchased. From Exhibits 10–4 and 10–5, this difference can be expressed by the formula

$$\text{Materials price variance} = (AQ \times AP) - (AQ \times SP)$$

Actual   Actual   Standard
Quantity   Price   Price
Purchased

The formula can be factored into simpler form as follows:

$$\text{Materials price variance} = AQ(AP - SP)$$

This simpler formula permits variance computations to be made very quickly. Using the data from Exhibits 10–4 and 10–5 in this formula, we have

6,500 kilograms ($3.80 per kilogram − $4.00 per kilogram) = −$1,300 F

Notice that the answer is the same as that yielded in Exhibit 10–4. Also note that because of the order of the calculation, a negative variance is always labelled as *favourable* (F) and a positive variance is always labelled as *unfavourable* (U) when the formula approach is used. This is true of all variance formulas in this and later chapters.

Variance reports are often issued in a tabular format that shows the details and explanation of particular variances. Following is an example of such a report that has been provided by the purchasing manager:

HEIRLOOM PEWTER COMPANY						
Performance Report—Purchasing Department						
	(1)	**(2)**	**(3)**	**(4)**	**(5)**	
				Difference in Price	**Total Price Variance**	
Item Purchased	**Quantity Purchased**	**Actual Price**	**Standard Price**	**(2) − (3)**	**(1) × (4)**	**Explanation**
Pewter.	6,500 kilograms	$3.80	$4.00	−$0.20	−$1,300 F	Negotiated for an especially favourable price.
F = Favourable						

Isolation of Variances

Variances should be isolated and brought to the attention of management as quickly as possible so that problems can be identified and corrected on a timely basis. The most significant variances should be viewed as red flags; an exception has occurred that requires explanation by the responsible manager and perhaps follow-up effort. The performance report itself may contain explanations for the variances, as illustrated above. In the case of Heirloom Pewter Company, the purchasing manager said that the favourable price variance resulted from negotiating an especially good price.

Responsibility for the Variance

Who is responsible for the materials price variance? Generally speaking, the purchasing manager has control over the price paid for goods and is therefore responsible for any price variances. Many factors influence the prices paid for goods, including how many units are ordered in a lot, how the order is delivered, whether the order is a rush order, and the quality of materials purchased. A deviation in any of these factors from what was assumed when the standards were set can result in a price variance. For example, purchase of second-grade materials rather than top-grade materials may result in a favourable price variance, since the lower-grade materials will generally be less costly (but perhaps less suitable for production).

However, someone other than the purchasing manager could be responsible for a materials price variance. Production may be scheduled in such a way, for example, that the purchasing manager must request delivery by air freight, rather than by truck. In these cases, the production manager bears responsibility for the resulting price variances.

A word of caution is in order. Variance analysis should not be used to assign blame. The emphasis must be on the control function in the sense of *supporting* the line managers and *assisting* them in meeting the goals that they have participated in setting for the company. In short, the emphasis should be positive rather than negative. Excessive focus on what has already happened, particularly in terms of assigning blame, can be destructive to the functioning of an organization.

Toy Mountain has developed a new toy called the Braingame. The company has a standard costing system to help control costs and has established the following standards for the Braingame:

Direct materials: 8 diodes per toy at $0.30 per diode

Direct labour: 1.2 hours per toy at $7 per hour

During August, the company produced 5,000 Braingames. Production data on the toy for August follow:

Direct materials: 70,000 diodes were purchased at a cost of $0.28 per diode. 20,000 of these diodes were still in inventory at the end of the month. (There was no opening inventory.)

Direct labour: 6,400 direct labour-hours were worked at a cost of $48,000.

Compute the direct materials price variance for August. What is a possible cause of this variance?

Materials Quantity Variance—A Closer Look

Materials quantity variance

A measure of the difference between the actual quantity of materials used in production and the standard quantity allowed, multiplied by the standard price per unit of materials.

A **materials quantity variance** measures the difference between the quantity of materials used in production and the quantity that should have been used, according to the standard that has been set. Although the variance is concerned with the physical usage of materials, it is generally stated in dollar terms, as shown in Exhibit 10–4. The formula for the materials quantity variance is

$$\text{Materials quantity variance} = (AQ \times SP) - (SQ \times SP)$$

where AQ = Actual Quantity Used, SP = Standard Price, and SQ = Standard Quantity Allowed for Actual Output.

Again, the formula can be factored into simpler terms:

$$\text{Materials quantity variance} = SP(AQ - SQ)$$

Using the data from Exhibit 10–4 in the formula, we have

$$\$4.00 \text{ per kilogram } (6{,}500 \text{ kilograms} - 6{,}000 \text{ kilograms*}) = \$2{,}000 \text{ U}$$

*2,000 units × 3.0 kilograms per unit = 6,000 kilograms

The answer, of course, is the same as that yielded in Exhibit 10–4. The data might appear as follows if a formal performance report were prepared:

	(1)	(2)	(3)	(4)	(5)	
HEIRLOOM PEWTER COMPANY Performance Report—Purchasing Department						
Type of Materials	**Standard Price**	**Actual Quantity**	**Standard Quantity Allowed**	**Difference in Quantity (2) − (3)**	**Total Quantity Variance (1) × (4)**	**Explanation**
Pewter............	$4.00	6,500 kg	6,000 kg	500 kg	$2,000 U	Low-quality materials unsuitable for production
U = Unfavourable						

The materials quantity variance is best isolated at the time that materials are placed into production. Materials are requisitioned for the number of units to be produced, according to the standard bill of materials for each unit. Any additional materials are usually drawn with an excess materials requisition, which is different from the normal requisition. This procedure calls attention to the excessive usage of materials *while production is still in process* and provides an opportunity for early identification and correction of any developing problem.

Excessive usage of materials can result from many factors, including faulty machines, inferior quality of materials, untrained workers, and poor supervision. Generally speaking, it is the responsibility of the production department to see that materials usage is kept in line with standards. There may be times, however, when the *purchasing* department is responsible for an unfavourable materials quantity variance. If the purchasing department obtains inferior-quality materials in an effort to reduce costs, the materials may be unsuitable for use and may result in excessive waste. Thus, purchasing rather than production will be responsible for the quantity variance. Indeed, at Heirloom Pewter, the production manager said that low-quality materials were the cause of the unfavourable materials quantity variance for June.

INSTANT QUIZ 10-3
Using the information supplied for Toy Mountain in Instant Quiz 10-2, calculate the materials quantity variance and indicate a possible cause.

■ USING STANDARD COSTS—DIRECT LABOUR VARIANCES

> **LEARNING OBJECTIVE** ③
> Compute the direct labour rate and efficiency variances, and explain their significance.

Hanlon's next step in determining Heirloom Pewter's variances for June was to compute the direct labour variances for the month. Recall from Exhibit 10–2 that the standard direct labour cost per unit of product is $52.50, computed as

2.5 hours per unit × $21 per hour = $52.50 per unit

During June, the company paid its direct labour workers $108,000, including employment taxes and benefits, for 5,400 hours of work. This was an average of $20 per hour. Using these data and the standard costs from Exhibit 10–2, Hanlon computed the direct labour rate and efficiency variances that appear in Exhibit 10–6.

EXHIBIT 10–6   Variance Analysis—Direct Labour

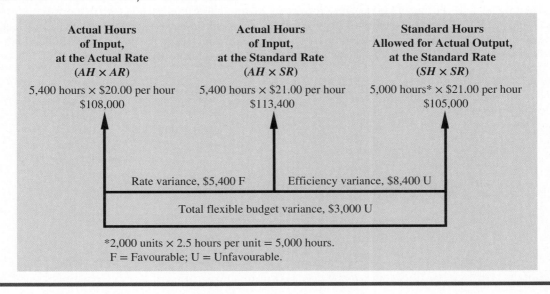

Actual Hours of Input, at the Actual Rate (*AH* × *AR*)	Actual Hours of Input, at the Standard Rate (*AH* × *SR*)	Standard Hours Allowed for Actual Output, at the Standard Rate (*SH* × *SR*)
5,400 hours × $20.00 per hour	5,400 hours × $21.00 per hour	5,000 hours* × $21.00 per hour
$108,000	$113,400	$105,000

Rate variance, $5,400 F   Efficiency variance, $8,400 U

Total flexible budget variance, $3,000 U

*2,000 units × 2.5 hours per unit = 5,000 hours.
F = Favourable; U = Unfavourable.

Notice that the column headings in Exhibit 10–6 are the same as those used in the prior two exhibits, except that in Exhibit 10–6 the terms *hours* and *rate* are used in place of the terms *quantity* and *price*.

Labour Rate Variance—A Closer Look

Labour rate variance
A measure of the difference between the actual hourly labour rate and the standard rate, multiplied by the number of hours worked during the period.

As explained earlier, the price variance for direct labour is commonly termed a **labour rate variance**. This variance measures any deviation from standard in the average hourly rate paid to direct labour workers. The formula for the labour rate variance is

$$\text{Labour rate variance} = (AH \times AR) - (AH \times SR)$$

$$\begin{matrix} \text{Actual} & \text{Actual} & \text{Standard} \\ \text{Hours} & \text{Rate} & \text{Rate} \end{matrix}$$

The formula can be factored into simpler form as

$$\text{Labour rate variance} = AH(AR - SR)$$

Using the data from Exhibit 10–6 in the formula, we have

$$5{,}400 \text{ hours } (\$20.00 \text{ per hour} - \$21.00 \text{ per hour}) = -\$5{,}400 \text{ F}$$

In most companies, the rates paid to workers are quite predictable. Nevertheless, rate variances can arise through the way labour is used. Skilled workers with high hourly rates of pay may be given duties that require less skill and call for low hourly rates of pay. This will result in unfavourable labour rate variances, since the actual hourly rate of pay will exceed the standard rate specified for the particular task being performed. A reverse situation exists when unskilled or untrained workers are assigned to jobs that require higher levels of skill or training. The lower pay scale for these workers will result in favourable rate variances, although the workers may be less efficient. Finally, unfavourable rate variances can arise from overtime work paid at premium rates if any portion of the overtime premium is added to the direct labour account.

Who is responsible for controlling the labour rate variance? Since rate variances generally arise as a result of how labour is used, production supervisors are responsible for controlling them.

Labour Efficiency Variance—A Closer Look

Labour efficiency variance
A measure of the difference between the actual hours taken to complete a task and the standard hours allowed, multiplied by the standard hourly labour rate.

The quantity variance for direct labour, more commonly called the **labour efficiency variance**, measures the productivity of labour time. No variance is more closely watched by management, since it is widely believed that increasing the productivity of direct labour time is vital to reducing costs. The formula for the labour efficiency variance is

$$\text{Labour efficiency variance} = (AH \times SR) - (SH \times SR)$$

$$\begin{matrix} \text{Actual} & \text{Standard} & \text{Standard} \\ \text{Hours} & \text{Rate} & \text{Hours} \\ & & \text{Allowed for} \\ & & \text{Actual Output} \end{matrix}$$

Factored into simpler terms, the formula is

$$\text{Labour efficiency variance} = SR(AH - SH)$$

Using the data from Exhibit 10–6 in the formula, we have

$$\$21.00 \text{ per hour} (5{,}400 \text{ hours} - 5{,}000 \text{ hours*}) = \$8{,}400 \text{ U}$$

$$\text{*}2{,}000 \text{ units} \times 2.5 \text{ hours per unit} = 5{,}000 \text{ hours}$$

Possible causes of an unfavourable labour efficiency variance are poorly trained or motivated workers; poor-quality materials, requiring more labour time for processing; faulty equipment, causing breakdowns and work interruptions; poor supervision of workers; and inaccurate standards. The manager in charge of production is generally responsible for the labour efficiency variance. However, an unfavourable variance might be attributed to purchasing if the acquisition of lower-quality materials results in excessive labour processing time.

Insufficient demand for the company's products may be another important cause of an unfavourable labour efficiency variance. Managers in some companies argue that it is difficult, and perhaps unwise, to constantly adjust the workforce in response to changes in the amount of work that needs to be done. In such companies, the direct labour workforce is essentially fixed in the short run. If demand is insufficient to keep everyone busy, workers are not laid off. In this case, if demand falls below the level needed to keep everyone busy, an unfavourable labour efficiency variance will often be recorded because the actual quantity of hours for which employees are paid will exceed what is required for the actual output.

If the volume of customer orders is insufficient to keep employees busy, a manager has two options—either accept an unfavourable labour efficiency variance or utilize the employees to produce quantities of goods that exceed demand, resulting in a buildup of inventory. A central principle of lean production (JIT) is that building inventory with no immediate prospect of sale is a bad idea. Excessive inventory—particularly work in process inventory—can lead to damaged or obsolete goods and therefore to generally inefficient operations. As a consequence, when the workforce is basically fixed in the short term, managers must be cautious about how labour efficiency variances are interpreted and used. Some advocate dispensing with labour efficiency variances entirely in such situations—at least for motivating and controlling workers on the shop floor.

INSTANT QUIZ 10-4
Using the information supplied for Toy Mountain in Instant Quiz 10-2, calculate the direct labour rate and efficiency variances, and indicate possible causes for each.

■ USING STANDARD COSTS—VARIABLE MANUFACTURING OVERHEAD VARIANCES

LEARNING OBJECTIVE 4
Compute the variable manufacturing overhead spending and efficiency variances, and explain their significance.

The next step in Hanlon's analysis of Heirloom Pewter's variances for June is to compute the variable manufacturing overhead variances. The variable portion of manufacturing overhead can be analyzed with the same basic formulas used to analyze direct materials and direct labour. Recall from Exhibit 10–2 that the standard variable manufacturing overhead is $7.50 per unit of product, computed as follows:

$$2.5 \text{ hours per unit} \times \$3.00 \text{ per hour} = \$7.50 \text{ per unit}$$

Heirloom Pewter's cost records showed that the total actual variable manufacturing overhead cost for June was $15,390. Recall from the earlier discussion of the direct labour variances that 5,400 hours of direct labour time was recorded during the month and that the company produced 2,000 pairs of bookends. Hanlon's analysis of this overhead data appears in Exhibit 10–7.

Notice the similarities between Exhibits 10–6 and 10–7. These similarities arise from the fact that direct labour-hours are being used as a base for allocating overhead cost to units of product; thus, the same hourly figures appear in Exhibit 10–7 for variable manufacturing overhead as in Exhibit 10–6 for direct labour. The main difference between the two exhibits is in the standard hourly rate being used, which in this company is much lower for variable manufacturing overhead. However, the format of the variance analysis for variable manufacturing overhead is the same if machine-hours or material quantities or some other base is used.

EXHIBIT 10–7
Variance Analysis—
Variable
Manufacturing
Overhead

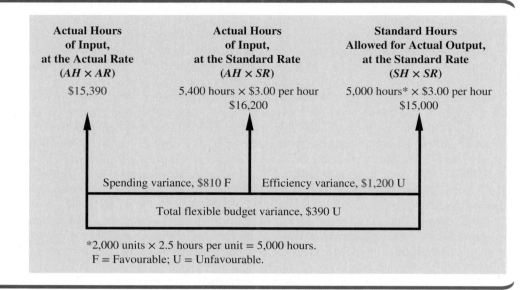

Actual Hours of Input, at the Actual Rate ($AH \times AR$)	Actual Hours of Input, at the Standard Rate ($AH \times SR$)	Standard Hours Allowed for Actual Output, at the Standard Rate ($SH \times SR$)
$15,390	5,400 hours × $3.00 per hour $16,200	5,000 hours* × $3.00 per hour $15,000

Spending variance, $810 F ⟷ Efficiency variance, $1,200 U

Total flexible budget variance, $390 U

*2,000 units × 2.5 hours per unit = 5,000 hours.
F = Favourable; U = Unfavourable.

Variable Manufacturing Overhead Variances—A Closer Look

Variable overhead spending variance
The difference between the actual variable overhead cost incurred during a period and the standard cost that should have been incurred based on the actual activity of the period.

The formula for the **variable overhead spending variance** is

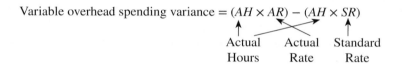

$$\text{Variable overhead spending variance} = (AH \times AR) - (AH \times SR)$$

Actual Hours   Actual Rate   Standard Rate

Using the data from Exhibit 10–7, we have

$$(5,400 \times \$2.85) - (5,400 \times \$3.00) = -\$810 \text{ F}$$

Or, factored into simpler terms:

$$\text{Variable overhead spending variance} = AH(AR - SR)$$

Using the data from Exhibit 10–7 in the formula, we have

$$5,400 \text{ hours } (\$2.85 \text{ per hour*} - \$3.00 \text{ per hour}) = -\$810 \text{ F}$$

*$15,390 ÷ 5,400 hours = $2.85 per hour

As will be explained below, the actual rate of $2.85 per hour incorporates both the price and the quantity of all actual variable overhead items used during the period. As such it represents a mixture of many individual actual rates (cost per kilogram of indirect materials, rate per hour of indirect labour, etc.) and cannot be interpreted in the same way as the actual price for direct materials or the actual rate for direct labour.

Variable overhead efficiency variance
The difference between the actual activity (direct labour-hours, machine-hours, or some other base) of a period and the standard activity allowed, multiplied by the variable part of the predetermined overhead rate.

    The formula for the **variable overhead efficiency variance** is

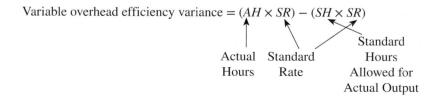

$$\text{Variable overhead efficiency variance} = (AH \times SR) - (SH \times SR)$$

Actual Hours   Standard Rate   Standard Hours Allowed for Actual Output

Or, factored into simpler terms:

$$\text{Variable overhead efficiency variance} = SR(AH - SH)$$

Again using the data from Exhibit 10–7, the computation of the variance is

$$\$3 \text{ per hour } (5,400 \text{ hours} - 5,000 \text{ hours*}) = \$1,200 \text{ U}$$

$$*2,000 \text{ units} \times 2.5 \text{ hours per unit} = 5,000 \text{ hours}$$

Interpreting the Spending Variance

The variable overhead spending variance is most useful to managers when the cost driver for variable overhead really is the actual number of labour-hours or machine-hours worked. In other words, when the actual variable overhead costs vary in proportion with the actual number of hours worked in a period, the variable overhead spending variance can be informative. An overhead spending variance can occur if either (a) the actual purchase price of the variable overhead items differs from the standards or (b) the actual quantity of variable overhead items used differs from the standards.

To illustrate the two distinct components of the spending variance, we will further consider the Heirloom Pewter Company example. Assume that the variable manufacturing overhead rate of $3 per hour shown in Exhibit 10–2 is calculated as follows:

$$\text{Predetermined variable overhead rate} = \frac{\text{Estimated June total variable overhead cost}}{\text{Estimated June total direct labour-hours}}$$

$$\$3 = \$15,000 \div 5,000*$$

$$*2,000 \text{ units} \times 2.5 \text{ per hours per unit}$$

Further assume that the $15,000 of total variable manufacturing overhead costs consists of the following three items:

Indirect labour.	$ 7,500
Indirect materials	5,000
Utilities	2,500
Total variable overhead.	$15,000

The rate of $3 per hour incorporates estimates of both the *price* per unit that will be paid for each item included in variable overhead (e.g., indirect materials) and the *quantity* of those items that will be used for each direct labour-hour worked on the product. For example, assume that Hanlon's estimate of $5,000 for indirect materials is based on expected usage of 200 kilograms of finishing materials at a cost of $25 per kilogram. This implies that 0.04 kilograms of indirect materials will be used for *each hour* worked on a pair of bookends (200 kilograms ÷ 5,000 hours). Given these characteristics of the predetermined overhead rate, two factors can cause the budgeted rate of $3 per hour to differ from the actual rate of $2.85 ($15,390 ÷ 5,400 hours) per hour implied by Exhibit 10–7. First, given the favourable spending variance for June, it may be that the actual cost of indirect materials was less than $25 per kilogram. Second, less than 0.04 kilograms of indirect materials may have been used per hour in producing 2,000 pairs of bookends in June. Of course, various combinations of these factors can also lead to the favourable spending variance, such as lower prices *and* more efficient use of indirect materials. Alternatively, higher prices could be more than offset by more efficient use of indirect materials.

In principle, the price and quantity components of the spending variance could be separately reported. However, this is seldom done because, typically, the price element is small so the variance is mainly influenced by how efficiently the quantities of variable overhead resources are used, such as indirect materials. Even though the price and quantity components are rarely broken out, the spending variance is useful to managers. For example, an unfavourable spending variance tells managers they must find ways to acquire overhead items at cheaper prices, use lower quantities of them, or both.

INSTANT QUIZ 10-5

OrderUp Company provides customer help centre services for online merchants. According to the company's standards, 0.15 direct labour-hours are required to fulfill a help request for one customer, and the variable overhead rate is $1.30 per direct labour-hour. This month, 35,000 help requests were responded to using 5,700 direct labour-hours. The company incurred a total of $7,125 in variable overhead costs.

What variable overhead cost should have been incurred to fill the service requests for the 35,000 items? How much does this differ from the actual variable overhead cost?

Interpreting the Efficiency Variance

Like the variable overhead spending variance, the variable overhead efficiency variance is useful only if the cost driver for variable overhead really is the actual hours worked. Then any increase or decrease in hours actually worked should result in an increase or decrease in variable overhead costs actually incurred. The variable overhead efficiency variance is an estimate of the effect on variable overhead costs of efficiencies or inefficiencies in the use of the base (i.e., hours). In a sense, the term *variable overhead efficiency variance* is a misnomer. It seems to suggest that it measures the efficiency with which variable overhead resources were used. It does not. It is an estimate of the indirect effect on variable overhead costs of efficiency or inefficiency in the use of the activity base.

This point can be illustrated by looking again at Exhibit 10–7. During June, 400 more labour-hours were used than should have been used to produce the period's output. Each of these hours presumably required the incurrence of $3.00 of variable overhead cost, resulting in an unfavourable variance of $1,200 (400 hours × $3.00 = $1,200). Although this $1,200 variance is called an *overhead efficiency variance*, it could better be called a *labour-hours efficiency variance*, since it results from using too many labour-hours rather than from inefficient use of overhead resources. Accordingly, be careful to interpret the variance with a clear understanding of what it really measures. It is worth noting that the efficiency variance for variable overhead can be calculated only if a standard exists for hours (or other quantities) *allowed* for the actual quantity of output achieved for a period. In the absence of a quantity standard for inputs, only the spending variance can be calculated, as will be illustrated later in this chapter.

Control of the Efficiency Variance

Who is responsible for control of the overhead efficiency variance? Since the variance really reflects efficiency in the utilization of the base underlying the flexible budget, whoever is responsible for control of this base is responsible for control of the variance. If the base is direct labour-hours, then the supervisor or manager responsible for the use of labour time will be responsible for any overhead efficiency variance.

In preparation for the scheduled meeting to discuss his analysis of Heirloom Pewter's standard costs and variances, Hanlon distributed Exhibits 10–2 through 10–7 to the management group of Heirloom Pewter. This included Wriston, the president of the company; Kuchel, the production manager; and Warner, the purchasing manager. Wriston opened the meeting with the following question:

Wriston: George, I think I understand the report you distributed, but just to make sure, would you mind summarizing what you found?

Hanlon: As you can see, the biggest problems are the unfavourable materials quantity variance of $2,000 and the unfavourable labour efficiency variance of $8,400.

Wriston: Tom, you're the production boss. What do you think is causing the unfavourable labour efficiency variance?

Kuchel: It has to be the new production workers. Our experienced workers shouldn't have much problem meeting the standard of 2.5 hours per unit. We all knew that there would be some inefficiency for a while as we brought new people on board. My plan for overcoming the problem is to pair up each of the new workers with one of our old-timers and have them work together for a while. It would slow down our old-timers a bit, but I'll bet the unfavourable variance disappears and our new workers would learn a lot.

Wriston: Sounds good. Now, what about that $2,000 unfavourable materials quantity variance?

Hanlon: Tom, are the new workers generating a lot of scrap?

Kuchel: Yeah, I guess so.

Wriston: I think that could be part of the problem. Can you do anything about it?

Kuchel: I can watch the scrap closely for a few days to see where it's being generated. If it is the new workers, I can have the old-timers work with them on the problem when I team them up.

Wriston: Janet, the favourable materials price variance of $1,300 isn't helping us if it is contributing to the unfavourable materials quantity and labour efficiency variances. Let's make sure that our raw material purchases conform to our quality standards.

Warner: Fair enough.

Wriston: Good. Let's reconvene in a few weeks to see what has happened. Hopefully, we can get those unfavourable variances under control.

LEARNING AID

Summary of Variance Formulas for Variable Costs

1. **Direct Materials**

   Price variance: $\quad AQ^*(AP - SP)$

   Quantity variance: $\quad SP(AQ - SQ)$

   where AQ^* = Actual quantity *purchased*, AP = Actual price, SP = Standard price, AQ = Actual quantity used, and SQ = Standard quantity

2. **Direct Labour**

   Rate variance: $\quad AH(AR - SR)$

   Efficiency variance: $\quad SR(AH - SH)$

   where AH = Actual hours, AR = Actual direct labour rate, SR = Standard direct labour rate, and SH = Standard direct labour-hours

3. **Variable Overhead**

   Spending variance: $\quad AH^*(AR^* - SR^*)$

   Efficiency variance: $\quad SR^*(AH^* - SH^*)$

   where AH^* = Actual hours of activity base, AR^* = Actual variable overhead rate, SR^* = Standard variable overhead rate, and SH^* = Standard hours of activity base

---

Before proceeding further, we suggest that you pause at this point and go back and review the data contained in Exhibits 10–2 through 10–7. These exhibits and the accompanying text discussion provide a comprehensive, integrated illustration of standard setting and variance analysis.

Standard Costs and Variances in the Service Industry

While standard costing has its roots in the manufacturing industry, standard costing techniques can also help firms in the service industry understand and better manage their costs. The main differences between standard costing in the manufacturing and service industries are the terminology used and the manner in which the cost of goods sold account is constructed. A manufacturer's cost of goods manufactured is the sum of direct materials, direct labour, and manufacturing overhead cost. A merchandising company (e.g., a retail department store) calculates its cost of goods sold as the net purchase price paid for the products sold during the period. The cost of services provided in other service-based businesses mainly consists of labour, indirect overhead costs, and perhaps a small amount of direct materials incurred to provide services to customers/clients.

Variance analysis can also be useful in service companies, although direct materials might be the computers, office equipment, and office supplies necessary to provide the service and direct labour might be the salary paid to the employees providing the service. For example, a senior accountant's salary is considered direct labour in an accounting firm, while the office receptionist's salary is considered an overhead cost.

Although usually framed in terms of production, variance analysis can be very useful to managers of companies in the service industry. Labour variances are particularly useful since salaries and wages of the employees providing services usually make up the bulk of a service company's costs. Labour rate variances may indicate excessive overtime worked or the use of a greater proportion than expected of more senior staff that results in an increase in the overall average wage for the period. Labour efficiency variances occur when staff spend more than the standard time providing a particular service.

LEARNING OBJECTIVE ⑤

Explain the significance of the denominator activity figure in determining the standard cost of a unit of product.

■ OVERHEAD RATES AND FIXED OVERHEAD ANALYSIS

The detailed analysis of fixed overhead differs considerably from that of variable overhead discussed in the previous section, simply because of the difference in the nature of the costs involved. To provide a background for our discussion, we will first review briefly the need for, and computation of, predetermined overhead rates. This review will be helpful, since the predetermined overhead rate plays a major role in fixed overhead analysis. We will then show how fixed overhead variances are computed and discuss their usefulness to managers.

Flexible Budgets and Overhead Rates

Fixed costs come in large, discrete amounts that by definition do not change with changes in the level of activity within the relevant range. As we learned in Chapter 5, this creates a problem in product costing, since a given level of fixed overhead cost spread over a small number of units will result in a higher cost per unit than if the same costs are spread over a large number of units. Consider the data in the following table:

Month	(1) Fixed Overhead Cost	(2) Number of Units Produced	(3) Unit Cost (1) ÷ (2)
January...............	$6,000	1,000	$6.00
February..............	6,000	1,500	4.00
March................	6,000	800	7.50

Notice that the large number of units produced in February results in a low unit cost ($4.00), whereas the small number of units produced in March results in a high unit cost ($7.50). This problem arises only in connection with the fixed portion of overhead, since by definition the variable portion of overhead remains constant on a per unit basis, with the total costs rising and falling in proportion to changes in the activity level. Most managers feel that the fixed portion of unit cost should be stabilized so that a single unit cost figure can be used throughout the year. As we learned in Chapter 5, this stability can be accomplished by using the predetermined overhead rate.

We will analyze the fixed overhead costs of Heirloom Pewter Company using the flexible budget of the company, as displayed in Exhibit 10–8. Note that the budgeted total fixed overhead costs amount to $300,000 within the relevant range of activity.

Overhead Costs	Cost Formula (per direct labour-hour)	Annual Activity (in direct labour-hours)		
		40,000	50,000	60,000
HEIRLOOM PEWTER COMPANY **Flexible Budgets at Various Levels of Activity**				
Variable overhead costs:				
Indirect labour	$1.50	$ 60,000	$ 75,000	$ 90,000
Lubricants	1.00	40,000	50,000	60,000
Power	0.50	20,000	25,000	30,000
Total variable overhead cost	$3.00	120,000	150,000	180,000
Fixed overhead costs:				
Depreciation.		120,000	120,000	120,000
Supervisory salaries.		144,000	144,000	144,000
Insurance		36,000	36,000	36,000
Total fixed overhead cost		300,000	300,000	300,000
Total overhead cost		$420,000	$450,000	$480,000

EXHIBIT 10–8
Flexible Budget Schedule

Denominator Activity

The formula that we used in Chapter 5 to compute the predetermined overhead rate is as follows (MH: machine-hours; DLH: direct labour-hours):

$$\text{Predetermined overhead rate} = \frac{\text{Estimated total manufacturing overhead cost}}{\text{Estimated total units in the base (MH, DLH, etc.)}}$$

The estimated total units in the base of the formula for the predetermined overhead rate is called the **denominator activity**. Recall from our discussion in Chapter 5 that once an estimated activity level (denominator activity) has been chosen, it remains unchanged throughout the year, even if the actual activity turns out to be different from the original estimate. The reason for not changing the denominator is to maintain stability in the amount of overhead applied to each unit of product, regardless of when it is produced during the year.

Denominator activity The activity figure used to compute the predetermined overhead rate.

Computing the Overhead Rate

When we discussed predetermined overhead rates in Chapter 5, we didn't explain how the estimated total manufacturing cost was determined. This figure can be derived from the flexible budget. Once the denominator level of activity is chosen, the flexible budget can be used to determine the total amount of overhead cost that should be incurred at that level of activity. The predetermined overhead rate can then be computed using the following variation on the basic formula for the predetermined overhead rate:

$$\frac{\text{Predetermined}}{\text{overhead rate}} = \frac{\text{Overhead from the flexible budget at the denominator level of activity}}{\text{Denominator level of activity}}$$

To illustrate, refer to Heirloom Pewter Company's flexible budget for manufacturing overhead in Exhibit 10–8. Suppose that the budgeted activity level for the year is 50,000 direct labour-hours (DLH) and that this will be used as the denominator activity in the formula for the predetermined overhead rate. The numerator in the formula is the estimated total overhead cost (variable and fixed) of $450,000 when the activity is 50,000 DLH. This figure is taken from

EXHIBIT 10–9
Standard Cost
Record—Absorption
Cost

Inputs	(1) Standard Quantity or Hours	(2) Standard Price or Rate	(3) Standard Cost (1) × (2)
Direct materials (from Exhibit 10–2)............	3.0 kilograms	$ 4.00	$12.00
Direct labour (from Exhibit 10–2).............	2.5 hours	21.00	52.50
Variable manufacturing overhead			
(from Exhibit 10–2).....................	2.5 hours	3.00	7.50
Fixed manufacturing overhead	2.5 hours	6.00	15.00
Total standard variable cost per unit			$87.00

the flexible budget in Exhibit 10–8. Therefore, the predetermined overhead rate for Heirloom Pewter Company is computed as follows:

$$\frac{\$450,000}{50,000 \text{ DLH}} = \$9.00 \text{ per direct labour-hour}$$

The company can also break its predetermined overhead rate down into variable and fixed elements rather than using a single combined figure:

$$\text{Variable element}: \frac{\$150,000}{50,000 \text{ DLH}} = \$3.00 \text{ per direct labour-hour}$$

$$\text{Fixed element}: \frac{\$300,000}{50,000 \text{ DLH}} = \$6.00 \text{ per direct labour-hour}$$

For every direct labour-hour of operation, work in process will be charged with $9.00 of overhead, of which $3.00 will be variable overhead and $6.00 will be fixed overhead. If a pair of bookends takes two and one-half direct labour-hours to complete, then its cost will include $7.50 variable overhead and $15 fixed overhead, as per the revised standard cost record shown in Exhibit 10–9, which now includes fixed manufacturing overhead.

In summary, the flexible budget provides the estimated overhead cost needed to compute the predetermined overhead rate. Thus, the flexible budget plays a key role in determining the amount of fixed and variable overhead cost that will be charged to units of product.

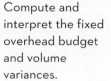

LEARNING OBJECTIVE 6
Compute and interpret the fixed overhead budget and volume variances.

■ OVERHEAD APPLICATION AND FIXED OVERHEAD VARIANCES

To understand the fixed overhead variances, it is necessary first to understand how overhead is applied to work in process in a standard costing system. Therefore, we examine the details of the application process next.

Overhead Application in a Standard Costing System

Normal cost system
A costing system in which overhead costs are applied to jobs by multiplying a predetermined overhead rate by the actual amount of the allocation base incurred by the job.

In Chapter 5, recall that we applied overhead to work in process on the basis of actual hours of activity (multiplied by the predetermined overhead rate). This procedure was correct, since at the time we were dealing with a **normal cost system** that applies overhead using the actual levels of the activity base. However, we are now dealing with a standard costing system. In such a system, overhead is applied to work in process on the basis of the *standard hours allowed for the actual output of the period* (taken from the flexible budget) rather than on the basis of the actual number of hours worked. This point is illustrated in Exhibit 10–10. In a standard costing system, every unit of a particular product is charged with the same amount of overhead cost, regardless of how much time the unit actually requires for processing.

Normal Costing System		Standard Costing System	
Manufacturing Overhead		**Manufacturing Overhead**	
Actual overhead costs incurred.	Applied overhead costs: Actual hours × Predetermined overhead rate.	Actual overhead costs incurred.	Applied overhead costs: Standard hours allowed for actual output × Predetermined overhead rate.
Under- or overapplied overhead		Under- or overapplied overhead	

EXHIBIT 10–10
Applied Overhead Costs: Normal Costing System versus Standard Costing System

To illustrate the computation of fixed overhead variances, we again refer to the data for Heirloom Pewter Company:

Denominator activity in direct labour-hours	50,000
Budgeted annual fixed overhead costs	$300,000
Fixed portion of the predetermined overhead rate (computed earlier)	$ 6

Let us assume that the following actual operating results were recorded for the month of June:

Actual direct labour-hours	5,400
Standard direct labour-hours allowed*	5,000
Actual fixed overhead costs:	
Depreciation	$10,000
Supervisory salaries.	14,000
Insurance	3,500
Total actual cost.	$27,500

*For the actual production in June

From these data, two variances can be computed for fixed overhead—a *budget variance* and a *volume variance*. The variances for the month of June are shown in Exhibit 10–11.

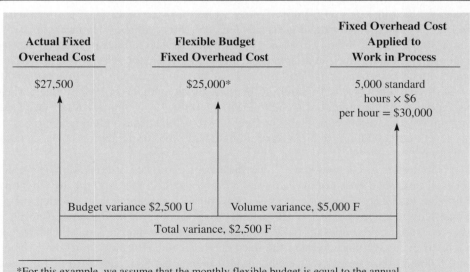

EXHIBIT 10–11
Computation of the June Fixed Overhead Variances

*For this example, we assume that the monthly flexible budget is equal to the annual budget divided by 12: $300,000 ÷ 12 = $25,000 per month.

Notice from the exhibit that overhead has been applied to work in process on the basis of 5,000 standard hours allowed for the actual output of June rather than on the basis of 5,400 actual hours worked. As stated earlier, this keeps unit costs from being affected by any variations in efficiency.

Budget Variance

Budget variance
A measure of the difference between the actual fixed overhead costs incurred during the period and the budgeted fixed overhead costs as contained in the flexible budget.

The **budget variance** is the difference between the actual fixed overhead costs incurred during the period and the budgeted fixed overhead costs as contained in the flexible budget. It can be computed as shown in Exhibit 10–11 or by using the formula

Budget variance = Actual fixed overhead cost − Flexible budget fixed overhead cost

Applying this formula to Heirloom Pewter Company, the budget variance is

$$\$27,500 - \$25,000 = \$2,500 \text{ U}$$

Budget variances for fixed overhead can be very useful, since they represent the difference between how much should have been spent (according to the flexible budget) and how much was actually spent. For the month of June, Heirloom Pewter's actual fixed costs were $2,500 higher than budget, and management may want to identify which specific fixed overhead items caused this variance. We will present a detailed performance report for overhead costs later in the chapter.

Volume Variance

The volume variance is a measure of utilization of plant facilities. The variance arises whenever the standard hours allowed for the actual output of a period are different from the denominator activity level that was planned when the period began. It can be computed as shown in Exhibit 10–11 or by the following formula:

$$\begin{array}{l} \text{Volume} \\ \text{variance} \end{array} = \begin{array}{l} \text{Fixed portion of} \\ \text{the predetermined} \\ \text{overhead rate} \end{array} \times \left(\begin{array}{l} \text{Denominator} \\ \text{hours} \end{array} - \begin{array}{l} \text{Standard hours} \\ \text{allowed} \end{array} \right)$$

Applying this formula to Heirloom Pewter Company, the volume variance is

$$\$6 \text{ per DLH}(4{,}167 - 5{,}000) = -\$4{,}998 \text{ F}$$

As discussed in Chapter 5, predetermined overhead rates are often prepared on an annual basis to avoid distortions in product costs caused by seasonal fluctuations in overhead items (e.g., heating costs). Heirloom Pewter's rate of $6 per hour for fixed overhead is based on estimated annual fixed costs of $300,000 and an annual denominator activity level of 50,000 labour-hours. However, to facilitate the calculation of a volume variance for the *month* of June, Hanlon assigned the annual denominator activity of 50,000 direct labour-hours evenly to each month. Therefore, denominator activity for June is 50,000 ÷ 12 = 4,167. Except for a $2 rounding difference, the favourable $4,998 volume variance above agrees with the amount of $5,000 shown in Exhibit 10–11. Importantly, when calculating the volume variance for the year, Hanlon will use the total annual denominator activity level of 50,000 hours and the standard hours allowed for the total production output for the year.

It is important to note that the volume variance is a measure of utilization of available plant facilities, not a measure of overspending or underspending. A company would normally incur the same dollar amount of fixed overhead cost regardless of whether the period's activity was above or below the planned (denominator) level because, after all, the costs are fixed over the relevant range of activity. Also note that fixed overhead does not have an efficiency variance because the fixed overhead budget for the actual direct labour-hours, 5,400, is the same as the fixed overhead budget for 5,000 standard direct labour-hours, namely $25,000. The volume variance occurs only as a result of the standard (5,000) and denominator (4,167) direct labour-hours difference, 833 direct labour-hours. In short, the volume variance is an activity-related variance. It is explainable only by activity and is controllable only through activity.

To summarize:

1. If the denominator activity and the standard hours allowed for the actual output of the period are the same, then there is no volume variance.
2. If the denominator activity is greater than the standard hours allowed for the actual output of the period, then the volume variance is unfavourable, signifying an underutilization of available facilities.
3. If the denominator activity is less than the standard hours allowed for the actual output of the period, then the volume variance is favourable, signifying a higher utilization of available facilities than was planned.

INSTANT QUIZ 10–6

Carlton Corporation uses a standard costing system that applies overhead to products based on the standard direct labour-hours allowed for the actual output of the period. Data concerning the most recent year appear below:

Total budgeted fixed overhead cost for the year...............................	$400,000
Actual fixed overhead cost for the year......................................	$ 394,000
Budgeted standard direct labour-hours (denominator level of activity)	50,000
Actual direct labour-hours	51,000
Standard direct labour-hours allowed for the actual output	48,000

Compute the fixed portion of the predetermined overhead rate for the year and the fixed overhead budget and volume variances.

Graphic Analysis of Fixed Overhead Variances

Some insights into the budget and volume variances can be gained through graphic analysis. A graph containing these variances is presented in Exhibit 10–12.

EXHIBIT 10–12   Graphic Analysis of Fixed Overhead Variances

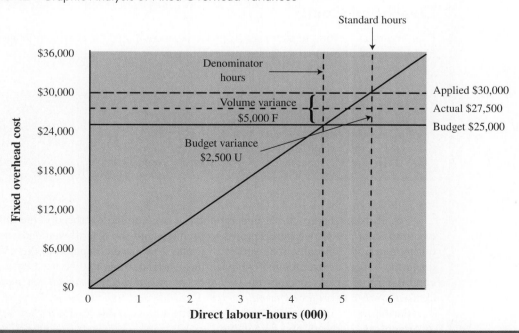

As shown in the graph, fixed overhead cost is applied to work in process at the predetermined rate of $6 for each standard hour of activity. (The applied cost line is the upward-sloping line on the graph.) Since a denominator level of 4,167 direct labour-hours was used for June, the applied cost line crosses the budget cost line at exactly the 4,167 direct labour-hours point. Thus, if the denominator hours and the standard hours allowed for the output are the same, there can be no volume variance, since the applied cost line and the budget cost line will be the same on the graph. It is only when the standard hours differ from the denominator hours that a volume variance can arise.

In this case, more standard hours are allowed for the actual June output (5,000 hours) than denominator hours (4,167 hours); the result is a favourable volume variance, since more cost was applied to production than was originally budgeted. If the situation had been reversed and fewer standard hours than denominator hours had been allowed for the actual output, then the volume variance on the graph would have been unfavourable.

Cautions in Fixed Overhead Analysis

A volume variance arises for fixed overhead because when applying the costs to work in process, we act *as if* the fixed costs were variable. This point can be seen from the graph in Exhibit 10–12. Notice from the graph that the fixed overhead costs are applied to work in process at a rate of $6 per hour *as if* they were variable. Treating these costs as if they were variable is necessary for product costing purposes, but there are some real dangers here. The manager can easily become misled and start thinking of the fixed costs as if they were *in fact* variable.

Keep in mind that fixed overhead costs come in large chunks. Expressing fixed costs on a per unit or per hour basis, although necessary for product costing for external reports, is artificial. Increases or decreases in activity in fact have no effect on total fixed costs within the relevant range of activity. Even though fixed costs are expressed on a unit or per hour basis, they are *not* proportional to activity. In a sense, the volume variance is the error that occurs as a result of treating fixed costs as variable costs in the costing system.

Because of the confusion that can arise concerning the interpretation of the volume variance, some companies present the volume variance in physical units (hours) rather than in dollars, or express utilization as a percentage of capacity utilized.

Overhead Variances and Under- or Overapplied Overhead Cost

Four variances relating to overhead cost have been computed for Heirloom Pewter Company in this chapter. These four variances are as follows:

Variable overhead spending variance (Exhibit 10–7)	$ 810 F
Variable overhead efficiency variance (Exhibit 10–7)	1,200 U
Fixed overhead budget variance (Exhibit 10–11)	2,500 U
Fixed overhead volume variance (Exhibit 10–11).........................	5,000 F
Total overhead variance (equals total overapplied overhead)	$2,110 F

Recall from Chapter 5 that underapplied or overapplied overhead is the difference between the amount of overhead applied to products and the actual overhead costs incurred during a period. Basically, the overhead variances we have computed in this chapter break down the under- or overapplied overhead into variances that can be used by managers for control purposes. Consequently, *the sum of the overhead variances equals the under- or overapplied overhead cost for a period.*

Furthermore, in a standard costing system, unfavourable variances are equivalent to underapplied overhead, and favourable variances are equivalent to overapplied overhead.

Unfavourable variances occur because more was spent on overhead than the standards allow. Underapplied overhead occurs when more was spent on overhead than was applied to products during the period. But in a standard costing system, the standard amount of overhead allowed is exactly the same as the amount of overhead applied to products. Therefore, in a standard costing system, unfavourable variances and underapplied overhead are the same thing, as are favourable variances and overapplied overhead.

For Heirloom Pewter Company, the total overhead variance was $2,110 favourable. Therefore, its overhead cost was overapplied by $2,110 for the year. To reinforce this concept, carefully study the review problem at the end of the chapter.

■ OVERHEAD REPORTING, VARIANCE INVESTIGATIONS, AND CAPACITY ANALYSIS

LEARNING OBJECTIVE 7
Prepare a performance report for manufacturing overhead, decide which variances to investigate, and perform an analysis of capacity utilization.

Hanlon completes his analysis of overhead spending at Heirloom Pewter Company in June by preparing the performance report shown in Exhibit 10–13. The report builds on the analysis of variable and fixed overhead presented, respectively, in Exhibits 10–7 and Exhibit 10–11 by providing details on the individual items included in each category. This additional level of detail allows managers to determine the amount that each overhead item contributes to the spending (budget) and efficiency variances.

Two things should be noted about Exhibit 10–13. First, because Hanlon has developed a standard costing system and wants to report both the spending and efficiency variances for variable overhead costs, he has included budgeted costs for both the actual direct labour-hours used (5,400) and the standard direct labour-hours allowed (5,000) for the 2,000 units produced in June. As a result, the sum of the individual spending ($810 F) and efficiency ($1,200 U) variances reported in Exhibit 10–13 corresponds to the variances shown in Exhibit 10–7. The second issue to note in Exhibit 10–13 is that for fixed overhead costs, no efficiency variances are included; only budget variances are calculated. This is consistent with Exhibit 10–11, which illustrates that for fixed overhead, it is not possible to calculate an efficiency variance. As discussed earlier, this is because within the relevant range of activity, fixed costs do not change as the activity level changes. Therefore, the budget for each fixed overhead item is the same in columns (2) and (3) of Exhibit 10–13, even though the activity level differs by 400 hours (5,400 − 5,000) across these two columns. For control purposes, the budget variance for fixed overhead is the key tool. By comparing what was actually spent on each fixed overhead item to the budget, Hanlon can determine how well the managers responsible for these line items did in controlling costs.

Preparing an overhead performance report that contains both spending and efficiency variances is possible only if a standard costing system is in place. In the absence of a standard costing system, column (3) in Exhibit 10–13 would not exist since it represents the standard direct labour-hours allowed for the actual output achieved. However, even if a standard costing system is not being used, an overhead performance report can still be prepared, but it will include *only* the spending and budget variances. An example of this type of report is presented in Exhibit 10–14. Note that the spending and budget variances in Exhibit 10–14 are the same as those in Exhibit 10–13. The only difference between the two performance reports is that Exhibit 10–13, based on the standard costing system developed at Heirloom Pewter, also includes efficiency variances.

After preparing the performance report, managers still have to decide whether the variances that have been calculated require further action. For example, the $2,000 unfavourable fixed overhead budget variance for supervisory salaries is the largest single variance for the month of June. Should it be investigated? Should answers be sought as to the cause of the variance? Identifying which variances to target for investigation is an important part of the variance analysis cycle presented in Exhibit 10–1. In the next section, we examine how managers make these decisions.

EXHIBIT 10–13 An Overhead Performance Report

HEIRLOOM PEWTER CORPORATION
Overhead Performance Report
For the Month Ended June 30

Actual production (units)................. 2,000
Actual direct labour-hours.............. 5,400
Standard direct labour-hours allowed 5,000

> Budget allowances are based on the direct labour-hours that should have been used (5,000) to produce 2,000 units and the hours actually worked (5,400).

> This approach yields both a spending and an efficiency variance for variable manufacturing overhead.

		Breakdown of the Total Flexible Budget Variance	

Overhead Costs	Cost Formula (per Direct Labour-Hour)	(1) Actual Costs 5,400 Direct Labour-Hours	(2) Budget Based on 5,400 Direct Labour-Hours*	(3) Budget Based on 5,000 Direct Labour-Hours*	Total Flexible Budget Variance (1) – (3)†	Spending (Budget) Variance (1) – (2)	Efficiency Variance (2) – (3)
Variable overhead costs:							
Indirect labour	$ 1.50	$ 7,830	$ 8,100	$ 7,500	$ 330 U	$ 270 F	$ 600 U
Lubricants	1.00	5,022	5,400	5,000	22 U	378 F	400 U
Power....................	0.50	2,538	2,700	2,500	38 U	162 F	200 U
Total variable overhead cost	$3.00	15,390	16,200	15,000	390 U	810 F	1,200 U
Fixed overhead costs:							
Depreciation		10,000	10,000	10,000	0	0	—
Supervisory salaries........		14,000	12,000	12,000	2,000 U	2,000 U	—
Insurance		3,500	3,000	3,000	500 U	500 U	—
Total fixed overhead cost.....		27,500	25,000	25,000	2,500 U	2,500 U	—
Total overhead cost..........		$42,890	$41,200	$40,000	$2,890 U	$1,690 U	$1,200 U

*Budget amounts for variable overhead costs are determined by multiplying budgeted direct labour-hours by the cost formula amount (per direct labour-hour). For example, indirect labour costs of $8,100 for 5,400 hours = $1.50 × 5,400.

†Total variable and fixed overhead variances as per Exhibits 10–7 (variable overhead) and 10–11 (fixed overhead).

EXHIBIT 10–14 An Overhead Performance Report with Only Spending or Budget Variances

	HEIRLOOM PEWTER CORPORATION Overhead Performance Report For the Month Ended June 30			
Actual production (units). 2,000				
Actual direct labour-hours. 5,400				
Overhead Costs	**Cost Formula (per Direct Labour-Hour)**	**(1) Actual Costs 5,400 Direct Labour-Hours**	**(2) Budget Based on 5,400 Direct Labour-Hours***	**Spending (Budget) Variance (1) − (2)**
Variable overhead costs:				
Indirect labour	$1.50	$ 7,830	$ 8,100	$ 270 F
Lubricants	1.00	5,022	5,400	378 F
Power.	0.50	2,538	2,700	162 F
Total variable overhead cost	$3.00	15,390	16,200	810 F
Fixed overhead costs:				
Depreciation		10,000	10,000	0
Supervisory salaries		14,000	12,000	2,000 U
Insurance		3,500	3,000	500 U
Total fixed overhead cost		27,500	25,000	2,500 U
Total overhead cost		$42,890	$41,200	$1,690 U

*Budget amounts for variable overhead costs are determined by multiplying budgeted direct labour-hours by the cost formula amount (per direct labour-hour). For example, indirect labour costs of $8,100 for 5,400 hours = $1.50 × 5,400.

Variance Investigation Decisions

Variance analysis and performance reports are important elements of **management by exception**, which focuses on those areas of responsibility where goals and expectations are not being met.

    The budgets and standards discussed in this chapter and in the preceding chapter reflect management's plans. If all goes according to plan, there will be little difference between actual results and the budgets and standards. However, if actual results do not conform to the budget and to standards, the performance reporting system sends a signal to the manager that an "exception" has occurred. This signal is in the form of a variance from the budget or standards.

    However, are all variances worth investigating? The answer is no. Differences between actual results and what was expected will almost always occur. If every variance were investigated, management would spend a great deal of time tracking down immaterial differences. Variances may occur for any of a variety of reasons—only some of which warrant management attention. For example, hotter than normal weather in the summer may result in higher than expected electricity bills for air conditioning. Because of unpredictable random factors, every cost category will produce a variance of some kind.

    How should managers decide which variances are worth investigating? One indicator is the dollar amount of the variance. A variance of $5 is probably not big enough to warrant attention, whereas a variance of $5,000 might well be worth investigating. Another indicator is the size of the variance relative to the amount of spending involved. A variance that is only 0.1% of spending on an item is likely due to random factors, while a variance of 10% of spending is more indicative that something is wrong and should be investigated.

    Another approach is to plot variance data on a statistical control chart, as illustrated in Exhibit 10–15. The basic idea of a statistical control chart is that some random fluctuations in variances from period to period are to be expected even when costs are under control. A variance should be investigated only when it is unusual relative to the normal level of random fluctuation. Typically, the standard deviation of the variances is used as the measure of the

Management by exception

A system of management in which standards are set for various operating activities that are then periodically compared to actual results. Any differences that are deemed significant are brought to the attention of management as "exceptions."

EXHIBIT 10–15
A Statistical Control Chart

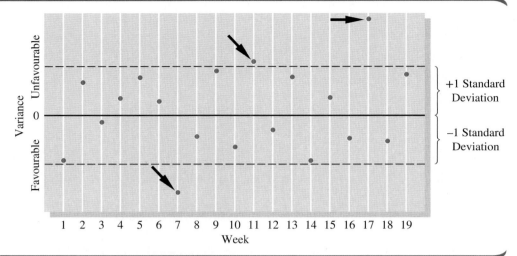

normal level of fluctuations. Often a simple decision rule is adopted, such as "investigate all variances that are more than X standard deviations from zero." In the control chart in Exhibit 10–15, X is 1.0. That is, the decision rule in this company is to investigate all variances that are more than one standard deviation above (unfavourable) or below (favourable) zero. This means that the variances in weeks 7, 11, and 17 would have been investigated, but none of the others.

What value of X should be chosen? The greater the value of X, the wider the band of acceptable variances that would not be investigated. Thus, the greater the value of X, the less time will be spent tracking down variances, but the more likely it is that a truly out-of-control situation will be overlooked. Ordinarily, if X is selected to be 1.0, roughly 30% of all variances will trigger an investigation even when there is no real problem. If X is set at 1.5, the figure drops to about 13%. If X is set at 2.0, the figure drops to about 5%.

In addition to watching for unusually large variances, the pattern of the variances should be monitored. For example, a series of steadily increasing variances should trigger an investigation even if no variance is large enough by itself to warrant investigation.

Capacity Analysis

Capacity analysis allows managers to evaluate the financial impact of not fully utilizing available productive capacity, making it an important strategic tool for management. However, increasing the utilization of capacity by eliminating bottlenecks or increasing demand for products can take time. Similarly, reducing capacity because of insufficient long-term demand cannot be done overnight, so it is important that capacity analysis be conducted on an ongoing basis.

We use Heirloom Pewter Company to illustrate a basic approach to capacity analysis. Recall that the company has a budgeted production level of 20,000 pairs of bookends for the year. This denominator level of activity was used earlier in this chapter to determine a standard cost per pair of bookends of $87.00, based on 20,000 units or 50,000 direct labour-hours (see Exhibit 10–9). Assume now that the year has ended and 16,000 pairs of bookends have been sold.

Theoretical capacity
The volume of activity resulting from operations conducted 24 hours per day, 7 days per week, 365 days per year, with no downtime.

Practical capacity
The productive capacity possible after subtracting unavoidable downtime from theoretical capacity.

If all available production time were used and no waste occurred, Heirloom Pewter could reach a level of capacity known as **theoretical capacity**. This level of capacity would require operations to be conducted around the clock, 365 days per year, with no downtime, similar to the definition of an ideal standard presented earlier in this chapter. If the denominator level of 20,000 units or 50,000 direct labour-hours represented 50% of the theoretical capacity, then Heirloom Pewter could produce 40,000 units (20,000 ÷ 0.50) in 100,000 hours.

Practical capacity represents what could be produced if unavoidable downtime were subtracted from theoretical capacity. Maintenance, breakdowns, and setup times for new operations are considered to be unavoidable downtime. If the denominator level were 80% of practical capacity, then 25,000 units (20,000 ÷ 0.80) could be produced using 62,500 direct labour-hours.

Capacity analysis proceeds by first examining the overhead cost (variable + fixed) at each level of capacity:

		Total Overhead Costs
Theoretical....................	(100,000 DLH × $3.00) × $300,000 =	$600,000
Practical......................	(62,500 DLH × $3.00) × $300,000 =	$487,500
Denominator	(50,000 DLH × $3.00) × $300,000 =	$450,000
Actual	(40,000 DLH × $3.00) × $300,000 =	$420,000

If Heirloom Pewter can sell all that it can produce at $105 per unit, then an indication of the opportunity cost incurred of not operating at the various levels of capacity can be computed as follows:

	Contribution Margin*	Total Overhead	Operating Income
Theoretical...........	40,000 units × ($105.00 − $64.50) −	$600,000 =	$1,020,000
Practical.............	25,000 units × ($105.00 − $64.50) −	$487,500 =	$ 525,000
Denominator	20,000 units × ($105.00 − $64.50) −	$450,000 =	$ 360,000
Actual	16,000 units × ($105.00 − $64.50) −	$420,000 =	$ 228,000

*$64.50 variable costs exclude $7.50 per unit variable overhead because it is included in the total overhead amount.

Note that $64.50 is composed of the standard materials cost of $12 per unit and the standard direct labour cost of $52.50 per unit shown in Exhibit 10–9. The remaining variable production cost of $7.50 per unit for overhead is included in the overhead charges calculated above.

To calculate the opportunity cost of operating at 16,000 units (a profit of $228,000), we begin by looking at what additional profit would have been possible at the theoretical capacity: $1,020,000 − $228,000, or $792,000 in lost profits. By examining marketing strategies or product design changes necessary to sell an additional 24,000 units (40,000 − 16,000), management might be able to significantly improve its profit picture. Analysis would also have to be conducted to evaluate the potential impact of any additional unit sales on setup costs, maintenance, wastage, etc. However, before making a decision to increase productive capacity, managers should conduct the type of analysis discussed in Chapter 13, where we examine capital budgeting decisions. Alternatively, if the long-term demand for bookends is expected to be only 16,000 units, management may consider reducing productive capacity, since only 64% (16,000 ÷ 25,000) of practical capacity is required to meet this level of demand. Reducing the fixed costs, such as insurance, taxes, and maintenance, associated with the unused capacity can lead to improvements in operating profits.

■ EVALUATION OF CONTROLS BASED ON STANDARD COSTS

Advantages of Standard Costs

Standard costing systems have a number of advantages:

1. Standard costs are a key element in a management by exception approach. If costs remain within the standards, managers can focus on other issues. When costs fall significantly outside the standards, managers are alerted that problems may exist. This approach helps managers focus on important issues.

2. Standards that are viewed as reasonable by employees can promote efficiency. They provide benchmarks that individuals can use to judge their own performance.

3. Standard costs can greatly simplify bookkeeping. Instead of recording actual costs for each job, the standard costs for materials, labour, and overhead can be charged to jobs.

4. Standard costs fit naturally in an integrated system of responsibility accounting. The standards establish what costs should be, who should be responsible for them, and whether actual costs are under control.

Potential Problems with the Use of Standard Costs

The use of standard costs can present a number of potential problems:

1. Standard cost variance reports are usually prepared on a monthly basis and often are released days or even weeks after the end of the month. As a consequence, the information in the reports may be very outdated. Timely, frequent reports that are approximately correct are better than infrequent reports that are very precise but out of date by the time they are released. Some companies are now reporting variances and other key operating data daily or even more frequently.

2. Labour quantity standards and efficiency variances make two important assumptions. First, they assume that the production process is labour-paced: If labour works faster, output will go up. However, output in many companies is no longer determined by how fast labour works; rather, it is determined by the processing speed of machines. Second, the computations assume that labour is a variable cost. However, as discussed, direct labour may essentially be fixed in many companies. If labour is fixed, then an undue emphasis on labour efficiency variances creates pressure to build excess inventories.

3. In some cases, a favourable variance can be as bad as or worse than an unfavourable variance. For example, Harvey's has a standard for the amount of hamburger meat that should be in a burger. If there is a favourable variance, it means that less meat was used than the standard specifies. The result is a substandard burger and possibly a dissatisfied customer.

4. There may be a tendency with standard cost reporting systems to emphasize meeting the standards to the exclusion of other important objectives, such as maintaining and improving quality, on-time delivery, and customer satisfaction. This tendency can be reduced by using supplemental performance measures that focus on these other objectives.

5. Just meeting standards may not be sufficient; continuous improvement may be necessary to survive in the current competitive environment. For this reason, some companies focus on trends in standard cost variances—aiming for continuous improvement rather than just meeting the standards. In other companies, engineered standards are being replaced either by a rolling average of actual costs, which is expected to decline, or by very challenging target costs.

BEYOND THE BOTTOM LINE

If managers are insensitive and use variance reports to lay blame, morale may suffer and subordinates may be tempted to cover up unfavourable variances. For example, workers may intensify their efforts to increase output at the end of the month to avoid an unfavourable labour efficiency variance. In the rush to increase output, quality may suffer. Therefore, variance investigation should be done with care and should be framed as finding ways to improve performance in future periods rather than as laying blame for poor performance in prior periods.

In summary, managers should exercise considerable care in their use of a standard costing system. It is particularly important that managers go out of their way to focus on the positive, rather than just on the negative, and to be aware of possible unintended consequences.

KNOWLEDGE IN ACTION

Managers prepare cost and quantity standards to evaluate the efficiency of their production or service provision processes. Standard costs are useful for the following reasons:

- By comparing actual to standard, managers can easily identify where to focus their cost control efforts
- Standards that are viewed as reasonable by employees act as benchmarks by which employees can evaluate their own performance and potentially identify the need to work more efficiently
- Analysis of variances fits with the idea of responsibility accounting, in which divisional managers' performance is evaluated relative to their ability to manage costs of the products produced or services provided by the division for which they are responsible

SUMMARY

- A standard is a benchmark or norm for measuring performance. Standards are set for both the cost and the quantity of inputs needed to manufacture goods or to provide services. Quantity standards indicate how much of a cost element, such as labour time or raw materials, should be used in manufacturing a unit of product or in providing a unit of service. Cost standards indicate what the cost of the time or the materials should be. [LO1]

- Standards are normally practical in nature, meaning that they can be attained by reasonable, although highly efficient, efforts. Such standards are generally felt to have a favourable motivational impact on employees. Ideal standards are those attainable only under the best circumstances by the most skilled and efficient workers. While serving as a reminder that continuous improvement is needed, ideal standards can be discouraging. [LO1]

- The difference between actual cost and standard cost is referred to as a *variance*. Variances are computed for both the price and the quantity elements of materials, labour, and variable overhead. Price, rate, and spending variances for inputs are computed by taking the difference between the actual and standard prices of the inputs and multiplying the result by the amount of input purchased or used. Quantity and efficiency variances are computed by taking the difference between the actual amount of the input used and the amount of input that is allowed for the actual output, and then multiplying the result by the standard price of the input. [LO2, LO3, LO4]

- The denominator activity is the figure used to calculate the predetermined overhead rate for variable and fixed overhead. The overhead rate is used to determine the total standard cost per unit of a product by multiplying the rate by the quantity of the activity required to produce each unit. [LO5]

- Two variances exist for fixed overhead. The budget variance is simply the difference between the actual and budgeted amounts for total fixed overhead costs. The volume variance is the difference between the amount of fixed overhead cost applied to inventory and the total amount of fixed overhead that was originally budgeted for the period. [LO6]

- An overhead performance report provides details on each item that makes up total variable and fixed overhead. Both actual and budget figures are included in the report. Companies that use a standard costing system can prepare a performance report that includes both spending and efficiency variances for variable overhead and the budget variance for fixed overhead. Managers use the performance report to understand which specific overhead items are contributing the most to the overall variances for variable and fixed overhead. [LO7]

- Only unusual or particularly *significant* variances should be investigated—otherwise, a great deal of time could be spent investigating unimportant matters. Variance investigation decisions can be based on the dollar amount of the variance or the size of the variance relative to the amount of spending. A statistical control approach can also be employed, whereby only variances that are a certain number of standard deviations above or below zero are investigated. [LO7]

- Capacity analysis is a useful strategic tool that allows managers to evaluate the financial impact of operating at less than full productive capacity. Different definitions of "full capacity" exist, including theoretical capacity and practical capacity. Theoretical capacity is the volume of activity that would result from conducting operations with no downtime, 365 days a year, 24 hours per day. Practical capacity is determined by deducting unavoidable downtime from theoretical capacity. **[LO7]**

REVIEW PROBLEM: STANDARD COSTS

Fun Unlimited Corp. produces a toy called the Challenge. Overhead is applied to products on the basis of direct labour-hours. The company recently implemented a standard costing system to help control costs and has established the following standards for the Challenge toys:

Direct materials: 6 microns per toy at $0.50 per micron
Direct labour: 1.3 hours per toy at $15 per hour
Variable manufacturing overhead: 1.3 hours per toy at $4 per hour
Fixed manufacturing overhead: 1.3 hours per toy at $6 per hour

During July, the company produced 3,000 Challenge toys. The fixed overhead expense budget for July was $24,180, with 4,030 direct labour-hours as the denominator level of activity. Production data for the month on the toys follow:

Direct materials: 25,000 microns were purchased at a cost of $0.48 per micron; 5,000 of these microns were still in inventory at the end of the month.
Direct labour: 4,000 direct labour-hours were worked, at a cost of $64,000.
Variable overhead: Actual cost in July was $17,000.
Fixed overhead: Actual cost in July was $25,000.

Required:
1. Compute the materials, labour, variable manufacturing overhead, and fixed manufacturing overhead variances.
2. Calculate total overapplied or underapplied overhead for July.

Solution to Review Problem

1. Materials variances:

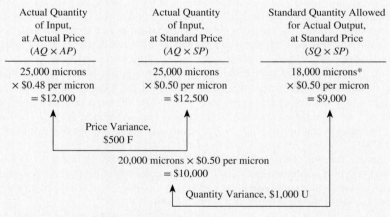

*3,000 toys × 6 microns per toy = 18,000 microns

A total variance is not computed in this situation because the amount of materials purchased (25,000 microns) differs from the amount of materials used in production (20,000 microns).

Using the formulas in the chapter, the same variances are computed as

$$\text{Materials price variance} = AQ(AP - SP)$$
$$25{,}000 \text{ microns } (\$0.48 \text{ per micron} - \$0.50 \text{ per micron}) = -\$500 \text{ F}$$

$$\text{Materials quantity variance} = SP(AQ - SQ)$$
$$\$0.50 \text{ per micron } (20{,}000 \text{ microns} - 18{,}000 \text{ microns}) = \$1{,}000 \text{ U}$$

Direct labour variances:

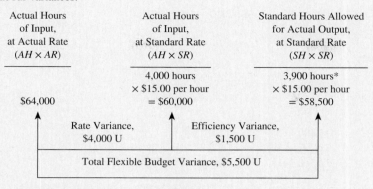

*3,000 toys × 1.3 hours per toy = 3,900 hours

Using the formulas in the chapter, the same variances are computed as

$$\text{Labour rate variance} = AH(AR - SR)$$
$$4,000 \text{ hours } (\$16.00 \text{ per hour* } - \$15.00 \text{ per hour}) = \$4,000 \text{ U}$$

*$64,000 ÷ 4,000 hours = $16.00 per hour

$$\text{Labour efficiency variance} = SR(AH - SH)$$
$$\$15.00 \text{ per hour } (4,000 \text{ hours } - 3,900 \text{ hours}) = \$1,500 \text{ U}$$

Variable manufacturing overhead variances:

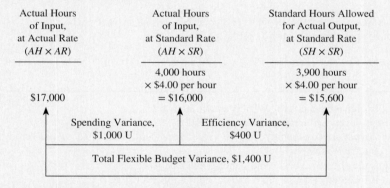

Using the formulas in the chapter, the same variances are computed as

$$\text{Variable overhead spending variance} = AH(AR - SR)$$
$$4,000 \text{ hours } (\$4.25 \text{ per hour* } - \$4.00 \text{ per hour}) = \$1,000 \text{ U}$$

*$17,000 ÷ 4,000 hours = $4.25 per hour

$$\text{Variable overhead efficiency variance} = SR(AH - SH)$$
$$\$4.00 \text{ per hour } (4,000 \text{ hours } - 3,900 \text{ hours}) = \$400 \text{ U}$$

Fixed manufacturing overhead variances:

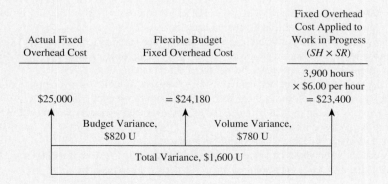

Using the formula in the chapter, the volume variance is computed as

$$\$6(4{,}030 - 3900) = \$780 \text{ U}$$

2. Actual overhead costs incurred:

Variable	$17,000
Fixed	25,000
Total	$42,000

Overhead costs applied:

Variable	$15,600
Fixed	23,400
Total	$39,000

Therefore, overhead is underapplied by $3,000 ($42,000 − $39,000).

DISCUSSION CASE

DISCUSSION CASE 10–1
Standard costing systems are helpful to managers, as they provide signals of poor quality or exceptional performance. Using standard costs on a management-by-exception basis can help managers to pinpoint areas that they need to pay particular attention to in the following periods, either in an attempt to improve performance or to better understand what is going well in that area that might be transferable to other areas in the organization. Even so, standard costing systems also facilitate other less positive outcomes, such as assigning blame and failing to work to improve efficiency beyond that dictated by the standard.

Required:
Discuss these and other potential negative consequences, as well as what can be done to overcome them when designing and utilizing standard costing systems.

QUESTIONS

10–1 What is a quantity standard? What is a price standard?

10–2 Distinguish between ideal and practical standards.

10–3 If employees are consistently unable to meet a standard, what effect would you expect this to have on their productivity?

10–4 What is the difference between a standard and a budget?

10–5 What is included in the standard rate per hour for direct labour?

10–6 Why are variances generally segregated in terms of a price variance and a quantity variance?

10–7 Who is generally responsible for the materials price variance? The materials quantity variance? The labour efficiency variance?

10–8 What are some possible causes of an unfavourable labour efficiency variance?

10–9 What does the term *standard hours allowed* mean?

10–10 What are the two factors that can cause a variable overhead spending variance?

10–11 What is meant by the term *denominator level of activity*?

10–12 Why do we apply overhead to work in process on the basis of standard hours allowed in Chapter 10, when we applied it on the basis of actual hours in Chapter 5? What is the difference in costing systems between the two chapters?

10–13 In a standard costing system, what two variances are computed for fixed manufacturing overhead?

10–14 What does the fixed overhead budget variance measure?

10–15 Under what circumstances would you expect the volume variance to be favourable? Unfavourable? Does the volume variance measure deviations in spending for fixed overhead items? Explain.

10–16 How might the volume variance be measured other than in dollars?

10–17 In Chapter 5, you became acquainted with the concept of under- or overapplied overhead. The under- or overapplied overhead can be broken down into what four variances?

10–18 "If factory overhead in total is underapplied, the overhead variances will be unfavourable." Do you agree? Why or why not?

10–19 How do managers decide which variances to investigate?

10–20 Why can undue emphasis on labour efficiency variances lead to excess work in process inventories?

10–21 What is the difference between theoretical capacity and practical capacity?

FOUNDATIONAL EXERCISES

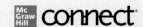

[LO2, LO3, LO4]

Preble Company manufactures one product. Its variable manufacturing overhead is applied to production based on direct labour-hours, and its standard costs per unit are as follows:

Direct materials: 5 kg at $8.00 per kg	$40.00
Direct labour: 2 hours at $14 per hour	28.00
Variable overhead: 2 hours at $5 per hour	10.00
Total standard cost per unit	$78.00

The company planned to produce and sell 25,000 units in March. However, during March the company actually produced and sold 30,000 units and incurred the following costs:

- Purchased 160,000 kg of raw materials at a cost of $7.50 per kg. All of this material was used in production.
- Direct labour: 55,000 hours at a rate of $15.00 per hour.
- Total variable manufacturing overhead for the month was $280,500.

Required:
10–1   What is the materials price variance for March?
10–2   What is the materials quantity variance for March?
10–3   If Preble had purchased 170,000 kg of materials at $7.50 per kg and used 160,000 kg in production, what would be the materials price variance for March?
10–4   If Preble had purchased 170,000 kg of materials at $7.50 per kg and used 160,000 kg in production, what would be the materials quantity variance for March?
10–5   What is the labour rate variance for March?
10–6   What is the labour efficiency variance for March?
10–7   What is the variable overhead spending variance for March?
10–8   What is the variable overhead efficiency variance for March?

EXERCISES

EXERCISE 10–1   Setting Standards; Preparing a Standard Cost Card [LO1]

Specialty Chemicals Ltd. makes a special powder coating for metal surfaces sold in envelope-style pouches. The main ingredient of this powder coating is a chemical known as X43. Information concerning the purchase and use of X43 follows:

> *Purchase of X43:* The raw material X43 is purchased in 50-kilogram containers at a cost of $125 per kilogram. A discount of 2% is offered by the supplier for payment within 10 days, and Specialty Chemicals takes all discounts. Shipping costs, which Specialty Chemicals must pay, amount to $250 for an average shipment of ten 50-kilogram containers.
>
> *Use of X43:* The bill of materials calls for 480 grams of X43 per pouch of powder coating. About 4% of all X43 purchased is rejected as unsuitable and is not used to make the powder coating. Thus, on average the 480 grams of suitable X43 required for each pouch of powder coating represents 96% of the amount that initially goes into production.

Required:
1. Compute the standard purchase price for one kilogram of X43.
2. Compute the standard quantity of X43 (in grams) per pouch that passes final inspection.
3. Using the data from (1) and (2) above, prepare a standard cost card showing the standard cost of X43 per pouch of powder coating.

EXERCISE 10–2   Material Variances [LO2]

Fantastic Feeder Products Inc. manufactures high-quality wooden cutting boards sold to restaurants and gourmet home cooks. One of these boards, the CertiPro II, requires an expensive hardwood. During a recent month, the company manufactured 1,200 CertiPro II cutting boards using 540 metres of hardwood. The hardwood cost the company $2,970.

The company's standards for one CertiPro II cutting board are 0.4 metres of hardwood, at a cost of $5.00 per metre.

Required:
1. What cost for wood should have been incurred to make 1,200 CertiPro II cutting boards? How much greater or less is this than the cost that was incurred?
2. Break down the difference computed in (1) above into a materials price variance and a materials quantity variance.

EXERCISE 10–3 Direct Labour Variances [LO3]

SkyInc provides in-flight meals for a number of major airlines. One of the company's products is stuffed cannelloni with roasted pepper sauce, fresh baby corn, and spring salad. During the most recent week, the company prepared 6,000 of these meals, using 1,150 direct labour-hours. The company paid these direct labour workers a total of $17,250 for this work, or $15 per hour.

According to the standard cost card for this meal, it should require 0.20 direct labour-hours at a cost of $14 per hour.

Required:
1. What direct labour cost should have been incurred to prepare 6,000 meals? How much does this differ from the actual direct labour cost?
2. Break down the difference computed in (1) above into a labour rate variance and a labour efficiency variance.

EXERCISE 10–4 Variable Overhead Variances [LO4]

Claims Management Inc. provides claims processing services to several large health insurance providers. Customers who are covered by health insurance provided by one of Claims Management's partners submit their claims for health and dental services along with related documentation, and the employees at Claims Management compare their claims to the details of their benefit plans and calculate the value of the benefits owed. The company uses a predetermined variable overhead rate based on direct labour-hours.

In the month of September, 15,000 claims were processed using 4,500 direct labour-hours. The company incurred a total of $4,950 in variable overhead costs.

According to the company's standards, 0.25 direct labour-hours are required to process a claim, and the variable overhead rate is $1.20 per direct labour-hour.

Required:
1. What variable overhead cost should have been incurred to process the 15,000 claims? How much does this differ from the actual variable overhead cost?
2. Break down the difference computed in (1) above into a variable overhead spending variance and a variable overhead efficiency variance.

> **CHECK FIGURE**
> 1. Standard variable overhead cost = $4,500.

EXERCISE 10–5 Fixed Overhead Variances [LO5, LO6]

Happy Valley Pet Products uses a standard costing system that applies overhead to products based on standard direct labour-hours allowed for actual output of the period. During the recent year, the following data were collected:

Total budgeted fixed overhead cost for the year	$40,000
Actual fixed overhead cost for the year	$38,000
Budgeted standard direct labour-hours	10,000
Actual direct labour-hours	12,000
Standard direct labour-hours allowed for the actual output	9,000

Required:
1. Compute the fixed portion of the predetermined overhead rate for the year.
2. Compute the fixed overhead budget and volume variances.

EXERCISE 10–6 Variable Overhead Performance Report [LO7]

Hastings Company bases its variable overhead performance report on the actual direct labour-hours of the period. Data concerning the most recent year, which ended on December 31, are as follows:

Budgeted direct labour-hours..........................	42,000
Actual direct labour-hours	44,000
Standard direct labour-hours allowed	45,000
Cost formula (per direct labour-hour):	
Indirect labour	$ 0.90
Supplies	$ 0.15
Electricity..	$ 0.05
Actual costs incurred:	
Indirect labour	$42,000
Supplies	$ 6,900
Electricity..	$ 1,800

Required:

Prepare a variable overhead performance report using the format in Exhibit 10–13. Compute both variable overhead spending and efficiency variances.

EXERCISE 10–7 Setting Standards [LO1]

Agnessa Premium Chocolate Ltd. produces specialty chocolate confections in England. The owner of the company is setting up a standard costing system; the following data are for one of the company's products, the Truffle Supreme, made with the finest white chocolate and various fillings. The data below pertain only to the white chocolate used in the product. (The currency in the United Kingdom is the British pound sterling, which is denoted by £.)

Material requirements, kilograms of white chocolate per dozen truffles	0.80 kilograms
Allowance for waste, kilograms of white chocolate per dozen truffles....	0.02 kilograms
Allowance for rejects, kilograms of white chocolate per dozen truffles.....	0.03 kilograms
Purchase price, finest-grade white chocolate	£9.00 per kilogram
Purchase discount	5% of purchase price
Shipping cost from the supplier in Belgium.......................	£0.20 per kilogram
Receiving and handling cost....................................	£0.05 per kilogram

Required:

1. Determine the standard price of a kilogram of white chocolate.
2. Determine the standard quantity of white chocolate for a dozen truffles.
3. Determine the standard price of the white chocolate in a dozen truffles.

EXERCISE 10–8 Material and Labour Variances [LO2, LO3]

Camping Supply Company has developed a new camping lamp that runs on solar power. The solar cells charge in the sun all day and then the lamp is ready to run when the sun goes down. The company has a standard costing system to help control costs and has established the following standards related to the new camping lamp:

> Direct materials: 2 small solar cells per lamp at $0.50 per cell
> Direct labour: 0.50 hours per lamp at $15 per hour

During March, the company produced 4,000 camping lights. Production data for March are as follows:

> Direct materials: 12,000 small solar cells were purchased at a cost of $0.45 per cell; 5,500 of
>   these were still in inventory at the end of the month (there was no opening inventory).
> Direct labour: 1,600 direct labour-hours were worked at a cost of $25,600.

Required:
1. Compute the following variances for March:
   a. Direct materials price and quantity variances.
   b. Direct labour rate and efficiency variances.
2. Prepare a brief explanation of the possible causes of each variance.

EXERCISE 10–9 Material and Labour Variances [LO2, LO3]

The direct materials and direct labour standards for one bottle of Clean-All spray cleaner are given below:

	Standard Quantity or Hours	Standard Price or Rate	Standard Cost
Direct materials.	6.0 mL	$0.20 per mL	$1.20
Direct labour	0.2 hours	$15.00 per hour	$3.00

During the most recent month, the following activity was recorded:

a. 20,000 millilitres of material was purchased at a cost of $0.25 per millilitre.
b. All of the material was used to produce 3,000 bottles of Clean-All.
c. 625 hours of direct labour time was recorded at a total labour cost of $10,000.

Required:
1. Compute the direct materials price and quantity variances for the month.
2. Compute the direct labour rate and efficiency variances for the month.

EXERCISE 10–10 Material Variances [LO2]

Refer to the data in Exercise 10–9. Assume that instead of producing 3,000 bottles of Clean-All during the month, the company produced only 2,000 bottles, using 16,000 millilitres of material. (The rest of the material purchased remained in raw materials inventory.)

Required:
Compute the direct materials price and quantity variances for the month.

EXERCISE 10–11 Labour and Variable Manufacturing Overhead Variances [LO3, LO4]

Affordable Electronics Inc. manufactures medium-quality, reasonably priced wireless speakers for home use. The company uses standards to control its costs. The labour standards that have been set for one speaker are as follows:

Standard Hours	Standard Rate per Hour	Standard Cost
15 minutes (0.25 hours)	$16.00	$4.00

During July, 3,850 hours of direct labour time were recorded to make 16,000 units. The direct labour cost totalled $61,600 for the month.

Required:
1. What direct labour cost should have been incurred to make the 16,000 speakers? By how much does this differ from the cost that was incurred?
2. Break down the difference in cost from (1) above into a labour rate variance and a labour efficiency variance.
3. The budgeted variable manufacturing overhead rate is $3.00 per direct labour-hour. During July, the company incurred $13,475 in variable manufacturing overhead cost. Compute the variable overhead spending and efficiency variances for the month.

EXERCISE 10–12 Working Backward from Labour Variances [LO3]

Worldwide Credit Card Inc. uses standards to control the labour time involved in opening mail from cardholders and recording the enclosed remittances. Incoming mail is gathered into batches, and a standard time is set for opening and recording each batch. The labour standards relating to one batch are as follows:

	Standard Hours	Standard Rate	Standard Cost
Per batch	2.5	$12.00	$30.00

The record showing the time spent last week in opening batches of mail has been misplaced. However, the batch supervisor recalls that 168 batches were received and opened during the week, and the controller recalls the following variance data relating to these batches:

Total labour variance	$660 U
Labour rate variance	$300 F

Required:
1. Determine the number of actual labour-hours spent opening batches during the week.
2. Determine the actual hourly rate paid to employees for opening batches last week.

(*Hint:* A useful way to proceed is to work from known to unknown data, either by using the variance formulas or by using the columnar format shown in Exhibit 10–6.)

EXERCISE 10–13 Predetermined Overhead Rate; Overhead Variances [LO4, LO5, LO6]
The condensed form of Nordstrop Company's flexible budget for manufacturing overhead follows:

Overhead Costs	Cost Formula (per machine-hour)	Machine-Hours		
		8,000	9,000	10,000
Variable cost	$1.05	$ 8,400	$ 9,450	$10,500
Fixed cost		24,800	24,800	24,800
Total overhead cost		$33,200	$34,250	$35,300

The following information is available for a recent period:

a.   The denominator activity of 8,000 machine-hours was chosen to compute the predetermined overhead rate.
b.   At the 8,000 standard machine-hours level of activity, the company should produce 3,200 units of product.
c.   The company's actual operating results were as follows:

Number of units produced	3,500
Actual machine-hours	8,500
Actual variable overhead costs.	$ 9,860
Actual fixed overhead costs	$25,100

Required:
1. Compute the predetermined overhead rate and break it down into variable and fixed cost elements.
2. What were the standard hours allowed for the year's actual output?
3. Compute the variable overhead spending and efficiency variances and the fixed overhead budget and volume variances.

> **CHECK FIGURE**
> 3. Variable overhead spending variance = $935 U; Variable overhead efficiency variance = $262.50 F.

EXERCISE 10–14 Using Fixed Overhead Variances [LO5, LO6]
The standard cost card for the single product manufactured by Princess Company is given below:

Standard Cost Card—Per Unit	
Direct materials, 2.1 metres at $6 per metre	$12.60
Direct labour, 0.5 direct labour-hours at $25 per direct labour-hour.	12.50
Variable overhead, 0.5 direct labour-hours at $4 per direct labour-hour	2.00
Fixed overhead, 0.5 direct labour-hours at $8 per direct labour-hour	4.00
Total standard cost per unit	$31.10

Last year, the company produced 6,800 units of product and worked 5,225 actual direct labour-hours. Manufacturing overhead cost is applied to production on the basis of direct labour-hours. Selected data relating to the company's fixed manufacturing overhead cost for the year are shown below:

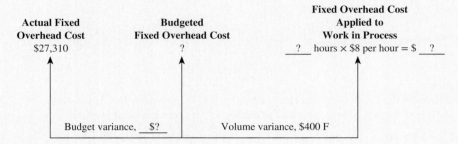

Actual Fixed Overhead Cost	Budgeted Fixed Overhead Cost	Fixed Overhead Cost Applied to Work in Process
$27,310	?	_?_ hours × $8 per hour = $ _?_

Budget variance, _$?_   Volume variance, $400 F

Required:
1. What were the standard hours allowed for the year's production?
2. What was the amount of budgeted fixed overhead cost for the year?
3. What was the budget variance for the year?
4. What denominator activity level did the company use in setting the predetermined overhead rate for the year?

EXERCISE 10–15 Fixed Overhead Variances [LO5, LO6]
Selected operating information on three different companies for a recent period is given below:

	Company		
	X	**Y**	**Z**
Full-capacity direct labour-hours	20,000	9,000	10,000
Budgeted direct labour-hours*	19,000	8,500	8,000
Actual direct labour-hours	19,500	8,000	9,000
Standard direct labour-hours allowed for actual output	18,500	8,250	9,500

*Denominator activity for computing the predetermined overhead rate.

Required:
For each company, state whether the volume variance would be favourable or unfavourable; also, explain in each case *why* the volume variance would be favourable or unfavourable.

EXERCISE 10–16 Overhead Performance Report with Both Spending and Efficiency Variances [LO4, LO7]
The cheque-clearing office of Pay Loans Company is responsible for processing all cheques that come to the company for payment. Managers at the company believe that variable overhead costs are essentially proportional to the number of labour-hours worked in the office, so labour-hours are used as the activity base when preparing variable overhead budgets and performance reports. Data for October, the most recent month, appear below:

Budgeted labour-hours.	1,300
Actual labour-hours	1,290
Standard labour-hours allowed for the actual number of cheques processed	1,320

	Cost Formula (per labour-hour)	Actual Costs Incurred in October
Variable overhead costs:		
Office supplies	$0.30	$ 219
Staff coffee lounge	0.10	186
Indirect labour.	3.90	3,348
Total variable overhead cost	$4.30	$3,753

Fixed overhead at Pay Loans Company consists entirely of supervisory salaries and is applied at a rate of $6 per direct labour-hour. Actual fixed overhead costs totalled $6,300 in October, while the flexible budget was $6,000 for the month.

Required:

Prepare an overhead performance report for October for the cheque-clearing office that includes both spending and efficiency variances for variable overhead and the budget variance for fixed overhead. Use Exhibit 10–13 as a guide in preparing the performance report.

EXERCISE 10–17 Capacity Analysis [LO7]

Comfort Company produces leather office chairs. The standard cost per chair is as follows:

Direct materials	$35
Direct labour	15
Variable overhead (2 machine-hours at $4.00)*	8
Fixed overhead (2 machine-hours at $8.00)*	16
Total standard cost per chair	$74

*Overhead rates are based on a denominator activity level of 30,000 machine-hours.

During 2017, Comfort Company produced and sold 12,000 office chairs. Management believes that the denominator level of activity represents 75% of theoretical capacity and 80% of practical capacity.

Required:

1. Calculate the total overhead costs at the following levels of activity: theoretical, practical, denominator, and actual (2017).
2. Assuming Comfort Company can sell all of the chairs it can produce for $100 per unit, calculate the opportunity loss of producing 12,000 chairs in 2017 compared to the following capacity utilization alternatives: theoretical, practical, and denominator.

EXERCISE 10–18 Predetermined Overhead Rate [LO5]

Operating at a normal level of 30,000 direct labour-hours, Lasser Company produces 12,000 units of product each year. The direct labour wage rate is $15 per hour. Two and one-half yards of direct materials go into each unit of product; the material costs $17.20 per yard. Variable manufacturing overhead should be $2 per standard direct labour-hour. Fixed manufacturing overhead should be $168,000 per period.

Required:

1. Using 30,000 direct labour-hours as the denominator activity, compute the predetermined overhead rate and break it down into variable and fixed elements.
2. Complete the standard cost card below for one unit of product:

Direct materials, 2.5 yards at $17.20 per yard	$43
Direct labour, ?	?
Variable manufacturing overhead, ?	?
Fixed manufacturing overhead, ?	?
Total standard cost per unit	$?

PROBLEMS

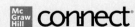

PROBLEM 10–19 Developing Standard Costs [LO1]

Maxime S.A. is a small company that processes wild mushrooms found in the forests of central France. For many years, Maxime's products have had strong sales in France. However, companies from other countries in Europe, such as Italy and Spain, have begun marketing similar products in France, and price competition has become intense. Jean Gauthier, the company's controller, is planning to implement a standard costing system for Maxime and has gathered considerable information from the purchasing and production managers concerning production and material requirements for Maxime's products. Gauthier believes that the use of standard costing will allow Maxime to improve cost control and thereby better compete with the new entrants into the French market.

Maxime's most popular product is dried chanterelle mushrooms, which are sold in small vacuum-packed jars. Each jar contains 15 grams of dried mushrooms. Fresh mushrooms are purchased for €60 per kilogram in bulk from individuals who gather them from local forests. (€ stands for euro, the currency used in France.) Because of imperfections in the mushrooms and normal spoilage, one-quarter of the fresh mushrooms are discarded. Fifteen minutes is the direct labour time required for inspecting and sorting per kilogram of fresh mushrooms. After sorting and inspecting, the acceptable mushrooms are flash-dried, which requires 10 minutes of direct labour time per kilogram of acceptable, sorted, and inspected fresh mushrooms. The flash-drying removes most of the moisture content of the mushrooms and therefore reduces the weight of the acceptable mushrooms by 80%. As a consequence, a kilogram of *acceptable* fresh mushrooms yields only about 150 grams of dried mushrooms. After drying, the mushrooms are vacuum-packed in small jars and labels are applied.

Direct labour is paid at a rate of €12 per hour. The cost of the glass jars, lids, and labels is €10 per 100 jars. The labour time required to pack 100 jars is 10 minutes.

CHECK FIGURE

1. Standard cost per jar of chanterelle mushrooms = €6.63.

Required:
1. Develop the standard cost for the direct labour and materials cost components of a single jar of dried chanterelle mushrooms, including the costs of the mushrooms, inspecting and sorting, drying, and packing.
2. Gauthier wonders who should be held responsible—the purchasing manager or the production manager—for the following:
   a. The materials price variances for the chanterelle mushrooms. Explain.
   b. The materials quantity variances for the chanterelle mushrooms. Explain.

PROBLEM 10–20 Materials and Labour Variances; Computations from Incomplete Data [LO1, LO2, LO3]

Talia Company produces a single product. The company has set standards as follows for materials and labour:

	Direct Materials	Direct Labour
Standard quantity or hours per unit	? kilograms	1.25 hours
Standard price or rate	? per kilogram	$10 per hour
Standard cost per unit	?	$12.50

During the past month, the company purchased 3,000 kilograms of direct materials at a cost of $8,250. All of this material was used in the production of 700 units of product. Direct labour cost totalled $6,825 for the month. The following variances have been computed:

Materials quantity variance.	$600 U
Total materials variance	$150 F
Labour efficiency variance	$2,250 F

Required:
1. For direct materials:
   a. Compute the standard price per kilogram for materials.
   b. Compute the standard quantity allowed for materials for the month's production.
   c. Compute the standard quantity of materials allowed per unit of product.
2. For direct labour:
   a. Compute the actual direct labour cost per hour for the month.
   b. Compute the labour rate variance.

(*Hint:* In completing the problem, it may be helpful to move from known to unknown data either by using the variance formulas or by using the columnar format shown in Exhibits 10–4 and 10–6.)

PROBLEM 10–21 Basic Variance Analysis [LO2, LO3, LO4]

VitalAid Inc. manufactures a vacuum-sealed high-protein food supplement that it sells to food aid organizations around the world. The company uses variable costing in conjunction with a standard costing system and has established the following standards for one package of VitalAid bars:

	Standard Quantity or Hours	Standard Price or Rate	Standard Cost
Direct materials	350 grams	$12.00 per kg	$4.20
Direct labour	0.25 hours	$13.00 per hour	$3.25
Variable manufacturing overhead	0.5 hours	$1.60 per hour	$0.80
Total standard variable cost			$8.25

During October, the company recorded the following activity relative to production of VitalAid:

a. The company produced 4,000 packages during October.
b. A total of 1,800 kilograms of material was purchased at a cost of $19,800.
c. There was no beginning inventory of materials; however, at the end of the month, 300 kilograms of material remained in ending inventory.
d. The company employs 5 people to work on the production of VitalAid. During October, each employee worked an average of 185 hours at an average rate of $14.00 per hour.
e. Variable manufacturing overhead is assigned to VitalAid on the basis of direct labour-hours. Variable manufacturing overhead costs during October totalled $1,850.

The company's management is anxious to determine the efficiency of the VitalAid production activities.

Required:
1. a. Compute the price and quantity variances for direct materials used in the production of VitalAid.
    b. The materials were purchased from a new supplier who is anxious to enter into a long-term purchase contract. Would you recommend that the company sign the contract? Explain.
2. a. Compute the rate and efficiency variances for labour employed in the production of VitalAid.
    b. In the past, the 5 people employed in the production of VitalAid consisted of 3 senior workers and 2 assistants. During October, the company experimented with 4 senior workers and 1 assistant. Would you recommend that the new labour mix be continued? Explain.
3. Compute the variable overhead spending and efficiency variances. What relationship can you see between this efficiency variance and the labour efficiency variance?

PROBLEM 10–22 Materials and Labour Variances; Computations from Incomplete Data [LO1, LO2, LO3]

Grand River Manufacturing produces a metal flange that it sells to several local home building supply retailers. The company has set standards as follows for materials and labour:

	Direct Materials	Direct Labour
Standard quantity or hours per unit	1.5 kilograms	? hours
Standard price or rate.	$4 per kilogram	$? per hour
Standard cost per unit.	$6	$?

During the past month, the company purchased 1,500 kilograms of direct materials at a cost of $6,375. All of this material was used in the production of 966 units of product using 425 hours of direct labour. Direct labour cost totalled $5,950 for the month. The following variances have been computed:

Labour rate variance	$425 F
Total labour variance	$350 F
Materials quantity variance.	$204 U

Required:
1. For direct labour:
    a. Compute the standard rate per hour for labour.
    b. Compute the standard quantity allowed for labour for the month's production.
    c. Compute the standard quantity of labour allowed per unit of product.

2. For direct materials:
   a. Compute the actual direct materials cost per kilogram for the month.
   b. Compute the materials price variance.

(*Hint:* In completing the problem, it may be helpful to move from known to unknown data either by using the variance formulas or by using the columnar format shown in Exhibits 10–4 and 10–6.)

PROBLEM 10–23 Multiple Products, Materials, and Processes [LO1, LO2, LO3, LO4]

Mickley Corporation produces two products, Alpha6 and Zeta7, which pass through two operations, Sintering and Finishing. Each of the products uses two raw materials, X442 and Y661. The company uses a standard cost system, with the following standards for each product (on a per unit basis):

| | Raw Material | | Standard Labour Time | |
	X442	Y661	Sintering	Finishing
Alpha6	1.8 kgs	2.0 litres	0.20 hrs	0.80 hrs
Zeta7	3.0 kgs	4.5 litres	0.35 hrs	0.90 hrs

Information relating to materials purchased and materials used in production during May follows:

	Purchases	Purchase Cost	Standard Price	Used in Production
X442	14,500 kg	$52,200	$3.50 per kg	8,500 kg
Y661	15,500 litres	$20,925	$1.40 per litre	13,000 litres

The following additional information is available:
1. The company recognizes price variances when materials are purchased.
2. The standard labour rate is $19.80 per hour in Sintering and $19.20 per hour in Finishing.
3. During May, 1,200 direct labour-hours were worked in Sintering at a total labour cost of $27,000, and 2,850 direct labour-hours were worked in Finishing at a total labour cost of $59,850.
4. Production during May was 1,500 Alpha6 and 2,000 Zeta7.

Required:
1. Prepare a standard cost card for each product, showing the standard cost of direct materials and direct labour.
2. Compute the materials price and quantity variances for each material.
3. Compute the labour rate and efficiency variances for each operation.

PROBLEM 10–24 Basic Variance Analysis; the Impact of Variances on Unit Costs [LO2, LO3, LO4]

Koontz Company manufactures a number of products. The standards relating to one of these products are shown below, along with actual cost data for May.

	Standard Cost per Unit	Actual Cost per Unit
Direct materials:		
Standard: 1.80 metres at $3.00 per metre	$ 5.40	
Actual: 1.80 metres at $3.30 per metre		$ 5.94
Direct labour:		
Standard: 0.90 hours at $18.00 hour	$16.20	
Actual: 0.92 hours at $17.50 per hour.		$16.10
Variable overhead:		
Standard: 0.90 hours at $5.00 per hour	$ 4.50	
Actual: 0.92 hours at $4.50 per hour.		$ 4.14
Total cost per unit	$26.10	$26.18
Excess of actual cost over standard		
cost per unit.	$0.08	

The production superintendent was pleased when he saw this report and commented: "This $0.08 excess cost is well within the 2% limit management has set for acceptable variances. It's obvious that there's not much to worry about with this product."

Actual production for the month was 12,000 units. Variable overhead cost is assigned to products on the basis of direct labour-hours. There were no beginning or ending inventories of materials.

Required:
1. Compute the following variances for May:
    a. Materials price and quantity variances.
    b. Labour rate and efficiency variances.
    c. Variable overhead spending and efficiency variances.
2. How much of the $0.08 excess unit cost is traceable to each of the variances computed in (1) above?
3. How much of the $0.08 excess unit cost is traceable to apparent inefficient use of labour time?
4. Do you agree that the excess unit cost is not of concern?

PROBLEM 10–25 Working Backward from Variance Data [LO2, LO3, LO4, LO6]

You have recently accepted a position with Sea-Jewels Inc., the manufacturer of a popular consumer product. When trying to open your variance analysis files, you find some of them have become corrupted. All you can retrieve is shown below:

Standard Cost Card

Direct materials, 9 kilograms at $3 per kilogram	$27.00
Direct labour, 1.2 direct labour-hours at $15 per direct labour-hour	18.00
Variable manufacturing overhead, 1.2 direct labour-hours at $3 per direct labour-hour	3.60
Fixed manufacturing overhead, 1.2 direct labour-hours at $7 per direct labour-hour	8.40
Standard cost per unit	$57.00

		Variances Reported			
	Total Standard Cost*	Price or Rate	Spending or Budget	Quantity or Efficiency	Volume
Direct materials.	$202,500	$3,450 F		$ 4,500 U	
Direct labour	$135,000	$7,275 U		$10,500 U	
Variable manufacturing overhead	$ 27,000		$650 F	$?† U	
Fixed manufacturing overhead	$ 63,000		$250 F		$7,000 U

*Applied to work in process during the period
†Data corrupted

Manufacturing overhead cost is applied to production on the basis of direct labour-hours and that all of the materials purchased during the period were used in production. Since the company uses JIT to control work flows, work in process inventories are insignificant and can be ignored. Use the information you do have to answer the following questions.

Required:
1. How many units were produced last period? (Think hard about this one!)
2. How many kilograms of direct material were purchased and used in production?
3. What was the actual cost per kilogram of material?
4. How many actual direct labour-hours were worked during the period?
5. What was the actual rate paid per direct labour-hour?
6. How much actual variable manufacturing overhead cost was incurred during the period?
7. What is the total fixed manufacturing overhead cost in the company's flexible budget?
8. What were the denominator direct labour-hours for last period?

PROBLEM 10–26 Comprehensive Variance Analysis [LO2, LO3, LO4]

Marvel Parts Inc. manufactures auto accessories. One of the company's products is a set of seat covers that can be adjusted to fit nearly any small car. The company has a standard cost system in use for all of its products. According to the standards that have been set for the seat covers, the factory should work

2,850 hours each month to produce 1,900 sets of covers. The standard costs associated with this level of production are as follows:

	Total	Per Set of Covers
Direct materials......................................	$42,560	$22.40
Direct labour...	$17,100	9.00
Variable manufacturing overhead (based on direct labour-hours)	$ 6,840	3.60
		$35.00

During August, the factory worked only 2,800 direct labour-hours and produced 2,000 sets of covers. The following actual costs were recorded during the month:

	Total	Per Set of Covers
Direct materials (12,000 metres).........................	$45,600	$22.80
Direct labour...	$18,200	9.10
Variable manufacturing overhead.........................	$ 7,000	3.50
....		$35.40

At standard, each set of covers should require 5.6 metres of material. All of the materials purchased during the month were used in production.

Required:
Compute the following variances for August:

1. The materials price and quantity variances.
2. The labour rate and efficiency variances.
3. The variable overhead spending and efficiency variances.

PROBLEM 10–27 Selection of a Denominator; Overhead Analysis; Standard Cost Card [LO1, LO4, LO5, LO6]
Flores Company's condensed flexible budget for manufacturing overhead is as follows:

Overhead Costs	Cost Formula (per DLH)	Direct Labour-Hours		
		30,000	40,000	50,000
Variable manufacturing overhead cost ...	$2.50	$ 75,000	$100,000	$125,000
Fixed manufacturing overhead cost......		320,000	320,000	320,000
Total manufacturing overhead cost		$395,000	$420,000	$445,000

The company produces a single product that requires 2.5 direct labour-hours to complete. The direct labour wage rate is $20 per hour. Three metres of raw material are required for each unit of product, at a cost of $5 per metre.

Demand for the company's product differs widely from year to year. Expected activity for this year is 50,000 direct labour-hours; normal activity is 40,000 direct labour-hours per year.

Required:
1. Assume that the company chooses 40,000 direct labour-hours as the denominator level of activity. Compute the predetermined overhead rate, breaking it down into fixed and variable cost components.
2. Assume that the company chooses 50,000 direct labour-hours as the denominator level of activity. Repeat the computations in (1) above.

3. Complete two standard cost cards as outlined below:

Denominator Activity: 40,000 DLHs

Direct materials, 3 metres at $5 per metre	$15.00
Direct labour, ?	?
Variable manufacturing overhead, ?...................	?
Fixed manufacturing overhead, ?	?
Total standard cost per unit.........................	$?

Denominator Activity: 50,000 DLHs

Direct materials, 3 metres at $5 per metre	$15.00
Direct labour, ?	?
Variable manufacturing overhead, ?...................	?
Fixed manufacturing overhead, ?	?
Total standard cost per unit.........................	$?

4. Assume that 48,000 actual hours are worked during the year, and that 18,500 units are produced. Actual manufacturing overhead costs for the year are as follows:

Variable manufacturing overhead cost	$124,800
Fixed manufacturing overhead cost	321,700
Total manufacturing overhead cost................	$446,500

   a.   Compute the standard hours allowed for the year's actual output.
   b.   Compute the missing items from the manufacturing overhead account below. Assume that the company uses 40,000 direct labour-hours (normal activity) as the denominator activity figure in computing overhead rates, as in (1) above:

Manufacturing Overhead

Actual costs	446,500	?
	?	?

   c.   Analyze your underapplied or overapplied overhead balance in terms of variable overhead spending and efficiency variances and fixed overhead budget and volume variances.
5. Looking at the variances that you have computed, what appears to be the major disadvantage of using normal activity rather than expected actual activity as a denominator in computing the pre-determined overhead rate? What advantages can you see to offset this disadvantage?

PROBLEM 10–28 Comprehensive Variance Analysis [LO2, LO3, LO4, LO5, LO6]

Helix Company produces costumes used in the television and movie industries. Recently the company received an ongoing order for Samurai robes to be worn in an upcoming Japanese historical action series made for television. The company uses a standard costing system to assist in the control of costs. According to the standards set for these robes, the factory has a denominator activity level of 780 direct labour-hours each month, which should result in the production of 1,950 robes. The standard costs associated with this level of production are as follows:

	Total	Per Unit of Product
Direct materials	$35,490	$18.20
Direct labour	$ 7,020	3.60
Variable manufacturing overhead*	$ 2,340	1.20
Fixed manufacturing overhead*........................	$ 4,680	2.40
		$25.40

*Based on direct labour-hours

During April, the factory worked only 760 direct labour-hours and produced 2,000 robes. The following actual costs were recorded during the month:

	Total	Per Unit of Product
Direct materials (6,000 metres)	$36,000	$18.00
Direct labour	$ 7,600	3.80
Variable manufacturing overhead	$ 3,800	1.90
Fixed manufacturing overhead.	$ 4,600	2.30
		$26.00

At standard, each robe should require 2.8 metres of material. All of the materials purchased during the month were used in production.

Required:

Compute the following variances for April:

1. The materials price and quantity variances.
2. The labour rate and efficiency variances.
3. The variable manufacturing overhead spending and efficiency variances.
4. The fixed manufacturing overhead budget and volume variances.

PROBLEM 10–29 Applying Overhead; Overhead Variances [LO4, LO5, LO6]

Ryder Company produces a single product, school backpacks made of a sturdy nylon fabric. The production of these bags requires a relatively large amount of labour time. Overhead cost is applied on the basis of standard direct labour-hours. The company's condensed flexible budget for manufacturing overhead is given below:

Overhead Costs	Cost Formula (per DLH)	Direct Labour-Hours		
		12,000	15,000	18,000
Variable manufacturing overhead cost	$2	$24,000	$ 30,000	$ 36,000
Fixed manufacturing overhead cost.		75,000	75,000	75,000
Total manufacturing overhead cost		$99,000	$105,000	$111,000

Each backpack requires 2 metres of direct material that has a standard cost of $1.50 per metre. The product requires 1.5 hours of direct labour time. The standard labour rate is $15 per hour.

During the year, the company had planned to operate at a denominator activity level of 15,000 direct labour-hours and to produce 10,000 units of product. Actual activity and costs for the year were as follows:

Number of units produced.	11,000
Actual direct labour-hours worked	17,500
Actual variable manufacturing overhead cost incurred . . .	$31,500
Actual fixed manufacturing overhead cost incurred	$76,500

Required:

1. Compute the predetermined overhead rate for the year. Break the rate down into variable and fixed components.
2. *a.* Compute the standard direct labour-hours allowed for the year's production.
   b. Complete the following manufacturing overhead T-account for the year:

Manufacturing Overhead

?	?
?	?

3. Determine the reason for the underapplied or overapplied overhead from (2) above by computing the variable overhead spending and efficiency variances and the fixed overhead budget and volume variances.
4. Suppose the company had chosen 18,000 direct labour-hours as the denominator activity rather than 15,000 hours. State which, if any, of the variances computed in (3) above would have changed, and explain how the variance(s) would have changed. No computations are necessary.

PROBLEM 10–30 Applying Overhead; Overhead Variances [LO4, LO5, LO6]
The Scottish firm of Cullen and MacNeil produces a single product and uses a standard costing system to help control costs. Manufacturing overhead is applied to production on the basis of standard machine-hours. The Scottish currency is the British pound. According to the company's flexible budget, the following overhead costs should be incurred at an activity level of 18,000 machine-hours (the denominator activity level chosen for the year):

Variable manufacturing overhead cost	£27,000
Fixed manufacturing overhead cost	54,000
Total manufacturing overhead cost	£81,000

During the year, the following operating results were recorded:

Actual machine-hours worked	15,000
Standard machine-hours allowed	16,000
Actual variable manufacturing overhead cost incurred	£24,000
Actual fixed manufacturing overhead cost incurred	£52,000

At the end of the year, the company's Manufacturing Overhead account contained the following data:

Manufacturing Overhead

Actual costs	76,000	Applied costs	72,000
	4,000		

Management would like to determine the cause of the £4,000 underapplied overhead.

Required:
1. Compute the predetermined overhead rate for the year. Break it down into variable and fixed cost elements.
2. Show how the £72,000 "Applied costs" figure in the manufacturing overhead account was computed.
3. Analyze the £4,000 underapplied overhead figure in terms of the variable overhead spending and efficiency variances and the fixed overhead budget and volume variances.
4. Explain the meaning of each variance that you computed in (3) above.

CHECK FIGURE
1. Predetermined overhead rate = £4.50/MH, with £1.50/MH variable and £3.00/MH fixed.

PROBLEM 10–31 Comprehensive Variance Analysis [LO2, LO3, LO4]
London Company's Forest City Plant produces precast ingots for industrial use. Anne-Marie Gosnell, who was recently appointed general manager of the Forest City Plant, has just been handed the plant's income statement for October. The statement is shown below.

Gosnell was shocked to see the poor results for the month, particularly since sales were exactly as budgeted. She stated, "I sure hope the plant has a standard costing system in operation. If it doesn't, I won't have the slightest idea of where to start looking for the problem."

	Budgeted	Actual
Sales (2,500 ingots)	$125,000	$125,000
Variable expenses:		
Variable cost of goods sold*	40,000	45,455
Variable selling expenses	10,000	10,000
Total variable expenses	50,000	55,455
Contribution margin	75,000	69,545
Fixed expenses:		
Manufacturing overhead	30,000	29,500
Selling and administrative	37,500	37,500
Total fixed expenses	67,500	67,000
Operating income (loss)	$ 7,500	$ 2,545

*Contains direct materials, direct labour, and variable manufacturing overhead

The plant uses a standard costing system, with the standard variable cost per ingot details shown below:

	Standard Quantity or Hours	Standard Price or Rate	Standard Cost
Direct materials	2.0 kilograms	$1.25 per kilogram	$2.50
Direct labour	0.54 hours	$10.00 per hour	5.40
Variable manufacturing overhead . .	0.27 hours*	$1.00 per hour	0.27
Total standard variable cost			$8.17

*Based on machine-hours

Gosnell has determined that during October the plant produced 2,500 ingots and incurred the following costs:

a. Purchased 6,300 kilograms of materials at a cost of $1.50 per kilogram. There were no raw materials in inventory at the beginning of the month.

b. Used 4,900 kilograms of materials in production. (Finished goods and work in process inventories are insignificant and can be ignored.)

c. Worked 1,800 direct labour-hours at a cost of $9.50 per hour.

d. Incurred a total variable manufacturing overhead cost of $1,080 for the month. A total of 900 machine-hours were recorded. It is the company's policy to close all variances to cost of goods sold on a monthly basis.

Required:

1. Compute the following variances for October:
   a. Direct materials price and quantity variances.
   b. Direct labour rate and efficiency variances.
   c. Variable manufacturing overhead spending and efficiency variances.
2. Summarize the variances that you computed in (1) above by showing the net overall favourable or unfavourable variance for October. What impact did this figure have on the company's income statement?
3. Pick out the two most significant variances that you computed in (1) above. Explain to Gosnell possible causes of these variances.

PROBLEM 10–32 Comprehensive Variance Analysis in a Hospital [LO2, LO3, LO4, LO5, LO6]
Marc Goudreau, administrator of Clearwater Hospital, was puzzled by the prior month's reports. "Every month, it's anyone's guess whether the lab will show a profit or a loss. Perhaps the only answer is to increase our lab fees again."

"We can't," replied Rhoda Groves, the controller. "There are still a lot of complaints about the last increase, particularly from the insurance companies and government health units. They're now paying only about 80% of what we bill. I'm beginning to think the problem is on the cost side."

To determine if the Clearwater lab costs are in line with those of other hospital labs, Goudreau has asked you to evaluate the costs for the past month. Groves has provided you with the following information:

a. Two basic types of tests are performed in the lab—smears and blood tests. During the past month, 2,700 smears and 900 blood tests were performed in the lab.

b. Small glass plates are used in both types of tests. During the past month, the hospital purchased 16,000 plates at a cost of $38,400. This cost is net of a 4% purchase discount. A total of 2,000 of these plates were unused at the end of the month; no plates were on hand at the beginning of the month.

c. During the past month, 1,800 hours of labour time were used in performing smears and blood tests. The cost of this labour time was $18,450.

d. The lab's variable overhead cost last month totalled $11,700.

e. Fixed overhead cost last month totalled $10,400.

Clearwater Hospital has never used standard costs. By searching industry literature, however, you have determined the following nationwide averages for hospital labs:

Plates: Three plates are required per lab test. These plates cost $2.50 each and are disposed of after the test is completed.

Labour: Each smear should require 0.3 hours to complete, and each blood test should require 0.6 hours to complete. The average cost of this lab time is $12 per hour.

Overhead: Overhead cost is based on direct labour-hours. The average rate of variable overhead is $6 per hour. The average rate of fixed overhead is $8 per hour. These rates are based on a denominator activity level of 1,250 hours per month.

Required:
1. Compute the materials price variance for the plates purchased last month, and compute a materials quantity variance for the plates used last month.
2. *a.* Compute a labour rate variance and a labour efficiency variance for the lab.
   b. In most hospitals, three-quarters of the workers in the lab are certified technicians and one-quarter are assistants. In an effort to reduce costs, Clearwater Hospital employs only one-half certified technicians and one-half assistants. Would you recommend that this policy be continued? Explain.
3. Compute the variable overhead spending and efficiency variances. Is there any relationship between the variable overhead efficiency variance and the labour efficiency variance? Explain.
4. Compute the fixed overhead budget and volume variances.

PROBLEM 10–33 Comprehensive Standard Cost Variances [LO2, LO3, LO4, LO5, LO6]
Clarissa McWhirter, vice-president of Cyprus Company, was pleased to see a small variance on the income statement after the trouble the company had been having in controlling manufacturing costs. She noted that the $18,500 overall manufacturing variance reported last period was well below the 3% limit that had been set for variances. The company produces and sells a single product. The standard cost card for the product follows:

Standard Cost Card—Per Unit	
Direct materials, 4 metres at $3.00 per metre	$12
Direct labour, 1.5 direct labour-hour at $16 per direct labour-hour	24
Variable overhead, 1.5 direct labour-hour at $4 per direct labour-hour	6
Fixed overhead, 1.5 direct labour-hour at $6 per direct labour-hour	9
Standard cost per unit	$51

The following additional information is available for the year just completed:

a. The company manufactured 20,000 units of product during the year.
b. A total of 78,000 metres of material was purchased during the year at a cost of $3.25 per metre. All of this material was used to manufacture the 20,000 units. There were no beginning or ending inventories for the year.
c. The company worked 32,500 direct labour-hours during the year at a cost of $15 per hour.
d. Overhead cost is applied to products on the basis of standard direct labour-hours. Data relating to manufacturing overhead costs follow:

Denominator activity level (direct labour-hours)	25,000
Budgeted fixed overhead costs (from the flexible budget)	$150,000
Actual fixed overhead costs	$148,000
Actual variable overhead costs	$123,500

Required:
1. Compute the direct materials price and quantity variances for the year.
2. Compute the direct labour rate and efficiency variances for the year.
3. For manufacturing overhead, compute the following:
   a. The variable overhead spending and efficiency variances for the year.
   b. The fixed overhead budget and volume variances for the year.
4. Total the variances you have computed, and compare the net amount with the $18,500 mentioned by the vice-president. Do you think that everyone should be congratulated for a job well done? Explain.

PROBLEM 10–34 Overhead Performance Report [LO7]
Asper Company has recently introduced budgeting as an integral part of its corporate planning process. An inexperienced member of the accounting staff was given the assignment of constructing a flexible budget for manufacturing overhead costs and prepared it in the format that follows:

Percentage of Capacity	80%	100%
Machine-hours	40,000	50,000
Utilities	$ 41,000	$ 49,000
Supplies	4,000	5,000
Indirect labour	8,000	10,000
Maintenance	37,000	41,000
Supervision	10,000	10,000
Total manufacturing overhead cost	$100,000	$115,000

The company assigns manufacturing overhead costs to production on the basis of standard machine-hours. The cost formulas used to prepare the budgeted figures above are relevant over a range of 80% to 100% of capacity in a month. The managers who will be working under these budgets have control over both fixed and variable manufacturing overhead costs.

Required:
1. Use the high-low method (see Chapter 3) to separate fixed and variable costs.
2. Come up with a single cost formula for all overhead costs based on your analysis in (1) above. (*Hint:* Your cost formula should be of the form $y = a + bx$.)
3. During May, the company operated at 86% of machine-hour capacity. Actual manufacturing overhead costs incurred during the month were as follows:

Utilities	$ 42,540
Supplies	6,450
Indirect labour	9,890
Maintenance	35,190
Supervision	10,000
Total actual manufacturing overhead cost	$104,070

Fixed costs had no budget variances. Prepare an overhead performance report for May. Include both fixed and variable costs in your report (in separate sections). Structure your report so that it shows only a spending variance for variable overhead. The company originally budgeted to work 40,000 machine-hours during the month; standard hours allowed for the month's production totalled 41,000 machine-hours. (Use Exhibit 10–14 as a guide.)
4. Explain possible causes of the spending variance for supplies.

PROBLEM 10–35 Flexible Budget and Overhead Performance Report [LO4, LO5, LO6, LO7]
Groschl Company has had great difficulty in controlling manufacturing overhead costs. At a recent convention, the president heard about a control device for overhead costs known as a *flexible budget*, and he has hired you to implement this budgeting program in Groschl Company. After some effort, you have developed the following cost formulas for the company's Machining Department. These costs are based on a normal operating range of 10,000 to 20,000 machine-hours per month:

Overhead Cost	Cost Formula
Utilities	$0.70 per machine-hour
Lubricants	$1.00 per machine-hour plus $8,000 per month
Machine setup	$0.20 per machine-hour
Indirect labour	$0.60 per machine-hour plus $120,000 per month
Depreciation	$32,000 per month

During March, the first month after your preparation of the above data, the Machining Department worked 18,000 machine-hours and produced 9,000 units of product. The actual manufacturing overhead costs for March were as follows:

Utilities	$ 12,000
Lubricants	24,500
Machine setup	4,800
Indirect labour.	132,500
Depreciation	32,000
Total manufacturing overhead cost	$205,800

Fixed costs had no budget variances. The department had originally been budgeted to work 20,000 machine-hours during March.

Required:
1. Prepare an overhead performance report for the Machining Department for the month of March. Include both variable and fixed costs in the report (in separate sections). Show only a spending variance on the report. (Use Exhibit 10–14 as your guide.)
2. What additional information would you need to compute an overhead efficiency variance for the department?

PROBLEM 10–36 Evaluating an Overhead Performance Report [LO5, LO6, LO7]
Timothy Hawkins, superintendent of Kal-Tubing Company's Machining Department, is very happy with his performance report for the past month. The report follows:

KAL-TUBING COMPANY Overhead Performance Report—Machining Department			
	Actual	**Budget**	**Variance**
Machine-hours	22,500	26,250	
Variable manufacturing overhead:			
Indirect labour	$ 59,100	$ 63,000	$ 3,900 F
Utilities	152,400	178,500	26,100 F
Supplies	37,800	42,000	4,200 F
Maintenance.	74,700	84,000	9,300 F
Total variable manufacturing overhead	324,000	367,500	43,500 F
Fixed manufacturing overhead:			
Maintenance.	$117,000	$117,000	0
Supervision	247,500	247,500	0
Depreciation.	180,000	180,000	0
Total fixed manufacturing overhead	544,500	544,500	0
Total manufacturing overhead	$868,500	$912,000	$43,500 F

When he received a copy of this report, Wayne Lockhart, the production manager, commented, "I've been getting these reports for months now, and I still can't see how they help me assess efficiency and cost control in that department. I agree that the budget for the month was 26,250 machine-hours, but that represents 8,750 units of product, since it should take three hours to produce one unit. The department produced only 5,250 units during the month, and took 22,500 machine-hours to do it. Why do all the variances turn up favourable?"

Required:
1. In answer to Lockhart's question, why are all the variances favourable? Is the performance report useful? Explain.
2. Prepare a new overhead performance report that will help Lockhart assess efficiency and cost control in the Machining Department. (*Hint:* Exhibit 10–13 may be helpful in structuring your report.)

PROBLEM 10–37 Overhead Performance Report [LO7]

Reagan Products Ltd., an Australian company, has the following cost formulas (expressed in Australian dollars) for variable overhead costs in one of its machine shops:

Variable Overhead Cost	Cost Formula (per machine-hour)
Supplies	$1.20
Power	2.10
Lubrication	0.90
Wearing tools	5.40
Total	$9.60

The flexible budget amounts for fixed overhead costs in July are as follows:

Fixed Overhead Cost	Flexible Budget
Depreciation	$17,500
Supervisory salaries	24,500
Maintenance	5,250
Total	$47,250

During July, the machine shop was scheduled to work 5,600 machine-hours and to produce 28,000 units of product. The standard machine time per unit of product is 0.2 hours. A severe storm during the month forced the company to close for several days, which reduced the level of output for the month. Actual results for July were as follows:

Actual machine-hours worked	4,700
Actual number of units produced	24,500

Actual costs for July were as follows:

Overhead Costs	Total Actual Cost	Per Machine-Hour
Variable overhead costs:		
Supplies	$ 5,593	$1.19
Power	10,199	2.17
Lubrication	4,512	0.96
Wearing tools	24,863	5.29
Total variable overhead	45,167	$9.61
Fixed overhead costs:		
Depreciation	17,500	—
Supervisory salaries	25,550	—
Maintenance	4,375	—
Total fixed overhead	47,425	—
Total overhead	$92,592	

Required:

Prepare an overhead performance report including both variable and fixed overhead for the machine shop for July. Use column headings in your report as shown below:

Overhead Costs	Cost Formula (per MH)	Actual Costs Incurred, 4,700 MHs	Flexible Budget Based on 4,700 MHs	Flexible Budget Based on Standard 4,900 MHs	Total Variance	Breakdown of the Total Variance	
						Spending Variance	Efficiency Variance

PROBLEM 10–38 Capacity Analysis [LO7]

The Yardman Company produces electric weed trimmers, among other products. The following standard costs per unit are associated with the trimmers:

Item	Quantity	Cost per Unit
Direct materials	4 pieces at $6.00	$24.00
Direct labour	2 hours at $15.00	30.00
Variable overhead.	2 hours at $3.00	6.00
Fixed overhead.	2 hours at $5.00	10.00
Total		$70.00

Normal activity of 60,000 hours was used as the denominator level. Other possible capacity levels were as follows:

Expected annual	55,000 hours
Practical annual.	75,000 hours
Theoretical annual.	100,000 hours

An analysis of the difference between practical and theoretical capacity for the past year showed the following: 10,000 hours were not used because management decided not to employ two crews of workers. A further 5,000 hours of capacity had to be assigned to setup when machines were switched from one product to another. Another 5,000 hours were not used because scheduled maintenance of production equipment was required. Finally, the remaining 5,000 hours of theoretical capacity were not used because existing markets could not use all of the theoretical capacity without a substantial reduction in selling price. Management approached the Marketing Department to determine what pricing policy would be needed to move from the denominator level of activity (30,000 units) to practical capacity (37,500 units). Marketing suggested that a price reduction of 10% below the existing selling price of $80 would increase demand from 30,000 units to 37,500 units.

Marketing also indicated that to move from practical capacity (37,500 units) to theoretical capacity (50,000 units), two crews would need to be hired, setups eliminated, and maintenance deferred. A further 10% price reduction below the existing $80 would also be needed to increase demand by another 12,500 units.

Required:

Calculate gross profit at the following levels of capacity utilization: (*a*) expected annual, (*b*) denominator, (*c*) practical, and (*d*) theoretical. *Note:* Be sure to incorporate the selling price reductions necessary to sell all units produced at practical and theoretical levels of capacity utilization.

CASES

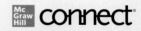

CASE 10–39 Ethics and Possible Dysfunctional Consequences of Managing to Standards [LO1]

Road Gear manufactures accessories for road and mountain bicycles. The market for cycling accessories is very competitive, so Road Gear uses a standard costing system to control costs. The day-to-day management of each major line of accessories is the responsibility of a product line manager. These managers are responsible for all major production decisions, including purchasing direct materials, hiring and training production staff, scheduling production, and quality inspections. Monthly performance reports are prepared showing variances for direct materials, direct labour, variable overhead, and fixed overhead for each product line. The performance reports are prepared and distributed five business days after month-end and are reviewed at a monthly meeting attended by all of the product line managers, the vice-president of manufacturing, and the chief financial officer. The product line managers are responsible for explaining all significant unfavourable variances each month, and their annual performance review is based in part on how well they manage actual costs relative to the standard costs for their products. The performance reviews affect the managers' annual merit pay increases and bonus.

One of Road Gear's product lines is a high-quality bicycle computer, the Speed Tracker, that records speed, distance, time, cadence, and a variety of other metrics. Dan Roth is the product line manager for the Speed Tracker and has been with Road Gear for only about 14 months. Prior to joining the company, Roth worked at one of Road Gear's main competitors as a production foreman. Roth's first fiscal year at Road Gear was not very successful. Due to a variety of factors, the monthly variances for the Speed Tracker, particularly those for direct materials and direct labour, were unfavourable the majority of months. Even though Road Gear uses practical standards, Roth felt that the standard prices and quantities for direct materials, and the standard rates and hours for direct labour, were too tight. Moreover, increases in direct material costs during the year made matters worse, and as Roth repeatedly pointed out during the monthly meetings, he had no control over the prices charged by suppliers. Senior management was not convinced by Roth's explanations, so his merit pay increase was well below that of the average given to the other product line managers; his annual bonus was equally low.

In the current fiscal year, Roth decided to take a more active role in managing production costs for the Speed Tracker. He found a cheaper microprocessor, the Zip, for the Speed Tracker that cost 20% less per unit than the previous processor, the Zap, which was used in last year's model. Although Roth knew that the Zip was of lower quality and considerably less reliable than the Zap, he figured the tradeoff was worth it since it would result in a favourable price variance for the Speed Tracker and would have no impact on the quantity variance. Moreover, since the causes of favourable variances typically weren't discussed at the monthly meetings, Roth was pretty sure he wouldn't have to explain the price–quality tradeoff he had made. Roth also began hiring less-experienced production employees in an effort to eliminate the unfavourable labour rate variance for the Speed Tracker. Although the quality of workmanship was lower with these less-experienced workers and they took longer to produce each unit, the unfavourable labour efficiency variance was more than offset by the favourable rate variance.

Roth was pleased with his performance for the first three months of the current year. His variances for direct materials and direct labour were favourable in total, and senior management seemed satisfied that he was doing a better job managing costs. Although the number of Speed Trackers being returned under warranty was up nearly 15% over the same period last year, Roth attributed this to random events that likely wouldn't recur over the remaining months of the year.

Required:
1. Were the actions taken by Roth in the current fiscal year to improve his performance on direct materials and direct labour costs ethical? Explain.
2. What are some longer-term consequences of Roth's behaviour for Road Gear?
3. What steps could senior management at Road Gear take to reduce the type of behaviour exhibited by Roth?

CASE 10–40 Ethics and the Manager [LO7]
Lance Prating is the controller of the Colchester manufacturing facility of Tech Systems Incorporated. Among the many reports that must be filed with corporate headquarters is the annual overhead performance report. The report covers the year that ends on December 31 and is due at corporate headquarters shortly after the beginning of the new year. Prating does not like putting work off until the last minute, so just before Christmas, he put together a preliminary draft of the overhead performance report. Some adjustments would later be required for the few transactions that occur between Christmas and New Year's Day. A copy of the preliminary draft report, which Prating completed on December 21, is shown below:

COLCHESTER MANUFACTURING FACILITY
Overhead Performance Report
December 21 Preliminary Draft

Budgeted machine-hours   100,000
Actual machine-hours   90,000

Overhead Costs	Cost Formula (per machine-hour)	Actual Costs for 90,000 Machine-Hours	Flexible Budget Based on 90,000 Machine-Hours	Spending or Budget Variance
Variable overhead costs:				
Power.....................	$0.03	$ 2,840	$ 2,700	$ 140 U
Supplies.................	0.86	79,060	77,400	1,660 U
Abrasives...............	0.34	32,580	30,600	1,980 U
	$1.23	114,480	110,700	3,780 U
Fixed overhead costs:				
Depreciation		228,300	226,500	1,800 U
Supervisory salaries		187,300	189,000	1,700 F
Insurance................		23,000	23,000	0
Industrial engineering......		154,000	160,000	6,000 F
Factory building lease......		46,000	46,000	0
Total fixed overhead cost		638,600	644,500	5,900 F
Total overhead cost..........		$753,080	$755,200	$2,120 F

Tab Kapp, the general manager at the Colchester facility, asked to see a copy of the preliminary draft report at 4:45 p.m. on December 23. Prating carried a copy of the report to Kapp's office, where the following discussion took place:

> *Kapp:* Wow! Almost all of the variances on the report are unfavourable. The only thing that looks good at all are the favourable variances for supervisory salaries and for industrial engineering. How did we have an unfavourable variance for depreciation?
>
> *Prating:* Do you remember that milling machine that broke down because the wrong lubricant was used by the machine operator?
>
> *Kapp:* Only vaguely.
>
> *Prating:* It turned out we couldn't fix it. We had to scrap the machine and buy a new one.
>
> *Kapp:* This report doesn't look good. I was raked over the coals last year when we had just a few unfavourable variances.
>
> *Prating:* I'm afraid the final report is going to look even worse.
>
> *Kapp:* Oh?
>
> *Prating:* The line item for industrial engineering on the report is for work we hired Klein Engineering to do for us on a contract basis. The original contract was for $160,000, but we asked them to do some additional work that was not in the contract. Under the terms of the contract, we have to reimburse Klein Engineering for the costs of the additional work. The $154,000 in actual costs that appear on the preliminary draft report reflects only their billings through December 21. The last bill they had sent us was on November 28, and they completed the project just last week. Yesterday I got a call from Maria over at Klein and she said they would be sending us a final bill for the project before the end of the year. The total bill, including the reimbursements for the additional work, is going to be…
>
> *Kapp:* I am not sure I want to hear this.
>
> *Prating:* … $176,000.
>
> *Kapp:* Ouch!
>
> *Prating:* The additional work we asked them to do added $16,000 to the cost of the project.
>
> *Kapp:* No way can I turn in a performance report with an overall unfavourable variance. They'll really get on my back at corporate headquarters. Call Maria at Klein and ask her not to send the bill until after the first of the year. We have to have that $6,000 favourable variance for industrial engineering on the performance report.

Required:

What should Lance Prating do? Explain.

INSTANT QUIZ SOLUTIONS

10–1

Ideal standards are measures of performance that can typically be attained only under ideal circumstances. While firms might strive to attain ideal standards, they do not take into account regular machine downtime and employee rest periods. Practical standards, on the other hand, do take these things into account and reflect efficient levels of production that should be achievable on a day-to-day basis. Variances from practical standards should be investigated since they represent unexpected events that have not been already taken into account when practical standards were set.

10–2

Materials price variance $= AQ(AP - SP)$, so 70,000 diodes ($0.28 per diode $-$ $0.30 per diode) $=$ $-$1,400 F. The actual price paid per unit for the material was less than the standard price, which could occur if the company purchased a lower-grade material at a discount or bought an unusually large quantity to take advantage of quantity discounts. A favourable variance would also be experienced if the market price of the material changed or if the purchasing department did some particularly sharp bargaining.

10–3

Materials quantity variance $= SP(AQ - SQ)$, so $0.30 per diode (50,000 diodes $-$ 40,000 diodes) $=$ $3,000 U. More materials were used to produce the actual output than were called for by the standard perhaps due to poorly trained or supervised workers, improperly adjusted machines, or defective materials.

10–4

Labour rate variance = $AH(AR - SR)$, so 6,400 hours ($7.50* per hour − $7.00 per hour) = $3,200 U.
*$48,000 ÷ 6,400 hours = $7.50 per hour

The average wage rate was higher than the standard wage rate. Possible explanations are an increase in wages that has not been reflected in the standards, unanticipated overtime, or a shift toward more highly paid workers.

Labour efficiency variance = $SR(AH - SH)$, so $7 per hour (6,400 hours − 6,000 hours) = $2,800 U. The actual number of labour-hours was greater than the standard labour-hours allowed for the actual output, which could be due to poor supervision, poorly trained workers, low-quality materials requiring more labour time to process, or machine breakdowns.

10–5

Total direct labour-hours allowed = 35,000 requests × 0.15 standard direct labour-hours per request = 5,250 DLH. Standard variable overhead cost = 5,250 DLH × $1.30 per DLH = $6,825. Actual variable overhead cost incurred = $7,125 − $6,825 = $300 U.

10–6

Fixed portion of the predetermined overhead rate = Fixed overhead ÷ Denominator level of activity = $400,000 ÷ 50,000 DLHs = $8.00 per DLH.

Budget variance = Actual fixed overhead cost − Flexible budget fixed overhead cost = $394,000 − $400,000 = −$6,000 F.

Volume variance = Fixed portion of predetermined rate × (Denominator hours − Standard hours) = $8.00 per DLH (50,000 DLHs − 48,000 DLHs) = $16,000 U.

■ APPENDIX 10A: FURTHER ANALYSIS OF MATERIALS VARIANCES

LEARNING OBJECTIVE 8
Compute the mix and yield variances for materials, and explain their significance.

In this appendix, we will consider subcomponents of the materials quantity variance: a *materials mix* and *materials yield variance*. The extended model for calculating these variances is presented in Exhibit 10A–1.

The production of most goods generally requires more than one type of direct materials input. Chemical firms use varying proportions of interchangeable materials, and the same is true of food processing companies. For example, a company that produces flour with a mixture of red and white wheat may, on occasion, substitute one kind of wheat for another. When legally permitted, a manufacturer of canned fruit cocktail may substitute peaches for pears and a manufacturer of sausages may substitute beef for pork. The calculation of mix and yield variances is appropriate *only* if different types of materials can be substituted for one another. A **mix variance** results if the actual mix of materials inputs differs from the standard mix of materials. The standard mix reflects the proportional mix of materials that is expected to be used to produce a given product. A mix variance is calculated to determine the effects of a change in the materials mix on the total materials cost. The mix variance is favourable if the actual mix of materials inputs is cheaper than the standard mix. This means that a greater proportion of less-expensive materials was used in production. The mix variance is unfavourable if the actual mix of materials inputs is more expensive than the standard mix because a greater proportion of more-expensive materials was used. Where a manager has control over the composition of the mix, the mix variance can be a useful measure of the manager's performance.

A **yield variance** occurs when the total quantity of inputs actually used generates a different rate of output from what would have been achieved using standard quantities of inputs at the standard mix. To isolate the effects of the yield variance from the mix variance, the yield variance is calculated using the standard mix of materials inputs. By so doing, managers can calculate the dollar impact on total materials costs of the actual total quantity of inputs differing from the quantities that should have been used according to the standard costing system. A favourable yield variance means a lower total quantity of inputs was used than planned, while an unfavourable yield variance means more inputs were used in total than planned.

To illustrate the calculation of the mix and yield variances, assume that Cape Breton Chemical Company combines secret ingredients A and B to make a product known as Super-Cleaner Bjax. The standard mix calls for 2 kilograms of A and 3 kilograms of B to produce one unit of Bjax. The standard mix for A and B is therefore 2/5 and 3/5, respectively. Assume that 150 units were produced in July using 350 kilograms of A and 450 kilograms of B. Material A has a standard unit price of $1.50, and material B has a standard unit price of $2.50.

Mix variance
The dollar effect on total materials cost of a difference between the actual mix of materials inputs and the standard mix of materials.

Yield variance
The dollar effect on total materials costs of the total quantity of inputs actually used generating a different output from what would have been achieved using standard quantities of inputs at the standard mix.

EXHIBIT 10A–1   Extended Model for Variance Analysis—Materials

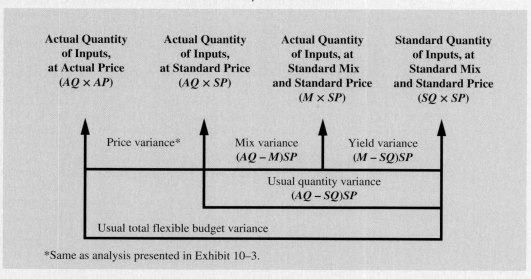

*Same as analysis presented in Exhibit 10–3.

We begin by calculating the materials quantity variance for each type of material input and in total, using the formula presented earlier in the chapter: $SP(AQ - SQ)$:

Material A: $1.50(350 - 300^*) = \$75$ U
Material B: $2.50(450 - 450^*) = \$0$

*Material A: 2 kilograms per unit $\times$ 150 units;
Material B: 3 kilograms per unit $\times$ 150 units

Thus, the total quantity variance to be further analyzed into its mix and yield components is $75 unfavourable.

For each type of input, the mix variance can be calculated in two steps. First, multiply the budgeted mix percentage for that input by the actual *total* inputs of all types and subtract the result from the actual quantity of that input used in production for the period. This is the mix variance expressed in physical terms for each type of input. Second, multiply your answer from step one by the standard price of that input. The formula for the mix variance that is applied to *each* type of material input is shown below:

$$\text{Mix variance} = \left[\text{Actual quantity} - \left(\frac{\text{Budgeted}}{\%} \times \text{Total input} \right) \right] \times \text{Standard price}$$

or for each input used in production:

$$\text{Mix variance} = (AQ_A - M_A) \, SP_A$$

where

AQ_A is the actual quantity used of material A.
M_A is the standard mix of material A given the total quantity of material actually used.
SP_A is the standard price of material A.

For material A, the mix variance in July is

$$\left[350 - \frac{2}{5}(350 + 450) \right] \times \$1.50 = \$45 \text{ U}$$

Similarly, for material B, the mix variance in July is

$$\left[450 - \frac{3}{5}(350 + 450) \right] \times \$2.50 = \$75 \text{ F}$$

The result of multiplying the budgeted mix percentage for material A by the total quantity of inputs actually used in July is 320 kilograms [⅖(350 + 450)]. This is the amount of material A that would have been used if the budgeted mix had been adhered to. Since the amount of material actually used, 350 kilograms, exceeds the budgeted amount, the mix variance is unfavourable. If the budgeted mix had been adhered to for material B, 480 kilograms [⅗(350 + 450)] would have been used in July. Since the actual usage of material B was only 450 kilograms, the materials mix variance of material B is favourable. Note that the mix variances are calculated using the total quantity of materials inputs actually used (800 kilograms) and thus focus on the effects of the actual mix of inputs differing from the standard mix of inputs.

Overall, the mix variance is $30 favourable, which is the result of using a higher percentage of the less expensive material A in July (350 ÷ 800 = 43.75%) than planned in the budget (2 ÷ 5 = 40%). If the opposite had been true and a higher percentage of the more expensive material B had been used in July compared to the budgeted mix, the overall mix variance would have been unfavourable.

The yield variance is also calculated in two steps for each type of input. First, multiply the total quantity of all inputs used for the period by the standard mix percentage for that input, and, from this result, subtract the standard quantity of the input allowed for the output achieved. Note that this approach holds mix constant at the standard proportions, allowing the yield variance to be isolated from any differences between the actual and standard mix. Second, multiply the result of the first step by the standard price for that input. The formula for the yield variance that is applied to *each* type of material input is shown below:

Yield variance = [(Budgeted percentage $\times$ Total input) − Standard quantity] $\times$ Standard price

or, for each input used in production,

$$\text{Yield variance} = (M_A - SQ_A) \, SP_A$$

where

SQ_A is the standard quantity of material A, with the other items in the formula as defined above.

For material A, the yield variance in July is

$$\left[\frac{2}{5}(350 + 450) - 2(150)\right] \$1.50 = \$30 \text{ U}$$

Similarly, for material B, the yield variance in July is

$$\left[\frac{3}{5}(350 + 450) - 3(150)\right] \$2.50 = \$75 \text{ U}$$

Note that the yield variances are calculated using the standard mix of materials (40% A, 60% B) and thus focus on the effects of the actual quantity of inputs (at the standard mix) differing from the standard quantity of inputs. Overall, the yield variance for July is $105 unfavourable, comprising the individual amounts shown above. This indicates that, in total, more inputs were used for production than should have been according to the standards.

It is important to note how the sum of the mix and yield variances is equal to the total materials quantity variance calculated above:

Variance	Amount
Mix:	
Material A...............................	$45 U
Material B...............................	75 F
Total mix variance	$30 F
Yield:	
Material A...............................	$30 U
Material B...............................	75 U
Total yield variance......................	$105 U
Total mix and yield variances..................	$ 75 U

Collectively, the mix and yield variances explain why the total quantity variance occurred. In our example, using an actual mix of inputs that favoured the less expensive material A resulted in a favourable mix variance. However, this was offset by the fact that more inputs in total (particularly for material B) were required to produce the output for the period. Specifically, 800 kilograms of materials inputs was actually used (350 kilograms of material A and 450 kilograms of material B), while the standard amount allowed for the output achieved was 750 kilograms (300 kilograms of material A and 450 kilograms of material B). This resulted in a $105 unfavourable yield variance. It could be that the less expensive material A was more easily damaged, was harder to work with, or had other characteristics that led to the unfavourable yield variance. Whatever the reason, the manager's decision to increase the proportion of material A used in July production led to an unfavourable yield variance and an unfavourable total materials quantity variance. By separately examining the mix and yield components of the total quantity variance, the effects of the tradeoffs between mix and yield effects can be detected. Moreover, there may be implications for other variances that arise from using an actual mix of inputs that differs from the standard. In our example, if material A is harder to work with, this could lead to an unfavourable labour efficiency variance if employees need to spend more time working with substandard material. So calculating the mix and yield variances may help managers understand the causes of other variances for the period.

Labour efficiency variances, described earlier in the chapter, can be analyzed in a similar manner if the composition of a work group is provided in the standard. The effects of departing from the standard mix of skilled and unskilled workers or experienced and less experienced employees can be broken down into mix and yield components. As with our example above, this allows managers to quantify the financial impact of changing the mix of labour inputs.

■ APPENDIX 10A SUMMARY

- When the production of a good requires more than one type of direct materials input, the total materials quantity variance can be further analyzed into mix and yield components if those inputs are substituted for each other. **[LO8]**
- A mix variance quantifies the dollar impact on materials costs of using an actual mix of inputs that differs from the standard mix. A yield variance quantifies the dollar impact of the actual total quantity of inputs differing from the standard quantity allowed for the output achieved. Because the yield variance is calculated using the standard mix of inputs, it permits the isolation of quantity differences (actual versus standard) from the mix differences (actual versus standard) calculated for the mix variance. **[LO8]**
- Calculating the mix and yield variances allows for a more complete evaluation of managers' decisions to change the mix of inputs in any given period. Because changing the mix of inputs can often affect the yield generated by those inputs, the dollar impact of this tradeoff becomes clear after calculating the mix and yield variances. Changing the mix of inputs can also affect other variances, such as labour efficiency, and thus may help explain outcomes on those variances. **[LO8]**
- Mix and yield variances can also be calculated when different types of labour inputs are required to produce a product or deliver a service and can be substituted for each other. **[LO8]**

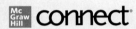

■ APPENDIX 10A EXERCISES AND PROBLEMS

EXERCISE 10A–1 Mix and Yield Variances [LO8]

The Grayson Company uses standard costs to account for its production of a specialty cleaning product called Green Clean. The standard cost of materials and direct labour to produce one bottle of Green Clean is as follows:

Material A	1.5 litres at $0.80 per litre	$1.20
Material B	0.5 litres at $2.00 per litre	1.00
Direct labour	0.25 hours at $10.00 per hour	2.50

Both material A and material B are added at the start of the process. Production data for June 2016 are as follows:

a. Beginning work in process, 5,000 units, 25% complete.
b. Started during June, 18,000 units.
c. Ending work in process, 6,000 units, 60% complete.
d. No units were spoiled.
e. 28,000 litres of material A was issued to production.
f. 12,000 litres of material B was used during June.
g. Direct labour worked totalled 4,800 hours at a cost of $50,000 for the month.

Required:
Determine all of the material and labour variances possible from the preceding data for the month of June.

EXERCISE 10A–2 Mix and Yield Variances [LO8]

Davis Division uses two raw materials—X33 and Z42—to produce its product called Base 23, a chemical base for interior house paint. The materials are mixed in the following standard proportions to yield 100 litres of Base 23:

Material	Quantity (litres)	Cost per Litre
X33	80	$1
Z42	20	$5

It requires 5 hours of direct labour at $15 per hour to produce 100 litres of Base 23.

On average, the division can produce and sell 20,000 litres of Base 23 per month. In a recent month, the division used the following amounts of materials and labour to produce 18,000 litres of Base 23:

Material	Quantity (litres)	Total Actual Cost
X33	16,200	$16,200
Z42	5,400	27,500
	21,600	$43,700
Direct labour	1,050 hours	$15,750

Required:
1. Calculate the following materials variances for Base 23:
   a. Price.
   b. Quantity.
   c. Mix.
   d. Yield.

■ APPENDIX 10B: GENERAL LEDGER ENTRIES TO RECORD VARIANCES

LEARNING OBJECTIVE 9
Prepare journal entries to record standard costs and variances.

Although standard costs and variances can be computed and used by management without being formally entered into the accounting records, most organizations prefer to make formal entries. Formal entry tends to give variances a greater emphasis than informal, off-the-record computations. This emphasis gives a clear signal of management's desire to keep costs within the standards that have been set. In addition, formal use of standard costs considerably simplifies the bookkeeping process. Inventories and cost of goods sold can be valued at their standard costs—eliminating the need to keep track of the actual cost of each unit.

Direct Materials Variances

To illustrate the general ledger entries needed to record standard cost variances, we will return to the data contained in the review problem at the end of the main body of the chapter. The entry to record the purchase of direct materials is as follows:

Raw materials (25,000 microns at $0.50 per micron).	12,500	
Materials price variance (25,000 microns at $0.02 per micron F)		500
Accounts payable (25,000 microns at $0.48 per micron)		12,000

Notice that the price variance is recognized when purchases are made, rather than when materials are actually used in production. This permits the price variance to be isolated early, and it also permits the materials to be carried in the Inventory account at standard cost. As direct materials are later drawn from inventory and used in production, the quantity variance is isolated as follows:

Work in process (18,000 microns at $0.50 per micron)	9,000	
Materials quantity variance (2,000 microns U at $0.50 per micron)	1,000	
Raw materials (20,000 microns at $0.50 per micron).		10,000

Thus, direct materials enter into the Work in Process account at standard cost, in terms of both price and quantity. Notice that the favourable price variance is a credit and the unfavourable quantity variance is a debit.

The term *direct materials* is not the same as *raw materials*, even though they are often used interchangeably. Technically, *raw materials* refer to materials that are basic to the production process and usually no processing has been done that changes their nature. *Direct materials* refer to materials identified in the product as opposed to indirect supplies or materials that are not identified in the product. For example, oil is a direct material for the production of electricity and it is considered a raw material by most. Steel is a direct material in the production of automobiles. However, a car seat is a direct material, not a raw material. Because of the confusion, we will consider the two terms interchangeable unless an obvious distinction is necessary.

Direct Labour Variances

Referring again to the cost data in the review problem at the end of the chapter, the general ledger entry to record the incurrence of direct labour cost is as follows:

Work in process (3,900 hours at $15.00 per hour)	58,500	
Labour efficiency variance (100 hours U at $15.00 per hour)	1,500	
Labour rate variance (4,000 hours at $1.00 per hour U)	4,000	
Wages payable (4,000 hours at $16.00 per hour)		64,000

Thus, as with direct materials, direct labour costs enter into the Work in Process account at standard, both in terms of the rate and in terms of the hours allowed for the actual production of the period.

Variable and Fixed Manufacturing Overhead Variances

Referring to the cost data in the review problem at the end of the chapter, the entries to record actual overhead, the application of overhead, the overhead variances, and the disposition of underapplied overhead for July are shown below.

To record actual variable and fixed overhead for July:

Overhead costs ($17,000 + $25,000)	42,000	
Various credits, such as accounts payable		42,000

To record the application of variable overhead (3,900 × $4) and fixed overhead (3,900 × $6) in July:

Work in progress ($15,600 + $23,400)	39,000	
Overhead costs		39,000

To record the overhead variances and the disposition of underapplied overhead for July:

Variable overhead spending variance U	1,000	
Variable overhead efficiency variance U	400	
Fixed overhead budget variance U	820	
Fixed overhead volume variance U	780	
Overhead costs		3,000

Cost Flows in a Standard Costing System

The flows of costs through the company's accounts are illustrated for direct materials and direct labour in Exhibit 10B–1. Note that entries into the various inventory accounts are made at standard cost—not actual cost. The differences between actual and standard costs are entered into special accounts that accumulate the various standard cost variances. Ordinarily, these standard cost variance accounts are closed out to cost of goods sold at the end of the period. Unfavourable variances increase cost of goods sold, and favourable variances decrease cost of goods sold.

EXHIBIT 10B–1 Cash Flows in a Standard Costing System

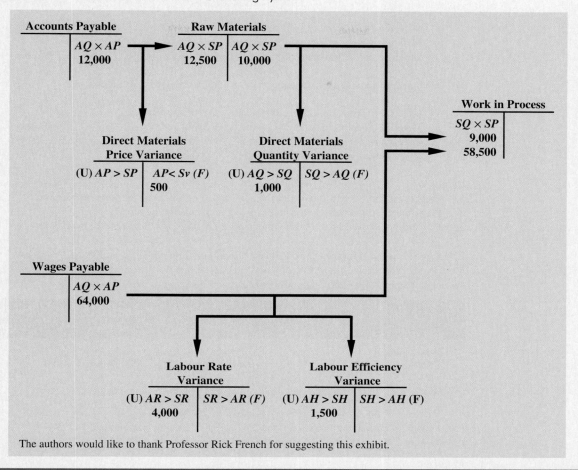

The authors would like to thank Professor Rick French for suggesting this exhibit.

APPENDIX 10B SUMMARY

- Entering standard costs and variances into the accounting records emphasizes management's desire to keep actual costs as close to standard as possible. It also simplifies the bookkeeping process because inventories and cost of goods sold can be valued at standard costs, negating the need to keep track of the actual costs of each unit. **[LO9]**
- Differences between the actual amounts paid for materials, labour, and overhead and standard costs are charged to accounts for price, rate, quantity, and efficiency variances. At the end of each reporting period, the variance accounts are closed out to cost of goods sold. Unfavourable variances increase cost of goods sold, while favourable variances decrease cost of goods sold. **[LO9]**

APPENDIX 10B EXERCISES AND PROBLEMS

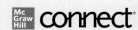

EXERCISE 10B–1 Recording Variances in the General Ledger [LO9]

Wannabe Corporation makes a product with the following standard costs for direct materials and direct labour:

Direct materials: 1.90 metres at $6.70 per metre	$12.73
Direct labour: 0.35 hours at $17.00 per hour	$ 5.95

During the most recent month, 10,000 units were produced. The costs associated with the month's production of this product were as follows:

Materials purchased: 19,500 metres at $7.00 per metre $136,500
Materials used in production: 17,400 metres . . . .   —
Direct labour: 2,540 hours at $17.75 per hour $45,085

The standard cost variances for direct materials and direct labour are as follows:

Materials price variance: 19,500 metres at $0.30 per metre U . . . . $ 5,850 U
Materials quantity variance: 1,600 metres at $6.70 per metre F . . . . $10,720 F
Labour rate variance: 2,540 hours at $0.75 per hour U . . . . $ 1,905 U
Labour efficiency variance: 960 hours at $17.00 per hour F . . . . $16,320 F

Required:
1.   Prepare the journal entry to record the purchase of materials on account for the month.
2.   Prepare the journal entry to record the use of materials for the month.
3.   Prepare the journal entry to record the incurrence of direct labour cost for the month.

EXERCISE 10B–2 Materials and Labour Variances; Journal Entries [LO2, LO3, LO9]
Marmot Products began production of a new product on April 1. The company uses a standard costing system and has established the following standards for one unit of the new product:

	Standard Quantity or Hours	Standard Price or Rate	Standard Cost
Direct materials.	3.5 metres	$ 6 per metre	$21
Direct labour	0.4 hours	$10 per hour	$ 4

During April, the following activity was recorded regarding the new product:

a.   Purchased 7,000 metres of materials at a cost of $5.75 per metre.
b.   Used 6,000 metres of materials to produce 1,500 units of the new product.
c.   Worked 725 direct labour-hours on the new product at a cost of $8,120.

Required:
1.   For direct materials:
    a.   Compute the direct materials price and quantity variances.
    b.   Prepare journal entries to record the purchase of materials and the use of materials in production.
2.   For direct labour:
    a.   Compute the direct labour rate and efficiency variances.
    b.   Prepare journal entries to record the incurrence of direct labour cost for the month.
3.   Post the entries you have prepared to the T-accounts below:

Raw Materials		Accounts Payable
? | ?		
Bal. ?		

Materials Price Variance		Wages Payable

Materials Quantity Variance		Labour Rate Variance

Work in Process		Labour Efficiency Variance
Materials used ?		
Labour cost ? | ?		

PROBLEM 10B–3 Comprehensive Variance Analysis; Journal Entries
[LO2, LO3, LO4, LO5, LO6, LO9]

Haliburton Mills Inc. is a large producer of men's and women's clothing. The company uses standard costs for all of its products. The standard costs and actual costs for a recent period are given below for one of the company's product lines (per unit of product):

	Standard Cost	Actual Cost
Direct materials:		
Standard: 4.0 metres at $3.60 per metre	$14.40	
Actual: 4.4 metres at $3.35 per metre		$14.74
Direct labour:		
Standard: 1.6 hours at $4.50 per hour	7.20	
Actual: 1.4 hours at $4.85 per hour.		6.79
Variable manufacturing overhead:		
Standard: 1.6 hours at $1.80 per hour	2.88	
Actual: 1.4 hours at $2.15 per hour.		3.01
Fixed manufacturing overhead:		
Standard: 1.6 hours at $3.00 per hour	4.80	
Actual: 1.4 hours at $3.05 per hour.		4.27
Total cost per unit	$29.28	$28.81

Actual costs: 4,800 units at $28.81	$138,288
Standard costs: 4,800 units at $29.28	140,544
Difference in cost—favourable	$ 2,256

During this period, the company produced 4,800 units of product. A comparison of standard and actual costs for the period on a total cost basis is also given above.

There was no inventory of materials on hand to start the period. During the period, 21,120 metres of materials was purchased and used in production. The denominator level of activity for the period was 6,860 hours.

Required:
1. For direct materials:
    a. Compute the price and quantity variances for the period.
    b. Prepare journal entries to record all activity relating to direct materials for the period.
2. For direct labour:
    a. Compute the rate and efficiency variances.
    b. Prepare a journal entry to record the incurrence of direct labour cost for the period.
3. Compute the variable manufacturing overhead spending and efficiency variances.
4. Compute the fixed overhead budget and volume variances.
5. On seeing the $2,256 total cost variance, the company's president stated, "It's obvious that our costs are well under control." Do you agree? Explain.
6. State possible causes of each variance that you have computed.

PROBLEM 10B–4 Comprehensive Variance Analysis with Incomplete Data; Journal Entries
[LO2, LO3, LO4, LO5, LO6, LO9]

Topline Surf Boards manufactures a single product. The standard cost of one unit of this product is as follows:

Direct materials: 2 metres at $3 per metre	$6.00
Direct labour: 1 hour at $4.50 per hour.	4.50
Variable manufacturing overhead: 1 hour at $3 per hour	3.00
Fixed manufacturing overhead: 1 hour at $5 per hour	5.00
Total standard variable cost per unit	$18.50

During October, 6,000 units were produced. Selected data relating to the month's production follow:

Materials purchased: 20,000 metres at $2.85 per metre	$57,000
Materials used in production: 12,650 metres	—
Direct labour: ? hours at $? per hour	$27,950
Variable manufacturing overhead cost incurred	$20,475
Variable manufacturing overhead efficiency variance	$ 1,500 U
Denominator level of activity for October	6,200 hours
Fixed manufacturing overhead budget variance	1,000 U

There was no beginning inventory of raw materials. The variable and fixed manufacturing overhead rates are based on direct labour-hours.

Required:
1. For direct materials:
   a. Compute the price and quantity variances for October.
   b. Prepare journal entries to record activity for October.
2. For direct labour:
   a. Compute the rate and efficiency variances for October.
   b. Prepare a journal entry to record labour activity for October.
3. For variable manufacturing overhead:
   a. Compute the spending variance for October, and verify the efficiency variance given above.
   b. If manufacturing overhead is applied to production on the basis of direct labour-hours, is it possible to have a favourable direct labour efficiency variance and an unfavourable variable overhead efficiency variance? Explain.
4. For fixed manufacturing overhead:
   a. Compute the volume variance for October.
   b. Compute actual costs for October.
5. State possible causes of each variance that you have computed.

LEARNING OBJECTIVE   ⑩

Analyze variances from sales budgets.

■ APPENDIX 10C: SALES VARIANCE ANALYSIS

Sales Variance Analysis

The interaction of price and quantity represents important information for businesses to analyze to determine why the strategic goals and specific budgeted targets were not achieved. Managers want to know the effects of market volume changes, market penetration or share changes, sales mix changes, and price changes. Each of these elements can be isolated, but the true test of management is to reconstitute the combination needed for a new marketing strategy. Variances from previous results can provide a valuable starting point for this process.

To illustrate the nature of variance reporting in the revenue area, consider the following example for Ace Video Company:

Budget sales in units:		
Deluxe video game		10,000
Standard video game.		5,000
Budget price:		
Deluxe.	$	60
Standard	$	30
Market volume expected:		
Deluxe.		70,000
Standard		90,000
Budget variable expense:		
Deluxe.	$	24
Standard	$	15

The sales price for the deluxe video game was reduced to $54 from the anticipated $60. This resulted in a $48,000 increase in revenue. The standard video game price was increased by $3 per unit, resulting in a revenue decrease of $18,000. The reasoning behind the price and revenue changes is something marketing management should explain, so that a new pricing strategy can be considered.

Actual results for the period were as follows:

Unit sales:	
Deluxe.....................................	12,000
Standard	4,000
Sales prices:	
Deluxe.....................................	$ 54
Standard	$ 33
Market volume:	
Deluxe.....................................	75,000
Standard	85,000

Exhibit 10C–1 summarizes the relationships among budgeted and actual results. Revenue variance analysis can proceed as follows:

$$\text{Sales price variance} = \left[\text{Actual sales price} - \text{Budgeted sales price} \right] \times \text{Actual sales volume}$$

Deluxe: ($54 − $60) × 12,000 units = $72,000 U
Standard: ($33 − $30) × 4,000 units = 12,000 F

Total sales price variance = $60,000 U

Note in Exhibit 10C–1 that the total $60,000 unfavourable **sales price variance** in contribution margin resulting from the change in sales price is calculated using actual sales volume in units times the difference in sales price (actual versus budget) because actual and budgeted variable costs per unit are the same.

Firms often want to know how well they are performing compared to the market for their product. If the total market demand changes, they want to evaluate the impact on profits. Importantly, the variances that follow focus on the effects of volume, quantity, and mix changes on contribution margin. If these changes also affected the fixed costs, managers would also want to analyze these effects, but this is beyond the scope of our discussion. *Market volume variances* and *market share variances* can provide a method of seeing the contribution margin effects of market volume changes or changes in the portion of the market, termed *market share* or *market penetration*, captured by the firm.

Sales price variance
Actual sales price minus budgeted sales price, multiplied by actual sales quantity.

EXHIBIT 10C–1 Actual and Budgeted Results—Ace Video Company

	Actual Results			Flexible Budget			Master Budget	
Revenue:								
Deluxe	(12,000 × $54)	$648,000		(12,000 × $60)	$720,000		(10,000 × $60)	$600,000
Standard	(4,000 × $33)	132,000		(4,000 × $30)	120,000		(5,000 × $30)	150,000
		780,000			840,000			750,000
Variable expenses:								
Deluxe	(12,000 × $24)	288,000		(12,000 × $24)	288,000		(10,000 × $24)	240,000
Standard	(4,000 × $15)	60,000		(4,000 × $15)	60,000		(5,000 × $15)	75,000
		348,000			348,000			315,000
Contribution margin		$432,000			$492,000			$435,000
			Sales Price Variance				**Sales Volume Variance**	
Total variances			$60,000 U				$57,000 F	

Market volume variance
Actual market volume minus budget market volume, times anticipated market share, multiplied by budgeted contribution margin.

We begin with the **market volume variance**, holding market share constant:

$$\begin{matrix} \text{Market} \\ \text{volume} \\ \text{variance} \end{matrix} = \left(\begin{matrix} \text{Actual} \\ \text{market} \\ \text{volume} \end{matrix} - \begin{matrix} \text{Budget} \\ \text{market} \\ \text{volume} \end{matrix} \right) \times \begin{matrix} \text{Anticipated market} \\ \text{share percentage} \end{matrix} \times \begin{matrix} \text{Budgeted} \\ \text{contribution} \\ \text{margin per unit} \end{matrix}$$

Deluxe: $(75{,}000 - 70{,}000) \times (10{,}000 \div 70{,}000) \times (\$60 - \$24) = \$25{,}714$ F
Standard: $(85{,}000 - 90{,}000) \times (5{,}000 \div 90{,}000) \times (\$30 - \$15) = \underline{\$\ 4{,}167}$ U
Total $\underline{\underline{\$21{,}547\ \text{F}}}$

The market volume variance represents the effect on contribution margin of the total market size (demand) differing from what was anticipated. Using Ace Video's budgeted market share percentages for each product, the analysis above indicates that the net effect of higher than anticipated total market demand for Deluxe video games and lower than anticipated total market demand for Standard video games is an increase in contribution margin of $21,547. This variance, although favourable, is not the result of any actions taken by Ace Video managers; instead it simply reflects the impact on contribution margin of the total market demand for video games differing from the estimates prepared by the company.

Market share variance
Actual sales volume minus the anticipated portion of the actual market volume, multiplied by budgeted contribution margin per unit.

To calculate the impact on contribution margin of Ace Video's market share differing from budget, holding the effects of total market demand constant, we use the following **market share variance** approach:

$$\begin{matrix} \text{Market} \\ \text{share} \\ \text{variance} \end{matrix} = \begin{matrix} \text{Actual} \\ \text{sales} \\ \text{quantity} \end{matrix} - \left(\begin{matrix} \text{Actual} \\ \text{market} \\ \text{volume} \end{matrix} \times \begin{matrix} \text{Anticipated} \\ \text{market share} \\ \text{percentage} \end{matrix} \right) \times \begin{matrix} \text{Budgeted} \\ \text{contribution} \\ \text{margin per unit} \end{matrix}$$

Deluxe: $\{12{,}000 - [75{,}000 \times (10{,}000 \div 70{,}000)]\} \times (\$60 - \$24) = \$46{,}286$ F
Standard: $\{4{,}000 - [85{,}000 \times (5{,}000 \div 90{,}000)]\} \times (\$30 - \$15) = \underline{\ 10{,}833}$ U
Total $\underline{\underline{\$35{,}453\ \text{F}}}$

The favourable market share variance of $35,453 reflects the net effect of Ace Video enjoying a higher than budgeted market share for Deluxe video games (16% actual versus 14.3% budgeted) but a lower than budgeted market share for Standard video games (4.7% versus 5.6%).[1] The market share variance can be influenced by actions taken by managers. For example, the favourable market share variance for Deluxe video games is likely in part attributable to the $6 per unit price decrease. Another controllable factor that could influence the market share variance is a change to the company's marketing campaign.

Two aspects of the market volume variance and market share variance are worth emphasizing. First, each variance was calculated at the contribution margin level rather than individually analyzing revenues and variable expenses. This permits a direct evaluation of the profit effect of actual sales volumes differing from the master budget. Second, the use of the budgeted contribution margin per unit isolates the effects of volume variances from those of price (or cost) variances. The impact of actual selling prices differing from budget is captured by the sales price variance, while the impact of actual variable costs per unit differing from budget was analyzed in the main chapter text.

Sales mix variance
Quantifies the effects on contribution margin of selling the two products in a mix that differs from the original budget.

The market volume variance and the market share variance help managers understand why actual sales quantities were 12,000 units for Deluxe and 4,000 units for Standard compared to budgeted unit sales of 10,000 and 5,000, respectively. In total, these volume differences resulted in the following contribution margin variances:

Deluxe: $(12{,}000 - 10{,}000) \times (\$60 - \$24) = \$72{,}000$ F
Standard: $(4{,}000 - 5{,}000) \times (\$30 - \$15) = \underline{\ 15{,}000}$ U
Total $\underline{\$57{,}000\ \text{F}}$

Composition: Market volume $= \$21{,}547$ F
Market share $= \underline{\ 35{,}453}$ F
$\underline{\underline{\$57{,}000\ \text{F}}}$

Sales quantity variance
Quantifies the effects on contribution margin of unit sales differing from the budget, holding constant the sales mix at the budgeted proportions.

An alternative view of sales volume variances can be generated by examining **sales mix variance** and **sales quantity variance** in terms of their relationship to the budgeted contribution margin. For this approach to be meaningful, management must be in a position to control the mix of products it sells in the market. While alternative formulations are possible using gross margins, sales prices, or weighted-average contribution margins, the straightforward use of contributions will be used in the illustration that follows, so that the principle can be understood:

$$\begin{matrix} \text{Sales} \\ \text{mix} \\ \text{variance} \end{matrix} = \begin{pmatrix} \begin{matrix} \text{Actual} \\ \text{sales} \\ \text{quantity} \end{matrix} - \begin{matrix} \text{Actual sales} \\ \text{quantity at} \\ \text{anticipated} \\ \text{sales mix} \end{matrix} \end{pmatrix} \times \begin{matrix} \text{Budgeted} \\ \text{contribution} \\ \text{margin per unit} \end{matrix}$$

Deluxe: $\{[12{,}000 - 16{,}000^* \times (10/15)]\} \times (\$60 - \$24) = \$48{,}000$ F
Standard: $\{[4{,}000 - 16{,}000 \times (5/15)]\} \times (\$30 - \$15) \quad = \underline{\ 20{,}000\ \text{U}}$
Total sales mix variance $\qquad\qquad \underline{\underline{\$28{,}000\ \text{F}}}$

*16,000 units = (12,000 + 4,000), 10/15 is the anticipated proportion of Deluxe sales, and 5/15 is the anticipated Standard mix proportion.

$$\begin{matrix} \text{Sales} \\ \text{quantity} \\ \text{variance} \end{matrix} = \begin{Bmatrix} \begin{bmatrix} \text{Actual sales} \\ \text{quantity at} \\ \text{anticipated} \\ \text{sales mix} \end{bmatrix} - \begin{matrix} \text{Anticipated} \\ \text{sales} \\ \text{quantity} \end{matrix} \end{Bmatrix} \times \begin{matrix} \text{Budgeted} \\ \text{contribution} \\ \text{margin per unit} \end{matrix}$$

Deluxe: $\{[16{,}000 \times (10/15)] - 10{,}000\} \times (\$60 - \$24) = \$24{,}000$ F
Standard: $\{[16{,}000 \times (5/15)] - 5{,}000\} \times (\$30 - \$15) \ = \underline{\$\ 5{,}000\ \text{F}}$
Total sales quantity variance $\qquad\qquad \underline{\underline{\$29{,}000\ \text{F}}}$

The total sales volume variance is \$57,000 favourable, composed of the following:

Sales mix.........................	\$28,000 F
Sales quantity	29,000 F
Total	\$57,000 F

The sales mix variance quantifies the effects on contribution margin of selling the two products in a mix that differs from the original budget. As shown in the analysis above, Ace Video had a budgeted mix of 66.7% Deluxe games (10,000/15,000) and 33.3% Standard games (5,000/15,000). However, the actual mix turned out to be 75% Deluxe games (12,000/16,000) and 25% Standard games (4,000/16,000). Selling a higher proportion of Deluxe games generates a favourable total sales mix variance because Deluxe has a contribution margin of \$36 per unit compared to \$15 per unit for Standard. The sales quantity variance isolates the effects on contribution margin of unit sales differing from the budget, holding constant the sales mix at the budgeted proportions. Because total sales quantity was 16,000 units compared to the budget of 15,000 units, the total quantity variance is favourable.[2]

■ APPENDIX 10C SUMMARY

- Increases in sales value do not necessarily equate to increases in profitability if selling and administrative costs related to providing the product that customers demand are higher than expected. [LO10]

■ APPENDIX 10C REVIEW PROBLEM: SALES VARIANCE ANALYSIS

The Leo Company produces and sells two product lines with budgeted revenues and expenses as follows:

	Spars	Masts
Expected total industry sales.........................	48,000 units	85,000 units
Expected Leo Company sales......................	4,200 units	17,000 units
Expected selling price..............................	$200 per unit	$300 per unit
Expected cost of manufacturing (40% fixed)...........	110 per unit	180 per unit
Expected selling and administrative costs (70% fixed)....	60 per unit	70 per unit
Expected product profit margin	$30 per unit	$50 per unit
Actual results for 2021 included:		
Actual total industry sales......................	60,000 units	100,000 units
Actual Leo Company sales	6,000 units	18,000 units
Actual selling price.............................	$180 per unit	$300 per unit

All costs behaved exactly as expected.

W. Gallant, vice-president of marketing and sales, has requested that the employees of his department be paid a bonus for the year based on the fact that they have been able to increase sales by 2,800 units over budget level for the year, an increase of over 13%.

Required:
1. Calculate the changes in overall company profits caused by the following factors:
    a. Sales price.
    b. Sales mix.
    c. Sales quantity.
    d. Market share.
    e. Market volume.

Solution to Appendix 10C Review Problem

1. **Budgeted Contribution Margin:**	Spars	Masts
Selling price	$200	$300
Variable costs:		
Manufacturing..	66	108
Selling and administrative.................................	18	21
Total variable costs	84	129
Budgeted contribution margin per unit........................	$116	$171

a. Sales Price Variance:

Spars ($180 − $200) × 6,000...........................	$120,000 U
Masts ($300 − $300) × 18,000	–0–
Total..	$120,000 U

b. Sales Mix Variance:

Spars [6,000 − (4,200 ÷ 21,200 × 24,000)] × $116	$144,453 F
Masts [18,000 − (17,000 ÷ 21,200 × 24,000)] × $171	212,943 U
Total..	$ 68,490 U

c. Sales Quantity Variance:

Spars [(4,200 ÷ 21,200 × 24,000) − 4,200] × $116	$ 64,347 F
Masts [(17,000 ÷ 21,200 × 24,000) − 17,000] × $171	383,943 F
Total..	$448,290 F

d. Market Share Variance:

Spars [6,000 − (4,200 ÷ 48,000 × 60,000)] × $116	$ 87,000 F
Masts [18,000 − (17,000 ÷ 85,000 × 100,000)] × $171	342,000 U
Total..	$255,000 U

e. Market Volume Variance:

Spars [(60,000 − 48,000) × (4,200 ÷ 48,000)] × $116	$121,800 F
Masts [(100,000 − 85,000) × (17,000 ÷ 85,000)] × $171.........	513,000 F
Total..	$634,800 F

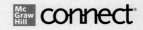

■ APPENDIX 10C QUESTIONS, EXERCISES, AND PROBLEMS

10C–1 What is the *market share variance*, and is it controllable by managers?
10C–2 What is the *sales mix variance*, and is it controllable by managers?

EXERCISE 10C–1 Variance Analysis [LO10]

Johnston Company (JC) sells two types of bicycles with details as follows for 2022:

	Mountain	Road
Plan		
Expected total industry unit sales	96,000	170,000
Budgeted JC unit sales	8,400	34,000
Budgeted selling price per unit	$ 1,200	$ 1,600
Budgeted variable costs per unit	$ 968	$ 1,258
Actuals		
Actual total industry unit sales	120,000	200,000
Actual JC unit sales	12,000	36,000
Actual selling price per unit	$ 1,240	$ 1,575
Actual variable cost per unit	$ 1,000	$ 1,275

Required:
1. Calculate the budgeted contribution margin for each model.
2. Calculate the following variances:
   a. Sales price.
   b. Market volume.
   c. Market share.
   d. Sales mix.
   e. Sales quantity.

PROBLEM 10C–2 Variance Analysis [LO10]

Rest Easy produces two types of mattresses: Regular and Heavenly. Budgeted and actual data for 2021 were as follows:

	Master Budget		Actual	
	Regular	Heavenly	Regular	Heavenly
Price per unit.	$ 300	$ 800	$ 325	$ 700
Variable costs per unit.	$ 220	$ 590	$ 238	$ 583
Unit sales.	4,500	5,500	7,200	4,800

Market Data for 2022:

Expected total market unit sales of mattresses: Regular 300,000; Heavenly 200,000

Actual total market sales of beds: Regular 444,444; Heavenly 222,223

Required:
1. Calculate the following variances:
   a. Sales price.
   b. Market volume.
   c. Market share.
   d. Sales mix.
   e. Sales quantity.
2. During 2022, Big Sleep, one of Rest Easy's key competitors, introduced an aggressive new marketing campaign that included online advertising. Big Sleep also reduced prices on its mattress that competes directly with Rest Easy's Heavenly model. Management at Rest Easy decided to follow suit by reducing the price on the Heavenly model but decided against changing the marketing approach. Using any of the variances that you believe are relevant from (1) above, evaluate the decisions made by Rest Easy's managers regarding the Heavenly model.

ENDNOTES

1. Actual market shares for Deluxe and Standard video games are calculated as follows: Deluxe 16% = 12,000 ÷ 75,000; Standard 4.7% = 4,000 ÷ 85,000. Budgeted market shares for Deluxe and Standard video games are calculated as follows: Deluxe 14.3% = 10,000 ÷ 70,000; Standard 5.6% = 5,000 ÷ 90,000.

2. Because the sales quantity variance holds sales mix constant at the budgeted proportions, it can also be calculated using a weighted-average contribution margin approach. The weighted-average contribution margin, using the budgeted sales mix, is $29 per unit: (10/15 × $36) + (5/15 × $15). Total sales quantity variance = (Actual total sales quantity − Budgeted total sales quantity) × Budgeted average contribution margin per unit. Using the data from our example, (16,000 − 15,000) × $29 = $29,000 F.

CHAPTER

11

REPORTING FOR CONTROL

LEARNING OBJECTIVES

After studying Chapter 11, you should be able to

1 Prepare a segmented income statement using the contribution format, and explain the difference between traceable fixed costs and common fixed costs.

2 Differentiate among responsibility centres such as cost centres, profit centres, and investment centres, and explain how performance is measured in each.

3 Analyze the return on investment.

4 Compute residual income, and describe the strengths and weaknesses of this method of measuring performance.

5 Explain the use of balanced scorecards to assess performance.

6 (Appendix 11A) Determine the range, if any, within which a negotiated transfer price should fall, and explain approaches to setting the transfer price.

7 (Appendix 11A) Identify the four types of quality costs, explain their interaction, and prepare a quality cost report.

8 (Appendix 11A) Allocate service department costs to operating departments using the direct method.

9 (Appendix 11A) Allocate service department costs to operating department costs using the step-down method.

■ MANAGING PERFORMANCE: HOW WELL ARE WE DOING?

Jonathan Weiss / Shutterstock

In 2011 Target announced it had purchased more than 200 Zellers locations from Hudson's Bay Company, allowing it to expand into Canada. Consumers were excited for this upscale discount retailer to shake up the retail industry in Canada. Unfortunately, Target's Canadian business segment reported significant losses from the point the first store opened until January 2015 when Target announced it would be exiting the Canadian market altogether. Value for money, a narrower product selection than in the U.S. stores, and a softening Canadian dollar all added to decline of the Canadian business segment. In this chapter, we will learn how organizations like Target that have multiple geographic or industry segments keep track of the financial returns on investment in those segments and how they determine which segments are doing well and which segments need significant attention.

T hrough a combination of feedback from actual results, comparisons to budgets, comparisons to results of previous periods, and even comparisons to other organizations, managers attempt to ensure that the organization moves in the planned direction using *performance assessment* or *control.*

Managers control the organization using a variety of approaches. Accounting reports of financial results represent one important approach to controlling operations because such reports provide a means of obtaining comparisons to budgets, to previous results, and to the results of other organizations, as well as providing knowledge of actual financial results. Such financial comparisons also serve as a base for reward schemes or contracts used to motivate managers to work toward planned goals and objectives.

These financial performance reports can be constructed in various ways so that they better serve the specific control functions that management desires. As this chapter illustrates, segment reporting, responsibility centre reporting, and investment performance are commonly used reporting structures that provide somewhat different types of information. Each presents information in a manner that permits a different view of the organization and a different aspect of organizational control. Understanding how the aspects change and why managers would want these changes will permit you to integrate the concepts of control with reports about standard cost variances, cost of production, and flexible budget analyses described in earlier chapters.

The modern manufacturing environment has promoted the need for flexibility in management to accompany flexibility in production. Flexibility in management requires timely and accurate decisions by members of the organization ranging from top management to the production worker. Accounting formats often represent approaches that are not well understood by production workers. Increasingly, companies are using non-financial indicators of performance, such as scrap levels, rework efforts, market share, employee morale, pollutant discharges, and customer satisfaction. The process of collecting and presenting these data on a real-time basis is assisted by computer systems. Properly configured enterprise resource planning systems enable the operational and financial data to be maintained consistently by using a common interactive database.

■ DECENTRALIZATION IN ORGANIZATIONS

Decentralized organization
An organization in which decision making is spread throughout the organization rather than being confined to a few top executives.

In a **decentralized organization**, decision making is spread throughout the organization rather than being confined to a few top executives. All large organizations are decentralized to some extent, out of necessity. At one extreme, a strongly decentralized organization is one in which there are few, if any, constraints on the freedom of even the lowest-level managers and employees to make decisions. At the other extreme, in a strongly centralized organization, lower-level managers have little freedom to make decisions. Most organizations fall somewhere between these two extremes.

Advantages and Disadvantages of Decentralization

The major advantages of decentralization include:

1. By delegating day-to-day problem solving to lower-level managers, top management can concentrate on bigger issues, such as overall strategy.
2. Empowering lower-level managers to make decisions puts the decision-making authority in the hands of those who tend to have the most detailed and up-to-date information about day-to-day operations.
3. By eliminating layers of decision making and approvals, organizations can respond more quickly to customers and to changes in the operating environment.
4. Granting decision-making authority helps train lower-level managers for higher-level positions.
5. Empowering lower-level managers to make decisions can increase their motivation and job satisfaction.

The major disadvantages of decentralization include:

1. Lower-level managers may make decisions without fully understanding the company's overall strategy.
2. If lower-level managers make their own decisions independently of each other, coordination may be lacking.
3. Spreading innovative ideas may be difficult in a decentralized organization. Someone in one part of the organization may have a terrific idea that would benefit other parts of the organization, but without strong central direction the idea may not be shared with, and adopted by, other parts of the organization.
4. Lower-level managers may have objectives that clash with the objectives of the entire organization. For example, a manager may be more interested in increasing the size of his or her department, leading to more power and prestige, than in increasing the department's effectiveness.

BEYOND THE BOTTOM LINE

The advantages of decentralization need to be considered relative to the potential disadvantages. For example, the shareholders of the company delegate their decision-making authority to the top managers. Unfortunately, top managers may abuse that trust by rewarding themselves and their friends too generously, spending too much company money on palatial offices, and so on. The issue of how to ensure that top managers act in the best interests of the company's owners continues to challenge experts. To a large extent, the owners rely on performance evaluation using return on investment and residual income measures, as discussed later in the chapter, and on bonuses and stock options. The stock market is also an important disciplining mechanism. If top managers squander the company's resources, the price of the company's stock will almost surely fall—possibly resulting in a loss of prestige, bonuses, and a job. And, of course, particularly outrageous self-dealing may land a CEO in court.

Decentralization and Segment Reporting

Effective decentralization requires *segment reporting* to permit analysis and evaluation of the decisions made by the segment managers. In addition to the companywide income statement, reports are needed for individual segments of the organization. A *segment* is defined as a part or activity of an organization about which managers would like cost, revenue, or profit data. A company's operations can be segmented in many ways. For example, a grocery store chain like Loblaws or Sobeys can segment its business by geographic region, by individual store, by the nature of the merchandise (i.e., fresh foods, canned goods, paper goods), by brand name, and so on. As we will see, it is possible to classify segments according to managers' ability to control revenues, costs, and profits. Importantly, the tools used to evaluate segment managers' performance depend directly on what they have control over.

■ SEGMENT REPORTING

To operate effectively, managers and decision makers must have a great deal more information available to them than the information provided by a single companywide income statement. Whether prepared on a variable costing or absorption basis, such statements usually provide only a summary of overall operations; as such, they typically do not contain enough detail to allow the manager or investor to detect problems that may exist in the organization. For example, some product lines may be profitable while others are unprofitable; some sales

LEARNING OBJECTIVE ❶

Prepare a segmented income statement using the contribution format, and explain the difference between traceable fixed costs and common fixed costs.

territories may have a poor sales mix, or salespeople may be overlooking sales opportunities. Managers may want to analyze the results at a more detailed level to see if some salespeople are more effective than others, or to see if some producing divisions are effectively or ineffectively using their capacity and/or resources. To uncover such problems the manager may need not one but several income statements that focus on the segments of a company. The preparation of income statements of this type is known as *segmented reporting*.

An operating segment for financial accounting purposes is a component of an enterprise

- That engages in business activities from which it may earn revenues and incur expenses.
- Whose operating results are regularly reviewed by the enterprise's chief operating officer to make decisions about resources to be allocated to the segment and assess its performance.
- For which discrete financial information is available.

Different Levels of Segmented Statements

Segmented statements can be prepared for different levels of activity in an organization and in different formats; Exhibit 11–1 illustrates three levels of segmented statements for Cassalatta Inc., presented in a widely used format. The contribution format income statement for the entire company appears at the very top of the exhibit under the column labelled Total Company. Immediately to the right of this column are two columns—one for each of the two divisions. We can see that the Business Products Division's segment margin is $60,000 and the Consumer Products Division's is $40,000. These segment margins show the company's divisional managers how much each of their divisions is contributing to the company's profits.

Segmented income statements can be prepared for activities at many levels in a company. The divisions are segmented according to their major product lines. In the case of the Consumer Products Division, the product lines are computer animation and computer games. Going even further, each of the product lines is segmented according to how it is sold—in retail stores or by online sales. Notice that as we go from one segmented statement to another, we are looking at smaller and smaller pieces of the company. While not shown in Exhibit 11–1, segmented income statements could also have been prepared for the major product lines in the Business Products Division.

The benefits accruing to the manager from a series of statements such as those contained in Exhibit 11–1 are substantial. By carefully examining trends and results in each segment, the manager can gain considerable insight into the company as a whole and perhaps discover opportunities and courses of action that would otherwise have remained hidden from view. Advanced computer-based information systems make it easier to construct such statements and to keep them continuously current.

One obvious question becomes evident from a careful review of Exhibit 11–1: Why break down results by divisions first, product lines next, and then sales territories? The order of breakdown depends on what information is desired. Certainly it might be advantageous to begin with each sales territory. Then it would be possible to examine product lines for each sales territory, and then divisions for each product line. This alternative would permit a product-line comparison between divisions. What management wants to learn and the types of comparisons desired are factors used for deciding the order of the breakdown. The order of the breakdown should not affect the numbers, but it can alter what appears on a given report and the ease of review.

Assigning Costs to Segments

Segmented statements for internal use are typically prepared in the contribution format, as described in Chapter 3. The same costing guidelines are used in preparing these statements as are used in preparing a contribution statement generally, with one exception. This lies in the handling of fixed costs. Notice from Exhibit 11–1 that the fixed costs are divided into two parts on a segmented statement—one part labelled *traceable* and the other part labelled *common*. Only those fixed costs labelled *traceable* are charged to the various segments. If a fixed

Segments Defined as Divisions

	Total Company	Division Business Products Division	Division Consumer Products Division
Sales	$500,000	$300,000	$200,000
Variable expenses:			
Variable cost of goods sold	180,000	120,000	60,000
Other variable expenses	50,000	30,000	20,000
Total variable expenses	230,000	150,000	80,000
Contribution margin	270,000	150,000	120,000
Traceable fixed expenses	170,000	90,000	80,000*
Divisional segment margin	100,000	$ 60,000	$ 40,000
Common fixed expenses not traceable to individual divisions	85,000		
Operating income	$ 15,000		

EXHIBIT 11–1
Cassalatta Inc.—Segmented Income Statements in the Contribution Format

Segments Defined as Product Lines of the Consumer Products Division

	Consumer Products Division	Product Line Computer Animation	Product Line Computer Games
Sales	$200,000	$75,000	$125,000
Variable expenses:			
Variable cost of goods sold	60,000	20,000	40,000
Other variable expenses	20,000	5,000	15,000
Total variable expenses	80,000	25,000	55,000
Contribution margin	120,000	50,000	70,000
Traceable fixed expenses	70,000	30,000	40,000
Product-line segment margin	50,000	$20,000	$ 30,000
Common fixed expenses not traceable to individual product lines	10,000		
Divisional segment margin	$ 40,000		

Segments Defined as Sales Territories for One Product Line—Computer Games—of the Consumer Products Division

	Computer Games	Sales Territory Online Sales	Sales Territory Retail Stores
Sales	$125,000	$100,000	$25,000
Variable expenses:			
Variable cost of goods sold	40,000	32,000	8,000
Other variable expenses	15,000	5,000	10,000
Total variable expenses	55,000	37,000	18,000
Contribution margin	70,000	63,000	7,000
Traceable fixed expenses	25,000	15,000	10,000
Sales channel segment margin	45,000	$ 48,000	$ (3,000)
Common fixed expenses not traceable to individual sales channels	15,000		
Product-line segment margin	$ 30,000		

*Notice that this $80,000 in traceable fixed expenses is divided into two parts when the Consumer Products Division is broken down into product lines—$70,000 traceable and $10,000 common. The reasons for this are discussed later in the section "Traceable Costs Can Become Common."

cost is not traceable directly to some segment, then it is treated as a common cost and kept separate from the segments themselves. Thus, under the contribution approach, a cost is never arbitrarily assigned to a segment of an organization.

In summary, two guidelines are followed in assigning costs to the various segments of a company under the contribution approach:

1. First, according to cost behaviour patterns (i.e., variable and fixed).
2. Second, according to whether the costs are directly traceable to the segments involved.

We now consider various aspects of Exhibit 11–1 in more depth.

Sales and Contribution Margin

To prepare segmented statements for management purposes, it is necessary to keep records of sales by individual segment, as well as in total for the organization. After deducting related variable expenses, a contribution margin (CM) figure can be computed for each segment, as illustrated in Exhibit 11–1.

Recall from our discussion of variable costing that the CM is an extremely useful piece of data for the manager—particularly for determining the effect on net income of increases or decreases in sales volume. If sales volume goes up or down, the effect on operating income can easily be computed by simply multiplying the unit CM by the change in units sold or by multiplying the change in sales dollars by the CM ratio. One assumption implicit here is that selling prices and variable costs do not change with changes in volume. Segmented statements give the manager the ability to make such computations on a product-by-product, division-by-division, or territory-by-territory basis, thereby providing the information needed to highlight areas of weakness or to capitalize on areas of strength.

The CM is basically a short-run planning tool. As such, it is especially valuable in decisions relating to temporary uses of capacity, to special orders, or to short-run product-line promotion. Decisions relative to the short run usually involve only variable costs and revenues, which of course are the very elements involved in CM. By carefully monitoring segment CM and segment CM ratios, the manager is in a position to make those short-run decisions that maximize each segment's contribution to the overall profitability of the organization. Such decisions will be discussed in detail in Chapter 12.

The Importance of Fixed Costs

The emphasis we place on the usefulness of the CM should not be taken as a suggestion that fixed costs are not important. Fixed costs are very important in any organization. What the contribution approach does imply is that *different costs are needed for different purposes*. For one purpose, variable costs and revenues alone may be adequate for a manager's needs; for another purpose, the manager's needs may encompass the fixed costs as well.

The breaking apart of fixed and variable costs also emphasizes to management that the costs are controlled differently and that these differences must be kept clearly in mind for both short-run and long-run planning. Moreover, the grouping of fixed costs under the contribution approach highlights the fact that, after the fixed costs have been covered, operating income increases to the extent of the CM generated on each additional unit sold. All of these concepts are useful to the manager *internally* for planning purposes.

Traceable and Common Fixed Costs

Traceable fixed costs
Fixed costs that can be identified with a particular segment and that arise because of the existence of the segment.

Traceable fixed costs can be defined as those fixed costs that can be identified with a particular segment and that arise because of the existence of the segment—if the segment had never existed, the fixed cost would not have been incurred, and/or if the segment were eliminated, the fixed cost would disappear. Only the traceable fixed costs are charged to particular segments. If a cost is not traceable to a segment, then it is not assigned to the segment. For example, the maintenance cost for the building in which a Challenger jet is assembled is a *traceable* fixed cost of the Challenger business segment of Bombardier Ltd.

A **common fixed cost** is a fixed cost that supports the operations of more than one segment but is not traceable in whole or in part to any one segment. Even if the segment were entirely eliminated, there would be no change in a true common fixed cost. Note the following:

- The salary of the Frito-Lay product manager at PepsiCo is a *traceable* fixed cost of the Frito-Lay business segment of PepsiCo.
- The salary of the CEO of General Motors Canada is a *common* fixed cost of the various divisions of General Motors Canada.
- The cost of the automatic bar-coding machine at Cassalatta is a *common* fixed cost of the Consumer Products Division and the Business Products Division.
- The cost of the receptionist's salary at an office shared by a number of doctors is a *common* fixed cost of the doctors. The cost is traceable to the office, but not to any one of the doctors individually.

Common fixed costs are not allocated to segments—the total amount is deducted to arrive at the income for the company as a whole (see Exhibit 11–1). The management accountant may contend that nothing is added to the overall usefulness of a segmented statement by allocating the common costs among segments. The accountant would argue that such allocations tend to reduce the usefulness of segmented statements. The reason is that arbitrary allocations draw attention away from those costs that are traceable to a segment and that should form a basis for appraising performance.

It is argued that any attempt to allocate common fixed costs among segments may result in misleading data or may obscure important relationships between segment revenues and segment earnings. Arbitrary allocation of common fixed costs often results in a segment appearing to be unprofitable, whereas it may be contributing substantially above its own traceable costs toward the overall profitability of a firm. In such cases, the allocated costs may lead to the unwise elimination of a segment and to a decrease in profits for the company as a whole because common costs do not disappear if the segment is closed down.

A word of caution is necessary here. Management reaction to common costs may help control the growth of such costs. Managers may use common cost allocation as a form of cost price or as a signal about the benefits received from headquarters and thus modify their actions for the common good of the organization. Empirical investigations suggest firms often allocate common costs to segments for a number of reasons. Rigorous analysis of the treatment of uncontrollable costs and allocated common costs suggests there may be some benefit to charging managers with uncontrollable costs or allocating common costs to segments. Managerial behaviour is complex, and investigation of it often finds results that were previously thought to be fallacious but may not be so.

Identifying Traceable Fixed Costs

The distinction between traceable and common fixed costs is crucial in segmented reporting, because traceable fixed costs are charged to the segments, but common fixed costs are not. In an actual situation, it is sometimes hard to determine whether a cost should be classified as traceable or common.

The general guideline is to treat as traceable costs *only those costs that would disappear over time if the segment itself disappeared.* For example, if the Consumer Products Division in Exhibit 11–1 were sold or discontinued, it would no longer be necessary to pay the division manager's salary. Therefore, the division manager's salary should be classified as a traceable fixed cost of the Consumer Products Division. On the other hand, the president of the company undoubtedly would continue to be paid even if the Consumer Products Division were dropped. In fact, he or she might even be paid more if dropping the division was a good idea. Therefore, the president's salary is common to both divisions and should not be charged to either division.

There will always be some costs that fall between the traceable and common categories, and considerable care and good judgment are required for their proper classification. The important point is to resist the temptation to allocate costs (such as depreciation of corporate facilities) that are clearly common and that will continue regardless of whether the segment exists or not. *Any allocation of common costs to segments reduces the value of the segment margin as a guide to long-run segment profitability and segment performance.*

Breakdown of Traceable Fixed Costs

In preparing segmented income statements, some managers like to separate the traceable fixed costs into two classes—discretionary and committed. As discussed in Chapter 3, discretionary fixed costs are under the immediate control of the manager, whereas committed fixed costs are not. Therefore, a breakdown of the traceable fixed costs into these two classes allows a company to distinguish between the performance of the segment manager and the performance of the segment as a long-term investment.

In some situations, this distinction in performance can be very important. A top-flight manager, for example, may be assigned to a division that has an antiquated plant or that is saddled with other committed fixed costs that are beyond the segment manager's control. Under these conditions, it is unfair to judge the segment manager's performance simply on the basis of overall margin generated by the segment. Rather, in these circumstances, the discretionary fixed costs should be separated from the committed fixed costs and deducted as a separate group from the segment's CM. The amount remaining after deducting the discretionary fixed costs, sometimes called a *segment performance margin*, should then be used as a basis for evaluating the segment manager's performance. This would be a valid measure of performance, as the amount involved would represent the margin generated by the segment after deducting all costs controllable by the segment manager. The committed fixed costs of a segment can be broken down in still other ways. However, the preceding discussion is adequate for our purposes.

Activity-Based Costing

Some costs are easy to identify as traceable costs. For example, the costs of advertising Procter & Gamble's Crest toothpaste on television are clearly traceable to Crest. A more difficult situation arises when a building, machine, or other resource is shared by two or more segments. For example, assume that a multi-product company leases warehouse space that is used for storing the full range of its products. Would the lease cost of the warehouse be a traceable or a common cost of the products? Managers familiar with activity-based costing (ABC) might argue that the lease is traceable and should be assigned to the products according to how much space the products use in the warehouse. In like manner, these managers would argue that order-processing costs, sales support costs, and other selling and administrative expenses should also be charged to segments according to the segments' consumption of selling and administrative resources.

To illustrate, consider the Holt Corporation, a company that manufactures concrete pipe for industrial uses. The company has three products—9-inch pipe, 12-inch pipe, and 18-inch pipe. Space is leased in a large warehouse on a yearly basis as needed. The lease cost of this space is $10 per square metre per year. The 9-inch pipe occupies 400 square metres of space, the 12-inch pipe occupies 1,600 square metres, and the 18-inch pipe occupies 2,000 square metres. The company also has an order-processing department that incurred $150,000 in order-processing costs last year. Management believes that order-processing costs are driven by the number of orders placed by customers in a year. Last year, 2,500 orders were placed, of which 1,200 were for 9-inch pipe, 800 were for 12-inch pipe, and 500 were for 18-inch pipe. Given these data, the following costs would be assigned to each product using the ABC approach:

Warehouse space cost:	
9-inch pipe: $10 × 400 square metres	$ 4,000
12-inch pipe: $10 × 1,600 square metres	16,000
18-inch pipe: $10 × 2,000 square metres	20,000
Total cost assigned	$ 40,000
Order-processing costs:	
$150,000 ÷ 2,500 orders = $60 per order	
9-inch pipe: $60 × 1,200 orders	$ 72,000
12-inch pipe: $60 × 800 orders	48,000
18-inch pipe: $60 × 500 orders	30,000
Total cost assigned	$150,000

This method of assigning costs combines the strength of ABC with the power of the contribution approach and greatly enhances the manager's ability to measure the profitability and performance of segments. However, managers must still ask themselves if the costs would in fact disappear over time if the segment itself disappeared. In the case of Holt Corporation, it is clear that the $20,000 in warehousing costs for 18-inch pipe would be eliminated if 18-inch pipe were no longer being produced. The company would simply rent less warehouse space the following year. However, suppose the company owns the warehouse. Then it is not so clear that the $20,000 of the cost of the warehouse would really disappear if 18-inch pipe were discontinued as a product. That part of the company warehouse might simply be empty while the costs of the warehouse continue to be incurred.

Traceable Costs Can Become Common

Fixed costs that are traceable to one segment may be common costs of another segment. This is because there are limits to how finely a cost can be separated without resorting to arbitrary allocation. The more finely segments are defined, the more costs they have in common.

This concept can be seen in Exhibit 11–2. Notice that when segments are defined as divisions, the Consumer Products Division has $80,000 in traceable fixed expenses. Only $70,000 of this amount remains traceable, however, when we narrow our definition to that of

	Total Company	Segment Business Products Division	Segment Consumer Products Division
Contribution margin	$270,000	$150,000	$120,000
Traceable fixed expenses	170,000	90,000	80,000

	Consumer Products Division	Segment Computer Animation	Segment Computer Games
Contribution margin	$120,000	$50,000	$70,000
Traceable fixed expenses	70,000	30,000	40,000
Product-line segment margin	50,000	$20,000	$30,000
Common fixed expenses	10,000		
Divisional segment margin	$ 40,000		

EXHIBIT 11–2
Reclassification of Traceable Fixed Expenses from Exhibit 11–1

the product lines. Notice that the other $10,000 then becomes a common cost of these product lines of the Consumer Products Division.

Why would $10,000 of traceable fixed cost become a common cost when the division is divided into product lines? The $10,000 is the monthly salary of the manager of the Consumer Products Division. This salary is a traceable cost of the division as a whole but is a common cost of the division's product lines. The manager's salary is a necessary cost of having the two product lines, but even if one of the product lines were discontinued entirely, the manager's salary would probably not be cut. Therefore, none of the manager's salary can really be traced to the individual products.

The $70,000 traceable fixed cost of the product lines consists of the cost of product-specific advertising. A total of $30,000 was spent on advertising animation software and $40,000 was spent on advertising computer games. These costs can clearly be traced to the individual product lines.

Segment Margin

Segment margin
A margin obtained by deducting a segment's traceable fixed costs from the segment's contribution margin.

Observe from Exhibit 11–1 that the **segment margin** is obtained by deducting a segment's traceable fixed costs from the segment's CM. It represents the margin available after a segment has covered all of its own costs. The segment margin is the best gauge of the long-run profitability of a segment, because it includes only those costs that are caused by the segment. The term *long-run* is applied here because fixed costs could be altered if the segment were eliminated. If a segment cannot cover its own costs, that segment should probably be dropped (unless it is essential to sales of other segments). Notice from Exhibit 11–1, for example, that the Retail Stores sales channel has a negative segment margin. This means that the segment is not generating enough revenue to cover its own costs. In fact, it is detracting from profits in that its $3,000 loss must be covered by other segments. Retention or elimination of product lines and other segments is covered in more depth in Chapter 12.

From a decision-making point of view, the segment margin is most useful in major decisions that affect capacity, such as dropping a segment. By contrast, as noted earlier, the CM is most useful in decisions relating to short-run changes, such as pricing of special orders that involve temporary use of existing capacity.

Segment Reporting for Financial Accounting

Differences in segment profits reports for internal management decision making and those required for external reporting are minimized given *International Financial Reporting Standard (IFRS) 8—Operating Segments*. This standard requires that segmented reports prepared for external users use the same methods and definitions used for internal segmented reports that are prepared to aid in making operating decisions. This is a very unusual requirement. Companies are not ordinarily required to report the same data to external users that are reported internally for decision-making purposes. This requirement has some serious drawbacks. First, segmented data are often highly sensitive, so companies are reluctant to release such data to the public for the simple reason that their competitors will then have access to the data. Second, segmented statements prepared in accordance with GAAP do not distinguish between fixed and variable costs and between traceable and common costs. Indeed, the segmented income statements illustrated earlier in this chapter do not conform to GAAP for that reason. To avoid the complications of reconciling non-GAAP segment earnings with GAAP consolidated earnings, it is likely that at least some managers will choose to construct their segmented financial statements to conform to GAAP. This will result in more occurrences of the problems discussed in the following section.

Hindrances to Proper Cost Assignment

Costs must be properly assigned to segments. All of the costs attributable to a segment—and only those costs—should be assigned to the segment. Unfortunately, companies often make mistakes when assigning costs to segments. They omit some costs, inappropriately assign traceable fixed costs, and arbitrarily allocate common fixed costs.

Omission of Costs

The costs assigned to a segment should include all costs attributable to that segment from the company's entire value chain, as discussed in Chapter 1. All of these functions, from research and development through product design, manufacturing, marketing, distribution, and customer service, are required to bring a product or service to the customer and generate revenues.

However, as discussed in Chapters 2, 5, and 8, only manufacturing costs are included in product costs under absorption costing, which is widely regarded as required for financial reporting. To avoid having to maintain two costing systems and to provide consistency between internal and external reports, many companies also use absorption costing for their internal reports, such as segmented income statements. As a result, such companies omit from their profitability analysis part or all of the *upstream* costs in the value chain, which consist of research and development and product design, and the *downstream* costs, which consist of marketing, distribution, and customer service. Yet these non-manufacturing costs are just as essential as manufacturing costs in determining product profitability. These upstream and downstream costs, which are usually included in selling and administrative expenses on the income statement, can represent half or more of the total costs of an organization. If either the upstream or downstream costs are omitted in profitability analysis, then the product is undercosted and management may unwittingly develop and maintain products that result in losses in the long run.

Inappropriate Methods for Assigning Traceable Costs among Segments

In addition to omitting costs, many companies do not correctly handle traceable fixed expenses on segmented income statements. First, they may not trace fixed expenses to segments even when it is feasible to do so. Second, they may use inappropriate allocation bases to allocate traceable fixed expenses to segments.

Failure to Trace Costs Directly

Costs that can be traced directly to a specific company segment should be charged directly to that segment. Failure to trace these costs directly results in these costs being placed in a companywide overhead pool. While a portion of these costs would then be allocated to the segment generating the costs, the rest would be incorrectly allocated to other segments. For example, the rent for a branch office of an insurance company should be charged directly against the branch to which it relates rather than included in a companywide overhead pool and then spread throughout the company.

Inappropriate Allocation Base

Some companies allocate costs to segments using arbitrary bases such as sales dollars or cost of goods sold. For example, under the sales dollars approach, costs are allocated to the various segments according to the percentage of company sales generated by each segment. Thus, if a segment generates 20% of the company's sales, it is allocated 20% of the company's selling and administrative expenses as its "fair share." This same basic procedure is followed if costs of goods sold or some other measure is used as the allocation base.

Costs should be allocated to segments for internal decision-making purposes only when the allocation base actually drives the cost being allocated (or is very highly correlated with the real cost driver). For example, sales should be used to allocate selling and administrative expenses only if a 10% increase in sales will result in a 10% increase in selling and administrative expenses. To the extent that selling and administrative expenses are not driven by sales volume, these expenses will be improperly allocated—with a disproportionately high percentage of the selling and administrative expenses assigned to the segments with the largest sales.

Arbitrarily Dividing Common Costs among Segments

Another business practice that leads to distorted segment costs is the practice of assigning non-traceable costs to segments. For example, some companies allocate the costs of the corporate headquarters building to products on segment reports. However, in a multi-product company, no single product is likely to be responsible for any significant amount of this cost. Even if a product were eliminated entirely, there would usually be no significant effect on any of the costs of the corporate headquarters building. In short, there is no cause-and-effect relationship between the cost of the corporate headquarters building and the existence of any one product. As a consequence, any allocation of the costs of the corporate headquarters building to the products must be arbitrary.

Common costs like the costs of the corporate headquarters building are necessary, of course, to have a functioning organization. The common practice of arbitrarily allocating these costs to segments is often justified on the grounds that "someone" has to "cover the common costs." While it is undeniably true that the common costs must be covered, arbitrarily allocating common costs to segments does not ensure that this will happen. In fact, adding a share of common costs to the real costs of a segment may make an otherwise profitable segment appear to be unprofitable. If a manager eliminates the apparently unprofitable segment, the real traceable costs of the segment will be saved, but its revenues will be lost. What happens to the common fixed costs that were allocated to the segment? They don't disappear; they are reallocated to the remaining segments of the company. That makes all of the remaining segments appear to be less profitable—possibly resulting in dropping other segments. The net effect will be to reduce the profits of the company as a whole and make it even more difficult to cover the common costs.

Additionally, common fixed costs are not manageable by the manager to whom they are arbitrarily allocated; they are the responsibility of higher-level managers. Allocating common fixed costs to responsibility centres is counterproductive in a responsibility accounting system. When common fixed costs are allocated to managers, they are held responsible for those costs even though they cannot control them.

In summary, the way many companies handle segment reporting results in cost distortion. This distortion results from three practices—the failure to trace costs directly to a specific segment when it is feasible to do so, the use of inappropriate bases for allocating costs, and the allocation of common costs to segments. The examples of segment reporting provided in Exhibit 11–1 and 11–2 avoid many of the problems encountered by companies that do not use variable costing. Variable costing permits a clearer allocation of costs to segments because it avoids the distortions created by the allocation of fixed manufacturing overhead that would be present with the use of absorption costing. Thus, our suggestions are to use variable costing for segment reports and allocate fixed manufacturing overhead as a period expense based on the criterion of traceability; that is, *fixed costs will disappear over time if the segment itself disappears.*

Responsibility centre
Any business segment whose manager has control over cost or profit or the use of investment funds.

LEARNING OBJECTIVE ❷
Differentiate among responsibility centres such as cost centres, profit centres, and investment centres, and explain how performance is measured in each.

■ RESPONSIBILITY CENTRES

A **responsibility centre** is broadly defined as any part of an organization whose manager has control over and is accountable for cost, profit, or investments. The three primary types of responsibility centres are cost centres, profit centres, and investment centres.[1] As discussed below, organizations categorize responsibility centres into one of these three types based on the manager's authority to control cost, revenue, and investment funds.

Cost Centre

Cost centre
A business segment whose manager has control over cost but has no control over revenue or the use of investment funds.

A **cost centre** is a business segment whose manager has control over costs but not over revenue or investment funds. Service departments, such as accounting, finance, selling and administrative, legal, and personnel, are usually considered to be cost centres. In addition, manufacturing facilities are often considered to be cost centres. The managers of cost centres are expected to minimize cost while providing the level of services or the amount of product demanded by the other parts of the organization. For example, the manager of a production facility would be evaluated at least in part by comparing actual costs to how much the costs should have been for the actual number of units produced during the period. Flexible budget variances and standard cost variances, discussed in Chapters 9 and 10, are often used to evaluate cost centre performance. However, managers should not be held accountable for controlling common costs arbitrarily allocated to their segment.

Profit Centre

In contrast to a cost centre, a **profit centre** is any business segment whose manager has control over both cost and revenue. Like a cost centre, however, a profit centre manager generally does not have control over investment funds. For example, the manager in charge of one of six resorts would be responsible for both the revenues and costs, and hence the profits, of the resort but might not have control over major investments in the resort. Profit centre managers are often evaluated by comparing actual profit to targeted or budgeted profit.

Profit centre
A business segment whose manager has control over cost and revenue but has no control over the use of investment funds.

Investment Centre

An **investment centre** is any segment of an organization whose manager has control over cost, revenue, and investments in operating assets. For example, the president of General Motors Canada, a division of the General Motors Company, would have a great deal of discretion over investments in the division. The president of the division would be responsible for initiating investment proposals, such as funding research into more fuel-efficient engines for sport-utility vehicles. Once the proposal has been approved by General Motors Company's top-level executives and the board of directors, the president of General Motors Canada would then be responsible for making sure that the investment pays off. Investment centre managers are usually evaluated using return on investment or residual income measures, as discussed later in the chapter.

Investment centre
A business segment whose manager has control over cost and revenue and also has control over the use of investment funds.

A partial organization chart for Universal Foods Corporation, a company in the snack food and beverage industry, appears in Exhibit 11–3. This partial organization chart indicates

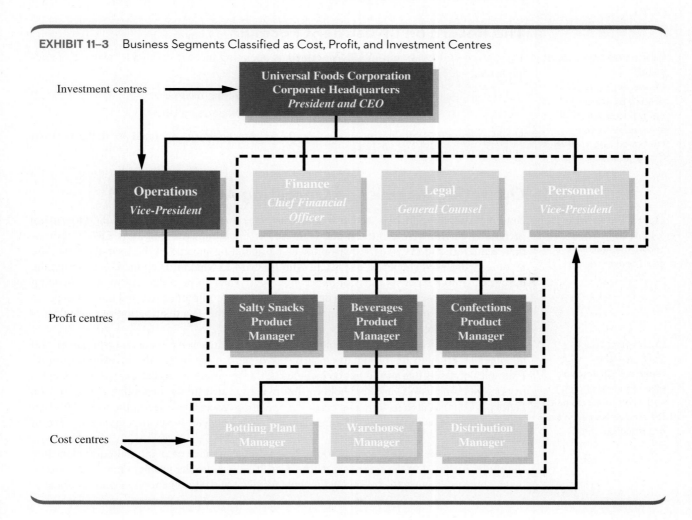

EXHIBIT 11–3 Business Segments Classified as Cost, Profit, and Investment Centres

how the various business segments of the company are classified in terms of responsibility. Note that the cost centres are the departments and work centres that do not generate significant revenues by themselves. These are staff departments such as Finance, Legal, and Personnel, and operating units such as the bottling plant, warehouse, and beverage distribution centre. The profit centres are business segments that generate revenues and costs and include the Beverage, Salty Snacks, and Confections product segments. The vice-president of Operations oversees allocation of investment funds across the product segments and is also responsible for revenues and costs; therefore, Operations is treated as an investment centre. And, finally, corporate headquarters is an investment centre, since it is responsible for all revenues, costs, and investments.

LEARNING OBJECTIVE ❸

Analyze the return on investment.

◼ EVALUATING INVESTMENT CENTRE PERFORMANCE—RETURN ON INVESTMENT

So far in this chapter we have focused on how to assign costs properly to responsibility centres. This is an important issue when evaluating cost and profit centres. However, evaluating an investment centre's performance requires more than accurate cost and segment margin reporting. In addition, an investment centre is responsible for earning an adequate return on investment. The next two sections of this chapter present two methods for evaluating this aspect of an investment centre's performance. The first method is called *return on investment (ROI)*. The second method is called *residual income*.

The Return on Investment Formula

Return on investment (ROI)

Operating income divided by average operating assets. ROI also equals margin multiplied by turnover.

The **return on investment (ROI)** is defined as operating income divided by average operating assets:

$$\text{Return on Investment} = \frac{\text{Operating income}}{\text{Average operating assets}}$$

The higher the ROI of a business segment, the greater the profit generated per dollar invested in the segment's operating assets.

Operating Income and Operating Assets Defined

Operating income

Income before interest and income taxes have been deducted.

Note that *operating income*, rather than net income, is used in the ROI formula. **Operating income** is income before interest and taxes and is sometimes referred to as *EBIT* (earnings before interest and taxes). The reason for using operating income in the formula is that the income figure used should be consistent with the base to which it is applied. Notice that the base (i.e., denominator) consists of *operating assets*. Thus, to be consistent we use operating income in the numerator because no debt is included in the denominator, and interest expense is paid for by the profits from the operating assets and thus is a distribution of those profits rather than an expense.

Operating assets

Cash, accounts receivable, inventory, plant and equipment, and all other assets held for productive use in an organization.

Operating assets include cash, accounts receivable, inventory, plant and equipment, and all other assets held for productive use in the organization and/or the investment centre. Examples of assets that would not be included in the operating assets category (i.e., examples of non-operating assets) are land held for future use, an investment in another company, or a factory building rented to someone else. The operating assets base used in the formula is typically computed as the average of the operating assets between the beginning and the end of the year.

A major issue in ROI computations is the dollar amount of plant and equipment that should be included in the operating assets base. To illustrate the problem involved, assume that a company reports the following amounts for plant and equipment on its balance sheet:

Plant and equipment	$3,000,000
Less accumulated depreciation	900,000
Net book value	$2,100,000

What dollar amount of plant and equipment should the company include with its operating assets in computing ROI? One widely used approach is to include only the plant and equipment's *net book value*—that is, the plant and equipment's original cost less accumulated depreciation ($2,100,000 in the example above). A second approach is to ignore depreciation and include the plant and equipment's entire *gross cost* in the operating assets base ($3,000,000 in the example above). Both of these approaches are used in actual practice, even though they will obviously yield very different operating asset, operating income, and ROI figures.

The following arguments can be raised for using net book value to measure operating assets and for using gross cost to measure operating assets in ROI computation.

Arguments for using net book value to measure operating assets in return on investment computations:
1. The net book value method is consistent with how plant and equipment are reported on the balance sheet (i.e., cost less accumulated depreciation to date).
2. The net book value method is consistent with the computation of operating income, which includes depreciation as an operating expense.

Arguments for using gross cost to measure operating assets in return on investment computations:
1. The gross cost method eliminates both the age of equipment and the method of depreciation as factors in ROI computations. (Under the net book value method, ROI tends to increase over time as net book value declines due to depreciation.)
2. The gross cost method does not discourage replacement of old, worn-out equipment. (Under the net book value method, replacing fully depreciated equipment with new equipment can have a dramatic adverse effect on ROI.)

Managers generally view consistency as the most important of the considerations above. As a result, a majority of companies use the net book value approach in ROI computations. In this text, we will also use the net book value approach unless a specific exercise or problem directs otherwise.

Understanding Return on Investment

The equation for ROI, operating income divided by average operating assets, does not provide much help to managers interested in taking action to improve their ROI. It offers only two levers for improving performance—operating income and average operating assets. Fortunately, ROI can also be expressed as follows:

$$\text{Return on Investment} = \text{Margin} \times \text{Turnover}$$

where

$$\text{Margin} = \frac{\text{Operating income}}{\text{Sales}}$$

and

$$\text{Turnover} = \frac{\text{Sales}}{\text{Average operating assets}}$$

The **margin** is a measure of management's ability to control operating expenses in relation to sales. The lower operating expenses are per dollar of sales, the higher the margin earned. **Turnover** is a measure of the sales that are generated for each dollar invested in operating

Margin
Operating income divided by sales.

Turnover
The amount of sales generated in an investment centre for each dollar invested in operating assets. Sales divided by average operating assets.

assets. Note that the sales terms in the margin and turnover formulas cancel out when they are multiplied together, yielding the original formula for ROI stated in terms of operating income and average operating assets. So either formula for ROI will give the same answer. However, the margin and turnover formulation provides some additional insights.

From a manager's perspective, margin and turnover are very important concepts. Margin is ordinarily improved by increasing sales or reducing operating expenses, including cost of goods sold and selling and administrative expenses. Some managers tend to focus too much on margin and ignore turnover. However, turnover incorporates a crucial area of a manager's responsibility—the investment in operating assets. Excessive funds tied up in operating assets (e.g., cash, accounts receivable, inventories, plant and equipment, and other assets) depress turnover and lower ROI. In fact, inefficient use of operating assets can be just as much of a drag on profitability as excessive operating expenses, which depress margin.

INSTANT QUIZ 11–2

Tamarind Services Company, a division of a major oil company, provides various services to the operators of an oil field in northern Alberta. Data concerning the most recent year are as follows:

Sales	$12,000,000
Operating income	3,600,000
Average operating assets	24,000,000

Compute the margin, turnover, and ROI for Tamarind Services Company.

E.I. du Pont de Nemours and Company (better known as DuPont) pioneered the use of ROI and recognized the importance of looking at both margin and turnover in assessing a manager's performance. ROI is now widely used as the key measure of investment centre performance. ROI reflects in a single figure many aspects of the manager's responsibilities. It can be compared to the returns of other investment centres in the organization, the returns of other companies in the industry, and the past returns of the investment centre itself.

DuPont also developed the diagram that appears in the Learning Aid below. This diagram helps managers understand how they can improve ROI. Any increase in ROI must involve at least one of the following:

1. Increased sales.
2. Reduced operating expenses.
3. Reduced operating assets.

Many actions involve combinations of changes in sales, expenses, and operating assets. For example, a manager may make an investment in (i.e., increase) operating assets to reduce operating expenses or increase sales. Whether the net effect is favourable or not is judged in terms of its overall impact on ROI.

To illustrate how ROI is affected by various actions, we will use the Monthaven outlet of the Burger Grill chain as an example. Burger Grill is a small chain of upscale casual restaurants that has been rapidly adding outlets via franchising. The Monthaven franchise is owned by a group of local surgeons who have little time to devote to management and little expertise in business matters. Therefore, they delegate operating decisions—including decisions concerning investments in operating assets such as inventories—to a professional manager they have hired. The manager is evaluated largely based on the ROI the franchise generates.

The following data represent the results of operations for the most recent month:

Sales	$100,000
Operating expenses	90,000
Operating income	10,000
Average operating assets	50,000

LEARNING AID

Elements of Return on Investment

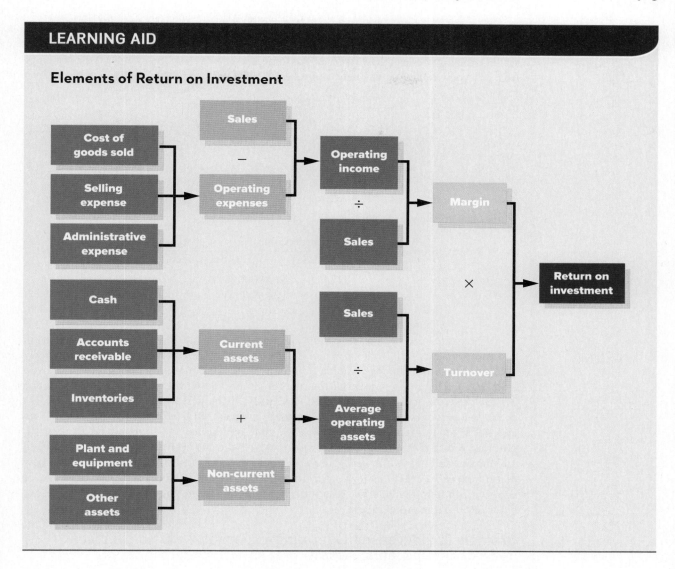

The ROI for the month is computed as follows:

$$\text{Return on Investment} = \frac{\text{Operating income}}{\text{Sales}} \times \frac{\text{Sales}}{\text{Average operating assets}}$$

$$= \frac{\$10,000}{\$100,000} \times \frac{\$100,000}{\$50,000}$$

$$= 10\% \times 2 = 20\%$$

INSTANT QUIZ 11-3
Describe the performance signals provided by the margin and turnover elements of the ROI formula. Identify the elements of each that would contribute to an improvement in ROI.

Example 1: Increased Sales without Any Increase in Operating Assets

Assume that the manager of the Monthaven Burger Grill can increase sales by 10% without any increase in operating assets. The increase in sales will require additional operating expenses. However, operating expenses include some fixed expenses, which would probably not be affected by a 10% increase in sales. Therefore, the increase in operating expenses would probably be less than 10%; let's assume the increase is 7.8%. Under these assumptions, the new operating income would be $12,980, an increase of 29.8%, determined as follows:

Sales (1.10 × $100,000)	$110,000
Operating expenses (1.078 × $90,000)	97,020
Operating income	$ 12,980

In this case, the new ROI would be

$$\text{Return on Investment} = \frac{\text{Operating income}}{\text{Sales}} \times \frac{\text{Sales}}{\text{Average operating assets}}$$

$$= \frac{\$12,980}{\$110,000} \times \frac{\$100,000}{\$50,000}$$

$$= 11.8\% \times 2.2 = 25.96\% \text{ (as compared to 20\% originally)}$$

When sales are increased *without* an increase in operating assets, both the margin and turnover are likely to be affected. In the example above, because sales increased by 10% and operating expenses increased by only 7.8%, the margin increased to 11.8% (up from 10%). This improvement in the margin, combined with the increase in turnover to 2.2 (up from 2), led to the gain in ROI. Clearly, if the percentage increase in sales exceeds the percentage increase in operating expenses, ROI will always improve, if no additional operating assets are required to generate the new sales. However, it is worth pointing out that given the increase in turnover, the old ROI of 20% could have been maintained as long as the new margin did not fall below 9.09% (20% ÷ 2.2). If the new margin exceeds 9.09%, as it does in the example, ROI will increase. Using this type of analysis can help managers assess the extent to which operating expenses can increase before ROI begins to decrease.

Example 2: Decreased Operating Expenses with No Change in Sales or Operating Assets

Assume that by improving business processes, the manager of the Monthaven Burger Grill can reduce operating expenses by $1,000 without any effect on sales or operating assets. This reduction in operating expenses would result in increasing operating income by $1,000, from $10,000 to $11,000. The new ROI is

$$\text{Return on Investment} = \frac{\text{Operating income}}{\text{Sales}} \times \frac{\text{Sales}}{\text{Average operating assets}}$$

$$= \frac{\$11,000}{\$100,000} \times \frac{\$100,000}{\$50,000}$$

$$= 11\% \times 2 = 22\% \text{ (as compared to 20\% originally)}$$

When margins or profits are being squeezed, the first line of attack is often to cut costs. Discretionary fixed costs are particularly vulnerable to cuts. However, managers must be careful not to cut too much or in the wrong place. Inappropriate cost cutting can lead to decreased sales, increased costs elsewhere, and a drop in morale.

Example 3: Invest in Operating Assets to Increase Sales

Assume that the manager of the Monthaven Burger Grill invests $2,000 in a state-of-the-art soft-serve ice cream machine that can dispense a number of different flavours. This new machine will boost sales by $4,000 but will require additional operating expenses of $1,000. Thus, operating income will increase by $3,000, to $13,000. The new ROI is

$$\text{Return on Investment} = \frac{\text{Operating income}}{\text{Sales}} \times \frac{\text{Sales}}{\text{Average operating assets}}$$

$$= \frac{\$13,000}{\$104,000} \times \frac{\$104,000}{\$52,000}$$

$$= 12.5\% \times 2 = 25\% \text{ (as compared to 20\% originally)}$$

In this example, the investment had no effect on turnover, which remained at 2, so there had to be an increase in margin in order to improve the ROI.

Criticisms of Return on Investment

Although ROI is widely used in evaluating performance, it is not a perfect tool. The method is subject to the following criticisms:

1. Just telling managers to increase ROI may not be enough. Managers may not know how to increase ROI; they may increase ROI in a way that is inconsistent with the company's strategy; or they may take actions that increase ROI in the short run but harm the company in the long run (such as cutting back on research and development).
2. A manager who takes over a business segment typically inherits many committed costs over which the manager has no control. These committed costs may be relevant in assessing the performance of the business segment as an investment but make it difficult to fairly assess the performance of the manager relative to other managers.
3. As discussed in the next section, a manager who is evaluated based on ROI may reject profitable investment opportunities.

■ RESIDUAL INCOME

LEARNING OBJECTIVE ④
Compute residual income, and describe the strengths and weaknesses of this method of measuring performance.

Another approach to measuring an investment centre's performance focuses on a concept known as *residual income*. **Residual income** is the operating income that an investment centre earns above the minimum required return on its operating assets. Thus, we use operating income as defined with ROI but reduce it by a special charge computed as a percentage of average operating assets. In equation form, residual income is calculated as follows:

$$\text{Residual income} = \text{Operating income} - \left(\text{Average operating assets} \times \text{Minimum required rate of return}\right)$$

Economic value added (EVA®) is a similar concept that differs in some details from residual income. EVA® has been popularized and trademarked by the consulting firm Stern, Stewart & Co. For example, under the economic value-added concept, funds used for research and development are treated as investments rather than as expenses. However, for our purposes, we will illustrate residual income because the adjustments for EVA® are complex and would create more confusion than is appropriate for this introduction.

When residual income is used to measure performance, the purpose is to maximize the total amount of residual income, not to maximize overall ROI. Organizations as diverse as Loblaws, Quaker Oats, and Domtar have embraced some version of residual income in recent years.

For illustration, consider the following data for an investment centre—the Whitehorse Division of Yukon Marine Services Corporation:

Residual income
The operating income that an investment centre earns above the required return on its operating assets.

Economic value added (EVA®)
A concept similar to residual income.

YUKON MARINE SERVICES CORPORATION
Whitehorse Division
Basic Data for Performance Evaluation

Average operating assets	$100,000
Operating income	$ 20,000
Minimum required rate of return	15%

Yukon Marine Services Corporation has long had a policy of evaluating investment centre managers based on ROI but is considering a switch to residual income. The controller of the company, who is in favour of the change to residual income, has provided the following table, which shows how the performance of the division would be evaluated under each of the two methods:

YUKON MARINE SERVICES CORPORATION
Whitehorse Division
Alternative Performance Measures

	Return on Investment	Residual Income
Average operating assets.............................	$100,000 (a)	$100,000
Operating income	$ 20,000 (b)	$ 20,000
Return on investment, (b) ÷ (a)......................	20%	
Minimum required return (15% × $100,000)		15,000
Residual income		$ 5,000

The reasoning underlying the residual income calculation is straightforward. The company is able to earn a rate of return of at least 15% on its investments. Since the company has invested $100,000 in the Whitehorse Division in the form of operating assets, the company should be able to earn at least $15,000 (15% × $100,000) on this investment. Since the Whitehorse Division's operating income is $20,000, the residual income exceeds the minimum required return by $5,000. If residual income is adopted as the performance measure to replace ROI, then the manager of the Whitehorse Division will be evaluated based on the growth from year to year in residual income.

INSTANT QUIZ 11–4

British firm Midlands Design Ltd. specializes in providing design services to residential developers. Last year the company had operating income of £600,000 on sales of £2,400,000. The company's average operating assets for the year were £4,400,000, and its minimum required rate of return was 9%. Compute the company's residual income for the year.

Motivation and Residual Income

One of the primary reasons why the controller of Yukon Marine Services Corporation would like to switch from ROI to residual income has to do with how managers view new investments under the two performance measurement schemes. The residual income approach encourages managers to make investments that are profitable for the entire company but that would be rejected by managers who are evaluated by the ROI formula.

To illustrate this problem, suppose that the manager of the Whitehorse Division is considering purchasing a computerized diagnostic machine to aid in servicing marine diesel engines. The machine would cost $25,000 and is expected to generate additional operating income of $4,500 a year. From the standpoint of the company, this would be a good investment since it promises a rate of return of 18% ($4,500 ÷ $25,000), which is in excess of the company's minimum required rate of return of 15%.

If the manager of the Whitehorse Division is evaluated based on residual income, she would be in favour of the investment in the diagnostic machine evaluated below:

YUKON MARINE SERVICES CORPORATION
Whitehorse Division
Performance Evaluated Using Residual Income

	Present	New Project	Overall
Average operating assets....................	$100,000	$25,000	$125,000
Operating income	$ 20,000	$ 4,500	$ 24,500
Minimum required return	15,000	3,750*	18,750
Residual income	$ 5,000	$ 750	$ 5,750

*$25,000 × 15% = $3,750

Since the project would increase the residual income of the Whitehorse Division, the manager would want to invest in the new diagnostic machine.

Now suppose that the manager of the Whitehorse Division is evaluated based on ROI. The effect of the diagnostic machine on the division's ROI is computed below:

YUKON MARINE SERVICES CORPORATION
Whitehorse Division
Performance Evaluated Using Return on Investment

	Present	New Project	Overall
Average operating assets (a)	$100,000	$25,000	$125,000
Operating income (b)	$ 20,000	$ 4,500*	$ 24,500
Return on investment, (b) ÷ (a)	20%	18%	19.6%

*$25,000 × 18% = $4,500

The new project reduces the division's ROI from 20% to 19.6%. This happens because the 18% rate of return on the new diagnostic machine, while above the company's 15% minimum rate of return, is below the division's current ROI of 20%. Therefore, the new diagnostic machine would reduce the division's ROI, even though it would be a good investment from the standpoint of the company as a whole. If the manager of the division is evaluated based on ROI, she will be reluctant to even propose such an investment.

Generally, a manager who is evaluated based on ROI will want to reject any project whose rate of return is below the division's current ROI even if the rate of return on the project is above the minimum required rate of return for the entire company. In contrast, any project whose rate of return is above the minimum required rate of return for the company will result in an increase in residual income and thus add value for the shareholders. Since it is in the best interests of the company as a whole to accept any project whose rate of return is above the minimum required rate of return, managers who are evaluated based on residual income will tend to make better decisions concerning investment projects than managers who are evaluated based on ROI.

Divisional Comparison and Residual Income

The residual income approach has one major disadvantage. It cannot be used to compare the performance of divisions of different sizes. You would expect larger divisions to have more residual income than smaller divisions, not necessarily because they are better managed but simply because they are bigger.

As an example, consider the following residual income computations for Division X and Division Y:

	Division	
	X	Y
Average operating assets (a)	$1,000,000	$250,000
Operating income	$ 120,000	$ 40,000
Minimum required return: 10% × (a)	100,000	25,000
Residual income	$ 20,000	$ 15,000

Observe that Division X has slightly more residual income than Division Y, but that Division X has $1,000,000 in operating assets as compared to only $250,000 in operating assets for Division Y. Thus, Division X's greater residual income is probably more a result of its size than the quality of its management. In fact, it appears that the smaller division is better managed, since it has been able to generate nearly as much residual income with only one-fourth as much in operating assets with which to work. This problem can be reduced to some degree by focusing on the percentage change in residual income from year to year rather than on the absolute amount of the residual income.

Criticisms of Residual Income

As shown above, compared to ROI, the use of residual income can lead managers to make decisions more consistent with shareholders' objectives. Further, some claim that residual income is more closely related to shareholder returns than other metrics, such as sales growth, net income, and ROI. However, the following criticisms of residual income are worth noting:

1. Residual income is based on historical accounting data, which means that in particular, the accounting values used for capital assets can suffer from being out of date when costs are rising. This can lead to inflated amounts for residual income.
2. The residual income approach does not indicate what earnings *should* be for a particular business unit. A means of comparison is needed, which could involve using external benchmarks based on key competitors or evaluating trends in residual income over time (e.g., tracking the percentage change over several periods).
3. Residual income is a financial metric that does not incorporate important leading non-financial indicators of success, such as employee motivation and customer satisfaction.

LEARNING OBJECTIVE ⑤

Explain the use of balanced score-cards to assess performance.

Balanced scorecard
An integrated set of performance measures that is derived from and supports the organization's strategy.

■ BALANCED SCORECARD

A **balanced scorecard** consists of an integrated set of performance measures that is derived from the company's strategy and that supports the company's strategy throughout the organization. A strategy is essentially a theory about how to achieve the organization's goals and deals with issues such as how to attract customers, what products or services to sell, what markets to enter, and how to compete with rivals. According to some experts, there are three potentially successful generic strategic approaches to outperforming competitors:

1. **Cost leadership:** By maintaining low cost through efficiency relative to competitors, a company can make superior profits at current industry prices. Alternatively, the company can become a price leader because other firms are unable to undercut its prices. Low costs may also serve as a barrier against potential new market entrants and thereby protect long-term profitability. However, technological change or imitation of low-cost techniques by rivals can threaten the success of this strategy.
2. **Differentiation:** For products or services that are perceived as unique, customers will sometimes pay premium prices, giving the company higher profit margins. This cushion of higher profits reduces the effect of supplier or buyer power. Brand loyalty, however, may fail if the cost differential between the firm and the cost leader in the industry becomes too wide.
3. **Focus or niche:** By serving a narrow, strategic target market more effectively than rivals who are competing more broadly, a firm may be able to achieve superior profitability. The risk of being overtaken by broad-target firms who have economies of scale is a constant threat to the success of this strategy.

Under the balanced scorecard approach, top management translates its strategy into performance measures that employees can understand and can do something about. For example, the length of time passengers have to wait in line to have their baggage checked might be a performance measure for the supervisor in charge of the Air Canada check-in counter at the Vancouver airport. This performance measure is easily understood by the supervisor and can be improved by the supervisor's actions.

Common Characteristics of Balanced Scorecards

Performance measures used in the balanced scorecard approach tend to fall into the four groups illustrated in Exhibit 11–4: financial, customer, internal business processes, and learning and growth. Internal business processes are what the company does in an attempt to satisfy customers. For example, in a manufacturing company, assembling a product is an internal

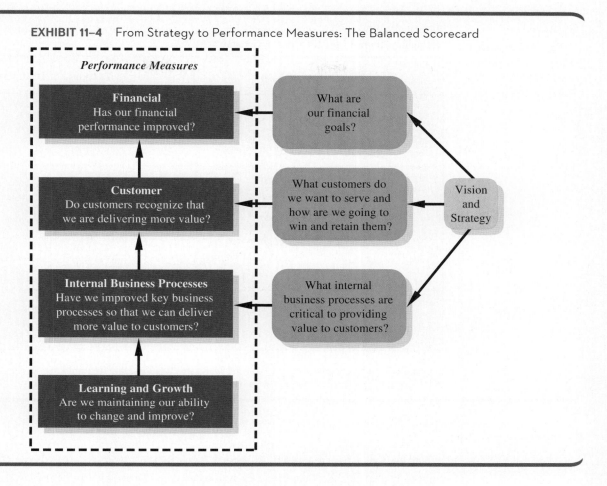

EXHIBIT 11–4 From Strategy to Performance Measures: The Balanced Scorecard

business process. For an airline, handling baggage is an internal business process. The basic idea is that learning is necessary to improve internal business processes, improving business processes is necessary to improve customer satisfaction, and improving customer satisfaction is necessary to improve financial results.

Note that the emphasis in Exhibit 11–4 is on *improvement*—not on just attaining some specific objective such as profits of $10 million. In the balanced scorecard approach, continuous improvement is encouraged. In many industries, this is a matter of survival. If an organization does not continuously improve, it will eventually lose out to competitors that do.

Financial performance measures appear at the top of Exhibit 11–4. Ultimately, most companies exist to provide financial rewards to owners. There are exceptions. Some companies—for example, The Body Shop—may have loftier goals, such as providing environmentally friendly products to consumers. However, these types of organizations must generate enough financial resources to stay in operation.

However, for several reasons, financial performance measures (even ROI or EVA®) are not sufficient in themselves—they should be integrated with non-financial measures in a well-designed balanced scorecard. First, financial measures are lagging indicators that report on the results of past actions. In contrast, non-financial measures of key success drivers, such as customer satisfaction, are leading indicators of future financial performance. Second, top managers are ordinarily responsible for the financial performance measures—not lower-level managers—so it may be easier for lower-level managers to have greater control and impact on non-financial than financial performance.

Consider a regional airline with the following strategy: to uniquely position ourselves by focusing on being a short-haul, low-fare, high-frequency, point-to-point carrier in eastern North America. Exhibit 11–5 suggests how the airline might reflect this strategy in its balanced scorecard.

EXHIBIT 11–5
A Possible Strategy
Map for a Regional
Airline and the
Balanced Scorecard

Vision: Continue building on our unique position—the *only* short-haul, low-fare, high-frequency, point-to-point carrier in Canada.

Simplified Strategy Map	Performance Measures	Targets	Initiatives
Financial — Increase Profitability, Lower Costs, Increase Revenue	· Market value · Seat revenue · Plane lease cost	· 25% per year · 20% per year · 5% per year	· Optimize routes · Standardize planes
Customer — More Customers, On-time Flights, Lowest Prices	· On-time arrival rating · Customer ranking · Number of customers	· First in industry · 98% Satisfaction · % change	· Quality management · Customer loyalty program
Internal — Improve Turnaround Time	· On-ground time · On-time departure	· <25 minutes · 93%	· Cycle time optimization program
Learning — Align Ground Crews	· % ground crew shareholders · % ground crew trained	· Yr. 1 70% Yr. 4 90% Yr. 6 100%	· Stock ownership plan · Ground crew training

Source: Developed from material by the Balanced Scorecard Collaborative and *Harvard Business Review* (Kaplan & Norton). © Balanced Scorecard Institute, a Strategy Management Group company.

If the balanced scorecard is correctly constructed, the performance measures should be linked on a cause-and-effect basis. Each link can then be read as a hypothesis in the form "If we improve this performance measure, then this other performance measure should also improve." Starting from the bottom of Exhibit 11–5, we can read the links between performance measures as follows: If ground crews acquire the skills to perform better and become shareholders, they will perform better and be motivated to increase turnaround times, ensuring more on-time flights. More on-time flights when accompanied by low prices should increase customer satisfaction and loyalty, leading to increased revenues and decreased costs, resulting in an increase in profits.

In essence, the balanced scorecard illustrates a theory of how the company can attain its desired outcomes (financial, in this case) by taking concrete actions. While the strategy laid out in Exhibit 11–5 seems plausible, it should be regarded as only a theory that should be discarded if it proves to be invalid. One of the advantages of the balanced scorecard is that it can be used to continuously test the theories underlying management's strategy. If a strategy is not working, it should become evident when some of the predicted effects (i.e., more repeat customers) do not occur. Without this feedback, management may drift on indefinitely with an ineffective strategy based on faulty assumptions.

Exhibit 11–5 includes some examples of performance measures that can be found in the customer, internal business process, and learning and growth categories of the balanced scorecards of a regional airline. However, companies in other industries would likely highlight other performance measures that are of more relevance to organizations in their industries. Managers should carefully select the performance measures for their company's balanced scorecard, keeping the following points in mind. First, the performance measures should be consistent with, and follow from, the company's strategy. If the performance measures are not consistent with the company's strategy, people will find themselves working at cross-purposes. Second, the scorecard should not have too many performance measures. This can lead to a lack of focus and confusion.

INSTANT QUIZ 11-5
Why does the balanced scorecard include financial performance measures as well as measures of non-financial performance? Why do the measures in a balanced scorecard differ from company to company?

While the entire organization will have an overall balanced scorecard, each responsible individual may have his or her own personal scorecard as well. This scorecard should consist of items the individual can personally influence that relate directly to the performance measures on the overall balanced scorecard (e.g., hours spent in training courses). The performance measures on this personal scorecard should not be overly influenced by actions taken by others in the company or by events that are outside the individual's control. Also, the personal scorecard measures should not lead an individual to take actions that are inconsistent with the organization's objectives.

IN BUSINESS

In February 2018 the Province of Manitoba announced it would implement a balanced scorecard system to "align actions with established priorities, identify key measures of performance and report on progress through a public outcomes dashboard." This system includes four main components customized for a public-sector context: Quality of Life, Value for Money, Working Smarter, and Public Service. Details can be accessed at mbmeasuringprogress.ca. Within each balanced scorecard component, citizens can click through to find what is being measured, how it is being measured, what targets have been set, and progress toward meeting these targets. For example, one Quality of Life indicator is K–12 literacy, measured using the K–12 Literacy Index produced by the public and independent school systems in Manitoba. For the year 2018/19 the index measured 64%, while the province's stated goal is to be at or above 75% by 2024. The balanced scorecard system allows for goal setting and accountability for the province's public service.

Tying Compensation to the Balanced Scorecard

Incentive compensation for employees, such as bonuses, can, and probably should, be tied to balanced scorecard performance measures. However, this should be done only after the organization has been successfully managed with the scorecard for some time—perhaps a year or more. Managers must be confident that the performance measures are reliable, sensible, understood by those who are being evaluated, and not easily manipulated. As argued by Robert Kaplan and David Norton, the promoters of the balanced scorecard concept, before linking compensation to achieving balanced scorecard targets boards of directors must be sure that they are using the right measures and that the data collected concerning performance relative to target are reliable.

Advantages of Timely Feedback

Whatever performance measures are used, they should be reported on a frequent and timely basis. For example, data about defects should be reported to the responsible managers at least once a day so that action can be taken quickly if an unusual number of defects occur. In the most advanced companies, any defect is reported *immediately*, and its cause is tracked down before any more defects occur. Another common characteristic of the performance measures under the balanced scorecard approach is that managers focus on *trends* in the performance measures over time. The emphasis is on progress and *improvement* rather than on meeting any specific standard.

Corporate Social Responsibility and the Balanced Scorecard

As stated in the introduction to this chapter, companies are responsible for creating strategies that produce financial results that satisfy shareholders. However, they also have a *corporate social responsibility* to serve other stakeholders—such as customers, employees, suppliers, communities, and environmental and human rights advocates—whose interests are tied to the company's performance. **Corporate social responsibility (CSR)** is a concept whereby organizations consider the needs of all stakeholders when making decisions. CSR extends beyond legal compliance to include voluntary actions that satisfy stakeholder expectations.

Many of the world's largest companies prepare corporate social responsibility performance reports (also called sustainability reports) that are shared with their external stakeholders. In addition, a growing percentage of these companies are hiring public accounting firms to provide assurance services that lend additional credibility to the disclosures contained in those reports. While many of these companies undoubtedly feel a moral obligation to serve diverse stakeholders, these same companies also understand that social and environmental issues provide them with immense *opportunities* and *risks*.

From an opportunity management standpoint, some companies have responded to social and environmental challenges by making strategic investments in product, service, and process innovations that increase stakeholder satisfaction and profits. For example, Toyota developed the hybrid-engine Prius to respond to societal concerns about auto emissions and to grow shareholder wealth. Procter & Gamble decided to consolidate its distribution centres, thereby lowering its transportation costs while simultaneously reducing its fuel consumption and the associated emissions.

From a risk management standpoint, most companies understand that if they overlook their social and environmental responsibilities it will damage their reputation. For example, if a company discharges lethal pollutants into the environment, purchases products from an overseas supplier that employs child labour, or systematically discriminates against a group of its employees, the adverse consequences of those actions will cause negative publicity. This, in turn, will trigger undesirable after-effects such as customer boycotts or defections, a decline in job applications from top-notch candidates, an increase in employee turnover, disenchanted investors, and possibly even lawsuits and government-imposed fines.

Whether a company's interest in CSR is grounded in morality, opportunism, risk management, or a combination of all three, it needs to accompany this interest with measures and reports that can be tracked by managers and shared with external stakeholders.

Global Reporting Initiative

The Global Reporting Initiative (GRI) is a leading organization in the field of social and environmental performance measurement. It has created a widely adopted sustainability reporting framework that includes three universal standards and three sets of topic-specific standards related to economic, environmental, and social performance.

The universal standards require companies to provide disclosures related to topics such as strategy and analysis, stakeholder engagement, and governance. More specifically, they require a company's most senior decision maker (such as its CEO) to describe her company's strategic priorities, plans, and achievements with respect to corporate social performance. They also mandate that a company identify its stakeholders and summarize the means and frequency of its communications with them. Finally, the universal standards ask a company to describe the role of its highest governing body (such as its board of directors) in managing risks, evaluating social, environmental, and economic performance, and reporting results to external stakeholders.

Corporate social responsibility (CSR)
A concept whereby organizations consider the needs of all stakeholders when making decisions.

The three topic-specific standards parallel the phrases "triple bottom line" and "people, planet, and profit" that are commonly used to summarize a company's expanded set of corporate social responsibilities. The economic standards pertain to topics such as funding employee retirement benefits, procuring supplies and hiring senior managers from the local community, analyzing entry-level wages by gender, and assessing the financial implications of climate change. The environmental standards relate to issues such as water usage, waste management, energy consumption, biodiversity preservation, and emissions control. Finally, the social standards focus on a range of topics including occupational health and safety, human rights, training and education, diversity and equal opportunity, customer health and safety, as well as marketing and labelling.

While some companies incorporate social and environmental performance measures into their existing balanced scorecards, others implement a variety of adaptations. For example, some companies add a fifth category to their scorecards that purposely focuses on an expanded set of stakeholders. Other companies establish separate scorecards dedicated to their own and/or their suppliers' social and environmental performance. Exhibit 11–6 provides examples of social and environmental performance measures for each of the four balanced scorecard categories.

EXHIBIT 11–6
Examples of Corporate Social Responsibility Measures for the Balanced Scorecard

Learning and Growth:
- Number of occupational injuries/accidents (–)
- Average compensation for female employees ÷ average compensation for male employees (+)
- Number of job applicants from under-represented groups (+)
- Average community service hours per employee (+)

Internal Business Processes:
- Average water consumed per unit produced (–)
- Percent of raw material inputs that have been recycled (+)
- Average carbon emissions per unit produced (–)
- Kilograms of waste produced (–)

Customer:
- Percent of customers that strongly agree with the statement "Your company cares about the communities where it operates" (+)
- Percent of customers that strongly agree with the statement "Your company has a superior commitment to product safety" (+)
- Percent of customers that strongly agree with the statement "Your company is committed to environmental stewardship" (+)
- Percent of customers that strongly agree with the statement "Your company provides me with the information that I need to assess its social and environmental performance" (+)

Financial:
- Percent of revenue from eco-conscious products (+)
- Average fuel cost per sales dollar (–)
- Total workers' compensation costs
- Capital expenditures on "green" products and processes

KNOWLEDGE IN ACTION

Managers can apply their knowledge about process costing when

- Using segmented reports to examine trends and results in each segment at a level of detail that allows them to better determine what may underlie results that are more positive or more negative than expected. Segment reports break down results of an organization into more manageable parts on the basis of product lines, geography, sales territory, etc.
- Accounting for the performance of their divisions. Responsibility centre managers are held accountable for the performance of their decentralized divisions. The results for which these managers are accountable depend on the degree to which they control costs, revenues, and investments for their division. Profit centre managers are held accountable for their division's achievement of profit targets, while investment centre managers are held accountable for their division's achievement of ROI or residual income targets.
- Accounting for their division's generation of profit or ROI. Managers may choose to use a balanced scorecard to communicate with employees in their organizations the means by which profit or ROI should be improved. The non-financial measures and targets included in the balanced scorecard provide guidance concerning the actions employees at the operational level in the division can take to help the division achieve its financial targets and for the organization as a whole to achieve its strategic objectives.

SUMMARY

- Segmented income statements provide information for evaluating the profitability and performance of divisions, product lines, sales territories, and other company segments. Under the contribution approach, variable costs and fixed costs are clearly distinguished from each other, and only those costs that are traceable to a segment are assigned to the segment. **[LO1]**
- A responsibility centre is any segment of an organization whose manager has control over and is accountable for cost, profit, or investments. Responsibility centre managers are evaluated based on what they can control. **[LO2]**
- A cost centre is a business segment whose manager has control over costs only. A profit centre is a segment whose manager controls revenues and costs but not investments in operating assets. An investment centre manager controls profits and investments in operating assets. **[LO2]**
- Return on investment (ROI), residual income, and economic value added (EVA®) can be used to evaluate investment centre performance. **[LO3, LO4]**
- The balanced scorecard consists of an integrated system of performance measures that are derived from and support the company's strategy. It has four main categories of performance measures: financial, customer, internal business processes, and learning and growth. Different companies will have different balanced scorecards because they have different strategies. **[LO5]**

REVIEW PROBLEM 1: SEGMENTED STATEMENTS

The business staff of the law firm Frampton, Davis, & Smythe have constructed the following report, which breaks down the firm's overall results for last month into two main business segments—family law and commercial law:

	Total	Family Law	Commercial Law
Revenues from clients....................	$1,000,000	$400,000	$600,000
Variable expenses	220,000	100,000	120,000
Contribution margin	780,000	300,000	480,000
Traceable fixed expenses	670,000	280,000	390,000
Segment margin	110,000	20,000	90,000
Common fixed expenses.................	60,000	24,000	36,000
Operating income	$ 50,000	$ (4,000)	$ 54,000

However, this report is not quite correct. The common fixed expenses, such as the managing partner's salary, selling and administrative expenses, and general firm advertising, have been allocated to the two segments based on revenues from clients.

Required:
1. Redo the segment report, eliminating the allocation of common fixed expenses. Would the firm be better off financially if the family law segment were dropped? (*Note:* Many of the firm's commercial law clients also use the firm for their family law requirements, such as drawing up wills.)
2. The firm's advertising agency has proposed an ad campaign targeted at boosting the revenues of the family law segment. The ad campaign would cost $20,000, and the advertising agency claims that it would increase family law revenues by $100,000. The managing partner of Frampton, Davis, & Smythe believes this increase in business could be accommodated without any increase in fixed expenses. What effect would this ad campaign have on the family law segment margin and on the firm's overall operating income?

Solution to Review Problem 1

1. The corrected segmented income statement appears below:

	Total	Family Law	Commercial Law
Revenues from clients....................	$1,000,000	$400,000	$600,000
Variable expenses	220,000	100,000	120,000
Contribution margin	780,000	300,000	480,000
Traceable fixed expenses	670,000	280,000	390,000
Segment margin	110,000	$ 20,000	$ 90,000
Common fixed expenses.................	60,000		
Operating income	$ 50,000		

The firm would not be financially better off if the family law practice were dropped. The family law segment is covering all of its own costs and is contributing $20,000 per month to covering the common fixed expenses of the firm. While the segment margin for family law is much lower than for commercial law, it is still profitable.

2. The ad campaign would increase the family law segment margin by $55,000, as follows:

Increased revenues from clients...........................	$100,000
Family law contribution margin ratio ($300,000 ÷ $400,000)....	× 75%
Incremental contribution margin	$ 75,000
Less cost of the ad campaign.............................	20,000
Increased segment margin	$ 55,000

Since there would be no increase in fixed expenses (including common fixed expenses), the increase in overall operating income is also $55,000.

REVIEW PROBLEM 2: RETURN ON INVESTMENT AND RESIDUAL INCOME

Selected operating data for two divisions of Outback Brewing Ltd. are given below:

	Queensland	New South Wales
Sales	$4,000,000	$7,000,000
Average total operating assets	$2,000,000	$2,000,000
Operating income	$ 360,000	$ 420,000
Plant and equipment (net)	$ 950,000	$ 800,000

Required:
1. Compute the rate of return for each division using the ROI formula stated in terms of margin and turnover.
2. Compute residual income for each division, assuming the required rate of return is 15%.

Solution to Review Problem 2

1. ROI computations:

$$\text{ROI} = \text{Margin} \times \text{Turnover}$$
$$= \frac{\text{Operating income}}{\text{Sales}} \times \frac{\text{Sales}}{\text{Average operating assets}}$$

Queensland Division:

$$\text{ROI} = \frac{\$360,000}{\$4,000,000} \times \frac{\$4,000,000}{\$2,000,000}$$
$$= 9\% \times 2 = 18\%$$

New South Wales Division:

$$\text{ROI} = \frac{\$420,000}{\$7,000,000} \times \frac{\$7,000,000}{\$2,000,000}$$
$$= 6\% \times 3.5 = 21\%$$

2. Residual income for each division is calculated as follows:
Queensland Division:

$$\$360,000 - (\$2,000,000 \times 15\%) = \$60,000$$

New South Wales Division:

$$\$420,000 - (\$2,000,000 \times 15\%) = \$120,000$$

DISCUSSION CASE

DISCUSSION CASE 11–1

Mason Paper Company (MPC) manufactures large quantities of standard white 8½ × 11 inch paper for use in computer printers and photocopiers. MPC has reported operating losses for the last two years due to intense price pressure from much larger competitors. The MPC management team is contemplating a change in strategy to reverse the trend of losses experienced over the last several years. The VP Finance, Don Townsend, has made the following argument concerning the new strategy:

> As we all know, the commodity paper manufacturing business is all about economies of scale. The largest competitors with the lowest cost per unit win. We have limited-capacity machines that keep us from producing high volumes of paper like our closest competitors. Therefore, I propose that we abandon cost reduction as a strategic goal and instead pursue manufacturing flexibility as the key to our future success.
>
> Manufacturing flexibility means we have to abandon our "crank out as many tonnes of paper as possible" mentality. Instead, we need to look for customers interested in lower-volume, specialty papers for which we can charge a higher price. To succeed in this new market, we first need to improve our ability to switch our equipment to produce different paper grades. Right now, we require an average of four hours to change over to another

paper grade. Timely customer deliveries are a function of changeover performance. Second, we need to expand the range of paper grades that we can manufacture. Currently, we can manufacture only one paper grade. Our customers must perceive that we are a one-stop shop that can meet all of their specialty-grade paper needs. Third, we will need to improve our yields (e.g., tonnes of acceptable output relative to total tonnes processed) in the non-standard paper grades. Our percentage of waste within these grades will be unacceptably high unless we do something to improve our processes. Our variable costs will go through the roof if we cannot increase our yields!

Required:

Why would a company that changes its strategic goals need to change its performance measurement system as well? What are some examples of measures that would have been appropriate for MPC prior to its change in strategy? Why would those measures fail to support MPC's new strategy? What new measures would you suggest be adopted to support the new strategy at MPC?

QUESTIONS

11–1 What is meant by the term *decentralization*?

11–2 What is a segment of an organization? Give several examples of segments.

11–3 What costs are assigned to a segment under the contribution approach?

11–4 Explain how the segment margin differs from the CM.

11–5 Why aren't common costs allocated to segments under the contribution approach?

11–6 How is it possible for a cost that is traceable to a segment to become a common cost if the segment is divided into further segments?

11–7 Identify three inappropriate methods for assigning traceable costs among segments.

11–8 Identify three types of responsibility centres, and describe how performance is measured for each one.

11–9 What is meant by the terms *margin* and *turnover*?

11–10 What are the three approaches to improving ROI?

11–11 What is meant by the term *residual income*?

11–12 In what way can the use of ROI for investment centres lead to bad decisions? How does the residual income approach overcome this problem?

11–13 Should residual income be used to compare divisions of different sizes? Why or why not?

11–14 What are the four groups of performance measures typically included in a balanced scorecard?

FOUNDATIONAL EXERCISES

[LO2, LO3, LO4]

Westerville Company reported the following results from last year's operations:

Sales	$1,000,000
Variable expenses	300,000
Contribution margin	700,000
Fixed expenses	500,000
Net operating income	$ 200,000
Average operating assets	$ 625,000

This year, the company has a $120,000 investment opportunity with the following cost and revenue characteristics:

Sales	$200,000
Contribution margin ratio	60% of sales
Fixed expenses	$ 90,000

The company's minimum required rate of return is 15%.

Required:

11–1 What is last year's margin?

11–2 What is last year's turnover?

11–3 What is last year's return on investment (ROI)?

11–4 What is the margin related to this year's investment opportunity?

11–5 What is the turnover related to this year's investment opportunity?

11–6 What is the ROI related to this year's investment opportunity?

11–7   If the company pursues the investment opportunity and otherwise performs the same as last year, what margin will it earn this year?

11–8   If the company pursues the investment opportunity and otherwise performs the same as last year, what turnover will it earn this year?

11–9   If the company pursues the investment opportunity and otherwise performs the same as last year, what ROI will it earn this year?

11–10   If Westerville's chief executive officer will earn a bonus only if her ROI from this year exceeds her ROI from last year, would she pursue the investment opportunity? Would the owners of the company want her to pursue the investment opportunity?

11–11   What is last year's residual income?

11–12   What is the residual income of this year's investment opportunity?

11–13   If the company pursues the investment opportunity and otherwise performs the same as last year, what residual income will it earn this year?

11–14   If Westerville's chief executive officer will earn a bonus only if her residual income from this year exceeds her residual income from last year, would she pursue the investment opportunity?

11–15   Assume that the contribution margin ratio of the investment opportunity was 50% instead of 60%. If Westerville's chief executive officer will earn a bonus only if her residual income from this year exceeds her residual income from last year, would she pursue the investment opportunity? Would the owners of the company want her to pursue the investment opportunity?

EXERCISES

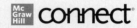

EXERCISE 11–1   Basic Segmented Income Statement [LO1]

Royal Lawncare produces and sells two packaged products, Weedban and Greengrow. Revenue and cost information relating to the products is as follows:

	Product	
	Weedban	**Greengrow**
Selling price per unit..................................	$ 6.00	$ 7.50
Variable expenses per unit	$ 2.40	$ 5.25
Traceable fixed expenses per year	$45,000	$21,000

Common fixed expenses in the company total $33,000 annually. Last year the company produced and sold 15,000 units of Weedban and 28,000 units of Greengrow.

Required:

Prepare a contribution format income statement for the year, segmented by product lines.

EXERCISE 11–2   Segmented Income Statement [LO1]

Bovine Company, a wholesale distributor of umbrellas, has been experiencing losses for some time, as shown by its most recent monthly contribution format income statement:

Sales	$1,000,000
Variable expenses	396,000
Contribution margin	604,000
Fixed expenses	652,000
Operating loss.....................................	$ (48,000)

In an effort to isolate the problem, the president has asked for an income statement segmented by geographic market. Accordingly, the Accounting Department has developed the following:

	Geographic Market		
	South	**Central**	**North**
Sales	$300,000	$400,000	$300,000
Variable expenses as a percentage of sales........	52%	30%	40%
Traceable fixed expenses	$160,000	$265,000	$150,000

Required:

1. Prepare a contribution format income statement segmented by geographic market, as requested by the president.

2. The company's sales manager believes that sales in the Central geographic market could be increased by 15% if monthly advertising is increased by $13,000. Would you recommend the increased advertising? Show computations to support your answer.

EXERCISE 11–3 Working with a Segmented Income Statement [LO1]

Middleton Associates is a consulting firm that specializes in information systems for construction and landscaping companies. The firm has two offices—one in Toronto and one in Vancouver. The firm classifies the direct costs of consulting jobs as variable costs. A segmented contribution format income statement for the company's most recent year is given below:

| | Total Company | | Office | | | |
			Toronto		Vancouver	
Sales	$750,000	100.0%	$150,000	100%	$600,000	100%
Variable expenses	405,000	54.0	45,000	30	360,000	60
Contribution margin	345,000	46.0	105,000	70	240,000	40
Traceable fixed expenses	168,000	22.4	78,000	52	90,000	15
Office segment margin	177,000	23.6	$ 27,000	18%	$150,000	25%
Common fixed expenses						
not traceable to offices	120,000	16.0				
Operating income	$ 57,000	7.6%				

Required:

1. By how much would the company's operating income increase if Vancouver increased its sales by $75,000 per year? Assume no change in cost behaviour patterns.

2. Refer to the original data. Assume that sales in Toronto increase by $50,000 next year and that sales in Vancouver remain unchanged. Assume no change in fixed costs.

   a. Prepare a new segmented income statement for the company using the above format. Show both amounts and percentages.

   b. Observe from the income statement you have prepared that the CM ratio for Toronto has remained unchanged at 70% (the same as in the above data) but that the segment margin ratio has changed. How do you explain the change in the segment margin ratio?

EXERCISE 11–4 Working with a Segmented Income Statement [LO1]

Refer to the data in Exercise 11–3. Assume that Vancouver's sales by major market are as follows:

| | Vancouver | | Market | | | |
			Construction Clients		Landscaping Clients	
Sales	$600,000	100.0%	$400,000	100%	$200,000	100%
Variable expenses	360,000	60	260,000	65	100,000	50
Contribution margin	240,000	40	140,000	35	100,000	50
Traceable fixed expenses	72,000	12	20,000	5	52,000	26
Market segment margin.......	168,000	28	$120,000	30%	$ 48,000	24%
Common fixed expenses						
not traceable to offices	18,000	3				
Office segment margin	$150,000	25%				

The company would like to initiate an intensive advertising campaign in one of the two markets during the next month. The campaign would cost $8,000. Marketing studies indicate that such a campaign would increase sales in the construction market by $70,000 or increase sales in the landscaping market by $60,000.

Required:
1. In which of the markets would you recommend that the company focus its advertising campaign? Show computations to support your answer.
2. In Exercise 11–3, Vancouver shows $90,000 in traceable fixed expenses. What happened to the $90,000 in this exercise?

EXERCISE 11–5 Segmented Income Statement [LO1]
Shannon Company segments its income statement in its North and South Division. The company's overall sales, contribution margin ratio, and net operating income are $500,000, 46%, and $10,000, respectively. The North Division's contribution margin and contribution margin ratio are $150,000 and 50%, respectively. The South Division's segment margin is $30,000. The company has $90,000 of common fixed expenses that cannot be traced to either division.

Required:
Prepare an income statement for Shannon Company that uses the contribution format and is segmented by divisions. In addition, for the company as a whole and for each segment, show each item on the segmented income statements as a percent of sales.

EXERCISE 11–6 Decentralization and Responsibility Centres [LO2]
Listed below are terms relating to decentralization and responsibility centres.

Cost centre	Cost
Accountable	Investment
Profit	Flexible
Revenue	Residual income

Choose the term or terms that most appropriately complete the following statements. The terms can be used more than once. (Note that a blank can hold more than one word.)

1. A responsibility centre is any part of an organization for which a manager is _____ for performance.
2. A profit centre is a business segment where the manager has control over _____ and _____.
3. An investment centre manager is held responsible for the _____ of the segment.
4. A(n) _____ is often evaluated using _____ budget variances.
5. _____ centre managers are responsible for initiating investment proposals.

EXERCISE 11–7 Computing and Interpreting Return on Investment [LO3]
Selected operating data on the two divisions of Prism Company are given below:

	Division	
	Western	**Eastern**
Sales	$1,040,000	$2,400,000
Average operating assets	400,000	400,000
Operating income	91,000	96,000
Plant and equipment	125,000	200,000

Required:
1. Compute the rate of return for each division using the ROI formula stated in terms of margin and turnover.
2. Which divisional manager seems to be doing the better job? Why?

EXERCISE 11–8 Contrasting Return on Investment and Residual Income [LO3, LO4]

Ferris Ltd. of Australia has two divisions, one in Perth and one in Darwin. Selected data on the two divisions follow:

	Division	
	Perth	**Darwin**
Sales	$9,000,000	$20,000,000
Operating income	630,000	1,800,000
Average operating assets	3,000,000	10,000,000

Required:
1. Compute the ROI for each division.
2. Assume that the company evaluates performance using residual income and that the minimum required rate of return for any division is 16%. Compute the residual income for each division.
3. Is the Darwin Division's greater residual income an indication that it is better managed? Explain.

EXERCISE 11–9 Return on Investment and Residual Income Relationships [LO3, LO4]

A family friend has asked for your help in analyzing the operations of three companies operating in the same service sector industry. Supply the missing data in the following table:

	Company		
	A	**B**	**C**
Sales	$400,000	$750,000	$600,000
Operating income	$?	$ 45,000	$?
Average operating assets	$160,000	$?	$150,000
Return on investment	20%	18%	?
Minimum required rate of return:			
Percentage	15%	?	12%
Dollar amount	$?	$ 50,000	$?
Residual income	$?	$?	$ 6,000

EXERCISE 11–10 Return on Investment Relationships [LO3]

Provide the missing data in the following table:

	Division		
	Fab	**Consulting**	**IT**
Sales	$800,000	$?	$?
Operating income	$ 72,000	$?	$40,000
Average operating assets	$?	$130,000	$?
Margin	?	4%	8%
Turnover	?	5	?
Return on investment	18%	?	20%

EXERCISE 11–11 Effects of Changes in Profits and Assets on Return on Investment [LO3]

FitPlus is a regional chain of health clubs. Each club's manager has the authority to make investments as needed and is evaluated based largely on ROI. FitPlus Club 52 reported the following results for the past year:

Sales	$750,000
Operating income	26,250
Average operating assets	80,000

Required:
The following questions are to be considered independently. Carry out all computations to two decimal places.

1. Compute the club's ROI.
2. Assume that the manager of the club is able to increase sales by $80,000 and that as a result operating income increases by $6,000. Further assume that this is possible without any increase in operating assets. What would the club's ROI be?
3. Assume that the manager of the club is able to reduce expenses by $3,200 without any change in sales or operating assets. What would the club's ROI be?
4. Assume that the manager of the club is able to reduce operating assets by $20,000 without any change in sales or operating income. What would the club's ROI be?

EXERCISE 11–12 Evaluating New Investments Using Return on Investment and Residual Income [LO3, LO4]
Three divisions of Jameson Co. report the following sales and operating data:

	Fitness Training	Spa Services	Athletic Wear
Sales	$600,000	$750,000	$400,000
Average operating assets....................	$200,000	$250,000	$100,000
Operating income	$ 30,000	$ 37,500	$ 24,000
Minimum required rate of return	10%	12%	10%

Required:
1. Compute the ROI for each division, using the formula stated in terms of margin and turnover.
2. Compute the residual income for each division.
3. Assume that each division is presented with an investment opportunity that would yield a rate of return of 17%.
    a. If performance is being measured by ROI, which division or divisions will probably accept the opportunity? Reject it? Why?
    b. If performance is being measured by residual income, which division or divisions will probably accept the opportunity? Reject it? Why?

CHECK FIGURE
Fitness training:
ROI = 15%; Residual income = $10,000.

EXERCISE 11–13 Effects of Changes in Sales, Expenses, and Assets on ROI [LO3]
CommercialServices.com provides business-to-business services on the Internet. Data concerning the most recent year appear below:

Sales	$3,000,000
Net operating income	$ 150,000
Average operating assets............................	$ 750,000

Required:
Consider each question below independently. Carry out all computations to two decimal places:

1. Compute the company's return on investment (ROI).
2. The entrepreneur who founded the company is convinced that sales will increase next year by 50% and that net operating income will increase by 200%, with no increase in average operating assets. What would be the company's ROI?
3. The chief financial officer of the company believes a more realistic scenario would be a $1,000,000 increase in sales, requiring a $250,000 increase in average operating assets, with a resulting $200,000 increase in net operating income. What would be the company's ROI in this scenario?

EXERCISE 11–14 Examples of Balanced Scorecard Performance Measures [LO5]
Reid Company would like to implement a balanced scorecard performance measurement system. Its senior management team has assembled the measures shown below for possible inclusion in its scorecard.

Required:
For each measure, indicate by placing an X in the appropriate column whether it would most likely be classified in the learning and growth, internal business process, customer, or financial category of the company's balanced scorecard.

	Learning and Growth	Internal Business Process	Customer	Financial
Example: Employee absenteeism rate	X			
Sales from new customers				
Customer defection rate				
Average number of workplace accidents per employee.				
Delivery cycle time				
Average training hours per employee.				
Number of job applicants from underrepresented groups				
Percent of customers that strongly agree with the statement "your employees treated me courteously"				
Return on assets				
Percent of customers that strongly agree with the statement "Your company has a superior commitment to product safety"				
Number of modular product designs				
Lost sales due to out-of-stock merchandise				
Kilograms of waste produced				
Number of customer referrals				
Residual income.				
Average mentorship hours per employee.				

EXERCISE 11–15 Defining Balanced Scorecard Measures [LO5]

Askew Company is interested in adopting the balanced scorecard. As a first step, the company just completed a brainstorming activity to define areas where it needs to improve with respect to learning and growth, internal business process performance, customer satisfaction, and financial results. The results of its brainstorming session are summarized below:

Learning and Growth	Internal Business Process
"Too many customer service employees leave our company to work for other employers"	"Too many customer service employees leave our company to work for other employers"
"We are not providing enough training to our employees"	"It is taking too long to make products and ship them to customers"
"Our employees are not generating enough ideas to help improve what we do"	"Customers have to call us repeatedly to get problems solved"

Customer	Financial
"The number of customers we are serving seems to be shrinking"	"Wall Street is becoming very concerned about our future"
"Customers are complaining about excessive delays with respect to receiving what they ordered"	"Sales are decreasing instead of increasing"
"We are acquiring fewer new customers from our current customers' word-of-mouth"	"It takes too long to convert customer orders into cash"

The company has asked you to guide its balanced scorecard implementation process from this point forward.

Required:

1. As a first step, you decide to explain that the insights from the company's brainstorming session need to be translated into performance measures that can be tracked and managed. To illustrate this point, provide one example of a plausible performance measure for each comment raised during the company's brainstorming session.

2. As a second step, you decide to highlight the importance of defining a strategy and then link-ing performance measures together using if-then hypothesis statements in a manner that reflects the chosen strategy. To illustrate this point, choose a strategy for the company based on its brainstorming goals (either product leadership, operational excellence, or customer intimacy) and define three plausible if-then hypothesis statements using some of your meas-ures from Requirement 1. Use a + or − to indicate whether each performance measure should increase or decrease.

PROBLEMS

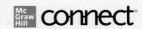

PROBLEM 11–16 Restructuring a Segmented Income Statement [LO1]
Brabant NV of the Netherlands is a wholesale distributor of Dutch cheeses that it sells throughout the European Union. Unfortunately, the company's profits have been declining, which has caused consider-able concern. To help understand the condition of the company, the managing director of the company has requested that the monthly income statement be segmented by sales territory. Accordingly, the com-pany's accounting department has prepared the following statement for March, the more recent month. (The Dutch currency is the euro, which is designated by €.)

	Sales Territory		
	Southern Europe	**Middle Europe**	**Northern Europe**
Sales	€300,000	€800,000	€ 700,000
Territorial expenses (traceable):			
Cost of goods sold	93,000	240,000	315,000
Salaries	54,000	56,000	112,000
Insurance	9,000	16,000	14,000
Advertising	105,000	240,000	245,000
Depreciation	21,000	32,000	28,000
Shipping	15,000	32,000	42,000
Total territorial expenses	297,000	616,000	756,000
Territorial income (loss) before corporate expenses	3,000	184,000	(56,000)
Corporate expenses:			
Advertising (general)	15,000	40,000	35,000
Selling and administrative	20,000	20,000	20,000
Total corporate expenses	35,000	60,000	55,000
Operating income (loss)	€ (32,000)	€124,000	€(111,000)

Cost of goods sold and shipping expenses are both variable; other costs are all fixed. Brabant NV purchases cheeses at auction and from farmers' cooperatives, and it distributes them in the three territories shown in the statement above. Each of the three sales territories has its own manager and sales staff. The cheeses vary widely in profitability; some have a high margin and some have a low margin. (Certain cheeses, after having been aged for long periods, are the most expensive and carry the highest margins.)

Required:
1. List any disadvantages or weaknesses of the statement format illustrated above.
2. Explain the base that is apparently being used to allocate the corporate expenses to the territories. Do you agree with these allocations? Explain.
3. Prepare a new segmented contribution format income statement for May. Show a Total column as well as data for each territory. Include percentages on your statement for all columns. Carry per-centages to one decimal place.
4. Analyze the statement that you prepared in (3) above. What points that might help to improve the company's performance would you bring to management's attention?

PROBLEM 11–17 Segment Reporting and Decision Making [LO1]
Creaston Limited's most recent monthly contribution format income statement is given below:

CREASTON LIMITED Income Statement For the Month Ended May 31		
Sales	$900,000	100.0%
Variable expenses	408,000	45.3
Contribution margin	492,000	54.7
Fixed expenses	465,000	51.7
Operating income	$ 27,000	3.0%

Management is disappointed with the company's performance and is wondering what can be done to improve profits. By examining sales and cost records, you have determined the following:

a. The company is divided into two sales territories—Central and Eastern. Central Territory recorded $400,000 in sales and $208,000 in variable expenses during May. The remaining sales and variable expenses were recorded in Eastern Territory. Fixed expenses of $160,000 and $130,000 are traceable to Central and Eastern Territories, respectively. The rest of the fixed expenses are common to the two territories.

b. The company is the exclusive distributor for two products—Kiks and Dows. Sales of Kiks and Dows totalled $100,000 and $300,000, respectively, in Central Territory during May. Variable expenses are 25% of the selling price for Kiks and 61% for Dows. Cost records show that $60,000 of Central Territory's fixed expenses are traceable to Kiks and $54,000 to Dows, with the remainder common to the two products.

Required:
1. Prepare contribution format segmented income statements, first showing the total company broken down between sales territories and then showing Central Territory broken down by product line. Show both Amount and Percentage columns for the company in total and for each segment. Round percentage computations to one decimal place.
2. Look at the statement you have prepared showing the total company segmented by sales territory. Which points revealed by this statement should be brought to management's attention?
3. Look at the statement you have prepared showing Central Territory segmented by product lines. Which points revealed by this statement should be brought to management's attention?

PROBLEM 11–18 Basic Segmented Statement; Activity-Based Cost Assignment [LO1]
Vega Foods Inc. recently purchased a small mill that it intends to operate as one of its subsidiaries. The newly acquired mill offers three products for sale—wheat cereal, pancake mix, and flour. Each product sells for $10 per package. Materials, labour, and other variable production costs are $3.00 per bag of wheat cereal, $4.20 per bag of pancake mix, and $1.80 per bag of flour. Sales commissions are 10% of sales for any product. All other costs are fixed.

The mill's income statement for the most recent month is given below:

	Total Company	Product Line		
		Wheat Cereal	Pancake Mix	Flour
Sales	$600,000	$200,000	$300,000	$100,000
Expenses:				
Materials, labour, and other	204,000	60,000	126,000	18,000
Sales commissions	60,000	20,000	30,000	10,000
Advertising	123,000	48,000	60,000	15,000
Salaries	66,000	34,000	21,000	11,000
Equipment depreciation	30,000	10,000	15,000	5,000
Warehouse rent	12,000	4,000	6,000	2,000
Selling and administrative	90,000	30,000	30,000	30,000
Total expenses	585,000	206,000	288,000	91,000
Operating income (loss)	$ 15,000	$ (6,000)	$ 12,000	$ 9,000

The following additional information about the company is available:

a.   The same equipment is used to mill and package all three products. In the above income statement, equipment depreciation has been allocated on the basis of sales dollars. An analysis of equipment usage indicates that it is used 40% of the time to make wheat cereal, 50% of the time to make pancake mix, and 10% of the time to make flour.

b.   All three products are stored in the same warehouse. In the above income statement, the warehouse rent has been allocated on the basis of sales dollars. The warehouse contains 24,000 square metres of space, of which 8,000 square metres are used for wheat cereal, 14,000 square metres are used for pancake mix, and 2,000 square metres are used for flour. The warehouse space costs the company $0.50 per square metre to rent.

c.   The selling and administrative costs relate to the administration of the company as a whole. In the above income statement, these costs have been divided equally among the three product lines.

d.   All other costs are traceable to the product lines.

Management at Vega Foods is anxious to improve the mill's 2.5% margin on sales.

Required:

1.   Prepare a new contribution format segmented income statement for the month. Adjust the allocations as required.

2.   After seeing the income statement in the main body of the problem, management has decided to eliminate the wheat cereal, because it is not returning a profit, and to focus all available resources on promoting the pancake mix.

a.   Based on the statement you have prepared, do you agree with the decision to eliminate the wheat cereal? Explain.

b.   Based on the statement you have prepared, do you agree with the decision to focus all available resources on promoting the pancake mix? Assume that an ample market is available for all three products. (*Hint:* Compute the CM ratio for each product.)

PROBLEM 11–19   Finely Segmented Income Statements [LO1]
Severo S.A. of Sao Paulo, Brazil, is organized into two divisions. The company's contribution format segmented income statement (in terms of the Brazilian currency, the real, R) for last month is given below:

	Total Company	Division	
		Cloth	Leather
Sales	R3,500,000	R2,000,000	R1,500,000
Variable expenses	1,721,000	960,000	761,000
Contribution margin	1,779,000	1,040,000	739,000
Traceable fixed expenses:			
Advertising	612,000	300,000	312,000
Selling and administrative	427,000	210,000	217,000
Depreciation	229,000	115,000	114,000
Total traceable fixed expenses	1,268,000	625,000	643,000
Divisional segment margin	511,000	R 415,000	R 96,000
Common fixed expenses	390,000		
Operating income	R 121,000		

Top management can't understand why the Leather Division has such a low segment margin when its sales are only 25% less than sales in the Cloth Division. As one step in isolating the problem, management has directed that the Leather Division be further segmented into product lines. The following information is available on the product lines in the Leather Division:

	Leather Division Product Line		
	Garments	Shoes	Handbags
Sales	R500,000	R700,000	R300,000
Traceable fixed expenses:			
Advertising	R 80,000	R112,000	R120,000
Selling and administrative	R 30,000	R 35,000	R 42,000
Depreciation	R 25,000	R 56,000	R 33,000
Variable expenses as a percentage of sales	65%	40%	52%

Analysis shows that R110,000 of the Leather Division's selling and administrative expenses are common to the product lines.

Required:

1. Prepare a contribution format segmented income statement for the Leather Division, with segments defined as product lines.
2. Management is surprised by the handbag product line's poor showing and would like to have the product line segmented by market. The following information is available about the markets in which the handbag line is sold:

	Handbag Markets	
	Domestic	Foreign
Sales..................................	R200,000	R100,000
Traceable fixed expenses:		
Advertising.........................	R 40,000	R 80,000
Variable expenses as a percentage		
of sales	43%	70%

All of the handbag product line's selling and administrative expenses and depreciation are common to the markets in which the product is sold. Prepare a contribution format segmented income statement for the handbag product line with segments defined as markets.

3. Refer to the statement prepared in (1) above. The sales manager wants to run a special promotional campaign on one of the product lines over the next month. A marketing study indicates that such a campaign would increase sales of the Garments product line by R200,000 or sales of the Shoes product line by R145,000. The campaign would cost R30,000. Show computations to determine which product line should be chosen.

PROBLEM 11–20   Comparison of Performance Using Return on Investment [LO3]

The following are comparative data submitted by three companies in the food services:

	Company		
	A	B	C
Sales	$500,000	$150,000	$?
Operating income.......................	$ 70,000	$ 21,000	$?
Average operating assets	$250,000	?	$300,000
Margin	?	?	4%
Turnover................................	?	?	2
Return on investment....................	?	7%	?

Required:

1. What advantages are there to breaking down the ROI computation into two separate elements, margin and turnover?
2. Fill in the missing information above, and comment on the relative performance of the three companies in as much detail as the data permit. Make *specific recommendations* about how to improve the ROI.

(Adapted from National Association of Accountants, *Research Report No. 35*, p. 34.)

> **CHECK FIGURE**
> Company A ROI =
> 28%; Company C
> sales = $600,000.

PROBLEM 11–21   Return on Investment and Residual Income [LO3, LO4]

Faced with headquarters' desire to add a new product line, Stefan Grenier, manager of Bilti Products' East Division, felt that he had to see the numbers before he made a move. His division's ROI has led the company for three years, and he doesn't want any letdown.

Bilti Products is a decentralized wholesaler with four autonomous divisions. The divisions are evaluated on the basis of ROI, with year-end bonuses given to divisional managers who have the highest ROI. Operating results for the company's East Division for last year are given below:

Sales.....................................	$21,000,000
Variable expenses........................	13,400,000
Contribution margin......................	7,600,000
Fixed expenses...........................	5,920,000
Operating income........................	$ 1,680,000
Divisional operating assets	$ 5,250,000

The company had an overall ROI of 18% last year (considering all divisions). The new product line that headquarters wants Grenier's East Division to add would require an investment of $3,000,000. The cost and revenue characteristics of the new product line per year would be as follows:

Sales...........................	$9,000,000
Variable expenses..................	65% of sales
Fixed expenses....................	$2,520,000

Required:
1. Compute the East Division's ROI for last year; also compute the ROI as it would appear if the new product line were added.
2. If you were in Grenier's position, would you accept or reject the new product line? Explain.
3. Why do you suppose headquarters is anxious for the East Division to add the new product line?
4. Suppose that the company's minimum required rate of return on operating assets is 18% and that performance is evaluated using residual income.
    a. Compute East Division's residual income for last year; also compute the residual income as it would appear if the new product line were added.
    b. Under these circumstances, if you were in Grenier's position, would you accept or reject the new product line? Explain.

PROBLEM 11–22 Return on Investment and Residual Income [LO3, LO4]
Financial data for Bridger Inc. for last year are as follows:

BRIDGER INC. Balance Sheet		
	Ending Balance	**Beginning Balance**
Assets		
Cash	$ 150,000	$ 145,000
Accounts receivable	500,000	360,000
Inventory................................	510,000	590,000
Plant and equipment, net....................	840,000	865,000
Investment in Brier Company................	450,000	420,000
Land (undeveloped)	270,000	270,000
Total assets	$2,720,000	$2,650,000
Liabilities and shareholders' equity		
Accounts payable	$ 340,000	$ 380,000
Long-term debt...........................	1,000,000	1,000,000
Shareholders' equity.......................	1,380,000	1,270,000
Total liabilities and shareholders' equity	$2,720,000	$2,650,000

BRIDGER INC. Income Statement		
Sales		$2,090,000
Operating expenses........................		1,776,500
Operating income		313,500
Interest and taxes:		
Interest expense	$90,000	
Tax expense	85,000	175,000
Net income		$ 138,500

The company paid dividends of $85,000 last year. The "Investment in Brier Company" on the balance sheet represents an investment in the common shares of another company.

Required:
1. Compute the company's margin, turnover, and ROI for last year.
2. The board of directors of Bridger Inc. has set a minimum required return of 14%. What was the company's residual income last year?

PROBLEM 11–23 Cost–Volume–Profit Analysis; Return on Investment [LO3, LO4]

The Switch Division of Tornax Inc. produces a small switch that is used by various companies as a component part in their products. Tornax operates its divisions as autonomous units, giving its divisional managers great discretion in pricing and other decisions. Each division is expected to generate a minimum required rate of return of at least 14% on its operating assets. The Switch Division has average operating assets of $700,000. The switches are sold for $5 each. Variable costs are $3 per switch, and fixed costs total $462,000 per year. The division has a capacity of 300,000 switches each year.

Required:

1. How many switches must the Switch Division sell each year to generate the desired rate of return on its assets?
   a. What is the margin earned at this level of sales?
   b. What is the turnover at this level of sales?
2. Assume that the Switch Division's current ROI equals the minimum required rate of 14%. In order to increase the division's ROI, the divisional manager wants to increase the selling price per switch by 4%. Market studies indicate that an increase in the selling price would cause sales to drop by 20,000 units each year. However, operating assets could be reduced by $50,000 due to decreased needs for accounts receivable and inventory. Compute the margin, turnover, and ROI if these changes are made.
3. Refer to the original data. Assume again that the Switch Division's current ROI equals the minimum required rate of 14%. Rather than increase the selling price, the sales manager wants to reduce the selling price per switch by 4%. Market studies indicate that this would fill the plant to capacity. In order to carry the greater level of sales, however, operating assets would increase by $50,000. Compute the margin, turnover, and ROI if these changes are made.

PROBLEM 11–24 Return on Investment Analysis [LO3]

The contribution format income statement for Smith & Company for its most recent period is given below:

	Total	Unit
Sales.....................................	$1,000,000	$100.00
Less variable expenses...................	600,000	60.00
Contribution margin.....................	400,000	40.00
Less fixed expenses	320,000	
Operating income........................	80,000	
Less income taxes at 40%	32,000	
Net income.............................	$ 48,000	

The company had average operating assets of $500,000 during the period.

Required:

1. Compute the company's ROI for the period using the ROI formula stated in terms of margin and turnover.

   For each of the following questions, indicate whether the margin and turnover will increase, decrease, or remain unchanged as a result of the events described, and then compute the new ROI figure. Consider each question separately, starting in each case from the original ROI computed in (1) above.

2. The company achieves cost savings of $20,000 per period by using less costly materials.
3. Using lean production, the company is able to reduce the average level of inventory by $100,000. (The released funds are used to pay off bank loans.)
4. Sales are increased by $100,000; operating assets remain unchanged.
5. The company issues bonds and uses the proceeds to purchase $150,000 in machinery and equipment at the beginning of the period. Interest on the bonds is $2,000 per period. Sales remain unchanged. The new, more efficient equipment reduces production costs by $8,000 per period.
6. The company invests $100,000 in cash (received on accounts receivable) in a plot of land that is to be held for possible future use as a plant site.
7. Obsolete inventory carried on the books at a cost of $10,000 is scrapped and written off as a loss.

> **CHECK FIGURE**
> 2. increase;
> 4. increase;
> 7. decrease

PROBLEM 11–25   Balanced Scorecards; Customer Metrics [LO5]

Many organizations focus their strategy on providing high-quality customer service and consequently place metrics concerning customer relationship management on their balanced scorecards. Consider Sam's Pita Pit and the Classic Steakhouse, two restaurants with different target markets and different strategies. Sam's Pita Pit is located near a college campus and serves mainly students looking for a healthy meal, quick service, and low prices. While there are several tables in the restaurant where customers can dine in, most of Sam's business is on a take-out basis. Classic Steak House, on the other hand, is an upscale restaurant targeting business lunches and special occasion dinners. Customers value good-quality food and service and spend on average $150 per table. Both restaurants are considering implementing balanced scorecards.

Required:

What kind of measures might Sam's Pita Pit and the Classic Steakhouse include in the customer category of their new balanced scorecards? Create a table with one column for each set of measures. Which measures would be similar and which would be different across scorecards and why?

PROBLEM 11–26   Balanced Scorecards and Incentives [LO5]

Smith's Family Fashions implemented a balanced scorecard performance measurement system several years ago. Smith's is a locally owned clothing retailer with fashions for men, women, teens, and children. At the beginning of the year, John Smith took over the management of the Women's Wear department from his mother when she retired. John recognized there was a need for trendy clothing appealing to fashionable local women. Since taking over the department, John has changed the fashion lines he carries to be more appealing to this new target market while still offering well-priced, high-quality clothing that appeals to the store's more traditional customers.

The management of Smith's Family Fashions is overseen by a board of directors, including several members of the Smith family. John and other department heads have agreed to be evaluated by the board on the basis of performance relative to targets set across balanced scorecard categories. John's targets and actual performance since taking over as department head are provided below. The board decides on year-end bonuses based on each department head's performance relative to target:

	Target	Actual
Return on assets employed by department........	14%	15%
Proportion of repeat customers	60%	57%
Sales generated by new product lines as a percentage of total departmental sales.........	65%	64%
Average discount on goods sold.	10%	18%

Required:

Take on the role of a member of the board of directors preparing for a board meeting at which decisions will be made about the payment of annual bonuses to department heads. Discuss the performance of the Women's Wear department as compared to actual based on the metric provided. Where has performance been better (worse) than actual? What do the actual results, taken together, say about the likely success of John's new strategy?

PROBLEM 11–27   Perverse Effects of Some Performance Measures [LO4]

There is often more than one way to improve a performance measure. Unfortunately, some of the actions taken by managers to make their performance look better may actually harm the organization. For example, suppose the marketing department is held responsible only for increasing the performance measure "total revenues." Increases in total revenues may be achieved by working harder and smarter, but they can also usually be achieved by simply cutting prices. The increase in volume from cutting prices almost always results in greater total revenues; however, it does not always lead to greater total profits. Those who design performance measurement systems need to keep in mind that managers who are under pressure to perform may take actions to improve performance measures that have negative consequences elsewhere.

Required:

For each of the following situations, describe actions that managers might take to show improvement in the performance measure but which do not actually lead to improvement in the organization's overall performance.

1. Concerned with the slow rate at which new products are brought to market, top management of a consumer electronics company introduces a new performance measure—speed-to-market. The research and development department is given responsibility for this performance measure, which measures the average amount of time a product is in development before it is released to the market for sale.

2. The CEO of an airline company is dissatisfied with the amount of time that her ground crews are taking to unload luggage from airplanes. To solve the problem, she decides to measure the average elapsed time from when an airplane parks at the gate to when all pieces of luggage are unloaded from the airplane. For each month that an airport's ground crew can lower its "average elapsed time" relative to the prior month, the CEO pays a lump-sum bonus to be split equally among members of the crew.

3. A manufacturing company has been plagued by the chronic failure to ship orders to customers by the promised date. To solve this problem, the production manager has been given the responsibility of increasing the percentage of orders shipped on time. When a customer calls in an order, the production manager and the customer agree to a delivery date. If the order is not completed by that date, it is counted as a late shipment.

PROBLEM 11–28 Building a Balanced Scorecard; Service Industry [LO5]
Lost Peak ski resort was for many years a small, family-owned resort serving day skiers from nearby towns. Lost Peak was recently acquired by Western Resorts, a major ski resort operator. The new owners have plans to upgrade the resort into a destination resort for vacationers. As part of this plan, the new owners would like to make major improvements in the Powder 8 Lodge, the resort's on-the-hill cafeteria. The menu at the lodge is very limited—hamburgers, hot dogs, chili, tuna fish sandwiches, pizzas, french fries, and packaged snacks. With little competition, the previous owners of the resort had felt no urgency to upgrade the food service at the lodge. If skiers want lunch on the mountain, the only alternatives are the Powder 8 Lodge or a brown bag lunch brought from home.

As part of the deal when acquiring Lost Peak, Western Resorts agreed to retain all of the current employees of the resort. The manager of the lodge, while hardworking and enthusiastic, has very little experience in the restaurant business. The manager is responsible for selecting the menu, finding and training employees, and overseeing daily operations. The kitchen staff prepare food and wash dishes. The dining room staff take orders, serve as cashiers, and clean the dining room area.

Shortly after taking over Lost Peak, management of Western Resorts held a day-long meeting with all of the employees of the Powder 8 Lodge to discuss the future of the ski resort and the new management's plans for the lodge. At the end of this meeting, management and lodge employees created a balanced scorecard for the lodge that would help guide operations for the coming ski season. Almost everyone who participated in the meeting seemed to be enthusiastic about the scorecard and management's plans for the lodge.

The following performance measures were included on the balanced scorecard for the Powder 8 Lodge:

a. Weekly Powder 8 Lodge sales
b. Weekly Powder 8 Lodge profit
c. Number of menu items
d. Dining area cleanliness as rated by a representative from Western Resorts management
e. Customer satisfaction with menu choices as measured by customer surveys
f. Customer satisfaction with service as measured by customer surveys
g. Average time to take an order
h. Average time to prepare an order
i. Percentage of kitchen staff completing a basic cooking course at the local community college
j. Percentage of dining room staff completing a basic hospitality course at the local community college

Western Resorts will pay for the costs of staff attending courses at the local community college.

Required:
1. Using the above performance measures, construct a balanced scorecard for the Powder 8 Lodge. Use Exhibit 11–5 as a guide. Use arrows to show causal links and indicate with a + or – whether the performance measure should increase or decrease.
2. What hypotheses are built into the balanced scorecard for the Powder 8 Lodge? Which of these hypotheses do you believe are most questionable? Why?
3. How will management know if one of the hypotheses underlying the balanced scorecard is false?

CASES

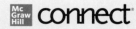

CASE 11–29 Creating Balanced Scorecards That Support Different Strategies [LO5]
The Performance Enhancement Group (PEG) helps companies to build balanced scorecards. As part of its marketing efforts, PEG conducts an annual balanced scorecard workshop for prospective clients. You are PEG's newest employee, so your boss has asked you to participate in this year's workshop by explaining to attendees how a company's strategy determines the measures that are appropriate for its

balanced scorecard. Your boss has provided you with the excerpts below from the annual reports of two current PEG clients. She has asked you to use these excerpts in your portion of the workshop.

Excerpt from Applied Pharmaceuticals' annual report:

> The keys to our business are consistent and timely new-product introductions and manufacturing process integrity. The new-product introduction side of the equation is a function of research and development (R&D) yield (e.g., the number of marketable drug compounds created relative to the total number of potential compounds pursued). We seek to optimize our R&D yield and first-to-market capability by investing in state-of-the-art technology, hiring the highest possible percentage of the "best and the brightest" engineers, and providing world-class training to those engineers. Manufacturing process integrity is all about establishing world-class quality specifications and then relentlessly engaging in prevention and appraisal activities to minimize defect rates. Our customers must have an awareness of and respect for our brand image of being "first to market and first in quality." If we deliver on this pledge to our customers, then our financial goal of increasing our return on shareholders' equity should take care of itself.

Excerpt from Destination Resorts International's annual report:

> Our business succeeds or fails based on the quality of the service that our front-line employees provide to customers. Therefore, it is imperative that we strive to maintain high employee morale and minimize employee turnover. In addition, it is critical that we train our employees to use technology to create one seamless worldwide experience for our repeat customers. Once an employee enters a customer preference (e.g., provide two extra pillows in the room, deliver fresh brewed coffee to the room at 8:00 A.M., etc.) into our database, our worldwide workforce strives to ensure that a customer will never need to repeat this preference at any of our destination resorts. If we properly train and retain a motivated workforce, we should see continuous improvement in our percentage of error-free repeat customer check-ins, the time taken to resolve customer complaints, and our independently assessed room cleanliness. This in turn should drive improvement in our customer retention, which is the key to meeting our revenue growth goals.

Required:
1. Based on the excerpts above, compare and contrast the strategies of Applied Pharmaceuticals and Destination Resorts International.
2. Select balanced scorecard measures for each company and link the scorecard measures using the framework from Exhibit 11–5. Use arrows to show the causal links between the performance measures and show whether the performance measure should increase or decrease over time. Feel free to create measures that may not be specifically mentioned in the chapter, but nonetheless make sense given the strategic goals of each company.
3. What hypotheses are built into each balanced scorecard? Why do the hypotheses differ between the two companies?

CASE 11–30 Performance Evaluation; Return on Investment and Residual Income [LO3, LO4]
Convenient Food Markets (CFM) is a chain of more than 100 convenience stores. The company has faced increasing competition over the past several years, mainly because department store chains have been adding grocery departments and gas stations have been adding full-service convenience stores to their locations. As a consequence, the company has lost market share recently to competitors. The company has set a target minimum rate of return for its stores of 22%.

John Nicholson is the district manager of the 17 CFM stores in Bailingham. Nicholson's district happens to include the original store, the first in the CFM chain, which opened more than 40 years ago. In fact, Nicholson's first summer job was as a stock boy at the original store in the year that it opened. After university, he returned to CFM as a store manager, has worked his way up to district manager, and plans to retire in about five years.

CFM leases store buildings, investing significantly in the interior design, display, and decoration. The original CFM store remains profitable, in part because the fixtures and fittings are almost fully depreciated. While the company has invested in significant leasehold improvements in other newer stores, little has changed in the original store since opening day. While Nicholson has a sense of nostalgia for the original store, in reality, sales volumes have been falling and foot traffic has declined significantly in recent years. Fewer people are moving to the neighbourhood, as more and more people are moving to the suburbs.

All 17 stores in the district report to Nicholson, who is evaluated on the basis of average ROI for the stores in his district. For this calculation, the net book value of investment in furnishings and fixtures represents the operating assets of each of the stores. Operating income after depreciation on leasehold improvements represents the numerator for this calculation.

Nicholson is considering a proposal from a developer to open a new store in a newly developed residential neighbourhood. The developer has completed about 60% of the new homes planned for this neighbourhood and will complete the other 40% within the next 18 months. Due to limited capital to invest, Nicholson realizes that opening the new store would mean closing down an old store, and the original store seems to be the best candidate. To aid in his decision, Nicholson has collected the following information:

	Original Store (prior-year actual)	New Store (forecast)
Operating income less depreciation.....	$ 75,000	$145,000
Net book value of operating assets......	195,000	475,000

Required:
1. Calculate the ROI and residual income for both the original store and the new store.
2. Take on the role of an internal auditor at CFM. Assume that your task is to evaluate the effectiveness of the performance evaluation system for CFM district managers. In this capacity, write a short memo to the CFO of CFM to discuss your findings. In the memo, you should indicate whether you believe Nicholson will want to open the new store, whether your analysis indicates that Nicholson should open the new store, and why or why not. You should also include your observations about the effect of the performance evaluation system on the decisions made by CFM district managers and what might be done to improve it.

CONNECTING CONCEPTS

SECTION 3

PLANNING AND CONTROL

Over the past several years, Claire Jackson, CEO and founder of Easy Learning (EL), has been working to expand operations outside of Canada. In particular, she has placed two long-time, trusted managers in Paris and Buenos Aires in order to develop the European and South American markets. Competition is less fierce in these parts of the world and the supply of skilled technical and education staff is in good supply.

Claire was deeply involved in the development and expansion activities for the first few years. Now that the new divisions are up and running, she has decided to decentralize by creating a European and a South American division and putting their current local managers in charge.

After the first full year of operations under the decentralized structure, the contribution format income statement for the company as a whole is as follows:

Sales...................................	$8,250,000
Variable expenses.......................	4,134,000
Contribution margin.....................	4,116,000
Fixed expenses..........................	4,412,000
Operating Loss..........................	$ (296,000)

When the divisions were created, EL invested heavily in operating assets to set up and organize the new operations. Therefore, Claire decided to make these divisions investment centres and to require each division to generate a return on investment on operating assets of at least 12%, which is the company's minimum required rate of return. The divisional managers' bonuses are also based on ROI. Average operating assets of the European division are $1,000,000 and $485,000 for the South American division.

Claire is concerned that the company has incurred an operating loss for the first time this year, although she is not completely surprised given her decision to expand. She would like to isolate the problem and decide how to respond. She is concerned that one problem may be her lack of direct supervision of the newly created divisions.

Required:

1. Use the following information to help the CEO better understand the profitability of each geographic segment. What does your analysis suggest she should do?

	Geographic Segment		
	Canada	**Europe**	**South America**
Sales	$6,950,000	$825,000	$475,000
Variable expenses as a % of sales	52%	40%	40%
Traceable fixed expenses	$3,622,000	$375,000	$270,000

2. Calculate the ROI for each of the European and South American divisions. Will the divisional managers receive a bonus this year? If not, what can the CEO suggest to help these managers raise their ROI next year?

INSTANT QUIZ SOLUTIONS

11–1

A traceable cost of a segment is a cost that arises specifically because of the existence of that segment. If the segment were eliminated, the cost would disappear. A common cost, by contrast, is a cost that supports more than one segment, but is not traceable in whole or in part to any one of the segments. If the departments of a company are treated as segments, then examples of the traceable costs of a department could include the salary of the department's supervisor, depreciation of machines used exclusively by the department, and the costs of supplies used by the department. Examples of common costs are the lease cost of the headquarters building, corporate image advertising, and periodic depreciation of machines shared by several departments.

11–2

Margin = Operating income ÷ Sales = $3,600,000 ÷ $12,000,000 = 30%
Turnover = Sales ÷ Average operating assets = $12,000,000 ÷ $24,000,000 = 0.5
Return on Investment = Margin × Turnover = 30% × 0.5 = 15%

11–3

Margin is a measure of management's ability to control operating expenses relative to sales. Turnover is a measure of the sales generated for each dollar invested in operating assets. To increase ROI, the manager would try to increase sales, decrease operating expenses, and/or decrease operating assets.

11–4

Average operating assets (a).	£4,400,000
Net operating income	£ 600,000
Minimum required return: 9% × (a).	396,000
Residual income.	£ 204,000

11–5

The balanced scorecard is constructed to support the company's strategy, which is a theory about what actions will further the company's goals. Assuming that the company has financial goals, measures of financial performance must be included in the balanced scorecard as a check on the reality of the theory. If the non-financial measures show improvement, but the financial outcomes do not improve, the theory may be flawed and the strategy should be changed. Since different companies have different strategies, their balanced scorecards should be different.

■ APPENDIX 11A: ADDITIONAL CONTROL TOPICS

■ TRANSFER PRICING

In this appendix, we discuss a key issue that arises when segments of the same company (often referred to as *divisions*) supply goods and services to each other. The issue is determining the transfer price of the goods or services being sold between segments. A **transfer price** is the price charged when one segment sells goods or services to another segment of the same company. Because the dollar amount of these transfers can be very large, the transfer price at which they occur can have a significant impact on the profits of both the buying and selling segment. As a result, managers are very interested in how transfer prices are set.

As an example of a transfer pricing scenario, most companies in the oil industry, such as Imperial, Shell, and Petro-Canada, have petroleum-refining and retail sales divisions that are evaluated on the basis of return on investment (ROI) or residual income, two performance measures that were discussed in the main body of the chapter. The petroleum-refining division processes crude oil into gasoline, kerosene, lubricants, and other end products. The retail sales division takes gasoline and other products from the refining division and sells them through the company's chain of service stations. Each product has a price for transfers within the company. Suppose the transfer price for gasoline is $1.00 per litre. Then the refining division gets credit for $1.00 per litre of revenue on its segment report and the retailing division must deduct $1.00 per litre as an expense on its segment report. Clearly, the refining division would like the transfer price to be as high as possible, whereas the retailing division would like the transfer price to be as low as possible. However, the transaction has no direct effect on the entire company's reported profit because the revenue recorded for the transfer by the selling division is exactly offset by the cost recorded by the buying division.

Three common approaches are used to set transfer prices:

1. Allow the managers involved in the transfers to negotiate their own transfer prices.
2. Set transfer prices at cost, using either variable cost or full absorption cost.
3. Set transfer prices at the market price.

We consider each of these approaches in turn, beginning with negotiated transfer prices. Throughout the discussion, keep in mind that *the fundamental objective in setting transfer prices is to motivate the managers to act in the best interests of the overall company.*

Negotiated Transfer Prices

A **negotiated transfer price** is a transfer price that is agreed on between the selling and purchasing segments or divisions. Negotiated transfer prices have several important advantages. First, this approach preserves the autonomy of the divisions and is consistent with the spirit of decentralization. Second, the managers of the divisions are likely to have much better information about the potential costs and benefits of the transfer than others in the company.

When negotiated transfer prices are used, the managers who are involved in a proposed transfer within the company meet to discuss the terms and conditions of the transfer. Perhaps most important, they must agree to a transfer price: (1) the selling division will agree to the transfer only if the profits of the selling division increase as a result of the transfer, and (2) the purchasing division will agree to the transfer only if the profits of the purchasing division also increase as a result of the transfer.

Clearly, if the transfer price is below the selling division's cost, a loss will occur on the transaction and the selling division will refuse to agree to the transfer. If the transfer price is set too high, it will be impossible for the purchasing division to make any profit on the transferred item. For any given proposed transfer, the transfer price has a lower limit (determined by the situation of the selling division) and an upper limit (determined by the situation of the purchasing division). These limits determine the **range of acceptable transfer prices**—the range of transfer prices within which the profits of both divisions participating in a transfer would increase, or at least not decrease.

We consider the range of acceptable transfer prices that might be considered by the divisional managers of Harrison Ltd. to help illustrate the issues. Assume that Harrison Ltd. owns fast-food restaurants and snack food and beverage manufacturers in Atlantic Canada. One of the restaurants, Pizza Place, serves a variety of beverages along with pizzas. One of the beverages is ginger beer, which is served on tap. Harrison has just purchased a new division, Cumberland Beverages, that produces ginger beer. The managing director of Cumberland Beverages has approached the managing director of Pizza Place about purchasing Cumberland Beverages ginger beer for sale at Pizza

LEARNING OBJECTIVE

Determine the range, if any, within which a negotiated transfer price should fall, and explain approaches to setting the transfer price.

Transfer price
The price charged when one division or segment provides goods or services to another division or segment of an organization.

Negotiated transfer price
A transfer price agreed on between buying and selling divisions.

Range of acceptable transfer prices
The range of transfer prices within which the profits of both the selling division and the purchasing division would increase as a result of a transfer.

Place restaurants rather than its usual brand of ginger beer. Managers at Pizza Place agree that the quality of Cumberland Beverages' ginger beer is comparable to the quality of their regular brand. It is just a question of price. The basic facts follow:

Cumberland Beverages:	
Ginger beer production capacity per month..............	10,000 kegs
Variable cost per keg of ginger beer	$8 per keg
Fixed costs per month	$70,000
Selling price of Cumberland Beverages ginger beer on the outside market..................................	$20 per keg
Pizza Place:	
Purchase price of regular brand of ginger beer	$18 per keg
Monthly consumption of ginger beer....................	2,000 kegs

The Selling Division's Lowest Acceptable Transfer Price

The selling division, Cumberland Beverages, will be interested in a proposed transfer only if its profit increases. Clearly, the transfer price must not fall below the variable cost per keg of $8. In addition, if Cumberland Beverages has insufficient capacity to fill the Pizza Place order, then it will have to give up some of its regular sales. Cumberland Beverages would expect to be compensated for the contribution margin on these lost sales. In summary, if the transfer has no effect on fixed costs, then from the selling division's standpoint the transfer price must cover both the variable costs of producing the transferred units and any opportunity costs from lost sales:

Seller's perspective:

$$\text{Transfer price} \geq \text{Variable cost per unit} + \frac{\text{Total contribution margin on lost sales}}{\text{Number of units transferred}}$$

The Purchasing Division's Highest Acceptable Transfer Price

The purchasing division, Pizza Place, will be interested in the proposal only if its profit increases. In cases like this where a purchasing division has an outside supplier, the purchasing division's decision is simple—buy from the inside supplier if the price is less than the price offered by the outside supplier:

Purchaser's perspective:

$$\text{Transfer price} \leq \text{Cost of buying from outside supplier}$$

We will consider several different hypothetical situations and see what the range of acceptable transfer prices is in each situation.

Selling Division with Idle Capacity

Suppose that Cumberland Beverages has sufficient idle capacity to satisfy the demand for ginger beer from Pizza Place without cutting into sales of ginger beer to its regular customers. To be specific, let's suppose that Cumberland Beverages is selling only 7,000 kegs of ginger beer per month on the outside market. That leaves unused capacity of 3,000 kegs per month—more than enough to satisfy Pizza Place's requirement of 2,000 kegs per month. What range of transfer prices, if any, would make both divisions better off with the transfer of 2,000 kegs per month?

1. The selling division, Cumberland Beverages, will be interested in the proposal only if

$$\text{Transfer price} \geq \text{Variable cost per unit} + \frac{\text{Total contribution margin on lost sales}}{\text{Number of units transferred}}$$

Since Cumberland Beverages has ample idle capacity, there are no lost outside sales. And since the variable cost per unit is $8, the lowest acceptable transfer price as far as the selling division is concerned is also $8:

$$\text{Transfer price} \geq \$8 + \frac{\$0}{2,000} = \$8$$

2.   The purchasing division, Pizza Place, can buy similar ginger beer from an outside vendor for $18 per keg. Therefore, Pizza Place would be unwilling to pay more than $18 per keg for Cumberland Beverages' ginger beer:

$$\text{Transfer price} \leq \text{Cost of buying from outside supplier} = \$18$$

3.   Combining the requirements of both the selling division and the purchasing division, the acceptable range of transfer prices in this situation is

$$\$8 \leq \text{Transfer price} \leq \$18$$

Assuming that the managers understand their own businesses and that they are cooperative, they should be able to agree on a transfer price within this range.

Selling Division with No Idle Capacity

Suppose that Cumberland Beverages has *no* idle capacity; it is selling 10,000 kegs of ginger beer a month on the outside market at $20 per keg. To fill the order from Pizza Place, Cumberland Beverages would have to divert 2,000 kegs from its regular customers. What range of transfer prices, if any, would make both divisions better off transferring the 2,000 kegs within the company?

1.   The selling division, Cumberland Beverages, will be interested in the proposal only if

$$\text{Transfer price} \geq \text{Variable cost per unit} + \frac{\text{Total contribution margin on lost sales}}{\text{Number of units transferred}}$$

Since Cumberland Beverages has no idle capacity, there *are* lost outside sales. The contribution margin per barrel on these outside sales is $12 ($20 − $8):

$$\text{Transfer price} \geq \$8 + \frac{(\$20 - \$8) \times 2,000}{2,000} = \$8 + (\$20 - \$8) = \$20$$

Thus, as far as the selling division is concerned, the transfer price must at least cover the revenue on the lost sales, which is $20 per keg. This makes sense since the cost of producing the 2,000 kegs is the same whether they are sold on the inside market or on the outside. The only difference is that the selling division loses the revenue of $20 per keg if it transfers the kegs to Pizza Place.

2.   As before, the purchasing division, Pizza Place, would be unwilling to pay more than the $18 per keg it is already paying for similar ginger beer from its regular supplier:

$$\text{Transfer price} \leq \text{Cost of buying from outside supplier} = \$18$$

3.   Therefore, the selling division would insist on a transfer price of at least $20, but the purchasing division would refuse any transfer price above $18. It is impossible to satisfy both division managers simultaneously; there can be no agreement on a transfer price, and no transfer will take place. Is this good? The answer is yes. From the standpoint of the entire company, the transfer does not make sense. Why give up sales of $20 to save $18?

Basically, the transfer price is a mechanism for dividing between the two divisions any profit the entire company earns as a result of the transfer. If the company loses money on the transfer, there will be no profit to divide up, and it will be impossible for the two divisions to come to an agreement. On the other hand, if the company as a whole makes money on the transfer, there will be a potential profit to share, and it will always be possible for the two divisions to find a mutually agreeable transfer price that increases the profits of both divisions. If the pie is bigger, it is always possible to divide it up so that everyone has a bigger piece.

Selling Division with Some Idle Capacity

Suppose now that Cumberland Beverages is selling 9,000 kegs of ginger beer per month on the outside market. Assume that Pizza Place can sell only one kind of ginger beer on tap. It cannot buy 1,000 kegs from Cumberland Beverages and 1,000 kegs from its regular supplier; it must buy all of its ginger beer from one source.

To fill the entire 2,000-keg-per-month order from Pizza Place, Cumberland Beverages would have to divert 1,000 kegs from its regular customers, who are paying $20 per keg. The other 1,000 kegs can be made using idle capacity. What range of transfer prices, if any, would make both divisions better off transferring the 2,000 kegs within the company?

1. As before, the selling division, Cumberland Beverages, will insist on a transfer price that at least covers its variable cost and opportunity cost:

$$\text{Transfer price} \geq \text{Variable cost per unit} + \frac{\text{Total contribution margin on lost sales}}{\text{Number of units transferred}}$$

Since Cumberland Beverages does not have enough idle capacity to fill the entire order for 2,000 kegs, there *are* lost outside sales. The contribution margin per keg on the 1,000 kegs of lost outside sales is $12 ($20 − $8):

$$\text{Transfer price} \geq \$8 + \frac{(\$20 - \$8) \times 1,000}{2,000} = \$8 + \$6 = \$14$$

Thus, as far as the selling division is concerned, the transfer price must cover the variable cost of $8 plus the average opportunity cost of lost sales of $6.

2. As before, the purchasing division, Pizza Place, would be unwilling to pay more than the $18 per keg it pays its regular supplier:

$$\text{Transfer price} \leq \text{Cost of buying from outside supplier} = \$18$$

3. Combining the requirements for both the selling and purchasing divisions, the range of acceptable transfer prices is

$$\$14 \leq \text{Transfer price} \leq \$18$$

Again, assuming that the managers understand their own businesses and that they are cooperative, they should be able to agree on a transfer price within this range.

No Outside Supplier

If Pizza Place has no outside supplier for the ginger beer, the highest price the purchasing division would be willing to pay depends on how much the purchasing division expects to make on the transferred units— excluding the transfer price. If, for example, Pizza Place expects to earn $30 per keg of ginger beer after paying its own expenses, then it should be willing to pay up to $30 per keg to Cumberland Beverages. Remember, however, that this assumes Pizza Place cannot buy ginger beer from other sources.

The Learning Aid below summarizes the range of acceptable transfer prices for selling and buying divisions under the various scenarios used in our examples. Examples from Cumberland Beverages are included in the learning aid.

LEARNING AID

Range of Negotiated Transfer Prices

Minimum price selling division would accept

1. *Selling division with idle capacity:*

   Transfer price ≥ Variable cost per unit

   Cumberland Beverages minimum transfer price:

   $$\text{Transfer price} \geq \$8 + \frac{\$0}{2,000} = \$8$$

2. *Selling division with no idle capacity:*

   $$\text{Transfer price} \geq \text{Variable cost per unit} + \frac{\text{Total contribution margin on lost sales}}{\text{Number of units transferred}}$$

   Cumberland Beverages minimum transfer price:

   $$\text{Transfer price} \geq \$8 + \frac{(\$20 - \$8) \times 2,000}{2,000} = \$8 + (\$20 - \$8) = \$20$$

3. *Selling division with some idle capacity:*

   $$\text{Transfer price} \geq \text{Variable cost per unit} + \frac{\text{Total contribution margin on lost sales}}{\text{Number of units transferred}}$$

   Cumberland Beverages minimum transfer price:

   $$\text{Transfer price} \geq \$8 + \frac{(\$20 - \$8) \times 1,000}{2,000} = \$8 + \$6 = \$14$$

Maximum price buying division would pay

1. *If outside supplier exists:* Transfer price ≤ Cost of buying from outside supplier

2. *If no outside supplier exists:* Transfer price ≤ Expected net profit from sale to final customer

Transfers to the Selling Division at Cost

Many companies set transfer prices at either the variable cost or full absorption cost incurred by the selling division. Although the cost approach to setting transfer prices is relatively simple to apply, it has some major weaknesses, which are explained below.

First, the use of cost—particularly full cost—as a transfer price can lead to bad decisions. Let's return to the example involving the ginger beer to illustrate the problem. The full cost of ginger beer can never be less than $15 per keg ($8 per keg variable cost + $7 per keg fixed cost at capacity). What if the cost of buying the ginger beer from an outside supplier is less than $15—for example, $14 per keg? If the transfer price were automatically set at full cost, then Pizza Place would never want to buy ginger beer from Cumberland Beverages, since it could buy its ginger beer from the outside supplier at a lower cost. However, from the standpoint of the company as a whole, ginger beer should be transferred from Cumberland Beverages to Pizza Place whenever Cumberland Beverages has more than 1,000 kegs of idle capacity. Why? Because when Cumberland Beverages has more than 1,000 kegs of idle capacity, the total transfer price (including the opportunity cost) will be less than the $14 per keg to buy from outside suppliers.[2]

Second, if cost is used as the transfer price, the selling division will never show a profit on any internal transfer. The only division that shows a profit is the division that makes the final sale to an outside party.

Third, cost-based prices do not provide any incentive to control costs. If the costs of one division are simply passed on to the next, then there is little incentive to reduce costs. This problem can be overcome to some extent by using standard costs rather than actual costs for transfer prices.

Despite these shortcomings, cost-based transfer prices are commonly used in practice. Advocates argue that they are easily understood, are convenient to use, and avoid the potential behavioural problems with negotiated transfer prices.

Transfers at Market Price

Some form of competitive **market price** (i.e., the price charged for an item on the open market) is often regarded as the best approach to establishing transfer prices—particularly if transfer price negotiations are causing problems between sellers and buyers.

The market price approach is designed for situations in which there is an *intermediate market* for the transferred product or service. By **intermediate market**, we mean a market in which the product or service is sold in its present form to outside customers. If the selling division has no idle capacity, the market price in the intermediate market is the perfect choice for the transfer price. This is because if the selling division can sell a transferred item on the outside market instead, then the real cost of the transfer as far as the company is concerned is the opportunity cost of the lost revenue on the outside sale.

Whether the item is transferred internally or sold on the outside intermediate market, the production costs are exactly the same. If the market price is used as the transfer price, the selling division manager will not lose anything by making the transfer, and the purchasing division manager will get the correct signal about how much it really costs the company for the transfer to take place.

While the market price works well when there is no idle capacity, difficulties can occur when the selling division has idle capacity. Recalling once again the ginger beer example, the outside market price for the ginger beer produced by Cumberland Beverages is $20 per keg. However, Pizza Place can purchase all of the ginger beer it wants from outside suppliers for $18 per keg. Why would Pizza Place ever buy ginger beer from Cumberland Beverages if Pizza Place is forced to pay Cumberland Beverages' market price? In some market price–based transfer pricing schemes, the transfer price would be lowered to $18, the outside vendor's market price, and Pizza Place would be directed to buy from Cumberland Beverages, as long as Cumberland Beverages is willing to sell. This approach can work reasonably well, but a drawback is that managers at Pizza Place will regard the cost of ginger beer as $18 rather than the $8, which is the real cost to the company when the selling division has sufficient idle capacity to fill the entire order. Consequently, the managers of Pizza Place may make pricing and other decisions based on an incorrect cost.

Market price
The price being charged for an item on the open (intermediate) market.

Intermediate market
A market in which a transferred product or service is sold in its present form to outside customers.

Divisional Autonomy

The principles of decentralization suggest that companies should grant managers autonomy to set transfer prices and to decide whether to sell internally or externally. It may be very difficult for top managers to accept this principle when their subordinate managers are about to make a decision that is not in the best interests of the company overall. However, if top management intervenes, the purposes of decentralization are defeated. Furthermore, to impose the correct transfer price, top managers would have to know details about the buying and selling divisions' outside market, variable costs, and capacity utilization. The whole premise of decentralization is that local managers have access to better information for operational decisions than top managers at corporate headquarters.

Of course, if a division manager consistently makes suboptimal decisions, the performance of the division will suffer. The offending manager's compensation will be adversely affected and promotion will become less likely. However, if top managers really want to create a culture of autonomy and independent profit responsibility, they must allow their subordinate managers to control their own destiny—even to the extent of granting their managers the right to make mistakes.

LEARNING OBJECTIVE ⑦
Identify the four types of quality costs, explain their interaction, and prepare a quality cost report.

■ OPERATING PERFORMANCE MEASURES—QUALITY COSTS

One type of internal business process measure that might be used in a firm's balanced scorecard is the cost of quality. This is usually a summary metric made up of different types or categories of quality costs. Increasingly, managers at both manufacturing and service companies are emphasizing the importance of understanding the various kinds of quality costs and how they can be managed. In this section, we discuss the types of quality costs and their interaction as well as illustrate how some companies extend the reporting of these costs beyond the summary metrics included in their performance measurement system.

A company may have a product with a high-quality design that uses high-quality components, but if the product is poorly assembled or has other defects, the company will have high warranty repair costs and dissatisfied customers. People who are dissatisfied with a product are unlikely to buy the product again and may tell others about their bad experiences. This is the worst possible sort of advertising. To prevent such problems, companies have been expending a great deal of effort to reduce defects. The objective is to have high *quality of conformance*.

Quality of Conformance

Quality of conformance
The degree to which a product or service meets or exceeds its design specifications and is free of defects or other problems that mar its appearance or degrade its performance.

A product that meets or exceeds its design specifications and is free of defects that mar its appearance or degrade its performance is said to have high **quality of conformance**. Note that if an economy car is free of defects, it can have a quality of conformance that is just as high as a defect-free luxury car. The purchasers of economy cars cannot expect their cars to be as lavishly equipped as luxury cars, but they can and do expect them to be free of defects.

Preventing, detecting, and dealing with defects cause costs that are called *quality costs* or the *cost of quality*. The use of the term *quality cost* is confusing to some people. It does not refer to costs such as using a higher grade of leather to make a wallet or using 14-karat gold instead of gold-plating in jewellery. Instead, the term **quality cost** refers to all of the costs that are incurred to prevent defects or that are incurred as a result of defects occurring.

Quality cost
Costs that are incurred to prevent defective products from reaching customers or that are incurred as a result of defective units.

Quality costs can be broken down into four broad groups. Two of these groups—known as *prevention costs* and *appraisal costs*—are incurred in an effort to keep defective products from reaching customers. The other two groups—known as *internal failure costs* and *external failure costs*—are incurred because defects are produced despite efforts to prevent them. Examples of specific costs involved in each of these four groups are given in Exhibit 11A–1.

Several things should be noted about the quality costs shown in the exhibit. First, quality costs do not relate to just manufacturing; rather, they relate to all of the activities in a company, from initial research and development through customer service. Second, the number and nature of costs associated with quality is very large. Therefore, total quality costs can be quite high unless management gives this area special attention.

Prevention Costs

Prevention costs
Costs incurred to keep defects from occurring.

Generally the most effective way to minimize quality costs while maintaining high-quality output is to avoid having quality problems arise in the first place. This is the purpose of **prevention costs**. Such costs relate to any activity that reduces the number of defects in products or services. Companies have learned that it is much less costly to prevent a problem from happening than it is to diagnose and correct the problem after it has occurred.

Prevention Costs	**Internal Failure Costs**	**EXHIBIT 11A–1**
Systems development	Net cost of scrap or spoilage	Typical Quality Costs
Quality engineering	Rework materials, labour, and overhead	
Quality training	Reinspection of reworked products	
Quality circles	Retesting of reworked products	
Statistical process control activities	Downtime caused by quality problems	
Supervision of prevention activities	Disposal of defective products	
Quality data gathering, analysis, and reporting	Analysis of the cause of defects in production	
Quality improvement projects	Re-entering data because of keying errors	
Technical support provided to suppliers	Debugging software costs	
Audits of the effectiveness of the quality system		
	External Failure Costs	
Appraisal Costs	Cost of field servicing and handling complaints	
Test and inspection of incoming materials	Warranty repairs and replacements	
Test and inspection of in-process goods	Repairs/replacements beyond warranty period	
Final product testing and inspection	Product recalls	
Supplies used in testing and inspection	Liability arising from defective products	
Supervision of testing and inspection activities	Returns and allowances arising from quality problems	
Depreciation of test equipment	Lost sales arising from a reputation for poor quality	
Maintenance of test equipment		
Plant utilities in the inspection area		
Field testing and appraisal at customer site		

Note from Exhibit 11A–1 that prevention costs include activities relating to quality circles and statistical process control. **Quality circles** consist of small groups of employees who meet on a regular basis to discuss ways to improve the quality of output (products or services). Both management and workers are usually included in these circles.

Statistical process control is an analytical technique used to detect whether a process is in or out of control. An out-of-control process results in defective units and may be caused by a malfunctioning machine or some other factor. In statistical process control, workers use charts and analysis to monitor the quality of units that pass through their workstations. Using these charts, workers can quickly spot processes that are out of control and that are creating defects.

Note also from the list of prevention costs in Exhibit 11A–1 that some companies provide technical support to their suppliers as a way of preventing defects. Particularly in just-in-time (JIT) systems, such support to suppliers is vital. In a JIT system, parts are delivered from suppliers just in time and in just the correct quantity to fill customer orders. If a defective part is received from a supplier, the part cannot be used and the order for the ultimate customer may not be filled on time. Hence, it is critical that every part received from a supplier be free of defects. Consequently, companies that use JIT often require their suppliers to certify that they will deliver parts and materials that are free of defects.

Appraisal Costs

Any defective parts and products should be caught as early as possible. **Appraisal costs**, which are sometimes called *inspection costs*, are incurred to identify defective products *before* the products are shipped to customers. Unfortunately, performing appraisal activities doesn't keep defects from happening again so it can be a costly approach to quality control.

Employees are increasingly being asked to be responsible for their own quality control. This approach, along with designing products to be easy to manufacture properly, allows quality to be built into products rather than relying on inspection to get the defects out.

Internal Failure Costs

Failure costs are incurred when a product fails to conform to its design specifications. Failure costs can be either internal or external. **Internal failure costs** result from identification of defects during the appraisal process. Such costs include scrap, rejected products, reworking of defective units, and downtime caused by quality problems. It is crucial that defects be discovered before a product is shipped to customers. Of course, the more effective a company's appraisal activities, the greater the chance of

Quality circles
Small groups of employees who meet on a regular basis to discuss ways of improving quality.

Statistical process control
A charting technique used to monitor the quality of work being done at a workstation for the purpose of immediately correcting any problems.

Appraisal costs
Costs that are incurred to identify defective products before the products are shipped to customers.

Internal failure costs
Costs that are incurred as a result of identifying defective products before they are shipped to customers.

catching defects internally and the greater the level of internal failure costs as compared to external failure costs. Unfortunately, appraisal activities typically focus on symptoms rather than on causes and do nothing to reduce the number of defective items. However, appraisal activities do bring defects to the attention of management, which should lead to efforts to increase prevention activities so that the defects do not happen.

External Failure Costs

External failure costs
Costs that are incurred when a product or service that is defective is delivered to a customer.

External failure costs result when a defective product is delivered to a customer. As shown in Exhibit 11A–1, external failure costs include warranty repairs and replacements, product recalls, liability arising from legal action against a company, and lost sales arising from a reputation for poor quality. Such costs can significantly reduce profits.

Distribution of Quality Costs

How does a company reduce its total quality cost? The answer lies in how the quality costs are distributed. Refer to the graph in Exhibit 11A–2, which shows total quality costs as a function of the quality of conformance.

The graph shows that when the quality of conformance is low, total quality cost is high, and most of this cost consists of internal and external failure costs. A low quality of conformance means that a high percentage of units are defective and hence the company must incur high failure costs. However, as a company spends more on prevention and appraisal activities, the percentage of defective units will drop. This results in lower costs of internal and external failure. Ordinarily, total quality cost drops as the quality of conformance increases. Thus, a company can reduce its total quality cost by focusing its efforts on prevention and appraisal.

As a company's quality program becomes more refined and as its failure costs begin to fall, prevention activities usually become more effective than appraisal activities. Appraisal can only find defects, whereas prevention can eliminate them. The best way to prevent defects from happening is to design processes that reduce the likelihood of defects and to continuously monitor processes using statistical process control methods.

EXHIBIT 11A–2
Effect of Quality Costs on Quality of Conformance

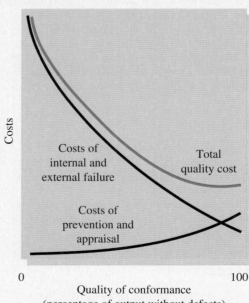

Quality Cost Reports

As an initial step in quality improvement programs, companies often construct a *quality cost report*, which provides an estimate of the financial consequences of the company's current level of defects. A **quality cost report** details the prevention costs, appraisal costs, and costs of internal and external failures that arise from the company's current level of defective products and services. An example of a quality cost report is shown in Exhibit 11A–3.

Quality cost report
A report that details prevention costs, appraisal costs, and the costs of internal and external failures.

Several things should be noted from the data in Exhibit 11A–3. First, Ventura Company's quality costs are poorly distributed in both years, with most of the costs being traceable to either internal failure or external failure. The external failure costs are particularly high in year 1 in comparison to other costs.

Second, the company increased its spending on prevention and appraisal activities in year 2. As a result, internal failure costs go up in that year (from $2 million in year 1 to $3 million in year 2), but external failure costs drop sharply (from $5.15 million in year 1 to only $2 million in year 2). Because of the increase in appraisal activity in year 2, more defects are being caught inside the company before goods are shipped to customers. This results in more cost for scrap, rework, and so forth, but saves warranty repairs, warranty replacements, and other external failure costs.

Third, as a result of greater emphasis on prevention and appraisal, *total* quality cost has decreased in year 2. As continued emphasis is placed on prevention and appraisal in future years, total quality cost should continue to decrease. Moreover, appraisal costs should also decrease as more effort is put into prevention.

EXHIBIT 11A–3   Quality Cost Report

VENTURA COMPANY Quality Cost Report For Years 1 and 2				
	Year 1		**Year 2**	
	Amount	**Percentage***	**Amount**	**Percentage***
Prevention costs:				
Systems development	$ 270,000	0.54%	$ 400,000	0.80%
Quality training.	130,000	0.26%	210,000	0.42%
Supervision of prevention activities	40,000	0.08%	70,000	0.14%
Quality improvement projects.	210,000	0.42%	320,000	0.64%
Total prevention cost.	650,000	1.30%	1,000,000	2.00%
Appraisal costs:				
Inspection	560,000	1.12%	600,000	1.20%
Reliability testing	420,000	0.84%	580,000	1.16%
Supervision of testing and inspection	80,000	0.16%	120,000	0.24%
Depreciation of test equipment	140,000	0.28%	200,000	0.40%
Total appraisal cost	1,200,000	2.40%	1,500,000	3.00%
Internal failure costs:				
Net cost of scrap	750,000	1.50%	900,000	1.80%
Rework materials, labour, and overhead.	810,000	1.62%	1,430,000	2.86%
Downtime due to defects in quality.	100,000	0.20%	170,000	0.34%
Disposal of defective products	340,000	0.68%	500,000	1.00%
Total internal failure cost	2,000,000	4.00%	3,000,000	6.00%
External failure costs:				
Warranty repairs	900,000	1.80%	400,000	0.80%
Warranty replacements	2,300,000	4.60%	870,000	1.74%
Allowances	630,000	1.26%	130,000	0.26%
Cost of servicing at customer location	1,320,000	2.64%	600,000	1.20%
Total external failure cost	5,150,000	10.30%	2,000,000	4.00%
Total quality cost.	**$9,000,000**	**18.00%**	**$7,500,000**	**15.00%**

*As a percentage of total sales. Assume that in each year, sales totalled $50,000,000.

EXHIBIT 11A–4
Quality Costs in
Graphic Form

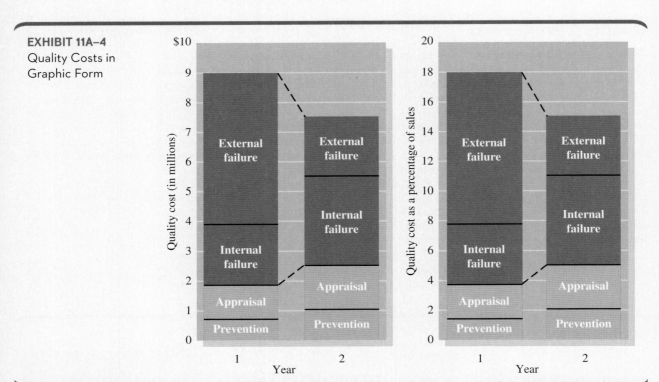

Quality Cost Reports in Graphic Form

As a supplement to the quality cost report shown in Exhibit 11A–3, companies frequently prepare quality cost information in graphic form. Graphic presentations include pie charts, bar graphs, trend lines, and so on. The data for Ventura Company from Exhibit 11A–3 are presented in bar graph form in Exhibit 11A–4.

The first bar graph in Exhibit 11A–4 is scaled in terms of dollars of quality cost, and the second is scaled in terms of quality cost as a percentage of sales. The percentage figures in the second graph show that total quality cost equals 18% of sales in year 1 and 15% of sales in year 2, the same as reported earlier in Exhibit 11A–3.

Data in graphic form help managers to see trends more clearly and to see the magnitude of the various costs relative to each other.

Uses of Quality Cost Information

The information provided by a quality cost report is used by managers in several ways. First, quality cost information helps managers see the financial significance of defects. Managers are usually not aware of the magnitude of their quality costs because they span several departments and are not normally tracked and accumulated by the cost system.

Second, quality cost information helps managers identify the relative importance of the quality problems faced by the firm. For example, the quality cost report may show that scrap is a major quality problem or that the company is incurring significant warranty costs. With this information, managers have a better idea of where to focus improvement efforts.

Third, quality cost information helps managers see whether their quality costs are poorly distributed. In general, quality costs should be distributed more toward prevention and appraisal activities and less toward failures.

Counterbalancing these benefits, several limitations of quality cost information should be recognized. First, simply measuring and reporting quality costs will not solve quality-related problems. Action must be taken to solve problems. Second, results usually lag behind quality improvement programs. Initially, total quality costs may even increase as quality control systems are designed and installed.

Decreases in these costs may not begin to occur until the quality program has been in effect for a year or more. Third, the most important quality cost, lost sales arising from customer ill will, is usually omitted from the quality cost report because it is difficult to estimate.

■ SERVICE DEPARTMENT COST ALLOCATIONS

Most large organizations have both operating departments and service departments. The central purposes of the organization are carried out in the operating departments. In contrast, service departments do not directly engage in operating activities. Instead, they provide services or assistance to the operating departments. Examples of service departments include internal auditing, human resources, financial reporting, accounts receivable, and purchasing.

Service department costs are charged to operating departments for a variety of reasons, including:

- To encourage operating departments to make wise use of service department resources. If the services were provided for free, operating managers might be inclined to use excessive amounts of these resources.
- To provide operating departments with more complete cost data for making decisions. Actions taken by operating departments impact service department costs. For example, hiring another employee will increase costs in the human resources department. Such service department costs should be charged to the operating departments, otherwise the operating departments will not take them into account when making decisions.
- To help measure the profitability of operating departments. Charging service department costs to operating departments provides a more complete accounting of the costs incurred as a consequence of activities in the operating departments.
- To create an incentive for service departments to operate efficiently. Charging service department costs will motivate managers in operating departments to take an active interest in keeping service department costs low.

Earlier in this appendix, we discussed transfer prices that are charged within an organization when one part of an organization provides a product or service to another part of the organization. Service department charges can be viewed as transfer prices that are charged for services provided by service departments to operating departments.

Three different approaches have traditionally been used to allocate the costs of service departments to other departments: the direct method, the step-down method, and the reciprocal method. These three methods are discussed in the following sections. However, before getting into the details of these methods, a few words are in order concerning *interdepartmental services*.

Interdepartmental Services

Many service departments provide services to each other, as well as to operating departments. For example, the human resources department often provides training for all employees, including those working in other service departments, as well as to employees of the operating departments. In turn, the human resources department may receive services from other service departments, such as financial reporting. Services provided between service departments are known as *interdepartmental* or *reciprocal services*.

Direct Method

The *direct method* is the simplest of the three cost allocation methods. It ignores the services provided by a service department to other service departments (e.g., reciprocal services) and allocates all service department costs directly to operating departments. Even if a service department (such as human resources) provides a large amount of service to another service department (such as internal audit), no allocations are made between the two departments. Rather, all costs are allocated *directly* to the operating departments, bypassing the other service departments. Hence the term *direct method*.

For an example of the direct method, assume the Grand Ocean Hospital has two service departments and two operating departments, as shown below. The hospital allocates its Hospital

LEARNING OBJECTIVE

Allocate service department costs to operating departments using the direct method.

EXHIBIT 11A–5   Direct Method of Allocation

	Service Departments		Operating Departments		
	Hospital Administration	Custodial Services	Laboratory	Patient Care	Total
Departmental costs before allocation	$360,000	$90,000	$261,000	$689,000	$1,400,000
Allocation:					
Hospital Administration costs ($^{18}/_{48}$, $^{30}/_{48}$)*	(360,000)		135,000	225,000	
Custodial Services costs ($^{5}/_{50}$, $^{45}/_{50}$)†	—	(90,000)	9,000	81,000	
Total cost after allocation	$ 0	$ 0	$405,000	$995,000	$1,400,000

*Based on the employee-hours in the two operating departments, which are 18,000 + 30,000 = 48,000.
†Based on the space occupied by the two operating departments, which is 500 + 4,500 = 5,000.

Administration costs on the basis of employee-hours and its Custodial Services costs on the basis of square metres occupied:

	Service Departments		Operating Departments		
	Hospital Administration	Custodial Services	Laboratory	Patient Care	Total
Departmental costs before allocation . . .	$360,000	$90,000	$261,000	$689,000	$1,400,000
Employee hours.	12,000	6,000	18,000	30,000	66,000
Space occupied— square metres.	1,000	20	500	4,500	6,020

The direct method of allocating the hospital's service department costs to the operating departments is shown in Exhibit 11A–5. Two things should be noted in this exhibit. First, the employee-hours of the Hospital Administration Department and the Custodial Services Department are ignored when allocating the costs of Hospital Administration using the direct method. Note that the same rule is used when allocating the costs of the Custodial Services Department. Even though the Hospital Administration and Custodial Services Departments occupy some space, this is ignored when the Custodial Services costs are allocated. Second, note that after all allocations have been completed, all of the service department costs are contained in the two operating departments. Although the direct method is simple, it is less accurate than the other methods because it ignores interdepartmental services.

Step-Down Method

LEARNING OBJECTIVE 9

Allocate service department costs to operating department costs using the step-down method.

Unlike the direct method, the *step-down method* provides for allocation of a service department's costs to other service departments, as well as to operating departments. The step-down method is sequential. The sequence typically begins with the department that provides the greatest amount of service to other service departments. After its costs have been allocated, the process continues, step by step, ending with the department that provides the least amount of services to other service departments.

Exhibit 11A–6 shows the details of the step-down method. Note the following three key points about these allocations. First, you see two allocations, or steps. In the first step, the costs of Hospital

EXHIBIT 11A–6   Step-Down Method of Allocation

	Service Departments		Operating Departments		
	Hospital Administration	Custodial Services	Laboratory	Patient Care	Total
Departmental costs before allocation	$360,000	$ 90,000	$261,000	$ 689,000	$1,400,000
Allocation:					
Hospital Administration costs ($6/54$, $18/54$, $30/54$)*	(360,000)	40,000	120,000	120,000	
Custodial Services costs ($5/50$, $45/50$)†		(130,000)	13,000	117,000	
Total cost after allocation	$ 0	$ 0	$394,000	$1,006,000	$1,400,000

*Based on the employee-hours in Custodial Services and the two operating departments, which are 6,000 + 18,000 + 30,000 = 54,000.
†As in Exhibit 11A–5, this allocation is based on the space occupied by the two operating departments.

Administration are allocated to another service department (Custodial Services) as well as to the operating departments. In contrast to the direct method, the allocation base for Hospital Administration costs now includes the employee-hours for Custodial Services as well as for the operating departments. However, the allocation base still excludes the employee-hours for Hospital Administration itself. Second, note that in the second step under the Allocation heading, the cost of Custodial Services is allocated to the two operating departments, but none of the cost is allocated to Hospital Administration even though Hospital Administration occupies space in the building. In the step-down method, after a service department's costs have been allocated, costs of other service departments are not reallocated back to it. Third, note that the cost of Custodial Services allocated to other departments in the second step ($130,000) includes the costs of Hospital Administration that were allocated to Custodial Services in the first step.

Reciprocal Method

The **reciprocal method** gives full recognition to interdepartmental services. Under the step-down method discussed above, only partial recognition of interdepartmental services is possible, since the step-down method always allocates costs forward—never backward among service departments. The reciprocal method, by contrast, allocates service department costs in *both* directions. Thus, since Custodial Services in the prior example provides service for Hospital Administration, part of Custodial Services' costs will be allocated *back* to Hospital Administration if the reciprocal method is used. At the same time, part of Hospital Administration's costs will be allocated *forward* to Custodial Services. This type of reciprocal allocation requires the use of simultaneous linear equations.

The reciprocal method is rarely used in practice primarily because the step-down method usually provides results that are a reasonable approximation of the results that the reciprocal method would provide. Thus, companies have had little motivation to use the more complex reciprocal method.

Reciprocal method A method of allocating service department costs that gives full recognition to interdepartmental services.

Revenue-Producing Department

To conclude our discussion of allocation methods, it is important to note that even though most service departments are cost centres and therefore generate no revenues, a few service departments, such as the cafeteria, may charge for the services they perform. If a service department generates revenues, these revenues should be offset against the department's costs, and only the net amount of cost remaining after this offset should be allocated to other departments within the organization. In this manner, the other departments will not be required to bear costs for which the service department has already been reimbursed.

■ APPENDIX 11A QUESTIONS, EXERCISES, PROBLEMS, AND CASES

11A–1 From the standpoint of a selling division that has idle capacity, what is the minimum acceptable transfer price for an item?

11A–2 What are the advantages and disadvantages of negotiated transfer prices?

11A–3 If a market price for a product can be determined, why is it usually the best transfer price?

11A–4 Quality cost reports typically break down types of quality costs into four broad groups. What are these four groups, and how do they differ?

11A–5 In their efforts to reduce the total cost of quality, should companies generally focus on decreasing prevention and appraisal costs?

11A–6 What is the difference between a service department and an operating department?

11A–7 How are service department costs assigned to products?

11A–8 What are interdepartmental services?

11A–9 How do the direct and step-down methods of service department cost allocation differ?

EXERCISE 11A–1 Transfer Pricing Basics [LO6]

Collyer Products Inc. has a Valve Division that manufactures and sells a standard valve as follows:

Capacity in units	100,000
Selling price to outside customers on the intermediate market	$15
Variable costs per unit.	$8
Fixed costs per unit (based on capacity)	$5

The company has a Pump Division that could use this valve in the manufacture of one of its pumps. The Pump Division is currently purchasing 10,000 valves per year from an overseas supplier at a cost of $14 per valve.

Required:

1. Assume that the Valve Division has ample idle capacity to handle all of the Pump Division's needs. What is the acceptable range, if any, for the transfer price between the two divisions?
2. Assume that the Valve Division is selling all that it can produce to outside customers on the intermediate market. What is the acceptable range, if any, for the transfer price between the two divisions?
3. Assume again that the Valve Division is selling all that it can produce to outside customers on the intermediate market. Also assume that $2 in variable expenses can be avoided on transfers within the company, due to reduced selling costs. What is the acceptable range, if any, for the transfer price between the two divisions?
4. Assume the Pump Division needs 20,000 special high-pressure valves per year. The Valve Division's variable costs to manufacture and ship the special valve would be $10 per unit. To produce these special valves, the Valve Division would have to reduce its production and sales of regular valves from 100,000 units per year to 70,000 units per year. As far as the Valve Division is concerned, what is the lowest acceptable transfer price?

EXERCISE 11A–2 Transfer Pricing Situations [LO6]

In each of the cases below, assume that Division X has a product that can be sold either to outside customers or to Division Y of the same company for use in its production process. The managers of the divisions are evaluated based on their divisional profits:

	Case	
	A	**B**
Division X:		
Capacity in units	100,000	100,000
Number of units being sold to outside customers	100,000	80,000
Selling price per unit to outside customers	$50	$35
Variable costs per unit.	$30	$20
Fixed costs per unit (based on capacity)	$ 8	$ 6
Division Y:		
Number of units needed for production	20,000	20,000
Purchase price per unit now being paid to an outside supplier.	$47	$34

Required:

1. Refer to the data in Case A above. Assume that $2 per unit in variable selling costs can be avoided on intracompany sales. If the managers are free to negotiate and make decisions on their own, will a transfer take place? If so, within what range will the transfer price fall? Explain.

2. Refer to the data in Case B above. In this case there will be no reduction in variable selling costs on intracompany sales. If the managers are free to negotiate and make decisions on their own, will a transfer take place? If so, within what range will the transfer price fall? Explain.

EXERCISE 11A–3 Transfer Pricing from the Viewpoint of the Entire Company [LO6]

The Components Division manufactures components used in GPS devices. The components can be sold either to the Watch Division of the same company or to outside customers. Last year, the following activity was recorded in the Components Division:

Selling price per component.	$25
Variable cost per component.	$10
Number of components:	
Produced during the year	10,000
Sold to outside customers	8,000
Sold to Watch Division	2,000

Sales to the Watch Division were at the same price as sales to outside customers. The components purchased by the Watch Division were used in a sports watch manufactured by that division. The Watch Division incurred $30 in additional variable cost per watch and then sold them for $100 each.

Required:

1. Prepare income statements for last year for each division and the company as a whole.

2. Assume that the Components Division's manufacturing capacity is 10,000 components per year. Next year, the Watch Division wants to purchase 3,000 components from the Components Division, rather than only 2,000 components, as it did last year. Components of this specific type are not currently available from outside sources. From the standpoint of the company as a whole, should the Components Division sell the 1,000 additional components to the Watch Division, or should it continue to sell them to outside customers? Explain.

EXERCISE 11A–4 Using Quality Management Terms [LO7]

Listed below are terms relating to quality management.

Appraisal costs	Quality circles
Quality cost report	Prevention costs
Quality	External failure costs
Internal failure costs	Quality of conformance

Required:

Choose the terms that most appropriately complete the following statements. Terms can be used more than once, and a blank can hold more than one word.

1. When a product or service does not conform to customer expectations in terms of features or performance, it is viewed as being poor in _____.

2. A product or service will have a low _____ if it does not function the way its designers intended, or if it has many defects as a result of sloppy manufacture.

3. A company incurs _____ and _____ in an effort to keep poor quality of conformance from occurring.

4. A company incurs _____ and _____ because poor quality of conformance has occurred.

5. Of the four groups of costs associated with quality of conformance, _____ are generally the most damaging to a company.

6. Inspection, testing, and other costs incurred to keep defective products from being shipped to customers are known as _____.

7. _____ are incurred in an effort to eliminate poor product design, defective manufacturing practices, and the provision of substandard service.

8. The costs relating to defects, rejected products, and downtime caused by quality problems are known as _____.

9. When a product that is defective in some way is delivered to a customer, then _____ are incurred.

10. Over time, a company's total quality costs should decrease if it redistributes its quality costs by placing its greatest emphasis on _____ and _____.

11. In many companies, small groups of employees, known as _____, meet on a regular basis to discuss ways to improve the quality of output.

12. The way to ensure that management is aware of the costs associated with quality is to summarize such costs on a(n) _____.

EXERCISE 11A–5 Classification of Quality Costs [LO7]

A number of activities that are a part of a company's quality control system are listed below:

a. Quality improvement initiatives
b. Cost of spoilage
c. Inspecting raw materials
d. Lawsuit arising from defective products
e. Handling customer complaints
f. Reprogramming customer database software
g. Training finished goods quality inspectors
h. Repairs to quality testing equipment
i. Disposal of scrap material
j. Training instructors of quality programs
k. Lost sales arising from product quality concerns
l. Insurance on quality testing equipment
m. Training final product testers
n. Installing software for use in statistical process control
o. Shipping costs for product returns from customers
p. Overtime paid for a rush order caused by quality problems with raw materials

Required:
1. Classify the costs associated with each of these activities into one of the following categories: prevention cost, appraisal cost, internal failure cost, or external failure cost.
2. Which of the four types of costs in (1) above are incurred in an effort to keep poor quality of conformance from occurring? Which of the four types of costs in (1) above are incurred because poor quality of conformance has occurred?

EXERCISE 11A–6 Direct Method [LO8]

Okanagan College has provided the following data to be used in its service department cost allocations:

	Service Departments		Operating Departments	
	Administration	Physical Plant Services	Undergraduate Programs	Graduate Programs
Departmental costs before allocations	$1,500,000	$654,000	$32,650,000	$1,890,000
Student credit-hours			40,000	10,000
Space occupied in square metres........	2,500	750	25,000	5,000

Required:
Using the direct method, allocate the costs of the service departments to the two operating departments. Allocate the costs of the Administration Department based on student credit-hours and the costs of the Physical Plant Services Department based on space occupied.

EXERCISE 11A–7 Step-Down Method [LO9]

Books and Java, a book store and coffee shop, has provided the following data to be used in its service department cost allocations:

	Service Departments		Operating Departments	
	Administration	Cleaning	Book Store	Coffee Shop
Departmental costs before allocations ...	$300,000	$80,000	$4,640,000	$1,900,000
Employee-hours	640	320	6,200	1,480
Space occupied in square metres.......	500	100	4,000	1,000

Required:

Using the step-down method, allocate the costs of the service departments to the two operating departments. Allocate the costs of the Administration Department first on the basis of employee-hours and then on the costs of the Cleaning Services Department on the basis of space occupied.

EXERCISE 11A–8 Step-Down Method [LO9]

Arbon Company has three service departments and two operating departments. Selected data concerning the five departments are presented below:

	Service Departments			Operating Departments		
	Administrative	**Janitorial**	**Equipment Maintenance**	**Prep**	**Finishing**	**Total**
Costs	$84,000	$67,800	$36,000	$256,100	$498,600	$942,500
Number of employees	80	60	240	600	300	1,280
Square metres of space occupied	300	1,200	1,000	2,000	7,000	11,500
Machine-hours				10,000	30,000	40,000

The company allocates service department costs by the step-down method in the following order: Administrative (number of employees), Janitorial (space occupied), and Equipment Maintenance (machine-hours).

Required:

Using the step-down method, allocate the service department costs to the operating departments.

EXERCISE 11A–9 Direct Method [LO8]

Refer to the data for Arbon Company in Exercise 11A–8.

Required:

Assuming that the company uses the direct method rather than the step-down method to allocate service department costs, how much overhead cost would be assigned to each operating department?

PROBLEM 11A–10 Basic Transfer Pricing [LO6]

In Cases 1 to 3 below, assume that Division A has a product that can be sold either to Division B of the same company or to outside customers. The managers of both divisions are evaluated based on their own division's ROI. The managers are free to decide if they will participate in any internal transfers. All transfer prices are negotiated. Treat each case independently:

	Case			
	1	**2**	**3**	**4**
Division A:				
Capacity in units	50,000	300,000	100,000	200,000
Number of units now being sold to outside customers	50,000	300,000	75,000	200,000
Selling price per unit to outside customers . . .	$ 100	$ 40	$ 60	$ 45
Variable costs per unit	$ 63	$ 19	$ 35	$ 30
Fixed costs per unit (based on capacity)	$ 25	$ 8	$ 17	$ 6
Division B:				
Number of units needed annually	10,000	70,000	20,000	60,000
Purchase price now being paid to an outside supplier	$ 92	$ 39	$ 60*	—

*Before any purchase discount

Required:

1. Refer to Case 1. A study has indicated that Division A can avoid $5 per unit in variable costs on any sales to Division B. Will the managers agree to a transfer, and, if so, within what range will the transfer price be? Explain.

2.   Refer to Case 2. Assume that Division A can avoid $4 per unit in variable costs on any sales to Division B.
    a.   Would you expect any disagreement between the two divisional managers over what the transfer price should be? Explain.
    b.   Assume that Division A offers to sell 70,000 units to Division B for $38 per unit and that Division B refuses this price. What will be the loss in potential profits for the company as a whole?

3.   Refer to Case 3. Assume that Division B is now receiving a 5% price discount from the outside supplier.
    a.   Will the managers agree to a transfer? If so, within what range will the transfer price be?
    b.   Assume that Division B offers to purchase 20,000 units from Division A at $52 per unit. If Division A accepts this price, would you expect its ROI to increase, decrease, or remain unchanged? Why?

4.   Refer to Case 4. Assume that Division B wants Division A to provide it with 60,000 units of a *different* product from the one that Division A is now producing. The new product would require $25 per unit in variable costs and would require that Division A cut back production of its present product by 30,000 units annually. What is the lowest acceptable transfer price from Division A's perspective?

PROBLEM 11A–11   Transfer Pricing with an Outside Market [LO6]
Hrubec Products Inc. operates a Pulp Division that manufactures wood pulp for use in the production of various paper goods. Revenue and costs associated with a tonne of pulp follow:

Selling price		$70
Expenses:		
Variable...	$42	
Fixed (based on a capacity of 50,000 tonnes per year)........	18	60
Operating income		$10

Hrubec Products has just acquired a small company that manufactures paper cartons. Hrubec plans to treat its newly acquired Carton Division as a profit centre. The manager of the Carton Division is currently purchasing 5,000 tonnes of pulp per year from a supplier at a cost of $63 per tonne. Hrubec's president is anxious for the Carton Division to begin purchasing its pulp from the Pulp Division if the managers of the two divisions can negotiate an acceptable transfer price.

Required:
For (1) and (2) below, assume the Pulp Division can sell all of its pulp to outside customers for $70 per tonne.

1.   What is the Pulp Division's lowest acceptable transfer price? What is the Carton Division's highest acceptable transfer price? What is the range of acceptable transfer prices (if any) between the two divisions? Are the managers of the Carton and Pulp Divisions likely to voluntarily agree to a transfer price for 5,000 tonnes of pulp next year? Why or why not?

2.   If the Pulp Division meets the price that the Carton Division is currently paying to its supplier and sells 5,000 tonnes of pulp to the Carton Division each year, what will be the effect on the profits of the Pulp Division, the Carton Division, and the company as a whole?

For (3)–(6) below, assume that the Pulp Division is currently selling only 30,000 tonnes of pulp each year to outside customers at the stated $70 price.

3.   What is the Pulp Division's lowest acceptable transfer price? What is the Carton Division's highest acceptable transfer price? What is the range of acceptable transfer prices (if any) between the two divisions? Are the managers of the Carton and Pulp Divisions likely to voluntarily agree to a transfer price for 5,000 tonnes of pulp next year? Why or why not?

4.   Suppose the Carton Division's outside supplier drops its price to only $59 per tonne. Should the Pulp Division meet this price? Explain. If the Pulp Division does *not* meet the $59 price, what will be the effect on the profits of the company as a whole?

5.   Refer to (4) above. If the Pulp Division refuses to meet the $59 price, should the Carton Division be required to purchase from the Pulp Division at a higher price for the good of the company as a whole?

6.   Refer to (4) above. Assume that due to inflexible management policies, the Carton Division is required to purchase 5,000 tonnes of pulp each year from the Pulp Division at $70 per tonne. What will be the effect on the profits of the company as a whole?

PROBLEM 11A–12 Transfer Pricing Basics [LO6]

Nelcro Company's Electrical Division produces a high-quality transformer. Sales and cost data on the transformer follow:

Selling price per unit on the outside market	$40
Variable costs per unit.	$21
Fixed costs per unit (based on capacity)	$9
Capacity in units	60,000

Nelcro Company has a Motor Division that would like to begin purchasing this transformer from the Electrical Division. The Motor Division is currently purchasing 10,000 transformers each year from another company at a cost of $38 per transformer. Nelcro Company evaluates its division managers on the basis of divisional profits.

Required:
1. Assume that the Electrical Division is now selling only 50,000 transformers each year to outside customers.
   a. From the standpoint of the Electrical Division, what is the lowest acceptable transfer price for transformers sold to the Motor Division?
   b. From the standpoint of the Motor Division, what is the highest acceptable transfer price for transformers acquired from the Electrical Division?
   c. If left free to negotiate without interference, would you expect the division managers to voluntarily agree to the transfer of 10,000 transformers from the Electrical Division to the Motor Division? Why or why not?
   d. From the standpoint of the entire company, should a transfer take place? Why or why not?
2. Assume that the Electrical Division is now selling all of the transformers it can produce to outside customers.
   a. From the standpoint of the Electrical Division, what is the lowest acceptable transfer price for transformers sold to the Motor Division?
   b. From the standpoint of the Motor Division, what is the highest acceptable transfer price for transformers acquired from the Electrical Division?
   c. If left free to negotiate without interference, would you expect the division managers to voluntarily agree to the transfer of 10,000 transformers from the Electrical Division to the Motor Division? Why or why not?
   d. From the standpoint of the entire company, should a transfer take place? Why or why not?

PROBLEM 11A–13 Transfer Pricing and Inefficiency [LO6]

Airflow Inc. produces ceiling fans for home and industrial use. The parts for the different styles of fans are produced and sold by the Parts Division to the Assembly Division of Airflow Inc. The cost to the Parts Division is $12 per fan. The Assembly Division assembles the purchased parts into finished fans at a cost of $6 per unit and sells the assembled product to an outside wholesaler for $25 per unit. Due to the proprietary technology used to make the Airflow fans operate particularly quietly, the Parts Division is not allowed to sell the parts it produces to external customers. Both divisions have some idle capacity. The managers of both divisions are evaluated based on the profitability of their divisions.

Required:
1. What is the profit per unit of the two divisions if the transfer price is $15 per unit?
2. What is the profit per unit of the two divisions if the transfer price is $12 per unit?
3. If the Parts Division operates inefficiently, causing the cost of the parts to rise to $13 per unit, and that cost is used as the transfer price, what is the profit of the two divisions?
4. Take on the role of the Assembly Division manager and evaluate the answer in (3) above. Would you agree or disagree with the $13 transfer price? Why?
5. Which transfer price is best from the point of view of the company as a whole? Why?

PROBLEM 11A–14 Quality Cost Report [LO7]

Mercury Inc. produces cell phones at its plant in Texas. In recent years, the company's market share has been eroded by stiff competition from overseas. Price and product quality are the two key areas in which companies compete in this market.

A year ago, the company's cell phones had been ranked low in product quality in a consumer survey. Shocked by this result, Jorge Gomez, Mercury's president, initiated an intense effort to improve product quality. Gomez set up a task force to implement a formal quality improvement program. Included on this task force were representatives from the Engineering, Marketing, Customer Service, Production, and Accounting departments. The broad representation was needed because Gomez believed that this was a companywide program and that all employees should share the responsibility for its success.

After the first meeting of the task force, Holly Elsoe, manager of the Marketing Department, asked John Tran, production manager, what he thought of the proposed program. Tran replied, "I have reservations. Quality is too abstract to be attaching costs to it and then to be holding you and me responsible for cost improvements. I like to work with goals that I can see and count! I'm nervous about having my annual bonus based on a decrease in quality costs; there are too many variables that we have no control over."

Mercury's quality improvement program has now been in operation for one year. The company's quality related costs are shown below.

MERCURY INC. Quality Cost Report (in thousands)	Last Year	This Year
Prevention costs:		
Machine maintenance	$ 70	$ 120
Training suppliers	0	10
Quality circles	0	20
Total prevention cost	70	150
Appraisal costs:		
Incoming inspection	20	40
Final testing	80	90
Total appraisal cost	100	130
Internal failure costs:		
Rework	50	130
Scrap	40	70
Total internal failure cost	90	200
External failure costs:		
Warranty repairs	90	30
Customer returns	320	80
Total external failure cost	410	110
Total quality cost	$ 670	$ 590
Total production cost	$4,200	$4,800

As they were reviewing the report, Elsoe asked Tran what he now thought of the quality improvement program. Tran replied. "I'm relieved that the new quality improvement program hasn't hurt our bonuses, but the program has increased the workload in the Production Department. It is true that customer returns are way down, but the cell phones that were returned by customers to retail outlets were rarely sent back to us for rework."

Required:

1. Prepare a quality cost report for both this year and last year. Include two percentage columns for quality costs. Calculate each quality cost as a percentage of total production costs. Calculate each quality cost as a percentage of total quality costs. Carry percentage computations to one decimal place. By analyzing the report, determine if Mercury Inc.'s quality improvement program has been successful. List specific evidence to support your answer.

2. Do you expect the improvement program as it progresses to continue to increase the workload in the Production Department?

3. Jorge Gomez believed that the quality improvement program was essential and that Mercury Inc. could no longer afford to ignore the importance of product quality. Discuss how Mercury Inc. could measure the cost of *not* implementing the quality improvement program.

PROBLEM 11A–15 Step-Down Method [LO9]
Pleasant View Clinic has three service departments—Food Services, Administrative Services, and X-ray Services. The costs of these departments are allocated by the step-down method, using the allocation bases and in the order shown below:

Service Department	Costs Incurred	Base for Allocation
Food Services	Variable	Meals served
	Fixed	Peak-period needs
Administrative Services	Variable	Files processed
	Fixed	10% X-ray Services, 20% Outpatient Clinic, 30% OB Care, and 40% General Clinic
X-ray Services.	Variable	X-rays taken
	Fixed	Peak-period needs

Estimated cost and operating data for all departments in the clinic for the forthcoming month are presented below:

	Food Services	Admin. Services	X-ray Services	Outpatient Clinic	OB Care	General Clinic	Total
Variable costs	$ 73,150	$ 6,800	$38,100	$11,700	$ 14,850	$ 53,400	$198,000
Fixed costs.	48,000	33,040	59,520	26,958	99,738	344,744	612,000
Total costs	$121,150	$39,840	$97,620	$38,658	$114,588	$398,144	$810,000
Meals served		1,000	500		7,000	30,000	38,500
Percent of peak-period Food Services needs . . .		2%	1%		17%	80%	100%
Files processed			1,500	3,000	900	12,000	17,400
X-rays taken				1,200	350	8,400	9,950
Percent of peak-period X-ray Services needs.				13%	3%	84%	100%

All billing in the clinic is done through the Outpatient Clinic, OB Care, or General Clinic. The clinic's administrator wants the costs of the three service departments allocated to these three billing centres.

Required:
Prepare the cost allocation desired by the clinic administrator. Include under each billing centre the direct costs of the centre as well as the costs allocated from the service departments.

PROBLEM 11A–16 Direct and Step-Down Method [LO8, LO9]

At the end of last year, a group of architects and engineers in Squamish, B.C., decided to join efforts in providing one-stop design and engineering consulting services to the construction industry.

The founding partners decided to divide the operation into three parts: the Consulting Department, the Legal Department, and the Accounting Department.

The consulting department deals directly with the clients, providing two somewhat distinct services, design consulting (DC) and engineering consulting (EC). In its first full month of operations, the consulting department incurred costs of $40,000, with 40% attributed to design consultations and 60% to engineering consultations. Billings to clients amounted to $80,000 and $51,000 for design and engineering consultations, respectively. This department made use of the other two departments' services in preparing work for the external clients.

The accounting and legal departments also provided professional services for each other and for the two consulting departments on the basis of time according to the following schedule:

	Accounting Department	Legal Department	Consulting	
			DC	EC
Departmental costs before allocation	$20,000	$30,000	?	?
Proportion of Accounting Department services used.		20%	60%	20%
Proportion of Legal Department services used	50%		10%	40%

Having completed the first month's activity, the partners are ready to evaluate the performance of the group and of the individual areas.

Required:

Prepare an income statement for DC and EC using (1) the direct allocation method and (2) the step-down method. Recommend one of the two methods to the partners and justify your choice.

CASE 11A–17 Step-Down Method versus Direct Method [LO8, LO9]

"I can't understand what's happening here," said Mike Holt, president of Severson Products Inc. "We always seem to bid too high on jobs that require a lot of labour time in the Finishing Department, and we always seem to get every job we bid on that requires a lot of machine time in the Milling Department. Yet we don't seem to be making much money on those Milling Department jobs. I wonder if the problem is in our overhead rates."

Severson Products manufactures high-quality wood products to customers' specifications. Some jobs take a large amount of machine work in the Milling Department, and other jobs take a large amount of hand-finishing work in the Finishing Department. In addition to the Milling and Finishing Departments, the company has three service departments. The costs of these service departments are allocated to other departments *in the order listed below*. For each service department, use the most appropriate allocation base:

	Total Labour-Hours	Square Metres of Space Occupied	Number of Employees	Machine-Hours	Labour-Hours
Cafeteria	16,000	12,000	25		
Custodial Services.	9,000	3,000	40		
Machinery Maintenance	15,000	10,000	60		
Milling.	30,000	40,000	100	160,000	20,000
Finishing	100,000	20,000	300	40,000	70,000
	170,000	85,000	525	200,000	90,000

Budgeted overhead costs in each department for the current year are as follows:

Cafeteria	$ 320,000*
Custodial Services.	65,400
Machinery Maintenance	93,600
Milling.	416,000
Finishing	166,000
Total budgeted cost	$1,061,000

*This represents the amount of cost subsidized by the company

The company has always allocated service department costs to the operating departments (Milling and Finishing) using the direct method of allocation, because of its simplicity.

Required:

1. Allocate service department costs to operating departments by the step-down method. Then compute predetermined overhead rates in the operating departments for the current year, using machine-hours as the allocation base in the Milling Department and direct labour-hours as the allocation base in the Finishing Department.
2. Repeat (1) above, this time using the direct method. Again compute predetermined overhead rates in the Milling and Finishing Departments.
3. Assume that during the current year the company bids on a job that requires machine and labour time as follows:

	Machine-Hours	Direct Labour-Hours
Milling Department.	2,000	1,600
Finishing Department	800	13,000
Total hours	2,800	14,600

  a. Determine the amount of overhead that would be assigned to the job if the company used the overhead rates developed in (1) above. Then determine the amount of overhead that would be assigned to the job if the company used the overhead rates developed in (2) above.

  b. Explain to the president why the step-down method provides a better basis for computing predetermined overhead rates than the direct method.

ENDNOTES

1. Some companies classify business segments that are responsible mainly for generating revenue, such as an insurance sales office, as *revenue centres*. Other companies consider this to be just another type of profit centre, since costs of some kind (salaries, rent, utilities) are usually deducted from the revenues in the segment's income statement.

2. Recall that when Cumberland Beverages has 1,000 kegs of idle capacity, the minimum transfer price is calculated to be \$14 ($\$8 + [(\$20 - \$8) \times 1,000/2,000]$). Therefore, if idle capacity is greater than 1,000 kegs, then the transfer price will always be less than the outside purchase price of \$14 and the transfer should occur. For example, if idle capacity is 1,200 kegs, then the transfer price is \$12.80, calculated as ($\$8 + [(\$20 - \$8) \times 800/2,000]$).

SECTION 4

SHORT-TERM AND LONG-TERM DECISIONS

Chapters 12 and 13

Two time frames are commonly used to characterize the types of decision analysis covered in this final section. Chapter 12 presents a framework for making short-term decisions where the analysis involves examining those revenues and costs that differ across the alternatives under consideration. Several commonly encountered decision situations are presented, along with the approach used to identify and use relevant costs and benefits. However, the situations examined in this chapter do not involve long-term capital expenditures for items such as plant and equipment, so the time value of money (cost of interest) does not need to be incorporated into the analysis.

Long-term decision analysis typically involves significant capital expenditures and requires explicit consideration of the time value of money. The approach presented in Chapter 13 is commonly described as *capital budgeting*. The concept of using only relevant costs and benefits in the analysis still holds in this chapter. The chapter also introduces corporate income taxes to the analysis because of their effects on cash flows.

RELEVANT COSTS FOR DECISION MAKING

■ ENHANCING PRODUCT OFFERINGS TO STAY COMPETITIVE AT WESTJET

Skycolors / Shutterstock

WestJet, founded in 1996, is Canada's leading "high-value, low-fare" airline. Stiff competition in the Canadian airline industry has forced WestJet to re-think its product offerings. In 2018 WestJet introduced Swoop, an ultra-low-cost airline focused on flights within Canada and from Canada to popular warm-weather destinations in the United States, Mexico, and the Caribbean. The strategy seems to be working, as Swoop reported a load factor of 95% compared to WestJet's overall load factor of 79.2% at the end of 2018. The popularity of the new airline has continued to grow as Swoop welcomed its two millionth passenger at the beginning of 2020.

Which revenues and costs are relevant when evaluating the financial effects of adding or discontinuing a product line? This and other related topics are considered in this chapter.

Decision making is a critical aspect of managing an organization. Managers must constantly decide which products or services to offer, which production methods to use, whether to make or buy component parts, what prices to charge, whether to accept special orders at special prices, how to allocate limited resources, and so on. In each case, the decision should lead to outcomes that contribute to achieving the performance goals identified as part of the organization's strategic objectives (e.g., grow revenues, reduce costs, improve return on investment). However, decision making is a complex process. Numerous alternatives may exist for each decision situation, and large amounts of data must be analyzed, only some of which are relevant.

How can managers cope with these complexities in an effort to consistently make good decisions? The key is to identify and compare *only* the relevant costs and benefits for each alternative. A **relevant cost** is a cost that differs among the alternatives under consideration *and* that will be incurred in the future (i.e., the cost has not already been incurred). A key challenge for managers, and fundamental to good decision making, is differentiating between relevant and irrelevant costs. This is critical because consideration of irrelevant costs wastes managers' time and effort and can lead to the wrong decisions. Further complicating matters is the fact that the relevance of specific costs and benefits depends on the decision situation. For example, a product supervisor's salary is typically irrelevant in deciding whether or not to accept a special order from a customer but can be relevant when deciding whether to keep or drop that product line. The purpose of this chapter is to provide a framework for distinguishing between relevant and irrelevant costs by illustrating their use in a wide range of decision-making situations.

We begin the chapter by developing a general framework for identifying relevant costs and benefits. We then apply this framework to a variety of non-recurring situations to illustrate how the relevance of a cost or benefit depends on the type of decision being made. Next we turn our attention to analyzing situations where managers must decide how to allocate a limited resource such as labour-hours. Finally, the relationship between relevant costs and pricing issues is further examined in the appendix.

Two aspects of the decision situations and the related analysis presented in this chapter are important to emphasize. First, none of the situations involve capital expenditures (e.g., replacing production equipment), where the time value of money can be an important factor in the analysis. This type of analysis, termed *capital budgeting*, is covered in Chapter 13. Second, the key criterion used in the various decision situations presented in this chapter is the maximization of operating income. However, in practice, managers may also consider qualitative factors when making decisions. For example, when deciding whether to keep or drop a product or segment, the effect on employee morale and the impact on the company's reputation with its customers may be important but very difficult or costly to quantify. The extent to which qualitative factors influence a decision will vary from situation to situation, but these factors are often taken into account.

Relevant cost
A cost that differs among the alternatives in a particular decision and will be incurred in the future. In managerial accounting, this term is synonymous with **avoidable cost** and **differential cost**.

LEARNING OBJECTIVE ❶
Distinguish between relevant and irrelevant costs in decision making.

■ COST CONCEPTS FOR DECISION MAKING

Four cost terms discussed in Chapter 2 are particularly applicable to this chapter. These terms are *differential costs*, *incremental costs*, *opportunity costs*, and *sunk costs*. You may find it helpful to turn back to Chapter 2 and review the concepts before reading on.

Identifying Relevant Costs and Benefits

Because it is fundamental to the proper analysis of the various decision situations covered in this chapter, we begin by identifying the nature of relevant costs and benefits. Only those costs and benefits that differ in total among alternatives and that will be incurred in the future are relevant in a decision. If a cost will be the same regardless of the alternative selected, then it can be ignored. For example, if you are trying to decide whether to go to a movie or to download a movie for the evening, the lease payments on your car are irrelevant. Whether you go to a movie or stay home, the lease payments will be exactly the same and are therefore irrelevant in the decision. On the other hand, the cost of the movie ticket and the cost of downloading the movie are relevant in the decision because they are *avoidable costs*.

An **avoidable cost** is a cost that can be eliminated in whole or in part by choosing one alternative over another. By choosing the alternative of going to the movie, the cost of downloading a movie can be avoided. By choosing the alternative of downloading a movie, the cost of the movie ticket can be avoided. Therefore, the cost of the movie ticket and the cost of downloading a movie are both avoidable costs. On the other hand, the lease payments on the car are not an avoidable cost because you would continue to lease your car under either alternative. Avoidable costs are relevant costs. Unavoidable costs are irrelevant costs.

Two broad categories of costs are never relevant in decisions. These irrelevant costs are

1. sunk costs (e.g., a previously owned computer used to download the movie), and
2. future costs that do not differ between the alternatives (e.g., car lease payments when making a "go to a movie" versus "download a movie" decision).

As we learned in Chapter 2, a *sunk cost* is a cost that has already been incurred and that cannot be avoided, regardless of what a manager decides to do. Sunk costs do not change, regardless of the alternatives being considered, and they are therefore always irrelevant and should be ignored. Similarly, future costs that are the same under each alternative being considered are also irrelevant since they will not affect the decision. The cost of the car lease next month is a future cost but will be the same whether you go to the movie or download a movie. On the other hand, future costs that do differ between alternatives *are* relevant. For example, when deciding whether to go to a movie or download a movie, the cost of buying a movie ticket and the cost of downloading a movie have not yet been incurred. These are future costs that differ between alternatives when the decision is being made and therefore are relevant.

Along with sunk cost, the term *differential cost* was introduced in Chapter 2. In managerial accounting, the terms *avoidable cost*, *differential cost*, *incremental cost*, and *relevant cost* are often used interchangeably. To identify the costs and benefits that are relevant in a particular decision situation, these steps can be followed:

1. Eliminate costs and benefits that do not differ between alternatives. These irrelevant costs consist of (a) sunk costs and (b) future costs and benefits that do not differ between alternatives.
2. Use the remaining costs and benefits that do differ between alternatives in making the decision. The costs that remain are the differential, or avoidable, costs.

Different Costs for Different Purposes

It is important to recognize that costs that are relevant in one decision situation are not necessarily relevant in another. Simply put, this means that *the manager needs different costs for different purposes*. For one purpose, a particular group of costs may be relevant; for another purpose, an entirely different group of costs may be relevant. Thus, in *each* decision situation the manager must examine the data at hand and isolate the relevant costs. Otherwise, the manager runs the risk of being misled by irrelevant data.

The concept of "different costs for different purposes" is basic to managerial accounting; we will see its application frequently in the remainder of this chapter.

An Example of Identifying Relevant Costs and Benefits

Cynthia is currently a student in an MBA program in Halifax and would like to visit a friend in Moncton over the weekend. She is trying to decide whether to drive or take the train.

Avoidable cost
Any cost that can be eliminated (in whole or in part) by choosing one alternative over another in a decision-making situation. In managerial accounting, this term is synonymous with **relevant cost** and **differential cost**.

Because she is on a tight budget, she wants to carefully consider the costs of the two alternatives. If one alternative is far less expensive than the other, that may determine her choice. By car, the distance between her apartment in Halifax and her friend's apartment in Moncton is 265 kilometres. Cynthia has compiled a list of items to consider in the table below:

Automobile Costs

	Item	Annual Cost of Fixed Items	Cost per Kilometre (based on 16,000 kilometres per year)
(a)	Annual straight-line depreciation on car [($24,000 original cost − $10,000 estimated resale value in 5 years)/5 years]	$2,800	$0.175
(b)	Cost of gasoline ($1.20 per litre ÷ 10 kilometres per litre)		0.120
(c)	Annual cost of auto insurance and licence	2,000	0.125
(d)	Maintenance and repairs		0.050
(e)	Parking fees at university ($45 per month × 8 months)	360	0.023
(f)	Tires ($600 to replace all 4 tires every 50,000 kilometres)		0.012
(g)	Total average cost per kilometre		$0.505

Additional Data

	Item	
(h)	Cost of round-trip VIA ticket	$85
(i)	Benefit of relaxing and being able to study during the train ride rather than having to drive	?
(j)	Cost of putting the cat in a kennel while gone	$40
(k)	Benefit of having a car available in Moncton	?
(l)	Hassle of parking the car in Moncton	?
(m)	Cost of parking the car in Moncton	$25 per day

Which costs and benefits are relevant in this decision? Remember, only those costs and benefits that differ between alternatives are relevant. Everything else is irrelevant and can be ignored. Starting at the top of the list, we consider the relevance of each item:

- Item (a): The original cost of the car is a sunk cost. This cost has already been incurred and therefore can never differ between alternatives. Consequently, it is irrelevant and can be ignored. The same is true of the accounting depreciation of $2,800 per year, which simply spreads the sunk cost across the useful life of the asset.
- Item (b): The cost of gasoline consumed by driving to Moncton is clearly a relevant cost in this decision. If Cynthia takes the train, this cost will not be incurred. Hence, the cost differs between alternatives and is therefore relevant.
- Item (c): The annual cost of auto insurance and licence is not relevant. Whether Cynthia takes the train or drives on this particular trip, her annual auto insurance premium and her auto licence fee will remain the same. If Cynthia has an accident while driving to Moncton and back, this might affect her insurance premium when the policy is renewed. If the expected cost of the increase in the insurance premium could be estimated, it would be a relevant cost of this particular trip, but the normal amount of the insurance premium is not relevant in any case.

- Item (*d*): The cost of maintenance and repairs is relevant. While maintenance and repair costs have a large random component, over the long run they are typically proportional to the amount the car is driven. Thus, the average cost of $0.05 per kilometre is a reasonable estimate to use.
- Item (*e*): The monthly fee that Cynthia pays to park at her university during the academic year is not relevant in the decision of how to get to Moncton. Regardless of which alternative she selects—driving or taking the train—she will still need to pay for parking at school.
- Item (*f*): The cost of replacing all four tires ($600) every 50,000 kilometres is relevant. The more often Cynthia uses her car, the sooner she will have to replace the tires. Therefore, the $0.012 per kilometre for tires is appropriate to use in deciding whether to drive or take the train.
- Item (*g*): Some elements of the total average cost of $0.505 per kilometre are relevant, but some are not relevant. Since it contains some irrelevant costs, it would be incorrect to estimate the cost of driving to Moncton and back by simply multiplying the $0.505 by 530 kilometres (265 kilometres each way × 2). This erroneous approach would yield a cost of driving of $267.65. Unfortunately, such mistakes are often made in both personal life and in business. Since the total cost is stated on a per kilometre basis, people are easily misled. Often people think that if the cost is stated as $0.505 per kilometre, the cost of driving 100 kilometres is $50.50. But it is not. Many of the costs included in the $0.505 cost per kilometre are sunk and/or fixed and will not increase if the car is driven another 100 kilometres. The $0.505 is an average cost, not an incremental cost. Study such unitized costs carefully (i.e., costs stated in terms of a dollar amount per unit, per kilometre, per direct labour-hour, per machine-hour, and so on)—they are often misleading.
- Item (*h*): The $85 cost of a round-trip ticket on VIA is clearly relevant in this decision. If Cynthia drives, she will not have to buy the ticket.
- Item (*i*): Although it is difficult to put a dollar value on relaxing and being able to study while on the train, this item is relevant to the decision. It is relevant because it is a benefit that is available only if she takes the train.
- Item (*j*): The cost of putting Cynthia's cat in the kennel while she is gone is clearly irrelevant to this decision. Whether she takes the train or drives to Moncton she will still need to put her cat in a kennel.
- Items (*k*) and (*l*): Like item (*i*), they are relevant to the decision even if it is difficult to measure their dollar impacts.
- Item (*m*): The cost of parking in Moncton is relevant to the decision since it will be incurred only if Cynthia takes her car.

Bringing together all of the relevant data, Cynthia would estimate the relative costs of driving and taking the train as follows:

Relevant financial cost of driving to Moncton:	
Gasoline (530 kilometres at $0.12 per km)	$ 63.60
Maintenance and repairs (530 kilometres @ $0.05 per km)	26.50
Tires (530 kilometres @ $0.012 per km)	6.36
Cost of parking the car in Moncton (2 days @ $25 per day)	50.00
Total	$146.46
Relevant financial cost of taking the train to Moncton:	
Cost of round-trip VIA ticket from Halifax to Moncton	$ 85.00

What should Cynthia do? From a purely financial standpoint, it would be cheaper by $61.46 ($146.46 − $85.00) to take the train. Cynthia has to decide whether the benefit of having the car available in Moncton justifies the higher cost of driving.

In this example, we focused on identifying the relevant costs and benefits—everything else was ignored. In the next example, we will begin the analysis by including all of the costs and benefits—relevant or not. We will see that if we are very careful, we will still get the correct answer because the irrelevant costs and benefits will cancel out when we compare the alternatives.

Reconciling the Total and Differential Approaches

OfficeMate Company is considering a new labour-saving machine that rents for $3,000 per year. The machine will be used in the production of the company's best-selling heavy-duty stapler. Data concerning the company's annual sales and costs of producing these staplers with and without the new machine are shown in the following table:

	Current Situation	Situation with the New Machine
Units produced and sold	5,000	5,000
Selling price per unit	$ 40	$ 40
Direct materials cost per unit	14	14
Direct labour cost per unit	8	5
Variable overhead cost per unit	2	2
Fixed costs, other	62,000	62,000
Fixed costs, new machine	—	3,000

Given the annual sales and the price and cost data in this table, the operating income for the product under the two alternatives can be computed as shown in Exhibit 12–1.

Note that the operating income is higher by $12,000 with the new machine, so it is the better alternative. Note also that the $12,000 advantage for the new machine can be obtained in two different ways. It is the difference between the $30,000 operating income with the new machine and the $18,000 operating income for the current situation. It is also the sum of

EXHIBIT 12–1
Total and Differential Costs

	Current Situation	Situation with New Machine	Differential Costs and Benefits
Sales (5,000 units @ $40 per unit)	$200,000	$200,000	$ 0
Less variable expenses:			
Direct materials (5,000 units @ $14 per unit)	70,000	70,000	0
Direct labour (5,000 units @ $8 and $5 per unit)	40,000	25,000	15,000
Variable overhead (5,000 units @ $2 per unit)	10,000	10,000	0
Total variable expenses	120,000	105,000	
Contribution margin	80,000	95,000	
Less fixed expenses:			
Other	62,000	62,000	0
Rent of new machine	0	3,000	(3,000)
Total fixed expenses	62,000	65,000	
Operating income	$ 18,000	$ 30,000	$12,000

the differential costs and benefits as shown in the last column of Exhibit 12–1. A positive number in the Differential Costs and Benefits column indicates that the difference between the alternatives favours the new machine; a negative number indicates that the difference favours the current situation. A zero in that column simply means that the total amount for the item is exactly the same for both alternatives. So, since the difference in the operating incomes equals the sum of the differences for the individual items, any cost or benefit that is the same for both alternatives will have no impact on which alternative is preferred. This is why we stated earlier that costs and benefits that do not differ between alternatives are irrelevant and can be ignored. If we properly account for them, they will cancel out when we compare the alternatives.

We could have arrived at the same solution more quickly by ignoring the irrelevant costs and benefits:

- The selling price per unit and the number of units sold do not differ between the alternatives. Therefore, the total sales revenues are exactly the same for the two alternatives, as shown in Exhibit 12–1. Since the sales revenues are exactly the same, they have no effect on the difference in operating income between the two alternatives. That is shown in the last column in Exhibit 12–1, which indicates a $0 differential benefit.
- The direct materials cost per unit, the variable overhead cost per unit, and the number of units produced and sold do not differ between the alternatives. Consequently, the direct materials cost and the variable overhead cost will be the same for the two alternatives and can be ignored.
- The "other" fixed expenses do not differ between the alternatives, so they can be ignored as well.

Indeed, the only costs that do differ between the alternatives are direct labour costs and the fixed rental cost of the new machine. Hence, these are the only relevant costs. The two alternatives can be compared based on just these relevant costs:

Net advantage to renting the new machine:	
Decrease in direct labour costs (5,000 units at a cost savings of $3 per unit)	$15,000
Increase in fixed expenses (rent).	(3,000)
Net annual cost savings from renting the new machine	$12,000

If we focus on just the relevant costs and benefits, therefore, we get exactly the same answer that we got when we listed all of the costs and benefits—including those that do not differ between the alternatives and hence are irrelevant. We get the same answer because the only costs and benefits that matter in the final comparison of the operating incomes are those that differ between the two alternatives and therefore are not zero in the last column of Exhibit 12–1. Those two relevant costs are both listed in the above analysis, showing the net advantage to renting the new machine.

Why Isolate Relevant Costs?

In the preceding example, we used two different approaches to analyze the alternatives. First, we considered only the relevant costs. Second, we considered all costs, both those that were relevant and those that were not. We obtained the same answer under both approaches. It would be natural to ask, "Why bother isolating relevant costs when total costs will do the job just as well?" Isolating relevant costs is desirable for at least two reasons.

First, only rarely will enough information be available to prepare a detailed income statement for both alternatives as we have done in the preceding examples. Assume, for example, that you are called on to make a decision relating to a *single product* of a multi-departmental, multi-product firm. Under these circumstances, it would be virtually impossible to prepare an income statement of any type. You would have to rely on your ability to recognize which costs are relevant and which are not in order to assemble the data necessary to make a decision.

Second, combining irrelevant costs with relevant costs may cause confusion and distract attention from the matters that are really critical. Furthermore, the danger always exists that an irrelevant piece of data may be used improperly, resulting in an incorrect decision. Indeed, research shows that managers will often attempt to use *all* information provided, relevant and irrelevant, when making a decision.[1] The best approach is to discard irrelevant data and base the decision entirely on the relevant data.

INSTANT QUIZ 12–1

"All future costs are relevant in decision making." Do you agree? Why or why not?

Relevant cost analysis, combined with the contribution approach to the income statement, provides a powerful tool for making decisions. We will investigate various uses of this tool in the remaining sections of this chapter.

<table>
<tr><td>**LEARNING OBJECTIVE**   **2**
Prepare analyses for various decision situations.</td></tr>
</table>

■ ANALYSIS OF VARIOUS DECISION SITUATIONS

Periodically, managers are faced with making non-routine or special decisions. Should a product line or segment be kept or dropped? Should a product component be made internally or purchased from an external supplier (outsourced)? Should special orders be accepted or rejected? Should a product be sold as is or processed further? While on the surface these may appear to be very different decision situations, the approach to the analysis is similar in each case. For each situation, the relevant costs and benefits must be quantified and the alternative with the most favourable impact on operating income selected. In some situations, the analysis will consist only of a comparison of relevant costs (make versus buy), while in others, both relevant benefits and relevant costs will be involved (keep or drop a product). As will be illustrated in the examples of each decision situation that follows, the challenge for managers is identifying and quantifying the relevant costs and benefits.

Adding and Dropping Product Lines and Other Segments

Decisions relating to whether existing product lines or other segments of a company should be dropped and new ones added are among the most difficult that a manager has to make. In such decisions, many qualitative and quantitative factors must be considered. Ultimately, however, any final decision to drop an old segment or to add a new one will hinge primarily on the impact the decision will have on operating income. To assess this impact, it is necessary to prepare a careful analysis of the costs involved.

Consider the three major product lines of AFM Electronics—TVs, tablets, and digital cameras. Sales and cost information for the preceding month for each separate product line and for the company in total are given in Exhibit 12–2.

What can be done to improve the company's overall performance? One product line—digital cameras—shows an operating loss for the month. Perhaps dropping this line would cause profits in the company as a whole to improve. In deciding whether the line should be dropped, management should employ the reasoning that follows.

If the digital camera line is dropped, then the company will lose $16,000 per month in contribution margin. By dropping the line, however, it may be possible to avoid some fixed costs by, for example, laying off certain employees or reducing advertising costs. If by dropping the digital camera line the company is able to avoid more in fixed costs than it

EXHIBIT 12–2
AFM Electronics
Product Lines

| | Total | Product Line | | |
		TVs	Tablets	Digital Cameras
Sales..........................	$340,000	$187,500	$112,500	$40,000
Less variable expenses	136,500	75,000	37,500	24,000
Contribution margin	203,500	112,500	75,000	16,000
Less fixed expenses:				
Salaries........................	69,400	44,250	18,750	6,400
Advertising....................	17,950	1,500	11,250	5,200
Utilities......................	2,300	750	750	800
Depreciation—fixtures............	6,100	1,500	3,000	1,600
Rent	27,200	15,000	9,000	3,200
Insurance	4,150	3,000	750	400
Selling and administrative	40,800	22,500	13,500	4,800
Total fixed expenses	167,900	88,500	57,000	22,400
Operating income (loss)	$ 35,600	$ 24,000	$ 18,000	$(6,400)

loses in contribution margin, then it will be better off if the line is eliminated, because overall operating income should improve. On the other hand, if the company is not able to avoid as much in fixed costs as it loses in contribution margin, then the digital camera line should be retained. In short, the manager should ask, "What costs can I avoid if I drop this product line?"

As we have seen from our earlier discussion, not all costs are avoidable. For example, some of the costs associated with a product line may be sunk costs. Other costs may be allocated common costs that will not differ in total regardless of whether the product line is dropped or retained. As discussed in Chapter 7, an activity-based costing analysis may be used to help identify the relevant costs.

To show how the manager should proceed in a product-line analysis, suppose that the management of AFM Electronics has analyzed the costs being charged to the three product lines and has determined the following:

1. The salaries expense represents salaries paid to employees working directly in each product-line area. All of the employees working in digital camera–related activities will be laid off if the line is dropped.
2. The advertising expense represents direct advertising of each product line and is avoidable if the line is dropped.
3. The utilities expense represents utilities costs for the entire company. The amount charged to each product line is an allocation based on space occupied and is not avoidable if the product line is dropped.
4. The depreciation expense represents depreciation on fixtures used for display of the various product lines. Although the fixtures are nearly new, they are custom built and will have little resale value if the digital camera line is dropped.
5. The rent expense represents rent on the entire building housing the company; it is allocated to the product lines on the basis of sales dollars. The monthly rent of $27,200 is fixed under a long-term lease agreement.
6. The insurance expense represents insurance carried on inventories within each of the three product-line areas.
7. The selling and administrative expense represents the costs of accounting, purchasing, and general management, which are allocated to the product lines on the basis of sales dollars. Total administrative costs will not change if the digital camera line is dropped.

With this information, management can identify costs that can and cannot be avoided if the product line is dropped:

	Total Cost	Not Avoidable*	Avoidable
Salaries....................................	$ 6,400		$ 6,400
Advertising..............................	5,200		5,200
Utilities...................................	800	$ 800	
Depreciation—fixtures.....................	1,600	1,600	
Rent	3,200	3,200	
Insurance	400		400
Selling and administrative	4,800	4,800	
Total fixed expenses...................	$22,400	$10,400	$12,000

*These costs represent either (1) sunk costs or (2) future costs that will not change if the digital camera line is retained or discontinued.

To determine how dropping the line will affect the overall profits of the company, we can compare the contribution margin that will be lost to the costs that can be avoided if the line is dropped:

Contribution margin lost if the digital camera line is discontinued (see Exhibit 12–2)	$(16,000)
Less fixed costs that can be avoided if the digital camera line is discontinued (see above)	12,000
Decrease in overall company operating income	$ (4,000)

In this case, the fixed costs that can be avoided by dropping the product line are less than the contribution margin that will be lost. Therefore, based on the data given, the digital camera line should not be discontinued unless a more profitable use can be found for the floor and counter space that it is occupying.

A Comparative Format

Some managers prefer to approach decisions of this type by preparing comparative income statements showing the effects on the company as a whole of either keeping or dropping the product line in question. A comparative analysis of this type for AFM Electronics is shown in Exhibit 12–3.

As shown by column 3 in the exhibit, overall company operating income will decrease by $4,000 each period if the digital camera line is dropped. This is the same answer, of course, as we obtained in our earlier analysis.

Beware of Allocated Fixed Costs

Our conclusion that the digital camera line should not be dropped seems to conflict with the data shown earlier in Exhibit 12–2. Recall from the exhibit that the digital camera line is showing a loss rather than a profit. Why keep a line that is showing a loss? The explanation for this apparent inconsistency lies at least in part with the common fixed costs that are being allocated to the product lines. As we observed in Chapter 11, one of the great dangers in allocating common fixed costs is that such allocations can make a product line (or other segment of a business) *look* less profitable than it really is. By allocating the common fixed costs

EXHIBIT 12–3
A Comparative
Format for Product-
Line Analysis

	Keep Digital Cameras	Drop Digital Cameras	Difference: Operating Income Increase or (Decrease)
Sales....................................	$40,000	$ 0	$(40,000)
Less variable expenses.....................	24,000	0	24,000
Contribution margin......................	16,000	0	(16,000)
Less fixed expenses:			
Salaries.............................	6,400	0	6,400
Advertising..........................	5,200	0	5,200
Utilities..............................	800	800	0
Depreciation—fixtures..................	1,600	1,600	0
Rent	3,200	3,200	0
Insurance	400	0	400
Selling and administrative	4,800	4,800	0
Total fixed expenses	22,400	10,400	12,000
Operating income (loss)	$(6,400)	$(10,400)	$ (4,000)

among all product lines, the digital camera line has been made to *look* as if it were unprofitable, whereas in fact dropping the line would result in a decrease in overall company operating income. This point can be seen clearly if we recast the data in Exhibit 12–2 by eliminating the allocation of the common fixed costs. This recasting of data—using the segmented approach from Chapter 11—is shown in Exhibit 12–4.

EXHIBIT 12–4
AFM Electronics
Product Lines—
Recast in
Contribution
Format (from
Exhibit 12-2)

		Product Line		
	Total	TVs	Tablets	Digital Cameras
Sales.............................	$340,000	$187,500	$112,500	$40,000
Less variable expenses	136,500	75,000	37,500	24,000
Contribution margin.................	203,500	112,500	75,000	16,000
Less traceable fixed expenses:				
Salaries........................	69,400	44,250	18,750	6,400
Advertising.....................	17,950	1,500	11,250	5,200
Depreciation—fixtures............	6,100	1,500	3,000	1,600
Insurance	4,150	3,000	750	400
Total fixed expenses............	97,600	50,250	33,750	13,600
Product-line segment margin..........	105,900	$ 62,250	$ 41,250	$ 2,400*
Less common fixed expenses:				
Utilities........................	2,300			
Rent	27,200			
Selling and administrative	40,800			
Total	70,300			
Operating income	$ 35,600			

*If the digital camera line is dropped, this $2,400 in segment margin will be lost to the company. In addition, we have seen that the $1,600 depreciation on the fixtures is a sunk cost that cannot be avoided. The sum of these two figures ($2,400 + $1,600 = $4,000) is the decrease in the company's overall profits if the digital camera line is discontinued.

Exhibit 12–4 gives us a much different perspective of the profitability of the digital camera line compared to Exhibit 12–2. As shown in Exhibit 12–4, the digital camera line is covering all of its own traceable fixed costs and is generating a $2,400 segment margin toward covering the common fixed costs of the company. Unless another product line can be found that will generate a greater segment margin than this, the company would be better off keeping the digital camera line. By keeping the line, the company's overall operating income will be higher than if the product line is dropped. An alternative way of formulating the analysis is to start with the digital camera net loss of $(6,400) from Exhibit 12–2 and add back the non-avoidable (irrelevant) expenses of $10,400 to arrive at the relevant benefit (segment margin) of $4,000 that would be forgone if the product line were discontinued.

Additionally, we should note that managers may choose to retain an unprofitable product line if the line is necessary to the sale of other products or if it serves as a "magnet" to attract customers. Bread, for example, is not an especially profitable line in food stores, but customers expect it to be available, and many would undoubtedly shift their buying elsewhere if a particular store decided to stop carrying bread. Accordingly, to the extent that dropping a product line or segment results in decreases (or increases) to sales of other products or segments, the related impact on contribution margin should be included in the keep versus drop analysis.

LEARNING AID

Keep or Drop a Product/Segment

Relevant Costs and Benefits
- Contribution margin (CM) lost if dropped
- Fixed costs avoided if dropped
- CM lost/gained on other products/segments

Irrelevant Costs
- Allocated common costs
- Sunk costs

Decision Rule:

Keep if   CM lost (all products/segments) > Fixed costs avoided + CM gained (other products/segments).

Drop if   CM lost (all products/segments) < Fixed costs avoided + CM gained (other products/segments).

INSTANT QUIZ 12–2

Able Supply Co. is considering dropping a high-pressure water line from its product mix based on the following information:

Revenue from high-pressure water line.........	$100,000
Less: Direct costs	(83,000)
Indirect costs.........................	(22,000)
Loss from high-pressure water line.............	$ (5,000)

What factors should Able Supply consider before deciding to drop this product line?

The Make or Buy Decision

Many steps may be involved in getting a finished product into the hands of a consumer. First, raw materials may have to be obtained through mining, drilling, growing crops, raising animals, and so forth. Second, these raw materials may have to be processed to remove impurities and to extract the desirable and usable materials. Third, the usable materials may have to undergo some preliminary conversion so as to be usable in final products. For example, cotton must be made into thread and textiles before being made into clothing. Fourth, the actual manufacturing of the finished product must take place. And, finally, the finished product must be distributed to the ultimate consumer. Each of these steps is part of the value chain discussed in Chapter 1.

Separate companies may carry out each step in the value chain, or a single company may carry out several of the steps. When a single company is involved in more than one of these steps in the value chain, it is following a policy of **vertical integration**. Vertical integration is very common. Some firms control *all* of the activities in the value chain, from producing basic raw materials right up to the manufacture and final distribution of finished goods. Other firms integrate on a smaller scale by purchasing many of the parts and materials that go into their finished products.

A decision to produce internally, rather than to buy externally from a supplier, is called a **make or buy decision**. Indeed, any decision relating to vertical integration is a make or buy decision, since the company is deciding whether to meet its own needs internally or to buy externally.

Vertical integration
The involvement by a single company in more than one of the steps of the value chain, from production of basic raw materials to the manufacture and distribution of a finished product.

Make or buy decision
A decision as to whether an item should be produced internally or purchased from an outside supplier.

Strategic Aspects of the Make or Buy Decision

Integration provides certain advantages. An integrated firm is less dependent on its suppliers and may be able to ensure a smoother flow of parts and materials for production than a non-integrated firm. For example, a strike against a major parts supplier can interrupt the operations of a non-integrated firm for many months, whereas an integrated firm that is producing its own parts might be able to continue operations. Also, many firms feel that they can control quality better by producing their own parts and materials, rather than by relying on the quality control standards of outside suppliers.

The positive aspects of integration are counterbalanced by some advantages of using external suppliers. By pooling demand from a number of firms, a supplier may be able to realize economies of scale in research and development and in manufacturing. These economies of scale can result in higher quality and lower unit costs than would be possible if the firm were to attempt to make the parts on its own. However, companies must be careful to retain control over activities that are essential to maintaining their competitive position.

An Example of Make or Buy

To illustrate a make or buy decision, let's consider OSN Cycles. The company is now producing the heavy-duty gear shifters used in its most popular line of mountain bikes. The company's accounting department reports the following costs of producing the shifter internally:

	Per Unit	8,000 Units
Direct materials	$ 6	$ 48,000
Direct labour	4	32,000
Variable overhead	1	8,000
Supervisor's salary	3	24,000
Depreciation of special equipment	2	16,000
Allocated general overhead	5	40,000
Total cost	$21	$168,000

An outside supplier has offered to sell OSN Cycles 8,000 shifters per year at a price of only $19 each. Should the company stop producing the shifters internally and start purchasing them from the outside supplier? To approach the decision from a financial point of view, the manager should again focus on the differential costs. As we have seen, the differential costs can be obtained by eliminating those costs that are not avoidable—that is, by eliminating (1) the sunk costs and (2) the future costs that will continue regardless of whether the shifters are produced internally or purchased outside. The costs that remain after making these eliminations are the costs that are avoidable to the company by purchasing outside. If these avoidable costs are less than the outside purchase price, then the company should continue to manufacture its own shifters and reject the outside supplier's offer. That is, the company should purchase outside only if the outside purchase price is less than the costs that can be avoided internally as a result of stopping production of the shifters.

Looking at the data above, note first that depreciation of special equipment is listed as one of the costs of producing the shifters internally. Since the equipment has already been purchased, this depreciation is a sunk cost and is therefore irrelevant. If the equipment could be sold, its salvage value would be relevant. Or if the machine could be used to make other products, this could be relevant as well. However, we will assume that the equipment has no salvage value and that it has no other use except in making the heavy-duty gear shifters.

Also note that the company is allocating a portion of its general overhead costs to the shifters. Any portion of this general overhead cost that would actually be eliminated if the gear shifters were purchased rather than made is relevant in the analysis. However, it is likely that the general overhead costs allocated to the gear shifters are in fact common to all items produced in the factory and would continue unchanged even if the shifters were purchased from outside. Such allocated common costs are not differential costs (because they do not differ between the make and buy alternatives) and should be eliminated from the analysis along with the sunk costs.

The variable costs of producing the shifters (materials, labour, and variable overhead) are differential costs, because they can be avoided by buying the shifters from the outside supplier. If the supervisor can be laid off and her salary avoided by buying the shifters, then her salary will be a differential cost and relevant to the decision. Assuming that both the variable costs and the supervisor's salary can be avoided by buying from the outside supplier, the analysis takes the form shown in Exhibit 12–5.

EXHIBIT 12–5   OSN Cycles Make or Buy Analysis

	Production "Cost" per Unit	Per Unit Differential Costs		Total Differential Costs—8,000 Units	
		Make	**Buy**	**Make**	**Buy**
Direct materials.	$ 6	$ 6		$ 48,000	
Direct labour	4	4		32,000	
Variable overhead	1	1		8,000	
Supervisor's salary	3	3		24,000	
Depreciation of special equipment	2	–		–	
Allocated general overhead.	5	–		–	
Outside purchase price			$19		$152,000
Total cost.	$21	$14	$19	$112,000	$152,000
Difference in favour of continuing to make		$ 5		$ 40,000	

Since it costs $5 less per unit to continue to make the shifters, OSN Cycles should reject the outside supplier's offer. However, there is one additional factor that the company may wish to consider before coming to a final decision. This factor is the opportunity cost of the space now being used to produce the shifters.

Opportunity Cost

If the space now being used to produce the shifters *would otherwise be idle*, then OSN Cycles should continue to produce its own shifters and the supplier's offer should be rejected, as stated above. Idle space that has no alternative use has an opportunity cost of zero.

But what if the space now being used to produce shifters could be used for some other purpose? In that case, the space has an opportunity cost that must be considered in assessing the desirability of the supplier's offer. What is this opportunity cost? It is the segment margin that could be derived from the best alternative use of the space.

To illustrate, assume that the space now being used to produce shifters could be used to produce disc brakes that would generate a segment margin of $60,000 per year. Under these conditions, OSN Cycles would be better off to accept the supplier's offer and to use the available space to produce the new product line:

	Make	**Buy**
Differential cost per unit (see Exhibit 12–5).........	$ 14	$ 19
Number of units needed annually	× 8,000	× 8,000
Total annual cost.........................	112,000	152,000
Opportunity cost—segment margin forgone on a potential new product line	60,000	—
Total cost.............................	$172,000	$152,000
Difference in favour of purchasing from the outside supplier.........................		$20,000[2]

INSTANT QUIZ 12–3

Susan Jones owns a local coffee shop. She and her staff have been producing baked goods in-house for several years. The bakery products are good sellers, but the margins are quite low. The owner has been approached by a large commercial bakery that can provide baked goods daily to the coffee shop at prices much below Jones's current production costs due to economies of scale rather than the use of poor-quality products. Jones has sampled the baked goods offered and has found them to be as good as her current product offering. What factors should Jones consider before deciding whether to accept the contract to outsource production of baked goods?

Opportunity costs are not recorded in the accounts of an organization because they do not represent actual dollar outlays. Rather, they represent economic benefits that are *forgone* as a result of pursuing a particular course of action. Because of this, opportunity costs are often erroneously ignored by managers when making decisions. The opportunity costs of OSN Cycles are sufficiently large in this case to make continued production of the shifters very costly from an economic point of view.

LEARNING AID

Make or Buy

Relevant Costs
- Incremental costs of making the product (variable and fixed)
- Opportunity cost of utilizing space to make the product
- Outside purchase price

Irrelevant Costs
- Allocated common costs
- Sunk costs

Total relevant costs of making = Incremental costs + Opportunity costs

Decision Rule:

Make if   Total relevant costs of making < Outside purchase price

Buy if   Total relevant costs of making > Outside purchase price

---

Special Orders

Special order
A one-time order that is not considered part of the company's normal ongoing business.

Managers must often evaluate whether a *special order* should be accepted and, if the order is accepted, what price should be charged. A **special order** is a one-time order that is not considered part of the company's normal ongoing business. The objective in setting a price for special orders is to achieve positive incremental operating income. To illustrate, OSN Cycles has just received a request from the police department of a large Canadian city to produce 100 specially modified mountain bikes at a price of $560 each. The bikes would be used to patrol some of the more densely populated residential sections of the city. OSN Cycles can easily modify its City Cruiser model to fit the specifications of the police department. The normal selling price of the City Cruiser bike is $700, and its unit product cost is $564, as shown below:

Direct materials.	$372
Direct labour.	90
Manufacturing overhead.	102
Unit product cost.	$564

The variable portion of the above manufacturing overhead is $12 per unit. The order would have no effect on the company's total fixed manufacturing overhead costs.

The modifications to the bikes consist of welded brackets to hold radios, nightsticks, and other gear. These modifications would require $34 in incremental variable costs per unit. In addition, the company would have to pay a graphic design studio $1,200 to design and cut stencils that would be used for spray painting the police department's logo and other identifying marks on the bikes.

This order should have no effect on the company's other sales. The production manager says that he can handle the special order without disrupting any of the regular scheduled production.

What effect would accepting this order have on the company's operating income?

Only the incremental costs and benefits are relevant. Since the existing fixed manufacturing overhead costs would not be affected by the order, they are not incremental costs and therefore are not relevant. The incremental operating income can be computed as follows:

	Per Unit	**Total for 100 Bikes**
Incremental revenue	$560	$56,000
Incremental costs:		
Variable costs:		
Direct materials.	372	37,200
Direct labour	90	9,000
Variable manufacturing overhead	12	1,200
Special modifications	34	3,400
Total variable cost.	$508	50,800
Fixed cost:		
Purchase of stencils.		1,200
Total incremental cost.		52,000
Incremental operating income.		$ 4,000

Therefore, even though the price on the special order ($560) is below the normal unit product cost ($564) and the order would require incurring additional costs, it would result in an increase in operating income. In general, a special order is profitable as long as the incremental revenue from the special order exceeds the incremental costs of the order.

INSTANT QUIZ 12–4

Continental Floral Design creates simple floral arrangements made from fresh, long-lasting flowers and greenery. Gino's Trattoria, an upscale Italian restaurant, buys 40 simple floral centrepieces that Continental delivers each week to decorate the tables in the restaurant's dining room. Continental Floral employs five staff, who are all paid fixed salaries, and the company leases space in a large local warehouse. Gino Adduci, the owner of Gino's Trattoria, has approached Continental's owner, Tom Smythe, with a special request for a one-time order of 10 additional arrangements that he will use for a private party at his own home this week. Adduci has requested a special low price of $20 per arrangement. What should Smythe consider before agreeing to provide the extra arrangements at this special low price?

However, in performing the analysis it is important to make sure that there is indeed idle capacity and that the special order does not affect the company's ability to meet normal demand. For example, what if OSN Cycles is already operating at 100% of capacity and normally sells all the bikes it can produce for $700 each? What is the opportunity cost of accepting the order? Should the company accept the $560 price? If not, what is the minimum price it should accept? To answer these questions, the analysis can be conducted as follows:

	Per Unit
(a) Opportunity Costs:	
Normal selling price	$700
Less variable costs:	
Direct materials.	372
Direct labour	90
Variable overhead	12
Total variable costs	474
Contribution margin forgone.	$226*
(b) Total relevant costs:	
Incremental costs:	
Variable ($474 + $34).	$508
Fixed ($1,200/100)	12
	520
Opportunity costs	226
Total.	$746

*If OSN Cycles is operating at 100% capacity, every bike it sells to the police department means forgoing the contribution margin of $226 the company would have earned on a sale to a regular customer. This is the per unit opportunity cost of accepting the special order.

LEARNING AID

Accept or Reject a Special Order

Relevant Costs and Benefits
• Incremental costs of filling the order (variable and fixed)
• Opportunity cost of filling the order
• Incremental revenues from the order

Irrelevant Costs
• Allocated common costs
• Sunk costs

Total relevant costs = Incremental costs + Opportunity costs

Decision Rule:
Accept if   Incremental revenues > Total relevant costs
Reject if   Incremental revenues < Total relevant costs

Since the total relevant costs of $746 exceed the offer price of $560, OSN Cycles should decline the offer. Indeed, to be no worse off from a financial perspective, the minimum price that should be charged on the special order is $746 per bike. At this price, management should be indifferent between filling the special order and continuing to sell all it can produce to regular customers.

Joint Product Costs and the Sell or Process Further Decision

In some industries, a number of end products are produced from a single raw material input. For example, in the petroleum-refining industry, a large number of products are extracted from crude oil, including gasoline, jet fuel, home heating oil, lubricants, asphalt, and various organic chemicals. Another example is provided by the St. Thomas Wool Cooperative. The company buys raw wool from local sheep-herders, separates the wool into three grades—coarse, fine, and superfine—and then dyes the wool using traditional methods that rely on pigments from local materials. Exhibit 12–6 contains a diagram of the production process.

Joint products
Two or more items that are produced from a common input.

As mentioned above, the St. Thomas Wool Cooperative produces coarse wool, fine wool, and superfine wool from one input—raw wool. Two or more products that are produced from a common input are known as **joint products**. The term **joint product costs** is used to describe those manufacturing costs that are incurred in producing joint products up to the split-off point. The **split-off point** is the point in the manufacturing process at which the joint products can be recognized as separate products. This does not occur at the St. Thomas Wool Cooperative until the raw wool has gone through the separating process. At the Cooperative, the joint costs are the $200,000 cost of the raw wool and the $40,000 cost of separating the wool. The undyed wool is called an *intermediate product* because it is not finished at this point. Nevertheless, a market does exist for undyed wool—although at a significantly lower price than finished dyed wool.

Joint product costs
Costs that are incurred up to the split-off point in producing joint products.

Split-off point
That point in the manufacturing process where some or all of the joint products can be recognized as individual products.

The Pitfalls of Allocation

Joint product costs are really common costs incurred to simultaneously produce a variety of end products. Traditional cost accounting books cover various approaches to allocating these common costs among the different products at the split-off point. A typical approach is to allocate the joint product costs according to the relative sales value of the end products.

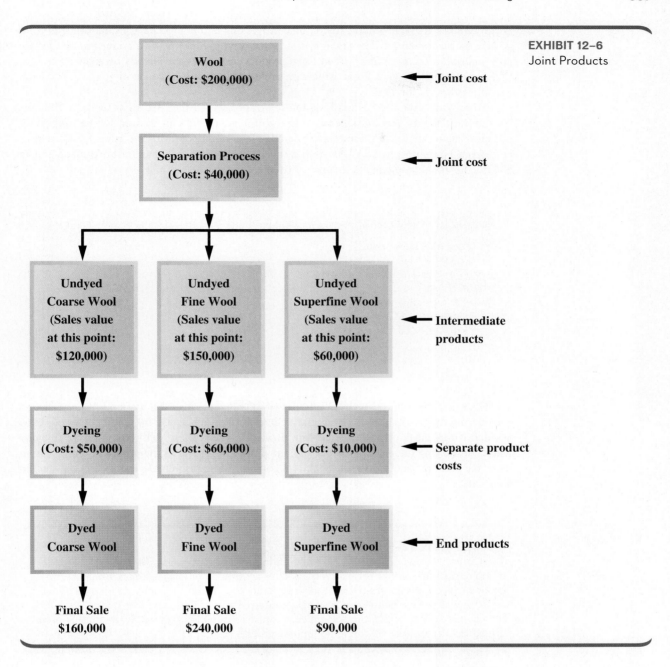

EXHIBIT 12–6
Joint Products

Although allocation of joint product costs is needed for some purposes, such as inventory valuation for financial reporting, allocations of this kind should be viewed with great caution *internally* in the decision-making process. As will be discussed in the next section, because allocated joint product costs are sunk costs, they should never be used when making decisions about what to do with the joint products beyond the split-off point (i.e., sell immediately or process further).

Sell or Process Further Decisions

Deciding what to do with a product from the split-off point forward is known as a **sell or process further decision**. Joint costs are irrelevant in these decisions because by the time the split-off point is reached, the joint product costs have already been incurred and therefore are sunk costs.

Sell or process further decision
A decision as to whether a joint product should be sold at the split-off point or processed further and sold at a later time in a different form.

It will always be profitable to continue processing a joint product after the split-off point *as long as the incremental revenue from such processing exceeds the incremental processing cost incurred after the split-off point.* Joint product costs that have already been incurred up to the split-off point are sunk costs, which are irrelevant in decisions concerning what to do from the split-off point forward.

To provide a detailed example of the sell or process further decision, return to the data for the St. Thomas Wool Cooperative in Exhibit 12–6. We can answer several important questions using these data. First, is the company generating a profit if it runs the entire process from beginning to end? Assuming there are no costs other than those displayed in Exhibit 12–6, the company is indeed profitable, determined as follows:

Analysis of the profitability of the overall operation:		
Combined final sales value		
($160,000 + $240,000 + $90,000)		$490,000
Less costs of producing the end products:		
Cost of wool	$200,000	
Cost of separating wool.	40,000	
Combined costs of dyeing		
($50,000 + $60,000 + $10,000)	120,000	360,000
Profit		$130,000

Note that the joint costs of buying the wool and separating the wool *are* relevant when considering the profitability of the entire operation. This is because these joint costs *could* be avoided if the entire operation were shut down. However, these joint costs are *not* relevant when considering the profitability of any one product. As long as the process is being run to make the other products, no additional joint costs are incurred to make the specific product in question.

INSTANT QUIZ 12–5

The Corner Hardware Store sells barbecues in spring and summer. The store manager is trying to decide whether to sell the barbecues assembled or unassembled. An unassembled barbecue is purchased from the supplier for $100 and can be sold unassembled for $200. Assembly of the barbecue requires 30 minutes of labour time, and the store pays its employees $15 per hour. Corner Hardware can sell assembled barbecues for $225. Should the barbecues be sold assembled or unassembled?

Even though the company is making money overall, it may be losing money on one or more of the products. If the company buys wool and runs the separation process, it will get all three intermediate products. Nothing can be done about that. However, each of these products can be sold *as is* without further processing. It may be that the company would be better off selling one or more of the products prior to dyeing to avoid the dyeing costs. The appropriate way to make this choice is to compare the incremental revenues to the incremental costs from further processing, as done in Exhibit 12–7.

As this analysis shows, the company would be better off selling the undyed coarse wool as is rather than processing it further. The other two products should be processed further and dyed before selling them.

Note that the joint costs of the wool ($200,000) and of the wool separation process ($40,000) play no role in the decision to sell or further process the intermediate products. These joint costs are relevant in a decision of whether to buy wool and to run the wool

	Coarse Wool	Fine Wool	Superfine Wool
Final sales value after further processing	$160,000	$240,000	$90,000
Less sales value at the split-off point	120,000	150,000	60,000
Incremental revenue from further processing	40,000	90,000	30,000
Less cost of further processing (dyeing)	50,000	60,000	10,000
Profit (loss) from further processing	$ (10,000)	$ 30,000	$20,000

EXHIBIT 12–7
Sell or Process
Further Decision

separation process, but they are not relevant in decisions about what to do with the intermediate products once they have been separated.

LEARNING AID

Sell or Process Further

Relevant Costs and Benefits
- Incremental costs of further processing
- Incremental revenues from further processing

Irrelevant Costs
- Allocated joint product costs

Decision Rule:

Process further if	Incremental revenues > Incremental costs of further processing
Sell at split-off point if	Incremental revenues < Incremental costs of further processing

---

■ UTILIZATION OF A CONSTRAINED RESOURCE

Another decision situation that managers often face is the problem of how to utilize a constrained resource. When a limited resource of some type restricts a company's ability to fully satisfy demand for its products or services, the company is said to have a **constraint**. A convenience store has limited shelf space, so it must decide which products to sell. Manufacturing firms may have constraints on machine-hours, labour-hours, or the amount of raw materials available for production. The **theory of constraints (TOC)** maintains that effectively managing a constraint is important to the financial success of an organization. The challenge for managers is deciding how best to utilize the constrained resource to maximize the company's profits. As will be illustrated below, fixed costs are usually unaffected by the allocation of the constrained resource in the short run, so the focus will be on analyzing and maximizing contribution margin.

Contribution Margin in Relation to a Constrained Resource

To maximize total contribution margin, a firm should not necessarily promote those products that have the highest *unit* contribution margin. Rather, total contribution margin will be maximized by promoting those products or accepting those orders that provide the highest unit contribution margin *in relation to the constrained resource*. To illustrate, OSN Cycles makes a line of panniers—saddlebags for bicycles. There are two models of panniers—a

Constraint
A limitation under which a company must operate (such as limited machine time available or limited raw materials available) that restricts the company's ability to satisfy demand for its products or services.

LEARNING OBJECTIVE ③
Determine the most profitable use of a constrained resource and the value of obtaining more of the constrained resource.

Theory of constraints (TOC)
A management approach that emphasizes the importance of managing constraints.

touring model and a mountain model. Cost and revenue data for the two models of panniers are given below:

	Model	
	Mountain Pannier	**Touring Pannier**
Selling price per unit.............................	$40	$50
Variable cost per unit	30	42
Contribution margin per unit	$10	$ 8
Contribution margin (CM) ratio	25%	16%

The mountain pannier appears to be much more profitable than the touring pannier. It has a $10 per unit contribution margin as compared to only $8 per unit for the touring model, and it has a 25% CM ratio as compared to only 16% for the touring model.

But now let's add one more piece of information—the plant that makes the panniers is operating at capacity. Ordinarily this does not mean that every machine and every person in the plant is working at the maximum possible rate. Because machines have different capacities, some machines will be operating at less than 100% of capacity. However, if the plant as a whole cannot produce any more units, some machine or process must be operating at capacity. The machine or process that is limiting overall output is called the *bottleneck*—it is the constraint.

At OSN Cycles, the bottleneck is a particular stitching machine. The mountain pannier requires four minutes of stitching time, and each unit of the touring pannier requires two minutes of stitching time. Since this stitching machine already has more work than it can handle, production will have to be cut back on one of the models. In this situation, which product is more profitable? To answer this question, the manager should look at the *contribution margin per unit of the constrained resource*, also known as the **profitability index**. This figure is computed by dividing the contribution margin by the quantity of the constrained resource required per unit. These calculations are carried out below for the mountain and touring panniers:

Profitability index
Contribution margin per unit ÷ Quantity of constrained resource required per unit

	Model	
	Mountain Pannier	**Touring Pannier**
Contribution margin per unit (a).....................	$10.00	$8.00
Time on the stitching machine required to produce one unit (b)	4 min.	2 min.
Contribution margin per unit of the constrained resource, (a) ÷ (b)	$2.50/min.	$4.00/min.

Using the profitability index, it is easy to decide which product is less profitable and should be de-emphasized. Each minute of processing time on the stitching machine that is devoted to the touring pannier results in an increase of $4 in contribution margin and profits. The comparable figure for the mountain pannier is only $2.50 per minute. Therefore, the touring model should be emphasized. Even though the mountain model has the larger per unit contribution margin and the larger CM ratio, the touring model provides the larger contribution margin in relation to the constrained resource.

INSTANT QUIZ 12-6

Safety Shoes Ltd. makes standard and premium quality safety boots. The contribution margin of a standard pair of boots is $20 and of a premium pair of boots is $35. The company has one machine that is used to sew the upper section of the boots to the soles. This machine is typically used each month at near capacity. It is now near the end of June. Assuming Safety Shoes can sell as many pairs of boots of either type as it produces in June, what information is most relevant to the decision about which products should be made using the remaining unused machine capacity?

To verify that the touring model is indeed the more profitable product when considering the constrained resource, suppose an hour of additional stitching time is available and that there are unfilled orders for both products. The additional hour on the stitching machine could be used to make either 15 mountain panniers (60 minutes ÷ 4 minutes) or 30 touring panniers (60 minutes ÷ 2 minutes), with the following consequences:

	Model	
	Mountain Pannier	**Touring Pannier**
Contribution margin per unit	$ 10	$ 8
Additional units that can be processed in one hour	× 15	× 30
Additional contribution margin.	$150	$240

The analysis illustrated in this example generalizes well to situations where demand exceeds capacity and managers must allocate a constrained resource to three or more products. Demand should be fully satisfied for the product with the highest profitability index. Any capacity that remains should then be allocated to the product with the second-highest profitability index, and so on until all available capacity has been utilized. Simply looking at unit contribution margins alone is not enough when constraints exist; contribution margin per unit of the scarce resource must guide decision making.

Managing Constraints

Profits can be increased by effectively managing an organization's constraints. One aspect of managing constraints is to decide how best to utilize them. If the constraint is a bottleneck in the production process, the manager should select the product mix that maximizes the total contribution margin. In addition, the manager should take an active role in managing the constraint itself. Management should focus efforts on increasing the efficiency of the bottleneck operation (constraint) and on increasing its capacity. Such efforts directly increase the output of finished goods and will often pay off in an almost immediate increase in profits.

It is often possible for a manager to effectively increase the capacity of the bottleneck by what is called **relaxing (or elevating) the constraint**. For example, the stitching machine operator could be asked to work overtime. This would result in more available stitching time and hence more finished goods that can be sold. The benefits from relaxing the constraint in such a manner are often enormous and can easily be quantified. The manager should first ask, "What would I do with additional capacity at the bottleneck if it was available?" In the bicycle pannier example, the additional capacity was worth $4 ($2.50) per minute or $240 ($150) per hour because adding an hour of capacity would

Relaxing (or elevating) the constraint
Increasing the capacity of a bottleneck.

generate an additional $240 ($150) of contribution margin if it were used solely to process more touring (mountain) panniers. Based on the profitability indices, additional capacity should first be allocated to production of touring panniers, followed by mountain panniers if any capacity remains. Since overtime pay for the operator is likely to be much less than $240 (or $150 for that matter!), running the stitching machine on overtime would be an excellent way to increase the company's profits while satisfying its customers at the same time.

The implications are clear: managers should focus much of their attention on managing bottlenecks. As we have discussed, managers should emphasize products that most profitably utilize the constrained resource. They should also make sure that products are processed smoothly through the bottlenecks, with minimal lost time due to breakdowns and setups. And they should try to find ways to increase the capacity at the bottlenecks, which can be accomplished in a number of ways:

- Working overtime on the bottleneck.
- Subcontracting some of the processing that would be done at the bottleneck.
- Shifting workers from processes that are not bottlenecks to the process that *is* a bottleneck.
- Focusing business process improvement efforts such as total quality management and business process re-engineering on the bottleneck.
- Reducing defective units. Each defective unit that is processed through the bottleneck and subsequently scrapped takes the place of a good unit that could be sold.

The last three methods of increasing the capacity of the bottleneck are particularly attractive, because they are low-cost interventions and may even yield additional cost savings.

INSTANT QUIZ 12–7
How should the relative profitability of products be determined when trying to decide how to allocate a constrained resource such as machine-hours?

The Problem of Multiple Constraints

What does a firm do if it has more than one potential constraint? For example, a firm may have limited raw materials, limited direct labour-hours available, limited floor space, and limited advertising dollars to spend on product promotion. How would it proceed to find the right combination of products to produce? The proper combination or "mix" of products can be found using a quantitative method known as *linear programming*, which is covered in quantitative methods and operations management courses.

KNOWLEDGE IN ACTION

Managers can apply their knowledge about relevant costs when

- deciding whether to add or drop a product line or service offering
- deciding whether to make a product/offer a service or buy it from an outside source
- deciding whether to accept a one-time special order at a lower than usual price
- deciding whether to sell a product as-is or process it further
- making product mix decisions given capacity constraints and bottlenecks

SUMMARY

- A framework was presented for distinguishing between relevant and irrelevant costs. Relevant costs and benefits are those that will be incurred in the future and that differ among the alternatives under consideration. As such, sunk costs are irrelevant (incurred in the past), while avoidable, differential, and opportunity costs are all relevant. **[LO1]**
- Application of relevant cost concepts was illustrated in several different decision situations often faced by managers: adding or dropping product lines/segments, making versus buying decisions, accepting or rejecting special orders, and selling versus processing joint products further. A learning aid was presented for each type of decision, identifying the relevant and irrelevant costs and the decision rule. **[LO2]**
- A simple approach was illustrated for allocating a constrained resource when demand exceeds production capacity because of a production bottleneck in the short run. The allocation approach is based on calculating the contribution margin per unit of the constrained resource, which is known as the *profitability index*. Demand should first be fully satisfied for the product with the highest profitability index, and then for the product with the next highest index, and so on, until all of the available capacity has been used. **[LO3]**

REVIEW PROBLEM: RELEVANT COSTS

The St. Albert Cycle Company manufactures three types of bicycles—dirt bikes, mountain bikes, and racing bikes. Data on sales and expenses for the past quarter follow:

	Total	Dirt Bikes	Mountain Bikes	Racing Bikes
Sales	$300,000	$90,000	$150,000	$60,000
Less variable manufacturing and selling expenses	120,000	27,000	60,000	33,000
Contribution margin	180,000	63,000	90,000	27,000
Less fixed expenses:				
Advertising, traceable	30,000	10,000	14,000	6,000
Depreciation of special equipment	23,000	6,000	9,000	8,000
Salaries of product-line managers	35,000	12,000	13,000	10,000
Allocated common fixed expenses*	60,000	18,000	30,000	12,000
Total fixed expenses	148,000	46,000	66,000	36,000
Operating income (loss)	$ 32,000	$17,000	$ 24,000	$ (9,000)

*Allocated on the basis of sales dollars

Management is concerned about the continued losses shown by the racing bikes and wants a recommendation as to whether or not the line should be discontinued. The special equipment used to produce racing bikes has no resale value and does not wear out.

Required:
1. Should production and sale of the racing bikes be discontinued? Explain. Show computations to support your answer.
2. Recast the above data in a format that would be more usable to management in assessing the long-run profitability of the various product lines.

Solution to Review Problem

1. No, production and sale of the racing bikes should not be discontinued. If the racing bikes were discontinued, then the operating income for the company as a whole would decrease by $11,000 each quarter:

Lost contribution margin		$(27,000)
Fixed costs that can be avoided:		
Advertising, traceable	$ 6,000	
Salary of the product-line manager	10,000	16,000
Decrease in operating income for the company as a whole		$(11,000)

The depreciation of the special equipment is a sunk cost and is not relevant to the decision. The common costs are allocated and will continue regardless of whether or not the racing bikes are discontinued; thus, they are not relevant to the decision.

Alternative Solution

	Current Total	Total If Racing Bikes Are Dropped	Difference: Operating Income Increase or (Decrease) If Dropped
Sales	$300,000	$240,000	$(60,000)
Less variable expenses	120,000	87,000	33,000
Contribution margin	180,000	153,000	(27,000)
Less fixed expenses:			
Advertising, traceable	30,000	24,000	6,000
Depreciation on special equipment	23,000	23,000	0
Salaries of product managers	35,000	25,000	10,000
Common allocated costs	60,000	60,000	0
Total fixed expenses	148,000	132,000	16,000
Operating income	$ 32,000	$ 21,000	$(11,000)

2. The segmented report can be improved by eliminating the allocation of the common fixed expenses. Following the format introduced in Chapter 11 for a segmented income statement, a better report is as follows:

	Total	Dirt Bikes	Mountain Bikes	Racing Bikes
Sales	$300,000	$90,000	$150,000	$60,000
Less variable manufacturing and selling expenses	120,000	27,000	60,000	33,000
Contribution margin	180,000	63,000	90,000	27,000
Less traceable fixed expenses:				
Advertising	30,000	10,000	14,000	6,000
Depreciation of special equipment	23,000	6,000	9,000	8,000
Salaries of the product-line managers	35,000	12,000	13,000	10,000
Total traceable fixed expenses	88,000	28,000	36,000	24,000
Product-line segment margin	92,000	$35,000	$ 54,000	$ 3,000
Less common fixed expenses	60,000			
Operating income	$ 32,000			

DISCUSSION CASE

DISCUSSION CASE 12–1

One of the decisions facing managers illustrated in this chapter is whether to keep or drop an existing product, service, or operating segment. The analysis presented indicates that if the costs avoided by dropping the product or segment exceed the contribution margin lost, then "drop" is the correct decision from a financial perspective. However, when companies such as General Motors or Chrysler decide to drop a major product, service, or operating segment, there may be non-financial consequences involving suppliers, creditors, employees, and customers.

Required:
What non-financial consequences might General Motors or Chrysler face if they decided to drop their parts and service divisions and, instead, focus only on selling new and used cars?

QUESTIONS

12–1 What is a *relevant cost*?

12–2 Define the following terms: *incremental cost*, *opportunity cost*, and *sunk cost*.

12–3 Are avoidable costs always relevant costs? Explain.

12–4 Depreciation (as shown on the income statement) is an expense to a company, but this same expense is irrelevant in decision making. Explain why this is so.

12–5 "Sunk costs are easy to spot—they're simply the fixed costs associated with a decision." Do you agree? Explain.

12–6 Are variable costs always relevant in decision making? Explain.

12–7 Davis Company is considering dropping one of its product lines. What costs of the product line would be relevant to this decision? Irrelevant?

12–8 "If a product line is generating a loss, then that's pretty good evidence that the product line should be discontinued." Do you agree? Explain.

12–9 How does opportunity cost enter into the make or buy decision?

12–10 Which costs are relevant to special-order decisions?

12–11 What is a constraint?

12–12 List four ways to increase capacity at bottlenecks.

12–13 Define the following terms: *joint products*, *joint product costs*, and *split-off point*.

12–14 From a decision-making point of view, what pitfalls are there in allocating common costs among joint products?

12–15 What guideline can be used in determining whether a joint product should be sold at the split-off point or processed further?

12–16 Why should relevant costs be isolated when analyzing a decision situation?

FOUNDATIONAL EXERCISES

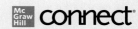

[LO1, LO2, LO3]

Cane Company manufactures two products called Alpha and Beta that sell for $120 and $80, respectively. Each product uses only one type of raw material that costs $6 per pound. The company has the capacity to annually produce 100,000 units of each product. Its unit costs for each product at this level of activity are given below:

	Alpha	Beta
Direct materials.	$ 30	$12
Direct labour	$ 20	$15
Variable manufacturing overhead	$ 7	$ 5
Traceable fixed manufacturing overhead	$ 16	$18
Variable selling expenses	$ 12	$ 8
Common fixed expenses	$ 15	$10
Cost per unit	100	$68

The company considers its traceable fixed manufacturing overhead to be avoidable, whereas its common fixed expenses are deemed unavoidable and have been allocated to products based on sales dollars.

Required:

(Answer each question independently unless instructed otherwise.)

12–1 What is the total amount of traceable fixed manufacturing overhead for the Alpha product line and for the Beta product line?

12–2 What is the company's total amount of common fixed expenses?

12–3 Assume that Cane expects to produce and sell 80,000 Alphas during the current year. One of Cane's sales representatives has found a new customer that is willing to buy 10,000 additional Alphas for a price of $80 per unit. If Cane accepts the customer's offer, how much will its profits increase or decrease?

12–4 Assume that Cane expects to produce and sell 90,000 Betas during the current year. One of Cane's sales representatives has found a new customer that is willing to buy 5,000 additional Betas for a price of $39 per unit. If Cane accepts the customer's offer, how much will its profits increase or decrease?

12–5 Assume that Cane expects to produce and sell 95,000 Alphas during the current year. One of Cane's sales representatives has found a new customer that is willing to buy 10,000 additional Alphas for a price of $80 per unit. If Cane accepts the customer's offer, it will decrease Alpha sales to regular customers by 5,000 units. Should Cane accept this special order?

12–6 Assume that Cane normally produces and sells 90,000 Betas per year. If Cane discontinues the Beta product line, how much will profits increase or decrease?

12–7 Assume that Cane normally produces and sells 40,000 Betas per year. If Cane discontinues the Beta product line, how much will profits increase or decrease?

12–8 Assume that Cane normally produces and sells 60,000 Betas and 80,000 Alphas per year. If Cane discontinues the Beta product line, its sales representatives could increase sales of Alpha by 15,000 units. If Cane discontinues the Beta product line, how much would profits increase or decrease?

12–9 Assume that Cane expects to produce and sell 80,000 Alphas during the current year. A supplier has offered to manufacture and deliver 80,000 Alphas to Cane for a price of $80 per unit. If Cane buys 80,000 units from the supplier instead of making those units, how much will profits increase or decrease?

12–10 Assume that Cane expects to produce and sell 50,000 Alphas during the current year. A supplier has offered to manufacture and deliver 50,000 Alphas to Cane for a price of $80 per unit. If Cane buys 50,000 units from the supplier instead of making those units, how much will profits increase or decrease?

12–11 How many pounds of raw material are needed to make one unit of Alpha and one unit of Beta?

12–12 What contribution margin per pound of raw material is earned by Alpha and Beta?

12–13 Assume that Cane's customers would buy a maximum of 80,000 units of Alpha and 60,000 units of Beta. Also assume that the company's raw material available for production is limited to 160,000 pounds. How many units of each product should Cane produce to maximize its profits?

12–14 If Cane follows your recommendation in requirement 13, what total contribution margin will it earn?

12–15 If Cane uses its 160,000 pounds of raw materials as you recommended in requirement 13, up to how much should it be willing to pay per pound for additional raw materials?

EXERCISES

EXERCISE 12–1 Identifying Relevant Costs [LO1]

The management of Boehm & De Graaf A/S, a Danish furniture manufacturer, must determine whether certain costs are relevant in two different cases:

Case 1: The company chronically runs at capacity, and the old Model A3000 machine is the company's constraint. Management is considering purchasing a new Model B3800 machine to use in addition to the Model A3000 machine. The old Model A3000 machine would continue to be used to capacity as before, with the new Model B3800 being used to expand production. The increase in volume would be large enough to require increases in fixed selling expenses and in general administrative overhead, but not in the general fixed manufacturing overhead.

Case 2: The old Model A3000 machine is not the company's constraint, but management is considering replacing it with a new Model B3800 machine because of the potential savings in direct materials cost with the new machine. The Model A3000 machine would be sold. This change would have no effect on production or sales, other than some savings in direct materials costs due to less waste.

Required:
Place an X in the appropriate column to indicate whether each item is relevant or not relevant to each of the two cases. Consider the two cases independently.

Item	Case 1 Relevant	Case 1 Not Relevant	Case 2 Relevant	Case 2 Not Relevant
a. Sales revenue........................				
b. Direct materials.....................				
c. Direct labour				
d. Variable manufacturing overhead				
e. Book value—Model A3000 machine				
f. Disposal value—Model A3000 machine...				
g. Depreciation—Model A3000 machine				
h. Market value—Model B3800 machine (cost)				
i. Fixed manufacturing overhead (general)...				
j. Variable selling expense				
k. Fixed selling expense.................				
l. General administrative overhead				

EXERCISE 12–2 Dropping or Retaining a Segment [LO2]

Cumberland County Senior Services is a non-profit organization devoted to providing essential services to seniors who live in their own homes within the Cumberland County area. Three services are provided for seniors—home nursing, Meals on Wheels, and housekeeping. In the home nursing program, nurses visit seniors on a regular basis to check on their general health and to perform tests ordered by their physicians. The Meals on Wheels program delivers a hot meal once a day to each senior enrolled in the program. The housekeeping service provides weekly housecleaning and maintenance services. Data on revenue and expenses for the past year follow:

	Total	Home Nursing	Meals on Wheels	Housekeeping
Revenues.........................	$900,000	$260,000	$400,000	$240,000
Variable expenses	490,000	120,000	210,000	160,000
Contribution margin	410,000	140,000	190,000	80,000
Fixed expenses:				
Depreciation	68,000	8,000	40,000	20,000
Liability insurance	42,000	20,000	7,000	15,000
Program administrators' salaries.......	115,000	40,000	38,000	37,000
General administrative overhead*......	180,000	52,000	80,000	48,000
Total fixed expenses	405,000	120,000	165,000	120,000
Operating income (loss)	$ 5,000	$ 20,000	$ 25,000	$ (40,000)

*Allocated on the basis of program revenues

The head administrator of Cumberland County Senior Services, Judith Ewa, is concerned about the organization's finances and considers the operating income of $5,000 last year to be razor-thin. (Last year's results were very similar to the results for previous years and are representative of what would be expected in the future.) She feels that the organization should be building its financial reserves at a more rapid rate in order to prepare for the next inevitable recession. After seeing the above report, Ewa asked for more information about the financial advisability of discontinuing the housekeeping program.

The depreciation in the housekeeping category is for a small van that is used to carry the housekeepers and their equipment from job to job. If the program were discontinued, the van would be donated to a charitable organization. Depreciation charges assume zero salvage value. None of the general administrative overhead would be avoided if the housekeeping program were dropped, but the liability insurance and the salary of the program administrator would be avoided.

Required:
1. Should the housekeeping program be discontinued? Explain. Show computations to support your answer.
2. Recast the above data in a format that would be more useful to management in assessing the long-run financial viability of the various services.

EXERCISE 12–3 Make or Buy a Component [LO2]

Current-Control Inc. manufactures a variety of electrical switches. The company is currently manufacturing all of its own component parts. An outside supplier has offered to sell a switch to Current-Control for $32 per unit. To evaluate this offer, Current-Control has gathered the following information relating to its own cost of producing the switch internally:

	Per Unit	12,000 Units per Year
Direct materials.	$12	$144,000
Direct labour.	10	120,000
Variable manufacturing overhead	3	36,000
Fixed manufacturing overhead, traceable	8*	96,000
Fixed manufacturing overhead, common, but allocated	16	192,000
Total cost.	$49	$588,000

*25% supervisory salaries; 75% depreciation of special equipment (no resale value)

CHECK FIGURE
Difference in favour of continuing to make switches = $5 per unit.

Required:

1. Assuming that the company has no alternative use for the facilities now being used to produce the switch, should the outside supplier's offer be accepted? Show all computations.

2. Suppose that if the switches were purchased, Current-Control could use the freed capacity to launch a new product. The segment margin of the new product would be $78,000 per year. Should Current-Control accept the offer to buy the switches from the outside supplier for $32 each? Show computations.

EXERCISE 12–4 Evaluating a Special Order [LO2]

Sato Awards has had a request for a special order of 10 silver-plated trophies from the provincial tennis association. The normal selling price of such a trophy is $249.95 and its unit product cost is $164.00, as shown below:

Direct materials	$ 93.00
Direct labour	56.00
Manufacturing overhead	15.00
Unit product cost	$164.00

Most of the manufacturing overhead is fixed and unaffected by variations in how many trophies are produced in any given period. However, $7 of the overhead is variable, depending on the number of trophies produced. The customer would like a special logo applied to the trophies requiring additional materials costing $6 per trophy and would also require acquisition of a special tool costing $195 that would have no other use once the special order was completed. This order would have no effect on the company's regular sales, and the order could be filled using the company's existing capacity without affecting any other order.

Required:

What effect would accepting this order have on the company's operating income if a special price of $199.95 is offered per trophy for this order? Should the special order be accepted at this price?

EXERCISE 12–5 Utilization of a Constrained Resource [LO3]

The following are the selling price, variable costs, and contribution margin for one unit of each of Banner Company's three products: A, B, and C:

	Product		
	A	B	C
Selling price	$60	$90	$80
Variable costs:			
Direct materials.	27	14	40
Direct labour.	12	32	16
Variable manufacturing overhead	3	8	4
Total variable cost.	42	54	60
Contribution margin	$18	$36	$20
Contribution margin ratio	30%	40%	25%

Due to a strike in the plant of one of its competitors, demand for the company's products far exceeds its capacity to produce. Management is trying to determine which product(s) to concentrate on next week in filling its backlog of orders. The direct labour rate is $8 per hour, and only 3,000 hours of labour time are available each week.

Required:

1. Compute the amount of contribution margin that will be obtained per hour of labour time spent on each product.
2. Which orders would you recommend that the company work on next week—the orders for product A, product B, or product C? Show computations.
3. By paying overtime wages, more than 3,000 hours of direct labour time can be made available next week. Up to how much should the company be willing to pay per hour in overtime wages as long as there is unfilled demand for the three products? Explain.

EXERCISE 12–6 Sell or Process Further [LO2]

In a joint processing operation, Nolen Company manufactures three grades of sugar from a common input, sugar cane. Joint processing costs up to the split-off point total $40,000 per year. The company allocates these costs to the joint products on the basis of their total sales value at the split-off point. These sales values are as follows: raw sugar, $20,000; brown sugar, $20,000; and white sugar, $21,000.

Each product may be sold at the split-off point or processed further. Additional processing requires no special facilities. The additional processing costs and the sales value after further processing for each product (on an annual basis) are shown below:

Product	Additional Processing Costs	Sales Value
Raw sugar	$21,000	$40,000
Brown sugar	$14,000	$35,000
White sugar	$ 6,000	$41,000

Required:

Which product or products should be sold at the split-off point, and which product or products should be processed further? Show computations.

EXERCISE 12–7 Identification of Relevant Costs [LO1]

Hart Company sells and delivers office furniture across Western Canada. The costs associated with the acquisition and annual operation of a delivery truck are given below:

Insurance	$1,750
Licences	$250
Taxes (vehicle)	$150
Garage rent for parking (per truck)	$1,350
Depreciation ($30,000 ÷ 5 years)	$6,000
Gasoline, oil, tires, and repairs	$0.16/km

Required:

1. Assume that Hart Company owns one truck that has been driven 50,000 kilometres during the first year. Compute the average cost per kilometre of owning and operating the truck.
2. At the beginning of the second year, Hart Company is unsure whether to use the truck or leave it parked in the garage and have all hauling done commercially. (The government requires the payment of vehicle taxes even if the vehicle isn't used.) What costs from the previous list are relevant to this decision? Explain.
3. Assume that the company decides to use the truck during the second year. Near year-end, an order is received from a customer over 1,000 kilometres away. What costs from the previous list are relevant in a decision between using the truck to make the delivery and having the delivery done commercially? Explain.
4. Occasionally, the company could use two trucks at the same time. For this reason, some thought is being given to purchasing a second truck. The total kilometres driven would be the same as if only one truck were owned. What costs from the previous list are relevant to a decision about whether to purchase the second truck? Explain.

EXERCISE 12–8 Utilizing a Constrained Resource [LO3]

Outdoor Luggage Inc. makes high-end, hard-sided luggage for sports equipment. Data concerning three of the company's most popular models appear below.

	Ski Guard	Golf Guard	Fishing Guard
Selling price per unit.	$200	$300	$255
Variable cost per unit	$ 60	$140	$ 55
Plastic injection moulding machine processing time required per unit	2 min.	5 min.	4 min.
Kgs of plastic pellets per unit	7 kg	4 kg	8 kg

Required:

1. The total time available on the plastic injection moulding machine is the constraint in the production process. Which product would be the most profitable use of this constraint? Which product would be the least profitable use of this constraint?
2. A severe shortage of plastic pellets has required the company to cut back its production so much that the plastic injection moulding machine is no longer the bottleneck. Instead, the constraint is the total available kilograms of plastic pellets. Which product would be the most profitable use of this constraint? Which product would be the least profitable use of this constraint?
3. Which product has the largest unit contribution margin? Why wouldn't this product be the most profitable use of the constrained resource in either case?

EXERCISE 12–9 Make or Buy a Component [LO2]

Delta Company produces a single product. The cost of producing and selling a single unit of this product at the company's normal activity level of 60,000 units per year is:

	Per Unit
Direct materials.	$6.10
Direct labour.	4.80
Variable manufacturing overhead.	2.00
Fixed manufacturing overhead.	4.20
Variable selling and administrative expenses.	1.50
Fixed selling and administrative expenses.	2.40

The normal selling price is $21 per unit. The company's capacity is 75,000 units per year. An order has been received from a mail-order house for 15,000 units at a special price of $14.00 per unit. This order would not affect regular sales.

Required:

1. If the order is accepted, by how much will annual profits be increased or decreased? (The order will not change the company's total fixed costs.)
2. Assume the company has 1,000 units of this product left over from last year that are inferior to the current model. The units must be sold through regular channels at reduced prices. What unit cost is relevant for establishing a minimum selling price for these units? Explain.

EXERCISE 12–10 Special Order [LO2]

At the Kicher Company's current activity level of 8,000 units per month, the costs of producing and selling one unit of the company's only product are as follows:

Direct materials.	$5.00
Direct labour.	$6.00
Variable manufacturing overhead.	$1.00
Fixed manufacturing overhead.	$9.00
Variable selling and administrative expenses.	$3.00
Fixed selling and administrative expenses.	$4.00

The normal selling price is $26 per unit. An order has been received from a potential customer overseas for 4,000 units at a price of $24.00 per unit. This order would not affect regular sales. The company's capacity is 10,000 units per month and enough excess capacity exists to fill this order.

Required:
1. If the order is accepted, by how much will monthly profits increase or decrease? (The order would not change the company's total fixed costs.)
2. Assume the company has 500 units of this product left over from last year that are inferior to the current model. The units must be sold through regular channels at reduced prices. What unit cost is relevant for establishing a minimum selling price for these units? Explain.

EXERCISE 12–11 Utilization of a Constrained Resource [LO3]
Westburne Company produces three products: Alpha, Omega, and Beta. Data (per unit) concerning the three products follow:

	Alpha	Omega	Beta
Selling price	$160	$112	$140
Less variable expenses:			
Direct materials	48	30	18
Labour and overhead	48	54	80
Total variable expenses	96	84	98
Contribution margin	$ 64	$ 28	$ 42
Contribution margin ratio	40%	25%	30%

Demand for the company's products is very strong, with far more orders each month than the company can produce with the available raw materials. The same material is used in each product. The material costs $6 per kilogram, with a maximum of 10,000 kilograms available each month.

Required:
Which orders would you advise the company to accept first, those for Alpha, Omega, or Beta? Which orders second? Third?

CHECK FIGURE
The company should accept orders first for Beta, second for Alpha, and third for Omega.

EXERCISE 12–12 Sell or Process Further [LO2]
Dorsey Company manufactures three products from a common input in a joint processing operation. Joint processing costs up to the split-off point total $350,000 per quarter. The company allocates these costs to the joint products on the basis of their relative sales value at the split-off point. Unit selling prices and total output at the split-off point are as follows:

	Selling Price	Quarterly Output
Product A	$16 per kg	15,000 kg
Product B	$ 8 per kg	20,000 kg
Product C	$25 per litre	4,000 litres

Each product can be processed further after the split-off point. Additional processing requires no special facilities. The additional processing costs (per quarter) and unit selling prices after further processing are given below:

	Additional Processing Costs	Selling Price
Product A	$63,000	$20 per kg
Product B	$80,000	$13 per kg
Product C	$36,000	$32 per litre

Required:
Which product or products should be sold at the split-off point and which product or products should be processed further? Show computations.

EXERCISE 12–13 Managing a Constrained Resource [LO3]

Portsmouth Company makes fine colonial reproduction furniture. Upholstered furniture is one of its major product lines and the bottleneck on this production line is time in the upholstery shop. Upholstering is a craft that takes years of experience to master and the demand for upholstered furniture far exceeds the company's capacity in the upholstering shop. Information concerning three of the company's upholstered chairs appears below:

	Recliner	Sofa	Love Seat
Selling price per unit..........................	$1,400	$1,800	$1,500
Variable cost per unit	$ 800	$1,200	$1,000
Upholstery shop time required to produce one unit ...	8 hrs	10 hrs	5 hrs

Required:
1. More time could be made available in the upholstery shop by asking the employees who work in this shop to work overtime. Assuming this extra time would be used to produce sofas, up to how much of a premium should the company be willing to pay these employees per hour to keep the upholstery shop open after hours?
2. A small nearby upholstering company has offered to upholster furniture for Portsmouth at a fixed charge of $45 per hour. The management of Portsmouth is confident that this upholstering company's work is high quality and their upholsterers should be able to work about as quickly as Portsmouth's own upholsterers on the simpler jobs such as the love seat. Should management accept the offer? Explain.

EXERCISE 12–14 Identification of Relevant Costs [LO1]

Jason brought home eight ducks from his last hunting trip in northern Ontario. His friend Harry dislikes any type of hunting, and to discourage Jason from further hunting, Harry has presented him with the following cost estimates:

Camper and equipment:	
Cost, $16,000; usable for eight seasons; 10 hunting trips per season.............	$200
Travel expense (pickup truck):	
100 kilometres at $0.35 per kilometre (gas, oil, and	
tires—$0.25 per kilometre; depreciation and	
insurance—$0.10 per kilometre)	35
Shotgun shells (two boxes)...	20
Boat:	
Cost, $4,000, usable for eight seasons; 10 hunting trips per season..............	50
Hunting licence:	
Cost, $30 for the season; 10 hunting trips per season........................	3
Money lost playing poker:	
Loss, $40 (Jason plays poker every weekend)	40
Coffee beans:	
Cost, $20...	20
Total cost of the trip	$368
Cost per duck ($368 ÷ 8 ducks)	$ 46

Required:
1. Assuming that the duck-hunting trip Jason has just completed is typical, what costs are relevant to a decision as to whether Jason should go duck hunting again this season?
2. Suppose that Jason gets lucky on his next hunting trip and shoots 10 ducks in the amount of time it took him to shoot 8 ducks on his last trip. How much would it have cost him to shoot the last 2 ducks? Explain.
3. Which costs are relevant in a decision of whether Jason should give up hunting? Explain.

EXERCISE 12–15 Dropping or Retaining a Segment [LO2]

Williams Products Inc. manufactures and sells a number of items, including school knapsacks. The company has been experiencing losses on the knapsacks for some time, as shown by the contribution format income statement below:

<table>
<tr><td colspan="3" style="text-align:center">WILLIAMS PRODUCTS INC.
Income Statement—School Knapsacks
For the Quarter Ended June 30</td></tr>
<tr><td>Sales</td><td></td><td>$225,000</td></tr>
<tr><td>Variable expenses:</td><td></td><td></td></tr>
<tr><td> Variable manufacturing expenses</td><td>$65,000</td><td></td></tr>
<tr><td> Sales commissions</td><td>24,000</td><td></td></tr>
<tr><td> Shipping</td><td>6,000</td><td></td></tr>
<tr><td>Total variable expenses</td><td></td><td>95,000</td></tr>
<tr><td>Contribution margin</td><td></td><td>130,000</td></tr>
<tr><td>Fixed expenses:</td><td></td><td></td></tr>
<tr><td> Salary of product-line manager</td><td>10,500</td><td></td></tr>
<tr><td> General factory overhead</td><td>52,000*</td><td></td></tr>
<tr><td> Depreciation of equipment (no resale value)</td><td>18,000</td><td></td></tr>
<tr><td> Advertising—traceable</td><td>55,000</td><td></td></tr>
<tr><td> Insurance on inventories</td><td>4,500</td><td></td></tr>
<tr><td> Purchasing department</td><td>25,000†</td><td></td></tr>
<tr><td>Total fixed expenses</td><td></td><td>165,000</td></tr>
<tr><td>Operating loss</td><td></td><td>$ (35,000)</td></tr>
</table>

*Allocated on the basis of machine-hours
†Allocated on the basis of sales dollars

Discontinuing the knapsacks would not affect sales of other product lines and would have no noticeable effect on the company's total general factory overhead or total purchasing department expenses.

Required:

Would you recommend that the company discontinue the manufacture and sale of school knapsacks? Support your answer with appropriate computations.

EXERCISE 12–16 Make or Buy a Component [LO2]

Royal Company manufactures 10,000 units of Part R-3 each year. At this level of activity, the cost per unit for Part R-3 follows:

Direct materials	$14.40
Direct labour	21.00
Variable manufacturing overhead	9.60
Fixed manufacturing overhead	25.00
Total cost per part	$70.00

An outside supplier has offered to sell 10,000 units of Part R-3 each year to Royal Company for $54 per part. If Royal Company accepts this offer, the facilities now being used to manufacture Part R-3 could be rented to another company at an annual rental of $150,000. However, Royal Company has determined that $15 of the fixed manufacturing overhead being applied to Part R-3 would continue even if the part were purchased from the outside supplier.

Required:

Prepare computations showing how much profits will increase or decrease if the outside supplier's offer is accepted.

EXERCISE 12–17 Sell or Process Further [LO2]

The Fraser Paper Company produces large rolls of white paper weighing 1,000 kilograms for wholesalers for $1,500 each. The wholesalers then cut the paper into standard-sized sheets and package it in 2-kilogram packages. These packages are sold to printers for $4 per package. There is no waste in the cutting process. Fraser Paper currently produces 5 million kilograms of paper annually at a fixed cost of $1 million and a variable cost of $0.80 per kilogram. If Fraser bypassed the wholesalers and cut its own paper for sale directly to printers, Fraser would have to add equipment and personnel with an annual fixed cost of $650,000. Incremental variable costs would be $0.10 per kilogram.

Required:
Should Fraser cut its own paper or continue to sell to wholesalers?

EXERCISE 12–18 Dropping a Product Line [LO2]
Bed & Bath, a retailing company, has two departments—Hardware and Linens. The company's most recent monthly contribution format income statement follows:

| | Total | Department | |
		Hardware	Linens
Sales	$4,000,000	$3,000,000	$1,000,000
Variable expenses	1,300,000	900,000	400,000
Contribution margin	2,700,000	2,100,000	600,000
Fixed expenses	2,200,000	1,400,000	800,000
Net operating income (loss)	$ 500,000	$ 700,000	$ (200,000)

A study indicates that $340,000 of the fixed expenses being charged to Linens are sunk costs or allocated costs that will continue even if the Linens Department is dropped. In addition, the elimination of the Linens Department will result in a 10% decrease in the sales of the Hardware Department.

Required:
What is the financial advantage (disadvantage) of discontinuing the Linens Department?

EXERCISE 12–19 Make or Buy [LO2]
Electric Scooter Co. makes motorized scooters for city commuters. The scooters can be charged using a regular household plug, and the batteries hold their charge for 24 hours. The manufacturing plant is currently operating at 70% capacity. The plant manager is considering manufacturing headlights for the scooters, which are currently being produced by an outside company and purchased by Electric Scooter for $14 each. Electric Scooter has the equipment and the workforce to produce the headlights. The engineers have suggested a variable cost of $3 in direct labour and $4 in direct materials. The plant overhead rate is 150% of direct labour dollars, and 20% of the overhead is fixed cost.

Required:
Should Electric Scooter make the headlights in-house?

EXERCISE 12–20 Dropping a Product Line [LO2]
A doughnut shop makes three basic types of doughnuts: cream filled, chocolate filled, and jam filled. The doughnut shop manager is analyzing the product mix and has collected the following information:

	Chocolate Filled	Cream Filled	Jam Filled
Sales price per dozen	$ 4.00	$ 3.00	$ 2.50
Direct cost per dozen	(2.10)	(0.90)	(2.00)
Fixed overhead per dozen	(0.40)	(0.50)	(1.00)
Profit per dozen	$ 1.50	$ 1.60	(0.50)

The fixed costs are unavoidable and are allocated to each doughnut type based on the quantity produced. The doughnut shop has excess capacity.

Required:
1. Which product should the doughnut shop promote if the promotion will result in an increase in sales of 50 dozen of the promoted product?
2. Should the jam-filled doughnuts be dropped from the product line? Why or why not?
3. How does the decision to drop the jam-filled doughnuts change if the shop is currently producing at capacity?

PROBLEMS

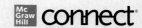

PROBLEM 12–21 Dropping or Retaining a Flight [LO2]

Profits have been decreasing for several years at Pegasus Airlines. In an effort to improve the company's performance, consideration is being given to dropping several flights that appear to be unprofitable. A typical income statement for one round-trip of one such flight (flight 482) is as follows:

Ticket revenue (175 = seat capacity × 40% occupancy × $200 ticket price per person).........	$14,000	100%
Variable expenses ($15 per person)	1,050	7.5
Contribution margin	12,950	92.5%
Flight expenses:		
Salaries, flight crew	1,800	
Flight promotion............................	750	
Depreciation of aircraft.......................	1,550	
Fuel for aircraft.............................	5,800	
Liability insurance	4,200	
Salaries, flight assistants.....................	1,500	
Baggage loading and flight preparation	1,700	
Overnight costs for flight crew at destination........	300	
Total flight expenses.............................	17,600	
Operating loss	$(4,650)	

The following additional information is available about the flight:

a. Members of the flight crew are paid fixed annual salaries, whereas the flight assistants are paid based on the number of round trips they complete.

b. One-third of the liability insurance is a special charge assessed against flight 482 because in the opinion of the insurance company, the destination of the flight is in a "high-risk" area. The remaining two-thirds would be unaffected by a decision to drop flight 482.

c. The baggage loading and flight preparation expense is an allocation of ground crews' salaries and depreciation of ground equipment. Dropping flight 482 would have no effect on the company's total baggage loading and flight preparation expenses.

d. If flight 482 is dropped, Pegasus Airlines has no authorization at present to replace it with another flight.

e. Aircraft depreciation is due entirely to obsolescence. Depreciation due to wear and tear is negligible.

f. Dropping flight 482 would not allow Pegasus Airlines to reduce the number of aircraft in its fleet or the number of flight crew on its payroll.

Required:

1. Prepare an analysis showing what impact dropping flight 482 would have on the airline's profits.

2. The airline's scheduling officer has been criticized because only about 50% of the seats on Pegasus's flights are being filled compared to an industry average of 60%. The scheduling officer has explained that Pegasus's average seat occupancy could be improved considerably by eliminating about 10% of its flights, but that doing so would reduce profits. Explain how this could happen.

PROBLEM 12–22 Sell or Process Further [LO2]

Valley Meat Processing Corporation is a major processor of beef and other meat products. The company has a large number of T-bone steaks on hand, and it is trying to decide whether to sell the T-bone steaks as is or to process them further into filet mignon and New York–cut steaks.

Management believes that a kilogram of T-bone steak would yield the following profit:

Wholesale selling price ($16.00 per kilogram)....................	$16.00
Less joint costs incurred up to the split-off point where T-bone steak can be identified as a separate product........................	12.00
Profit per kilogram	$ 4.00

As mentioned above, instead of being sold as is, the T-bone steaks could be further processed into filet mignon and New York–cut steaks. Cutting one side of a T-bone steak provides the filet mignon, and cutting the other side provides the New York cut. One 480-gram T-bone steak cut in this way will yield one 181-gram filet mignon and one 241-gram New York cut; the remaining grams are waste. The cost of processing the T-bone steaks into these cuts is $1.40 per kilogram. The filet mignon can be sold retail for $26 per kilogram, and the New York cut can be sold wholesale for $22 per kilogram.

Required:
1. Determine the profit for each 480-gram T-bone steak processed further into filet mignon and New York–cut steaks.
2. Would you recommend that the T-bone steaks be sold as is or processed further? Why?

(Prepared from a situation suggested by Professor John W. Hardy.)

PROBLEM 12–23 Close or Retain a Store [LO2]
The Tilots Corporation's segmented absorption costing income statement for the last quarter for its three metropolitan stores is given below:

	Total	Uptown Store	Downtown Store	Westpark Store
Sales	$2,500,000	$900,000	$600,000	$1,000,000
Cost of goods sold	1,450,000	513,000	372,000	565,000
Gross margin	1,050,000	387,000	228,000	435,000
Selling and administrative expenses:				
Selling expenses:				
Direct advertising	118,500	40,000	36,000	42,500
General advertising*	20,000	7,200	4,800	8,000
Sales salaries	157,000	52,000	45,000	60,000
Delivery salaries	30,000	10,000	10,000	10,000
Store rent	215,000	70,000	65,000	80,000
Depreciation of store fixtures	46,950	18,300	8,800	19,850
Depreciation of delivery equipment	27,000	9,000	9,000	9,000
Total selling expenses	614,450	206,500	178,600	229,350
Administrative expenses:				
Store management salaries	63,000	20,000	18,000	25,000
General office salaries*	50,000	18,000	12,000	20,000
Utilities	89,800	31,000	27,200	31,600
Insurance on fixtures and inventory	25,500	8,000	9,000	8,500
Employee benefits	36,000	12,000	10,200	13,800
General office expenses—other*	25,000	9,000	6,000	10,000
Total administrative expenses	289,300	98,000	82,400	108,900
Total operating expenses	903,750	304,500	261,000	338,250
Operating income (loss)	$ 146,250	$ 82,500	$(33,000)	$ 96,750

*Allocated on the basis of sales dollars

Management is very concerned about the Downtown Store's inability to show a profit, and consideration is being given to closing the store. The company has asked you recommend a course of action. Additional information available on the store is provided below:

a. The manager of the store has been with the company for many years; he would be retained and transferred to another position in the company if the Downtown Store were closed. His salary is $6,000 per month, or $18,000 per quarter. If the store were not closed, a new employee would be hired to fill the other position at a salary of $5,000 per month.
b. The lease on the building housing the Downtown Store can be broken with no penalty.
c. The fixtures being used in the Downtown Store would be transferred to the other two stores if the Downtown Store were closed.

d.   Employee benefits are 12% of salaries.

e.   A single delivery crew serves all three stores. One delivery person could be discharged if the Downtown Store were closed; this person's salary amounts to $7,000 per quarter. The delivery equipment would be distributed to the other stores. The equipment does not wear out through use, but it does eventually become obsolete.

f.   One-third of the Downtown Store's insurance relates to its fixtures.

g.   The general office salaries and other expenses relate to the general management of the Tilots Corporation. The employee in the general office who is responsible for the Downtown Store would be discharged if the store were closed. This employee's compensation amounts to $8,000 per quarter.

Required:

1.   Prepare a schedule showing the change in revenues and expenses and the impact on the overall company operating income that would result if the Downtown Store were closed.

2.   Based on your computations in (1) above, what would you recommend to the management of the Tilots Corporation?

3.   Assume that if the Downtown Store were closed, sales in the Uptown Store would increase by $200,000 per quarter due to loyal customers shifting their buying to the Uptown Store. The Uptown Store has ample capacity to handle the increased sales, and its gross margin is 43% of sales. What effect would these factors have on your recommendation concerning the Downtown Store? Show computations.

PROBLEM 12–24 Sell or Process Further [LO2]

The Scottie Sweater Company produces sweaters under the "Scottie" label. The company buys raw wool and processes it into wool yarn from which the sweaters are woven. One spindle of wool yarn is required to produce one sweater. The costs and revenues associated with the sweaters are given below:

Selling price per sweater...............		$30.00
Cost per sweater to manufacture:		
Raw materials:		
Wool yarn	$16.00	
Buttons, thread, lining...............	2.00	
Total raw materials	18.00	
Direct labour	5.80	
Manufacturing overhead	8.70	32.50
Manufacturing profit (loss).............		$(2.50)

Originally, all of the wool yarn was used to produce sweaters, but in recent years a market has developed for the wool yarn itself. Current cost and revenue data on the yarn are given below:

Selling price per spindle of yarn...........		$20.00
Cost to manufacture:		
Raw materials (raw wool)...............	$7.00	
Direct labour	3.60	
Manufacturing overhead	5.40	16.00
Manufacturing profit...................		$ 4.00

All of the manufacturing overhead costs are fixed and would not be affected even if sweaters were discontinued. Manufacturing overhead is assigned to products on the basis of 150% of direct labour cost. Materials and direct labour costs are variable.

Required:

1.   What is the incremental contribution margin (if any) from further processing the wool into sweaters?

2.   What is the lowest price that the company should accept for a sweater? Explain.

CHECK FIGURE
Incremental contribution margin from processing wool into sweaters = $2.20.

PROBLEM 12–25 Relevant Cost Analysis in a Variety of Situations [LO2]
Ovation Company has a single product called a Bit. The company normally produces and sells 60,000 Bits each year at a selling price of $32 per unit. The company's unit costs at this level of activity are given below:

Direct materials..........................	$10.00	
Direct labour.............................	4.50	
Variable manufacturing overhead	2.30	
Fixed manufacturing overhead	5.00	($300,000 total)
Variable selling expenses	1.20	
Fixed selling expenses......................	3.50	($210,000 total)
Total cost per unit	$26.50	

A number of questions relating to the production and sale of Bits follow. Each question is independent.

Required:
1. Assume that Ovation Company has sufficient capacity to produce 90,000 Bits each year without any increase in fixed manufacturing overhead costs. The company could increase its sales by 25% above the current 60,000 units each year if it were willing to increase the fixed selling expenses by $80,000. Would the increased fixed selling expenses be justified?
2. Assume again that Ovation Company has sufficient capacity to produce 90,000 Bits each year. A customer in a foreign market wants to purchase 20,000 Bits. Import duties on the Bits would be $1.70 per unit, and costs for permits and licences would be $9,000. The only selling costs that would be associated with the order are $3.20 per unit shipping cost. Compute the per unit break-even price on this order.
3. The company has 1,000 Bits on hand that have some irregularities and are therefore considered to be "seconds." Due to the irregularities, it will be impossible to sell these units at the normal price through regular distribution channels. What unit cost figure is relevant for setting a minimum selling price? Explain.
4. Due to a strike in its supplier's plant, Ovation Company is unable to purchase more material for the production of Bits. The strike is expected to last for two months. Ovation Company has enough material on hand to operate at 30% of normal levels for the two-month period. As an alternative, Ovation could close its plant down entirely for the two months. If the plant were closed, fixed manufacturing overhead costs would continue at 60% of their normal level during the two-month period and the fixed selling expenses would be reduced by 20%. What would be the impact on profits of closing the plant for the two-month period?
5. An outside manufacturer has offered to produce Bits and ship them directly to Ovation's customers. If Ovation Company accepts this offer, the facilities that it uses to produce Bits would be idle; however, fixed manufacturing overhead costs would be reduced by 75%. Since the outside manufacturer would pay for all shipping costs, the variable selling expenses would be only two-thirds of their current amount. Compute the unit cost that is relevant for comparison to the price quoted by the outside manufacturer.

PROBLEM 12–26 Shutting Down or Continuing to Operate a Plant [LO2]
(*Note:* This type of decision is similar to dropping a product line.) Nicholas Company manufactures a fast-bonding glue, normally producing and selling 40,000 litres of the glue each month. This glue, which is known as MJ-7, is used in the wood industry to manufacture plywood. The selling price of MJ-7 is $35 per litre, variable costs are $21 per litre, fixed manufacturing overhead costs in the plant total $230,000 per month, and the fixed selling costs total $310,000 per month.

Strikes in the mills that purchase the bulk of the MJ-7 glue have caused Nicholas Company's sales to temporarily drop to only 11,000 litres per month. Nicholas Company's management estimates that the strikes will last for two months, after which sales of MJ-7 should return to normal. Due to the current low level of sales, Nicholas Company's management is thinking about closing down the plant during the strike.

If Nicholas Company does close down the plant, fixed manufacturing overhead costs can be reduced by $60,000 per month and fixed selling costs can be reduced by 10%. Start-up costs at the end of the shutdown period would total $14,000. Since Nicholas Company uses lean production methods, no inventories are on hand.

Required:

1. Assuming that the strikes continue for two months, would you recommend that Nicholas Company close the plant? Explain. Show computations to support your answer.
2. At what level of sales (in litres) for the two-month period should Nicholas Company be indifferent between closing the plant and keeping it open? Show computations. (*Hint:* This is a type of break-even analysis, except that the fixed-cost portion of your break-even computation should include only those fixed costs that are relevant (i.e., avoidable) over the two-month period.)

PROBLEM 12–27 Make or Buy Analysis [LO2]

"That old equipment for producing oil drums is worn out," said Bill Seebach, president of Hondrich Company. "We need to make a decision quickly." The company is trying to decide whether it should rent new equipment and continue to make its oil drums internally or whether it should discontinue production and purchase them from an outside supplier. The alternatives follow:

Alternative 1: Rent new equipment for producing the oil drums for $120,000 per year.
Alternative 2: Purchase oil drums from an outside supplier for $16 each.

Hondrich Company's costs per unit of producing the oil drums internally (with the old equipment) are given below. These costs are based on a current activity level of 40,000 units per year:

Direct materials..	$ 5.50
Direct labour..	8.00
Variable overhead..	1.20
Fixed overhead ($1.50 supervision, $1.80 depreciation, and $4 general company overhead)............................	7.30
Total cost per unit..	$22.00

The new equipment would be more efficient and, according to the manufacturer, would reduce direct labour costs and variable overhead costs by 25%. Supervision cost ($60,000 per year) and direct materials cost per unit would not be affected by the new equipment. The new equipment's capacity would be 60,000 oil drums per year.

The total general company overhead would be unaffected by this decision.

Required:

1. Seebach is unsure what the company should do and would like an analysis showing the unit costs and total costs for each of the two alternatives given above. Assume that 40,000 oil drums are needed each year. Which course of action would you recommend to Seebach?
2. Would your recommendation in (1) above be the same if the company's needs were (*a*) 50,000 oil drums per year, or (*b*) 60,000 oil drums per year? Show computations in good form.
3. What other factors would you recommend that Seebach consider before making a decision?

> **CHECK FIGURE**
> Difference in favour of buying the oil drums = $0.90 per unit.

PROBLEM 12–28 Accept or Reject a Special Order [LO2]

Moore Company manufactures and sells a single product called a Lop. Operating at capacity, the company can produce and sell 30,000 Lops per year. Costs associated with this level of production and sales are given below:

	Unit	Total
Direct materials..	$15	$ 450,000
Direct labour...	8	240,000
Variable manufacturing overhead......................	3	90,000
Fixed manufacturing overhead	9	270,000
Variable selling expense	4	120,000
Fixed selling expense	6	180,000
Total cost...	$45	$1,350,000

The Lops normally sell for $50 each. Fixed manufacturing overhead is constant at $270,000 per year within the range of 25,000 through 30,000 Lops per year.

Required:
1. Assume that due to a recession, Moore Company expects to sell only 25,000 Lops through regular channels next year. A large retail chain has offered to purchase 5,000 Lops if Moore is willing to accept a 16% discount off the regular price. There would be no sales commissions on this order, so variable selling expenses would be slashed by 75%. However, Moore Company would have to purchase a special machine to engrave the retail chain's name on the 5,000 units. This machine would cost $10,000. Moore Company has no assurance that the retail chain will purchase additional units in the future. Determine the impact on profits next year if this special order is accepted.
2. Refer to the original data. Assume again that Moore Company expects to sell only 25,000 Lops through regular channels next year. The provincial government would like to make a one-time-only purchase of 5,000 Lops. The government would pay a fixed fee of $1.80 per Lop, and it would reimburse Moore Company for all costs of production (variable and fixed) associated with the units. Since the government would pick up the Lops with its own trucks, there would be no variable selling expenses associated with this order. If Moore Company accepts the order, by how much will profits increase or decrease for the year?
3. Assume the same situation as that described in (2) above, except that the company expects to sell 30,000 Lops through regular channels next year, so accepting the government's order would require giving up regular sales of 5,000 Lops. If the government's order is accepted, by how much will profits increase or decrease from what they would be if the 5,000 Lops were sold through regular channels?

PROBLEM 12–29 Sell or Process Further [LO2]

Clean and Shine Corporation produces several types of industrial and household cleaning compounds and solutions. While most of its products are processed independently a few are related, such as the company's Clean 236 and its Sparkle silver polish.

Clean 236 is a coarse cleaning powder with many industrial uses. It costs $3.20 a kilogram to make, and it has a selling price of $4.00 a kilogram. A small portion of the annual production of Clean 236 is retained in the factory for further processing. It is combined with several other ingredients to form a paste that is marketed as Sparkle silver polish. The silver polish sells for $8.00 per jar.

This further processing requires one-half kilogram of Clean 236 per jar of silver polish. The additional direct costs involved in the processing of a jar of silver polish are as follows:

Other ingredients..............................	$1.30
Direct labour.....................................	2.96
Total direct cost................................	$4.26

Overhead costs associated with the processing of the silver polish are as follows:

Variable manufacturing overhead cost..............	25% of direct labour cost
Fixed manufacturing overhead cost (per month):	
Production supervisor.........................	$6,000
Depreciation of mixing equipment..............	$2,800

The production supervisor has no duties other than to oversee production of the silver polish. The mixing equipment, purchased two years ago, is special-purpose equipment acquired specifically to produce the silver polish. Its resale value is negligible and it does not wear out through use.

Direct labour is a variable cost at Clean and Shine Corporation.

Advertising costs for the silver polish total $8,000 per month. Variable selling costs associated with the silver polish are 7.5% of sales.

Due to a recent decline in the demand for silver polish, the company is wondering whether its continued production is advisable. The sales manager feels that it would be more profitable to sell all of the Clean 236 as a cleaning powder.

Required:
1. What is the incremental contribution margin per jar from further processing Clean 236 into silver polish?
2. What is the minimum number of jars of silver polish that must be sold each month to justify the continued processing of Clean 236 into silver polish? Explain.

CASES

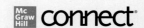

CASE 12–30 Integrative Case: Relevant Costs; Pricing [LO1, LO2]

Double Duty, a combination fertilizer–weed killer, is Alanco's only product. It is sold nationwide through normal marketing channels to retail nurseries and garden stores.

Taylor Nursery plans to sell a similar fertilizer–weed killer compound through its regional nursery chain under its own private label. Taylor does not have manufacturing facilities of its own, so it has asked Alanco (and several other companies) to submit a bid for manufacturing and delivering a 25,000-kilogram order of the private-brand compound to Taylor. While the chemical composition of the Taylor compound differs from that of Double Duty, the manufacturing processes are very similar.

The Taylor compound would be produced in 1,000-kilogram lots. Each lot would require 30 direct labour-hours and the following chemicals:

Chemical	Quantity in Kilograms
CW–3	400
JX–6	300
MZ–8	200
BE–7	100

The first three chemicals (CW–3, JX–6, and MZ–8) are all used in the production of Double Duty. BE–7 was used in another compound that Alanco discontinued several months ago. The supply of BE–7 that Alanco had on hand when the other compound was discontinued was not discarded. Alanco could sell its supply of BE–7 at the prevailing market price less $0.10 per kilogram selling and handling expenses.

Alanco also has on hand a chemical called CN–5, which was manufactured for use in another product that is no longer produced. CN–5, which cannot be used in Double Duty, can be substituted for CW–3 on a one-to-one basis without affecting the quality of the Taylor compound. The CN–5 in inventory has a salvage value of $500.

Inventory and cost data for the chemicals that can be used to produce the Taylor compound are as shown below:

Raw Material	Kilograms in Inventory	Actual Price per Kilogram When Purchased	Current Market Price per Kilogram
CW–3	22,000	$0.80	$0.90
JX–6	5,000	0.55	0.60
MZ–8	8,000	1.40	1.60
BE–7	4,000	0.60	0.65
CN–5	5,500	0.75	(salvage)

The current direct labour rate is $14 per hour. The predetermined overhead rate is based on direct labour-hours (DLH). The predetermined overhead rate for the current year, based on a two-shift capacity of 400,000 total DLH with no overtime, is as follows:

Variable manufacturing overhead	$ 4.50 per DLH
Fixed manufacturing overhead	7.50 per DLH
Combined rate	$12.00 per DLH

Alanco's production manager reports that the current equipment and facilities are adequate to manufacture the Taylor compound. Therefore, the order would have no effect on total fixed manufacturing overhead costs. However, Alanco is within 400 hours of its two-shift capacity this month. Any additional hours beyond 400 hours must be done in overtime. If need be, the Taylor compound could be produced on regular time by shifting a portion of Double Duty production to overtime. Alanco's rate for overtime hours is 1½ times the regular pay rate, or $21 per hour. There is no allowance for any overtime premium in the predetermined overhead rate.

Required:
1. Alanco has decided to submit a bid for a 25,000-kilogram order of Taylor Nursery's new compound. The order must be delivered by the end of the current month. Taylor Nursery has indicated that this is a one-time order that will not be repeated. Calculate the lowest price that Alanco could bid for the order without reducing its operating income.
2. Refer to the original data. Assume that Taylor Nursery plans to place regular orders for 25,000-kilogram lots of the new compound during the coming year. Alanco expects the demand for Double Duty to remain strong. Therefore, the recurring orders from Taylor Nursery would put Alanco over its two-shift capacity. However, production could be scheduled so that 60% of each Taylor Nursery order could be completed during regular hours. As another option, some Double Duty production could be shifted temporarily to overtime so that the Taylor Nursery orders could be produced on regular time. Current market prices are the best available estimates of future market prices.

    Alanco's standard markup policy for new products is 40% of the full manufacturing cost, including fixed manufacturing overhead. Calculate the price that Alanco would quote Taylor Nursery for each 25,000-kilogram lot of the new compound, assuming that it is to be treated as a new product and this pricing policy is followed.

CASE 12–31 Special Order and Constrained Resource [LO2, LO3]

East Coast Digital (ECD) produces high-quality audio and video equipment. One of the company's most popular products is a high-definition personal video recorder (PVR) for use with digital television systems. Demand has increased rapidly for the PVR over the past three years, given the appeal to customers of being able to easily record programs while they watch live television, watch recorded programs while they record a different program, and save dozens of programs for future viewing on the unit's large internal hard drive.

A complex production process is utilized for the PVR involving both laser and imaging equipment. ECD has a monthly production capacity of 4,000 hours on its laser machine and 1,000 hours on its image machine. However, given the recent increase in demand for the PVR, both machines are currently operating at 90% of capacity every month, based on existing orders from customers. Direct labour costs are $15 and $20 per hour to operate, respectively, the laser and image machines.

The revenue and costs on a per unit basis for the PVR are as follows:

Selling price		$320.00
Cost to manufacture:		
Direct materials	$50.00	
Direct labour—laser process	60.00	
Direct labour—image process	20.00	
Variable overhead	40.00	
Fixed overhead	50.00	
Variable selling costs	20.00	240.00
Operating profit		$ 80.00

On December 1, Dave Nance, vice-president of Sales and Marketing at ECD, received a special-order request from a prospective customer, Jay Limited, which has offered to buy 250 PVRs at $280 per unit if the product can be delivered by December 31. Jay Limited is a large retailer with outlets that specialize in audio and video equipment. This special order from Jay Limited is in addition to orders from existing customers that are utilizing 90% of the production capacity each month. Variable selling costs would not be incurred on this special order. Jay Limited is not willing to accept anything less than the 250 PVRs requested (i.e., ECD cannot partially fill the order).

Before responding to the customer, Nance decided to meet with Dianne Davis, the product manager for the PVR, to discuss whether to accept the offer from Jay Limited. An excerpt from their conversation follows:

Nance: I'm not sure we should accept the offer. This customer is really playing hardball with its terms and conditions.

Davis: Agreed, but it is a reputable company and I suspect this is the way it typically deals with its suppliers. Plus, this could be the beginning of a profitable relationship with Jay Limited since the company may be interested in some of our other product offerings in the future.

Nance: That may be true, but I'm not sure we should be willing to incur such a large opportunity cost just to get our foot in the door with this client.

Davis: Have you calculated the opportunity cost?

Nance: Sure, that was simple. Jay Limited is offering $280 per unit and we sell to our regular customers at $320 per unit. Therefore, we're losing $40 per unit, which at 250 units is $10,000 in lost revenue. That's our opportunity cost and it's clearly relevant to the decision.

Davis: I sort of follow your logic, but I think the fact that we're not currently operating at full capacity needs to be taken into consideration.

Nance: How so?

Davis: Well, your approach to calculating the opportunity cost ignores the fact that we aren't currently selling all of the PVRs that we could produce. So, in that sense we aren't really losing $40 per unit on all 250 units required by Jay Limited.

Nance: I see your point but I'm not clear on how we should calculate the opportunity cost.

Davis: This really isn't my area of expertise either, but it seems appropriate to start by trying to figure out how many of the 250 units required by Jay Limited we could produce without disrupting our ability to fill existing orders. Then we could determine how many units we would have to forgo selling to existing customers to make up the 250-unit order. That would then be our opportunity cost in terms of the number of physical units involved. Make sense?

Nance: I think so. So, to get the dollar amount of the opportunity cost of accepting the 250-unit order from Jay Limited we'd then simply multiply the number of units we'd have to forgo selling to existing customers by $40. Correct?

Davis: I'm not so sure about the $40. I think we somehow need to factor in the incremental profit we typically earn by selling each PVR to existing customers to really get to the true opportunity cost.

Nance: Now I'm getting really getting confused. Can you work through the numbers and get back to me?

Davis: I'll try.

Nance: Thanks. And by the way, Jay Limited is calling in an hour and wants our answer.

Required:

1. Is Davis's general approach to calculating the opportunity cost in terms of the physical units involved correct? Explain.
2. Assuming productive capacity cannot be increased for either machine in December, how many PVRs would ECD have to forgo selling to existing customers to fill the special order from Jay Limited?
3. Calculate the opportunity cost of accepting the special order.
4. Calculate the net effect on profits of accepting the special order.
5. Now assume that ECD is operating at 75% of capacity in December. What is the minimum price ECD should be willing to accept on the special order?
6. What are some qualitative issues that should be considered when accepting special orders such as that proposed by Jay Limited?

CASE 12–32 Sell or Process Further Decision [LO2]

Turnberry Tomatoes has a plant that can process vine-ripened tomatoes, along with other ingredients, into various tomato sauces and salsas. The company can sell all of its unprocessed vine-ripened tomatoes at a selling price of $6.15 per kilogram. In the past, the company has sold only part of its unprocessed vine-ripened tomatoes and has retained the rest for further processing into tomato sauces and salsas. The salsa has been selling for $8.75 per kilogram, but recently the price has become unstable and has dropped to $7.80 per kilogram. The costs and revenues associated with a kilogram of salsa follow:

		Per Kilogram of Salsa
Selling price		$ 7.80
Cost to manufacture:		
Raw materials:		
Extra salsa ingredients	$1.00	
Unprocessed tomatoes (1 kg)	5.90	6.90
Direct labour		0.25
Manufacturing overhead		0.75
Manufacturing profit (loss)		$(0.10)

Because of the weak price for the company's processed sauces and salsas, the sales manager believes that the company should discontinue processing the salsas and instead simply sell the unprocessed vine-ripened tomatoes. Current cost and revenue data on the unprocessed vine-ripened tomatoes follow:

		Per Kilogram of Tomatoes
Selling price		$6.15
Cost to manufacture:		
Seeds, pesticides, and fertilizers	$4.90	
Direct labour	0.25	
Manufacturing overhead	0.75	5.90
Manufacturing profit		$0.25

The sales manager argues that since the current $7.80 per kilogram price for the salsa results in a $0.10 per kilogram loss, the production of salsa should not be resumed until the price per kilogram rises above $7.90. The company assigns manufacturing overhead cost to the two products on the basis of labour-hours, but virtually all manufacturing overhead costs are fixed. Materials and labour costs are variable. The company can sell all of the unprocessed vine-ripened tomatoes and salsa it can produce at the current market prices.

Required:
1. Do you agree with the sales manager that the company should discontinue the processing of salsa and use the entire labour capacity to grow, sort, and package tomatoes if the price of salsa remains at $7.80 per kilogram? Support your answer with computations and explanations.
2. What is the lowest price that the company should accept for a kilogram of salsa? Again support your answer with computations and explanations.

CASE 12–33 Make or Buy; Utilization of a Constrained Resource [LO1, LO2, LO3]
Drums, bins, boxes, and other containers that are used in the petroleum industry are sold by Holden Inc. One of the company's products is a heavy-duty, environmentally friendly, corrosion-resistant metal drum, called the STR drum, used to store toxic wastes. Production is constrained by the capacity of an automated welding machine that is used to make precision welds. A total of 4,500 hours of welding time is available annually on the machine. Since each drum requires 0.6 hours of welding time, annual production is limited to 7,500 drums. At present, the welding machine is used exclusively to make the STR drums. The accounting department has provided the following financial data concerning the STR drums:

STR Drums		
Selling price per drum		$225.00
Cost per drum:		
Direct materials	$78.15	
Direct labour ($27 per hour)	5.40	
Manufacturing overhead	6.75	
Selling and administrative expenses	44.70	135.00
Margin per drum		$ 90.00

Management believes that 9,000 STR drums could be sold each year if the company had sufficient manufacturing capacity. As an alternative to adding another welding machine, management has considered buying additional drums from an outside supplier of quality products, Anderson Industries Inc. Anderson would be able to provide up to 6,000 STR-type drums per year at a price of $207 per drum, which Holden would relabel and sell to its customers at its normal selling price.

Candace Burke, Holden's production manager, has suggested that the company could make better use of the welding machine by manufacturing wrought iron park benches, which would require 0.75 hours of welding time per bench and yet sell for far more than the drums. Burke believes that Holden could sell up to 2,400 wrought iron park benches per year to municipalities and conservation areas at a price of $360 each. The Accounting Department has provided the following data concerning the proposed new product:

Wrought Iron Park Benches		
Selling price per bench		$360.00
Cost per bench:		
Direct materials.	$149.10	
Direct labour ($27 per hour)	43.20	
Manufacturing overhead	54.00	
Selling and administrative expenses	71.70	318.00
Margin per bench		$ 42.00

The park benches could be produced with existing equipment and personnel. Manufacturing overhead is allocated to products on the basis of direct labour-hours. Most of the manufacturing overhead consists of fixed common costs, such as rent on the factory building, but some of it is variable. The variable manufacturing overhead has been estimated at $2.00 per STR drum and $2.85 per park bench. The variable manufacturing overhead cost would not be incurred on drums acquired from the outside supplier.

Selling and administrative expenses are allocated to products on the basis of revenues. Almost all of the selling and administrative expenses are fixed common costs, but it has been estimated that variable selling and administrative expenses amount to $1.15 per STR drum whether made or purchased and $1.95 per park bench.

All of the company's employees—direct and indirect—are paid for full 40-hour workweeks and the company has a policy of laying off workers only in major recessions.

Required:
1. Should the financial analysis prepared by the company be used in deciding which product to sell? Why?
2. Compute the contribution margin per unit for
    a. Purchased STR drums.
    b. Manufactured STR drums.
    c. Manufactured park benches.
3. Determine the number of STR drums (if any) that should be purchased and the number of STR drums and/or park benches (if any) that should be manufactured. What is the increase in operating income that would result from this plan over current operations?

    As soon as your analysis was shown to the top management team at Holden, several managers got into an argument concerning how direct labour costs should be treated when making this decision. One manager argued that direct labour is always treated as a variable cost in textbooks and in practice and has always been considered a variable cost at Holden. After all, "direct" means you can directly trace the cost to products. "If direct labour is not a variable cost, what is?" Another manager argued just as strenuously that direct labour should be considered a fixed cost at Holden. No one had been laid off in over a decade, and for all practical purposes, everyone at the plant is on a monthly salary. Everyone classified as direct labour works a regular 40-hour workweek, and overtime has not been necessary since the company adopted just-in-time techniques. Whether the welding machine were used to make drums or park benches, the total payroll would be exactly the same. There is enough slack, in the form of idle time, to accommodate any increase in total direct labour time that the park benches would require.
4. Redo requirements (2) and (3) above, making the opposite assumption about direct labour from the one you originally made. In other words, if you treated direct labour as a variable cost, redo the analysis treating it as a fixed cost. If you treated direct labour as a fixed cost, redo the analysis treating it as a variable cost.
5. What do you think is the correct way to treat direct labour cost in this situation—as variable or as fixed?

INSTANT QUIZ SOLUTIONS

12–1

No. Only those future costs that differ between the alternatives under consideration are relevant costs in decision making.

12–2

Direct costs can usually be avoided, but some indirect costs might remain even after the product line is dropped. Another factor to consider is whether the company has an alternative use for the space taken up by the machinery and equipment used to produce this product. If so, then management needs to consider the opportunity cost of not putting the space to an alternative use in making a decision. Finally, management should also consider the effect of dropping this product on sales of Able's other products. Will customers expect to be able to buy this product from Able, and, if so, will they go elsewhere for all of their related needs since Able does not carry the full line of products that customers expect?

12–3

Jones must first consider which costs are avoidable by outsourcing baked goods production. For example, can some employees be laid off if products are no longer produced on-site? If so, how much cost savings will be generated? Jones should also consider the opportunity cost of the space currently taken up with bakery equipment. Could that space be put to a more productive use? For example, if she expanded her seating area, would she attract more customers to the shop? Factors other than potential cost savings must also be considered. For example, she would need to consider whether the supplier is dependable in terms of quality and delivery, and she should be concerned about the possibility that the supplier might raise the price soon after Jones signs the contract to a price greater than her original cost of production.

12–4

Smythe needs to consider the incremental costs of filling the special order. For example, will the additional cost of materials required to fill the special order be less than the $20 special price? Since Smythe's staff are paid fixed salaries, there should be no incremental fixed costs assuming they have time available to fill the order without working overtime. In addition, Smythe needs to consider the opportunity cost of filling this special order. Could he be generating more incremental revenue by filling a similar order at the regular price? If so, what is the likelihood a customer will place such an order before the end of the week?

12–5

The incremental revenue earned by assembling the barbecue is $225 − $200, or $25. The incremental cost is $15/hour × ½ hour = $7.50. Since the incremental revenue is greater than the incremental cost, Corner Hardware should sell the barbecues assembled.

12–6

The company needs to consider the contribution margin per unit of constrained resource provided by each product. To calculate this measure more information is needed—specifically, the machine time required to attach the upper part of each type of boot to the sole. With this information, the company can divide the contribution margin of each product by the machine time required and maximize production of the product with the higher contribution margin per minute.

12–7

When companies have a constraint on a production input such as labour-hours or machine-hours, the relative profitability of products should be determined by calculating the profitability index. The profitability index is determined by dividing the contribution margin per unit for each product by the amount of the good output. The result is the contribution margin per unit of the scarce resource. Production should be maximized for the product with the highest profitability index, and so on until all capacity has been utilized.

■ APPENDIX 12A: PRICING PRODUCTS AND SERVICES

LEARNING OBJECTIVE ④
Compute selling prices based on costs using the absorption and variable costing approaches.

Our consideration of special orders in the main body of this chapter focused on non-routine situations where companies receive an offer for a product or service at a specific price. By comparing to the offer price the relevant costs that would be incurred if the offer were accepted, managers can determine the incremental effect on operating income. In this appendix, we expand our discussion of the relationship between relevant costs and pricing issues to include two distinct pricing situations requiring ongoing analysis by managers. First, we examine situations where companies are faced with the problem of setting their own prices for products or services. In this setting, we present two approaches to setting prices based on costs. Second, we examine a setting where the company offers a product or service that competes with other similar products or services for which a market price already exists. In this setting, we introduce the concept of target costing. Importantly, in both settings managers must identify and use relevant cost information to make decisions that are in the best interests of the company. Setting prices is a critical decision for managers. If the price is set too high, customers will avoid purchasing the company's products. If the price is set too low, the company's costs may not be covered.

Cost-Plus Pricing

A common approach to pricing is to set prices based on a certain *markup* above cost.[3] A product's **markup** is the difference between its selling price and its cost. The markup is usually expressed as a percentage of cost. This approach is called **cost-plus pricing** because the predetermined markup percentage is applied to the cost base to determine a target selling price:

$$\text{Selling price} = \text{Cost} + (\text{Markup percentage} \times \text{Cost})$$

For example, if a company uses a markup of 50%, it adds 50% to the costs of its products to determine the selling price. If a product costs $10, then the company will charge $15 for the product.

There are two key issues when the cost-plus approach to pricing is used. First, what costs are relevant to the pricing decision? Second, how should the markup be determined? Several alternative approaches are considered in this appendix.

As discussed in Chapters 2 through 8 and Chapter 10, various definitions of *cost* exist, each of which could be used as the base for setting a selling price. To provide a coherent illustration of cost-plus pricing, absorption costing will be presented first. We will then present an example of cost-plus pricing using the total variable costing approach.

Markup
The difference between the selling price of a product or service and its cost. The markup is usually expressed as a percentage of cost.

Cost-plus pricing
A pricing method in which a predetermined markup is applied to a cost base to determine the target selling price.

Setting a Target Selling Price Using the Absorption Costing Approach

To illustrate, assume that the management of Roper Company wants to set the selling price on a product that has just undergone some design modifications. The Accounting Department has provided cost estimates for the redesigned product as shown below:

	Per Unit	Total
Direct materials.	$12	
Direct labour	8	
Variable manufacturing overhead	6	
Fixed manufacturing overhead	–	$140,000
Variable selling and administrative expenses	4	
Fixed selling and administrative expenses	–	120,000

The first step in the absorption costing approach to cost-plus pricing is to compute the unit product cost. For Roper Company, this amounts to $40 per unit at a volume of 10,000 units, as shown in the first part of Exhibit 12A–1.

Roper Company has a general policy of marking up unit product costs by 50%. A price quotation sheet for the company prepared using the absorption approach is also presented in Exhibit 12A–1. Note that selling and administrative costs are not included in the cost base. Instead, the markup is set at a level that will cover these expenses.

Next we examine how some companies compute markup percentages.

EXHIBIT 12A–1
Price Quotation
Sheet—Absorption
Basis (10,000 Units)

Direct materials.	$12
Direct labour	8
Variable manufacturing overhead	6
Fixed manufacturing overhead (based on 10,000 units)	14
Unit product cost.	40
Markup to cover selling and administrative expenses and	
desired profit—50% of unit manufacturing cost.	20
Target selling price	$60

Determining the Markup Percentage

How did Roper Company arrive at its markup percentage of 50%? This figure could be based on industry norms or just a company tradition that seems to work. The markup percentage may also be the result of an explicit computation. As we have discussed, the markup over cost should ideally be largely determined by market conditions. However, a popular approach is to at least start with a markup based on cost and desired profit. The reasoning is as follows: the markup must be large enough to cover selling and administrative expenses and provide an adequate return on investment (ROI). Given the forecast unit sales, the markup can be computed as follows:

$$\text{Markup percentage on absorption cost} = \frac{\left(\begin{array}{c}\text{Required ROI} \\ \times \text{ Investment}\end{array}\right) + \text{Selling and administrative expenses}}{\text{Unit sales} \times \text{Unit product cost}}$$

To show how the formula above is applied, assume Roper Company must invest $200,000 to produce and market 10,000 units of the product each year. The $200,000 investment covers the purchase of equipment and the funds needed for working capital items such as inventory and accounts receivable. If Roper Company requires a 20% ROI, then the markup for the product is determined as follows:

$$\text{Markup percentage on absorption cost} = \frac{(20\% \times \$200,000) + [(\$4 \times 10,000) + \$120,000]}{10,000 \times \$40}$$

$$\text{Markup percentage on absorption cost} = \frac{\$40,000 + \$160,000}{\$400,000} = 50\%$$

As shown earlier, this markup of 50% leads to a target selling price of $60 for the Roper Company product. As shown in Exhibit 12A–2, *if the company actually sells 10,000 units* of the product at this price, and actual costs are as expected, the company's ROI on this product will indeed be 20%. If it turns out that more than 10,000 units are sold at this price, the ROI will be greater than 20%. If fewer than 10,000 units are sold, the ROI will be less than 20%. *The required ROI will be attained only if the forecast unit sales volume is attained or exceeded at the expected unit price (or higher)*, and actual costs are equal to or less than expected costs for that level of sales activity.

Problems with the Absorption Costing Approach

Using the absorption costing approach, the pricing problem looks deceptively simple. All you have to do is compute your unit product cost, decide how much profit you want, and then set your price. It appears that you can ignore demand and arrive at a price that will safely yield whatever profit you want. However, as noted above, the absorption costing approach relies on a forecast of unit sales. Neither the markup nor the unit product cost can be computed without such a forecast.

The absorption costing approach essentially assumes that customers *need* the forecast unit sales and will pay whatever price the company decides to charge. However, customers have a choice. If the price is too high, they can buy from a competitor or they may choose not to buy at all. Suppose, for example, that when Roper Company sets its price at $60, it sells only 7,000 units rather than the 10,000 units forecast. As shown in Exhibit 12A–3, the company would then have a loss of $50,000 on the product instead of a profit of $40,000. Some managers believe that the absorption costing approach to pricing is safe. This is not necessarily so. The absorption costing approach is safe only as long as customers choose to buy at least as many units as managers forecast they would buy and costs behave as predicted or come in at lower levels.

EXHIBIT 12A–2
Income Statement and Return on Investment Analysis— Roper Company Actual Unit Sales = 10,000 Units; Selling Price = $60

Direct materials	$12
Direct labour	8
Variable manufacturing overhead	6
Fixed manufacturing overhead ($140,000 ÷ 10,000 units)	14
Unit product cost	$40

ROPER COMPANY
Absorption Costing Income Statement

Sales ($60 × 10,000 units)	$600,000
Less cost of goods sold ($40 × 10,000 units)	400,000
Gross margin	200,000
Less selling and administrative expenses ($4 × 10,000 units + $120,000)	160,000
Operating income	$ 40,000

ROI

$$\text{ROI} = \frac{\text{Operating income}}{\text{Average operating assets}}$$

$$= \frac{\$40,000}{\$200,000}$$

$$= 20\%$$

EXHIBIT 12A–3
Income Statement and ROI Analysis— Roper Company Actual Unit Sales = 7,000 Units; Selling Price = $60

Direct materials	$12
Direct labour	8
Variable manufacturing overhead	6
Fixed manufacturing overhead ($140,000 ÷ 7,000 units)	20
Unit product cost	$46

ROPER COMPANY
Absorption Costing Income Statement

Sales ($60 × 7,000 units)	$420,000
Less cost of goods sold ($46 × 7,000 units)	322,000
Gross margin	98,000
Less selling and administrative expenses ($4 × 7,000 units + $120,000)	148,000
Operating income	$(50,000)

ROI

$$\text{ROI} = \frac{\text{Operating income}}{\text{Average operating assets}}$$

$$= \frac{\$50,000}{\$200,000}$$

$$= -25\%$$

Setting a Target Selling Price Using the Variable Costing Approach

Some companies use a variable costing approach to determine the target selling price based on either variable manufacturing costs or total variable costs. The key advantages of the variable costing approach are (1) it is consistent with the cost–volume–profit analysis presented in Chapter 4, which allows managers to determine the profit effects of changes in price and volume, and (2) it avoids the need to arbitrarily allocate common fixed costs to specific products.

To illustrate the use of the variable costing approach using total variable costs, we return to the Roper Company example.[4] The revised formula for calculating the markup is as follows:

$$\text{Markup percentage on total variable cost} = \frac{(\text{Required ROI} \times \text{Investment}) + \text{Total fixed expenses}}{\text{Unit sales} \times \text{Unit total variable costs}}$$

The numerator now includes fixed manufacturing overhead costs, and the denominator includes both manufacturing and selling and administrative variable expenses. The reason for this approach is that the markup must result in a contribution margin that covers all fixed expenses *and* leads to the required level of profit.

The calculations for the Roper Company data are as follows:

$$\text{Markup percentage on total variable cost} = \frac{(20\% \times \$200{,}000) + \$140{,}000 + \$120{,}000}{10{,}000 \times (\$12 + \$8 + \$6 + \$4)}$$

$$\text{Markup percentage on total variable cost} = \frac{\$40{,}000 + \$260{,}000}{\$300{,}000} = 100\%$$

A markup of 100% under the total variable costing approach results in the same $60 per unit selling price as the absorption costing approach: $30 + (100% × $30) = $60. By comparison, the markup required under the absorption costing approach is only 50% because the cost base ($40) is higher by virtue of including *all* manufacturing costs (variable and fixed). This highlights the need for managers using the total variable costing approach to remember that the markup must cover all costs, variable *and* fixed. While the ROI method of determining the markup explicitly incorporates all fixed costs in the calculations, other approaches, such as industry norms or company tradition, may not. Regardless of the method used to calculate the cost base or the markup percentage, managers must be diligent in ensuring that all costs are covered.

Setting a Target Selling Price for Service Companies Using Time and Materials Pricing

Time and materials pricing
A pricing method, often used in service firms, in which two pricing rates are established—one based on direct labour time and the other based on direct materials used.

A variation of cost-plus pricing used by some companies, particularly in service industries, is called **time and materials pricing**. Under this approach, two pricing rates are established, one based on direct labour time and the other based on the cost of direct material used.

This pricing method is widely used in the service industry (e.g., repair shops and printing shops) and by many professionals, such as engineers and lawyers. The time and materials rates are usually market determined. In other words, the rates are determined by the interplay of supply and demand and by competitive conditions in the industry. However, some companies set the rates using a process similar to the process followed in the absorption costing approach to cost-plus pricing. In this case, the rates include allowances for selling and administrative expenses, for other direct and indirect costs, and for a desired profit. This section will show how the rates might be set using the cost-plus approach.

Time Component

The time component is typically expressed as a rate per hour of labour. The rate is computed by adding together three elements: (1) the direct costs of the employee, including salary and benefits; (2) a pro rata allowance for selling and administrative expenses of the organization; and (3) an allowance for a desired profit per hour of employee time. In some organizations (such as a repair shop), the same hourly rate will be charged regardless of which employee actually works on the job; in other organizations, the rate may vary by employee. For example, in a public accounting firm, the rate charged for a staff accountant's time will be less than the rate charged for an experienced senior accountant or for a partner.

Materials Component

Materials loading charge
A markup applied to the cost of materials that is designed to cover the costs of ordering, handling, and carrying materials in inventory and to provide for some profit.

The materials component is determined by adding a **materials loading charge** to the invoice price of any materials used on the job. The materials loading charge is designed to cover the costs of ordering, handling, and carrying materials in inventory, plus a profit margin on the materials themselves.

An Example of Time and Materials Pricing

To provide an example of time and materials pricing, we use data from The Quality Auto Shop. The following costs for repairs and parts have been budgeted for the coming year:

	Repairs	Parts
Mechanics' wages	$300,000	$ —
Service manager—salary	40,000	—
Parts manager—salary	—	36,000
Clerical assistant—salary	18,000	15,000
Employee benefits—16% of salaries and wages.	57,280	8,160
Supplies.	720	540
Utilities	36,000	20,800
Property taxes	8,400	1,900
Depreciation	91,600	37,600
Invoice cost of parts used		400,000
Total budgeted cost	$552,000	$520,000

The company expects to bill customers for 24,000 hours of repair time. A profit of $7 per hour of repair time is considered reasonable, given the competitive conditions in the market. For parts, the competitive markup on the invoice cost of parts used is 15%.

Exhibit 12A–4 shows the computation of the billing rate and the materials loading charge to be used for the next year. Note that the billing rate, or time component, is $30 per hour of repair time and the materials loading charge is 45% of the invoice cost of parts used. Using these rates, a repair job that requires 4.5 hours of mechanics' time and $200 in parts would be billed as follows:

Labour time: 4.5 hours × $30		$135
Parts used:		
Invoice cost	$200	
Materials loading charge: 45% × $200	90	290
Total price of the job.		$425

EXHIBIT 12A–4   Time and Materials Pricing

	Time Component: Repairs		Parts: Materials Loading Charge	
	Total	Per Hour*	Total	Percent†
Cost of mechanics' time:				
Mechanics' wages	$300,000			
Employee benefits (16% of wages)	48,000			
Total cost	348,000	$14.50		
For repairs—other cost of repair service. For parts— costs of ordering, handling, and storing parts:				
Repairs service manager—salary	40,000		$ —	
Parts manager—salary	—		36,000	
Clerical assistant—salary	18,000		15,000	
Employee benefits (16% of salaries)	9,280		8,160	
Supplies.	720		540	
Utilities	36,000		20,800	
Property taxes	8,400		1,900	
Depreciation	91,600		37,600	
Total cost.	204,000	8.50	20,000	30%
Desired profit:				
24,000 hours × $7	168,000	7.00	—	
15% × $400,000			60,000	15%
Total amount to be billed	$720,000	$30.00	$180,000	45%

*Based on 24,000 hours.
†Based on $400,000 invoice cost of parts. The charge for ordering, handling, and storing parts, for example, is computed as follows: $120,000 cost ÷ $400,000 invoice cost = 30%.

Rather than using labour-hours as the basis for computing the time rate, a machine shop, a printing shop, or a similar organization might use machine-hours.

This method of setting prices is a variation of the absorption costing approach. As such, it is not surprising that it suffers from the same problem: customers may not be willing to pay the rates that have been computed. Further, if the actual volume of business is less than the forecast 24,000 hours and $400,000 worth of parts, or actual costs exceed estimates, the profit objectives will not be met and the company may not even break even.

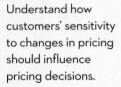

LEARNING OBJECTIVE

Understand how customers' sensitivity to changes in pricing should influence pricing decisions.

■ PRICING AND CUSTOMER LATITUDE

As discussed in the previous section, customers have latitude in their purchasing decisions. They can purchase a competitor's product or allocate their spending budget to some other product altogether. This latitude should be taken into account when setting prices. To illustrate, consider Nature's Garden, a company that sells many products including Apple-Almond Shampoo. The company has provided the following data regarding this product:

	Apple-Almond Shampoo
Unit sales (a)	200,000
Selling price per unit	$5.00
Variable cost per unit..........................	2.00
Contribution margin per unit (b)	$3.00
Total contribution margin (a × b)	$600,000
Traceable fixed expenses........................	570,000
Net operating income...........................	$ 30,000

Management is considering increasing the price of Apple-Almond Shampoo from $5.00 to $5.50, but is fully aware that this 10% increase in price [= ($5.50 − $5.00) ÷ $5.00] will result in a decline in unit sales because of the latitude that customers have in their purchasing decisions. If unit sales drop too much, profit (i.e., net operating income) may actually decline despite the increase in the selling price. The company's marketing managers have estimated that this price hike could decrease unit sales by as much as 15%, from 200,000 units to 170,000 units.

The question the company would like to answer is which price ($5.00 or $5.50) will generate higher profits? To answer this question, the company can use the following equation to calculate Apple-Almond Shampoo's profit at each price:

$$\text{Profit} = (P - V) \times Q - \text{Fixed expenses}$$

where P is the selling price per unit, V is the variable cost per unit, and Q is the unit sales.

At a price of $5.00 and a sales volume of 200,000 units, Apple-Almond Shampoo earns a profit of $30,000 as shown below:

$$
\begin{aligned}
\text{Profit} &= (P - V) \times Q - \text{Fixed expenses} \\
&= (\$5 - \$2) \times 200,000 - \$570,000 \\
&= \$3\,(200,000) - \$570,000 \\
&= \$30,000
\end{aligned}
$$

At a price of $5.50 and a sales volume of 170,000 units, assuming that fixed expenses are not affected by the decrease in unit sales, Apple-Almond Shampoo earns a profit of $25,000 as shown below:

$$
\begin{aligned}
\text{Profit} &= (P - V) \times Q - \text{Fixed expenses} \\
&= (\$5.50 - \$2) \times 170,000 - \$570,000 \\
&= \$3\,(200,000) - \$570,000 \\
&= \$25,000
\end{aligned}
$$

Given these results, Nature's Garden should not raise the price of this product to $5.50 because its profits would be $5,000 higher (= $30,000 − $25,000) at the lower price of $5.00.

Customer Latitude: A Closer Look

Thus far, our example has assumed that management has only two options: either keep the price of Apple-Almond Shampoo at $5.00 or increase it to $5.50 with a resulting drop in unit sales of 15%. However, keep in mind that the 15% figure is an estimate, not a certainty. Based on our previous calculations, we know that increasing the price from $5.00 to $5.50 would reduce profits if unit sales decrease by 15%. If unit sales decrease by more than 15%, profits will decline even more. But what would be the financial implications if unit sales actually decreased by something *less than* 15%?

Management could explore this possibility by calculating the unit sales (Q) needed at the higher price ($5.50) to achieve the same profit ($30,000) that is earned at the lower price ($5.00). Assuming that fixed expenses remain unchanged, that critical value of unit sales (Q) can be solved for as follows:

$$\text{Profit} = (P - V) \times Q - \text{Fixed expenses}$$
$$\$30,000 = (\$5.50 - \$2) \times Q - \$570,000$$
$$\$30,000 = \$3.50Q - \$570,000$$
$$\$600,000 = \$3.50Q$$
$$Q = 171,429 \text{ units (rounded)}$$

This calculation tells us that if the company sells 171,429 units at the selling price of $5.50, the company will earn the same profit that it earned at the lower price of $5.00. But if the company sells *more* than 171,429 units, then increasing the selling price by 10% will *increase* profit. However, if the company sells *fewer* than 171,429 units, then increasing the selling price by 10% will *decrease* profit. The critical value of 171,429 units is sort of a break-even in this situation.

The sales volume of 171,429 units reflects a percentage change in sales of –14.3% [= (171,429 – 200,000) ÷ 200,000]. Thus, if management believes unit sales will drop by *less* than 14.3% it should choose a price of $5.50. If management believes unit sales will drop by *more* than 14.3% it should choose a price of $5.00. Let's suppose that management believes unit sales will drop by less than 14.3% and therefore the selling price is increased to $5.50. Further suppose that management is correct, and after increasing the price unit sales drop by only 13%—from 200,000 units to 174,000 units. Then Apple-Almond Shampoo would earn a profit of $39,000 as shown below:

$$\text{Profit} = (P - V) \times Q - \text{Fixed expenses}$$
$$= (\$5.50 - \$2) \times 174,000 - \$570,000$$
$$= \$3.50 (174,000) - \$570,000$$
$$= \$39,000$$

In this case, because unit sales drop by only 13%, the higher price of $5.50 causes profits to increase by $9,000 (= $39,000 – $30,000).

Choosing Optimal Prices: The Influence of Customer Latitude

If we assume a 10% increase in the price of Apple-Almond Shampoo causes a 13% decrease in unit sales, then a price of $5.50 will generate $9,000 (= $39,000 – $30,000) of additional profit compared to a price of $5.00. However, it would be incorrect to conclude that $5.50 is the *optimal price* for Apple-Almond Shampoo; in other words, the price that would maximize profit.

A price of $5.50 is not necessarily the optimal price, because Nature's Garden is not limited to choosing a price of either $5.00 or $5.50. Perhaps the company would be better off considering an 8% or 12% price increase rather than just a 10% increase. For that matter, the company can establish any price it wants for Apple-Almond Shampoo. It could establish a very low price, such as $2.00 per unit, or a very high price, such as $50 per unit, or anything in between. The low price of $2.00 would be a bad idea because it equals the product's variable cost per unit and would lead to a loss of $570,000, whereas the high price of $50 per unit may be a bad idea because very few customers, if any, would pay $50 for a bottle of shampoo. Thus, the management challenge becomes leveraging knowledge of how customers will respond to changes in price to determine the selling price that will maximize profits—keeping in mind that this optimal price could be higher or lower than the current price of $5.00.

Exhibit 12A–5 uses Microsoft Excel Solver to illustrate a pricing model that calculates an optimal price for any product or service once the percentage change in price and percentage change in unit sales have been specified. This pricing model assumes a constant elasticity demand curve and fixed expenses that are unaffected by changes in unit sales.[5] The specific calculations shown in Exhibit 12A–5 relate to Nature Garden's Apple-Almond Shampoo assuming that a 10% increase in price causes a 13% decrease in unit sales.

EXHIBIT 12A–5
Nature's Garden
Apple-Almond
Shampoo: An
Optimal Pricing
Model

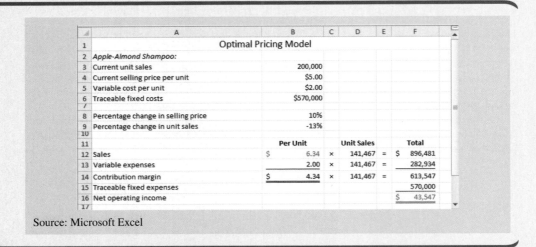

Source: Microsoft Excel

Note: The price shown in cell B12 is rounded to the nearest penny, whereas Excel used the unrounded price (which is approximately $6.337) to compute the total sales in cell F12.

The first thing to notice with respect to the output from our optimal price calculations shown in Exhibit 12A–5 is that the optimal price is not $5.00 or $5.50. It is $6.34 as shown in cell B12. At this price, the company earns a profit of $43,547 (cell F16), which is $4,547 (= $43,547 − $39,000) higher than the previously computed profit obtained at a price of $5.50. While the mathematics underlying this pricing model are beyond the scope of this course, if you choose to download the model and familiarize yourself with it, we want you to understand how to input data into the model and how to interpret the results.

To input data into the model, you should follow a four-step process. First, input the product's current unit sales (cell B3), current selling price (cell B4), variable cost per unit (cell B5), and traceable fixed costs (cell B6). Second, input the percentage change in selling price (cell B8) and the percentage change in unit sales (cell B9). Third, input the current selling price in cell B12. Fourth, click on the Data tab in Microsoft Excel and select Solver in the upper right-hand portion of your screen.[6] When the Solver window opens, click "Solve" and the optimal price will be calculated and automatically inserted into cell B12. In addition, the optimal profit will be automatically calculated in cell F16.

A Visual Perspective of the Optimal Pricing Model

Exhibit 12A–6 plots Apple-Almond Shampoo's net operating income as a function of the selling price when we assume that a 10% increase in price decreases unit sales by 13%.[7]

This plot provides a visual aid in understanding what the optimal pricing model is doing. Essentially, Excel Solver efficiently searches along this graph for the price that maximizes the profit, which in this case is a selling price of $6.34 that results in a total profit of $43,547.

For a variety of reasons, this optimal selling price should not be taken too literally. A prudent manager would make a small change in price in the direction of the optimal price and then observe what happens to unit sales and to the net operating income. Nevertheless, the Excel workbook can provide us with important insights into pricing. If we wanted to adjust the percentage change in unit sales or the percentage change in selling price, we could re-run the Solver function to automatically compute the revised optimal selling price.[8] For example, the table below summarizes the results for three scenarios illustrating different customer sensitivities to a 10% increase in price for Apple-Almond Shampoo:

Percentage change in selling price......................	+10%	+10%	+10%
Percentage change in unit sales	−12%	−13%	−15%
Optimal selling price	$7.86	$6.84	$4.84
Unit sales	109,009	141,467	211,685
Net operating income.................................	$68,908	$43,547	$30,390

In general, the more sensitive customers are to price the lower the optimal selling price will be, and the less sensitive customers are to price the higher the optimal selling price will be. For example, when customers respond to a 10% increase in price with a 12% decrease in unit sales the optimal price is $7.86, which is $2.86 above the current price of $5.00. Conversely, when customers respond to a 10%

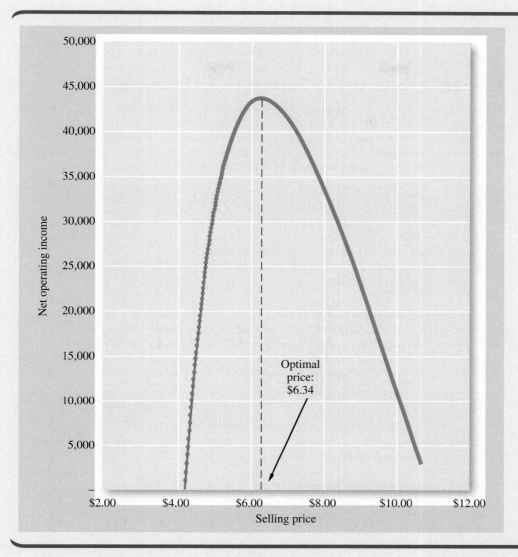

EXHIBIT 12A–6
Nature's Garden
Apple-Almond
Shampoo: Net
Operating Income
as a Function of
Selling Price

increase in price with a 15% decrease in unit sales the optimal price is $4.84, which is $0.16 below the current price of $5.00. This large swing in prices illustrates how a small change in customers' sensitivity to price can have a big impact on the optimal selling price.

■ VALUE-BASED PRICING

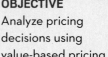

LEARNING OBJECTIVE 6
Analyze pricing decisions using value-based pricing.

An alternative to cost-plus pricing is **value-based pricing**. Companies that use value-based pricing establish selling prices based on the economic value of the benefits that their products and services provide to customers.

One approach to value-based pricing relies on a concept known as the **economic value to the customer (EVC)**. A product's economic value to the customer is the price of the customer's best available alternative plus the value of what differentiates the product from that alternative. The price of the best available alternative is known as the *reference value*, whereas the value of what differentiates a product from the best available alternative is known as the *differentiation value*.

A product's differentiation value can arise in either of two ways. First, a product may differentiate itself by enabling customers to generate more sales and contribution margin than the best available alternative. Second, a product may differentiate itself by enabling customers to realize greater cost savings than the best available alternative.

In equation form, the EVC is computed as follows:

$$\text{Economic value to the customer} = \text{Reference value} + \text{Differentiation value}$$

Value-based pricing
A pricing system in which a company establishes selling prices based on the economic value of the benefits that their products and services provide to customers.

Economic value to the customer (EVC)
The price of a customer's best alternative (called the reference value) plus the value of what differentiates the product from that alternative (called the differentiation value).

Once the seller computes the EVC, it seeks to negotiate a value-based selling price with the customer that falls within the following range:

$$\text{Reference value} \leq \text{Value-based price} \leq \text{EVC}$$

Economic Value to the Customer: An Example

The managers of *Hike America* magazine want to establish a selling price for a one-month full-page advertisement in their magazine. While their primary competitor, *Hiking Trails* magazine, charges $5,000 per month for a full-page ad, the managers of *Hike America* believe that they can justify a higher selling price by quantifying the EVC of a full-page ad in their magazine. To enable their analysis, the managers gathered the following data pertaining to the two magazines:

	Hike America	Hiking Trails
Number of readers	200,000	300,000
Percent of readers who buy advertised products each month	0.2%	0.1%
Monthly spending per reader who buys advertised products.	$100	$80
Contribution margin ratio of advertisers	25%	25%

Although *Hike America* has fewer readers than *Hiking Trails* magazine (200,000 vs. 300,000), a higher percentage of *Hike America*'s "hard core" subscribers buy advertised products each month (0.2% vs. 0.1%) and they spend more per person on advertised products ($100 vs. $80). Given the assumption that advertisers in both magazines earn a contribution margin ratio of 25% on all merchandise sales, *Hike America*'s managers computed the differentiation value of an ad placed in their magazine as follows:

	Hike America	Hiking Trails
Number of readers (a)	200,000	300,000
Percent of readers who buy advertised products each month (b).	0.2%	00.1%
Number of readers per month buying advertised products (a × b)	400	300
Monthly sales per reader who buys advertised products (a)	$100	$80
Contribution margin ratio (b).	25%	25%
Monthly contribution margin per reader who buys advertised products (a × b)	$25	$20
Number of readers buying advertised products (a)	400	300
Monthly contribution margin per reader who buys advertised products (b).	$25	$20
Contribution margin per month provided by a full-page ad (a) × (b)	$10,000	$6,000
Differentiation value	$4,000	

Given that *Hike America*'s reference value is $5,000—the price charged by *Hiking Trails* for a full-page ad—the EVC would be computed as follows:

$$\text{Economic value to customer} = \text{Reference value} + \text{Differentiation value}$$
$$= \$5,000 + \$4,000$$
$$= \$9,000$$

Hike America would seek to negotiate a value-based selling price for a full-page advertisement within the following range:

$$\text{Reference value} \leq \text{Value-based price} \leq \text{EVC}$$
$$\$5,000 \leq \text{Value-based price} \leq \$9,000$$

It bears emphasizing that the EVC of $9,000 does not necessarily represent the price that *Hike America* should charge customers for a full-page advertisement. Instead, it provides the magazine's managers a starting point for understanding the economic benefit (in terms of additional contribution margin) that a full-page ad in their magazine can offer to prospective customers. In fact, the data shown below suggest that *Hike America* probably needs to establish a price less than $9,000.

| | Hike America | | |
	Price = $9,000	Price = $8,000	Hiking Trails
Contribution margin provided by the ad....................	$10,000	$10,000	$6,000
Investment in the ad (a)	9,000	8,000	5,000
Incremental profit from the ad (b) ..	$ 1,000	$ 2,000	$1,000
Return on investment (b/a)........	11%	25%	20%

Notice that the right-hand column of numbers shows that *Hiking Trails* magazine provides its customers with a 20% ROI for a full-page advertisement. Conversely, the left-hand column of numbers shows that *Hike America*'s customers would earn only an 11% ROI if they paid $9,000 for a full-page ad. Thus, if *Hike America* established a price of $9,000 it would provide advertisers with a lower ROI than they could earn by placing a full-page ad in *Hiking Trails* magazine. However, *Hike America* might consider touting a lower price, such as $8,000, to its prospective customers. As shown in the middle column of data, this lower price would provide prospective advertisers with an ROI of 25%, which compares favourably with the *Hiking Trails* ROI of 20%.

■ TARGET COSTING

LEARNING OBJECTIVE ❼
Compute target costs based on selling prices.

Target costing
The process of determining the maximum allowable cost for a new product and then developing a prototype that can be profitably manufactured and distributed for that maximum target cost figure.

Our discussion so far has presumed that a product has already been developed, has been costed, and is ready to be marketed as soon as a price is set. In many cases, the sequence of events is just the reverse. That is, the company will already *know* what price should or can be charged, and the problem will be to *develop a product* that can be marketed profitably at the desired price. Even in this situation, where the normal sequence of events is reversed, cost is still a crucial factor. The company's approach will be to employ *target costing*. **Target costing** is the process of determining the maximum allowable cost for a new product and then developing a prototype that can be profitably made for that maximum target cost figure. Many companies use target costing, including Chrysler, Ford, Sharp, and Toyota.

The target cost for a product is computed by starting with the product's anticipated selling price and then deducting the desired profit, as follows:

$$\text{Target cost} = \text{Anticipated selling price} - \text{Desired profit}$$

The product development team is then given the responsibility of designing the product so that it can be made for no more than the target cost.

Reasons for Using Target Costing

The target costing approach was developed in recognition of two important characteristics of markets and costs. The first is that many companies have less control over price than they would like. The market (i.e., supply and demand) really determines prices, and a company that attempts to ignore this does so at its peril. Therefore, the anticipated market price is taken as a given in target costing. The second observation is that most of the cost of a product is determined in the design stage. Once a product has been designed and has gone into production, not much can be done to significantly reduce its cost. Most of the opportunities to reduce cost come from designing the product so that it is as simple to make as possible and uses cost-effective parts, while meeting the expectations of customers with respect to quality. If the company has little control over market price and limited control over cost once the product has gone into production, then it follows that the major opportunities for affecting profit come at the design stage, where valuable features for which customers are willing to pay can be added and where most of the costs are really determined. The difference between target costing and other approaches to product development is profound. Instead of designing the product, determining the cost, and setting the price, the target cost is set first and then the product is designed so that the target cost is attained.

Effective target costing requires a detailed understanding of what is valued by the customer; the full costs of production, including long-term investments; and a detailed breakdown of the target cost. A management philosophy of customer focus and cost reduction (Kaizen costing) will help a company to realize the full benefits of target costing.

An Example of Target Costing

For a simple numerical example of target costing, assume the following situation: AFM Electronics feels that there is a market niche for stereo headphones with certain new features. Surveying the features and prices of headphones already on the market, the Marketing Department believes that a price of $150 would be about right for the new headphones. At that price, Marketing estimates that 80,000 of the new headphones could be sold annually. To design, develop, and produce these new headphones, an investment of $8,000,000 would be required. The company wants a 30% ROI. Given these data, the target cost to manufacture, sell, distribute, and service one pair of headphones is $120, as shown below:

Projected sales (80,000 headphones × $150)	$12,000,000
Less desired profit (30% × $8,000,000)	2,400,000
Target cost for 80,000 headphones	$ 9,600,000
Target cost per pair of headphone ($9,600,000 ÷ 80,000 headphones)	$ 120.00

This $120 target cost would be broken down into target costs for the various functions: manufacturing, marketing, distribution, after-sales service, and so on. Each functional area would be responsible for keeping its actual costs within the target.

■ APPENDIX 12A SUMMARY

- Companies offering products and services where a market price is not readily available often use cost-plus pricing. One approach to cost-plus pricing uses absorption unit product costs as the cost base, with the markup calculated both to cover non-manufacturing costs and to provide an adequate return on investment (ROI). Another approach uses total variable costs as the base, with the markup covering all fixed costs and providing an adequate ROI. **[LO4]**
- Companies in the service industry often use a variation of the cost-plus approach called time and materials pricing. Two pricing rates are established: one for direct labour time and the other for direct material costs. **[LO4]**
- The degree to which either cost-plus pricing or time and materials pricing will lead to the desired profits critically depends on the accuracy of both the sales forecasts and the cost estimates. **[LO4]**
- Customers have latitude in their purchasing decisions. They can choose to buy your product, a competitor's product, or nothing at all. This latitude should be taken into account when setting prices. In general, the more sensitive customers are to price, the lower the optimal selling price will be and the less sensitive customers are to price, the higher the optimal selling price will be. **[LO5]**
- Companies that use value-based pricing establish selling prices based on the economic value of the benefits that their products and services provide to customers. Once the seller computes the EVC, it establishes a value-based selling price that falls between the reference value and the EVC. **[LO6]**
- Some companies develop and sell products or services for which an established market and price already exist. Target costing can be used in such situations. Desired profit is deducted from the estimated market price to determine the product's target cost. The product design and development team then has the responsibility of ensuring that the actual cost of the new product does not exceed the target cost. **[LO7]**

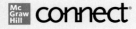 ## ■ APPENDIX 12A EXERCISES AND PROBLEMS

EXERCISE 12A–1 Absorption Costing and Total Variable Costing Approaches to Setting a Selling Price [LO4]

Nolan Limited is considering introducing a new product. Management has gathered the following information:

Number of units to be produced and sold each year	10,000
Unit product cost	$ 16
Projected annual selling and administrative expenses	$ 40,000
Estimated investment required by the company	$400,000
Desired return on investment (ROI)	8%

Required:

1. Using the absorption costing approach to cost-plus pricing, compute the markup the company will have to use to achieve the desired ROI.
2. Assume that the $16 unit product cost includes $3 per unit for fixed manufacturing overhead based on producing and selling 10,000 units each year. Also assume that $26,000 of the total selling and administrative expenses of $40,000 is fixed. The remainder is variable. Use the total variable costing approach to calculate the markup the company will have to use to achieve the desired ROI.
3. Compute the target selling price per unit under each pricing approach from (1) and (2) above.

EXERCISE 12A–2 Target Costing [LO7]

Little River Cycles (LRC) produces and distributes carbon fibre road bikes. Management is eager to take advantage of the growing market for these bikes. LRC's sales manager estimates that to be competitive the bike can't be priced at more than $2,000. At this price, management thinks the company can sell 1,000 bikes per year. Producing the bikes will require an initial investment of $2,000,000, and the company's target ROI is 25%.

Required:

Calculate the target cost of one carbon fibre road bike.

EXERCISE 12A–3 Time and Materials Pricing [LO4]

Ronnie's Repair Company provides repair services for small engines and uses time and materials pricing. The company has budgeted the following costs for next year:

Mechanics' wages and benefits........................	$900,000
Other repair costs, except for parts-related costs	$450,000
Costs of ordering, handling, and storing parts	40% of invoice cost

In total, the company expects to have 50,000 hours of billable repair time next year. According to competitive conditions, the company believes it should aim for a profit of $8 per hour of each mechanic's time. The competitive markup on parts is 40% of invoice cost.

Required:

1. Compute the time rate and the materials loading charge that would be used to bill jobs.
2. One of the company's mechanics has just completed a repair job that required 12 hours of time and $100 in parts (invoice cost). Compute the amount that would be billed for the job.

EXERCISE 12A–4 Customer Latitude and Pricing [LO5]

Maria Lorenzi owns an ice cream stand that she operates during the summer months in Port Elgin, Ontario. She is unsure how to price her ice cream cones and has experimented with two prices in successive weeks during the busy August season. The number of people who entered the store was roughly the same each week. During the first week, she priced the cones at $3.50 and 1,800 cones were sold. During the second week, she priced the cones at $4.00 and 1,400 cones were sold. The variable cost of a cone is $0.80 and consists solely of the costs of the ice cream and the cone itself. The fixed expenses of the ice cream stand are $2,675 per week.

Required:

1. What profit did Maria earn during the first week when her price was $3.50?
2. At the start of the second week, Maria increased her selling price by what percentage? What percentage did unit sales decrease? (Round your answers to one-tenth of a percent.)
3. What profit did Maria earn during the second week when her price was $4.00?
4. What was Maria's increase (decrease) in profits from the first week to the second week?

EXERCISE 12A–5 Value-Based Pricing [LO6]

McDermott Company has developed a new industrial component called IC-75. The company is excited about IC-75 because it offers superior performance relative to the comparable component sold by McDermott's primary competitor. The competing part sells for $1,200 and needs to be replaced after 2,000 hours of use. It also requires $200 of preventive maintenance during its useful life. The IC-75's performance capabilities are similar to its competing product with two important exceptions—it needs to be replaced after 4,000 hours of use and it requires $300 of preventive maintenance during its useful life.

Required:

From a value-based pricing standpoint:

1. What is the reference value that McDermott should consider when pricing IC-75?
2. What is the differentiation value offered by IC-75 relative to the competitor's offering for each 4,000 hours of usage?
3. What is IC-75's economic value to the customer over its 4,000-hour life?
4. What range of possible prices should McDermott consider when setting a price for IC-75?

PROBLEM 12A–6 Standard Costs; Absorption Costing and Total Variable Costing Approach to Setting Prices [LO4]

Gerber Clothing Inc. has designed a rain suit for outdoor enthusiasts that is about to be introduced on the market. A standard cost card has been prepared for the new suit, as follows:

	Standard Quantity or Hours	Standard Price or Rate	Standard Cost
Direct materials..........................	2.5 metres	$10.00 per metre	$25.00
Direct labour...........................	1.0 hours	28.00 per hour	28.00
Manufacturing overhead (¹⁄₆ variable)	1.0 hours	24.00 per hour	24.00
Total standard cost per suit.................			$77.00

a. The only variable selling and administrative costs will be $4 per suit for shipping. Fixed selling and administrative costs will be as follows (per year):

Salaries	$ 45,000
Advertising and other	200,000
Total	$245,000

b. Since the company manufactures many products, it is felt that no more than 10,000 hours of labour time per year can be devoted to production of the new suits.
c. An investment of $500,000 will be necessary to carry inventories and accounts receivable and to purchase some new equipment. The company wants a 20% ROI in new product lines.
d. Manufacturing overhead costs are allocated to products on the basis of direct labour-hours.

Required:

1. Assume that the company uses the absorption approach to cost-plus pricing.
    a. Compute the markup that the company needs on the rain suits to achieve a 20% ROI if it sells all of the suits it can produce using 10,000 hours of labour time.
    b. Using the markup you have computed, prepare a price quote sheet for a single rain suit.
    c. Assume that the company is able to sell all of the rain suits that it can produce. Prepare an income statement for the first year of activity, and compute the company's ROI for the year on the suits, using the ROI formula from Chapter 11.
2. Repeat 1(*a*) and 1(*b*) above, assuming that the company uses the total variable costing approach to cost-plus pricing.
3. After marketing the rain suits for several years, the company is experiencing a decrease in demand due to an economic recession. A large retail outlet will make a bulk purchase of suits if its company logo is affixed to each suit and if an acceptable price can be worked out. What is the minimum acceptable price per rain suit for this order?

PROBLEM 12A–7 Target Costing [LO7]

Free Riders Inc. is considering adding a scooter to its motorcycle lineup. Management will negotiate the price of the scooter with its manufacturer.

Management of Free Riders believes the scooters can be sold to its customers for $4,000 each. At that price, annual sales of the scooters should be 200 units. If the scooters are added to Free Riders' product lines, the company will have to invest $200,000 in inventories and special warehouse fixtures. The variable cost of selling the scooters will be $1,000 per unit.

Required:

1. If Free Riders requires a 20% ROI, what is the maximum amount the company would be willing to pay the manufacturer for the scooters?
2. After many hours of negotiations, management has concluded that the manufacturer is unwilling to sell the scooters at a low enough price for Free Riders to earn its 20% required ROI. Apart from simply giving up on the idea of adding the scooters to Free Riders' product lines, what could management do?

PROBLEM 12A–8 Time and Materials Pricing [LO4]

Computer Repair Inc. uses time and materials pricing, and each year it reviews its rates in light of the actual costs incurred in the prior year. Actual costs incurred last year in connection with repair work and in connection with the company's parts inventory are shown below:

	Repairs	Parts
Repair technicians—wages	$480,000	
Repair service manager—salary	56,000	
Parts manager—salary		$ 60,000
Repairs and parts assistant—salary	28,800	7,500
Retirement benefits (20% of salaries and wages)	112,960	13,500
Health insurance (5% of salaries and wages)	28,240	3,375
Utilities	120,000	24,000
Truck operating costs	19,200	
Property taxes	9,280	5,400
Liability and fire insurance	6,720	3,000
Supplies	1,200	225
Rent—building	38,400	33,000
Depreciation—trucks and equipment	59,200	
Invoice cost of parts used		600,000
Total costs for the year	$960,000	$750,000

Customers were billed for 20,000 hours of repair work last year.

The company has a target profit of $10 per hour of repair service time and a target profit of 40% of the invoice cost of parts used. During the past year, the company billed repair service time at $50 per hour and added a materials loading charge of 40% to parts. Management feels these rates may now be inadequate, since costs have risen somewhat over the last year.

Required:

1. Using the above data, compute the following:
    a.   The rate that would be charged per hour of repair service time using time and materials pricing.
    b.   The materials loading charge that would be used in billing jobs. The materials loading charge should be expressed as a percentage of the invoice cost.
2. Assume that the company adopts the rates that you have computed in (1) above. What should be the total price charged on a repair job that requires six hours of service time and parts with an invoice cost of $500?
3. If the company adopts the rates that you have computed in (1) above, would you expect the company's profits to improve?

PROBLEM 12A–9 Value-Based Pricing [LO6]

The managers of *Midwest Whitetails* magazine (a magazine dedicated to deer hunters) want to establish a price for customers wishing to place a full-page advertisement in their magazine for one month. To help with the price-setting decision, the managers intend to compute the economic value to the customer (EVC) of a full-page ad in their magazine. They have gathered the following data pertaining to *Midwest Whitetails* magazine as well as their primary competitor, *Trophy Whitetails* magazine:

	Midwest Whitetails	Trophy Whitetails
Number of readers	130,000	200,000
Percent of readers who buy advertised products each month	0.7%	0.5%
Monthly spending per reader who buys advertised products	$120	$100
Contribution margin ratio of advertisers	40%	40%

Trophy Whitetails magazine charges $4,000 per month for a full-page ad. Managers at *Midwest Whitetails* believe they can charge more than $4,000 by quantifying the economic value to customers of placing an ad in their magazine.

Although *Midwest Whitetails* has fewer readers than *Trophy Whitetails* (130,000 vs. 200,000), *Midwest Whitetails* attracts a segment of hunters that is more likely to buy advertisers' products than the casual hunters who tend to subscribe to *Trophy Whitetails*. Therefore, a higher percentage of *Midwest Whitetails* subscribers buy advertised products (0.7% vs. 0.5%) and they spend more per person on advertised products ($120 vs. $100). The managers of *Midwest Whitetails* assume that advertisers in both magazines earn an average contribution margin ratio of 40% on all of their merchandise sales.

Required:
From a value-based pricing standpoint:

1. What is the reference value that *Midwest Whitetails* should consider when setting the price of a full-page ad in its magazine?
2. What is the differentiation value offered by a full-page ad placed in *Midwest Whitetails* magazine?
3. What is the economic value to the customer (EVC) of a full-page ad in *Midwest Whitetails* magazine?
4. What range of possible prices should *Midwest Whitetails* consider when setting a price for a full-page ad?

ENDNOTES

1. K. Siegel-Jacobs and F. Yates, "Effects of Procedural and Outcome Accountability on Judgment Quality," *Organizational Behaviour and Human Decision Processes* 65:1, 1996, pp. 7–17.
2. An alternative approach to the analysis is to add the incremental unit cost of continuing to make the shifters of $14 (see Exhibit 12–5) to the opportunity cost per unit of $7.50 ($60,000 opportunity cost ÷ 8,000 units), giving a total of $21.50. Since $21.50 is greater than the purchase price of $19 per unit, OSN Cycle should buy the shifters.
3. There are some legal restrictions on prices. Competition laws prohibit "predatory" pricing, which is generally interpreted by the courts to mean a price below average variable cost. "Price discrimination"—charging different prices to customers in the same market for the same product or service—is also prohibited by law.
4. The variable manufacturing cost approach would exclude variable selling and administrative expenses from the cost base and instead include them in the numerator. Otherwise, it is the same as the total variable costing approach.
5. This pricing model assumes a constant elasticity demand curve and fixed expenses that are unaffected by the changes in unit sales. Other demand curves, such as a linear demand curve, could be assumed. While there is some empirical support for using the constant elasticity demand curve, it should be acknowledged that the "optimal" selling price will depend on the demand curve that is assumed. Because of this, as well as the uncertainty that usually surrounds estimates of customer responses to price changes, the "optimal" price produced by this model should be viewed as an estimate and not taken too literally.
6. Solver is an add-in offered within Microsoft Excel. To activate Solver if you do not see it in your Data tab, click the File tab and select Options. Within the Excel Options menu that appears on your screen click Add-ins and then select Solver Add-in and click OK.
7. As with the Solver solution to the optimal pricing problem, this graph assumes a constant elasticity demand curve and that the fixed expenses are constant throughout the entire range of unit sales that result from the various prices.
8. If Solver is unable to find a solution, the most likely cause is that the combination of the percentage change in price and the percentage change in unit sales that you have input has resulted in an infinite optimal price. For example, if a 10% increase in price always leads to only a 5% decrease in units sold and fixed costs are constant, then profits always go up when the price is increased. This obviously cannot happen in practice. At some point customers will stop buying the product altogether.

CHAPTER 13

CAPITAL BUDGETING DECISIONS

LEARNING OBJECTIVES

After studying Chapter 13, you should be able to

1. Evaluate the acceptability of an investment project using the net present value method.

2. Evaluate the acceptability of an investment project using the internal rate of return method.

3. Evaluate an investment project that has uncertain cash flows.

4. Rank investment projects in order of preference.

5. Determine the payback period for an investment.

6. Calculate the simple rate of return for an investment.

7. (Appendix 13A) Explain present value concepts and the underlying mathematics of interest.

8. (Appendix 13B) Incorporate income taxes into a capital budgeting analysis.

■ GOING FOR GOLD

THE CANADIAN PRESS / Frank Gunn

Barrick Gold Corporation is the largest gold mining company in the world. Founded in the early 1980s, Barrick has its company headquarters in Toronto and has mining and exploration projects in numerous countries worldwide. To facilitate growth in operations Barrick must continuously make significant capital investments to develop new projects, expand existing projects, and sustain operations. In 2018, the company spent over $1.4 billion on capital projects.

The challenge for capital-intensive companies such as Barrick is deciding from among many alternatives which projects to invest in and when. Because the funds companies have available for capital spending are usually limited, these decisions are extremely important. Moreover, making good capital budgeting decisions can have a considerable impact on the long-term profitability of a company.

Capital budgeting
The process of planning significant outlays on projects that have long-term implications, such as purchasing new equipment or introducing a new product.

Managers often consider decisions that involve an investment today in the hope of realizing future profits. For example, Tim Hortons makes an investment when it opens a new restaurant. McCain Foods makes an investment when it expands production facilities to increase processing capacity. Paradigm makes an investment when it redesigns a stereo speaker model and must retool its production lines. All of these investments require spending now with the expectation of additional future net cash flows.

The term **capital budgeting** is used to describe how managers plan significant outlays on projects that have long-term implications, such as purchasing new equipment and introducing new products. Most companies have many more potential projects than can actually be funded, so managers must carefully select those projects that promise the greatest future return. How well managers make these capital budgeting decisions can affect the long-run profitability of the company given the magnitude of the spending often involved.

■ CAPITAL BUDGETING—PLANNING INVESTMENTS

Typical Capital Budgeting Decisions

Any decision that involves an outlay now in order to obtain some return (increase in revenue or reduction in costs) in the future is a capital budgeting decision. Typical capital budgeting decisions are as follows:

1. *Cost-reduction decisions.* Should new equipment be purchased to reduce costs?
2. *Expansion decisions.* Should a new plant, warehouse, or other facility be acquired to increase capacity and production?
3. *Equipment selection decisions.* Which of several available machines should be purchased?
4. *Lease or buy decisions.* Should new equipment be leased or purchased?
5. *Equipment replacement decisions.* Should old equipment be replaced now or later?

Screening decisions
Decisions as to whether a proposed investment passes a pre-established profitability hurdle.

Preference decisions
Decisions as to which of several competing acceptable investment proposals is best.

Capital budgeting decisions tend to fall into two broad categories—*screening decisions* and *preference decisions*. **Screening decisions** are those relating to whether a proposed project is acceptable—whether it passes a pre-established profitability hurdle. For example, a firm may have a policy of accepting projects only if they promise a return of at least 10% on the investment.

Preference decisions, by contrast, relate to selecting from among several acceptable alternatives. To illustrate, a firm may be considering several different machines to replace an existing machine on the assembly line. The choice of which machine to purchase is a *preference* decision. In this chapter, we initially discuss screening decisions and then move on to preference decisions.

A point worth emphasizing is that the various analytical techniques described in this and the preceding chapters of the book are only as good as the data used as inputs for the calculations. Issues related to data quality and integrity have gained more attention in recent years given the vast amount of information now available to organizations for use in decision making from an ever-expanding variety of new sources. For example, customer feedback provided via social media could be used to estimate the impact of product or service enhancements on incremental cash flows. As will be illustrated below, incremental cash flows are a critical element in capital budgeting screening and preference decisions. However, managers must decide whether they are comfortable with the integrity of data collected from "new" sources such as social media given the possibility that such information may be biased, or at the extreme, fabricated. Thus, a fundamental step in the analytical approaches described in the following sections is assessing whether the data available for use in estimating cash inflows and outflows meet acceptable levels of quality and integrity.

The Time Value of Money

Capital investments usually result in cash inflows and outflows extending over fairly long periods of time. Therefore, when evaluating investment proposals, it is necessary to employ techniques that recognize the *time value of money*. A dollar today is worth more than a dollar a year from now. The same concept applies in choosing between investment alternatives. Projects that promise returns earlier in time are preferable to those that promise later returns.

The capital budgeting techniques that recognize the time value of money involve *discounted cash flows*. We will spend most of this chapter illustrating the use of discounted cash flow methods in making capital budgeting decisions. If you are not already familiar with discounting and the mathematics underlying interest rates and discount factors, you should read Appendix 13A at the end of this chapter before proceeding further.

■ DISCOUNTED CASH FLOWS— THE NET PRESENT VALUE METHOD

Two approaches to making capital budgeting decisions use discounted cash flows. One is the *net present value method*, and the other is the *internal rate of return method*. The net present value method is discussed in this section; the internal rate of return method is discussed in the following section.

The Net Present Value Method Illustrated

Under the net present value method, the present value of a project's cash inflows is compared to the present value of the project's cash outflows. The difference between the present value of these cash flows, called the **net present value**, determines whether the project is an acceptable investment. To illustrate, assume the data outlined in Example 1 below.

Net present value
The difference between the present value of the cash inflows and the present value of the cash outflows associated with an investment project.

Example 1

Management at Harper Company is thinking about buying a machine to perform certain operations that are now performed manually. The machine will cost $65,000, and it will last for five years. At the end of the five-year period, the machine will have a zero scrap value. Use of the machine will reduce labour costs by $18,000 per year. Harper Company requires a minimum return of 10% before taxes on all investment projects.[1]

Should the machine be purchased? Management must determine whether a cash investment now of $65,000 can be justified if it will result in an $18,000 reduction in cost each year over the next five years. It may appear that the answer is obvious since the total cost savings are $90,000 ($18,000 per year × 5 years). However, it is not enough that the cost reductions cover just the original cost of the machine; they must also yield at least a 10% return or the company would be better off investing the money elsewhere.

To determine whether the investment is desirable, the stream of annual $18,000 cost savings is discounted to its present value, which is then compared to the cost of the new machine. Since Harper Company requires a minimum return of 10% on all investment projects, this rate is used in the discounting process and is called the *discount rate*. In other words, the discount rate is the pre-established profitability hurdle used for screening decisions.

Appendix 13A provides a discussion of the various formulas used to calculate discount rates and future value factors when doing analysis that incorporates the time value of money. Two of these formulas, the present value of a single cash flow paid or received in the future (A3) and the present value of a series of equal cash flows to be paid or received in the future (A4), are used extensively in capital budgeting analysis.

Before software packages such as Microsoft Excel became so commonly used, preparers of capital budgeting analyses often relied on present value tables to provide the specific discount factors used in the calculations. These tables provided discount factors for a variety of required rates and time periods, based on the formulas presented in Appendix 13A.

EXHIBIT 13–1
Net Present Value
Analysis of a
Proposed Project

Initial cost	$65,000
Life of the project	5 years
Annual cost savings	$18,000
Salvage value	$ 0
Required rate of return	10%

Item	Year(s)	Amount of Cash Flow	Present Value of Cash Flows
Annual cost savings	1–5	$ 18,000	$68,234*
Initial investment	Now	$(65,000)	(65,000)
Net present value			$ 3,234

*Calculated using the NPV formula of Microsoft Excel and a required rate of return of 10%. Using Exhibit 13A–5 in Appendix 13A the factor used to calculate the present value of a five-year annuity (a series of equal cash flows) at a discount rate of 10% is 3.791. The present value of a five-year annuity of $18,000 is therefore: $18,000 × 3.791 = $68,238. This differs from the amount calculated by Microsoft Excel due to rounding.

Software packages are now readily available to perform the present value calculations quickly and without error, using these same formulas. Appendix 13A provides a list of Microsoft Excel formulas commonly used in net present value analysis. Because of its widespread use, Exhibit 13–1 shows the approach to the analysis with the present value of the annual cost savings calculated using the NPV formula in Microsoft Excel. We use Microsoft Excel rather than relying on present value tables in our presentation of the examples that follow throughout the rest of the chapter. However, we include the present value tables in Exhibit 13A–4 and Exhibit 13A–5 of Appendix 13A so that the calculations performed by Microsoft Excel can be verified. Moreover, we illustrate how using present value factors from Exhibit 13A–4 and Exhibit 13A–5 result in the same answers (except for rounding differences) as Microsoft Excel in Exhibit 13–1 and Exhibit 13–4 below.

According to the analysis, Harper Company should purchase the new machine. The present value of the cost savings is $68,234, compared to the present value of the required investment (cost of the machine) of only $65,000. Deducting the present value of the investment required from the present value of the cost savings gives a *net present value* of $3,234. Whenever the net present value is zero or greater, as in our example, an investment project is acceptable. Whenever the net present value is negative (the present value of the cash outflows exceeds the present value of the cash inflows), an investment project is unacceptable.

INSTANT QUIZ 13–1
Calculate the net present value of a project that requires an initial investment of $100,000 and will generate $20,000 per year in cost savings for 6 years. The required rate of return is 9%.

Emphasis on Cash Flows

In capital budgeting decisions, the focus is on cash flows and not on accounting income. Accounting income is based on accruals that ignore the timing of cash flows. From a capital budgeting standpoint, the timing of cash flows is critical, since a dollar received today is more valuable than a dollar received in the future. Therefore, instead of determining accounting income when making capital budgeting decisions, the manager must concentrate on identifying the specific cash flows associated with an investment project.

Although the specific cash flows will vary from project to project, certain types of cash flows tend to recur, as explained in the following paragraphs.

Typical Cash Outflows

Most projects will have at least three types of cash outflows. First, they often require an immediate cash outflow in the form of an initial investment in equipment or other assets. Any salvage value realized from the sale of old equipment or assets can be recognized as a cash inflow or as a reduction in the required investment. Second, some projects require that a company expand its working capital. **Working capital** is current assets (cash, accounts receivable, and inventory) less current liabilities. When a company takes on a new project, the balances in the current asset accounts will often increase. For example, opening a new Best Buy location would require additional cash in sales registers and more inventory to meet demand. These additional working capital needs should be treated as part of the initial investment in a project. Third, many projects require periodic outlays for repairs and maintenance and for additional operating costs. These should all be treated as cash outflows for capital budgeting purposes.

Working capital
The excess of current assets over current liabilities.

Typical Cash Inflows

Most projects will have at least three types of cash inflows. First, a project will normally increase revenues or reduce costs. In either case the amount involved should be treated as a cash inflow for capital budgeting purposes. Notice that from a cash flow standpoint, a reduction in costs is equivalent to an increase in revenues. Second, cash inflows are also frequently realized from selling equipment or assets for the salvage value when a project is terminated or from selling the old assets that are being replaced as part of the project. Third, any working capital that was tied up in an existing project can be released for use elsewhere at the end of the project and should be treated as a cash inflow. Working capital is released, for example, when a company sells off its inventory or collects its receivables.

In summary, the following types of cash flows are common in business investment projects:

Cash outflows:
> Initial investment in new assets (including installation costs).
> Increased working capital needs (e.g., accounts receivable).
> Periodic repairs and maintenance of new assets.
> Incremental operating costs of new assets.

Cash inflows:
> Incremental revenues from the new assets.
> Cost savings from the new assets.
> Salvage value of old assets sold when the new assets are acquired.
> Salvage value of new assets sold at the end of the new project's useful life.
> Release of working capital (e.g., inventory decreases).

Recovery of the Original Investment

When computing the present value of a project, depreciation is not deducted for two reasons. First, depreciation is not a current cash outflow.[2] As discussed previously, discounted cash flow methods of making capital budgeting decisions focus on *cash flows*. Although depreciation is used in computing net income for financial statements, it is not relevant in analysis that focuses on cash flows.

Second, discounted cash flow methods *automatically* provide for return of the original investment, thereby making a deduction for depreciation unnecessary. To demonstrate this point, consider the information given in Example 2.

Example 2

Carver Dental Clinic is considering purchasing an attachment for its X-ray machine that will cost $3,170. The attachment will be usable for four years, after which time it will have no salvage value. It will increase net cash inflows by $1,000 per year. The clinic's board of directors has decided that no investments are to be made unless they generate an annual return of at least 10%.

A present value analysis of the desirability of purchasing the X-ray attachment is presented in Exhibit 13–2. Notice that the attachment promises exactly a 10% return on the original investment, since the net present value is zero at a 10% discount rate.

EXHIBIT 13–2
Carver Dental
Clinic—Net Present
Value Analysis of
X-ray Attachment

Initial cost		$3,170
Life of the project		4 years
Annual cost savings......................		$1,000
Salvage value...........................		$ 0
Required rate of return		10%

Item	Year(s)	Amount of Cash Flow	Present Value of Cash Flows
Annual cost savings	1–4	$ 1,000	$ 3,170*
Initial investment	Now	$(3,170)	(3,170)
Net present value			$ 0

*Calculated using the NPV formula of Microsoft Excel and a required rate of return of 10%.

Each annual $1,000 cash inflow arising from use of the attachment is made up of two parts. One part represents a recovery of a portion of the original $3,170 paid for the attachment, and the other part represents a return on this investment. The breakdown of each year's $1,000 cash inflow between recovery *of* investment and return *on* investment is shown in Exhibit 13–3.

The first year's $1,000 cash inflow consists of a return *on* investment of $317 (a 10% return *on* the $3,170 original investment), plus a $683 return *of* that investment. Since the amount of the unrecovered investment decreases over the four years, the dollar amount of the return on investment also decreases each year. By the end of the fourth year, the entire $3,170 original investment has been recovered.

Simplifying Assumptions

Two simplifying assumptions are usually made in net present value analysis.

First, all cash flows other than the initial investment occur at the end of periods. This is somewhat unrealistic in that cash flows typically occur *throughout* a period—rather than just at the end. However, making this assumption simplifies computations without significantly affecting the accuracy of the analysis in most cases.

Second, all cash flows generated by an investment project are immediately reinvested at a rate of return equal to the discount rate. Unless these conditions are met, the return computed for the project will not be accurate. We used a discount rate of 10% for the Carver Dental Clinic in Exhibit 13–2. Unless the funds released each period are immediately reinvested at a 10% return, the net present value computed for the X-ray attachment will be misstated.

EXHIBIT 13–3   Carver Dental Clinic—Breakdown of Annual Cash Inflows

Year	(1) Investment Outstanding during the Year	(2) Cash Inflow	(3) Return on Investment (1) × 10%	(4) Recovery of Investment during the Year (2) − (3)	(5) Unrecovered Investment at the End of the Year (1) − (4)
1........................	$3,170	$1,000	$317	$ 683	$2,487
2........................	2,487	1,000	249	751	1,736
3........................	1,736	1,000	173	827	909
4........................	909	1,000	91	909	0
Total investment recovered ...				$3,170	

Choosing a Discount Rate

A positive net present value means that the project's return exceeds the discount rate. Therefore, if the company's minimum required rate of return is used as the discount rate, a project with a positive net present value has a return that exceeds the minimum required rate of return and is acceptable. Conversely, a project with a negative net present value has a return that is less than the minimum required rate of return and is unacceptable.

The firm's *weighted-average cost of capital* is usually regarded as the most appropriate choice for the discount rate. The **weighted-average cost of capital (WACC)** is the average rate of return the company must provide to its long-term creditors and shareholders for the use of their funds. WACC is based on the different returns required by the various providers of capital (e.g., creditors and shareholders) and the proportion of capital provided by each. The detailed calculations and assumptions involved in determining the WACC are covered in finance texts and will not be considered here.

The WACC is the minimum required rate of return, because if a project's rate of return is less than the cost of capital, company earnings will not be enough to compensate its creditors and shareholders. Therefore, any rate of return less than the WACC should not be accepted. Depending on the riskiness of the project under consideration, many companies may use a discount rate that differs from the WACC. For example, projects that are above the average level of risk taken on by the company (e.g., entering a new market in a developing country) will be analyzed using a discount rate that is higher than the WACC. The rationale for this approach is that riskier investments should generate higher returns. Decisions on the appropriate discount rate to use should always be made on a project-by-project basis, taking the risk of the project's underlying cash flows into consideration.

Weighted-average cost of capital (WACC)
The average rate of return companies must provide to long-term creditors and shareholders for the use of their funds.

An Extended Example of the Net Present Value Method

To continue our discussion, Example 3 presents an extended example of how the net present value method is used to analyze an investment proposal.

Example 3

Under a special licensing arrangement, Jones Company has an opportunity to market a new product in western Canada for a five-year period. The product would be purchased from the manufacturer, with Jones Company responsible for all costs of promotion and distribution. Jones Company has estimated that the following costs and revenues would be associated with the new product:

Cost of equipment needed.	$ 60,000
Working capital needed.	100,000
Maintenance of the equipment in four years	5,000
Salvage value of the equipment in five years	10,000
Straight-line depreciation per year (($60,000 – $10,000) ÷ 5)	10,000
Annual revenues and costs:	
Sales revenues	200,000
Cost of goods sold.	125,000
Out-of-pocket operating costs (for salaries,	
advertising and other direct costs).	35,000

At the end of the five-year period, the working capital would be released for investment elsewhere. Jones Company's discount rate is 14%. Would you recommend that the new product be introduced?

The solution is given in Exhibit 13–4.

Notice how the working capital is handled in the analysis. It is included as a cash outflow at the beginning of the project and as a cash inflow when it is released at the end of the project. Also notice that annual depreciation of $10,000 is *not* included in the analysis. This is because it is not an out-of-pocket cost, since it involves no current cash outlay. For this reason we ignore depreciation in the examples covered in the rest of the sections that follow. Since the net present value is positive, the new product is acceptable.

EXHIBIT 13–4 The Net Present Value Method—An Extended Example

Sales revenues.		$200,000
Less cost of goods sold.		125,000
Less out-of-pocket costs for salaries, advertising, etc.		35,000
Annual net cash inflows		$ 40,000

Item	Year(s)	Cash Flow	Present Value of Cash Flows*
Purchase of equipment.	Now	$ (60,000)	$ (60,000)
Working capital needed	Now	(100,000)	$(100,000)
Maintenance of equipment.	4	(5,000)	(2,960)
Annual net cash inflows from sales	1–5	40,000	137,323
Salvage value of equipment	5	10,000	5,194**
Working capital released	5	100,000	51,937
Net present value			$ 31,494

*Calculated using the NPV formula of Microsoft Excel and a required rate of return of 14%.
**Using Exhibit 13A–4 in Appendix 13A the factor used to calculate the present value of a single payment to be received in five years at a discount rate of 14% is 0.519. The present value of $10,000 to be received in Year 5 is therefore $10,000 × 0.519 = $5,190. This differs from the amount calculated by Microsoft Excel due to rounding.

INSTANT QUIZ 13–2
Calculate the net present value of a project that requires an initial investment in new machinery of $500,000 and $50,000 in working capital, generates annual net cash inflows of $70,000 for 10 years, and will require maintenance spending of $25,000 at the end of year 5. All of the working capital will be released at the end of year 10, and the machine will have a salvage value of $50,000 at the end of the project. The required rate of return is 10%.

To illustrate all of the elements included in the net present value method, we separately show the present value of each cash flow in Exhibit 13–4 and in the other examples that follow. However, when using software tools such as Microsoft Excel, all cash flows in a particular year can be combined and the present value of the total calculated. For example, in Year 5 in Exhibit 13–4, the present value of the total inflows of $118,000 (($40,000 ÷ 5) + $10,000 + $100,000) would be calculated in Microsoft Excel rather than doing three separate present value calculations.

So far, all of our examples have involved only a single investment alternative. We will now expand the net present value method to include two alternatives. In addition, we will integrate the concept of relevant costs into the discounted cash flow analysis.

The net present value method can be used to compare competing investment projects in two ways: the *total-cost approach* and the *incremental-cost approach*. These approaches are illustrated in the following two sections.

The Total-Cost Approach

The total-cost approach is the most flexible method for comparing competing projects. To illustrate the mechanics of the approach, assume the data provided in Example 4.

Example 4

Harris Ferry Company provides a ferry service across Harris Harbour. One of its ferryboats is in poor condition. This ferry can be renovated at an immediate cost of $200,000. Further repairs and an overhaul of the motor will be needed 5 years from now at a cost of $80,000. The ferry will be usable for 10 more

EXHIBIT 13–5   The Total-Cost Approach to Project Selection

	New Ferry	Old Ferry
Annual revenue.	$400,000	$400,000
Annual cash operating costs	210,000	300,000
Net annual cash inflows	$190,000	$100,000

Item	Year(s)	Amount of Cash Flow	Present Value of Cash Flows*
Buy the new ferry:			
Initial investment	Now	$(360,000)	$(360,000)
Repairs in five years.	5	(30,000)	(15,581)
Net annual cash inflows.	1–10	190,000	991,062
Salvage of the old ferry	Now	70,000	70,000
Salvage of the new ferry	10	60,000	16,185
Net present value			701,666
Keep the old ferry:			
Initial repairs	Now	$(200,000)	(200,000)
Repairs in five years.	5	(80,000)	(41,549)
Net annual cash inflows.	1–10	100,000	521,612
Salvage of the old ferry	10	60,000	16,185
Net present value			296,248
Net present value in favour of buying the new ferry			$ 405,418

*Calculated using the NPV formula of Microsoft Excel and a required rate of return of 14%

years if this work is done. At the end of 10 years, the ferry will have to be scrapped at a salvage value of approximately $60,000. The scrap value of the ferry right now is $70,000. It will cost $300,000 each year to operate the ferry, and revenues will total $400,000 annually.

As an alternative, Harris Ferry Company can purchase a new ferryboat at a cost of $360,000. The new ferry will have a life of 10 years, but it will require repairs at the end of 5 years estimated to cost $30,000. At the end of 10 years, it is estimated that the ferry will have a scrap value of $60,000. It will cost $210,000 each year to operate the ferry, and revenues will total $400,000 annually.

Harris Ferry Company requires a return of at least 14% before taxes on all investment projects.

Should the company purchase the new ferry or renovate the old ferry? Using the total-cost approach, Exhibit 13–5 gives the solution.

Two points should be noted from Exhibit 13–5. First, *all* cash inflows and *all* cash outflows are included in the solution under each alternative. No effort has been made to isolate those cash flows that are relevant to the decision and those that are not relevant.

Second, a net present value figure is computed for each of the two alternatives. This is a distinct advantage of the total-cost approach in that an unlimited number of alternatives can be compared to determine the best action. For example, another alternative for Harris Ferry Company is to get out of the ferry business entirely. The net present value of this alternative could be computed to compare with the alternatives shown in Exhibit 13–5. Once management has determined the net present value of each alternative to consider, they can select the course of action likely to be the most profitable. In this case the data indicate that the most profitable course is to purchase the new ferry.[3]

The Incremental-Cost Approach

When only two alternatives are being considered, the incremental-cost approach offers a simpler approach to the analysis. Unlike the total-cost approach, it focuses only on differential costs.[4] The approach includes only those costs and revenues that *differ* between the

EXHIBIT 13–6
The Incremental-
Cost Approach to
Project Selection

Item	Year(s)	Amount of Cash Flow	Present Value of Cash Flows*
Incremental initial investment to buy the new ferry	Now	$(160,000)	$(160,000)
Repairs in five years avoided	5	50,000	25,968
Increased net annual cash inflows	1–10	90,000	469,450
Salvage of the old ferry	Now	70,000	70,000
Net present value in favour of buying the new ferry			$ 405,418

*Calculated using the NPV formula of Microsoft Excel and a required rate of return of 14%

two alternatives being considered. To illustrate, refer again to the data in Example 4 relating to Harris Ferry Company. The solution using only differential costs is presented in Exhibit 13–6.

Two things should be noted from the data in Exhibit 13–6. First, the net present value of $405,418 in favour of buying shown in this exhibit agrees with the net present value shown under the total-cost approach in Exhibit 13–5. This is expected since the two approaches are just different ways of analyzing the same underlying set of facts.

Second, the only costs used in Exhibit 13–6 are those for which there are differences between the two alternatives in the prior exhibit. For example, the $160,000 incremental investment required to purchase the new ferry in Exhibit 13–6 is the difference between the $360,000 cost of the new ferry and the $200,000 cost required to renovate the old ferry shown in Exhibit 13–5. The other figures in Exhibit 13–6 were computed in the same way.

Least-Cost Decisions

Some decisions do not involve revenues. For example, a company may be trying to decide whether to lease or to buy an executive jet. In situations such as this, where no revenues are involved, the most desirable alternative will be the one that requires the *least total cost* from the present value perspective. Hence, these are known as *least-cost decisions*. To illustrate a least-cost decision, assume the data provided in Example 5.

Example 5

Athena Company is considering replacing an old machine. A new machine is available that could substantially reduce annual operating costs. Selected data relating to the old and new machines are presented below:

	Old Machine	New Machine
Purchase cost when new............................	$200,000	$250,000
Salvage value now	30,000	0
Annual cash operating costs...........................	150,000	90,000
Overhaul needed immediately	40,000	0
Salvage value in six years	0	50,000
Remaining life	6 years	6 years

Athena Company's cost of capital is 10%.

Exhibit 13–7 presents the alternatives using the total-cost approach. As shown in the exhibit, the new machine has the lower total cost when the present value of the net cash outflows is considered. An analysis of the two alternatives using the incremental-cost approach is presented in Exhibit 13–8. As before, the data in this exhibit represent the differences between

Item	Year(s)	Amount of Cash Flow	Present Value of Cash Flows*
Buy the new machine:			
Initial investment	Now	$(250,000)	$(250,000)
Salvage of the old machine	Now	30,000	30,000
Annual cash operating costs.	1–6	(90,000)	(391,973)
Salvage of the new machine.	6	50,000	28,224
Present value of net cash outflows.			(583,749)
Keep the old machine:			
Overhaul needed now.	Now	$ (40,000)	(40,000)
Annual cash operating costs.	1–6	(150,000)	(653,289)
Present value of net cash outflows.			(693,289)
Net present value in favour of buying the new machine.			$ 109,540

*Calculated using the NPV formula of Microsoft Excel and a required rate of 10%

EXHIBIT 13–7
The Total-Cost Approach (Least-Cost Decision)

Item	Year(s)	Amount of Cash Flow	Present Value of Cash Flows*
Incremental initial investment to purchase the new machine.	Now	$(210,000)	$(210,000)
Salvage of the old machine	Now	30,000	30,000
Savings in annual cash operating costs	1–6	60,000	261,316
Difference in salvage value in six years.	6	50,000	28,224
Net present value in favour of buying the new machine.			$ 109,540

*Calculated using the NPV formula of Microsoft Excel and a required rate of return of 10%

EXHIBIT 13–8
The Incremental-Cost Approach (Least-Cost Decision)

the alternatives after all irrelevant cash flows have been eliminated, namely those that do not differ across the two alternatives.

IN BUSINESS

Air Canada's announcement to order 45 new Airbus A220 aircraft is a good example of a capital budgeting decision on a very large scale. The estimated total cost of the new aircraft is over CDN $3 billion.

In making this decision Air Canada management would likely have considered the incremental revenues from the routes these planes will be used to service as well as the incremental costs of operating the aircraft. For example, the A220 is touted as being considerably more fuel efficient than other planes of similar size, offering the potential for significant operating cost savings.

In press releases related to the purchase of the A220, Air Canada also made specific mention of the reduced greenhouse emissions that this model generates, its lower level of noise pollution, and the smaller environmental impact of the production process used in manufacturing the airplane.

This example is reflective of a growing trend by many organizations to consider and disclose both the financial and non-financial factors used in making capital budgeting and other key decisions.

LEARNING OBJECTIVE **2**

Evaluate the acceptability of an investment project using the internal rate of return method.

■ DISCOUNTED CASH FLOWS—THE INTERNAL RATE OF RETURN METHOD

The **internal rate of return (IRR)** is the return promised by an investment project over its useful life. The IRR is the discount rate that equates the present value of a project's cash outflows with the present value of its cash inflows. In other words, the IRR is the discount rate that results in a net present value of zero.

The Internal Rate of Return Method Illustrated

To illustrate the IRR method, assume the data shown in Example 6.

Internal rate of return (IRR)
The discount rate at which the net present value of an investment project is zero.

Example 6
Glendale School District is considering purchasing a zero-turn ride-on lawn mower. At present, the lawn is mowed using a small hand-pushed gas mower. The zero-turn mower will cost $16,950 and will have a useful life of 10 years. It will have only a negligible scrap value, which can be ignored. The zero-turn mower would do the job much more quickly than the old mower and would result in labour savings of $3,000 per year.

To compute the IRR promised by the new mower, we must find the discount rate that will cause the net present value of the project to be zero. How do we do this? As with the present value calculations discussed above, computer software programs such as Microsoft Excel can be used to easily determine the IRR. The Microsoft Excel formula we use to perform the calculation is IRR. Applying this formula to the cash flows related to the project, including the initial investment, will yield the discount rate that causes the net present value to be zero. For our example, the IRR is 12%.

INSTANT QUIZ 13–3
Calculate the IRR for a project that requires a $100,000 initial investment and is expected to generate annual net cash inflows of $16,000 for 10 years.

Exhibit 13–9 shows that using a 12% discount rate equates the present value of the annual cash inflows with the present value of the investment required in the project, leaving a zero net present value. The 12% rate therefore represents the IRR promised by the project. Our example did not involve a salvage value, and the cash flows are constant at $3,000 per year. However, software programs such as Microsoft Excel can easily handle IRR calculations involving salvage values and uneven cash flows.

EXHIBIT 13–9
Evaluation of the Mower Purchase Using a 12% Discount Rate

Initial cost			$16,950
Life of the project			10 years
Annual cost savings.......................			$3,000
Salvage value............................			$0
Internal rate of return			12%*

Item	Year(s)	Amount of Cash Flow	Present Value of Cash Flows**
Initial investment	Now	$(16,950)	$(16,950)
Annual cost savings	1–10	3,000	16,950
Net present value			$ 0

*Calculated using the IRR formula of Microsoft Excel
**Calculated using the NPV formula of Microsoft Excel and a discount rate of 12%

Using the Internal Rate of Return

Once the IRR has been computed, how does the manager use the information for screening decisions? The IRR is compared to the company's *required rate of return*. The **required rate of return** is the minimum rate of return that an investment project must yield to be acceptable. If the IRR is *equal to* or *greater than* the required rate of return, then the project is acceptable. If it is *less than* the required rate of return, then the project is rejected.

In the case of the Glendale School District example used earlier, assume that the district has set a minimum required rate of return of 10% on all projects. Since the mower's IRR is 12%, it meets the criterion and should be accepted as a project.

Required rate of return
The minimum rate of return that an investment project must yield to be acceptable.

The Weighted-Average Cost of Capital as a Screening Tool

As we have seen in the examples, the WACC is often used to screen investment projects. This screening is accomplished in different ways, depending on whether the company is using the IRR method or the net present value method in its capital budgeting analysis.

When the IRR method is used, the WACC is used as the *hurdle rate* that a project must meet for acceptance. If the IRR of a project is less than the WACC, then the project is ordinarily rejected. We saw the application of this approach in the Glendale School District example, where the hurdle rate was 10%.

When the net present value method is used, the WACC is the *discount rate* used to compute the net present value of a proposed project. Any project yielding a negative net present value is rejected unless other factors are significant enough to justify its acceptance. The use of the WACC as a screening tool is summarized in the Learning Aid below.

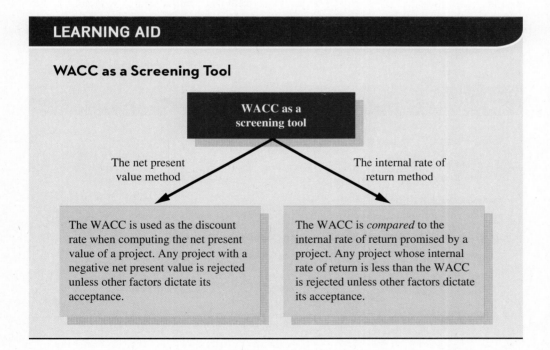

LEARNING AID

WACC as a Screening Tool

WACC as a screening tool

The net present value method

The internal rate of return method

The WACC is used as the discount rate when computing the net present value of a project. Any project with a negative net present value is rejected unless other factors dictate its acceptance.

The WACC is *compared* to the internal rate of return promised by a project. Any project whose internal rate of return is less than the WACC is rejected unless other factors dictate its acceptance.

Comparison of the Net Present Value and Internal Rate of Return Methods

The net present value method offers a key advantage over the IRR method because of the assumption each method makes about the reinvestment of cash flows generated by the project. Both methods assume that cash flows generated by a project during its useful life are immediately reinvested but make different assumptions about the return earned on the reinvested capital. The net present value method assumes that the rate of return is the discount rate, whereas the IRR method assumes that the rate of return is the IRR on the project. If the IRR of the project is high, this assumption may not be realistic. Instead, it is generally more conservative and realistic to assume that cash inflows can be reinvested at a rate of return equal to the discount rate—particularly if the discount rate is the company's WACC. In short, when the net present value method and the IRR method do not lead to the same conclusions concerning the attractiveness of a project, it is better to go with the net present value method. Of the two methods, it makes the more conservative assumption about the rate of return that can be earned on cash flows from the project.

Real Options

The analysis in this chapter has so far assumed that an investment cannot be postponed and that, once started, nothing can be done to alter the course of the project. In reality, investments can often be postponed. Postponement is a particularly attractive option when the net present value of the project is modest using current estimates of future cash flows, but the future cash flows involve a great deal of uncertainty that may be resolved over time.

Similarly, once an investment is made, management can often exploit changes in the business environment and take actions that enhance future cash flows. For example, buying a jet for use by company executives provides management with a number of options, some of which may become more attractive as time passes. Instead of just using the jet itself, the company may decide to rent it to other companies if the rental rates become high enough. In the case of an investment in automated equipment, management may initially buy only the basic model without costly add-ons, but keep the option open to add more capacity and capability later.

The ability to delay the start of a project, to expand it if conditions are favourable, and to otherwise modify usage plans as business conditions change, can add considerable value to many investments. These advantages can be quantified using what is called *real option analysis*, but the techniques are beyond the scope of this book.

LEARNING AID

Net Present Value and Internal Rate of Return Methods

Relevant cash inflows:
• Incremental revenues; reduction in costs; salvage value; release of working capital

Relevant cash outflows:
• Initial investment; increased working capital needs; incremental operating costs

Decision Rule (for determining project acceptability):

Acceptable if	Net present value ≥ $0; Internal rate of return ≥ Required rate of return
Not acceptable if	Net present value < $0; Internal rate of return < Required rate of return

---

LEARNING OBJECTIVE 3

Evaluate an investment project that has uncertain cash flows.

■ UNCERTAIN CASH FLOWS

The analysis to this point in the chapter has assumed that all of the future cash flows are known with a reasonable degree of certainty. However, future cash flows are often uncertain or difficult to estimate. A number of techniques are available for handling this complication. Some of these techniques are quite complex, involving computer simulations or advanced analytical techniques beyond the scope of this book. However, to provide a basic understanding of how uncertainty is incorporated in the analysis, we provide a basic illustration of the approach in the next section.

An Example of Uncertain Cash Flows

As an example of difficult to estimate future cash flows, consider the case of investments in automated equipment such as that used in manufacturing facilities. The up-front costs of automated equipment and the tangible benefits, such as reductions in operating costs and waste, tend to be relatively easy to estimate. However, the intangible benefits, such as greater reliability, greater speed, and higher quality, are more difficult to quantify in terms of future cash flows. These intangible benefits certainly affect future cash flows—particularly in terms of increased sales and perhaps higher selling prices—but the cash flow effects are difficult to estimate. What can be done?

A fairly simple procedure can be followed when the intangible benefits are expected to be significant. Suppose, for example, that a company with a 12% WACC is considering purchasing automated equipment that would have a 10-year useful life. Also suppose that a discounted cash flow analysis of just the tangible costs and benefits shows a negative net present value of $226,000. Clearly, if the intangible benefits are large enough, the company could turn this negative net present value into a positive net present value. In this case, the amount of additional cash flow per year from the intangible benefits that would be needed to make the project financially attractive can easily be computed using the PMT formula in Microsoft Excel (see Appendix 13A). This formula provides the annual amount of additional cash inflows for the 10-year life of the project that will have a present value of about $226,000 using a discount rate of 12%. The answer is an additional $40,000 per year (rounded), which as shown below has a present value of about $226,000:

Net present value excluding the intangible benefits (negative)	$(226,000)
Present value of $40,000 per year for 10 periods using a 12% discount rate	$ 226,009

So, if intangible benefits such as greater production scheduling flexibility or higher quality of output are worth at least $40,000 per year to the company, the automated equipment should be purchased. However, if management does not believe these intangible benefits are worth at least $40,000 per year, then the automated equipment should not be purchased.

This technique can be used in other situations in which the future benefits of a current investment are uncertain or intangible. For example, this technique can be used when the salvage value is difficult to estimate. To illustrate, suppose that all of the cash flows from an investment in a solar panel manufacturing facility have been estimated, other than the salvage value in 20 years. Using a discount rate of 12%, management has determined that the net present value of all these cash flows is negative $150,000. This negative net present value would be offset by the salvage value of the manufacturing facility. How much would the salvage value have to be to make this investment attractive? This time, the solution can easily be obtained using the FV formula in Microsoft Excel (see Appendix 13A). The objective is to find the amount to be received in 20 years that has a present value of $150,000, using a discount rate of 12%. As shown below, the amount is about $1,447,000:

Net present value excluding salvage value (negative)	$(150,000)
Present value of $1,447,000 to be received in 20 years using a discount rate of 12%	$ 150,006

So, if the salvage value of the manufacturing facility in 20 years is at least $1,447,000, its net present value will be at least zero (or positive if the salvage value is higher) and the investment should be made. However, if management believes the salvage value is unlikely to be that large, the investment should not be made.

■ PREFERENCE DECISIONS—THE RANKING OF INVESTMENT PROJECTS

Preference decisions come *after* screening decisions and attempt to answer the following question: "How do the remaining investment proposals, all of which have been screened and provide an acceptable rate of return, rank in terms of preference? That is, which one(s) would be *best* for the firm to accept?"

Preference decisions are more difficult to make than screening decisions because investment funds are usually limited. This often requires that some profitable investment opportunities be forgone. Sometimes preference decisions are called *ranking decisions*, or *rationing decisions*, because they ration limited investment funds among competing alternatives; hence, the alternatives must be ranked. Either the IRR method or the net present value method can be used in making preference decisions. However, as discussed earlier, if the two methods lead to different conclusions, it is best to use the more conservative net present value method.

Internal Rate of Return Method

When using the IRR method to rank competing investment projects, the preference rule is simple: *the higher the IRR, the more desirable the project*. An investment project with an IRR of 18% is preferable to another project that promises a return of only 15%. Because of the simplicity and understandability of this approach, the IRR is widely used to rank projects.

Net Present Value Method

Unfortunately, the net present value of one project cannot be compared directly to the net present value of another project unless the required investments in the projects are of equal size. For example, assume that a company is considering two competing investments, as shown below:

	Investment	
	A	**B**
Investment required.............................	$(10,000)	$(5,000)
Present value of cash inflows	11,000	6,000
Net present value...............................	$ 1,000	$ 1,000

Although each project has a net present value of $1,000, the projects are not equally desirable if funds available for investment are limited. The project requiring an investment of only $5,000 is much more desirable when funds are limited than the project requiring an investment of $10,000. To compare the two projects on a meaningful basis, the present value of the cash inflows should be divided by the investment required. The result is called the **project profitability index**. The formula for the project profitability index is

Project profitability index

The ratio of the present value of a project's cash inflows to the investment required.

$$\text{Project profitability index} = \frac{\text{Present value of cash inflows}}{\text{Investment required}} \qquad (1)$$

The project profitability indexes for the two investments above are computed as follows:

	Investment	
	A	**B**
Present value of cash inflows (a)	$11,000	$6,000
Investment required (b)...........................	$10,000	$5,000
Project profitability index, (a) ÷ (b)	1.1	1.2

When using the project profitability index to rank competing investment projects, the preference rule is as follows: *the higher the project profitability index, the more desirable the project*. Applying this rule to the two investments above, Investment B should be chosen over Investment A.

The project profitability index is an application of the techniques for utilizing scarce resources discussed in Chapter 12. In this case, the scarce resource is the limited funds available for investment, and the project profitability index is similar to the contribution margin per unit of the scarce resource.

A few details should be clarified with respect to the computation of the project profitability index. "Investment required" refers to any cash outflows that occur at the beginning of the project, reduced by any salvage value recovered from the disposal or sale of old equipment; it also includes any investment in working capital that the project may need.

Comparing the Preference Rules

The project profitability index is conceptually superior to the IRR as a method of making preference decisions. This is because the project profitability index will always give the correct signal as to the relative desirability of alternatives, even if the alternatives have different useful lives and different patterns of earnings. By contrast, if useful lives are unequal, the IRR method can lead the manager to make incorrect decisions. Assume the situation presented in Example 7.

Example 7

Parker Company is considering two investment proposals, only one of which can be accepted. Project A requires an investment of $5,000 and will provide a single cash inflow of $6,000 at the end of the first year. Therefore, it promises an IRR of 20%. Project B also requires an investment of $5,000. It will provide cash inflows of $1,360 each year for six years. Its IRR is 16%. Which project should be accepted?

Although Project A promises an IRR of 20%, compared to only 16% for Project B, Project A is not necessarily preferable to Project B. It is preferable only if the funds released at the end of the year under Project A can be reinvested at a high rate of return in some other project for the five remaining years. Otherwise, Project B, which promises a return of 16% over the entire six years, is more desirable.

Assume that the company in this example has an after-tax WACC of 12%. Employing the net present value method with the project profitability index would rank the two proposals as follows:

	Project A	Project B
Present value of cash inflows:		
$6,000 received at the end of one year at 12%	$5,357 (a)	
$1,360 received at the end of each year for six years at 12%		$5,592 (a)
Investment required	$5,000 (b)	$5,000 (b)
Project profitability index, (a) ÷ (b)	1.07	1.12

The project profitability index indicates that Project B is more desirable than Project A. This is in fact the case if the funds released from Project A at the end of one year can be reinvested at only 12% (the WACC). In short, the IRR method of ranking tends to favour short-term, high-yield projects, whereas the net present value method of ranking (using the project profitability index) tends to favour longer-term projects.

INSTANT QUIZ 13-4

Calculate the project profitability index of a project that requires an initial investment of $150,000 and is expected to generate cash inflows that will have a present value of $180,000.

Post-audit of Investment Projects

A *post-audit* should be conducted after an investment project has been approved and implemented. A **post-audit** involves evaluating the extent to which expected results are actually being realized. This is a key part of the capital budgeting process that helps keep managers committed to their investment proposals. Any tendency to inflate the benefits or understate the costs in a proposal should become evident after a few post-audits have been conducted. The post-audit also provides an opportunity to possibly expand successful projects or to reduce losses on unsuccessful projects by discontinuing them.

The same capital budgeting analysis should be used in the post-audit that was used in the original approval process. That is, if a project was approved on the basis of a net present value analysis, then the same procedure should be used in performing the post-audit. However, the data used in the post-audit analysis should be the *actual results* rather than the estimates used in the original proposal. This gives management an opportunity to compare how well the project has actually done relative to the original estimates. The accountability established by this approach also encourages managers to prepare realistic estimates when submitting capital budgets in the future, since they know that they will be compared to the actual results in the post-audit process.

Post-audits are not without their challenges. A proper review may be time-consuming, and it is often difficult to attribute incremental costs and revenues to a specific project. This is especially true if several projects were implemented around the same time and there is overlap among them with respect to their impact on operating results. Also, to ensure objectivity, the post-audit should be performed by an individual or team that has not been directly involved in developing or implementing the actual project. Importantly, the post-audit should not be aimed at placing blame; instead the objective should be to improve control over the capital budgeting process and to facilitate a learning process that will improve the estimates developed in support of future projects.

■ OTHER APPROACHES TO CAPITAL BUDGETING DECISIONS

Although conceptually inferior to the net present value or the IRR method, other techniques are often used by managers to make capital budgeting decisions. In this section, we examine two of these methods, known as *payback* and *simple rate of return*. Neither involves the use of discounted cash flows, but their use can be attributed to their simplicity.

The Payback Method

The payback method focuses on the *payback period*. The **payback period** is the length of time that it takes for a project to recover its initial cost from the net cash inflows that it generates. The premise of the payback method is that the more quickly the cost of an investment can be recovered, the more desirable the investment.

The payback period is usually expressed in years. *When the net annual cash inflow is the same every year*, the following formula can be used to compute the payback period:

$$\text{Payback period} = \frac{\text{Investment required}}{\text{Net annual cash inflow*}} \qquad (2)$$

*If new equipment is replacing old equipment, this becomes incremental net annual cash inflow.

To illustrate the payback method, assume the data given in Example 8.

Example 8

York Company needs a new machine. The company is considering two options: Machine A and Machine B. Machine A costs $15,000 and will reduce operating costs by $5,000 per year. Machine B costs only $12,000 but will also reduce operating costs by $5,000 per year.

Which machine should be purchased according to the payback method?

$$\text{Machine A payback period} = \frac{\$15,000}{\$5,000} = 3.0 \text{ years}$$

$$\text{Machine B payback period} = \frac{\$12,000}{\$5,000} = 2.4 \text{ years}$$

According to the payback calculations, York Company should purchase Machine B, since it has a shorter payback period than Machine A.

Evaluation of the Payback Method

The payback method is not a true measure of the profitability of an investment. Rather, it simply tells the manager how many years will be required to recover the original investment. Unfortunately, a shorter payback period does not always mean that one investment is more desirable than another.

To illustrate, refer to the example above. Since Machine B has a shorter payback period than Machine A, it *appears* that Machine B is more desirable than Machine A. But if we add one more piece of data, the conclusion will change. Now assume that Machine A has a projected 10-year life, and Machine B has a projected 5-year life. It would take two purchases of Machine B, costing $24,000 in total (assuming no inflation or other changes to the price), to provide the same length of service as would be provided by a single purchase of Machine A for $15,000. Under these circumstances, Machine A is a much better investment than Machine B, even though Machine B has a shorter payback period. Unfortunately, the payback method has no mechanism for highlighting differences in useful lives between investments. Such differences can be very important, and relying on payback alone may result in incorrect decisions.

A further criticism of the payback method is that it does not adequately consider the time value of money. A cash inflow to be received several years in the future is weighed equally with a cash inflow to be received now. To illustrate, assume that for an investment of $8,000 you can purchase either of the two following streams of cash inflows:

	Cash Inflows							
Year	1	2	3	4	5	6	7	8
Stream 1	$ 0	$ 0	$ 0	$8,000	$2,000	$2,000	$2,000	$2,000
Stream 2	$2,000	$2,000	$2,000	$2,000	$8,000	$ 0	$ 0	$ 0

Which stream of cash inflows would you prefer to receive in return for your $8,000 investment? Each stream has a payback period of 4.0 years. Therefore, if you relied on payback alone to make the decision, you would be forced to say that the streams are equally desirable. However, from the point of view of the time value of money, Stream 2 is much more desirable than Stream 1 because the return occurs sooner. You can check this logic by calculating the net present value of the two projects using the method discussed earlier in the chapter. Using any discount rate you like, Project B will always have a higher net present value than Project A.

On the other hand, under certain conditions, the payback method can be very useful as an initial screening tool to help answer the question, "Should I consider this proposal further?" If a proposal doesn't provide a payback within some specified period, then there may be no need to consider it further. In addition, the payback period is often of great importance to firms that are cash poor, such as start-up companies. When a firm is cash poor, a project with a short payback period but a low rate of return might be preferred over another project because the company may simply need a faster recovery of its cash investment. Finally, the payback method is sometimes used in industries where products become obsolete very rapidly—such as consumer electronics. Since products may last only a year or two, the payback period on investments must be very short.

INSTANT QUIZ 13-5

Calculate the payback period of a project that requires an initial investment of $150,000 and is expected to generate net annual cash inflows of $40,000.

An Extended Example of Payback

As shown by formula (2) above, the payback period is computed by dividing the investment in a project by the net annual cash inflows that the project will generate. If new equipment is replacing old equipment, then any salvage value to be received on disposal of the old equipment should be deducted from the cost of the new equipment, and only the *incremental* investment should be used in the payback computation. In addition, any depreciation deducted in arriving at the project's operating income must be added back to obtain the project's expected annual net cash inflow. To illustrate, consider the data in Example 9.

Example 9

Family Limited operates several theme parks in Ontario. Some of the vending machines in one of its parks provide very little revenue, so the company is considering removing the machines and installing equipment to dispense coffee. The equipment would cost $190,000 and have a five-year useful life with no salvage value. Incremental annual revenues and costs associated with the sale of coffee are as follows:

Sales	$300,000
Less cost of ingredients.	180,000
Contribution margin	120,000
Less fixed expenses:	
Salaries	54,000
Maintenance	6,000
Depreciation	20,000
Total fixed expenses	80,000
Operating income	$ 40,000

The old vending machines have a salvage value of $10,000. The company will not purchase equipment unless it has a payback period of four years or less. Does the coffee-making equipment pass this criterion?

Exhibit 13–10 shows the computation of the payback period for the coffee machines. Several things should be noted. First, depreciation is not a cash outlay, so it must be added back to adjust operating income to a cash basis. Second, the payback computation deducts the salvage value of the old machines from the cost of the new equipment so that only the incremental investment is used to compute the payback period.

EXHIBIT 13–10
Computation of the Payback Period

Step 1: Compute the net annual cash inflow. Since the net annual cash inflow is not given, it must be computed before the payback period can be determined:

Operating income (given in Example 9)	$40,000
Add: Non-cash deduction for depreciation	20,000
Net annual cash inflow.	$60,000

Step 2: Compute the payback period. Using the net annual cash inflow figure from above, the payback period can be determined as follows:

Cost of the new equipment.	$190,000
Less salvage value of old equipment	(10,000)
Investment required	$180,000

$$\text{Payback period} = \frac{\text{Investment required}}{\text{Net annual cash inflow}}$$

$$= \frac{\$180,000}{\$60,000} = 3 \text{ years}$$

Year	Investment (a)	Cash Inflow (b)	Unrecovered Investment* (c)
1................................	$4,000	$1,000	$3,000
2................................		0	$3,000
3................................		$2,000	$1,000
4................................	$2,000	$1,000	$2,000
5................................		$ 500	$1,500
6................................		$3,000	0
7................................		$2,000	0

*Year X unrecovered investment, column (c) = Year (X − 1) unrecovered investment (column c) + Year X investment (column a) − Year X cash inflow (column b). For example, the unrecovered investment in year 4 is calculated as follows: $1,000 (year 3 unrecovered investment) + $2,000 (year 4 investment) − $1,000 (year 4 cash inflow) = $2,000.

EXHIBIT 13–11
Payback Calculation and Uneven Cash Flows

As Exhibit 13–10 shows, the proposed equipment has a payback period of less than four years, so the company's payback requirement has been met.

Payback and Uneven Cash Flows

When the cash flows associated with an investment project change from year to year, the simple payback formula provided earlier cannot be used. Consider the following data:

Year	Investment	Cash Inflow
1.......................................	$4,000	$1,000
2.......................................		0
3.......................................		2,000
4.......................................	2,000	1,000
5.......................................		500
6.......................................		3,000
7.......................................		2,000
8.......................................		2,000

What is the payback period on this investment? The answer is 5.5 years, but to obtain this figure it is necessary to track the unrecovered investment year by year. The steps involved in this process are shown in Exhibit 13–11. By the middle of the sixth year, sufficient cash inflows will have been realized to recover the entire investment of $6,000 ($4,000 + $2,000).

Simple rate of return The rate of return computed by dividing a project's annual operating income by the initial investment required.

■ THE SIMPLE RATE OF RETURN METHOD

The **simple rate of return** method is another capital budgeting technique that does not involve discounted cash flows. The method is also known as the *accounting rate of return* or the *unadjusted rate of return.*

Unlike the other capital budgeting methods that we have discussed, the simple rate of return method does not focus on cash flows. Rather, it focuses on accounting-based operating income. The approach is to estimate the revenues that will be generated by a proposed investment and then deduct from these revenues all of the projected operating expenses associated with the project. This operating income figure is then divided by the

LEARNING OBJECTIVE **6**
Calculate the simple rate of return for an investment.

initial investment in the project less any expected salvage value, as shown in the following formula:

$$\text{Simple rate of return} = \frac{\begin{bmatrix}\text{Incremental} \\ \text{revenues}\end{bmatrix} - \begin{bmatrix}\text{Incremental expenses,} \\ \text{including depreciation}\end{bmatrix} = \begin{bmatrix}\text{Incremental} \\ \text{operating income}\end{bmatrix}}{\text{Initial investment} - \text{Salvage value}} \qquad (3)$$

The logic of deducting the salvage value from the initial investment in the denominator is that doing so incorporates the positive cash inflow from eventually selling the asset(s) in calculating the rate of return. As such, it is consistent with the other capital budgeting methods covered earlier in the chapter (NPV, IRR, cash payback), all of which incorporate salvage value in the calculations.

Or, if a cost reduction project is involved, the formula becomes

$$\text{Simple rate of return} = \frac{\begin{bmatrix}\text{Cost} \\ \text{savings}\end{bmatrix} - \begin{bmatrix}\text{Depreciation on} \\ \text{new equipment}\end{bmatrix}}{\text{Initial investment} - \text{Salvage value}} \qquad (4)$$

*The investment should be reduced by any salvage from the sale of old equipment.

The deduction of depreciation on the investment in new equipment in the numerator is subject to potential confusion, given how the initial investment was handled earlier in the chapter. However, deducting depreciation expense in formula (3) or (4) makes the calculation of the simple rate of return conceptually similar to the return on investment (ROI) performance metric illustrated in Chapter 11. Examples 10 and 11 demonstrate the calculation of the simple rate of return.

Example 10

Brigham Tea Company is a processor of herbal tea. The company is contemplating purchasing equipment for an additional processing line. The additional processing line would increase revenues by $90,000 per year. Incremental cash operating expenses would be $40,000 per year. The equipment would cost $180,000 and have a nine-year life. No salvage value is projected.

The simple rate of return for this example is calculated as follows:

$$\text{Simple rate of return} = \frac{\begin{bmatrix}\$90,000 \\ \text{incremental revenues}\end{bmatrix} - \begin{bmatrix}\$40,000 \text{ cash operating expenses} \\ + \$20,000 \text{ depreciation}\end{bmatrix}}{\$180,000 \text{ initial investment}}$$

$$= \frac{\$30,000}{\$180,000}$$

$$= 16.7\%$$

Example 11

Jackson Limited produces maple products such as maple syrup, maple butter, and maple cream using an evaporator to boil the sap. The cost of operating the existing evaporator is $60,000 per year. The company is investigating purchasing a new evaporator that would cost $180,000 and have a 20-year useful life with a salvage value of $20,000. The new machine would be far more efficient to operate, consuming considerably less electricity than the old machine. As a result, the new machine would cost $36,000 per year to operate and maintain. The evaporator currently being used has no scrap value.

A cost-reduction project is involved in Example 11. By applying formula (4), we can compute the simple rate of return as follows:

$$\text{Simple rate of return} = \frac{\$24,000 \text{ cost savings*} - \$8,000 \text{ depreciation on new equipment**}}{\$180,000 - \$20,000}$$

$$= 10\%$$

*$60,000 − $36,000 = $24,000 cost savings per year.
**($180,000 − $20,000) ÷ 20 years = $8,000 depreciation per year.

INSTANT QUIZ 13–6
Calculate the simple rate of return for an investment in equipment that would cost $400,000, have a 10-year useful life, have a salvage value of $40,000, and generate annual cost savings of $90,000.

Criticism of the Simple Rate of Return

The most important criticism of the simple rate of return is that it ignores the time value of money—it considers a dollar received 10 years from now just as valuable as a dollar received today. Thus, the simple rate of return can be misleading if the alternatives being considered have different cash flow patterns in terms of timing. In contrast, the net present value method explicitly incorporates the time value of money. However, as noted earlier, the appeal of the simple rate of return is its simplicity both in terms of the calculations involved and the understandability of the metric.

■ BEHAVIOURAL CONSIDERATIONS

So far, this chapter has emphasized the quantitative aspects of capital budgeting. Managers should also be mindful of important behavioural considerations. For example, estimates of cash flows, discount rates, and salvage values may be affected by the attitudes of individual managers toward risk. Risk-averse managers tend to be more conservative in their estimates and thus would be inclined to understate expected revenues or cost savings for a given project. Alternatively, managers may strongly favour their own project ideas and bias estimates of cash inflows and outflows to make their project proposals look more attractive. If so, this would render the resultant calculations of net present value or the internal rate of return less accurate.

Considerations other than the profitability of a project may also influence preference decisions. If only limited funds are available for capital investments, a division with several good investment proposals may be denied approval of some proposals in favour of the less profitable projects proposed by managers of other divisions. Such resource allocation decisions based on non-financial reasons may be deemed necessary to give the appearance of fairness across the organization.

Importantly, some projects are approved even though they may not generate a positive net present value. For example, projects involving employee, consumer, or environmental safety, or that otherwise impact a firm's ability to operate in a socially responsible manner, may be evaluated using criteria that are very difficult to quantify such as employee well-being or consumer perceptions of social responsibility. Other projects that cannot be justified on financial grounds may have to be undertaken in order to conform to municipal, provincial/territorial, or federal laws. For example, manufacturing companies may be required to invest in equipment to reduce emissions even though doing so will not result in cost savings.

BEYOND THE BOTTOM LINE

Companies are becoming increasingly sensitive to making decisions that align with stakeholder concerns both for the environment and social issues. For example, some companies have made capital investments in on-site fitness centres because exercise contributes to the mental and physical well-being of employees. These investments may not generate a positive net present value but they provide indirect benefits by making the organization more attractive to prospective and current employees. Such investments may also result in productivity gains (e.g., less absenteeism) as the result of having more satisfied and healthier employees.

In summary, the capital budgeting process often involves more than just the quantitative techniques presented in this chapter. A purely quantitative approach to capital budgeting is not representative of what actually happens in practice. Important qualitative factors within the firm often strongly influence capital budgeting decisions.

KNOWLEDGE IN ACTION

Managers can apply their knowledge about capital budgeting when

- Deciding whether or not to proceed with an individual investment project
- Comparing and choosing projects to invest in when capital funds are limited
- Estimating the number of periods required to recover a project's initial investment
- Quantifying the intangible benefits necessary to make an investment project attractive
- Identifying financing needs related to planned capital expenditures

SUMMARY

- Capital budgeting decisions fall into two categories: screening decisions and preference decisions. Screening decisions involve determining whether a proposed investment meets a predetermined standard of acceptability. Preference decisions involve selecting from among two or more acceptable investment proposals.
- Investment decisions should take into account the time value of money, since a dollar today is more valuable than a dollar received in the future. The net present value and internal rate of return (IRR) methods both reflect this fact. In the net present value method, the difference between the present value of the cash inflows and the present value of the cash outflows is called the project's *net present value*. The discount rate used to calculate the net present value method is usually a minimum required rate of return, such as the company's weighted-average cost of capital (WACC). Software programs such as Microsoft Excel can be used to quickly and accurately calculate present value amounts. **[LO1]**
- The IRR is the rate of return that equates the present value of the cash inflows and the present value of cash outflows, resulting in a zero net present value. If the IRR is less than the company's minimum required rate of return, the project is rejected (if decisions are based solely on quantitative criteria). Software programs such as Microsoft Excel can be used to quickly and accurately calculate a project's IRR. **[LO2]**
- Some projects have cash flows that are difficult to estimate. Intangible benefits that may result from upgrading production equipment such as improved quality or reliability can be difficult to quantify with any degree of certainty. However, management can cope with this uncertainty by estimating the dollar amount of intangible benefits that would be required to make a project attractive. If management believes the value of the intangible benefits will meet or exceed the required amount, the project should proceed. **[LO3]**
- After identifying projects that are estimated to provide an acceptable rate of return, managers can rank them using either the project profitability index or their IRRs. The project profitability index is conceptually superior to the IRR approach and is computed by dividing the net present value of the project by the required initial investment. **[LO4]**
- After a project has been approved, a post-audit should be performed to see whether expected results are actually being realized. This is a key part of the capital budgeting process, since it tends to improve the quality of the estimates going into future investment proposals and provides management with an opportunity to recognize any developing problems or opportunities with existing projects. **[LO4]**
- Some companies prefer to use the payback period as an approach to making capital budgeting decisions. The payback period is the number of periods (usually expressed in years) required to recover the cost of the initial investment from the net cash inflows generated by the project. The payback approach ignores the time value of money. **[LO5]**

- The simple rate of return is another approach to making capital budgeting decisions that also ignores the time value of money. It is determined by dividing a project's accounting income (incremental revenues and costs) by the initial investment in the project. **[LO6]**

REVIEW PROBLEM: COMPARISON OF CAPITAL BUDGETING METHODS

Bryant Limited is considering making a capital expenditure for a project that would have an eight-year life and require a $5,000,000 investment in equipment. At the end of eight years, the project would terminate and the equipment would have no salvage value. The project would provide operating income each year as follows:

Sales.....................................		$6,000,000
Variable expenses.........................		3,600,000
Contribution margin.......................		2,400,000
Fixed expenses:		
Advertising, salaries, and other		
fixed out-of-pocket costs	$1,400,000	
Depreciation...........................	600,000	
Total fixed expenses......................		2,000,000
Operating income.........................		$ 400,000

The company's discount rate is 8%.

Required:
1. Compute the net annual cash inflow from the project.
2. Compute the project's net present value. Is the project acceptable?
3. Find the project's IRR to the nearest whole percentage point.
4. Compute the project's payback period.
5. Compute the project's simple rate of return.

Solution to Review Problem

1. The net annual cash inflow can be computed by deducting the cash expenses from sales:

Sales...	$6,000,000
Variable expenses...............................	3,600,000
Contribution margin.............................	2,400,000
Advertising, salaries, and	
other fixed out-of-pocket costs..................	1,400,000
Net annual cash inflow..........................	$1,000,000

Or the net annual cash inflow can be computed by adding depreciation back to operating income:

Operating income.............................	$ 400,000
Add: Non-cash deduction for depreciation	600,000
Net annual cash inflow....................	$1,000,000

2. The net present value is computed as follows:

Item	Year(s)	Amount of Cash Flow	Present Value of Cash Flows*
Cost of new equipment	Now	$(5,000,000)	$(5,000,000)
Annual net cash inflows.............	1–8	1,000,000	5,746,639
Net present value			$ 746,639

*Calculated using the NPV formula of Microsoft Excel and a discount rate of 8%

Yes, the project is acceptable because it has a positive net present value.

3. The IRR using the IRR formula in Microsoft Excel is 12%.

4. The formula for the payback period is

$$\text{Payback period} = \frac{\text{Investment required}}{\text{Annual net cash flow}}$$

$$= \frac{\$5,000,000}{\$1,000,000} = 5.0 \text{ years}$$

5. The formula for the simple rate of return is

$$\text{Simple rate of return} = \frac{\text{Annual incremental operating income}}{\text{Initial investment}}$$

$$= \frac{\$400,000}{\$5,000,000} = 8\%$$

DISCUSSION CASE

DISCUSSION CASE 13–1

Many small and medium-sized companies tend not to use discounted cash flow techniques when analyzing capital expenditures. Instead, if any analysis of capital expenditures is performed, techniques such as the payback method or the simple rate of return are used.

Required:

1. Why might smaller companies prefer to use techniques such as cash payback or the simple rate of return over discounted cash flow techniques?

2. Do you think it is any less beneficial for smaller companies to use discounted cash flow techniques when analyzing capital expenditures than it is for larger companies? Why or why not?

QUESTIONS

13–1 What is the difference between capital budgeting screening decisions and capital budgeting preference decisions?

13–2 What is meant by the term *discounting*?

13–3 What is meant by the term *time value of money*?

13–4 Should the salvage value on equipment being replaced as part of a new project proposal be included as a cash inflow when calculating net present value and/or the internal rate of return for that project? Why or why not?

13–5 What is the main criticism of the simple rate of return method?

13–6 What are the two simplifying assumptions in net present value analysis?

13–7 If a post-audit shows that the actual cash inflows for a project are lower than the estimates used to originally determine a project's net present value, does this mean that the manager who prepared the estimates inflated them to make the project look better? Why or why not?

13–8 What is the weighted average cost of capital and how should it be used in capital budgeting decisions?

13–9 How is the IRR used to determine whether a project is acceptable or not?

13–10 When two alternatives are being considered when making a capital budgeting decision, what does it mean to use an incremental-cost approach for calculating the net present value?

13–11 "As the discount rate decreases, the present value of a given future cash flow also decreases." Do you agree? Explain.

13–12 What are some non-financial factors that might be considered when making capital budgeting decisions?

13–13 Conceptually, what does the project profitability index represent? How should it be used to compare competing investment projects?

13–14 Why is depreciation expense not included in the calculation of a project's payback period?

13–15 How is the eventual salvage value of new equipment being purchased as part of a capital project treated when calculating the simple rate of return?

FOUNDATIONAL EXERCISES

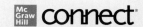

[LO1, LO2, LO4, LO5, LO6]

Cardinal Company is considering a five-year project that would require a $2,975,000 investment in equipment with a useful life of five years and no salvage value. The company's discount rate is 14%. The project would provide net operating income in each of five years as follows:

Sales.		$2,735,000
Variable expenses.		1,000,000
Contribution margin.		1,735,000
Fixed expenses:		
Advertising, salaries, and other out-of-pocket costs	$735,000	
Depreciation.	595,000	
Total fixed expenses.		1,330,000
Operating income.		$ 405,000

Required:

(Answer each question by referring to the original data unless instructed otherwise.)

13–1 Which item(s) in the income statement shown above will not affect cash flows?

13–2 What are the project's annual net cash inflows? What is the present value of the project's annual net cash inflows?

13–3 What is the project's net present value?

13–4 What is the project profitability index for this project? (Round your answer to the nearest whole percent.)

13–5 What is the project's internal rate of return to the nearest whole percent?

13–6 What is the project's payback period?

13–7 What is the project's simple rate of return for each of the five years?

13–8 If the company's discount rate was 16% instead of 14%, would you expect the project's net present value to be higher than, lower than, or the same as your answer to requirement 4? No computations are necessary.

13–9 If the equipment had a salvage value of $300,000 at the end of five years, would you expect the project's payback period to be higher than, lower than, or the same as your answer to requirement 7? No computations are necessary.

13–10 If the equipment had a salvage value of $300,000 at the end of five years, would you expect the project's net present value to be higher than, lower than, or the same as your answer to requirement 3? No computations are necessary.

13–11 If the equipment had a salvage value of $300,000 at the end of five years, would you expect the project's simple rate of return to be higher than, lower than, or the same as your answer to requirement 8? No computations are necessary.

13–12 Assume a post-audit showed that all estimates (including total sales) were exactly correct except for the variable expense ratio, which actually turned out to be 45%. What was the project's actual net present value?

13–13 Assume a post-audit showed that all estimates (including total sales) were exactly correct except for the variable expense ratio, which actually turned out to be 45%. What was the project's actual payback period?

13–14 Assume a post-audit showed that all estimates (including total sales) were exactly correct except for the variable expense ratio, which actually turned out to be 45%. What was the project's actual simple rate of return?

EXERCISES

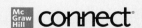

EXERCISE 13–1 Net Present Value Method [LO1]

The manager of the creative design department of a toy manufacturer is interested in purchasing a three-dimensional printer to use in designing prototypes for new toys. The cost is $80,000, but it will reduce labour and other costs by $25,000 per year. At the end of the printer's five-year useful life, it will have no scrap value. The company's required rate of return is 8%.

Required:
Ignore income taxes.

1. Determine the net present value of the investment in the printer.
2. What is the printer's internal rate of return?

EXERCISE 13–2 Internal Rate of Return [LO2]
Billy Brown, owner of Billy's Ice Cream On-the-Go, is investigating purchasing a new delivery van that would contain a custom-built refrigeration unit. The van would cost $90,000, have an eight-year useful life, and generate cost savings of $15,000 per year compared to the van currently being used. Also, Billy estimates the new van would result in the sale of 2,000 more litres of ice cream each year, which has a contribution margin of $1 per litre.

Required:
Ignore income taxes.

1. What would be the total annual cash inflows associated with the new van for capital budgeting purposes?
2. Find the IRR promised by the new van, rounded to one decimal place.
3. Now assume that in addition to the cash flows described above, the van will have a $10,000 salvage value at the end of eight years. Calculate the IRR rounded to one decimal place.

EXERCISE 13–3 Uncertain Future Cash Flows [LO3]
Jannsen Limited is contemplating investing in solar panels to reduce its need to purchase electricity from its local hydro company. The panels are estimated to cost $2,000,000 and will have a 15-year useful life with no salvage value. The electricity cost savings are expected to be about $200,000 per year. Management expects there will be some intangible benefits arising from purchasing the solar panels such as increased goodwill among its younger customers who are, on average, environmentally conscious. This could lead to increased repeat business with these customers in the future. Jannsen uses a discount rate of 10% when evaluating capital expenditures.

Required:
Ignore income taxes.

> **CHECK FIGURE**
> Net present value
> $(478,784).

1. Calculate the net present value of the investment in solar panels.
2. Approximately what would the intangible benefits need to be each year to make it worthwhile to invest in the solar panels?

EXERCISE 13–4 Preference Ranking [LO4]
Information on four potential projects is given below:

	Project			
	A	**B**	**C**	**D**
Investment required	$(350,000)	$(390,000)	$(450,000)	$(480,000)
Present value of cash inflows........	535,000	590,000	670,000	730,000
Net present value	$ 185,000	$ 200,000	$ 220,000	$ 250,000

Required:
Ignore income taxes.

1. Compute the project profitability index for each project.
2. Rank the projects in terms of preference.

EXERCISE 13–5 Payback Method [LO5]
The management of Unter Corporation, an architectural design firm, is considering an investment with the following cash flows:

Year		Investment	Cash Inflow
1	....	$15,000	$1,000
2	....	$ 8,000	$2,000
3	....		$2,500
4	....		$4,000
5	....		$5,000
6	....		$6,000
7	....		$5,000
8	....		$4,000
9	....		$3,000
10	....		$2,000

Required:

Ignore income taxes.

1.   Determine the payback period of the investment.
2.   Would the payback period be affected if the cash inflow in the last year was several times as large?

EXERCISE 13–6 Simple Rate of Return Method [LO6]

The CFO of The Fun Factory is investigating the possibility of investing in a three-dimensional printer that would cost $20,000. The printer would eliminate the need to have prototypes of new toys be produced by a third party. The cost of having the prototypes manufactured by the third party is about $8,000 per year. The printer would have a useful life of five years with no salvage value with expected annual operating costs of $3,000 per year.

Required:

Ignore income taxes. Compute the simple rate of return on the printer.

EXERCISE 13–7 Comparison of Projects Using Net Present Value [LO1]

Mitchell Company has $30,000 to invest and has two alternative uses of the funds, as shown below. Mitchell Company uses an 8% discount rate:

	Invest in Project Alpha	Invest in Project Beta
Investment required	$30,000	$ 30,000
Annual cash inflows...........................	$ 8,000	$ 0
Single cash inflow at the end of 10 years		$120,000
Life of the project............................	10 years	10 years

Required:

Ignore income taxes. Which investment would you recommend that the company accept? Show all computations using net present value. Prepare separate computations for each investment.

EXERCISE 13–8 Basic Net Present Value Analysis [LO1]

Jim Pooley operates a hot dog stand in downtown Toronto. He is considering purchasing a new stand that will cost $30,000. The new stand will be more efficient to run and Jim estimates it will save him $5,000 per year in operating costs. The new stand will have a 10-year useful life with a scrap value of $2,500 at the end of year 10. Jim thinks he can sell his old stand now for $1,000.

Required:

Ignore income taxes. Calculate the net present value of the new hot dog stand assuming Jim requires a 7% return.

EXERCISE 13–9 Internal Rate of Return [LO2]

Applecross Dental Services is investigating expanding its operations by acquiring additional teeth cleaning equipment. The equipment would cost $150,000 and management has estimated that it would result in net cash inflows of $15,000 per year. The equipment would have a 15-year useful life with an expected salvage value of $15,000.

Required:
Ignore income taxes.

1. Compute the equipment's IRR rounded to one decimal place.
2. Assume that instead of $15,000, the salvage value in 15 years for the new equipment will be $0. Compute the IRR under this new assumption. Why does the new IRR differ so little from the value calculated in requirement 1?

EXERCISE 13–10 Uncertain Benefits [LO3]

Darlington Limited is considering implementing a new online employee recognition system that will allow employees to recognize their peers for "going above and beyond" in helping the company achieve its goals. Employees who receive recognition from their peers using the new system will be eligible for small financial rewards. The new system has an up-front cost of $50,000 with the recognition awards expected to cost about $5,000 per year. The consulting firm that will help implement the new system has told management at Darlington Limited that it will likely generate significant cost savings vis-a-vis reduced turnover as the result of more engaged employees. Management plans to use the new system for a trial period of 5 years.

Required:
Ignore income taxes.

What annual cost savings related to reduced employee turnover will Darlington Limited need to achieve to generate an internal rate of return of 10% on the new system?

EXERCISE 13–11 Basic Payback Period and Simple Rate of Return Computations [LO5, LO6]

Sun Coast Tours is considering purchasing a new boat for use in its tour business. Relevant information concerning the boat is as follows:

Purchase cost	$210,000
Annual net cash inflows that will be provided by the boat	$ 50,000
Life of the boat	10 years

Required:
Ignore income taxes.

CHECK FIGURE
1. Payback period is 4.2 years; 2. Simple rate of return is 15%.

1. Compute the payback period for the boat. If the company rejects all proposals with a payback period of more than five years, will the boat be purchased?
2. Compute the simple rate of return on the boat. Use straight-line depreciation based on the boat's useful life, assuming $10,000 salvage value. Will the boat be purchased if the company's required rate of return is 12%?

EXERCISE 13–12 Working with Net Present Value [LO1]

Piccadilly Hospital has purchased new lab equipment for $200,000. The equipment is expected to last for three years and to provide cash inflows as follows:

Year 1	$60,000
Year 2	$70,000
Year 3	?

Required:
Assuming that the equipment will yield exactly a 10% rate of return, what is the expected cash inflow for year 3?

EXERCISE 13–13 Basic Net Present Value and Internal Rate of Return Analysis [LO1, LO2]

Henrie's Drapery Service is investigating the purchase of a new machine for cleaning and blocking drapes. The machine would cost $137,280, including freight and installation. Henrie's has estimated that the new machine would increase the company's cash inflows, net of expenses, by $40,000 per year. The machine would have a five-year useful life and no salvage value.

Required:
1. Compute the machine's internal rate of return to the nearest whole percent.
2. Compute the machine's net present value. Use a discount rate of 14%. Why is the NPV so close to zero?
3. Suppose that the new machine would increase the company's annual cash inflows, net of expenses, by only $37,150 per year. Under these conditions, compute the internal rate of return to the nearest whole percent.

EXERCISE 13–14 Net Present Value Analysis of Two Alternatives [LO1]
Top Notch Limited has $750,000 to invest and is trying to decide between two alternative uses of the funds. The alternatives are as follows:

	A	B
Cost of equipment required	$750,000	$ 0
Working capital investment required	$ 0	$750,000
Annual cash inflows	$210,000	$150,000
Salvage value of equipment in seven years	$ 50,000	$ 0
Life of the project	7 years	7 years

The working capital needed for Project B will be released for investment elsewhere at the end of seven years. Top Notch uses a 20% discount rate.

Required:
Ignore income taxes. Which investment alternative (if either) would you recommend that the company accept? Show all computations using the net present value format. Prepare separate computations for each project.

EXERCISE 13–15 Payback Period and Simple Rate of Return [LO5, LO6]
Jamieson Enterprises is considering the development of a go-kart track at an estimated total cost of $680,000. The go-karts would have a $50,000 salvage value at the end of their 10-year useful life. Estimated revenues and costs on an annual basis would be as follows:

Ticket revenues		$380,000
Less operating expenses:		
Maintenance and utilities	$ 71,000	
Salaries	130,000	
Depreciation*	63,000	
Insurance	43,000	
Total operating expenses		307,000
Operating income		$ 73,000

*($680,000 − $50,000) ÷ 10

Required:
Ignore income taxes.

1. Jamieson Enterprises will not proceed with development of the go-kart track unless the payback period is less than six years. Should they proceed?
2. Compute the simple rate of return for the go-kart track. If Jamieson Enterprises requires a simple rate of return of at least 10%, does the go-kart track meet this criterion?

PROBLEMS

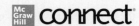

PROBLEM 13–16 Basic Net Present Value Analysis [LO1]

Windhoek Mines Ltd., of Namibia, is contemplating the purchase of equipment to exploit a mineral deposit on land to which the company has mineral rights. An engineering and cost analysis has been made, and it is expected that the following cash flows would be associated with opening and operating a mine in the area:

Cost of new equipment required and timbers	$275,000
Working capital required	$100,000
Annual net cash inflows*	$120,000
Cost to construct new roads in three years	$ 40,000
Salvage value of equipment in four years	$ 65,000

*Receipts from sales of ore, less out-of-pocket costs for salaries, utilities, insurance, etc.

The mineral deposit would be exhausted after four years of mining. At that point, the working capital would be released for reinvestment elsewhere. The company's required rate of return is 20%.

Required:

Ignore income taxes. Determine the net present value of the proposed mining project. Should the project be accepted? Explain.

PROBLEM 13–17 Basic Net Present Value Analysis [LO1, LO2]

Custom Cycles is looking at purchasing a new piece of equipment that would allow them to automate part of their production process now done manually. The equipment will cost $200,000 and would have a useful life of 10 years. At the end of year five, the equipment would require a $10,000 upgrade to replace major components. The equipment is expected to have a salvage value of $18,000 at the end of year ten.

Excluding depreciation, the new machine will have operating costs of $28,000 per year. The company uses straight-line depreciation for all production equipment. The cost of doing the work manually that the new machine will be able to do completely is $68,000 per year. Custom Cycles requires a 12% return on all investments in equipment.

Required:

Ignore income taxes.

1. What net annual cash inflows will be provided by the new equipment?
2. Compute the new equipment's net present value. Use the incremental cost approach, and round all dollar amounts to the nearest whole dollar.
3. What is the internal rate of return on the new equipment?

PROBLEM 13–18 Net Present Value Analysis; Uncertain Cash Flows [LO1, LO3]

Johnson Limited is contemplating the installation of a new system that would allow for automated handling of customer inquiries about their order status, account balances, etc. Currently all such inquiries are handled manually by customer service representatives. The software for the new system would cost $225,000. An additional $162,500 would be required for one-time installation costs. Management estimates that the new system would result in costs of $10,000 per year related to addressing software issues and other technological problems that may arise. However, the new system is expected to reduce labour costs by $84,000 per year.

Management estimates that the system would be used for five years. Severance costs related to the employees that would be laid off after implementing the new system would be $20,000. Johnson Limited requires a return of at least 15% on investments of this type.

Required:

Ignore income taxes.

1. Compute the net annual cost savings promised by the new system.
2. Using the data from (1) above and other data from the problem, compute the new system's net present value. Would you recommend that the system be implemented? Explain.

3.   Assume that there are intangible benefits associated with the new system related to having more satisfied customers. For example, shorter wait times for automated responses would increase the likelihood that customers will buy products from Johnson Limited again in the future. What dollar value per year would management have to attach to these intangible benefits in order to make the new system an acceptable investment?

PROBLEM 13–19 Preference Ranking of Investment Projects [LO4]
Information on four investment projects being investigated by Revco Products is as follows:

	Project Number			
	1	**2**	**3**	**4**
Investment required	$(270,000)	$(450,000)	$(360,000)	$(480,000)
Present value of cash inflows.	336,140	522,970	433,400	567,270
Net present value	$ 66,140	$ 72,970	$ 73,400	$ 87,270
Life of the project.	6 years	3 years	12 years	6 years
Internal rate of return.	18%	19%	14%	16%

A 10% discount rate has been used in the present value computations above. Limited funds are available for investment, so the company can't accept all of the available projects.

Required:
1.   Compute the project profitability index for each investment project.
2.   Rank the four projects according to preference, in terms of
    a.   Net present value.
    b.   Project profitability index.
    c.   IRR.
3.   Which ranking do you prefer? Why?

PROBLEM 13–20 Simple Rate of Return; Payback [LO5, LO6]
Sharkey's Fun Centre contains a number of electronic games as well as a miniature golf course and various rides located outside the building. Paul Sharkey, the owner, would like to construct a water slide on one portion of his property. Mr. Sharkey has gathered the following information about the slide:

a.   Water slide equipment could be purchased and installed at a cost of $330,000. According to the manufacturer, the slide would be usable for 12 years, after which it would have no salvage value.
b.   Mr. Sharkey would use straight-line depreciation on the slide equipment.
c.   To make room for the water slide, several rides would be dismantled and sold. These rides are fully depreciated, but they could be sold for $60,000 to an amusement park in a nearby city.
d.   Mr. Sharkey has concluded that about 50,000 more people would use the water slide each year than have been using the rides. The admission price would be $3.60 per person (the same price that the Fun Centre has been charging for the old rides).
e.   Based on experience at other water slides, Mr. Sharkey estimates that annual incremental operating expenses for the slide would be: salaries, $85,000; insurance, $4,200; utilities, $13,000; and maintenance, $9,800.

Required:
Ignore income taxes.

1.   Prepare an income statement showing the expected operating income each year from the water slide.
2.   Compute the simple rate of return expected from the water slide. Based on this computation, would the water slide be constructed if Mr. Sharkey requires a simple rate of return of at least 14% on all investments?
3.   Compute the payback period for the water slide. If Mr. Sharkey accepts any project with a payback period of five years or less, would the water slide be constructed?

PROBLEM 13–21 Keep or Sell a Property [LO1]
Ben Ryatt, a professor of languages at a university in western Canada, owns a small office building adjacent to the university campus. He acquired the property 12 years ago at a total cost of $560,000:

$52,000 for the land and $508,000 for the building. He has just received an offer from a real estate company that wants to purchase the property. However, the property has been a good source of income over the years, so Ryatt is unsure whether he should keep it or sell it. His alternatives are as follows:

Keep the property. Ryatt's accountant has kept careful records of the income realized from the property over the past 10 years. These records indicate the following annual revenues and expenses:

Rental receipts..		$150,000
Less building expenses:		
Utilities..	$28,600	
Depreciation of building...........................	17,800	
Property taxes and insurance	19,500	
Repairs and maintenance	10,500	
Custodial help and supplies	43,500	119,900
Operating income		$ 30,100

Ryatt makes a $12,600 mortgage payment each year on the property. The mortgage will be paid off in 10 more years. He has been depreciating the building by the straight-line method, assuming a salvage value of $9,600 for the building, which he still thinks is an appropriate figure. He feels sure that the building can be rented for another 16 years. He also feels sure that 16 years from now the land will be worth 2.5 times what he paid for it.

Sell the property. A real estate company has offered to purchase the property by paying $150,000 immediately and $23,000 per year for the next 16 years. Control of the property would go to the real estate company immediately. To sell the property, Ryatt would need to pay the mortgage off, which could be done by making a lump-sum payment of $71,000.

Required:
Ryatt requires a 14% rate of return. Would you recommend he keep or sell the property? Show computations using the total-cost approach to net present value. Ignore income taxes.

PROBLEM 13–22 Simple Rate of Return; Payback; Internal Rate of Return [LO2, LO5, LO6]
Chateau Beaune is a family-owned winery headed by Gerard Despinoy and located in the Burgundy region of France. The harvesting season in early fall is the busiest part of the year for the winery, and many part-time workers are hired to help pick and process grapes. Despinoy is investigating purchasing a harvesting machine that would significantly reduce the amount of labour required in the picking process. The harvesting machine is built to straddle grapevines, which are laid out in low-lying rows. Two workers are carried on the machine just above ground level, one on each side of the vine. As the machine slowly crawls through the vineyard, the workers cut bunches of grapes from the vines, which then fall into a hopper. The machine separates the grapes from the stems and other woody debris. The debris is then pulverized and spread behind the machine as a rich ground mulch. Despinoy has gathered the following information relating to the decision of whether to purchase the machine:

a. The winery would save €190,000 per year in labour costs with the new harvesting machine. In addition, the company would no longer have to purchase and spread ground mulch—at an annual savings of €10,000. (The French currency is the euro, which is denoted by the symbol €.)

b. The harvesting machine would cost €480,000. It would have an estimated 12-year useful life and zero salvage value. The winery uses straight-line depreciation.

c. Annual out-of-pocket costs associated with the harvesting machine would be insurance, €1,000; fuel, €9,000; and a maintenance contract, €12,000. In addition, two operators would be hired and trained for the machine, and they would be paid a total of €70,000 per year, including all benefits.

d. Despinoy feels that the investment in the harvesting machine should earn at least a 16% rate of return.

Required:
Ignore income taxes.

1. Determine the annual net savings in cash operating costs that would be realized if the harvesting machine were purchased.

2. Compute the simple rate of return expected from the harvesting machine.

3. Compute the payback period on the harvesting machine. Despinoy will not purchase equipment unless it has a payback period of five years or less. Under this criterion, should the harvesting machine be purchased?

4.   Compute (to the nearest whole percentage point) the IRR promised by the harvesting machine. Based on this computation, does it appear that the simple rate of return is an accurate guide in investment decisions?

PROBLEM 13–23   Net Present Value; Uncertain Future Cash Flows; Post-Audit [LO1, LO3]

"I really want to invest in the advanced production module to combine with our other manufacturing equipment, we'll have a complete flexible manufacturing system (FMS) in place in our Lakeland plant," said Karen Davis, production manager for Big Sounds Electronics.

"I'm hopeful that the reduced labour and inventory costs will justify its purchase," replied Pat Laplante, the controller. "The new CFO is insistent all capital spending needs to pay for itself out of cost reductions."

Analysis indicates that using the new production module will result in a savings of 20,000 direct labour-hours each year. The labour rate is $20 per hour. Also, the smoother work flow made possible by the FMS will allow the company to reduce the amount of inventory on hand by $450,000. The released funds will be available for use elsewhere in the company. This inventory reduction will take place in the first year of operation. The company's required rate of return is 15%:

Cost of the module	$2,400,000
Software and installation	$1,050,000
Annual savings in labour costs	?
Annual savings in inventory carrying costs	$ 200,000
Monthly increase in power and maintenance costs	$ 4,500
Salvage value in 15 years	$ 180,000
Useful life	15 years

Required:
Ignore income taxes.

1.   Determine the net *annual* cost savings if the module is purchased. (Do not include the $450,000 inventory reduction or the salvage value in this computation.)
2.   Compute the net present value of the proposed investment in the module. Based on these data, would you recommend that the module be purchased? Explain.
3.   Assume that the module is purchased. At the end of the first year, Laplante has found that some items didn't work out as planned. Due to unforeseen problems, software and installation costs were $200,000 more than estimated, and direct labour has been reduced by only 17,500 hours per year, rather than by 20,000 hours. Assuming that all other cost data were accurate, does it appear that the company made a wise investment? Show computations, using the net present value format as in (2) above. (*Hint:* It might be helpful to place yourself back at the beginning of the first year, with the new data.)
4.   On seeing your analysis in (3) above, the CFO stated, "That module was a really bad investment." Compute for the CFO the additional amount of cash inflows that would be needed each year in order for the equipment to yield a 15% rate of return.

PROBLEM 13–24   Internal Rate of Return; Sensitivity Analysis [LO2]

Jan Boothe is the CFO of the Laurelwood Sports Medicine Clinic. Boothe is trying to determine whether or not the clinic should move patient files and other items out of a spare room in the clinic and use the room for physiotherapy work. She has determined that it would require an investment of $286,000 for equipment and related costs of getting the room ready for use. Based on receipts being generated from other rooms in the clinic, Boothe estimates that the new room would generate a net cash inflow of $70,000 per year. The equipment purchased for the room would have a seven-year estimated useful life.

Required:
Ignore income taxes.

1.   Compute the IRR on the equipment for the new room to one decimal place. Verify your answer by computing the net present value of the equipment using the IRR you have computed as the discount rate.
2.   Assume that Boothe will not purchase the new equipment unless it promises a return of at least 14%. Compute the amount of annual cash inflow that would provide this return on the $286,000 investment.

3. Although seven years is the average life for physiotherapy equipment, Boothe knows that due to changing technology this life can vary substantially. Compute the IRR to one decimal place if the life of the equipment were (*a*) five years and (*b*) nine years, rather than seven years. Is there any information provided by these computations that you would be particularly anxious to show Boothe? Explain.

4. Boothe is unsure about the estimated $70,000 annual cash inflow from the room. She thinks that the actual cash inflow could be as much as 15% greater or less than this figure.

    a. Assume that the actual cash inflow each year is 15% greater than estimated. Recompute the IRR to one decimal place using the seven-year life.

    b. Assume that the actual cash inflow each year is 15% less than estimated. Recompute the IRR to one decimal place using the seven-year life.

5. Refer to the original data. Assume that the equipment is purchased and that the room is opened for use. However, due to an increasing number of physiotherapists in the area, the clinic is able to generate only $60,000 per year in net cash receipts from the new room. At the end of five years, the clinic closes the room and sells the equipment to a company for a cash price of $120,000. Compute the IRR to one decimal place that the clinic earned on its investment over the five-year period.

PROBLEM 13–25 Net Present Value Analysis of a Lease or Buy Decision [LO1]
The Riteway Ad Agency provides cars for its sales staff. In the past, the company has always purchased its cars from a dealer and then sold the cars after three years of use. The company's present fleet of cars is three years old and will be sold very shortly. To provide a replacement fleet, the company is considering two alternatives:

Purchase alternative. If the new cars are purchased, then the costs incurred by the company will be as follows:

Purchase cost of a new fleet: 10 cars at $17,000 each	$170,000
Annual cost of servicing, licences, and taxes for the fleet	$ 3,000
Repairs for the fleet:	
First year	$ 1,500
Second year	$ 4,000
Third year	$ 6,000

At the end of three years, the fleet could be sold for one-half of the original purchase price.

Lease alternative. The company can lease the cars under a three-year lease contract. The lease cost would be $55,000 per year (the first payment due at the end of Year 1). As part of this lease cost, the owner would provide all servicing and repairs, license the cars, and pay all the taxes. Riteway would be required to make a $10,000 security deposit at the beginning of the lease period, which would be refunded when the cars were returned to the owner at the end of the lease contract.

Riteway Ad Agency's required rate of return is 18%.

Required:
Ignore income taxes.

1. What is the net present value of the cash flows associated with the purchase alternative? Round all dollar amounts to the nearest whole dollar.
2. What is the net present value of the cash flows associated with the lease alternative? Round all dollar amounts to the nearest whole dollar.
3. Which alternative should the company accept?

PROBLEM 13–26 Preference Ranking of Investment Projects [LO4]
Since limited funds are available for investment, Riley & Tanner Limited must ration the funds among four competing projects. Selected information on the four projects follows:

Project	Investment Required	Present Value of Cash Inflows	Life of the Project (years)	Internal Rate of Return
1	$1,960,000	$ 2,457,621	7	18%
2	1,653,750	2,126,250	12	23%
3	1,225,000	1,619,144	7	20%
4	1,715,000	2,058,224	3	22%

The present values of the net cash inflows above have been computed using a 10% discount rate. The company wants your assistance in determining which project to accept first, which to accept second, and so forth. The company's investment funds are limited.

Required:
1. Compute the project profitability index for each project.
2. In order of preference, rank the four projects in terms of
    a. Net present value.
    b. Project profitability index.
    c. IRR.
3. Which ranking do you prefer? Why?

PROBLEM 13–27 Simple Rate of Return and Payback Analysis of Two Machines [LO5, LO6]

Blue Ridge Furniture is considering purchasing two different items of equipment, as described below:

Machine A. A machine has just come onto the market that compresses sawdust into various shelving products. Currently, the sawdust is disposed of as a waste product. The following information is available about the machine:

a. The machine would cost $780,000 and would have a 25% salvage value at the end of its 10-year useful life. The company uses straight-line depreciation and considers salvage value in computing depreciation deductions.
b. The shelving products produced by the machine would generate revenues of $350,000 per year. Variable manufacturing costs would be 20% of sales.
c. Fixed annual expenses associated with the new shelving products would be advertising, $42,000; salaries, $86,000; utilities, $9,000; and insurance, $13,000.

Machine B. A second machine has come onto the market that would automate a sanding process that is now done largely by hand. The following information is available about this machine:

a. The new sanding machine would cost $220,000 and would have no salvage value at the end of its 10-year useful life. The company would use straight-line depreciation.
b. Several old pieces of sanding equipment that are fully depreciated would be disposed of at a scrap value of $7,200.
c. The new sanding machine would provide substantial annual savings in cash operating costs. It would require an operator at an annual salary of $26,000 and $3,000 in annual maintenance costs. The current hand-operated sanding procedure costs the company $85,000 per year.

Blue Ridge Furniture requires a simple rate of return of 16% on all equipment purchases. Also, the company will not purchase equipment unless the equipment has a payback period of four years or less.

Required:
Ignore income taxes.

1. For Machine A:
    a. Prepare an income statement showing the expected operating income each year from the new shelving products. Use the contribution format.
    b. Compute the simple rate of return.
    c. Compute the payback period.
2. For Machine B:
    a. Compute the simple rate of return.
    b. Compute the payback period.
3. According to the company's criteria, which machine, if either, should the company purchase?

PROBLEM 13–28 Net Present Value Analysis of a New Product [LO1]

Secure Homes is pondering an opportunity to produce and sell a new smart home monitoring system that can be managed remotely using a smartphone app. The company has gathered the following data on probable costs and market potential:

a. New equipment would have to be acquired to produce the monitoring system. The equipment would cost $300,000 and be usable for 12 years. After 12 years, it would have a salvage value equal to 10% of the original cost.

b. Production and sales of the monitoring system would require a working capital investment of $120,000 to finance accounts receivable, inventories, and day-to-day cash needs. This working capital would be released for use elsewhere by the company after 12 years.

c. An extensive marketing study projects sales in units over the next 12 years as follows:

Year(s)	Sales in Units
1......	4,000
2......	7,000
3......	10,000
4–12 ...	12,000

d. The monitoring systems would sell for $135 each; variable costs for production, administration, and sales would be $75 per unit.

e. To gain entry into the market, the company would have to advertise heavily in the early years of sales. The advertising program follows:

Year(s)	Amount of Advertising
1–2	$210,000
3	150,000
4–12	120,000

f. Other fixed costs for salaries, insurance, maintenance, and straight-line depreciation on equipment would total $382,500 per year. (Depreciation is based on cost less salvage value.)

g. The company's required rate of return is 15%.

Required:

Ignore income taxes.

1. Compute the net cash inflow (cash receipts less yearly cash operating expenses) anticipated from sale of the monitoring systems for each year over the next 12 years.

2. Using the data computed in (1) above and other data provided in the problem, determine the net present value of the proposed investment. Would you recommend that Secure Homes invest in the new product?

3. What is the project's internal rate of return?

PROBLEM 13–29 Net Present Value; Total-Cost and Incremental-Cost Approaches [LO1]

Clean Duds Laundromat has an industrial water softener that enhances the water quality used in its washing machines. The water softener is approaching the end of its useful life and must be either overhauled or replaced. Details of the two alternatives are shown below.

If the company overhauls its current water softener, then it will be usable for eight more years. If, instead, a new water softener is purchased, it will be used for eight years, after which it will be replaced. The new water softener will be considerably more energy efficient, resulting in a substantial reduction in annual operating costs, as shown below:

	Current Water Softener	New Water Softener
Purchase cost new........................	$8,000	$10,000
Remaining book value	$4,500	—
Overhaul needed now	$4,000	—
Annual cash operating costs	$6,000	$ 4,500
Salvage value now.........................	$2,000	—
Salvage value eight years from now	$1,000	$ 3,000

Clean Duds computes depreciation on a straight-line basis. All equipment purchases are evaluated using a 12% discount rate.

CHECK FIGURE
1. Net cash inflow:
year 1 $(330,000),
year 2 $(150,000),
year 3 $90,000,
years 4–12 $240,000;
2. Net present value $19,808;
3. IRR = 15.4%.

Required:

Ignore income taxes.

1. Should Clean Duds Laundromat upgrade the old water softener or purchase the new one? Use the total-cost approach to net present value in making your decision.
2. Redo (1) above, this time using the incremental-cost approach.

PROBLEM 13–30 Net Present Value Analysis [LO1]

In five years, Kent Duncan will retire. He is exploring the possibility of opening a self-service car wash. The car wash could be managed in the free time he has available from his regular occupation, and it could be closed easily when he retires. After careful study, Mr. Duncan has determined the following:

- A building in which a car wash could be installed is available under a five-year lease at a cost of $1,700 per month.
- Purchase and installation costs of equipment would total $175,000. In five years the equipment could be sold for about 10% of its original cost.
- An investment of an additional $2,000 would be required to cover working capital needs for cleaning supplies, change funds, and so forth. After five years, this working capital would be released for investment elsewhere.
- Both a wash and a vacuum service would be offered with a wash costing $2.00 and the vacuum costing $1.00 per use.
- The only variable costs associated with the operation would be 20 cents per wash for water and 10 cents per use of the vacuum for electricity.
- In addition to rent, monthly costs of operation would be: cleaning, $450; insurance, $75; and maintenance, $500.
- Gross receipts from the wash would be about $1,350 per week. According to the experience of other car washes, 60% of the customers using the wash would also use the vacuum.

Mr. Duncan will not open the car wash unless it provides at least a 10% return.

Required:

1. Assuming that the car wash will be open 52 weeks a year, compute the expected annual net cash receipts (gross cash receipts less cash disbursements) from its operation. (Do not include the cost of the equipment, the working capital, or the salvage value in these computations.)
2. Would you advise Mr. Duncan to open the car wash? Show computations using the net present value method of investment analysis. Round all dollar figures to the nearest whole dollar.

CASES

CASE 13–31 Capital Budget Reviews and the Role of the Post-Audit [LO1]

Stephen Scott recently joined the Finance and Planning Division of the Bank of Ontario as an assistant chief financial officer (CFO). The Bank is a publicly owned company. Scott is a Chartered Professional Accountant and has spent the previous four years working in the accounting department of a large Canadian manufacturing company. He took the job at the bank because it provided an opportunity to get some international business experience.

One of Scott's responsibilities is to perform an initial review of the capital budgeting proposals developed by the various divisions at the bank. Because the bank's divisions are very large and have a high degree of operating autonomy, each division has its own divisional controller, who prepares the proposals with input from key managers in the division and other bank personnel. For 2021, the bank budgeted $500,000 for capital spending in each of the six major divisions for projects requiring less than $100,000 of expenditures. For projects of that size, the divisions are free to go ahead and spend the funds as they see fit, without the need for centralized review and approval. The bank budgeted a further $20 million in capital spending for 2021 to be allocated to the divisions on the basis of the project proposals submitted as part of the capital budget review process. These proposals are for individual projects requiring capital expenditures in excess of $100,000.

All project submissions are ranked from most to least profitable using the project profitability index: Present value of the net cash inflows ÷ Investment required. The bank uses a required return of 15% in determining the present value of net cash inflows from projects. The final review of the proposals is conducted by the CFO, the assistant CFO, and the vice-president of Finance (VPF). In addition to these three individuals, the review meeting is attended by the senior manager and controller of each division. Non-financial factors, such as the importance of the expenditure for maintaining the bank's competitive position and its impact on customer retention and growth, are considered as part of the review and approval process. However, these factors typically have a smaller impact on the final decision than the project profitability index, which senior management believes to be more objective and reliable.

As part of his initial review of the proposals, Scott was instructed by the CFO to evaluate the reasonableness of the assumptions and to check the accuracy of the calculations. Where necessary, he was to follow up with the divisional controllers if he had any questions about the details. As Scott began his review, he was struck by the relatively high project profitability index on the vast majority of the projects. In several instances, the assumptions underlying the proposal seemed very optimistic, so he decided to follow up with the individual divisional controllers.

Almost without fail, the controllers admitted to using highly optimistic cash inflows in order to make their proposals look as good as possible. The controllers also commented that the division managers viewed the capital budget review process as a game that they wanted to win by getting as many of their projects approved as possible. As one controller put it, "What's the harm in a little optimism as long as the estimates in all of the proposals are more or less equally overstated?" Scott also learned from the controllers that word had leaked out that last year only those projects with a project profitability index over 30% were funded, and that they had been instructed by their divisional managers to make sure that all current-year proposals met that threshold. Some of the divisional controllers also suggested that it was clear that senior management at the bank condoned the optimism included in their proposals since the use of post-audits had been discontinued several years ago after the CFO at the time (who has since been replaced) concluded that the cost of the audits exceeded their benefits.

As Scott sat in his office after a conversation with one of the divisional controllers, he wasn't sure what to do next. The divisional controllers told him he'd be wasting his time going to the CFO or the VPF, since they all knew how the capital budgeting game was being played. He was also concerned that rocking the boat would upset the divisional controllers, with whom he had to work closely on other aspects of his job. But he couldn't shake the feeling that this was an issue that deserved more attention.

Required:
Review pages 1–4 of the Chartered Professional Accountants of Ontario CPA Code of Professional Conduct at **https://media.cpaontario.ca/stewardship-of-the-profession/pdfs/CPA-Ontario-Code-of-professional-conduct.pdf**

1. Which principles of the Ontario CPA Code of Professional Conduct might Scott be in violation of if he takes no action?
2. What should Scott do?
3. What would be some benefits of post-audits for capital projects in excess of $100,000 at the Bank of Ontario?
4. Will post-audits eliminate the problem of inaccurate estimates and assumptions being experienced at the Bank of Ontario? Why or why not?

CASE 13–32 Net Present Value Analysis of Securities [LO1]
Anita Vasquez received $160,000 from her mother's estate. She placed the funds in the hands of a broker, who purchased the following securities on Vasquez's behalf:

a. Common shares were purchased at a cost of $80,000. The shares paid no dividends, but they were sold for $180,000 at the end of four years.
b. Preferred shares were purchased at their par value of $30,000. The shares paid a 6% dividend (based on par value) each year for four years. At the end of four years, the shares were sold for $24,000.
c. Bonds were purchased at a cost of $50,000. The bonds paid $3,000 in interest every six months. After four years, the bonds were sold for $58,500. (*Note:* In discounting a cash flow that occurs semi-annually, the procedure is to halve the discount rate and double the number of periods. Use the same procedure in discounting the proceeds from the sale.)

The securities were all sold at the end of four years so that Vasquez would have funds available to start a new business venture. The broker stated that the investments had earned more than a 20% return annually, and he gave Vasquez the following computation to support his statement:

Common shares:	
Gain on sale ($180,000 − $80,000)	$100,000
Preferred shares:	
Dividends paid (6% × $30,000 × 4 years)	7,200
Loss on sale ($24,000 − $30,000)	(6,000)
Bonds:	
Interest paid ($3,000 × 8 periods).	24,000
Gain on sale ($58,500 − $50,000)	8,500
Net gain on all investments	$133,700

Return: ($133,700 ÷ 4) ÷ $160,000 = 20.9%

Required:

Ignore income taxes.

1. Using a 20% discount rate, compute the net present value of each of the three investments. On which investment(s) did Anita earn a 20% rate of return? (Round computations to the nearest whole dollar.)
2. Considering all three investments together, did Anita earn a 20% rate of return? Explain.
3. Anita wants to use the $262,500 in proceeds ($180,000 + $24,000 + $58,500 = $262,500) from sale of the securities to open a fast-food franchise under a 10-year contract. What net annual cash inflow must the store generate for Anita to earn a 16% return over the 10-year period? Anita will not receive back her original investment at the end of the contract. (Round computations to the nearest whole dollar.)

CONNECTING CONCEPTS

SECTION 4

ANALYSIS OF SOUTH AMERICAN OPERATIONS

Claire Jackson (CEO) of Easy Learning (EL) is considering discontinuing operations in South America, which are based in Argentina. For a variety of reasons it has been a challenge for EL to grow the business in this region and costs continue to rise because of high inflation. Results from the most recent fiscal year just ended are shown below.

Sales	$400,000
Variable expenses	180,000
Contribution margin	$220,000
Fixed expenses	310,000
Operating income (loss)	($90,000)

If the South American operations are discontinued, Jackson has identified the following implications:

1. Assets with an original cost of $485,000, mostly leasehold improvements and computer equipment, can be sold for $15,000. Assume that the assets are completely written off for both accounting purposes and tax purposes (i.e., $0 NBV and UCC) and that the salvage proceeds of $15,000 are not taxable.
2. Severance pay for the three full-time employees will total $50,000. Severance pay is a tax deductible expense.
3. Of the total annual fixed expenses of $310,000, $40,000 represents an allocation from head office for computer support and will continue to be incurred even if the South American operations are discontinued.
4. The corporate tax rate in Argentina is 35%.

Jackson is also considering the option of trying to make the South American operations profitable. She believes that with more emphasis on marketing and sales, EL could be successful. Details and assumptions made by Jackson for this option are as follows:

1. To increase sales, an additional marketing specialist would be hired immediately at an annual cost of $110,000 including benefits. This is $20,000 higher than the next highest paid employee in EL's Argentina office.
2. The new marketing specialist should be able to acquire two new customers in each of the next two years and each customer will generate annual revenue of $100,000. One additional new customer will be acquired each year thereafter and each will generate annual revenue of $100,000.
3. Hiring a new marketing specialist will necessitate the purchase of office furniture with a total cost of $5,000. The CCA rate in Argentina for office furniture is 10%. Assume there is no CCA half-year rule in Argentina.
4. EL will not lose any existing customers over the next five years and will be able to retain all newly acquired customers over that same period. This contrasts with the typical churn rate for high-tech companies of about 20% per year.
5. Variable expenses will continue at the same rate as in the most recent fiscal period for the next five years.
6. The marketing specialist will receive a commission of 10% of revenue generated from new customer acquisitions.
7. Existing total fixed expenses of $310,000 per year, including the $40,000 allocation from head office for computer support, will be unchanged for the next five years.

Required:

1. Should the South American operations be discontinued or should Jackson hire a new marketing specialist in an attempt to grow the business? Because of the uncertainty in the South American operating environment, Jackson wants you to prepare your analysis of the two options for a five-year period. EL has a required return of 12%.

2. Regardless of your recommendation for part 1, what qualitative factors should Jackson consider when deciding whether or not to discontinue operations in South America?

3. Assume that the marketing specialist will be able to acquire two new customers in the first year, but thereafter only one new customer will be acquired each year. Each new customer will generate annual revenue of $100,000. Given this new assumption, revise your analysis of the option to continue operations in South America. Assume all other details and assumptions regarding this option remain unchanged. Should the operations be discontinued or should the new marketing specialist be hired?

4. What do the results of the revised analysis in part 3 above suggest about the riskiness of the option to hire a new marketing specialist? How could this risk be incorporated in your analysis?

INSTANT QUIZ SOLUTIONS

13–1

Net present value = $(100,000) + $89,718* = $(10,282)
*Present value of $20,000 cost savings for 6 years using a 9% required rate of return.

13–2

Item	Year(s)	Amount of Cash Flow	Present Value of Cash Flows
Purchase of equipment	Now	$(500,000)	$(500,000)
Working capital needed	Now	(50,000)	(50,000)
Overhaul of equipment	5	(25,000)	(15,523)
Annual net cash inflows	1–10	70,000	430,120
Salvage value of equipment	10	50,000	19,277
Working capital released	10	50,000	19,277
Net present value			$ (96,849)

13–3

The IRR is 9.61% using the IRR formula in Microsoft Excel.

13–4

Present value of cash inflows: $180,000 (a)
Investment required: $150,000 (b)
Project profitability index: $180,000 ÷ $150,000 = 1.2 (a) ÷ (b)

13–5

Initial investment = $150,000
Net annual cash inflows = $40,000
Payback: $150,000 ÷ $40,000 = 3.75 years

13–6

Simple rate of return = ($90,000 − $36,000*) ÷ ($400,000 − $40,000)
Simple rate of return = 15%
*Depreciation: ($400,000 − $40,000) ÷ 10 = $36,000 per year.

■ APPENDIX 13A: THE CONCEPT OF PRESENT VALUE

LEARNING OBJECTIVE

Explain present value concepts and the underlying mathematics of interest.

The point was made in Chapter 13 that a manager would rather receive a dollar today than a dollar a year from now. There are two reasons why this is true. First, a dollar received today can be invested immediately and by the end of the year it will typically have earned some return, making the total amount in hand at the end of the year *greater* than the initial investment. Conversely, the same person receiving a dollar a year from now will simply have a dollar in hand at that time.

Second, the future involves uncertainty. The longer we have to wait to receive a dollar, the more uncertain it becomes that we will actually get that dollar. As time passes, conditions change and future payment of the dollar might become impossible.

Since money has a time value, managers need a method of determining whether a cash outlay made now in an investment project can be justified in terms of the expected cash inflows from the project in future years. That is, the manager must have a means of expressing future receipts in present dollar terms so that the future receipts can be compared *on an equivalent basis* with whatever investment is required now in the project under consideration. The mathematics of interest provides managers with the means of making such a comparison.

The Mathematics of Interest

If a bank pays $102 one year from now in return for a deposit of $100 now, we say that the bank is paying interest at an annual rate of 2%. The relationships involved in this notion can be expressed in mathematical terms by means of the following equation:

$$F_1 = P(1 + r) \tag{A1}$$

where F_1 = the amount to be received in one year, P = the present outlay to be made now, and r = the rate of interest involved. If the present outlay is $100 deposited in a bank savings account that is to earn interest at 2%, then $P = \$100$ and $r = 0.02$. Under these conditions, $F_1 = \$102$, the amount to be received in one year.

The $100 present outlay is called the **present value** of the $102 amount to be received in one year. It is also known as the *discounted value* of the future $102 receipt. The $100 figure represents the value in present terms of a receipt of $102 to be received a year from now when the interest rate is 2%.

Present value
The value now of an amount that will be received in some future period.

Compound Interest

What if the investor leaves the money in the bank for a second year and continues to earn 2% per year? In that case, by the end of the second year, the original $100 deposit will have grown to $104.04, as shown below:

Original deposit	$100.00
Interest for the first year: $100 × 0.02	2.00
Amount at the end of the first year	102.00
Interest for the second year: $102 × 0.02	2.04
Amount at the end of the second year	$104.04

Notice that the interest for the second year is $2.04, as compared to only $2 for the first year. The reason for the greater amount of interest earned during the second year is that during the second year, interest is being paid *on interest*. That is, the $2 interest earned during the first year has been left in the account and has been added to the original $100 deposit in computing interest for the second year. This concept is known as **compound interest**. The compounding we have done is on an annual basis. However, interest can be compounded on a semi-annual, quarterly, or even more frequent basis. Many financial institutions are now compounding interest on a daily basis. The more frequently compounding is done, the more rapidly the invested balance will grow.

Compound interest
The process of paying interest on interest for an investment.

How is the concept of compound interest expressed in equation form? It is expressed by taking equation (A1) and adjusting it to state the number of years, n, that a sum is going to be left deposited in the bank:

$$F_n = P(1 + r)^n \tag{A2}$$

where n = number of years.

If $n = 2$ years, then our computation of the value of F two years hence is as follows:

$$F_2 = \$100(1 + .02)^2$$
$$F_2 = \$104.04$$

Present Value and Future Value

Exhibit 13A–1 shows the relationship between present value and future value as expressed in the interest equations. As shown in the exhibit, if $100 is deposited in a bank at 2% interest, it will grow to $110.40 by the end of five years if interest is compounded annually.

Exhibit 13A–1 illustrates that an investment can be viewed in two ways: either in terms of its future value or in terms of its present value. We have seen from our computations above that if we know the present value of a sum (such as our $100 deposit), it is a relatively simple task to compute the sum's future value in n years by using equation (A2). But what if the tables are reversed, and we know the *future* value of some amount but we do not know its present value?

For example, assume that you are to receive $200 two years from now. You know that the future value of this sum is $200, since this is the amount that you will be receiving in two years. But what is the sum's present value—what is it worth *right now*? The present value of any sum to be received in the future can be computed by rearranging equation (A2) and solving for P:

$$P = F_n(1 + r)^{-n}$$

or

$$P = F_n \frac{1}{(1 + r)^n} \qquad (A3)$$

Suppose that in our example, $F = \$200$ (the amount to be received in the future), $r = 0.05$ (the rate of interest), and $n = 2$ (the number of years in the future that the amount is to be received):

$$P = F_n(1 + r)^{-n}$$
$$P = \$200(1 + 0.05)^{-2}$$
$$P = \$181.41$$

As shown by the computation above, the present value of $200 to be received two years from now is $181.41 if the interest rate is 5%. In effect, we are saying that $181.41 received *right now* is equivalent to $200 received two years from now if the rate of return is 5%. The $181.41 and the $200 are just two ways of looking at the same amount at different points in time.

The expression $(1 + r)^{-n}$ in formula A3 is often referred to as the *discount factor* or the *present value factor*. Present value tables provide discount factors for various combinations of r and n. We have provided such a table in Exhibit 13A–4 at the end of this appendix. Using the table to determine the

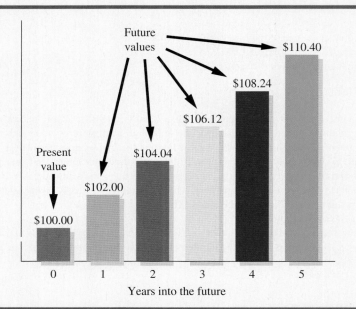

EXHIBIT 13A–1
The Relationship between Present Value and Future Value

present value of $200 to be received two years from now requires selecting the discount factor when $r =$ 5% and $n =2$. Per Exhibit 13A–4, the discount factor is .907. This factor can be used to calculate the present value as follows: $200 × .907 = 181.40. The small difference compared to the answer above is due to rounding the discount factor to three decimal places.

The process of finding the present value of a future cash flow, which we have just examined, is called **discounting**. We have *discounted* the $200 to its present value of $181.41. The 5% interest figure that we have used to find this present value is called the **discount rate**. As discussed in Chapter 13, companies typically use the weighted-average cost of capital (WACC) as the discount rate, with adjustments to the rate possible depending on the riskiness of the particular project under consideration. Discounting of future sums to their present value is a common practice in business. Knowing the present value of a sum to be received in the future can be very useful to a manager, particularly in making capital budgeting decisions such as those discussed in Chapter 13.

Some of the present value formulas we will be using are more complex and difficult to use. Fortunately, software programs such as Microsoft Excel and financial calculators incorporate these formulas.

Discounting
The process of finding the present value of a future cash flow.

Discount rate
The rate used to calculate the present value of future cash flows.

Example 1

A purchaser promises to pay $100,000 two years from now for a lot of land. This amount includes interest at an annual rate of 5%. What is the selling price of the land today? Round to the nearest hundred dollars.

Using formula (A3), the answer is

$$P = \$100{,}000(1 + 0.05)^{-2}$$
$$P = \$90{,}700$$

Example 2

A woman in Vancouver plans to take a trip four years from now. She estimates that she will need $18,000 at that time. At an annual interest rate of 4%, compounded semi-annually, how much must be deposited into a bank account today to accumulate the required $18,000?

Because interest is compounded semi-annually in this example, the interest per period is 2% (the annual rate divided by 2) and the number of periods is 8 (the number of years times 2). The formula solution is $18,000 × (1 + 0.02)^{-8} = $15,363$.

Present Value of a Series of Cash Flows (Annuity)

The present value of an **annuity** is the present value of a series of equal payments or receipts discounted at compound interest and made at regular intervals. Stated differently, it is the total amount that allows the withdrawal of a series of equal amounts at regular intervals if the balance remaining after each withdrawal earns compound interest.

The present value of $1 to be received at the end of each of four periods at 4% interest per period is shown graphically in Exhibit 13A–2.

Annuity
A series of equal cash payments or receipts.

EXHIBIT 13A–2   Illustration of Present Value of an Ordinary Annuity

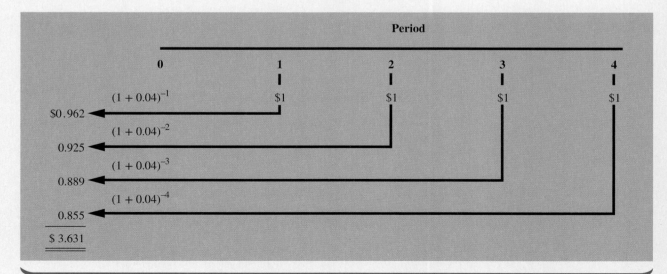

Two points are important in connection with Exhibit 13A–2. First, notice that the farther we go forward in time, the smaller the present value of the $1 interest receipt. The present value of $1 received a year from now is $0.962, compared to only $0.855 for the $1 interest payment to be received four periods from now.

The formula for the present value (P_n) of an annuity of $1 per period compounded at the rate of r for n periods is

$$P_n = \frac{1 - (1 + r)^{-n}}{r} \quad \text{or} \quad \frac{1}{r}\left(1 - \frac{1}{(1 + r)^n}\right) \tag{A4}$$

For the illustration in Exhibit 13A–2,

$$P_n = \frac{1 - (1 + 0.04)^{-4}}{0.04} = \$3.631$$

Tables containing discount factors for the present value of an annuity are also available for various combinations of r and n based on formula A4. We have provided such a table in Exhibit 13A–5 at the end of this appendix. Using the table to determine the present value of $1 to be received at the end of each of the next four years at an annual rate of 4% requires selecting the discount factor when $r = 4\%$ and $n = 4$. Per Exhibit 13A–5, the discount factor is 3.630. This factor can be used to calculate the present value of the annuity as follows: $1 \times 3.630 = \$3.63$. The small difference compared to the answer above is due to rounding the discount factor to three decimal places.

Example 3

What is the present value of receiving a series of six semi-annual payments of $2,000 at 4% interest compounded annually? Assume that it is now January 1, 2021, and the first payment is to be made on June 30, 2021.

The purpose of solving this problem could be to determine (1) the sum that will provide for six semi-annual withdrawals of $2,000 if invested at 2% per period (4% divided by two interest periods per year) and (2) the sum that is payable now in settlement of a series of obligations of $2,000 that are due at six semi-annual intervals and discounted at 2% per period. Using formula (A4), the solution is

$$P_n = \frac{1 - (1 + 0.02)^{-6}}{0.02} \times \$2,000 = \$11,203$$

Example 4

How much money would a company be willing to invest in a project that would return $3,000 every three months for three years and, in addition, a lump sum of $20,000 at the end of the third year? The receipts begin three months from now. Interest is 8% per annum.

The $3,000 to be received at the end of each three-month period is an ordinary annuity. The number of interest periods is 12 (4 per year for 3 years), and the quarterly interest rate is 2% (8% ÷ 4 periods). The present value of the ordinary annuity of $3,000, using formula (A4), and the present value of the $20,000 lump sum, using formula (A3), are as follows:

$$P_n = \frac{1 - (1 + 0.02)^{-12}}{0.02} \times \$3,000 + \$20,000(1 + 0.02)^{-12}$$

$$P_n = \$31,726 + \$15,770$$

$$P_n = \$47,496$$

Present Value of an Annuity Due

An annuity due is one in which the payments or receipts occur at the *beginning* of each period. Exhibit 13A–3 compares the present value of an ordinary annuity of $1 for four periods with the present value of an annuity due for $1 for four periods. The interest rate is assumed to be 8%.

Note that part B of Exhibit 13A–3 can be interpreted as an ordinary annuity of $1 for three periods ($0.926 + $0.857 + $0.794) to which we add $1. We can calculate the present value of an annuity due by subtracting one period from n and calculating the present value of an ordinary annuity for $n - 1$ periods. We then add 1 to this annuity factor, because the first payment is received immediately.

Example 5

On February 1, 2021, Davis Company signed an 18-month lease with Kelly Leasing Company. The lease payments begin immediately. Calculate the present value of the lease, assuming that $2,000 is paid each quarter and that the annual interest rate is 8%.

EXHIBIT 13A–3   Present Value of an Ordinary Annuity and an Annuity Due

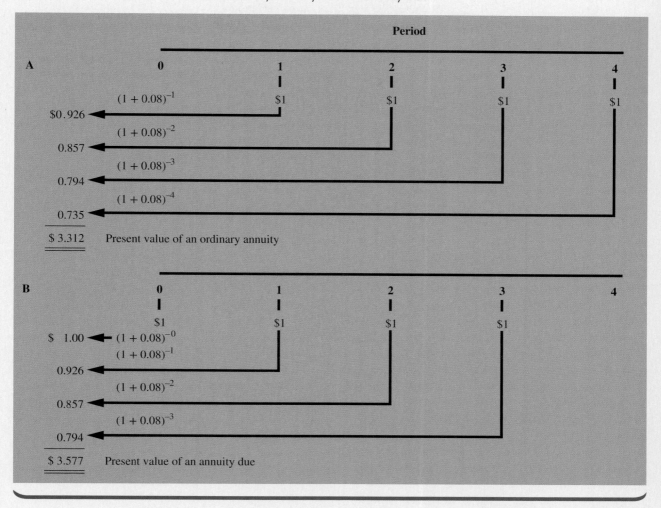

To determine the present value, we use formula (A4) adjusted for the fact that we now have an annuity due, where n is equal to six periods (18 months = 6 quarters) and the quarterly interest rate is 2% (8% ÷ 4):

$$PV \text{ (annuity due)} = \$2{,}000 \times \left[1 + \frac{1 - (1 + 0.02)^{-5}}{0.02}\right]$$

$$= \$2{,}000 \times (1 + 4.713)$$

$$= \$11{,}426$$

Deferred Annuities

A deferred annuity is one in which the first payment or receipt does not begin until more than one interest period has expired. This is common for capital expenditure decisions that may take several periods to become operational.

Example 6

What is the present value on December 31, 2021, of a series of five annual receipts of $1,000, the first of which is expected to be received December 31, 2023? The interest rate is 5% per annum.

The easiest way of solving this problem is to think about it as having two steps:

Step 1.   Calculate the present value on December 31, 2022, of an ordinary annuity of a series of five receipts of $1,000 beginning December 31, 2023, using an interest rate of 5%.

$$\frac{1 - (1 + 0.05)^{-5}}{0.05} \times \$1{,}000 = \$4{,}329$$

Step 2. The problem is now translated into a simple present value problem, where the present value on December 31, 2021, of the annuity beginning December 31 2023 can be computed by discounting the $4,329 back two interest periods (from December 31, 2023, to December 31, 2021):

$$PV \text{ (December 31, 2021)} = \$4,329 \, (1 + 0.05)^{-2}$$
$$= \$3,927$$

Future Value of an Annuity

Business transactions often involve a series of equal payments spaced evenly. As discussed earlier in this appendix, a series of equal payments at regular intervals is known as an *annuity*. The total that becomes due immediately after the last payment is the amount of an ordinary annuity or an annuity in arrears. If the payments are made or received at the beginning of the first interest period, the annuity is termed an *annuity due* or an *annuity in advance*.

The distinction between an ordinary annuity and an annuity due is presented graphically as follows:

Ordinary Annuity

	$1	$1	$1	$1

0   1   2   3   4

Annuity Due

$1	$1	$1	$1	$0

0   1   2   3   4

To illustrate how the future value of an ordinary annuity is determined, assume that $1 is deposited in a savings account at the end of each of four periods at 8% per period:

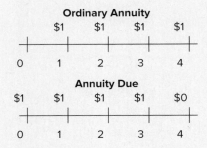

Thus, the value of an ordinary annuity of $1 due at the end of each period for four periods is

$$\$1 + \$1(1 + 0.08)^1 + \$1(1 + 0.08)^2 + \$1(1 + 0.08)^3$$
$$= \$1 + \$1.08 + \$1.1664 + \$1.2597$$
$$= \$4.5061$$

From the preceding illustration it can be seen that the $1 deposited at the end of the first year accumulates interest for a total of three periods, increasing to a value of $1.2597. The deposit at the end of the second year grows to $1.1664, and the $1 deposited at the end of the third period accumulates to $1.08. The $1 deposited at the end of the fourth period has not yet earned any interest. The series of four payments of $1 each period grows to $4.5061 at the end of the fourth period.

This problem can be solved quickly by using a mathematical expression based on a geometric progression. The future value of an annuity in arrears (F_n) compounded at an interest rate (r) for a given number of periods (n) is

$$F_n = \frac{(1 + r)^n - 1}{r} \tag{A5}$$

The value of a series of $1 deposits made at the end of each of four years compounded at 8% annually is

$$F_n = \$1 \times \frac{(1 + 0.08)^4 - 1}{0.08} = \$4.5061$$

The approach to finding the future value of an annuity of $1 where each payment is made at the beginning of each period is illustrated by the following diagram:

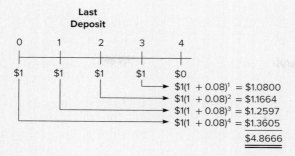

To find the future value of an annuity of $1 per period for four periods if each payment is made at the *beginning* of each period (an annuity due), we can modify the formula as follows:

$$F_n \text{ (annuity due)} = \$1 \times \frac{(1 + r)^n - 1}{r} \times (1 + r)$$

$$= \$1 \times \frac{(1 + 0.08)^4 - 1}{0.08} \times (1 + 0.08)$$

$$= \$4.867$$

Using Microsoft Excel

Microsoft Excel has numerous formulas that can be used to perform most of the calculations covered in Chapter 13 and the appendices. Some key formulas are as follows:

NPV(rate,value1,value2,…): *net present value*—allows for unequal cash flows.
PV(rate,nper,pmt,fv,type): *present value*—cash flows must be the same each period.
PV(rate,nper,,pmt): *present value of a single lump sum received at the end of a period.*
PMT(rate,nper,pv,type): the amount of an *equal series of payments* that will result in a specified present value.
FV(rate,nper,pmt,pv,type): *future value*—cash flows must be the same each period.
IRR(values,guess): *internal rate of return* of a series of cash flows.
NPER(rate,pmt,pv,type): the *number of periods* required to yield a required rate of return.

where

- *rate* is the interest rate per period (e.g., the required rate of return for capital expenditures).
- *value1, value2,* … are the cash inflows and outflows related to the asset.
- *nper* is the total number of payment periods in an annuity.
- *pmt* is the payment made each period and cannot change over the life of the annuity.
- *pv* is the present value, the total amount that a series of future payments is worth now.
- *fv* is the future value, or a cash balance you want to attain after the last payment is made. If *fv* is omitted, it is assumed to be 0 (the future value of a loan, for example, is 0).
- *principal* is the amount to be invested now.
- *type* is the number 0 or 1 and indicates when payments are due (0 or omitted, payment is at the end of the period; 1, payment is at the beginning of the period).
- *values* are the cash inflows and outflows related to the project.
- *guess* is an estimate of the project's IRR (can be left blank).

■ APPENDIX 13A SUMMARY

- The concept of present value is based on the concept that a dollar received today is worth more than a dollar received in the future. This is so because a dollar received today can be invested immediately and will earn a positive return and because the future involves uncertainty. This uncertainty results in the possibility that the dollar will not be received in the future. **[LO7]**
- Several key concepts were covered in this appendix. *Present value* is the value now of an amount that will be received in some future period; an *annuity* is a stream of identical cash flows; *compound interest* is the process of paying interest on interest in an investment; and *discount rate* is the rate of return used to find the present value of future cash flows or the future value of amounts received now. **[LO7]**
- The factors used in the various present value calculations can be determined by using the formulas presented throughout this appendix or by referring to tables such as those in Exhibits 13A–4 and 13A–5. However, financial calculators and spreadsheet programs such as Microsoft Excel are now commonly used to perform the calculations.

EXHIBIT 13A–4   Present Value of $1 $\frac{1}{(1+r)^n}$

Periods	4%	5%	6%	7%	8%	9%	10%	11%	12%	13%	14%	15%	16%	17%	18%	19%	20%	21%	22%	23%	24%	25%
1	0.962	0.952	0.943	0.935	0.926	0.917	0.909	0.901	0.893	0.885	0.877	0.870	0.862	0.855	0.847	0.840	0.833	0.826	0.820	0.813	0.806	0.800
2	0.925	0.907	0.890	0.873	0.857	0.842	0.826	0.812	0.797	0.783	0.769	0.756	0.743	0.731	0.718	0.706	0.694	0.683	0.672	0.661	0.650	0.640
3	0.889	0.864	0.840	0.816	0.794	0.772	0.751	0.731	0.712	0.693	0.675	0.658	0.641	0.624	0.609	0.593	0.579	0.564	0.551	0.537	0.524	0.512
4	0.855	0.823	0.792	0.763	0.735	0.708	0.683	0.659	0.636	0.613	0.592	0.572	0.552	0.534	0.516	0.499	0.482	0.467	0.451	0.437	0.423	0.410
5	0.822	0.784	0.747	0.713	0.681	0.650	0.621	0.593	0.567	0.543	0.519	0.497	0.476	0.456	0.437	0.419	0.402	0.386	0.370	0.355	0.341	0.328
6	0.790	0.746	0.705	0.666	0.630	0.596	0.564	0.535	0.507	0.480	0.456	0.432	0.410	0.390	0.370	0.352	0.335	0.319	0.303	0.289	0.275	0.262
7	0.760	0.711	0.665	0.623	0.583	0.547	0.513	0.482	0.452	0.425	0.400	0.376	0.354	0.333	0.314	0.296	0.279	0.263	0.249	0.235	0.222	0.210
8	0.731	0.677	0.627	0.582	0.540	0.502	0.467	0.434	0.404	0.376	0.351	0.327	0.305	0.285	0.266	0.249	0.233	0.218	0.204	0.191	0.179	0.168
9	0.703	0.645	0.592	0.544	0.500	0.460	0.424	0.391	0.361	0.333	0.308	0.284	0.263	0.243	0.225	0.209	0.194	0.180	0.167	0.155	0.144	0.134
10	0.676	0.614	0.558	0.508	0.463	0.422	0.386	0.352	0.322	0.295	0.270	0.247	0.227	0.208	0.191	0.176	0.162	0.149	0.137	0.126	0.116	0.107
11	0.650	0.585	0.527	0.475	0.429	0.388	0.350	0.317	0.287	0.261	0.237	0.215	0.195	0.178	0.162	0.148	0.135	0.123	0.112	0.103	0.094	0.086
12	0.625	0.557	0.497	0.444	0.397	0.356	0.319	0.286	0.257	0.231	0.208	0.187	0.168	0.152	0.137	0.124	0.112	0.102	0.092	0.083	0.076	0.069
13	0.601	0.530	0.469	0.415	0.368	0.326	0.290	0.258	0.229	0.204	0.182	0.163	0.145	0.130	0.116	0.104	0.093	0.084	0.075	0.068	0.061	0.055
14	0.577	0.505	0.442	0.388	0.340	0.299	0.263	0.232	0.205	0.181	0.160	0.141	0.125	0.111	0.099	0.088	0.078	0.069	0.062	0.055	0.049	0.044
15	0.555	0.481	0.417	0.362	0.315	0.275	0.239	0.209	0.183	0.160	0.140	0.123	0.108	0.095	0.084	0.074	0.065	0.057	0.051	0.045	0.040	0.035
16	0.534	0.458	0.394	0.339	0.292	0.252	0.218	0.188	0.163	0.141	0.123	0.107	0.093	0.081	0.071	0.062	0.054	0.047	0.042	0.036	0.032	0.028
17	0.513	0.436	0.371	0.317	0.270	0.231	0.198	0.170	0.146	0.125	0.108	0.093	0.080	0.069	0.060	0.052	0.045	0.039	0.034	0.030	0.026	0.023
18	0.494	0.416	0.350	0.296	0.250	0.212	0.180	0.153	0.130	0.111	0.095	0.081	0.069	0.059	0.051	0.044	0.038	0.032	0.028	0.024	0.021	0.018
19	0.475	0.396	0.331	0.277	0.232	0.194	0.164	0.138	0.116	0.098	0.083	0.070	0.060	0.051	0.043	0.037	0.031	0.027	0.023	0.020	0.017	0.014
20	0.456	0.377	0.312	0.258	0.215	0.178	0.149	0.124	0.104	0.087	0.073	0.061	0.051	0.043	0.037	0.031	0.026	0.022	0.019	0.016	0.014	0.012
21	0.439	0.359	0.294	0.242	0.199	0.164	0.135	0.112	0.093	0.077	0.064	0.053	0.044	0.037	0.031	0.026	0.022	0.018	0.015	0.013	0.011	0.009
22	0.422	0.342	0.278	0.226	0.184	0.150	0.123	0.101	0.083	0.068	0.056	0.046	0.038	0.032	0.026	0.022	0.018	0.015	0.013	0.011	0.009	0.007
23	0.406	0.326	0.262	0.211	0.170	0.138	0.112	0.091	0.074	0.060	0.049	0.040	0.033	0.027	0.022	0.018	0.015	0.012	0.010	0.009	0.007	0.006
24	0.390	0.310	0.247	0.197	0.158	0.126	0.102	0.082	0.066	0.053	0.043	0.035	0.028	0.023	0.019	0.015	0.013	0.010	0.008	0.007	0.006	0.005
25	0.375	0.295	0.233	0.184	0.146	0.116	0.092	0.074	0.059	0.047	0.038	0.030	0.024	0.020	0.016	0.013	0.010	0.009	0.007	0.006	0.005	0.004
26	0.361	0.281	0.220	0.172	0.135	0.106	0.084	0.066	0.053	0.042	0.033	0.026	0.021	0.017	0.014	0.011	0.009	0.007	0.006	0.005	0.004	0.003
27	0.347	0.268	0.207	0.161	0.125	0.098	0.076	0.060	0.047	0.037	0.029	0.023	0.018	0.014	0.011	0.009	0.007	0.006	0.005	0.004	0.003	0.002
28	0.333	0.255	0.196	0.150	0.116	0.090	0.069	0.054	0.042	0.033	0.026	0.020	0.016	0.012	0.010	0.008	0.006	0.005	0.004	0.003	0.002	0.002
29	0.321	0.243	0.185	0.141	0.107	0.082	0.063	0.048	0.037	0.029	0.022	0.017	0.014	0.011	0.008	0.006	0.005	0.004	0.003	0.002	0.002	0.002
30	0.308	0.231	0.174	0.131	0.099	0.075	0.057	0.044	0.033	0.026	0.020	0.015	0.012	0.009	0.007	0.005	0.004	0.003	0.003	0.002	0.002	0.001
40	0.208	0.142	0.097	0.067	0.046	0.032	0.022	0.015	0.011	0.008	0.005	0.004	0.003	0.002	0.001	0.001	0.001	0.000	0.000	0.000	0.000	0.000

EXHIBIT 13A–5 Present Value of an Annuity of \$1 in Arrears; $\dfrac{1}{r}\left[1 - \dfrac{1}{(1+r)^n}\right]$

Periods	4%	5%	6%	7%	8%	9%	10%	11%	12%	13%	14%	15%	16%	17%	18%	19%	20%	21%	22%	23%	24%	25%
1	0.962	0.952	0.943	0.935	0.926	0.917	0.909	0.901	0.893	0.885	0.877	0.870	0.862	0.855	0.847	0.840	0.833	0.826	0.820	0.813	0.806	0.800
2	1.886	1.859	1.833	1.808	1.783	1.759	1.736	1.713	1.690	1.668	1.647	1.626	1.605	1.585	1.566	1.547	1.528	1.509	1.492	1.474	1.457	1.440
3	2.775	2.723	2.673	2.624	2.577	2.531	2.487	2.444	2.402	2.361	2.322	2.283	2.246	2.210	2.174	2.140	2.106	2.074	2.042	2.011	1.981	1.952
4	3.630	3.546	3.465	3.387	3.312	3.240	3.170	3.102	3.037	2.974	2.914	2.855	2.798	2.743	2.690	2.639	2.589	2.540	2.494	2.448	2.404	2.362
5	4.452	4.329	4.212	4.100	3.993	3.890	3.791	3.696	3.605	3.517	3.433	3.352	3.274	3.199	3.127	3.058	2.991	2.926	2.864	2.803	2.745	2.689
6	5.242	5.076	4.917	4.767	4.623	4.486	4.355	4.231	4.111	3.998	3.889	3.784	3.685	3.589	3.498	3.410	3.326	3.245	3.167	3.092	3.020	2.951
7	6.002	5.786	5.582	5.389	5.206	5.033	4.868	4.712	4.564	4.423	4.288	4.160	4.039	3.922	3.812	3.706	3.605	3.508	3.416	3.327	3.242	3.161
8	6.733	6.463	6.210	5.971	5.747	5.535	5.335	5.146	4.968	4.799	4.639	4.487	4.344	4.207	4.078	3.954	3.837	3.726	3.619	3.518	3.421	3.329
9	7.435	7.108	6.802	6.515	6.247	5.995	5.759	5.537	5.328	5.132	4.946	4.772	4.607	4.451	4.303	4.163	4.031	3.905	3.786	3.673	3.566	3.463
10	8.111	7.722	7.360	7.024	6.710	6.418	6.145	5.889	5.650	5.426	5.216	5.019	4.833	4.659	4.494	4.339	4.192	4.054	3.923	3.799	3.682	3.571
11	8.760	8.306	7.887	7.499	7.139	6.805	6.495	6.207	5.938	5.687	5.453	5.234	5.029	4.836	4.656	4.486	4.327	4.177	4.035	3.902	3.776	3.656
12	9.385	8.863	8.384	7.943	7.536	7.161	6.814	6.492	6.194	5.918	5.660	5.421	5.197	4.988	4.793	4.611	4.439	4.278	4.127	3.985	3.851	3.725
13	9.986	9.394	8.853	8.358	7.904	7.487	7.103	6.750	6.424	6.122	5.842	5.583	5.342	5.118	4.910	4.715	4.533	4.362	4.203	4.053	3.912	3.780
14	10.563	9.899	9.295	8.745	8.244	7.786	7.367	6.982	6.628	6.302	6.002	5.724	5.468	5.229	5.008	4.802	4.611	4.432	4.265	4.108	3.962	3.824
15	11.118	10.380	9.712	9.108	8.559	8.061	7.606	7.191	6.811	6.462	6.142	5.847	5.575	5.324	5.092	4.876	4.675	4.489	4.315	4.153	4.001	3.859
16	11.652	10.838	10.106	9.447	8.851	8.313	7.824	7.379	6.974	6.604	6.265	5.954	5.668	5.405	5.162	4.938	4.730	4.536	4.357	4.189	4.033	3.887
17	12.166	11.274	10.477	9.763	9.122	8.544	8.022	7.549	7.120	6.729	6.373	6.047	5.749	5.475	5.222	4.990	4.775	4.576	4.391	4.219	4.059	3.910
18	12.659	11.690	10.828	10.059	9.372	8.756	8.201	7.702	7.250	6.840	6.467	6.128	5.818	5.534	5.273	5.033	4.812	4.608	4.419	4.243	4.080	3.928
19	13.134	12.085	11.158	10.336	9.604	8.950	8.365	7.839	7.366	6.938	6.550	6.198	5.877	5.584	5.316	5.070	4.843	4.635	4.442	4.263	4.097	3.942
20	13.590	12.462	11.470	10.594	9.818	9.129	8.514	7.963	7.469	7.025	6.623	6.259	5.929	5.628	5.353	5.101	4.870	4.657	4.460	4.279	4.110	3.954
21	14.029	12.821	11.764	10.836	10.017	9.292	8.649	8.075	7.562	7.102	6.687	6.312	5.973	5.665	5.384	5.127	4.891	4.675	4.476	4.292	4.121	3.963
22	14.451	13.163	12.042	11.061	10.201	9.442	8.772	8.176	7.645	7.170	6.743	6.359	6.011	5.696	5.410	5.149	4.909	4.690	4.488	4.302	4.130	3.970
23	14.857	13.489	12.303	11.272	10.371	9.580	8.883	8.266	7.718	7.230	6.792	6.399	6.044	5.723	5.432	5.167	4.925	4.703	4.499	4.311	4.137	3.976
24	15.247	13.799	12.550	11.469	10.529	9.707	8.985	8.348	7.784	7.283	6.835	6.434	6.073	5.746	5.451	5.182	4.937	4.713	4.507	4.318	4.143	3.981
25	15.622	14.094	12.783	11.654	10.675	9.823	9.077	8.422	7.843	7.330	6.873	6.464	6.097	5.766	5.467	5.195	4.948	4.721	4.514	4.323	4.147	3.985
26	15.983	14.375	13.003	11.826	10.810	9.929	9.161	8.488	7.896	7.372	6.906	6.491	6.118	5.783	5.480	5.206	4.956	4.728	4.520	4.328	4.151	3.988
27	16.330	14.643	13.211	11.987	10.935	10.027	9.237	8.548	7.943	7.409	6.935	6.514	6.136	5.798	5.492	5.215	4.964	4.734	4.524	4.332	4.154	3.990
28	16.663	14.898	13.406	12.137	11.051	10.116	9.307	8.602	7.984	7.441	6.961	6.534	6.152	5.810	5.502	5.223	4.970	4.739	4.528	4.335	4.157	3.992
29	16.984	15.141	13.591	12.278	11.158	10.198	9.370	8.650	8.022	7.470	6.983	6.551	6.166	5.820	5.510	5.229	4.975	4.743	4.531	4.337	4.159	3.994
30	17.292	15.372	13.765	12.409	11.258	10.274	9.427	8.694	8.055	7.496	7.003	6.566	6.177	5.829	5.517	5.235	4.979	4.746	4.534	4.339	4.160	3.995
40	19.793	17.159	15.046	13.332	11.925	10.757	9.779	8.951	8.244	7.634	7.105	6.642	6.233	5.871	5.548	5.258	4.997	4.760	4.544	4.347	4.166	3.999

■ APPENDIX 13A REVIEW PROBLEM: PRESENT VALUE EXERCISES

Each of the following situations is independent.

1. Greg plans to retire in 12 years. When he retires, he would like to take an extended vacation, which he expects will cost at least $40,000. What lump-sum amount must he invest now to have $40,000 at the end of 12 years if the rate of return is
   a. 8%?
   b. 12%?

2. The Morgans would like to send their daughter to a music camp at the end of each of the next five years. The camp costs $1,000 a year. What lump-sum amount would have to be invested now to have $1,000 at the end of each year if the rate of return is
   a. 8%?
   b. 12%?

3. You have just received an inheritance from a relative. You can either receive a $200,000 lump-sum amount at the end of 10 years or receive $14,000 at the end of each year for the next 10 years.
   a. If your annual rate of return is 4%, which alternative would you prefer?
   b. If your annual rate of return is 8%, which alternative would you prefer?

Solution to Appendix 13A Review Problem

In the solutions below we use the formulas presented in the appendix to demonstrate the calculations underlying software packages and financial calculators. We also present the solutions to requirements 1 and 2 using the discount factors from Exhibits 13A–4 and 13A–5. We suggest you check the answers to all the requirements using Microsoft Excel or a financial calculator.

1. a. The amount that must be invested now is the present value of the $40,000, using a discount rate of 8% and 12 periods. Using formula (A3), the answer is as follows:

$$P_n = \$40,000(1 + 0.08)^{-12}$$
$$P_n = \$15,885$$

or using the discount factor from Exhibit 13A–4 for 8% and 12 years:

$$P_n = \$40,000 \times .397$$
$$P_n = \$15,880 \text{ (difference due to rounding)}$$

   b. We will proceed as we did in (a) above, but this time we will use a discount rate of 12%.

$$P_n = \$40,000(1 + 0.12)^{-12}$$
$$P_n = \$10,267$$

or using the discount factor from Exhibit 13A–4 for 12% and 12 years:

$$P_n = \$40,000 \times .257$$
$$P_n = \$10,280 \text{ (difference due to rounding)}$$

   Notice that as the discount rate (desired rate of return) increases, the present value decreases.

2. This part differs from (1) above in that we are now dealing with an ordinary annuity rather than with a single future sum. The amount that must be invested now is the present value of the $1,000 needed at the end of each year for five years. Accordingly, we use formula (A4) to calculate the present values.

   a.
$$P_n = \$1,000 \times \frac{1 - (1 + 0.08)^{-5}}{0.08}$$
$$P_n = \$3,993$$

or using the discount factor from Exhibit 13A–5 for 8% and 5 years:

$$P_n = \$1,000 \times 3.993$$
$$P_n = \$3,993$$

b.

$$P_n = \$1,000 \times \frac{1(1 + 0.12)^{-5}}{0.12}$$
$$P_n = \$3,605$$

or using the discount factor from Exhibit 13A–5 for 12% and 5 years:

$$P_n = \$1,000 \times 3.603$$
$$P_n = \$3,603$$

Again, notice that as the discount rate increases, the present value decreases. When the rate of return increases, less must be invested today to yield a given amount in the future.

3. Whichever alternative has the higher present value is the one that should be selected.

   a. 4% rate of return:
      Present value of alternative 1 using formula (A3):

$$P_n = \$200,000(1 + 0.04)^{-10}$$
$$P_n = \$135,113$$

      Present value of alternative 2 using formula (A4):

$$P_n = \frac{1 - (1 + 0.04)^{-10}}{0.04} \times \$14,000$$
$$P_n = \$113,553$$

   Thus, you should prefer to receive the $200,000 at the end of year 10 rather than $14,000 per year as an annuity for 10 years if the annual return is 4%.

   b. 8% rate of return:
      Present value of alternative 1 using formula (A3):

$$P_n = \$200,000(1 + 0.08)^{-10}$$
$$P_n = \$92,639$$

      Present value of alternative 2 using formula (A4):

$$P_n = \frac{1 - (1 + 0.08)^{-10}}{0.08} \times \$14,000$$
$$P_n = \$93,941$$

   Now, you should prefer to receive the $14,000 annuity for 10 years if the annual return is 8% rather than the $200,000 lump-sum payment. Note how the preferred alternative is sensitive to the return that can be earned on an annual basis.

■ APPENDIX 13A EXERCISES

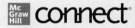

EXERCISE 13A–1 Basic Present Value Concepts [LO7]
Each of the following parts is independent. Ignore income taxes.

1. Express Delivery plans to build a new warehouse in four years to have more space for its products awaiting shipment. The warehouse will cost $500,000. What lump-sum amount should the company invest now to have the $500,000 available at the end of the four-year period? Assume that the company can invest money at
   a. 6%.
   b. 10%.

2. Washington Products Inc. can purchase a new electronic data storage server that will save $3,000 per year in paper storage and warehouse costs. The data server will last for five years and have no salvage value. What is the maximum purchase price that Washington Products would be willing to pay for the copier if the company's required rate of return is
   a. 9%?
   b. 15%?

3. Susan has just won the million-dollar Power Lottery jackpot at a gambling casino. The casino will pay her $50,000 per year for 20 years as the payoff. If Susan can invest money at a 5% rate of return, what is the present value of her winnings? Did she really win a million dollars? Explain.

EXERCISE 13A–2 Basic Present Value Concepts [LO7]
Consider each of the following situations independently.

1. Annual cash inflows from two competing investment opportunities are given below. Each investment opportunity will require the same initial investment. Compute the present value of the cash inflows for each investment using a 20% discount rate:

Year	Investment	
	X	Y
1.	$ 3,000	$12,000
2.	6,000	9,000
3.	9,000	6,000
4.	12,000	3,000
	$30,000	$30,000

2. At the end of four years, when you graduate from college, your parents have promised to give you a used car that will cost $10,000. What lump sum must they invest now to have the $10,000 at the end of four years if they can invest money at
   a. 6%?
   b. 12%?

3. Joanne has just won the grand prize on a popular quiz show. She has a choice between (a) receiving $250,000 immediately and (b) receiving $30,000 per year at the end of the year for eight years, plus a lump sum of $100,000 at the end of the eight-year period. If Joanne can get a return of 3% on her investments, which option would you recommend that she accept? Use present value analysis, and show all computations.

4. You have just learned that you are a beneficiary in the will of your late Uncle Sam. The executor of her estate has given you three options as to how you may receive your inheritance:
   a. You may receive $100,000 immediately.
   b. You may receive $150,000 at the end of five years.
   c. You may receive $24,000 at the end of each year for five years (a total of $120,000).

   If you can invest money at a 8% return, which option would you prefer?

CHECK FIGURE
1. Present value of investment X = $17,662; 2a. $7,921.

LEARNING OBJECTIVE ⑧
Incorporate income taxes into a capital budgeting analysis.

■ APPENDIX 13B: INCOME TAXES IN CAPITAL BUDGETING DECISIONS

In our discussion of capital budgeting, we ignored income taxes in the chapter for two reasons. First, some organizations do not pay income taxes. Not-for-profit organizations, such as hospitals and charitable foundations, and government agencies are exempt from income taxes. Second, capital budgeting is complex and is best covered in small steps. Now that we have covered the basic concepts of present value, we can examine the effects of income taxes on capital budgeting decisions.

Canadian income tax regulations are very complex, so we cover only the basics in this appendix. To keep the material as easy to understand as possible, we have made many simplifying assumptions about the tax regulations throughout this appendix. Among the most important of these assumptions are (1) taxable income equals net income before income tax expense as computed for financial reports, and (2) the tax rate is a flat percentage of taxable income.

The Concept of After-Tax Cost

For-profit businesses must pay income taxes, with the amount of income tax that must be paid determined by the company's net taxable income. Tax-deductible expenses (tax deductions) decrease the company's net taxable income and hence reduce the taxes the company must pay. For this reason, expenses are often stated on an *after-tax* basis. For example, if a company pays rent of $10 million per year but this expense results in a reduction in income taxes of $3 million (tax rate = 30%), the after-tax cost of the rent is said to be $7 million. The amount of an expenditure net of its tax effect is known as the **after-tax cost**.

> **After-tax cost**
> The net amount of cash outflow resulting from a tax-deductible cash expense after the income tax effects have been considered.

To illustrate, assume that a company with a tax rate of 30% is contemplating a training program that costs $60,000. What impact will this have on the company's taxes? To keep matters simple, let's assume the training program has no immediate effect on sales. How much does the company actually pay for the training program after taking into account the impact of this expense on taxes? The answer is $42,000, as shown in Exhibit 13B–1. While the training program costs $60,000 before taxes, it will reduce the company's taxes by $18,000, so its *after-tax* cost is only $42,000. This $18,000 reduction in taxes can also be calculated directly by simply multiplying $60,000 by the 30% tax rate.

The after-tax cost of any tax-deductible cash expense can be determined using the following formula:[5]

$$\text{After-tax cost (net cash outflow)} = (1 - \text{Tax rate}) \times \text{Tax-deductible cash expense} \qquad \text{(B1)}$$

We can verify the accuracy of this formula by applying it to the $60,000 training program expenditure:

$$(1 - 0.30) \times \$60,000 = \$42,000 \text{ after-tax cost of the training program}$$

This formula is very useful since it provides the actual amount of cash a company must pay after taking into consideration tax effects. It is this actual after-tax cash outflow that should be used in capital budgeting decisions.

Similar reasoning applies to revenues and other *taxable* cash inflows. Since these cash receipts are taxable, the company must pay tax on them. The **after-tax benefit**, or net cash inflow, realized from a particular cash receipt can be obtained by applying a simple variation of the cash expenditure formula used above:

> **After-tax benefit**
> The net amount of cash inflow realized from a taxable cash receipt after income tax effects have been considered.

$$\text{After-tax benefit (net cash inflow)} = (1 - \text{Tax rate}) \times \text{Taxable cash receipt} \qquad \text{(B2)}$$

We emphasize the term *taxable cash receipt* because not all cash inflows are taxable. For example, the release of working capital at the termination of a project is not a taxable cash inflow. It is not counted as income for either financial accounting or income tax reporting purposes since it is simply a recovery of the initial investment.

Capital Cost Allowance Tax Shield

Capital cost allowance (CCA) is the amount of depreciation expense allowed by the Canada Revenue Agency for tax purposes. Because CCA, like accounting depreciation, is not a cash outflow, it was ignored in the chapter in all discounted cash flow computations. However, CCA does affect the amount of taxes that must be paid and therefore has an indirect effect on the company's cash flows.

> **Capital cost allowance (CCA)**
> The amount of depreciation expense allowed by the Canada Revenue Agency for tax purposes.

To illustrate the effect of CCA deductions on tax payments, consider a company with annual cash sales of $500,000 and cash operating expenses of $310,000. In addition, the company has a depreciable

	Without Training Program	With Training Program
Sales	$850,000	$850,000
Less tax-deductible expenses:		
Salaries, insurance, and other	700,000	700,000
New training program...........................		60,000
Total expenses....................................	700,000	760,000
Taxable income....................................	$150,000	$ 90,000
Income taxes (30%)................................	$ 45,000	$ 27,000
Cost of new training program........................		$60,000
Less reduction in income taxes ($45,000 − $27,000).........		18,000
After-tax cost of the new training program................		$42,000

EXHIBIT 13B–1
The Computation of After-Tax Cost

EXHIBIT 13B–2
The Effect of Capital Cost Allowance Deductions on Tax Payments

	Without CCA Deduction	With CCA Deduction
Sales	$500,000	$500,000
Cash operating expenses.	310,000	310,000
Cash flow from operations	190,000	190,000
Capital cost allowance.	—	90,000
Taxable income.	$190,000	$100,000
Income taxes (30%).	$ 57,000	$ 30,000

$27,000 lower taxes with the CCA deduction

Cash flow comparison:		
Cash flow from operations (above).	$190,000	$190,000
Income taxes (above)	57,000	30,000
Net cash flow	$133,000	$160,000

$27,000 greater cash flow with the CCA deduction

Capital cost allowance tax shields
Reductions in tax payments caused by capital cost allowance deductions.

asset on which the CCA deduction is $90,000 per year. The tax rate is 30%. As shown in Exhibit 13B–2, the CCA deduction reduces the company's taxes by $27,000. In effect, the CCA deduction of $90,000 *shields* $90,000 in revenues from taxation and thereby *reduces* the amount of taxes that the company must pay. Because CCA deductions shield revenues from taxation, they are referred to as **capital cost allowance tax shields**.[6]

The reduction in tax payments created by the CCA tax shield illustrated in Exhibit 13B–2 is equal to the amount of the CCA deduction multiplied by the tax rate, as follows:

$$\text{Tax savings from the CCA tax shield} = \text{Tax rate} \times \text{CCA deduction} \qquad \text{(B3)}$$

We can verify this formula by applying it to the $90,000 CCA deduction in our example:

$$0.30 \times \$90,000 = \$27,000 \text{ reduction in tax payments}$$

In this appendix, when we estimate after-tax cash flows for capital budgeting decisions, we will include the tax savings provided by the CCA tax shield.

Rules for CCA are complex, and most companies take advantage of accelerated methods allowed under the tax regulations. These accelerated methods usually result in a reduction in current taxes because of higher CCA amounts and an offsetting increase in future taxes as CCA amounts fall. This shifting of part of the tax burden from the current year to future years is advantageous from a present value point of view, since tax savings received today are worth more than tax savings received in the future. A summary of the concepts we have introduced so far is given in the Learning Aid below.

LEARNING AID

Tax Adjustments Required in a Capital Budgeting Analysis

Item	Treatment
Tax-deductible cash expense*.	Multiply by (1 – Tax rate) to get after-tax cost.
Taxable cash receipt*.	Multiply by (1 – Tax rate) to get after-tax cash inflow.
CCA deduction	Multiply annual CCA deduction by the tax rate to get the tax savings from the CCA tax shield.

*Cash expenses can be deducted from the cash receipts and the difference multiplied by (1 – Tax rate). See the example at the top of Exhibit 13B–3.

Capital Cost Allowance Instead of Depreciation

As noted above, CCA is the Canada Revenue Agency's counterpart to depreciation. Depreciation is the allocation of the cost of an asset over its useful life. The amount deducted each period for financial statement reporting purposes is based on generally accepted accounting principles (GAAP). For income tax purposes, however, depreciation is not an allowable expense. Instead, a CCA is permitted by regulations that accompany the Canadian Income Tax Act. A CCA deduction is allowed for business-related capital property such as equipment and automobiles.

The income tax regulations group assets into classes, and each class is then assigned a maximum CCA rate for tax purposes. Maximum CCA rates are prescribed by the regulations in the Income Tax Act for numerous classes or pools of assets. A company has the option of deducting CCA for each asset class for any amount ranging from zero to the maximum amount prescribed by the Act. The CCA rate applicable to each class is usually intended to reflect the economic life of the assets of that class.

These prescribed rates are subject to government change. Examples of these asset pools and maximum prescribed rates as per the 2019 Canadian Income Tax Act follow:

Asset	Class	Maximum Rate
Non-residential buildings.	1	4%
Motor vehicles	10	30%
Computer hardware and software	52	100%
Assets not included in other classes such as furniture, appliances, etc..	8	20%

CCA is calculated by applying the prescribed rate to a declining balance called the **undepreciated capital cost (UCC)**. The UCC of an asset class or pool of assets is the remaining book value that is available for tax-deductible depreciation (CCA). The maximum amount of CCA that may be deducted in a taxation year is the UCC multiplied by the CCA rate for that asset class. However, for net additions made to each asset class during the year, only one-half of the prescribed rate is permitted. Under this half-year rule, only half of the normal CCA for most assets is allowed as a tax-deductible expense in the year the asset is acquired.

Undepreciated capital cost (UCC)
The remaining book value of an asset class or pool of assets that is available for tax-deductible depreciation (capital cost allowance).

Example 1

Saskatoon Ltd. has obtained a $30,000 loan to acquire a truck (Class 10 for CCA purposes). Assuming that the company will have taxable income for the foreseeable future, calculate the present value of the CCA tax shield for the first three years if the WACC is 10% and the tax rate is 40%.

(1) Year	(2) UCC	(3) CCA (2) × 30%	(4) Tax Savings (3) × 40%	(5) Present Value of Tax Savings†
1	$30,000	$4,500*	$1,800	$1,636
2	25,500	7,650	3,060	2,528
3	17,850	5,355	2,142	1,609

*Half-year rule applies in the year the asset is purchased; $30,000 × 0.30 × (½) = $4,500
†Calculated using the PV formula of Microsoft Excel and a required rate of return of 10%

Because the CCA is calculated on the declining UCC balance of a pool of assets rather than on a single asset, a business is able to obtain tax savings from a project even after its disposition. As long as there are other assets in the pool and the proceeds from disposal are less than the UCC for the class, tax savings can be realized in perpetuity.

It can be shown mathematically that the present value of this perpetual stream of tax savings from a declining balance CCA is calculated by using the *CCA tax shield formula*:

$$PV = \frac{Cdt}{d+k} \times \frac{1+0.5k}{1+k} \qquad \text{(B4)}$$

where

C = The capital cost of the asset added to the asset pool.

d = CCA rate.

t = The firm's marginal income tax rate.

k = The weighted-average cost of capital (required return).

$\dfrac{1 + 0.5k}{1 + k}$ = The correction factor to account for the provision that only one-half of the capital cost of an asset is included in UCC during the year of acquisition.

For the previous example, the present value of the CCA tax shield is

$$\frac{\$30,000 \times 0.3 \times 0.4}{0.3 + 0.10} \times \frac{1 + 0.5 \times 0.10}{1 + 0.10} = \$9,000 \times 0.95455 = \$8,591$$

Example 2

Using the data in the previous example, calculate the present value of the CCA tax shield, assuming that other assets remain in the pool and the asset is disposed of for \$6,000 after five years' use.

The sale of the asset results in a cash inflow at the end of year 5. This disposal results in the asset pool balance (UCC) being reduced by the \$6,000 proceeds. The present value of the CCA tax shield is also reduced, because from the end of year 5 onward CCA will be applied to a smaller UCC balance than it otherwise would have been without the asset disposal. If S represents salvage value, the CCA tax shield formula must be adjusted by deducting

$$\frac{Sdt}{d + k} \times (1 + k)^{-n}$$

where

$$\frac{Sdt}{d + k}$$

calculates the present value of the lost tax shield at the end of year 5 ($n = 5$). This lost tax shield is then discounted to time period zero by multiplying it by $(1 + k)^{-n}$ (see Appendix 13A for the present value formula, or Exhibit 13A–4 for the present value factor) or by using a software package or a financial calculator to perform the present value calculation. The present value of the tax shield lost is calculated as follows:

$$\frac{\$6,000 \times 0.3 \times 0.4}{0.3 + 0.1} \times (1 + 0.10)^{-5} = \$1,117.66$$

Therefore, the net present value of the CCA tax shields is $\$8,591 - \$1,117.66 = \$7,473.34$.

Example of Income Taxes and Capital Budgeting

Now that we have reviewed after-tax costs, after-tax benefits, and the CCA tax shield, we can examine a comprehensive example of income taxes and capital budgeting that incorporates all of these concepts.

Example 3

The mineral rights to land that has a deposit of ore are owned by Englund Company. The company is uncertain whether it should purchase equipment and open a mine on the property. After careful study, the following data have been assembled by the company:

Cost of equipment needed	\$300,000
Working capital needed	75,000
Estimated annual cash receipts from sales of ore	250,000
Estimated annual cash expenses for salaries, insurance, utilities, and other cash expenses of mining the ore	170,000
Cost of road repairs needed in 6 years	40,000
Salvage value of the equipment in 10 years	100,000

The ore in the mine would be exhausted after 10 years of mining activity, at which time the mine would be closed. The equipment would then be sold for its salvage value. Englund Company uses a 20% rate, assuming no salvage value, to compute CCA deductions for tax purposes. The company's after-tax WACC is 12% and its tax rate is 30%.

EXHIBIT 13B–3   Example of Income Taxes and Capital Budgeting

	Per Year
Cash receipts from sales of ore	$250,000
Less payments for salaries, insurance, utilities, and other cash expenses.	170,000
Net cash receipts	$ 80,000

Items and Computations	Year(s)	(1) Amount	(2) Tax Effect*	After-Tax Cash Flows (1) × (2)	Present Value of Cash Flows†
Cost of new equipment	Now	$(300,000)	—	$(300,000)	$(300,000)
Working capital needed	Now	(75,000)	—	(75,000)	(75,000)
Net annual cash receipts.	1–10	80,000	1 − 0.30	56,000	316,412
Road repairs	6	(40,000)	1 − 0.30	(28,000)	(14,186)
Salvage value of equipment	10	100,000	—	100,000	32,197
Release of working capital.	10	75,000	—	75,000	24,148
Subtotal					$ (16,429)

Present value of CCA tax shield:

$$PV = \left[\frac{Cdt}{d+k} \times \frac{1+0.5k}{1+k} \right] - \left[\frac{Sdt}{d+k} \times (1+k)^{-n} \right]$$

$$PV = \left[\frac{\$300,000 \times 0.2 \times 0.3}{0.2+0.12} \times \frac{1+0.06}{1+0.12} \right] - \left[\frac{\$100,000 \times 0.2 \times 0.3}{0.2+0.12} \times (1+0.12)^{-10} \right]$$

$$PV = (\$56,250 \times 0.9464) - (\$18,750 \times 0.3220)$$

$$PV = \$53,235 - \$6,037$$

$$PV = \$47,198$$

	47,198
Net present value	$ 30,769

*Taxable cash receipts and tax-deductible cash expenses are multiplied by (1 − Tax rate) to determine the after-tax cash flow. CCA deductions are multiplied by the tax rate itself to determine the after-tax cash flow (i.e., tax savings from the CCA tax shield).
†Except for the present value of the tax CCA shield, calculations use the NPV formula of Microsoft Excel and a required rate of return of 12%.

Should Englund Company purchase the equipment and open a mine on the property? The solution to the problem is given in Exhibit 13B–3. We suggest that you carefully work through the solution, noting the points that follow the exhibit.

Cost of new equipment. The initial investment of $300,000 in the new equipment is included in full, with no reductions for taxes. This represents an *investment*, not an expense, so no tax adjustment is made. Only revenues and expenses are adjusted for the effects of taxes. However, this investment does affect taxes through the CCA deductions that are considered below.

Working capital. The working capital needed for the project is included in full, with no reductions for taxes. As with the cost of new equipment, working capital is an investment and not an expense, so no tax adjustment is made. Also observe that no tax adjustment is made when the working capital is released at the end of the project's life. The release of working capital is not a taxable cash flow, since it merely represents a return of investment funds to the company.

Net annual cash receipts. The net annual cash receipts from sales of ore are adjusted for the effects of income taxes, as discussed earlier in this appendix. Note at the top of Exhibit 13B–3 that the annual cash expenses are deducted from the annual cash receipts to obtain the net cash receipts. This simplifies the computations.

Road repairs. Since the road repairs occur just once (in the sixth year), they are treated separately from other expenses. Road repairs would be a tax-deductible cash expense, and therefore they are adjusted for the effects of income taxes, as discussed earlier in this appendix.

Capital cost allowance deductions. The tax savings provided by CCA deductions are essentially an annuity that is included in the present value computations using the CCA tax shield formula.

Salvage value of equipment. The salvage value of $100,000 results in the present value inflow of $32,197. However, later in the analysis, note that the present value of the tax shield is reduced. The value of $18,750 is the present value at the end of year 10 of the lost CCA tax shield from the salvage. This amount must therefore be discounted to *the present*. To illustrate, we have used the present value formula presented in Appendix 13A to calculate the amount.

Since the net present value of the proposed mining project is positive, the equipment should be purchased and the mine opened.

LEARNING AID

Net Present Value and Internal Rate of Return Methods (with Taxes)

Relevant cash inflows:
- Incremental revenues (after tax); reduction in costs (after tax); salvage value; release of working capital; CCA tax shield.

Relevant cash outflows:
- Initial investment; increased working capital needs; incremental operating costs (after tax); CCA tax shield lost upon disposal of asset.

Decision Rule (for determining project acceptability):

Acceptable if Net present value ≥ $0; Internal rate of return ≥ Required rate of return

Not acceptable if Net present value < $0; Internal rate of return < Required rate of return

---

■ APPENDIX 13B SUMMARY

- Unless a company is a tax-exempt organization, such as a not-for-profit school or government unit, income taxes should be considered in making capital budgeting decisions. Tax-deductible cash expenditures and taxable cash receipts are placed on an after-tax basis by multiplying them by 1 − Tax rate. Only after-tax amounts should be used in determining the desirability of an investment proposal. **[LO8]**
- Although capital cost allowance is not a cash outflow, it is a valid deduction for tax purposes and therefore affects income tax payments. The CCA tax shield is computed by multiplying the CCA deduction by the tax rate and results in income tax savings. The present value of these tax savings is used in calculating the net present value of a project. **[LO8]**
- When an asset is sold, the undepreciated capital cost (UCC) is reduced by the amount of the sale proceeds. An adjustment must then also be made to the capital budgeting analysis to adjust for the present value of the CCA tax shields lost. **[LO8]**

■ APPENDIX 13B REVIEW PROBLEM: CAPITAL BUDGETING AND TAXES

Dade Company is considering investing $100,000 in a panel van for use in delivering groceries ordered online. The van is expected to generate net annual cash inflows of $20,000 over a six-year period. The van will have a salvage value of $10,000 in six years. The CCA is 30% and the income tax rate is 30%. Dade Company requires an after-tax return of 8% on all investments.

Required:
Compute the net present value of the investment in the van. Should the van be purchased?

Solution to Appendix 13B Review Problem

The net present value analysis is as follows:

Items and Computations	Year(s)	(1) Amount	(2) Tax Effect	(1) × (2) After-Tax Cash Flows	Present Value of Cash Flows[†]
Investment in panel van	Now	$(100,000)		$(100,000)	$(100,000)
Net annual cash receipts	1–6	20,000	1 − 0.30	14,000	43,213
CCA tax shield*	1–6				21,316
Salvage value of the van	6	10,000		10,000	6,301
Net present value					$ (29,170)

*CCA tax shield calculations:

$$PV = \left[\frac{Cdt}{d+k} \times \frac{1+0.5k}{1+k}\right] - \left[\frac{Sdt}{d+k} \times (1+k)^{-n}\right]$$

$$PV = \left[\frac{\$100,000 \times 0.3 \times 0.3}{0.3 + 0.08} \times \frac{1+0.04}{1+0.08}\right] - \left[\frac{\$10,000 \times 0.3 \times 0.3}{0.3 + 0.08} \times (1+0.10)^{-6}\right]$$

$$PV = [\$23,684 \times 0.9630] - [\$2,368 \times 0.6301]$$

$$PV = \$21,316$$

[†]Except for the present value of the CCA tax shield, calculations use the NPV formula of Microsoft Excel and a required rate of return of 10%.

No, the investment project should not be undertaken. It has a negative net present value when the company's cost of capital is used as the discount rate.

■ APPENDIX 13B EXERCISES AND PROBLEMS

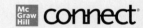

EXERCISE 13B–1 After-Tax Costs [LO8]
Solve each of the following parts independently.

1. Lowney Limited has hired a public accounting firm to identify opportunities to reduce their corporate income tax expense. The firm's tax advisory fee will be $250,000. What will be the after-tax cost of the firm's fee if Lowney's tax rate is 30%?
2. Cycling Accessories has introduced a new line of cold-weather apparel, and annual revenues have increased by $600,000. If the company's tax rate is 25%, what is the after-tax benefit from the increased revenues?
3. Solar Solutions has purchased new manufacturing equipment that cost $400,000. Calculate the yearly tax savings from the CCA tax shield for the next three years. Assume that the income tax rate is 30%, the CCA rate is 30%, and the weighted-average cost of capital (WACC) is 12%. Assume that CCA in the first year is subject to the half-year rule.

EXERCISE 13B–2 After-Tax Cash Flows in Net Present Value Analysis [LO8]
Courtney Limited has capital project opportunities each of which would require an initial investment of $400,000. Details for each opportunity are shown below:

	Investment 1	Investment 2
Investment in manufacturing equipment.............	$400,000	
Investment in working capital.....................		$400,000
Net annual cash inflows	$100,000	$100,000
Life of the project	10 years	10 years
CCA	30%	

The robotic equipment would have a salvage value of $75,000 in 12 years. The equipment would be depreciated over 12 years. At the end of 12 years, the investment in working capital would be released for use elsewhere. The company requires an after-tax return of 12% on all investments. The tax rate is 30%.

Required:
Compute the net present value of each investment project. (Round to the nearest whole dollar.)

EXERCISE 13B–3 Net Present Value Analysis Including Income Taxes [LO8]
The Hub Store at a university in eastern Canada is considering purchasing a self-serve checkout machine similar to those used in many grocery stores and other retail outlets. Currently the university pays part-time wages to students totalling $55,000 per year. A self-serve checkout machine would reduce part-time student wages by $35,000 per year. The machine would cost $240,000 and has a 10-year useful life. Total costs of operating the checkout machine would be $5,000 per year, including maintenance. Major maintenance would be needed on the machine in five years at a total cost of $10,000. The salvage value of the checkout machine in 10 years would be $40,000.

The CCA rate is 30%. Management requires a 10% after-tax return on all equipment purchases. The company's tax rate is 30%.

Required:
1.   Determine the before-tax net annual cost savings that the new checkout machine will provide.
2.   Using the data from (1) above and other data from the exercise, compute the checkout machine's net present value. (Round all dollar amounts to the nearest whole dollar.) Would you recommend that the machine be purchased?

PROBLEM 13B–4 Basic Net Present Value Analysis Including Income Taxes [LO8]
Rosman Company has an opportunity to pursue a capital budgeting project with a five-year time horizon. After careful study, Rosman estimated the following costs and revenues for the project:

Cost of new equipment	$420,000
Sale of old equipment no longer needed.	$ 80,000
Annual cash inflows	$135,000
Working capital needed.	$ 65,000
Equipment maintenance in each of Years 3 and 4	$ 20,000

The new piece of equipment mentioned above has a useful life of five years and zero salvage value. The old piece of equipment mentioned above would be sold at the beginning of the project and there would be no gain or loss realized on its sale. Rosman uses the straight-line depreciation method for financial reporting and the CCA rate for tax purposes is 20%. The company's tax rate is 30% and its after-tax cost of capital is 12%. When the project concludes in five years the working capital will be released for investment elsewhere within the company.

Required:
Compute the net present value of this investment opportunity. Round all dollar amounts to the nearest whole dollar. Would you recommend that the contract be accepted?

PROBLEM 13B–5 A Comparison of Investment Alternatives Including Income Taxes [LO8]
Kim Huang, an expert in architectural design and restoration of historical buildings, has just received a $160,000 after-tax bonus for the successful completion of a project on time and under budget. Business has been so good that she is planning to retire in 15 years, spending her time travelling, enjoying outdoor activities, and doing charitable work. Huang is considering purchasing a small discount perfume shop that is available at a nearby factory outlet centre. The business can be purchased from its current owner for $160,000. The following information relates to this alternative:

a.   Of the purchase price, $64,000 would be for fixtures and other depreciable items. The remainder would be for the company's working capital (inventory, accounts receivable, and cash). The fixtures and other depreciable items would have a remaining useful life of at least 15 years but would be depreciated for tax-reporting purposes using a CCA of 20%. Salvage value is expected to be negligible at the end of 15 years, but the working capital would be released for reinvestment elsewhere.

b.   Store records indicate that sales have averaged $325,000 per year and out-of-pocket costs have averaged $295,000 per year (before income taxes). These out-of-pocket costs include rent on the building, cost of goods sold, utilities, and wages and salaries for the sales staff and the store manager. Huang plans to entrust the day-to-day operations of the store to the manager.

c. Huang's tax rate is 40%, and she wishes to use an after-tax discount rate of 10%, given the risk involved.

Required:

Should Huang purchase the perfume shop? Use the total-cost approach to discounted cash flow in your analysis and a discount rate of 10%. (Round all dollar amounts to the nearest whole dollar.)

PROBLEM 13B–6 Net Present Value Analysis Including Income Taxes [LO8]

Winthrop Company has an opportunity to manufacture and sell a new product for a five-year period. To pursue this opportunity, the company would need to purchase a piece of equipment for $130,000. The equipment would have a useful life of five years and a $10,000 salvage value. The CCA rate for the equipment is 30%. After careful study, Winthrop estimated the following annual costs and revenues for the new product:

Sales revenues....................................	$250,000
Variable expenses	$130,000
Fixed expenses	$ 70,000

The company's tax rate is 30% and its after-tax cost of capital is 10%.

Required:

1. Compute the net present value of the project. Round all dollar amounts to the nearest whole dollar.
2. Would you recommend that the project be undertaken?

ENDNOTES

1. For simplicity, we ignore inflation and taxes. The impact of income taxes on capital budgeting decisions is discussed in Appendix 13B.
2. Although depreciation itself is not a cash outflow, it does have an effect on cash outflows for income taxes. We will take a look at this effect when we discuss the impact of income taxes on capital budgeting in Appendix 13B.
3. The alternative with the highest net present value is not always the best choice, although it is the best choice in this case. For further discussion, see the section Preference Decisions—The Ranking of Investment Projects later in this chapter.
4. Technically, the incremental-cost approach is misnamed, since it focuses on differential costs (that is, on both cost increases and decreases) rather than just on incremental costs. As used here, the term *incremental costs* should be interpreted broadly to include both cost increases and cost decreases.
5. This formula assumes that a company is operating at a profit; if it is operating at a loss, the tax situation can be very complex. For simplicity, we assume in all examples, exercises, and problems that the company is operating at a profit.
6. The term *capital cost allowance (CCA) tax shield* may convey the impression that there is something underhanded about CCA deductions—that companies are getting some sort of a special tax break. However, to use the CCA deduction, a company must have already acquired a depreciable asset—which typically requires a cash outflow. Essentially, the tax regulations require companies to delay recognizing the cash outflow as an expense until CCA charges are recorded.

EXTERNAL REPORTING AND ANALYSIS

Chapter 14

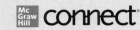

Online **Chapter 14** presents an approach for conducting financial statement analysis that will be of use to an organization's external stakeholders, such as shareholders and creditors, and to internal users, such as managers. Shareholders are concerned about future earnings and dividends; creditors are concerned about the organization's ability to repay existing or new debt. Managers are concerned about the short- and long-term impacts of operating, investing, and financing decisions. Financial statement analysis, although based on historical information, can provide useful signals about an organization's prospects with respect to profitability and cash flow. Financial statement analysis can also highlight areas in need of managerial attention, such as inventory turnover, working capital management, and capital structure. Where possible, an effective approach to financial statement analysis also incorporates comparative information related to industry trends and specific results for leading competitors.

Chapter 14 is available on the *Managerial Accounting*, Twelfth Canadian Edition Connect site.

Chapter Sources

Chapter 1

In Business: Wearable Technology Source: Adapted from Dom Nicastro, "Examining the Role of Wearables Technology in the Workplace." CMSWire.com, August 27, 2018. Retrieved from https://www.cmswire.com/digital-workplace/examining-the-role-of-wearables-technology-in-the-workplace/.

In Business: CSR Source: Adapted from Canadian Tire, "Social Responsibility." Retrieved from https://corp.canadiantire.ca/sustainability/social-responsibility/default.aspx; strategy™, "MEC, Canadian Tire Most Reputable Brands for CSR." Retrieved from http://strategyonline.ca/2018/10/26/mec-canadian-tire-among-most-reputable-brands-for-csr/.

Problem 1.4 Source: Adapted from Dan Lovallo and Daniel Kahneman, "Delusions of Success: How Optimism Undermines Executives' Decisions," *Harvard Business Review*, July 2003, pp. 56–63.

Chapter 2

Introduction Source: Adapted from Nathaniel Bullard, "Electric Car Price Tag Shrinks Along with Battery Cost," *Bloomberg Opinion*, April 12, 2019, https://www.bloomberg.com/opinion/articles/2019-04-12/electric-vehicle-battery-shrinks-and-so-does-the-total-cost.

Chapter 3

In Business: Internet Service Providers Source: Adapted from "Telecom Order CRTC 2019-288." Canadian Radio-television and Telecommunications Commission. Ottawa: August 15, 2019. Retrieved from https://crtc.gc.ca/eng/archive/2019/2019-288.htm.

Chapter 5

In Business: RFIDs Source: Adapted from "Air Canada Cargo Increases Process Efficiency & Big Data Capabilities with Piece-Level RFID Tracking," *RFID World*, May 16, 2016. Retrieved from http://www.rfidworld.ca/air-canada-cargo-increases-process-efficiency-big-data-capabilities-with-piece-level-rfid-tracking/2579.

In Business: Streaming Services Source: Adapted from Christine Persaud, "The show cost how much?! The Priciest Original Series on Netflix," *Digital Trends*, January 21, 2019. Retrieved from https://www.digitaltrends.com/movies/most-expensive-netflix.

Chapter 6

Introduction Source: Conversation with Brad Bays, formerly a Procter & Gamble financial executive.

In Business: The Coca-Cola Company Sources: "The Coca-Cola System," accessed at https://www.coca-colacompany.com/our-company/the-coca-cola-system; and "Ingredients in Coke and Their Function," accessed at https://www.thoughtco.com/the-ingredients-and-their-function-in-coke-explained-3976096.

In Business: The Trappist Monks of St. Sixtus Monastery Source: Adapted material from Melissa Stanger's "How a Tiny Brewery Run by Monks Came to Make the Best Beer in the World," *Business Insider.com*, January 26, 2015.

Chapter 7

Introduction Source: Adapted material from "Toyota Targets Fewer Parts, Complexity to Speed Product Creation," *Automotive News*, June 15, 2013, http://www.autonews.com/apps/pbcs.dll/article?AID=/20130615/OEM/306159999#ixzz2YmgrOPIV.

In Business: Canadian River Expeditions Source: Adapted material from Canadian River Expeditions & Nahanni River Adventures, http://nahanni.com/about/.

In Business: Activity-Based Costing Sources: Alnoor Bhimani, Maurice Gosselin, Mthuli Ncube, and Hiroshi Okano, "Activity-Based Costing: How Far Have We Come Internationally?" *Cost Management*, May–June 2007, pp. 12–17; Robert Kaplan and Steven Anderson, "The Innovation of Time-Driven Activity-Based Costing," *Cost Management*, March–April 2007, pp. 5–15.

Chapter 8

Introduction Source: Adapted from A. Brüggen, R. Krishnan, and K. L. Sedatole (2011). Drivers and Consequences of Short-Term Production Decisions: Evidence from the Auto Industry. *Contemporary Accounting Research*, 28(1), 83–123.

In Business: Conmed Source: Adapted from Pete Engardio, "Lean and Mean Gets Extreme," *Businessweek*, March 23 and 30, 2009, pp. 60–62. Used with permission of Bloomberg L.P. Copyright © 2017. All rights reserved.

Chapter 9

Introduction Source: Discussions with Dave Pooley, Chief Financial Officer of Axonify.

Chapter 10

Introduction Source: Adapted from Kevin Gaffney, Valeri Gladkikh, and Alan Webb, "A Case Study of a Variance Analysis Framework for Managing Distribution Costs," *Accounting Perspectives, 6*, 2007, pp. 167–190.

In Business: Vale S.A. Sources: "A Tale of Two Countries," *SteelOrbis Blog*, April 13, 2013. Retrieved from http://blog.steelorbis.com/2013/04/15/a-tale-of-two-countries/; "Brazil's Iron Ore Ship Finally Comes in," *Little Red Blog China News and Analysis*, April 19, 2013, Retrieved from http://little-red-blog.com/brazils-iron-ore-ship-finally-comes-in/.

Chapter 11

Introduction Source: Adapted from "Target Leaving Canada: 'Losing Money Every Day.'" Accessed at https://www.ctvnews.ca/business/target-leaving-canada-losing-money-every-day-1.2189973, February 15, 2020.

In Business: The Province of Manitoba's Balance Scorecard System Source: "Our Plan" and "K–12 Literacy Index" at mbmeasuringprogress.ca.

Chapter 12

Introduction Sources: Alicja Siekierska, "WestJet CEO: Swoop 'Has Significantly Exceeded Our Expectations,'" *Yahoo Finance*, October 10, 2018; https://finance.yahoo.com/news/westjet-ceo-swoop-significantly-exceeded-expectations-185950067.html; http://www.swoop.com News and Press Releases.

Chapter 13

Introduction Source: Barrick Gold Corporation, *2018 Annual Report*.

In Business: Air Canada Sources: "The First A220 for Air Canada Rolls out of the Painting Hangar," https://www.travelindustrywire.com/article108007.html; "Air Canada's new made-in-Quebec A220 aircraft won't relieve capacity crunch from Boeing groundings," https://business.financialpost.com/transportation/airlines/air-canadas-new-made-in-quebec-a220-aircraft-wont-relieve-capacity-crunch-from-boeing-groundings; "Air Canada's Airbus A220 is the next generation of sustainable travel," https://www.aircanada.com/ca/en/aco/home/about/media/media-features/airbus-A220.html.

Company/Name Index

Subject Index